REA

ACPL ITEM
DISCARDED

Health Care State Rankings 2009

Other titles in the State Fact Finder series

City Crime Rankings

Crime State Rankings

Education State Rankings

State Rankings

Health Care State Rankings 2009

Health Care Across America

Kathleen O'Leary Morgan

and

Scott Morgan

Editors

CQ PRESS

A Division of SAGE

Washington, D.C.

CQ Press
2300 N Street, NW, Suite 800
Washington, DC 20037

Phone: 202-729-1900; toll-free, 1-866-4CQ-PRESS (1-866-427-7737)

Web: www.cqpress.com

Cover design: Silverander Communications

⊗The paper used in this publication exceeds the requirements of the American
National Standard for Information Sciences—Permanence of Paper for Printed
Library Materials, ANSI Z39.48-1992.

Printed and bound in the United States of America

13 12 11 10 09   1 2 3 4 5

ISBN 978-1-60426-526-2
ISSN 1065-1403

Contents

Detailed Table of Contents

III. FACILITIES

IV. FINANCE

VII. PHYSICAL FITNESS

APPENDIX

Introduction and Methodology

Health Care State Rankings 2009 analyzes the latest health care data for each of the fifty states and the District of Columbia. The book provides state-by-state rankings of roughly 500 health care factors in the following seven categories: births and reproductive health, deaths, facilities, finance, incidence of disease, providers, and physical fitness.

Purpose of This Book

The purpose of *Health Care State Rankings 2009* is to serve as a resource for researchers, health policy professionals, and the community. The book provides the means by which individuals can compare the status of their state's health care to that of other states and the nation as a whole.

These data and rankings can be used in a variety of ways, by a variety of audiences, including the following examples:

- Health care policymakers can use them to help identify health care problems for further study.
- State governments can determine whether their health care levels are on par with the rest of the nation.
- The federal government can use this type of analysis to allocate grant funding (Bauer, 2004).
- The media can rely upon these results to report and compare health care rankings across states and years.

In addition to the data and rankings, the volume offers numerous information-finding tools, including a thorough table of contents, table listings at the beginning of each chapter, and a detailed index. A directory of the data sources used by the editors is included, providing addresses, telephone numbers, and Web sites. The Appendix consists of four charts: Population in 2008, Population in 2007, Male Population in 2007, and Female Population in 2007.

The Data and Their Limitations

The data featured in *Health Care State Rankings 2009* were chosen specifically by the editors from a variety of government and private-sector sources. Although the data provide more than a snapshot of the status of health care across the nation, they are not inclusive of all the possible health care data that might be available.

Previous editions of *Health Care State Rankings* have used the term "healthiest" when describing some states' place within the overall rankings. We no longer use this term because it is purely descriptive. At no point do we attempt to explain *why* a particular state is doing better or less well in health care than other states or against the national average. Such an explanation—currently sought by health policy experts and other social science researchers—is beyond the scope of this book. While our selection of factors clearly affects the rankings, we believe the rankings provide a solid measurement of how the fifty states and Washington, D.C., are faring with regard to health care. Researchers, practitioners, and others can confidently use the data to understand health care issues and guide policy decisions.

Methodology

As noted previously, the rankings in *Health Care State Rankings 2009* are based on seven overall categories, which are broken down into twenty-one factors that reflect access to health care providers, affordability of health care, and the general health of the population. These factors are divided into two groups: those that are "negative," for which a high ranking would be considered troublesome for a state, and those that are "positive," for which a high ranking would be considered a good sign for a state:

Negative Factors

- Births of Low Birthweight as a Percent of All Births in 2006
- Teenage Birth Rate in 2006
- Percent of Mothers Receiving Late or No Prenatal Care in 2006
- Age-Adjusted Death Rate in 2006
- Infant Mortality Rate in 2005
- Age-Adjusted Death Rate by Malignant Neoplasms in 2005
- Age-Adjusted Death Rate by Suicide in 2005
- Average Annual Family Coverage Health Insurance Premium per Enrolled Employee in 2006
- Percent of Population Not Covered by Health Insurance in 2007

- Percent of Children Not Covered by Health Insurance in 2007
- Estimated Rate of New Cancer Cases in 2008
- AIDS Rate in 2006
- Sexually Transmitted Disease Rate in 2007
- Percent of Population Lacking Access to Primary Care in 2008
- Percent of Adults Who Are Binge Drinkers: 2007
- Percent of Adults Who Smoke: 2007
- Percent of Adults Obese: 2007
- Percent of Adults Who Do Not Exercise: 2007

Positive Factors

- Rate of Beds in Community Hospitals in 2007
- Percent of Children Aged 19 to 35 Months Fully Immunized in 2007
- Safety Belt Usage Rate in 2007

The twenty-one factors involve a rate or percent of frequency so the numbers are not biased toward population size, and the positive and negative nature of each factor is taken into account as part of the formula. Once we calculate the score for each individual factor, we add the scores to determine the state's overall ranking, with a positive score indicating a positive outlook for a state and demonstrating that the state is above the national average.

"Comparison Score" Methodology

The methodology for determining the state health care rate rankings involves a multi-step process in which rates for each of the twenty-one factors listed above is processed through a formula that measures how a state compares to the national average for a given category. The end result is that the farther below the national average a state's health ranking is, the lower it ranks overall. The farther above the national average a state's health ranking is, the higher it ranks overall. The methodology used for the most recent edition of the book has been used for the previous editions of *Health Care State Rankings*. The editors subjectively determine which factors are "negative" and which are "positive," as negative and positive factors are treated differently in the formula.

The methodology for *Health Care State Rankings* is described here in detail. The formula below is used for these calculations:

$$\frac{\text{State Rate} - \text{National Rate}}{\text{National Rate}} \times 100$$

The following are steps for the "comparison score" calculation and examples that illustrate the calculations. Negative values are given in parentheses.

1. Using the state of Vermont as an example, consider the following two factors, one positive and one negative: *Positive Factor:* Percent of Children Aged 19 to 35 Months Fully Immunized in 2007 is 67.3; *Negative Factor:* Births of Low Birthweight as a Percent of All Births in 2006 is 6.9.

2. The percent difference between the state rate and the national rate for all twenty-one factors is then computed. For the positive factor of percent of fully immunized children, Vermont's rate of 67.3 is divided by the national rate of 77.4 for a percent difference of 0.8695. For the negative factor of low birthweight, Vermont's rate of 6.9 is divided by the national rate of 8.3 for a percent difference of 0.8313.

3. The number "1" is then subtracted from the percent difference for each factor so that states whose results match the national average will equal 0 instead of 1. The results are then multiplied by 100 for a more manageable number. For the positive factor in our example, 1 is subtracted from .8695 to equal (.1305), which is then multiplied by 100 to equal (13.05). For the negative factor, 1 is subtracted from 0.8313 to equal (.1687), which is then multiplied by 100 to equal (16.87).

4. These numbers are then scaled to be 1/21 of the index by multiplying each score by 4.76% (because there are twenty-one equally weighted factors, each factor is multiplied by 4.76% or 1/21). For the positive factor, (13.05) times .0476 equals (.62). For the negative factor, (16.87) times .0476 equals (.80).

5. The negative factors are then multiplied by negative one (–1). Positive factors are not multiplied by anything. Therefore, Vermont's score for the positive factor of Percent of Children Aged 19 to 35 Months Fully Immunized in 2007 remains (.62). Vermont's score for the negative factor of Births of Low Birthweight as a Percent of all Births in 2006 is .80, or (.80) multiplied by –1. Remember that a positive score illustrates that the state scored higher than the national average on a positive factor and lower than the national average on a negative factor. Therefore, Vermont's score of (.62) for the positive factor of fully immunized children (a negative score on a positive factor) illustrates that Vermont has a lower than the national average score. Vermont's score of .80 for the negative factor of low birthweight (a positive score on a negative factor) illustrates that Vermont has a lower than the national average score for babies being born with a low birthweight.

6. The final comparison score for each state is the sum of the individual scores for the twenty-one equally weighted factors ("SUM" on the 2009 Health Care State Rankings table on page xvi). This way, the states are assessed on how they stack up against the national average. In the case of Vermont, the SUM is 15.13 (note that we only illustrated the calculations of two of the twenty-one factors here). The interpretation of these scores is that the higher the state score, the further above the national score; the lower the score, the further below the national score; and a score of zero is equal to the national score. With a SUM of 15.13, Vermont is significantly above the national average.

The scores are then sorted to produce the rankings. Note that the rankings do not indicate the actual difference between the scores, only their order, providing a means by which health care trends can be gauged in differing communities.

The 2009 Health Care State Rankings table on page xvi provides the results of the state scores. All states are ranked from highest to lowest, with any ties among the states listed alphabetically for a given ranking. Negative numbers are reported in parentheses. Data reported as "NA" are not available or could not be calculated. In tables with national totals (as opposed to rates, per capita data, or the like), a separate column shows the percentage of the national total represented by each state. This "% of USA" column is particularly interesting when compared with a state's share of the nation's population for a particular year. Source information and other important notes are shown clearly at the bottom of each page.

References

Bauer, L. 2004. *Local Law Enforcement Block Grant Program, 1996–2004*. Technical Report. Washington, D.C.: Bureau of Justice Statistics.

The 2009 Health Care State Rankings

RANK	STATE	SUM	08 RANK	CHANGE
42	Alabama	(10.33)	42	0
37	Alaska	(3.82)	38	1
41	Arizona	(9.82)	40	-1
38	Arkansas	(4.75)	37	-1
17	California	7.06	17	0
27	Colorado	1.15	29	2
9	Connecticut	14.16	11	2
35	Delaware	(2.73)	41	6
45	Florida	(12.87)	46	1
40	Georgia	(8.08)	45	5
3	Hawaii	17.25	8	5
23	Idaho	4.00	23	0
28	Illinois	1.08	33	5
25	Indiana	3.27	27	2
4	Iowa	15.84	6	2
16	Kansas	7.66	15	-1
29	Kentucky	1.02	32	3
49	Louisiana	(23.46)	49	0
8	Maine	14.59	4	-4
33	Maryland	(1.09)	35	2
2	Massachusetts	17.91	5	3
20	Michigan	5.19	22	2
1	Minnesota	22.66	1	0
50	Mississippi	(25.28)	50	0
36	Missouri	(3.25)	34	-2
32	Montana	(0.41)	25	-7
10	Nebraska	13.15	7	-3
47	Nevada	(16.06)	47	0
5	New Hampshire	15.76	2	-3
14	New Jersey	9.16	16	2
48	New Mexico	(18.48)	48	0
31	New York	0.04	30	-1
34	North Carolina	(1.90)	31	-3
13	North Dakota	10.10	9	-4
26	Ohio	1.98	21	-5
44	Oklahoma	(11.12)	43	-1
19	Oregon	5.52	19	0
21	Pennsylvania	4.84	18	-3
11	Rhode Island	11.71	10	-1
46	South Carolina	(13.67)	44	-2
22	South Dakota	4.17	24	2
39	Tennessee	(5.15)	36	-3
43	Texas	(10.45)	39	-4
7	Utah	14.87	12	5
6	Vermont	15.13	3	-3
24	Virginia	3.77	20	-4
12	Washington	10.60	13	1
18	West Virginia	5.87	26	8
15	Wisconsin	8.47	14	-1
30	Wyoming	0.78	28	-2

RANK	STATE	SUM	08 RANK	CHANGE
1	Minnesota	22.66	1	0
2	Massachusetts	17.91	5	3
3	Hawaii	17.25	8	5
4	Iowa	15.84	6	2
5	New Hampshire	15.76	2	-3
6	Vermont	15.13	3	-3
7	Utah	14.87	12	5
8	Maine	14.59	4	-4
9	Connecticut	14.16	11	2
10	Nebraska	13.15	7	-3
11	Rhode Island	11.71	10	-1
12	Washington	10.60	13	1
13	North Dakota	10.10	9	-4
14	New Jersey	9.16	16	2
15	Wisconsin	8.47	14	-1
16	Kansas	7.66	15	-1
17	California	7.06	17	0
18	West Virginia	5.87	26	8
19	Oregon	5.52	19	0
20	Michigan	5.19	22	2
21	Pennsylvania	4.84	18	-3
22	South Dakota	4.17	24	2
23	Idaho	4.00	23	0
24	Virginia	3.77	20	-4
25	Indiana	3.27	27	2
26	Ohio	1.98	21	-5
27	Colorado	1.15	29	2
28	Illinois	1.08	33	5
29	Kentucky	1.02	32	3
30	Wyoming	0.78	28	-2
31	New York	0.04	30	-1
32	Montana	(0.41)	25	-7
33	Maryland	(1.09)	35	2
34	North Carolina	(1.90)	31	-3
35	Delaware	(2.73)	41	6
36	Missouri	(3.25)	34	-2
37	Alaska	(3.82)	38	1
38	Arkansas	(4.75)	37	-1
39	Tennessee	(5.15)	36	-3
40	Georgia	(8.08)	45	5
41	Arizona	(9.82)	40	-1
42	Alabama	(10.33)	42	0
43	Texas	(10.45)	39	-4
44	Oklahoma	(11.12)	43	-1
45	Florida	(12.87)	46	1
46	South Carolina	(13.67)	44	-2
47	Nevada	(16.06)	47	0
48	New Mexico	(18.48)	48	0
49	Louisiana	(23.46)	49	0
50	Mississippi	(25.28)	50	0

I. Births and Reproductive Health

Births in 2007

National Total = 4,314,658 Live Births*

ALPHA ORDER

RANK	STATE	BIRTHS	% of USA
23	Alabama	65,219	1.5%
47	Alaska	11,060	0.3%
13	Arizona	103,646	2.4%
34	Arkansas	40,939	0.9%
1	California	566,388	13.1%
22	Colorado	70,992	1.6%
32	Connecticut	41,684	1.0%
46	Delaware	11,774	0.3%
4	Florida	239,273	5.5%
8	Georgia	147,294	3.4%
40	Hawaii	19,110	0.4%
38	Idaho	25,053	0.6%
5	Illinois	182,135	4.2%
14	Indiana	89,916	2.1%
35	Iowa	40,778	0.9%
31	Kansas	42,268	1.0%
26	Kentucky	59,127	1.4%
23	Louisiana	65,219	1.5%
42	Maine	14,177	0.3%
18	Maryland	79,476	1.8%
19	Massachusetts	77,731	1.8%
10	Michigan	125,880	2.9%
20	Minnesota	73,599	1.7%
30	Mississippi	46,690	1.1%
17	Missouri	81,827	1.9%
44	Montana	12,407	0.3%
37	Nebraska	26,967	0.6%
33	Nevada	41,041	1.0%
41	New Hampshire	14,397	0.3%
11	New Jersey	115,294	2.7%
36	New Mexico	30,392	0.7%
3	New York	258,249	6.0%
9	North Carolina	131,314	3.0%
48	North Dakota	8,837	0.2%
6	Ohio	150,892	3.5%
27	Oklahoma	55,372	1.3%
29	Oregon	48,957	1.1%
7	Pennsylvania	149,970	3.5%
43	Rhode Island	12,503	0.3%
25	South Carolina	62,851	1.5%
45	South Dakota	12,344	0.3%
16	Tennessee	85,894	2.0%
2	Texas	405,376	9.4%
28	Utah	55,002	1.3%
50	Vermont	6,492	0.2%
12	Virginia	109,615	2.5%
15	Washington	89,387	2.1%
39	West Virginia	21,432	0.5%
21	Wisconsin	72,932	1.7%
49	Wyoming	7,858	0.2%

RANK ORDER

RANK	STATE	BIRTHS	% of USA
1	California	566,388	13.1%
2	Texas	405,376	9.4%
3	New York	258,249	6.0%
4	Florida	239,273	5.5%
5	Illinois	182,135	4.2%
6	Ohio	150,892	3.5%
7	Pennsylvania	149,970	3.5%
8	Georgia	147,294	3.4%
9	North Carolina	131,314	3.0%
10	Michigan	125,880	2.9%
11	New Jersey	115,294	2.7%
12	Virginia	109,615	2.5%
13	Arizona	103,646	2.4%
14	Indiana	89,916	2.1%
15	Washington	89,387	2.1%
16	Tennessee	85,894	2.0%
17	Missouri	81,827	1.9%
18	Maryland	79,476	1.8%
19	Massachusetts	77,731	1.8%
20	Minnesota	73,599	1.7%
21	Wisconsin	72,932	1.7%
22	Colorado	70,992	1.6%
23	Alabama	65,219	1.5%
23	Louisiana	65,219	1.5%
25	South Carolina	62,851	1.5%
26	Kentucky	59,127	1.4%
27	Oklahoma	55,372	1.3%
28	Utah	55,002	1.3%
29	Oregon	48,957	1.1%
30	Mississippi	46,690	1.1%
31	Kansas	42,268	1.0%
32	Connecticut	41,684	1.0%
33	Nevada	41,041	1.0%
34	Arkansas	40,939	0.9%
35	Iowa	40,778	0.9%
36	New Mexico	30,392	0.7%
37	Nebraska	26,967	0.6%
38	Idaho	25,053	0.6%
39	West Virginia	21,432	0.5%
40	Hawaii	19,110	0.4%
41	New Hampshire	14,397	0.3%
42	Maine	14,177	0.3%
43	Rhode Island	12,503	0.3%
44	Montana	12,407	0.3%
45	South Dakota	12,344	0.3%
46	Delaware	11,774	0.3%
47	Alaska	11,060	0.3%
48	North Dakota	8,837	0.2%
49	Wyoming	7,858	0.2%
50	Vermont	6,492	0.2%
	District of Columbia	7,628	0.2%

Source: U.S. Department of Health and Human Services, National Center for Health Statistics
"National Vital Statistics Reports" (Vol. 56, No. 21, July 14, 2008, http://www.cdc.gov/nchs/births.htm)
*Preliminary data by state of residence.

Birth Rate in 2007

National Rate = 14.3 Live Births per 1,000 Population*

ALPHA ORDER

RANK	STATE	RATE
26	Alabama	14.1
5	Alaska	16.2
4	Arizona	16.3
19	Arkansas	14.5
8	California	15.6
18	Colorado	14.7
45	Connecticut	11.9
33	Delaware	13.7
37	Florida	13.1
9	Georgia	15.5
15	Hawaii	15.0
3	Idaho	16.7
22	Illinois	14.2
22	Indiana	14.2
33	Iowa	13.7
13	Kansas	15.2
28	Kentucky	14.0
17	Louisiana	14.9
49	Maine	10.8
26	Maryland	14.1
44	Massachusetts	12.0
42	Michigan	12.5
22	Minnesota	14.2
7	Mississippi	16.0
30	Missouri	13.9
40	Montana	13.0
13	Nebraska	15.2
6	Nevada	16.1
48	New Hampshire	11.0
35	New Jersey	13.3
9	New Mexico	15.5
35	New York	13.3
19	North Carolina	14.5
30	North Dakota	13.9
37	Ohio	13.1
12	Oklahoma	15.3
37	Oregon	13.1
43	Pennsylvania	12.1
45	Rhode Island	11.9
21	South Carolina	14.3
9	South Dakota	15.5
28	Tennessee	14.0
2	Texas	17.0
1	Utah	20.6
50	Vermont	10.5
22	Virginia	14.2
30	Washington	13.9
47	West Virginia	11.8
40	Wisconsin	13.0
15	Wyoming	15.0

RANK ORDER

RANK	STATE	RATE
1	Utah	20.6
2	Texas	17.0
3	Idaho	16.7
4	Arizona	16.3
5	Alaska	16.2
6	Nevada	16.1
7	Mississippi	16.0
8	California	15.6
9	Georgia	15.5
9	New Mexico	15.5
9	South Dakota	15.5
12	Oklahoma	15.3
13	Kansas	15.2
13	Nebraska	15.2
15	Hawaii	15.0
15	Wyoming	15.0
17	Louisiana	14.9
18	Colorado	14.7
19	Arkansas	14.5
19	North Carolina	14.5
21	South Carolina	14.3
22	Illinois	14.2
22	Indiana	14.2
22	Minnesota	14.2
22	Virginia	14.2
26	Alabama	14.1
26	Maryland	14.1
28	Kentucky	14.0
28	Tennessee	14.0
30	Missouri	13.9
30	North Dakota	13.9
30	Washington	13.9
33	Delaware	13.7
33	Iowa	13.7
35	New Jersey	13.3
35	New York	13.3
37	Florida	13.1
37	Ohio	13.1
37	Oregon	13.1
40	Montana	13.0
40	Wisconsin	13.0
42	Michigan	12.5
43	Pennsylvania	12.1
44	Massachusetts	12.0
45	Connecticut	11.9
45	Rhode Island	11.9
47	West Virginia	11.8
48	New Hampshire	11.0
49	Maine	10.8
50	Vermont	10.5

District of Columbia	13.0

Source: CQ Press using data from U.S. Department of Health and Human Services, National Center for Health Statistics "National Vital Statistics Reports" (Vol. 56, No. 21, July 14, 2008, http://www.cdc.gov/nchs/births.htm)

*Preliminary data by state of residence.

Percent Change in Birth Rate: 1998 to 2007

National Percent Change = 0.0% Change*

ALPHA ORDER

RANK	STATE	PERCENT CHANGE
31	Alabama	0.0
28	Alaska	1.3
24	Arizona	1.9
15	Arkansas	3.6
36	California	(1.3)
26	Colorado	1.4
50	Connecticut	(8.5)
38	Delaware	(1.4)
13	Florida	4.0
34	Georgia	(0.6)
18	Hawaii	3.4
5	Idaho	7.7
46	Illinois	(4.7)
31	Indiana	0.0
7	Iowa	7.0
8	Kansas	5.6
19	Kentucky	2.9
36	Louisiana	(1.3)
35	Maine	(0.9)
21	Maryland	2.2
47	Massachusetts	(7.7)
48	Michigan	(8.1)
10	Minnesota	5.2
11	Mississippi	4.6
21	Missouri	2.2
6	Montana	7.4
4	Nebraska	9.4
14	Nevada	3.9
49	New Hampshire	(8.3)
43	New Jersey	(3.6)
23	New Mexico	2.0
43	New York	(3.6)
26	North Carolina	1.4
2	North Dakota	13.9
41	Ohio	(3.0)
9	Oklahoma	5.5
41	Oregon	(3.0)
25	Pennsylvania	1.7
40	Rhode Island	(2.5)
12	South Carolina	4.4
3	South Dakota	12.3
29	Tennessee	0.7
31	Texas	0.0
38	Utah	(1.4)
45	Vermont	(4.5)
15	Virginia	3.6
29	Washington	0.7
17	West Virginia	3.5
20	Wisconsin	2.4
1	Wyoming	18.1

RANK ORDER

RANK	STATE	PERCENT CHANGE
1	Wyoming	18.1
2	North Dakota	13.9
3	South Dakota	12.3
4	Nebraska	9.4
5	Idaho	7.7
6	Montana	7.4
7	Iowa	7.0
8	Kansas	5.6
9	Oklahoma	5.5
10	Minnesota	5.2
11	Mississippi	4.6
12	South Carolina	4.4
13	Florida	4.0
14	Nevada	3.9
15	Arkansas	3.6
15	Virginia	3.6
17	West Virginia	3.5
18	Hawaii	3.4
19	Kentucky	2.9
20	Wisconsin	2.4
21	Maryland	2.2
21	Missouri	2.2
23	New Mexico	2.0
24	Arizona	1.9
25	Pennsylvania	1.7
26	Colorado	1.4
26	North Carolina	1.4
28	Alaska	1.3
29	Tennessee	0.7
29	Washington	0.7
31	Alabama	0.0
31	Indiana	0.0
31	Texas	0.0
34	Georgia	(0.6)
35	Maine	(0.9)
36	California	(1.3)
36	Louisiana	(1.3)
38	Delaware	(1.4)
38	Utah	(1.4)
40	Rhode Island	(2.5)
41	Ohio	(3.0)
41	Oregon	(3.0)
43	New Jersey	(3.6)
43	New York	(3.6)
45	Vermont	(4.5)
46	Illinois	(4.7)
47	Massachusetts	(7.7)
48	Michigan	(8.1)
49	New Hampshire	(8.3)
50	Connecticut	(8.5)

| | District of Columbia | (4.4) |

Source: CQ Press using data from U.S. Department of Health and Human Services, National Center for Health Statistics
   "National Vital Statistics Reports" (Vol. 56, No. 21, July 14, 2008, http://www.cdc.gov/nchs/births.htm)
   "VitalStats" (http://www.cdc.gov/nchs/datawh/vitalstats/VitalStats.htm)
*By state of residence.

Births in 2006

National Total = 4,265,555 Live Births*

RANK	STATE	BIRTHS	% of USA
24	Alabama	63,232	1.5%
47	Alaska	10,996	0.3%
13	Arizona	102,429	2.4%
33	Arkansas	40,961	1.0%
1	California	562,440	13.2%
22	Colorado	70,751	1.7%
31	Connecticut	41,820	1.0%
45	Delaware	11,989	0.3%
4	Florida	236,802	5.6%
8	Georgia	148,633	3.5%
40	Hawaii	18,982	0.4%
38	Idaho	24,184	0.6%
5	Illinois	180,572	4.2%
14	Indiana	88,631	2.1%
34	Iowa	40,607	1.0%
32	Kansas	40,968	1.0%
26	Kentucky	58,250	1.4%
23	Louisiana	63,376	1.5%
42	Maine	14,151	0.3%
19	Maryland	77,494	1.8%
18	Massachusetts	77,676	1.8%
10	Michigan	127,483	3.0%
20	Minnesota	73,525	1.7%
30	Mississippi	46,056	1.1%
17	Missouri	81,385	1.9%
43	Montana	12,508	0.3%
37	Nebraska	26,727	0.6%
35	Nevada	40,027	0.9%
41	New Hampshire	14,378	0.3%
11	New Jersey	115,020	2.7%
36	New Mexico	29,936	0.7%
3	New York	250,104	5.9%
9	North Carolina	127,859	3.0%
48	North Dakota	8,621	0.2%
6	Ohio	150,593	3.5%
27	Oklahoma	54,016	1.3%
29	Oregon	48,689	1.1%
7	Pennsylvania	149,090	3.5%
44	Rhode Island	12,372	0.3%
25	South Carolina	62,171	1.5%
46	South Dakota	11,919	0.3%
16	Tennessee	84,355	2.0%
2	Texas	399,603	9.4%
28	Utah	53,504	1.3%
50	Vermont	6,511	0.2%
12	Virginia	107,817	2.5%
15	Washington	86,876	2.0%
39	West Virginia	20,931	0.5%
21	Wisconsin	72,340	1.7%
49	Wyoming	7,672	0.2%

RANK	STATE	BIRTHS	% of USA
1	California	562,440	13.2%
2	Texas	399,603	9.4%
3	New York	250,104	5.9%
4	Florida	236,802	5.6%
5	Illinois	180,572	4.2%
6	Ohio	150,593	3.5%
7	Pennsylvania	149,090	3.5%
8	Georgia	148,633	3.5%
9	North Carolina	127,859	3.0%
10	Michigan	127,483	3.0%
11	New Jersey	115,020	2.7%
12	Virginia	107,817	2.5%
13	Arizona	102,429	2.4%
14	Indiana	88,631	2.1%
15	Washington	86,876	2.0%
16	Tennessee	84,355	2.0%
17	Missouri	81,385	1.9%
18	Massachusetts	77,676	1.8%
19	Maryland	77,494	1.8%
20	Minnesota	73,525	1.7%
21	Wisconsin	72,340	1.7%
22	Colorado	70,751	1.7%
23	Louisiana	63,376	1.5%
24	Alabama	63,232	1.5%
25	South Carolina	62,171	1.5%
26	Kentucky	58,250	1.4%
27	Oklahoma	54,016	1.3%
28	Utah	53,504	1.3%
29	Oregon	48,689	1.1%
30	Mississippi	46,056	1.1%
31	Connecticut	41,820	1.0%
32	Kansas	40,968	1.0%
33	Arkansas	40,961	1.0%
34	Iowa	40,607	1.0%
35	Nevada	40,027	0.9%
36	New Mexico	29,936	0.7%
37	Nebraska	26,727	0.6%
38	Idaho	24,184	0.6%
39	West Virginia	20,931	0.5%
40	Hawaii	18,982	0.4%
41	New Hampshire	14,378	0.3%
42	Maine	14,151	0.3%
43	Montana	12,508	0.3%
44	Rhode Island	12,372	0.3%
45	Delaware	11,989	0.3%
46	South Dakota	11,919	0.3%
47	Alaska	10,996	0.3%
48	North Dakota	8,621	0.2%
49	Wyoming	7,672	0.2%
50	Vermont	6,511	0.2%
	District of Columbia	8,523	0.2%

Source: U.S. Department of Health and Human Services, National Center for Health Statistics
"National Vital Statistics Reports" (Vol. 57, No. 7, January 7, 2009, http://www.cdc.gov/nchs/births.htm)
*Final data by state of residence.

Birth Rate in 2006

National Rate = 14.2 Live Births per 1,000 Population*

ALPHA ORDER

RANK	STATE	RATE
31	Alabama	13.7
5	Alaska	16.4
3	Arizona	16.6
19	Arkansas	14.6
9	California	15.4
14	Colorado	14.9
45	Connecticut	11.9
25	Delaware	14.0
38	Florida	13.1
7	Georgia	15.9
16	Hawaii	14.8
4	Idaho	16.5
23	Illinois	14.1
25	Indiana	14.0
32	Iowa	13.6
16	Kansas	14.8
29	Kentucky	13.8
16	Louisiana	14.8
49	Maine	10.7
29	Maryland	13.8
43	Massachusetts	12.1
42	Michigan	12.6
22	Minnesota	14.2
8	Mississippi	15.8
28	Missouri	13.9
35	Montana	13.2
12	Nebraska	15.1
6	Nevada	16.0
48	New Hampshire	10.9
35	New Jersey	13.2
10	New Mexico	15.3
40	New York	13.0
20	North Carolina	14.4
32	North Dakota	13.6
38	Ohio	13.1
12	Oklahoma	15.1
35	Oregon	13.2
44	Pennsylvania	12.0
46	Rhode Island	11.6
20	South Carolina	14.4
11	South Dakota	15.2
25	Tennessee	14.0
2	Texas	17.0
1	Utah	21.0
50	Vermont	10.4
23	Virginia	14.1
32	Washington	13.6
47	West Virginia	11.5
40	Wisconsin	13.0
14	Wyoming	14.9

RANK ORDER

RANK	STATE	RATE
1	Utah	21.0
2	Texas	17.0
3	Arizona	16.6
4	Idaho	16.5
5	Alaska	16.4
6	Nevada	16.0
7	Georgia	15.9
8	Mississippi	15.8
9	California	15.4
10	New Mexico	15.3
11	South Dakota	15.2
12	Nebraska	15.1
12	Oklahoma	15.1
14	Colorado	14.9
14	Wyoming	14.9
16	Hawaii	14.8
16	Kansas	14.8
16	Louisiana	14.8
19	Arkansas	14.6
20	North Carolina	14.4
20	South Carolina	14.4
22	Minnesota	14.2
23	Illinois	14.1
23	Virginia	14.1
25	Delaware	14.0
25	Indiana	14.0
25	Tennessee	14.0
28	Missouri	13.9
29	Kentucky	13.8
29	Maryland	13.8
31	Alabama	13.7
32	Iowa	13.6
32	North Dakota	13.6
32	Washington	13.6
35	Montana	13.2
35	New Jersey	13.2
35	Oregon	13.2
38	Florida	13.1
38	Ohio	13.1
40	New York	13.0
40	Wisconsin	13.0
42	Michigan	12.6
43	Massachusetts	12.1
44	Pennsylvania	12.0
45	Connecticut	11.9
46	Rhode Island	11.6
47	West Virginia	11.5
48	New Hampshire	10.9
49	Maine	10.7
50	Vermont	10.4
	District of Columbia	14.7

Source: U.S. Department of Health and Human Services, National Center for Health Statistics
"National Vital Statistics Reports" (Vol. 57, No. 7, January 7, 2009, http://www.cdc.gov/nchs/births.htm)
*Final data by state of residence.

Fertility Rate in 2006

National Rate = 68.5 Live Births per 1,000 Women 15 to 44 Years Old*

<table>
<tr><th colspan="3">ALPHA ORDER</th><th colspan="3">RANK ORDER</th></tr>
<tr><th>RANK</th><th>STATE</th><th>RATE</th><th>RANK</th><th>STATE</th><th>RATE</th></tr>
<tr><td>32</td><td>Alabama</td><td>67.0</td><td>1</td><td>Utah</td><td>94.1</td></tr>
<tr><td>7</td><td>Alaska</td><td>76.7</td><td>2</td><td>Arizona</td><td>81.6</td></tr>
<tr><td>2</td><td>Arizona</td><td>81.6</td><td>3</td><td>Idaho</td><td>80.9</td></tr>
<tr><td>16</td><td>Arkansas</td><td>72.2</td><td>4</td><td>Texas</td><td>78.8</td></tr>
<tr><td>17</td><td>California</td><td>71.8</td><td>5</td><td>South Dakota</td><td>78.5</td></tr>
<tr><td>19</td><td>Colorado</td><td>70.2</td><td>6</td><td>Nevada</td><td>77.9</td></tr>
<tr><td>45</td><td>Connecticut</td><td>58.8</td><td>7</td><td>Alaska</td><td>76.7</td></tr>
<tr><td>29</td><td>Delaware</td><td>67.3</td><td>8</td><td>Wyoming</td><td>75.9</td></tr>
<tr><td>29</td><td>Florida</td><td>67.3</td><td>9</td><td>Mississippi</td><td>75.7</td></tr>
<tr><td>15</td><td>Georgia</td><td>72.4</td><td>10</td><td>Nebraska</td><td>75.1</td></tr>
<tr><td>13</td><td>Hawaii</td><td>73.9</td><td>11</td><td>New Mexico</td><td>74.7</td></tr>
<tr><td>3</td><td>Idaho</td><td>80.9</td><td>11</td><td>Oklahoma</td><td>74.7</td></tr>
<tr><td>33</td><td>Illinois</td><td>66.8</td><td>13</td><td>Hawaii</td><td>73.9</td></tr>
<tr><td>26</td><td>Indiana</td><td>68.3</td><td>14</td><td>Kansas</td><td>73.3</td></tr>
<tr><td>22</td><td>Iowa</td><td>69.1</td><td>15</td><td>Georgia</td><td>72.4</td></tr>
<tr><td>14</td><td>Kansas</td><td>73.3</td><td>16</td><td>Arkansas</td><td>72.2</td></tr>
<tr><td>31</td><td>Kentucky</td><td>67.1</td><td>17</td><td>California</td><td>71.8</td></tr>
<tr><td>18</td><td>Louisiana</td><td>70.6</td><td>18</td><td>Louisiana</td><td>70.6</td></tr>
<tr><td>48</td><td>Maine</td><td>54.5</td><td>19</td><td>Colorado</td><td>70.2</td></tr>
<tr><td>39</td><td>Maryland</td><td>64.2</td><td>20</td><td>South Carolina</td><td>69.6</td></tr>
<tr><td>46</td><td>Massachusetts</td><td>56.9</td><td>21</td><td>Montana</td><td>69.5</td></tr>
<tr><td>41</td><td>Michigan</td><td>61.7</td><td>22</td><td>Iowa</td><td>69.1</td></tr>
<tr><td>24</td><td>Minnesota</td><td>68.7</td><td>23</td><td>North Carolina</td><td>69.0</td></tr>
<tr><td>9</td><td>Mississippi</td><td>75.7</td><td>24</td><td>Minnesota</td><td>68.7</td></tr>
<tr><td>27</td><td>Missouri</td><td>67.9</td><td>24</td><td>North Dakota</td><td>68.7</td></tr>
<tr><td>21</td><td>Montana</td><td>69.5</td><td>26</td><td>Indiana</td><td>68.3</td></tr>
<tr><td>10</td><td>Nebraska</td><td>75.1</td><td>27</td><td>Missouri</td><td>67.9</td></tr>
<tr><td>6</td><td>Nevada</td><td>77.9</td><td>28</td><td>Tennessee</td><td>67.5</td></tr>
<tr><td>49</td><td>New Hampshire</td><td>53.4</td><td>29</td><td>Delaware</td><td>67.3</td></tr>
<tr><td>38</td><td>New Jersey</td><td>64.5</td><td>29</td><td>Florida</td><td>67.3</td></tr>
<tr><td>11</td><td>New Mexico</td><td>74.7</td><td>31</td><td>Kentucky</td><td>67.1</td></tr>
<tr><td>42</td><td>New York</td><td>61.1</td><td>32</td><td>Alabama</td><td>67.0</td></tr>
<tr><td>23</td><td>North Carolina</td><td>69.0</td><td>33</td><td>Illinois</td><td>66.8</td></tr>
<tr><td>24</td><td>North Dakota</td><td>68.7</td><td>34</td><td>Virginia</td><td>66.3</td></tr>
<tr><td>37</td><td>Ohio</td><td>64.7</td><td>35</td><td>Oregon</td><td>65.4</td></tr>
<tr><td>11</td><td>Oklahoma</td><td>74.7</td><td>36</td><td>Washington</td><td>65.2</td></tr>
<tr><td>35</td><td>Oregon</td><td>65.4</td><td>37</td><td>Ohio</td><td>64.7</td></tr>
<tr><td>43</td><td>Pennsylvania</td><td>60.6</td><td>38</td><td>New Jersey</td><td>64.5</td></tr>
<tr><td>47</td><td>Rhode Island</td><td>54.6</td><td>39</td><td>Maryland</td><td>64.2</td></tr>
<tr><td>20</td><td>South Carolina</td><td>69.6</td><td>40</td><td>Wisconsin</td><td>64.0</td></tr>
<tr><td>5</td><td>South Dakota</td><td>78.5</td><td>41</td><td>Michigan</td><td>61.7</td></tr>
<tr><td>28</td><td>Tennessee</td><td>67.5</td><td>42</td><td>New York</td><td>61.1</td></tr>
<tr><td>4</td><td>Texas</td><td>78.8</td><td>43</td><td>Pennsylvania</td><td>60.6</td></tr>
<tr><td>1</td><td>Utah</td><td>94.1</td><td>44</td><td>West Virginia</td><td>59.4</td></tr>
<tr><td>50</td><td>Vermont</td><td>52.2</td><td>45</td><td>Connecticut</td><td>58.8</td></tr>
<tr><td>34</td><td>Virginia</td><td>66.3</td><td>46</td><td>Massachusetts</td><td>56.9</td></tr>
<tr><td>36</td><td>Washington</td><td>65.2</td><td>47</td><td>Rhode Island</td><td>54.6</td></tr>
<tr><td>44</td><td>West Virginia</td><td>59.4</td><td>48</td><td>Maine</td><td>54.5</td></tr>
<tr><td>40</td><td>Wisconsin</td><td>64.0</td><td>49</td><td>New Hampshire</td><td>53.4</td></tr>
<tr><td>8</td><td>Wyoming</td><td>75.9</td><td>50</td><td>Vermont</td><td>52.2</td></tr>
<tr><td></td><td></td><td></td><td></td><td>District of Columbia</td><td>58.4</td></tr>
</table>

Source: U.S. Department of Health and Human Services, National Center for Health Statistics
"National Vital Statistics Reports" (Vol. 57, No. 7, January 7, 2009, http://www.cdc.gov/nchs/births.htm)
*Final data by state of residence.

Births to White Women in 2006

National Total = 3,310,308 Live Births to White Women*

ALPHA ORDER

ALPHA ORDER

RANK	STATE	BIRTHS	% of USA
26	Alabama	42,801	1.3%
48	Alaska	6,944	0.2%
11	Arizona	88,443	2.7%
34	Arkansas	32,068	1.0%
1	California	453,916	13.7%
17	Colorado	64,570	2.0%
32	Connecticut	33,746	1.0%
45	Delaware	8,393	0.3%
4	Florida	171,579	5.2%
9	Georgia	93,749	2.8%
50	Hawaii	5,532	0.2%
38	Idaho	23,272	0.7%
5	Illinois	139,213	4.2%
13	Indiana	76,469	2.3%
29	Iowa	37,781	1.1%
31	Kansas	36,034	1.1%
22	Kentucky	51,719	1.6%
30	Louisiana	37,334	1.1%
41	Maine	13,527	0.4%
24	Maryland	43,961	1.3%
19	Massachusetts	62,402	1.9%
8	Michigan	99,020	3.0%
21	Minnesota	59,189	1.8%
36	Mississippi	24,205	0.7%
16	Missouri	66,593	2.0%
42	Montana	10,703	0.3%
37	Nebraska	23,569	0.7%
33	Nevada	32,590	1.0%
40	New Hampshire	13,561	0.4%
12	New Jersey	82,570	2.5%
35	New Mexico	24,815	0.7%
3	New York	172,921	5.2%
10	North Carolina	92,430	2.8%
46	North Dakota	7,357	0.2%
6	Ohio	121,614	3.7%
27	Oklahoma	41,839	1.3%
25	Oregon	43,898	1.3%
7	Pennsylvania	117,653	3.6%
43	Rhode Island	10,445	0.3%
28	South Carolina	39,122	1.2%
44	South Dakota	9,510	0.3%
18	Tennessee	63,710	1.9%
2	Texas	334,526	10.1%
23	Utah	50,621	1.5%
49	Vermont	6,306	0.2%
14	Virginia	75,843	2.3%
15	Washington	71,234	2.2%
39	West Virginia	20,032	0.6%
20	Wisconsin	61,258	1.9%
47	Wyoming	7,155	0.2%

RANK ORDER

RANK	STATE	BIRTHS	% of USA
1	California	453,916	13.7%
2	Texas	334,526	10.1%
3	New York	172,921	5.2%
4	Florida	171,579	5.2%
5	Illinois	139,213	4.2%
6	Ohio	121,614	3.7%
7	Pennsylvania	117,653	3.6%
8	Michigan	99,020	3.0%
9	Georgia	93,749	2.8%
10	North Carolina	92,430	2.8%
11	Arizona	88,443	2.7%
12	New Jersey	82,570	2.5%
13	Indiana	76,469	2.3%
14	Virginia	75,843	2.3%
15	Washington	71,234	2.2%
16	Missouri	66,593	2.0%
17	Colorado	64,570	2.0%
18	Tennessee	63,710	1.9%
19	Massachusetts	62,402	1.9%
20	Wisconsin	61,258	1.9%
21	Minnesota	59,189	1.8%
22	Kentucky	51,719	1.6%
23	Utah	50,621	1.5%
24	Maryland	43,961	1.3%
25	Oregon	43,898	1.3%
26	Alabama	42,801	1.3%
27	Oklahoma	41,839	1.3%
28	South Carolina	39,122	1.2%
29	Iowa	37,781	1.1%
30	Louisiana	37,334	1.1%
31	Kansas	36,034	1.1%
32	Connecticut	33,746	1.0%
33	Nevada	32,590	1.0%
34	Arkansas	32,068	1.0%
35	New Mexico	24,815	0.7%
36	Mississippi	24,205	0.7%
37	Nebraska	23,569	0.7%
38	Idaho	23,272	0.7%
39	West Virginia	20,032	0.6%
40	New Hampshire	13,561	0.4%
41	Maine	13,527	0.4%
42	Montana	10,703	0.3%
43	Rhode Island	10,445	0.3%
44	South Dakota	9,510	0.3%
45	Delaware	8,393	0.3%
46	North Dakota	7,357	0.2%
47	Wyoming	7,155	0.2%
48	Alaska	6,944	0.2%
49	Vermont	6,306	0.2%
50	Hawaii	5,532	0.2%
	District of Columbia	2,566	0.1%

Source: U.S. Department of Health and Human Services, National Center for Health Statistics
   "National Vital Statistics Reports" (Vol. 57, No. 7, January 7, 2009, http://www.cdc.gov/nchs/births.htm)
*Final data by state of residence. By race of mother.

White Births as a Percent of All Births in 2006

National Percent = 76.7% of Live Births*

<table>
<tr><td colspan="3"><u>ALPHA ORDER</u></td><td colspan="3"><u>RANK ORDER</u></td></tr>
<tr><th>RANK</th><th>STATE</th><th>PERCENT</th><th>RANK</th><th>STATE</th><th>PERCENT</th></tr>
<tr><td>43</td><td>Alabama</td><td>65.6</td><td>1</td><td>Vermont</td><td>97.1</td></tr>
<tr><td>45</td><td>Alaska</td><td>62.8</td><td>2</td><td>Maine</td><td>95.4</td></tr>
<tr><td>14</td><td>Arizona</td><td>85.3</td><td>3</td><td>New Hampshire</td><td>94.2</td></tr>
<tr><td>32</td><td>Arkansas</td><td>78.3</td><td>4</td><td>West Virginia</td><td>93.5</td></tr>
<tr><td>27</td><td>California</td><td>80.1</td><td>5</td><td>Idaho</td><td>92.9</td></tr>
<tr><td>9</td><td>Colorado</td><td>91.0</td><td>6</td><td>Iowa</td><td>92.7</td></tr>
<tr><td>23</td><td>Connecticut</td><td>81.0</td><td>7</td><td>Utah</td><td>92.0</td></tr>
<tr><td>39</td><td>Delaware</td><td>71.3</td><td>8</td><td>Wyoming</td><td>91.1</td></tr>
<tr><td>37</td><td>Florida</td><td>71.7</td><td>9</td><td>Colorado</td><td>91.0</td></tr>
<tr><td>44</td><td>Georgia</td><td>63.6</td><td>10</td><td>Oregon</td><td>89.7</td></tr>
<tr><td>50</td><td>Hawaii</td><td>28.9</td><td>11</td><td>Kentucky</td><td>87.5</td></tr>
<tr><td>5</td><td>Idaho</td><td>92.9</td><td>12</td><td>Nebraska</td><td>87.4</td></tr>
<tr><td>34</td><td>Illinois</td><td>76.4</td><td>13</td><td>Montana</td><td>86.3</td></tr>
<tr><td>16</td><td>Indiana</td><td>85.0</td><td>14</td><td>Arizona</td><td>85.3</td></tr>
<tr><td>6</td><td>Iowa</td><td>92.7</td><td>14</td><td>Kansas</td><td>85.3</td></tr>
<tr><td>14</td><td>Kansas</td><td>85.3</td><td>16</td><td>Indiana</td><td>85.0</td></tr>
<tr><td>11</td><td>Kentucky</td><td>87.5</td><td>17</td><td>Wisconsin</td><td>84.0</td></tr>
<tr><td>47</td><td>Louisiana</td><td>57.2</td><td>18</td><td>Rhode Island</td><td>83.5</td></tr>
<tr><td>2</td><td>Maine</td><td>95.4</td><td>19</td><td>North Dakota</td><td>83.3</td></tr>
<tr><td>48</td><td>Maryland</td><td>55.3</td><td>20</td><td>Texas</td><td>82.5</td></tr>
<tr><td>26</td><td>Massachusetts</td><td>80.3</td><td>21</td><td>New Mexico</td><td>81.6</td></tr>
<tr><td>30</td><td>Michigan</td><td>78.7</td><td>22</td><td>Missouri</td><td>81.4</td></tr>
<tr><td>25</td><td>Minnesota</td><td>80.4</td><td>23</td><td>Connecticut</td><td>81.0</td></tr>
<tr><td>49</td><td>Mississippi</td><td>51.8</td><td>24</td><td>Ohio</td><td>80.6</td></tr>
<tr><td>22</td><td>Missouri</td><td>81.4</td><td>25</td><td>Minnesota</td><td>80.4</td></tr>
<tr><td>13</td><td>Montana</td><td>86.3</td><td>26</td><td>Massachusetts</td><td>80.3</td></tr>
<tr><td>12</td><td>Nebraska</td><td>87.4</td><td>27</td><td>California</td><td>80.1</td></tr>
<tr><td>29</td><td>Nevada</td><td>79.4</td><td>28</td><td>Washington</td><td>79.7</td></tr>
<tr><td>3</td><td>New Hampshire</td><td>94.2</td><td>29</td><td>Nevada</td><td>79.4</td></tr>
<tr><td>38</td><td>New Jersey</td><td>71.6</td><td>30</td><td>Michigan</td><td>78.7</td></tr>
<tr><td>21</td><td>New Mexico</td><td>81.6</td><td>31</td><td>Pennsylvania</td><td>78.5</td></tr>
<tr><td>42</td><td>New York</td><td>67.0</td><td>32</td><td>Arkansas</td><td>78.3</td></tr>
<tr><td>40</td><td>North Carolina</td><td>70.4</td><td>33</td><td>South Dakota</td><td>77.0</td></tr>
<tr><td>19</td><td>North Dakota</td><td>83.3</td><td>34</td><td>Illinois</td><td>76.4</td></tr>
<tr><td>24</td><td>Ohio</td><td>80.6</td><td>35</td><td>Oklahoma</td><td>75.6</td></tr>
<tr><td>35</td><td>Oklahoma</td><td>75.6</td><td>36</td><td>Tennessee</td><td>74.2</td></tr>
<tr><td>10</td><td>Oregon</td><td>89.7</td><td>37</td><td>Florida</td><td>71.7</td></tr>
<tr><td>31</td><td>Pennsylvania</td><td>78.5</td><td>38</td><td>New Jersey</td><td>71.6</td></tr>
<tr><td>18</td><td>Rhode Island</td><td>83.5</td><td>39</td><td>Delaware</td><td>71.3</td></tr>
<tr><td>46</td><td>South Carolina</td><td>62.2</td><td>40</td><td>North Carolina</td><td>70.4</td></tr>
<tr><td>33</td><td>South Dakota</td><td>77.0</td><td>41</td><td>Virginia</td><td>69.2</td></tr>
<tr><td>36</td><td>Tennessee</td><td>74.2</td><td>42</td><td>New York</td><td>67.0</td></tr>
<tr><td>20</td><td>Texas</td><td>82.5</td><td>43</td><td>Alabama</td><td>65.6</td></tr>
<tr><td>7</td><td>Utah</td><td>92.0</td><td>44</td><td>Georgia</td><td>63.6</td></tr>
<tr><td>1</td><td>Vermont</td><td>97.1</td><td>45</td><td>Alaska</td><td>62.8</td></tr>
<tr><td>41</td><td>Virginia</td><td>69.2</td><td>46</td><td>South Carolina</td><td>62.2</td></tr>
<tr><td>28</td><td>Washington</td><td>79.7</td><td>47</td><td>Louisiana</td><td>57.2</td></tr>
<tr><td>4</td><td>West Virginia</td><td>93.5</td><td>48</td><td>Maryland</td><td>55.3</td></tr>
<tr><td>17</td><td>Wisconsin</td><td>84.0</td><td>49</td><td>Mississippi</td><td>51.8</td></tr>
<tr><td>8</td><td>Wyoming</td><td>91.1</td><td>50</td><td>Hawaii</td><td>28.9</td></tr>
<tr><td></td><td></td><td></td><td></td><td>District of Columbia</td><td>33.6</td></tr>
</table>

Source: CQ Press using data from U.S. Department of Health and Human Services, National Center for Health Statistics
"National Vital Statistics Reports" (Vol. 57, No. 7, January 7, 2009, http://www.cdc.gov/nchs/births.htm)
*Final data by state of residence. By race of mother.

Births to Black Women in 2006

National Total = 666,481 Live Births to Black Women*

RANK	STATE (ALPHA ORDER)	BIRTHS	% of USA
17	Alabama	19,408	2.9%
42	Alaska	438	0.1%
29	Arizona	4,075	0.6%
22	Arkansas	7,952	1.2%
5	California	34,284	5.1%
32	Colorado	3,148	0.5%
25	Connecticut	5,619	0.8%
33	Delaware	3,076	0.5%
1	Florida	56,904	8.5%
3	Georgia	49,439	7.4%
39	Hawaii	611	0.1%
46	Idaho	147	0.0%
6	Illinois	31,583	4.7%
20	Indiana	10,449	1.6%
35	Iowa	1,622	0.2%
31	Kansas	3,169	0.5%
26	Kentucky	5,465	0.8%
11	Louisiana	24,588	3.7%
43	Maine	299	0.0%
8	Maryland	28,181	4.2%
21	Massachusetts	9,390	1.4%
13	Michigan	23,085	3.5%
23	Minnesota	7,570	1.1%
15	Mississippi	21,089	3.2%
19	Missouri	12,470	1.9%
50	Montana	63	0.0%
34	Nebraska	1,885	0.3%
30	Nevada	3,566	0.5%
44	New Hampshire	263	0.0%
16	New Jersey	20,994	3.1%
40	New Mexico	601	0.1%
2	New York	54,467	8.2%
7	North Carolina	29,959	4.5%
47	North Dakota	133	0.0%
9	Ohio	25,436	3.8%
27	Oklahoma	5,002	0.8%
37	Oregon	1,154	0.2%
10	Pennsylvania	25,046	3.8%
36	Rhode Island	1,194	0.2%
14	South Carolina	21,514	3.2%
45	South Dakota	219	0.0%
18	Tennessee	18,363	2.8%
4	Texas	49,205	7.4%
41	Utah	518	0.1%
48	Vermont	80	0.0%
12	Virginia	24,394	3.7%
28	Washington	4,747	0.7%
38	West Virginia	700	0.1%
24	Wisconsin	7,112	1.1%
49	Wyoming	66	0.0%

RANK	STATE (RANK ORDER)	BIRTHS	% of USA
1	Florida	56,904	8.5%
2	New York	54,467	8.2%
3	Georgia	49,439	7.4%
4	Texas	49,205	7.4%
5	California	34,284	5.1%
6	Illinois	31,583	4.7%
7	North Carolina	29,959	4.5%
8	Maryland	28,181	4.2%
9	Ohio	25,436	3.8%
10	Pennsylvania	25,046	3.8%
11	Louisiana	24,588	3.7%
12	Virginia	24,394	3.7%
13	Michigan	23,085	3.5%
14	South Carolina	21,514	3.2%
15	Mississippi	21,089	3.2%
16	New Jersey	20,994	3.1%
17	Alabama	19,408	2.9%
18	Tennessee	18,363	2.8%
19	Missouri	12,470	1.9%
20	Indiana	10,449	1.6%
21	Massachusetts	9,390	1.4%
22	Arkansas	7,952	1.2%
23	Minnesota	7,570	1.1%
24	Wisconsin	7,112	1.1%
25	Connecticut	5,619	0.8%
26	Kentucky	5,465	0.8%
27	Oklahoma	5,002	0.8%
28	Washington	4,747	0.7%
29	Arizona	4,075	0.6%
30	Nevada	3,566	0.5%
31	Kansas	3,169	0.5%
32	Colorado	3,148	0.5%
33	Delaware	3,076	0.5%
34	Nebraska	1,885	0.3%
35	Iowa	1,622	0.2%
36	Rhode Island	1,194	0.2%
37	Oregon	1,154	0.2%
38	West Virginia	700	0.1%
39	Hawaii	611	0.1%
40	New Mexico	601	0.1%
41	Utah	518	0.1%
42	Alaska	438	0.1%
43	Maine	299	0.0%
44	New Hampshire	263	0.0%
45	South Dakota	219	0.0%
46	Idaho	147	0.0%
47	North Dakota	133	0.0%
48	Vermont	80	0.0%
49	Wyoming	66	0.0%
50	Montana	63	0.0%
	District of Columbia	5,739	0.9%

Source: U.S. Department of Health and Human Services, National Center for Health Statistics
"National Vital Statistics Reports" (Vol. 57, No. 7, January 7, 2009, http://www.cdc.gov/nchs/births.htm)
*Final data by state of residence. By race of mother.

Black Births as a Percent of All Births in 2006

National Percent = 15.4% of Live Births*

ALPHA ORDER

RANK	STATE	PERCENT
6	Alabama	29.8
35	Alaska	4.0
37	Arizona	3.9
13	Arkansas	19.4
32	California	6.1
34	Colorado	4.4
20	Connecticut	13.5
7	Delaware	26.1
8	Florida	23.8
5	Georgia	33.6
39	Hawaii	3.2
49	Idaho	0.6
16	Illinois	17.3
23	Indiana	11.6
35	Iowa	4.0
30	Kansas	7.5
27	Kentucky	9.2
2	Louisiana	37.7
41	Maine	2.1
3	Maryland	35.5
21	Massachusetts	12.1
14	Michigan	18.3
24	Minnesota	10.3
1	Mississippi	45.2
19	Missouri	15.2
50	Montana	0.5
31	Nebraska	7.0
29	Nevada	8.7
43	New Hampshire	1.8
15	New Jersey	18.2
42	New Mexico	2.0
12	New York	21.1
9	North Carolina	22.8
45	North Dakota	1.5
17	Ohio	16.9
28	Oklahoma	9.0
40	Oregon	2.4
18	Pennsylvania	16.7
26	Rhode Island	9.5
4	South Carolina	34.2
43	South Dakota	1.8
11	Tennessee	21.4
21	Texas	12.1
47	Utah	0.9
46	Vermont	1.2
10	Virginia	22.3
33	Washington	5.3
38	West Virginia	3.3
25	Wisconsin	9.8
48	Wyoming	0.8

RANK ORDER

RANK	STATE	PERCENT
1	Mississippi	45.2
2	Louisiana	37.7
3	Maryland	35.5
4	South Carolina	34.2
5	Georgia	33.6
6	Alabama	29.8
7	Delaware	26.1
8	Florida	23.8
9	North Carolina	22.8
10	Virginia	22.3
11	Tennessee	21.4
12	New York	21.1
13	Arkansas	19.4
14	Michigan	18.3
15	New Jersey	18.2
16	Illinois	17.3
17	Ohio	16.9
18	Pennsylvania	16.7
19	Missouri	15.2
20	Connecticut	13.5
21	Massachusetts	12.1
21	Texas	12.1
23	Indiana	11.6
24	Minnesota	10.3
25	Wisconsin	9.8
26	Rhode Island	9.5
27	Kentucky	9.2
28	Oklahoma	9.0
29	Nevada	8.7
30	Kansas	7.5
31	Nebraska	7.0
32	California	6.1
33	Washington	5.3
34	Colorado	4.4
35	Alaska	4.0
35	Iowa	4.0
37	Arizona	3.9
38	West Virginia	3.3
39	Hawaii	3.2
40	Oregon	2.4
41	Maine	2.1
42	New Mexico	2.0
43	New Hampshire	1.8
43	South Dakota	1.8
45	North Dakota	1.5
46	Vermont	1.2
47	Utah	0.9
48	Wyoming	0.8
49	Idaho	0.6
50	Montana	0.5

District of Columbia	75.2

Source: CQ Press using data from U.S. Department of Health and Human Services, National Center for Health Statistics
"National Vital Statistics Reports" (Vol. 57, No. 7, January 7, 2009, http://www.cdc.gov/nchs/births.htm)
*Final data by state of residence. By race of mother.

Births to Hispanic Women in 2006

National Total = 1,039,077 Live Births to Hispanic Women*

ALPHA ORDER					RANK ORDER			
RANK	STATE	BIRTHS	% of USA		RANK	STATE	BIRTHS	% of USA
30	Alabama	4,724	0.5%		1	California	293,322	28.2%
43	Alaska	752	0.1%		2	Texas	198,259	19.1%
5	Arizona	45,521	4.4%		3	Florida	70,059	6.7%
32	Arkansas	4,397	0.4%		4	New York	59,331	5.7%
1	California	293,322	28.2%		5	Arizona	45,521	4.4%
9	Colorado	22,813	2.2%		6	Illinois	44,342	4.3%
20	Connecticut	8,485	0.8%		7	New Jersey	29,210	2.8%
40	Delaware	1,883	0.2%		8	Georgia	23,657	2.3%
3	Florida	70,059	6.7%		9	Colorado	22,813	2.2%
8	Georgia	23,657	2.3%		10	North Carolina	21,217	2.0%
36	Hawaii	3,039	0.3%		11	New Mexico	16,514	1.6%
34	Idaho	3,792	0.4%		12	Washington	15,796	1.5%
6	Illinois	44,342	4.3%		13	Nevada	15,600	1.5%
21	Indiana	8,454	0.8%		14	Virginia	14,467	1.4%
35	Iowa	3,226	0.3%		15	Pennsylvania	13,279	1.3%
27	Kansas	6,587	0.6%		16	Massachusetts	10,749	1.0%
37	Kentucky	2,774	0.3%		17	Maryland	10,087	1.0%
39	Louisiana	2,344	0.2%		18	Oregon	9,939	1.0%
49	Maine	218	0.0%		19	Michigan	8,682	0.8%
17	Maryland	10,087	1.0%		20	Connecticut	8,485	0.8%
16	Massachusetts	10,749	1.0%		21	Indiana	8,454	0.8%
19	Michigan	8,682	0.8%		22	Utah	8,224	0.8%
28	Minnesota	6,027	0.6%		23	Tennessee	7,939	0.8%
41	Mississippi	1,556	0.1%		24	Oklahoma	7,065	0.7%
31	Missouri	4,556	0.4%		25	Wisconsin	6,870	0.7%
45	Montana	401	0.0%		26	Ohio	6,737	0.6%
33	Nebraska	3,999	0.4%		27	Kansas	6,587	0.6%
13	Nevada	15,600	1.5%		28	Minnesota	6,027	0.6%
44	New Hampshire	585	0.1%		29	South Carolina	5,874	0.6%
7	New Jersey	29,210	2.8%		30	Alabama	4,724	0.5%
11	New Mexico	16,514	1.6%		31	Missouri	4,556	0.4%
4	New York	59,331	5.7%		32	Arkansas	4,397	0.4%
10	North Carolina	21,217	2.0%		33	Nebraska	3,999	0.4%
47	North Dakota	249	0.0%		34	Idaho	3,792	0.4%
26	Ohio	6,737	0.6%		35	Iowa	3,226	0.3%
24	Oklahoma	7,065	0.7%		36	Hawaii	3,039	0.3%
18	Oregon	9,939	1.0%		37	Kentucky	2,774	0.3%
15	Pennsylvania	13,279	1.3%		38	Rhode Island	2,557	0.2%
38	Rhode Island	2,557	0.2%		39	Louisiana	2,344	0.2%
29	South Carolina	5,874	0.6%		40	Delaware	1,883	0.2%
45	South Dakota	401	0.0%		41	Mississippi	1,556	0.1%
23	Tennessee	7,939	0.8%		42	Wyoming	896	0.1%
2	Texas	198,259	19.1%		43	Alaska	752	0.1%
22	Utah	8,224	0.8%		44	New Hampshire	585	0.1%
50	Vermont	74	0.0%		45	Montana	401	0.0%
14	Virginia	14,467	1.4%		45	South Dakota	401	0.0%
12	Washington	15,796	1.5%		47	North Dakota	249	0.0%
48	West Virginia	219	0.0%		48	West Virginia	219	0.0%
25	Wisconsin	6,870	0.7%		49	Maine	218	0.0%
42	Wyoming	896	0.1%		50	Vermont	74	0.0%
						District of Columbia	1,329	0.1%

Source: U.S. Department of Health and Human Services, National Center for Health Statistics
"National Vital Statistics Reports" (Vol. 57, No. 7, January 7, 2009, http://www.cdc.gov/nchs/births.htm)
*Final data by state of residence. By race of mother. Persons of Hispanic origin may be of any race.

Hispanic Births as a Percent of All Births in 2006

National Percent = 24.1% of Live Births*

ALPHA ORDER

RANK	STATE	PERCENT
36	Alabama	7.2
38	Alaska	6.8
4	Arizona	43.9
28	Arkansas	10.7
2	California	51.8
6	Colorado	32.1
12	Connecticut	20.4
17	Delaware	16.0
7	Florida	29.3
16	Georgia	16.1
18	Hawaii	15.9
20	Idaho	15.1
9	Illinois	24.3
29	Indiana	9.4
35	Iowa	7.9
19	Kansas	15.6
40	Kentucky	4.7
43	Louisiana	3.6
48	Maine	1.5
26	Maryland	12.7
23	Massachusetts	13.8
37	Michigan	6.9
34	Minnesota	8.2
44	Mississippi	3.3
39	Missouri	5.6
45	Montana	3.2
22	Nebraska	14.8
5	Nevada	38.0
42	New Hampshire	4.1
8	New Jersey	25.3
1	New Mexico	54.3
10	New York	23.0
15	North Carolina	16.2
47	North Dakota	2.8
41	Ohio	4.5
25	Oklahoma	12.8
13	Oregon	20.3
33	Pennsylvania	8.9
11	Rhode Island	20.5
31	South Carolina	9.3
45	South Dakota	3.2
32	Tennessee	9.2
3	Texas	48.9
21	Utah	15.0
49	Vermont	1.1
24	Virginia	13.2
14	Washington	17.7
50	West Virginia	1.0
29	Wisconsin	9.4
27	Wyoming	11.4

RANK ORDER

RANK	STATE	PERCENT
1	New Mexico	54.3
2	California	51.8
3	Texas	48.9
4	Arizona	43.9
5	Nevada	38.0
6	Colorado	32.1
7	Florida	29.3
8	New Jersey	25.3
9	Illinois	24.3
10	New York	23.0
11	Rhode Island	20.5
12	Connecticut	20.4
13	Oregon	20.3
14	Washington	17.7
15	North Carolina	16.2
16	Georgia	16.1
17	Delaware	16.0
18	Hawaii	15.9
19	Kansas	15.6
20	Idaho	15.1
21	Utah	15.0
22	Nebraska	14.8
23	Massachusetts	13.8
24	Virginia	13.2
25	Oklahoma	12.8
26	Maryland	12.7
27	Wyoming	11.4
28	Arkansas	10.7
29	Indiana	9.4
29	Wisconsin	9.4
31	South Carolina	9.3
32	Tennessee	9.2
33	Pennsylvania	8.9
34	Minnesota	8.2
35	Iowa	7.9
36	Alabama	7.2
37	Michigan	6.9
38	Alaska	6.8
39	Missouri	5.6
40	Kentucky	4.7
41	Ohio	4.5
42	New Hampshire	4.1
43	Louisiana	3.6
44	Mississippi	3.3
45	Montana	3.2
45	South Dakota	3.2
47	North Dakota	2.8
48	Maine	1.5
49	Vermont	1.1
50	West Virginia	1.0

District of Columbia 17.4

Source: CQ Press using data from U.S. Department of Health and Human Services, National Center for Health Statistics
    "National Vital Statistics Reports" (Vol. 57, No. 7, January 7, 2009, http://www.cdc.gov/nchs/births.htm)
*Final data by state of residence. By race of mother. Persons of Hispanic origin may be of any race.

Births of Low Birthweight in 2006

National Total = 351,974 Live Births*

ALPHA ORDER RANK	STATE	BIRTHS	% of USA	RANK ORDER RANK	STATE	BIRTHS	% of USA
18	Alabama	6,624	1.9%	1	California	38,411	10.9%
48	Alaska	654	0.2%	2	Texas	33,727	9.6%
14	Arizona	7,289	2.1%	3	New York	20,790	5.9%
29	Arkansas	3,749	1.1%	4	Florida	20,614	5.9%
1	California	38,411	10.9%	5	Illinois	15,577	4.4%
20	Colorado	6,317	1.8%	6	Georgia	14,232	4.0%
31	Connecticut	3,395	1.0%	7	Ohio	13,180	3.7%
41	Delaware	1,108	0.3%	8	Pennsylvania	12,562	3.6%
4	Florida	20,614	5.9%	9	North Carolina	11,585	3.3%
6	Georgia	14,232	4.0%	10	Michigan	10,637	3.0%
40	Hawaii	1,531	0.4%	11	New Jersey	9,882	2.8%
39	Idaho	1,671	0.5%	12	Virginia	8,914	2.5%
5	Illinois	15,577	4.4%	13	Tennessee	8,108	2.3%
16	Indiana	7,268	2.1%	14	Arizona	7,289	2.1%
35	Iowa	2,809	0.8%	15	Maryland	7,269	2.1%
34	Kansas	2,933	0.8%	16	Indiana	7,268	2.1%
25	Kentucky	5,327	1.5%	17	Louisiana	7,231	2.1%
17	Louisiana	7,231	2.1%	18	Alabama	6,624	1.9%
44	Maine	967	0.3%	19	Missouri	6,555	1.9%
15	Maryland	7,269	2.1%	20	Colorado	6,317	1.8%
22	Massachusetts	6,138	1.7%	21	South Carolina	6,292	1.8%
10	Michigan	10,637	3.0%	22	Massachusetts	6,138	1.7%
27	Minnesota	4,807	1.4%	23	Mississippi	5,698	1.6%
23	Mississippi	5,698	1.6%	24	Washington	5,641	1.6%
19	Missouri	6,555	1.9%	25	Kentucky	5,327	1.5%
45	Montana	912	0.3%	26	Wisconsin	4,974	1.4%
38	Nebraska	1,900	0.5%	27	Minnesota	4,807	1.4%
32	Nevada	3,335	0.9%	28	Oklahoma	4,503	1.3%
42	New Hampshire	994	0.3%	29	Arkansas	3,749	1.1%
11	New Jersey	9,882	2.8%	30	Utah	3,700	1.1%
36	New Mexico	2,668	0.8%	31	Connecticut	3,395	1.0%
3	New York	20,790	5.9%	32	Nevada	3,335	0.9%
9	North Carolina	11,585	3.3%	33	Oregon	2,963	0.8%
49	North Dakota	576	0.2%	34	Kansas	2,933	0.8%
7	Ohio	13,180	3.7%	35	Iowa	2,809	0.8%
28	Oklahoma	4,503	1.3%	36	New Mexico	2,668	0.8%
33	Oregon	2,963	0.8%	37	West Virginia	2,024	0.6%
8	Pennsylvania	12,562	3.6%	38	Nebraska	1,900	0.5%
43	Rhode Island	988	0.3%	39	Idaho	1,671	0.5%
21	South Carolina	6,292	1.8%	40	Hawaii	1,531	0.4%
46	South Dakota	836	0.2%	41	Delaware	1,108	0.3%
13	Tennessee	8,108	2.3%	42	New Hampshire	994	0.3%
2	Texas	33,727	9.6%	43	Rhode Island	988	0.3%
30	Utah	3,700	1.1%	44	Maine	967	0.3%
50	Vermont	447	0.1%	45	Montana	912	0.3%
12	Virginia	8,914	2.5%	46	South Dakota	836	0.2%
24	Washington	5,641	1.6%	47	Wyoming	682	0.2%
37	West Virginia	2,024	0.6%	48	Alaska	654	0.2%
26	Wisconsin	4,974	1.4%	49	North Dakota	576	0.2%
47	Wyoming	682	0.2%	50	Vermont	447	0.1%
					District of Columbia	980	0.3%

Source: U.S. Department of Health and Human Services, National Center for Health Statistics
"National Vital Statistics Reports" (Vol. 57, No. 7, January 7, 2009, http://www.cdc.gov/nchs/births.htm)
*Final data by state of residence. Births of less than 2,500 grams (5 pounds 8 ounces).

Births of Low Birthweight as a Percent of All Births in 2006

National Percent = 8.3% of Live Births*

ALPHA ORDER				RANK ORDER		
RANK	STATE	PERCENT		RANK	STATE	PERCENT
3	Alabama	10.5		1	Mississippi	12.4
50	Alaska	0.0		2	Louisiana	11.4
35	Arizona	7.1		3	Alabama	10.5
10	Arkansas	9.2		4	South Carolina	10.1
44	California	6.8		5	West Virginia	9.7
13	Colorado	8.9		6	Georgia	9.6
28	Connecticut	8.1		6	Tennessee	9.6
9	Delaware	9.3		8	Maryland	9.4
17	Florida	8.7		9	Delaware	9.3
6	Georgia	9.6		10	Arkansas	9.2
28	Hawaii	8.1		11	Kentucky	9.1
38	Idaho	6.9		11	North Carolina	9.1
18	Illinois	8.6		13	Colorado	8.9
27	Indiana	8.2		13	New Mexico	8.9
38	Iowa	6.9		13	Wyoming	8.9
34	Kansas	7.2		16	Ohio	8.8
11	Kentucky	9.1		17	Florida	8.7
2	Louisiana	11.4		18	Illinois	8.6
44	Maine	6.8		18	New Jersey	8.6
8	Maryland	9.4		20	Pennsylvania	8.5
32	Massachusetts	7.9		21	Michigan	8.4
21	Michigan	8.4		21	Texas	8.4
47	Minnesota	6.5		23	Nevada	8.3
1	Mississippi	12.4		23	New York	8.3
28	Missouri	8.1		23	Oklahoma	8.3
33	Montana	7.3		23	Virginia	8.3
35	Nebraska	7.1		27	Indiana	8.2
23	Nevada	8.3		28	Connecticut	8.1
38	New Hampshire	6.9		28	Hawaii	8.1
18	New Jersey	8.6		28	Missouri	8.1
13	New Mexico	8.9		31	Rhode Island	8.0
23	New York	8.3		32	Massachusetts	7.9
11	North Carolina	9.1		33	Montana	7.3
46	North Dakota	6.7		34	Kansas	7.2
16	Ohio	8.8		35	Arizona	7.1
23	Oklahoma	8.3		35	Nebraska	7.1
49	Oregon	6.1		37	South Dakota	7.0
20	Pennsylvania	8.5		38	Idaho	6.9
31	Rhode Island	8.0		38	Iowa	6.9
4	South Carolina	10.1		38	New Hampshire	6.9
37	South Dakota	7.0		38	Utah	6.9
6	Tennessee	9.6		38	Vermont	6.9
21	Texas	8.4		38	Wisconsin	6.9
38	Utah	6.9		44	California	6.8
38	Vermont	6.9		44	Maine	6.8
23	Virginia	8.3		46	North Dakota	6.7
47	Washington	6.5		47	Minnesota	6.5
5	West Virginia	9.7		47	Washington	6.5
38	Wisconsin	6.9		49	Oregon	6.1
13	Wyoming	8.9		50	Alaska	0.0
					District of Columbia	11.5

Source: U.S. Department of Health and Human Services, National Center for Health Statistics
"National Vital Statistics Reports" (Vol. 57, No. 7, January 7, 2009, http://www.cdc.gov/nchs/births.htm)
*Final data by state of residence. Births of less than 2,500 grams (5 pounds 8 ounces).

Births of Low Birthweight to White Women in 2006

National Total = 168,871 Live Births*

RANK	STATE	BIRTHS	% of USA
22	Alabama	3,251	1.9%
49	Alaska	377	0.2%
24	Arizona	2,930	1.7%
30	Arkansas	2,192	1.3%
2	California	10,056	6.0%
18	Colorado	3,654	2.2%
35	Connecticut	1,782	1.1%
45	Delaware	506	0.3%
5	Florida	8,134	4.8%
10	Georgia	5,234	3.1%
50	Hawaii	269	0.2%
37	Idaho	1,368	0.8%
7	Illinois	7,033	4.2%
11	Indiana	5,114	3.0%
29	Iowa	2,339	1.4%
31	Kansas	2,047	1.2%
15	Kentucky	4,275	2.5%
23	Louisiana	2,994	1.8%
39	Maine	901	0.5%
25	Maryland	2,807	1.7%
17	Massachusetts	3,855	2.3%
8	Michigan	6,144	3.6%
21	Minnesota	3,264	1.9%
33	Mississippi	2,006	1.2%
14	Missouri	4,439	2.6%
42	Montana	716	0.4%
38	Nebraska	1,313	0.8%
36	Nevada	1,400	0.8%
40	New Hampshire	875	0.5%
16	New Jersey	4,241	2.5%
41	New Mexico	744	0.4%
4	New York	8,853	5.2%
9	North Carolina	5,547	3.3%
46	North Dakota	478	0.3%
3	Ohio	8,860	5.2%
27	Oklahoma	2,757	1.6%
32	Oregon	2,016	1.2%
6	Pennsylvania	7,875	4.7%
47	Rhode Island	473	0.3%
28	South Carolina	2,674	1.6%
43	South Dakota	617	0.4%
12	Tennessee	4,823	2.9%
1	Texas	10,681	6.3%
26	Utah	2,805	1.7%
48	Vermont	413	0.2%
13	Virginia	4,446	2.6%
20	Washington	3,340	2.0%
34	West Virginia	1,877	1.1%
19	Wisconsin	3,356	2.0%
44	Wyoming	564	0.3%

RANK	STATE	BIRTHS	% of USA
1	Texas	10,681	6.3%
2	California	10,056	6.0%
3	Ohio	8,860	5.2%
4	New York	8,853	5.2%
5	Florida	8,134	4.8%
6	Pennsylvania	7,875	4.7%
7	Illinois	7,033	4.2%
8	Michigan	6,144	3.6%
9	North Carolina	5,547	3.3%
10	Georgia	5,234	3.1%
11	Indiana	5,114	3.0%
12	Tennessee	4,823	2.9%
13	Virginia	4,446	2.6%
14	Missouri	4,439	2.6%
15	Kentucky	4,275	2.5%
16	New Jersey	4,241	2.5%
17	Massachusetts	3,855	2.3%
18	Colorado	3,654	2.2%
19	Wisconsin	3,356	2.0%
20	Washington	3,340	2.0%
21	Minnesota	3,264	1.9%
22	Alabama	3,251	1.9%
23	Louisiana	2,994	1.8%
24	Arizona	2,930	1.7%
25	Maryland	2,807	1.7%
26	Utah	2,805	1.7%
27	Oklahoma	2,757	1.6%
28	South Carolina	2,674	1.6%
29	Iowa	2,339	1.4%
30	Arkansas	2,192	1.3%
31	Kansas	2,047	1.2%
32	Oregon	2,016	1.2%
33	Mississippi	2,006	1.2%
34	West Virginia	1,877	1.1%
35	Connecticut	1,782	1.1%
36	Nevada	1,400	0.8%
37	Idaho	1,368	0.8%
38	Nebraska	1,313	0.8%
39	Maine	901	0.5%
40	New Hampshire	875	0.5%
41	New Mexico	744	0.4%
42	Montana	716	0.4%
43	South Dakota	617	0.4%
44	Wyoming	564	0.3%
45	Delaware	506	0.3%
46	North Dakota	478	0.3%
47	Rhode Island	473	0.3%
48	Vermont	413	0.2%
49	Alaska	377	0.2%
50	Hawaii	269	0.2%
	District of Columbia	156	0.1%

Source: U.S. Department of Health and Human Services, National Center for Health Statistics
"National Vital Statistics Reports" (Vol. 57, No. 7, January 7, 2009, http://www.cdc.gov/nchs/births.htm)
*Final data by state of residence. Births of less than 2,500 grams (5 pounds 8 ounces). Includes only non-Hispanic whites.

Births of Low Birthweight to White Women
as a Percent of All Births to White Women in 2006
National Percent = 7.3% of Live Births to White Women*

RANK	STATE	PERCENT
7	Alabama	8.5
46	Alaska	6.0
35	Arizona	6.8
11	Arkansas	7.9
44	California	6.4
4	Colorado	8.7
33	Connecticut	6.9
15	Delaware	7.7
18	Florida	7.6
22	Georgia	7.5
50	Hawaii	5.9
32	Idaho	7.0
23	Illinois	7.4
18	Indiana	7.6
35	Iowa	6.8
33	Kansas	6.9
4	Kentucky	8.7
7	Louisiana	8.5
35	Maine	6.8
18	Maryland	7.6
27	Massachusetts	7.2
28	Michigan	7.1
46	Minnesota	6.0
3	Mississippi	8.9
28	Missouri	7.1
26	Montana	7.3
42	Nebraska	6.6
10	Nevada	8.3
35	New Hampshire	6.8
23	New Jersey	7.4
4	New Mexico	8.7
28	New York	7.1
13	North Carolina	7.8
39	North Dakota	6.7
15	Ohio	7.7
11	Oklahoma	7.9
46	Oregon	6.0
23	Pennsylvania	7.4
15	Rhode Island	7.7
13	South Carolina	7.8
39	South Dakota	6.7
9	Tennessee	8.4
18	Texas	7.6
42	Utah	6.6
39	Vermont	6.7
28	Virginia	7.1
46	Washington	6.0
1	West Virginia	9.5
45	Wisconsin	6.2
2	Wyoming	9.1

RANK	STATE	PERCENT
1	West Virginia	9.5
2	Wyoming	9.1
3	Mississippi	8.9
4	Colorado	8.7
4	Kentucky	8.7
4	New Mexico	8.7
7	Alabama	8.5
7	Louisiana	8.5
9	Tennessee	8.4
10	Nevada	8.3
11	Arkansas	7.9
11	Oklahoma	7.9
13	North Carolina	7.8
13	South Carolina	7.8
15	Delaware	7.7
15	Ohio	7.7
15	Rhode Island	7.7
18	Florida	7.6
18	Indiana	7.6
18	Maryland	7.6
18	Texas	7.6
22	Georgia	7.5
23	Illinois	7.4
23	New Jersey	7.4
23	Pennsylvania	7.4
26	Montana	7.3
27	Massachusetts	7.2
28	Michigan	7.1
28	Missouri	7.1
28	New York	7.1
28	Virginia	7.1
32	Idaho	7.0
33	Connecticut	6.9
33	Kansas	6.9
35	Arizona	6.8
35	Iowa	6.8
35	Maine	6.8
35	New Hampshire	6.8
39	North Dakota	6.7
39	South Dakota	6.7
39	Vermont	6.7
42	Nebraska	6.6
42	Utah	6.6
44	California	6.4
45	Wisconsin	6.2
46	Alaska	6.0
46	Minnesota	6.0
46	Oregon	6.0
46	Washington	6.0
50	Hawaii	5.9

	District of Columbia	7.3

Source: U.S. Department of Health and Human Services, National Center for Health Statistics
"National Vital Statistics Reports" (Vol. 57, No. 7, January 7, 2009, http://www.cdc.gov/nchs/births.htm)
*Final data by state of residence. Births of less than 2,500 grams (5 pounds 8 ounces). Includes only non-Hispanic whites.

Births of Low Birthweight to Black Women in 2006

National Total = 86,122 Live Births*

RANK	STATE	BIRTHS	% of USA
15	Alabama	3,001	3.5%
42	Alaska	38	0.0%
30	Arizona	459	0.5%
21	Arkansas	1,172	1.4%
8	California	3,850	4.5%
29	Colorado	467	0.5%
27	Connecticut	646	0.8%
31	Delaware	442	0.5%
2	Florida	6,862	8.0%
1	Georgia	7,021	8.2%
40	Hawaii	51	0.1%
46	Idaho	17	0.0%
5	Illinois	4,474	5.2%
20	Indiana	1,459	1.7%
35	Iowa	168	0.2%
33	Kansas	371	0.4%
24	Kentucky	769	0.9%
7	Louisiana	3,934	4.6%
45	Maine	22	0.0%
11	Maryland	3,393	3.9%
23	Massachusetts	859	1.0%
12	Michigan	3,224	3.7%
26	Minnesota	651	0.8%
9	Mississippi	3,514	4.1%
19	Missouri	1,673	1.9%
50	Montana	3	0.0%
34	Nebraska	239	0.3%
28	Nevada	470	0.5%
44	New Hampshire	23	0.0%
18	New Jersey	2,464	2.9%
39	New Mexico	76	0.1%
4	New York	5,343	6.2%
6	North Carolina	4,218	4.9%
48	North Dakota	9	0.0%
10	Ohio	3,432	4.0%
25	Oklahoma	753	0.9%
38	Oregon	93	0.1%
16	Pennsylvania	2,877	3.3%
36	Rhode Island	115	0.1%
13	South Carolina	3,099	3.6%
43	South Dakota	24	0.0%
17	Tennessee	2,578	3.0%
3	Texas	6,518	7.6%
40	Utah	51	0.1%
47	Vermont	10	0.0%
14	Virginia	3,031	3.5%
32	Washington	399	0.5%
37	West Virginia	112	0.1%
22	Wisconsin	938	1.1%
49	Wyoming	7	0.0%

RANK	STATE	BIRTHS	% of USA
1	Georgia	7,021	8.2%
2	Florida	6,862	8.0%
3	Texas	6,518	7.6%
4	New York	5,343	6.2%
5	Illinois	4,474	5.2%
6	North Carolina	4,218	4.9%
7	Louisiana	3,934	4.6%
8	California	3,850	4.5%
9	Mississippi	3,514	4.1%
10	Ohio	3,432	4.0%
11	Maryland	3,393	3.9%
12	Michigan	3,224	3.7%
13	South Carolina	3,099	3.6%
14	Virginia	3,031	3.5%
15	Alabama	3,001	3.5%
16	Pennsylvania	2,877	3.3%
17	Tennessee	2,578	3.0%
18	New Jersey	2,464	2.9%
19	Missouri	1,673	1.9%
20	Indiana	1,459	1.7%
21	Arkansas	1,172	1.4%
22	Wisconsin	938	1.1%
23	Massachusetts	859	1.0%
24	Kentucky	769	0.9%
25	Oklahoma	753	0.9%
26	Minnesota	651	0.8%
27	Connecticut	646	0.8%
28	Nevada	470	0.5%
29	Colorado	467	0.5%
30	Arizona	459	0.5%
31	Delaware	442	0.5%
32	Washington	399	0.5%
33	Kansas	371	0.4%
34	Nebraska	239	0.3%
35	Iowa	168	0.2%
36	Rhode Island	115	0.1%
37	West Virginia	112	0.1%
38	Oregon	93	0.1%
39	New Mexico	76	0.1%
40	Hawaii	51	0.1%
40	Utah	51	0.1%
42	Alaska	38	0.0%
43	South Dakota	24	0.0%
44	New Hampshire	23	0.0%
45	Maine	22	0.0%
46	Idaho	17	0.0%
47	Vermont	10	0.0%
48	North Dakota	9	0.0%
49	Wyoming	7	0.0%
50	Montana	3	0.0%
	District of Columbia	703	0.8%

Source: U.S. Department of Health and Human Services, National Center for Health Statistics
"National Vital Statistics Reports" (Vol. 57, No. 7, January 7, 2009, http://www.cdc.gov/nchs/births.htm)
*Final data by state of residence. Births of less than 2,500 grams (5 pounds 8 ounces). Includes only non-Hispanic blacks.

Births of Low Birthweight to Black Women
as a Percent of All Births to Black Women in 2006
National Percent = 14.0% of Live Births to Black Women*

RANK	STATE	PERCENT
5	Alabama	15.5
44	Alaska	9.6
30	Arizona	12.8
8	Arkansas	15.0
35	California	12.0
4	Colorado	15.7
32	Connecticut	12.5
11	Delaware	14.8
26	Florida	13.4
15	Georgia	14.4
43	Hawaii	10.2
NA	Idaho**	NA
16	Illinois	14.3
20	Indiana	14.1
41	Iowa	10.6
33	Kansas	12.4
13	Kentucky	14.6
3	Louisiana	16.2
45	Maine	7.5
26	Maryland	13.4
34	Massachusetts	12.1
17	Michigan	14.2
42	Minnesota	10.3
1	Mississippi	16.7
25	Missouri	13.6
NA	Montana**	NA
23	Nebraska	14.0
20	Nevada	14.1
39	New Hampshire	10.8
20	New Jersey	14.1
8	New Mexico	15.0
31	New York	12.6
17	North Carolina	14.2
NA	North Dakota**	NA
14	Ohio	14.5
6	Oklahoma	15.4
8	Oregon	15.0
23	Pennsylvania	14.0
36	Rhode Island	11.6
7	South Carolina	15.2
37	South Dakota	11.2
11	Tennessee	14.8
17	Texas	14.2
38	Utah	11.0
NA	Vermont**	NA
29	Virginia	13.0
40	Washington	10.7
2	West Virginia	16.3
26	Wisconsin	13.4
NA	Wyoming**	NA

RANK	STATE	PERCENT
1	Mississippi	16.7
2	West Virginia	16.3
3	Louisiana	16.2
4	Colorado	15.7
5	Alabama	15.5
6	Oklahoma	15.4
7	South Carolina	15.2
8	Arkansas	15.0
8	New Mexico	15.0
8	Oregon	15.0
11	Delaware	14.8
11	Tennessee	14.8
13	Kentucky	14.6
14	Ohio	14.5
15	Georgia	14.4
16	Illinois	14.3
17	Michigan	14.2
17	North Carolina	14.2
17	Texas	14.2
20	Indiana	14.1
20	Nevada	14.1
20	New Jersey	14.1
23	Nebraska	14.0
23	Pennsylvania	14.0
25	Missouri	13.6
26	Florida	13.4
26	Maryland	13.4
26	Wisconsin	13.4
29	Virginia	13.0
30	Arizona	12.8
31	New York	12.6
32	Connecticut	12.5
33	Kansas	12.4
34	Massachusetts	12.1
35	California	12.0
36	Rhode Island	11.6
37	South Dakota	11.2
38	Utah	11.0
39	New Hampshire	10.8
40	Washington	10.7
41	Iowa	10.6
42	Minnesota	10.3
43	Hawaii	10.2
44	Alaska	9.6
45	Maine	7.5
NA	Idaho**	NA
NA	Montana**	NA
NA	North Dakota**	NA
NA	Vermont**	NA
NA	Wyoming**	NA
	District of Columbia	14.5

Source: U.S. Department of Health and Human Services, National Center for Health Statistics
"National Vital Statistics Reports" (Vol. 57, No. 7, January 7, 2009, http://www.cdc.gov/nchs/births.htm)
*Final data by state of residence. Births of less than 2,500 grams (5 pounds 8 ounces). Includes only non-Hispanic blacks.
**Not available. Fewer than 20 births of low birthweight to black women.

Births of Low Birthweight to Hispanic Women in 2006

National Total = 72,538 Live Births*

ALPHA ORDER

RANK	STATE	BIRTHS	% of USA
31	Alabama	287	0.4%
44	Alaska	37	0.1%
6	Arizona	3,128	4.3%
30	Arkansas	303	0.4%
1	California	18,332	25.3%
8	Colorado	1,914	2.6%
17	Connecticut	747	1.0%
40	Delaware	117	0.2%
3	Florida	4,936	6.8%
10	Georgia	1,452	2.0%
34	Hawaii	238	0.3%
35	Idaho	232	0.3%
5	Illinois	3,180	4.4%
22	Indiana	564	0.8%
36	Iowa	205	0.3%
28	Kansas	371	0.5%
38	Kentucky	201	0.3%
39	Louisiana	169	0.2%
48	Maine	21	0.0%
18	Maryland	681	0.9%
15	Massachusetts	906	1.2%
20	Michigan	605	0.8%
29	Minnesota	357	0.5%
41	Mississippi	111	0.2%
32	Missouri	266	0.4%
46	Montana	27	0.0%
32	Nebraska	266	0.4%
13	Nevada	1,037	1.4%
43	New Hampshire	54	0.1%
7	New Jersey	2,197	3.0%
9	New Mexico	1,499	2.1%
4	New York	4,738	6.5%
11	North Carolina	1,315	1.8%
47	North Dakota	22	0.0%
24	Ohio	481	0.7%
25	Oklahoma	465	0.6%
21	Oregon	583	0.8%
12	Pennsylvania	1,148	1.6%
37	Rhode Island	204	0.3%
27	South Carolina	373	0.5%
45	South Dakota	33	0.0%
23	Tennessee	526	0.7%
2	Texas	15,139	20.9%
19	Utah	618	0.9%
50	Vermont	4	0.0%
16	Virginia	862	1.2%
14	Washington	987	1.4%
49	West Virginia	10	0.0%
26	Wisconsin	427	0.6%
42	Wyoming	61	0.1%

RANK ORDER

RANK	STATE	BIRTHS	% of USA
1	California	18,332	25.3%
2	Texas	15,139	20.9%
3	Florida	4,936	6.8%
4	New York	4,738	6.5%
5	Illinois	3,180	4.4%
6	Arizona	3,128	4.3%
7	New Jersey	2,197	3.0%
8	Colorado	1,914	2.6%
9	New Mexico	1,499	2.1%
10	Georgia	1,452	2.0%
11	North Carolina	1,315	1.8%
12	Pennsylvania	1,148	1.6%
13	Nevada	1,037	1.4%
14	Washington	987	1.4%
15	Massachusetts	906	1.2%
16	Virginia	862	1.2%
17	Connecticut	747	1.0%
18	Maryland	681	0.9%
19	Utah	618	0.9%
20	Michigan	605	0.8%
21	Oregon	583	0.8%
22	Indiana	564	0.8%
23	Tennessee	526	0.7%
24	Ohio	481	0.7%
25	Oklahoma	465	0.6%
26	Wisconsin	427	0.6%
27	South Carolina	373	0.5%
28	Kansas	371	0.5%
29	Minnesota	357	0.5%
30	Arkansas	303	0.4%
31	Alabama	287	0.4%
32	Missouri	266	0.4%
32	Nebraska	266	0.4%
34	Hawaii	238	0.3%
35	Idaho	232	0.3%
36	Iowa	205	0.3%
37	Rhode Island	204	0.3%
38	Kentucky	201	0.3%
39	Louisiana	169	0.2%
40	Delaware	117	0.2%
41	Mississippi	111	0.2%
42	Wyoming	61	0.1%
43	New Hampshire	54	0.1%
44	Alaska	37	0.1%
45	South Dakota	33	0.0%
46	Montana	27	0.0%
47	North Dakota	22	0.0%
48	Maine	21	0.0%
49	West Virginia	10	0.0%
50	Vermont	4	0.0%
	District of Columbia	102	0.1%

Source: U.S. Department of Health and Human Services, National Center for Health Statistics
"National Vital Statistics Reports" (Vol. 57, No. 7, January 7, 2009, http://www.cdc.gov/nchs/births.htm)
*Final data. Births of less than 2,500 grams (5 pounds 8 ounces). Hispanic can be of any race.

Births of Low Birthweight to Hispanic Women
as a Percent of All Births to Hispanic Women in 2006
National Percent = 7.0% of Live Births to Hispanic Women*

ALPHA ORDER				RANK ORDER		
RANK	STATE	PERCENT		RANK	STATE	PERCENT
40	Alabama	6.1		1	Maine	9.6
48	Alaska	4.9		2	New Hampshire	9.3
23	Arizona	6.9		3	New Mexico	9.1
23	Arkansas	6.9		4	Connecticut	8.8
35	California	6.3		4	North Dakota	8.8
7	Colorado	8.4		6	Pennsylvania	8.7
4	Connecticut	8.8		7	Colorado	8.4
37	Delaware	6.2		7	Massachusetts	8.4
21	Florida	7.0		9	South Dakota	8.3
40	Georgia	6.1		10	New York	8.0
12	Hawaii	7.8		10	Rhode Island	8.0
40	Idaho	6.1		12	Hawaii	7.8
16	Illinois	7.2		13	Texas	7.6
28	Indiana	6.7		14	New Jersey	7.5
33	Iowa	6.4		14	Utah	7.5
47	Kansas	5.6		16	Illinois	7.2
16	Kentucky	7.2		16	Kentucky	7.2
16	Louisiana	7.2		16	Louisiana	7.2
1	Maine	9.6		16	Ohio	7.2
25	Maryland	6.8		20	Mississippi	7.1
7	Massachusetts	8.4		21	Florida	7.0
21	Michigan	7.0		21	Michigan	7.0
44	Minnesota	5.9		23	Arizona	6.9
20	Mississippi	7.1		23	Arkansas	6.9
46	Missouri	5.8		25	Maryland	6.8
25	Montana	6.8		25	Montana	6.8
28	Nebraska	6.7		25	Wyoming	6.8
30	Nevada	6.6		28	Indiana	6.7
2	New Hampshire	9.3		28	Nebraska	6.7
14	New Jersey	7.5		30	Nevada	6.6
3	New Mexico	9.1		30	Oklahoma	6.6
10	New York	8.0		30	Tennessee	6.6
37	North Carolina	6.2		33	Iowa	6.4
4	North Dakota	8.8		33	South Carolina	6.4
16	Ohio	7.2		35	California	6.3
30	Oklahoma	6.6		35	Washington	6.3
44	Oregon	5.9		37	Delaware	6.2
6	Pennsylvania	8.7		37	North Carolina	6.2
10	Rhode Island	8.0		37	Wisconsin	6.2
33	South Carolina	6.4		40	Alabama	6.1
9	South Dakota	8.3		40	Georgia	6.1
30	Tennessee	6.6		40	Idaho	6.1
13	Texas	7.6		43	Virginia	6.0
14	Utah	7.5		44	Minnesota	5.9
NA	Vermont**	NA		44	Oregon	5.9
43	Virginia	6.0		46	Missouri	5.8
35	Washington	6.3		47	Kansas	5.6
NA	West Virginia**	NA		48	Alaska	4.9
37	Wisconsin	6.2		NA	Vermont**	NA
25	Wyoming	6.8		NA	West Virginia**	NA
					District of Columbia	7.7

Source: U.S. Department of Health and Human Services, National Center for Health Statistics
"National Vital Statistics Reports" (Vol. 57, No. 7, January 7, 2009, http://www.cdc.gov/nchs/births.htm)
*Final data. Births of less than 2,500 grams (5 pounds 8 ounces). Hispanic can be of any race.
**Not available. Fewer than 20 births of low birthweight to Hispanic women.

Births to Unmarried Women in 2006

National Total = 1,641,946 Live Births*

ALPHA ORDER

RANK	STATE	BIRTHS	% of USA
25	Alabama	23,163	1.4%
47	Alaska	4,047	0.2%
11	Arizona	45,089	2.7%
29	Arkansas	17,114	1.0%
1	California	211,501	12.9%
28	Colorado	19,535	1.2%
34	Connecticut	14,209	0.9%
41	Delaware	5,456	0.3%
3	Florida	105,111	6.4%
6	Georgia	62,996	3.8%
39	Hawaii	6,832	0.4%
40	Idaho	5,878	0.4%
5	Illinois	69,961	4.3%
13	Indiana	36,703	2.2%
35	Iowa	13,720	0.8%
33	Kansas	14,430	0.9%
27	Kentucky	20,562	1.3%
17	Louisiana	31,543	1.9%
42	Maine	5,253	0.3%
18	Maryland	30,730	1.9%
21	Massachusetts	24,984	1.5%
10	Michigan	48,880	3.0%
24	Minnesota	23,341	1.4%
23	Mississippi	24,330	1.5%
16	Missouri	32,009	1.9%
44	Montana	4,500	0.3%
37	Nebraska	8,631	0.5%
31	Nevada	16,525	1.0%
46	New Hampshire	4,231	0.3%
12	New Jersey	37,900	2.3%
32	New Mexico	15,323	0.9%
4	New York	100,115	6.1%
9	North Carolina	51,271	3.1%
48	North Dakota	2,732	0.2%
7	Ohio	61,008	3.7%
26	Oklahoma	22,090	1.3%
30	Oregon	16,703	1.0%
8	Pennsylvania	57,065	3.5%
43	Rhode Island	5,013	0.3%
19	South Carolina	28,365	1.7%
45	South Dakota	4,422	0.3%
15	Tennessee	34,944	2.1%
2	Texas	157,302	9.6%
36	Utah	10,071	0.6%
50	Vermont	2,244	0.1%
14	Virginia	36,415	2.2%
20	Washington	27,690	1.7%
38	West Virginia	7,937	0.5%
22	Wisconsin	24,636	1.5%
49	Wyoming	2,530	0.2%

RANK ORDER

RANK	STATE	BIRTHS	% of USA
1	California	211,501	12.9%
2	Texas	157,302	9.6%
3	Florida	105,111	6.4%
4	New York	100,115	6.1%
5	Illinois	69,961	4.3%
6	Georgia	62,996	3.8%
7	Ohio	61,008	3.7%
8	Pennsylvania	57,065	3.5%
9	North Carolina	51,271	3.1%
10	Michigan	48,880	3.0%
11	Arizona	45,089	2.7%
12	New Jersey	37,900	2.3%
13	Indiana	36,703	2.2%
14	Virginia	36,415	2.2%
15	Tennessee	34,944	2.1%
16	Missouri	32,009	1.9%
17	Louisiana	31,543	1.9%
18	Maryland	30,730	1.9%
19	South Carolina	28,365	1.7%
20	Washington	27,690	1.7%
21	Massachusetts	24,984	1.5%
22	Wisconsin	24,636	1.5%
23	Mississippi	24,330	1.5%
24	Minnesota	23,341	1.4%
25	Alabama	23,163	1.4%
26	Oklahoma	22,090	1.3%
27	Kentucky	20,562	1.3%
28	Colorado	19,535	1.2%
29	Arkansas	17,114	1.0%
30	Oregon	16,703	1.0%
31	Nevada	16,525	1.0%
32	New Mexico	15,323	0.9%
33	Kansas	14,430	0.9%
34	Connecticut	14,209	0.9%
35	Iowa	13,720	0.8%
36	Utah	10,071	0.6%
37	Nebraska	8,631	0.5%
38	West Virginia	7,937	0.5%
39	Hawaii	6,832	0.4%
40	Idaho	5,878	0.4%
41	Delaware	5,456	0.3%
42	Maine	5,253	0.3%
43	Rhode Island	5,013	0.3%
44	Montana	4,500	0.3%
45	South Dakota	4,422	0.3%
46	New Hampshire	4,231	0.3%
47	Alaska	4,047	0.2%
48	North Dakota	2,732	0.2%
49	Wyoming	2,530	0.2%
50	Vermont	2,244	0.1%
	District of Columbia	4,906	0.3%

Source: U.S. Department of Health and Human Services, National Center for Health Statistics
"National Vital Statistics Reports" (Vol. 57, No. 7, January 7, 2009, http://www.cdc.gov/nchs/births.htm)
*Final data by state of residence.

Births to Unmarried Women as a Percent of All Births in 2006

National Percent = 38.5% of Live Births*

ALPHA ORDER				RANK ORDER		
RANK	STATE	PERCENT		RANK	STATE	PERCENT
29	Alabama	36.6		1	Mississippi	52.8
28	Alaska	36.8		2	New Mexico	51.2
7	Arizona	44.0		3	Louisiana	49.8
9	Arkansas	41.8		4	South Carolina	45.6
25	California	37.6		5	Delaware	45.5
48	Colorado	27.6		6	Florida	44.4
37	Connecticut	34.0		7	Arizona	44.0
5	Delaware	45.5		8	Georgia	42.4
6	Florida	44.4		9	Arkansas	41.8
8	Georgia	42.4		10	Indiana	41.4
30	Hawaii	36.0		10	Tennessee	41.4
49	Idaho	24.3		12	Nevada	41.3
21	Illinois	38.7		13	Oklahoma	40.9
10	Indiana	41.4		14	Ohio	40.5
38	Iowa	33.8		14	Rhode Island	40.5
33	Kansas	35.2		16	North Carolina	40.1
32	Kentucky	35.3		17	New York	40.0
3	Louisiana	49.8		18	Maryland	39.7
26	Maine	37.1		19	Texas	39.4
18	Maryland	39.7		20	Missouri	39.3
43	Massachusetts	32.2		21	Illinois	38.7
22	Michigan	38.3		22	Michigan	38.3
45	Minnesota	31.7		22	Pennsylvania	38.3
1	Mississippi	52.8		24	West Virginia	37.9
20	Missouri	39.3		25	California	37.6
30	Montana	36.0		26	Maine	37.1
42	Nebraska	32.3		26	South Dakota	37.1
12	Nevada	41.3		28	Alaska	36.8
47	New Hampshire	29.4		29	Alabama	36.6
40	New Jersey	33.0		30	Hawaii	36.0
2	New Mexico	51.2		30	Montana	36.0
17	New York	40.0		32	Kentucky	35.3
16	North Carolina	40.1		33	Kansas	35.2
45	North Dakota	31.7		34	Vermont	34.5
14	Ohio	40.5		35	Oregon	34.3
13	Oklahoma	40.9		36	Wisconsin	34.1
35	Oregon	34.3		37	Connecticut	34.0
22	Pennsylvania	38.3		38	Iowa	33.8
14	Rhode Island	40.5		38	Virginia	33.8
4	South Carolina	45.6		40	New Jersey	33.0
26	South Dakota	37.1		40	Wyoming	33.0
10	Tennessee	41.4		42	Nebraska	32.3
19	Texas	39.4		43	Massachusetts	32.2
50	Utah	18.8		44	Washington	31.9
34	Vermont	34.5		45	Minnesota	31.7
38	Virginia	33.8		45	North Dakota	31.7
44	Washington	31.9		47	New Hampshire	29.4
24	West Virginia	37.9		48	Colorado	27.6
36	Wisconsin	34.1		49	Idaho	24.3
40	Wyoming	33.0		50	Utah	18.8
					District of Columbia	57.6

Source: U.S. Department of Health and Human Services, National Center for Health Statistics
"National Vital Statistics Reports" (Vol. 57, No. 7, January 7, 2009, http://www.cdc.gov/nchs/births.htm)
*Final data by state of residence.

Births to Unmarried White Women in 2006

National Total = 614,522 Live Births*

ALPHA ORDER

RANK	STATE	BIRTHS	% of USA
30	Alabama	8,473	1.4%
49	Alaska	1,535	0.2%
20	Arizona	12,108	2.0%
28	Arkansas	8,628	1.4%
3	California	35,506	5.8%
31	Colorado	7,950	1.3%
35	Connecticut	5,088	0.8%
45	Delaware	2,095	0.3%
4	Florida	35,027	5.7%
13	Georgia	17,364	2.8%
50	Hawaii	1,086	0.2%
39	Idaho	4,011	0.7%
9	Illinois	22,858	3.7%
8	Indiana	23,648	3.8%
23	Iowa	10,604	1.7%
29	Kansas	8,551	1.4%
14	Kentucky	15,234	2.5%
22	Louisiana	11,118	1.8%
38	Maine	4,941	0.8%
26	Maryland	9,016	1.5%
19	Massachusetts	12,602	2.1%
7	Michigan	25,033	4.1%
18	Minnesota	13,272	2.2%
33	Mississippi	6,438	1.0%
10	Missouri	19,637	3.2%
41	Montana	2,891	0.5%
36	Nebraska	5,067	0.8%
37	Nevada	5,013	0.8%
40	New Hampshire	3,751	0.6%
27	New Jersey	8,821	1.4%
42	New Mexico	2,611	0.4%
6	New York	28,392	4.6%
11	North Carolina	17,479	2.8%
47	North Dakota	1,782	0.3%
1	Ohio	37,756	6.1%
21	Oklahoma	11,542	1.9%
24	Oregon	10,317	1.7%
5	Pennsylvania	30,738	5.0%
46	Rhode Island	1,839	0.3%
25	South Carolina	9,751	1.6%
43	South Dakota	2,452	0.4%
12	Tennessee	17,379	2.8%
2	Texas	35,631	5.8%
34	Utah	5,485	0.9%
44	Vermont	2,146	0.3%
17	Virginia	13,552	2.2%
15	Washington	15,095	2.5%
32	West Virginia	7,261	1.2%
16	Wisconsin	14,042	2.3%
48	Wyoming	1,780	0.3%

RANK ORDER

RANK	STATE	BIRTHS	% of USA
1	Ohio	37,756	6.1%
2	Texas	35,631	5.8%
3	California	35,506	5.8%
4	Florida	35,027	5.7%
5	Pennsylvania	30,738	5.0%
6	New York	28,392	4.6%
7	Michigan	25,033	4.1%
8	Indiana	23,648	3.8%
9	Illinois	22,858	3.7%
10	Missouri	19,637	3.2%
11	North Carolina	17,479	2.8%
12	Tennessee	17,379	2.8%
13	Georgia	17,364	2.8%
14	Kentucky	15,234	2.5%
15	Washington	15,095	2.5%
16	Wisconsin	14,042	2.3%
17	Virginia	13,552	2.2%
18	Minnesota	13,272	2.2%
19	Massachusetts	12,602	2.1%
20	Arizona	12,108	2.0%
21	Oklahoma	11,542	1.9%
22	Louisiana	11,118	1.8%
23	Iowa	10,604	1.7%
24	Oregon	10,317	1.7%
25	South Carolina	9,751	1.6%
26	Maryland	9,016	1.5%
27	New Jersey	8,821	1.4%
28	Arkansas	8,628	1.4%
29	Kansas	8,551	1.4%
30	Alabama	8,473	1.4%
31	Colorado	7,950	1.3%
32	West Virginia	7,261	1.2%
33	Mississippi	6,438	1.0%
34	Utah	5,485	0.9%
35	Connecticut	5,088	0.8%
36	Nebraska	5,067	0.8%
37	Nevada	5,013	0.8%
38	Maine	4,941	0.8%
39	Idaho	4,011	0.7%
40	New Hampshire	3,751	0.6%
41	Montana	2,891	0.5%
42	New Mexico	2,611	0.4%
43	South Dakota	2,452	0.4%
44	Vermont	2,146	0.3%
45	Delaware	2,095	0.3%
46	Rhode Island	1,839	0.3%
47	North Dakota	1,782	0.3%
48	Wyoming	1,780	0.3%
49	Alaska	1,535	0.2%
50	Hawaii	1,086	0.2%
	District of Columbia	126	0.0%

Source: U.S. Department of Health and Human Services, National Center for Health Statistics
"National Vital Statistics Reports" (Vol. 57, No. 7, January 7, 2009, http://www.cdc.gov/nchs/births.htm)
*Final data by state of residence. By race of mother. Includes only non-Hispanic whites.

Births to Unmarried White Women
as a Percent of All Births to White Women in 2006
National Percent = 26.6% of Live Births*

ALPHA ORDER

RANK	STATE	PERCENT
44	Alabama	22.2
37	Alaska	24.4
27	Arizona	27.9
11	Arkansas	31.2
43	California	22.4
48	Colorado	18.9
47	Connecticut	19.8
8	Delaware	31.8
6	Florida	32.6
34	Georgia	25.0
40	Hawaii	23.7
46	Idaho	20.6
39	Illinois	24.0
3	Indiana	34.8
13	Iowa	30.7
21	Kansas	28.8
12	Kentucky	30.9
9	Louisiana	31.6
1	Maine	37.2
37	Maryland	24.4
41	Massachusetts	23.5
22	Michigan	28.7
35	Minnesota	24.6
26	Mississippi	28.4
9	Missouri	31.6
19	Montana	29.4
32	Nebraska	25.4
18	Nevada	29.8
20	New Hampshire	29.2
49	New Jersey	15.5
15	New Mexico	30.4
42	New York	22.6
36	North Carolina	24.5
33	North Dakota	25.1
6	Ohio	32.6
5	Oklahoma	33.1
14	Oregon	30.5
23	Pennsylvania	28.6
17	Rhode Island	30.1
25	South Carolina	28.5
29	South Dakota	26.7
15	Tennessee	30.4
31	Texas	25.5
50	Utah	13.0
4	Vermont	34.6
45	Virginia	21.7
28	Washington	26.8
2	West Virginia	36.7
30	Wisconsin	25.7
23	Wyoming	28.6

RANK ORDER

RANK	STATE	PERCENT
1	Maine	37.2
2	West Virginia	36.7
3	Indiana	34.8
4	Vermont	34.6
5	Oklahoma	33.1
6	Florida	32.6
6	Ohio	32.6
8	Delaware	31.8
9	Louisiana	31.6
9	Missouri	31.6
11	Arkansas	31.2
12	Kentucky	30.9
13	Iowa	30.7
14	Oregon	30.5
15	New Mexico	30.4
15	Tennessee	30.4
17	Rhode Island	30.1
18	Nevada	29.8
19	Montana	29.4
20	New Hampshire	29.2
21	Kansas	28.8
22	Michigan	28.7
23	Pennsylvania	28.6
23	Wyoming	28.6
25	South Carolina	28.5
26	Mississippi	28.4
27	Arizona	27.9
28	Washington	26.8
29	South Dakota	26.7
30	Wisconsin	25.7
31	Texas	25.5
32	Nebraska	25.4
33	North Dakota	25.1
34	Georgia	25.0
35	Minnesota	24.6
36	North Carolina	24.5
37	Alaska	24.4
37	Maryland	24.4
39	Illinois	24.0
40	Hawaii	23.7
41	Massachusetts	23.5
42	New York	22.6
43	California	22.4
44	Alabama	22.2
45	Virginia	21.7
46	Idaho	20.6
47	Connecticut	19.8
48	Colorado	18.9
49	New Jersey	15.5
50	Utah	13.0

District of Columbia	5.9

Source: U.S. Department of Health and Human Services, National Center for Health Statistics
"National Vital Statistics Reports" (Vol. 57, No. 7, January 7, 2009, http://www.cdc.gov/nchs/births.htm)
*Final data by state of residence. By race of mother. Includes only non-Hispanic whites.

Births to Unmarried Black Women in 2006

National Total = 436,227 Live Births*

ALPHA ORDER

ALPHA ORDER				RANK ORDER			
RANK	STATE	BIRTHS	% of USA	RANK	STATE	BIRTHS	% of USA
16	Alabama	13,506	3.1%	1	Florida	35,001	8.0%
41	Alaska	176	0.0%	2	Georgia	33,038	7.6%
29	Arizona	2,238	0.5%	3	Texas	30,345	7.0%
21	Arkansas	6,146	1.4%	4	New York	29,293	6.7%
7	California	20,838	4.8%	5	Illinois	24,560	5.6%
33	Colorado	1,589	0.4%	6	North Carolina	20,926	4.8%
27	Connecticut	3,517	0.8%	7	California	20,838	4.8%
31	Delaware	2,141	0.5%	8	Louisiana	18,768	4.3%
1	Florida	35,001	8.0%	9	Ohio	18,363	4.2%
2	Georgia	33,038	7.6%	10	Michigan	17,442	4.0%
42	Hawaii	125	0.0%	11	Mississippi	16,670	3.8%
46	Idaho	49	0.0%	12	Pennsylvania	16,040	3.7%
5	Illinois	24,560	5.6%	13	Maryland	15,752	3.6%
20	Indiana	8,109	1.9%	14	South Carolina	15,452	3.5%
35	Iowa	1,147	0.3%	15	Virginia	14,951	3.4%
30	Kansas	2,184	0.5%	16	Alabama	13,506	3.1%
24	Kentucky	3,812	0.9%	17	Tennessee	13,057	3.0%
8	Louisiana	18,768	4.3%	18	New Jersey	11,721	2.7%
43	Maine	101	0.0%	19	Missouri	9,568	2.2%
13	Maryland	15,752	3.6%	20	Indiana	8,109	1.9%
23	Massachusetts	4,273	1.0%	21	Arkansas	6,146	1.4%
10	Michigan	17,442	4.0%	22	Wisconsin	5,857	1.3%
25	Minnesota	3,793	0.9%	23	Massachusetts	4,273	1.0%
11	Mississippi	16,670	3.8%	24	Kentucky	3,812	0.9%
19	Missouri	9,568	2.2%	25	Minnesota	3,793	0.9%
50	Montana	18	0.0%	26	Oklahoma	3,699	0.8%
34	Nebraska	1,191	0.3%	27	Connecticut	3,517	0.8%
28	Nevada	2,322	0.5%	28	Nevada	2,322	0.5%
45	New Hampshire	89	0.0%	29	Arizona	2,238	0.5%
18	New Jersey	11,721	2.7%	30	Kansas	2,184	0.5%
39	New Mexico	285	0.1%	31	Delaware	2,141	0.5%
4	New York	29,293	6.7%	32	Washington	1,979	0.5%
6	North Carolina	20,926	4.8%	33	Colorado	1,589	0.4%
47	North Dakota	40	0.0%	34	Nebraska	1,191	0.3%
9	Ohio	18,363	4.2%	35	Iowa	1,147	0.3%
26	Oklahoma	3,699	0.8%	36	Oregon	688	0.2%
36	Oregon	688	0.2%	37	Rhode Island	631	0.1%
12	Pennsylvania	16,040	3.7%	38	West Virginia	507	0.1%
37	Rhode Island	631	0.1%	39	New Mexico	285	0.1%
14	South Carolina	15,452	3.5%	40	Utah	227	0.1%
43	South Dakota	101	0.0%	41	Alaska	176	0.0%
17	Tennessee	13,057	3.0%	42	Hawaii	125	0.0%
3	Texas	30,345	7.0%	43	Maine	101	0.0%
40	Utah	227	0.1%	43	South Dakota	101	0.0%
49	Vermont	26	0.0%	45	New Hampshire	89	0.0%
15	Virginia	14,951	3.4%	46	Idaho	49	0.0%
32	Washington	1,979	0.5%	47	North Dakota	40	0.0%
38	West Virginia	507	0.1%	48	Wyoming	33	0.0%
22	Wisconsin	5,857	1.3%	49	Vermont	26	0.0%
48	Wyoming	33	0.0%	50	Montana	18	0.0%
					District of Columbia	3,843	0.9%

Source: U.S. Department of Health and Human Services, National Center for Health Statistics
"National Vital Statistics Reports" (Vol. 57, No. 7, January 7, 2009, http://www.cdc.gov/nchs/births.htm)
*Final data by state of residence. By race of mother. Includes only non-Hispanic blacks.

Births to Unmarried Black Women
as a Percent of All Births to Black Women in 2006
National Percent = 70.7% of Live Births*

ALPHA ORDER

RANK	STATE	PERCENT
20	Alabama	69.9
43	Alaska	44.3
33	Arizona	62.3
4	Arkansas	78.4
29	California	65.0
39	Colorado	53.4
25	Connecticut	68.0
18	Delaware	71.5
24	Florida	68.5
26	Georgia	67.8
49	Hawaii	25.1
45	Idaho	40.8
3	Illinois	78.7
5	Indiana	78.2
17	Iowa	72.4
15	Kansas	72.9
16	Kentucky	72.6
7	Louisiana	77.3
47	Maine	34.6
34	Maryland	62.0
35	Massachusetts	60.1
9	Michigan	76.9
35	Minnesota	60.1
2	Mississippi	79.1
6	Missouri	77.6
NA	Montana**	NA
22	Nebraska	69.4
21	Nevada	69.6
44	New Hampshire	41.8
27	New Jersey	67.1
38	New Mexico	56.0
23	New York	69.0
19	North Carolina	70.4
48	North Dakota	34.2
8	Ohio	77.2
11	Oklahoma	75.7
32	Oregon	62.8
9	Pennsylvania	76.9
31	Rhode Island	63.6
12	South Carolina	75.5
42	South Dakota	47.2
13	Tennessee	74.9
28	Texas	65.9
41	Utah	49.0
46	Vermont	35.1
30	Virginia	63.9
40	Washington	52.8
14	West Virginia	73.6
1	Wisconsin	83.4
37	Wyoming	60.0

RANK ORDER

RANK	STATE	PERCENT
1	Wisconsin	83.4
2	Mississippi	79.1
3	Illinois	78.7
4	Arkansas	78.4
5	Indiana	78.2
6	Missouri	77.6
7	Louisiana	77.3
8	Ohio	77.2
9	Michigan	76.9
9	Pennsylvania	76.9
11	Oklahoma	75.7
12	South Carolina	75.5
13	Tennessee	74.9
14	West Virginia	73.6
15	Kansas	72.9
16	Kentucky	72.6
17	Iowa	72.4
18	Delaware	71.5
19	North Carolina	70.4
20	Alabama	69.9
21	Nevada	69.6
22	Nebraska	69.4
23	New York	69.0
24	Florida	68.5
25	Connecticut	68.0
26	Georgia	67.8
27	New Jersey	67.1
28	Texas	65.9
29	California	65.0
30	Virginia	63.9
31	Rhode Island	63.6
32	Oregon	62.8
33	Arizona	62.3
34	Maryland	62.0
35	Massachusetts	60.1
35	Minnesota	60.1
37	Wyoming	60.0
38	New Mexico	56.0
39	Colorado	53.4
40	Washington	52.8
41	Utah	49.0
42	South Dakota	47.2
43	Alaska	44.3
44	New Hampshire	41.8
45	Idaho	40.8
46	Vermont	35.1
47	Maine	34.6
48	North Dakota	34.2
49	Hawaii	25.1
NA	Montana**	NA

District of Columbia   79.3

Source: U.S. Department of Health and Human Services, National Center for Health Statistics
    "National Vital Statistics Reports" (Vol. 57, No. 7, January 7, 2009, http://www.cdc.gov/nchs/births.htm)
*Final data by state of residence. By race of mother. Includes only non-Hispanic blacks.
**Insufficient data.

Births to Unmarried Hispanic Women in 2006

National Total = 518,125 Live Births*

ALPHA ORDER					RANK ORDER			
RANK	STATE	BIRTHS	% of USA		RANK	STATE	BIRTHS	% of USA
40	Alabama	1,012	0.2%		1	California	141,410	27.3%
43	Alaska	277	0.1%		2	Texas	89,404	17.3%
5	Arizona	25,277	4.9%		3	New York	38,069	7.3%
31	Arkansas	2,044	0.4%		4	Florida	33,454	6.5%
1	California	141,410	27.3%		5	Arizona	25,277	4.9%
11	Colorado	9,441	1.8%		6	Illinois	21,702	4.2%
18	Connecticut	5,354	1.0%		7	New Jersey	16,682	3.2%
39	Delaware	1,158	0.2%		8	Georgia	11,507	2.2%
4	Florida	33,454	6.5%		9	North Carolina	11,278	2.2%
8	Georgia	11,507	2.2%		10	New Mexico	9,448	1.8%
36	Hawaii	1,442	0.3%		11	Colorado	9,441	1.8%
35	Idaho	1,512	0.3%		12	Pennsylvania	8,404	1.6%
6	Illinois	21,702	4.2%		13	Nevada	7,684	1.5%
19	Indiana	4,646	0.9%		14	Washington	7,490	1.4%
33	Iowa	1,583	0.3%		15	Virginia	7,260	1.4%
28	Kansas	3,266	0.6%		16	Massachusetts	7,085	1.4%
37	Kentucky	1,342	0.3%		17	Maryland	5,434	1.0%
38	Louisiana	1,164	0.2%		18	Connecticut	5,354	1.0%
49	Maine	93	0.0%		19	Indiana	4,646	0.9%
17	Maryland	5,434	1.0%		20	Oregon	4,621	0.9%
16	Massachusetts	7,085	1.4%		21	Michigan	4,187	0.8%
21	Michigan	4,187	0.8%		22	Tennessee	4,151	0.8%
27	Minnesota	3,371	0.7%		23	Ohio	3,833	0.7%
41	Mississippi	873	0.2%		24	Utah	3,549	0.7%
30	Missouri	2,290	0.4%		25	Wisconsin	3,447	0.7%
45	Montana	194	0.0%		26	Oklahoma	3,427	0.7%
32	Nebraska	1,953	0.4%		27	Minnesota	3,371	0.7%
13	Nevada	7,684	1.5%		28	Kansas	3,266	0.6%
44	New Hampshire	268	0.1%		29	South Carolina	2,695	0.5%
7	New Jersey	16,682	3.2%		30	Missouri	2,290	0.4%
10	New Mexico	9,448	1.8%		31	Arkansas	2,044	0.4%
3	New York	38,069	7.3%		32	Nebraska	1,953	0.4%
9	North Carolina	11,278	2.2%		33	Iowa	1,583	0.3%
47	North Dakota	116	0.0%		34	Rhode Island	1,572	0.3%
23	Ohio	3,833	0.7%		35	Idaho	1,512	0.3%
26	Oklahoma	3,427	0.7%		36	Hawaii	1,442	0.3%
20	Oregon	4,621	0.9%		37	Kentucky	1,342	0.3%
12	Pennsylvania	8,404	1.6%		38	Louisiana	1,164	0.2%
34	Rhode Island	1,572	0.3%		39	Delaware	1,158	0.2%
29	South Carolina	2,695	0.5%		40	Alabama	1,012	0.2%
46	South Dakota	190	0.0%		41	Mississippi	873	0.2%
22	Tennessee	4,151	0.8%		42	Wyoming	442	0.1%
2	Texas	89,404	17.3%		43	Alaska	277	0.1%
24	Utah	3,549	0.7%		44	New Hampshire	268	0.1%
50	Vermont	27	0.0%		45	Montana	194	0.0%
15	Virginia	7,260	1.4%		46	South Dakota	190	0.0%
14	Washington	7,490	1.4%		47	North Dakota	116	0.0%
48	West Virginia	100	0.0%		48	West Virginia	100	0.0%
25	Wisconsin	3,447	0.7%		49	Maine	93	0.0%
42	Wyoming	442	0.1%		50	Vermont	27	0.0%
						District of Columbia	897	0.2%

Source: U.S. Department of Health and Human Services, National Center for Health Statistics
   "National Vital Statistics Reports" (Vol. 57, No. 7, January 7, 2009, http://www.cdc.gov/nchs/births.htm)
*Final data by state of residence. Hispanic can be of any race.

Births to Unmarried Hispanic Women
as a Percent of All Births to Hispanic Women in 2006
National Percent = 49.9% of Live Births*

ALPHA ORDER

RANK	STATE	PERCENT
50	Alabama	21.4
48	Alaska	36.8
12	Arizona	55.5
38	Arkansas	46.5
31	California	48.2
46	Colorado	41.4
4	Connecticut	63.1
5	Delaware	61.5
33	Florida	47.8
27	Georgia	48.6
34	Hawaii	47.4
47	Idaho	39.9
25	Illinois	48.9
13	Indiana	55.0
24	Iowa	49.1
21	Kansas	49.6
29	Kentucky	48.4
20	Louisiana	49.7
45	Maine	42.7
14	Maryland	53.9
1	Massachusetts	65.9
31	Michigan	48.2
11	Minnesota	55.9
10	Mississippi	56.1
17	Missouri	50.3
29	Montana	48.4
26	Nebraska	48.8
22	Nevada	49.3
41	New Hampshire	45.8
8	New Jersey	57.1
7	New Mexico	57.2
2	New York	64.2
15	North Carolina	53.2
37	North Dakota	46.6
9	Ohio	56.9
28	Oklahoma	48.5
38	Oregon	46.5
3	Pennsylvania	63.3
5	Rhode Island	61.5
40	South Carolina	45.9
34	South Dakota	47.4
16	Tennessee	52.3
43	Texas	45.1
44	Utah	43.2
49	Vermont	36.5
18	Virginia	50.2
34	Washington	47.4
42	West Virginia	45.7
18	Wisconsin	50.2
22	Wyoming	49.3

RANK ORDER

RANK	STATE	PERCENT
1	Massachusetts	65.9
2	New York	64.2
3	Pennsylvania	63.3
4	Connecticut	63.1
5	Delaware	61.5
5	Rhode Island	61.5
7	New Mexico	57.2
8	New Jersey	57.1
9	Ohio	56.9
10	Mississippi	56.1
11	Minnesota	55.9
12	Arizona	55.5
13	Indiana	55.0
14	Maryland	53.9
15	North Carolina	53.2
16	Tennessee	52.3
17	Missouri	50.3
18	Virginia	50.2
18	Wisconsin	50.2
20	Louisiana	49.7
21	Kansas	49.6
22	Nevada	49.3
22	Wyoming	49.3
24	Iowa	49.1
25	Illinois	48.9
26	Nebraska	48.8
27	Georgia	48.6
28	Oklahoma	48.5
29	Kentucky	48.4
29	Montana	48.4
31	California	48.2
31	Michigan	48.2
33	Florida	47.8
34	Hawaii	47.4
34	South Dakota	47.4
34	Washington	47.4
37	North Dakota	46.6
38	Arkansas	46.5
38	Oregon	46.5
40	South Carolina	45.9
41	New Hampshire	45.8
42	West Virginia	45.7
43	Texas	45.1
44	Utah	43.2
45	Maine	42.7
46	Colorado	41.4
47	Idaho	39.9
48	Alaska	36.8
49	Vermont	36.5
50	Alabama	21.4

	District of Columbia	67.5

Source: U.S. Department of Health and Human Services, National Center for Health Statistics
   "National Vital Statistics Reports" (Vol. 57, No. 7, January 7, 2009, http://www.cdc.gov/nchs/births.htm)
*Final data by state of residence. Hispanic can be of any race.

Pregnancy Rate in 2005

National Rate = 69.1 Births and Abortions per 1,000 Women 15 to 49 Years Old*

ALPHA ORDER

RANK	STATE	RATE
30	Alabama	64.3
11	Alaska	72.4
7	Arizona	75.5
23	Arkansas	66.3
NA	California**	NA
19	Colorado	68.1
33	Connecticut	63.0
8	Delaware	75.3
4	Florida	77.3
10	Georgia	73.8
13	Hawaii	71.0
14	Idaho	70.6
15	Illinois	69.9
31	Indiana	63.8
29	Iowa	64.6
6	Kansas	75.7
44	Kentucky	58.4
NA	Louisiana**	NA
47	Maine	52.9
42	Maryland	59.8
38	Massachusetts	61.1
36	Michigan	61.4
23	Minnesota	66.3
33	Mississippi	63.0
39	Missouri	60.9
35	Montana	62.5
16	Nebraska	69.5
2	Nevada	83.1
NA	New Hampshire**	NA
20	New Jersey	67.9
9	New Mexico	74.2
5	New York	76.1
12	North Carolina	71.8
32	North Dakota	63.1
28	Ohio	65.0
17	Oklahoma	68.6
26	Oregon	65.9
40	Pennsylvania	60.8
27	Rhode Island	65.8
37	South Carolina	61.3
22	South Dakota	66.9
25	Tennessee	66.1
3	Texas	80.2
1	Utah	86.0
45	Vermont	53.3
20	Virginia	67.9
18	Washington	68.4
46	West Virginia	53.0
43	Wisconsin	59.6
41	Wyoming	59.9

RANK ORDER

RANK	STATE	RATE
1	Utah	86.0
2	Nevada	83.1
3	Texas	80.2
4	Florida	77.3
5	New York	76.1
6	Kansas	75.7
7	Arizona	75.5
8	Delaware	75.3
9	New Mexico	74.2
10	Georgia	73.8
11	Alaska	72.4
12	North Carolina	71.8
13	Hawaii	71.0
14	Idaho	70.6
15	Illinois	69.9
16	Nebraska	69.5
17	Oklahoma	68.6
18	Washington	68.4
19	Colorado	68.1
20	New Jersey	67.9
20	Virginia	67.9
22	South Dakota	66.9
23	Arkansas	66.3
23	Minnesota	66.3
25	Tennessee	66.1
26	Oregon	65.9
27	Rhode Island	65.8
28	Ohio	65.0
29	Iowa	64.6
30	Alabama	64.3
31	Indiana	63.8
32	North Dakota	63.1
33	Connecticut	63.0
33	Mississippi	63.0
35	Montana	62.5
36	Michigan	61.4
37	South Carolina	61.3
38	Massachusetts	61.1
39	Missouri	60.9
40	Pennsylvania	60.8
41	Wyoming	59.9
42	Maryland	59.8
43	Wisconsin	59.6
44	Kentucky	58.4
45	Vermont	53.3
46	West Virginia	53.0
47	Maine	52.9
NA	California**	NA
NA	Louisiana**	NA
NA	New Hampshire**	NA

District of Columbia 63.6

Source: CQ Press using data from U.S. Department of Health and Human Services, Centers for Disease Control and Prevention "Abortion Surveillance-United States, 2005" (Morbidity and Mortality Weekly Report, Vol. 57, No. SS-13, 11/28/08)

*The sum of live births and legal induced abortions per 1,000 women 15 to 49 years old. Births by state of residence, abortions by state of occurrence. Miscarriages are not included in these rates. National rate includes only states reporting abortions and births.

**Not available.

Teenage Pregnancy Rate in 2005

National Rate = 56.0 Births and Abortions per 1,000 Women 15 to 19 Years Old*

ALPHA ORDER

RANK ORDER

RANK	STATE	RATE	RANK	STATE	RATE
11	Alabama	62.8	1	New Mexico	79.4
17	Alaska	57.0	2	Nevada	78.4
4	Arizona	69.5	3	Texas	75.1
7	Arkansas	68.3	4	Arizona	69.5
NA	California**	NA	5	Tennessee	69.1
15	Colorado	57.9	6	Georgia	68.8
33	Connecticut	42.6	7	Arkansas	68.3
12	Delaware	60.5	8	North Carolina	66.1
NA	Florida**	NA	9	Oklahoma	64.7
6	Georgia	68.8	10	Mississippi	64.3
18	Hawaii	56.1	11	Alabama	62.8
36	Idaho	41.9	12	Delaware	60.5
NA	Illinois**	NA	13	Kansas	59.8
22	Indiana	52.1	14	New York	58.9
36	Iowa	41.9	15	Colorado	57.9
13	Kansas	59.8	16	South Carolina	57.8
20	Kentucky	54.3	17	Alaska	57.0
NA	Louisiana**	NA	18	Hawaii	56.1
41	Maine	37.2	19	Ohio	54.8
NA	Maryland**	NA	20	Kentucky	54.3
40	Massachusetts	37.6	21	Washington	53.8
29	Michigan	45.7	22	Indiana	52.1
41	Minnesota	37.2	23	Rhode Island	50.9
10	Mississippi	64.3	24	Montana	50.6
27	Missouri	49.6	25	Oregon	50.2
24	Montana	50.6	26	Virginia	49.9
34	Nebraska	42.5	27	Missouri	49.6
2	Nevada	78.4	28	West Virginia	48.9
NA	New Hampshire**	NA	29	Michigan	45.7
30	New Jersey	44.8	30	New Jersey	44.8
1	New Mexico	79.4	31	Wyoming	44.4
14	New York	58.9	32	Pennsylvania	43.5
8	North Carolina	66.1	33	Connecticut	42.6
39	North Dakota	38.2	34	Nebraska	42.5
19	Ohio	54.8	34	South Dakota	42.5
9	Oklahoma	64.7	36	Idaho	41.9
25	Oregon	50.2	36	Iowa	41.9
32	Pennsylvania	43.5	38	Wisconsin	39.8
23	Rhode Island	50.9	39	North Dakota	38.2
16	South Carolina	57.8	40	Massachusetts	37.6
34	South Dakota	42.5	41	Maine	37.2
5	Tennessee	69.1	41	Minnesota	37.2
3	Texas	75.1	43	Utah	36.7
43	Utah	36.7	44	Vermont	33.0
44	Vermont	33.0	NA	California**	NA
26	Virginia	49.9	NA	Florida**	NA
21	Washington	53.8	NA	Illinois**	NA
28	West Virginia	48.9	NA	Louisiana**	NA
38	Wisconsin	39.8	NA	Maryland**	NA
31	Wyoming	44.4	NA	New Hampshire**	NA

District of Columbia 64.5

Source: CQ Press using data from U.S. Department of Health and Human Services, Centers for Disease Control and Prevention "Abortion Surveillance-United States, 2005" (MMWR, Vol. 57, No. SS-13, 11/28/08, http://www.cdc.gov/mmwr/mmwr_ss.html)
*The sum of live births and legal induced abortions per 1,000 women 15 to 19 years old. Births by state of residence, abortions by state of occurrence. Miscarriages are not included in these rates. National rate includes only states reporting abortions and births.
**Not available.

Percent Change in Teenage Pregnancy Rate: 2001 to 2005

National Percent Change = 9.7% Decrease*

ALPHA ORDER				RANK ORDER		
RANK	STATE	PERCENT CHANGE		RANK	STATE	PERCENT CHANGE
31	Alabama	(12.5)		1	Wyoming	13.6
NA	Alaska**	NA		2	Colorado	7.0
8	Arizona	(4.7)		3	New Mexico	1.3
19	Arkansas	(7.8)		4	Montana	(0.8)
NA	California**	NA		5	North Dakota	(1.3)
2	Colorado	7.0		6	Kentucky	(3.2)
43	Connecticut	(20.2)		7	South Dakota	(4.5)
40	Delaware	(18.5)		8	Arizona	(4.7)
NA	Florida**	NA		9	Iowa	(4.8)
29	Georgia	(11.8)		10	Idaho	(5.0)
32	Hawaii	(12.6)		11	Tennessee	(5.1)
10	Idaho	(5.0)		12	Maine	(5.3)
NA	Illinois**	NA		13	Missouri	(5.7)
16	Indiana	(6.6)		13	Oklahoma	(5.7)
9	Iowa	(4.8)		15	Texas	(6.4)
27	Kansas	(11.5)		16	Indiana	(6.6)
6	Kentucky	(3.2)		17	Nevada	(6.7)
NA	Louisiana**	NA		18	Ohio	(7.4)
12	Maine	(5.3)		19	Arkansas	(7.8)
NA	Maryland**	NA		20	West Virginia	(8.3)
37	Massachusetts	(14.0)		21	Washington	(9.7)
34	Michigan	(13.3)		22	Wisconsin	(9.8)
24	Minnesota	(10.8)		23	Pennsylvania	(10.7)
26	Mississippi	(11.4)		24	Minnesota	(10.8)
13	Missouri	(5.7)		25	North Carolina	(11.0)
4	Montana	(0.8)		26	Mississippi	(11.4)
35	Nebraska	(13.6)		27	Kansas	(11.5)
17	Nevada	(6.7)		27	Virginia	(11.5)
NA	New Hampshire**	NA		29	Georgia	(11.8)
33	New Jersey	(12.8)		30	South Carolina	(12.0)
3	New Mexico	1.3		31	Alabama	(12.5)
36	New York	(13.9)		32	Hawaii	(12.6)
25	North Carolina	(11.0)		33	New Jersey	(12.8)
5	North Dakota	(1.3)		34	Michigan	(13.3)
18	Ohio	(7.4)		35	Nebraska	(13.6)
13	Oklahoma	(5.7)		36	New York	(13.9)
41	Oregon	(19.6)		37	Massachusetts	(14.0)
23	Pennsylvania	(10.7)		38	Vermont	(14.3)
41	Rhode Island	(19.6)		39	Utah	(16.6)
30	South Carolina	(12.0)		40	Delaware	(18.5)
7	South Dakota	(4.5)		41	Oregon	(19.6)
11	Tennessee	(5.1)		41	Rhode Island	(19.6)
15	Texas	(6.4)		43	Connecticut	(20.2)
39	Utah	(16.6)		NA	Alaska**	NA
38	Vermont	(14.3)		NA	California**	NA
27	Virginia	(11.5)		NA	Florida**	NA
21	Washington	(9.7)		NA	Illinois**	NA
20	West Virginia	(8.3)		NA	Louisiana**	NA
22	Wisconsin	(9.8)		NA	Maryland**	NA
1	Wyoming	13.6		NA	New Hampshire**	NA

District of Columbia   (52.6)

Source: CQ Press using data from U.S. Department of Health and Human Services, Centers for Disease Control and Prevention
    "Abortion Surveillance-United States, 2005" (MMWR, Vol. 57, No. SS-13, 11/28/08, http://www.cdc.gov/mmwr/mmwr_ss.html)
*The sum of live births and legal induced abortions per 1,000 women 15 to 19 years old. Births by state of residence, abortions
by state of occurrence. Miscarriages are not included in these rates. National rate includes only states reporting abortions and
births.
**Not available.

Births to Teenage Mothers in 2006

National Total = 435,436 Births*

ALPHA ORDER

RANK	STATE	BIRTHS	% of USA
17	Alabama	8,537	2.0%
46	Alaska	1,101	0.3%
10	Arizona	12,824	2.9%
27	Arkansas	5,946	1.4%
2	California	52,800	12.1%
24	Colorado	6,719	1.5%
36	Connecticut	2,875	0.7%
42	Delaware	1,263	0.3%
3	Florida	25,384	5.8%
5	Georgia	17,693	4.1%
40	Hawaii	1,619	0.4%
38	Idaho	2,140	0.5%
4	Illinois	17,752	4.1%
13	Indiana	9,549	2.2%
35	Iowa	3,495	0.8%
33	Kansas	4,109	0.9%
19	Kentucky	7,412	1.7%
16	Louisiana	8,628	2.0%
43	Maine	1,133	0.3%
25	Maryland	6,705	1.5%
29	Massachusetts	4,724	1.1%
11	Michigan	12,322	2.8%
28	Minnesota	5,090	1.2%
20	Mississippi	7,404	1.7%
14	Missouri	9,183	2.1%
41	Montana	1,283	0.3%
39	Nebraska	2,112	0.5%
31	Nevada	4,287	1.0%
47	New Hampshire	865	0.2%
22	New Jersey	7,159	1.6%
30	New Mexico	4,628	1.1%
6	New York	17,442	4.0%
8	North Carolina	14,701	3.4%
49	North Dakota	633	0.1%
7	Ohio	15,872	3.6%
21	Oklahoma	7,227	1.7%
32	Oregon	4,285	1.0%
9	Pennsylvania	13,599	3.1%
44	Rhode Island	1,127	0.3%
18	South Carolina	8,175	1.9%
45	South Dakota	1,123	0.3%
12	Tennessee	10,784	2.5%
1	Texas	53,093	12.2%
34	Utah	3,498	0.8%
50	Vermont	468	0.1%
15	Virginia	9,105	2.1%
23	Washington	7,110	1.6%
37	West Virginia	2,589	0.6%
26	Wisconsin	6,015	1.4%
48	Wyoming	850	0.2%

RANK ORDER

RANK	STATE	BIRTHS	% of USA
1	Texas	53,093	12.2%
2	California	52,800	12.1%
3	Florida	25,384	5.8%
4	Illinois	17,752	4.1%
5	Georgia	17,693	4.1%
6	New York	17,442	4.0%
7	Ohio	15,872	3.6%
8	North Carolina	14,701	3.4%
9	Pennsylvania	13,599	3.1%
10	Arizona	12,824	2.9%
11	Michigan	12,322	2.8%
12	Tennessee	10,784	2.5%
13	Indiana	9,549	2.2%
14	Missouri	9,183	2.1%
15	Virginia	9,105	2.1%
16	Louisiana	8,628	2.0%
17	Alabama	8,537	2.0%
18	South Carolina	8,175	1.9%
19	Kentucky	7,412	1.7%
20	Mississippi	7,404	1.7%
21	Oklahoma	7,227	1.7%
22	New Jersey	7,159	1.6%
23	Washington	7,110	1.6%
24	Colorado	6,719	1.5%
25	Maryland	6,705	1.5%
26	Wisconsin	6,015	1.4%
27	Arkansas	5,946	1.4%
28	Minnesota	5,090	1.2%
29	Massachusetts	4,724	1.1%
30	New Mexico	4,628	1.1%
31	Nevada	4,287	1.0%
32	Oregon	4,285	1.0%
33	Kansas	4,109	0.9%
34	Utah	3,498	0.8%
35	Iowa	3,495	0.8%
36	Connecticut	2,875	0.7%
37	West Virginia	2,589	0.6%
38	Idaho	2,140	0.5%
39	Nebraska	2,112	0.5%
40	Hawaii	1,619	0.4%
41	Montana	1,283	0.3%
42	Delaware	1,263	0.3%
43	Maine	1,133	0.3%
44	Rhode Island	1,127	0.3%
45	South Dakota	1,123	0.3%
46	Alaska	1,101	0.3%
47	New Hampshire	865	0.2%
48	Wyoming	850	0.2%
49	North Dakota	633	0.1%
50	Vermont	468	0.1%
	District of Columbia	999	0.2%

Source: U.S. Department of Health and Human Services, National Center for Health Statistics
    "Vital Stats" (http://www.cdc.gov/nchs/VitalStats.htm)
*Final data. Live births to women 15 to 19 years old by state of residence of mother.

Births to Teenage Mothers as a Percent of All Births in 2006

National Percent = 10.2% of Live Births*

ALPHA ORDER

RANK	STATE	PERCENT
5	Alabama	13.5
23	Alaska	10.0
11	Arizona	12.5
3	Arkansas	14.5
28	California	9.4
27	Colorado	9.5
45	Connecticut	6.9
20	Delaware	10.5
18	Florida	10.7
13	Georgia	11.9
36	Hawaii	8.5
32	Idaho	8.8
25	Illinois	9.8
17	Indiana	10.8
35	Iowa	8.6
23	Kansas	10.0
10	Kentucky	12.7
4	Louisiana	13.6
40	Maine	8.0
34	Maryland	8.7
49	Massachusetts	6.1
26	Michigan	9.7
45	Minnesota	6.9
1	Mississippi	16.1
15	Missouri	11.3
22	Montana	10.3
41	Nebraska	7.9
18	Nevada	10.7
50	New Hampshire	6.0
48	New Jersey	6.2
2	New Mexico	15.5
44	New York	7.0
14	North Carolina	11.5
42	North Dakota	7.3
20	Ohio	10.5
6	Oklahoma	13.4
32	Oregon	8.8
30	Pennsylvania	9.1
30	Rhode Island	9.1
8	South Carolina	13.1
28	South Dakota	9.4
9	Tennessee	12.8
7	Texas	13.3
47	Utah	6.5
43	Vermont	7.2
37	Virginia	8.4
39	Washington	8.2
12	West Virginia	12.4
38	Wisconsin	8.3
16	Wyoming	11.1

RANK ORDER

RANK	STATE	PERCENT
1	Mississippi	16.1
2	New Mexico	15.5
3	Arkansas	14.5
4	Louisiana	13.6
5	Alabama	13.5
6	Oklahoma	13.4
7	Texas	13.3
8	South Carolina	13.1
9	Tennessee	12.8
10	Kentucky	12.7
11	Arizona	12.5
12	West Virginia	12.4
13	Georgia	11.9
14	North Carolina	11.5
15	Missouri	11.3
16	Wyoming	11.1
17	Indiana	10.8
18	Florida	10.7
18	Nevada	10.7
20	Delaware	10.5
20	Ohio	10.5
22	Montana	10.3
23	Alaska	10.0
23	Kansas	10.0
25	Illinois	9.8
26	Michigan	9.7
27	Colorado	9.5
28	California	9.4
28	South Dakota	9.4
30	Pennsylvania	9.1
30	Rhode Island	9.1
32	Idaho	8.8
32	Oregon	8.8
34	Maryland	8.7
35	Iowa	8.6
36	Hawaii	8.5
37	Virginia	8.4
38	Wisconsin	8.3
39	Washington	8.2
40	Maine	8.0
41	Nebraska	7.9
42	North Dakota	7.3
43	Vermont	7.2
44	New York	7.0
45	Connecticut	6.9
45	Minnesota	6.9
47	Utah	6.5
48	New Jersey	6.2
49	Massachusetts	6.1
50	New Hampshire	6.0

District of Columbia   11.7

Source: CQ Press using data from U.S. Department of Health and Human Services, National Center for Health Statistics
"National Vital Statistics Reports" (Vol. 57, No. 7, January 7, 2009, http://www.cdc.gov/nchs/births.htm) and
"Vital Stats" (http://www.cdc.gov/nchs/VitalStats.htm)
*Final data. Live births to women 15 to 19 years old by state of residence.

Teenage Birth Rate in 2006

National Rate = 41.9 Live Births per 1,000 Women 15 to 19 Years Old*

ALPHA ORDER

RANK	STATE	RATE
12	Alabama	53.5
19	Alaska	44.3
5	Arizona	62.0
4	Arkansas	62.3
27	California	39.9
20	Colorado	43.8
47	Connecticut	23.5
23	Delaware	41.9
17	Florida	45.2
10	Georgia	54.2
24	Hawaii	40.5
30	Idaho	39.2
29	Illinois	39.5
21	Indiana	43.5
38	Iowa	32.9
22	Kansas	42.0
9	Kentucky	54.6
11	Louisiana	53.9
44	Maine	25.8
35	Maryland	33.6
48	Massachusetts	21.3
34	Michigan	33.8
41	Minnesota	27.9
1	Mississippi	68.4
16	Missouri	45.7
28	Montana	39.6
36	Nebraska	33.4
7	Nevada	55.8
50	New Hampshire	18.7
46	New Jersey	24.9
2	New Mexico	64.1
45	New York	25.7
14	North Carolina	49.7
43	North Dakota	26.5
26	Ohio	40.0
6	Oklahoma	59.6
31	Oregon	35.7
39	Pennsylvania	31.0
42	Rhode Island	27.8
13	South Carolina	53.0
25	South Dakota	40.2
8	Tennessee	54.7
3	Texas	63.1
33	Utah	34.0
49	Vermont	20.8
32	Virginia	35.2
36	Washington	33.4
18	West Virginia	44.9
40	Wisconsin	30.9
15	Wyoming	47.3

RANK ORDER

RANK	STATE	RATE
1	Mississippi	68.4
2	New Mexico	64.1
3	Texas	63.1
4	Arkansas	62.3
5	Arizona	62.0
6	Oklahoma	59.6
7	Nevada	55.8
8	Tennessee	54.7
9	Kentucky	54.6
10	Georgia	54.2
11	Louisiana	53.9
12	Alabama	53.5
13	South Carolina	53.0
14	North Carolina	49.7
15	Wyoming	47.3
16	Missouri	45.7
17	Florida	45.2
18	West Virginia	44.9
19	Alaska	44.3
20	Colorado	43.8
21	Indiana	43.5
22	Kansas	42.0
23	Delaware	41.9
24	Hawaii	40.5
25	South Dakota	40.2
26	Ohio	40.0
27	California	39.9
28	Montana	39.6
29	Illinois	39.5
30	Idaho	39.2
31	Oregon	35.7
32	Virginia	35.2
33	Utah	34.0
34	Michigan	33.8
35	Maryland	33.6
36	Nebraska	33.4
36	Washington	33.4
38	Iowa	32.9
39	Pennsylvania	31.0
40	Wisconsin	30.9
41	Minnesota	27.9
42	Rhode Island	27.8
43	North Dakota	26.5
44	Maine	25.8
45	New York	25.7
46	New Jersey	24.9
47	Connecticut	23.5
48	Massachusetts	21.3
49	Vermont	20.8
50	New Hampshire	18.7

	District of Columbia	48.4

Source: U.S. Department of Health and Human Services, National Center for Health Statistics
   "National Vital Statistics Reports" (Vol. 57, No. 7, January 7, 2009, http://www.cdc.gov/nchs/births.htm)
*Final data by state of residence.

Percent Change in Teenage Birth Rate: 2002 to 2006

National Percent Change = 2.6% Decrease*

ALPHA ORDER				RANK ORDER		
RANK	STATE	PERCENT CHANGE		RANK	STATE	PERCENT CHANGE
24	Alabama	(1.8)		1	Wyoming	18.5
2	Alaska	12.2		2	Alaska	12.2
16	Arizona	1.3		3	Montana	8.8
8	Arkansas	4.0		4	Kentucky	7.1
31	California	(2.9)		5	Hawaii	6.0
40	Colorado	(6.8)		6	South Dakota	5.8
45	Connecticut	(8.9)		7	Mississippi	5.7
46	Delaware	(9.5)		8	Arkansas	4.0
13	Florida	1.6		9	Missouri	3.6
30	Georgia	(2.7)		10	Nevada	3.5
5	Hawaii	6.0		11	Oklahoma	2.8
21	Idaho	0.3		12	New Mexico	2.7
37	Illinois	(6.4)		13	Florida	1.6
28	Indiana	(2.5)		13	Maine	1.6
18	Iowa	1.2		15	Minnesota	1.5
27	Kansas	(2.3)		16	Arizona	1.3
4	Kentucky	7.1		16	Ohio	1.3
42	Louisiana	(7.2)		18	Iowa	1.2
13	Maine	1.6		18	Washington	1.2
36	Maryland	(5.1)		20	Tennessee	0.7
44	Massachusetts	(8.6)		21	Idaho	0.3
31	Michigan	(2.9)		22	South Carolina	0.0
15	Minnesota	1.5		23	West Virginia	(1.3)
7	Mississippi	5.7		24	Alabama	(1.8)
9	Missouri	3.6		25	Pennsylvania	(1.9)
3	Montana	8.8		26	Texas	(2.0)
47	Nebraska	(9.7)		27	Kansas	(2.3)
10	Nevada	3.5		28	Indiana	(2.5)
39	New Hampshire	(6.5)		29	North Dakota	(2.6)
41	New Jersey	(7.1)		30	Georgia	(2.7)
12	New Mexico	2.7		31	California	(2.9)
48	New York	(12.9)		31	Michigan	(2.9)
35	North Carolina	(4.8)		33	Oregon	(3.0)
29	North Dakota	(2.6)		34	Wisconsin	(4.3)
16	Ohio	1.3		35	North Carolina	(4.8)
11	Oklahoma	2.8		36	Maryland	(5.1)
33	Oregon	(3.0)		37	Illinois	(6.4)
25	Pennsylvania	(1.9)		37	Virginia	(6.4)
50	Rhode Island	(21.9)		39	New Hampshire	(6.5)
22	South Carolina	0.0		40	Colorado	(6.8)
6	South Dakota	5.8		41	New Jersey	(7.1)
20	Tennessee	0.7		42	Louisiana	(7.2)
26	Texas	(2.0)		43	Utah	(7.6)
43	Utah	(7.6)		44	Massachusetts	(8.6)
49	Vermont	(14.0)		45	Connecticut	(8.9)
37	Virginia	(6.4)		46	Delaware	(9.5)
18	Washington	1.2		47	Nebraska	(9.7)
23	West Virginia	(1.3)		48	New York	(12.9)
34	Wisconsin	(4.3)		49	Vermont	(14.0)
1	Wyoming	18.5		50	Rhode Island	(21.9)

District of Columbia (30.0)

Source: CQ Press using data from U.S. Department of Health and Human Services, National Center for Health Statistics
"National Vital Statistics Reports" (Vol. 57, No. 7, January 7, 2009, http://www.cdc.gov/nchs/births.htm)
*Final data by state of residence. Births to women 15 to 19 years old.

Births to White Teenage Mothers in 2006

National Total = 308,344 Live Births*

ALPHA ORDER

RANK	STATE	BIRTHS	% of USA
20	Alabama	4,820	1.6%
47	Alaska	477	0.2%
5	Arizona	10,834	3.5%
22	Arkansas	4,182	1.4%
1	California	45,483	14.8%
16	Colorado	6,098	2.0%
37	Connecticut	2,051	0.7%
45	Delaware	731	0.2%
3	Florida	16,049	5.2%
8	Georgia	9,582	3.1%
50	Hawaii	347	0.1%
38	Idaho	2,032	0.7%
4	Illinois	11,039	3.6%
12	Indiana	7,512	2.4%
33	Iowa	3,133	1.0%
30	Kansas	3,389	1.1%
15	Kentucky	6,323	2.1%
27	Louisiana	3,772	1.2%
40	Maine	1,087	0.4%
35	Maryland	2,828	0.9%
28	Massachusetts	3,620	1.2%
11	Michigan	7,612	2.5%
31	Minnesota	3,346	1.1%
34	Mississippi	3,014	1.0%
14	Missouri	6,616	2.1%
41	Montana	916	0.3%
39	Nebraska	1,634	0.5%
29	Nevada	3,423	1.1%
43	New Hampshire	841	0.3%
21	New Jersey	4,252	1.4%
26	New Mexico	3,824	1.2%
7	New York	10,689	3.5%
9	North Carolina	8,947	2.9%
49	North Dakota	410	0.1%
6	Ohio	10,819	3.5%
19	Oklahoma	5,072	1.6%
25	Oregon	3,887	1.3%
10	Pennsylvania	8,461	2.7%
42	Rhode Island	891	0.3%
23	South Carolina	4,099	1.3%
46	South Dakota	658	0.2%
13	Tennessee	7,243	2.3%
2	Texas	44,177	14.3%
32	Utah	3,223	1.0%
48	Vermont	458	0.1%
18	Virginia	5,322	1.7%
17	Washington	5,802	1.9%
36	West Virginia	2,454	0.8%
24	Wisconsin	4,033	1.3%
44	Wyoming	765	0.2%

RANK ORDER

RANK	STATE	BIRTHS	% of USA
1	California	45,483	14.8%
2	Texas	44,177	14.3%
3	Florida	16,049	5.2%
4	Illinois	11,039	3.6%
5	Arizona	10,834	3.5%
6	Ohio	10,819	3.5%
7	New York	10,689	3.5%
8	Georgia	9,582	3.1%
9	North Carolina	8,947	2.9%
10	Pennsylvania	8,461	2.7%
11	Michigan	7,612	2.5%
12	Indiana	7,512	2.4%
13	Tennessee	7,243	2.3%
14	Missouri	6,616	2.1%
15	Kentucky	6,323	2.1%
16	Colorado	6,098	2.0%
17	Washington	5,802	1.9%
18	Virginia	5,322	1.7%
19	Oklahoma	5,072	1.6%
20	Alabama	4,820	1.6%
21	New Jersey	4,252	1.4%
22	Arkansas	4,182	1.4%
23	South Carolina	4,099	1.3%
24	Wisconsin	4,033	1.3%
25	Oregon	3,887	1.3%
26	New Mexico	3,824	1.2%
27	Louisiana	3,772	1.2%
28	Massachusetts	3,620	1.2%
29	Nevada	3,423	1.1%
30	Kansas	3,389	1.1%
31	Minnesota	3,346	1.1%
32	Utah	3,223	1.0%
33	Iowa	3,133	1.0%
34	Mississippi	3,014	1.0%
35	Maryland	2,828	0.9%
36	West Virginia	2,454	0.8%
37	Connecticut	2,051	0.7%
38	Idaho	2,032	0.7%
39	Nebraska	1,634	0.5%
40	Maine	1,087	0.4%
41	Montana	916	0.3%
42	Rhode Island	891	0.3%
43	New Hampshire	841	0.3%
44	Wyoming	765	0.2%
45	Delaware	731	0.2%
46	South Dakota	658	0.2%
47	Alaska	477	0.2%
48	Vermont	458	0.1%
49	North Dakota	410	0.1%
50	Hawaii	347	0.1%
	District of Columbia	67	0.0%

Source: U.S. Department of Health and Human Services, National Center for Health Statistics
   "Vital Stats" (http://www.cdc.gov/nchs/VitalStats.htm)
*Final data. Live births to women 15 to 19 years old by state of residence.

White Teenage Birth Rate in 2006

National Rate = 38.2 Births per 1,000 White Teenage Women*

ALPHA ORDER

RANK	STATE	RATE
11	Alabama	46.8
34	Alaska	28.9
3	Arizona	62.0
4	Arkansas	57.3
14	California	44.5
16	Colorado	44.2
46	Connecticut	20.3
25	Delaware	34.3
23	Florida	38.5
9	Georgia	49.1
32	Hawaii	29.8
22	Idaho	38.8
29	Illinois	32.1
20	Indiana	39.4
31	Iowa	31.3
21	Kansas	39.1
8	Kentucky	52.4
18	Louisiana	40.1
38	Maine	25.6
41	Maryland	23.6
48	Massachusetts	19.2
37	Michigan	26.7
45	Minnesota	20.9
7	Mississippi	52.8
19	Missouri	39.8
30	Montana	32.0
35	Nebraska	28.5
6	Nevada	55.1
50	New Hampshire	18.8
47	New Jersey	19.8
1	New Mexico	65.3
43	New York	22.1
15	North Carolina	44.4
49	North Dakota	19.1
27	Ohio	32.9
5	Oklahoma	55.6
24	Oregon	35.8
42	Pennsylvania	23.2
39	Rhode Island	25.5
17	South Carolina	43.2
36	South Dakota	27.9
10	Tennessee	48.6
2	Texas	64.3
26	Utah	33.5
44	Vermont	21.0
33	Virginia	29.4
28	Washington	32.2
13	West Virginia	44.9
40	Wisconsin	23.7
12	Wyoming	45.2

RANK ORDER

RANK	STATE	RATE
1	New Mexico	65.3
2	Texas	64.3
3	Arizona	62.0
4	Arkansas	57.3
5	Oklahoma	55.6
6	Nevada	55.1
7	Mississippi	52.8
8	Kentucky	52.4
9	Georgia	49.1
10	Tennessee	48.6
11	Alabama	46.8
12	Wyoming	45.2
13	West Virginia	44.9
14	California	44.5
15	North Carolina	44.4
16	Colorado	44.2
17	South Carolina	43.2
18	Louisiana	40.1
19	Missouri	39.8
20	Indiana	39.4
21	Kansas	39.1
22	Idaho	38.8
23	Florida	38.5
24	Oregon	35.8
25	Delaware	34.3
26	Utah	33.5
27	Ohio	32.9
28	Washington	32.2
29	Illinois	32.1
30	Montana	32.0
31	Iowa	31.3
32	Hawaii	29.8
33	Virginia	29.4
34	Alaska	28.9
35	Nebraska	28.5
36	South Dakota	27.9
37	Michigan	26.7
38	Maine	25.6
39	Rhode Island	25.5
40	Wisconsin	23.7
41	Maryland	23.6
42	Pennsylvania	23.2
43	New York	22.1
44	Vermont	21.0
45	Minnesota	20.9
46	Connecticut	20.3
47	New Jersey	19.8
48	Massachusetts	19.2
49	North Dakota	19.1
50	New Hampshire	18.8

District of Columbia   9.6

Source: CQ Press using data from U.S. Department of Health and Human Services, National Center for Health Statistics
"Vital Stats" (http://www.cdc.gov/nchs/VitalStats.htm)
*Final data. Live births to women 15 to 19 years old by state of residence.

Births to White Teenage Mothers as a Percent of All White Births in 2006

National Percent = 9.3% of White Live Births*

RANK	STATE	PERCENT
10	Alabama	11.3
37	Alaska	6.9
6	Arizona	12.2
3	Arkansas	13.0
16	California	10.0
20	Colorado	9.4
46	Connecticut	6.1
25	Delaware	8.7
20	Florida	9.4
14	Georgia	10.2
43	Hawaii	6.3
25	Idaho	8.7
32	Illinois	7.9
18	Indiana	9.8
29	Iowa	8.3
20	Kansas	9.4
6	Kentucky	12.2
15	Louisiana	10.1
31	Maine	8.0
41	Maryland	6.4
47	Massachusetts	5.8
33	Michigan	7.7
48	Minnesota	5.7
4	Mississippi	12.5
17	Missouri	9.9
27	Montana	8.6
37	Nebraska	6.9
12	Nevada	10.5
44	New Hampshire	6.2
50	New Jersey	5.1
1	New Mexico	15.4
44	New York	6.2
19	North Carolina	9.7
49	North Dakota	5.6
23	Ohio	8.9
8	Oklahoma	12.1
23	Oregon	8.9
35	Pennsylvania	7.2
28	Rhode Island	8.5
12	South Carolina	10.5
37	South Dakota	6.9
9	Tennessee	11.4
2	Texas	13.2
41	Utah	6.4
34	Vermont	7.3
36	Virginia	7.0
30	Washington	8.1
5	West Virginia	12.3
40	Wisconsin	6.6
11	Wyoming	10.7

RANK	STATE	PERCENT
1	New Mexico	15.4
2	Texas	13.2
3	Arkansas	13.0
4	Mississippi	12.5
5	West Virginia	12.3
6	Arizona	12.2
6	Kentucky	12.2
8	Oklahoma	12.1
9	Tennessee	11.4
10	Alabama	11.3
11	Wyoming	10.7
12	Nevada	10.5
12	South Carolina	10.5
14	Georgia	10.2
15	Louisiana	10.1
16	California	10.0
17	Missouri	9.9
18	Indiana	9.8
19	North Carolina	9.7
20	Colorado	9.4
20	Florida	9.4
20	Kansas	9.4
23	Ohio	8.9
23	Oregon	8.9
25	Delaware	8.7
25	Idaho	8.7
27	Montana	8.6
28	Rhode Island	8.5
29	Iowa	8.3
30	Washington	8.1
31	Maine	8.0
32	Illinois	7.9
33	Michigan	7.7
34	Vermont	7.3
35	Pennsylvania	7.2
36	Virginia	7.0
37	Alaska	6.9
37	Nebraska	6.9
37	South Dakota	6.9
40	Wisconsin	6.6
41	Maryland	6.4
41	Utah	6.4
43	Hawaii	6.3
44	New Hampshire	6.2
44	New York	6.2
46	Connecticut	6.1
47	Massachusetts	5.8
48	Minnesota	5.7
49	North Dakota	5.6
50	New Jersey	5.1

District of Columbia   2.6

Source: CQ Press using data from U.S. Department of Health and Human Services, National Center for Health Statistics
"Vital Stats" (http://www.cdc.gov/nchs/VitalStats.htm)
*Final data. Live births to women 15 to 19 years old by state of residence.

Births to Black Teenage Mothers in 2006

National Total = 111,019 Live Births*

ALPHA ORDER

RANK	STATE	BIRTHS	% of USA
15	Alabama	3,666	3.3%
41	Alaska	61	0.1%
28	Arizona	629	0.6%
21	Arkansas	1,676	1.5%
9	California	4,843	4.4%
33	Colorado	444	0.4%
27	Connecticut	793	0.7%
32	Delaware	522	0.5%
1	Florida	8,951	8.1%
3	Georgia	7,977	7.2%
42	Hawaii	56	0.1%
47	Idaho	12	0.0%
4	Illinois	6,556	5.9%
20	Indiana	1,995	1.8%
35	Iowa	286	0.3%
29	Kansas	612	0.6%
23	Kentucky	1,038	0.9%
10	Louisiana	4,758	4.3%
43	Maine	23	0.0%
14	Maryland	3,741	3.4%
25	Massachusetts	925	0.8%
11	Michigan	4,479	4.0%
25	Minnesota	925	0.8%
12	Mississippi	4,314	3.9%
19	Missouri	2,443	2.2%
49	Montana	10	0.0%
34	Nebraska	338	0.3%
30	Nevada	603	0.5%
45	New Hampshire	13	0.0%
18	New Jersey	2,812	2.5%
39	New Mexico	105	0.1%
5	New York	6,361	5.7%
6	North Carolina	5,264	4.7%
45	North Dakota	13	0.0%
7	Ohio	4,937	4.4%
24	Oklahoma	968	0.9%
37	Oregon	154	0.1%
8	Pennsylvania	4,862	4.4%
36	Rhode Island	163	0.1%
13	South Carolina	3,971	3.6%
44	South Dakota	21	0.0%
17	Tennessee	3,407	3.1%
2	Texas	8,397	7.6%
40	Utah	71	0.1%
50	Vermont	8	0.0%
16	Virginia	3,643	3.3%
31	Washington	599	0.5%
38	West Virginia	129	0.1%
22	Wisconsin	1,515	1.4%
48	Wyoming	11	0.0%

RANK ORDER

RANK	STATE	BIRTHS	% of USA
1	Florida	8,951	8.1%
2	Texas	8,397	7.6%
3	Georgia	7,977	7.2%
4	Illinois	6,556	5.9%
5	New York	6,361	5.7%
6	North Carolina	5,264	4.7%
7	Ohio	4,937	4.4%
8	Pennsylvania	4,862	4.4%
9	California	4,843	4.4%
10	Louisiana	4,758	4.3%
11	Michigan	4,479	4.0%
12	Mississippi	4,314	3.9%
13	South Carolina	3,971	3.6%
14	Maryland	3,741	3.4%
15	Alabama	3,666	3.3%
16	Virginia	3,643	3.3%
17	Tennessee	3,407	3.1%
18	New Jersey	2,812	2.5%
19	Missouri	2,443	2.2%
20	Indiana	1,995	1.8%
21	Arkansas	1,676	1.5%
22	Wisconsin	1,515	1.4%
23	Kentucky	1,038	0.9%
24	Oklahoma	968	0.9%
25	Massachusetts	925	0.8%
25	Minnesota	925	0.8%
27	Connecticut	793	0.7%
28	Arizona	629	0.6%
29	Kansas	612	0.6%
30	Nevada	603	0.5%
31	Washington	599	0.5%
32	Delaware	522	0.5%
33	Colorado	444	0.4%
34	Nebraska	338	0.3%
35	Iowa	286	0.3%
36	Rhode Island	163	0.1%
37	Oregon	154	0.1%
38	West Virginia	129	0.1%
39	New Mexico	105	0.1%
40	Utah	71	0.1%
41	Alaska	61	0.1%
42	Hawaii	56	0.1%
43	Maine	23	0.0%
44	South Dakota	21	0.0%
45	New Hampshire	13	0.0%
45	North Dakota	13	0.0%
47	Idaho	12	0.0%
48	Wyoming	11	0.0%
49	Montana	10	0.0%
50	Vermont	8	0.0%
	District of Columbia	919	0.8%

Source: U.S. Department of Health and Human Services, National Center for Health Statistics
   "Vital Stats" (http://www.cdc.gov/nchs/VitalStats.htm)
*Final data. Live births to women 15 to 19 years old by state of residence.

Black Teenage Birth Rate in 2006

National Rate = 64.6 Births per 1,000 Black Teenage Women*

ALPHA ORDER			RANK ORDER

RANK	STATE	RATE	RANK	STATE	RATE
21	Alabama	67.8	1	Wisconsin	90.8
35	Alaska	46.7	2	Nebraska	87.5
26	Arizona	59.6	3	Mississippi	86.9
4	Arkansas	82.6	4	Arkansas	82.6
43	California	41.7	5	Minnesota	81.4
33	Colorado	51.6	6	Ohio	80.0
34	Connecticut	47.3	7	Missouri	79.0
24	Delaware	64.7	8	Indiana	78.4
18	Florida	69.8	9	Kansas	78.2
23	Georgia	65.4	10	Pennsylvania	77.9
46	Hawaii	37.6	11	Kentucky	76.5
49	Idaho	21.5	12	Tennessee	76.4
14	Illinois	75.4	13	Louisiana	76.2
8	Indiana	78.4	14	Illinois	75.4
15	Iowa	74.8	15	Iowa	74.8
9	Kansas	78.2	16	Oklahoma	72.4
11	Kentucky	76.5	17	Nevada	70.5
13	Louisiana	76.2	18	Florida	69.8
47	Maine	36.6	19	South Carolina	69.7
28	Maryland	53.8	19	Texas	69.7
37	Massachusetts	44.2	21	Alabama	67.8
22	Michigan	66.0	22	Michigan	66.0
5	Minnesota	81.4	23	Georgia	65.4
3	Mississippi	86.9	24	Delaware	64.7
7	Missouri	79.0	25	North Carolina	62.7
45	Montana	37.7	26	Arizona	59.6
2	Nebraska	87.5	27	Virginia	55.8
17	Nevada	70.5	28	Maryland	53.8
50	New Hampshire	18.7	29	Washington	52.8
30	New Jersey	52.7	30	New Jersey	52.7
37	New Mexico	44.2	31	South Dakota	52.2
40	New York	43.1	32	West Virginia	51.8
25	North Carolina	62.7	33	Colorado	51.6
44	North Dakota	40.8	34	Connecticut	47.3
6	Ohio	80.0	35	Alaska	46.7
16	Oklahoma	72.4	36	Rhode Island	45.7
40	Oregon	43.1	37	Massachusetts	44.2
10	Pennsylvania	77.9	37	New Mexico	44.2
36	Rhode Island	45.7	39	Wyoming	43.7
19	South Carolina	69.7	40	New York	43.1
31	South Dakota	52.2	40	Oregon	43.1
12	Tennessee	76.4	42	Utah	42.6
19	Texas	69.7	43	California	41.7
42	Utah	42.6	44	North Dakota	40.8
48	Vermont	28.3	45	Montana	37.7
27	Virginia	55.8	46	Hawaii	37.6
29	Washington	52.8	47	Maine	36.6
32	West Virginia	51.8	48	Vermont	28.3
1	Wisconsin	90.8	49	Idaho	21.5
39	Wyoming	43.7	50	New Hampshire	18.7
				District of Columbia	70.6

Source: CQ Press using data from U.S. Department of Health and Human Services, National Center for Health Statistics
   "Vital Stats" (http://www.cdc.gov/nchs/VitalStats.htm)
*Final data. Live births to women 15 to 19 years old by state of residence.

Births to Black Teenage Mothers as a Percent of All Black Births in 2006

National Percent = 16.7% of Black Live Births*

ALPHA ORDER				RANK ORDER		
RANK	STATE	PERCENT		RANK	STATE	PERCENT
14	Alabama	18.9		1	Wisconsin	21.3
34	Alaska	13.9		2	Arkansas	21.1
29	Arizona	15.4		3	Illinois	20.8
2	Arkansas	21.1		4	Mississippi	20.5
31	California	14.1		5	Missouri	19.6
31	Colorado	14.1		6	Louisiana	19.4
31	Connecticut	14.1		6	Michigan	19.4
23	Delaware	17.0		6	Ohio	19.4
28	Florida	15.7		6	Oklahoma	19.4
26	Georgia	16.1		6	Pennsylvania	19.4
47	Hawaii	9.2		11	Kansas	19.3
48	Idaho	8.2		12	Indiana	19.1
3	Illinois	20.8		13	Kentucky	19.0
12	Indiana	19.1		14	Alabama	18.9
19	Iowa	17.6		15	Tennessee	18.6
11	Kansas	19.3		16	South Carolina	18.5
13	Kentucky	19.0		17	West Virginia	18.4
6	Louisiana	19.4		18	Nebraska	17.9
49	Maine	7.7		19	Iowa	17.6
38	Maryland	13.3		19	North Carolina	17.6
44	Massachusetts	9.9		21	New Mexico	17.5
6	Michigan	19.4		22	Texas	17.1
41	Minnesota	12.2		23	Delaware	17.0
4	Mississippi	20.5		24	Nevada	16.9
5	Missouri	19.6		25	Wyoming	16.7
27	Montana	15.9		26	Georgia	16.1
18	Nebraska	17.9		27	Montana	15.9
24	Nevada	16.9		28	Florida	15.7
50	New Hampshire	4.9		29	Arizona	15.4
37	New Jersey	13.4		30	Virginia	14.9
21	New Mexico	17.5		31	California	14.1
42	New York	11.7		31	Colorado	14.1
19	North Carolina	17.6		31	Connecticut	14.1
45	North Dakota	9.8		34	Alaska	13.9
6	Ohio	19.4		35	Rhode Island	13.7
6	Oklahoma	19.4		35	Utah	13.7
38	Oregon	13.3		37	New Jersey	13.4
6	Pennsylvania	19.4		38	Maryland	13.3
35	Rhode Island	13.7		38	Oregon	13.3
16	South Carolina	18.5		40	Washington	12.6
46	South Dakota	9.6		41	Minnesota	12.2
15	Tennessee	18.6		42	New York	11.7
22	Texas	17.1		43	Vermont	10.0
35	Utah	13.7		44	Massachusetts	9.9
43	Vermont	10.0		45	North Dakota	9.8
30	Virginia	14.9		46	South Dakota	9.6
40	Washington	12.6		47	Hawaii	9.2
17	West Virginia	18.4		48	Idaho	8.2
1	Wisconsin	21.3		49	Maine	7.7
25	Wyoming	16.7		50	New Hampshire	4.9
					District of Columbia	16.0

Source: CQ Press using data from U.S. Department of Health and Human Services, National Center for Health Statistics
"Vital Stats" (http://www.cdc.gov/nchs/VitalStats.htm)
*Final data. Live births to women 15 to 19 years old by state of residence.

Births to Young Teenagers: 2004 to 2006

National Total = 19,899 Live Births*

ALPHA ORDER

RANK	STATE	BIRTHS	% of USA
15	Alabama	475	2.4%
44	Alaska	29	0.1%
11	Arizona	547	2.7%
23	Arkansas	305	1.5%
2	California	2,133	10.7%
22	Colorado	308	1.5%
35	Connecticut	102	0.5%
39	Delaware	61	0.3%
3	Florida	1,163	5.8%
4	Georgia	980	4.9%
42	Hawaii	48	0.2%
41	Idaho	51	0.3%
5	Illinois	890	4.5%
20	Indiana	339	1.7%
37	Iowa	86	0.4%
33	Kansas	151	0.8%
27	Kentucky	259	1.3%
11	Louisiana	547	2.7%
48	Maine	20	0.1%
18	Maryland	361	1.8%
31	Massachusetts	157	0.8%
10	Michigan	581	2.9%
30	Minnesota	186	0.9%
13	Mississippi	534	2.7%
19	Missouri	357	1.8%
45	Montana	28	0.1%
36	Nebraska	87	0.4%
29	Nevada	194	1.0%
49	New Hampshire	14	0.1%
24	New Jersey	287	1.4%
28	New Mexico	211	1.1%
7	New York	753	3.8%
6	North Carolina	796	4.0%
47	North Dakota	22	0.1%
8	Ohio	718	3.6%
21	Oklahoma	312	1.6%
32	Oregon	153	0.8%
9	Pennsylvania	639	3.2%
40	Rhode Island	55	0.3%
17	South Carolina	404	2.0%
43	South Dakota	32	0.2%
14	Tennessee	526	2.6%
1	Texas	2,786	14.0%
34	Utah	105	0.5%
50	Vermont	10	0.1%
16	Virginia	405	2.0%
26	Washington	261	1.3%
38	West Virginia	69	0.3%
25	Wisconsin	269	1.4%
46	Wyoming	24	0.1%

RANK ORDER

RANK	STATE	BIRTHS	% of USA
1	Texas	2,786	14.0%
2	California	2,133	10.7%
3	Florida	1,163	5.8%
4	Georgia	980	4.9%
5	Illinois	890	4.5%
6	North Carolina	796	4.0%
7	New York	753	3.8%
8	Ohio	718	3.6%
9	Pennsylvania	639	3.2%
10	Michigan	581	2.9%
11	Arizona	547	2.7%
11	Louisiana	547	2.7%
13	Mississippi	534	2.7%
14	Tennessee	526	2.6%
15	Alabama	475	2.4%
16	Virginia	405	2.0%
17	South Carolina	404	2.0%
18	Maryland	361	1.8%
19	Missouri	357	1.8%
20	Indiana	339	1.7%
21	Oklahoma	312	1.6%
22	Colorado	308	1.5%
23	Arkansas	305	1.5%
24	New Jersey	287	1.4%
25	Wisconsin	269	1.4%
26	Washington	261	1.3%
27	Kentucky	259	1.3%
28	New Mexico	211	1.1%
29	Nevada	194	1.0%
30	Minnesota	186	0.9%
31	Massachusetts	157	0.8%
32	Oregon	153	0.8%
33	Kansas	151	0.8%
34	Utah	105	0.5%
35	Connecticut	102	0.5%
36	Nebraska	87	0.4%
37	Iowa	86	0.4%
38	West Virginia	69	0.3%
39	Delaware	61	0.3%
40	Rhode Island	55	0.3%
41	Idaho	51	0.3%
42	Hawaii	48	0.2%
43	South Dakota	32	0.2%
44	Alaska	29	0.1%
45	Montana	28	0.1%
46	Wyoming	24	0.1%
47	North Dakota	22	0.1%
48	Maine	20	0.1%
49	New Hampshire	14	0.1%
50	Vermont	10	0.1%
	District of Columbia	69	0.3%

Source: CQ Press using data from U.S. Department of Health and Human Services, National Center for Health Statistics
   "Vital Stats" (http://www.cdc.gov/nchs/VitalStats.htm)
*Final data. Births to 10- to 14-year-olds during the three years of 2004 to 2006 by state of residence.

Young Teen Birthrate: 2004 to 2006

National Rate = 0.7 Live Births per 1,000 10- to 14-Year-Old Females*

ALPHA ORDER

RANK	STATE	RATE
5	Alabama	1.0
32	Alaska	0.4
8	Arizona	0.9
3	Arkansas	1.1
22	California	0.5
17	Colorado	0.6
42	Connecticut	0.3
14	Delaware	0.7
14	Florida	0.7
5	Georgia	1.0
32	Hawaii	0.4
42	Idaho	0.3
14	Illinois	0.7
22	Indiana	0.5
42	Iowa	0.3
22	Kansas	0.5
17	Kentucky	0.6
2	Louisiana	1.2
48	Maine	0.2
17	Maryland	0.6
42	Massachusetts	0.3
22	Michigan	0.5
32	Minnesota	0.4
1	Mississippi	1.7
17	Missouri	0.6
42	Montana	0.3
22	Nebraska	0.5
13	Nevada	0.8
NA	New Hampshire**	NA
42	New Jersey	0.3
5	New Mexico	1.0
32	New York	0.4
8	North Carolina	0.9
32	North Dakota	0.4
17	Ohio	0.6
8	Oklahoma	0.9
32	Oregon	0.4
22	Pennsylvania	0.5
22	Rhode Island	0.5
8	South Carolina	0.9
32	South Dakota	0.4
8	Tennessee	0.9
3	Texas	1.1
32	Utah	0.4
NA	Vermont**	NA
22	Virginia	0.5
32	Washington	0.4
32	West Virginia	0.4
22	Wisconsin	0.5
22	Wyoming	0.5

RANK ORDER

RANK	STATE	RATE
1	Mississippi	1.7
2	Louisiana	1.2
3	Arkansas	1.1
3	Texas	1.1
5	Alabama	1.0
5	Georgia	1.0
5	New Mexico	1.0
8	Arizona	0.9
8	North Carolina	0.9
8	Oklahoma	0.9
8	South Carolina	0.9
8	Tennessee	0.9
13	Nevada	0.8
14	Delaware	0.7
14	Florida	0.7
14	Illinois	0.7
17	Colorado	0.6
17	Kentucky	0.6
17	Maryland	0.6
17	Missouri	0.6
17	Ohio	0.6
22	California	0.5
22	Indiana	0.5
22	Kansas	0.5
22	Michigan	0.5
22	Nebraska	0.5
22	Pennsylvania	0.5
22	Rhode Island	0.5
22	Virginia	0.5
22	Wisconsin	0.5
22	Wyoming	0.5
32	Alaska	0.4
32	Hawaii	0.4
32	Minnesota	0.4
32	New York	0.4
32	North Dakota	0.4
32	Oregon	0.4
32	South Dakota	0.4
32	Utah	0.4
32	Washington	0.4
32	West Virginia	0.4
42	Connecticut	0.3
42	Idaho	0.3
42	Iowa	0.3
42	Massachusetts	0.3
42	Montana	0.3
42	New Jersey	0.3
48	Maine	0.2
NA	New Hampshire**	NA
NA	Vermont**	NA

District of Columbia 1.5

Source: CQ Press using data from U.S. Department of Health and Human Services, National Center for Health Statistics
"Vital Stats" (http://www.cdc.gov/nchs/VitalStats.htm)
*Final data. Births to 10- to 14-year-olds during the three years of 2004 to 2006 by state of residence.
**Insufficient data for a reliable rate.

Births to Women 35 to 54 Years Old in 2006

National Total = 611,129 Live Births*

<table>
<tr><td colspan="4">ALPHA ORDER</td><td colspan="4">RANK ORDER</td></tr>
<tr><td>RANK</td><td>STATE</td><td>BIRTHS</td><td>% of USA</td><td>RANK</td><td>STATE</td><td>BIRTHS</td><td>% of USA</td></tr>
<tr><td>26</td><td>Alabama</td><td>5,770</td><td>0.9%</td><td>1</td><td>California</td><td>97,880</td><td>16.0%</td></tr>
<tr><td>45</td><td>Alaska</td><td>1,463</td><td>0.2%</td><td>2</td><td>New York</td><td>50,259</td><td>8.2%</td></tr>
<tr><td>16</td><td>Arizona</td><td>11,992</td><td>2.0%</td><td>3</td><td>Texas</td><td>45,476</td><td>7.4%</td></tr>
<tr><td>38</td><td>Arkansas</td><td>3,114</td><td>0.5%</td><td>4</td><td>Florida</td><td>34,444</td><td>5.6%</td></tr>
<tr><td>1</td><td>California</td><td>97,880</td><td>16.0%</td><td>5</td><td>Illinois</td><td>28,033</td><td>4.6%</td></tr>
<tr><td>18</td><td>Colorado</td><td>10,935</td><td>1.8%</td><td>6</td><td>New Jersey</td><td>25,296</td><td>4.1%</td></tr>
<tr><td>20</td><td>Connecticut</td><td>9,433</td><td>1.5%</td><td>7</td><td>Pennsylvania</td><td>23,705</td><td>3.9%</td></tr>
<tr><td>44</td><td>Delaware</td><td>1,653</td><td>0.3%</td><td>8</td><td>Georgia</td><td>18,604</td><td>3.0%</td></tr>
<tr><td>4</td><td>Florida</td><td>34,444</td><td>5.6%</td><td>9</td><td>Ohio</td><td>18,592</td><td>3.0%</td></tr>
<tr><td>8</td><td>Georgia</td><td>18,604</td><td>3.0%</td><td>10</td><td>Massachusetts</td><td>18,221</td><td>3.0%</td></tr>
<tr><td>35</td><td>Hawaii</td><td>3,284</td><td>0.5%</td><td>11</td><td>Virginia</td><td>17,859</td><td>2.9%</td></tr>
<tr><td>40</td><td>Idaho</td><td>2,315</td><td>0.4%</td><td>12</td><td>Michigan</td><td>16,973</td><td>2.8%</td></tr>
<tr><td>5</td><td>Illinois</td><td>28,033</td><td>4.6%</td><td>13</td><td>North Carolina</td><td>16,069</td><td>2.6%</td></tr>
<tr><td>21</td><td>Indiana</td><td>9,219</td><td>1.5%</td><td>14</td><td>Maryland</td><td>14,594</td><td>2.4%</td></tr>
<tr><td>33</td><td>Iowa</td><td>4,440</td><td>0.7%</td><td>15</td><td>Washington</td><td>13,713</td><td>2.2%</td></tr>
<tr><td>31</td><td>Kansas</td><td>4,563</td><td>0.7%</td><td>16</td><td>Arizona</td><td>11,992</td><td>2.0%</td></tr>
<tr><td>28</td><td>Kentucky</td><td>5,521</td><td>0.9%</td><td>17</td><td>Minnesota</td><td>11,260</td><td>1.8%</td></tr>
<tr><td>27</td><td>Louisiana</td><td>5,570</td><td>0.9%</td><td>18</td><td>Colorado</td><td>10,935</td><td>1.8%</td></tr>
<tr><td>42</td><td>Maine</td><td>2,014</td><td>0.3%</td><td>19</td><td>Wisconsin</td><td>9,903</td><td>1.6%</td></tr>
<tr><td>14</td><td>Maryland</td><td>14,594</td><td>2.4%</td><td>20</td><td>Connecticut</td><td>9,433</td><td>1.5%</td></tr>
<tr><td>10</td><td>Massachusetts</td><td>18,221</td><td>3.0%</td><td>21</td><td>Indiana</td><td>9,219</td><td>1.5%</td></tr>
<tr><td>12</td><td>Michigan</td><td>16,973</td><td>2.8%</td><td>22</td><td>Tennessee</td><td>8,681</td><td>1.4%</td></tr>
<tr><td>17</td><td>Minnesota</td><td>11,260</td><td>1.8%</td><td>23</td><td>Missouri</td><td>8,641</td><td>1.4%</td></tr>
<tr><td>34</td><td>Mississippi</td><td>3,390</td><td>0.6%</td><td>24</td><td>Oregon</td><td>6,698</td><td>1.1%</td></tr>
<tr><td>23</td><td>Missouri</td><td>8,641</td><td>1.4%</td><td>25</td><td>South Carolina</td><td>6,568</td><td>1.1%</td></tr>
<tr><td>46</td><td>Montana</td><td>1,439</td><td>0.2%</td><td>26</td><td>Alabama</td><td>5,770</td><td>0.9%</td></tr>
<tr><td>36</td><td>Nebraska</td><td>3,134</td><td>0.5%</td><td>27</td><td>Louisiana</td><td>5,570</td><td>0.9%</td></tr>
<tr><td>29</td><td>Nevada</td><td>5,321</td><td>0.9%</td><td>28</td><td>Kentucky</td><td>5,521</td><td>0.9%</td></tr>
<tr><td>39</td><td>New Hampshire</td><td>2,668</td><td>0.4%</td><td>29</td><td>Nevada</td><td>5,321</td><td>0.9%</td></tr>
<tr><td>6</td><td>New Jersey</td><td>25,296</td><td>4.1%</td><td>30</td><td>Utah</td><td>4,848</td><td>0.8%</td></tr>
<tr><td>37</td><td>New Mexico</td><td>3,118</td><td>0.5%</td><td>31</td><td>Kansas</td><td>4,563</td><td>0.7%</td></tr>
<tr><td>2</td><td>New York</td><td>50,259</td><td>8.2%</td><td>32</td><td>Oklahoma</td><td>4,548</td><td>0.7%</td></tr>
<tr><td>13</td><td>North Carolina</td><td>16,069</td><td>2.6%</td><td>33</td><td>Iowa</td><td>4,440</td><td>0.7%</td></tr>
<tr><td>49</td><td>North Dakota</td><td>926</td><td>0.2%</td><td>34</td><td>Mississippi</td><td>3,390</td><td>0.6%</td></tr>
<tr><td>9</td><td>Ohio</td><td>18,592</td><td>3.0%</td><td>35</td><td>Hawaii</td><td>3,284</td><td>0.5%</td></tr>
<tr><td>32</td><td>Oklahoma</td><td>4,548</td><td>0.7%</td><td>36</td><td>Nebraska</td><td>3,134</td><td>0.5%</td></tr>
<tr><td>24</td><td>Oregon</td><td>6,698</td><td>1.1%</td><td>37</td><td>New Mexico</td><td>3,118</td><td>0.5%</td></tr>
<tr><td>7</td><td>Pennsylvania</td><td>23,705</td><td>3.9%</td><td>38</td><td>Arkansas</td><td>3,114</td><td>0.5%</td></tr>
<tr><td>41</td><td>Rhode Island</td><td>2,269</td><td>0.4%</td><td>39</td><td>New Hampshire</td><td>2,668</td><td>0.4%</td></tr>
<tr><td>25</td><td>South Carolina</td><td>6,568</td><td>1.1%</td><td>40</td><td>Idaho</td><td>2,315</td><td>0.4%</td></tr>
<tr><td>47</td><td>South Dakota</td><td>1,212</td><td>0.2%</td><td>41</td><td>Rhode Island</td><td>2,269</td><td>0.4%</td></tr>
<tr><td>22</td><td>Tennessee</td><td>8,681</td><td>1.4%</td><td>42</td><td>Maine</td><td>2,014</td><td>0.3%</td></tr>
<tr><td>3</td><td>Texas</td><td>45,476</td><td>7.4%</td><td>43</td><td>West Virginia</td><td>1,955</td><td>0.3%</td></tr>
<tr><td>30</td><td>Utah</td><td>4,848</td><td>0.8%</td><td>44</td><td>Delaware</td><td>1,653</td><td>0.3%</td></tr>
<tr><td>48</td><td>Vermont</td><td>1,187</td><td>0.2%</td><td>45</td><td>Alaska</td><td>1,463</td><td>0.2%</td></tr>
<tr><td>11</td><td>Virginia</td><td>17,859</td><td>2.9%</td><td>46</td><td>Montana</td><td>1,439</td><td>0.2%</td></tr>
<tr><td>15</td><td>Washington</td><td>13,713</td><td>2.2%</td><td>47</td><td>South Dakota</td><td>1,212</td><td>0.2%</td></tr>
<tr><td>43</td><td>West Virginia</td><td>1,955</td><td>0.3%</td><td>48</td><td>Vermont</td><td>1,187</td><td>0.2%</td></tr>
<tr><td>19</td><td>Wisconsin</td><td>9,903</td><td>1.6%</td><td>49</td><td>North Dakota</td><td>926</td><td>0.2%</td></tr>
<tr><td>50</td><td>Wyoming</td><td>676</td><td>0.1%</td><td>50</td><td>Wyoming</td><td>676</td><td>0.1%</td></tr>
<tr><td></td><td></td><td></td><td></td><td></td><td>District of Columbia</td><td>1,683</td><td>0.3%</td></tr>
</table>

Source: CQ Press using data from U.S. Department of Health and Human Services, National Center for Health Statistics
"Vital Stats" (http://www.cdc.gov/nchs/VitalStats.htm)
*Final data by state of residence.

Births to Women 35 to 54 Years Old as a Percent of All Births in 2006

National Percent = 14.3% of Live Births*

ALPHA ORDER			RANK ORDER		
RANK	STATE	PERCENT	RANK	STATE	PERCENT
44	Alabama	9.1	1	Massachusetts	23.5
22	Alaska	13.3	2	Connecticut	22.6
28	Arizona	11.7	3	New Jersey	22.0
49	Arkansas	7.6	4	New York	20.1
9	California	17.4	5	Maryland	18.8
14	Colorado	15.5	6	New Hampshire	18.6
2	Connecticut	22.6	7	Rhode Island	18.3
19	Delaware	13.8	8	Vermont	18.2
17	Florida	14.5	9	California	17.4
26	Georgia	12.5	10	Hawaii	17.3
10	Hawaii	17.3	11	Virginia	16.6
41	Idaho	9.6	12	Pennsylvania	15.9
14	Illinois	15.5	13	Washington	15.8
37	Indiana	10.4	14	Colorado	15.5
33	Iowa	10.9	14	Illinois	15.5
32	Kansas	11.1	16	Minnesota	15.3
42	Kentucky	9.5	17	Florida	14.5
46	Louisiana	8.8	18	Maine	14.2
18	Maine	14.2	19	Delaware	13.8
5	Maryland	18.8	19	Oregon	13.8
1	Massachusetts	23.5	21	Wisconsin	13.7
22	Michigan	13.3	22	Alaska	13.3
16	Minnesota	15.3	22	Michigan	13.3
50	Mississippi	7.4	22	Nevada	13.3
35	Missouri	10.6	25	North Carolina	12.6
30	Montana	11.5	26	Georgia	12.5
28	Nebraska	11.7	27	Ohio	12.3
22	Nevada	13.3	28	Arizona	11.7
6	New Hampshire	18.6	28	Nebraska	11.7
3	New Jersey	22.0	30	Montana	11.5
37	New Mexico	10.4	31	Texas	11.4
4	New York	20.1	32	Kansas	11.1
25	North Carolina	12.6	33	Iowa	10.9
34	North Dakota	10.7	34	North Dakota	10.7
27	Ohio	12.3	35	Missouri	10.6
48	Oklahoma	8.4	35	South Carolina	10.6
19	Oregon	13.8	37	Indiana	10.4
12	Pennsylvania	15.9	37	New Mexico	10.4
7	Rhode Island	18.3	39	Tennessee	10.3
35	South Carolina	10.6	40	South Dakota	10.2
40	South Dakota	10.2	41	Idaho	9.6
39	Tennessee	10.3	42	Kentucky	9.5
31	Texas	11.4	43	West Virginia	9.3
44	Utah	9.1	44	Alabama	9.1
8	Vermont	18.2	44	Utah	9.1
11	Virginia	16.6	46	Louisiana	8.8
13	Washington	15.8	46	Wyoming	8.8
43	West Virginia	9.3	48	Oklahoma	8.4
21	Wisconsin	13.7	49	Arkansas	7.6
46	Wyoming	8.8	50	Mississippi	7.4

District of Columbia 19.7

Source: CQ Press using data from U.S. Department of Health and Human Services, National Center for Health Statistics
"Vital Stats" (http://www.cdc.gov/nchs/VitalStats.htm)
*Final data by state of residence.

Births by Vaginal Delivery in 2006

National Total = 2,938,967 Live Births*

ALPHA ORDER

RANK	STATE	BIRTHS	% of USA
23	Alabama	42,113	1.4%
46	Alaska	8,467	0.3%
11	Arizona	76,207	2.6%
34	Arkansas	27,362	0.9%
1	California	386,396	13.1%
20	Colorado	52,851	1.8%
33	Connecticut	27,559	0.9%
47	Delaware	8,308	0.3%
4	Florida	151,316	5.1%
8	Georgia	102,260	3.5%
39	Hawaii	14,123	0.5%
38	Idaho	18,670	0.6%
5	Illinois	127,123	4.3%
14	Indiana	62,928	2.1%
31	Iowa	29,359	1.0%
32	Kansas	28,964	1.0%
27	Kentucky	38,154	1.3%
26	Louisiana	40,878	1.4%
42	Maine	9,920	0.3%
21	Maryland	52,541	1.8%
22	Massachusetts	51,888	1.8%
10	Michigan	89,493	3.0%
18	Minnesota	54,850	1.9%
30	Mississippi	29,752	1.0%
17	Missouri	56,807	1.9%
43	Montana	9,006	0.3%
37	Nebraska	19,030	0.6%
35	Nevada	27,138	0.9%
41	New Hampshire	10,079	0.3%
13	New Jersey	72,003	2.4%
36	New Mexico	22,961	0.8%
3	New York	168,570	5.7%
9	North Carolina	89,629	3.0%
48	North Dakota	6,224	0.2%
6	Ohio	106,469	3.6%
28	Oklahoma	36,029	1.2%
29	Oregon	34,959	1.2%
7	Pennsylvania	104,810	3.6%
45	Rhode Island	8,524	0.3%
25	South Carolina	41,717	1.4%
44	South Dakota	8,701	0.3%
16	Tennessee	57,024	1.9%
2	Texas	266,935	9.1%
24	Utah	42,001	1.4%
50	Vermont	4,818	0.2%
12	Virginia	72,884	2.5%
15	Washington	62,203	2.1%
40	West Virginia	13,563	0.5%
19	Wisconsin	54,544	1.9%
49	Wyoming	5,662	0.2%

RANK ORDER

RANK	STATE	BIRTHS	% of USA
1	California	386,396	13.1%
2	Texas	266,935	9.1%
3	New York	168,570	5.7%
4	Florida	151,316	5.1%
5	Illinois	127,123	4.3%
6	Ohio	106,469	3.6%
7	Pennsylvania	104,810	3.6%
8	Georgia	102,260	3.5%
9	North Carolina	89,629	3.0%
10	Michigan	89,493	3.0%
11	Arizona	76,207	2.6%
12	Virginia	72,884	2.5%
13	New Jersey	72,003	2.4%
14	Indiana	62,928	2.1%
15	Washington	62,203	2.1%
16	Tennessee	57,024	1.9%
17	Missouri	56,807	1.9%
18	Minnesota	54,850	1.9%
19	Wisconsin	54,544	1.9%
20	Colorado	52,851	1.8%
21	Maryland	52,541	1.8%
22	Massachusetts	51,888	1.8%
23	Alabama	42,113	1.4%
24	Utah	42,001	1.4%
25	South Carolina	41,717	1.4%
26	Louisiana	40,878	1.4%
27	Kentucky	38,154	1.3%
28	Oklahoma	36,029	1.2%
29	Oregon	34,959	1.2%
30	Mississippi	29,752	1.0%
31	Iowa	29,359	1.0%
32	Kansas	28,964	1.0%
33	Connecticut	27,559	0.9%
34	Arkansas	27,362	0.9%
35	Nevada	27,138	0.9%
36	New Mexico	22,961	0.8%
37	Nebraska	19,030	0.6%
38	Idaho	18,670	0.6%
39	Hawaii	14,123	0.5%
40	West Virginia	13,563	0.5%
41	New Hampshire	10,079	0.3%
42	Maine	9,920	0.3%
43	Montana	9,006	0.3%
44	South Dakota	8,701	0.3%
45	Rhode Island	8,524	0.3%
46	Alaska	8,467	0.3%
47	Delaware	8,308	0.3%
48	North Dakota	6,224	0.2%
49	Wyoming	5,662	0.2%
50	Vermont	4,818	0.2%
	District of Columbia	5,915	0.2%

Source: CQ Press using data from U.S. Department of Health and Human Services, National Center for Health Statistics
"National Vital Statistics Reports" (Vol. 57, No. 7, January 7, 2009, http://www.cdc.gov/nchs/births.htm)
*Estimates by state of residence.

Percent of Births by Vaginal Delivery in 2006

National Percent = 68.9% of Live Births*

ALPHA ORDER

RANK	STATE	PERCENT
43	Alabama	66.6
3	Alaska	77.0
8	Arizona	74.4
39	Arkansas	66.8
32	California	68.7
6	Colorado	74.7
44	Connecticut	65.9
29	Delaware	69.3
49	Florida	63.9
31	Georgia	68.8
8	Hawaii	74.4
2	Idaho	77.2
22	Illinois	70.4
19	Indiana	71.0
13	Iowa	72.3
20	Kansas	70.7
45	Kentucky	65.5
48	Louisiana	64.5
25	Maine	70.1
33	Maryland	67.8
39	Massachusetts	66.8
24	Michigan	70.2
7	Minnesota	74.6
47	Mississippi	64.6
28	Missouri	69.8
15	Montana	72.0
18	Nebraska	71.2
33	Nevada	67.8
25	New Hampshire	70.1
50	New Jersey	62.6
4	New Mexico	76.7
37	New York	67.4
25	North Carolina	70.1
14	North Dakota	72.2
20	Ohio	70.7
42	Oklahoma	66.7
16	Oregon	71.8
23	Pennsylvania	70.3
30	Rhode Island	68.9
38	South Carolina	67.1
12	South Dakota	73.0
35	Tennessee	67.6
39	Texas	66.8
1	Utah	78.5
10	Vermont	74.0
35	Virginia	67.6
17	Washington	71.6
46	West Virginia	64.8
5	Wisconsin	75.4
11	Wyoming	73.8

RANK ORDER

RANK	STATE	PERCENT
1	Utah	78.5
2	Idaho	77.2
3	Alaska	77.0
4	New Mexico	76.7
5	Wisconsin	75.4
6	Colorado	74.7
7	Minnesota	74.6
8	Arizona	74.4
8	Hawaii	74.4
10	Vermont	74.0
11	Wyoming	73.8
12	South Dakota	73.0
13	Iowa	72.3
14	North Dakota	72.2
15	Montana	72.0
16	Oregon	71.8
17	Washington	71.6
18	Nebraska	71.2
19	Indiana	71.0
20	Kansas	70.7
20	Ohio	70.7
22	Illinois	70.4
23	Pennsylvania	70.3
24	Michigan	70.2
25	Maine	70.1
25	New Hampshire	70.1
25	North Carolina	70.1
28	Missouri	69.8
29	Delaware	69.3
30	Rhode Island	68.9
31	Georgia	68.8
32	California	68.7
33	Maryland	67.8
33	Nevada	67.8
35	Tennessee	67.6
35	Virginia	67.6
37	New York	67.4
38	South Carolina	67.1
39	Arkansas	66.8
39	Massachusetts	66.8
39	Texas	66.8
42	Oklahoma	66.7
43	Alabama	66.6
44	Connecticut	65.9
45	Kentucky	65.5
46	West Virginia	64.8
47	Mississippi	64.6
48	Louisiana	64.5
49	Florida	63.9
50	New Jersey	62.6

District of Columbia   69.4

Source: CQ Press using data from U.S. Department of Health and Human Services, National Center for Health Statistics
   "National Vital Statistics Reports" (Vol. 57, No. 7, January 7, 2009, http://www.cdc.gov/nchs/births.htm)
*Estimates by state of residence.

Births by Cesarean Delivery in 2006

National Total = 1,326,588 Live Cesarean Births*

<table>
<tr><td colspan="4">ALPHA ORDER</td><td colspan="4">RANK ORDER</td></tr>
<tr><th>RANK</th><th>STATE</th><th>BIRTHS</th><th>% of USA</th><th>RANK</th><th>STATE</th><th>BIRTHS</th><th>% of USA</th></tr>
<tr><td>21</td><td>Alabama</td><td>21,119</td><td>1.6%</td><td>1</td><td>California</td><td>176,044</td><td>13.3%</td></tr>
<tr><td>47</td><td>Alaska</td><td>2,529</td><td>0.2%</td><td>2</td><td>Texas</td><td>132,668</td><td>10.0%</td></tr>
<tr><td>14</td><td>Arizona</td><td>26,222</td><td>2.0%</td><td>3</td><td>Florida</td><td>85,486</td><td>6.4%</td></tr>
<tr><td>31</td><td>Arkansas</td><td>13,599</td><td>1.0%</td><td>4</td><td>New York</td><td>81,534</td><td>6.1%</td></tr>
<tr><td>1</td><td>California</td><td>176,044</td><td>13.3%</td><td>5</td><td>Illinois</td><td>53,449</td><td>4.0%</td></tr>
<tr><td>26</td><td>Colorado</td><td>17,900</td><td>1.3%</td><td>6</td><td>Georgia</td><td>46,373</td><td>3.5%</td></tr>
<tr><td>29</td><td>Connecticut</td><td>14,261</td><td>1.1%</td><td>7</td><td>Pennsylvania</td><td>44,280</td><td>3.3%</td></tr>
<tr><td>44</td><td>Delaware</td><td>3,681</td><td>0.3%</td><td>8</td><td>Ohio</td><td>44,124</td><td>3.3%</td></tr>
<tr><td>3</td><td>Florida</td><td>85,486</td><td>6.4%</td><td>9</td><td>New Jersey</td><td>43,017</td><td>3.2%</td></tr>
<tr><td>6</td><td>Georgia</td><td>46,373</td><td>3.5%</td><td>10</td><td>North Carolina</td><td>38,230</td><td>2.9%</td></tr>
<tr><td>40</td><td>Hawaii</td><td>4,859</td><td>0.4%</td><td>11</td><td>Michigan</td><td>37,990</td><td>2.9%</td></tr>
<tr><td>39</td><td>Idaho</td><td>5,514</td><td>0.4%</td><td>12</td><td>Virginia</td><td>34,933</td><td>2.6%</td></tr>
<tr><td>5</td><td>Illinois</td><td>53,449</td><td>4.0%</td><td>13</td><td>Tennessee</td><td>27,331</td><td>2.1%</td></tr>
<tr><td>16</td><td>Indiana</td><td>25,703</td><td>1.9%</td><td>14</td><td>Arizona</td><td>26,222</td><td>2.0%</td></tr>
<tr><td>35</td><td>Iowa</td><td>11,248</td><td>0.8%</td><td>15</td><td>Massachusetts</td><td>25,788</td><td>1.9%</td></tr>
<tr><td>33</td><td>Kansas</td><td>12,004</td><td>0.9%</td><td>16</td><td>Indiana</td><td>25,703</td><td>1.9%</td></tr>
<tr><td>23</td><td>Kentucky</td><td>20,096</td><td>1.5%</td><td>17</td><td>Maryland</td><td>24,953</td><td>1.9%</td></tr>
<tr><td>20</td><td>Louisiana</td><td>22,498</td><td>1.7%</td><td>18</td><td>Washington</td><td>24,673</td><td>1.9%</td></tr>
<tr><td>42</td><td>Maine</td><td>4,231</td><td>0.3%</td><td>19</td><td>Missouri</td><td>24,578</td><td>1.9%</td></tr>
<tr><td>17</td><td>Maryland</td><td>24,953</td><td>1.9%</td><td>20</td><td>Louisiana</td><td>22,498</td><td>1.7%</td></tr>
<tr><td>15</td><td>Massachusetts</td><td>25,788</td><td>1.9%</td><td>21</td><td>Alabama</td><td>21,119</td><td>1.6%</td></tr>
<tr><td>11</td><td>Michigan</td><td>37,990</td><td>2.9%</td><td>22</td><td>South Carolina</td><td>20,454</td><td>1.5%</td></tr>
<tr><td>24</td><td>Minnesota</td><td>18,675</td><td>1.4%</td><td>23</td><td>Kentucky</td><td>20,096</td><td>1.5%</td></tr>
<tr><td>28</td><td>Mississippi</td><td>16,304</td><td>1.2%</td><td>24</td><td>Minnesota</td><td>18,675</td><td>1.4%</td></tr>
<tr><td>19</td><td>Missouri</td><td>24,578</td><td>1.9%</td><td>25</td><td>Oklahoma</td><td>17,987</td><td>1.4%</td></tr>
<tr><td>45</td><td>Montana</td><td>3,502</td><td>0.3%</td><td>26</td><td>Colorado</td><td>17,900</td><td>1.3%</td></tr>
<tr><td>36</td><td>Nebraska</td><td>7,697</td><td>0.6%</td><td>27</td><td>Wisconsin</td><td>17,796</td><td>1.3%</td></tr>
<tr><td>32</td><td>Nevada</td><td>12,889</td><td>1.0%</td><td>28</td><td>Mississippi</td><td>16,304</td><td>1.2%</td></tr>
<tr><td>41</td><td>New Hampshire</td><td>4,299</td><td>0.3%</td><td>29</td><td>Connecticut</td><td>14,261</td><td>1.1%</td></tr>
<tr><td>9</td><td>New Jersey</td><td>43,017</td><td>3.2%</td><td>30</td><td>Oregon</td><td>13,730</td><td>1.0%</td></tr>
<tr><td>38</td><td>New Mexico</td><td>6,975</td><td>0.5%</td><td>31</td><td>Arkansas</td><td>13,599</td><td>1.0%</td></tr>
<tr><td>4</td><td>New York</td><td>81,534</td><td>6.1%</td><td>32</td><td>Nevada</td><td>12,889</td><td>1.0%</td></tr>
<tr><td>10</td><td>North Carolina</td><td>38,230</td><td>2.9%</td><td>33</td><td>Kansas</td><td>12,004</td><td>0.9%</td></tr>
<tr><td>48</td><td>North Dakota</td><td>2,397</td><td>0.2%</td><td>34</td><td>Utah</td><td>11,503</td><td>0.9%</td></tr>
<tr><td>8</td><td>Ohio</td><td>44,124</td><td>3.3%</td><td>35</td><td>Iowa</td><td>11,248</td><td>0.8%</td></tr>
<tr><td>25</td><td>Oklahoma</td><td>17,987</td><td>1.4%</td><td>36</td><td>Nebraska</td><td>7,697</td><td>0.6%</td></tr>
<tr><td>30</td><td>Oregon</td><td>13,730</td><td>1.0%</td><td>37</td><td>West Virginia</td><td>7,368</td><td>0.6%</td></tr>
<tr><td>7</td><td>Pennsylvania</td><td>44,280</td><td>3.3%</td><td>38</td><td>New Mexico</td><td>6,975</td><td>0.5%</td></tr>
<tr><td>43</td><td>Rhode Island</td><td>3,848</td><td>0.3%</td><td>39</td><td>Idaho</td><td>5,514</td><td>0.4%</td></tr>
<tr><td>22</td><td>South Carolina</td><td>20,454</td><td>1.5%</td><td>40</td><td>Hawaii</td><td>4,859</td><td>0.4%</td></tr>
<tr><td>46</td><td>South Dakota</td><td>3,218</td><td>0.2%</td><td>41</td><td>New Hampshire</td><td>4,299</td><td>0.3%</td></tr>
<tr><td>13</td><td>Tennessee</td><td>27,331</td><td>2.1%</td><td>42</td><td>Maine</td><td>4,231</td><td>0.3%</td></tr>
<tr><td>2</td><td>Texas</td><td>132,668</td><td>10.0%</td><td>43</td><td>Rhode Island</td><td>3,848</td><td>0.3%</td></tr>
<tr><td>34</td><td>Utah</td><td>11,503</td><td>0.9%</td><td>44</td><td>Delaware</td><td>3,681</td><td>0.3%</td></tr>
<tr><td>50</td><td>Vermont</td><td>1,693</td><td>0.1%</td><td>45</td><td>Montana</td><td>3,502</td><td>0.3%</td></tr>
<tr><td>12</td><td>Virginia</td><td>34,933</td><td>2.6%</td><td>46</td><td>South Dakota</td><td>3,218</td><td>0.2%</td></tr>
<tr><td>18</td><td>Washington</td><td>24,673</td><td>1.9%</td><td>47</td><td>Alaska</td><td>2,529</td><td>0.2%</td></tr>
<tr><td>37</td><td>West Virginia</td><td>7,368</td><td>0.6%</td><td>48</td><td>North Dakota</td><td>2,397</td><td>0.2%</td></tr>
<tr><td>27</td><td>Wisconsin</td><td>17,796</td><td>1.3%</td><td>49</td><td>Wyoming</td><td>2,010</td><td>0.2%</td></tr>
<tr><td>49</td><td>Wyoming</td><td>2,010</td><td>0.2%</td><td>50</td><td>Vermont</td><td>1,693</td><td>0.1%</td></tr>
<tr><td></td><td></td><td></td><td></td><td></td><td>District of Columbia</td><td>2,608</td><td>0.2%</td></tr>
</table>

Source: CQ Press using data from U.S. Department of Health and Human Services, National Center for Health Statistics
"National Vital Statistics Reports" (Vol. 57, No. 7, January 7, 2009, http://www.cdc.gov/nchs/births.htm)
*Estimates by state of residence.

Percent of Births by Cesarean Delivery in 2006

National Percent = 31.1% of Live Births*

ALPHA ORDER

RANK ORDER

RANK	STATE	PERCENT	RANK	STATE	PERCENT
8	Alabama	33.4	1	New Jersey	37.4
48	Alaska	23.0	2	Florida	36.1
42	Arizona	25.6	3	Louisiana	35.5
10	Arkansas	33.2	4	Mississippi	35.4
19	California	31.3	5	West Virginia	35.2
45	Colorado	25.3	6	Kentucky	34.5
7	Connecticut	34.1	7	Connecticut	34.1
22	Delaware	30.7	8	Alabama	33.4
2	Florida	36.1	9	Oklahoma	33.3
20	Georgia	31.2	10	Arkansas	33.2
42	Hawaii	25.6	10	Massachusetts	33.2
49	Idaho	22.8	10	Texas	33.2
29	Illinois	29.6	13	South Carolina	32.9
32	Indiana	29.0	14	New York	32.6
38	Iowa	27.7	15	Tennessee	32.4
30	Kansas	29.3	15	Virginia	32.4
6	Kentucky	34.5	17	Maryland	32.2
3	Louisiana	35.5	17	Nevada	32.2
24	Maine	29.9	19	California	31.3
17	Maryland	32.2	20	Georgia	31.2
10	Massachusetts	33.2	21	Rhode Island	31.1
27	Michigan	29.8	22	Delaware	30.7
44	Minnesota	25.4	23	Missouri	30.2
4	Mississippi	35.4	24	Maine	29.9
23	Missouri	30.2	24	New Hampshire	29.9
36	Montana	28.0	24	North Carolina	29.9
33	Nebraska	28.8	27	Michigan	29.8
17	Nevada	32.2	28	Pennsylvania	29.7
24	New Hampshire	29.9	29	Illinois	29.6
1	New Jersey	37.4	30	Kansas	29.3
47	New Mexico	23.3	30	Ohio	29.3
14	New York	32.6	32	Indiana	29.0
24	North Carolina	29.9	33	Nebraska	28.8
37	North Dakota	27.8	34	Washington	28.4
30	Ohio	29.3	35	Oregon	28.2
9	Oklahoma	33.3	36	Montana	28.0
35	Oregon	28.2	37	North Dakota	27.8
28	Pennsylvania	29.7	38	Iowa	27.7
21	Rhode Island	31.1	39	South Dakota	27.0
13	South Carolina	32.9	40	Wyoming	26.2
39	South Dakota	27.0	41	Vermont	26.0
15	Tennessee	32.4	42	Arizona	25.6
10	Texas	33.2	42	Hawaii	25.6
50	Utah	21.5	44	Minnesota	25.4
41	Vermont	26.0	45	Colorado	25.3
15	Virginia	32.4	46	Wisconsin	24.6
34	Washington	28.4	47	New Mexico	23.3
5	West Virginia	35.2	48	Alaska	23.0
46	Wisconsin	24.6	49	Idaho	22.8
40	Wyoming	26.2	50	Utah	21.5

	District of Columbia	30.6

Source: U.S. Department of Health and Human Services, National Center for Health Statistics
  "National Vital Statistics Reports" (Vol. 57, No. 7, January 7, 2009, http://www.cdc.gov/nchs/births.htm)
*Final data by state of residence.

Percent Change in Rate of Cesarean Births: 2002 to 2006

National Percent Change = 19.2% Increase*

ALPHA ORDER				RANK ORDER		
RANK	STATE	PERCENT CHANGE		RANK	STATE	PERCENT CHANGE
38	Alabama	16.4		1	Connecticut	30.7
31	Alaska	17.9		2	Florida	26.7
18	Arizona	20.2		3	Nevada	25.3
43	Arkansas	14.1		4	Vermont	24.4
36	California	16.8		5	Ohio	24.2
20	Colorado	19.9		5	Wyoming	24.2
1	Connecticut	30.7		7	Illinois	23.8
47	Delaware	12.5		8	New Hampshire	23.6
2	Florida	26.7		9	Kentucky	23.2
14	Georgia	20.5		10	Montana	22.3
23	Hawaii	19.6		11	New Mexico	22.0
40	Idaho	15.7		12	New Jersey	21.0
7	Illinois	23.8		13	Virginia	20.9
35	Indiana	16.9		14	Georgia	20.5
48	Iowa	11.7		14	Oregon	20.5
30	Kansas	18.1		16	New York	20.3
9	Kentucky	23.2		16	North Dakota	20.3
36	Louisiana	16.8		18	Arizona	20.2
39	Maine	16.3		19	West Virginia	20.1
34	Maryland	17.1		20	Colorado	19.9
27	Massachusetts	18.6		21	Pennsylvania	19.8
22	Michigan	19.7		22	Michigan	19.7
42	Minnesota	14.4		23	Hawaii	19.6
44	Mississippi	13.8		24	Wisconsin	19.4
33	Missouri	17.5		25	Texas	19.0
10	Montana	22.3		26	Rhode Island	18.7
50	Nebraska	7.9		27	Massachusetts	18.6
3	Nevada	25.3		28	Oklahoma	18.5
8	New Hampshire	23.6		29	Washington	18.3
12	New Jersey	21.0		30	Kansas	18.1
11	New Mexico	22.0		31	Alaska	17.9
16	New York	20.3		32	Tennessee	17.8
45	North Carolina	13.3		33	Missouri	17.5
16	North Dakota	20.3		34	Maryland	17.1
5	Ohio	24.2		35	Indiana	16.9
28	Oklahoma	18.5		36	California	16.8
14	Oregon	20.5		36	Louisiana	16.8
21	Pennsylvania	19.8		38	Alabama	16.4
26	Rhode Island	18.7		39	Maine	16.3
41	South Carolina	15.0		40	Idaho	15.7
49	South Dakota	9.8		41	South Carolina	15.0
32	Tennessee	17.8		42	Minnesota	14.4
25	Texas	19.0		43	Arkansas	14.1
46	Utah	12.6		44	Mississippi	13.8
4	Vermont	24.4		45	North Carolina	13.3
13	Virginia	20.9		46	Utah	12.6
29	Washington	18.3		47	Delaware	12.5
19	West Virginia	20.1		48	Iowa	11.7
24	Wisconsin	19.4		49	South Dakota	9.8
5	Wyoming	24.2		50	Nebraska	7.9
					District of Columbia	15.5

Source: CQ Press using data from U.S. Department of Health and Human Services, National Center for Health Statistics
"National Vital Statistics Reports" (Vol. 57, No. 7, January 7, 2009, http://www.cdc.gov/nchs/births.htm)
*Estimates by state of residence.

Percent of Births That Are Pre-Term in 2006

National Percent = 12.8% of Births*

ALPHA ORDER

RANK	STATE	PERCENT		RANK	STATE	PERCENT
2	Alabama	17.1		1	Mississippi	18.8
42	Alaska	11.2		2	Alabama	17.1
20	Arizona	13.2		3	Louisiana	16.4
13	Arkansas	13.7		4	South Carolina	15.4
45	California	10.7		5	Kentucky	15.1
30	Colorado	12.2		6	Tennessee	14.8
47	Connecticut	10.4		7	Nevada	14.4
13	Delaware	13.7		8	Georgia	14.1
12	Florida	13.8		8	New Mexico	14.1
8	Georgia	14.1		10	West Virginia	14.0
31	Hawaii	12.1		11	Oklahoma	13.9
37	Idaho	11.6		12	Florida	13.8
18	Illinois	13.3		13	Arkansas	13.7
20	Indiana	13.2		13	Delaware	13.7
37	Iowa	11.6		13	Texas	13.7
35	Kansas	11.8		16	North Carolina	13.6
5	Kentucky	15.1		17	Maryland	13.5
3	Louisiana	16.4		18	Illinois	13.3
43	Maine	11.1		18	Ohio	13.3
17	Maryland	13.5		20	Arizona	13.2
41	Massachusetts	11.3		20	Indiana	13.2
27	Michigan	12.5		22	New Jersey	12.9
46	Minnesota	10.5		23	Missouri	12.8
1	Mississippi	18.8		23	Wyoming	12.8
23	Missouri	12.8		25	South Dakota	12.7
34	Montana	11.9		26	Rhode Island	12.6
27	Nebraska	12.5		27	Michigan	12.5
7	Nevada	14.4		27	Nebraska	12.5
47	New Hampshire	10.4		29	New York	12.4
22	New Jersey	12.9		30	Colorado	12.2
8	New Mexico	14.1		31	Hawaii	12.1
29	New York	12.4		31	North Dakota	12.1
16	North Carolina	13.6		33	Virginia	12.0
31	North Dakota	12.1		34	Montana	11.9
18	Ohio	13.3		35	Kansas	11.8
11	Oklahoma	13.9		35	Pennsylvania	11.8
49	Oregon	10.3		37	Idaho	11.6
35	Pennsylvania	11.8		37	Iowa	11.6
26	Rhode Island	12.6		39	Utah	11.5
4	South Carolina	15.4		40	Wisconsin	11.4
25	South Dakota	12.7		41	Massachusetts	11.3
6	Tennessee	14.8		42	Alaska	11.2
13	Texas	13.7		43	Maine	11.1
39	Utah	11.5		44	Washington	11.0
50	Vermont	9.6		45	California	10.7
33	Virginia	12.0		46	Minnesota	10.5
44	Washington	11.0		47	Connecticut	10.4
10	West Virginia	14.0		47	New Hampshire	10.4
40	Wisconsin	11.4		49	Oregon	10.3
23	Wyoming	12.8		50	Vermont	9.6
					District of Columbia	16.0

Source: U.S. Department of Health and Human Services, National Center for Health Statistics
   "National Vital Statistics Reports" (Vol. 57, No. 7, January 7, 2009, http://www.cdc.gov/nchs/births.htm)
*Final data by state of residence. Births before 37 weeks of gestation.

Twin Birth Rate: 2004 to 2006

National Rate = 32.2 Twins Born per 1,000 Live Births*

ALPHA ORDER			RANK ORDER		
RANK	**STATE**	**RATE**	**RANK**	**STATE**	**RATE**
14	Alabama	33.5	1	Massachusetts	44.2
48	Alaska	26.7	2	New Jersey	42.7
49	Arizona	26.5	3	Connecticut	41.8
35	Arkansas	29.7	4	New Hampshire	39.0
38	California	29.5	5	Rhode Island	38.5
27	Colorado	31.3	6	Maryland	38.0
3	Connecticut	41.8	7	New York	36.6
9	Delaware	35.6	8	Illinois	35.7
33	Florida	30.0	9	Delaware	35.6
26	Georgia	31.4	10	Michigan	34.3
44	Hawaii	28.0	11	Pennsylvania	34.2
34	Idaho	29.8	12	Virginia	34.0
8	Illinois	35.7	13	Ohio	33.9
21	Indiana	32.2	14	Alabama	33.5
17	Iowa	33.1	15	Minnesota	33.4
35	Kansas	29.7	16	Mississippi	33.3
29	Kentucky	30.5	17	Iowa	33.1
23	Louisiana	32.0	18	North Dakota	32.9
22	Maine	32.1	19	Missouri	32.5
6	Maryland	38.0	20	Nebraska	32.4
1	Massachusetts	44.2	21	Indiana	32.2
10	Michigan	34.3	22	Maine	32.1
15	Minnesota	33.4	23	Louisiana	32.0
16	Mississippi	33.3	24	North Carolina	31.8
19	Missouri	32.5	24	South Carolina	31.8
40	Montana	29.0	26	Georgia	31.4
20	Nebraska	32.4	27	Colorado	31.3
41	Nevada	28.9	28	Tennessee	31.0
4	New Hampshire	39.0	29	Kentucky	30.5
2	New Jersey	42.7	30	Wisconsin	30.4
50	New Mexico	24.3	31	South Dakota	30.2
7	New York	36.6	32	Vermont	30.1
24	North Carolina	31.8	33	Florida	30.0
18	North Dakota	32.9	34	Idaho	29.8
13	Ohio	33.9	35	Arkansas	29.7
45	Oklahoma	27.5	35	Kansas	29.7
39	Oregon	29.3	35	Washington	29.7
11	Pennsylvania	34.2	38	California	29.5
5	Rhode Island	38.5	39	Oregon	29.3
24	South Carolina	31.8	40	Montana	29.0
31	South Dakota	30.2	41	Nevada	28.9
28	Tennessee	31.0	42	Texas	28.4
42	Texas	28.4	43	Wyoming	28.3
46	Utah	27.1	44	Hawaii	28.0
32	Vermont	30.1	45	Oklahoma	27.5
12	Virginia	34.0	46	Utah	27.1
35	Washington	29.7	46	West Virginia	27.1
46	West Virginia	27.1	48	Alaska	26.7
30	Wisconsin	30.4	49	Arizona	26.5
43	Wyoming	28.3	50	New Mexico	24.3
				District of Columbia	36.8

Source: U.S. Department of Health and Human Services, National Center for Health Statistics
 "National Vital Statistics Reports" (Vol. 57, No. 7, January 7, 2009, http://www.cdc.gov/nchs/births.htm)
*Final data by state of residence. Number of live births in twin deliveries.

Assisted Reproductive Technology Procedures in 2005

National Total = 133,459 Procedures*

ALPHA ORDER

RANK	STATE	PROCEDURES	% of USA
33	Alabama	736	0.6%
49	Alaska	150	0.1%
16	Arizona	2,117	1.6%
38	Arkansas	483	0.4%
1	California	18,655	14.0%
19	Colorado	1,810	1.4%
14	Connecticut	2,749	2.1%
41	Delaware	346	0.3%
7	Florida	6,364	4.8%
13	Georgia	2,938	2.2%
28	Hawaii	849	0.6%
40	Idaho	399	0.3%
3	Illinois	9,449	7.1%
18	Indiana	1,854	1.4%
29	Iowa	839	0.6%
36	Kansas	625	0.5%
27	Kentucky	929	0.7%
32	Louisiana	751	0.6%
43	Maine	217	0.2%
9	Maryland	4,685	3.5%
5	Massachusetts	8,571	6.4%
12	Michigan	3,183	2.4%
17	Minnesota	1,864	1.4%
39	Mississippi	439	0.3%
20	Missouri	1,703	1.3%
48	Montana	165	0.1%
35	Nebraska	656	0.5%
23	Nevada	1,184	0.9%
31	New Hampshire	774	0.6%
4	New Jersey	9,325	7.0%
42	New Mexico	311	0.2%
2	New York	16,713	12.5%
15	North Carolina	2,587	1.9%
45	North Dakota	204	0.2%
11	Ohio	3,361	2.5%
37	Oklahoma	569	0.4%
25	Oregon	1,010	0.8%
8	Pennsylvania	5,071	3.8%
30	Rhode Island	833	0.6%
26	South Carolina	974	0.7%
46	South Dakota	176	0.1%
24	Tennessee	1,031	0.8%
6	Texas	6,582	4.9%
34	Utah	662	0.5%
47	Vermont	174	0.1%
10	Virginia	4,232	3.2%
21	Washington	1,668	1.2%
44	West Virginia	209	0.2%
22	Wisconsin	1,570	1.2%
50	Wyoming	71	0.1%

RANK ORDER

RANK	STATE	PROCEDURES	% of USA
1	California	18,655	14.0%
2	New York	16,713	12.5%
3	Illinois	9,449	7.1%
4	New Jersey	9,325	7.0%
5	Massachusetts	8,571	6.4%
6	Texas	6,582	4.9%
7	Florida	6,364	4.8%
8	Pennsylvania	5,071	3.8%
9	Maryland	4,685	3.5%
10	Virginia	4,232	3.2%
11	Ohio	3,361	2.5%
12	Michigan	3,183	2.4%
13	Georgia	2,938	2.2%
14	Connecticut	2,749	2.1%
15	North Carolina	2,587	1.9%
16	Arizona	2,117	1.6%
17	Minnesota	1,864	1.4%
18	Indiana	1,854	1.4%
19	Colorado	1,810	1.4%
20	Missouri	1,703	1.3%
21	Washington	1,668	1.2%
22	Wisconsin	1,570	1.2%
23	Nevada	1,184	0.9%
24	Tennessee	1,031	0.8%
25	Oregon	1,010	0.8%
26	South Carolina	974	0.7%
27	Kentucky	929	0.7%
28	Hawaii	849	0.6%
29	Iowa	839	0.6%
30	Rhode Island	833	0.6%
31	New Hampshire	774	0.6%
32	Louisiana	751	0.6%
33	Alabama	736	0.6%
34	Utah	662	0.5%
35	Nebraska	656	0.5%
36	Kansas	625	0.5%
37	Oklahoma	569	0.4%
38	Arkansas	483	0.4%
39	Mississippi	439	0.3%
40	Idaho	399	0.3%
41	Delaware	346	0.3%
42	New Mexico	311	0.2%
43	Maine	217	0.2%
44	West Virginia	209	0.2%
45	North Dakota	204	0.2%
46	South Dakota	176	0.1%
47	Vermont	174	0.1%
48	Montana	165	0.1%
49	Alaska	150	0.1%
50	Wyoming	71	0.1%
	District of Columbia	642	0.5%

Source: U.S. Department of Health and Human Services, Centers for Disease Control and Prevention
    "Assisted Reproductive Technology, 2005" (MMWR, Vol. 57, No. SS-05, 06/20/08, http://www.cdc.gov/mmwr/mmwr_ss.html)
*By patient's residence. Does not include 792 procedures for patients with residences outside the U.S. Assisted reproductive technology (ART) includes treatments in which both eggs and sperm are handled in the laboratory. In 2005, 73% of ART treatments were freshly fertilized embryos using the patient's eggs, 15% were thawed embryos using the patient's eggs, 8% were freshly fertilized embryos from donor eggs, and 4% were thawed embryos from donor eggs.

Infants Born from Assisted Reproductive Technology Procedures in 2005

National Total = 52,041 Live Births*

<u>ALPHA ORDER</u>

RANK	STATE	BIRTHS	% of USA
30	Alabama	338	0.7%
48	Alaska	63	0.1%
19	Arizona	767	1.5%
39	Arkansas	215	0.4%
1	California	7,159	13.8%
16	Colorado	999	1.9%
15	Connecticut	1,025	2.0%
42	Delaware	148	0.3%
7	Florida	2,418	4.7%
12	Georgia	1,286	2.5%
36	Hawaii	264	0.5%
38	Idaho	241	0.5%
4	Illinois	3,211	6.2%
22	Indiana	669	1.3%
27	Iowa	414	0.8%
35	Kansas	271	0.5%
28	Kentucky	403	0.8%
32	Louisiana	301	0.6%
43	Maine	95	0.2%
9	Maryland	1,656	3.2%
6	Massachusetts	2,964	5.7%
13	Michigan	1,285	2.5%
17	Minnesota	971	1.9%
40	Mississippi	187	0.4%
20	Missouri	740	1.4%
46	Montana	79	0.2%
37	Nebraska	255	0.5%
24	Nevada	526	1.0%
33	New Hampshire	292	0.6%
3	New Jersey	3,459	6.7%
41	New Mexico	169	0.3%
2	New York	5,411	10.5%
14	North Carolina	1,029	2.0%
45	North Dakota	84	0.2%
11	Ohio	1,365	2.6%
34	Oklahoma	288	0.6%
23	Oregon	533	1.0%
8	Pennsylvania	1,808	3.5%
31	Rhode Island	331	0.6%
25	South Carolina	513	1.0%
47	South Dakota	74	0.1%
26	Tennessee	511	1.0%
5	Texas	3,103	6.0%
29	Utah	371	0.7%
49	Vermont	47	0.1%
10	Virginia	1,572	3.0%
18	Washington	811	1.6%
44	West Virginia	92	0.2%
21	Wisconsin	685	1.3%
50	Wyoming	39	0.1%

<u>RANK ORDER</u>

RANK	STATE	BIRTHS	% of USA
1	California	7,159	13.8%
2	New York	5,411	10.5%
3	New Jersey	3,459	6.7%
4	Illinois	3,211	6.2%
5	Texas	3,103	6.0%
6	Massachusetts	2,964	5.7%
7	Florida	2,418	4.7%
8	Pennsylvania	1,808	3.5%
9	Maryland	1,656	3.2%
10	Virginia	1,572	3.0%
11	Ohio	1,365	2.6%
12	Georgia	1,286	2.5%
13	Michigan	1,285	2.5%
14	North Carolina	1,029	2.0%
15	Connecticut	1,025	2.0%
16	Colorado	999	1.9%
17	Minnesota	971	1.9%
18	Washington	811	1.6%
19	Arizona	767	1.5%
20	Missouri	740	1.4%
21	Wisconsin	685	1.3%
22	Indiana	669	1.3%
23	Oregon	533	1.0%
24	Nevada	526	1.0%
25	South Carolina	513	1.0%
26	Tennessee	511	1.0%
27	Iowa	414	0.8%
28	Kentucky	403	0.8%
29	Utah	371	0.7%
30	Alabama	338	0.7%
31	Rhode Island	331	0.6%
32	Louisiana	301	0.6%
33	New Hampshire	292	0.6%
34	Oklahoma	288	0.6%
35	Kansas	271	0.5%
36	Hawaii	264	0.5%
37	Nebraska	255	0.5%
38	Idaho	241	0.5%
39	Arkansas	215	0.4%
40	Mississippi	187	0.4%
41	New Mexico	169	0.3%
42	Delaware	148	0.3%
43	Maine	95	0.2%
44	West Virginia	92	0.2%
45	North Dakota	84	0.2%
46	Montana	79	0.2%
47	South Dakota	74	0.1%
48	Alaska	63	0.1%
49	Vermont	47	0.1%
50	Wyoming	39	0.1%
	District of Columbia	202	0.4%

Source: U.S. Department of Health and Human Services, Centers for Disease Control and Prevention
    "Assisted Reproductive Technology, 2005" (MMWR, Vol. 57, No. SS-05, 06/20/08, http://www.cdc.gov/mmwr/mmwr_ss.html)
*By patient's residence. Does not include 300 births for patients with residences outside the U.S. Assisted reproductive technology (ART) includes treatments in which both eggs and sperm are handled in the laboratory. In 2005, 73% of ART treatments were freshly fertilized embryos using the patient's eggs, 15% were thawed embryos using the patient's eggs, 8% were freshly fertilized embryos from donor eggs, and 4% were thawed embryos from donor eggs.

Percent of Assisted Reproductive Technology Procedures That Resulted in Live Births in 2005
National Percent = 29.0%*

ALPHA ORDER

RANK	STATE	PERCENT
16	Alabama	33.2
28	Alaska	31.3
42	Arizona	27.6
17	Arkansas	33.1
40	California	28.3
3	Colorado	40.4
38	Connecticut	28.4
19	Delaware	32.7
36	Florida	28.6
25	Georgia	32.0
49	Hawaii	22.7
1	Idaho	43.1
47	Illinois	25.8
46	Indiana	26.3
10	Iowa	37.2
27	Kansas	31.4
28	Kentucky	31.3
33	Louisiana	29.6
19	Maine	32.7
43	Maryland	26.9
43	Massachusetts	26.9
32	Michigan	29.7
7	Minnesota	38.5
23	Mississippi	32.1
15	Missouri	33.8
14	Montana	33.9
34	Nebraska	29.3
17	Nevada	33.1
36	New Hampshire	28.6
41	New Jersey	27.7
5	New Mexico	38.9
48	New York	24.7
30	North Carolina	29.8
22	North Dakota	32.4
30	Ohio	29.8
7	Oklahoma	38.5
9	Oregon	37.8
45	Pennsylvania	26.5
34	Rhode Island	29.3
6	South Carolina	38.6
26	South Dakota	31.8
12	Tennessee	36.6
13	Texas	34.1
4	Utah	39.9
50	Vermont	22.4
38	Virginia	28.4
11	Washington	36.7
23	West Virginia	32.1
21	Wisconsin	32.5
2	Wyoming	40.8

RANK ORDER

RANK	STATE	PERCENT
1	Idaho	43.1
2	Wyoming	40.8
3	Colorado	40.4
4	Utah	39.9
5	New Mexico	38.9
6	South Carolina	38.6
7	Minnesota	38.5
7	Oklahoma	38.5
9	Oregon	37.8
10	Iowa	37.2
11	Washington	36.7
12	Tennessee	36.6
13	Texas	34.1
14	Montana	33.9
15	Missouri	33.8
16	Alabama	33.2
17	Arkansas	33.1
17	Nevada	33.1
19	Delaware	32.7
19	Maine	32.7
21	Wisconsin	32.5
22	North Dakota	32.4
23	Mississippi	32.1
23	West Virginia	32.1
25	Georgia	32.0
26	South Dakota	31.8
27	Kansas	31.4
28	Alaska	31.3
28	Kentucky	31.3
30	North Carolina	29.8
30	Ohio	29.8
32	Michigan	29.7
33	Louisiana	29.6
34	Nebraska	29.3
34	Rhode Island	29.3
36	Florida	28.6
36	New Hampshire	28.6
38	Connecticut	28.4
38	Virginia	28.4
40	California	28.3
41	New Jersey	27.7
42	Arizona	27.6
43	Maryland	26.9
43	Massachusetts	26.9
45	Pennsylvania	26.5
46	Indiana	26.3
47	Illinois	25.8
48	New York	24.7
49	Hawaii	22.7
50	Vermont	22.4

District of Columbia 23.5

Source: CQ Press using data from U.S. Department of Health and Human Services, Centers for Disease Control and Prevention "Assisted Reproductive Technology, 2005" (MMWR, Vol. 57, No. SS-05, 06/20/08, http://www.cdc.gov/mmwr/mmwr_ss.html)
*By patient's residence. Assisted reproductive technology (ART) includes treatments in which both eggs and sperm are handled in the laboratory. In 2005, 73% of ART treatments were freshly fertilized embryos using the patient's eggs, 15% were thawed embryos using the patient's eggs, 8% were freshly fertilized embryos from donor eggs, and 4% were thawed embryos from donor eggs.

Percent of Total Live Births Resulting from
Assisted Reproductive Technology Procedures in 2005
National Percent = 1.3% of Live Births*

ALPHA ORDER				RANK ORDER		
RANK	STATE	PERCENT		RANK	STATE	PERCENT
40	Alabama	0.6		1	Massachusetts	3.9
40	Alaska	0.6		2	New Jersey	3.0
30	Arizona	0.8		3	Rhode Island	2.6
46	Arkansas	0.5		4	Connecticut	2.5
14	California	1.3		5	Maryland	2.2
11	Colorado	1.4		5	New York	2.2
4	Connecticut	2.5		7	New Hampshire	2.0
14	Delaware	1.3		8	Illinois	1.8
18	Florida	1.1		9	Hawaii	1.5
26	Georgia	0.9		9	Virginia	1.5
9	Hawaii	1.5		11	Colorado	1.4
20	Idaho	1.0		11	Minnesota	1.4
8	Illinois	1.8		11	Nevada	1.4
30	Indiana	0.8		14	California	1.3
18	Iowa	1.1		14	Delaware	1.3
34	Kansas	0.7		16	Oregon	1.2
34	Kentucky	0.7		16	Pennsylvania	1.2
46	Louisiana	0.5		18	Florida	1.1
34	Maine	0.7		18	Iowa	1.1
5	Maryland	2.2		20	Idaho	1.0
1	Massachusetts	3.9		20	Michigan	1.0
20	Michigan	1.0		20	Nebraska	1.0
11	Minnesota	1.4		20	North Dakota	1.0
49	Mississippi	0.4		20	Washington	1.0
26	Missouri	0.9		20	Wisconsin	1.0
34	Montana	0.7		26	Georgia	0.9
20	Nebraska	1.0		26	Missouri	0.9
11	Nevada	1.4		26	Ohio	0.9
7	New Hampshire	2.0		26	South Carolina	0.9
2	New Jersey	3.0		30	Arizona	0.8
40	New Mexico	0.6		30	Indiana	0.8
5	New York	2.2		30	North Carolina	0.8
30	North Carolina	0.8		30	Texas	0.8
20	North Dakota	1.0		34	Kansas	0.7
26	Ohio	0.9		34	Kentucky	0.7
40	Oklahoma	0.6		34	Maine	0.7
16	Oregon	1.2		34	Montana	0.7
16	Pennsylvania	1.2		34	Utah	0.7
3	Rhode Island	2.6		34	Vermont	0.7
26	South Carolina	0.9		40	Alabama	0.6
40	South Dakota	0.6		40	Alaska	0.6
40	Tennessee	0.6		40	New Mexico	0.6
30	Texas	0.8		40	Oklahoma	0.6
34	Utah	0.7		40	South Dakota	0.6
34	Vermont	0.7		40	Tennessee	0.6
9	Virginia	1.5		46	Arkansas	0.5
20	Washington	1.0		46	Louisiana	0.5
49	West Virginia	0.4		46	Wyoming	0.5
20	Wisconsin	1.0		49	Mississippi	0.4
46	Wyoming	0.5		49	West Virginia	0.4

District of Columbia 2.5

Source: CQ Press using data from U.S. Department of Health and Human Services, Centers for Disease Control and Prevention
"Assisted Reproductive Technology, 2005" (MMWR, Vol. 57, No. SS-05, 06/20/08, http://www.cdc.gov/mmwr/mmwr_ss.html)
"National Vital Statistics Reports" (Vol. 56, No. 6, December 5, 2007, http://www.cdc.gov/nchs/births.htm)
*By patient's residence. Does not include births or procedures to patients with residences outside the U.S. Assisted reproductive technology (ART) includes treatments in which both eggs and sperm are handled in the laboratory (that is, in vitro fertilization and related procedures).

Percent of Assisted Reproductive Technology Procedure Infants Born in Multiple Birth Deliveries in 2005
National Percent = 48.9% of Assisted Reproductive Technology Births*

ALPHA ORDER

RANK	STATE	PERCENT
7	Alabama	53.6
19	Alaska	50.8
46	Arizona	45.2
22	Arkansas	50.7
19	California	50.8
9	Colorado	52.6
40	Connecticut	46.8
42	Delaware	46.6
33	Florida	48.0
13	Georgia	51.6
15	Hawaii	51.5
5	Idaho	54.4
41	Illinois	46.7
12	Indiana	51.9
36	Iowa	47.6
8	Kansas	53.5
13	Kentucky	51.6
19	Louisiana	50.8
29	Maine	49.5
43	Maryland	46.4
47	Massachusetts	43.6
23	Michigan	50.6
15	Minnesota	51.5
36	Mississippi	47.6
48	Missouri	43.0
4	Montana	55.7
39	Nebraska	47.5
27	Nevada	49.8
36	New Hampshire	47.6
30	New Jersey	48.9
1	New Mexico	56.2
43	New York	46.4
32	North Carolina	48.4
49	North Dakota	40.5
24	Ohio	50.4
34	Oklahoma	47.9
3	Oregon	55.9
28	Pennsylvania	49.6
9	Rhode Island	52.6
18	South Carolina	50.9
26	South Dakota	50.0
17	Tennessee	51.1
6	Texas	53.7
2	Utah	56.1
50	Vermont	34.0
45	Virginia	45.4
35	Washington	47.7
11	West Virginia	52.2
25	Wisconsin	50.2
31	Wyoming	48.7

RANK ORDER

RANK	STATE	PERCENT
1	New Mexico	56.2
2	Utah	56.1
3	Oregon	55.9
4	Montana	55.7
5	Idaho	54.4
6	Texas	53.7
7	Alabama	53.6
8	Kansas	53.5
9	Colorado	52.6
9	Rhode Island	52.6
11	West Virginia	52.2
12	Indiana	51.9
13	Georgia	51.6
13	Kentucky	51.6
15	Hawaii	51.5
15	Minnesota	51.5
17	Tennessee	51.1
18	South Carolina	50.9
19	Alaska	50.8
19	California	50.8
19	Louisiana	50.8
22	Arkansas	50.7
23	Michigan	50.6
24	Ohio	50.4
25	Wisconsin	50.2
26	South Dakota	50.0
27	Nevada	49.8
28	Pennsylvania	49.6
29	Maine	49.5
30	New Jersey	48.9
31	Wyoming	48.7
32	North Carolina	48.4
33	Florida	48.0
34	Oklahoma	47.9
35	Washington	47.7
36	Iowa	47.6
36	Mississippi	47.6
36	New Hampshire	47.6
39	Nebraska	47.5
40	Connecticut	46.8
41	Illinois	46.7
42	Delaware	46.6
43	Maryland	46.4
43	New York	46.4
45	Virginia	45.4
46	Arizona	45.2
47	Massachusetts	43.6
48	Missouri	43.0
49	North Dakota	40.5
50	Vermont	34.0
	District of Columbia	50.0

Source: U.S. Department of Health and Human Services, Centers for Disease Control and Prevention
    "Assisted Reproductive Technology, 2005" (MMWR, Vol. 57, No. SS-05, 06/20/08, http://www.cdc.gov/mmwr/mmwr_ss.html)
*By patient's residence. Includes births and procedures to patients with residences outside the U.S. Assisted reproductive technology (ART) includes treatments in which both eggs and sperm are handled in the laboratory (that is, in vitro fertilization and related procedures).

Percent of Mothers Beginning Prenatal Care in First Trimester in 2006

National Percent = 83.2% of Mothers*

ALPHA ORDER			RANK ORDER		
RANK	STATE	PERCENT	RANK	STATE	PERCENT
20	Alabama	81.7	1	Massachusetts	88.6
22	Alaska	81.1	2	Maine	87.7
29	Arizona	77.7	3	Missouri	87.2
26	Arkansas	79.5	4	Louisiana	87.0
8	California	85.9	5	Minnesota	86.5
25	Colorado	79.7	6	Iowa	86.4
9	Connecticut	85.8	7	Illinois	86.2
NA	Delaware**	NA	8	California	85.9
NA	Florida**	NA	9	Connecticut	85.8
15	Georgia	83.3	10	Michigan	85.4
19	Hawaii	81.8	11	Rhode Island	84.5
NA	Idaho**	NA	11	Wisconsin	84.5
7	Illinois	86.2	13	Virginia	84.2
28	Indiana	79.0	14	Montana	83.7
6	Iowa	86.4	15	Georgia	83.3
NA	Kansas**	NA	16	Mississippi	83.2
NA	Kentucky**	NA	17	West Virginia	82.8
4	Louisiana	87.0	18	North Carolina	82.6
2	Maine	87.7	19	Hawaii	81.8
20	Maryland	81.7	20	Alabama	81.7
1	Massachusetts	88.6	20	Maryland	81.7
10	Michigan	85.4	22	Alaska	81.1
5	Minnesota	86.5	23	Utah	80.2
16	Mississippi	83.2	24	New York*	79.9
3	Missouri	87.2	25	Colorado	79.7
14	Montana	83.7	26	Arkansas	79.5
NA	Nebraska**	NA	27	Oregon	79.2
33	Nevada	71.5	28	Indiana	79.0
NA	New Hampshire**	NA	29	Arizona	77.7
30	New Jersey	77.6	30	New Jersey	77.6
32	New Mexico	74.7	31	Oklahoma	75.6
24	New York*	79.9	32	New Mexico	74.7
18	North Carolina	82.6	33	Nevada	71.5
NA	North Dakota**	NA	NA	Delaware**	NA
NA	Ohio**	NA	NA	Florida**	NA
31	Oklahoma	75.6	NA	Idaho**	NA
27	Oregon	79.2	NA	Kansas**	NA
NA	Pennsylvania**	NA	NA	Kentucky**	NA
11	Rhode Island	84.5	NA	Nebraska**	NA
NA	South Carolina**	NA	NA	New Hampshire**	NA
NA	South Dakota**	NA	NA	North Dakota**	NA
NA	Tennessee**	NA	NA	Ohio**	NA
NA	Texas**	NA	NA	Pennsylvania**	NA
23	Utah	80.2	NA	South Carolina**	NA
NA	Vermont**	NA	NA	South Dakota**	NA
13	Virginia	84.2	NA	Tennessee**	NA
NA	Washington**	NA	NA	Texas**	NA
17	West Virginia	82.8	NA	Vermont**	NA
11	Wisconsin	84.5	NA	Washington**	NA
NA	Wyoming**	NA	NA	Wyoming**	NA
			District of Columbia		78.9

Source: U.S. Department of Health and Human Services, National Center for Health Statistics
   "National Vital Statistics Reports" (Vol. 57, No. 7, January 7, 2009, http://www.cdc.gov/nchs/births.htm)
*Final data by state of residence. New York's figure is for New York City only.
**Not available. These states have implemented the 2003 Revision of the U.S. Certificate of Live Birth and their prenatal care data are not comparable with those based on the 1989 revision.

Percent of White Mothers Beginning Prenatal Care in First Trimester in 2006

National Percent = 88.1% of White Mothers*

ALPHA ORDER

RANK	STATE	PERCENT
15	Alabama	88.5
25	Alaska	85.0
21	Arizona	86.8
28	Arkansas	83.0
7	California	89.8
23	Colorado	85.7
2	Connecticut	91.4
NA	Delaware**	NA
NA	Florida**	NA
13	Georgia	89.4
24	Hawaii	85.2
NA	Idaho**	NA
4	Illinois	90.7
29	Indiana	82.8
15	Iowa	88.5
NA	Kansas**	NA
NA	Kentucky**	NA
1	Louisiana	92.3
17	Maine	88.3
14	Maryland	89.2
2	Massachusetts	91.4
11	Michigan	89.5
5	Minnesota	90.4
10	Mississippi	89.6
11	Missouri	89.5
22	Montana	86.5
NA	Nebraska**	NA
32	Nevada	79.9
NA	New Hampshire**	NA
20	New Jersey	87.1
31	New Mexico	81.4
19	New York*	87.7
7	North Carolina	89.8
NA	North Dakota**	NA
NA	Ohio**	NA
33	Oklahoma	79.5
30	Oregon	82.4
NA	Pennsylvania**	NA
6	Rhode Island	90.0
NA	South Carolina**	NA
NA	South Dakota**	NA
NA	Tennessee**	NA
NA	Texas**	NA
26	Utah	84.1
NA	Vermont**	NA
9	Virginia	89.7
NA	Washington**	NA
27	West Virginia	83.5
18	Wisconsin	88.0
NA	Wyoming**	NA

RANK ORDER

RANK	STATE	PERCENT
1	Louisiana	92.3
2	Connecticut	91.4
2	Massachusetts	91.4
4	Illinois	90.7
5	Minnesota	90.4
6	Rhode Island	90.0
7	California	89.8
7	North Carolina	89.8
9	Virginia	89.7
10	Mississippi	89.6
11	Michigan	89.5
11	Missouri	89.5
13	Georgia	89.4
14	Maryland	89.2
15	Alabama	88.5
15	Iowa	88.5
17	Maine	88.3
18	Wisconsin	88.0
19	New York*	87.7
20	New Jersey	87.1
21	Arizona	86.8
22	Montana	86.5
23	Colorado	85.7
24	Hawaii	85.2
25	Alaska	85.0
26	Utah	84.1
27	West Virginia	83.5
28	Arkansas	83.0
29	Indiana	82.8
30	Oregon	82.4
31	New Mexico	81.4
32	Nevada	79.9
33	Oklahoma	79.5
NA	Delaware**	NA
NA	Florida**	NA
NA	Idaho**	NA
NA	Kansas**	NA
NA	Kentucky**	NA
NA	Nebraska**	NA
NA	New Hampshire**	NA
NA	North Dakota**	NA
NA	Ohio**	NA
NA	Pennsylvania**	NA
NA	South Carolina**	NA
NA	South Dakota**	NA
NA	Tennessee**	NA
NA	Texas**	NA
NA	Vermont**	NA
NA	Washington**	NA
NA	Wyoming**	NA

District of Columbia — 92.2

Source: U.S. Department of Health and Human Services, National Center for Health Statistics
"National Vital Statistics Reports" (Vol. 57, No. 7, January 7, 2009, http://www.cdc.gov/nchs/births.htm)
*Final data by state of residence. New York's figure is for New York City only. Does not include whites of Hispanic origin.
**Not available. These states have implemented the 2003 Revision of the U.S. Certificate of Live Birth and their prenatal care data are not comparable with those based on the 1989 revision.

Percent of Black Mothers Beginning Prenatal Care in First Trimester in 2006

National Percent = 76.1% of Black Mothers*

ALPHA ORDER				RANK ORDER		
RANK	STATE	PERCENT		RANK	STATE	PERCENT
15	Alabama	76.0		1	Montana	86.7
3	Alaska	82.9		2	Hawaii	85.5
10	Arizona	77.9		3	Alaska	82.9
24	Arkansas	72.6		4	California	81.9
4	California	81.9		5	Massachusetts	80.4
22	Colorado	73.7		6	Louisiana	79.9
18	Connecticut	75.0		7	Virginia	79.4
NA	Delaware**	NA		8	Missouri	79.2
NA	Florida**	NA		9	Georgia	78.9
9	Georgia	78.9		10	Arizona	77.9
2	Hawaii	85.5		11	Mississippi	77.3
NA	Idaho**	NA		12	Illinois	76.7
12	Illinois	76.7		13	New Mexico	76.3
30	Indiana	66.5		14	Maryland	76.2
23	Iowa	73.0		15	Alabama	76.0
NA	Kansas**	NA		15	North Carolina	76.0
NA	Kentucky**	NA		17	Wisconsin	75.5
6	Louisiana	79.9		18	Connecticut	75.0
27	Maine	69.8		18	New York*	75.0
14	Maryland	76.2		20	Minnesota	74.5
5	Massachusetts	80.4		21	Rhode Island	74.2
26	Michigan	71.9		22	Colorado	73.7
20	Minnesota	74.5		23	Iowa	73.0
11	Mississippi	77.3		24	Arkansas	72.6
8	Missouri	79.2		25	Oregon	72.1
1	Montana	86.7		26	Michigan	71.9
NA	Nebraska**	NA		27	Maine	69.8
31	Nevada	66.3		28	Oklahoma	69.7
NA	New Hampshire**	NA		29	West Virginia	68.4
32	New Jersey	62.4		30	Indiana	66.5
13	New Mexico	76.3		31	Nevada	66.3
18	New York*	75.0		32	New Jersey	62.4
15	North Carolina	76.0		33	Utah	57.4
NA	North Dakota**	NA		NA	Delaware**	NA
NA	Ohio**	NA		NA	Florida**	NA
28	Oklahoma	69.7		NA	Idaho**	NA
25	Oregon	72.1		NA	Kansas**	NA
NA	Pennsylvania**	NA		NA	Kentucky**	NA
21	Rhode Island	74.2		NA	Nebraska**	NA
NA	South Carolina**	NA		NA	New Hampshire**	NA
NA	South Dakota**	NA		NA	North Dakota**	NA
NA	Tennessee**	NA		NA	Ohio**	NA
NA	Texas**	NA		NA	Pennsylvania**	NA
33	Utah	57.4		NA	South Carolina**	NA
NA	Vermont**	NA		NA	South Dakota**	NA
7	Virginia	79.4		NA	Tennessee**	NA
NA	Washington**	NA		NA	Texas**	NA
29	West Virginia	68.4		NA	Vermont**	NA
17	Wisconsin	75.5		NA	Washington**	NA
NA	Wyoming**	NA		NA	Wyoming**	NA
					District of Columbia	74.9

Source: U.S. Department of Health and Human Services, National Center for Health Statistics
"National Vital Statistics Reports" (Vol. 57, No. 7, January 7, 2009, http://www.cdc.gov/nchs/births.htm)
*Final data by state of residence. New York's figure is for New York City only. Does not include blacks of Hispanic origin.
**Not available. These states have implemented the 2003 Revision of the U.S. Certificate of Live Birth and their prenatal care data are not comparable with those based on the 1989 revision.

Percent of Hispanic Mothers Beginning Prenatal Care in First Trimester in 2006

National Percent = 77.3% of Hispanic Mothers*

ALPHA ORDER

RANK	STATE	PERCENT
33	Alabama	50.6
4	Alaska	82.4
21	Arizona	70.2
23	Arkansas	69.7
1	California	83.8
24	Colorado	69.4
14	Connecticut	75.1
NA	Delaware**	NA
NA	Florida**	NA
16	Georgia	73.3
5	Hawaii	82.0
NA	Idaho**	NA
2	Illinois	82.5
31	Indiana	64.1
20	Iowa	71.7
NA	Kansas**	NA
NA	Kentucky**	NA
8	Louisiana	79.9
2	Maine	82.5
29	Maryland	65.0
6	Massachusetts	81.4
9	Michigan	78.6
19	Minnesota	72.1
18	Mississippi	73.1
11	Missouri	77.6
7	Montana	80.2
NA	Nebraska**	NA
32	Nevada	62.5
NA	New Hampshire**	NA
28	New Jersey	66.1
15	New Mexico	74.3
10	New York*	77.9
26	North Carolina	67.6
NA	North Dakota**	NA
NA	Ohio**	NA
30	Oklahoma	64.5
22	Oregon	70.1
NA	Pennsylvania**	NA
13	Rhode Island	75.7
NA	South Carolina**	NA
NA	South Dakota**	NA
NA	Tennessee**	NA
NA	Texas**	NA
27	Utah	66.4
NA	Vermont**	NA
25	Virginia	69.0
NA	Washington**	NA
12	West Virginia	76.1
17	Wisconsin	73.2
NA	Wyoming**	NA

RANK ORDER

RANK	STATE	PERCENT
1	California	83.8
2	Illinois	82.5
2	Maine	82.5
4	Alaska	82.4
5	Hawaii	82.0
6	Massachusetts	81.4
7	Montana	80.2
8	Louisiana	79.9
9	Michigan	78.6
10	New York*	77.9
11	Missouri	77.6
12	West Virginia	76.1
13	Rhode Island	75.7
14	Connecticut	75.1
15	New Mexico	74.3
16	Georgia	73.3
17	Wisconsin	73.2
18	Mississippi	73.1
19	Minnesota	72.1
20	Iowa	71.7
21	Arizona	70.2
22	Oregon	70.1
23	Arkansas	69.7
24	Colorado	69.4
25	Virginia	69.0
26	North Carolina	67.6
27	Utah	66.4
28	New Jersey	66.1
29	Maryland	65.0
30	Oklahoma	64.5
31	Indiana	64.1
32	Nevada	62.5
33	Alabama	50.6
NA	Delaware**	NA
NA	Florida**	NA
NA	Idaho**	NA
NA	Kansas**	NA
NA	Kentucky**	NA
NA	Nebraska**	NA
NA	New Hampshire**	NA
NA	North Dakota**	NA
NA	Ohio**	NA
NA	Pennsylvania**	NA
NA	South Carolina**	NA
NA	South Dakota**	NA
NA	Tennessee**	NA
NA	Texas**	NA
NA	Vermont**	NA
NA	Washington**	NA
NA	Wyoming**	NA
	District of Columbia	67.0

Source: U.S. Department of Health and Human Services, National Center for Health Statistics
   "National Vital Statistics Reports" (Vol. 57, No. 7, January 7, 2009, http://www.cdc.gov/nchs/births.htm)
*Final data by state of residence. New York's figure is for New York City only. Persons of Hispanic origin may be of any race.
**Not available. These states have implemented the 2003 Revision of the U.S. Certificate of Live Birth and their prenatal care data are not comparable with those based on the 1989 revision.

Percent of Mothers Receiving Late or No Prenatal Care in 2006

National Percent = 3.6% of Mothers*

ALPHA ORDER			RANK ORDER		
RANK	STATE	PERCENT	RANK	STATE	PERCENT
9	Alabama	4.5	1	Nevada	8.8
6	Alaska	4.9	2	New Mexico	6.7
3	Arizona	6.1	3	Arizona	6.1
8	Arkansas	4.7	3	Oklahoma	6.1
24	California	2.8	5	New Jersey	5.0
9	Colorado	4.5	6	Alaska	4.9
32	Connecticut	1.8	6	New York*	4.9
NA	Delaware**	NA	8	Arkansas	4.7
NA	Florida**	NA	9	Alabama	4.5
14	Georgia	4.1	9	Colorado	4.5
17	Hawaii	3.6	9	Indiana	4.5
NA	Idaho**	NA	12	Maryland	4.3
27	Illinois	2.4	12	Oregon	4.3
9	Indiana	4.5	14	Georgia	4.1
26	Iowa	2.5	14	Virginia	4.1
NA	Kansas**	NA	16	Utah	3.9
NA	Kentucky**	NA	17	Hawaii	3.6
25	Louisiana	2.6	18	Mississippi	3.2
32	Maine	1.8	18	West Virginia	3.2
12	Maryland	4.3	20	Michigan	3.1
28	Massachusetts	2.3	20	Montana	3.1
20	Michigan	3.1	20	North Carolina	3.1
30	Minnesota	2.1	20	Wisconsin	3.1
18	Mississippi	3.2	24	California	2.8
28	Missouri	2.3	25	Louisiana	2.6
20	Montana	3.1	26	Iowa	2.5
NA	Nebraska**	NA	27	Illinois	2.4
1	Nevada	8.8	28	Massachusetts	2.3
NA	New Hampshire**	NA	28	Missouri	2.3
5	New Jersey	5.0	30	Minnesota	2.1
2	New Mexico	6.7	31	Rhode Island	1.9
6	New York*	4.9	32	Connecticut	1.8
20	North Carolina	3.1	32	Maine	1.8
NA	North Dakota**	NA	NA	Delaware**	NA
NA	Ohio**	NA	NA	Florida**	NA
3	Oklahoma	6.1	NA	Idaho**	NA
12	Oregon	4.3	NA	Kansas**	NA
NA	Pennsylvania**	NA	NA	Kentucky**	NA
31	Rhode Island	1.9	NA	Nebraska**	NA
NA	South Carolina**	NA	NA	New Hampshire**	NA
NA	South Dakota**	NA	NA	North Dakota**	NA
NA	Tennessee**	NA	NA	Ohio**	NA
NA	Texas**	NA	NA	Pennsylvania**	NA
16	Utah	3.9	NA	South Carolina**	NA
NA	Vermont**	NA	NA	South Dakota**	NA
14	Virginia	4.1	NA	Tennessee**	NA
NA	Washington**	NA	NA	Texas**	NA
18	West Virginia	3.2	NA	Vermont**	NA
20	Wisconsin	3.1	NA	Washington**	NA
NA	Wyoming**	NA	NA	Wyoming**	NA

District of Columbia   5.5

Source: U.S. Department of Health and Human Services, National Center for Health Statistics
     "National Vital Statistics Reports" (Vol. 57, No. 7, January 7, 2009, http://www.cdc.gov/nchs/births.htm)
*Final data by state of residence. "Late" means care begun in third trimester. New York's figure is for New York City only.
**Not available. These states have implemented the 2003 Revision of the U.S. Certificate of Live Birth and their prenatal care data are not comparable with those based on the 1989 revision.

Percent of White Mothers Receiving Late or No Prenatal Care in 2006

National Percent = 2.3% of White Mothers*

<table>
<tr><td colspan="3">ALPHA ORDER</td><td colspan="3">RANK ORDER</td></tr>
<tr><td>RANK</td><td>STATE</td><td>PERCENT</td><td>RANK</td><td>STATE</td><td>PERCENT</td></tr>
<tr><td>17</td><td>Alabama</td><td>2.2</td><td>1</td><td>Nevada</td><td>6.4</td></tr>
<tr><td>4</td><td>Alaska</td><td>3.8</td><td>2</td><td>Oklahoma</td><td>5.4</td></tr>
<tr><td>8</td><td>Arizona</td><td>3.0</td><td>3</td><td>New Mexico</td><td>4.5</td></tr>
<tr><td>6</td><td>Arkansas</td><td>3.6</td><td>4</td><td>Alaska</td><td>3.8</td></tr>
<tr><td>22</td><td>California</td><td>2.1</td><td>5</td><td>Oregon</td><td>3.7</td></tr>
<tr><td>10</td><td>Colorado</td><td>2.8</td><td>6</td><td>Arkansas</td><td>3.6</td></tr>
<tr><td>32</td><td>Connecticut</td><td>1.1</td><td>7</td><td>Indiana</td><td>3.4</td></tr>
<tr><td>NA</td><td>Delaware**</td><td>NA</td><td>8</td><td>Arizona</td><td>3.0</td></tr>
<tr><td>NA</td><td>Florida**</td><td>NA</td><td>8</td><td>West Virginia</td><td>3.0</td></tr>
<tr><td>13</td><td>Georgia</td><td>2.3</td><td>10</td><td>Colorado</td><td>2.8</td></tr>
<tr><td>13</td><td>Hawaii</td><td>2.3</td><td>11</td><td>New Jersey</td><td>2.7</td></tr>
<tr><td>NA</td><td>Idaho**</td><td>NA</td><td>11</td><td>Utah</td><td>2.7</td></tr>
<tr><td>29</td><td>Illinois</td><td>1.5</td><td>13</td><td>Georgia</td><td>2.3</td></tr>
<tr><td>7</td><td>Indiana</td><td>3.4</td><td>13</td><td>Hawaii</td><td>2.3</td></tr>
<tr><td>23</td><td>Iowa</td><td>2.0</td><td>13</td><td>Virginia</td><td>2.3</td></tr>
<tr><td>NA</td><td>Kansas**</td><td>NA</td><td>13</td><td>Wisconsin</td><td>2.3</td></tr>
<tr><td>NA</td><td>Kentucky**</td><td>NA</td><td>17</td><td>Alabama</td><td>2.2</td></tr>
<tr><td>30</td><td>Louisiana</td><td>1.3</td><td>17</td><td>Maryland</td><td>2.2</td></tr>
<tr><td>25</td><td>Maine</td><td>1.7</td><td>17</td><td>Michigan</td><td>2.2</td></tr>
<tr><td>17</td><td>Maryland</td><td>2.2</td><td>17</td><td>Montana</td><td>2.2</td></tr>
<tr><td>28</td><td>Massachusetts</td><td>1.6</td><td>17</td><td>New York*</td><td>2.2</td></tr>
<tr><td>17</td><td>Michigan</td><td>2.2</td><td>22</td><td>California</td><td>2.1</td></tr>
<tr><td>30</td><td>Minnesota</td><td>1.3</td><td>23</td><td>Iowa</td><td>2.0</td></tr>
<tr><td>25</td><td>Mississippi</td><td>1.7</td><td>24</td><td>Missouri</td><td>1.8</td></tr>
<tr><td>24</td><td>Missouri</td><td>1.8</td><td>25</td><td>Maine</td><td>1.7</td></tr>
<tr><td>17</td><td>Montana</td><td>2.2</td><td>25</td><td>Mississippi</td><td>1.7</td></tr>
<tr><td>NA</td><td>Nebraska**</td><td>NA</td><td>25</td><td>North Carolina</td><td>1.7</td></tr>
<tr><td>1</td><td>Nevada</td><td>6.4</td><td>28</td><td>Massachusetts</td><td>1.6</td></tr>
<tr><td>NA</td><td>New Hampshire**</td><td>NA</td><td>29</td><td>Illinois</td><td>1.5</td></tr>
<tr><td>11</td><td>New Jersey</td><td>2.7</td><td>30</td><td>Louisiana</td><td>1.3</td></tr>
<tr><td>3</td><td>New Mexico</td><td>4.5</td><td>30</td><td>Minnesota</td><td>1.3</td></tr>
<tr><td>17</td><td>New York*</td><td>2.2</td><td>32</td><td>Connecticut</td><td>1.1</td></tr>
<tr><td>25</td><td>North Carolina</td><td>1.7</td><td>33</td><td>Rhode Island</td><td>1.0</td></tr>
<tr><td>NA</td><td>North Dakota**</td><td>NA</td><td>NA</td><td>Delaware**</td><td>NA</td></tr>
<tr><td>NA</td><td>Ohio**</td><td>NA</td><td>NA</td><td>Florida**</td><td>NA</td></tr>
<tr><td>2</td><td>Oklahoma</td><td>5.4</td><td>NA</td><td>Idaho**</td><td>NA</td></tr>
<tr><td>5</td><td>Oregon</td><td>3.7</td><td>NA</td><td>Kansas**</td><td>NA</td></tr>
<tr><td>NA</td><td>Pennsylvania**</td><td>NA</td><td>NA</td><td>Kentucky**</td><td>NA</td></tr>
<tr><td>33</td><td>Rhode Island</td><td>1.0</td><td>NA</td><td>Nebraska**</td><td>NA</td></tr>
<tr><td>NA</td><td>South Carolina**</td><td>NA</td><td>NA</td><td>New Hampshire**</td><td>NA</td></tr>
<tr><td>NA</td><td>South Dakota**</td><td>NA</td><td>NA</td><td>North Dakota**</td><td>NA</td></tr>
<tr><td>NA</td><td>Tennessee**</td><td>NA</td><td>NA</td><td>Ohio**</td><td>NA</td></tr>
<tr><td>NA</td><td>Texas**</td><td>NA</td><td>NA</td><td>Pennsylvania**</td><td>NA</td></tr>
<tr><td>11</td><td>Utah</td><td>2.7</td><td>NA</td><td>South Carolina**</td><td>NA</td></tr>
<tr><td>NA</td><td>Vermont**</td><td>NA</td><td>NA</td><td>South Dakota**</td><td>NA</td></tr>
<tr><td>13</td><td>Virginia</td><td>2.3</td><td>NA</td><td>Tennessee**</td><td>NA</td></tr>
<tr><td>NA</td><td>Washington**</td><td>NA</td><td>NA</td><td>Texas**</td><td>NA</td></tr>
<tr><td>8</td><td>West Virginia</td><td>3.0</td><td>NA</td><td>Vermont**</td><td>NA</td></tr>
<tr><td>13</td><td>Wisconsin</td><td>2.3</td><td>NA</td><td>Washington**</td><td>NA</td></tr>
<tr><td>NA</td><td>Wyoming**</td><td>NA</td><td>NA</td><td>Wyoming**</td><td>NA</td></tr>
<tr><td></td><td></td><td></td><td></td><td>District of Columbia</td><td>1.8</td></tr>
</table>

Source: U.S. Department of Health and Human Services, National Center for Health Statistics
"National Vital Statistics Reports" (Vol. 57, No. 7, January 7, 2009, http://www.cdc.gov/nchs/births.htm)
*Final data by state of residence. "Late" means care begun in third trimester. New York's figure is for New York City only.
Does not include whites of Hispanic origin.
**Not available. These states have implemented the 2003 Revision of the U.S. Certificate of Live Birth and their prenatal care
data are not comparable with those based on the 1989 revision.

Percent of Black Mothers Receiving Late or No Prenatal Care in 2006

National Percent = 5.7% of Black Mothers*

ALPHA ORDER			RANK ORDER		
RANK	STATE	PERCENT	RANK	STATE	PERCENT
21	Alabama	4.8	1	Utah	16.8
NA	Alaska**	NA	2	Nevada	11.6
21	Arizona	4.8	3	New Jersey	10.5
7	Arkansas	7.3	4	Indiana	8.5
29	California	3.8	5	Oklahoma	7.5
8	Colorado	7.0	6	New York*	7.4
28	Connecticut	3.9	7	Arkansas	7.3
NA	Delaware**	NA	8	Colorado	7.0
NA	Florida**	NA	9	West Virginia	6.8
20	Georgia	4.9	10	Michigan	6.6
NA	Hawaii**	NA	11	Iowa	6.2
NA	Idaho**	NA	11	Wisconsin	6.2
15	Illinois	5.4	13	Oregon	6.1
4	Indiana	8.5	14	Maryland	6.0
11	Iowa	6.2	15	Illinois	5.4
NA	Kansas**	NA	15	Minnesota	5.4
NA	Kentucky**	NA	17	New Mexico	5.3
26	Louisiana	4.2	18	Virginia	5.2
NA	Maine**	NA	19	Massachusetts	5.0
14	Maryland	6.0	20	Georgia	4.9
19	Massachusetts	5.0	21	Alabama	4.8
10	Michigan	6.6	21	Arizona	4.8
15	Minnesota	5.4	23	North Carolina	4.7
25	Mississippi	4.3	24	Missouri	4.5
24	Missouri	4.5	25	Mississippi	4.3
NA	Montana**	NA	26	Louisiana	4.2
NA	Nebraska**	NA	27	Rhode Island	4.0
2	Nevada	11.6	28	Connecticut	3.9
NA	New Hampshire**	NA	29	California	3.8
3	New Jersey	10.5	NA	Alaska**	NA
17	New Mexico	5.3	NA	Delaware**	NA
6	New York*	7.4	NA	Florida**	NA
23	North Carolina	4.7	NA	Hawaii**	NA
NA	North Dakota**	NA	NA	Idaho**	NA
NA	Ohio**	NA	NA	Kansas**	NA
5	Oklahoma	7.5	NA	Kentucky**	NA
13	Oregon	6.1	NA	Maine**	NA
NA	Pennsylvania**	NA	NA	Montana**	NA
27	Rhode Island	4.0	NA	Nebraska**	NA
NA	South Carolina**	NA	NA	New Hampshire**	NA
NA	South Dakota**	NA	NA	North Dakota**	NA
NA	Tennessee**	NA	NA	Ohio**	NA
NA	Texas**	NA	NA	Pennsylvania**	NA
1	Utah	16.8	NA	South Carolina**	NA
NA	Vermont**	NA	NA	South Dakota**	NA
18	Virginia	5.2	NA	Tennessee**	NA
NA	Washington**	NA	NA	Texas**	NA
9	West Virginia	6.8	NA	Vermont**	NA
11	Wisconsin	6.2	NA	Washington**	NA
NA	Wyoming**	NA	NA	Wyoming**	NA
				District of Columbia	7.4

Source: U.S. Department of Health and Human Services, National Center for Health Statistics
    "National Vital Statistics Reports" (Vol. 57, No. 7, January 7, 2009, http://www.cdc.gov/nchs/births.htm)
*Final data by state of residence. "Late" means care begun in third trimester. New York's figure is for New York City only.
Does not include blacks of Hispanic origin. **Not available. With the exception of Alaska, Hawaii, Maine, and Montana, these
states have implemented the 2003 Revision of the U.S. Certificate of Live Birth and their prenatal care data are not comparable
with those based on the 1989 revision.

Percent of Hispanic Mothers Receiving Late or No Prenatal Care in 2006

National Percent = 5.0% of Hispanic Mothers*

ALPHA ORDER

RANK	STATE	PERCENT
1	Alabama	22.4
22	Alaska	4.8
5	Arizona	8.7
11	Arkansas	7.2
28	California	3.2
11	Colorado	7.2
29	Connecticut	3.0
NA	Delaware**	NA
NA	Florida**	NA
6	Georgia	8.1
26	Hawaii	3.4
NA	Idaho**	NA
31	Illinois	2.4
8	Indiana	8.0
20	Iowa	4.9
NA	Kansas**	NA
NA	Kentucky**	NA
20	Louisiana	4.9
NA	Maine**	NA
6	Maryland	8.1
26	Massachusetts	3.4
24	Michigan	4.0
23	Minnesota	4.4
3	Mississippi	9.0
25	Missouri	3.8
19	Montana	5.1
NA	Nebraska**	NA
2	Nevada	11.1
NA	New Hampshire**	NA
13	New Jersey	6.8
13	New Mexico	6.8
18	New York*	5.3
15	North Carolina	5.7
NA	North Dakota**	NA
NA	Ohio**	NA
9	Oklahoma	7.7
16	Oregon	5.6
NA	Pennsylvania**	NA
29	Rhode Island	3.0
NA	South Carolina**	NA
NA	South Dakota**	NA
NA	Tennessee**	NA
NA	Texas**	NA
10	Utah	7.5
NA	Vermont**	NA
3	Virginia	9.0
NA	Washington**	NA
NA	West Virginia**	NA
17	Wisconsin	5.4
NA	Wyoming**	NA

RANK ORDER

RANK	STATE	PERCENT
1	Alabama	22.4
2	Nevada	11.1
3	Mississippi	9.0
3	Virginia	9.0
5	Arizona	8.7
6	Georgia	8.1
6	Maryland	8.1
8	Indiana	8.0
9	Oklahoma	7.7
10	Utah	7.5
11	Arkansas	7.2
11	Colorado	7.2
13	New Jersey	6.8
13	New Mexico	6.8
15	North Carolina	5.7
16	Oregon	5.6
17	Wisconsin	5.4
18	New York*	5.3
19	Montana	5.1
20	Iowa	4.9
20	Louisiana	4.9
22	Alaska	4.8
23	Minnesota	4.4
24	Michigan	4.0
25	Missouri	3.8
26	Hawaii	3.4
26	Massachusetts	3.4
28	California	3.2
29	Connecticut	3.0
29	Rhode Island	3.0
31	Illinois	2.4
NA	Delaware**	NA
NA	Florida**	NA
NA	Idaho**	NA
NA	Kansas**	NA
NA	Kentucky**	NA
NA	Maine**	NA
NA	Nebraska**	NA
NA	New Hampshire**	NA
NA	North Dakota**	NA
NA	Ohio**	NA
NA	Pennsylvania**	NA
NA	South Carolina**	NA
NA	South Dakota**	NA
NA	Tennessee**	NA
NA	Texas**	NA
NA	Vermont**	NA
NA	Washington**	NA
NA	West Virginia**	NA
NA	Wyoming**	NA

District of Columbia   6.3

Source: U.S. Department of Health and Human Services, National Center for Health Statistics
    "National Vital Statistics Reports" (Vol. 57, No. 7, January 7, 2009, http://www.cdc.gov/nchs/births.htm)
*Final data by state of residence. "Late" means care begun in third trimester. New York's figure is for New York City only.
Persons of Hispanic origin may be of any race. **Not available. With the exception of Maine and West Virginia, these states have implemented the 2003 Revision of the U.S. Certificate of Live Birth and their prenatal care data are not comparable with those based on the 1989 revision.

Reported Legal Abortions in 2005

Reporting States' Total = 820,151 Abortions*

ALPHA ORDER

RANK	STATE	ABORTIONS	% of USA
19	Alabama	11,211	1.4%
41	Alaska	1,955	0.2%
21	Arizona	10,723	1.3%
32	Arkansas	4,695	0.6%
NA	California**	NA	NA
17	Colorado	11,682	1.4%
16	Connecticut	12,110	1.5%
33	Delaware	4,148	0.5%
2	Florida	92,513	11.3%
8	Georgia	31,680	3.9%
36	Hawaii	3,548	0.4%
45	Idaho	1,099	0.1%
4	Illinois	43,409	5.3%
22	Indiana	10,686	1.3%
30	Iowa	5,881	0.7%
24	Kansas	10,462	1.3%
34	Kentucky	3,776	0.5%
NA	Louisiana**	NA	NA
39	Maine	2,653	0.3%
20	Maryland	10,797	1.3%
13	Massachusetts	23,268	2.8%
11	Michigan	25,209	3.1%
15	Minnesota	13,362	1.6%
38	Mississippi	3,041	0.4%
26	Missouri	7,977	1.0%
40	Montana	2,155	0.3%
37	Nebraska	3,173	0.4%
23	Nevada	10,565	1.3%
NA	New Hampshire**	NA	NA
9	New Jersey	31,230	3.8%
29	New Mexico	5,934	0.7%
1	New York	124,849	15.2%
7	North Carolina	32,335	3.9%
44	North Dakota	1,231	0.2%
6	Ohio	34,128	4.2%
28	Oklahoma	6,641	0.8%
18	Oregon	11,602	1.4%
5	Pennsylvania	34,909	4.3%
31	Rhode Island	5,091	0.6%
27	South Carolina	6,716	0.8%
46	South Dakota	805	0.1%
14	Tennessee	16,178	2.0%
3	Texas	77,108	9.4%
35	Utah	3,556	0.4%
43	Vermont	1,620	0.2%
10	Virginia	26,309	3.2%
12	Washington	24,108	2.9%
42	West Virginia	1,674	0.2%
25	Wisconsin	9,817	1.2%
47	Wyoming	14	0.0%

RANK ORDER

RANK	STATE	ABORTIONS	% of USA
1	New York	124,849	15.2%
2	Florida	92,513	11.3%
3	Texas	77,108	9.4%
4	Illinois	43,409	5.3%
5	Pennsylvania	34,909	4.3%
6	Ohio	34,128	4.2%
7	North Carolina	32,335	3.9%
8	Georgia	31,680	3.9%
9	New Jersey	31,230	3.8%
10	Virginia	26,309	3.2%
11	Michigan	25,209	3.1%
12	Washington	24,108	2.9%
13	Massachusetts	23,268	2.8%
14	Tennessee	16,178	2.0%
15	Minnesota	13,362	1.6%
16	Connecticut	12,110	1.5%
17	Colorado	11,682	1.4%
18	Oregon	11,602	1.4%
19	Alabama	11,211	1.4%
20	Maryland	10,797	1.3%
21	Arizona	10,723	1.3%
22	Indiana	10,686	1.3%
23	Nevada	10,565	1.3%
24	Kansas	10,462	1.3%
25	Wisconsin	9,817	1.2%
26	Missouri	7,977	1.0%
27	South Carolina	6,716	0.8%
28	Oklahoma	6,641	0.8%
29	New Mexico	5,934	0.7%
30	Iowa	5,881	0.7%
31	Rhode Island	5,091	0.6%
32	Arkansas	4,695	0.6%
33	Delaware	4,148	0.5%
34	Kentucky	3,776	0.5%
35	Utah	3,556	0.4%
36	Hawaii	3,548	0.4%
37	Nebraska	3,173	0.4%
38	Mississippi	3,041	0.4%
39	Maine	2,653	0.3%
40	Montana	2,155	0.3%
41	Alaska	1,955	0.2%
42	West Virginia	1,674	0.2%
43	Vermont	1,620	0.2%
44	North Dakota	1,231	0.2%
45	Idaho	1,099	0.1%
46	South Dakota	805	0.1%
47	Wyoming	14	0.0%
NA	California**	NA	NA
NA	Louisiana**	NA	NA
NA	New Hampshire**	NA	NA
	District of Columbia	2,518	0.3%

Source: U.S. Department of Health and Human Services, Centers for Disease Control and Prevention
   "Abortion Surveillance-United States, 2005" (MMWR, Vol. 57, No. SS-13, 11/28/08, http://www.cdc.gov/mmwr/mmwr_ss.html)
*By state of occurrence. Total is for reporting states only.
**Not reported.

Percent Change in Reported Legal Abortions: 2001 to 2005

National Percent Change = 2.9% Decrease*

RANK	STATE	PERCENT CHANGE	RANK	STATE	PERCENT CHANGE
41	Alabama	(16.2)	1	Wyoming	250.0
NA	Alaska**	NA	2	Colorado	152.1
4	Arizona	29.2	3	Idaho	48.9
45	Arkansas	(20.7)	4	Arizona	29.2
NA	California**	NA	5	New Mexico	14.9
2	Colorado	152.1	6	Florida	8.1
29	Connecticut	(8.7)	7	Virginia	7.0
39	Delaware	(14.8)	8	Vermont	6.6
6	Florida	8.1	9	North Carolina	6.3
20	Georgia	(4.7)	10	Maine	5.5
36	Hawaii	(11.3)	11	Nevada	4.5
3	Idaho	48.9	12	Iowa	2.8
24	Illinois	(6.7)	13	Missouri	2.3
32	Indiana	(10.0)	14	North Dakota	1.2
12	Iowa	2.8	15	Kentucky	0.3
39	Kansas	(14.8)	16	Texas	(0.4)
15	Kentucky	0.3	17	Utah	(1.1)
NA	Louisiana**	NA	18	New York	(1.8)
10	Maine	5.5	19	South Carolina	(4.2)
43	Maryland	(20.0)	20	Georgia	(4.7)
37	Massachusetts	(11.5)	21	Pennsylvania	(5.2)
35	Michigan	(10.7)	22	Oklahoma	(5.6)
31	Minnesota	(9.9)	23	Washington	(5.9)
38	Mississippi	(14.7)	24	Illinois	(6.7)
13	Missouri	2.3	24	Rhode Island	(6.7)
28	Montana	(8.3)	26	Tennessee	(7.0)
44	Nebraska	(20.3)	27	New Jersey	(7.1)
11	Nevada	4.5	28	Montana	(8.3)
NA	New Hampshire**	NA	29	Connecticut	(8.7)
27	New Jersey	(7.1)	30	Ohio	(8.9)
5	New Mexico	14.9	31	Minnesota	(9.9)
18	New York	(1.8)	32	Indiana	(10.0)
9	North Carolina	6.3	33	South Dakota	(10.1)
14	North Dakota	1.2	33	Wisconsin	(10.1)
30	Ohio	(8.9)	35	Michigan	(10.7)
22	Oklahoma	(5.6)	36	Hawaii	(11.3)
42	Oregon	(18.7)	37	Massachusetts	(11.5)
21	Pennsylvania	(5.2)	38	Mississippi	(14.7)
24	Rhode Island	(6.7)	39	Delaware	(14.8)
19	South Carolina	(4.2)	39	Kansas	(14.8)
33	South Dakota	(10.1)	41	Alabama	(16.2)
26	Tennessee	(7.0)	42	Oregon	(18.7)
16	Texas	(0.4)	43	Maryland	(20.0)
17	Utah	(1.1)	44	Nebraska	(20.3)
8	Vermont	6.6	45	Arkansas	(20.7)
7	Virginia	7.0	46	West Virginia	(28.2)
23	Washington	(5.9)	NA	Alaska**	NA
46	West Virginia	(28.2)	NA	California**	NA
33	Wisconsin	(10.1)	NA	Louisiana**	NA
1	Wyoming	250.0	NA	New Hampshire**	NA

District of Columbia   (53.2)

Source: CQ Press using data from U.S. Department of Health and Human Services, Centers for Disease Control and Prevention
   "Abortion Surveillance-United States, 2005" (MMWR, Vol. 57, No. SS-13, 11/28/08, http://www.cdc.gov/mmwr/mmwr_ss.html)
   "Abortion Surveillance-United States, 2001" (MMWR, Vol. 53, No. SS-9, 11/26/04)
*By state of occurrence. National percent change is only for states reporting in both years.
**Not reported.

Reported Legal Abortions per 1,000 Live Births in 2005

Reporting States' Ratio = 233 Abortions per 1,000 Live Births*

ALPHA ORDER

RANK	STATE	RATIO
28	Alabama	185
26	Alaska	187
39	Arizona	111
37	Arkansas	120
NA	California**	NA
29	Colorado	169
7	Connecticut	290
4	Delaware	356
2	Florida	409
18	Georgia	223
21	Hawaii	198
46	Idaho	48
15	Illinois	242
35	Indiana	123
30	Iowa	150
11	Kansas	262
45	Kentucky	67
NA	Louisiana**	NA
24	Maine	188
32	Maryland	144
5	Massachusetts	303
23	Michigan	197
24	Minnesota	188
42	Mississippi	72
40	Missouri	101
27	Montana	186
36	Nebraska	121
8	Nevada	283
NA	New Hampshire**	NA
9	New Jersey	274
19	New Mexico	206
1	New York	507
10	North Carolina	263
31	North Dakota	147
17	Ohio	230
34	Oklahoma	128
13	Oregon	253
16	Pennsylvania	240
3	Rhode Island	401
38	South Carolina	116
43	South Dakota	70
21	Tennessee	198
20	Texas	200
44	Utah	69
12	Vermont	257
14	Virginia	252
6	Washington	292
41	West Virginia	80
33	Wisconsin	138
47	Wyoming	2

RANK ORDER

RANK	STATE	RATIO
1	New York	507
2	Florida	409
3	Rhode Island	401
4	Delaware	356
5	Massachusetts	303
6	Washington	292
7	Connecticut	290
8	Nevada	283
9	New Jersey	274
10	North Carolina	263
11	Kansas	262
12	Vermont	257
13	Oregon	253
14	Virginia	252
15	Illinois	242
16	Pennsylvania	240
17	Ohio	230
18	Georgia	223
19	New Mexico	206
20	Texas	200
21	Hawaii	198
21	Tennessee	198
23	Michigan	197
24	Maine	188
24	Minnesota	188
26	Alaska	187
27	Montana	186
28	Alabama	185
29	Colorado	169
30	Iowa	150
31	North Dakota	147
32	Maryland	144
33	Wisconsin	138
34	Oklahoma	128
35	Indiana	123
36	Nebraska	121
37	Arkansas	120
38	South Carolina	116
39	Arizona	111
40	Missouri	101
41	West Virginia	80
42	Mississippi	72
43	South Dakota	70
44	Utah	69
45	Kentucky	67
46	Idaho	48
47	Wyoming	2
NA	California**	NA
NA	Louisiana**	NA
NA	New Hampshire**	NA

District of Columbia   316

Source: U.S. Department of Health and Human Services, Centers for Disease Control and Prevention
"Abortion Surveillance-United States, 2005" (MMWR, Vol. 57, No. SS-13, 11/28/08, http://www.cdc.gov/mmwr/mmwr_ss.html)
*By state of occurrence. National figure is for reporting states only.
**Not reported.

Reported Legal Abortions per 1,000 Women 15 to 44 Years Old in 2005

Reporting States' Rate = 15 Abortions per 1,000 Women 15 to 44 Years Old*

ALPHA ORDER				RANK ORDER		
RANK	STATE	RATE		RANK	STATE	RATE
24	Alabama	12		1	New York	30
19	Alaska	14		2	Florida	27
32	Arizona	9		3	Delaware	23
37	Arkansas	8		4	Rhode Island	22
NA	California**	NA		5	Nevada	21
24	Colorado	12		6	Kansas	19
9	Connecticut	17		7	North Carolina	18
3	Delaware	23		7	Washington	18
2	Florida	27		9	Connecticut	17
12	Georgia	16		9	Massachusetts	17
19	Hawaii	14		9	New Jersey	17
45	Idaho	4		12	Georgia	16
12	Illinois	16		12	Illinois	16
37	Indiana	8		12	Oregon	16
29	Iowa	10		12	Virginia	16
6	Kansas	19		16	New Mexico	15
45	Kentucky	4		16	Ohio	15
NA	Louisiana**	NA		16	Texas	15
29	Maine	10		19	Alaska	14
32	Maryland	9		19	Hawaii	14
9	Massachusetts	17		19	Pennsylvania	14
24	Michigan	12		22	Tennessee	13
24	Minnesota	12		22	Vermont	13
42	Mississippi	5		24	Alabama	12
40	Missouri	7		24	Colorado	12
24	Montana	12		24	Michigan	12
32	Nebraska	9		24	Minnesota	12
5	Nevada	21		24	Montana	12
NA	New Hampshire**	NA		29	Iowa	10
9	New Jersey	17		29	Maine	10
16	New Mexico	15		29	North Dakota	10
1	New York	30		32	Arizona	9
7	North Carolina	18		32	Maryland	9
29	North Dakota	10		32	Nebraska	9
16	Ohio	15		32	Oklahoma	9
32	Oklahoma	9		32	Wisconsin	9
12	Oregon	16		37	Arkansas	8
19	Pennsylvania	14		37	Indiana	8
4	Rhode Island	22		37	South Carolina	8
37	South Carolina	8		40	Missouri	7
42	South Dakota	5		41	Utah	6
22	Tennessee	13		42	Mississippi	5
16	Texas	15		42	South Dakota	5
41	Utah	6		42	West Virginia	5
22	Vermont	13		45	Idaho	4
12	Virginia	16		45	Kentucky	4
7	Washington	18		47	Wyoming	0
42	West Virginia	5		NA	California**	NA
32	Wisconsin	9		NA	Louisiana**	NA
47	Wyoming	0		NA	New Hampshire**	NA
				District of Columbia		17

Source: U.S. Department of Health and Human Services, Centers for Disease Control and Prevention
  "Abortion Surveillance-United States, 2005" (MMWR, Vol. 57, No. SS-13, 11/28/08, http://www.cdc.gov/mmwr/mmwr_ss.html)
*By state of occurrence. National figure is for reporting states only.
**Not reported.

Percent of Legal Abortions Obtained by Out-of-State Residents in 2005

Reporting States' Percent = 8.3% of Abortions*

ALPHA ORDER

RANK	STATE	PERCENT
8	Alabama	16.8
43	Alaska	0.3
36	Arizona	3.1
11	Arkansas	13.5
NA	California**	NA
17	Colorado	9.7
36	Connecticut	3.1
3	Delaware	26.9
NA	Florida**	NA
14	Georgia	11.6
42	Hawaii	0.5
36	Idaho	3.1
21	Illinois	7.9
33	Indiana	3.9
15	Iowa	11.3
1	Kansas	47.0
NA	Kentucky**	NA
NA	Louisiana**	NA
27	Maine	5.2
9	Maryland	14.7
30	Massachusetts	4.3
39	Michigan	2.8
21	Minnesota	7.9
39	Mississippi	2.8
18	Missouri	8.2
19	Montana	8.1
9	Nebraska	14.7
24	Nevada	6.3
NA	New Hampshire**	NA
26	New Jersey	5.5
25	New Mexico	5.6
NA	New York**	NA
7	North Carolina	16.9
2	North Dakota	36.8
19	Ohio	8.1
32	Oklahoma	4.0
13	Oregon	12.3
31	Pennsylvania	4.1
4	Rhode Island	23.0
33	South Carolina	3.9
6	South Dakota	18.3
5	Tennessee	21.3
35	Texas	3.5
23	Utah	7.8
16	Vermont	10.6
29	Virginia	4.7
28	Washington	5.0
12	West Virginia	13.3
41	Wisconsin	2.6
44	Wyoming	0.0

RANK ORDER

RANK	STATE	PERCENT
1	Kansas	47.0
2	North Dakota	36.8
3	Delaware	26.9
4	Rhode Island	23.0
5	Tennessee	21.3
6	South Dakota	18.3
7	North Carolina	16.9
8	Alabama	16.8
9	Maryland	14.7
9	Nebraska	14.7
11	Arkansas	13.5
12	West Virginia	13.3
13	Oregon	12.3
14	Georgia	11.6
15	Iowa	11.3
16	Vermont	10.6
17	Colorado	9.7
18	Missouri	8.2
19	Montana	8.1
19	Ohio	8.1
21	Illinois	7.9
21	Minnesota	7.9
23	Utah	7.8
24	Nevada	6.3
25	New Mexico	5.6
26	New Jersey	5.5
27	Maine	5.2
28	Washington	5.0
29	Virginia	4.7
30	Massachusetts	4.3
31	Pennsylvania	4.1
32	Oklahoma	4.0
33	Indiana	3.9
33	South Carolina	3.9
35	Texas	3.5
36	Arizona	3.1
36	Connecticut	3.1
36	Idaho	3.1
39	Michigan	2.8
39	Mississippi	2.8
41	Wisconsin	2.6
42	Hawaii	0.5
43	Alaska	0.3
44	Wyoming	0.0
NA	California**	NA
NA	Florida**	NA
NA	Kentucky**	NA
NA	Louisiana**	NA
NA	New Hampshire**	NA
NA	New York**	NA

District of Columbia	50.7

Source: U.S. Department of Health and Human Services, Centers for Disease Control and Prevention
   "Abortion Surveillance-United States, 2005" (MMWR, Vol. 57, No. SS-13, 11/28/08, http://www.cdc.gov/mmwr/mmwr_ss.html)
*By state of occurrence. National figure is for reporting states only.
**Not reported.

Percent of Reported Legal Abortions That Were First-Time Abortions: 2005

Reporting States' Percent = 53.5% of Abortions*

ALPHA ORDER				RANK ORDER		
RANK	STATE	PERCENT		RANK	STATE	PERCENT
7	Alabama	66.1		1	Wyoming	85.7
8	Alaska	65.5		2	Idaho	77.9
19	Arizona	62.2		3	South Dakota	69.4
18	Arkansas	62.4		4	West Virginia	68.2
NA	California**	NA		5	North Dakota	67.8
16	Colorado	63.3		6	Maine	66.5
NA	Connecticut**	NA		7	Alabama	66.1
13	Delaware	63.9		8	Alaska	65.5
NA	Florida**	NA		9	Utah	64.9
23	Georgia	58.0		10	Oklahoma	64.7
26	Hawaii	56.4		11	New Jersey	64.6
2	Idaho	77.9		12	Mississippi	64.2
NA	Illinois**	NA		13	Delaware	63.9
31	Indiana	53.6		13	Iowa	63.9
13	Iowa	63.9		15	Nebraska	63.6
20	Kansas	61.5		16	Colorado	63.3
27	Kentucky	55.7		17	South Carolina	63.0
NA	Louisiana**	NA		18	Arkansas	62.4
6	Maine	66.5		19	Arizona	62.2
41	Maryland	24.8		20	Kansas	61.5
38	Massachusetts	48.1		21	Vermont	59.4
36	Michigan	51.1		22	Minnesota	58.1
22	Minnesota	58.1		23	Georgia	58.0
12	Mississippi	64.2		24	Missouri	56.5
24	Missouri	56.5		24	Texas	56.5
34	Montana	52.5		26	Hawaii	56.4
15	Nebraska	63.6		27	Kentucky	55.7
32	Nevada	52.8		28	Oregon	55.5
NA	New Hampshire**	NA		29	Pennsylvania	55.1
11	New Jersey	64.6		30	Virginia	54.9
NA	New Mexico**	NA		31	Indiana	53.6
39	New York	45.4		32	Nevada	52.8
37	North Carolina	49.6		33	Washington	52.7
5	North Dakota	67.8		34	Montana	52.5
NA	Ohio**	NA		35	Rhode Island	51.5
10	Oklahoma	64.7		36	Michigan	51.1
28	Oregon	55.5		37	North Carolina	49.6
29	Pennsylvania	55.1		38	Massachusetts	48.1
35	Rhode Island	51.5		39	New York	45.4
17	South Carolina	63.0		40	Tennessee	35.3
3	South Dakota	69.4		41	Maryland	24.8
40	Tennessee	35.3		NA	California**	NA
24	Texas	56.5		NA	Connecticut**	NA
9	Utah	64.9		NA	Florida**	NA
21	Vermont	59.4		NA	Illinois**	NA
30	Virginia	54.9		NA	Louisiana**	NA
33	Washington	52.7		NA	New Hampshire**	NA
4	West Virginia	68.2		NA	New Mexico**	NA
NA	Wisconsin**	NA		NA	Ohio**	NA
1	Wyoming	85.7		NA	Wisconsin**	NA
					District of Columbia**	NA

Source: U.S. Department of Health and Human Services, Centers for Disease Control and Prevention
   "Abortion Surveillance-United States, 2005" (MMWR, Vol. 57, No. SS-13, 11/28/08, http://www.cdc.gov/mmwr/mmwr_ss.html)
*By state of occurrence. National figure is for reporting states only. Percent of abortions to women who had no previous abortions.
**Not reported.

Percent of Reported Legal Abortions Obtained by White Women in 2005

Reporting States' Percent = 53.0% of Abortions*

ALPHA ORDER				RANK ORDER		
RANK	STATE	PERCENT		RANK	STATE	PERCENT
30	Alabama	42.7		1	Vermont	95.2
20	Alaska	59.4		2	Idaho	92.6
NA	Arizona**	NA		3	West Virginia	86.9
19	Arkansas	60.4		4	Maine	85.8
NA	California**	NA		5	Oregon	83.4
11	Colorado	71.8		6	Montana	81.9
NA	Connecticut**	NA		7	North Dakota	80.4
26	Delaware	53.8		8	Iowa	79.6
NA	Florida**	NA		9	South Dakota	79.5
33	Georgia	37.4		10	Oklahoma	72.0
35	Hawaii	25.5		11	Colorado	71.8
2	Idaho	92.6		12	Texas	70.9
NA	Illinois**	NA		13	Wisconsin	69.2
17	Indiana	64.6		14	Kentucky	68.9
8	Iowa	79.6		15	Kansas	66.7
15	Kansas	66.7		16	Rhode Island	65.1
14	Kentucky	68.9		17	Indiana	64.6
NA	Louisiana**	NA		18	Minnesota	63.8
4	Maine	85.8		19	Arkansas	60.4
36	Maryland	22.9		20	Alaska	59.4
28	Massachusetts	49.9		21	South Carolina	59.0
25	Michigan	55.9		22	Ohio	57.6
18	Minnesota	63.8		23	Pennsylvania	56.8
37	Mississippi	22.1		24	Missouri	56.3
24	Missouri	56.3		25	Michigan	55.9
6	Montana	81.9		26	Delaware	53.8
NA	Nebraska**	NA		27	Tennessee	51.2
NA	Nevada**	NA		28	Massachusetts	49.9
NA	New Hampshire**	NA		29	Virginia	43.3
34	New Jersey	31.6		30	Alabama	42.7
NA	New Mexico**	NA		31	North Carolina	41.5
32	New York**	39.0		32	New York**	39.0
31	North Carolina	41.5		33	Georgia	37.4
7	North Dakota	80.4		34	New Jersey	31.6
22	Ohio	57.6		35	Hawaii	25.5
10	Oklahoma	72.0		36	Maryland	22.9
5	Oregon	83.4		37	Mississippi	22.1
23	Pennsylvania	56.8		NA	Arizona**	NA
16	Rhode Island	65.1		NA	California**	NA
21	South Carolina	59.0		NA	Connecticut**	NA
9	South Dakota	79.5		NA	Florida**	NA
27	Tennessee	51.2		NA	Illinois**	NA
12	Texas	70.9		NA	Louisiana**	NA
NA	Utah**	NA		NA	Nebraska**	NA
1	Vermont	95.2		NA	Nevada**	NA
29	Virginia	43.3		NA	New Hampshire**	NA
NA	Washington**	NA		NA	New Mexico**	NA
3	West Virginia	86.9		NA	Utah**	NA
13	Wisconsin	69.2		NA	Washington**	NA
NA	Wyoming**	NA		NA	Wyoming**	NA
				District of Columbia		20.3

Source: U.S. Department of Health and Human Services, Centers for Disease Control and Prevention
   "Abortion Surveillance-United States, 2005" (MMWR, Vol. 57, No. SS-13, 11/28/08, http://www.cdc.gov/mmwr/mmwr_ss.html)
*By state of occurrence. Includes those of Hispanic ethnicity. National percent is for reporting states only.
**Not reported. New York's number is for New York City only.

Percent of Reported Legal Abortions Obtained by Black Women in 2005

Reporting States' Percent = 35.5% of Abortions*

ALPHA ORDER				RANK ORDER		
RANK	STATE	PERCENT		RANK	STATE	PERCENT
4	Alabama	54.7		1	Mississippi	77.2
28	Alaska	6.7		2	Maryland	65.4
NA	Arizona**	NA		3	Georgia	57.8
16	Arkansas	31.8		4	Alabama	54.7
NA	California**	NA		5	New York**	47.2
29	Colorado	6.6		6	Tennessee	44.9
NA	Connecticut**	NA		7	New Jersey	44.8
9	Delaware	42.0		8	North Carolina	44.2
NA	Florida**	NA		9	Delaware	42.0
3	Georgia	57.8		10	Virginia	41.6
32	Hawaii	2.8		11	Missouri	38.7
36	Idaho	1.5		12	South Carolina	38.1
NA	Illinois**	NA		13	Pennsylvania	38.0
17	Indiana	28.9		14	Michigan	37.0
27	Iowa	9.2		15	Ohio	35.4
20	Kansas	22.3		16	Arkansas	31.8
22	Kentucky	19.4		17	Indiana	28.9
NA	Louisiana**	NA		18	Wisconsin	23.9
34	Maine	2.3		19	Texas	23.3
2	Maryland	65.4		20	Kansas	22.3
23	Massachusetts	19.3		21	Minnesota	21.2
14	Michigan	37.0		22	Kentucky	19.4
21	Minnesota	21.2		23	Massachusetts	19.3
1	Mississippi	77.2		24	Oklahoma	19.2
11	Missouri	38.7		25	Rhode Island	15.2
37	Montana	0.8		26	West Virginia	10.9
NA	Nebraska**	NA		27	Iowa	9.2
NA	Nevada**	NA		28	Alaska	6.7
NA	New Hampshire**	NA		29	Colorado	6.6
7	New Jersey	44.8		30	Oregon	6.1
NA	New Mexico**	NA		31	South Dakota	5.7
5	New York**	47.2		32	Hawaii	2.8
8	North Carolina	44.2		33	North Dakota	2.5
33	North Dakota	2.5		34	Maine	2.3
15	Ohio	35.4		35	Vermont	1.7
24	Oklahoma	19.2		36	Idaho	1.5
30	Oregon	6.1		37	Montana	0.8
13	Pennsylvania	38.0		NA	Arizona**	NA
25	Rhode Island	15.2		NA	California**	NA
12	South Carolina	38.1		NA	Connecticut**	NA
31	South Dakota	5.7		NA	Florida**	NA
6	Tennessee	44.9		NA	Illinois**	NA
19	Texas	23.3		NA	Louisiana**	NA
NA	Utah**	NA		NA	Nebraska**	NA
35	Vermont	1.7		NA	Nevada**	NA
10	Virginia	41.6		NA	New Hampshire**	NA
NA	Washington**	NA		NA	New Mexico**	NA
26	West Virginia	10.9		NA	Utah**	NA
18	Wisconsin	23.9		NA	Washington**	NA
NA	Wyoming**	NA		NA	Wyoming**	NA
				District of Columbia		49.4

Source: U.S. Department of Health and Human Services, Centers for Disease Control and Prevention
"Abortion Surveillance-United States, 2005" (MMWR, Vol. 57, No. SS-13, 11/28/08, http://www.cdc.gov/mmwr/mmwr_ss.html)
*By state of occurrence. National percent is for reporting states only.
**Not reported. New York's number is for New York City only.

Percent of Reported Legal Abortions Obtained by Hispanic Women in 2005

Reporting States' Percent = 19.4%*

ALPHA ORDER

RANK	STATE	PERCENT
22	Alabama	2.8
NA	Alaska**	NA
2	Arizona	38.2
20	Arkansas	4.2
NA	California**	NA
6	Colorado	21.0
NA	Connecticut**	NA
11	Delaware	9.1
NA	Florida**	NA
NA	Georgia**	NA
15	Hawaii	6.2
8	Idaho	12.1
NA	Illinois**	NA
13	Indiana	7.0
NA	Iowa**	NA
10	Kansas	10.0
NA	Kentucky**	NA
NA	Louisiana**	NA
24	Maine	2.0
NA	Maryland**	NA
NA	Massachusetts**	NA
NA	Michigan**	NA
16	Minnesota	5.6
27	Mississippi	0.5
23	Missouri	2.3
NA	Montana**	NA
NA	Nebraska**	NA
NA	Nevada**	NA
NA	New Hampshire**	NA
5	New Jersey	23.8
1	New Mexico	52.5
4	New York	25.4
NA	North Carolina**	NA
NA	North Dakota**	NA
21	Ohio	3.3
NA	Oklahoma**	NA
9	Oregon	11.1
14	Pennsylvania	6.4
NA	Rhode Island**	NA
18	South Carolina	4.7
17	South Dakota	5.5
19	Tennessee	4.5
3	Texas	36.3
7	Utah	19.7
25	Vermont	1.7
NA	Virginia**	NA
NA	Washington**	NA
26	West Virginia	0.6
11	Wisconsin	9.1
NA	Wyoming**	NA

RANK ORDER

RANK	STATE	PERCENT
1	New Mexico	52.5
2	Arizona	38.2
3	Texas	36.3
4	New York	25.4
5	New Jersey	23.8
6	Colorado	21.0
7	Utah	19.7
8	Idaho	12.1
9	Oregon	11.1
10	Kansas	10.0
11	Delaware	9.1
11	Wisconsin	9.1
13	Indiana	7.0
14	Pennsylvania	6.4
15	Hawaii	6.2
16	Minnesota	5.6
17	South Dakota	5.5
18	South Carolina	4.7
19	Tennessee	4.5
20	Arkansas	4.2
21	Ohio	3.3
22	Alabama	2.8
23	Missouri	2.3
24	Maine	2.0
25	Vermont	1.7
26	West Virginia	0.6
27	Mississippi	0.5
NA	Alaska**	NA
NA	California**	NA
NA	Connecticut**	NA
NA	Florida**	NA
NA	Georgia**	NA
NA	Illinois**	NA
NA	Iowa**	NA
NA	Kentucky**	NA
NA	Louisiana**	NA
NA	Maryland**	NA
NA	Massachusetts**	NA
NA	Michigan**	NA
NA	Montana**	NA
NA	Nebraska**	NA
NA	Nevada**	NA
NA	New Hampshire**	NA
NA	North Carolina**	NA
NA	North Dakota**	NA
NA	Oklahoma**	NA
NA	Rhode Island**	NA
NA	Virginia**	NA
NA	Washington**	NA
NA	Wyoming**	NA

District of Columbia 14.3

Source: U.S. Department of Health and Human Services, Centers for Disease Control and Prevention
    "Abortion Surveillance-United States, 2005" (MMWR, Vol. 57, No. SS-13, 11/28/08, http://www.cdc.gov/mmwr/mmwr_ss.html)
*By state of occurrence. National percent is for reporting states only. Hispanic can be of any race.
**Not reported.

Percent of Reported Legal Abortions Obtained by Married Women in 2005

Reporting States' Percent = 16.5% of Abortions*

ALPHA ORDER

RANK	STATE	PERCENT
39	Alabama	12.7
19	Alaska	17.4
15	Arizona	17.8
NA	Arkansas**	NA
NA	California**	NA
12	Colorado	18.4
NA	Connecticut**	NA
40	Delaware	12.5
NA	Florida**	NA
15	Georgia	17.8
28	Hawaii	16.0
6	Idaho	19.9
26	Illinois	16.5
29	Indiana	15.8
9	Iowa	19.1
13	Kansas	18.2
31	Kentucky	15.3
NA	Louisiana**	NA
22	Maine	16.8
8	Maryland	19.5
33	Massachusetts	14.4
38	Michigan	13.2
23	Minnesota	16.6
41	Mississippi	8.8
14	Missouri	18.1
23	Montana	16.6
NA	Nebraska**	NA
6	Nevada	19.9
NA	New Hampshire**	NA
36	New Jersey	14.0
35	New Mexico	14.2
34	New York**	14.3
4	North Carolina	20.4
26	North Dakota	16.5
30	Ohio	15.5
3	Oklahoma	20.8
4	Oregon	20.4
32	Pennsylvania	15.0
20	Rhode Island	17.0
23	South Carolina	16.6
2	South Dakota	22.0
20	Tennessee	17.0
10	Texas	18.8
1	Utah	23.2
15	Vermont	17.8
18	Virginia	17.5
NA	Washington**	NA
10	West Virginia	18.8
36	Wisconsin	14.0
42	Wyoming	0.0

RANK ORDER

RANK	STATE	PERCENT
1	Utah	23.2
2	South Dakota	22.0
3	Oklahoma	20.8
4	North Carolina	20.4
4	Oregon	20.4
6	Idaho	19.9
6	Nevada	19.9
8	Maryland	19.5
9	Iowa	19.1
10	Texas	18.8
10	West Virginia	18.8
12	Colorado	18.4
13	Kansas	18.2
14	Missouri	18.1
15	Arizona	17.8
15	Georgia	17.8
15	Vermont	17.8
18	Virginia	17.5
19	Alaska	17.4
20	Rhode Island	17.0
20	Tennessee	17.0
22	Maine	16.8
23	Minnesota	16.6
23	Montana	16.6
23	South Carolina	16.6
26	Illinois	16.5
26	North Dakota	16.5
28	Hawaii	16.0
29	Indiana	15.8
30	Ohio	15.5
31	Kentucky	15.3
32	Pennsylvania	15.0
33	Massachusetts	14.4
34	New York**	14.3
35	New Mexico	14.2
36	New Jersey	14.0
36	Wisconsin	14.0
38	Michigan	13.2
39	Alabama	12.7
40	Delaware	12.5
41	Mississippi	8.8
42	Wyoming	0.0
NA	Arkansas**	NA
NA	California**	NA
NA	Connecticut**	NA
NA	Florida**	NA
NA	Louisiana**	NA
NA	Nebraska**	NA
NA	New Hampshire**	NA
NA	Washington**	NA

District of Columbia   7.5

Source: U.S. Department of Health and Human Services, Centers for Disease Control and Prevention
   "Abortion Surveillance-United States, 2005" (MMWR, Vol. 57, No. SS-13, 11/28/08, http://www.cdc.gov/mmwr/mmwr_ss.html)
*By state of occurrence. National percent is for reporting states only.
**Not reported. New York's number is for New York City only.

Percent of Reported Legal Abortions Obtained by Unmarried Women in 2005

Reporting States' Percent = 81.0% of Abortions*

ALPHA ORDER			RANK ORDER		
RANK	STATE	PERCENT	RANK	STATE	PERCENT
4	Alabama	86.3	1	Wyoming	100.0
24	Alaska	80.4	2	Mississippi	91.1
16	Arizona	82.2	3	Delaware	87.5
NA	Arkansas**	NA	4	Alabama	86.3
NA	California**	NA	4	Michigan	86.3
37	Colorado	76.4	6	New Jersey	85.7
NA	Connecticut**	NA	7	Wisconsin	85.5
3	Delaware	87.5	8	Pennsylvania	85.0
NA	Florida**	NA	9	Kentucky	84.7
36	Georgia	77.3	10	New Mexico	83.6
11	Hawaii	83.5	11	Hawaii	83.5
27	Idaho	79.9	12	South Carolina	83.3
20	Illinois	81.6	13	North Dakota	83.2
17	Indiana	82.0	14	New York**	83.0
24	Iowa	80.4	15	Minnesota	82.3
19	Kansas	81.7	16	Arizona	82.2
9	Kentucky	84.7	17	Indiana	82.0
NA	Louisiana**	NA	18	Ohio	81.9
32	Maine	79.0	19	Kansas	81.7
34	Maryland	77.6	20	Illinois	81.6
21	Massachusetts	81.2	21	Massachusetts	81.2
4	Michigan	86.3	22	Tennessee	81.1
15	Minnesota	82.3	23	Vermont	81.0
2	Mississippi	91.1	24	Alaska	80.4
24	Missouri	80.4	24	Iowa	80.4
39	Montana	73.5	24	Missouri	80.4
NA	Nebraska**	NA	27	Idaho	79.9
40	Nevada	73.2	27	Texas	79.9
NA	New Hampshire**	NA	29	West Virginia	79.3
6	New Jersey	85.7	30	Oklahoma	79.2
10	New Mexico	83.6	31	Rhode Island	79.1
14	New York**	83.0	32	Maine	79.0
38	North Carolina	75.0	33	South Dakota	78.0
13	North Dakota	83.2	34	Maryland	77.6
18	Ohio	81.9	35	Oregon	77.5
30	Oklahoma	79.2	36	Georgia	77.3
35	Oregon	77.5	37	Colorado	76.4
8	Pennsylvania	85.0	38	North Carolina	75.0
31	Rhode Island	79.1	39	Montana	73.5
12	South Carolina	83.3	40	Nevada	73.2
33	South Dakota	78.0	41	Virginia	71.9
22	Tennessee	81.1	42	Utah	68.0
27	Texas	79.9	NA	Arkansas**	NA
42	Utah	68.0	NA	California**	NA
23	Vermont	81.0	NA	Connecticut**	NA
41	Virginia	71.9	NA	Florida**	NA
NA	Washington**	NA	NA	Louisiana**	NA
29	West Virginia	79.3	NA	Nebraska**	NA
7	Wisconsin	85.5	NA	New Hampshire**	NA
1	Wyoming	100.0	NA	Washington**	NA
				District of Columbia	91.7

Source: U.S. Department of Health and Human Services, Centers for Disease Control and Prevention
   "Abortion Surveillance-United States, 2005" (MMWR, Vol. 57, No. SS-13, 11/28/08, http://www.cdc.gov/mmwr/mmwr_ss.html)
*By state of occurrence. National percent is for reporting states only.
**Not reported. New York's number is for New York City only.

Reported Legal Abortions Obtained by Teenagers in 2005

Reporting States' Total = 113,993 Abortions Obtained by Teenagers*

ALPHA ORDER

RANK	STATE	ABORTIONS	% of USA
15	Alabama	2,089	1.8%
38	Alaska	386	0.3%
18	Arizona	1,923	1.7%
29	Arkansas	785	0.7%
NA	California**	NA	NA
14	Colorado	2,156	1.9%
13	Connecticut	2,303	2.0%
32	Delaware	575	0.5%
NA	Florida**	NA	NA
7	Georgia	4,902	4.3%
30	Hawaii	697	0.6%
42	Idaho	214	0.2%
NA	Illinois**	NA	NA
20	Indiana	1,757	1.5%
27	Iowa	1,087	1.0%
19	Kansas	1,827	1.6%
33	Kentucky	566	0.5%
NA	Louisiana**	NA	NA
35	Maine	522	0.5%
NA	Maryland**	NA	NA
11	Massachusetts	3,809	3.3%
8	Michigan	4,672	4.1%
16	Minnesota	2,025	1.8%
36	Mississippi	504	0.4%
23	Missouri	1,285	1.1%
37	Montana	474	0.4%
34	Nebraska	549	0.5%
21	Nevada	1,732	1.5%
NA	New Hampshire**	NA	NA
5	New Jersey	5,777	5.1%
25	New Mexico	1,158	1.0%
1	New York	22,763	20.0%
6	North Carolina	5,050	4.4%
41	North Dakota	257	0.2%
3	Ohio	6,057	5.3%
26	Oklahoma	1,133	1.0%
17	Oregon	1,947	1.7%
4	Pennsylvania	5,986	5.3%
28	Rhode Island	887	0.8%
24	South Carolina	1,261	1.1%
43	South Dakota	136	0.1%
12	Tennessee	2,621	2.3%
2	Texas	10,119	8.9%
31	Utah	583	0.5%
39	Vermont	333	0.3%
10	Virginia	4,056	3.6%
9	Washington	4,536	4.0%
40	West Virginia	308	0.3%
22	Wisconsin	1,726	1.5%
44	Wyoming	2	0.0%

RANK ORDER

RANK	STATE	ABORTIONS	% of USA
1	New York	22,763	20.0%
2	Texas	10,119	8.9%
3	Ohio	6,057	5.3%
4	Pennsylvania	5,986	5.3%
5	New Jersey	5,777	5.1%
6	North Carolina	5,050	4.4%
7	Georgia	4,902	4.3%
8	Michigan	4,672	4.1%
9	Washington	4,536	4.0%
10	Virginia	4,056	3.6%
11	Massachusetts	3,809	3.3%
12	Tennessee	2,621	2.3%
13	Connecticut	2,303	2.0%
14	Colorado	2,156	1.9%
15	Alabama	2,089	1.8%
16	Minnesota	2,025	1.8%
17	Oregon	1,947	1.7%
18	Arizona	1,923	1.7%
19	Kansas	1,827	1.6%
20	Indiana	1,757	1.5%
21	Nevada	1,732	1.5%
22	Wisconsin	1,726	1.5%
23	Missouri	1,285	1.1%
24	South Carolina	1,261	1.1%
25	New Mexico	1,158	1.0%
26	Oklahoma	1,133	1.0%
27	Iowa	1,087	1.0%
28	Rhode Island	887	0.8%
29	Arkansas	785	0.7%
30	Hawaii	697	0.6%
31	Utah	583	0.5%
32	Delaware	575	0.5%
33	Kentucky	566	0.5%
34	Nebraska	549	0.5%
35	Maine	522	0.5%
36	Mississippi	504	0.4%
37	Montana	474	0.4%
38	Alaska	386	0.3%
39	Vermont	333	0.3%
40	West Virginia	308	0.3%
41	North Dakota	257	0.2%
42	Idaho	214	0.2%
43	South Dakota	136	0.1%
44	Wyoming	2	0.0%
NA	California**	NA	NA
NA	Florida**	NA	NA
NA	Illinois**	NA	NA
NA	Louisiana**	NA	NA
NA	Maryland**	NA	NA
NA	New Hampshire**	NA	NA
	District of Columbia	458	0.4%

Source: U.S. Department of Health and Human Services, Centers for Disease Control and Prevention
  "Abortion Surveillance-United States, 2005" (MMWR, Vol. 57, No. SS-13, 11/28/08, http://www.cdc.gov/mmwr/mmwr_ss.html)
*19 years old and younger by state of occurrence. National total is for reporting states only.
**Not reported.

Percent of Reported Legal Abortions Obtained by Teenagers in 2005

Reporting States' Percent = 16.9% of Abortions*

ALPHA ORDER

RANK ORDER

RANK	STATE	PERCENT	RANK	STATE	PERCENT
12	Alabama	18.6	1	Montana	22.0
4	Alaska	19.7	2	North Dakota	20.9
19	Arizona	17.9	3	Vermont	20.6
29	Arkansas	16.7	4	Alaska	19.7
NA	California**	NA	4	Maine	19.7
13	Colorado	18.5	6	Hawaii	19.6
9	Connecticut	19.0	7	Idaho	19.5
43	Delaware	13.9	7	New Mexico	19.5
NA	Florida**	NA	9	Connecticut	19.0
38	Georgia	15.5	10	South Carolina	18.8
6	Hawaii	19.6	10	Washington	18.8
7	Idaho	19.5	12	Alabama	18.6
NA	Illinois**	NA	13	Colorado	18.5
31	Indiana	16.4	13	Iowa	18.5
13	Iowa	18.5	13	Michigan	18.5
22	Kansas	17.5	13	New Jersey	18.5
41	Kentucky	15.0	17	West Virginia	18.4
NA	Louisiana**	NA	18	New York	18.2
4	Maine	19.7	19	Arizona	17.9
NA	Maryland**	NA	20	Ohio	17.7
31	Massachusetts	16.4	21	Wisconsin	17.6
13	Michigan	18.5	22	Kansas	17.5
40	Minnesota	15.2	23	Rhode Island	17.4
30	Mississippi	16.6	24	Nebraska	17.3
36	Missouri	16.1	25	Oklahoma	17.1
1	Montana	22.0	25	Pennsylvania	17.1
24	Nebraska	17.3	27	South Dakota	16.9
31	Nevada	16.4	28	Oregon	16.8
NA	New Hampshire**	NA	29	Arkansas	16.7
13	New Jersey	18.5	30	Mississippi	16.6
7	New Mexico	19.5	31	Indiana	16.4
18	New York	18.2	31	Massachusetts	16.4
37	North Carolina	15.6	31	Nevada	16.4
2	North Dakota	20.9	31	Utah	16.4
20	Ohio	17.7	35	Tennessee	16.2
25	Oklahoma	17.1	36	Missouri	16.1
28	Oregon	16.8	37	North Carolina	15.6
25	Pennsylvania	17.1	38	Georgia	15.5
23	Rhode Island	17.4	39	Virginia	15.4
10	South Carolina	18.8	40	Minnesota	15.2
27	South Dakota	16.9	41	Kentucky	15.0
35	Tennessee	16.2	42	Wyoming	14.3
44	Texas	13.1	43	Delaware	13.9
31	Utah	16.4	44	Texas	13.1
3	Vermont	20.6	NA	California**	NA
39	Virginia	15.4	NA	Florida**	NA
10	Washington	18.8	NA	Illinois**	NA
17	West Virginia	18.4	NA	Louisiana**	NA
21	Wisconsin	17.6	NA	Maryland**	NA
42	Wyoming	14.3	NA	New Hampshire**	NA

District of Columbia   18.2

Source: CQ Press using data from U.S. Department of Health and Human Services, Centers for Disease Control and Prevention
   "Abortion Surveillance-United States, 2005" (MMWR, Vol. 57, No. SS-13, 11/28/08, http://www.cdc.gov/mmwr/mmwr_ss.html)
*19 years old and younger by state of occurrence. National percent is for reporting states only.
**Not reported.

Reported Legal Abortions Obtained by Teenagers 17 Years and Younger in 2005

Reporting States' Total = 43,653 Abortions*

ALPHA ORDER

RANK	STATE	ABORTIONS	% of USA
14	Alabama	802	1.8%
38	Alaska	140	0.3%
20	Arizona	643	1.5%
28	Arkansas	343	0.8%
NA	California**	NA	NA
15	Colorado	786	1.8%
12	Connecticut	996	2.3%
32	Delaware	235	0.5%
NA	Florida**	NA	NA
6	Georgia	1,943	4.5%
29	Hawaii	318	0.7%
41	Idaho	79	0.2%
NA	Illinois**	NA	NA
22	Indiana	591	1.4%
27	Iowa	398	0.9%
17	Kansas	695	1.6%
31	Kentucky	241	0.6%
NA	Louisiana**	NA	NA
36	Maine	200	0.5%
NA	Maryland**	NA	NA
11	Massachusetts	1,326	3.0%
9	Michigan	1,758	4.0%
18	Minnesota	682	1.6%
37	Mississippi	174	0.4%
25	Missouri	426	1.0%
33	Montana	213	0.5%
34	Nebraska	207	0.5%
19	Nevada	664	1.5%
NA	New Hampshire**	NA	NA
3	New Jersey	2,497	5.7%
24	New Mexico	488	1.1%
1	New York	9,747	22.3%
7	North Carolina	1,859	4.3%
NA	North Dakota**	NA	NA
4	Ohio	2,364	5.4%
26	Oklahoma	421	1.0%
16	Oregon	741	1.7%
5	Pennsylvania	2,083	4.8%
30	Rhode Island	285	0.7%
23	South Carolina	550	1.3%
NA	South Dakota**	NA	NA
13	Tennessee	956	2.2%
2	Texas	3,287	7.5%
35	Utah	203	0.5%
39	Vermont	115	0.3%
10	Virginia	1,348	3.1%
8	Washington	1,782	4.1%
40	West Virginia	105	0.2%
21	Wisconsin	630	1.4%
NA	Wyoming**	NA	NA

RANK ORDER

RANK	STATE	ABORTIONS	% of USA
1	New York	9,747	22.3%
2	Texas	3,287	7.5%
3	New Jersey	2,497	5.7%
4	Ohio	2,364	5.4%
5	Pennsylvania	2,083	4.8%
6	Georgia	1,943	4.5%
7	North Carolina	1,859	4.3%
8	Washington	1,782	4.1%
9	Michigan	1,758	4.0%
10	Virginia	1,348	3.1%
11	Massachusetts	1,326	3.0%
12	Connecticut	996	2.3%
13	Tennessee	956	2.2%
14	Alabama	802	1.8%
15	Colorado	786	1.8%
16	Oregon	741	1.7%
17	Kansas	695	1.6%
18	Minnesota	682	1.6%
19	Nevada	664	1.5%
20	Arizona	643	1.5%
21	Wisconsin	630	1.4%
22	Indiana	591	1.4%
23	South Carolina	550	1.3%
24	New Mexico	488	1.1%
25	Missouri	426	1.0%
26	Oklahoma	421	1.0%
27	Iowa	398	0.9%
28	Arkansas	343	0.8%
29	Hawaii	318	0.7%
30	Rhode Island	285	0.7%
31	Kentucky	241	0.6%
32	Delaware	235	0.5%
33	Montana	213	0.5%
34	Nebraska	207	0.5%
35	Utah	203	0.5%
36	Maine	200	0.5%
37	Mississippi	174	0.4%
38	Alaska	140	0.3%
39	Vermont	115	0.3%
40	West Virginia	105	0.2%
41	Idaho	79	0.2%
NA	California**	NA	NA
NA	Florida**	NA	NA
NA	Illinois**	NA	NA
NA	Louisiana**	NA	NA
NA	Maryland**	NA	NA
NA	New Hampshire**	NA	NA
NA	North Dakota**	NA	NA
NA	South Dakota**	NA	NA
NA	Wyoming**	NA	NA
	District of Columbia	220	0.5%

Source: U.S. Department of Health and Human Services, Centers for Disease Control and Prevention
   "Abortion Surveillance-United States, 2005" (MMWR, Vol. 57, No. SS-13, 11/28/08, http://www.cdc.gov/mmwr/mmwr_ss.html)
*By state of occurrence. National total is for reporting states only.
**Not reported.

Percent of Reported Legal Abortions Obtained by Teenagers 17 Years and Younger in 2005
Reporting States' Percent = 6.5% of Abortions*

ALPHA ORDER				RANK ORDER		
RANK	STATE	PERCENT		RANK	STATE	PERCENT
11	Alabama	7.2		1	Montana	9.9
11	Alaska	7.2		2	Hawaii	9.0
28	Arizona	6.0		3	Connecticut	8.2
10	Arkansas	7.3		3	New Mexico	8.2
NA	California**	NA		3	South Carolina	8.2
18	Colorado	6.7		6	New Jersey	8.0
3	Connecticut	8.2		7	New York	7.8
31	Delaware	5.7		8	Maine	7.5
NA	Florida**	NA		9	Washington	7.4
27	Georgia	6.1		10	Arkansas	7.3
2	Hawaii	9.0		11	Alabama	7.2
11	Idaho	7.2		11	Alaska	7.2
NA	Illinois**	NA		11	Idaho	7.2
37	Indiana	5.5		14	Vermont	7.1
17	Iowa	6.8		15	Michigan	7.0
19	Kansas	6.6		16	Ohio	6.9
21	Kentucky	6.4		17	Iowa	6.8
NA	Louisiana**	NA		18	Colorado	6.7
8	Maine	7.5		19	Kansas	6.6
NA	Maryland**	NA		20	Nebraska	6.5
31	Massachusetts	5.7		21	Kentucky	6.4
15	Michigan	7.0		21	Oregon	6.4
39	Minnesota	5.1		21	Wisconsin	6.4
31	Mississippi	5.7		24	Nevada	6.3
38	Missouri	5.3		24	Oklahoma	6.3
1	Montana	9.9		24	West Virginia	6.3
20	Nebraska	6.5		27	Georgia	6.1
24	Nevada	6.3		28	Arizona	6.0
NA	New Hampshire**	NA		28	Pennsylvania	6.0
6	New Jersey	8.0		30	Tennessee	5.9
3	New Mexico	8.2		31	Delaware	5.7
7	New York	7.8		31	Massachusetts	5.7
31	North Carolina	5.7		31	Mississippi	5.7
NA	North Dakota**	NA		31	North Carolina	5.7
16	Ohio	6.9		31	Utah	5.7
24	Oklahoma	6.3		36	Rhode Island	5.6
21	Oregon	6.4		37	Indiana	5.5
28	Pennsylvania	6.0		38	Missouri	5.3
36	Rhode Island	5.6		39	Minnesota	5.1
3	South Carolina	8.2		39	Virginia	5.1
NA	South Dakota**	NA		41	Texas	4.3
30	Tennessee	5.9		NA	California**	NA
41	Texas	4.3		NA	Florida**	NA
31	Utah	5.7		NA	Illinois**	NA
14	Vermont	7.1		NA	Louisiana**	NA
39	Virginia	5.1		NA	Maryland**	NA
9	Washington	7.4		NA	New Hampshire**	NA
24	West Virginia	6.3		NA	North Dakota**	NA
21	Wisconsin	6.4		NA	South Dakota**	NA
NA	Wyoming**	NA		NA	Wyoming**	NA

District of Columbia 8.7

Source: CQ Press using data from U.S. Department of Health and Human Services, Centers for Disease Control and Prevention "Abortion Surveillance-United States, 2005" (MMWR, Vol. 57, No. SS-13, 11/28/08, http://www.cdc.gov/mmwr/mmwr_ss.html)
*By state of occurrence. National percent is for reporting states only.
**Not reported.

Percent of Teenage Abortions Obtained
by Teenagers 17 Years and Younger in 2005
Reporting States' Percent = 38.4% of Teenage Abortions*

ALPHA ORDER

RANK	STATE	PERCENT
14	Alabama	38.4
28	Alaska	36.3
37	Arizona	33.4
3	Arkansas	43.7
NA	California**	NA
25	Colorado	36.5
5	Connecticut	43.2
10	Delaware	40.9
NA	Florida**	NA
11	Georgia	39.6
1	Hawaii	45.6
22	Idaho	36.9
NA	Illinois**	NA
36	Indiana	33.6
24	Iowa	36.6
18	Kansas	38.0
8	Kentucky	42.6
NA	Louisiana**	NA
15	Maine	38.3
NA	Maryland**	NA
29	Massachusetts	34.8
20	Michigan	37.6
35	Minnesota	33.7
32	Mississippi	34.5
38	Missouri	33.2
2	Montana	44.9
19	Nebraska	37.7
15	Nevada	38.3
NA	New Hampshire**	NA
5	New Jersey	43.2
9	New Mexico	42.1
7	New York	42.8
23	North Carolina	36.8
NA	North Dakota**	NA
13	Ohio	39.0
21	Oklahoma	37.2
17	Oregon	38.1
29	Pennsylvania	34.8
41	Rhode Island	32.1
4	South Carolina	43.6
NA	South Dakota**	NA
25	Tennessee	36.5
40	Texas	32.5
29	Utah	34.8
32	Vermont	34.5
38	Virginia	33.2
12	Washington	39.3
34	West Virginia	34.1
25	Wisconsin	36.5
NA	Wyoming**	NA

RANK ORDER

RANK	STATE	PERCENT
1	Hawaii	45.6
2	Montana	44.9
3	Arkansas	43.7
4	South Carolina	43.6
5	Connecticut	43.2
5	New Jersey	43.2
7	New York	42.8
8	Kentucky	42.6
9	New Mexico	42.1
10	Delaware	40.9
11	Georgia	39.6
12	Washington	39.3
13	Ohio	39.0
14	Alabama	38.4
15	Maine	38.3
15	Nevada	38.3
17	Oregon	38.1
18	Kansas	38.0
19	Nebraska	37.7
20	Michigan	37.6
21	Oklahoma	37.2
22	Idaho	36.9
23	North Carolina	36.8
24	Iowa	36.6
25	Colorado	36.5
25	Tennessee	36.5
25	Wisconsin	36.5
28	Alaska	36.3
29	Massachusetts	34.8
29	Pennsylvania	34.8
29	Utah	34.8
32	Mississippi	34.5
32	Vermont	34.5
34	West Virginia	34.1
35	Minnesota	33.7
36	Indiana	33.6
37	Arizona	33.4
38	Missouri	33.2
38	Virginia	33.2
40	Texas	32.5
41	Rhode Island	32.1
NA	California**	NA
NA	Florida**	NA
NA	Illinois**	NA
NA	Louisiana**	NA
NA	Maryland**	NA
NA	New Hampshire**	NA
NA	North Dakota**	NA
NA	South Dakota**	NA
NA	Wyoming**	NA

District of Columbia 48.0

Source: CQ Press using data from U.S. Department of Health and Human Services, Centers for Disease Control and Prevention
"Abortion Surveillance-United States, 2005" (MMWR, Vol. 57, No. SS-13, 11/28/08, http://www.cdc.gov/mmwr/mmwr_ss.html)
*By state of occurrence. National percent is for reporting states only.
**Not reported.

Reported Legal Abortions Performed at 12 Weeks or Less of Gestation in 2005

Reporting States' Total = 547,888 Abortions*

ALPHA ORDER

RANK	STATE	ABORTIONS	% of USA
17	Alabama	9,753	1.8%
33	Alaska	1,857	0.3%
19	Arizona	8,782	1.6%
27	Arkansas	3,908	0.7%
NA	California**	NA	NA
14	Colorado	10,245	1.9%
13	Connecticut	10,765	2.0%
31	Delaware	2,718	0.5%
NA	Florida**	NA	NA
5	Georgia	26,912	4.9%
29	Hawaii	3,038	0.6%
38	Idaho	1,066	0.2%
NA	Illinois**	NA	NA
16	Indiana	9,852	1.8%
24	Iowa	5,501	1.0%
18	Kansas	8,925	1.6%
28	Kentucky	3,155	0.6%
NA	Louisiana**	NA	NA
32	Maine	2,543	0.5%
NA	Maryland**	NA	NA
NA	Massachusetts**	NA	NA
9	Michigan	22,378	4.1%
12	Minnesota	11,803	2.2%
NA	Mississippi**	NA	NA
21	Missouri	7,268	1.3%
34	Montana	1,836	0.3%
NA	Nebraska**	NA	NA
NA	Nevada**	NA	NA
NA	New Hampshire**	NA	NA
7	New Jersey	25,097	4.6%
25	New Mexico	4,914	0.9%
1	New York	103,018	18.8%
8	North Carolina	24,403	4.5%
37	North Dakota	1,135	0.2%
4	Ohio	29,096	5.3%
23	Oklahoma	6,023	1.1%
15	Oregon	10,151	1.9%
3	Pennsylvania	30,907	5.6%
26	Rhode Island	4,578	0.8%
22	South Carolina	6,609	1.2%
39	South Dakota	760	0.1%
11	Tennessee	15,413	2.8%
2	Texas	71,017	13.0%
30	Utah	3,017	0.6%
35	Vermont	1,531	0.3%
6	Virginia	25,108	4.6%
10	Washington	21,058	3.8%
36	West Virginia	1,518	0.3%
20	Wisconsin	8,103	1.5%
40	Wyoming	12	0.0%

RANK ORDER

RANK	STATE	ABORTIONS	% of USA
1	New York	103,018	18.8%
2	Texas	71,017	13.0%
3	Pennsylvania	30,907	5.6%
4	Ohio	29,096	5.3%
5	Georgia	26,912	4.9%
6	Virginia	25,108	4.6%
7	New Jersey	25,097	4.6%
8	North Carolina	24,403	4.5%
9	Michigan	22,378	4.1%
10	Washington	21,058	3.8%
11	Tennessee	15,413	2.8%
12	Minnesota	11,803	2.2%
13	Connecticut	10,765	2.0%
14	Colorado	10,245	1.9%
15	Oregon	10,151	1.9%
16	Indiana	9,852	1.8%
17	Alabama	9,753	1.8%
18	Kansas	8,925	1.6%
19	Arizona	8,782	1.6%
20	Wisconsin	8,103	1.5%
21	Missouri	7,268	1.3%
22	South Carolina	6,609	1.2%
23	Oklahoma	6,023	1.1%
24	Iowa	5,501	1.0%
25	New Mexico	4,914	0.9%
26	Rhode Island	4,578	0.8%
27	Arkansas	3,908	0.7%
28	Kentucky	3,155	0.6%
29	Hawaii	3,038	0.6%
30	Utah	3,017	0.6%
31	Delaware	2,718	0.5%
32	Maine	2,543	0.5%
33	Alaska	1,857	0.3%
34	Montana	1,836	0.3%
35	Vermont	1,531	0.3%
36	West Virginia	1,518	0.3%
37	North Dakota	1,135	0.2%
38	Idaho	1,066	0.2%
39	South Dakota	760	0.1%
40	Wyoming	12	0.0%
NA	California**	NA	NA
NA	Florida**	NA	NA
NA	Illinois**	NA	NA
NA	Louisiana**	NA	NA
NA	Maryland**	NA	NA
NA	Massachusetts**	NA	NA
NA	Mississippi**	NA	NA
NA	Nebraska**	NA	NA
NA	Nevada**	NA	NA
NA	New Hampshire**	NA	NA
	District of Columbia	2,115	0.4%

Source: CQ Press using data from U.S. Department of Health and Human Services, Centers for Disease Control and Prevention
   "Abortion Surveillance-United States, 2005" (MMWR, Vol. 57, No. SS-13, 11/28/08, http://www.cdc.gov/mmwr/mmwr_ss.html)
*By state of occurrence. National total is for reporting states only.
**Not reported.

Percent of Reported Legal Abortions Performed
at 12 Weeks or Less of Gestation in 2005
Reporting States' Percent = 86.5% of Abortions*

ALPHA ORDER

RANK	STATE	PERCENT
24	Alabama	87.0
6	Alaska	95.0
37	Arizona	81.9
33	Arkansas	83.2
NA	California**	NA
21	Colorado	87.7
17	Connecticut	88.9
40	Delaware	65.5
NA	Florida**	NA
30	Georgia	84.9
26	Hawaii	85.6
2	Idaho	97.0
NA	Illinois**	NA
10	Indiana	92.2
9	Iowa	93.5
27	Kansas	85.3
32	Kentucky	83.6
NA	Louisiana**	NA
3	Maine	95.9
NA	Maryland**	NA
NA	Massachusetts**	NA
18	Michigan	88.8
20	Minnesota	88.3
NA	Mississippi**	NA
13	Missouri	91.1
29	Montana	85.2
NA	Nebraska**	NA
NA	Nevada**	NA
NA	New Hampshire**	NA
38	New Jersey	80.4
34	New Mexico	82.8
35	New York	82.5
39	North Carolina	75.5
10	North Dakota	92.2
27	Ohio	85.3
14	Oklahoma	90.7
22	Oregon	87.5
19	Pennsylvania	88.5
16	Rhode Island	89.9
1	South Carolina	98.4
8	South Dakota	94.4
5	Tennessee	95.3
12	Texas	92.1
31	Utah	84.8
7	Vermont	94.5
4	Virginia	95.4
23	Washington	87.3
14	West Virginia	90.7
35	Wisconsin	82.5
25	Wyoming	85.7

RANK ORDER

RANK	STATE	PERCENT
1	South Carolina	98.4
2	Idaho	97.0
3	Maine	95.9
4	Virginia	95.4
5	Tennessee	95.3
6	Alaska	95.0
7	Vermont	94.5
8	South Dakota	94.4
9	Iowa	93.5
10	Indiana	92.2
10	North Dakota	92.2
12	Texas	92.1
13	Missouri	91.1
14	Oklahoma	90.7
14	West Virginia	90.7
16	Rhode Island	89.9
17	Connecticut	88.9
18	Michigan	88.8
19	Pennsylvania	88.5
20	Minnesota	88.3
21	Colorado	87.7
22	Oregon	87.5
23	Washington	87.3
24	Alabama	87.0
25	Wyoming	85.7
26	Hawaii	85.6
27	Kansas	85.3
27	Ohio	85.3
29	Montana	85.2
30	Georgia	84.9
31	Utah	84.8
32	Kentucky	83.6
33	Arkansas	83.2
34	New Mexico	82.8
35	New York	82.5
35	Wisconsin	82.5
37	Arizona	81.9
38	New Jersey	80.4
39	North Carolina	75.5
40	Delaware	65.5
NA	California**	NA
NA	Florida**	NA
NA	Illinois**	NA
NA	Louisiana**	NA
NA	Maryland**	NA
NA	Massachusetts**	NA
NA	Mississippi**	NA
NA	Nebraska**	NA
NA	Nevada**	NA
NA	New Hampshire**	NA

District of Columbia 84.0

Source: CQ Press using data from U.S. Department of Health and Human Services, Centers for Disease Control and Prevention
"Abortion Surveillance-United States, 2005" (MMWR, Vol. 57, No. SS-13, 11/28/08, http://www.cdc.gov/mmwr/mmwr_ss.html)
*By state of occurrence. National percent is for reporting states only.
**Not reported.

Reported Legal Abortions Performed at or after 21 Weeks of Gestation in 2005

Reporting States' Total = 8,482 Abortions*

ALPHA ORDER

RANK	STATE	ABORTIONS	% of USA
18	Alabama	34	0.4%
33	Alaska	0	0.0%
13	Arizona	133	1.6%
33	Arkansas	0	0.0%
NA	California**	NA	NA
8	Colorado	273	3.2%
20	Connecticut	32	0.4%
30	Delaware	6	0.1%
NA	Florida**	NA	NA
2	Georgia	1,094	12.9%
23	Hawaii	16	0.2%
32	Idaho	5	0.1%
NA	Illinois**	NA	NA
33	Indiana	0	0.0%
24	Iowa	13	0.2%
5	Kansas	459	5.4%
16	Kentucky	54	0.6%
NA	Louisiana**	NA	NA
33	Maine	0	0.0%
NA	Maryland**	NA	NA
NA	Massachusetts**	NA	NA
12	Michigan	181	2.1%
17	Minnesota	48	0.6%
NA	Mississippi**	NA	NA
18	Missouri	34	0.4%
21	Montana	22	0.3%
NA	Nebraska**	NA	NA
NA	Nevada**	NA	NA
NA	New Hampshire**	NA	NA
3	New Jersey	850	10.0%
14	New Mexico	106	1.2%
1	New York	2,956	34.9%
33	North Carolina	0	0.0%
33	North Dakota	0	0.0%
4	Ohio	577	6.8%
28	Oklahoma	8	0.1%
9	Oregon	227	2.7%
11	Pennsylvania	192	2.3%
25	Rhode Island	11	0.1%
22	South Carolina	17	0.2%
27	South Dakota	10	0.1%
25	Tennessee	11	0.1%
7	Texas	395	4.7%
29	Utah	7	0.1%
33	Vermont	0	0.0%
15	Virginia	58	0.7%
6	Washington	444	5.2%
30	West Virginia	6	0.1%
10	Wisconsin	203	2.4%
33	Wyoming	0	0.0%

RANK ORDER

RANK	STATE	ABORTIONS	% of USA
1	New York	2,956	34.9%
2	Georgia	1,094	12.9%
3	New Jersey	850	10.0%
4	Ohio	577	6.8%
5	Kansas	459	5.4%
6	Washington	444	5.2%
7	Texas	395	4.7%
8	Colorado	273	3.2%
9	Oregon	227	2.7%
10	Wisconsin	203	2.4%
11	Pennsylvania	192	2.3%
12	Michigan	181	2.1%
13	Arizona	133	1.6%
14	New Mexico	106	1.2%
15	Virginia	58	0.7%
16	Kentucky	54	0.6%
17	Minnesota	48	0.6%
18	Alabama	34	0.4%
18	Missouri	34	0.4%
20	Connecticut	32	0.4%
21	Montana	22	0.3%
22	South Carolina	17	0.2%
23	Hawaii	16	0.2%
24	Iowa	13	0.2%
25	Rhode Island	11	0.1%
25	Tennessee	11	0.1%
27	South Dakota	10	0.1%
28	Oklahoma	8	0.1%
29	Utah	7	0.1%
30	Delaware	6	0.1%
30	West Virginia	6	0.1%
32	Idaho	5	0.1%
33	Alaska	0	0.0%
33	Arkansas	0	0.0%
33	Indiana	0	0.0%
33	Maine	0	0.0%
33	North Carolina	0	0.0%
33	North Dakota	0	0.0%
33	Vermont	0	0.0%
33	Wyoming	0	0.0%
NA	California**	NA	NA
NA	Florida**	NA	NA
NA	Illinois**	NA	NA
NA	Louisiana**	NA	NA
NA	Maryland**	NA	NA
NA	Massachusetts**	NA	NA
NA	Mississippi**	NA	NA
NA	Nebraska**	NA	NA
NA	Nevada**	NA	NA
NA	New Hampshire**	NA	NA
	District of Columbia	0	0.0%

Source: U.S. Department of Health and Human Services, Centers for Disease Control and Prevention
    "Abortion Surveillance-United States, 2005" (MMWR, Vol. 57, No. SS-13, 11/28/08, http://www.cdc.gov/mmwr/mmwr_ss.html)
*By state of occurrence. National total is for reporting states only.
**Not reported.

Percent of Reported Legal Abortions Performed at or after
21 Weeks of Gestation in 2005
Reporting States' Percent = 1.3% of Abortions*

ALPHA ORDER

RANK	STATE	PERCENT
23	Alabama	0.3
33	Alaska	0.0
12	Arizona	1.2
33	Arkansas	0.0
NA	California**	NA
5	Colorado	2.3
23	Connecticut	0.3
30	Delaware	0.1
NA	Florida**	NA
2	Georgia	3.5
17	Hawaii	0.5
17	Idaho	0.5
NA	Illinois**	NA
33	Indiana	0.0
26	Iowa	0.2
1	Kansas	4.4
11	Kentucky	1.4
NA	Louisiana**	NA
33	Maine	0.0
NA	Maryland**	NA
NA	Massachusetts**	NA
15	Michigan	0.7
20	Minnesota	0.4
NA	Mississippi**	NA
20	Missouri	0.4
14	Montana	1.0
NA	Nebraska**	NA
NA	Nevada**	NA
NA	New Hampshire**	NA
3	New Jersey	2.7
8	New Mexico	1.8
4	New York	2.4
33	North Carolina	0.0
33	North Dakota	0.0
10	Ohio	1.7
30	Oklahoma	0.1
7	Oregon	2.0
16	Pennsylvania	0.6
26	Rhode Island	0.2
23	South Carolina	0.3
12	South Dakota	1.2
30	Tennessee	0.1
17	Texas	0.5
26	Utah	0.2
33	Vermont	0.0
26	Virginia	0.2
8	Washington	1.8
20	West Virginia	0.4
6	Wisconsin	2.1
33	Wyoming	0.0

RANK ORDER

RANK	STATE	PERCENT
1	Kansas	4.4
2	Georgia	3.5
3	New Jersey	2.7
4	New York	2.4
5	Colorado	2.3
6	Wisconsin	2.1
7	Oregon	2.0
8	New Mexico	1.8
8	Washington	1.8
10	Ohio	1.7
11	Kentucky	1.4
12	Arizona	1.2
12	South Dakota	1.2
14	Montana	1.0
15	Michigan	0.7
16	Pennsylvania	0.6
17	Hawaii	0.5
17	Idaho	0.5
17	Texas	0.5
20	Minnesota	0.4
20	Missouri	0.4
20	West Virginia	0.4
23	Alabama	0.3
23	Connecticut	0.3
23	South Carolina	0.3
26	Iowa	0.2
26	Rhode Island	0.2
26	Utah	0.2
26	Virginia	0.2
30	Delaware	0.1
30	Oklahoma	0.1
30	Tennessee	0.1
33	Alaska	0.0
33	Arkansas	0.0
33	Indiana	0.0
33	Maine	0.0
33	North Carolina	0.0
33	North Dakota	0.0
33	Vermont	0.0
33	Wyoming	0.0
NA	California**	NA
NA	Florida**	NA
NA	Illinois**	NA
NA	Louisiana**	NA
NA	Maryland**	NA
NA	Massachusetts**	NA
NA	Mississippi**	NA
NA	Nebraska**	NA
NA	Nevada**	NA
NA	New Hampshire**	NA
	District of Columbia	0.0

Source: U.S. Department of Health and Human Services, Centers for Disease Control and Prevention
   "Abortion Surveillance-United States, 2005" (MMWR, Vol. 57, No. SS-13, 11/28/08, http://www.cdc.gov/mmwr/mmwr_ss.html)
*By state of occurrence. National percent is for reporting states only.
**Not reported.

II. Deaths

Deaths in 2007

National Total = 2,415,251 Deaths*

RANK	STATE	DEATHS	% of USA
18	Alabama	46,764	1.9%
50	Alaska	3,486	0.1%
20	Arizona	45,215	1.9%
30	Arkansas	28,324	1.2%
1	California	237,059	9.8%
27	Colorado	30,077	1.2%
29	Connecticut	28,536	1.2%
45	Delaware	7,332	0.3%
2	Florida	167,196	6.9%
11	Georgia	65,913	2.7%
43	Hawaii	9,319	0.4%
40	Idaho	10,967	0.5%
7	Illinois	100,049	4.1%
15	Indiana	54,246	2.2%
32	Iowa	27,304	1.1%
33	Kansas	24,307	1.0%
22	Kentucky	39,315	1.6%
23	Louisiana	38,611	1.6%
39	Maine	12,398	0.5%
21	Maryland	43,715	1.8%
16	Massachusetts	53,109	2.2%
8	Michigan	86,740	3.6%
25	Minnesota	37,116	1.5%
31	Mississippi	28,236	1.2%
14	Missouri	54,463	2.3%
44	Montana	8,616	0.4%
36	Nebraska	15,280	0.6%
35	Nevada	19,771	0.8%
41	New Hampshire	10,178	0.4%
10	New Jersey	69,172	2.9%
37	New Mexico	15,261	0.6%
4	New York	148,378	6.1%
9	North Carolina	76,093	3.2%
47	North Dakota	5,648	0.2%
6	Ohio	106,772	4.4%
26	Oklahoma	36,074	1.5%
28	Oregon	29,186	1.2%
5	Pennsylvania	124,485	5.2%
42	Rhode Island	9,751	0.4%
24	South Carolina	37,763	1.6%
46	South Dakota	6,821	0.3%
13	Tennessee	56,948	2.4%
3	Texas	158,740	6.6%
38	Utah	14,142	0.6%
48	Vermont	4,919	0.2%
12	Virginia	57,954	2.4%
17	Washington	47,043	1.9%
34	West Virginia	20,912	0.9%
19	Wisconsin	46,130	1.9%
49	Wyoming	4,200	0.2%

RANK	STATE	DEATHS	% of USA
1	California	237,059	9.8%
2	Florida	167,196	6.9%
3	Texas	158,740	6.6%
4	New York	148,378	6.1%
5	Pennsylvania	124,485	5.2%
6	Ohio	106,772	4.4%
7	Illinois	100,049	4.1%
8	Michigan	86,740	3.6%
9	North Carolina	76,093	3.2%
10	New Jersey	69,172	2.9%
11	Georgia	65,913	2.7%
12	Virginia	57,954	2.4%
13	Tennessee	56,948	2.4%
14	Missouri	54,463	2.3%
15	Indiana	54,246	2.2%
16	Massachusetts	53,109	2.2%
17	Washington	47,043	1.9%
18	Alabama	46,764	1.9%
19	Wisconsin	46,130	1.9%
20	Arizona	45,215	1.9%
21	Maryland	43,715	1.8%
22	Kentucky	39,315	1.6%
23	Louisiana	38,611	1.6%
24	South Carolina	37,763	1.6%
25	Minnesota	37,116	1.5%
26	Oklahoma	36,074	1.5%
27	Colorado	30,077	1.2%
28	Oregon	29,186	1.2%
29	Connecticut	28,536	1.2%
30	Arkansas	28,324	1.2%
31	Mississippi	28,236	1.2%
32	Iowa	27,304	1.1%
33	Kansas	24,307	1.0%
34	West Virginia	20,912	0.9%
35	Nevada	19,771	0.8%
36	Nebraska	15,280	0.6%
37	New Mexico	15,261	0.6%
38	Utah	14,142	0.6%
39	Maine	12,398	0.5%
40	Idaho	10,967	0.5%
41	New Hampshire	10,178	0.4%
42	Rhode Island	9,751	0.4%
43	Hawaii	9,319	0.4%
44	Montana	8,616	0.4%
45	Delaware	7,332	0.3%
46	South Dakota	6,821	0.3%
47	North Dakota	5,648	0.2%
48	Vermont	4,919	0.2%
49	Wyoming	4,200	0.2%
50	Alaska	3,486	0.1%
	District of Columbia	5,217	0.2%

Source: U.S. Department of Health and Human Services, National Center for Health Statistics
  "National Vital Statistics Reports" (Vol. 56, No. 21, July 14, 2008, http://www.cdc.gov/nchs/deaths.htm)
*Provisional data for 12 months ending with December by state of residence.

Death Rate in 2007

National Rate = 801.6 Deaths per 100,000 Population*

<table>
<tr><th colspan="3">ALPHA ORDER</th><th colspan="3">RANK ORDER</th></tr>
<tr><th>RANK</th><th>STATE</th><th>RATE</th><th>RANK</th><th>STATE</th><th>RATE</th></tr>
<tr><td>2</td><td>Alabama</td><td>1,010.8</td><td>1</td><td>West Virginia</td><td>1,155.5</td></tr>
<tr><td>50</td><td>Alaska</td><td>511.8</td><td>2</td><td>Alabama</td><td>1,010.8</td></tr>
<tr><td>44</td><td>Arizona</td><td>711.7</td><td>3</td><td>Pennsylvania</td><td>1,002.3</td></tr>
<tr><td>4</td><td>Arkansas</td><td>1,000.7</td><td>4</td><td>Arkansas</td><td>1,000.7</td></tr>
<tr><td>47</td><td>California</td><td>651.7</td><td>5</td><td>Oklahoma</td><td>999.8</td></tr>
<tr><td>48</td><td>Colorado</td><td>621.1</td><td>6</td><td>Mississippi</td><td>966.6</td></tr>
<tr><td>28</td><td>Connecticut</td><td>817.7</td><td>7</td><td>Maine</td><td>942.5</td></tr>
<tr><td>24</td><td>Delaware</td><td>850.6</td><td>8</td><td>Ohio</td><td>930.3</td></tr>
<tr><td>13</td><td>Florida</td><td>918.7</td><td>9</td><td>Kentucky</td><td>928.0</td></tr>
<tr><td>45</td><td>Georgia</td><td>692.1</td><td>10</td><td>Missouri</td><td>926.5</td></tr>
<tr><td>41</td><td>Hawaii</td><td>729.6</td><td>11</td><td>Tennessee</td><td>926.1</td></tr>
<tr><td>40</td><td>Idaho</td><td>733.0</td><td>12</td><td>Rhode Island</td><td>925.9</td></tr>
<tr><td>33</td><td>Illinois</td><td>780.1</td><td>13</td><td>Florida</td><td>918.7</td></tr>
<tr><td>23</td><td>Indiana</td><td>856.2</td><td>14</td><td>Iowa</td><td>915.2</td></tr>
<tr><td>14</td><td>Iowa</td><td>915.2</td><td>15</td><td>Montana</td><td>900.7</td></tr>
<tr><td>18</td><td>Kansas</td><td>875.2</td><td>16</td><td>North Dakota</td><td>885.4</td></tr>
<tr><td>9</td><td>Kentucky</td><td>928.0</td><td>17</td><td>Louisiana</td><td>882.9</td></tr>
<tr><td>17</td><td>Louisiana</td><td>882.9</td><td>18</td><td>Kansas</td><td>875.2</td></tr>
<tr><td>7</td><td>Maine</td><td>942.5</td><td>19</td><td>Nebraska</td><td>863.5</td></tr>
<tr><td>34</td><td>Maryland</td><td>778.0</td><td>20</td><td>Michigan</td><td>863.1</td></tr>
<tr><td>27</td><td>Massachusetts</td><td>821.1</td><td>21</td><td>South Carolina</td><td>857.3</td></tr>
<tr><td>20</td><td>Michigan</td><td>863.1</td><td>22</td><td>South Dakota</td><td>857.2</td></tr>
<tr><td>43</td><td>Minnesota</td><td>716.2</td><td>23</td><td>Indiana</td><td>856.2</td></tr>
<tr><td>6</td><td>Mississippi</td><td>966.6</td><td>24</td><td>Delaware</td><td>850.6</td></tr>
<tr><td>10</td><td>Missouri</td><td>926.5</td><td>25</td><td>North Carolina</td><td>841.6</td></tr>
<tr><td>15</td><td>Montana</td><td>900.7</td><td>26</td><td>Wisconsin</td><td>823.9</td></tr>
<tr><td>19</td><td>Nebraska</td><td>863.5</td><td>27</td><td>Massachusetts</td><td>821.1</td></tr>
<tr><td>37</td><td>Nevada</td><td>774.0</td><td>28</td><td>Connecticut</td><td>817.7</td></tr>
<tr><td>36</td><td>New Hampshire</td><td>775.6</td><td>29</td><td>Wyoming</td><td>802.7</td></tr>
<tr><td>30</td><td>New Jersey</td><td>799.4</td><td>30</td><td>New Jersey</td><td>799.4</td></tr>
<tr><td>35</td><td>New Mexico</td><td>776.9</td><td>31</td><td>Vermont</td><td>792.4</td></tr>
<tr><td>38</td><td>New York</td><td>763.7</td><td>32</td><td>Oregon</td><td>781.3</td></tr>
<tr><td>25</td><td>North Carolina</td><td>841.6</td><td>33</td><td>Illinois</td><td>780.1</td></tr>
<tr><td>16</td><td>North Dakota</td><td>885.4</td><td>34</td><td>Maryland</td><td>778.0</td></tr>
<tr><td>8</td><td>Ohio</td><td>930.3</td><td>35</td><td>New Mexico</td><td>776.9</td></tr>
<tr><td>5</td><td>Oklahoma</td><td>999.8</td><td>36</td><td>New Hampshire</td><td>775.6</td></tr>
<tr><td>32</td><td>Oregon</td><td>781.3</td><td>37</td><td>Nevada</td><td>774.0</td></tr>
<tr><td>3</td><td>Pennsylvania</td><td>1,002.3</td><td>38</td><td>New York</td><td>763.7</td></tr>
<tr><td>12</td><td>Rhode Island</td><td>925.9</td><td>39</td><td>Virginia</td><td>752.8</td></tr>
<tr><td>21</td><td>South Carolina</td><td>857.3</td><td>40</td><td>Idaho</td><td>733.0</td></tr>
<tr><td>22</td><td>South Dakota</td><td>857.2</td><td>41</td><td>Hawaii</td><td>729.6</td></tr>
<tr><td>11</td><td>Tennessee</td><td>926.1</td><td>42</td><td>Washington</td><td>729.4</td></tr>
<tr><td>46</td><td>Texas</td><td>665.8</td><td>43</td><td>Minnesota</td><td>716.2</td></tr>
<tr><td>49</td><td>Utah</td><td>529.9</td><td>44</td><td>Arizona</td><td>711.7</td></tr>
<tr><td>31</td><td>Vermont</td><td>792.4</td><td>45</td><td>Georgia</td><td>692.1</td></tr>
<tr><td>39</td><td>Virginia</td><td>752.8</td><td>46</td><td>Texas</td><td>665.8</td></tr>
<tr><td>42</td><td>Washington</td><td>729.4</td><td>47</td><td>California</td><td>651.7</td></tr>
<tr><td>1</td><td>West Virginia</td><td>1,155.5</td><td>48</td><td>Colorado</td><td>621.1</td></tr>
<tr><td>26</td><td>Wisconsin</td><td>823.9</td><td>49</td><td>Utah</td><td>529.9</td></tr>
<tr><td>29</td><td>Wyoming</td><td>802.7</td><td>50</td><td>Alaska</td><td>511.8</td></tr>
<tr><td></td><td></td><td></td><td></td><td>District of Columbia</td><td>887.4</td></tr>
</table>

Source: CQ Press using data from U.S. Department of Health and Human Services, National Center for Health Statistics
"National Vital Statistics Reports" (Vol. 56, No. 21, July 14, 2008, http://www.cdc.gov/nchs/deaths.htm)
*Provisional data for 12 months ending with December by state of residence. Not age-adjusted.

Deaths in 2006

National Total = 2,425,900 Deaths*

RANK	STATE	DEATHS	% of USA
17	Alabama	46,973	1.9%
50	Alaska	3,344	0.1%
18	Arizona	46,367	1.9%
31	Arkansas	27,891	1.1%
1	California	237,069	9.8%
28	Colorado	29,519	1.2%
29	Connecticut	29,275	1.2%
45	Delaware	7,206	0.3%
2	Florida	170,069	7.0%
11	Georgia	67,507	2.8%
43	Hawaii	9,451	0.4%
40	Idaho	10,610	0.4%
7	Illinois	102,183	4.2%
14	Indiana	55,575	2.3%
32	Iowa	27,360	1.1%
33	Kansas	24,549	1.0%
22	Kentucky	40,072	1.7%
23	Louisiana	39,974	1.6%
39	Maine	12,295	0.5%
21	Maryland	43,575	1.8%
16	Massachusetts	53,453	2.2%
8	Michigan	86,033	3.5%
25	Minnesota	37,031	1.5%
30	Mississippi	28,562	1.2%
15	Missouri	54,682	2.3%
44	Montana	8,474	0.3%
37	Nebraska	14,897	0.6%
35	Nevada	18,448	0.8%
41	New Hampshire	10,058	0.4%
10	New Jersey	70,336	2.9%
36	New Mexico	15,261	0.6%
4	New York	148,808	6.1%
9	North Carolina	74,714	3.1%
47	North Dakota	5,868	0.2%
6	Ohio	106,863	4.4%
26	Oklahoma	35,430	1.5%
27	Oregon	31,566	1.3%
5	Pennsylvania	125,713	5.2%
42	Rhode Island	9,687	0.4%
24	South Carolina	38,802	1.6%
46	South Dakota	7,081	0.3%
13	Tennessee	56,833	2.3%
3	Texas	157,365	6.5%
38	Utah	13,736	0.6%
48	Vermont	5,042	0.2%
12	Virginia	57,696	2.4%
20	Washington	46,108	1.9%
34	West Virginia	20,676	0.9%
19	Wisconsin	46,153	1.9%
49	Wyoming	4,311	0.2%

RANK	STATE	DEATHS	% of USA
1	California	237,069	9.8%
2	Florida	170,069	7.0%
3	Texas	157,365	6.5%
4	New York	148,808	6.1%
5	Pennsylvania	125,713	5.2%
6	Ohio	106,863	4.4%
7	Illinois	102,183	4.2%
8	Michigan	86,033	3.5%
9	North Carolina	74,714	3.1%
10	New Jersey	70,336	2.9%
11	Georgia	67,507	2.8%
12	Virginia	57,696	2.4%
13	Tennessee	56,833	2.3%
14	Indiana	55,575	2.3%
15	Missouri	54,682	2.3%
16	Massachusetts	53,453	2.2%
17	Alabama	46,973	1.9%
18	Arizona	46,367	1.9%
19	Wisconsin	46,153	1.9%
20	Washington	46,108	1.9%
21	Maryland	43,575	1.8%
22	Kentucky	40,072	1.7%
23	Louisiana	39,974	1.6%
24	South Carolina	38,802	1.6%
25	Minnesota	37,031	1.5%
26	Oklahoma	35,430	1.5%
27	Oregon	31,566	1.3%
28	Colorado	29,519	1.2%
29	Connecticut	29,275	1.2%
30	Mississippi	28,562	1.2%
31	Arkansas	27,891	1.1%
32	Iowa	27,360	1.1%
33	Kansas	24,549	1.0%
34	West Virginia	20,676	0.9%
35	Nevada	18,448	0.8%
36	New Mexico	15,261	0.6%
37	Nebraska	14,897	0.6%
38	Utah	13,736	0.6%
39	Maine	12,295	0.5%
40	Idaho	10,610	0.4%
41	New Hampshire	10,058	0.4%
42	Rhode Island	9,687	0.4%
43	Hawaii	9,451	0.4%
44	Montana	8,474	0.3%
45	Delaware	7,206	0.3%
46	South Dakota	7,081	0.3%
47	North Dakota	5,868	0.2%
48	Vermont	5,042	0.2%
49	Wyoming	4,311	0.2%
50	Alaska	3,344	0.1%
	District of Columbia	5,353	0.2%

Source: U.S. Department of Health and Human Services, National Center for Health Statistics
"Deaths: Preliminary Data for 2006" (http://www.cdc.gov/nchs/deaths.htm)
*Preliminary data by state of residence.

Death Rate in 2006

National Rate = 810.3 Deaths per 100,000 Population*

ALPHA ORDER

RANK	STATE	RATE
2	Alabama	1,021.4
50	Alaska	499.1
39	Arizona	751.9
4	Arkansas	992.3
47	California	650.3
48	Colorado	621.0
28	Connecticut	835.3
24	Delaware	844.3
9	Florida	940.1
43	Georgia	720.9
41	Hawaii	735.2
42	Idaho	723.5
33	Illinois	796.3
21	Indiana	880.3
15	Iowa	917.5
20	Kansas	888.1
7	Kentucky	952.7
11	Louisiana	932.3
13	Maine	930.3
35	Maryland	775.9
30	Massachusetts	830.4
23	Michigan	852.2
45	Minnesota	716.7
6	Mississippi	981.3
10	Missouri	935.9
19	Montana	897.1
26	Nebraska	842.4
40	Nevada	739.2
37	New Hampshire	764.9
32	New Jersey	806.2
34	New Mexico	780.8
36	New York	770.8
25	North Carolina	843.6
14	North Dakota	922.8
12	Ohio	931.0
5	Oklahoma	989.9
22	Oregon	853.0
3	Pennsylvania	1,010.5
16	Rhode Island	907.4
18	South Carolina	897.9
17	South Dakota	905.6
8	Tennessee	941.1
46	Texas	669.4
49	Utah	538.7
31	Vermont	808.1
38	Virginia	754.9
43	Washington	720.9
1	West Virginia	1,137.0
29	Wisconsin	830.6
27	Wyoming	837.1

RANK ORDER

RANK	STATE	RATE
1	West Virginia	1,137.0
2	Alabama	1,021.4
3	Pennsylvania	1,010.5
4	Arkansas	992.3
5	Oklahoma	989.9
6	Mississippi	981.3
7	Kentucky	952.7
8	Tennessee	941.1
9	Florida	940.1
10	Missouri	935.9
11	Louisiana	932.3
12	Ohio	931.0
13	Maine	930.3
14	North Dakota	922.8
15	Iowa	917.5
16	Rhode Island	907.4
17	South Dakota	905.6
18	South Carolina	897.9
19	Montana	897.1
20	Kansas	888.1
21	Indiana	880.3
22	Oregon	853.0
23	Michigan	852.2
24	Delaware	844.3
25	North Carolina	843.6
26	Nebraska	842.4
27	Wyoming	837.1
28	Connecticut	835.3
29	Wisconsin	830.6
30	Massachusetts	830.4
31	Vermont	808.1
32	New Jersey	806.2
33	Illinois	796.3
34	New Mexico	780.8
35	Maryland	775.9
36	New York	770.8
37	New Hampshire	764.9
38	Virginia	754.9
39	Arizona	751.9
40	Nevada	739.2
41	Hawaii	735.2
42	Idaho	723.5
43	Georgia	720.9
43	Washington	720.9
45	Minnesota	716.7
46	Texas	669.4
47	California	650.3
48	Colorado	621.0
49	Utah	538.7
50	Alaska	499.1
	District of Columbia	920.5

Source: U.S. Department of Health and Human Services, National Center for Health Statistics
"Deaths: Preliminary Data for 2006" (http://www.cdc.gov/nchs/deaths.htm)
*Preliminary data by state of residence. Not age-adjusted.

Age-Adjusted Death Rate in 2006

National Rate = 776.4 Deaths per 100,000 Population*

ALPHA ORDER

RANK	STATE	RATE
2	Alabama	952.3
28	Alaska	774.4
39	Arizona	724.2
8	Arkansas	888.5
48	California	700.2
43	Colorado	716.8
44	Connecticut	715.1
22	Delaware	783.4
45	Florida	711.3
10	Georgia	855.5
50	Hawaii	631.0
30	Idaho	747.2
24	Illinois	781.2
12	Indiana	846.8
36	Iowa	730.2
19	Kansas	794.6
6	Kentucky	914.5
4	Louisiana	928.5
26	Maine	774.8
20	Maryland	792.9
42	Massachusetts	719.8
17	Michigan	813.6
49	Minnesota	672.8
1	Mississippi	961.1
11	Missouri	848.3
23	Montana	781.5
35	Nebraska	735.1
15	Nevada	824.0
38	New Hampshire	724.7
34	New Jersey	736.4
29	New Mexico	774.0
47	New York	701.2
13	North Carolina	843.6
37	North Dakota	726.7
14	Ohio	841.1
5	Oklahoma	920.4
27	Oregon	774.7
18	Pennsylvania	801.8
31	Rhode Island	746.9
9	South Carolina	865.5
33	South Dakota	740.1
7	Tennessee	908.2
21	Texas	784.8
46	Utah	705.0
41	Vermont	720.7
25	Virginia	781.1
40	Washington	722.4
3	West Virginia	941.3
32	Wisconsin	746.6
16	Wyoming	822.7

RANK ORDER

RANK	STATE	RATE
1	Mississippi	961.1
2	Alabama	952.3
3	West Virginia	941.3
4	Louisiana	928.5
5	Oklahoma	920.4
6	Kentucky	914.5
7	Tennessee	908.2
8	Arkansas	888.5
9	South Carolina	865.5
10	Georgia	855.5
11	Missouri	848.3
12	Indiana	846.8
13	North Carolina	843.6
14	Ohio	841.1
15	Nevada	824.0
16	Wyoming	822.7
17	Michigan	813.6
18	Pennsylvania	801.8
19	Kansas	794.6
20	Maryland	792.9
21	Texas	784.8
22	Delaware	783.4
23	Montana	781.5
24	Illinois	781.2
25	Virginia	781.1
26	Maine	774.8
27	Oregon	774.7
28	Alaska	774.4
29	New Mexico	774.0
30	Idaho	747.2
31	Rhode Island	746.9
32	Wisconsin	746.6
33	South Dakota	740.1
34	New Jersey	736.4
35	Nebraska	735.1
36	Iowa	730.2
37	North Dakota	726.7
38	New Hampshire	724.7
39	Arizona	724.2
40	Washington	722.4
41	Vermont	720.7
42	Massachusetts	719.8
43	Colorado	716.8
44	Connecticut	715.1
45	Florida	711.3
46	Utah	705.0
47	New York	701.2
48	California	700.2
49	Minnesota	672.8
50	Hawaii	631.0

	District of Columbia	894.5

Source: U.S. Department of Health and Human Services, National Center for Health Statistics
    "Deaths: Preliminary Data for 2006" (http://www.cdc.gov/nchs/deaths.htm)
*Preliminary data by state of residence. Age-adjusted rates eliminate the distorting effects of the aging of the population. Rates based on the year 2000 standard population.

Percent Change in Death Rate: 1997 to 2006

National Percent Change = 6.3% Decrease*

ALPHA ORDER				RANK ORDER		
RANK	STATE	PERCENT CHANGE		RANK	STATE	PERCENT CHANGE
5	Alabama	2.0		1	Alaska	18.1
1	Alaska	18.1		2	Hawaii	10.5
40	Arizona	(7.6)		3	Wyoming	7.2
48	Arkansas	(10.1)		4	New Mexico	6.7
35	California	(6.6)		5	Alabama	2.0
33	Colorado	(5.7)		6	Montana	1.5
37	Connecticut	(7.1)		7	Louisiana	1.4
26	Delaware	(5.1)		8	North Dakota	0.4
49	Florida	(10.8)		9	South Carolina	0.2
46	Georgia	(9.1)		10	Michigan	0.0
2	Hawaii	10.5		11	Ohio	(1.1)
15	Idaho	(2.5)		11	West Virginia	(1.1)
41	Illinois	(8.0)		13	Kentucky	(2.0)
18	Indiana	(2.8)		14	Washington	(2.4)
31	Iowa	(5.5)		15	Idaho	(2.5)
19	Kansas	(3.0)		16	Mississippi	(2.6)
13	Kentucky	(2.0)		17	South Dakota	(2.7)
7	Louisiana	1.4		18	Indiana	(2.8)
21	Maine	(3.7)		19	Kansas	(3.0)
30	Maryland	(5.4)		20	Oklahoma	(3.3)
37	Massachusetts	(7.1)		21	Maine	(3.7)
10	Michigan	0.0		22	Oregon	(3.8)
45	Minnesota	(9.0)		23	Tennessee	(4.1)
16	Mississippi	(2.6)		24	Utah	(4.2)
36	Missouri	(6.9)		25	Wisconsin	(4.4)
6	Montana	1.5		26	Delaware	(5.1)
42	Nebraska	(8.7)		26	North Carolina	(5.1)
39	Nevada	(7.4)		26	Pennsylvania	(5.1)
29	New Hampshire	(5.2)		29	New Hampshire	(5.2)
47	New Jersey	(10.0)		30	Maryland	(5.4)
4	New Mexico	6.7		31	Iowa	(5.5)
50	New York	(11.9)		32	Virginia	(5.6)
26	North Carolina	(5.1)		33	Colorado	(5.7)
8	North Dakota	0.4		34	Vermont	(5.8)
11	Ohio	(1.1)		35	California	(6.6)
20	Oklahoma	(3.3)		36	Missouri	(6.9)
22	Oregon	(3.8)		37	Connecticut	(7.1)
26	Pennsylvania	(5.1)		37	Massachusetts	(7.1)
43	Rhode Island	(8.8)		39	Nevada	(7.4)
9	South Carolina	0.2		40	Arizona	(7.6)
17	South Dakota	(2.7)		41	Illinois	(8.0)
23	Tennessee	(4.1)		42	Nebraska	(8.7)
44	Texas	(8.9)		43	Rhode Island	(8.8)
24	Utah	(4.2)		44	Texas	(8.9)
34	Vermont	(5.8)		45	Minnesota	(9.0)
32	Virginia	(5.6)		46	Georgia	(9.1)
14	Washington	(2.4)		47	New Jersey	(10.0)
11	West Virginia	(1.1)		48	Arkansas	(10.1)
25	Wisconsin	(4.4)		49	Florida	(10.8)
3	Wyoming	7.2		50	New York	(11.9)
					District of Columbia	(20.6)

Source: CQ Press using data from U.S. Department of Health and Human Services, National Center for Health Statistics
   "Deaths: Preliminary Data for 2006" (http://www.cdc.gov/nchs/deaths.htm)
   "National Vital Statistics Report" (Vol. 47, No. 19, June 30, 1999)
*By state of residence. Not age-adjusted.

Deaths in 2005

National Total = 2,448,017 Deaths*

ALPHA ORDER

ALPHA ORDER

RANK	STATE	DEATHS	% of USA
17	Alabama	47,090	1.9%
50	Alaska	3,168	0.1%
20	Arizona	45,827	1.9%
31	Arkansas	28,055	1.1%
1	California	237,037	9.7%
28	Colorado	29,627	1.2%
29	Connecticut	29,467	1.2%
45	Delaware	7,472	0.3%
2	Florida	170,791	7.0%
11	Georgia	66,736	2.7%
43	Hawaii	9,136	0.4%
40	Idaho	10,556	0.4%
7	Illinois	103,974	4.2%
14	Indiana	55,675	2.3%
32	Iowa	27,811	1.1%
33	Kansas	24,682	1.0%
23	Kentucky	40,223	1.6%
21	Louisiana	44,355	1.8%
39	Maine	12,868	0.5%
22	Maryland	43,892	1.8%
16	Massachusetts	53,874	2.2%
8	Michigan	86,867	3.5%
25	Minnesota	37,535	1.5%
30	Mississippi	29,196	1.2%
15	Missouri	54,656	2.2%
44	Montana	8,528	0.3%
37	Nebraska	14,963	0.6%
35	Nevada	19,029	0.8%
41	New Hampshire	10,194	0.4%
10	New Jersey	71,963	2.9%
36	New Mexico	14,983	0.6%
4	New York	152,427	6.2%
9	North Carolina	74,638	3.0%
47	North Dakota	5,744	0.2%
6	Ohio	109,031	4.5%
26	Oklahoma	36,180	1.5%
27	Oregon	31,091	1.3%
5	Pennsylvania	129,532	5.3%
42	Rhode Island	10,007	0.4%
24	South Carolina	38,707	1.6%
46	South Dakota	7,086	0.3%
13	Tennessee	57,260	2.3%
3	Texas	156,457	6.4%
38	Utah	13,432	0.5%
48	Vermont	5,066	0.2%
12	Virginia	57,855	2.4%
19	Washington	46,203	1.9%
34	West Virginia	20,780	0.8%
18	Wisconsin	46,709	1.9%
49	Wyoming	4,099	0.2%

RANK ORDER

RANK	STATE	DEATHS	% of USA
1	California	237,037	9.7%
2	Florida	170,791	7.0%
3	Texas	156,457	6.4%
4	New York	152,427	6.2%
5	Pennsylvania	129,532	5.3%
6	Ohio	109,031	4.5%
7	Illinois	103,974	4.2%
8	Michigan	86,867	3.5%
9	North Carolina	74,638	3.0%
10	New Jersey	71,963	2.9%
11	Georgia	66,736	2.7%
12	Virginia	57,855	2.4%
13	Tennessee	57,260	2.3%
14	Indiana	55,675	2.3%
15	Missouri	54,656	2.2%
16	Massachusetts	53,874	2.2%
17	Alabama	47,090	1.9%
18	Wisconsin	46,709	1.9%
19	Washington	46,203	1.9%
20	Arizona	45,827	1.9%
21	Louisiana	44,355	1.8%
22	Maryland	43,892	1.8%
23	Kentucky	40,223	1.6%
24	South Carolina	38,707	1.6%
25	Minnesota	37,535	1.5%
26	Oklahoma	36,180	1.5%
27	Oregon	31,091	1.3%
28	Colorado	29,627	1.2%
29	Connecticut	29,467	1.2%
30	Mississippi	29,196	1.2%
31	Arkansas	28,055	1.1%
32	Iowa	27,811	1.1%
33	Kansas	24,682	1.0%
34	West Virginia	20,780	0.8%
35	Nevada	19,029	0.8%
36	New Mexico	14,983	0.6%
37	Nebraska	14,963	0.6%
38	Utah	13,432	0.5%
39	Maine	12,868	0.5%
40	Idaho	10,556	0.4%
41	New Hampshire	10,194	0.4%
42	Rhode Island	10,007	0.4%
43	Hawaii	9,136	0.4%
44	Montana	8,528	0.3%
45	Delaware	7,472	0.3%
46	South Dakota	7,086	0.3%
47	North Dakota	5,744	0.2%
48	Vermont	5,066	0.2%
49	Wyoming	4,099	0.2%
50	Alaska	3,168	0.1%
	District of Columbia	5,483	0.2%

Source: U.S. Department of Health and Human Services, National Center for Health Statistics
"National Vital Statistics Reports" (http://www.cdc.gov/nchs/deaths.htm)
*Final data by state of residence.

Death Rate in 2005

National Rate = 825.9 Deaths per 100,000 Population*

<table>
<tr><td colspan="3">ALPHA ORDER</td><td colspan="3">RANK ORDER</td></tr>
<tr><td>RANK</td><td>STATE</td><td>RATE</td><td>RANK</td><td>STATE</td><td>RATE</td></tr>
<tr><td>3</td><td>Alabama</td><td>1,033.2</td><td>1</td><td>West Virginia</td><td>1,143.7</td></tr>
<tr><td>50</td><td>Alaska</td><td>477.4</td><td>2</td><td>Pennsylvania</td><td>1,042.1</td></tr>
<tr><td>39</td><td>Arizona</td><td>771.6</td><td>3</td><td>Alabama</td><td>1,033.2</td></tr>
<tr><td>5</td><td>Arkansas</td><td>1,009.5</td><td>4</td><td>Oklahoma</td><td>1,019.8</td></tr>
<tr><td>47</td><td>California</td><td>656.0</td><td>5</td><td>Arkansas</td><td>1,009.5</td></tr>
<tr><td>48</td><td>Colorado</td><td>635.1</td><td>6</td><td>Mississippi</td><td>999.5</td></tr>
<tr><td>29</td><td>Connecticut</td><td>839.4</td><td>7</td><td>Louisiana</td><td>980.5</td></tr>
<tr><td>22</td><td>Delaware</td><td>885.8</td><td>8</td><td>Maine</td><td>973.7</td></tr>
<tr><td>11</td><td>Florida</td><td>960.0</td><td>9</td><td>Kentucky</td><td>963.8</td></tr>
<tr><td>42</td><td>Georgia</td><td>735.6</td><td>10</td><td>Tennessee</td><td>960.3</td></tr>
<tr><td>45</td><td>Hawaii</td><td>716.4</td><td>11</td><td>Florida</td><td>960.0</td></tr>
<tr><td>41</td><td>Idaho</td><td>738.6</td><td>12</td><td>Ohio</td><td>951.1</td></tr>
<tr><td>31</td><td>Illinois</td><td>814.6</td><td>13</td><td>Missouri</td><td>942.3</td></tr>
<tr><td>21</td><td>Indiana</td><td>887.7</td><td>14</td><td>Iowa</td><td>937.6</td></tr>
<tr><td>14</td><td>Iowa</td><td>937.6</td><td>15</td><td>Rhode Island</td><td>929.9</td></tr>
<tr><td>20</td><td>Kansas</td><td>899.3</td><td>16</td><td>South Dakota</td><td>913.2</td></tr>
<tr><td>9</td><td>Kentucky</td><td>963.8</td><td>17</td><td>Montana</td><td>911.4</td></tr>
<tr><td>7</td><td>Louisiana</td><td>980.5</td><td>18</td><td>South Carolina</td><td>909.7</td></tr>
<tr><td>8</td><td>Maine</td><td>973.7</td><td>19</td><td>North Dakota</td><td>902.2</td></tr>
<tr><td>36</td><td>Maryland</td><td>783.7</td><td>20</td><td>Kansas</td><td>899.3</td></tr>
<tr><td>28</td><td>Massachusetts</td><td>841.9</td><td>21</td><td>Indiana</td><td>887.7</td></tr>
<tr><td>24</td><td>Michigan</td><td>858.3</td><td>22</td><td>Delaware</td><td>885.8</td></tr>
<tr><td>44</td><td>Minnesota</td><td>731.3</td><td>23</td><td>North Carolina</td><td>859.6</td></tr>
<tr><td>6</td><td>Mississippi</td><td>999.5</td><td>24</td><td>Michigan</td><td>858.3</td></tr>
<tr><td>13</td><td>Missouri</td><td>942.3</td><td>25</td><td>Oregon</td><td>853.9</td></tr>
<tr><td>17</td><td>Montana</td><td>911.4</td><td>26</td><td>Nebraska</td><td>850.8</td></tr>
<tr><td>26</td><td>Nebraska</td><td>850.8</td><td>27</td><td>Wisconsin</td><td>843.7</td></tr>
<tr><td>35</td><td>Nevada</td><td>788.0</td><td>28</td><td>Massachusetts</td><td>841.9</td></tr>
<tr><td>37</td><td>New Hampshire</td><td>778.2</td><td>29</td><td>Connecticut</td><td>839.4</td></tr>
<tr><td>30</td><td>New Jersey</td><td>825.5</td><td>30</td><td>New Jersey</td><td>825.5</td></tr>
<tr><td>38</td><td>New Mexico</td><td>777.0</td><td>31</td><td>Illinois</td><td>814.6</td></tr>
<tr><td>34</td><td>New York</td><td>791.6</td><td>32</td><td>Vermont</td><td>813.1</td></tr>
<tr><td>23</td><td>North Carolina</td><td>859.6</td><td>33</td><td>Wyoming</td><td>804.8</td></tr>
<tr><td>19</td><td>North Dakota</td><td>902.2</td><td>34</td><td>New York</td><td>791.6</td></tr>
<tr><td>12</td><td>Ohio</td><td>951.1</td><td>35</td><td>Nevada</td><td>788.0</td></tr>
<tr><td>4</td><td>Oklahoma</td><td>1,019.8</td><td>36</td><td>Maryland</td><td>783.7</td></tr>
<tr><td>25</td><td>Oregon</td><td>853.9</td><td>37</td><td>New Hampshire</td><td>778.2</td></tr>
<tr><td>2</td><td>Pennsylvania</td><td>1,042.1</td><td>38</td><td>New Mexico</td><td>777.0</td></tr>
<tr><td>15</td><td>Rhode Island</td><td>929.9</td><td>39</td><td>Arizona</td><td>771.6</td></tr>
<tr><td>18</td><td>South Carolina</td><td>909.7</td><td>40</td><td>Virginia</td><td>764.5</td></tr>
<tr><td>16</td><td>South Dakota</td><td>913.2</td><td>41</td><td>Idaho</td><td>738.6</td></tr>
<tr><td>10</td><td>Tennessee</td><td>960.3</td><td>42</td><td>Georgia</td><td>735.6</td></tr>
<tr><td>46</td><td>Texas</td><td>684.4</td><td>43</td><td>Washington</td><td>734.8</td></tr>
<tr><td>49</td><td>Utah</td><td>543.9</td><td>44</td><td>Minnesota</td><td>731.3</td></tr>
<tr><td>32</td><td>Vermont</td><td>813.1</td><td>45</td><td>Hawaii</td><td>716.4</td></tr>
<tr><td>40</td><td>Virginia</td><td>764.5</td><td>46</td><td>Texas</td><td>684.4</td></tr>
<tr><td>43</td><td>Washington</td><td>734.8</td><td>47</td><td>California</td><td>656.0</td></tr>
<tr><td>1</td><td>West Virginia</td><td>1,143.7</td><td>48</td><td>Colorado</td><td>635.1</td></tr>
<tr><td>27</td><td>Wisconsin</td><td>843.7</td><td>49</td><td>Utah</td><td>543.9</td></tr>
<tr><td>33</td><td>Wyoming</td><td>804.8</td><td>50</td><td>Alaska</td><td>477.4</td></tr>
<tr><td></td><td></td><td></td><td></td><td>District of Columbia</td><td>996.0</td></tr>
</table>

Source: U.S. Department of Health and Human Services, National Center for Health Statistics
"National Vital Statistics Reports" (http://www.cdc.gov/nchs/deaths.htm)
*Final data by state of residence. Not age-adjusted.

Age-Adjusted Death Rate in 2005

National Rate = 798.8 Deaths per 100,000 Population*

ALPHA ORDER				RANK ORDER		
RANK	STATE	RATE		RANK	STATE	RATE
3	Alabama	998.0		1	Mississippi	1,026.9
33	Alaska	750.5		2	Louisiana	1,020.8
29	Arizona	771.7		3	Alabama	998.0
8	Arkansas	930.2		4	Oklahoma	980.8
46	California	713.0		5	West Virginia	960.4
38	Colorado	742.8		6	Tennessee	959.8
48	Connecticut	696.2		7	Kentucky	958.4
16	Delaware	830.5		8	Arkansas	930.2
35	Florida	749.4		9	Georgia	905.8
9	Georgia	905.8		10	South Carolina	904.4
50	Hawaii	609.0		11	Nevada	892.0
30	Idaho	766.7		12	North Carolina	876.0
25	Illinois	798.2		13	Missouri	869.4
14	Indiana	858.7		14	Indiana	858.7
39	Iowa	742.0		15	Ohio	856.8
21	Kansas	806.8		16	Delaware	830.5
7	Kentucky	958.4		17	Texas	828.7
2	Louisiana	1,020.8		18	Pennsylvania	814.7
19	Maine	813.0		19	Maine	813.0
26	Maryland	796.4		20	Michigan	812.3
44	Massachusetts	722.0		21	Kansas	806.8
20	Michigan	812.3		22	Virginia	801.5
49	Minnesota	683.9		23	Wyoming	801.4
1	Mississippi	1,026.9		24	Montana	798.4
13	Missouri	869.4		25	Illinois	798.2
24	Montana	798.4		26	Maryland	796.4
34	Nebraska	749.5		27	New Mexico	795.0
11	Nevada	892.0		28	Oregon	773.5
41	New Hampshire	732.4		29	Arizona	771.7
37	New Jersey	745.9		30	Idaho	766.7
27	New Mexico	795.0		31	South Dakota	757.0
45	New York	718.0		32	Wisconsin	752.2
12	North Carolina	876.0		33	Alaska	750.5
47	North Dakota	699.1		34	Nebraska	749.5
15	Ohio	856.8		35	Florida	749.4
4	Oklahoma	980.8		36	Rhode Island	747.3
28	Oregon	773.5		37	New Jersey	745.9
18	Pennsylvania	814.7		38	Colorado	742.8
36	Rhode Island	747.3		39	Iowa	742.0
10	South Carolina	904.4		40	Washington	738.1
31	South Dakota	757.0		41	New Hampshire	732.4
6	Tennessee	959.8		42	Utah	731.2
17	Texas	828.7		43	Vermont	728.4
42	Utah	731.2		44	Massachusetts	722.0
43	Vermont	728.4		45	New York	718.0
22	Virginia	801.5		46	California	713.0
40	Washington	738.1		47	North Dakota	699.1
5	West Virginia	960.4		48	Connecticut	696.2
32	Wisconsin	752.2		49	Minnesota	683.9
23	Wyoming	801.4		50	Hawaii	609.0
					District of Columbia	971.4

Source: U.S. Department of Health and Human Services, National Center for Health Statistics
   "National Vital Statistics Reports" (http://www.cdc.gov/nchs/deaths.htm)
*Final data by state of residence. Age-adjusted rates eliminate the distorting effects of the aging of the population. Rates based
on the year 2000 standard population.

Infant Deaths in 2005

National Total = 28,440 Infant Deaths*

ALPHA ORDER

RANK	STATE	DEATHS	% of USA
18	Alabama	568	2.0%
47	Alaska	62	0.2%
14	Arizona	662	2.3%
29	Arkansas	309	1.1%
1	California	2,930	10.3%
23	Colorado	444	1.6%
32	Connecticut	243	0.9%
41	Delaware	105	0.4%
3	Florida	1,629	5.7%
7	Georgia	1,159	4.1%
40	Hawaii	116	0.4%
39	Idaho	141	0.5%
5	Illinois	1,328	4.7%
13	Indiana	698	2.5%
35	Iowa	210	0.7%
30	Kansas	294	1.0%
27	Kentucky	375	1.3%
15	Louisiana	613	2.2%
42	Maine	97	0.3%
19	Maryland	547	1.9%
26	Massachusetts	396	1.4%
10	Michigan	1,012	3.6%
28	Minnesota	362	1.3%
21	Mississippi	481	1.7%
17	Missouri	590	2.1%
45	Montana	81	0.3%
38	Nebraska	147	0.5%
34	Nevada	215	0.8%
46	New Hampshire	76	0.3%
16	New Jersey	595	2.1%
36	New Mexico	177	0.6%
4	New York	1,431	5.0%
8	North Carolina	1,083	3.8%
48	North Dakota	50	0.2%
6	Ohio	1,225	4.3%
25	Oklahoma	417	1.5%
31	Oregon	269	0.9%
9	Pennsylvania	1,061	3.7%
44	Rhode Island	82	0.3%
20	South Carolina	543	1.9%
43	South Dakota	83	0.3%
12	Tennessee	724	2.5%
2	Texas	2,537	8.9%
33	Utah	230	0.8%
50	Vermont	42	0.1%
11	Virginia	781	2.7%
24	Washington	421	1.5%
37	West Virginia	169	0.6%
22	Wisconsin	469	1.6%
49	Wyoming	49	0.2%

RANK ORDER

RANK	STATE	DEATHS	% of USA
1	California	2,930	10.3%
2	Texas	2,537	8.9%
3	Florida	1,629	5.7%
4	New York	1,431	5.0%
5	Illinois	1,328	4.7%
6	Ohio	1,225	4.3%
7	Georgia	1,159	4.1%
8	North Carolina	1,083	3.8%
9	Pennsylvania	1,061	3.7%
10	Michigan	1,012	3.6%
11	Virginia	781	2.7%
12	Tennessee	724	2.5%
13	Indiana	698	2.5%
14	Arizona	662	2.3%
15	Louisiana	613	2.2%
16	New Jersey	595	2.1%
17	Missouri	590	2.1%
18	Alabama	568	2.0%
19	Maryland	547	1.9%
20	South Carolina	543	1.9%
21	Mississippi	481	1.7%
22	Wisconsin	469	1.6%
23	Colorado	444	1.6%
24	Washington	421	1.5%
25	Oklahoma	417	1.5%
26	Massachusetts	396	1.4%
27	Kentucky	375	1.3%
28	Minnesota	362	1.3%
29	Arkansas	309	1.1%
30	Kansas	294	1.0%
31	Oregon	269	0.9%
32	Connecticut	243	0.9%
33	Utah	230	0.8%
34	Nevada	215	0.8%
35	Iowa	210	0.7%
36	New Mexico	177	0.6%
37	West Virginia	169	0.6%
38	Nebraska	147	0.5%
39	Idaho	141	0.5%
40	Hawaii	116	0.4%
41	Delaware	105	0.4%
42	Maine	97	0.3%
43	South Dakota	83	0.3%
44	Rhode Island	82	0.3%
45	Montana	81	0.3%
46	New Hampshire	76	0.3%
47	Alaska	62	0.2%
48	North Dakota	50	0.2%
49	Wyoming	49	0.2%
50	Vermont	42	0.1%
	District of Columbia	112	0.4%

Source: U.S. Department of Health and Human Services, National Center for Health Statistics
   "National Vital Statistics Reports" (Vol. 56, No. 10, April 24, 2008, http://www.cdc.gov/nchs/deaths.htm)
*Final data. Deaths of infants under 1 year old by state of residence.

Infant Mortality Rate in 2005

National Rate = 6.9 Infant Deaths per 1,000 Live Births*

ALPHA ORDER

RANK	STATE	RATE
3	Alabama	9.4
37	Alaska	5.9
24	Arizona	6.9
13	Arkansas	7.9
43	California	5.3
33	Colorado	6.4
39	Connecticut	5.8
5	Delaware	9.0
21	Florida	7.2
9	Georgia	8.2
31	Hawaii	6.5
34	Idaho	6.1
17	Illinois	7.4
12	Indiana	8.0
43	Iowa	5.3
17	Kansas	7.4
28	Kentucky	6.6
2	Louisiana	10.1
24	Maine	6.9
19	Maryland	7.3
46	Massachusetts	5.2
13	Michigan	7.9
48	Minnesota	5.1
1	Mississippi	11.4
15	Missouri	7.5
23	Montana	7.0
42	Nebraska	5.6
39	Nevada	5.8
43	New Hampshire	5.3
46	New Jersey	5.2
34	New Mexico	6.1
39	New York	5.8
7	North Carolina	8.8
36	North Dakota	6.0
8	Ohio	8.3
10	Oklahoma	8.1
37	Oregon	5.9
19	Pennsylvania	7.3
31	Rhode Island	6.5
3	South Carolina	9.4
21	South Dakota	7.2
6	Tennessee	8.9
28	Texas	6.6
50	Utah	4.5
27	Vermont	6.7
15	Virginia	7.5
48	Washington	5.1
10	West Virginia	8.1
28	Wisconsin	6.6
26	Wyoming	6.8

RANK ORDER

RANK	STATE	RATE
1	Mississippi	11.4
2	Louisiana	10.1
3	Alabama	9.4
3	South Carolina	9.4
5	Delaware	9.0
6	Tennessee	8.9
7	North Carolina	8.8
8	Ohio	8.3
9	Georgia	8.2
10	Oklahoma	8.1
10	West Virginia	8.1
12	Indiana	8.0
13	Arkansas	7.9
13	Michigan	7.9
15	Missouri	7.5
15	Virginia	7.5
17	Illinois	7.4
17	Kansas	7.4
19	Maryland	7.3
19	Pennsylvania	7.3
21	Florida	7.2
21	South Dakota	7.2
23	Montana	7.0
24	Arizona	6.9
24	Maine	6.9
26	Wyoming	6.8
27	Vermont	6.7
28	Kentucky	6.6
28	Texas	6.6
28	Wisconsin	6.6
31	Hawaii	6.5
31	Rhode Island	6.5
33	Colorado	6.4
34	Idaho	6.1
34	New Mexico	6.1
36	North Dakota	6.0
37	Alaska	5.9
37	Oregon	5.9
39	Connecticut	5.8
39	Nevada	5.8
39	New York	5.8
42	Nebraska	5.6
43	California	5.3
43	Iowa	5.3
43	New Hampshire	5.3
46	Massachusetts	5.2
46	New Jersey	5.2
48	Minnesota	5.1
48	Washington	5.1
50	Utah	4.5

	District of Columbia	14.1

Source: U.S. Department of Health and Human Services, National Center for Health Statistics
   "National Vital Statistics Reports" (Vol. 56, No. 10, April 24, 2008, http://www.cdc.gov/nchs/deaths.htm)
*Final data. Deaths of infants under 1 year old by state of residence.

White Infant Mortality Rate in 2005

National Rate = 5.7 White Infant Deaths per 1,000 White Live Births*

ALPHA ORDER

RANK	STATE	RATE
4	Alabama	7.2
47	Alaska	4.7
12	Arizona	6.6
16	Arkansas	6.4
41	California	5.0
22	Colorado	6.0
44	Connecticut	4.9
22	Delaware	6.0
32	Florida	5.7
26	Georgia	5.9
19	Hawaii	6.3
21	Idaho	6.1
32	Illinois	5.7
6	Indiana	7.0
39	Iowa	5.1
12	Kansas	6.6
22	Kentucky	6.0
6	Louisiana	7.0
8	Maine	6.9
39	Maryland	5.1
45	Massachusetts	4.8
28	Michigan	5.8
48	Minnesota	4.5
12	Mississippi	6.6
16	Missouri	6.4
10	Montana	6.7
37	Nebraska	5.2
37	Nevada	5.2
41	New Hampshire	5.0
50	New Jersey	4.0
35	New Mexico	5.6
41	New York	5.0
15	North Carolina	6.5
28	North Dakota	5.8
10	Ohio	6.7
3	Oklahoma	7.3
26	Oregon	5.9
20	Pennsylvania	6.2
28	Rhode Island	5.8
5	South Carolina	7.1
22	South Dakota	6.0
2	Tennessee	7.4
32	Texas	5.7
49	Utah	4.4
16	Vermont	6.4
28	Virginia	5.8
45	Washington	4.8
1	West Virginia	7.9
36	Wisconsin	5.4
8	Wyoming	6.9

RANK ORDER

RANK	STATE	RATE
1	West Virginia	7.9
2	Tennessee	7.4
3	Oklahoma	7.3
4	Alabama	7.2
5	South Carolina	7.1
6	Indiana	7.0
6	Louisiana	7.0
8	Maine	6.9
8	Wyoming	6.9
10	Montana	6.7
10	Ohio	6.7
12	Arizona	6.6
12	Kansas	6.6
12	Mississippi	6.6
15	North Carolina	6.5
16	Arkansas	6.4
16	Missouri	6.4
16	Vermont	6.4
19	Hawaii	6.3
20	Pennsylvania	6.2
21	Idaho	6.1
22	Colorado	6.0
22	Delaware	6.0
22	Kentucky	6.0
22	South Dakota	6.0
26	Georgia	5.9
26	Oregon	5.9
28	Michigan	5.8
28	North Dakota	5.8
28	Rhode Island	5.8
28	Virginia	5.8
32	Florida	5.7
32	Illinois	5.7
32	Texas	5.7
35	New Mexico	5.6
36	Wisconsin	5.4
37	Nebraska	5.2
37	Nevada	5.2
39	Iowa	5.1
39	Maryland	5.1
41	California	5.0
41	New Hampshire	5.0
41	New York	5.0
44	Connecticut	4.9
45	Massachusetts	4.8
45	Washington	4.8
47	Alaska	4.7
48	Minnesota	4.5
49	Utah	4.4
50	New Jersey	4.0

	District of Columbia	8.8

Source: U.S. Department of Health and Human Services, National Center for Health Statistics
   "National Vital Statistics Reports" (Vol. 56, No. 10, April 24, 2008, http://www.cdc.gov/nchs/deaths.htm)
*Final data. Deaths of infants under 1 year old, exclusive of fetal deaths. Based on race of the mother.

Black Infant Mortality Rate in 2005

National Rate = 13.7 Black Infant Deaths per 1,000 Black Live Births*

ALPHA ORDER

RANK	STATE	RATE
14	Alabama	14.7
NA	Alaska**	NA
26	Arizona	12.6
12	Arkansas	14.9
23	California	13.6
10	Colorado	16.3
24	Connecticut	13.5
1	Delaware	18.9
28	Florida	12.0
26	Georgia	12.6
NA	Hawaii**	NA
NA	Idaho**	NA
8	Illinois	16.4
6	Indiana	17.0
20	Iowa	13.9
4	Kansas	17.6
25	Kentucky	13.2
12	Louisiana	14.9
NA	Maine**	NA
29	Maryland	11.6
34	Massachusetts	8.2
2	Michigan	18.3
32	Minnesota	10.6
5	Mississippi	17.2
15	Missouri	14.6
NA	Montana**	NA
NA	Nebraska**	NA
22	Nevada	13.7
NA	New Hampshire**	NA
30	New Jersey	11.0
NA	New Mexico**	NA
33	New York	9.3
8	North Carolina	16.4
NA	North Dakota**	NA
7	Ohio	16.9
11	Oklahoma	15.4
NA	Oregon**	NA
16	Pennsylvania	14.1
NA	Rhode Island**	NA
21	South Carolina	13.8
NA	South Dakota**	NA
19	Tennessee	14.0
16	Texas	14.1
NA	Utah**	NA
NA	Vermont**	NA
16	Virginia	14.1
31	Washington	10.9
NA	West Virginia**	NA
3	Wisconsin	17.7
NA	Wyoming**	NA

RANK ORDER

RANK	STATE	RATE
1	Delaware	18.9
2	Michigan	18.3
3	Wisconsin	17.7
4	Kansas	17.6
5	Mississippi	17.2
6	Indiana	17.0
7	Ohio	16.9
8	Illinois	16.4
8	North Carolina	16.4
10	Colorado	16.3
11	Oklahoma	15.4
12	Arkansas	14.9
12	Louisiana	14.9
14	Alabama	14.7
15	Missouri	14.6
16	Pennsylvania	14.1
16	Texas	14.1
16	Virginia	14.1
19	Tennessee	14.0
20	Iowa	13.9
21	South Carolina	13.8
22	Nevada	13.7
23	California	13.6
24	Connecticut	13.5
25	Kentucky	13.2
26	Arizona	12.6
26	Georgia	12.6
28	Florida	12.0
29	Maryland	11.6
30	New Jersey	11.0
31	Washington	10.9
32	Minnesota	10.6
33	New York	9.3
34	Massachusetts	8.2
NA	Alaska**	NA
NA	Hawaii**	NA
NA	Idaho**	NA
NA	Maine**	NA
NA	Montana**	NA
NA	Nebraska**	NA
NA	New Hampshire**	NA
NA	New Mexico**	NA
NA	North Dakota**	NA
NA	Oregon**	NA
NA	Rhode Island**	NA
NA	South Dakota**	NA
NA	Utah**	NA
NA	Vermont**	NA
NA	West Virginia**	NA
NA	Wyoming**	NA

	District of Columbia	17.0

Source: U.S. Department of Health and Human Services, National Center for Health Statistics
"National Vital Statistics Reports" (Vol. 56, No. 10, April 24, 2008, http://www.cdc.gov/nchs/deaths.htm)
*Final data. Deaths of infants under 1 year old, exclusive of fetal deaths. Based on race of the mother.
**Not available, fewer than 20 black infant deaths.

Neonatal Deaths in 2005

National Total = 18,770 Deaths*

ALPHA ORDER

RANK	STATE	DEATHS	% of USA
19	Alabama	347	1.8%
49	Alaska	31	0.2%
14	Arizona	433	2.3%
30	Arkansas	188	1.0%
1	California	1,991	10.6%
21	Colorado	329	1.8%
31	Connecticut	175	0.9%
40	Delaware	78	0.4%
3	Florida	1,024	5.5%
7	Georgia	770	4.1%
41	Hawaii	75	0.4%
38	Idaho	93	0.5%
5	Illinois	891	4.7%
12	Indiana	476	2.5%
34	Iowa	136	0.7%
29	Kansas	195	1.0%
28	Kentucky	226	1.2%
18	Louisiana	351	1.9%
42	Maine	68	0.4%
16	Maryland	394	2.1%
23	Massachusetts	286	1.5%
10	Michigan	699	3.7%
27	Minnesota	231	1.2%
24	Mississippi	284	1.5%
17	Missouri	371	2.0%
46	Montana	48	0.3%
39	Nebraska	86	0.5%
35	Nevada	130	0.7%
44	New Hampshire	62	0.3%
15	New Jersey	395	2.1%
37	New Mexico	105	0.6%
4	New York	992	5.3%
8	North Carolina	755	4.0%
47	North Dakota	36	0.2%
6	Ohio	828	4.4%
26	Oklahoma	248	1.3%
32	Oregon	174	0.9%
9	Pennsylvania	751	4.0%
43	Rhode Island	64	0.3%
20	South Carolina	336	1.8%
45	South Dakota	52	0.3%
13	Tennessee	462	2.5%
2	Texas	1,595	8.5%
33	Utah	155	0.8%
50	Vermont	26	0.1%
11	Virginia	537	2.9%
25	Washington	254	1.4%
36	West Virginia	106	0.6%
22	Wisconsin	318	1.7%
48	Wyoming	34	0.2%

RANK ORDER

RANK	STATE	DEATHS	% of USA
1	California	1,991	10.6%
2	Texas	1,595	8.5%
3	Florida	1,024	5.5%
4	New York	992	5.3%
5	Illinois	891	4.7%
6	Ohio	828	4.4%
7	Georgia	770	4.1%
8	North Carolina	755	4.0%
9	Pennsylvania	751	4.0%
10	Michigan	699	3.7%
11	Virginia	537	2.9%
12	Indiana	476	2.5%
13	Tennessee	462	2.5%
14	Arizona	433	2.3%
15	New Jersey	395	2.1%
16	Maryland	394	2.1%
17	Missouri	371	2.0%
18	Louisiana	351	1.9%
19	Alabama	347	1.8%
20	South Carolina	336	1.8%
21	Colorado	329	1.8%
22	Wisconsin	318	1.7%
23	Massachusetts	286	1.5%
24	Mississippi	284	1.5%
25	Washington	254	1.4%
26	Oklahoma	248	1.3%
27	Minnesota	231	1.2%
28	Kentucky	226	1.2%
29	Kansas	195	1.0%
30	Arkansas	188	1.0%
31	Connecticut	175	0.9%
32	Oregon	174	0.9%
33	Utah	155	0.8%
34	Iowa	136	0.7%
35	Nevada	130	0.7%
36	West Virginia	106	0.6%
37	New Mexico	105	0.6%
38	Idaho	93	0.5%
39	Nebraska	86	0.5%
40	Delaware	78	0.4%
41	Hawaii	75	0.4%
42	Maine	68	0.4%
43	Rhode Island	64	0.3%
44	New Hampshire	62	0.3%
45	South Dakota	52	0.3%
46	Montana	48	0.3%
47	North Dakota	36	0.2%
48	Wyoming	34	0.2%
49	Alaska	31	0.2%
50	Vermont	26	0.1%
	District of Columbia	79	0.4%

Source: U.S. Department of Health and Human Services, National Center for Health Statistics
   "National Vital Statistics Reports" (Vol. 56, No. 10, January 2008, http://www.cdc.gov/nchs/deaths.htm)
*Final data. Deaths of infants under 28 days old, exclusive of fetal deaths.

Neonatal Death Rate in 2005

National Rate = 4.5 Deaths per 1,000 Live Births*

ALPHA ORDER

RANK	STATE	RATE
6	Alabama	5.7
49	Alaska	3.0
25	Arizona	4.5
19	Arkansas	4.8
41	California	3.6
19	Colorado	4.8
31	Connecticut	4.2
1	Delaware	6.7
25	Florida	4.5
11	Georgia	5.4
31	Hawaii	4.2
36	Idaho	4.0
16	Illinois	5.0
9	Indiana	5.5
43	Iowa	3.5
18	Kansas	4.9
36	Kentucky	4.0
4	Louisiana	5.8
19	Maine	4.8
12	Maryland	5.3
40	Massachusetts	3.7
9	Michigan	5.5
46	Minnesota	3.3
1	Mississippi	6.7
23	Missouri	4.7
33	Montana	4.1
46	Nebraska	3.3
43	Nevada	3.5
29	New Hampshire	4.3
43	New Jersey	3.5
41	New Mexico	3.6
36	New York	4.0
3	North Carolina	6.1
29	North Dakota	4.3
8	Ohio	5.6
19	Oklahoma	4.8
39	Oregon	3.8
13	Pennsylvania	5.2
16	Rhode Island	5.0
4	South Carolina	5.8
25	South Dakota	4.5
6	Tennessee	5.7
33	Texas	4.1
49	Utah	3.0
33	Vermont	4.1
14	Virginia	5.1
48	Washington	3.1
14	West Virginia	5.1
25	Wisconsin	4.5
23	Wyoming	4.7

RANK ORDER

RANK	STATE	RATE
1	Delaware	6.7
1	Mississippi	6.7
3	North Carolina	6.1
4	Louisiana	5.8
4	South Carolina	5.8
6	Alabama	5.7
6	Tennessee	5.7
8	Ohio	5.6
9	Indiana	5.5
9	Michigan	5.5
11	Georgia	5.4
12	Maryland	5.3
13	Pennsylvania	5.2
14	Virginia	5.1
14	West Virginia	5.1
16	Illinois	5.0
16	Rhode Island	5.0
18	Kansas	4.9
19	Arkansas	4.8
19	Colorado	4.8
19	Maine	4.8
19	Oklahoma	4.8
23	Missouri	4.7
23	Wyoming	4.7
25	Arizona	4.5
25	Florida	4.5
25	South Dakota	4.5
25	Wisconsin	4.5
29	New Hampshire	4.3
29	North Dakota	4.3
31	Connecticut	4.2
31	Hawaii	4.2
33	Montana	4.1
33	Texas	4.1
33	Vermont	4.1
36	Idaho	4.0
36	Kentucky	4.0
36	New York	4.0
39	Oregon	3.8
40	Massachusetts	3.7
41	California	3.6
41	New Mexico	3.6
43	Iowa	3.5
43	Nevada	3.5
43	New Jersey	3.5
46	Minnesota	3.3
46	Nebraska	3.3
48	Washington	3.1
49	Alaska	3.0
49	Utah	3.0
	District of Columbia	9.9

Source: U.S. Department of Health and Human Services, National Center for Health Statistics
"National Vital Statistics Reports" (Vol. 56, No. 10, April 24, 2008, http://www.cdc.gov/nchs/deaths.htm)
*Final data. Deaths of infants under 28 days old, exclusive of fetal deaths.

White Neonatal Death Rate in 2005

National Rate = 3.8 White Neonatal Deaths per 1,000 White Live Births*

ALPHA ORDER

RANK	STATE	RATE
5	Alabama	4.6
NA	Alaska**	NA
7	Arizona	4.5
32	Arkansas	3.7
38	California	3.5
7	Colorado	4.5
29	Connecticut	3.8
7	Delaware	4.5
38	Florida	3.5
32	Georgia	3.7
25	Hawaii	3.9
21	Idaho	4.0
25	Illinois	3.9
5	Indiana	4.6
43	Iowa	3.2
12	Kansas	4.4
32	Kentucky	3.7
18	Louisiana	4.1
2	Maine	4.7
38	Maryland	3.5
38	Massachusetts	3.5
25	Michigan	3.9
47	Minnesota	2.9
44	Mississippi	3.1
21	Missouri	4.0
18	Montana	4.1
44	Nebraska	3.1
42	Nevada	3.3
18	New Hampshire	4.1
49	New Jersey	2.8
32	New Mexico	3.7
36	New York	3.6
16	North Carolina	4.3
21	North Dakota	4.0
7	Ohio	4.5
12	Oklahoma	4.4
29	Oregon	3.8
12	Pennsylvania	4.4
2	Rhode Island	4.7
12	South Carolina	4.4
7	South Dakota	4.5
16	Tennessee	4.3
36	Texas	3.6
46	Utah	3.0
25	Vermont	3.9
21	Virginia	4.0
47	Washington	2.9
1	West Virginia	5.1
29	Wisconsin	3.8
2	Wyoming	4.7

RANK ORDER

RANK	STATE	RATE
1	West Virginia	5.1
2	Maine	4.7
2	Rhode Island	4.7
2	Wyoming	4.7
5	Alabama	4.6
5	Indiana	4.6
7	Arizona	4.5
7	Colorado	4.5
7	Delaware	4.5
7	Ohio	4.5
7	South Dakota	4.5
12	Kansas	4.4
12	Oklahoma	4.4
12	Pennsylvania	4.4
12	South Carolina	4.4
16	North Carolina	4.3
16	Tennessee	4.3
18	Louisiana	4.1
18	Montana	4.1
18	New Hampshire	4.1
21	Idaho	4.0
21	Missouri	4.0
21	North Dakota	4.0
21	Virginia	4.0
25	Hawaii	3.9
25	Illinois	3.9
25	Michigan	3.9
25	Vermont	3.9
29	Connecticut	3.8
29	Oregon	3.8
29	Wisconsin	3.8
32	Arkansas	3.7
32	Georgia	3.7
32	Kentucky	3.7
32	New Mexico	3.7
36	New York	3.6
36	Texas	3.6
38	California	3.5
38	Florida	3.5
38	Maryland	3.5
38	Massachusetts	3.5
42	Nevada	3.3
43	Iowa	3.2
44	Mississippi	3.1
44	Nebraska	3.1
46	Utah	3.0
47	Minnesota	2.9
47	Washington	2.9
49	New Jersey	2.8
NA	Alaska**	NA
	District of Columbia**	NA

Source: U.S. Department of Health and Human Services, National Center for Health Statistics
   "National Vital Statistics Reports" (Vol. 56, No. 10, April 24, 2008, http://www.cdc.gov/nchs/deaths.htm)
*Final data. Deaths of infants under 28 days old, exclusive of fetal deaths. Based on race of the mother.
**Not available. Fewer than 20 white neonatal deaths.

Black Neonatal Death Rate in 2005

National Rate = 9.1 Black Neonatal Deaths per 1,000 Black Live Births*

ALPHA ORDER

RANK	STATE	RATE
19	Alabama	8.6
NA	Alaska**	NA
33	Arizona	5.8
14	Arkansas	9.6
23	California	8.3
4	Colorado	12.2
24	Connecticut	8.1
1	Delaware	13.7
25	Florida	7.7
17	Georgia	8.8
NA	Hawaii**	NA
NA	Idaho**	NA
9	Illinois	10.8
3	Indiana	12.5
NA	Iowa**	NA
10	Kansas	10.6
25	Kentucky	7.7
22	Louisiana	8.4
NA	Maine**	NA
19	Maryland	8.6
31	Massachusetts	6.1
2	Michigan	13.1
27	Minnesota	7.5
8	Mississippi	11.2
16	Missouri	9.3
NA	Montana**	NA
NA	Nebraska**	NA
27	Nevada	7.5
NA	New Hampshire**	NA
29	New Jersey	7.0
NA	New Mexico**	NA
32	New York	6.0
5	North Carolina	12.0
NA	North Dakota**	NA
6	Ohio	11.8
12	Oklahoma	9.8
NA	Oregon**	NA
13	Pennsylvania	9.7
NA	Rhode Island**	NA
19	South Carolina	8.6
NA	South Dakota**	NA
11	Tennessee	10.3
17	Texas	8.8
NA	Utah**	NA
NA	Vermont**	NA
14	Virginia	9.6
30	Washington	6.2
NA	West Virginia**	NA
7	Wisconsin	11.5
NA	Wyoming**	NA

RANK ORDER

RANK	STATE	RATE
1	Delaware	13.7
2	Michigan	13.1
3	Indiana	12.5
4	Colorado	12.2
5	North Carolina	12.0
6	Ohio	11.8
7	Wisconsin	11.5
8	Mississippi	11.2
9	Illinois	10.8
10	Kansas	10.6
11	Tennessee	10.3
12	Oklahoma	9.8
13	Pennsylvania	9.7
14	Arkansas	9.6
14	Virginia	9.6
16	Missouri	9.3
17	Georgia	8.8
17	Texas	8.8
19	Alabama	8.6
19	Maryland	8.6
19	South Carolina	8.6
22	Louisiana	8.4
23	California	8.3
24	Connecticut	8.1
25	Florida	7.7
25	Kentucky	7.7
27	Minnesota	7.5
27	Nevada	7.5
29	New Jersey	7.0
30	Washington	6.2
31	Massachusetts	6.1
32	New York	6.0
33	Arizona	5.8
NA	Alaska**	NA
NA	Hawaii**	NA
NA	Idaho**	NA
NA	Iowa**	NA
NA	Maine**	NA
NA	Montana**	NA
NA	Nebraska**	NA
NA	New Hampshire**	NA
NA	New Mexico**	NA
NA	North Dakota**	NA
NA	Oregon**	NA
NA	Rhode Island**	NA
NA	South Dakota**	NA
NA	Utah**	NA
NA	Vermont**	NA
NA	West Virginia**	NA
NA	Wyoming**	NA

District of Columbia	11.9

Source: U.S. Department of Health and Human Services, National Center for Health Statistics
"National Vital Statistics Reports" (Vol. 56, No. 10, April 24, 2008, http://www.cdc.gov/nchs/deaths.htm)
*Final data. Deaths of infants under 28 days old, exclusive of fetal deaths. Based on race of the mother.
**Not available. Fewer than 20 black neonatal deaths.

Estimated Deaths by Cancer in 2008

National Estimated Total = 565,650 Deaths

RANK	STATE	DEATHS	% of USA		RANK	STATE	DEATHS	% of USA
21	Alabama	9,920	1.8%		1	California	55,550	9.8%
50	Alaska	810	0.1%		2	Florida	41,660	7.4%
20	Arizona	10,290	1.8%		3	Texas	34,960	6.2%
31	Arkansas	6,350	1.1%		4	New York	34,870	6.2%
1	California	55,550	9.8%		5	Pennsylvania	29,370	5.2%
29	Colorado	6,700	1.2%		6	Ohio	24,410	4.3%
28	Connecticut	6,970	1.2%		7	Illinois	23,660	4.2%
45	Delaware	1,870	0.3%		8	Michigan	21,210	3.7%
2	Florida	41,660	7.4%		9	North Carolina	17,450	3.1%
11	Georgia	15,040	2.7%		10	New Jersey	16,800	3.0%
43	Hawaii	2,260	0.4%		11	Georgia	15,040	2.7%
41	Idaho	2,470	0.4%		12	Virginia	13,990	2.5%
7	Illinois	23,660	4.2%		13	Tennessee	13,260	2.3%
15	Indiana	12,780	2.3%		14	Massachusetts	13,070	2.3%
30	Iowa	6,480	1.1%		15	Indiana	12,780	2.3%
33	Kansas	5,360	0.9%		16	Missouri	12,630	2.2%
22	Kentucky	9,500	1.7%		17	Washington	11,370	2.0%
23	Louisiana	9,350	1.7%		18	Wisconsin	11,220	2.0%
38	Maine	3,270	0.6%		19	Maryland	10,360	1.8%
19	Maryland	10,360	1.8%		20	Arizona	10,290	1.8%
14	Massachusetts	13,070	2.3%		21	Alabama	9,920	1.8%
8	Michigan	21,210	3.7%		22	Kentucky	9,500	1.7%
24	Minnesota	9,100	1.6%		23	Louisiana	9,350	1.7%
32	Mississippi	6,010	1.1%		24	Minnesota	9,100	1.6%
16	Missouri	12,630	2.2%		25	South Carolina	8,860	1.6%
44	Montana	1,970	0.3%		26	Oregon	7,450	1.3%
36	Nebraska	3,330	0.6%		27	Oklahoma	7,420	1.3%
34	Nevada	4,690	0.8%		28	Connecticut	6,970	1.2%
40	New Hampshire	2,640	0.5%		29	Colorado	6,700	1.2%
10	New Jersey	16,800	3.0%		30	Iowa	6,480	1.1%
37	New Mexico	3,310	0.6%		31	Arkansas	6,350	1.1%
4	New York	34,870	6.2%		32	Mississippi	6,010	1.1%
9	North Carolina	17,450	3.1%		33	Kansas	5,360	0.9%
47	North Dakota	1,220	0.2%		34	Nevada	4,690	0.8%
6	Ohio	24,410	4.3%		35	West Virginia	4,580	0.8%
27	Oklahoma	7,420	1.3%		36	Nebraska	3,330	0.6%
26	Oregon	7,450	1.3%		37	New Mexico	3,310	0.6%
5	Pennsylvania	29,370	5.2%		38	Maine	3,270	0.6%
42	Rhode Island	2,310	0.4%		39	Utah	2,730	0.5%
25	South Carolina	8,860	1.6%		40	New Hampshire	2,640	0.5%
46	South Dakota	1,620	0.3%		41	Idaho	2,470	0.4%
13	Tennessee	13,260	2.3%		42	Rhode Island	2,310	0.4%
3	Texas	34,960	6.2%		43	Hawaii	2,260	0.4%
39	Utah	2,730	0.5%		44	Montana	1,970	0.3%
48	Vermont	1,140	0.2%		45	Delaware	1,870	0.3%
12	Virginia	13,990	2.5%		46	South Dakota	1,620	0.3%
17	Washington	11,370	2.0%		47	North Dakota	1,220	0.2%
35	West Virginia	4,580	0.8%		48	Vermont	1,140	0.2%
18	Wisconsin	11,220	2.0%		49	Wyoming	990	0.2%
49	Wyoming	990	0.2%		50	Alaska	810	0.1%
						District of Columbia	990	0.2%

ALPHA ORDER (left) / RANK ORDER (right)

Source: American Cancer Society
"Cancer Facts & Figures 2008" (Copyright 2008, American Cancer Society, http://www.cancer.org/docroot/stt/stt_0.asp)

Estimated Death Rate by Cancer in 2008

National Estimated Rate = 186.0 Deaths per 100,000 Population*

ALPHA ORDER

RANK	STATE	RATE
12	Alabama	212.8
49	Alaska	118.0
44	Arizona	158.3
6	Arkansas	222.4
46	California	151.1
48	Colorado	135.6
24	Connecticut	199.1
9	Delaware	214.2
4	Florida	227.3
45	Georgia	155.3
39	Hawaii	175.4
43	Idaho	162.1
35	Illinois	183.4
22	Indiana	200.4
8	Iowa	215.8
28	Kansas	191.3
5	Kentucky	222.5
14	Louisiana	212.0
2	Maine	248.4
33	Maryland	183.9
20	Massachusetts	201.1
14	Michigan	212.0
40	Minnesota	174.3
16	Mississippi	204.5
10	Missouri	213.6
18	Montana	203.6
31	Nebraska	186.7
36	Nevada	180.4
21	New Hampshire	200.6
27	New Jersey	193.5
42	New Mexico	166.8
38	New York	178.9
30	North Carolina	189.2
29	North Dakota	190.2
13	Ohio	212.5
17	Oklahoma	203.7
26	Oregon	196.6
3	Pennsylvania	235.9
7	Rhode Island	219.8
25	South Carolina	197.8
19	South Dakota	201.4
11	Tennessee	213.4
47	Texas	143.7
50	Utah	99.8
34	Vermont	183.5
37	Virginia	180.1
41	Washington	173.6
1	West Virginia	252.4
23	Wisconsin	199.4
32	Wyoming	185.9

RANK ORDER

RANK	STATE	RATE
1	West Virginia	252.4
2	Maine	248.4
3	Pennsylvania	235.9
4	Florida	227.3
5	Kentucky	222.5
6	Arkansas	222.4
7	Rhode Island	219.8
8	Iowa	215.8
9	Delaware	214.2
10	Missouri	213.6
11	Tennessee	213.4
12	Alabama	212.8
13	Ohio	212.5
14	Louisiana	212.0
14	Michigan	212.0
16	Mississippi	204.5
17	Oklahoma	203.7
18	Montana	203.6
19	South Dakota	201.4
20	Massachusetts	201.1
21	New Hampshire	200.6
22	Indiana	200.4
23	Wisconsin	199.4
24	Connecticut	199.1
25	South Carolina	197.8
26	Oregon	196.6
27	New Jersey	193.5
28	Kansas	191.3
29	North Dakota	190.2
30	North Carolina	189.2
31	Nebraska	186.7
32	Wyoming	185.9
33	Maryland	183.9
34	Vermont	183.5
35	Illinois	183.4
36	Nevada	180.4
37	Virginia	180.1
38	New York	178.9
39	Hawaii	175.4
40	Minnesota	174.3
41	Washington	173.6
42	New Mexico	166.8
43	Idaho	162.1
44	Arizona	158.3
45	Georgia	155.3
46	California	151.1
47	Texas	143.7
48	Colorado	135.6
49	Alaska	118.0
50	Utah	99.8
	District of Columbia	167.3

Source: CQ Press using data from American Cancer Society
   "Cancer Facts & Figures 2008" (Copyright 2008, American Cancer Society, http://www.cancer.org/docroot/stt/stt_0.asp)
*Rates calculated using 2008 Census resident population estimates. Not age-adjusted.

Age-Adjusted Death Rate by Cancer for Males in 2004

National Rate = 238.7 Deaths per 100,000 Male Population*

ALPHA ORDER

RANK	STATE	RATE
4	Alabama	279.0
27	Alaska	236.9
46	Arizona	208.2
6	Arkansas	271.3
45	California	209.1
48	Colorado	203.7
39	Connecticut	224.8
16	Delaware	252.6
37	Florida	226.0
10	Georgia	259.0
49	Hawaii	191.8
44	Idaho	210.8
17	Illinois	250.9
9	Indiana	262.0
29	Iowa	233.6
31	Kansas	231.7
1	Kentucky	291.8
2	Louisiana	291.0
14	Maine	255.6
20	Maryland	244.7
23	Massachusetts	242.0
22	Michigan	243.1
38	Minnesota	225.3
3	Mississippi	290.7
15	Missouri	254.2
35	Montana	227.3
41	Nebraska	223.0
25	Nevada	238.8
24	New Hampshire	241.0
28	New Jersey	236.7
47	New Mexico	207.4
42	New York	221.9
11	North Carolina	258.6
40	North Dakota	224.1
12	Ohio	257.4
13	Oklahoma	256.8
32	Oregon	231.4
19	Pennsylvania	247.7
20	Rhode Island	244.7
7	South Carolina	270.7
33	South Dakota	231.2
5	Tennessee	277.6
26	Texas	238.6
50	Utah	176.5
34	Vermont	228.5
18	Virginia	249.1
35	Washington	227.3
8	West Virginia	269.1
29	Wisconsin	233.6
43	Wyoming	218.4

RANK ORDER

RANK	STATE	RATE
1	Kentucky	291.8
2	Louisiana	291.0
3	Mississippi	290.7
4	Alabama	279.0
5	Tennessee	277.6
6	Arkansas	271.3
7	South Carolina	270.7
8	West Virginia	269.1
9	Indiana	262.0
10	Georgia	259.0
11	North Carolina	258.6
12	Ohio	257.4
13	Oklahoma	256.8
14	Maine	255.6
15	Missouri	254.2
16	Delaware	252.6
17	Illinois	250.9
18	Virginia	249.1
19	Pennsylvania	247.7
20	Maryland	244.7
20	Rhode Island	244.7
22	Michigan	243.1
23	Massachusetts	242.0
24	New Hampshire	241.0
25	Nevada	238.8
26	Texas	238.6
27	Alaska	236.9
28	New Jersey	236.7
29	Iowa	233.6
29	Wisconsin	233.6
31	Kansas	231.7
32	Oregon	231.4
33	South Dakota	231.2
34	Vermont	228.5
35	Montana	227.3
35	Washington	227.3
37	Florida	226.0
38	Minnesota	225.3
39	Connecticut	224.8
40	North Dakota	224.1
41	Nebraska	223.0
42	New York	221.9
43	Wyoming	218.4
44	Idaho	210.8
45	California	209.1
46	Arizona	208.2
47	New Mexico	207.4
48	Colorado	203.7
49	Hawaii	191.8
50	Utah	176.5

District of Columbia — 289.7

Source: American Cancer Society
"Cancer Facts & Figures 2008" (Copyright 2008, American Cancer Society, http://www.cancer.org/docroot/stt/stt_0.asp)
*For 2000 to 2004. Age-adjusted to the 2000 U.S. standard population.

Age-Adjusted Death Rate by Cancer for Females in 2004

National Rate = 162.2 Deaths per 100,000 Female Population*

ALPHA ORDER

RANK	STATE	RATE
25	Alabama	164.8
28	Alaska	161.8
47	Arizona	145.9
18	Arkansas	167.9
43	California	152.4
46	Colorado	146.6
32	Connecticut	159.0
8	Delaware	172.2
42	Florida	152.8
26	Georgia	163.0
50	Hawaii	120.6
44	Idaho	149.0
12	Illinois	170.1
6	Indiana	173.8
37	Iowa	156.9
35	Kansas	157.9
1	Kentucky	182.1
3	Louisiana	179.5
5	Maine	175.6
13	Maryland	170.0
14	Massachusetts	169.5
21	Michigan	166.3
39	Minnesota	156.1
17	Mississippi	168.3
11	Missouri	170.2
29	Montana	161.7
40	Nebraska	153.8
4	Nevada	176.2
22	New Hampshire	165.9
10	New Jersey	171.9
48	New Mexico	140.8
32	New York	159.0
27	North Carolina	162.0
45	North Dakota	146.9
7	Ohio	173.2
20	Oklahoma	166.8
15	Oregon	169.2
15	Pennsylvania	169.2
19	Rhode Island	167.6
30	South Carolina	161.5
41	South Dakota	153.0
9	Tennessee	172.0
38	Texas	156.6
49	Utah	120.8
31	Vermont	160.1
23	Virginia	165.5
24	Washington	165.1
2	West Virginia	181.2
36	Wisconsin	157.5
32	Wyoming	159.0

RANK ORDER

RANK	STATE	RATE
1	Kentucky	182.1
2	West Virginia	181.2
3	Louisiana	179.5
4	Nevada	176.2
5	Maine	175.6
6	Indiana	173.8
7	Ohio	173.2
8	Delaware	172.2
9	Tennessee	172.0
10	New Jersey	171.9
11	Missouri	170.2
12	Illinois	170.1
13	Maryland	170.0
14	Massachusetts	169.5
15	Oregon	169.2
15	Pennsylvania	169.2
17	Mississippi	168.3
18	Arkansas	167.9
19	Rhode Island	167.6
20	Oklahoma	166.8
21	Michigan	166.3
22	New Hampshire	165.9
23	Virginia	165.5
24	Washington	165.1
25	Alabama	164.8
26	Georgia	163.0
27	North Carolina	162.0
28	Alaska	161.8
29	Montana	161.7
30	South Carolina	161.5
31	Vermont	160.1
32	Connecticut	159.0
32	New York	159.0
32	Wyoming	159.0
35	Kansas	157.9
36	Wisconsin	157.5
37	Iowa	156.9
38	Texas	156.6
39	Minnesota	156.1
40	Nebraska	153.8
41	South Dakota	153.0
42	Florida	152.8
43	California	152.4
44	Idaho	149.0
45	North Dakota	146.9
46	Colorado	146.6
47	Arizona	145.9
48	New Mexico	140.8
49	Utah	120.8
50	Hawaii	120.6

District of Columbia   181.9

Source: American Cancer Society
   "Cancer Facts & Figures 2008" (Copyright 2008, American Cancer Society, http://www.cancer.org/docroot/stt/stt_0.asp)
*For 2000 to 2004. Age-adjusted to the 2000 U.S. standard population.

Estimated Deaths by Brain Cancer in 2008

National Estimated Total = 13,070 Deaths

ALPHA ORDER

RANK	STATE	DEATHS	% of USA
24	Alabama	200	1.5%
NA	Alaska*	NA	NA
16	Arizona	270	2.1%
33	Arkansas	140	1.1%
1	California	1,500	11.5%
24	Colorado	200	1.5%
30	Connecticut	150	1.1%
NA	Delaware*	NA	NA
3	Florida	820	6.3%
14	Georgia	300	2.3%
NA	Hawaii*	NA	NA
38	Idaho	80	0.6%
8	Illinois	470	3.6%
19	Indiana	250	1.9%
29	Iowa	160	1.2%
30	Kansas	150	1.1%
30	Kentucky	150	1.1%
23	Louisiana	210	1.6%
38	Maine	80	0.6%
21	Maryland	220	1.7%
16	Massachusetts	270	2.1%
7	Michigan	490	3.7%
20	Minnesota	240	1.8%
28	Mississippi	170	1.3%
15	Missouri	280	2.1%
43	Montana	50	0.4%
36	Nebraska	90	0.7%
34	Nevada	110	0.8%
41	New Hampshire	70	0.5%
12	New Jersey	330	2.5%
38	New Mexico	80	0.6%
4	New York	800	6.1%
10	North Carolina	350	2.7%
NA	North Dakota*	NA	NA
6	Ohio	550	4.2%
27	Oklahoma	180	1.4%
21	Oregon	220	1.7%
5	Pennsylvania	560	4.3%
42	Rhode Island	60	0.5%
26	South Carolina	190	1.5%
43	South Dakota	50	0.4%
10	Tennessee	350	2.7%
2	Texas	850	6.5%
36	Utah	90	0.7%
NA	Vermont*	NA	NA
13	Virginia	310	2.4%
9	Washington	380	2.9%
35	West Virginia	100	0.8%
16	Wisconsin	270	2.1%
NA	Wyoming*	NA	NA

RANK ORDER

RANK	STATE	DEATHS	% of USA
1	California	1,500	11.5%
2	Texas	850	6.5%
3	Florida	820	6.3%
4	New York	800	6.1%
5	Pennsylvania	560	4.3%
6	Ohio	550	4.2%
7	Michigan	490	3.7%
8	Illinois	470	3.6%
9	Washington	380	2.9%
10	North Carolina	350	2.7%
10	Tennessee	350	2.7%
12	New Jersey	330	2.5%
13	Virginia	310	2.4%
14	Georgia	300	2.3%
15	Missouri	280	2.1%
16	Arizona	270	2.1%
16	Massachusetts	270	2.1%
16	Wisconsin	270	2.1%
19	Indiana	250	1.9%
20	Minnesota	240	1.8%
21	Maryland	220	1.7%
21	Oregon	220	1.7%
23	Louisiana	210	1.6%
24	Alabama	200	1.5%
24	Colorado	200	1.5%
26	South Carolina	190	1.5%
27	Oklahoma	180	1.4%
28	Mississippi	170	1.3%
29	Iowa	160	1.2%
30	Connecticut	150	1.1%
30	Kansas	150	1.1%
30	Kentucky	150	1.1%
33	Arkansas	140	1.1%
34	Nevada	110	0.8%
35	West Virginia	100	0.8%
36	Nebraska	90	0.7%
36	Utah	90	0.7%
38	Idaho	80	0.6%
38	Maine	80	0.6%
38	New Mexico	80	0.6%
41	New Hampshire	70	0.5%
42	Rhode Island	60	0.5%
43	Montana	50	0.4%
43	South Dakota	50	0.4%
NA	Alaska*	NA	NA
NA	Delaware*	NA	NA
NA	Hawaii*	NA	NA
NA	North Dakota*	NA	NA
NA	Vermont*	NA	NA
NA	Wyoming*	NA	NA
	District of Columbia*	NA	NA

Source: American Cancer Society
"Cancer Facts & Figures 2008" (Copyright 2008, American Cancer Society, http://www.cancer.org/docroot/stt/stt_0.asp)
*Fewer than 50 deaths.

Estimated Death Rate by Brain Cancer in 2008

National Estimated Rate = 4.3 Deaths per 100,000 Population*

ALPHA ORDER

RANK	STATE	RATE
25	Alabama	4.3
NA	Alaska**	NA
27	Arizona	4.2
15	Arkansas	4.9
31	California	4.1
33	Colorado	4.0
25	Connecticut	4.3
NA	Delaware**	NA
23	Florida	4.5
44	Georgia	3.1
NA	Hawaii**	NA
12	Idaho	5.2
40	Illinois	3.6
36	Indiana	3.9
10	Iowa	5.3
9	Kansas	5.4
41	Kentucky	3.5
18	Louisiana	4.8
2	Maine	6.1
36	Maryland	3.9
27	Massachusetts	4.2
15	Michigan	4.9
22	Minnesota	4.6
3	Mississippi	5.8
21	Missouri	4.7
12	Montana	5.2
14	Nebraska	5.0
27	Nevada	4.2
10	New Hampshire	5.3
38	New Jersey	3.8
33	New Mexico	4.0
31	New York	4.1
38	North Carolina	3.8
NA	North Dakota**	NA
18	Ohio	4.8
15	Oklahoma	4.9
3	Oregon	5.8
23	Pennsylvania	4.5
6	Rhode Island	5.7
27	South Carolina	4.2
1	South Dakota	6.2
7	Tennessee	5.6
41	Texas	3.5
43	Utah	3.3
NA	Vermont**	NA
33	Virginia	4.0
3	Washington	5.8
8	West Virginia	5.5
18	Wisconsin	4.8
NA	Wyoming**	NA

RANK ORDER

RANK	STATE	RATE
1	South Dakota	6.2
2	Maine	6.1
3	Mississippi	5.8
3	Oregon	5.8
3	Washington	5.8
6	Rhode Island	5.7
7	Tennessee	5.6
8	West Virginia	5.5
9	Kansas	5.4
10	Iowa	5.3
10	New Hampshire	5.3
12	Idaho	5.2
12	Montana	5.2
14	Nebraska	5.0
15	Arkansas	4.9
15	Michigan	4.9
15	Oklahoma	4.9
18	Louisiana	4.8
18	Ohio	4.8
18	Wisconsin	4.8
21	Missouri	4.7
22	Minnesota	4.6
23	Florida	4.5
23	Pennsylvania	4.5
25	Alabama	4.3
25	Connecticut	4.3
27	Arizona	4.2
27	Massachusetts	4.2
27	Nevada	4.2
27	South Carolina	4.2
31	California	4.1
31	New York	4.1
33	Colorado	4.0
33	New Mexico	4.0
33	Virginia	4.0
36	Indiana	3.9
36	Maryland	3.9
38	New Jersey	3.8
38	North Carolina	3.8
40	Illinois	3.6
41	Kentucky	3.5
41	Texas	3.5
43	Utah	3.3
44	Georgia	3.1
NA	Alaska**	NA
NA	Delaware**	NA
NA	Hawaii**	NA
NA	North Dakota**	NA
NA	Vermont**	NA
NA	Wyoming**	NA
	District of Columbia**	NA

Source: CQ Press using data from American Cancer Society
   "Cancer Facts & Figures 2008" (Copyright 2008, American Cancer Society, http://www.cancer.org/docroot/stt/stt_0.asp)
*Rates calculated using 2008 Census resident population estimates. Not age-adjusted.
**Fewer than 50 deaths.

Estimated Deaths by Female Breast Cancer in 2008

National Estimated Total = 40,480 Deaths

ALPHA ORDER

RANK	STATE	DEATHS	% of USA
21	Alabama	730	1.8%
50	Alaska	50	0.1%
22	Arizona	700	1.7%
31	Arkansas	410	1.0%
1	California	4,150	10.3%
26	Colorado	530	1.3%
29	Connecticut	480	1.2%
45	Delaware	110	0.3%
2	Florida	2,760	6.8%
12	Georgia	1,110	2.7%
42	Hawaii	140	0.3%
41	Idaho	160	0.4%
7	Illinois	1,750	4.3%
17	Indiana	820	2.0%
32	Iowa	400	1.0%
33	Kansas	370	0.9%
25	Kentucky	590	1.5%
20	Louisiana	750	1.9%
39	Maine	190	0.5%
16	Maryland	830	2.1%
15	Massachusetts	860	2.1%
9	Michigan	1,310	3.2%
23	Minnesota	630	1.6%
30	Mississippi	440	1.1%
14	Missouri	890	2.2%
44	Montana	130	0.3%
38	Nebraska	230	0.6%
34	Nevada	340	0.8%
39	New Hampshire	190	0.5%
8	New Jersey	1,400	3.5%
36	New Mexico	240	0.6%
3	New York	2,650	6.5%
10	North Carolina	1,300	3.2%
48	North Dakota	80	0.2%
6	Ohio	1,800	4.4%
27	Oklahoma	510	1.3%
27	Oregon	510	1.3%
5	Pennsylvania	2,180	5.4%
42	Rhode Island	140	0.3%
24	South Carolina	620	1.5%
46	South Dakota	100	0.2%
13	Tennessee	920	2.3%
4	Texas	2,520	6.2%
36	Utah	240	0.6%
47	Vermont	90	0.2%
11	Virginia	1,140	2.8%
18	Washington	780	1.9%
35	West Virginia	310	0.8%
19	Wisconsin	760	1.9%
49	Wyoming	60	0.1%

RANK ORDER

RANK	STATE	DEATHS	% of USA
1	California	4,150	10.3%
2	Florida	2,760	6.8%
3	New York	2,650	6.5%
4	Texas	2,520	6.2%
5	Pennsylvania	2,180	5.4%
6	Ohio	1,800	4.4%
7	Illinois	1,750	4.3%
8	New Jersey	1,400	3.5%
9	Michigan	1,310	3.2%
10	North Carolina	1,300	3.2%
11	Virginia	1,140	2.8%
12	Georgia	1,110	2.7%
13	Tennessee	920	2.3%
14	Missouri	890	2.2%
15	Massachusetts	860	2.1%
16	Maryland	830	2.1%
17	Indiana	820	2.0%
18	Washington	780	1.9%
19	Wisconsin	760	1.9%
20	Louisiana	750	1.9%
21	Alabama	730	1.8%
22	Arizona	700	1.7%
23	Minnesota	630	1.6%
24	South Carolina	620	1.5%
25	Kentucky	590	1.5%
26	Colorado	530	1.3%
27	Oklahoma	510	1.3%
27	Oregon	510	1.3%
29	Connecticut	480	1.2%
30	Mississippi	440	1.1%
31	Arkansas	410	1.0%
32	Iowa	400	1.0%
33	Kansas	370	0.9%
34	Nevada	340	0.8%
35	West Virginia	310	0.8%
36	New Mexico	240	0.6%
36	Utah	240	0.6%
38	Nebraska	230	0.6%
39	Maine	190	0.5%
39	New Hampshire	190	0.5%
41	Idaho	160	0.4%
42	Hawaii	140	0.3%
42	Rhode Island	140	0.3%
44	Montana	130	0.3%
45	Delaware	110	0.3%
46	South Dakota	100	0.2%
47	Vermont	90	0.2%
48	North Dakota	80	0.2%
49	Wyoming	60	0.1%
50	Alaska	50	0.1%
	District of Columbia	70	0.2%

Source: American Cancer Society
"Cancer Facts & Figures 2008" (Copyright 2008, American Cancer Society, http://www.cancer.org/docroot/stt/stt_0.asp)

Age-Adjusted Death Rate by Female Breast Cancer in 2004

National Rate = 25.5 Deaths per 100,000 Female Population*

ALPHA ORDER

RANK	STATE	RATE
16	Alabama	26.0
48	Alaska	22.4
44	Arizona	23.4
31	Arkansas	24.4
32	California	24.2
49	Colorado	21.0
25	Connecticut	25.2
9	Delaware	26.6
43	Florida	23.5
22	Georgia	25.5
50	Hawaii	17.3
38	Idaho	23.7
8	Illinois	27.0
12	Indiana	26.2
41	Iowa	23.6
25	Kansas	25.2
12	Kentucky	26.2
1	Louisiana	29.8
38	Maine	23.7
5	Maryland	27.6
20	Massachusetts	25.6
18	Michigan	25.8
36	Minnesota	23.9
4	Mississippi	27.8
9	Missouri	26.6
33	Montana	24.0
41	Nebraska	23.6
12	Nevada	26.2
28	New Hampshire	24.8
2	New Jersey	28.5
47	New Mexico	22.6
12	New York	26.2
23	North Carolina	25.4
33	North Dakota	24.0
3	Ohio	28.0
20	Oklahoma	25.6
25	Oregon	25.2
6	Pennsylvania	27.5
33	Rhode Island	24.0
17	South Carolina	25.9
38	South Dakota	23.7
11	Tennessee	26.3
29	Texas	24.5
46	Utah	23.0
18	Vermont	25.8
7	Virginia	27.2
37	Washington	23.8
23	West Virginia	25.4
29	Wisconsin	24.5
45	Wyoming	23.2

RANK ORDER

RANK	STATE	RATE
1	Louisiana	29.8
2	New Jersey	28.5
3	Ohio	28.0
4	Mississippi	27.8
5	Maryland	27.6
6	Pennsylvania	27.5
7	Virginia	27.2
8	Illinois	27.0
9	Delaware	26.6
9	Missouri	26.6
11	Tennessee	26.3
12	Indiana	26.2
12	Kentucky	26.2
12	Nevada	26.2
12	New York	26.2
16	Alabama	26.0
17	South Carolina	25.9
18	Michigan	25.8
18	Vermont	25.8
20	Massachusetts	25.6
20	Oklahoma	25.6
22	Georgia	25.5
23	North Carolina	25.4
23	West Virginia	25.4
25	Connecticut	25.2
25	Kansas	25.2
25	Oregon	25.2
28	New Hampshire	24.8
29	Texas	24.5
29	Wisconsin	24.5
31	Arkansas	24.4
32	California	24.2
33	Montana	24.0
33	North Dakota	24.0
33	Rhode Island	24.0
36	Minnesota	23.9
37	Washington	23.8
38	Idaho	23.7
38	Maine	23.7
38	South Dakota	23.7
41	Iowa	23.6
41	Nebraska	23.6
43	Florida	23.5
44	Arizona	23.4
45	Wyoming	23.2
46	Utah	23.0
47	New Mexico	22.6
48	Alaska	22.4
49	Colorado	21.0
50	Hawaii	17.3
	District of Columbia	32.1

Source: American Cancer Society
   "Cancer Facts & Figures 2008" (Copyright 2008, American Cancer Society, http://www.cancer.org/docroot/stt/stt_0.asp)
*For 2000 to 2004. Age-adjusted to the 2000 U.S. standard population.

Estimated Deaths by Colon and Rectum Cancer in 2008

National Estimated Total = 49,960 Deaths

ALPHA ORDER

RANK	STATE	DEATHS	% of USA
22	Alabama	870	1.7%
50	Alaska	70	0.1%
17	Arizona	950	1.9%
30	Arkansas	580	1.2%
1	California	5,070	10.1%
27	Colorado	660	1.3%
32	Connecticut	560	1.1%
46	Delaware	150	0.3%
2	Florida	3,420	6.8%
11	Georgia	1,330	2.7%
40	Hawaii	210	0.4%
42	Idaho	200	0.4%
6	Illinois	2,250	4.5%
13	Indiana	1,130	2.3%
31	Iowa	570	1.1%
33	Kansas	520	1.0%
23	Kentucky	840	1.7%
20	Louisiana	920	1.8%
38	Maine	260	0.5%
18	Maryland	940	1.9%
15	Massachusetts	1,100	2.2%
8	Michigan	1,700	3.4%
24	Minnesota	760	1.5%
29	Mississippi	590	1.2%
15	Missouri	1,100	2.2%
44	Montana	160	0.3%
36	Nebraska	340	0.7%
34	Nevada	490	1.0%
40	New Hampshire	210	0.4%
9	New Jersey	1,590	3.2%
37	New Mexico	310	0.6%
3	New York	3,140	6.3%
10	North Carolina	1,400	2.8%
47	North Dakota	120	0.2%
7	Ohio	2,200	4.4%
26	Oklahoma	710	1.4%
28	Oregon	630	1.3%
5	Pennsylvania	2,560	5.1%
43	Rhode Island	190	0.4%
25	South Carolina	730	1.5%
44	South Dakota	160	0.3%
13	Tennessee	1,130	2.3%
4	Texas	3,020	6.0%
39	Utah	240	0.5%
47	Vermont	120	0.2%
12	Virginia	1,260	2.5%
18	Washington	940	1.9%
35	West Virginia	450	0.9%
21	Wisconsin	910	1.8%
49	Wyoming	100	0.2%

RANK ORDER

RANK	STATE	DEATHS	% of USA
1	California	5,070	10.1%
2	Florida	3,420	6.8%
3	New York	3,140	6.3%
4	Texas	3,020	6.0%
5	Pennsylvania	2,560	5.1%
6	Illinois	2,250	4.5%
7	Ohio	2,200	4.4%
8	Michigan	1,700	3.4%
9	New Jersey	1,590	3.2%
10	North Carolina	1,400	2.8%
11	Georgia	1,330	2.7%
12	Virginia	1,260	2.5%
13	Indiana	1,130	2.3%
13	Tennessee	1,130	2.3%
15	Massachusetts	1,100	2.2%
15	Missouri	1,100	2.2%
17	Arizona	950	1.9%
18	Maryland	940	1.9%
18	Washington	940	1.9%
20	Louisiana	920	1.8%
21	Wisconsin	910	1.8%
22	Alabama	870	1.7%
23	Kentucky	840	1.7%
24	Minnesota	760	1.5%
25	South Carolina	730	1.5%
26	Oklahoma	710	1.4%
27	Colorado	660	1.3%
28	Oregon	630	1.3%
29	Mississippi	590	1.2%
30	Arkansas	580	1.2%
31	Iowa	570	1.1%
32	Connecticut	560	1.1%
33	Kansas	520	1.0%
34	Nevada	490	1.0%
35	West Virginia	450	0.9%
36	Nebraska	340	0.7%
37	New Mexico	310	0.6%
38	Maine	260	0.5%
39	Utah	240	0.5%
40	Hawaii	210	0.4%
40	New Hampshire	210	0.4%
42	Idaho	200	0.4%
43	Rhode Island	190	0.4%
44	Montana	160	0.3%
44	South Dakota	160	0.3%
46	Delaware	150	0.3%
47	North Dakota	120	0.2%
47	Vermont	120	0.2%
49	Wyoming	100	0.2%
50	Alaska	70	0.1%
	District of Columbia	90	0.2%

Source: American Cancer Society
"Cancer Facts & Figures 2008" (Copyright 2008, American Cancer Society, http://www.cancer.org/docroot/stt/stt_0.asp)

Estimated Death Rate by Colon and Rectum Cancer in 2008

National Estimated Rate = 16.4 Deaths per 100,000 Population*

ALPHA ORDER

RANK	STATE	RATE
16	Alabama	18.7
49	Alaska	10.2
41	Arizona	14.6
4	Arkansas	20.3
44	California	13.8
46	Colorado	13.4
37	Connecticut	16.0
26	Delaware	17.2
16	Florida	18.7
45	Georgia	13.7
32	Hawaii	16.3
47	Idaho	13.1
25	Illinois	17.4
24	Indiana	17.7
13	Iowa	19.0
19	Kansas	18.6
7	Kentucky	19.7
2	Louisiana	20.9
7	Maine	19.7
29	Maryland	16.7
28	Massachusetts	16.9
27	Michigan	17.0
41	Minnesota	14.6
5	Mississippi	20.1
19	Missouri	18.6
31	Montana	16.5
12	Nebraska	19.1
14	Nevada	18.8
37	New Hampshire	16.0
21	New Jersey	18.3
39	New Mexico	15.6
36	New York	16.1
40	North Carolina	15.2
16	North Dakota	18.7
11	Ohio	19.2
9	Oklahoma	19.5
30	Oregon	16.6
3	Pennsylvania	20.6
23	Rhode Island	18.1
32	South Carolina	16.3
6	South Dakota	19.9
22	Tennessee	18.2
48	Texas	12.4
50	Utah	8.8
10	Vermont	19.3
34	Virginia	16.2
43	Washington	14.4
1	West Virginia	24.8
34	Wisconsin	16.2
14	Wyoming	18.8

RANK ORDER

RANK	STATE	RATE
1	West Virginia	24.8
2	Louisiana	20.9
3	Pennsylvania	20.6
4	Arkansas	20.3
5	Mississippi	20.1
6	South Dakota	19.9
7	Kentucky	19.7
7	Maine	19.7
9	Oklahoma	19.5
10	Vermont	19.3
11	Ohio	19.2
12	Nebraska	19.1
13	Iowa	19.0
14	Nevada	18.8
14	Wyoming	18.8
16	Alabama	18.7
16	Florida	18.7
16	North Dakota	18.7
19	Kansas	18.6
19	Missouri	18.6
21	New Jersey	18.3
22	Tennessee	18.2
23	Rhode Island	18.1
24	Indiana	17.7
25	Illinois	17.4
26	Delaware	17.2
27	Michigan	17.0
28	Massachusetts	16.9
29	Maryland	16.7
30	Oregon	16.6
31	Montana	16.5
32	Hawaii	16.3
32	South Carolina	16.3
34	Virginia	16.2
34	Wisconsin	16.2
36	New York	16.1
37	Connecticut	16.0
37	New Hampshire	16.0
39	New Mexico	15.6
40	North Carolina	15.2
41	Arizona	14.6
41	Minnesota	14.6
43	Washington	14.4
44	California	13.8
45	Georgia	13.7
46	Colorado	13.4
47	Idaho	13.1
48	Texas	12.4
49	Alaska	10.2
50	Utah	8.8

District of Columbia 15.2

Source: CQ Press using data from American Cancer Society
"Cancer Facts & Figures 2008" (Copyright 2008, American Cancer Society, http://www.cancer.org/docroot/stt/stt_0.asp)
*Rates calculated using 2008 Census resident population estimates. Not age-adjusted.

Estimated Deaths by Leukemia in 2008

National Estimated Total = 21,710 Deaths

ALPHA ORDER

RANK	STATE	DEATHS	% of USA
22	Alabama	360	1.7%
NA	Alaska*	NA	NA
19	Arizona	400	1.8%
31	Arkansas	240	1.1%
1	California	2,170	10.0%
27	Colorado	290	1.3%
29	Connecticut	270	1.2%
45	Delaware	70	0.3%
2	Florida	1,640	7.6%
11	Georgia	540	2.5%
43	Hawaii	80	0.4%
38	Idaho	120	0.6%
6	Illinois	980	4.5%
12	Indiana	510	2.3%
25	Iowa	310	1.4%
32	Kansas	220	1.0%
23	Kentucky	320	1.5%
25	Louisiana	310	1.4%
40	Maine	110	0.5%
20	Maryland	390	1.8%
15	Massachusetts	480	2.2%
8	Michigan	790	3.6%
20	Minnesota	390	1.8%
32	Mississippi	220	1.0%
16	Missouri	470	2.2%
43	Montana	80	0.4%
35	Nebraska	150	0.7%
34	Nevada	160	0.7%
41	New Hampshire	100	0.5%
9	New Jersey	640	2.9%
38	New Mexico	120	0.6%
4	New York	1,370	6.3%
10	North Carolina	600	2.8%
NA	North Dakota*	NA	NA
7	Ohio	900	4.1%
27	Oklahoma	290	1.3%
29	Oregon	270	1.2%
5	Pennsylvania	1,060	4.9%
42	Rhode Island	90	0.4%
23	South Carolina	320	1.5%
45	South Dakota	70	0.3%
16	Tennessee	470	2.2%
3	Texas	1,420	6.5%
37	Utah	130	0.6%
47	Vermont	50	0.2%
13	Virginia	500	2.3%
18	Washington	460	2.1%
35	West Virginia	150	0.7%
13	Wisconsin	500	2.3%
NA	Wyoming*	NA	NA

RANK ORDER

RANK	STATE	DEATHS	% of USA
1	California	2,170	10.0%
2	Florida	1,640	7.6%
3	Texas	1,420	6.5%
4	New York	1,370	6.3%
5	Pennsylvania	1,060	4.9%
6	Illinois	980	4.5%
7	Ohio	900	4.1%
8	Michigan	790	3.6%
9	New Jersey	640	2.9%
10	North Carolina	600	2.8%
11	Georgia	540	2.5%
12	Indiana	510	2.3%
13	Virginia	500	2.3%
13	Wisconsin	500	2.3%
15	Massachusetts	480	2.2%
16	Missouri	470	2.2%
16	Tennessee	470	2.2%
18	Washington	460	2.1%
19	Arizona	400	1.8%
20	Maryland	390	1.8%
20	Minnesota	390	1.8%
22	Alabama	360	1.7%
23	Kentucky	320	1.5%
23	South Carolina	320	1.5%
25	Iowa	310	1.4%
25	Louisiana	310	1.4%
27	Colorado	290	1.3%
27	Oklahoma	290	1.3%
29	Connecticut	270	1.2%
29	Oregon	270	1.2%
31	Arkansas	240	1.1%
32	Kansas	220	1.0%
32	Mississippi	220	1.0%
34	Nevada	160	0.7%
35	Nebraska	150	0.7%
35	West Virginia	150	0.7%
37	Utah	130	0.6%
38	Idaho	120	0.6%
38	New Mexico	120	0.6%
40	Maine	110	0.5%
41	New Hampshire	100	0.5%
42	Rhode Island	90	0.4%
43	Hawaii	80	0.4%
43	Montana	80	0.4%
45	Delaware	70	0.3%
45	South Dakota	70	0.3%
47	Vermont	50	0.2%
NA	Alaska*	NA	NA
NA	North Dakota*	NA	NA
NA	Wyoming*	NA	NA
	District of Columbia*	NA	NA

Source: American Cancer Society
"Cancer Facts & Figures 2008" (Copyright 2008, American Cancer Society, http://www.cancer.org/docroot/stt/stt_0.asp)
*Fewer than 50 deaths.

Estimated Death Rate by Leukemia in 2008

National Estimated Rate = 7.1 Deaths per 100,000 Population*

ALPHA ORDER

RANK	STATE	DEATHS
21	Alabama	7.7
NA	Alaska**	NA
39	Arizona	6.2
7	Arkansas	8.4
43	California	5.9
43	Colorado	5.9
21	Connecticut	7.7
12	Delaware	8.0
2	Florida	8.9
46	Georgia	5.6
39	Hawaii	6.2
17	Idaho	7.9
23	Illinois	7.6
12	Indiana	8.0
1	Iowa	10.3
17	Kansas	7.9
26	Kentucky	7.5
33	Louisiana	7.0
7	Maine	8.4
36	Maryland	6.9
29	Massachusetts	7.4
17	Michigan	7.9
26	Minnesota	7.5
26	Mississippi	7.5
12	Missouri	8.0
10	Montana	8.3
7	Nebraska	8.4
39	Nevada	6.2
23	New Hampshire	7.6
29	New Jersey	7.4
42	New Mexico	6.0
33	New York	7.0
37	North Carolina	6.5
NA	North Dakota**	NA
20	Ohio	7.8
12	Oklahoma	8.0
31	Oregon	7.1
6	Pennsylvania	8.5
5	Rhode Island	8.6
31	South Carolina	7.1
4	South Dakota	8.7
23	Tennessee	7.6
45	Texas	5.8
47	Utah	4.8
12	Vermont	8.0
38	Virginia	6.4
33	Washington	7.0
10	West Virginia	8.3
2	Wisconsin	8.9
NA	Wyoming**	NA

RANK ORDER

RANK	STATE	DEATHS
1	Iowa	10.3
2	Florida	8.9
2	Wisconsin	8.9
4	South Dakota	8.7
5	Rhode Island	8.6
6	Pennsylvania	8.5
7	Arkansas	8.4
7	Maine	8.4
7	Nebraska	8.4
10	Montana	8.3
10	West Virginia	8.3
12	Delaware	8.0
12	Indiana	8.0
12	Missouri	8.0
12	Oklahoma	8.0
12	Vermont	8.0
17	Idaho	7.9
17	Kansas	7.9
17	Michigan	7.9
20	Ohio	7.8
21	Alabama	7.7
21	Connecticut	7.7
23	Illinois	7.6
23	New Hampshire	7.6
23	Tennessee	7.6
26	Kentucky	7.5
26	Minnesota	7.5
26	Mississippi	7.5
29	Massachusetts	7.4
29	New Jersey	7.4
31	Oregon	7.1
31	South Carolina	7.1
33	Louisiana	7.0
33	New York	7.0
33	Washington	7.0
36	Maryland	6.9
37	North Carolina	6.5
38	Virginia	6.4
39	Arizona	6.2
39	Hawaii	6.2
39	Nevada	6.2
42	New Mexico	6.0
43	California	5.9
43	Colorado	5.9
45	Texas	5.8
46	Georgia	5.6
47	Utah	4.8
NA	Alaska**	NA
NA	North Dakota**	NA
NA	Wyoming**	NA
	District of Columbia**	NA

Source: CQ Press using data from American Cancer Society
"Cancer Facts & Figures 2008" (Copyright 2008, American Cancer Society, http://www.cancer.org/docroot/stt/stt_0.asp)
*Rates calculated using 2008 Census resident population estimates. Not age-adjusted.
**Fewer than 50 deaths.

Estimated Deaths by Liver Cancer in 2008

National Estimated Total = 18,410 Deaths

ALPHA ORDER

RANK	STATE	DEATHS	% of USA
21	Alabama	310	1.7%
NA	Alaska*	NA	NA
15	Arizona	370	2.0%
29	Arkansas	200	1.1%
1	California	2,510	13.6%
26	Colorado	220	1.2%
27	Connecticut	210	1.1%
44	Delaware	50	0.3%
3	Florida	1,310	7.1%
13	Georgia	400	2.2%
36	Hawaii	120	0.7%
40	Idaho	70	0.4%
6	Illinois	720	3.9%
19	Indiana	350	1.9%
33	Iowa	150	0.8%
35	Kansas	140	0.8%
25	Kentucky	250	1.4%
16	Louisiana	360	2.0%
38	Maine	80	0.4%
22	Maryland	300	1.6%
11	Massachusetts	420	2.3%
8	Michigan	560	3.0%
23	Minnesota	270	1.5%
31	Mississippi	180	1.0%
16	Missouri	360	2.0%
NA	Montana*	NA	NA
40	Nebraska	70	0.4%
32	Nevada	160	0.9%
40	New Hampshire	70	0.4%
9	New Jersey	540	2.9%
33	New Mexico	150	0.8%
4	New York	1,210	6.6%
10	North Carolina	460	2.5%
NA	North Dakota*	NA	NA
7	Ohio	650	3.5%
29	Oklahoma	200	1.1%
27	Oregon	210	1.1%
5	Pennsylvania	830	4.5%
43	Rhode Island	60	0.3%
24	South Carolina	260	1.4%
44	South Dakota	50	0.3%
16	Tennessee	360	2.0%
2	Texas	1,680	9.1%
38	Utah	80	0.4%
NA	Vermont*	NA	NA
14	Virginia	390	2.1%
12	Washington	410	2.2%
36	West Virginia	120	0.7%
20	Wisconsin	340	1.8%
NA	Wyoming*	NA	NA

RANK ORDER

RANK	STATE	DEATHS	% of USA
1	California	2,510	13.6%
2	Texas	1,680	9.1%
3	Florida	1,310	7.1%
4	New York	1,210	6.6%
5	Pennsylvania	830	4.5%
6	Illinois	720	3.9%
7	Ohio	650	3.5%
8	Michigan	560	3.0%
9	New Jersey	540	2.9%
10	North Carolina	460	2.5%
11	Massachusetts	420	2.3%
12	Washington	410	2.2%
13	Georgia	400	2.2%
14	Virginia	390	2.1%
15	Arizona	370	2.0%
16	Louisiana	360	2.0%
16	Missouri	360	2.0%
16	Tennessee	360	2.0%
19	Indiana	350	1.9%
20	Wisconsin	340	1.8%
21	Alabama	310	1.7%
22	Maryland	300	1.6%
23	Minnesota	270	1.5%
24	South Carolina	260	1.4%
25	Kentucky	250	1.4%
26	Colorado	220	1.2%
27	Connecticut	210	1.1%
27	Oregon	210	1.1%
29	Arkansas	200	1.1%
29	Oklahoma	200	1.1%
31	Mississippi	180	1.0%
32	Nevada	160	0.9%
33	Iowa	150	0.8%
33	New Mexico	150	0.8%
35	Kansas	140	0.8%
36	Hawaii	120	0.7%
36	West Virginia	120	0.7%
38	Maine	80	0.4%
38	Utah	80	0.4%
40	Idaho	70	0.4%
40	Nebraska	70	0.4%
40	New Hampshire	70	0.4%
43	Rhode Island	60	0.3%
44	Delaware	50	0.3%
44	South Dakota	50	0.3%
NA	Alaska*	NA	NA
NA	Montana*	NA	NA
NA	North Dakota*	NA	NA
NA	Vermont*	NA	NA
NA	Wyoming*	NA	NA
	District of Columbia*	NA	NA

Source: American Cancer Society
"Cancer Facts & Figures 2008" (Copyright 2008, American Cancer Society, http://www.cancer.org/docroot/stt/stt_0.asp)
*Fewer than 50 deaths.

Estimated Death Rate by Liver Cancer in 2008

National Estimated Rate = 6.1 Deaths per 100,000 Population*

ALPHA ORDER

RANK	STATE	RATE
9	Alabama	6.6
NA	Alaska**	NA
25	Arizona	5.7
5	Arkansas	7.0
7	California	6.8
42	Colorado	4.5
20	Connecticut	6.0
25	Delaware	5.7
4	Florida	7.1
43	Georgia	4.1
1	Hawaii	9.3
41	Idaho	4.6
29	Illinois	5.6
31	Indiana	5.5
37	Iowa	5.0
37	Kansas	5.0
22	Kentucky	5.9
2	Louisiana	8.2
17	Maine	6.1
34	Maryland	5.3
11	Massachusetts	6.5
29	Michigan	5.6
36	Minnesota	5.2
17	Mississippi	6.1
17	Missouri	6.1
NA	Montana**	NA
44	Nebraska	3.9
13	Nevada	6.2
34	New Hampshire	5.3
13	New Jersey	6.2
3	New Mexico	7.6
13	New York	6.2
37	North Carolina	5.0
NA	North Dakota**	NA
25	Ohio	5.7
31	Oklahoma	5.5
31	Oregon	5.5
8	Pennsylvania	6.7
25	Rhode Island	5.7
23	South Carolina	5.8
13	South Dakota	6.2
23	Tennessee	5.8
6	Texas	6.9
45	Utah	2.9
NA	Vermont**	NA
37	Virginia	5.0
12	Washington	6.3
9	West Virginia	6.6
20	Wisconsin	6.0
NA	Wyoming**	NA

RANK ORDER

RANK	STATE	RATE
1	Hawaii	9.3
2	Louisiana	8.2
3	New Mexico	7.6
4	Florida	7.1
5	Arkansas	7.0
6	Texas	6.9
7	California	6.8
8	Pennsylvania	6.7
9	Alabama	6.6
9	West Virginia	6.6
11	Massachusetts	6.5
12	Washington	6.3
13	Nevada	6.2
13	New Jersey	6.2
13	New York	6.2
13	South Dakota	6.2
17	Maine	6.1
17	Mississippi	6.1
17	Missouri	6.1
20	Connecticut	6.0
20	Wisconsin	6.0
22	Kentucky	5.9
23	South Carolina	5.8
23	Tennessee	5.8
25	Arizona	5.7
25	Delaware	5.7
25	Ohio	5.7
25	Rhode Island	5.7
29	Illinois	5.6
29	Michigan	5.6
31	Indiana	5.5
31	Oklahoma	5.5
31	Oregon	5.5
34	Maryland	5.3
34	New Hampshire	5.3
36	Minnesota	5.2
37	Iowa	5.0
37	Kansas	5.0
37	North Carolina	5.0
37	Virginia	5.0
41	Idaho	4.6
42	Colorado	4.5
43	Georgia	4.1
44	Nebraska	3.9
45	Utah	2.9
NA	Alaska**	NA
NA	Montana**	NA
NA	North Dakota**	NA
NA	Vermont**	NA
NA	Wyoming**	NA
	District of Columbia**	NA

Source: CQ Press using data from American Cancer Society
    "Cancer Facts & Figures 2008" (Copyright 2008, American Cancer Society, http://www.cancer.org/docroot/stt/stt_0.asp)
*Rates calculated using 2008 Census resident population estimates. Not age-adjusted.
**Fewer than 50 deaths.

Estimated Deaths by Lung Cancer in 2008

National Estimated Total = 161,840 Deaths

ALPHA ORDER

RANK	STATE	DEATHS	% of USA
18	Alabama	3,340	2.1%
50	Alaska	230	0.1%
24	Arizona	2,800	1.7%
27	Arkansas	2,210	1.4%
1	California	13,100	8.1%
32	Colorado	1,670	1.0%
30	Connecticut	1,850	1.1%
42	Delaware	590	0.4%
2	Florida	12,490	7.7%
11	Georgia	4,570	2.8%
44	Hawaii	570	0.4%
40	Idaho	630	0.4%
7	Illinois	6,600	4.1%
15	Indiana	3,990	2.5%
31	Iowa	1,810	1.1%
33	Kansas	1,610	1.0%
17	Kentucky	3,480	2.2%
20	Louisiana	2,980	1.8%
36	Maine	980	0.6%
22	Maryland	2,920	1.8%
16	Massachusetts	3,600	2.2%
8	Michigan	5,890	3.6%
26	Minnesota	2,380	1.5%
29	Mississippi	2,030	1.3%
14	Missouri	4,140	2.6%
43	Montana	580	0.4%
37	Nebraska	910	0.6%
35	Nevada	1,340	0.8%
38	New Hampshire	760	0.5%
13	New Jersey	4,300	2.7%
39	New Mexico	730	0.5%
4	New York	8,990	5.6%
9	North Carolina	5,470	3.4%
48	North Dakota	330	0.2%
6	Ohio	7,350	4.5%
25	Oklahoma	2,400	1.5%
28	Oregon	2,160	1.3%
5	Pennsylvania	8,230	5.1%
41	Rhode Island	600	0.4%
23	South Carolina	2,860	1.8%
46	South Dakota	450	0.3%
12	Tennessee	4,490	2.8%
3	Texas	9,890	6.1%
45	Utah	480	0.3%
47	Vermont	350	0.2%
10	Virginia	4,600	2.8%
19	Washington	3,180	2.0%
34	West Virginia	1,450	0.9%
21	Wisconsin	2,940	1.8%
49	Wyoming	260	0.2%

RANK ORDER

RANK	STATE	DEATHS	% of USA
1	California	13,100	8.1%
2	Florida	12,490	7.7%
3	Texas	9,890	6.1%
4	New York	8,990	5.6%
5	Pennsylvania	8,230	5.1%
6	Ohio	7,350	4.5%
7	Illinois	6,600	4.1%
8	Michigan	5,890	3.6%
9	North Carolina	5,470	3.4%
10	Virginia	4,600	2.8%
11	Georgia	4,570	2.8%
12	Tennessee	4,490	2.8%
13	New Jersey	4,300	2.7%
14	Missouri	4,140	2.6%
15	Indiana	3,990	2.5%
16	Massachusetts	3,600	2.2%
17	Kentucky	3,480	2.2%
18	Alabama	3,340	2.1%
19	Washington	3,180	2.0%
20	Louisiana	2,980	1.8%
21	Wisconsin	2,940	1.8%
22	Maryland	2,920	1.8%
23	South Carolina	2,860	1.8%
24	Arizona	2,800	1.7%
25	Oklahoma	2,400	1.5%
26	Minnesota	2,380	1.5%
27	Arkansas	2,210	1.4%
28	Oregon	2,160	1.3%
29	Mississippi	2,030	1.3%
30	Connecticut	1,850	1.1%
31	Iowa	1,810	1.1%
32	Colorado	1,670	1.0%
33	Kansas	1,610	1.0%
34	West Virginia	1,450	0.9%
35	Nevada	1,340	0.8%
36	Maine	980	0.6%
37	Nebraska	910	0.6%
38	New Hampshire	760	0.5%
39	New Mexico	730	0.5%
40	Idaho	630	0.4%
41	Rhode Island	600	0.4%
42	Delaware	590	0.4%
43	Montana	580	0.4%
44	Hawaii	570	0.4%
45	Utah	480	0.3%
46	South Dakota	450	0.3%
47	Vermont	350	0.2%
48	North Dakota	330	0.2%
49	Wyoming	260	0.2%
50	Alaska	230	0.1%
	District of Columbia	250	0.2%

Source: American Cancer Society
"Cancer Facts & Figures 2008" (Copyright 2008, American Cancer Society, http://www.cancer.org/docroot/stt/stt_0.asp)

Estimated Death Rate by Lung Cancer in 2008

National Estimated Rate = 53.2 Deaths per 100,000 Population*

<table>
<tr><td colspan="3">ALPHA ORDER</td><td colspan="3">RANK ORDER</td></tr>
<tr><th>RANK</th><th>STATE</th><th>RATE</th><th>RANK</th><th>STATE</th><th>RATE</th></tr>
<tr><td>6</td><td>Alabama</td><td>71.6</td><td>1</td><td>Kentucky</td><td>81.5</td></tr>
<tr><td>49</td><td>Alaska</td><td>33.5</td><td>2</td><td>West Virginia</td><td>79.9</td></tr>
<tr><td>43</td><td>Arizona</td><td>43.1</td><td>3</td><td>Arkansas</td><td>77.4</td></tr>
<tr><td>3</td><td>Arkansas</td><td>77.4</td><td>4</td><td>Maine</td><td>74.4</td></tr>
<tr><td>47</td><td>California</td><td>35.6</td><td>5</td><td>Tennessee</td><td>72.2</td></tr>
<tr><td>48</td><td>Colorado</td><td>33.8</td><td>6</td><td>Alabama</td><td>71.6</td></tr>
<tr><td>29</td><td>Connecticut</td><td>52.8</td><td>7</td><td>Missouri</td><td>70.0</td></tr>
<tr><td>10</td><td>Delaware</td><td>67.6</td><td>8</td><td>Mississippi</td><td>69.1</td></tr>
<tr><td>9</td><td>Florida</td><td>68.1</td><td>9</td><td>Florida</td><td>68.1</td></tr>
<tr><td>39</td><td>Georgia</td><td>47.2</td><td>10</td><td>Delaware</td><td>67.6</td></tr>
<tr><td>42</td><td>Hawaii</td><td>44.2</td><td>10</td><td>Louisiana</td><td>67.6</td></tr>
<tr><td>44</td><td>Idaho</td><td>41.3</td><td>12</td><td>Pennsylvania</td><td>66.1</td></tr>
<tr><td>34</td><td>Illinois</td><td>51.2</td><td>13</td><td>Oklahoma</td><td>65.9</td></tr>
<tr><td>16</td><td>Indiana</td><td>62.6</td><td>14</td><td>Ohio</td><td>64.0</td></tr>
<tr><td>17</td><td>Iowa</td><td>60.3</td><td>15</td><td>South Carolina</td><td>63.8</td></tr>
<tr><td>23</td><td>Kansas</td><td>57.5</td><td>16</td><td>Indiana</td><td>62.6</td></tr>
<tr><td>1</td><td>Kentucky</td><td>81.5</td><td>17</td><td>Iowa</td><td>60.3</td></tr>
<tr><td>10</td><td>Louisiana</td><td>67.6</td><td>18</td><td>Montana</td><td>60.0</td></tr>
<tr><td>4</td><td>Maine</td><td>74.4</td><td>19</td><td>North Carolina</td><td>59.3</td></tr>
<tr><td>31</td><td>Maryland</td><td>51.8</td><td>20</td><td>Virginia</td><td>59.2</td></tr>
<tr><td>28</td><td>Massachusetts</td><td>55.4</td><td>21</td><td>Michigan</td><td>58.9</td></tr>
<tr><td>21</td><td>Michigan</td><td>58.9</td><td>22</td><td>New Hampshire</td><td>57.8</td></tr>
<tr><td>41</td><td>Minnesota</td><td>45.6</td><td>23</td><td>Kansas</td><td>57.5</td></tr>
<tr><td>8</td><td>Mississippi</td><td>69.1</td><td>24</td><td>Rhode Island</td><td>57.1</td></tr>
<tr><td>7</td><td>Missouri</td><td>70.0</td><td>25</td><td>Oregon</td><td>57.0</td></tr>
<tr><td>18</td><td>Montana</td><td>60.0</td><td>26</td><td>Vermont</td><td>56.3</td></tr>
<tr><td>35</td><td>Nebraska</td><td>51.0</td><td>27</td><td>South Dakota</td><td>56.0</td></tr>
<tr><td>32</td><td>Nevada</td><td>51.5</td><td>28</td><td>Massachusetts</td><td>55.4</td></tr>
<tr><td>22</td><td>New Hampshire</td><td>57.8</td><td>29</td><td>Connecticut</td><td>52.8</td></tr>
<tr><td>36</td><td>New Jersey</td><td>49.5</td><td>30</td><td>Wisconsin</td><td>52.2</td></tr>
<tr><td>46</td><td>New Mexico</td><td>36.8</td><td>31</td><td>Maryland</td><td>51.8</td></tr>
<tr><td>40</td><td>New York</td><td>46.1</td><td>32</td><td>Nevada</td><td>51.5</td></tr>
<tr><td>19</td><td>North Carolina</td><td>59.3</td><td>33</td><td>North Dakota</td><td>51.4</td></tr>
<tr><td>33</td><td>North Dakota</td><td>51.4</td><td>34</td><td>Illinois</td><td>51.2</td></tr>
<tr><td>14</td><td>Ohio</td><td>64.0</td><td>35</td><td>Nebraska</td><td>51.0</td></tr>
<tr><td>13</td><td>Oklahoma</td><td>65.9</td><td>36</td><td>New Jersey</td><td>49.5</td></tr>
<tr><td>25</td><td>Oregon</td><td>57.0</td><td>37</td><td>Wyoming</td><td>48.8</td></tr>
<tr><td>12</td><td>Pennsylvania</td><td>66.1</td><td>38</td><td>Washington</td><td>48.6</td></tr>
<tr><td>24</td><td>Rhode Island</td><td>57.1</td><td>39</td><td>Georgia</td><td>47.2</td></tr>
<tr><td>15</td><td>South Carolina</td><td>63.8</td><td>40</td><td>New York</td><td>46.1</td></tr>
<tr><td>27</td><td>South Dakota</td><td>56.0</td><td>41</td><td>Minnesota</td><td>45.6</td></tr>
<tr><td>5</td><td>Tennessee</td><td>72.2</td><td>42</td><td>Hawaii</td><td>44.2</td></tr>
<tr><td>45</td><td>Texas</td><td>40.7</td><td>43</td><td>Arizona</td><td>43.1</td></tr>
<tr><td>50</td><td>Utah</td><td>17.5</td><td>44</td><td>Idaho</td><td>41.3</td></tr>
<tr><td>26</td><td>Vermont</td><td>56.3</td><td>45</td><td>Texas</td><td>40.7</td></tr>
<tr><td>20</td><td>Virginia</td><td>59.2</td><td>46</td><td>New Mexico</td><td>36.8</td></tr>
<tr><td>38</td><td>Washington</td><td>48.6</td><td>47</td><td>California</td><td>35.6</td></tr>
<tr><td>2</td><td>West Virginia</td><td>79.9</td><td>48</td><td>Colorado</td><td>33.8</td></tr>
<tr><td>30</td><td>Wisconsin</td><td>52.2</td><td>49</td><td>Alaska</td><td>33.5</td></tr>
<tr><td>37</td><td>Wyoming</td><td>48.8</td><td>50</td><td>Utah</td><td>17.5</td></tr>
<tr><td></td><td></td><td></td><td></td><td>District of Columbia</td><td>42.2</td></tr>
</table>

Source: CQ Press using data from American Cancer Society
"Cancer Facts & Figures 2008" (Copyright 2008, American Cancer Society, http://www.cancer.org/docroot/stt/stt_0.asp)
*Rates calculated using 2008 Census resident population estimates. Not age-adjusted.

Estimated Deaths by Non-Hodgkin's Lymphoma in 2008

National Estimated Total = 19,160 Deaths

ALPHA ORDER

RANK	STATE	DEATHS	% of USA
22	Alabama	320	1.7%
NA	Alaska*	NA	NA
21	Arizona	340	1.8%
32	Arkansas	190	1.0%
1	California	1,910	10.0%
29	Colorado	200	1.0%
28	Connecticut	230	1.2%
45	Delaware	60	0.3%
2	Florida	1,410	7.4%
11	Georgia	480	2.5%
42	Hawaii	80	0.4%
39	Idaho	100	0.5%
6	Illinois	800	4.2%
13	Indiana	450	2.3%
26	Iowa	290	1.5%
29	Kansas	200	1.0%
24	Kentucky	300	1.6%
24	Louisiana	300	1.6%
39	Maine	100	0.5%
20	Maryland	350	1.8%
13	Massachusetts	450	2.3%
7	Michigan	740	3.9%
22	Minnesota	320	1.7%
33	Mississippi	180	0.9%
12	Missouri	460	2.4%
42	Montana	80	0.4%
35	Nebraska	130	0.7%
37	Nevada	110	0.6%
41	New Hampshire	90	0.5%
9	New Jersey	550	2.9%
37	New Mexico	110	0.6%
5	New York	1,110	5.8%
10	North Carolina	500	2.6%
NA	North Dakota*	NA	NA
8	Ohio	660	3.4%
29	Oklahoma	200	1.0%
19	Oregon	380	2.0%
4	Pennsylvania	1,160	6.1%
46	Rhode Island	50	0.3%
27	South Carolina	270	1.4%
44	South Dakota	70	0.4%
15	Tennessee	430	2.2%
3	Texas	1,320	6.9%
35	Utah	130	0.7%
NA	Vermont*	NA	NA
16	Virginia	420	2.2%
17	Washington	400	2.1%
34	West Virginia	170	0.9%
18	Wisconsin	390	2.0%
NA	Wyoming*	NA	NA

RANK ORDER

RANK	STATE	DEATHS	% of USA
1	California	1,910	10.0%
2	Florida	1,410	7.4%
3	Texas	1,320	6.9%
4	Pennsylvania	1,160	6.1%
5	New York	1,110	5.8%
6	Illinois	800	4.2%
7	Michigan	740	3.9%
8	Ohio	660	3.4%
9	New Jersey	550	2.9%
10	North Carolina	500	2.6%
11	Georgia	480	2.5%
12	Missouri	460	2.4%
13	Indiana	450	2.3%
13	Massachusetts	450	2.3%
15	Tennessee	430	2.2%
16	Virginia	420	2.2%
17	Washington	400	2.1%
18	Wisconsin	390	2.0%
19	Oregon	380	2.0%
20	Maryland	350	1.8%
21	Arizona	340	1.8%
22	Alabama	320	1.7%
22	Minnesota	320	1.7%
24	Kentucky	300	1.6%
24	Louisiana	300	1.6%
26	Iowa	290	1.5%
27	South Carolina	270	1.4%
28	Connecticut	230	1.2%
29	Colorado	200	1.0%
29	Kansas	200	1.0%
29	Oklahoma	200	1.0%
32	Arkansas	190	1.0%
33	Mississippi	180	0.9%
34	West Virginia	170	0.9%
35	Nebraska	130	0.7%
35	Utah	130	0.7%
37	Nevada	110	0.6%
37	New Mexico	110	0.6%
39	Idaho	100	0.5%
39	Maine	100	0.5%
41	New Hampshire	90	0.5%
42	Hawaii	80	0.4%
42	Montana	80	0.4%
44	South Dakota	70	0.4%
45	Delaware	60	0.3%
46	Rhode Island	50	0.3%
NA	Alaska*	NA	NA
NA	North Dakota*	NA	NA
NA	Vermont*	NA	NA
NA	Wyoming*	NA	NA
	District of Columbia*	NA	NA

Source: American Cancer Society
   "Cancer Facts & Figures 2008" (Copyright 2008, American Cancer Society, http://www.cancer.org/docroot/stt/stt_0.asp)
*Fewer than 50 deaths.

Estimated Death Rate by Non-Hodgkin's Lymphoma in 2008

National Estimated Rate = 6.3 Deaths per 100,000 Population*

ALPHA ORDER

RANK	STATE	RATE
15	Alabama	6.9
NA	Alaska**	NA
40	Arizona	5.2
22	Arkansas	6.7
40	California	5.2
46	Colorado	4.0
23	Connecticut	6.6
15	Delaware	6.9
8	Florida	7.7
42	Georgia	5.0
26	Hawaii	6.2
23	Idaho	6.6
26	Illinois	6.2
12	Indiana	7.1
2	Iowa	9.7
12	Kansas	7.1
14	Kentucky	7.0
20	Louisiana	6.8
9	Maine	7.6
26	Maryland	6.2
15	Massachusetts	6.9
10	Michigan	7.4
29	Minnesota	6.1
29	Mississippi	6.1
7	Missouri	7.8
6	Montana	8.3
11	Nebraska	7.3
45	Nevada	4.2
20	New Hampshire	6.8
25	New Jersey	6.3
35	New Mexico	5.5
33	New York	5.7
37	North Carolina	5.4
NA	North Dakota**	NA
33	Ohio	5.7
35	Oklahoma	5.5
1	Oregon	10.0
4	Pennsylvania	9.3
43	Rhode Island	4.8
32	South Carolina	6.0
5	South Dakota	8.7
15	Tennessee	6.9
37	Texas	5.4
43	Utah	4.8
NA	Vermont**	NA
37	Virginia	5.4
29	Washington	6.1
3	West Virginia	9.4
15	Wisconsin	6.9
NA	Wyoming**	NA

RANK ORDER

RANK	STATE	RATE
1	Oregon	10.0
2	Iowa	9.7
3	West Virginia	9.4
4	Pennsylvania	9.3
5	South Dakota	8.7
6	Montana	8.3
7	Missouri	7.8
8	Florida	7.7
9	Maine	7.6
10	Michigan	7.4
11	Nebraska	7.3
12	Indiana	7.1
12	Kansas	7.1
14	Kentucky	7.0
15	Alabama	6.9
15	Delaware	6.9
15	Massachusetts	6.9
15	Tennessee	6.9
15	Wisconsin	6.9
20	Louisiana	6.8
20	New Hampshire	6.8
22	Arkansas	6.7
23	Connecticut	6.6
23	Idaho	6.6
25	New Jersey	6.3
26	Hawaii	6.2
26	Illinois	6.2
26	Maryland	6.2
29	Minnesota	6.1
29	Mississippi	6.1
29	Washington	6.1
32	South Carolina	6.0
33	New York	5.7
33	Ohio	5.7
35	New Mexico	5.5
35	Oklahoma	5.5
37	North Carolina	5.4
37	Texas	5.4
37	Virginia	5.4
40	Arizona	5.2
40	California	5.2
42	Georgia	5.0
43	Rhode Island	4.8
43	Utah	4.8
45	Nevada	4.2
46	Colorado	4.0
NA	Alaska**	NA
NA	North Dakota**	NA
NA	Vermont**	NA
NA	Wyoming**	NA
	District of Columbia**	NA

Source: CQ Press using data from American Cancer Society
   "Cancer Facts & Figures 2008" (Copyright 2008, American Cancer Society, http://www.cancer.org/docroot/stt/stt_0.asp)
*Rates calculated using 2008 Census resident population estimates. Not age-adjusted.
**Fewer than 50 deaths.

Estimated Deaths by Ovarian Cancer in 2008

National Estimated Total = 15,520 Deaths

RANK	STATE	DEATHS	% of USA
20	Alabama	280	1.8%
NA	Alaska*	NA	NA
17	Arizona	310	2.0%
33	Arkansas	140	0.9%
1	California	1,690	10.9%
23	Colorado	240	1.5%
29	Connecticut	180	1.2%
43	Delaware	50	0.3%
2	Florida	1,040	6.7%
11	Georgia	430	2.8%
43	Hawaii	50	0.3%
NA	Idaho*	NA	NA
6	Illinois	650	4.2%
13	Indiana	360	2.3%
28	Iowa	190	1.2%
31	Kansas	150	1.0%
26	Kentucky	210	1.4%
25	Louisiana	220	1.4%
39	Maine	80	0.5%
20	Maryland	280	1.8%
13	Massachusetts	360	2.3%
8	Michigan	550	3.5%
22	Minnesota	260	1.7%
31	Mississippi	150	1.0%
17	Missouri	310	2.0%
40	Montana	60	0.4%
36	Nebraska	90	0.6%
34	Nevada	130	0.8%
40	New Hampshire	60	0.4%
9	New Jersey	480	3.1%
36	New Mexico	90	0.6%
2	New York	1,040	6.7%
10	North Carolina	460	3.0%
NA	North Dakota*	NA	NA
7	Ohio	630	4.1%
29	Oklahoma	180	1.2%
24	Oregon	230	1.5%
5	Pennsylvania	810	5.2%
40	Rhode Island	60	0.4%
26	South Carolina	210	1.4%
43	South Dakota	50	0.3%
13	Tennessee	360	2.3%
4	Texas	930	6.0%
36	Utah	90	0.6%
NA	Vermont*	NA	NA
12	Virginia	390	2.5%
13	Washington	360	2.3%
34	West Virginia	130	0.8%
17	Wisconsin	310	2.0%
NA	Wyoming*	NA	NA

RANK	STATE	DEATHS	% of USA
1	California	1,690	10.9%
2	Florida	1,040	6.7%
2	New York	1,040	6.7%
4	Texas	930	6.0%
5	Pennsylvania	810	5.2%
6	Illinois	650	4.2%
7	Ohio	630	4.1%
8	Michigan	550	3.5%
9	New Jersey	480	3.1%
10	North Carolina	460	3.0%
11	Georgia	430	2.8%
12	Virginia	390	2.5%
13	Indiana	360	2.3%
13	Massachusetts	360	2.3%
13	Tennessee	360	2.3%
13	Washington	360	2.3%
17	Arizona	310	2.0%
17	Missouri	310	2.0%
17	Wisconsin	310	2.0%
20	Alabama	280	1.8%
20	Maryland	280	1.8%
22	Minnesota	260	1.7%
23	Colorado	240	1.5%
24	Oregon	230	1.5%
25	Louisiana	220	1.4%
26	Kentucky	210	1.4%
26	South Carolina	210	1.4%
28	Iowa	190	1.2%
29	Connecticut	180	1.2%
29	Oklahoma	180	1.2%
31	Kansas	150	1.0%
31	Mississippi	150	1.0%
33	Arkansas	140	0.9%
34	Nevada	130	0.8%
34	West Virginia	130	0.8%
36	Nebraska	90	0.6%
36	New Mexico	90	0.6%
36	Utah	90	0.6%
39	Maine	80	0.5%
40	Montana	60	0.4%
40	New Hampshire	60	0.4%
40	Rhode Island	60	0.4%
43	Delaware	50	0.3%
43	Hawaii	50	0.3%
43	South Dakota	50	0.3%
NA	Alaska*	NA	NA
NA	Idaho*	NA	NA
NA	North Dakota*	NA	NA
NA	Vermont*	NA	NA
NA	Wyoming*	NA	NA
	District of Columbia*	NA	NA

Source: American Cancer Society
"Cancer Facts & Figures 2008" (Copyright 2008, American Cancer Society, http://www.cancer.org/docroot/stt/stt_0.asp)
*Fewer than 50 deaths.

Estimated Death Rate by Ovarian Cancer in 2008

National Estimated Rate = 10.1 Deaths per 100,000 Female Population*

ALPHA ORDER

RANK	STATE	RATE
8	Alabama	11.7
NA	Alaska**	NA
33	Arizona	9.8
35	Arkansas	9.7
39	California	9.2
25	Colorado	10.0
25	Connecticut	10.0
10	Delaware	11.2
10	Florida	11.2
42	Georgia	8.9
43	Hawaii	7.8
NA	Idaho**	NA
25	Illinois	10.0
10	Indiana	11.2
3	Iowa	12.6
19	Kansas	10.7
35	Kentucky	9.7
25	Louisiana	10.0
7	Maine	11.9
35	Maryland	9.7
16	Massachusetts	10.8
16	Michigan	10.8
25	Minnesota	10.0
25	Mississippi	10.0
22	Missouri	10.3
4	Montana	12.5
24	Nebraska	10.1
22	Nevada	10.3
40	New Hampshire	9.0
16	New Jersey	10.8
40	New Mexico	9.0
21	New York	10.5
31	North Carolina	9.9
NA	North Dakota**	NA
19	Ohio	10.7
33	Oklahoma	9.8
6	Oregon	12.2
2	Pennsylvania	12.7
14	Rhode Island	11.0
38	South Carolina	9.3
4	South Dakota	12.5
9	Tennessee	11.4
43	Texas	7.8
45	Utah	6.9
NA	Vermont**	NA
31	Virginia	9.9
13	Washington	11.1
1	West Virginia	14.1
14	Wisconsin	11.0
NA	Wyoming**	NA

RANK ORDER

RANK	STATE	RATE
1	West Virginia	14.1
2	Pennsylvania	12.7
3	Iowa	12.6
4	Montana	12.5
4	South Dakota	12.5
6	Oregon	12.2
7	Maine	11.9
8	Alabama	11.7
9	Tennessee	11.4
10	Delaware	11.2
10	Florida	11.2
10	Indiana	11.2
13	Washington	11.1
14	Rhode Island	11.0
14	Wisconsin	11.0
16	Massachusetts	10.8
16	Michigan	10.8
16	New Jersey	10.8
19	Kansas	10.7
19	Ohio	10.7
21	New York	10.5
22	Missouri	10.3
22	Nevada	10.3
24	Nebraska	10.1
25	Colorado	10.0
25	Connecticut	10.0
25	Illinois	10.0
25	Louisiana	10.0
25	Minnesota	10.0
25	Mississippi	10.0
31	North Carolina	9.9
31	Virginia	9.9
33	Arizona	9.8
33	Oklahoma	9.8
35	Arkansas	9.7
35	Kentucky	9.7
35	Maryland	9.7
38	South Carolina	9.3
39	California	9.2
40	New Hampshire	9.0
40	New Mexico	9.0
42	Georgia	8.9
43	Hawaii	7.8
43	Texas	7.8
45	Utah	6.9
NA	Alaska**	NA
NA	Idaho**	NA
NA	North Dakota**	NA
NA	Vermont**	NA
NA	Wyoming**	NA
	District of Columbia**	NA

Source: CQ Press using data from American Cancer Society
"Cancer Facts & Figures 2008" (Copyright 2008, American Cancer Society, http://www.cancer.org/docroot/stt/stt_0.asp)
*Rates calculated using 2007 Census female population estimates. Not age-adjusted.
**Fewer than 50 deaths.

Estimated Deaths by Pancreatic Cancer in 2008

National Estimated Total = 34,290 Deaths

ALPHA ORDER

RANK	STATE	DEATHS	% of USA
23	Alabama	530	1.5%
50	Alaska	50	0.1%
20	Arizona	650	1.9%
30	Arkansas	370	1.1%
1	California	3,720	10.8%
28	Colorado	420	1.2%
24	Connecticut	520	1.5%
44	Delaware	110	0.3%
2	Florida	2,400	7.0%
12	Georgia	850	2.5%
40	Hawaii	170	0.5%
38	Idaho	180	0.5%
6	Illinois	1,530	4.5%
14	Indiana	750	2.2%
29	Iowa	380	1.1%
33	Kansas	320	0.9%
26	Kentucky	470	1.4%
22	Louisiana	540	1.6%
37	Maine	200	0.6%
19	Maryland	660	1.9%
11	Massachusetts	880	2.6%
8	Michigan	1,190	3.5%
21	Minnesota	560	1.6%
32	Mississippi	330	1.0%
17	Missouri	710	2.1%
44	Montana	110	0.3%
40	Nebraska	170	0.5%
34	Nevada	270	0.8%
42	New Hampshire	160	0.5%
9	New Jersey	1,060	3.1%
35	New Mexico	210	0.6%
3	New York	2,340	6.8%
10	North Carolina	1,020	3.0%
47	North Dakota	80	0.2%
7	Ohio	1,380	4.0%
30	Oklahoma	370	1.1%
27	Oregon	450	1.3%
5	Pennsylvania	1,820	5.3%
43	Rhode Island	130	0.4%
24	South Carolina	520	1.5%
46	South Dakota	100	0.3%
15	Tennessee	720	2.1%
4	Texas	2,060	6.0%
38	Utah	180	0.5%
48	Vermont	70	0.2%
13	Virginia	840	2.4%
15	Washington	720	2.1%
35	West Virginia	210	0.6%
18	Wisconsin	680	2.0%
49	Wyoming	60	0.2%

RANK ORDER

RANK	STATE	DEATHS	% of USA
1	California	3,720	10.8%
2	Florida	2,400	7.0%
3	New York	2,340	6.8%
4	Texas	2,060	6.0%
5	Pennsylvania	1,820	5.3%
6	Illinois	1,530	4.5%
7	Ohio	1,380	4.0%
8	Michigan	1,190	3.5%
9	New Jersey	1,060	3.1%
10	North Carolina	1,020	3.0%
11	Massachusetts	880	2.6%
12	Georgia	850	2.5%
13	Virginia	840	2.4%
14	Indiana	750	2.2%
15	Tennessee	720	2.1%
15	Washington	720	2.1%
17	Missouri	710	2.1%
18	Wisconsin	680	2.0%
19	Maryland	660	1.9%
20	Arizona	650	1.9%
21	Minnesota	560	1.6%
22	Louisiana	540	1.6%
23	Alabama	530	1.5%
24	Connecticut	520	1.5%
24	South Carolina	520	1.5%
26	Kentucky	470	1.4%
27	Oregon	450	1.3%
28	Colorado	420	1.2%
29	Iowa	380	1.1%
30	Arkansas	370	1.1%
30	Oklahoma	370	1.1%
32	Mississippi	330	1.0%
33	Kansas	320	0.9%
34	Nevada	270	0.8%
35	New Mexico	210	0.6%
35	West Virginia	210	0.6%
37	Maine	200	0.6%
38	Idaho	180	0.5%
38	Utah	180	0.5%
40	Hawaii	170	0.5%
40	Nebraska	170	0.5%
42	New Hampshire	160	0.5%
43	Rhode Island	130	0.4%
44	Delaware	110	0.3%
44	Montana	110	0.3%
46	South Dakota	100	0.3%
47	North Dakota	80	0.2%
48	Vermont	70	0.2%
49	Wyoming	60	0.2%
50	Alaska	50	0.1%
	District of Columbia	60	0.2%

Source: American Cancer Society
"Cancer Facts & Figures 2008" (Copyright 2008, American Cancer Society, http://www.cancer.org/docroot/stt/stt_0.asp)

Estimated Death Rate by Pancreatic Cancer in 2008

National Estimated Rate = 11.3 Deaths per 100,000 Population*

ALPHA ORDER

RANK	STATE	RATE
29	Alabama	11.4
49	Alaska	7.3
44	Arizona	10.0
7	Arkansas	13.0
43	California	10.1
47	Colorado	8.5
2	Connecticut	14.9
9	Delaware	12.6
6	Florida	13.1
46	Georgia	8.8
5	Hawaii	13.2
23	Idaho	11.8
20	Illinois	11.9
23	Indiana	11.8
8	Iowa	12.7
29	Kansas	11.4
36	Kentucky	11.0
13	Louisiana	12.2
1	Maine	15.2
25	Maryland	11.7
4	Massachusetts	13.5
20	Michigan	11.9
39	Minnesota	10.7
34	Mississippi	11.2
17	Missouri	12.0
29	Montana	11.4
45	Nebraska	9.5
41	Nevada	10.4
13	New Hampshire	12.2
13	New Jersey	12.2
40	New Mexico	10.6
17	New York	12.0
35	North Carolina	11.1
10	North Dakota	12.5
17	Ohio	12.0
42	Oklahoma	10.2
20	Oregon	11.9
3	Pennsylvania	14.6
11	Rhode Island	12.4
26	South Carolina	11.6
11	South Dakota	12.4
26	Tennessee	11.6
47	Texas	8.5
50	Utah	6.6
32	Vermont	11.3
38	Virginia	10.8
36	Washington	11.0
26	West Virginia	11.6
16	Wisconsin	12.1
32	Wyoming	11.3

RANK ORDER

RANK	STATE	RATE
1	Maine	15.2
2	Connecticut	14.9
3	Pennsylvania	14.6
4	Massachusetts	13.5
5	Hawaii	13.2
6	Florida	13.1
7	Arkansas	13.0
8	Iowa	12.7
9	Delaware	12.6
10	North Dakota	12.5
11	Rhode Island	12.4
11	South Dakota	12.4
13	Louisiana	12.2
13	New Hampshire	12.2
13	New Jersey	12.2
16	Wisconsin	12.1
17	Missouri	12.0
17	New York	12.0
17	Ohio	12.0
20	Illinois	11.9
20	Michigan	11.9
20	Oregon	11.9
23	Idaho	11.8
23	Indiana	11.8
25	Maryland	11.7
26	South Carolina	11.6
26	Tennessee	11.6
26	West Virginia	11.6
29	Alabama	11.4
29	Kansas	11.4
29	Montana	11.4
32	Vermont	11.3
32	Wyoming	11.3
34	Mississippi	11.2
35	North Carolina	11.1
36	Kentucky	11.0
36	Washington	11.0
38	Virginia	10.8
39	Minnesota	10.7
40	New Mexico	10.6
41	Nevada	10.4
42	Oklahoma	10.2
43	California	10.1
44	Arizona	10.0
45	Nebraska	9.5
46	Georgia	8.8
47	Colorado	8.5
47	Texas	8.5
49	Alaska	7.3
50	Utah	6.6

	District of Columbia	10.1

Source: CQ Press using data from American Cancer Society
"Cancer Facts & Figures 2008" (Copyright 2008, American Cancer Society, http://www.cancer.org/docroot/stt/stt_0.asp)
*Rates calculated using 2008 Census resident population estimates. Not age-adjusted.

Estimated Deaths by Prostate Cancer in 2008

National Estimated Total = 28,660 Deaths

ALPHA ORDER

RANK	STATE	DEATHS	% of USA
20	Alabama	490	1.7%
NA	Alaska*	NA	NA
14	Arizona	640	2.2%
27	Arkansas	360	1.3%
1	California	3,400	11.9%
29	Colorado	350	1.2%
25	Connecticut	400	1.4%
45	Delaware	100	0.3%
2	Florida	2,520	8.8%
11	Georgia	730	2.5%
42	Hawaii	130	0.5%
38	Idaho	170	0.6%
7	Illinois	1,100	3.8%
17	Indiana	550	1.9%
30	Iowa	340	1.2%
34	Kansas	220	0.8%
27	Kentucky	360	1.3%
23	Louisiana	420	1.5%
37	Maine	180	0.6%
17	Maryland	550	1.9%
19	Massachusetts	530	1.8%
8	Michigan	850	3.0%
22	Minnesota	450	1.6%
31	Mississippi	290	1.0%
21	Missouri	460	1.6%
43	Montana	120	0.4%
35	Nebraska	210	0.7%
33	Nevada	240	0.8%
40	New Hampshire	140	0.5%
9	New Jersey	800	2.8%
36	New Mexico	200	0.7%
4	New York	1,590	5.5%
10	North Carolina	750	2.6%
45	North Dakota	100	0.3%
6	Ohio	1,350	4.7%
31	Oklahoma	290	1.0%
26	Oregon	380	1.3%
5	Pennsylvania	1,430	5.0%
43	Rhode Island	120	0.4%
23	South Carolina	420	1.5%
45	South Dakota	100	0.3%
16	Tennessee	560	2.0%
3	Texas	1,730	6.0%
40	Utah	140	0.5%
48	Vermont	70	0.2%
15	Virginia	630	2.2%
12	Washington	700	2.4%
39	West Virginia	150	0.5%
12	Wisconsin	700	2.4%
49	Wyoming	50	0.2%

RANK ORDER

RANK	STATE	DEATHS	% of USA
1	California	3,400	11.9%
2	Florida	2,520	8.8%
3	Texas	1,730	6.0%
4	New York	1,590	5.5%
5	Pennsylvania	1,430	5.0%
6	Ohio	1,350	4.7%
7	Illinois	1,100	3.8%
8	Michigan	850	3.0%
9	New Jersey	800	2.8%
10	North Carolina	750	2.6%
11	Georgia	730	2.5%
12	Washington	700	2.4%
12	Wisconsin	700	2.4%
14	Arizona	640	2.2%
15	Virginia	630	2.2%
16	Tennessee	560	2.0%
17	Indiana	550	1.9%
17	Maryland	550	1.9%
19	Massachusetts	530	1.8%
20	Alabama	490	1.7%
21	Missouri	460	1.6%
22	Minnesota	450	1.6%
23	Louisiana	420	1.5%
23	South Carolina	420	1.5%
25	Connecticut	400	1.4%
26	Oregon	380	1.3%
27	Arkansas	360	1.3%
27	Kentucky	360	1.3%
29	Colorado	350	1.2%
30	Iowa	340	1.2%
31	Mississippi	290	1.0%
31	Oklahoma	290	1.0%
33	Nevada	240	0.8%
34	Kansas	220	0.8%
35	Nebraska	210	0.7%
36	New Mexico	200	0.7%
37	Maine	180	0.6%
38	Idaho	170	0.6%
39	West Virginia	150	0.5%
40	New Hampshire	140	0.5%
40	Utah	140	0.5%
42	Hawaii	130	0.5%
43	Montana	120	0.4%
43	Rhode Island	120	0.4%
45	Delaware	100	0.3%
45	North Dakota	100	0.3%
45	South Dakota	100	0.3%
48	Vermont	70	0.2%
49	Wyoming	50	0.2%
NA	Alaska*	NA	NA
	District of Columbia	70	0.2%

Source: American Cancer Society
   "Cancer Facts & Figures 2008" (Copyright 2008, American Cancer Society, http://www.cancer.org/docroot/stt/stt_0.asp)
*Fewer than 50 deaths.

Age-Adjusted Death Rate by Prostate Cancer in 2004

National Rate = 27.9 Deaths per 100,000 Male Population*

ALPHA ORDER

RANK	STATE	RATE
2	Alabama	35.6
26	Alaska	28.2
48	Arizona	25.3
9	Arkansas	30.5
47	California	25.4
35	Colorado	27.3
43	Connecticut	26.4
27	Delaware	28.1
49	Florida	23.7
5	Georgia	32.7
50	Hawaii	19.6
11	Idaho	30.1
17	Illinois	29.2
19	Indiana	29.1
23	Iowa	28.4
44	Kansas	25.9
21	Kentucky	28.6
4	Louisiana	33.5
22	Maine	28.5
14	Maryland	29.9
34	Massachusetts	27.4
29	Michigan	27.7
11	Minnesota	30.1
1	Mississippi	39.2
46	Missouri	25.6
20	Montana	29.0
45	Nebraska	25.7
29	Nevada	27.7
17	New Hampshire	29.2
37	New Jersey	27.0
29	New Mexico	27.7
36	New York	27.2
6	North Carolina	32.4
16	North Dakota	29.3
23	Ohio	28.4
42	Oklahoma	26.5
25	Oregon	28.3
29	Pennsylvania	27.7
41	Rhode Island	26.7
3	South Carolina	34.5
11	South Dakota	30.1
8	Tennessee	31.1
37	Texas	27.0
33	Utah	27.6
27	Vermont	28.1
7	Virginia	31.2
37	Washington	27.0
40	West Virginia	26.9
15	Wisconsin	29.6
10	Wyoming	30.4

RANK ORDER

RANK	STATE	RATE
1	Mississippi	39.2
2	Alabama	35.6
3	South Carolina	34.5
4	Louisiana	33.5
5	Georgia	32.7
6	North Carolina	32.4
7	Virginia	31.2
8	Tennessee	31.1
9	Arkansas	30.5
10	Wyoming	30.4
11	Idaho	30.1
11	Minnesota	30.1
11	South Dakota	30.1
14	Maryland	29.9
15	Wisconsin	29.6
16	North Dakota	29.3
17	Illinois	29.2
17	New Hampshire	29.2
19	Indiana	29.1
20	Montana	29.0
21	Kentucky	28.6
22	Maine	28.5
23	Iowa	28.4
23	Ohio	28.4
25	Oregon	28.3
26	Alaska	28.2
27	Delaware	28.1
27	Vermont	28.1
29	Michigan	27.7
29	Nevada	27.7
29	New Mexico	27.7
29	Pennsylvania	27.7
33	Utah	27.6
34	Massachusetts	27.4
35	Colorado	27.3
36	New York	27.2
37	New Jersey	27.0
37	Texas	27.0
37	Washington	27.0
40	West Virginia	26.9
41	Rhode Island	26.7
42	Oklahoma	26.5
43	Connecticut	26.4
44	Kansas	25.9
45	Nebraska	25.7
46	Missouri	25.6
47	California	25.4
48	Arizona	25.3
49	Florida	23.7
50	Hawaii	19.6

District of Columbia 46.5

Source: American Cancer Society
"Cancer Facts & Figures 2008" (Copyright 2008, American Cancer Society, http://www.cancer.org/docroot/stt/stt_0.asp)
*For 2000 to 2004. Age-adjusted to the 2000 U.S. standard population.

Deaths by AIDS in 2005

National Total = 12,543 Deaths*

ALPHA ORDER

RANK	STATE	DEATHS	% of USA
19	Alabama	172	1.4%
45	Alaska	7	0.1%
21	Arizona	138	1.1%
27	Arkansas	86	0.7%
3	California	1,291	10.3%
25	Colorado	93	0.7%
20	Connecticut	148	1.2%
29	Delaware	63	0.5%
1	Florida	1,718	13.7%
5	Georgia	666	5.3%
39	Hawaii	18	0.1%
44	Idaho	8	0.1%
9	Illinois	410	3.3%
24	Indiana	102	0.8%
40	Iowa	16	0.1%
35	Kansas	32	0.3%
30	Kentucky	62	0.5%
10	Louisiana	403	3.2%
43	Maine	11	0.1%
7	Maryland	528	4.2%
18	Massachusetts	184	1.5%
15	Michigan	224	1.8%
33	Minnesota	53	0.4%
17	Mississippi	191	1.5%
23	Missouri	130	1.0%
45	Montana	7	0.1%
36	Nebraska	26	0.2%
27	Nevada	86	0.7%
42	New Hampshire	13	0.1%
6	New Jersey	604	4.8%
34	New Mexico	34	0.3%
2	New York	1,644	13.1%
8	North Carolina	416	3.3%
50	North Dakota	3	0.0%
16	Ohio	223	1.8%
25	Oklahoma	93	0.7%
32	Oregon	57	0.5%
11	Pennsylvania	360	2.9%
37	Rhode Island	23	0.2%
13	South Carolina	249	2.0%
48	South Dakota	6	0.0%
12	Tennessee	281	2.2%
4	Texas	980	7.8%
41	Utah	15	0.1%
45	Vermont	7	0.1%
14	Virginia	233	1.9%
21	Washington	138	1.1%
38	West Virginia	22	0.2%
31	Wisconsin	60	0.5%
49	Wyoming	5	0.0%

RANK ORDER

RANK	STATE	DEATHS	% of USA
1	Florida	1,718	13.7%
2	New York	1,644	13.1%
3	California	1,291	10.3%
4	Texas	980	7.8%
5	Georgia	666	5.3%
6	New Jersey	604	4.8%
7	Maryland	528	4.2%
8	North Carolina	416	3.3%
9	Illinois	410	3.3%
10	Louisiana	403	3.2%
11	Pennsylvania	360	2.9%
12	Tennessee	281	2.2%
13	South Carolina	249	2.0%
14	Virginia	233	1.9%
15	Michigan	224	1.8%
16	Ohio	223	1.8%
17	Mississippi	191	1.5%
18	Massachusetts	184	1.5%
19	Alabama	172	1.4%
20	Connecticut	148	1.2%
21	Arizona	138	1.1%
21	Washington	138	1.1%
23	Missouri	130	1.0%
24	Indiana	102	0.8%
25	Colorado	93	0.7%
25	Oklahoma	93	0.7%
27	Arkansas	86	0.7%
27	Nevada	86	0.7%
29	Delaware	63	0.5%
30	Kentucky	62	0.5%
31	Wisconsin	60	0.5%
32	Oregon	57	0.5%
33	Minnesota	53	0.4%
34	New Mexico	34	0.3%
35	Kansas	32	0.3%
36	Nebraska	26	0.2%
37	Rhode Island	23	0.2%
38	West Virginia	22	0.2%
39	Hawaii	18	0.1%
40	Iowa	16	0.1%
41	Utah	15	0.1%
42	New Hampshire	13	0.1%
43	Maine	11	0.1%
44	Idaho	8	0.1%
45	Alaska	7	0.1%
45	Montana	7	0.1%
45	Vermont	7	0.1%
48	South Dakota	6	0.0%
49	Wyoming	5	0.0%
50	North Dakota	3	0.0%
	District of Columbia	204	1.6%

Source: U.S. Department of Health and Human Services, National Center for Health Statistics
  "National Vital Statistics Reports" (Vol. 56, No. 10, April 24, 2008, http://www.cdc.gov/nchs/deaths.htm)
*AIDS is Acquired Immunodeficiency Syndrome. It is a specific group of diseases or conditions which are indicative of severe immunosuppression related to infection with the Human Immunodeficiency Virus (HIV).

Death Rate by AIDS in 2005

National Rate = 4.2 Deaths per 100,000 Population*

ALPHA ORDER

RANK	STATE	RATE
14	Alabama	3.8
NA	Alaska**	NA
23	Arizona	2.3
18	Arkansas	3.1
15	California	3.6
28	Colorado	2.0
13	Connecticut	4.2
5	Delaware	7.5
1	Florida	9.7
6	Georgia	7.3
NA	Hawaii**	NA
NA	Idaho**	NA
17	Illinois	3.2
31	Indiana	1.6
NA	Iowa**	NA
35	Kansas	1.2
33	Kentucky	1.5
3	Louisiana	8.9
NA	Maine**	NA
2	Maryland	9.4
20	Massachusetts	2.9
24	Michigan	2.2
38	Minnesota	1.0
8	Mississippi	6.5
24	Missouri	2.2
NA	Montana**	NA
33	Nebraska	1.5
15	Nevada	3.6
NA	New Hampshire**	NA
7	New Jersey	6.9
30	New Mexico	1.8
4	New York	8.5
10	North Carolina	4.8
NA	North Dakota**	NA
29	Ohio	1.9
22	Oklahoma	2.6
31	Oregon	1.6
20	Pennsylvania	2.9
27	Rhode Island	2.1
9	South Carolina	5.9
NA	South Dakota**	NA
11	Tennessee	4.7
12	Texas	4.3
NA	Utah**	NA
NA	Vermont**	NA
18	Virginia	3.1
24	Washington	2.2
35	West Virginia	1.2
37	Wisconsin	1.1
NA	Wyoming**	NA

RANK ORDER

RANK	STATE	RATE
1	Florida	9.7
2	Maryland	9.4
3	Louisiana	8.9
4	New York	8.5
5	Delaware	7.5
6	Georgia	7.3
7	New Jersey	6.9
8	Mississippi	6.5
9	South Carolina	5.9
10	North Carolina	4.8
11	Tennessee	4.7
12	Texas	4.3
13	Connecticut	4.2
14	Alabama	3.8
15	California	3.6
15	Nevada	3.6
17	Illinois	3.2
18	Arkansas	3.1
18	Virginia	3.1
20	Massachusetts	2.9
20	Pennsylvania	2.9
22	Oklahoma	2.6
23	Arizona	2.3
24	Michigan	2.2
24	Missouri	2.2
24	Washington	2.2
27	Rhode Island	2.1
28	Colorado	2.0
29	Ohio	1.9
30	New Mexico	1.8
31	Indiana	1.6
31	Oregon	1.6
33	Kentucky	1.5
33	Nebraska	1.5
35	Kansas	1.2
35	West Virginia	1.2
37	Wisconsin	1.1
38	Minnesota	1.0
NA	Alaska**	NA
NA	Hawaii**	NA
NA	Idaho**	NA
NA	Iowa**	NA
NA	Maine**	NA
NA	Montana**	NA
NA	New Hampshire**	NA
NA	North Dakota**	NA
NA	South Dakota**	NA
NA	Utah**	NA
NA	Vermont**	NA
NA	Wyoming**	NA

District of Columbia   37.1

Source: U.S. Department of Health and Human Services, National Center for Health Statistics
"National Vital Statistics Reports" (Vol. 56, No. 10, April 24, 2008, http://www.cdc.gov/nchs/deaths.htm)
*AIDS is Acquired Immunodeficiency Syndrome. It is a specific group of diseases or conditions which are indicative of severe immunosuppression related to infection with the Human Immunodeficiency Virus (HIV). Not age-adjusted.
**Insufficient data to determine a reliable rate.

Age-Adjusted Death Rate by AIDS in 2005

National Rate = 4.2 Deaths per 100,000 Population*

ALPHA ORDER

RANK	STATE	RATE
14	Alabama	3.8
NA	Alaska**	NA
23	Arizona	2.5
17	Arkansas	3.2
15	California	3.7
27	Colorado	2.0
13	Connecticut	4.0
5	Delaware	7.3
1	Florida	9.8
5	Georgia	7.3
NA	Hawaii**	NA
NA	Idaho**	NA
17	Illinois	3.2
31	Indiana	1.7
NA	Iowa**	NA
35	Kansas	1.2
34	Kentucky	1.5
2	Louisiana	9.2
NA	Maine**	NA
3	Maryland	9.0
21	Massachusetts	2.7
24	Michigan	2.2
37	Minnesota	1.0
7	Mississippi	6.8
24	Missouri	2.2
NA	Montana**	NA
32	Nebraska	1.6
16	Nevada	3.6
NA	New Hampshire**	NA
8	New Jersey	6.6
30	New Mexico	1.8
4	New York	8.2
10	North Carolina	4.8
NA	North Dakota**	NA
29	Ohio	1.9
21	Oklahoma	2.7
32	Oregon	1.6
20	Pennsylvania	2.8
27	Rhode Island	2.0
9	South Carolina	5.9
NA	South Dakota**	NA
11	Tennessee	4.6
12	Texas	4.5
NA	Utah**	NA
NA	Vermont**	NA
19	Virginia	3.0
26	Washington	2.1
35	West Virginia	1.2
37	Wisconsin	1.0
NA	Wyoming**	NA

RANK ORDER

RANK	STATE	RATE
1	Florida	9.8
2	Louisiana	9.2
3	Maryland	9.0
4	New York	8.2
5	Delaware	7.3
5	Georgia	7.3
7	Mississippi	6.8
8	New Jersey	6.6
9	South Carolina	5.9
10	North Carolina	4.8
11	Tennessee	4.6
12	Texas	4.5
13	Connecticut	4.0
14	Alabama	3.8
15	California	3.7
16	Nevada	3.6
17	Arkansas	3.2
17	Illinois	3.2
19	Virginia	3.0
20	Pennsylvania	2.8
21	Massachusetts	2.7
21	Oklahoma	2.7
23	Arizona	2.5
24	Michigan	2.2
24	Missouri	2.2
26	Washington	2.1
27	Colorado	2.0
27	Rhode Island	2.0
29	Ohio	1.9
30	New Mexico	1.8
31	Indiana	1.7
32	Nebraska	1.6
32	Oregon	1.6
34	Kentucky	1.5
35	Kansas	1.2
35	West Virginia	1.2
37	Minnesota	1.0
37	Wisconsin	1.0
NA	Alaska**	NA
NA	Hawaii**	NA
NA	Idaho**	NA
NA	Iowa**	NA
NA	Maine**	NA
NA	Montana**	NA
NA	New Hampshire**	NA
NA	North Dakota**	NA
NA	South Dakota**	NA
NA	Utah**	NA
NA	Vermont**	NA
NA	Wyoming**	NA

District of Columbia	37.1

Source: U.S. Department of Health and Human Services, National Center for Health Statistics
   "National Vital Statistics Reports" (Vol. 56, No. 10, April 24, 2008, http://www.cdc.gov/nchs/deaths.htm)
*AIDS is Acquired Immunodeficiency Syndrome. It is a specific group of diseases or conditions which are indicative of severe immunosuppression related to infection with the Human Immunodeficiency Virus (HIV). Age-adjusted rates based on the year 2000 standard population.
**Insufficient data to determine a reliable rate.

Deaths by Alzheimer's Disease in 2005

National Total = 71,599 Deaths*

ALPHA ORDER

RANK	STATE	DEATHS	% of USA
20	Alabama	1,501	2.1%
50	Alaska	61	0.1%
12	Arizona	1,831	2.6%
33	Arkansas	686	1.0%
1	California	7,706	10.8%
27	Colorado	1,064	1.5%
31	Connecticut	777	1.1%
48	Delaware	180	0.3%
3	Florida	4,608	6.4%
14	Georgia	1,745	2.4%
46	Hawaii	192	0.3%
37	Idaho	407	0.6%
6	Illinois	2,827	3.9%
15	Indiana	1,651	2.3%
26	Iowa	1,082	1.5%
30	Kansas	912	1.3%
25	Kentucky	1,147	1.6%
21	Louisiana	1,405	2.0%
35	Maine	476	0.7%
29	Maryland	958	1.3%
16	Massachusetts	1,638	2.3%
8	Michigan	2,359	3.3%
22	Minnesota	1,320	1.8%
32	Mississippi	721	1.0%
17	Missouri	1,635	2.3%
45	Montana	267	0.4%
36	Nebraska	473	0.7%
41	Nevada	310	0.4%
38	New Hampshire	376	0.5%
13	New Jersey	1,815	2.5%
40	New Mexico	327	0.5%
10	New York	2,065	2.9%
7	North Carolina	2,417	3.4%
44	North Dakota	287	0.4%
4	Ohio	3,478	4.9%
28	Oklahoma	1,012	1.4%
24	Oregon	1,239	1.7%
5	Pennsylvania	3,429	4.8%
42	Rhode Island	298	0.4%
23	South Carolina	1,316	1.8%
43	South Dakota	290	0.4%
11	Tennessee	2,033	2.8%
2	Texas	4,629	6.5%
39	Utah	368	0.5%
47	Vermont	184	0.3%
18	Virginia	1,550	2.2%
9	Washington	2,309	3.2%
34	West Virginia	504	0.7%
19	Wisconsin	1,512	2.1%
49	Wyoming	110	0.2%

RANK ORDER

RANK	STATE	DEATHS	% of USA
1	California	7,706	10.8%
2	Texas	4,629	6.5%
3	Florida	4,608	6.4%
4	Ohio	3,478	4.9%
5	Pennsylvania	3,429	4.8%
6	Illinois	2,827	3.9%
7	North Carolina	2,417	3.4%
8	Michigan	2,359	3.3%
9	Washington	2,309	3.2%
10	New York	2,065	2.9%
11	Tennessee	2,033	2.8%
12	Arizona	1,831	2.6%
13	New Jersey	1,815	2.5%
14	Georgia	1,745	2.4%
15	Indiana	1,651	2.3%
16	Massachusetts	1,638	2.3%
17	Missouri	1,635	2.3%
18	Virginia	1,550	2.2%
19	Wisconsin	1,512	2.1%
20	Alabama	1,501	2.1%
21	Louisiana	1,405	2.0%
22	Minnesota	1,320	1.8%
23	South Carolina	1,316	1.8%
24	Oregon	1,239	1.7%
25	Kentucky	1,147	1.6%
26	Iowa	1,082	1.5%
27	Colorado	1,064	1.5%
28	Oklahoma	1,012	1.4%
29	Maryland	958	1.3%
30	Kansas	912	1.3%
31	Connecticut	777	1.1%
32	Mississippi	721	1.0%
33	Arkansas	686	1.0%
34	West Virginia	504	0.7%
35	Maine	476	0.7%
36	Nebraska	473	0.7%
37	Idaho	407	0.6%
38	New Hampshire	376	0.5%
39	Utah	368	0.5%
40	New Mexico	327	0.5%
41	Nevada	310	0.4%
42	Rhode Island	298	0.4%
43	South Dakota	290	0.4%
44	North Dakota	287	0.4%
45	Montana	267	0.4%
46	Hawaii	192	0.3%
47	Vermont	184	0.3%
48	Delaware	180	0.3%
49	Wyoming	110	0.2%
50	Alaska	61	0.1%
	District of Columbia	112	0.2%

Source: U.S. Department of Health and Human Services, National Center for Health Statistics
"National Vital Statistics Reports" (Vol. 56, No. 10, April 24, 2008, http://www.cdc.gov/nchs/deaths.htm)
*Final data by state of residence. A degenerative disease of the brain cells producing loss of memory and general intellectual impairment. It usually affects people over age 65. As the disease progresses, a variety of symptoms may become apparent, including confusion, irritability, and restlessness, as well as disorientation and impaired judgment and concentration.

Death Rate by Alzheimer's Disease in 2005

National Rate = 24.2 Deaths per 100,000 Population*

ALPHA ORDER

RANK	STATE	RATE
9	Alabama	32.9
50	Alaska	9.2
12	Arizona	30.8
31	Arkansas	24.7
38	California	21.3
34	Colorado	22.8
35	Connecticut	22.1
38	Delaware	21.3
28	Florida	25.9
43	Georgia	19.2
46	Hawaii	15.1
16	Idaho	28.5
35	Illinois	22.1
27	Indiana	26.3
4	Iowa	36.5
8	Kansas	33.2
24	Kentucky	27.5
10	Louisiana	31.1
5	Maine	36.0
44	Maryland	17.1
30	Massachusetts	25.6
33	Michigan	23.3
29	Minnesota	25.7
31	Mississippi	24.7
19	Missouri	28.2
16	Montana	28.5
26	Nebraska	26.9
48	Nevada	12.8
15	New Hampshire	28.7
40	New Jersey	20.8
45	New Mexico	17.0
49	New York	10.7
20	North Carolina	27.8
1	North Dakota	45.1
13	Ohio	30.3
16	Oklahoma	28.5
7	Oregon	34.0
23	Pennsylvania	27.6
21	Rhode Island	27.7
11	South Carolina	30.9
2	South Dakota	37.4
6	Tennessee	34.1
42	Texas	20.2
47	Utah	14.9
14	Vermont	29.5
41	Virginia	20.5
3	Washington	36.7
21	West Virginia	27.7
25	Wisconsin	27.3
37	Wyoming	21.6

RANK ORDER

RANK	STATE	RATE
1	North Dakota	45.1
2	South Dakota	37.4
3	Washington	36.7
4	Iowa	36.5
5	Maine	36.0
6	Tennessee	34.1
7	Oregon	34.0
8	Kansas	33.2
9	Alabama	32.9
10	Louisiana	31.1
11	South Carolina	30.9
12	Arizona	30.8
13	Ohio	30.3
14	Vermont	29.5
15	New Hampshire	28.7
16	Idaho	28.5
16	Montana	28.5
16	Oklahoma	28.5
19	Missouri	28.2
20	North Carolina	27.8
21	Rhode Island	27.7
21	West Virginia	27.7
23	Pennsylvania	27.6
24	Kentucky	27.5
25	Wisconsin	27.3
26	Nebraska	26.9
27	Indiana	26.3
28	Florida	25.9
29	Minnesota	25.7
30	Massachusetts	25.6
31	Arkansas	24.7
31	Mississippi	24.7
33	Michigan	23.3
34	Colorado	22.8
35	Connecticut	22.1
35	Illinois	22.1
37	Wyoming	21.6
38	California	21.3
38	Delaware	21.3
40	New Jersey	20.8
41	Virginia	20.5
42	Texas	20.2
43	Georgia	19.2
44	Maryland	17.1
45	New Mexico	17.0
46	Hawaii	15.1
47	Utah	14.9
48	Nevada	12.8
49	New York	10.7
50	Alaska	9.2

District of Columbia	20.3

Source: U.S. Department of Health and Human Services, National Center for Health Statistics
    "National Vital Statistics Reports" (Vol. 56, No. 10, April 24, 2008, http://www.cdc.gov/nchs/deaths.htm)
*Final data by state of residence. A degenerative disease of the brain cells producing loss of memory and general intellectual impairment. It usually affects people over age 65. As the disease progresses, a variety of symptoms may become apparent, including confusion, irritability, and restlessness, as well as disorientation and impaired judgment and concentration. Not age-adjusted.

Age-Adjusted Death Rate by Alzheimer's Disease in 2005

National Rate = 22.9 Deaths per 100,000 Population*

ALPHA ORDER

RANK	STATE	RATE
4	Alabama	33.2
36	Alaska	21.3
6	Arizona	31.3
30	Arkansas	22.6
27	California	23.2
13	Colorado	28.5
48	Connecticut	16.1
39	Delaware	20.0
43	Florida	18.4
18	Georgia	27.0
49	Hawaii	11.4
9	Idaho	29.4
38	Illinois	20.8
25	Indiana	24.7
23	Iowa	25.4
16	Kansas	27.2
11	Kentucky	28.9
3	Louisiana	34.2
10	Maine	29.1
46	Maryland	17.5
40	Massachusetts	19.8
37	Michigan	21.2
31	Minnesota	22.5
19	Mississippi	26.7
23	Missouri	25.4
26	Montana	23.9
34	Nebraska	21.8
47	Nevada	17.1
20	New Hampshire	26.1
45	New Jersey	17.6
44	New Mexico	18.3
50	New York	9.2
8	North Carolina	29.5
7	North Dakota	29.8
21	Ohio	26.0
14	Oklahoma	28.1
11	Oregon	28.9
41	Pennsylvania	18.9
42	Rhode Island	18.8
5	South Carolina	32.4
15	South Dakota	27.3
1	Tennessee	36.2
16	Texas	27.2
35	Utah	21.5
22	Vermont	25.7
31	Virginia	22.5
2	Washington	35.9
27	West Virginia	23.2
33	Wisconsin	22.4
29	Wyoming	22.7

RANK ORDER

RANK	STATE	RATE
1	Tennessee	36.2
2	Washington	35.9
3	Louisiana	34.2
4	Alabama	33.2
5	South Carolina	32.4
6	Arizona	31.3
7	North Dakota	29.8
8	North Carolina	29.5
9	Idaho	29.4
10	Maine	29.1
11	Kentucky	28.9
11	Oregon	28.9
13	Colorado	28.5
14	Oklahoma	28.1
15	South Dakota	27.3
16	Kansas	27.2
16	Texas	27.2
18	Georgia	27.0
19	Mississippi	26.7
20	New Hampshire	26.1
21	Ohio	26.0
22	Vermont	25.7
23	Iowa	25.4
23	Missouri	25.4
25	Indiana	24.7
26	Montana	23.9
27	California	23.2
27	West Virginia	23.2
29	Wyoming	22.7
30	Arkansas	22.6
31	Minnesota	22.5
31	Virginia	22.5
33	Wisconsin	22.4
34	Nebraska	21.8
35	Utah	21.5
36	Alaska	21.3
37	Michigan	21.2
38	Illinois	20.8
39	Delaware	20.0
40	Massachusetts	19.8
41	Pennsylvania	18.9
42	Rhode Island	18.8
43	Florida	18.4
44	New Mexico	18.3
45	New Jersey	17.6
46	Maryland	17.5
47	Nevada	17.1
48	Connecticut	16.1
49	Hawaii	11.4
50	New York	9.2

| | District of Columbia | 19.1 |

Source: U.S. Department of Health and Human Services, National Center for Health Statistics
   "National Vital Statistics Reports" (Vol. 56, No. 10, April 24, 2008, http://www.cdc.gov/nchs/deaths.htm)
*Final data by state of residence. A degenerative disease of the brain cells producing loss of memory and general intellectual impairment. It usually affects people over age 65. As the disease progresses, a variety of symptoms may become apparent, including confusion, irritability, and restlessness, as well as disorientation and impaired judgment and concentration. Age-adjusted rates based on the year 2000 standard population.

Deaths by Cerebrovascular Diseases in 2005

National Total = 143,579 Deaths*

ALPHA ORDER

RANK	STATE	DEATHS	% of USA
18	Alabama	2,952	2.1%
50	Alaska	178	0.1%
24	Arizona	2,364	1.6%
29	Arkansas	1,847	1.3%
1	California	15,585	10.9%
31	Colorado	1,599	1.1%
33	Connecticut	1,528	1.1%
46	Delaware	384	0.3%
3	Florida	9,361	6.5%
10	Georgia	3,854	2.7%
41	Hawaii	688	0.5%
39	Idaho	718	0.5%
7	Illinois	6,252	4.4%
15	Indiana	3,296	2.3%
28	Iowa	1,902	1.3%
32	Kansas	1,571	1.1%
27	Kentucky	2,168	1.5%
21	Louisiana	2,469	1.7%
40	Maine	693	0.5%
20	Maryland	2,476	1.7%
16	Massachusetts	2,977	2.1%
8	Michigan	5,057	3.5%
23	Minnesota	2,379	1.7%
30	Mississippi	1,622	1.1%
14	Missouri	3,347	2.3%
43	Montana	522	0.4%
35	Nebraska	986	0.7%
36	Nevada	945	0.7%
45	New Hampshire	497	0.3%
13	New Jersey	3,614	2.5%
38	New Mexico	730	0.5%
5	New York	6,622	4.6%
9	North Carolina	4,861	3.4%
47	North Dakota	368	0.3%
6	Ohio	6,279	4.4%
26	Oklahoma	2,235	1.6%
25	Oregon	2,289	1.6%
4	Pennsylvania	7,650	5.3%
42	Rhode Island	533	0.4%
22	South Carolina	2,458	1.7%
44	South Dakota	511	0.4%
12	Tennessee	3,659	2.5%
2	Texas	9,366	6.5%
37	Utah	794	0.6%
48	Vermont	260	0.2%
11	Virginia	3,675	2.6%
19	Washington	2,895	2.0%
34	West Virginia	1,151	0.8%
17	Wisconsin	2,960	2.1%
49	Wyoming	221	0.2%

RANK ORDER

RANK	STATE	DEATHS	% of USA
1	California	15,585	10.9%
2	Texas	9,366	6.5%
3	Florida	9,361	6.5%
4	Pennsylvania	7,650	5.3%
5	New York	6,622	4.6%
6	Ohio	6,279	4.4%
7	Illinois	6,252	4.4%
8	Michigan	5,057	3.5%
9	North Carolina	4,861	3.4%
10	Georgia	3,854	2.7%
11	Virginia	3,675	2.6%
12	Tennessee	3,659	2.5%
13	New Jersey	3,614	2.5%
14	Missouri	3,347	2.3%
15	Indiana	3,296	2.3%
16	Massachusetts	2,977	2.1%
17	Wisconsin	2,960	2.1%
18	Alabama	2,952	2.1%
19	Washington	2,895	2.0%
20	Maryland	2,476	1.7%
21	Louisiana	2,469	1.7%
22	South Carolina	2,458	1.7%
23	Minnesota	2,379	1.7%
24	Arizona	2,364	1.6%
25	Oregon	2,289	1.6%
26	Oklahoma	2,235	1.6%
27	Kentucky	2,168	1.5%
28	Iowa	1,902	1.3%
29	Arkansas	1,847	1.3%
30	Mississippi	1,622	1.1%
31	Colorado	1,599	1.1%
32	Kansas	1,571	1.1%
33	Connecticut	1,528	1.1%
34	West Virginia	1,151	0.8%
35	Nebraska	986	0.7%
36	Nevada	945	0.7%
37	Utah	794	0.6%
38	New Mexico	730	0.5%
39	Idaho	718	0.5%
40	Maine	693	0.5%
41	Hawaii	688	0.5%
42	Rhode Island	533	0.4%
43	Montana	522	0.4%
44	South Dakota	511	0.4%
45	New Hampshire	497	0.3%
46	Delaware	384	0.3%
47	North Dakota	368	0.3%
48	Vermont	260	0.2%
49	Wyoming	221	0.2%
50	Alaska	178	0.1%
	District of Columbia	231	0.2%

Source: U.S. Department of Health and Human Services, National Center for Health Statistics
   "National Vital Statistics Reports" (Vol. 56, No. 10, April 24, 2008, http://www.cdc.gov/nchs/deaths.htm)
*Final data by state of residence. Cerebrovascular diseases include stroke and other disorders of the blood vessels of the brain.

Death Rate by Cerebrovascular Diseases in 2005

National Rate = 48.4 Deaths per 100,000 Population*

ALPHA ORDER

RANK	STATE	RATE
3	Alabama	64.8
50	Alaska	26.8
43	Arizona	39.8
1	Arkansas	66.5
38	California	43.1
48	Colorado	34.3
36	Connecticut	43.5
34	Delaware	45.5
22	Florida	52.6
39	Georgia	42.5
20	Hawaii	54.0
26	Idaho	50.2
29	Illinois	49.0
22	Indiana	52.6
4	Iowa	64.1
13	Kansas	57.2
25	Kentucky	51.9
19	Louisiana	54.6
24	Maine	52.4
35	Maryland	44.2
31	Massachusetts	46.5
27	Michigan	50.0
32	Minnesota	46.3
17	Mississippi	55.5
12	Missouri	57.7
16	Montana	55.8
14	Nebraska	56.1
44	Nevada	39.1
45	New Hampshire	37.9
41	New Jersey	41.5
45	New Mexico	37.9
47	New York	34.4
15	North Carolina	56.0
10	North Dakota	57.8
18	Ohio	54.8
6	Oklahoma	63.0
7	Oregon	62.9
8	Pennsylvania	61.5
28	Rhode Island	49.5
10	South Carolina	57.8
2	South Dakota	65.9
9	Tennessee	61.4
42	Texas	41.0
49	Utah	32.2
40	Vermont	41.7
30	Virginia	48.6
33	Washington	46.0
5	West Virginia	63.4
21	Wisconsin	53.5
37	Wyoming	43.4

RANK ORDER

RANK	STATE	RATE
1	Arkansas	66.5
2	South Dakota	65.9
3	Alabama	64.8
4	Iowa	64.1
5	West Virginia	63.4
6	Oklahoma	63.0
7	Oregon	62.9
8	Pennsylvania	61.5
9	Tennessee	61.4
10	North Dakota	57.8
10	South Carolina	57.8
12	Missouri	57.7
13	Kansas	57.2
14	Nebraska	56.1
15	North Carolina	56.0
16	Montana	55.8
17	Mississippi	55.5
18	Ohio	54.8
19	Louisiana	54.6
20	Hawaii	54.0
21	Wisconsin	53.5
22	Florida	52.6
22	Indiana	52.6
24	Maine	52.4
25	Kentucky	51.9
26	Idaho	50.2
27	Michigan	50.0
28	Rhode Island	49.5
29	Illinois	49.0
30	Virginia	48.6
31	Massachusetts	46.5
32	Minnesota	46.3
33	Washington	46.0
34	Delaware	45.5
35	Maryland	44.2
36	Connecticut	43.5
37	Wyoming	43.4
38	California	43.1
39	Georgia	42.5
40	Vermont	41.7
41	New Jersey	41.5
42	Texas	41.0
43	Arizona	39.8
44	Nevada	39.1
45	New Hampshire	37.9
45	New Mexico	37.9
47	New York	34.4
48	Colorado	34.3
49	Utah	32.2
50	Alaska	26.8

District of Columbia   42.0

Source: U.S. Department of Health and Human Services, National Center for Health Statistics
   "National Vital Statistics Reports" (Vol. 56, No. 10, April 24, 2008, http://www.cdc.gov/nchs/deaths.htm)
*Final data by state of residence. Cerebrovascular diseases include stroke and other disorders of the blood vessels of the brain.
Not age-adjusted.

Age-Adjusted Death Rate by Cerebrovascular Diseases in 2005

National Rate = 46.6 Deaths per 100,000 Population*

ALPHA ORDER

RANK	STATE	RATE
1	Alabama	63.1
11	Alaska	53.2
41	Arizona	40.1
3	Arkansas	61.0
26	California	47.4
39	Colorado	41.7
49	Connecticut	34.7
37	Delaware	42.5
43	Florida	39.2
10	Georgia	55.2
35	Hawaii	44.1
15	Idaho	52.2
25	Illinois	47.5
19	Indiana	50.4
22	Iowa	47.7
20	Kansas	49.4
12	Kentucky	52.8
8	Louisiana	57.6
36	Maine	42.8
33	Maryland	45.1
44	Massachusetts	38.1
28	Michigan	46.5
38	Minnesota	42.2
6	Mississippi	58.0
13	Missouri	52.6
22	Montana	47.7
22	Nebraska	47.7
27	Nevada	46.8
48	New Hampshire	35.5
46	New Jersey	36.7
42	New Mexico	39.6
50	New York	30.6
6	North Carolina	58.0
40	North Dakota	41.5
21	Ohio	48.3
3	Oklahoma	61.0
9	Oregon	55.5
31	Pennsylvania	45.5
45	Rhode Island	37.4
5	South Carolina	58.5
18	South Dakota	51.4
2	Tennessee	63.0
16	Texas	52.1
32	Utah	45.4
47	Vermont	36.5
16	Virginia	52.1
29	Washington	46.3
13	West Virginia	52.6
30	Wisconsin	46.1
34	Wyoming	44.8

RANK ORDER

RANK	STATE	RATE
1	Alabama	63.1
2	Tennessee	63.0
3	Arkansas	61.0
3	Oklahoma	61.0
5	South Carolina	58.5
6	Mississippi	58.0
6	North Carolina	58.0
8	Louisiana	57.6
9	Oregon	55.5
10	Georgia	55.2
11	Alaska	53.2
12	Kentucky	52.8
13	Missouri	52.6
13	West Virginia	52.6
15	Idaho	52.2
16	Texas	52.1
16	Virginia	52.1
18	South Dakota	51.4
19	Indiana	50.4
20	Kansas	49.4
21	Ohio	48.3
22	Iowa	47.7
22	Montana	47.7
22	Nebraska	47.7
25	Illinois	47.5
26	California	47.4
27	Nevada	46.8
28	Michigan	46.5
29	Washington	46.3
30	Wisconsin	46.1
31	Pennsylvania	45.5
32	Utah	45.4
33	Maryland	45.1
34	Wyoming	44.8
35	Hawaii	44.1
36	Maine	42.8
37	Delaware	42.5
38	Minnesota	42.2
39	Colorado	41.7
40	North Dakota	41.5
41	Arizona	40.1
42	New Mexico	39.6
43	Florida	39.2
44	Massachusetts	38.1
45	Rhode Island	37.4
46	New Jersey	36.7
47	Vermont	36.5
48	New Hampshire	35.5
49	Connecticut	34.7
50	New York	30.6
	District of Columbia	40.9

Source: U.S. Department of Health and Human Services, National Center for Health Statistics
   "National Vital Statistics Reports" (Vol. 56, No. 10, April 24, 2008, http://www.cdc.gov/nchs/deaths.htm)
*Final data by state of residence. Cerebrovascular diseases include stroke and other disorders of the blood vessels of the brain.
Age-adjusted rates based on the year 2000 standard population.

Deaths by Chronic Liver Disease and Cirrhosis in 2005

National Total = 27,530 Deaths*

ALPHA ORDER

RANK	STATE	DEATHS	% of USA
19	Alabama	478	1.7%
49	Alaska	52	0.2%
10	Arizona	757	2.7%
33	Arkansas	228	0.8%
1	California	3,822	13.9%
22	Colorado	436	1.6%
30	Connecticut	283	1.0%
47	Delaware	67	0.2%
3	Florida	2,139	7.8%
12	Georgia	689	2.5%
44	Hawaii	96	0.3%
39	Idaho	126	0.5%
8	Illinois	1,002	3.6%
17	Indiana	496	1.8%
34	Iowa	215	0.8%
36	Kansas	200	0.7%
26	Kentucky	380	1.4%
26	Louisiana	380	1.4%
41	Maine	116	0.4%
21	Maryland	459	1.7%
16	Massachusetts	505	1.8%
7	Michigan	1,010	3.7%
28	Minnesota	317	1.2%
32	Mississippi	272	1.0%
24	Missouri	419	1.5%
40	Montana	120	0.4%
37	Nebraska	133	0.5%
31	Nevada	275	1.0%
42	New Hampshire	114	0.4%
11	New Jersey	730	2.7%
29	New Mexico	285	1.0%
4	New York	1,224	4.4%
9	North Carolina	782	2.8%
46	North Dakota	68	0.2%
5	Ohio	1,105	4.0%
23	Oklahoma	428	1.6%
25	Oregon	394	1.4%
6	Pennsylvania	1,058	3.8%
43	Rhode Island	107	0.4%
18	South Carolina	480	1.7%
45	South Dakota	83	0.3%
13	Tennessee	631	2.3%
2	Texas	2,459	8.9%
38	Utah	127	0.5%
50	Vermont	48	0.2%
14	Virginia	570	2.1%
15	Washington	558	2.0%
35	West Virginia	213	0.8%
20	Wisconsin	467	1.7%
48	Wyoming	60	0.2%

RANK ORDER

RANK	STATE	DEATHS	% of USA
1	California	3,822	13.9%
2	Texas	2,459	8.9%
3	Florida	2,139	7.8%
4	New York	1,224	4.4%
5	Ohio	1,105	4.0%
6	Pennsylvania	1,058	3.8%
7	Michigan	1,010	3.7%
8	Illinois	1,002	3.6%
9	North Carolina	782	2.8%
10	Arizona	757	2.7%
11	New Jersey	730	2.7%
12	Georgia	689	2.5%
13	Tennessee	631	2.3%
14	Virginia	570	2.1%
15	Washington	558	2.0%
16	Massachusetts	505	1.8%
17	Indiana	496	1.8%
18	South Carolina	480	1.7%
19	Alabama	478	1.7%
20	Wisconsin	467	1.7%
21	Maryland	459	1.7%
22	Colorado	436	1.6%
23	Oklahoma	428	1.6%
24	Missouri	419	1.5%
25	Oregon	394	1.4%
26	Kentucky	380	1.4%
26	Louisiana	380	1.4%
28	Minnesota	317	1.2%
29	New Mexico	285	1.0%
30	Connecticut	283	1.0%
31	Nevada	275	1.0%
32	Mississippi	272	1.0%
33	Arkansas	228	0.8%
34	Iowa	215	0.8%
35	West Virginia	213	0.8%
36	Kansas	200	0.7%
37	Nebraska	133	0.5%
38	Utah	127	0.5%
39	Idaho	126	0.5%
40	Montana	120	0.4%
41	Maine	116	0.4%
42	New Hampshire	114	0.4%
43	Rhode Island	107	0.4%
44	Hawaii	96	0.3%
45	South Dakota	83	0.3%
46	North Dakota	68	0.2%
47	Delaware	67	0.2%
48	Wyoming	60	0.2%
49	Alaska	52	0.2%
50	Vermont	48	0.2%
	District of Columbia	67	0.2%

Source: U.S. Department of Health and Human Services, National Center for Health Statistics
   "National Vital Statistics Reports" (Vol. 56, No. 10, April 24, 2008, http://www.cdc.gov/nchs/deaths.htm)
*Final data by state of residence. Cirrhosis of the liver is characterized by the replacement of normal tissue with fibrous tissue and the loss of functional liver cells. It can result from alcohol abuse, nutritional deprivation, or infection especially by the hepatitis virus.

Death Rate by Chronic Liver Disease and Cirrhosis in 2005

National Rate = 9.3 Deaths per 100,000 Population*

ALPHA ORDER

RANK	STATE	RATE
16	Alabama	10.5
39	Alaska	7.8
3	Arizona	12.7
32	Arkansas	8.2
14	California	10.6
20	Colorado	9.3
34	Connecticut	8.1
35	Delaware	7.9
5	Florida	12.0
41	Georgia	7.6
43	Hawaii	7.5
25	Idaho	8.8
35	Illinois	7.9
35	Indiana	7.9
46	Iowa	7.2
45	Kansas	7.3
22	Kentucky	9.1
29	Louisiana	8.4
25	Maine	8.8
32	Maryland	8.2
35	Massachusetts	7.9
17	Michigan	10.0
49	Minnesota	6.2
20	Mississippi	9.3
46	Missouri	7.2
2	Montana	12.8
41	Nebraska	7.6
8	Nevada	11.4
27	New Hampshire	8.7
29	New Jersey	8.4
1	New Mexico	14.8
48	New York	6.4
23	North Carolina	9.0
12	North Dakota	10.7
19	Ohio	9.6
4	Oklahoma	12.1
10	Oregon	10.8
28	Pennsylvania	8.5
18	Rhode Island	9.9
9	South Carolina	11.3
12	South Dakota	10.7
14	Tennessee	10.6
10	Texas	10.8
50	Utah	5.1
40	Vermont	7.7
43	Virginia	7.5
24	Washington	8.9
7	West Virginia	11.7
29	Wisconsin	8.4
6	Wyoming	11.8

RANK ORDER

RANK	STATE	RATE
1	New Mexico	14.8
2	Montana	12.8
3	Arizona	12.7
4	Oklahoma	12.1
5	Florida	12.0
6	Wyoming	11.8
7	West Virginia	11.7
8	Nevada	11.4
9	South Carolina	11.3
10	Oregon	10.8
10	Texas	10.8
12	North Dakota	10.7
12	South Dakota	10.7
14	California	10.6
14	Tennessee	10.6
16	Alabama	10.5
17	Michigan	10.0
18	Rhode Island	9.9
19	Ohio	9.6
20	Colorado	9.3
20	Mississippi	9.3
22	Kentucky	9.1
23	North Carolina	9.0
24	Washington	8.9
25	Idaho	8.8
25	Maine	8.8
27	New Hampshire	8.7
28	Pennsylvania	8.5
29	Louisiana	8.4
29	New Jersey	8.4
29	Wisconsin	8.4
32	Arkansas	8.2
32	Maryland	8.2
34	Connecticut	8.1
35	Delaware	7.9
35	Illinois	7.9
35	Indiana	7.9
35	Massachusetts	7.9
39	Alaska	7.8
40	Vermont	7.7
41	Georgia	7.6
41	Nebraska	7.6
43	Hawaii	7.5
43	Virginia	7.5
45	Kansas	7.3
46	Iowa	7.2
46	Missouri	7.2
48	New York	6.4
49	Minnesota	6.2
50	Utah	5.1

| | District of Columbia | 12.2 |

Source: U.S. Department of Health and Human Services, National Center for Health Statistics
"National Vital Statistics Reports" (Vol. 56, No. 10, April 24, 2008, http://www.cdc.gov/nchs/deaths.htm)
*Final data by state of residence. Cirrhosis of the liver is characterized by the replacement of normal tissue with fibrous tissue and the loss of functional liver cells. It can result from alcohol abuse, nutritional deprivation, or infection especially by the hepatitis virus. Not age-adjusted.

Age-Adjusted Death Rate by Chronic Liver Disease and Cirrhosis in 2005

National Rate = 9.0 Deaths per 100,000 Population*

ALPHA ORDER				RANK ORDER		
RANK	STATE	RATE		RANK	STATE	RATE
15	Alabama	9.7		1	New Mexico	14.4
20	Alaska	9.0		2	Arizona	12.8
2	Arizona	12.8		3	Texas	11.7
35	Arkansas	7.5		4	Montana	11.5
7	California	11.0		5	Nevada	11.4
15	Colorado	9.7		6	Oklahoma	11.3
41	Connecticut	7.2		7	California	11.0
36	Delaware	7.3		8	South Carolina	10.6
10	Florida	10.2		9	Wyoming	10.5
27	Georgia	8.3		10	Florida	10.2
44	Hawaii	6.7		10	South Dakota	10.2
22	Idaho	8.8		12	Oregon	10.1
31	Illinois	7.8		13	Tennessee	9.9
34	Indiana	7.7		14	West Virginia	9.8
48	Iowa	6.5		15	Alabama	9.7
43	Kansas	7.0		15	Colorado	9.7
26	Kentucky	8.5		17	North Dakota	9.6
27	Louisiana	8.3		18	Michigan	9.5
42	Maine	7.1		19	Mississippi	9.2
30	Maryland	7.9		20	Alaska	9.0
36	Massachusetts	7.3		20	Rhode Island	9.0
18	Michigan	9.5		22	Idaho	8.8
49	Minnesota	6.0		22	North Carolina	8.8
19	Mississippi	9.2		22	Ohio	8.8
44	Missouri	6.7		25	Washington	8.6
4	Montana	11.5		26	Kentucky	8.5
36	Nebraska	7.3		27	Georgia	8.3
5	Nevada	11.4		27	Louisiana	8.3
29	New Hampshire	8.0		29	New Hampshire	8.0
31	New Jersey	7.8		30	Maryland	7.9
1	New Mexico	14.4		31	Illinois	7.8
50	New York	5.9		31	New Jersey	7.8
22	North Carolina	8.8		31	Wisconsin	7.8
17	North Dakota	9.6		34	Indiana	7.7
22	Ohio	8.8		35	Arkansas	7.5
6	Oklahoma	11.3		36	Delaware	7.3
12	Oregon	10.1		36	Massachusetts	7.3
36	Pennsylvania	7.3		36	Nebraska	7.3
20	Rhode Island	9.0		36	Pennsylvania	7.3
8	South Carolina	10.6		36	Virginia	7.3
10	South Dakota	10.2		41	Connecticut	7.2
13	Tennessee	9.9		42	Maine	7.1
3	Texas	11.7		43	Kansas	7.0
44	Utah	6.7		44	Hawaii	6.7
44	Vermont	6.7		44	Missouri	6.7
36	Virginia	7.3		44	Utah	6.7
25	Washington	8.6		44	Vermont	6.7
14	West Virginia	9.8		48	Iowa	6.5
31	Wisconsin	7.8		49	Minnesota	6.0
9	Wyoming	10.5		50	New York	5.9
					District of Columbia	11.9

Source: U.S. Department of Health and Human Services, National Center for Health Statistics
"National Vital Statistics Reports" (Vol. 56, No. 10, April 24, 2008, http://www.cdc.gov/nchs/deaths.htm)
*Final data by state of residence. Cirrhosis of the liver is characterized by the replacement of normal tissue with fibrous tissue and the loss of functional liver cells. It can result from alcohol abuse, nutritional deprivation, or infection especially by the hepatitis virus. Age-adjusted rates based on the year 2000 standard population.

Deaths by Chronic Lower Respiratory Diseases in 2005

National Total = 130,933 Deaths*

ALPHA ORDER					RANK ORDER			

RANK	STATE	DEATHS	% of USA		RANK	STATE	DEATHS	% of USA
21	Alabama	2,382	1.8%		1	California	13,188	10.1%
50	Alaska	158	0.1%		2	Florida	9,482	7.2%
16	Arizona	2,821	2.2%		3	Texas	7,988	6.1%
31	Arkansas	1,559	1.2%		4	New York	6,818	5.2%
1	California	13,188	10.1%		5	Ohio	6,580	5.0%
25	Colorado	1,914	1.5%		6	Pennsylvania	6,149	4.7%
33	Connecticut	1,471	1.1%		7	Illinois	5,067	3.9%
45	Delaware	411	0.3%		8	Michigan	4,466	3.4%
2	Florida	9,482	7.2%		9	North Carolina	4,149	3.2%
11	Georgia	3,411	2.6%		10	Indiana	3,471	2.7%
48	Hawaii	287	0.2%		11	Georgia	3,411	2.6%
39	Idaho	717	0.5%		12	Tennessee	3,185	2.4%
7	Illinois	5,067	3.9%		13	New Jersey	3,148	2.4%
10	Indiana	3,471	2.7%		14	Missouri	3,085	2.4%
29	Iowa	1,703	1.3%		15	Virginia	2,897	2.2%
30	Kansas	1,567	1.2%		16	Arizona	2,821	2.2%
19	Kentucky	2,578	2.0%		17	Washington	2,699	2.1%
27	Louisiana	1,906	1.5%		18	Massachusetts	2,647	2.0%
38	Maine	830	0.6%		19	Kentucky	2,578	2.0%
26	Maryland	1,908	1.5%		20	Wisconsin	2,449	1.9%
18	Massachusetts	2,647	2.0%		21	Alabama	2,382	1.8%
8	Michigan	4,466	3.4%		22	Oklahoma	2,368	1.8%
24	Minnesota	1,965	1.5%		23	South Carolina	1,977	1.5%
32	Mississippi	1,473	1.1%		24	Minnesota	1,965	1.5%
14	Missouri	3,085	2.4%		25	Colorado	1,914	1.5%
42	Montana	580	0.4%		26	Maryland	1,908	1.5%
36	Nebraska	949	0.7%		27	Louisiana	1,906	1.5%
35	Nevada	1,227	0.9%		28	Oregon	1,837	1.4%
40	New Hampshire	630	0.5%		29	Iowa	1,703	1.3%
13	New Jersey	3,148	2.4%		30	Kansas	1,567	1.2%
37	New Mexico	855	0.7%		31	Arkansas	1,559	1.2%
4	New York	6,818	5.2%		32	Mississippi	1,473	1.1%
9	North Carolina	4,149	3.2%		33	Connecticut	1,471	1.1%
49	North Dakota	272	0.2%		34	West Virginia	1,350	1.0%
5	Ohio	6,580	5.0%		35	Nevada	1,227	0.9%
22	Oklahoma	2,368	1.8%		36	Nebraska	949	0.7%
28	Oregon	1,837	1.4%		37	New Mexico	855	0.7%
6	Pennsylvania	6,149	4.7%		38	Maine	830	0.6%
43	Rhode Island	523	0.4%		39	Idaho	717	0.5%
23	South Carolina	1,977	1.5%		40	New Hampshire	630	0.5%
44	South Dakota	440	0.3%		41	Utah	592	0.5%
12	Tennessee	3,185	2.4%		42	Montana	580	0.4%
3	Texas	7,988	6.1%		43	Rhode Island	523	0.4%
41	Utah	592	0.5%		44	South Dakota	440	0.3%
46	Vermont	381	0.3%		45	Delaware	411	0.3%
15	Virginia	2,897	2.2%		46	Vermont	381	0.3%
17	Washington	2,699	2.1%		47	Wyoming	291	0.2%
34	West Virginia	1,350	1.0%		48	Hawaii	287	0.2%
20	Wisconsin	2,449	1.9%		49	North Dakota	272	0.2%
47	Wyoming	291	0.2%		50	Alaska	158	0.1%
						District of Columbia	132	0.1%

Source: U.S. Department of Health and Human Services, National Center for Health Statistics
"National Vital Statistics Reports" (Vol. 56, No. 10, April 24, 2008, http://www.cdc.gov/nchs/deaths.htm)
*Final data by state of residence. Chronic lower respiratory diseases are diseases of the lungs including bronchitis, emphysema, and asthma. Includes allied conditions.

Death Rate by Chronic Lower Respiratory Diseases in 2005

National Rate = 44.2 Deaths per 100,000 Population*

ALPHA ORDER

RANK	STATE	RATE
18	Alabama	52.3
49	Alaska	23.8
28	Arizona	47.5
12	Arkansas	56.1
43	California	36.5
38	Colorado	41.0
36	Connecticut	41.9
24	Delaware	48.7
16	Florida	53.3
42	Georgia	37.6
50	Hawaii	22.5
22	Idaho	50.2
39	Illinois	39.7
13	Indiana	55.3
7	Iowa	57.4
9	Kansas	57.1
5	Kentucky	61.8
35	Louisiana	42.1
3	Maine	62.8
47	Maryland	34.1
37	Massachusetts	41.4
32	Michigan	44.1
40	Minnesota	38.3
21	Mississippi	50.4
17	Missouri	53.2
4	Montana	62.0
14	Nebraska	54.0
19	Nevada	50.8
26	New Hampshire	48.1
44	New Jersey	36.1
30	New Mexico	44.3
45	New York	35.4
27	North Carolina	47.8
34	North Dakota	42.7
7	Ohio	57.4
2	Oklahoma	66.7
20	Oregon	50.5
23	Pennsylvania	49.5
25	Rhode Island	48.6
29	South Carolina	46.5
11	South Dakota	56.7
15	Tennessee	53.4
46	Texas	34.9
48	Utah	24.0
6	Vermont	61.2
40	Virginia	38.3
33	Washington	42.9
1	West Virginia	74.3
31	Wisconsin	44.2
9	Wyoming	57.1

RANK ORDER

RANK	STATE	RATE
1	West Virginia	74.3
2	Oklahoma	66.7
3	Maine	62.8
4	Montana	62.0
5	Kentucky	61.8
6	Vermont	61.2
7	Iowa	57.4
7	Ohio	57.4
9	Kansas	57.1
9	Wyoming	57.1
11	South Dakota	56.7
12	Arkansas	56.1
13	Indiana	55.3
14	Nebraska	54.0
15	Tennessee	53.4
16	Florida	53.3
17	Missouri	53.2
18	Alabama	52.3
19	Nevada	50.8
20	Oregon	50.5
21	Mississippi	50.4
22	Idaho	50.2
23	Pennsylvania	49.5
24	Delaware	48.7
25	Rhode Island	48.6
26	New Hampshire	48.1
27	North Carolina	47.8
28	Arizona	47.5
29	South Carolina	46.5
30	New Mexico	44.3
31	Wisconsin	44.2
32	Michigan	44.1
33	Washington	42.9
34	North Dakota	42.7
35	Louisiana	42.1
36	Connecticut	41.9
37	Massachusetts	41.4
38	Colorado	41.0
39	Illinois	39.7
40	Minnesota	38.3
40	Virginia	38.3
42	Georgia	37.6
43	California	36.5
44	New Jersey	36.1
45	New York	35.4
46	Texas	34.9
47	Maryland	34.1
48	Utah	24.0
49	Alaska	23.8
50	Hawaii	22.5

District of Columbia — 24.0

Source: U.S. Department of Health and Human Services, National Center for Health Statistics
"National Vital Statistics Reports" (Vol. 56, No. 10, April 24, 2008, http://www.cdc.gov/nchs/deaths.htm)
*Final data by state of residence. Chronic lower respiratory diseases are diseases of the lungs including bronchitis, emphysema, and asthma. Includes allied conditions. Not age-adjusted.

Age-Adjusted Death Rate by Chronic Lower Respiratory Diseases in 2005

National Rate = 43.2 Deaths per 100,000 Population*

ALPHA ORDER

RANK ORDER

RANK	STATE	RATE	RANK	STATE	RATE
17	Alabama	50.0	1	Oklahoma	63.5
34	Alaska	42.2	2	Kentucky	61.3
23	Arizona	47.4	3	West Virginia	60.5
15	Arkansas	51.2	4	Nevada	59.4
36	California	40.9	5	Wyoming	57.2
16	Colorado	50.3	6	Vermont	55.6
45	Connecticut	35.3	7	Montana	55.1
28	Delaware	46.1	8	Indiana	54.1
38	Florida	39.8	9	Idaho	53.9
20	Georgia	48.4	10	Tennessee	53.3
50	Hawaii	18.7	11	Kansas	52.4
9	Idaho	53.9	12	Maine	52.3
39	Illinois	39.7	13	Mississippi	51.9
8	Indiana	54.1	14	Ohio	51.7
25	Iowa	46.6	15	Arkansas	51.2
11	Kansas	52.4	16	Colorado	50.3
2	Kentucky	61.3	17	Alabama	50.0
31	Louisiana	44.5	18	Missouri	49.2
12	Maine	52.3	19	North Carolina	49.1
44	Maryland	35.4	20	Georgia	48.4
43	Massachusetts	35.8	21	Nebraska	48.3
33	Michigan	42.3	22	South Dakota	47.5
42	Minnesota	36.9	23	Arizona	47.4
13	Mississippi	51.9	24	Oregon	46.9
18	Missouri	49.2	25	Iowa	46.6
7	Montana	55.1	26	New Hampshire	46.2
21	Nebraska	48.3	26	South Carolina	46.2
4	Nevada	59.4	28	Delaware	46.1
26	New Hampshire	46.2	29	New Mexico	46.0
48	New Jersey	32.9	30	Washington	44.7
29	New Mexico	46.0	31	Louisiana	44.5
49	New York	32.4	32	Texas	43.9
19	North Carolina	49.1	33	Michigan	42.3
46	North Dakota	34.0	34	Alaska	42.2
14	Ohio	51.7	35	Virginia	41.2
1	Oklahoma	63.5	36	California	40.9
24	Oregon	46.9	37	Wisconsin	40.4
41	Pennsylvania	38.1	38	Florida	39.8
40	Rhode Island	39.0	39	Illinois	39.7
26	South Carolina	46.2	40	Rhode Island	39.0
22	South Dakota	47.5	41	Pennsylvania	38.1
10	Tennessee	53.3	42	Minnesota	36.9
32	Texas	43.9	43	Massachusetts	35.8
47	Utah	33.9	44	Maryland	35.4
6	Vermont	55.6	45	Connecticut	35.3
35	Virginia	41.2	46	North Dakota	34.0
30	Washington	44.7	47	Utah	33.9
3	West Virginia	60.5	48	New Jersey	32.9
37	Wisconsin	40.4	49	New York	32.4
5	Wyoming	57.2	50	Hawaii	18.7
				District of Columbia	23.9

Source: U.S. Department of Health and Human Services, National Center for Health Statistics
    "National Vital Statistics Reports" (Vol. 56, No. 10, April 24, 2008, http://www.cdc.gov/nchs/deaths.htm)
*Final data by state of residence. Chronic lower respiratory diseases are diseases of the lungs including bronchitis, emphysema,
and asthma. Includes allied conditions. Age-adjusted rates based on the year 2000 standard population.

Deaths by Diabetes Mellitus in 2005

National Total = 75,119 Deaths*

ALPHA ORDER

RANK	STATE	DEATHS	% of USA
18	Alabama	1,429	1.9%
50	Alaska	93	0.1%
24	Arizona	1,208	1.6%
28	Arkansas	824	1.1%
1	California	7,697	10.2%
31	Colorado	753	1.0%
29	Connecticut	811	1.1%
45	Delaware	233	0.3%
3	Florida	5,193	6.9%
12	Georgia	1,742	2.3%
46	Hawaii	218	0.3%
41	Idaho	299	0.4%
7	Illinois	3,034	4.0%
13	Indiana	1,719	2.3%
32	Iowa	727	1.0%
33	Kansas	710	0.9%
25	Kentucky	1,187	1.6%
14	Louisiana	1,695	2.3%
38	Maine	385	0.5%
19	Maryland	1,388	1.8%
21	Massachusetts	1,271	1.7%
8	Michigan	2,842	3.8%
22	Minnesota	1,258	1.7%
34	Mississippi	677	0.9%
17	Missouri	1,549	2.1%
42	Montana	285	0.4%
37	Nebraska	449	0.6%
39	Nevada	336	0.4%
40	New Hampshire	310	0.4%
9	New Jersey	2,540	3.4%
35	New Mexico	595	0.8%
4	New York	4,051	5.4%
10	North Carolina	2,261	3.0%
47	North Dakota	204	0.3%
5	Ohio	3,794	5.1%
23	Oklahoma	1,217	1.6%
27	Oregon	1,149	1.5%
6	Pennsylvania	3,553	4.7%
43	Rhode Island	282	0.4%
25	South Carolina	1,187	1.6%
44	South Dakota	241	0.3%
11	Tennessee	1,844	2.5%
2	Texas	5,605	7.5%
36	Utah	541	0.7%
48	Vermont	173	0.2%
15	Virginia	1,642	2.2%
16	Washington	1,554	2.1%
30	West Virginia	766	1.0%
20	Wisconsin	1,276	1.7%
49	Wyoming	130	0.2%

RANK ORDER

RANK	STATE	DEATHS	% of USA
1	California	7,697	10.2%
2	Texas	5,605	7.5%
3	Florida	5,193	6.9%
4	New York	4,051	5.4%
5	Ohio	3,794	5.1%
6	Pennsylvania	3,553	4.7%
7	Illinois	3,034	4.0%
8	Michigan	2,842	3.8%
9	New Jersey	2,540	3.4%
10	North Carolina	2,261	3.0%
11	Tennessee	1,844	2.5%
12	Georgia	1,742	2.3%
13	Indiana	1,719	2.3%
14	Louisiana	1,695	2.3%
15	Virginia	1,642	2.2%
16	Washington	1,554	2.1%
17	Missouri	1,549	2.1%
18	Alabama	1,429	1.9%
19	Maryland	1,388	1.8%
20	Wisconsin	1,276	1.7%
21	Massachusetts	1,271	1.7%
22	Minnesota	1,258	1.7%
23	Oklahoma	1,217	1.6%
24	Arizona	1,208	1.6%
25	Kentucky	1,187	1.6%
25	South Carolina	1,187	1.6%
27	Oregon	1,149	1.5%
28	Arkansas	824	1.1%
29	Connecticut	811	1.1%
30	West Virginia	766	1.0%
31	Colorado	753	1.0%
32	Iowa	727	1.0%
33	Kansas	710	0.9%
34	Mississippi	677	0.9%
35	New Mexico	595	0.8%
36	Utah	541	0.7%
37	Nebraska	449	0.6%
38	Maine	385	0.5%
39	Nevada	336	0.4%
40	New Hampshire	310	0.4%
41	Idaho	299	0.4%
42	Montana	285	0.4%
43	Rhode Island	282	0.4%
44	South Dakota	241	0.3%
45	Delaware	233	0.3%
46	Hawaii	218	0.3%
47	North Dakota	204	0.3%
48	Vermont	173	0.2%
49	Wyoming	130	0.2%
50	Alaska	93	0.1%
	District of Columbia	192	0.3%

Source: U.S. Department of Health and Human Services, National Center for Health Statistics
  "National Vital Statistics Reports" (Vol. 56, No. 10, April 24, 2008, http://www.cdc.gov/nchs/deaths.htm)
*Final data by state of residence. A severe, chronic form of diabetes caused by insufficient production of insulin and resulting in abnormal metabolism of carbohydrates, fats, and proteins. The disease, which typically appears in childhood or adolescence, is characterized by increased sugar levels in the blood and urine, excessive thirst, and frequent urination.

Death Rate by Diabetes Mellitus in 2005

National Rate = 25.3 Deaths per 100,000 Population*

ALPHA ORDER

RANK	STATE	RATE
7	Alabama	31.4
49	Alaska	14.0
44	Arizona	20.3
12	Arkansas	29.6
41	California	21.3
48	Colorado	16.1
37	Connecticut	23.1
21	Delaware	27.6
13	Florida	29.2
46	Georgia	19.2
47	Hawaii	17.1
43	Idaho	20.9
34	Illinois	23.8
22	Indiana	27.4
31	Iowa	24.5
26	Kansas	25.9
17	Kentucky	28.4
2	Louisiana	37.5
14	Maine	29.1
29	Maryland	24.8
45	Massachusetts	19.9
18	Michigan	28.1
31	Minnesota	24.5
36	Mississippi	23.2
23	Missouri	26.7
11	Montana	30.5
27	Nebraska	25.5
50	Nevada	13.9
35	New Hampshire	23.7
14	New Jersey	29.1
9	New Mexico	30.9
42	New York	21.0
25	North Carolina	26.0
5	North Dakota	32.0
4	Ohio	33.1
3	Oklahoma	34.3
6	Oregon	31.6
16	Pennsylvania	28.6
24	Rhode Island	26.2
19	South Carolina	27.9
8	South Dakota	31.1
9	Tennessee	30.9
31	Texas	24.5
39	Utah	21.9
20	Vermont	27.8
40	Virginia	21.7
30	Washington	24.7
1	West Virginia	42.2
38	Wisconsin	23.0
27	Wyoming	25.5

RANK ORDER

RANK	STATE	RATE
1	West Virginia	42.2
2	Louisiana	37.5
3	Oklahoma	34.3
4	Ohio	33.1
5	North Dakota	32.0
6	Oregon	31.6
7	Alabama	31.4
8	South Dakota	31.1
9	New Mexico	30.9
9	Tennessee	30.9
11	Montana	30.5
12	Arkansas	29.6
13	Florida	29.2
14	Maine	29.1
14	New Jersey	29.1
16	Pennsylvania	28.6
17	Kentucky	28.4
18	Michigan	28.1
19	South Carolina	27.9
20	Vermont	27.8
21	Delaware	27.6
22	Indiana	27.4
23	Missouri	26.7
24	Rhode Island	26.2
25	North Carolina	26.0
26	Kansas	25.9
27	Nebraska	25.5
27	Wyoming	25.5
29	Maryland	24.8
30	Washington	24.7
31	Iowa	24.5
31	Minnesota	24.5
31	Texas	24.5
34	Illinois	23.8
35	New Hampshire	23.7
36	Mississippi	23.2
37	Connecticut	23.1
38	Wisconsin	23.0
39	Utah	21.9
40	Virginia	21.7
41	California	21.3
42	New York	21.0
43	Idaho	20.9
44	Arizona	20.3
45	Massachusetts	19.9
46	Georgia	19.2
47	Hawaii	17.1
48	Colorado	16.1
49	Alaska	14.0
50	Nevada	13.9

District of Columbia	34.9

Source: U.S. Department of Health and Human Services, National Center for Health Statistics
"National Vital Statistics Reports" (Vol. 56, No. 10, April 24, 2008, http://www.cdc.gov/nchs/deaths.htm)
*Final data by state of residence. A severe, chronic form of diabetes caused by insufficient production of insulin and resulting in abnormal metabolism of carbohydrates, fats, and proteins. The disease, which typically appears in childhood or adolescence, is characterized by increased sugar levels in the blood and urine, excessive thirst, and frequent urination. Not age-adjusted.

Age-Adjusted Death Rate by Diabetes Mellitus in 2005

National Rate = 24.6 Deaths per 100,000 Population*

ALPHA ORDER

RANK	STATE	RATE
8	Alabama	29.8
39	Alaska	22.2
43	Arizona	20.2
13	Arkansas	27.1
30	California	23.5
47	Colorado	19.2
45	Connecticut	19.7
19	Delaware	25.9
35	Florida	22.6
32	Georgia	23.3
50	Hawaii	14.7
40	Idaho	22.1
28	Illinois	23.6
14	Indiana	26.7
44	Iowa	19.8
28	Kansas	23.6
11	Kentucky	27.9
1	Louisiana	38.7
27	Maine	24.2
23	Maryland	25.5
48	Massachusetts	17.4
14	Michigan	26.7
33	Minnesota	23.2
30	Mississippi	23.5
26	Missouri	24.7
17	Montana	26.5
33	Nebraska	23.2
49	Nevada	15.3
38	New Hampshire	22.5
14	New Jersey	26.7
4	New Mexico	31.2
46	New York	19.3
18	North Carolina	26.3
20	North Dakota	25.8
7	Ohio	30.0
3	Oklahoma	32.6
10	Oregon	29.0
35	Pennsylvania	22.6
41	Rhode Island	21.6
12	South Carolina	27.2
20	South Dakota	25.8
5	Tennessee	30.4
9	Texas	29.6
5	Utah	30.4
24	Vermont	25.1
35	Virginia	22.6
24	Washington	25.1
2	West Virginia	34.4
42	Wisconsin	20.8
22	Wyoming	25.7

RANK ORDER

RANK	STATE	RATE
1	Louisiana	38.7
2	West Virginia	34.4
3	Oklahoma	32.6
4	New Mexico	31.2
5	Tennessee	30.4
5	Utah	30.4
7	Ohio	30.0
8	Alabama	29.8
9	Texas	29.6
10	Oregon	29.0
11	Kentucky	27.9
12	South Carolina	27.2
13	Arkansas	27.1
14	Indiana	26.7
14	Michigan	26.7
14	New Jersey	26.7
17	Montana	26.5
18	North Carolina	26.3
19	Delaware	25.9
20	North Dakota	25.8
20	South Dakota	25.8
22	Wyoming	25.7
23	Maryland	25.5
24	Vermont	25.1
24	Washington	25.1
26	Missouri	24.7
27	Maine	24.2
28	Illinois	23.6
28	Kansas	23.6
30	California	23.5
30	Mississippi	23.5
32	Georgia	23.3
33	Minnesota	23.2
33	Nebraska	23.2
35	Florida	22.6
35	Pennsylvania	22.6
35	Virginia	22.6
38	New Hampshire	22.5
39	Alaska	22.2
40	Idaho	22.1
41	Rhode Island	21.6
42	Wisconsin	20.8
43	Arizona	20.2
44	Iowa	19.8
45	Connecticut	19.7
46	New York	19.3
47	Colorado	19.2
48	Massachusetts	17.4
49	Nevada	15.3
50	Hawaii	14.7

District of Columbia	34.6

Source: U.S. Department of Health and Human Services, National Center for Health Statistics
 "National Vital Statistics Reports" (Vol. 56, No. 10, April 24, 2008, http://www.cdc.gov/nchs/deaths.htm)
*Final data by state of residence. A severe, chronic form of diabetes caused by insufficient production of insulin and resulting in abnormal metabolism of carbohydrates, fats, and proteins. The disease, which typically appears in childhood or adolescence, is characterized by increased sugar levels in the blood and urine, excessive thirst, and frequent urination. Age-adjusted rates based on the year 2000 standard population.

Deaths by Diseases of the Heart in 2005

National Total = 652,091 Deaths*

ALPHA ORDER

RANK	STATE	DEATHS	% of USA
17	Alabama	12,869	2.0%
50	Alaska	627	0.1%
22	Arizona	10,966	1.7%
29	Arkansas	7,575	1.2%
1	California	64,916	10.0%
32	Colorado	6,307	1.0%
28	Connecticut	7,650	1.2%
44	Delaware	2,031	0.3%
3	Florida	46,279	7.1%
11	Georgia	16,781	2.6%
43	Hawaii	2,319	0.4%
42	Idaho	2,450	0.4%
7	Illinois	28,226	4.3%
14	Indiana	14,542	2.2%
30	Iowa	7,437	1.1%
33	Kansas	5,960	0.9%
23	Kentucky	10,782	1.7%
20	Louisiana	11,008	1.7%
39	Maine	2,941	0.5%
19	Maryland	11,594	1.8%
16	Massachusetts	13,280	2.0%
8	Michigan	25,128	3.9%
27	Minnesota	7,926	1.2%
26	Mississippi	8,637	1.3%
12	Missouri	14,974	2.3%
45	Montana	1,855	0.3%
36	Nebraska	3,640	0.6%
35	Nevada	5,094	0.8%
41	New Hampshire	2,530	0.4%
9	New Jersey	20,655	3.2%
37	New Mexico	3,435	0.5%
2	New York	51,985	8.0%
10	North Carolina	17,765	2.7%
47	North Dakota	1,512	0.2%
6	Ohio	29,003	4.4%
24	Oklahoma	10,043	1.5%
31	Oregon	6,791	1.0%
5	Pennsylvania	36,207	5.6%
38	Rhode Island	3,005	0.5%
25	South Carolina	9,359	1.4%
46	South Dakota	1,776	0.3%
13	Tennessee	14,946	2.3%
4	Texas	40,152	6.2%
40	Utah	2,872	0.4%
48	Vermont	1,234	0.2%
15	Virginia	14,192	2.2%
21	Washington	10,985	1.7%
34	West Virginia	5,538	0.8%
18	Wisconsin	11,842	1.8%
49	Wyoming	952	0.1%

RANK ORDER

RANK	STATE	DEATHS	% of USA
1	California	64,916	10.0%
2	New York	51,985	8.0%
3	Florida	46,279	7.1%
4	Texas	40,152	6.2%
5	Pennsylvania	36,207	5.6%
6	Ohio	29,003	4.4%
7	Illinois	28,226	4.3%
8	Michigan	25,128	3.9%
9	New Jersey	20,655	3.2%
10	North Carolina	17,765	2.7%
11	Georgia	16,781	2.6%
12	Missouri	14,974	2.3%
13	Tennessee	14,946	2.3%
14	Indiana	14,542	2.2%
15	Virginia	14,192	2.2%
16	Massachusetts	13,280	2.0%
17	Alabama	12,869	2.0%
18	Wisconsin	11,842	1.8%
19	Maryland	11,594	1.8%
20	Louisiana	11,008	1.7%
21	Washington	10,985	1.7%
22	Arizona	10,966	1.7%
23	Kentucky	10,782	1.7%
24	Oklahoma	10,043	1.5%
25	South Carolina	9,359	1.4%
26	Mississippi	8,637	1.3%
27	Minnesota	7,926	1.2%
28	Connecticut	7,650	1.2%
29	Arkansas	7,575	1.2%
30	Iowa	7,437	1.1%
31	Oregon	6,791	1.0%
32	Colorado	6,307	1.0%
33	Kansas	5,960	0.9%
34	West Virginia	5,538	0.8%
35	Nevada	5,094	0.8%
36	Nebraska	3,640	0.6%
37	New Mexico	3,435	0.5%
38	Rhode Island	3,005	0.5%
39	Maine	2,941	0.5%
40	Utah	2,872	0.4%
41	New Hampshire	2,530	0.4%
42	Idaho	2,450	0.4%
43	Hawaii	2,319	0.4%
44	Delaware	2,031	0.3%
45	Montana	1,855	0.3%
46	South Dakota	1,776	0.3%
47	North Dakota	1,512	0.2%
48	Vermont	1,234	0.2%
49	Wyoming	952	0.1%
50	Alaska	627	0.1%
	District of Columbia	1,518	0.2%

Source: U.S. Department of Health and Human Services, National Center for Health Statistics
"National Vital Statistics Reports" (Vol. 56, No. 10, April 24, 2008, http://www.cdc.gov/nchs/deaths.htm)
*Final data by state of residence.

Death Rate by Diseases of the Heart in 2005

National Rate = 220.0 Deaths per 100,000 Population*

ALPHA ORDER				RANK ORDER		
RANK	STATE	RATE		RANK	STATE	RATE
5	Alabama	282.4		1	West Virginia	304.8
50	Alaska	94.5		2	Mississippi	295.7
40	Arizona	184.6		3	Pennsylvania	291.3
7	Arkansas	272.6		4	Oklahoma	283.1
42	California	179.7		5	Alabama	282.4
48	Colorado	135.2		6	Rhode Island	279.2
25	Connecticut	217.9		7	Arkansas	272.6
17	Delaware	240.8		8	New York	270.0
9	Florida	260.1		9	Florida	260.1
39	Georgia	185.0		10	Kentucky	258.4
41	Hawaii	181.9		11	Missouri	258.2
46	Idaho	171.4		12	Ohio	253.0
23	Illinois	221.1		13	Iowa	250.7
20	Indiana	231.9		14	Tennessee	250.6
13	Iowa	250.7		15	Michigan	248.3
26	Kansas	217.1		16	Louisiana	243.3
10	Kentucky	258.4		17	Delaware	240.8
16	Louisiana	243.3		18	North Dakota	237.5
22	Maine	222.5		19	New Jersey	236.9
30	Maryland	207.0		20	Indiana	231.9
29	Massachusetts	207.5		21	South Dakota	228.9
15	Michigan	248.3		22	Maine	222.5
47	Minnesota	154.4		23	Illinois	221.1
2	Mississippi	295.7		24	South Carolina	219.9
11	Missouri	258.2		25	Connecticut	217.9
33	Montana	198.3		26	Kansas	217.1
30	Nebraska	207.0		27	Wisconsin	213.9
28	Nevada	210.9		28	Nevada	210.9
35	New Hampshire	193.1		29	Massachusetts	207.5
19	New Jersey	236.9		30	Maryland	207.0
43	New Mexico	178.1		30	Nebraska	207.0
8	New York	270.0		32	North Carolina	204.6
32	North Carolina	204.6		33	Montana	198.3
18	North Dakota	237.5		34	Vermont	198.1
12	Ohio	253.0		35	New Hampshire	193.1
4	Oklahoma	283.1		36	Virginia	187.5
38	Oregon	186.5		37	Wyoming	186.9
3	Pennsylvania	291.3		38	Oregon	186.5
6	Rhode Island	279.2		39	Georgia	185.0
24	South Carolina	219.9		40	Arizona	184.6
21	South Dakota	228.9		41	Hawaii	181.9
14	Tennessee	250.6		42	California	179.7
44	Texas	175.6		43	New Mexico	178.1
49	Utah	116.3		44	Texas	175.6
34	Vermont	198.1		45	Washington	174.7
36	Virginia	187.5		46	Idaho	171.4
45	Washington	174.7		47	Minnesota	154.4
1	West Virginia	304.8		48	Colorado	135.2
27	Wisconsin	213.9		49	Utah	116.3
37	Wyoming	186.9		50	Alaska	94.5
					District of Columbia	275.7

Source: U.S. Department of Health and Human Services, National Center for Health Statistics
   "National Vital Statistics Reports" (Vol. 56, No. 10, April 24, 2008, http://www.cdc.gov/nchs/deaths.htm)
*Final data by state of residence. Not age-adjusted.

Age-Adjusted Death Rate by Diseases of the Heart in 2005

National Rate = 211.1 Deaths per 100,000 Population*

ALPHA ORDER

RANK	STATE	RATE
2	Alabama	273.5
46	Alaska	162.6
32	Arizona	185.0
8	Arkansas	249.5
26	California	196.3
48	Colorado	162.0
42	Connecticut	172.9
14	Delaware	224.3
27	Florida	194.6
12	Georgia	234.8
49	Hawaii	152.0
37	Idaho	177.9
20	Illinois	214.3
16	Indiana	222.3
28	Iowa	191.4
29	Kansas	189.2
4	Kentucky	258.5
5	Louisiana	255.7
34	Maine	182.7
22	Maryland	210.3
43	Massachusetts	172.7
13	Michigan	231.4
50	Minnesota	141.5
1	Mississippi	306.8
11	Missouri	235.5
44	Montana	169.4
38	Nebraska	176.7
9	Nevada	242.1
36	New Hampshire	179.4
24	New Jersey	208.9
33	New Mexico	184.5
10	New York	239.6
23	North Carolina	209.6
39	North Dakota	175.3
14	Ohio	224.3
3	Oklahoma	272.6
45	Oregon	164.7
19	Pennsylvania	218.5
21	Rhode Island	213.8
18	South Carolina	218.9
35	South Dakota	182.1
6	Tennessee	252.1
17	Texas	219.5
46	Utah	162.6
41	Vermont	173.6
25	Virginia	198.0
40	Washington	174.3
7	West Virginia	251.8
31	Wisconsin	185.8
30	Wyoming	186.9

RANK ORDER

RANK	STATE	RATE
1	Mississippi	306.8
2	Alabama	273.5
3	Oklahoma	272.6
4	Kentucky	258.5
5	Louisiana	255.7
6	Tennessee	252.1
7	West Virginia	251.8
8	Arkansas	249.5
9	Nevada	242.1
10	New York	239.6
11	Missouri	235.5
12	Georgia	234.8
13	Michigan	231.4
14	Delaware	224.3
14	Ohio	224.3
16	Indiana	222.3
17	Texas	219.5
18	South Carolina	218.9
19	Pennsylvania	218.5
20	Illinois	214.3
21	Rhode Island	213.8
22	Maryland	210.3
23	North Carolina	209.6
24	New Jersey	208.9
25	Virginia	198.0
26	California	196.3
27	Florida	194.6
28	Iowa	191.4
29	Kansas	189.2
30	Wyoming	186.9
31	Wisconsin	185.8
32	Arizona	185.0
33	New Mexico	184.5
34	Maine	182.7
35	South Dakota	182.1
36	New Hampshire	179.4
37	Idaho	177.9
38	Nebraska	176.7
39	North Dakota	175.3
40	Washington	174.3
41	Vermont	173.6
42	Connecticut	172.9
43	Massachusetts	172.7
44	Montana	169.4
45	Oregon	164.7
46	Alaska	162.6
46	Utah	162.6
48	Colorado	162.0
49	Hawaii	152.0
50	Minnesota	141.5

District of Columbia	268.2

Source: U.S. Department of Health and Human Services, National Center for Health Statistics
"National Vital Statistics Reports" (Vol. 56, No. 10, April 24, 2008, http://www.cdc.gov/nchs/deaths.htm)
*Final data by state of residence. Age-adjusted rates based on the year 2000 standard population.

Deaths by Malignant Neoplasms in 2005

National Total = 559,312 Deaths*

ALPHA ORDER

RANK ORDER

RANK	STATE	DEATHS	% of USA
20	Alabama	9,913	1.8%
50	Alaska	732	0.1%
21	Arizona	9,820	1.8%
31	Arkansas	6,361	1.1%
1	California	54,732	9.8%
30	Colorado	6,395	1.1%
28	Connecticut	7,052	1.3%
45	Delaware	1,799	0.3%
2	Florida	40,592	7.3%
11	Georgia	14,358	2.6%
43	Hawaii	2,169	0.4%
41	Idaho	2,368	0.4%
7	Illinois	24,250	4.3%
15	Indiana	12,796	2.3%
29	Iowa	6,453	1.2%
33	Kansas	5,428	1.0%
22	Kentucky	9,505	1.7%
23	Louisiana	9,249	1.7%
37	Maine	3,218	0.6%
19	Maryland	10,371	1.9%
13	Massachusetts	13,182	2.4%
8	Michigan	20,094	3.6%
24	Minnesota	8,823	1.6%
32	Mississippi	6,065	1.1%
16	Missouri	12,419	2.2%
44	Montana	1,956	0.3%
36	Nebraska	3,355	0.6%
35	Nevada	4,238	0.8%
39	New Hampshire	2,549	0.5%
9	New Jersey	17,171	3.1%
38	New Mexico	3,141	0.6%
3	New York	35,556	6.4%
10	North Carolina	16,724	3.0%
47	North Dakota	1,302	0.2%
6	Ohio	24,702	4.4%
26	Oklahoma	7,446	1.3%
27	Oregon	7,326	1.3%
5	Pennsylvania	29,616	5.3%
42	Rhode Island	2,292	0.4%
25	South Carolina	8,652	1.5%
46	South Dakota	1,612	0.3%
14	Tennessee	12,995	2.3%
4	Texas	34,291	6.1%
40	Utah	2,520	0.5%
48	Vermont	1,202	0.2%
12	Virginia	13,877	2.5%
17	Washington	11,048	2.0%
34	West Virginia	4,617	0.8%
18	Wisconsin	10,943	2.0%
49	Wyoming	886	0.2%

RANK	STATE	DEATHS	% of USA
1	California	54,732	9.8%
2	Florida	40,592	7.3%
3	New York	35,556	6.4%
4	Texas	34,291	6.1%
5	Pennsylvania	29,616	5.3%
6	Ohio	24,702	4.4%
7	Illinois	24,250	4.3%
8	Michigan	20,094	3.6%
9	New Jersey	17,171	3.1%
10	North Carolina	16,724	3.0%
11	Georgia	14,358	2.6%
12	Virginia	13,877	2.5%
13	Massachusetts	13,182	2.4%
14	Tennessee	12,995	2.3%
15	Indiana	12,796	2.3%
16	Missouri	12,419	2.2%
17	Washington	11,048	2.0%
18	Wisconsin	10,943	2.0%
19	Maryland	10,371	1.9%
20	Alabama	9,913	1.8%
21	Arizona	9,820	1.8%
22	Kentucky	9,505	1.7%
23	Louisiana	9,249	1.7%
24	Minnesota	8,823	1.6%
25	South Carolina	8,652	1.5%
26	Oklahoma	7,446	1.3%
27	Oregon	7,326	1.3%
28	Connecticut	7,052	1.3%
29	Iowa	6,453	1.2%
30	Colorado	6,395	1.1%
31	Arkansas	6,361	1.1%
32	Mississippi	6,065	1.1%
33	Kansas	5,428	1.0%
34	West Virginia	4,617	0.8%
35	Nevada	4,238	0.8%
36	Nebraska	3,355	0.6%
37	Maine	3,218	0.6%
38	New Mexico	3,141	0.6%
39	New Hampshire	2,549	0.5%
40	Utah	2,520	0.5%
41	Idaho	2,368	0.4%
42	Rhode Island	2,292	0.4%
43	Hawaii	2,169	0.4%
44	Montana	1,956	0.3%
45	Delaware	1,799	0.3%
46	South Dakota	1,612	0.3%
47	North Dakota	1,302	0.2%
48	Vermont	1,202	0.2%
49	Wyoming	886	0.2%
50	Alaska	732	0.1%
	District of Columbia	1,151	0.2%

Source: U.S. Department of Health and Human Services, National Center for Health Statistics
"National Vital Statistics Reports" (Vol. 56, No. 10, April 24, 2008, http://www.cdc.gov/nchs/deaths.htm)
*Final data by state of residence. Neoplasms are abnormal tissue, tumors. Includes many cancers.

Death Rate by Malignant Neoplasms in 2005

National Rate = 188.7 Deaths per 100,000 Population*

ALPHA ORDER

RANK	STATE	RATE
8	Alabama	217.5
49	Alaska	110.3
43	Arizona	165.3
4	Arkansas	228.9
46	California	151.5
48	Colorado	137.1
24	Connecticut	200.9
12	Delaware	213.3
5	Florida	228.2
45	Georgia	158.3
41	Hawaii	170.1
42	Idaho	165.7
33	Illinois	190.0
21	Indiana	204.0
8	Iowa	217.5
26	Kansas	197.8
6	Kentucky	227.8
19	Louisiana	204.5
2	Maine	243.5
34	Maryland	185.2
18	Massachusetts	206.0
25	Michigan	198.5
40	Minnesota	171.9
17	Mississippi	207.6
11	Missouri	214.1
15	Montana	209.0
32	Nebraska	190.8
38	Nevada	175.5
29	New Hampshire	194.6
28	New Jersey	197.0
44	New Mexico	162.9
35	New York	184.7
31	North Carolina	192.6
19	North Dakota	204.5
10	Ohio	215.5
14	Oklahoma	209.9
23	Oregon	201.2
3	Pennsylvania	238.3
13	Rhode Island	213.0
22	South Carolina	203.3
16	South Dakota	207.7
7	Tennessee	217.9
47	Texas	150.0
50	Utah	102.0
30	Vermont	192.9
36	Virginia	183.4
37	Washington	175.7
1	West Virginia	254.1
27	Wisconsin	197.7
39	Wyoming	174.0

RANK ORDER

RANK	STATE	RATE
1	West Virginia	254.1
2	Maine	243.5
3	Pennsylvania	238.3
4	Arkansas	228.9
5	Florida	228.2
6	Kentucky	227.8
7	Tennessee	217.9
8	Alabama	217.5
8	Iowa	217.5
10	Ohio	215.5
11	Missouri	214.1
12	Delaware	213.3
13	Rhode Island	213.0
14	Oklahoma	209.9
15	Montana	209.0
16	South Dakota	207.7
17	Mississippi	207.6
18	Massachusetts	206.0
19	Louisiana	204.5
19	North Dakota	204.5
21	Indiana	204.0
22	South Carolina	203.3
23	Oregon	201.2
24	Connecticut	200.9
25	Michigan	198.5
26	Kansas	197.8
27	Wisconsin	197.7
28	New Jersey	197.0
29	New Hampshire	194.6
30	Vermont	192.9
31	North Carolina	192.6
32	Nebraska	190.8
33	Illinois	190.0
34	Maryland	185.2
35	New York	184.7
36	Virginia	183.4
37	Washington	175.7
38	Nevada	175.5
39	Wyoming	174.0
40	Minnesota	171.9
41	Hawaii	170.1
42	Idaho	165.7
43	Arizona	165.3
44	New Mexico	162.9
45	Georgia	158.3
46	California	151.5
47	Texas	150.0
48	Colorado	137.1
49	Alaska	110.3
50	Utah	102.0
	District of Columbia	209.1

Source: U.S. Department of Health and Human Services, National Center for Health Statistics
"National Vital Statistics Reports" (Vol. 56, No. 10, April 24, 2008, http://www.cdc.gov/nchs/deaths.htm)
*Final data by state of residence. Neoplasms are abnormal tissue, tumors. Includes many cancers. Not age-adjusted.

Age-Adjusted Death Rate by Malignant Neoplasms in 2005

National Rate = 183.8 Deaths per 100,000 Population*

ALPHA ORDER

RANK	STATE	RATE
7	Alabama	204.1
41	Alaska	169.2
46	Arizona	163.7
5	Arkansas	208.3
45	California	167.0
48	Colorado	159.6
36	Connecticut	175.7
10	Delaware	197.8
35	Florida	178.1
19	Georgia	190.4
49	Hawaii	148.9
38	Idaho	174.1
20	Illinois	190.1
9	Indiana	199.3
29	Iowa	182.5
24	Kansas	185.4
1	Kentucky	219.9
3	Louisiana	209.3
8	Maine	201.9
22	Maryland	188.3
25	Massachusetts	185.2
18	Michigan	190.8
43	Minnesota	167.8
4	Mississippi	208.4
11	Missouri	197.7
26	Montana	184.4
37	Nebraska	174.8
17	Nevada	191.0
28	New Hampshire	183.7
31	New Jersey	182.1
47	New Mexico	162.6
40	New York	170.8
16	North Carolina	192.8
42	North Dakota	168.9
14	Ohio	196.5
12	Oklahoma	197.6
23	Oregon	186.9
15	Pennsylvania	193.3
27	Rhode Island	184.1
13	South Carolina	197.3
32	South Dakota	180.9
2	Tennessee	211.5
34	Texas	178.5
50	Utah	139.4
39	Vermont	172.9
21	Virginia	188.8
33	Washington	179.5
6	West Virginia	207.7
30	Wisconsin	182.3
44	Wyoming	167.7

RANK ORDER

RANK	STATE	RATE
1	Kentucky	219.9
2	Tennessee	211.5
3	Louisiana	209.3
4	Mississippi	208.4
5	Arkansas	208.3
6	West Virginia	207.7
7	Alabama	204.1
8	Maine	201.9
9	Indiana	199.3
10	Delaware	197.8
11	Missouri	197.7
12	Oklahoma	197.6
13	South Carolina	197.3
14	Ohio	196.5
15	Pennsylvania	193.3
16	North Carolina	192.8
17	Nevada	191.0
18	Michigan	190.8
19	Georgia	190.4
20	Illinois	190.1
21	Virginia	188.8
22	Maryland	188.3
23	Oregon	186.9
24	Kansas	185.4
25	Massachusetts	185.2
26	Montana	184.4
27	Rhode Island	184.1
28	New Hampshire	183.7
29	Iowa	182.5
30	Wisconsin	182.3
31	New Jersey	182.1
32	South Dakota	180.9
33	Washington	179.5
34	Texas	178.5
35	Florida	178.1
36	Connecticut	175.7
37	Nebraska	174.8
38	Idaho	174.1
39	Vermont	172.9
40	New York	170.8
41	Alaska	169.2
42	North Dakota	168.9
43	Minnesota	167.8
44	Wyoming	167.7
45	California	167.0
46	Arizona	163.7
47	New Mexico	162.6
48	Colorado	159.6
49	Hawaii	148.9
50	Utah	139.4

District of Columbia 206.0

Source: U.S. Department of Health and Human Services, National Center for Health Statistics
"National Vital Statistics Reports" (Vol. 56, No. 10, April 24, 2008, http://www.cdc.gov/nchs/deaths.htm)
*Final data by state of residence. Neoplasms are abnormal tissue, tumors. Includes many cancers. Age-adjusted rates based on the year 2000 standard population.

Deaths by Nephritis and Other Kidney Diseases in 2005

National Total = 43,901 Deaths*

ALPHA ORDER

RANK	STATE	DEATHS	% of USA
17	Alabama	1,036	2.4%
50	Alaska	38	0.1%
26	Arizona	608	1.4%
25	Arkansas	624	1.4%
3	California	2,482	5.7%
30	Colorado	470	1.1%
27	Connecticut	580	1.3%
43	Delaware	128	0.3%
4	Florida	2,416	5.5%
11	Georgia	1,520	3.5%
42	Hawaii	150	0.3%
44	Idaho	110	0.3%
5	Illinois	2,402	5.5%
13	Indiana	1,284	2.9%
35	Iowa	250	0.6%
29	Kansas	517	1.2%
19	Kentucky	912	2.1%
15	Louisiana	1,187	2.7%
35	Maine	250	0.6%
21	Maryland	752	1.7%
12	Massachusetts	1,410	3.2%
8	Michigan	1,681	3.8%
23	Minnesota	669	1.5%
24	Mississippi	667	1.5%
16	Missouri	1,156	2.6%
45	Montana	109	0.2%
37	Nebraska	245	0.6%
33	Nevada	438	1.0%
40	New Hampshire	173	0.4%
9	New Jersey	1,597	3.6%
38	New Mexico	239	0.5%
6	New York	2,360	5.4%
10	North Carolina	1,561	3.6%
46	North Dakota	67	0.2%
7	Ohio	1,902	4.3%
28	Oklahoma	564	1.3%
34	Oregon	295	0.7%
1	Pennsylvania	3,108	7.1%
41	Rhode Island	156	0.4%
20	South Carolina	823	1.9%
48	South Dakota	55	0.1%
22	Tennessee	719	1.6%
2	Texas	2,729	6.2%
39	Utah	177	0.4%
49	Vermont	52	0.1%
14	Virginia	1,277	2.9%
31	Washington	450	1.0%
32	West Virginia	442	1.0%
18	Wisconsin	930	2.1%
47	Wyoming	66	0.2%

RANK ORDER

RANK	STATE	DEATHS	% of USA
1	Pennsylvania	3,108	7.1%
2	Texas	2,729	6.2%
3	California	2,482	5.7%
4	Florida	2,416	5.5%
5	Illinois	2,402	5.5%
6	New York	2,360	5.4%
7	Ohio	1,902	4.3%
8	Michigan	1,681	3.8%
9	New Jersey	1,597	3.6%
10	North Carolina	1,561	3.6%
11	Georgia	1,520	3.5%
12	Massachusetts	1,410	3.2%
13	Indiana	1,284	2.9%
14	Virginia	1,277	2.9%
15	Louisiana	1,187	2.7%
16	Missouri	1,156	2.6%
17	Alabama	1,036	2.4%
18	Wisconsin	930	2.1%
19	Kentucky	912	2.1%
20	South Carolina	823	1.9%
21	Maryland	752	1.7%
22	Tennessee	719	1.6%
23	Minnesota	669	1.5%
24	Mississippi	667	1.5%
25	Arkansas	624	1.4%
26	Arizona	608	1.4%
27	Connecticut	580	1.3%
28	Oklahoma	564	1.3%
29	Kansas	517	1.2%
30	Colorado	470	1.1%
31	Washington	450	1.0%
32	West Virginia	442	1.0%
33	Nevada	438	1.0%
34	Oregon	295	0.7%
35	Iowa	250	0.6%
35	Maine	250	0.6%
37	Nebraska	245	0.6%
38	New Mexico	239	0.5%
39	Utah	177	0.4%
40	New Hampshire	173	0.4%
41	Rhode Island	156	0.4%
42	Hawaii	150	0.3%
43	Delaware	128	0.3%
44	Idaho	110	0.3%
45	Montana	109	0.2%
46	North Dakota	67	0.2%
47	Wyoming	66	0.2%
48	South Dakota	55	0.1%
49	Vermont	52	0.1%
50	Alaska	38	0.1%
	District of Columbia	68	0.2%

Source: U.S. Department of Health and Human Services, National Center for Health Statistics
   "National Vital Statistics Reports" (Vol. 56, No. 10, April 24, 2008, http://www.cdc.gov/nchs/deaths.htm)
*Final data by state of residence. Includes nephrotic syndrome and nephrosis.

Death Rate by Nephritis and Other Kidney Diseases in 2005

National Rate = 14.8 Deaths per 100,000 Population*

ALPHA ORDER

RANK	STATE	RATE
5	Alabama	22.7
50	Alaska	5.7
40	Arizona	10.2
6	Arkansas	22.5
49	California	6.9
41	Colorado	10.1
23	Connecticut	16.5
25	Delaware	15.2
28	Florida	13.6
19	Georgia	16.8
37	Hawaii	11.8
45	Idaho	7.7
13	Illinois	18.8
9	Indiana	20.5
42	Iowa	8.4
13	Kansas	18.8
8	Kentucky	21.9
1	Louisiana	26.2
12	Maine	18.9
29	Maryland	13.4
7	Massachusetts	22.0
21	Michigan	16.6
31	Minnesota	13.0
4	Mississippi	22.8
10	Missouri	19.9
38	Montana	11.6
27	Nebraska	13.9
16	Nevada	18.1
30	New Hampshire	13.2
15	New Jersey	18.3
33	New Mexico	12.4
34	New York	12.3
17	North Carolina	18.0
39	North Dakota	10.5
21	Ohio	16.6
24	Oklahoma	15.9
44	Oregon	8.1
2	Pennsylvania	25.0
26	Rhode Island	14.5
11	South Carolina	19.3
48	South Dakota	7.1
35	Tennessee	12.1
36	Texas	11.9
46	Utah	7.2
43	Vermont	8.3
18	Virginia	16.9
46	Washington	7.2
3	West Virginia	24.3
19	Wisconsin	16.8
31	Wyoming	13.0

RANK ORDER

RANK	STATE	RATE
1	Louisiana	26.2
2	Pennsylvania	25.0
3	West Virginia	24.3
4	Mississippi	22.8
5	Alabama	22.7
6	Arkansas	22.5
7	Massachusetts	22.0
8	Kentucky	21.9
9	Indiana	20.5
10	Missouri	19.9
11	South Carolina	19.3
12	Maine	18.9
13	Illinois	18.8
13	Kansas	18.8
15	New Jersey	18.3
16	Nevada	18.1
17	North Carolina	18.0
18	Virginia	16.9
19	Georgia	16.8
19	Wisconsin	16.8
21	Michigan	16.6
21	Ohio	16.6
23	Connecticut	16.5
24	Oklahoma	15.9
25	Delaware	15.2
26	Rhode Island	14.5
27	Nebraska	13.9
28	Florida	13.6
29	Maryland	13.4
30	New Hampshire	13.2
31	Minnesota	13.0
31	Wyoming	13.0
33	New Mexico	12.4
34	New York	12.3
35	Tennessee	12.1
36	Texas	11.9
37	Hawaii	11.8
38	Montana	11.6
39	North Dakota	10.5
40	Arizona	10.2
41	Colorado	10.1
42	Iowa	8.4
43	Vermont	8.3
44	Oregon	8.1
45	Idaho	7.7
46	Utah	7.2
46	Washington	7.2
48	South Dakota	7.1
49	California	6.9
50	Alaska	5.7

District of Columbia	12.4

Source: U.S. Department of Health and Human Services, National Center for Health Statistics
"National Vital Statistics Reports" (Vol. 56, No. 10, April 24, 2008, http://www.cdc.gov/nchs/deaths.htm)
*Final data by state of residence. Includes nephrotic syndrome and nephrosis. Not age-adjusted.

Age-Adjusted Death Rate by Nephritis and Other Kidney Diseases in 2005

National Rate = 14.3 Deaths per 100,000 Population*

ALPHA ORDER

RANK	STATE	RATE
3	Alabama	22.0
37	Alaska	10.3
38	Arizona	10.2
7	Arkansas	20.5
45	California	7.5
31	Colorado	12.3
28	Connecticut	13.1
25	Delaware	14.2
38	Florida	10.2
6	Georgia	21.2
40	Hawaii	10.1
43	Idaho	7.9
13	Illinois	18.4
9	Indiana	19.8
49	Iowa	6.2
17	Kansas	16.7
3	Kentucky	22.0
1	Louisiana	27.6
20	Maine	15.5
26	Maryland	13.8
13	Massachusetts	18.4
19	Michigan	15.6
33	Minnesota	12.0
2	Mississippi	23.7
15	Missouri	18.3
40	Montana	10.1
32	Nebraska	12.2
5	Nevada	21.4
30	New Hampshire	12.4
18	New Jersey	16.5
29	New Mexico	12.9
36	New York	11.0
12	North Carolina	18.5
44	North Dakota	7.6
23	Ohio	14.8
21	Oklahoma	15.3
47	Oregon	7.2
11	Pennsylvania	19.0
35	Rhode Island	11.2
10	South Carolina	19.3
50	South Dakota	5.7
33	Tennessee	12.0
22	Texas	14.9
40	Utah	10.1
46	Vermont	7.4
16	Virginia	17.9
47	Washington	7.2
8	West Virginia	20.2
24	Wisconsin	14.7
27	Wyoming	13.5

RANK ORDER

RANK	STATE	RATE
1	Louisiana	27.6
2	Mississippi	23.7
3	Alabama	22.0
3	Kentucky	22.0
5	Nevada	21.4
6	Georgia	21.2
7	Arkansas	20.5
8	West Virginia	20.2
9	Indiana	19.8
10	South Carolina	19.3
11	Pennsylvania	19.0
12	North Carolina	18.5
13	Illinois	18.4
13	Massachusetts	18.4
15	Missouri	18.3
16	Virginia	17.9
17	Kansas	16.7
18	New Jersey	16.5
19	Michigan	15.6
20	Maine	15.5
21	Oklahoma	15.3
22	Texas	14.9
23	Ohio	14.8
24	Wisconsin	14.7
25	Delaware	14.2
26	Maryland	13.8
27	Wyoming	13.5
28	Connecticut	13.1
29	New Mexico	12.9
30	New Hampshire	12.4
31	Colorado	12.3
32	Nebraska	12.2
33	Minnesota	12.0
33	Tennessee	12.0
35	Rhode Island	11.2
36	New York	11.0
37	Alaska	10.3
38	Arizona	10.2
38	Florida	10.2
40	Hawaii	10.1
40	Montana	10.1
40	Utah	10.1
43	Idaho	7.9
44	North Dakota	7.6
45	California	7.5
46	Vermont	7.4
47	Oregon	7.2
47	Washington	7.2
49	Iowa	6.2
50	South Dakota	5.7
	District of Columbia	12.1

Source: U.S. Department of Health and Human Services, National Center for Health Statistics
"National Vital Statistics Reports" (Vol. 56, No. 10, April 24, 2008, http://www.cdc.gov/nchs/deaths.htm)
*Final data by state of residence. Includes nephrotic syndrome and nephrosis. Age-adjusted rates based on the year 2000 standard population.

Deaths by Influenza and Pneumonia in 2005

National Total = 63,001 Deaths*

ALPHA ORDER

RANK ORDER

RANK	STATE	DEATHS	% of USA
21	Alabama	1,011	1.6%
50	Alaska	44	0.1%
17	Arizona	1,297	2.1%
27	Arkansas	886	1.4%
1	California	7,553	12.0%
31	Colorado	666	1.1%
23	Connecticut	956	1.5%
47	Delaware	162	0.3%
6	Florida	2,802	4.4%
12	Georgia	1,596	2.5%
43	Hawaii	241	0.4%
40	Idaho	289	0.5%
5	Illinois	2,949	4.7%
16	Indiana	1,317	2.1%
26	Iowa	896	1.4%
30	Kansas	730	1.2%
20	Kentucky	1,021	1.6%
22	Louisiana	996	1.6%
38	Maine	352	0.6%
19	Maryland	1,194	1.9%
9	Massachusetts	1,935	3.1%
8	Michigan	1,950	3.1%
28	Minnesota	846	1.3%
32	Mississippi	645	1.0%
14	Missouri	1,527	2.4%
45	Montana	213	0.3%
36	Nebraska	370	0.6%
35	Nevada	454	0.7%
41	New Hampshire	273	0.4%
11	New Jersey	1,637	2.6%
37	New Mexico	353	0.6%
2	New York	5,521	8.8%
10	North Carolina	1,830	2.9%
46	North Dakota	172	0.3%
7	Ohio	2,416	3.8%
24	Oklahoma	948	1.5%
33	Oregon	614	1.0%
4	Pennsylvania	3,068	4.9%
42	Rhode Island	253	0.4%
29	South Carolina	771	1.2%
43	South Dakota	241	0.4%
13	Tennessee	1,588	2.5%
3	Texas	3,654	5.8%
39	Utah	333	0.5%
49	Vermont	97	0.2%
15	Virginia	1,464	2.3%
25	Washington	927	1.5%
34	West Virginia	458	0.7%
18	Wisconsin	1,268	2.0%
48	Wyoming	119	0.2%

RANK	STATE	DEATHS	% of USA
1	California	7,553	12.0%
2	New York	5,521	8.8%
3	Texas	3,654	5.8%
4	Pennsylvania	3,068	4.9%
5	Illinois	2,949	4.7%
6	Florida	2,802	4.4%
7	Ohio	2,416	3.8%
8	Michigan	1,950	3.1%
9	Massachusetts	1,935	3.1%
10	North Carolina	1,830	2.9%
11	New Jersey	1,637	2.6%
12	Georgia	1,596	2.5%
13	Tennessee	1,588	2.5%
14	Missouri	1,527	2.4%
15	Virginia	1,464	2.3%
16	Indiana	1,317	2.1%
17	Arizona	1,297	2.1%
18	Wisconsin	1,268	2.0%
19	Maryland	1,194	1.9%
20	Kentucky	1,021	1.6%
21	Alabama	1,011	1.6%
22	Louisiana	996	1.6%
23	Connecticut	956	1.5%
24	Oklahoma	948	1.5%
25	Washington	927	1.5%
26	Iowa	896	1.4%
27	Arkansas	886	1.4%
28	Minnesota	846	1.3%
29	South Carolina	771	1.2%
30	Kansas	730	1.2%
31	Colorado	666	1.1%
32	Mississippi	645	1.0%
33	Oregon	614	1.0%
34	West Virginia	458	0.7%
35	Nevada	454	0.7%
36	Nebraska	370	0.6%
37	New Mexico	353	0.6%
38	Maine	352	0.6%
39	Utah	333	0.5%
40	Idaho	289	0.5%
41	New Hampshire	273	0.4%
42	Rhode Island	253	0.4%
43	Hawaii	241	0.4%
43	South Dakota	241	0.4%
45	Montana	213	0.3%
46	North Dakota	172	0.3%
47	Delaware	162	0.3%
48	Wyoming	119	0.2%
49	Vermont	97	0.2%
50	Alaska	44	0.1%
	District of Columbia	98	0.2%

Source: U.S. Department of Health and Human Services, National Center for Health Statistics
    "National Vital Statistics Reports" (Vol. 56, No. 10, April 24, 2008, http://www.cdc.gov/nchs/deaths.htm)
*Final data by state of residence.

Death Rate by Influenza and Pneumonia in 2005

National Rate = 21.3 Deaths per 100,000 Population*

ALPHA ORDER				RANK ORDER		
RANK	STATE	RATE		RANK	STATE	RATE
21	Alabama	22.2		1	Arkansas	31.9
50	Alaska	6.6		2	South Dakota	31.1
24	Arizona	21.8		3	Iowa	30.2
1	Arkansas	31.9		3	Massachusetts	30.2
30	California	20.9		5	New York	28.7
48	Colorado	14.3		6	Connecticut	27.2
6	Connecticut	27.2		7	North Dakota	27.0
35	Delaware	19.2		8	Oklahoma	26.7
45	Florida	15.8		9	Kansas	26.6
41	Georgia	17.6		9	Maine	26.6
36	Hawaii	18.9		9	Tennessee	26.6
32	Idaho	20.2		12	Missouri	26.3
18	Illinois	23.1		13	West Virginia	25.2
28	Indiana	21.0		14	Pennsylvania	24.7
3	Iowa	30.2		15	Kentucky	24.5
9	Kansas	26.6		16	Rhode Island	23.5
15	Kentucky	24.5		17	Wyoming	23.4
23	Louisiana	22.0		18	Illinois	23.1
9	Maine	26.6		19	Wisconsin	22.9
25	Maryland	21.3		20	Montana	22.8
3	Massachusetts	30.2		21	Alabama	22.2
33	Michigan	19.3		22	Mississippi	22.1
43	Minnesota	16.5		23	Louisiana	22.0
22	Mississippi	22.1		24	Arizona	21.8
12	Missouri	26.3		25	Maryland	21.3
20	Montana	22.8		26	North Carolina	21.1
28	Nebraska	21.0		26	Ohio	21.1
37	Nevada	18.8		28	Indiana	21.0
31	New Hampshire	20.8		28	Nebraska	21.0
37	New Jersey	18.8		30	California	20.9
39	New Mexico	18.3		31	New Hampshire	20.8
5	New York	28.7		32	Idaho	20.2
26	North Carolina	21.1		33	Michigan	19.3
7	North Dakota	27.0		33	Virginia	19.3
26	Ohio	21.1		35	Delaware	19.2
8	Oklahoma	26.7		36	Hawaii	18.9
42	Oregon	16.9		37	Nevada	18.8
14	Pennsylvania	24.7		37	New Jersey	18.8
16	Rhode Island	23.5		39	New Mexico	18.3
40	South Carolina	18.1		40	South Carolina	18.1
2	South Dakota	31.1		41	Georgia	17.6
9	Tennessee	26.6		42	Oregon	16.9
44	Texas	16.0		43	Minnesota	16.5
49	Utah	13.5		44	Texas	16.0
46	Vermont	15.6		45	Florida	15.8
33	Virginia	19.3		46	Vermont	15.6
47	Washington	14.7		47	Washington	14.7
13	West Virginia	25.2		48	Colorado	14.3
19	Wisconsin	22.9		49	Utah	13.5
17	Wyoming	23.4		50	Alaska	6.6
					District of Columbia	17.8

Source: U.S. Department of Health and Human Services, National Center for Health Statistics
"National Vital Statistics Reports" (Vol. 56, No. 10, April 24, 2008, http://www.cdc.gov/nchs/deaths.htm)
*Final data by state of residence. Not age-adjusted.

Age-Adjusted Death Rate by Influenza and Pneumonia in 2005

National Rate = 20.3 Deaths per 100,000 Population*

<u>ALPHA ORDER</u>   <u>RANK ORDER</u>

RANK	STATE	RATE		RANK	STATE	RATE
18	Alabama	21.9		1	Arkansas	29.2
49	Alaska	12.3		2	Tennessee	27.6
18	Arizona	21.9		3	Oklahoma	26.1
1	Arkansas	29.2		4	New York	25.3
13	California	22.8		5	Kentucky	25.1
41	Colorado	17.2		6	Wyoming	24.4
25	Connecticut	20.5		7	Massachusetts	24.2
37	Delaware	18.0		8	Missouri	23.9
50	Florida	11.8		9	Louisiana	23.7
12	Georgia	23.3		10	Mississippi	23.5
44	Hawaii	15.0		11	South Dakota	23.4
25	Idaho	20.5		12	Georgia	23.3
16	Illinois	22.0		13	California	22.8
28	Indiana	20.0		14	Kansas	22.5
22	Iowa	21.4		15	Nevada	22.4
14	Kansas	22.5		16	Illinois	22.0
5	Kentucky	25.1		16	North Carolina	22.0
9	Louisiana	23.7		18	Alabama	21.9
20	Maine	21.8		18	Arizona	21.9
21	Maryland	21.7		20	Maine	21.8
7	Massachusetts	24.2		21	Maryland	21.7
39	Michigan	17.8		22	Iowa	21.4
45	Minnesota	14.5		23	West Virginia	21.0
10	Mississippi	23.5		24	Virginia	20.9
8	Missouri	23.9		25	Connecticut	20.5
32	Montana	18.9		25	Idaho	20.5
40	Nebraska	17.3		27	Texas	20.4
15	Nevada	22.4		28	Indiana	20.0
29	New Hampshire	19.4		29	New Hampshire	19.4
43	New Jersey	16.3		30	New Mexico	19.2
30	New Mexico	19.2		31	Wisconsin	19.1
4	New York	25.3		32	Montana	18.9
16	North Carolina	22.0		33	Utah	18.8
35	North Dakota	18.5		34	Ohio	18.6
34	Ohio	18.6		35	North Dakota	18.5
3	Oklahoma	26.1		36	South Carolina	18.4
45	Oregon	14.5		37	Delaware	18.0
37	Pennsylvania	18.0		37	Pennsylvania	18.0
41	Rhode Island	17.2		39	Michigan	17.8
36	South Carolina	18.4		40	Nebraska	17.3
11	South Dakota	23.4		41	Colorado	17.2
2	Tennessee	27.6		41	Rhode Island	17.2
27	Texas	20.4		43	New Jersey	16.3
33	Utah	18.8		44	Hawaii	15.0
48	Vermont	13.7		45	Minnesota	14.5
24	Virginia	20.9		45	Oregon	14.5
45	Washington	14.5		45	Washington	14.5
23	West Virginia	21.0		48	Vermont	13.7
31	Wisconsin	19.1		49	Alaska	12.3
6	Wyoming	24.4		50	Florida	11.8

District of Columbia   17.0

Source: U.S. Department of Health and Human Services, National Center for Health Statistics
  "National Vital Statistics Reports" (Vol. 56, No. 10, April 24, 2008, http://www.cdc.gov/nchs/deaths.htm)
*Final data by state of residence. Age-adjusted rates based on the year 2000 standard population.

Deaths by Injury in 2005

National Total = 173,753 Deaths*

ALPHA ORDER

ALPHA ORDER

RANK	STATE	DEATHS	% of USA
20	Alabama	3,440	2.0%
46	Alaska	498	0.3%
11	Arizona	4,802	2.8%
30	Arkansas	2,094	1.2%
1	California	17,336	10.0%
23	Colorado	3,049	1.8%
35	Connecticut	1,563	0.9%
47	Delaware	441	0.3%
3	Florida	12,382	7.1%
10	Georgia	5,433	3.1%
43	Hawaii	638	0.4%
39	Idaho	908	0.5%
7	Illinois	6,226	3.6%
16	Indiana	3,802	2.2%
34	Iowa	1,610	0.9%
33	Kansas	1,651	1.0%
21	Kentucky	3,257	1.9%
13	Louisiana	4,298	2.5%
41	Maine	789	0.5%
24	Maryland	3,045	1.8%
27	Massachusetts	2,664	1.5%
9	Michigan	5,484	3.2%
26	Minnesota	2,687	1.5%
28	Mississippi	2,609	1.5%
14	Missouri	4,073	2.3%
40	Montana	792	0.5%
38	Nebraska	972	0.6%
31	Nevada	1,808	1.0%
42	New Hampshire	671	0.4%
18	New Jersey	3,605	2.1%
32	New Mexico	1,770	1.0%
5	New York	6,888	4.0%
8	North Carolina	5,849	3.4%
49	North Dakota	395	0.2%
6	Ohio	6,502	3.7%
25	Oklahoma	2,820	1.6%
29	Oregon	2,223	1.3%
4	Pennsylvania	7,756	4.5%
45	Rhode Island	551	0.3%
22	South Carolina	3,168	1.8%
44	South Dakota	553	0.3%
12	Tennessee	4,675	2.7%
2	Texas	12,772	7.4%
36	Utah	1,472	0.8%
50	Vermont	371	0.2%
15	Virginia	4,046	2.3%
17	Washington	3,692	2.1%
37	West Virginia	1,317	0.8%
19	Wisconsin	3,442	2.0%
48	Wyoming	416	0.2%

RANK ORDER

RANK	STATE	DEATHS	% of USA
1	California	17,336	10.0%
2	Texas	12,772	7.4%
3	Florida	12,382	7.1%
4	Pennsylvania	7,756	4.5%
5	New York	6,888	4.0%
6	Ohio	6,502	3.7%
7	Illinois	6,226	3.6%
8	North Carolina	5,849	3.4%
9	Michigan	5,484	3.2%
10	Georgia	5,433	3.1%
11	Arizona	4,802	2.8%
12	Tennessee	4,675	2.7%
13	Louisiana	4,298	2.5%
14	Missouri	4,073	2.3%
15	Virginia	4,046	2.3%
16	Indiana	3,802	2.2%
17	Washington	3,692	2.1%
18	New Jersey	3,605	2.1%
19	Wisconsin	3,442	2.0%
20	Alabama	3,440	2.0%
21	Kentucky	3,257	1.9%
22	South Carolina	3,168	1.8%
23	Colorado	3,049	1.8%
24	Maryland	3,045	1.8%
25	Oklahoma	2,820	1.6%
26	Minnesota	2,687	1.5%
27	Massachusetts	2,664	1.5%
28	Mississippi	2,609	1.5%
29	Oregon	2,223	1.3%
30	Arkansas	2,094	1.2%
31	Nevada	1,808	1.0%
32	New Mexico	1,770	1.0%
33	Kansas	1,651	1.0%
34	Iowa	1,610	0.9%
35	Connecticut	1,563	0.9%
36	Utah	1,472	0.8%
37	West Virginia	1,317	0.8%
38	Nebraska	972	0.6%
39	Idaho	908	0.5%
40	Montana	792	0.5%
41	Maine	789	0.5%
42	New Hampshire	671	0.4%
43	Hawaii	638	0.4%
44	South Dakota	553	0.3%
45	Rhode Island	551	0.3%
46	Alaska	498	0.3%
47	Delaware	441	0.3%
48	Wyoming	416	0.2%
49	North Dakota	395	0.2%
50	Vermont	371	0.2%
	District of Columbia	448	0.3%

Source: U.S. Department of Health and Human Services, National Center for Health Statistics
(http://wonder.cdc.gov)
*By state of residence. Injury as used here includes accidents (including motor vehicle), suicides, homicides, and "other" undetermined.

Death Rate by Injury in 2005

National Rate = 58.6 Deaths per 100,000 Population*

ALPHA ORDER

RANK	STATE	RATE
10	Alabama	75.6
12	Alaska	75.1
6	Arizona	80.7
11	Arkansas	75.4
46	California	48.0
20	Colorado	65.4
47	Connecticut	44.6
40	Delaware	52.4
18	Florida	69.7
30	Georgia	59.5
44	Hawaii	50.1
21	Idaho	63.5
45	Illinois	48.8
26	Indiana	60.7
37	Iowa	54.3
27	Kansas	60.1
9	Kentucky	78.1
1	Louisiana	95.4
28	Maine	59.9
36	Maryland	54.5
48	Massachusetts	41.4
37	Michigan	54.3
40	Minnesota	52.4
3	Mississippi	89.7
17	Missouri	70.3
4	Montana	84.7
35	Nebraska	55.3
13	Nevada	74.9
42	New Hampshire	51.3
48	New Jersey	41.4
2	New Mexico	91.9
50	New York	35.7
19	North Carolina	67.4
24	North Dakota	62.2
33	Ohio	56.7
7	Oklahoma	79.6
25	Oregon	61.1
22	Pennsylvania	62.5
42	Rhode Island	51.3
14	South Carolina	74.6
16	South Dakota	71.4
8	Tennessee	78.5
34	Texas	55.7
31	Utah	59.1
29	Vermont	59.6
39	Virginia	53.5
32	Washington	58.7
15	West Virginia	72.6
23	Wisconsin	62.3
5	Wyoming	81.8

RANK ORDER

RANK	STATE	RATE
1	Louisiana	95.4
2	New Mexico	91.9
3	Mississippi	89.7
4	Montana	84.7
5	Wyoming	81.8
6	Arizona	80.7
7	Oklahoma	79.6
8	Tennessee	78.5
9	Kentucky	78.1
10	Alabama	75.6
11	Arkansas	75.4
12	Alaska	75.1
13	Nevada	74.9
14	South Carolina	74.6
15	West Virginia	72.6
16	South Dakota	71.4
17	Missouri	70.3
18	Florida	69.7
19	North Carolina	67.4
20	Colorado	65.4
21	Idaho	63.5
22	Pennsylvania	62.5
23	Wisconsin	62.3
24	North Dakota	62.2
25	Oregon	61.1
26	Indiana	60.7
27	Kansas	60.1
28	Maine	59.9
29	Vermont	59.6
30	Georgia	59.5
31	Utah	59.1
32	Washington	58.7
33	Ohio	56.7
34	Texas	55.7
35	Nebraska	55.3
36	Maryland	54.5
37	Iowa	54.3
37	Michigan	54.3
39	Virginia	53.5
40	Delaware	52.4
40	Minnesota	52.4
42	New Hampshire	51.3
42	Rhode Island	51.3
44	Hawaii	50.1
45	Illinois	48.8
46	California	48.0
47	Connecticut	44.6
48	Massachusetts	41.4
48	New Jersey	41.4
50	New York	35.7
	District of Columbia	77.0

Source: U.S. Department of Health and Human Services, National Center for Health Statistics
(http://wonder.cdc.gov)
*By state of residence. Injury as used here includes accidents (including motor vehicle), suicides, homicides, and "other" undetermined. Not age-adjusted.

Age-Adjusted Death Rate by Injury in 2005

National Rate = 57.8 Deaths per 100,000 Population*

ALPHA ORDER

RANK	STATE	RATE
12	Alabama	74.5
8	Alaska	78.6
5	Arizona	80.8
13	Arkansas	74.3
43	California	48.5
19	Colorado	67.1
47	Connecticut	42.4
39	Delaware	51.8
20	Florida	66.0
23	Georgia	62.0
45	Hawaii	47.7
22	Idaho	64.9
44	Illinois	48.4
24	Indiana	60.0
41	Iowa	50.1
27	Kansas	58.7
10	Kentucky	77.3
1	Louisiana	96.0
33	Maine	56.3
35	Maryland	54.5
49	Massachusetts	39.3
36	Michigan	53.8
40	Minnesota	50.5
3	Mississippi	90.2
16	Missouri	68.6
4	Montana	81.1
38	Nebraska	52.7
11	Nevada	76.3
42	New Hampshire	49.8
48	New Jersey	40.5
2	New Mexico	92.8
50	New York	34.4
18	North Carolina	67.3
32	North Dakota	56.4
34	Ohio	55.2
7	Oklahoma	78.8
28	Oregon	58.6
26	Pennsylvania	59.1
46	Rhode Island	47.1
14	South Carolina	74.1
17	South Dakota	67.7
9	Tennessee	77.7
29	Texas	58.2
21	Utah	65.0
31	Vermont	57.3
37	Virginia	53.6
30	Washington	57.7
15	West Virginia	69.4
25	Wisconsin	59.8
5	Wyoming	80.8

RANK ORDER

RANK	STATE	RATE
1	Louisiana	96.0
2	New Mexico	92.8
3	Mississippi	90.2
4	Montana	81.1
5	Arizona	80.8
5	Wyoming	80.8
7	Oklahoma	78.8
8	Alaska	78.6
9	Tennessee	77.7
10	Kentucky	77.3
11	Nevada	76.3
12	Alabama	74.5
13	Arkansas	74.3
14	South Carolina	74.1
15	West Virginia	69.4
16	Missouri	68.6
17	South Dakota	67.7
18	North Carolina	67.3
19	Colorado	67.1
20	Florida	66.0
21	Utah	65.0
22	Idaho	64.9
23	Georgia	62.0
24	Indiana	60.0
25	Wisconsin	59.8
26	Pennsylvania	59.1
27	Kansas	58.7
28	Oregon	58.6
29	Texas	58.2
30	Washington	57.7
31	Vermont	57.3
32	North Dakota	56.4
33	Maine	56.3
34	Ohio	55.2
35	Maryland	54.5
36	Michigan	53.8
37	Virginia	53.6
38	Nebraska	52.7
39	Delaware	51.8
40	Minnesota	50.5
41	Iowa	50.1
42	New Hampshire	49.8
43	California	48.5
44	Illinois	48.4
45	Hawaii	47.7
46	Rhode Island	47.1
47	Connecticut	42.4
48	New Jersey	40.5
49	Massachusetts	39.3
50	New York	34.4

District of Columbia	72.9

Source: U.S. Department of Health and Human Services, National Center for Health Statistics
     (http://wonder.cdc.gov)
*By state of residence. Injury as used here includes accidents (including motor vehicle), suicides, homicides, and "other"
undetermined. Age-adjusted rates based on the year 2000 standard population.

Deaths by Accidents in 2005

National Total = 117,809 Deaths*

ALPHA ORDER

RANK	STATE	DEATHS	% of USA
21	Alabama	2,395	2.0%
46	Alaska	313	0.3%
11	Arizona	3,150	2.7%
30	Arkansas	1,329	1.1%
1	California	11,129	9.4%
24	Colorado	1,947	1.7%
34	Connecticut	1,134	1.0%
48	Delaware	293	0.2%
2	Florida	8,868	7.5%
9	Georgia	3,762	3.2%
43	Hawaii	436	0.4%
39	Idaho	606	0.5%
7	Illinois	4,182	3.5%
19	Indiana	2,480	2.1%
32	Iowa	1,202	1.0%
33	Kansas	1,149	1.0%
20	Kentucky	2,405	2.0%
13	Louisiana	3,072	2.6%
40	Maine	579	0.5%
29	Maryland	1,376	1.2%
27	Massachusetts	1,907	1.6%
10	Michigan	3,451	2.9%
26	Minnesota	1,922	1.6%
25	Mississippi	1,936	1.6%
14	Missouri	2,848	2.4%
41	Montana	524	0.4%
38	Nebraska	704	0.6%
35	Nevada	1,104	0.9%
42	New Hampshire	477	0.4%
16	New Jersey	2,561	2.2%
31	New Mexico	1,267	1.1%
5	New York	4,645	3.9%
8	North Carolina	4,123	3.5%
49	North Dakota	287	0.2%
6	Ohio	4,438	3.8%
23	Oklahoma	2,005	1.7%
28	Oregon	1,469	1.2%
4	Pennsylvania	5,446	4.6%
45	Rhode Island	334	0.3%
22	South Carolina	2,272	1.9%
44	South Dakota	402	0.3%
12	Tennessee	3,147	2.7%
3	Texas	8,598	7.3%
37	Utah	743	0.6%
50	Vermont	272	0.2%
15	Virginia	2,638	2.2%
17	Washington	2,543	2.2%
36	West Virginia	940	0.8%
18	Wisconsin	2,490	2.1%
47	Wyoming	302	0.3%

RANK ORDER

RANK	STATE	DEATHS	% of USA
1	California	11,129	9.4%
2	Florida	8,868	7.5%
3	Texas	8,598	7.3%
4	Pennsylvania	5,446	4.6%
5	New York	4,645	3.9%
6	Ohio	4,438	3.8%
7	Illinois	4,182	3.5%
8	North Carolina	4,123	3.5%
9	Georgia	3,762	3.2%
10	Michigan	3,451	2.9%
11	Arizona	3,150	2.7%
12	Tennessee	3,147	2.7%
13	Louisiana	3,072	2.6%
14	Missouri	2,848	2.4%
15	Virginia	2,638	2.2%
16	New Jersey	2,561	2.2%
17	Washington	2,543	2.2%
18	Wisconsin	2,490	2.1%
19	Indiana	2,480	2.1%
20	Kentucky	2,405	2.0%
21	Alabama	2,395	2.0%
22	South Carolina	2,272	1.9%
23	Oklahoma	2,005	1.7%
24	Colorado	1,947	1.7%
25	Mississippi	1,936	1.6%
26	Minnesota	1,922	1.6%
27	Massachusetts	1,907	1.6%
28	Oregon	1,469	1.2%
29	Maryland	1,376	1.2%
30	Arkansas	1,329	1.1%
31	New Mexico	1,267	1.1%
32	Iowa	1,202	1.0%
33	Kansas	1,149	1.0%
34	Connecticut	1,134	1.0%
35	Nevada	1,104	0.9%
36	West Virginia	940	0.8%
37	Utah	743	0.6%
38	Nebraska	704	0.6%
39	Idaho	606	0.5%
40	Maine	579	0.5%
41	Montana	524	0.4%
42	New Hampshire	477	0.4%
43	Hawaii	436	0.4%
44	South Dakota	402	0.3%
45	Rhode Island	334	0.3%
46	Alaska	313	0.3%
47	Wyoming	302	0.3%
48	Delaware	293	0.2%
49	North Dakota	287	0.2%
50	Vermont	272	0.2%
	District of Columbia	207	0.2%

Source: U.S. Department of Health and Human Services, National Center for Health Statistics
"National Vital Statistics Reports" (Vol. 56, No. 10, April 24, 2008, http://www.cdc.gov/nchs/deaths.htm)
*Final data by state of residence. Includes motor vehicle deaths, poisoning, falls, drowning, and other accidents.

Death Rate by Accidents in 2005

National Rate = 39.7 Deaths per 100,000 Population*

ALPHA ORDER

RANK	STATE	RATE
11	Alabama	52.5
18	Alaska	47.2
9	Arizona	53.0
16	Arkansas	47.8
45	California	30.8
27	Colorado	41.7
43	Connecticut	32.3
39	Delaware	34.7
14	Florida	49.8
28	Georgia	41.5
40	Hawaii	34.2
25	Idaho	42.4
42	Illinois	32.8
33	Indiana	39.5
29	Iowa	40.5
26	Kansas	41.9
5	Kentucky	57.6
1	Louisiana	67.9
22	Maine	43.8
49	Maryland	24.6
47	Massachusetts	29.8
41	Michigan	34.1
36	Minnesota	37.4
2	Mississippi	66.3
15	Missouri	49.1
7	Montana	56.0
32	Nebraska	40.0
19	Nevada	45.7
37	New Hampshire	36.4
48	New Jersey	29.4
3	New Mexico	65.7
50	New York	24.1
17	North Carolina	47.5
20	North Dakota	45.1
34	Ohio	38.7
6	Oklahoma	56.5
31	Oregon	40.3
22	Pennsylvania	43.8
44	Rhode Island	31.0
8	South Carolina	53.4
12	South Dakota	51.8
10	Tennessee	52.8
35	Texas	37.6
46	Utah	30.1
24	Vermont	43.7
38	Virginia	34.9
30	Washington	40.4
13	West Virginia	51.7
21	Wisconsin	45.0
4	Wyoming	59.3

RANK ORDER

RANK	STATE	RATE
1	Louisiana	67.9
2	Mississippi	66.3
3	New Mexico	65.7
4	Wyoming	59.3
5	Kentucky	57.6
6	Oklahoma	56.5
7	Montana	56.0
8	South Carolina	53.4
9	Arizona	53.0
10	Tennessee	52.8
11	Alabama	52.5
12	South Dakota	51.8
13	West Virginia	51.7
14	Florida	49.8
15	Missouri	49.1
16	Arkansas	47.8
17	North Carolina	47.5
18	Alaska	47.2
19	Nevada	45.7
20	North Dakota	45.1
21	Wisconsin	45.0
22	Maine	43.8
22	Pennsylvania	43.8
24	Vermont	43.7
25	Idaho	42.4
26	Kansas	41.9
27	Colorado	41.7
28	Georgia	41.5
29	Iowa	40.5
30	Washington	40.4
31	Oregon	40.3
32	Nebraska	40.0
33	Indiana	39.5
34	Ohio	38.7
35	Texas	37.6
36	Minnesota	37.4
37	New Hampshire	36.4
38	Virginia	34.9
39	Delaware	34.7
40	Hawaii	34.2
41	Michigan	34.1
42	Illinois	32.8
43	Connecticut	32.3
44	Rhode Island	31.0
45	California	30.8
46	Utah	30.1
47	Massachusetts	29.8
48	New Jersey	29.4
49	Maryland	24.6
50	New York	24.1
	District of Columbia	37.6

Source: U.S. Department of Health and Human Services, National Center for Health Statistics
   "National Vital Statistics Reports" (Vol. 56, No. 10, April 24, 2008, http://www.cdc.gov/nchs/deaths.htm)
*Final data by state of residence. Includes motor vehicle deaths, poisoning, falls, drowning, and other accidents. Not age-adjusted.

Age-Adjusted Death Rate by Accidents in 2005

National Rate = 39.1 Deaths per 100,000 Population*

ALPHA ORDER

RANK	STATE	RATE
11	Alabama	51.8
12	Alaska	51.3
7	Arizona	53.8
19	Arkansas	46.8
44	California	31.4
21	Colorado	43.8
45	Connecticut	29.8
40	Delaware	33.9
18	Florida	47.1
20	Georgia	44.4
43	Hawaii	31.7
22	Idaho	43.1
42	Illinois	32.4
31	Indiana	38.9
35	Iowa	36.1
28	Kansas	40.2
5	Kentucky	57.3
1	Louisiana	68.8
25	Maine	41.1
49	Maryland	24.7
47	Massachusetts	27.7
41	Michigan	33.3
36	Minnesota	35.4
2	Mississippi	66.6
16	Missouri	47.4
10	Montana	52.4
33	Nebraska	37.1
17	Nevada	47.3
38	New Hampshire	35.2
46	New Jersey	28.3
2	New Mexico	66.6
50	New York	22.9
15	North Carolina	47.8
30	North Dakota	39.3
33	Ohio	37.1
6	Oklahoma	55.8
32	Oregon	38.1
26	Pennsylvania	40.3
48	Rhode Island	26.7
8	South Carolina	53.1
14	South Dakota	48.1
9	Tennessee	52.5
26	Texas	40.3
39	Utah	34.0
24	Vermont	41.2
37	Virginia	35.3
29	Washington	39.6
13	West Virginia	49.4
23	Wisconsin	42.2
4	Wyoming	58.6

RANK ORDER

RANK	STATE	RATE
1	Louisiana	68.8
2	Mississippi	66.6
2	New Mexico	66.6
4	Wyoming	58.6
5	Kentucky	57.3
6	Oklahoma	55.8
7	Arizona	53.8
8	South Carolina	53.1
9	Tennessee	52.5
10	Montana	52.4
11	Alabama	51.8
12	Alaska	51.3
13	West Virginia	49.4
14	South Dakota	48.1
15	North Carolina	47.8
16	Missouri	47.4
17	Nevada	47.3
18	Florida	47.1
19	Arkansas	46.8
20	Georgia	44.4
21	Colorado	43.8
22	Idaho	43.1
23	Wisconsin	42.2
24	Vermont	41.2
25	Maine	41.1
26	Pennsylvania	40.3
26	Texas	40.3
28	Kansas	40.2
29	Washington	39.6
30	North Dakota	39.3
31	Indiana	38.9
32	Oregon	38.1
33	Nebraska	37.1
33	Ohio	37.1
35	Iowa	36.1
36	Minnesota	35.4
37	Virginia	35.3
38	New Hampshire	35.2
39	Utah	34.0
40	Delaware	33.9
41	Michigan	33.3
42	Illinois	32.4
43	Hawaii	31.7
44	California	31.4
45	Connecticut	29.8
46	New Jersey	28.3
47	Massachusetts	27.7
48	Rhode Island	26.7
49	Maryland	24.7
50	New York	22.9

District of Columbia	37.0

Source: U.S. Department of Health and Human Services, National Center for Health Statistics
   "National Vital Statistics Reports" (Vol. 56, No. 10, April 24, 2008, http://www.cdc.gov/nchs/deaths.htm)
*Final data by state of residence. Includes motor vehicle deaths, poisoning, falls, drowning, and other accidents. Age-adjusted
rates based on the year 2000 standard population.

Deaths by Motor Vehicle Accidents in 2005

National Total = 45,343 Deaths*

ALPHA ORDER

RANK	STATE	DEATHS	% of USA
14	Alabama	1,188	2.6%
48	Alaska	93	0.2%
13	Arizona	1,200	2.6%
25	Arkansas	696	1.5%
1	California	4,427	9.8%
26	Colorado	673	1.5%
37	Connecticut	293	0.6%
47	Delaware	119	0.3%
3	Florida	3,526	7.8%
5	Georgia	1,686	3.7%
45	Hawaii	141	0.3%
39	Idaho	283	0.6%
8	Illinois	1,469	3.2%
18	Indiana	975	2.2%
32	Iowa	468	1.0%
30	Kansas	498	1.1%
17	Kentucky	1,003	2.2%
16	Louisiana	1,029	2.3%
41	Maine	192	0.4%
28	Maryland	628	1.4%
31	Massachusetts	484	1.1%
11	Michigan	1,231	2.7%
27	Minnesota	642	1.4%
20	Mississippi	965	2.1%
12	Missouri	1,203	2.7%
40	Montana	236	0.5%
38	Nebraska	287	0.6%
34	Nevada	459	1.0%
43	New Hampshire	162	0.4%
24	New Jersey	760	1.7%
33	New Mexico	461	1.0%
7	New York	1,530	3.4%
6	North Carolina	1,666	3.7%
46	North Dakota	130	0.3%
9	Ohio	1,404	3.1%
22	Oklahoma	833	1.8%
29	Oregon	512	1.1%
4	Pennsylvania	1,771	3.9%
49	Rhode Island	87	0.2%
15	South Carolina	1,071	2.4%
42	South Dakota	176	0.4%
10	Tennessee	1,308	2.9%
2	Texas	3,780	8.3%
36	Utah	319	0.7%
50	Vermont	82	0.2%
19	Virginia	969	2.1%
23	Washington	762	1.7%
35	West Virginia	403	0.9%
21	Wisconsin	870	1.9%
44	Wyoming	155	0.3%

RANK ORDER

RANK	STATE	DEATHS	% of USA
1	California	4,427	9.8%
2	Texas	3,780	8.3%
3	Florida	3,526	7.8%
4	Pennsylvania	1,771	3.9%
5	Georgia	1,686	3.7%
6	North Carolina	1,666	3.7%
7	New York	1,530	3.4%
8	Illinois	1,469	3.2%
9	Ohio	1,404	3.1%
10	Tennessee	1,308	2.9%
11	Michigan	1,231	2.7%
12	Missouri	1,203	2.7%
13	Arizona	1,200	2.6%
14	Alabama	1,188	2.6%
15	South Carolina	1,071	2.4%
16	Louisiana	1,029	2.3%
17	Kentucky	1,003	2.2%
18	Indiana	975	2.2%
19	Virginia	969	2.1%
20	Mississippi	965	2.1%
21	Wisconsin	870	1.9%
22	Oklahoma	833	1.8%
23	Washington	762	1.7%
24	New Jersey	760	1.7%
25	Arkansas	696	1.5%
26	Colorado	673	1.5%
27	Minnesota	642	1.4%
28	Maryland	628	1.4%
29	Oregon	512	1.1%
30	Kansas	498	1.1%
31	Massachusetts	484	1.1%
32	Iowa	468	1.0%
33	New Mexico	461	1.0%
34	Nevada	459	1.0%
35	West Virginia	403	0.9%
36	Utah	319	0.7%
37	Connecticut	293	0.6%
38	Nebraska	287	0.6%
39	Idaho	283	0.6%
40	Montana	236	0.5%
41	Maine	192	0.4%
42	South Dakota	176	0.4%
43	New Hampshire	162	0.4%
44	Wyoming	155	0.3%
45	Hawaii	141	0.3%
46	North Dakota	130	0.3%
47	Delaware	119	0.3%
48	Alaska	93	0.2%
49	Rhode Island	87	0.2%
50	Vermont	82	0.2%
	District of Columbia	38	0.1%

Source: U.S. Department of Health and Human Services, National Center for Health Statistics
 "National Vital Statistics Reports" (Vol. 56, No. 10, April 24, 2008, http://www.cdc.gov/nchs/deaths.htm)
*Final data by state of residence. These numbers are compiled from death certificates by the Centers for Disease Control and Prevention. They may differ from motor vehicle deaths collected by the U.S. Department of Transportation from other sources.

Death Rate by Motor Vehicle Accidents in 2005

National Rate = 15.3 Deaths per 100,000 Population*

ALPHA ORDER

RANK	STATE	RATE
3	Alabama	26.1
33	Alaska	14.0
16	Arizona	20.2
6	Arkansas	25.0
39	California	12.3
29	Colorado	14.4
47	Connecticut	8.3
31	Delaware	14.1
17	Florida	19.8
21	Georgia	18.6
45	Hawaii	11.1
17	Idaho	19.8
43	Illinois	11.5
27	Indiana	15.5
25	Iowa	15.8
22	Kansas	18.1
7	Kentucky	24.0
10	Louisiana	22.7
28	Maine	14.5
44	Maryland	11.2
50	Massachusetts	7.6
40	Michigan	12.2
37	Minnesota	12.5
1	Mississippi	33.0
14	Missouri	20.7
4	Montana	25.2
24	Nebraska	16.3
20	Nevada	19.0
38	New Hampshire	12.4
46	New Jersey	8.7
8	New Mexico	23.9
49	New York	7.9
19	North Carolina	19.2
15	North Dakota	20.4
40	Ohio	12.2
9	Oklahoma	23.5
31	Oregon	14.1
30	Pennsylvania	14.2
48	Rhode Island	8.1
4	South Carolina	25.2
10	South Dakota	22.7
13	Tennessee	21.9
23	Texas	16.5
35	Utah	12.9
34	Vermont	13.2
36	Virginia	12.8
42	Washington	12.1
12	West Virginia	22.2
26	Wisconsin	15.7
2	Wyoming	30.4

RANK ORDER

RANK	STATE	RATE
1	Mississippi	33.0
2	Wyoming	30.4
3	Alabama	26.1
4	Montana	25.2
4	South Carolina	25.2
6	Arkansas	25.0
7	Kentucky	24.0
8	New Mexico	23.9
9	Oklahoma	23.5
10	Louisiana	22.7
10	South Dakota	22.7
12	West Virginia	22.2
13	Tennessee	21.9
14	Missouri	20.7
15	North Dakota	20.4
16	Arizona	20.2
17	Florida	19.8
17	Idaho	19.8
19	North Carolina	19.2
20	Nevada	19.0
21	Georgia	18.6
22	Kansas	18.1
23	Texas	16.5
24	Nebraska	16.3
25	Iowa	15.8
26	Wisconsin	15.7
27	Indiana	15.5
28	Maine	14.5
29	Colorado	14.4
30	Pennsylvania	14.2
31	Delaware	14.1
31	Oregon	14.1
33	Alaska	14.0
34	Vermont	13.2
35	Utah	12.9
36	Virginia	12.8
37	Minnesota	12.5
38	New Hampshire	12.4
39	California	12.3
40	Michigan	12.2
40	Ohio	12.2
42	Washington	12.1
43	Illinois	11.5
44	Maryland	11.2
45	Hawaii	11.1
46	New Jersey	8.7
47	Connecticut	8.3
48	Rhode Island	8.1
49	New York	7.9
50	Massachusetts	7.6

District of Columbia   6.9

Source: U.S. Department of Health and Human Services, National Center for Health Statistics
    "National Vital Statistics Reports" (Vol. 56, No. 10, April 24, 2008, http://www.cdc.gov/nchs/deaths.htm)
*Final data by state of residence. These numbers are compiled from death certificates by the Centers for Disease Control and Prevention. They may differ from motor vehicle deaths collected by the U.S. Department of Transportation from other sources. Not age-adjusted.

Age-Adjusted Death Rate by Motor Vehicle Accidents in 2005

National Rate = 15.2 Deaths per 100,000 Population*

ALPHA ORDER

RANK	STATE	RATE
3	Alabama	25.7
28	Alaska	14.6
14	Arizona	20.4
6	Arkansas	24.6
37	California	12.3
29	Colorado	14.3
47	Connecticut	8.3
31	Delaware	13.8
17	Florida	19.7
21	Georgia	18.8
45	Hawaii	11.0
16	Idaho	19.8
43	Illinois	11.5
25	Indiana	15.4
27	Iowa	15.2
22	Kansas	17.9
7	Kentucky	23.7
10	Louisiana	22.4
30	Maine	14.1
44	Maryland	11.2
50	Massachusetts	7.3
40	Michigan	12.1
38	Minnesota	12.2
1	Mississippi	32.9
15	Missouri	20.3
5	Montana	24.7
24	Nebraska	15.9
19	Nevada	19.3
38	New Hampshire	12.2
46	New Jersey	8.7
8	New Mexico	23.6
49	New York	7.8
20	North Carolina	19.1
18	North Dakota	19.6
40	Ohio	12.1
9	Oklahoma	23.0
31	Oregon	13.8
31	Pennsylvania	13.8
48	Rhode Island	7.9
4	South Carolina	25.0
10	South Dakota	22.4
13	Tennessee	21.7
23	Texas	16.8
34	Utah	13.6
35	Vermont	12.9
36	Virginia	12.7
42	Washington	12.0
12	West Virginia	21.9
26	Wisconsin	15.3
2	Wyoming	30.0

RANK ORDER

RANK	STATE	RATE
1	Mississippi	32.9
2	Wyoming	30.0
3	Alabama	25.7
4	South Carolina	25.0
5	Montana	24.7
6	Arkansas	24.6
7	Kentucky	23.7
8	New Mexico	23.6
9	Oklahoma	23.0
10	Louisiana	22.4
10	South Dakota	22.4
12	West Virginia	21.9
13	Tennessee	21.7
14	Arizona	20.4
15	Missouri	20.3
16	Idaho	19.8
17	Florida	19.7
18	North Dakota	19.6
19	Nevada	19.3
20	North Carolina	19.1
21	Georgia	18.8
22	Kansas	17.9
23	Texas	16.8
24	Nebraska	15.9
25	Indiana	15.4
26	Wisconsin	15.3
27	Iowa	15.2
28	Alaska	14.6
29	Colorado	14.3
30	Maine	14.1
31	Delaware	13.8
31	Oregon	13.8
31	Pennsylvania	13.8
34	Utah	13.6
35	Vermont	12.9
36	Virginia	12.7
37	California	12.3
38	Minnesota	12.2
38	New Hampshire	12.2
40	Michigan	12.1
40	Ohio	12.1
42	Washington	12.0
43	Illinois	11.5
44	Maryland	11.2
45	Hawaii	11.0
46	New Jersey	8.7
47	Connecticut	8.3
48	Rhode Island	7.9
49	New York	7.8
50	Massachusetts	7.3
	District of Columbia	6.9

Source: U.S. Department of Health and Human Services, National Center for Health Statistics
"National Vital Statistics Reports" (Vol. 56, No. 10, April 24, 2008, http://www.cdc.gov/nchs/deaths.htm)
*Final data by state of residence. These numbers are compiled from death certificates by the Centers for Disease Control and Prevention. They may differ from motor vehicle deaths collected by the U.S. Department of Transportation from other sources. Age-adjusted rates based on the year 2000 standard population.

Deaths by Firearm Injury in 2005

National Total = 30,694 Deaths*

ALPHA ORDER

RANK	STATE	DEATHS	% of USA
16	Alabama	736	2.4%
41	Alaska	116	0.4%
12	Arizona	934	3.0%
26	Arkansas	439	1.4%
1	California	3,453	11.2%
22	Colorado	535	1.7%
38	Connecticut	187	0.6%
45	Delaware	75	0.2%
3	Florida	1,838	6.0%
8	Georgia	1,064	3.5%
50	Hawaii	28	0.1%
37	Idaho	195	0.6%
9	Illinois	1,019	3.3%
17	Indiana	705	2.3%
36	Iowa	201	0.7%
33	Kansas	257	0.8%
21	Kentucky	548	1.8%
14	Louisiana	858	2.8%
42	Maine	109	0.4%
18	Maryland	657	2.1%
35	Massachusetts	224	0.7%
7	Michigan	1,074	3.5%
30	Minnesota	361	1.2%
25	Mississippi	455	1.5%
15	Missouri	752	2.4%
39	Montana	161	0.5%
40	Nebraska	135	0.4%
29	Nevada	390	1.3%
43	New Hampshire	88	0.3%
27	New Jersey	434	1.4%
31	New Mexico	267	0.9%
9	New York	1,019	3.3%
5	North Carolina	1,119	3.6%
47	North Dakota	61	0.2%
6	Ohio	1,116	3.6%
24	Oklahoma	468	1.5%
28	Oregon	402	1.3%
4	Pennsylvania	1,352	4.4%
49	Rhode Island	39	0.1%
19	South Carolina	589	1.9%
44	South Dakota	82	0.3%
11	Tennessee	976	3.2%
2	Texas	2,490	8.1%
34	Utah	227	0.7%
48	Vermont	44	0.1%
13	Virginia	888	2.9%
20	Washington	567	1.8%
32	West Virginia	261	0.9%
23	Wisconsin	474	1.5%
46	Wyoming	71	0.2%

RANK ORDER

RANK	STATE	DEATHS	% of USA
1	California	3,453	11.2%
2	Texas	2,490	8.1%
3	Florida	1,838	6.0%
4	Pennsylvania	1,352	4.4%
5	North Carolina	1,119	3.6%
6	Ohio	1,116	3.6%
7	Michigan	1,074	3.5%
8	Georgia	1,064	3.5%
9	Illinois	1,019	3.3%
9	New York	1,019	3.3%
11	Tennessee	976	3.2%
12	Arizona	934	3.0%
13	Virginia	888	2.9%
14	Louisiana	858	2.8%
15	Missouri	752	2.4%
16	Alabama	736	2.4%
17	Indiana	705	2.3%
18	Maryland	657	2.1%
19	South Carolina	589	1.9%
20	Washington	567	1.8%
21	Kentucky	548	1.8%
22	Colorado	535	1.7%
23	Wisconsin	474	1.5%
24	Oklahoma	468	1.5%
25	Mississippi	455	1.5%
26	Arkansas	439	1.4%
27	New Jersey	434	1.4%
28	Oregon	402	1.3%
29	Nevada	390	1.3%
30	Minnesota	361	1.2%
31	New Mexico	267	0.9%
32	West Virginia	261	0.9%
33	Kansas	257	0.8%
34	Utah	227	0.7%
35	Massachusetts	224	0.7%
36	Iowa	201	0.7%
37	Idaho	195	0.6%
38	Connecticut	187	0.6%
39	Montana	161	0.5%
40	Nebraska	135	0.4%
41	Alaska	116	0.4%
42	Maine	109	0.4%
43	New Hampshire	88	0.3%
44	South Dakota	82	0.3%
45	Delaware	75	0.2%
46	Wyoming	71	0.2%
47	North Dakota	61	0.2%
48	Vermont	44	0.1%
49	Rhode Island	39	0.1%
50	Hawaii	28	0.1%
	District of Columbia	154	0.5%

Source: U.S. Department of Health and Human Services, National Center for Health Statistics
"National Vital Statistics Reports" (Vol. 56, No. 10, April 24, 2008, http://www.cdc.gov/nchs/deaths.htm)
*Final data by state of residence.

Death Rate by Firearm Injury in 2005

National Rate = 10.4 Deaths per 100,000 Population*

ALPHA ORDER			RANK ORDER		
RANK	STATE	RATE	RANK	STATE	RATE
6	Alabama	16.1	1	Louisiana	19.0
2	Alaska	17.5	2	Alaska	17.5
8	Arizona	15.7	3	Montana	17.2
7	Arkansas	15.8	4	Tennessee	16.4
31	California	9.6	5	Nevada	16.2
22	Colorado	11.5	6	Alabama	16.1
45	Connecticut	5.3	7	Arkansas	15.8
36	Delaware	8.9	8	Arizona	15.7
29	Florida	10.3	9	Mississippi	15.6
19	Georgia	11.7	10	West Virginia	14.4
50	Hawaii	2.2	11	Wyoming	13.9
14	Idaho	13.6	12	New Mexico	13.8
39	Illinois	8.0	12	South Carolina	13.8
23	Indiana	11.2	14	Idaho	13.6
43	Iowa	6.8	15	Oklahoma	13.2
33	Kansas	9.4	16	Kentucky	13.1
16	Kentucky	13.1	17	Missouri	13.0
1	Louisiana	19.0	18	North Carolina	12.9
38	Maine	8.2	19	Georgia	11.7
19	Maryland	11.7	19	Maryland	11.7
49	Massachusetts	3.5	19	Virginia	11.7
27	Michigan	10.6	22	Colorado	11.5
42	Minnesota	7.0	23	Indiana	11.2
9	Mississippi	15.6	24	Oregon	11.0
17	Missouri	13.0	25	Pennsylvania	10.9
3	Montana	17.2	25	Texas	10.9
40	Nebraska	7.7	27	Michigan	10.6
5	Nevada	16.2	27	South Dakota	10.6
44	New Hampshire	6.7	29	Florida	10.3
47	New Jersey	5.0	30	Ohio	9.7
12	New Mexico	13.8	31	California	9.6
45	New York	5.3	31	North Dakota	9.6
18	North Carolina	12.9	33	Kansas	9.4
31	North Dakota	9.6	34	Utah	9.2
30	Ohio	9.7	35	Washington	9.0
15	Oklahoma	13.2	36	Delaware	8.9
24	Oregon	11.0	37	Wisconsin	8.6
25	Pennsylvania	10.9	38	Maine	8.2
48	Rhode Island	3.6	39	Illinois	8.0
12	South Carolina	13.8	40	Nebraska	7.7
27	South Dakota	10.6	41	Vermont	7.1
4	Tennessee	16.4	42	Minnesota	7.0
25	Texas	10.9	43	Iowa	6.8
34	Utah	9.2	44	New Hampshire	6.7
41	Vermont	7.1	45	Connecticut	5.3
19	Virginia	11.7	45	New York	5.3
35	Washington	9.0	47	New Jersey	5.0
10	West Virginia	14.4	48	Rhode Island	3.6
37	Wisconsin	8.6	49	Massachusetts	3.5
11	Wyoming	13.9	50	Hawaii	2.2
				District of Columbia	28.0

Source: U.S. Department of Health and Human Services, National Center for Health Statistics
   "National Vital Statistics Reports" (Vol. 56, No. 10, April 24, 2008, http://www.cdc.gov/nchs/deaths.htm)
*Final data by state of residence. Not age-adjusted.

Age-Adjusted Death Rate by Firearm Injury in 2005

National Rate = 10.2 Deaths per 100,000 Population*

<table>
<tr><td colspan="3">ALPHA ORDER</td><td colspan="3">RANK ORDER</td></tr>
<tr><td>RANK</td><td>STATE</td><td>RATE</td><td>RANK</td><td>STATE</td><td>RATE</td></tr>
<tr><td>6</td><td>Alabama</td><td>15.9</td><td>1</td><td>Louisiana</td><td>18.6</td></tr>
<tr><td>2</td><td>Alaska</td><td>17.8</td><td>2</td><td>Alaska</td><td>17.8</td></tr>
<tr><td>7</td><td>Arizona</td><td>15.8</td><td>3</td><td>Montana</td><td>16.7</td></tr>
<tr><td>9</td><td>Arkansas</td><td>15.6</td><td>4</td><td>Nevada</td><td>16.3</td></tr>
<tr><td>31</td><td>California</td><td>9.6</td><td>5</td><td>Tennessee</td><td>16.0</td></tr>
<tr><td>21</td><td>Colorado</td><td>11.6</td><td>6</td><td>Alabama</td><td>15.9</td></tr>
<tr><td>45</td><td>Connecticut</td><td>5.3</td><td>7</td><td>Arizona</td><td>15.8</td></tr>
<tr><td>34</td><td>Delaware</td><td>8.8</td><td>8</td><td>Mississippi</td><td>15.7</td></tr>
<tr><td>28</td><td>Florida</td><td>10.1</td><td>9</td><td>Arkansas</td><td>15.6</td></tr>
<tr><td>19</td><td>Georgia</td><td>11.9</td><td>10</td><td>Idaho</td><td>13.9</td></tr>
<tr><td>50</td><td>Hawaii</td><td>2.2</td><td>11</td><td>New Mexico</td><td>13.8</td></tr>
<tr><td>10</td><td>Idaho</td><td>13.9</td><td>11</td><td>South Carolina</td><td>13.8</td></tr>
<tr><td>38</td><td>Illinois</td><td>7.9</td><td>13</td><td>West Virginia</td><td>13.7</td></tr>
<tr><td>23</td><td>Indiana</td><td>11.2</td><td>14</td><td>Wyoming</td><td>13.4</td></tr>
<tr><td>43</td><td>Iowa</td><td>6.6</td><td>15</td><td>Oklahoma</td><td>13.0</td></tr>
<tr><td>33</td><td>Kansas</td><td>9.2</td><td>16</td><td>Kentucky</td><td>12.9</td></tr>
<tr><td>16</td><td>Kentucky</td><td>12.9</td><td>17</td><td>Missouri</td><td>12.8</td></tr>
<tr><td>1</td><td>Louisiana</td><td>18.6</td><td>17</td><td>North Carolina</td><td>12.8</td></tr>
<tr><td>39</td><td>Maine</td><td>7.7</td><td>19</td><td>Georgia</td><td>11.9</td></tr>
<tr><td>19</td><td>Maryland</td><td>11.9</td><td>19</td><td>Maryland</td><td>11.9</td></tr>
<tr><td>49</td><td>Massachusetts</td><td>3.4</td><td>21</td><td>Colorado</td><td>11.6</td></tr>
<tr><td>27</td><td>Michigan</td><td>10.6</td><td>21</td><td>Virginia</td><td>11.6</td></tr>
<tr><td>41</td><td>Minnesota</td><td>6.9</td><td>23</td><td>Indiana</td><td>11.2</td></tr>
<tr><td>8</td><td>Mississippi</td><td>15.7</td><td>24</td><td>Texas</td><td>11.1</td></tr>
<tr><td>17</td><td>Missouri</td><td>12.8</td><td>25</td><td>Pennsylvania</td><td>10.8</td></tr>
<tr><td>3</td><td>Montana</td><td>16.7</td><td>26</td><td>Oregon</td><td>10.7</td></tr>
<tr><td>40</td><td>Nebraska</td><td>7.6</td><td>27</td><td>Michigan</td><td>10.6</td></tr>
<tr><td>4</td><td>Nevada</td><td>16.3</td><td>28</td><td>Florida</td><td>10.1</td></tr>
<tr><td>44</td><td>New Hampshire</td><td>6.5</td><td>28</td><td>South Dakota</td><td>10.1</td></tr>
<tr><td>47</td><td>New Jersey</td><td>5.1</td><td>30</td><td>Utah</td><td>9.9</td></tr>
<tr><td>11</td><td>New Mexico</td><td>13.8</td><td>31</td><td>California</td><td>9.6</td></tr>
<tr><td>46</td><td>New York</td><td>5.2</td><td>31</td><td>Ohio</td><td>9.6</td></tr>
<tr><td>17</td><td>North Carolina</td><td>12.8</td><td>33</td><td>Kansas</td><td>9.2</td></tr>
<tr><td>34</td><td>North Dakota</td><td>8.8</td><td>34</td><td>Delaware</td><td>8.8</td></tr>
<tr><td>31</td><td>Ohio</td><td>9.6</td><td>34</td><td>North Dakota</td><td>8.8</td></tr>
<tr><td>15</td><td>Oklahoma</td><td>13.0</td><td>36</td><td>Washington</td><td>8.7</td></tr>
<tr><td>26</td><td>Oregon</td><td>10.7</td><td>37</td><td>Wisconsin</td><td>8.5</td></tr>
<tr><td>25</td><td>Pennsylvania</td><td>10.8</td><td>38</td><td>Illinois</td><td>7.9</td></tr>
<tr><td>48</td><td>Rhode Island</td><td>3.6</td><td>39</td><td>Maine</td><td>7.7</td></tr>
<tr><td>11</td><td>South Carolina</td><td>13.8</td><td>40</td><td>Nebraska</td><td>7.6</td></tr>
<tr><td>28</td><td>South Dakota</td><td>10.1</td><td>41</td><td>Minnesota</td><td>6.9</td></tr>
<tr><td>5</td><td>Tennessee</td><td>16.0</td><td>42</td><td>Vermont</td><td>6.7</td></tr>
<tr><td>24</td><td>Texas</td><td>11.1</td><td>43</td><td>Iowa</td><td>6.6</td></tr>
<tr><td>30</td><td>Utah</td><td>9.9</td><td>44</td><td>New Hampshire</td><td>6.5</td></tr>
<tr><td>42</td><td>Vermont</td><td>6.7</td><td>45</td><td>Connecticut</td><td>5.3</td></tr>
<tr><td>21</td><td>Virginia</td><td>11.6</td><td>46</td><td>New York</td><td>5.2</td></tr>
<tr><td>36</td><td>Washington</td><td>8.7</td><td>47</td><td>New Jersey</td><td>5.1</td></tr>
<tr><td>13</td><td>West Virginia</td><td>13.7</td><td>48</td><td>Rhode Island</td><td>3.6</td></tr>
<tr><td>37</td><td>Wisconsin</td><td>8.5</td><td>49</td><td>Massachusetts</td><td>3.4</td></tr>
<tr><td>14</td><td>Wyoming</td><td>13.4</td><td>50</td><td>Hawaii</td><td>2.2</td></tr>
<tr><td></td><td></td><td></td><td></td><td>District of Columbia</td><td>27.0</td></tr>
</table>

Source: U.S. Department of Health and Human Services, National Center for Health Statistics
    "National Vital Statistics Reports" (Vol. 56, No. 10, April 24, 2008, http://www.cdc.gov/nchs/deaths.htm)
*Final data by state of residence. Age-adjusted rates based on the year 2000 standard population.

Deaths by Homicide in 2005

National Total = 18,124 Homicides*

ALPHA ORDER

RANK	STATE	DEATHS	% of USA
16	Alabama	433	2.4%
41	Alaska	37	0.2%
13	Arizona	532	2.9%
25	Arkansas	219	1.2%
1	California	2,540	14.0%
28	Colorado	182	1.0%
32	Connecticut	107	0.6%
37	Delaware	55	0.3%
3	Florida	998	5.5%
9	Georgia	649	3.6%
44	Hawaii	25	0.1%
38	Idaho	45	0.2%
5	Illinois	866	4.8%
19	Indiana	368	2.0%
39	Iowa	44	0.2%
33	Kansas	106	0.6%
24	Kentucky	222	1.2%
11	Louisiana	592	3.3%
45	Maine	22	0.1%
12	Maryland	576	3.2%
29	Massachusetts	178	1.0%
7	Michigan	677	3.7%
31	Minnesota	139	0.8%
21	Mississippi	254	1.4%
18	Missouri	417	2.3%
42	Montana	33	0.2%
39	Nebraska	44	0.2%
27	Nevada	190	1.0%
47	New Hampshire	19	0.1%
17	New Jersey	427	2.4%
30	New Mexico	152	0.8%
4	New York	901	5.0%
8	North Carolina	661	3.6%
50	North Dakota	11	0.1%
10	Ohio	630	3.5%
26	Oklahoma	214	1.2%
34	Oregon	102	0.6%
6	Pennsylvania	749	4.1%
43	Rhode Island	32	0.2%
20	South Carolina	337	1.9%
45	South Dakota	22	0.1%
14	Tennessee	495	2.7%
2	Texas	1,501	8.3%
36	Utah	63	0.3%
49	Vermont	12	0.1%
15	Virginia	490	2.7%
23	Washington	231	1.3%
35	West Virginia	93	0.5%
22	Wisconsin	236	1.3%
48	Wyoming	16	0.1%

RANK ORDER

RANK	STATE	DEATHS	% of USA
1	California	2,540	14.0%
2	Texas	1,501	8.3%
3	Florida	998	5.5%
4	New York	901	5.0%
5	Illinois	866	4.8%
6	Pennsylvania	749	4.1%
7	Michigan	677	3.7%
8	North Carolina	661	3.6%
9	Georgia	649	3.6%
10	Ohio	630	3.5%
11	Louisiana	592	3.3%
12	Maryland	576	3.2%
13	Arizona	532	2.9%
14	Tennessee	495	2.7%
15	Virginia	490	2.7%
16	Alabama	433	2.4%
17	New Jersey	427	2.4%
18	Missouri	417	2.3%
19	Indiana	368	2.0%
20	South Carolina	337	1.9%
21	Mississippi	254	1.4%
22	Wisconsin	236	1.3%
23	Washington	231	1.3%
24	Kentucky	222	1.2%
25	Arkansas	219	1.2%
26	Oklahoma	214	1.2%
27	Nevada	190	1.0%
28	Colorado	182	1.0%
29	Massachusetts	178	1.0%
30	New Mexico	152	0.8%
31	Minnesota	139	0.8%
32	Connecticut	107	0.6%
33	Kansas	106	0.6%
34	Oregon	102	0.6%
35	West Virginia	93	0.5%
36	Utah	63	0.3%
37	Delaware	55	0.3%
38	Idaho	45	0.2%
39	Iowa	44	0.2%
39	Nebraska	44	0.2%
41	Alaska	37	0.2%
42	Montana	33	0.2%
43	Rhode Island	32	0.2%
44	Hawaii	25	0.1%
45	Maine	22	0.1%
45	South Dakota	22	0.1%
47	New Hampshire	19	0.1%
48	Wyoming	16	0.1%
49	Vermont	12	0.1%
50	North Dakota	11	0.1%
	District of Columbia	180	1.0%

Source: U.S. Department of Health and Human Services, National Center for Health Statistics
  "National Vital Statistics Reports" (Vol. 56, No. 10, April 24, 2008, http://www.cdc.gov/nchs/deaths.htm)
*By state of residence. Includes legal intervention. Homicide data shown here are collected by the Centers for Disease Control
and Prevention based on death certificates and differ from murder data collected by the F.B.I. from other sources.

Death Rate by Homicide in 2005

National Rate = 6.1 Deaths per 100,000 Population*

ALPHA ORDER			RANK ORDER		
RANK	STATE	RATE	RANK	STATE	RATE
3	Alabama	9.5	1	Louisiana	13.1
23	Alaska	5.6	2	Maryland	10.3
4	Arizona	9.0	3	Alabama	9.5
7	Arkansas	7.9	4	Arizona	9.0
14	California	7.0	5	Mississippi	8.7
31	Colorado	3.9	6	Tennessee	8.3
36	Connecticut	3.0	7	Arkansas	7.9
18	Delaware	6.5	7	Nevada	7.9
23	Florida	5.6	7	New Mexico	7.9
12	Georgia	7.2	7	South Carolina	7.9
44	Hawaii	2.0	11	North Carolina	7.6
35	Idaho	3.1	12	Georgia	7.2
15	Illinois	6.8	12	Missouri	7.2
22	Indiana	5.9	14	California	7.0
46	Iowa	1.5	15	Illinois	6.8
31	Kansas	3.9	16	Michigan	6.7
26	Kentucky	5.3	17	Texas	6.6
1	Louisiana	13.1	18	Delaware	6.5
45	Maine	1.7	18	Virginia	6.5
2	Maryland	10.3	20	Oklahoma	6.0
38	Massachusetts	2.8	20	Pennsylvania	6.0
16	Michigan	6.7	22	Indiana	5.9
41	Minnesota	2.7	23	Alaska	5.6
5	Mississippi	8.7	23	Florida	5.6
12	Missouri	7.2	25	Ohio	5.5
34	Montana	3.5	26	Kentucky	5.3
43	Nebraska	2.5	27	West Virginia	5.1
7	Nevada	7.9	28	New Jersey	4.9
NA	New Hampshire**	NA	29	New York	4.7
28	New Jersey	4.9	30	Wisconsin	4.3
7	New Mexico	7.9	31	Colorado	3.9
29	New York	4.7	31	Kansas	3.9
11	North Carolina	7.6	33	Washington	3.7
NA	North Dakota**	NA	34	Montana	3.5
25	Ohio	5.5	35	Idaho	3.1
20	Oklahoma	6.0	36	Connecticut	3.0
38	Oregon	2.8	36	Rhode Island	3.0
20	Pennsylvania	6.0	38	Massachusetts	2.8
36	Rhode Island	3.0	38	Oregon	2.8
7	South Carolina	7.9	38	South Dakota	2.8
38	South Dakota	2.8	41	Minnesota	2.7
6	Tennessee	8.3	42	Utah	2.6
17	Texas	6.6	43	Nebraska	2.5
42	Utah	2.6	44	Hawaii	2.0
NA	Vermont**	NA	45	Maine	1.7
18	Virginia	6.5	46	Iowa	1.5
33	Washington	3.7	NA	New Hampshire**	NA
27	West Virginia	5.1	NA	North Dakota**	NA
30	Wisconsin	4.3	NA	Vermont**	NA
NA	Wyoming**	NA	NA	Wyoming**	NA

District of Columbia   32.7

Source: U.S. Department of Health and Human Services, National Center for Health Statistics
 "National Vital Statistics Reports" (Vol. 56, No. 10, April 24, 2008, http://www.cdc.gov/nchs/deaths.htm)
*By state of residence. Includes legal intervention. Homicide data shown here are collected by the Centers for Disease Control and Prevention based on death certificates and differ from murder data collected by the F.B.I. from other sources. Not age-adjusted.
**Insufficient data to determine a reliable rate.

Age-Adjusted Death Rate by Homicide in 2005

National Rate = 6.1 Deaths per 100,000 Population*

ALPHA ORDER

RANK	STATE	RATE
3	Alabama	9.6
25	Alaska	5.4
4	Arizona	8.8
8	Arkansas	7.9
14	California	6.9
31	Colorado	3.8
35	Connecticut	3.2
17	Delaware	6.5
22	Florida	5.9
13	Georgia	7.0
44	Hawaii	2.0
35	Idaho	3.2
16	Illinois	6.7
22	Indiana	5.9
46	Iowa	1.5
31	Kansas	3.8
27	Kentucky	5.3
1	Louisiana	12.9
45	Maine	1.7
2	Maryland	10.4
39	Massachusetts	2.8
15	Michigan	6.8
41	Minnesota	2.7
4	Mississippi	8.8
12	Missouri	7.2
34	Montana	3.4
42	Nebraska	2.5
8	Nevada	7.9
NA	New Hampshire**	NA
28	New Jersey	5.1
7	New Mexico	8.0
29	New York	4.7
11	North Carolina	7.5
NA	North Dakota**	NA
24	Ohio	5.6
21	Oklahoma	6.0
39	Oregon	2.8
20	Pennsylvania	6.3
37	Rhode Island	3.0
8	South Carolina	7.9
38	South Dakota	2.9
6	Tennessee	8.3
17	Texas	6.5
43	Utah	2.4
NA	Vermont**	NA
19	Virginia	6.4
33	Washington	3.6
25	West Virginia	5.4
30	Wisconsin	4.3
NA	Wyoming**	NA

RANK ORDER

RANK	STATE	RATE
1	Louisiana	12.9
2	Maryland	10.4
3	Alabama	9.6
4	Arizona	8.8
4	Mississippi	8.8
6	Tennessee	8.3
7	New Mexico	8.0
8	Arkansas	7.9
8	Nevada	7.9
8	South Carolina	7.9
11	North Carolina	7.5
12	Missouri	7.2
13	Georgia	7.0
14	California	6.9
15	Michigan	6.8
16	Illinois	6.7
17	Delaware	6.5
17	Texas	6.5
19	Virginia	6.4
20	Pennsylvania	6.3
21	Oklahoma	6.0
22	Florida	5.9
22	Indiana	5.9
24	Ohio	5.6
25	Alaska	5.4
25	West Virginia	5.4
27	Kentucky	5.3
28	New Jersey	5.1
29	New York	4.7
30	Wisconsin	4.3
31	Colorado	3.8
31	Kansas	3.8
33	Washington	3.6
34	Montana	3.4
35	Connecticut	3.2
35	Idaho	3.2
37	Rhode Island	3.0
38	South Dakota	2.9
39	Massachusetts	2.8
39	Oregon	2.8
41	Minnesota	2.7
42	Nebraska	2.5
43	Utah	2.4
44	Hawaii	2.0
45	Maine	1.7
46	Iowa	1.5
NA	New Hampshire**	NA
NA	North Dakota**	NA
NA	Vermont**	NA
NA	Wyoming**	NA

District of Columbia   31.7

Source: U.S. Department of Health and Human Services, National Center for Health Statistics
    "National Vital Statistics Reports" (Vol. 56, No. 10, April 24, 2008, http://www.cdc.gov/nchs/deaths.htm)
*By state of residence. Includes legal intervention. Homicide data shown here are collected by the Centers for Disease Control and Prevention based on death certificates and differ from murder data collected by the F.B.I. from other sources. Age-adjusted rates based on the year 2000 standard population.
**Insufficient data to determine a reliable rate.

Deaths by Suicide in 2005

National Total = 32,637 Suicides*

ALPHA ORDER

RANK	STATE	DEATHS	% of USA
23	Alabama	535	1.6%
43	Alaska	131	0.4%
10	Arizona	945	2.9%
30	Arkansas	400	1.2%
1	California	3,206	9.8%
15	Colorado	800	2.5%
36	Connecticut	295	0.9%
48	Delaware	83	0.3%
3	Florida	2,347	7.2%
11	Georgia	924	2.8%
45	Hawaii	107	0.3%
38	Idaho	228	0.7%
8	Illinois	1,086	3.3%
16	Indiana	745	2.3%
35	Iowa	333	1.0%
32	Kansas	362	1.1%
19	Kentucky	566	1.7%
26	Louisiana	505	1.5%
41	Maine	175	0.5%
29	Maryland	472	1.4%
27	Massachusetts	480	1.5%
7	Michigan	1,108	3.4%
21	Minnesota	547	1.7%
31	Mississippi	363	1.1%
17	Missouri	727	2.2%
39	Montana	206	0.6%
40	Nebraska	187	0.6%
27	Nevada	480	1.5%
42	New Hampshire	162	0.5%
22	New Jersey	536	1.6%
34	New Mexico	342	1.0%
6	New York	1,189	3.6%
9	North Carolina	1,009	3.1%
46	North Dakota	92	0.3%
5	Ohio	1,341	4.1%
24	Oklahoma	522	1.6%
20	Oregon	560	1.7%
4	Pennsylvania	1,430	4.4%
50	Rhode Island	71	0.2%
25	South Carolina	510	1.6%
44	South Dakota	121	0.4%
13	Tennessee	856	2.6%
2	Texas	2,418	7.4%
33	Utah	348	1.1%
49	Vermont	78	0.2%
12	Virginia	866	2.7%
14	Washington	822	2.5%
37	West Virginia	255	0.8%
18	Wisconsin	643	2.0%
47	Wyoming	90	0.3%

RANK ORDER

RANK	STATE	DEATHS	% of USA
1	California	3,206	9.8%
2	Texas	2,418	7.4%
3	Florida	2,347	7.2%
4	Pennsylvania	1,430	4.4%
5	Ohio	1,341	4.1%
6	New York	1,189	3.6%
7	Michigan	1,108	3.4%
8	Illinois	1,086	3.3%
9	North Carolina	1,009	3.1%
10	Arizona	945	2.9%
11	Georgia	924	2.8%
12	Virginia	866	2.7%
13	Tennessee	856	2.6%
14	Washington	822	2.5%
15	Colorado	800	2.5%
16	Indiana	745	2.3%
17	Missouri	727	2.2%
18	Wisconsin	643	2.0%
19	Kentucky	566	1.7%
20	Oregon	560	1.7%
21	Minnesota	547	1.7%
22	New Jersey	536	1.6%
23	Alabama	535	1.6%
24	Oklahoma	522	1.6%
25	South Carolina	510	1.6%
26	Louisiana	505	1.5%
27	Massachusetts	480	1.5%
27	Nevada	480	1.5%
29	Maryland	472	1.4%
30	Arkansas	400	1.2%
31	Mississippi	363	1.1%
32	Kansas	362	1.1%
33	Utah	348	1.1%
34	New Mexico	342	1.0%
35	Iowa	333	1.0%
36	Connecticut	295	0.9%
37	West Virginia	255	0.8%
38	Idaho	228	0.7%
39	Montana	206	0.6%
40	Nebraska	187	0.6%
41	Maine	175	0.5%
42	New Hampshire	162	0.5%
43	Alaska	131	0.4%
44	South Dakota	121	0.4%
45	Hawaii	107	0.3%
46	North Dakota	92	0.3%
47	Wyoming	90	0.3%
48	Delaware	83	0.3%
49	Vermont	78	0.2%
50	Rhode Island	71	0.2%
	District of Columbia	33	0.1%

Source: U.S. Department of Health and Human Services, National Center for Health Statistics
   "National Vital Statistics Reports" (Vol. 56, No. 10, April 24, 2008, http://www.cdc.gov/nchs/deaths.htm)
*Final data by state of residence.

Death Rate by Suicide in 2005

National Rate = 11.0 Deaths per 100,000 Population*

ALPHA ORDER

RANK	STATE	RATE
28	Alabama	11.7
3	Alaska	19.7
8	Arizona	15.9
13	Arkansas	14.4
42	California	8.9
6	Colorado	17.1
44	Connecticut	8.4
41	Delaware	9.8
18	Florida	13.2
40	Georgia	10.2
44	Hawaii	8.4
7	Idaho	16.0
43	Illinois	8.5
27	Indiana	11.9
34	Iowa	11.2
18	Kansas	13.2
17	Kentucky	13.6
34	Louisiana	11.2
18	Maine	13.2
44	Maryland	8.4
47	Massachusetts	7.5
36	Michigan	10.9
37	Minnesota	10.7
24	Mississippi	12.4
22	Missouri	12.5
1	Montana	22.0
38	Nebraska	10.6
2	Nevada	19.9
24	New Hampshire	12.4
50	New Jersey	6.1
4	New Mexico	17.7
49	New York	6.2
30	North Carolina	11.6
12	North Dakota	14.5
28	Ohio	11.7
11	Oklahoma	14.7
10	Oregon	15.4
32	Pennsylvania	11.5
48	Rhode Island	6.6
26	South Carolina	12.0
9	South Dakota	15.6
13	Tennessee	14.4
38	Texas	10.6
15	Utah	14.1
22	Vermont	12.5
33	Virginia	11.4
21	Washington	13.1
16	West Virginia	14.0
30	Wisconsin	11.6
4	Wyoming	17.7

RANK ORDER

RANK	STATE	RATE
1	Montana	22.0
2	Nevada	19.9
3	Alaska	19.7
4	New Mexico	17.7
4	Wyoming	17.7
6	Colorado	17.1
7	Idaho	16.0
8	Arizona	15.9
9	South Dakota	15.6
10	Oregon	15.4
11	Oklahoma	14.7
12	North Dakota	14.5
13	Arkansas	14.4
13	Tennessee	14.4
15	Utah	14.1
16	West Virginia	14.0
17	Kentucky	13.6
18	Florida	13.2
18	Kansas	13.2
18	Maine	13.2
21	Washington	13.1
22	Missouri	12.5
22	Vermont	12.5
24	Mississippi	12.4
24	New Hampshire	12.4
26	South Carolina	12.0
27	Indiana	11.9
28	Alabama	11.7
28	Ohio	11.7
30	North Carolina	11.6
30	Wisconsin	11.6
32	Pennsylvania	11.5
33	Virginia	11.4
34	Iowa	11.2
34	Louisiana	11.2
36	Michigan	10.9
37	Minnesota	10.7
38	Nebraska	10.6
38	Texas	10.6
40	Georgia	10.2
41	Delaware	9.8
42	California	8.9
43	Illinois	8.5
44	Connecticut	8.4
44	Hawaii	8.4
44	Maryland	8.4
47	Massachusetts	7.5
48	Rhode Island	6.6
49	New York	6.2
50	New Jersey	6.1
	District of Columbia	6.0

Source: U.S. Department of Health and Human Services, National Center for Health Statistics
"National Vital Statistics Reports" (Vol. 56, No. 10, April 24, 2008, http://www.cdc.gov/nchs/deaths.htm)
*Final data by state of residence. Not age-adjusted.

Age-Adjusted Death Rate by Suicide in 2005

National Rate = 10.9 Deaths per 100,000 Population*

ALPHA ORDER				RANK ORDER		
RANK	STATE	RATE		RANK	STATE	RATE
28	Alabama	11.5		1	Montana	21.5
2	Alaska	20.2		2	Alaska	20.2
7	Arizona	16.2		3	Nevada	20.1
13	Arkansas	14.2		4	New Mexico	17.7
42	California	9.1		5	Colorado	17.3
5	Colorado	17.3		6	Wyoming	17.2
46	Connecticut	8.1		7	Arizona	16.2
41	Delaware	9.6		7	Idaho	16.2
20	Florida	12.6		9	South Dakota	15.3
39	Georgia	10.5		10	Utah	15.1
45	Hawaii	8.3		11	Oregon	14.8
7	Idaho	16.2		12	Oklahoma	14.7
43	Illinois	8.5		13	Arkansas	14.2
25	Indiana	11.9		14	Tennessee	14.0
35	Iowa	10.9		15	North Dakota	13.7
18	Kansas	13.1		16	Kentucky	13.3
16	Kentucky	13.3		17	West Virginia	13.2
33	Louisiana	11.1		18	Kansas	13.1
23	Maine	12.3		19	Washington	12.7
44	Maryland	8.4		20	Florida	12.6
47	Massachusetts	7.2		20	Mississippi	12.6
37	Michigan	10.8		22	Missouri	12.4
40	Minnesota	10.3		23	Maine	12.3
20	Mississippi	12.6		24	Vermont	12.2
22	Missouri	12.4		25	Indiana	11.9
1	Montana	21.5		26	New Hampshire	11.8
37	Nebraska	10.8		26	South Carolina	11.8
3	Nevada	20.1		28	Alabama	11.5
26	New Hampshire	11.8		28	North Carolina	11.5
49	New Jersey	6.0		28	Wisconsin	11.5
4	New Mexico	17.7		31	Ohio	11.4
49	New York	6.0		32	Virginia	11.2
28	North Carolina	11.5		33	Louisiana	11.1
15	North Dakota	13.7		33	Pennsylvania	11.1
31	Ohio	11.4		35	Iowa	10.9
12	Oklahoma	14.7		35	Texas	10.9
11	Oregon	14.8		37	Michigan	10.8
33	Pennsylvania	11.1		37	Nebraska	10.8
48	Rhode Island	6.3		39	Georgia	10.5
26	South Carolina	11.8		40	Minnesota	10.3
9	South Dakota	15.3		41	Delaware	9.6
14	Tennessee	14.0		42	California	9.1
35	Texas	10.9		43	Illinois	8.5
10	Utah	15.1		44	Maryland	8.4
24	Vermont	12.2		45	Hawaii	8.3
32	Virginia	11.2		46	Connecticut	8.1
19	Washington	12.7		47	Massachusetts	7.2
17	West Virginia	13.2		48	Rhode Island	6.3
28	Wisconsin	11.5		49	New Jersey	6.0
6	Wyoming	17.2		49	New York	6.0
					District of Columbia	5.5

Source: U.S. Department of Health and Human Services, National Center for Health Statistics
"National Vital Statistics Reports" (Vol. 56, No. 10, April 24, 2008, http://www.cdc.gov/nchs/deaths.htm)
*Final data by state of residence. Age-adjusted rates based on the year 2000 standard population.

Alcohol-Induced Deaths in 2005

National Total = 21,634 Deaths*

ALPHA ORDER

RANK ORDER

RANK	STATE	DEATHS	% of USA
27	Alabama	255	1.2%
40	Alaska	121	0.6%
7	Arizona	667	3.1%
35	Arkansas	146	0.7%
1	California	3,932	18.2%
13	Colorado	500	2.3%
32	Connecticut	186	0.9%
47	Delaware	58	0.3%
2	Florida	1,612	7.5%
12	Georgia	506	2.3%
50	Hawaii	49	0.2%
36	Idaho	135	0.6%
10	Illinois	572	2.6%
24	Indiana	319	1.5%
31	Iowa	193	0.9%
33	Kansas	177	0.8%
28	Kentucky	252	1.2%
30	Louisiana	216	1.0%
38	Maine	131	0.6%
26	Maryland	281	1.3%
18	Massachusetts	380	1.8%
6	Michigan	725	3.4%
21	Minnesota	345	1.6%
34	Mississippi	162	0.7%
23	Missouri	340	1.6%
39	Montana	125	0.6%
41	Nebraska	113	0.5%
29	Nevada	225	1.0%
43	New Hampshire	110	0.5%
15	New Jersey	486	2.2%
24	New Mexico	319	1.5%
4	New York	1,064	4.9%
8	North Carolina	616	2.8%
45	North Dakota	75	0.3%
5	Ohio	754	3.5%
21	Oklahoma	345	1.6%
11	Oregon	530	2.4%
14	Pennsylvania	490	2.3%
48	Rhode Island	56	0.3%
19	South Carolina	378	1.7%
44	South Dakota	87	0.4%
17	Tennessee	451	2.1%
3	Texas	1,271	5.9%
37	Utah	133	0.6%
49	Vermont	53	0.2%
20	Virginia	350	1.6%
8	Washington	616	2.8%
42	West Virginia	112	0.5%
16	Wisconsin	468	2.2%
46	Wyoming	64	0.3%

RANK	STATE	DEATHS	% of USA
1	California	3,932	18.2%
2	Florida	1,612	7.5%
3	Texas	1,271	5.9%
4	New York	1,064	4.9%
5	Ohio	754	3.5%
6	Michigan	725	3.4%
7	Arizona	667	3.1%
8	North Carolina	616	2.8%
8	Washington	616	2.8%
10	Illinois	572	2.6%
11	Oregon	530	2.4%
12	Georgia	506	2.3%
13	Colorado	500	2.3%
14	Pennsylvania	490	2.3%
15	New Jersey	486	2.2%
16	Wisconsin	468	2.2%
17	Tennessee	451	2.1%
18	Massachusetts	380	1.8%
19	South Carolina	378	1.7%
20	Virginia	350	1.6%
21	Minnesota	345	1.6%
21	Oklahoma	345	1.6%
23	Missouri	340	1.6%
24	Indiana	319	1.5%
24	New Mexico	319	1.5%
26	Maryland	281	1.3%
27	Alabama	255	1.2%
28	Kentucky	252	1.2%
29	Nevada	225	1.0%
30	Louisiana	216	1.0%
31	Iowa	193	0.9%
32	Connecticut	186	0.9%
33	Kansas	177	0.8%
34	Mississippi	162	0.7%
35	Arkansas	146	0.7%
36	Idaho	135	0.6%
37	Utah	133	0.6%
38	Maine	131	0.6%
39	Montana	125	0.6%
40	Alaska	121	0.6%
41	Nebraska	113	0.5%
42	West Virginia	112	0.5%
43	New Hampshire	110	0.5%
44	South Dakota	87	0.4%
45	North Dakota	75	0.3%
46	Wyoming	64	0.3%
47	Delaware	58	0.3%
48	Rhode Island	56	0.3%
49	Vermont	53	0.2%
50	Hawaii	49	0.2%
	District of Columbia	83	0.4%

Source: U.S. Department of Health and Human Services, National Center for Health Statistics
(http://wonder.cdc.gov)
*By state of residence. Includes excessive blood level of alcohol, accidental poisoning by alcohol and the following
alcohol-related causes: psychoses, dependence syndrome, polyneuropathy, cardiomyopathy, gastritis, chronic liver disease, and
cirrhosis. Excludes accidents, homicides, and other causes indirectly related to alcohol use.

Death Rate by Alcohol-Induced Deaths in 2005

National Rate = 7.3 Deaths per 100,000 Population*

ALPHA ORDER

RANK	STATE	RATE
34	Alabama	5.6
1	Alaska	18.2
7	Arizona	11.2
40	Arkansas	5.3
9	California	10.9
10	Colorado	10.7
40	Connecticut	5.3
24	Delaware	6.9
16	Florida	9.1
37	Georgia	5.5
50	Hawaii	3.8
14	Idaho	9.4
48	Illinois	4.5
44	Indiana	5.1
27	Iowa	6.5
28	Kansas	6.4
31	Kentucky	6.0
46	Louisiana	4.8
11	Maine	9.9
45	Maryland	5.0
32	Massachusetts	5.9
22	Michigan	7.2
25	Minnesota	6.7
34	Mississippi	5.6
32	Missouri	5.9
4	Montana	13.4
28	Nebraska	6.4
15	Nevada	9.3
20	New Hampshire	8.4
34	New Jersey	5.6
2	New Mexico	16.6
37	New York	5.5
23	North Carolina	7.1
6	North Dakota	11.8
26	Ohio	6.6
13	Oklahoma	9.7
3	Oregon	14.6
49	Pennsylvania	3.9
43	Rhode Island	5.2
17	South Carolina	8.9
7	South Dakota	11.2
21	Tennessee	7.6
37	Texas	5.5
40	Utah	5.3
18	Vermont	8.5
47	Virginia	4.6
12	Washington	9.8
30	West Virginia	6.2
18	Wisconsin	8.5
5	Wyoming	12.6

RANK ORDER

RANK	STATE	RATE
1	Alaska	18.2
2	New Mexico	16.6
3	Oregon	14.6
4	Montana	13.4
5	Wyoming	12.6
6	North Dakota	11.8
7	Arizona	11.2
7	South Dakota	11.2
9	California	10.9
10	Colorado	10.7
11	Maine	9.9
12	Washington	9.8
13	Oklahoma	9.7
14	Idaho	9.4
15	Nevada	9.3
16	Florida	9.1
17	South Carolina	8.9
18	Vermont	8.5
18	Wisconsin	8.5
20	New Hampshire	8.4
21	Tennessee	7.6
22	Michigan	7.2
23	North Carolina	7.1
24	Delaware	6.9
25	Minnesota	6.7
26	Ohio	6.6
27	Iowa	6.5
28	Kansas	6.4
28	Nebraska	6.4
30	West Virginia	6.2
31	Kentucky	6.0
32	Massachusetts	5.9
32	Missouri	5.9
34	Alabama	5.6
34	Mississippi	5.6
34	New Jersey	5.6
37	Georgia	5.5
37	New York	5.5
37	Texas	5.5
40	Arkansas	5.3
40	Connecticut	5.3
40	Utah	5.3
43	Rhode Island	5.2
44	Indiana	5.1
45	Maryland	5.0
46	Louisiana	4.8
47	Virginia	4.6
48	Illinois	4.5
49	Pennsylvania	3.9
50	Hawaii	3.8

District of Columbia 14.3

Source: U.S. Department of Health and Human Services, National Center for Health Statistics
(http://wonder.cdc.gov)

*By state of residence. Includes excessive blood level of alcohol, accidental poisoning by alcohol and the following alcohol-related causes: psychoses, dependence syndrome, polyneuropathy, cardiomyopathy, gastritis, chronic liver disease, and cirrhosis. Excludes accidents, homicides, and other causes indirectly related to alcohol use. Not age-adjusted.

Age-Adjusted Death Rate by Alcohol-Induced Deaths in 2005

National Rate = 7.0 Deaths per 100,000 Population*

ALPHA ORDER

RANK	STATE	RATE
38	Alabama	5.2
1	Alaska	19.7
6	Arizona	11.3
41	Arkansas	4.9
7	California	11.2
10	Colorado	10.5
44	Connecticut	4.8
27	Delaware	6.3
17	Florida	8.1
33	Georgia	5.5
49	Hawaii	3.6
11	Idaho	9.5
47	Illinois	4.4
41	Indiana	4.9
29	Iowa	6.1
27	Kansas	6.3
32	Kentucky	5.7
45	Louisiana	4.7
16	Maine	8.2
45	Maryland	4.7
33	Massachusetts	5.5
22	Michigan	6.8
25	Minnesota	6.5
33	Mississippi	5.5
33	Missouri	5.5
4	Montana	12.1
26	Nebraska	6.4
14	Nevada	9.0
19	New Hampshire	7.5
38	New Jersey	5.2
2	New Mexico	16.5
38	New York	5.2
23	North Carolina	6.7
8	North Dakota	11.1
29	Ohio	6.1
12	Oklahoma	9.4
3	Oregon	13.4
49	Pennsylvania	3.6
41	Rhode Island	4.9
15	South Carolina	8.3
9	South Dakota	11.0
21	Tennessee	7.0
31	Texas	5.9
24	Utah	6.6
20	Vermont	7.4
47	Virginia	4.4
12	Washington	9.4
37	West Virginia	5.4
18	Wisconsin	7.9
5	Wyoming	11.7

RANK ORDER

RANK	STATE	RATE
1	Alaska	19.7
2	New Mexico	16.5
3	Oregon	13.4
4	Montana	12.1
5	Wyoming	11.7
6	Arizona	11.3
7	California	11.2
8	North Dakota	11.1
9	South Dakota	11.0
10	Colorado	10.5
11	Idaho	9.5
12	Oklahoma	9.4
12	Washington	9.4
14	Nevada	9.0
15	South Carolina	8.3
16	Maine	8.2
17	Florida	8.1
18	Wisconsin	7.9
19	New Hampshire	7.5
20	Vermont	7.4
21	Tennessee	7.0
22	Michigan	6.8
23	North Carolina	6.7
24	Utah	6.6
25	Minnesota	6.5
26	Nebraska	6.4
27	Delaware	6.3
27	Kansas	6.3
29	Iowa	6.1
29	Ohio	6.1
31	Texas	5.9
32	Kentucky	5.7
33	Georgia	5.5
33	Massachusetts	5.5
33	Mississippi	5.5
33	Missouri	5.5
37	West Virginia	5.4
38	Alabama	5.2
38	New Jersey	5.2
38	New York	5.2
41	Arkansas	4.9
41	Indiana	4.9
41	Rhode Island	4.9
44	Connecticut	4.8
45	Louisiana	4.7
45	Maryland	4.7
47	Illinois	4.4
47	Virginia	4.4
49	Hawaii	3.6
49	Pennsylvania	3.6

District of Columbia — 14.2

Source: U.S. Department of Health and Human Services, National Center for Health Statistics
(http://wonder.cdc.gov)
*By state of residence. Includes excessive blood level of alcohol, accidental poisoning by alcohol and the following alcohol-related causes: psychoses, dependence syndrome, polyneuropathy, cardiomyopathy, gastritis, chronic liver disease, and cirrhosis. Excludes accidents, homicides, and other causes indirectly related to alcohol use. Age-adjusted rates based on the year 2000 standard population.

Drug-Induced Deaths in 2005

National Total = 33,541 Deaths*

ALPHA ORDER

RANK	STATE	DEATHS	% of USA
32	Alabama	332	1.0%
45	Alaska	85	0.3%
14	Arizona	849	2.5%
33	Arkansas	286	0.9%
1	California	3,821	11.4%
20	Colorado	640	1.9%
30	Connecticut	352	1.0%
46	Delaware	67	0.2%
2	Florida	2,664	7.9%
15	Georgia	820	2.4%
41	Hawaii	143	0.4%
44	Idaho	118	0.4%
8	Illinois	1,140	3.4%
18	Indiana	665	2.0%
39	Iowa	154	0.5%
34	Kansas	284	0.8%
19	Kentucky	662	2.0%
16	Louisiana	752	2.2%
37	Maine	168	0.5%
17	Maryland	696	2.1%
13	Massachusetts	867	2.6%
5	Michigan	1,398	4.2%
31	Minnesota	338	1.0%
35	Mississippi	263	0.8%
20	Missouri	640	1.9%
43	Montana	119	0.4%
42	Nebraska	129	0.4%
28	Nevada	464	1.4%
40	New Hampshire	152	0.5%
10	New Jersey	966	2.9%
29	New Mexico	385	1.1%
7	New York	1,175	3.5%
9	North Carolina	1,061	3.2%
50	North Dakota	13	0.0%
6	Ohio	1,382	4.1%
24	Oklahoma	533	1.6%
25	Oregon	513	1.5%
4	Pennsylvania	1,680	5.0%
38	Rhode Island	163	0.5%
26	South Carolina	486	1.4%
48	South Dakota	47	0.1%
11	Tennessee	936	2.8%
3	Texas	2,152	6.4%
27	Utah	481	1.4%
47	Vermont	55	0.2%
22	Virginia	617	1.8%
12	Washington	931	2.8%
36	West Virginia	197	0.6%
23	Wisconsin	561	1.7%
49	Wyoming	45	0.1%

RANK ORDER

RANK	STATE	DEATHS	% of USA
1	California	3,821	11.4%
2	Florida	2,664	7.9%
3	Texas	2,152	6.4%
4	Pennsylvania	1,680	5.0%
5	Michigan	1,398	4.2%
6	Ohio	1,382	4.1%
7	New York	1,175	3.5%
8	Illinois	1,140	3.4%
9	North Carolina	1,061	3.2%
10	New Jersey	966	2.9%
11	Tennessee	936	2.8%
12	Washington	931	2.8%
13	Massachusetts	867	2.6%
14	Arizona	849	2.5%
15	Georgia	820	2.4%
16	Louisiana	752	2.2%
17	Maryland	696	2.1%
18	Indiana	665	2.0%
19	Kentucky	662	2.0%
20	Colorado	640	1.9%
20	Missouri	640	1.9%
22	Virginia	617	1.8%
23	Wisconsin	561	1.7%
24	Oklahoma	533	1.6%
25	Oregon	513	1.5%
26	South Carolina	486	1.4%
27	Utah	481	1.4%
28	Nevada	464	1.4%
29	New Mexico	385	1.1%
30	Connecticut	352	1.0%
31	Minnesota	338	1.0%
32	Alabama	332	1.0%
33	Arkansas	286	0.9%
34	Kansas	284	0.8%
35	Mississippi	263	0.8%
36	West Virginia	197	0.6%
37	Maine	168	0.5%
38	Rhode Island	163	0.5%
39	Iowa	154	0.5%
40	New Hampshire	152	0.5%
41	Hawaii	143	0.4%
42	Nebraska	129	0.4%
43	Montana	119	0.4%
44	Idaho	118	0.4%
45	Alaska	85	0.3%
46	Delaware	67	0.2%
47	Vermont	55	0.2%
48	South Dakota	47	0.1%
49	Wyoming	45	0.1%
50	North Dakota	13	0.0%
	District of Columbia	94	0.3%

Source: U.S. Department of Health and Human Services, National Center for Health Statistics
(http://wonder.cdc.gov)

*By state of residence. Includes drug psychoses, drug dependence, nondependent use excluding alcohol and tobacco, accidental poisoning or suicide by drugs, medicaments and biologicals. Excludes accidents, homicides and other causes indirectly related to drug use.

Death Rate by Drug-Induced Deaths in 2005

National Rate = 11.3 Deaths per 100,000 Population*

ALPHA ORDER

RANK	STATE	RATE
44	Alabama	7.3
17	Alaska	12.8
11	Arizona	14.3
31	Arkansas	10.3
29	California	10.6
14	Colorado	13.7
33	Connecticut	10.1
43	Delaware	8.0
8	Florida	15.0
36	Georgia	9.0
25	Hawaii	11.2
41	Idaho	8.3
38	Illinois	8.9
29	Indiana	10.6
49	Iowa	5.2
31	Kansas	10.3
5	Kentucky	15.9
4	Louisiana	16.7
18	Maine	12.7
20	Maryland	12.5
15	Massachusetts	13.5
13	Michigan	13.8
46	Minnesota	6.6
36	Mississippi	9.0
27	Missouri	11.0
18	Montana	12.7
44	Nebraska	7.3
3	Nevada	19.2
23	New Hampshire	11.6
26	New Jersey	11.1
1	New Mexico	20.0
47	New York	6.1
21	North Carolina	12.2
50	North Dakota	2.0
22	Ohio	12.0
8	Oklahoma	15.0
12	Oregon	14.1
15	Pennsylvania	13.5
7	Rhode Island	15.2
24	South Carolina	11.4
47	South Dakota	6.1
6	Tennessee	15.7
35	Texas	9.4
2	Utah	19.3
39	Vermont	8.8
42	Virginia	8.2
10	Washington	14.8
28	West Virginia	10.9
33	Wisconsin	10.1
39	Wyoming	8.8

RANK ORDER

RANK	STATE	RATE
1	New Mexico	20.0
2	Utah	19.3
3	Nevada	19.2
4	Louisiana	16.7
5	Kentucky	15.9
6	Tennessee	15.7
7	Rhode Island	15.2
8	Florida	15.0
8	Oklahoma	15.0
10	Washington	14.8
11	Arizona	14.3
12	Oregon	14.1
13	Michigan	13.8
14	Colorado	13.7
15	Massachusetts	13.5
15	Pennsylvania	13.5
17	Alaska	12.8
18	Maine	12.7
18	Montana	12.7
20	Maryland	12.5
21	North Carolina	12.2
22	Ohio	12.0
23	New Hampshire	11.6
24	South Carolina	11.4
25	Hawaii	11.2
26	New Jersey	11.1
27	Missouri	11.0
28	West Virginia	10.9
29	California	10.6
29	Indiana	10.6
31	Arkansas	10.3
31	Kansas	10.3
33	Connecticut	10.1
33	Wisconsin	10.1
35	Texas	9.4
36	Georgia	9.0
36	Mississippi	9.0
38	Illinois	8.9
39	Vermont	8.8
39	Wyoming	8.8
41	Idaho	8.3
42	Virginia	8.2
43	Delaware	8.0
44	Alabama	7.3
44	Nebraska	7.3
46	Minnesota	6.6
47	New York	6.1
47	South Dakota	6.1
49	Iowa	5.2
50	North Dakota	2.0

District of Columbia	16.1

Source: U.S. Department of Health and Human Services, National Center for Health Statistics
(http://wonder.cdc.gov)

*By state of residence. Includes drug psychoses, drug dependence, nondependent use excluding alcohol and tobacco, accidental poisoning or suicide by drugs, medicaments and biologicals. Excludes accidents, homicides and other causes indirectly related to drug use. Not age-adjusted.

Age-Adjusted Death Rate by Drug-Induced Deaths in 2005

National Rate = 11.2 Deaths per 100,000 Population*

ALPHA ORDER

RANK	STATE	RATE
44	Alabama	7.4
19	Alaska	12.2
9	Arizona	14.8
29	Arkansas	10.7
31	California	10.6
15	Colorado	13.3
34	Connecticut	9.9
42	Delaware	8.2
8	Florida	15.1
37	Georgia	8.9
26	Hawaii	11.1
40	Idaho	8.5
37	Illinois	8.9
29	Indiana	10.7
49	Iowa	5.2
32	Kansas	10.5
5	Kentucky	15.8
4	Louisiana	17.0
17	Maine	12.7
20	Maryland	12.1
16	Massachusetts	13.2
12	Michigan	13.7
46	Minnesota	6.5
36	Mississippi	9.3
24	Missouri	11.2
18	Montana	12.3
45	Nebraska	7.3
3	Nevada	19.2
24	New Hampshire	11.2
28	New Jersey	10.9
2	New Mexico	20.9
48	New York	5.9
20	North Carolina	12.1
50	North Dakota	2.0
22	Ohio	12.0
7	Oklahoma	15.4
14	Oregon	13.6
12	Pennsylvania	13.7
9	Rhode Island	14.8
23	South Carolina	11.3
47	South Dakota	6.3
6	Tennessee	15.6
35	Texas	9.6
1	Utah	21.3
39	Vermont	8.7
43	Virginia	8.0
11	Washington	14.2
26	West Virginia	11.1
33	Wisconsin	10.0
40	Wyoming	8.5

RANK ORDER

RANK	STATE	RATE
1	Utah	21.3
2	New Mexico	20.9
3	Nevada	19.2
4	Louisiana	17.0
5	Kentucky	15.8
6	Tennessee	15.6
7	Oklahoma	15.4
8	Florida	15.1
9	Arizona	14.8
9	Rhode Island	14.8
11	Washington	14.2
12	Michigan	13.7
12	Pennsylvania	13.7
14	Oregon	13.6
15	Colorado	13.3
16	Massachusetts	13.2
17	Maine	12.7
18	Montana	12.3
19	Alaska	12.2
20	Maryland	12.1
20	North Carolina	12.1
22	Ohio	12.0
23	South Carolina	11.3
24	Missouri	11.2
24	New Hampshire	11.2
26	Hawaii	11.1
26	West Virginia	11.1
28	New Jersey	10.9
29	Arkansas	10.7
29	Indiana	10.7
31	California	10.6
32	Kansas	10.5
33	Wisconsin	10.0
34	Connecticut	9.9
35	Texas	9.6
36	Mississippi	9.3
37	Georgia	8.9
37	Illinois	8.9
39	Vermont	8.7
40	Idaho	8.5
40	Wyoming	8.5
42	Delaware	8.2
43	Virginia	8.0
44	Alabama	7.4
45	Nebraska	7.3
46	Minnesota	6.5
47	South Dakota	6.3
48	New York	5.9
49	Iowa	5.2
50	North Dakota	2.0

	District of Columbia	16.3

Source: U.S. Department of Health and Human Services, National Center for Health Statistics
 (http://wonder.cdc.gov)
*By state of residence. Includes drug psychoses, drug dependence, nondependent use excluding alcohol and tobacco, accidental poisoning or suicide by drugs, medicaments and biologicals. Excludes accidents, homicides and other causes indirectly related to drug use. Age-adjusted rates based on the year 2000 standard population.

Occupational Fatalities in 2007

National Total = 5,488 Deaths*

ALPHA ORDER

RANK	STATE	DEATHS	% of USA
23	Alabama	99	1.8%
41	Alaska	30	0.5%
25	Arizona	88	1.6%
28	Arkansas	87	1.6%
2	California	407	7.4%
16	Colorado	119	2.2%
40	Connecticut	38	0.7%
48	Delaware	10	0.2%
3	Florida	362	6.6%
7	Georgia	171	3.1%
43	Hawaii	23	0.4%
41	Idaho	30	0.5%
6	Illinois	182	3.3%
14	Indiana	127	2.3%
25	Iowa	88	1.6%
22	Kansas	100	1.8%
18	Kentucky	112	2.0%
13	Louisiana	134	2.4%
45	Maine	21	0.4%
29	Maryland	82	1.5%
31	Massachusetts	74	1.3%
15	Michigan	120	2.2%
32	Minnesota	72	1.3%
24	Mississippi	92	1.7%
10	Missouri	155	2.8%
37	Montana	54	1.0%
35	Nebraska	63	1.1%
34	Nevada	68	1.2%
47	New Hampshire	14	0.3%
19	New Jersey	106	1.9%
39	New Mexico	43	0.8%
5	New York	219	4.0%
9	North Carolina	158	2.9%
43	North Dakota	23	0.4%
8	Ohio	164	3.0%
20	Oklahoma	104	1.9%
33	Oregon	69	1.3%
4	Pennsylvania	220	4.0%
50	Rhode Island	5	0.1%
17	South Carolina	114	2.1%
45	South Dakota	21	0.4%
11	Tennessee	147	2.7%
1	Texas	527	9.6%
30	Utah	78	1.4%
48	Vermont	10	0.2%
12	Virginia	141	2.6%
25	Washington	88	1.6%
36	West Virginia	61	1.1%
21	Wisconsin	103	1.9%
38	Wyoming	48	0.9%

RANK ORDER

RANK	STATE	DEATHS	% of USA
1	Texas	527	9.6%
2	California	407	7.4%
3	Florida	362	6.6%
4	Pennsylvania	220	4.0%
5	New York	219	4.0%
6	Illinois	182	3.3%
7	Georgia	171	3.1%
8	Ohio	164	3.0%
9	North Carolina	158	2.9%
10	Missouri	155	2.8%
11	Tennessee	147	2.7%
12	Virginia	141	2.6%
13	Louisiana	134	2.4%
14	Indiana	127	2.3%
15	Michigan	120	2.2%
16	Colorado	119	2.2%
17	South Carolina	114	2.1%
18	Kentucky	112	2.0%
19	New Jersey	106	1.9%
20	Oklahoma	104	1.9%
21	Wisconsin	103	1.9%
22	Kansas	100	1.8%
23	Alabama	99	1.8%
24	Mississippi	92	1.7%
25	Arizona	88	1.6%
25	Iowa	88	1.6%
25	Washington	88	1.6%
28	Arkansas	87	1.6%
29	Maryland	82	1.5%
30	Utah	78	1.4%
31	Massachusetts	74	1.3%
32	Minnesota	72	1.3%
33	Oregon	69	1.3%
34	Nevada	68	1.2%
35	Nebraska	63	1.1%
36	West Virginia	61	1.1%
37	Montana	54	1.0%
38	Wyoming	48	0.9%
39	New Mexico	43	0.8%
40	Connecticut	38	0.7%
41	Alaska	30	0.5%
41	Idaho	30	0.5%
43	Hawaii	23	0.4%
43	North Dakota	23	0.4%
45	Maine	21	0.4%
45	South Dakota	21	0.4%
47	New Hampshire	14	0.3%
48	Delaware	10	0.2%
48	Vermont	10	0.2%
50	Rhode Island	5	0.1%
	District of Columbia	13	0.2%

Source: U.S. Department of Labor, Bureau of Labor Statistics
   "National Census of Fatal Occupational Injuries in 2007" (press release, August 20, 2008, http://www.bls.gov/iif/home.htm)
*Preliminary data. Includes four fatalities that occurred within the territorial boundaries of the United States but for which a state of incident could not be determined.

Occupational Fatality Rate in 2007

National Rate = 3.7 Deaths per 100,000 Workers*

ALPHA ORDER

RANK	STATE	RATE
22	Alabama	4.6
3	Alaska	9.2
35	Arizona	3.0
8	Arkansas	6.7
43	California	2.4
22	Colorado	4.6
48	Connecticut	2.1
46	Delaware	2.3
24	Florida	4.1
27	Georgia	3.7
27	Hawaii	3.7
24	Idaho	4.1
38	Illinois	2.8
24	Indiana	4.1
15	Iowa	5.5
6	Kansas	7.0
13	Kentucky	5.8
7	Louisiana	6.9
34	Maine	3.1
38	Maryland	2.8
46	Massachusetts	2.3
41	Michigan	2.6
41	Minnesota	2.6
5	Mississippi	7.3
16	Missouri	5.4
2	Montana	11.1
9	Nebraska	6.6
17	Nevada	5.3
49	New Hampshire	1.9
43	New Jersey	2.4
20	New Mexico	4.7
43	New York	2.4
27	North Carolina	3.7
10	North Dakota	6.5
36	Ohio	2.9
11	Oklahoma	6.3
27	Oregon	3.7
31	Pennsylvania	3.6
50	Rhode Island	0.9
14	South Carolina	5.7
19	South Dakota	4.9
18	Tennessee	5.1
20	Texas	4.7
12	Utah	5.9
36	Vermont	2.9
31	Virginia	3.6
40	Washington	2.7
4	West Virginia	7.8
33	Wisconsin	3.5
1	Wyoming	17.1

RANK ORDER

RANK	STATE	RATE
1	Wyoming	17.1
2	Montana	11.1
3	Alaska	9.2
4	West Virginia	7.8
5	Mississippi	7.3
6	Kansas	7.0
7	Louisiana	6.9
8	Arkansas	6.7
9	Nebraska	6.6
10	North Dakota	6.5
11	Oklahoma	6.3
12	Utah	5.9
13	Kentucky	5.8
14	South Carolina	5.7
15	Iowa	5.5
16	Missouri	5.4
17	Nevada	5.3
18	Tennessee	5.1
19	South Dakota	4.9
20	New Mexico	4.7
20	Texas	4.7
22	Alabama	4.6
22	Colorado	4.6
24	Florida	4.1
24	Idaho	4.1
24	Indiana	4.1
27	Georgia	3.7
27	Hawaii	3.7
27	North Carolina	3.7
27	Oregon	3.7
31	Pennsylvania	3.6
31	Virginia	3.6
33	Wisconsin	3.5
34	Maine	3.1
35	Arizona	3.0
36	Ohio	2.9
36	Vermont	2.9
38	Illinois	2.8
38	Maryland	2.8
40	Washington	2.7
41	Michigan	2.6
41	Minnesota	2.6
43	California	2.4
43	New Jersey	2.4
43	New York	2.4
46	Delaware	2.3
46	Massachusetts	2.3
48	Connecticut	2.1
49	New Hampshire	1.9
50	Rhode Island	0.9
	District of Columbia	4.3

Source: CQ Press using data from U.S. Department of Labor, Bureau of Labor Statistics
"National Census of Fatal Occupational Injuries in 2007" (press release, August 20, 2008, http://www.bls.gov/iif/home.htm)
*Preliminary data. Rates based on employed civilian labor force.

III. Facilities

Community Hospitals in 2007

National Total = 4,897 Hospitals*

ALPHA ORDER

RANK	STATE	HOSPITALS	% of USA
20	Alabama	109	2.2%
47	Alaska	22	0.4%
31	Arizona	66	1.3%
26	Arkansas	84	1.7%
2	California	355	7.2%
28	Colorado	75	1.5%
42	Connecticut	34	0.7%
50	Delaware	6	0.1%
4	Florida	200	4.1%
8	Georgia	147	3.0%
46	Hawaii	23	0.5%
39	Idaho	39	0.8%
5	Illinois	190	3.9%
17	Indiana	114	2.3%
15	Iowa	117	2.4%
13	Kansas	128	2.6%
21	Kentucky	104	2.1%
12	Louisiana	129	2.6%
40	Maine	37	0.8%
36	Maryland	49	1.0%
27	Massachusetts	78	1.6%
9	Michigan	143	2.9%
11	Minnesota	131	2.7%
22	Mississippi	95	1.9%
15	Missouri	117	2.4%
34	Montana	52	1.1%
25	Nebraska	85	1.7%
43	Nevada	33	0.7%
44	New Hampshire	28	0.6%
29	New Jersey	73	1.5%
41	New Mexico	35	0.7%
3	New York	202	4.1%
18	North Carolina	113	2.3%
37	North Dakota	41	0.8%
7	Ohio	171	3.5%
18	Oklahoma	113	2.3%
32	Oregon	58	1.2%
6	Pennsylvania	187	3.8%
49	Rhode Island	11	0.2%
30	South Carolina	67	1.4%
35	South Dakota	51	1.0%
10	Tennessee	133	2.7%
1	Texas	409	8.4%
37	Utah	41	0.8%
48	Vermont	14	0.3%
23	Virginia	87	1.8%
23	Washington	87	1.8%
33	West Virginia	56	1.1%
14	Wisconsin	124	2.5%
45	Wyoming	24	0.5%

RANK ORDER

RANK	STATE	HOSPITALS	% of USA
1	Texas	409	8.4%
2	California	355	7.2%
3	New York	202	4.1%
4	Florida	200	4.1%
5	Illinois	190	3.9%
6	Pennsylvania	187	3.8%
7	Ohio	171	3.5%
8	Georgia	147	3.0%
9	Michigan	143	2.9%
10	Tennessee	133	2.7%
11	Minnesota	131	2.7%
12	Louisiana	129	2.6%
13	Kansas	128	2.6%
14	Wisconsin	124	2.5%
15	Iowa	117	2.4%
15	Missouri	117	2.4%
17	Indiana	114	2.3%
18	North Carolina	113	2.3%
18	Oklahoma	113	2.3%
20	Alabama	109	2.2%
21	Kentucky	104	2.1%
22	Mississippi	95	1.9%
23	Virginia	87	1.8%
23	Washington	87	1.8%
25	Nebraska	85	1.7%
26	Arkansas	84	1.7%
27	Massachusetts	78	1.6%
28	Colorado	75	1.5%
29	New Jersey	73	1.5%
30	South Carolina	67	1.4%
31	Arizona	66	1.3%
32	Oregon	58	1.2%
33	West Virginia	56	1.1%
34	Montana	52	1.1%
35	South Dakota	51	1.0%
36	Maryland	49	1.0%
37	North Dakota	41	0.8%
37	Utah	41	0.8%
39	Idaho	39	0.8%
40	Maine	37	0.8%
41	New Mexico	35	0.7%
42	Connecticut	34	0.7%
43	Nevada	33	0.7%
44	New Hampshire	28	0.6%
45	Wyoming	24	0.5%
46	Hawaii	23	0.5%
47	Alaska	22	0.4%
48	Vermont	14	0.3%
49	Rhode Island	11	0.2%
50	Delaware	6	0.1%
	District of Columbia	10	0.2%

Source: American Hospital Association (Chicago, IL)
"Hospital Statistics" (2009 edition)
*Community hospitals are all nonfederal, short-term, general, and special hospitals whose facilities and services are available to the public.

Rate of Community Hospitals in 2007

National Rate = 1.6 Community Hospitals per 100,000 Population*

ALPHA ORDER

RANK	STATE	RATE
18	Alabama	2.4
9	Alaska	3.2
43	Arizona	1.0
12	Arkansas	3.0
43	California	1.0
29	Colorado	1.5
43	Connecticut	1.0
50	Delaware	0.7
41	Florida	1.1
29	Georgia	1.5
24	Hawaii	1.8
15	Idaho	2.6
29	Illinois	1.5
24	Indiana	1.8
7	Iowa	3.9
5	Kansas	4.6
16	Kentucky	2.5
13	Louisiana	2.9
14	Maine	2.8
48	Maryland	0.9
39	Massachusetts	1.2
36	Michigan	1.4
16	Minnesota	2.5
8	Mississippi	3.3
23	Missouri	2.0
3	Montana	5.4
4	Nebraska	4.8
37	Nevada	1.3
22	New Hampshire	2.1
49	New Jersey	0.8
24	New Mexico	1.8
43	New York	1.0
39	North Carolina	1.2
1	North Dakota	6.4
29	Ohio	1.5
10	Oklahoma	3.1
28	Oregon	1.6
29	Pennsylvania	1.5
43	Rhode Island	1.0
29	South Carolina	1.5
1	South Dakota	6.4
20	Tennessee	2.2
27	Texas	1.7
29	Utah	1.5
19	Vermont	2.3
41	Virginia	1.1
37	Washington	1.3
10	West Virginia	3.1
20	Wisconsin	2.2
5	Wyoming	4.6

RANK ORDER

RANK	STATE	RATE
1	North Dakota	6.4
1	South Dakota	6.4
3	Montana	5.4
4	Nebraska	4.8
5	Kansas	4.6
5	Wyoming	4.6
7	Iowa	3.9
8	Mississippi	3.3
9	Alaska	3.2
10	Oklahoma	3.1
10	West Virginia	3.1
12	Arkansas	3.0
13	Louisiana	2.9
14	Maine	2.8
15	Idaho	2.6
16	Kentucky	2.5
16	Minnesota	2.5
18	Alabama	2.4
19	Vermont	2.3
20	Tennessee	2.2
20	Wisconsin	2.2
22	New Hampshire	2.1
23	Missouri	2.0
24	Hawaii	1.8
24	Indiana	1.8
24	New Mexico	1.8
27	Texas	1.7
28	Oregon	1.6
29	Colorado	1.5
29	Georgia	1.5
29	Illinois	1.5
29	Ohio	1.5
29	Pennsylvania	1.5
29	South Carolina	1.5
29	Utah	1.5
36	Michigan	1.4
37	Nevada	1.3
37	Washington	1.3
39	Massachusetts	1.2
39	North Carolina	1.2
41	Florida	1.1
41	Virginia	1.1
43	Arizona	1.0
43	California	1.0
43	Connecticut	1.0
43	New York	1.0
43	Rhode Island	1.0
48	Maryland	0.9
49	New Jersey	0.8
50	Delaware	0.7
	District of Columbia	1.7

Source: CQ Press using data from American Hospital Association (Chicago, IL)
"Hospital Statistics" (2009 edition)

*Community hospitals are all nonfederal, short-term, general, and special hospitals whose facilities and services are available to the public.

Community Hospitals per 1,000 Square Miles in 2007

National Rate = 1.3 Community Hospitals*

ALPHA ORDER

RANK	STATE	RATE
20	Alabama	2.1
50	Alaska**	0.0
41	Arizona	0.6
29	Arkansas	1.6
19	California	2.2
39	Colorado	0.7
4	Connecticut	6.1
17	Delaware	2.4
12	Florida	3.0
15	Georgia	2.5
20	Hawaii	2.1
44	Idaho	0.5
9	Illinois	3.3
11	Indiana	3.1
20	Iowa	2.1
29	Kansas	1.6
14	Kentucky	2.6
15	Louisiana	2.5
38	Maine	1.0
6	Maryland	3.9
2	Massachusetts	7.4
32	Michigan	1.5
32	Minnesota	1.5
25	Mississippi	2.0
28	Missouri	1.7
46	Montana	0.4
37	Nebraska	1.1
47	Nevada	0.3
12	New Hampshire	3.0
1	New Jersey	8.4
47	New Mexico	0.3
8	New York	3.7
20	North Carolina	2.1
41	North Dakota	0.6
7	Ohio	3.8
29	Oklahoma	1.6
41	Oregon	0.6
5	Pennsylvania	4.1
3	Rhode Island	7.1
20	South Carolina	2.1
39	South Dakota	0.7
10	Tennessee	3.2
32	Texas	1.5
44	Utah	0.5
32	Vermont	1.5
25	Virginia	2.0
36	Washington	1.2
18	West Virginia	2.3
27	Wisconsin	1.9
49	Wyoming	0.2

RANK ORDER

RANK	STATE	RATE
1	New Jersey	8.4
2	Massachusetts	7.4
3	Rhode Island	7.1
4	Connecticut	6.1
5	Pennsylvania	4.1
6	Maryland	3.9
7	Ohio	3.8
8	New York	3.7
9	Illinois	3.3
10	Tennessee	3.2
11	Indiana	3.1
12	Florida	3.0
12	New Hampshire	3.0
14	Kentucky	2.6
15	Georgia	2.5
15	Louisiana	2.5
17	Delaware	2.4
18	West Virginia	2.3
19	California	2.2
20	Alabama	2.1
20	Hawaii	2.1
20	Iowa	2.1
20	North Carolina	2.1
20	South Carolina	2.1
25	Mississippi	2.0
25	Virginia	2.0
27	Wisconsin	1.9
28	Missouri	1.7
29	Arkansas	1.6
29	Kansas	1.6
29	Oklahoma	1.6
32	Michigan	1.5
32	Minnesota	1.5
32	Texas	1.5
32	Vermont	1.5
36	Washington	1.2
37	Nebraska	1.1
38	Maine	1.0
39	Colorado	0.7
39	South Dakota	0.7
41	Arizona	0.6
41	North Dakota	0.6
41	Oregon	0.6
44	Idaho	0.5
44	Utah	0.5
46	Montana	0.4
47	Nevada	0.3
47	New Mexico	0.3
49	Wyoming	0.2
50	Alaska**	0.0
	District of Columbia***	NA

Source: CQ Press using data from American Hospital Association (Chicago, IL)
"Hospital Statistics" (2009 edition)
*Based on land and water area figures. Community hospitals are nonfederal short-term general and other special hospitals, whose facilities and services are available to the public.
**Alaska has 22 community hospitals for its 663,267 square miles.
***The District of Columbia has 10 community hospitals for its 68 square miles.

Community Hospitals in Urban Areas in 2007

National Total = 2,900 Hospitals*

RANK	STATE	HOSPITALS	% of USA
17	Alabama	60	2.1%
47	Alaska	5	0.2%
22	Arizona	48	1.7%
28	Arkansas	35	1.2%
1	California	323	11.1%
27	Colorado	38	1.3%
30	Connecticut	29	1.0%
48	Delaware	4	0.1%
3	Florida	169	5.8%
9	Georgia	82	2.8%
40	Hawaii	13	0.4%
39	Idaho	14	0.5%
6	Illinois	126	4.3%
13	Indiana	74	2.6%
29	Iowa	33	1.1%
30	Kansas	29	1.0%
26	Kentucky	40	1.4%
10	Louisiana	79	2.7%
38	Maine	15	0.5%
24	Maryland	43	1.5%
12	Massachusetts	76	2.6%
8	Michigan	84	2.9%
21	Minnesota	49	1.7%
34	Mississippi	26	0.9%
16	Missouri	64	2.2%
45	Montana	6	0.2%
37	Nebraska	16	0.6%
36	Nevada	23	0.8%
42	New Hampshire	11	0.4%
14	New Jersey	73	2.5%
40	New Mexico	13	0.4%
4	New York	162	5.6%
19	North Carolina	55	1.9%
45	North Dakota	6	0.2%
7	Ohio	117	4.0%
22	Oklahoma	48	1.7%
30	Oregon	29	1.0%
5	Pennsylvania	139	4.8%
42	Rhode Island	11	0.4%
25	South Carolina	42	1.4%
44	South Dakota	10	0.3%
11	Tennessee	77	2.7%
2	Texas	260	9.0%
35	Utah	25	0.9%
49	Vermont	2	0.1%
18	Virginia	57	2.0%
20	Washington	53	1.8%
33	West Virginia	27	0.9%
15	Wisconsin	68	2.3%
49	Wyoming	2	0.1%

RANK	STATE	HOSPITALS	% of USA
1	California	323	11.1%
2	Texas	260	9.0%
3	Florida	169	5.8%
4	New York	162	5.6%
5	Pennsylvania	139	4.8%
6	Illinois	126	4.3%
7	Ohio	117	4.0%
8	Michigan	84	2.9%
9	Georgia	82	2.8%
10	Louisiana	79	2.7%
11	Tennessee	77	2.7%
12	Massachusetts	76	2.6%
13	Indiana	74	2.6%
14	New Jersey	73	2.5%
15	Wisconsin	68	2.3%
16	Missouri	64	2.2%
17	Alabama	60	2.1%
18	Virginia	57	2.0%
19	North Carolina	55	1.9%
20	Washington	53	1.8%
21	Minnesota	49	1.7%
22	Arizona	48	1.7%
22	Oklahoma	48	1.7%
24	Maryland	43	1.5%
25	South Carolina	42	1.4%
26	Kentucky	40	1.4%
27	Colorado	38	1.3%
28	Arkansas	35	1.2%
29	Iowa	33	1.1%
30	Connecticut	29	1.0%
30	Kansas	29	1.0%
30	Oregon	29	1.0%
33	West Virginia	27	0.9%
34	Mississippi	26	0.9%
35	Utah	25	0.9%
36	Nevada	23	0.8%
37	Nebraska	16	0.6%
38	Maine	15	0.5%
39	Idaho	14	0.5%
40	Hawaii	13	0.4%
40	New Mexico	13	0.4%
42	New Hampshire	11	0.4%
42	Rhode Island	11	0.4%
44	South Dakota	10	0.3%
45	Montana	6	0.2%
45	North Dakota	6	0.2%
47	Alaska	5	0.2%
48	Delaware	4	0.1%
49	Vermont	2	0.1%
49	Wyoming	2	0.1%
	District of Columbia	10	0.3%

Source: American Hospital Association (Chicago, IL)
    "Hospital Statistics" (2009 edition)

*Community hospitals are all nonfederal, short-term, general, and special hospitals whose facilities and services are available to the public. Urban is defined as any area inside a metropolitan statistical area as defined by the U.S. Office of Management and Budget.

Percent of Community Hospitals in Urban Areas in 2007

National Percent = 59.2% of Community Hospitals*

ALPHA ORDER

RANK	STATE	PERCENT
26	Alabama	55.0
43	Alaska	22.7
10	Arizona	72.7
34	Arkansas	41.7
4	California	91.0
29	Colorado	50.7
6	Connecticut	85.3
13	Delaware	66.7
7	Florida	84.5
25	Georgia	55.8
24	Hawaii	56.5
40	Idaho	35.9
14	Illinois	66.3
16	Indiana	64.9
41	Iowa	28.2
43	Kansas	22.7
37	Kentucky	38.5
19	Louisiana	61.2
35	Maine	40.5
5	Maryland	87.8
3	Massachusetts	97.4
22	Michigan	58.7
38	Minnesota	37.4
42	Mississippi	27.4
28	Missouri	54.7
49	Montana	11.5
46	Nebraska	18.8
11	Nevada	69.7
36	New Hampshire	39.3
1	New Jersey	100.0
39	New Mexico	37.1
8	New York	80.2
31	North Carolina	48.7
47	North Dakota	14.6
12	Ohio	68.4
33	Oklahoma	42.5
30	Oregon	50.0
9	Pennsylvania	74.3
1	Rhode Island	100.0
18	South Carolina	62.7
45	South Dakota	19.6
23	Tennessee	57.9
17	Texas	63.6
20	Utah	61.0
48	Vermont	14.3
15	Virginia	65.5
21	Washington	60.9
32	West Virginia	48.2
27	Wisconsin	54.8
50	Wyoming	8.3

RANK ORDER

RANK	STATE	PERCENT
1	New Jersey	100.0
1	Rhode Island	100.0
3	Massachusetts	97.4
4	California	91.0
5	Maryland	87.8
6	Connecticut	85.3
7	Florida	84.5
8	New York	80.2
9	Pennsylvania	74.3
10	Arizona	72.7
11	Nevada	69.7
12	Ohio	68.4
13	Delaware	66.7
14	Illinois	66.3
15	Virginia	65.5
16	Indiana	64.9
17	Texas	63.6
18	South Carolina	62.7
19	Louisiana	61.2
20	Utah	61.0
21	Washington	60.9
22	Michigan	58.7
23	Tennessee	57.9
24	Hawaii	56.5
25	Georgia	55.8
26	Alabama	55.0
27	Wisconsin	54.8
28	Missouri	54.7
29	Colorado	50.7
30	Oregon	50.0
31	North Carolina	48.7
32	West Virginia	48.2
33	Oklahoma	42.5
34	Arkansas	41.7
35	Maine	40.5
36	New Hampshire	39.3
37	Kentucky	38.5
38	Minnesota	37.4
39	New Mexico	37.1
40	Idaho	35.9
41	Iowa	28.2
42	Mississippi	27.4
43	Alaska	22.7
43	Kansas	22.7
45	South Dakota	19.6
46	Nebraska	18.8
47	North Dakota	14.6
48	Vermont	14.3
49	Montana	11.5
50	Wyoming	8.3
	District of Columbia	100.0

Source: CQ Press using data from American Hospital Association (Chicago, IL)
"Hospital Statistics" (2009 edition)
*Community hospitals are all nonfederal, short-term, general, and special hospitals whose facilities and services are available to the public. Urban is defined as any area inside a metropolitan statistical area as defined by the U.S. Office of Management and Budget.

Community Hospitals in Rural Areas in 2007

National Total = 1,997 Hospitals*

RANK	STATE	HOSPITALS	% of USA
18	Alabama	49	2.5%
39	Alaska	17	0.9%
38	Arizona	18	0.9%
18	Arkansas	49	2.5%
28	California	32	1.6%
25	Colorado	37	1.9%
46	Connecticut	5	0.3%
47	Delaware	2	0.1%
29	Florida	31	1.6%
7	Georgia	65	3.3%
43	Hawaii	10	0.5%
33	Idaho	25	1.3%
9	Illinois	64	3.2%
23	Indiana	40	2.0%
3	Iowa	84	4.2%
2	Kansas	99	5.0%
9	Kentucky	64	3.2%
17	Louisiana	50	2.5%
35	Maine	22	1.1%
45	Maryland	6	0.3%
47	Massachusetts	2	0.1%
11	Michigan	59	3.0%
4	Minnesota	82	4.1%
5	Mississippi	69	3.5%
16	Missouri	53	2.7%
21	Montana	46	2.3%
5	Nebraska	69	3.5%
43	Nevada	10	0.5%
39	New Hampshire	17	0.9%
49	New Jersey	0	0.0%
35	New Mexico	22	1.1%
23	New York	40	2.0%
12	North Carolina	58	2.9%
26	North Dakota	35	1.8%
15	Ohio	54	2.7%
7	Oklahoma	65	3.3%
31	Oregon	29	1.5%
20	Pennsylvania	48	2.4%
49	Rhode Island	0	0.0%
33	South Carolina	25	1.3%
22	South Dakota	41	2.1%
13	Tennessee	56	2.8%
1	Texas	149	7.5%
41	Utah	16	0.8%
42	Vermont	12	0.6%
30	Virginia	30	1.5%
27	Washington	34	1.7%
31	West Virginia	29	1.5%
13	Wisconsin	56	2.8%
35	Wyoming	22	1.1%

RANK	STATE	HOSPITALS	% of USA
1	Texas	149	7.5%
2	Kansas	99	5.0%
3	Iowa	84	4.2%
4	Minnesota	82	4.1%
5	Mississippi	69	3.5%
5	Nebraska	69	3.5%
7	Georgia	65	3.3%
7	Oklahoma	65	3.3%
9	Illinois	64	3.2%
9	Kentucky	64	3.2%
11	Michigan	59	3.0%
12	North Carolina	58	2.9%
13	Tennessee	56	2.8%
13	Wisconsin	56	2.8%
15	Ohio	54	2.7%
16	Missouri	53	2.7%
17	Louisiana	50	2.5%
18	Alabama	49	2.5%
18	Arkansas	49	2.5%
20	Pennsylvania	48	2.4%
21	Montana	46	2.3%
22	South Dakota	41	2.1%
23	Indiana	40	2.0%
23	New York	40	2.0%
25	Colorado	37	1.9%
26	North Dakota	35	1.8%
27	Washington	34	1.7%
28	California	32	1.6%
29	Florida	31	1.6%
30	Virginia	30	1.5%
31	Oregon	29	1.5%
31	West Virginia	29	1.5%
33	Idaho	25	1.3%
33	South Carolina	25	1.3%
35	Maine	22	1.1%
35	New Mexico	22	1.1%
35	Wyoming	22	1.1%
38	Arizona	18	0.9%
39	Alaska	17	0.9%
39	New Hampshire	17	0.9%
41	Utah	16	0.8%
42	Vermont	12	0.6%
43	Hawaii	10	0.5%
43	Nevada	10	0.5%
45	Maryland	6	0.3%
46	Connecticut	5	0.3%
47	Delaware	2	0.1%
47	Massachusetts	2	0.1%
49	New Jersey	0	0.0%
49	Rhode Island	0	0.0%
	District of Columbia	0	0.0%

Source: American Hospital Association (Chicago, IL)
    "Hospital Statistics" (2009 edition)
*Community hospitals are all nonfederal, short-term, general, and special hospitals whose facilities and services are available to the public. Rural is defined as any area outside a metropolitan statistical area as defined by the U.S. Office of Management and Budget.

Percent of Community Hospitals in Rural Areas in 2007

National Percent = 40.8% of Community Hospitals*

ALPHA ORDER

RANK	STATE	PERCENT
25	Alabama	45.0
7	Alaska	77.3
41	Arizona	27.3
17	Arkansas	58.3
47	California	9.0
22	Colorado	49.3
45	Connecticut	14.7
38	Delaware	33.3
44	Florida	15.5
26	Georgia	44.2
27	Hawaii	43.5
11	Idaho	64.1
37	Illinois	33.7
35	Indiana	35.1
10	Iowa	71.8
7	Kansas	77.3
14	Kentucky	61.5
32	Louisiana	38.8
16	Maine	59.5
46	Maryland	12.2
48	Massachusetts	2.6
29	Michigan	41.3
13	Minnesota	62.6
9	Mississippi	72.6
23	Missouri	45.3
2	Montana	88.5
5	Nebraska	81.2
40	Nevada	30.3
15	New Hampshire	60.7
49	New Jersey	0.0
12	New Mexico	62.9
43	New York	19.8
20	North Carolina	51.3
4	North Dakota	85.4
39	Ohio	31.6
18	Oklahoma	57.5
21	Oregon	50.0
42	Pennsylvania	25.7
49	Rhode Island	0.0
33	South Carolina	37.3
6	South Dakota	80.4
28	Tennessee	42.1
34	Texas	36.4
31	Utah	39.0
3	Vermont	85.7
36	Virginia	34.5
30	Washington	39.1
19	West Virginia	51.8
24	Wisconsin	45.2
1	Wyoming	91.7

RANK ORDER

RANK	STATE	PERCENT
1	Wyoming	91.7
2	Montana	88.5
3	Vermont	85.7
4	North Dakota	85.4
5	Nebraska	81.2
6	South Dakota	80.4
7	Alaska	77.3
7	Kansas	77.3
9	Mississippi	72.6
10	Iowa	71.8
11	Idaho	64.1
12	New Mexico	62.9
13	Minnesota	62.6
14	Kentucky	61.5
15	New Hampshire	60.7
16	Maine	59.5
17	Arkansas	58.3
18	Oklahoma	57.5
19	West Virginia	51.8
20	North Carolina	51.3
21	Oregon	50.0
22	Colorado	49.3
23	Missouri	45.3
24	Wisconsin	45.2
25	Alabama	45.0
26	Georgia	44.2
27	Hawaii	43.5
28	Tennessee	42.1
29	Michigan	41.3
30	Washington	39.1
31	Utah	39.0
32	Louisiana	38.8
33	South Carolina	37.3
34	Texas	36.4
35	Indiana	35.1
36	Virginia	34.5
37	Illinois	33.7
38	Delaware	33.3
39	Ohio	31.6
40	Nevada	30.3
41	Arizona	27.3
42	Pennsylvania	25.7
43	New York	19.8
44	Florida	15.5
45	Connecticut	14.7
46	Maryland	12.2
47	California	9.0
48	Massachusetts	2.6
49	New Jersey	0.0
49	Rhode Island	0.0
	District of Columbia	0.0

Source: CQ Press using data from American Hospital Association (Chicago, IL)
    "Hospital Statistics" (2009 edition)

*Community hospitals are all nonfederal, short-term, general, and special hospitals whose facilities and services are available to the public. Rural is defined as any area outside a metropolitan statistical area as defined by the U.S. Office of Management and Budget.

Nongovernment Not-For-Profit Hospitals in 2007

National Total = 2,913 Hospitals*

ALPHA ORDER

RANK	STATE	HOSPITALS	% of USA
38	Alabama	27	0.9%
46	Alaska	13	0.4%
24	Arizona	43	1.5%
23	Arkansas	45	1.5%
1	California	203	7.0%
32	Colorado	37	1.3%
35	Connecticut	32	1.1%
49	Delaware	6	0.2%
10	Florida	82	2.8%
18	Georgia	59	2.0%
42	Hawaii	16	0.5%
43	Idaho	15	0.5%
4	Illinois	150	5.1%
20	Indiana	56	1.9%
19	Iowa	58	2.0%
21	Kansas	55	1.9%
12	Kentucky	73	2.5%
31	Louisiana	38	1.3%
34	Maine	34	1.2%
22	Maryland	47	1.6%
13	Massachusetts	67	2.3%
7	Michigan	123	4.2%
9	Minnesota	91	3.1%
37	Mississippi	29	1.0%
16	Missouri	61	2.1%
28	Montana	42	1.4%
24	Nebraska	43	1.5%
46	Nevada	13	0.4%
39	New Hampshire	24	0.8%
14	New Jersey	65	2.2%
43	New Mexico	15	0.5%
2	New York	174	6.0%
11	North Carolina	75	2.6%
30	North Dakota	40	1.4%
6	Ohio	137	4.7%
33	Oklahoma	35	1.2%
24	Oregon	43	1.5%
3	Pennsylvania	158	5.4%
48	Rhode Island	11	0.4%
40	South Carolina	23	0.8%
24	South Dakota	43	1.5%
16	Tennessee	61	2.1%
4	Texas	150	5.1%
41	Utah	22	0.8%
45	Vermont	14	0.5%
15	Virginia	64	2.2%
29	Washington	41	1.4%
36	West Virginia	31	1.1%
8	Wisconsin	117	4.0%
50	Wyoming	5	0.2%

RANK ORDER

RANK	STATE	HOSPITALS	% of USA
1	California	203	7.0%
2	New York	174	6.0%
3	Pennsylvania	158	5.4%
4	Illinois	150	5.1%
4	Texas	150	5.1%
6	Ohio	137	4.7%
7	Michigan	123	4.2%
8	Wisconsin	117	4.0%
9	Minnesota	91	3.1%
10	Florida	82	2.8%
11	North Carolina	75	2.6%
12	Kentucky	73	2.5%
13	Massachusetts	67	2.3%
14	New Jersey	65	2.2%
15	Virginia	64	2.2%
16	Missouri	61	2.1%
16	Tennessee	61	2.1%
18	Georgia	59	2.0%
19	Iowa	58	2.0%
20	Indiana	56	1.9%
21	Kansas	55	1.9%
22	Maryland	47	1.6%
23	Arkansas	45	1.5%
24	Arizona	43	1.5%
24	Nebraska	43	1.5%
24	Oregon	43	1.5%
24	South Dakota	43	1.5%
28	Montana	42	1.4%
29	Washington	41	1.4%
30	North Dakota	40	1.4%
31	Louisiana	38	1.3%
32	Colorado	37	1.3%
33	Oklahoma	35	1.2%
34	Maine	34	1.2%
35	Connecticut	32	1.1%
36	West Virginia	31	1.1%
37	Mississippi	29	1.0%
38	Alabama	27	0.9%
39	New Hampshire	24	0.8%
40	South Carolina	23	0.8%
41	Utah	22	0.8%
42	Hawaii	16	0.5%
43	Idaho	15	0.5%
43	New Mexico	15	0.5%
45	Vermont	14	0.5%
46	Alaska	13	0.4%
46	Nevada	13	0.4%
48	Rhode Island	11	0.4%
49	Delaware	6	0.2%
50	Wyoming	5	0.2%
	District of Columbia	7	0.2%

Source: American Hospital Association (Chicago, IL)
"Hospital Statistics" (2009 edition)
*Nongovernment not-for-profit hospitals are a subset of community hospitals.

Investor-Owned (For-Profit) Hospitals in 2007

National Total = 873 Hospitals*

ALPHA ORDER

RANK	STATE	HOSPITALS	% of USA
6	Alabama	40	4.6%
36	Alaska	2	0.2%
14	Arizona	19	2.2%
10	Arkansas	25	2.9%
3	California	81	9.3%
25	Colorado	10	1.1%
41	Connecticut	1	0.1%
45	Delaware	0	0.0%
2	Florida	92	10.5%
8	Georgia	31	3.6%
45	Hawaii	0	0.0%
33	Idaho	3	0.3%
21	Illinois	13	1.5%
14	Indiana	19	2.2%
45	Iowa	0	0.0%
23	Kansas	11	1.3%
14	Kentucky	19	2.2%
5	Louisiana	41	4.7%
41	Maine	1	0.1%
36	Maryland	2	0.2%
26	Massachusetts	8	0.9%
31	Michigan	4	0.5%
45	Minnesota	0	0.0%
12	Mississippi	24	2.7%
13	Missouri	21	2.4%
41	Montana	1	0.1%
36	Nebraska	2	0.2%
20	Nevada	14	1.6%
31	New Hampshire	4	0.5%
28	New Jersey	5	0.6%
21	New Mexico	13	1.5%
36	New York	2	0.2%
27	North Carolina	6	0.7%
41	North Dakota	1	0.1%
23	Ohio	11	1.3%
7	Oklahoma	33	3.8%
36	Oregon	2	0.2%
9	Pennsylvania	27	3.1%
45	Rhode Island	0	0.0%
10	South Carolina	25	2.9%
33	South Dakota	3	0.3%
4	Tennessee	50	5.7%
1	Texas	142	16.3%
18	Utah	15	1.7%
45	Vermont	0	0.0%
14	Virginia	19	2.2%
28	Washington	5	0.6%
18	West Virginia	15	1.7%
28	Wisconsin	5	0.6%
33	Wyoming	3	0.3%

RANK ORDER

RANK	STATE	HOSPITALS	% of USA
1	Texas	142	16.3%
2	Florida	92	10.5%
3	California	81	9.3%
4	Tennessee	50	5.7%
5	Louisiana	41	4.7%
6	Alabama	40	4.6%
7	Oklahoma	33	3.8%
8	Georgia	31	3.6%
9	Pennsylvania	27	3.1%
10	Arkansas	25	2.9%
10	South Carolina	25	2.9%
12	Mississippi	24	2.7%
13	Missouri	21	2.4%
14	Arizona	19	2.2%
14	Indiana	19	2.2%
14	Kentucky	19	2.2%
14	Virginia	19	2.2%
18	Utah	15	1.7%
18	West Virginia	15	1.7%
20	Nevada	14	1.6%
21	Illinois	13	1.5%
21	New Mexico	13	1.5%
23	Kansas	11	1.3%
23	Ohio	11	1.3%
25	Colorado	10	1.1%
26	Massachusetts	8	0.9%
27	North Carolina	6	0.7%
28	New Jersey	5	0.6%
28	Washington	5	0.6%
28	Wisconsin	5	0.6%
31	Michigan	4	0.5%
31	New Hampshire	4	0.5%
33	Idaho	3	0.3%
33	South Dakota	3	0.3%
33	Wyoming	3	0.3%
36	Alaska	2	0.2%
36	Maryland	2	0.2%
36	Nebraska	2	0.2%
36	New York	2	0.2%
36	Oregon	2	0.2%
41	Connecticut	1	0.1%
41	Maine	1	0.1%
41	Montana	1	0.1%
41	North Dakota	1	0.1%
45	Delaware	0	0.0%
45	Hawaii	0	0.0%
45	Iowa	0	0.0%
45	Minnesota	0	0.0%
45	Rhode Island	0	0.0%
45	Vermont	0	0.0%

| District of Columbia | 3 | 0.3% |

Source: American Hospital Association (Chicago, IL)
    "Hospital Statistics" (2009 edition)
*Investor-owned (for-profit) hospitals are a subset of community hospitals.

State and Local Government-Owned Hospitals in 2007

National Total = 1,111 Hospitals*

ALPHA ORDER

RANK	STATE	HOSPITALS	% of USA
8	Alabama	42	3.8%
31	Alaska	7	0.6%
36	Arizona	4	0.4%
26	Arkansas	14	1.3%
2	California	71	6.4%
16	Colorado	28	2.5%
44	Connecticut	1	0.1%
45	Delaware	0	0.0%
18	Florida	26	2.3%
5	Georgia	57	5.1%
31	Hawaii	7	0.6%
22	Idaho	21	1.9%
17	Illinois	27	2.4%
13	Indiana	39	3.5%
4	Iowa	59	5.3%
3	Kansas	62	5.6%
28	Kentucky	12	1.1%
6	Louisiana	50	4.5%
41	Maine	2	0.2%
45	Maryland	0	0.0%
39	Massachusetts	3	0.3%
24	Michigan	16	1.4%
11	Minnesota	40	3.6%
8	Mississippi	42	3.8%
14	Missouri	35	3.2%
30	Montana	9	0.8%
11	Nebraska	40	3.6%
34	Nevada	6	0.5%
45	New Hampshire	0	0.0%
39	New Jersey	3	0.3%
31	New Mexico	7	0.6%
18	New York	26	2.3%
15	North Carolina	32	2.9%
45	North Dakota	0	0.0%
20	Ohio	23	2.1%
7	Oklahoma	45	4.1%
27	Oregon	13	1.2%
41	Pennsylvania	2	0.2%
45	Rhode Island	0	0.0%
23	South Carolina	19	1.7%
35	South Dakota	5	0.5%
21	Tennessee	22	2.0%
1	Texas	117	10.5%
36	Utah	4	0.4%
45	Vermont	0	0.0%
36	Virginia	4	0.4%
10	Washington	41	3.7%
29	West Virginia	10	0.9%
41	Wisconsin	2	0.2%
24	Wyoming	16	1.4%

RANK ORDER

RANK	STATE	HOSPITALS	% of USA
1	Texas	117	10.5%
2	California	71	6.4%
3	Kansas	62	5.6%
4	Iowa	59	5.3%
5	Georgia	57	5.1%
6	Louisiana	50	4.5%
7	Oklahoma	45	4.1%
8	Alabama	42	3.8%
8	Mississippi	42	3.8%
10	Washington	41	3.7%
11	Minnesota	40	3.6%
11	Nebraska	40	3.6%
13	Indiana	39	3.5%
14	Missouri	35	3.2%
15	North Carolina	32	2.9%
16	Colorado	28	2.5%
17	Illinois	27	2.4%
18	Florida	26	2.3%
18	New York	26	2.3%
20	Ohio	23	2.1%
21	Tennessee	22	2.0%
22	Idaho	21	1.9%
23	South Carolina	19	1.7%
24	Michigan	16	1.4%
24	Wyoming	16	1.4%
26	Arkansas	14	1.3%
27	Oregon	13	1.2%
28	Kentucky	12	1.1%
29	West Virginia	10	0.9%
30	Montana	9	0.8%
31	Alaska	7	0.6%
31	Hawaii	7	0.6%
31	New Mexico	7	0.6%
34	Nevada	6	0.5%
35	South Dakota	5	0.5%
36	Arizona	4	0.4%
36	Utah	4	0.4%
36	Virginia	4	0.4%
39	Massachusetts	3	0.3%
39	New Jersey	3	0.3%
41	Maine	2	0.2%
41	Pennsylvania	2	0.2%
41	Wisconsin	2	0.2%
44	Connecticut	1	0.1%
45	Delaware	0	0.0%
45	Maryland	0	0.0%
45	New Hampshire	0	0.0%
45	North Dakota	0	0.0%
45	Rhode Island	0	0.0%
45	Vermont	0	0.0%
	District of Columbia	0	0.0%

Source: American Hospital Association (Chicago, IL)
"Hospital Statistics" (2009 edition)
*State and local government-owned hospitals are a subset of community hospitals.

Beds in Community Hospitals in 2007

National Total = 800,892 Beds*

ALPHA ORDER					RANK ORDER			
RANK	STATE	HOSPITALS	% of USA		RANK	STATE	HOSPITALS	% of USA
18	Alabama	15,682	2.0%		1	California	69,325	8.7%
49	Alaska	1,554	0.2%		2	New York	62,367	7.8%
23	Arizona	12,157	1.5%		3	Texas	58,192	7.3%
31	Arkansas	9,502	1.2%		4	Florida	51,648	6.4%
1	California	69,325	8.7%		5	Pennsylvania	39,728	5.0%
30	Colorado	9,708	1.2%		6	Illinois	34,560	4.3%
32	Connecticut	7,483	0.9%		7	Ohio	32,866	4.1%
47	Delaware	2,288	0.3%		8	Georgia	25,483	3.2%
4	Florida	51,648	6.4%		9	Michigan	25,396	3.2%
8	Georgia	25,483	3.2%		10	North Carolina	23,158	2.9%
44	Hawaii	2,920	0.4%		11	Tennessee	21,688	2.7%
43	Idaho	3,296	0.4%		12	New Jersey	21,544	2.7%
6	Illinois	34,560	4.3%		13	Missouri	18,454	2.3%
14	Indiana	17,055	2.1%		14	Indiana	17,055	2.1%
28	Iowa	10,515	1.3%		15	Virginia	16,895	2.1%
29	Kansas	10,079	1.3%		16	Massachusetts	16,496	2.1%
20	Kentucky	14,423	1.8%		17	Minnesota	15,809	2.0%
19	Louisiana	15,516	1.9%		18	Alabama	15,682	2.0%
41	Maine	3,509	0.4%		19	Louisiana	15,516	1.9%
25	Maryland	11,743	1.5%		20	Kentucky	14,423	1.8%
16	Massachusetts	16,496	2.1%		21	Wisconsin	13,981	1.7%
9	Michigan	25,396	3.2%		22	Mississippi	12,712	1.6%
17	Minnesota	15,809	2.0%		23	Arizona	12,157	1.5%
22	Mississippi	12,712	1.6%		24	South Carolina	12,032	1.5%
13	Missouri	18,454	2.3%		25	Maryland	11,743	1.5%
39	Montana	4,002	0.5%		26	Washington	11,315	1.4%
33	Nebraska	7,468	0.9%		27	Oklahoma	10,862	1.4%
36	Nevada	5,051	0.6%		28	Iowa	10,515	1.3%
45	New Hampshire	2,841	0.4%		29	Kansas	10,079	1.3%
12	New Jersey	21,544	2.7%		30	Colorado	9,708	1.2%
40	New Mexico	3,695	0.5%		31	Arkansas	9,502	1.2%
2	New York	62,367	7.8%		32	Connecticut	7,483	0.9%
10	North Carolina	23,158	2.9%		33	Nebraska	7,468	0.9%
42	North Dakota	3,488	0.4%		34	West Virginia	7,436	0.9%
7	Ohio	32,866	4.1%		35	Oregon	6,841	0.9%
27	Oklahoma	10,862	1.4%		36	Nevada	5,051	0.6%
35	Oregon	6,841	0.9%		37	Utah	4,584	0.6%
5	Pennsylvania	39,728	5.0%		38	South Dakota	4,245	0.5%
46	Rhode Island	2,449	0.3%		39	Montana	4,002	0.5%
24	South Carolina	12,032	1.5%		40	New Mexico	3,695	0.5%
38	South Dakota	4,245	0.5%		41	Maine	3,509	0.4%
11	Tennessee	21,688	2.7%		42	North Dakota	3,488	0.4%
3	Texas	58,192	7.3%		43	Idaho	3,296	0.4%
37	Utah	4,584	0.6%		44	Hawaii	2,920	0.4%
50	Vermont	1,362	0.2%		45	New Hampshire	2,841	0.4%
15	Virginia	16,895	2.1%		46	Rhode Island	2,449	0.3%
26	Washington	11,315	1.4%		47	Delaware	2,288	0.3%
34	West Virginia	7,436	0.9%		48	Wyoming	2,071	0.3%
21	Wisconsin	13,981	1.7%		49	Alaska	1,554	0.2%
48	Wyoming	2,071	0.3%		50	Vermont	1,362	0.2%
						District of Columbia	3,418	0.4%

Source: American Hospital Association (Chicago, IL)
     "Hospital Statistics" (2009 edition)

*All nonfederal short-term general and other special hospitals, whose facilities and services are available to the public. Includes beds in hospital and nursing home units.

Rate of Beds in Community Hospitals in 2007

National Rate = 266 Beds per 100,000 Population*

ALPHA ORDER			RANK ORDER		
RANK	STATE	RATE	RANK	STATE	RATE
13	Alabama	339	1	North Dakota	547
36	Alaska	228	2	South Dakota	533
45	Arizona	191	3	Mississippi	435
14	Arkansas	336	4	Nebraska	422
45	California	191	5	Montana	418
43	Colorado	200	6	West Virginia	411
41	Connecticut	214	7	Wyoming	396
27	Delaware	265	8	Kansas	363
21	Florida	284	9	Louisiana	355
25	Georgia	268	10	Tennessee	353
35	Hawaii	229	11	Iowa	352
37	Idaho	220	12	Kentucky	340
23	Illinois	269	13	Alabama	339
23	Indiana	269	14	Arkansas	336
11	Iowa	352	15	New York	321
8	Kansas	363	16	Pennsylvania	320
12	Kentucky	340	17	Missouri	314
9	Louisiana	355	18	Minnesota	305
26	Maine	267	19	Oklahoma	301
42	Maryland	209	20	Ohio	286
29	Massachusetts	255	21	Florida	284
30	Michigan	253	22	South Carolina	273
18	Minnesota	305	23	Illinois	269
3	Mississippi	435	23	Indiana	269
17	Missouri	314	25	Georgia	268
5	Montana	418	26	Maine	267
4	Nebraska	422	27	Delaware	265
44	Nevada	198	28	North Carolina	256
40	New Hampshire	216	29	Massachusetts	255
32	New Jersey	249	30	Michigan	253
47	New Mexico	188	31	Wisconsin	250
15	New York	321	32	New Jersey	249
28	North Carolina	256	33	Texas	244
1	North Dakota	547	34	Rhode Island	233
20	Ohio	286	35	Hawaii	229
19	Oklahoma	301	36	Alaska	228
48	Oregon	183	37	Idaho	220
16	Pennsylvania	320	38	Vermont	219
34	Rhode Island	233	38	Virginia	219
22	South Carolina	273	40	New Hampshire	216
2	South Dakota	533	41	Connecticut	214
10	Tennessee	353	42	Maryland	209
33	Texas	244	43	Colorado	200
50	Utah	172	44	Nevada	198
38	Vermont	219	45	Arizona	191
38	Virginia	219	45	California	191
49	Washington	175	47	New Mexico	188
6	West Virginia	411	48	Oregon	183
31	Wisconsin	250	49	Washington	175
7	Wyoming	396	50	Utah	172
				District of Columbia	581

Source: CQ Press using data from American Hospital Association (Chicago, IL)
   "Hospital Statistics" (2009 edition)
*All nonfederal short-term general and other special hospitals, whose facilities and services are available to the public. Includes beds in hospital and nursing home units.

Average Number of Beds per Community Hospital in 2007

National Average = 164 Beds per Community Hospital*

ALPHA ORDER

RANK	STATE	RATE
23	Alabama	144
50	Alaska	71
14	Arizona	184
34	Arkansas	113
11	California	195
29	Colorado	129
7	Connecticut	220
1	Delaware	381
4	Florida	258
18	Georgia	173
30	Hawaii	127
45	Idaho	85
15	Illinois	182
22	Indiana	150
42	Iowa	90
48	Kansas	79
25	Kentucky	139
32	Louisiana	120
41	Maine	95
5	Maryland	240
9	Massachusetts	211
17	Michigan	178
31	Minnesota	121
26	Mississippi	134
20	Missouri	158
49	Montana	77
43	Nebraska	88
21	Nevada	153
38	New Hampshire	101
3	New Jersey	295
37	New Mexico	106
2	New York	309
10	North Carolina	205
45	North Dakota	85
13	Ohio	192
40	Oklahoma	96
33	Oregon	118
8	Pennsylvania	212
6	Rhode Island	223
16	South Carolina	180
47	South Dakota	83
19	Tennessee	163
24	Texas	142
36	Utah	112
39	Vermont	97
12	Virginia	194
28	Washington	130
27	West Virginia	133
34	Wisconsin	113
44	Wyoming	86

RANK ORDER

RANK	STATE	RATE
1	Delaware	381
2	New York	309
3	New Jersey	295
4	Florida	258
5	Maryland	240
6	Rhode Island	223
7	Connecticut	220
8	Pennsylvania	212
9	Massachusetts	211
10	North Carolina	205
11	California	195
12	Virginia	194
13	Ohio	192
14	Arizona	184
15	Illinois	182
16	South Carolina	180
17	Michigan	178
18	Georgia	173
19	Tennessee	163
20	Missouri	158
21	Nevada	153
22	Indiana	150
23	Alabama	144
24	Texas	142
25	Kentucky	139
26	Mississippi	134
27	West Virginia	133
28	Washington	130
29	Colorado	129
30	Hawaii	127
31	Minnesota	121
32	Louisiana	120
33	Oregon	118
34	Arkansas	113
34	Wisconsin	113
36	Utah	112
37	New Mexico	106
38	New Hampshire	101
39	Vermont	97
40	Oklahoma	96
41	Maine	95
42	Iowa	90
43	Nebraska	88
44	Wyoming	86
45	Idaho	85
45	North Dakota	85
47	South Dakota	83
48	Kansas	79
49	Montana	77
50	Alaska	71

	District of Columbia	342

Source: CQ Press using data from American Hospital Association (Chicago, IL)
"Hospital Statistics" (2009 edition)

*All nonfederal short-term general and other special hospitals, whose facilities and services are available to the public. Includes beds in hospital and nursing home units.

Admissions to Community Hospitals in 2007

National Total = 35,345,986 Admissions*

ALPHA ORDER

RANK	STATE	ADMISSIONS	% of USA
17	Alabama	696,131	2.0%
48	Alaska	56,584	0.2%
19	Arizona	675,216	1.9%
31	Arkansas	366,452	1.0%
1	California	3,276,372	9.3%
27	Colorado	425,959	1.2%
29	Connecticut	396,895	1.1%
44	Delaware	107,037	0.3%
4	Florida	2,387,525	6.8%
12	Georgia	963,583	2.7%
43	Hawaii	110,788	0.3%
40	Idaho	133,895	0.4%
6	Illinois	1,606,241	4.5%
18	Indiana	690,866	2.0%
30	Iowa	368,272	1.0%
33	Kansas	325,355	0.9%
23	Kentucky	611,689	1.7%
21	Louisiana	630,873	1.8%
39	Maine	151,877	0.4%
16	Maryland	698,057	2.0%
13	Massachusetts	842,417	2.4%
8	Michigan	1,204,263	3.4%
20	Minnesota	635,133	1.8%
28	Mississippi	417,929	1.2%
14	Missouri	833,114	2.4%
45	Montana	106,860	0.3%
37	Nebraska	214,628	0.6%
35	Nevada	244,187	0.7%
42	New Hampshire	121,747	0.3%
9	New Jersey	1,084,226	3.1%
38	New Mexico	170,081	0.5%
2	New York	2,540,711	7.2%
10	North Carolina	1,027,909	2.9%
47	North Dakota	89,010	0.3%
7	Ohio	1,542,176	4.4%
26	Oklahoma	453,977	1.3%
32	Oregon	347,089	1.0%
5	Pennsylvania	1,880,382	5.3%
41	Rhode Island	128,519	0.4%
25	South Carolina	518,994	1.5%
46	South Dakota	99,931	0.3%
11	Tennessee	969,763	2.7%
3	Texas	2,468,109	7.0%
36	Utah	223,971	0.6%
50	Vermont	49,892	0.1%
15	Virginia	787,319	2.2%
24	Washington	574,169	1.6%
34	West Virginia	286,892	0.8%
22	Wisconsin	613,356	1.7%
49	Wyoming	53,077	0.2%

RANK ORDER

RANK	STATE	ADMISSIONS	% of USA
1	California	3,276,372	9.3%
2	New York	2,540,711	7.2%
3	Texas	2,468,109	7.0%
4	Florida	2,387,525	6.8%
5	Pennsylvania	1,880,382	5.3%
6	Illinois	1,606,241	4.5%
7	Ohio	1,542,176	4.4%
8	Michigan	1,204,263	3.4%
9	New Jersey	1,084,226	3.1%
10	North Carolina	1,027,909	2.9%
11	Tennessee	969,763	2.7%
12	Georgia	963,583	2.7%
13	Massachusetts	842,417	2.4%
14	Missouri	833,114	2.4%
15	Virginia	787,319	2.2%
16	Maryland	698,057	2.0%
17	Alabama	696,131	2.0%
18	Indiana	690,866	2.0%
19	Arizona	675,216	1.9%
20	Minnesota	635,133	1.8%
21	Louisiana	630,873	1.8%
22	Wisconsin	613,356	1.7%
23	Kentucky	611,689	1.7%
24	Washington	574,169	1.6%
25	South Carolina	518,994	1.5%
26	Oklahoma	453,977	1.3%
27	Colorado	425,959	1.2%
28	Mississippi	417,929	1.2%
29	Connecticut	396,895	1.1%
30	Iowa	368,272	1.0%
31	Arkansas	366,452	1.0%
32	Oregon	347,089	1.0%
33	Kansas	325,355	0.9%
34	West Virginia	286,892	0.8%
35	Nevada	244,187	0.7%
36	Utah	223,971	0.6%
37	Nebraska	214,628	0.6%
38	New Mexico	170,081	0.5%
39	Maine	151,877	0.4%
40	Idaho	133,895	0.4%
41	Rhode Island	128,519	0.4%
42	New Hampshire	121,747	0.3%
43	Hawaii	110,788	0.3%
44	Delaware	107,037	0.3%
45	Montana	106,860	0.3%
46	South Dakota	99,931	0.3%
47	North Dakota	89,010	0.3%
48	Alaska	56,584	0.2%
49	Wyoming	53,077	0.2%
50	Vermont	49,892	0.1%
	District of Columbia	136,488	0.4%

Source: American Hospital Association (Chicago, IL)
"Hospital Statistics" (2009 edition)

*Admissions to all nonfederal short-term general and other special hospitals, whose facilities and services are available to the public. Includes admissions to hospital and nursing home units.

Inpatient Days in Community Hospitals in 2007

National Total = 194,549,348 Inpatient Days*

ALPHA ORDER

RANK	STATE	DAYS	% of USA
17	Alabama	3,551,293	1.8%
49	Alaska	337,028	0.2%
23	Arizona	3,041,795	1.6%
32	Arkansas	1,908,909	1.0%
2	California	17,154,514	8.8%
29	Colorado	2,169,902	1.1%
30	Connecticut	2,128,239	1.1%
45	Delaware	671,628	0.3%
4	Florida	12,351,368	6.3%
8	Georgia	6,278,894	3.2%
41	Hawaii	796,898	0.4%
47	Idaho	654,818	0.3%
6	Illinois	8,107,743	4.2%
18	Indiana	3,513,575	1.8%
28	Iowa	2,266,094	1.2%
31	Kansas	2,025,564	1.0%
21	Kentucky	3,188,902	1.6%
19	Louisiana	3,448,099	1.8%
40	Maine	839,900	0.4%
20	Maryland	3,243,033	1.7%
13	Massachusetts	4,391,528	2.3%
9	Michigan	6,275,096	3.2%
16	Minnesota	3,929,879	2.0%
25	Mississippi	2,675,307	1.4%
15	Missouri	4,310,130	2.2%
39	Montana	957,251	0.5%
34	Nebraska	1,619,546	0.8%
36	Nevada	1,275,671	0.7%
46	New Hampshire	659,511	0.3%
11	New Jersey	5,613,126	2.9%
43	New Mexico	764,458	0.4%
1	New York	18,344,398	9.4%
10	North Carolina	6,069,660	3.1%
42	North Dakota	772,643	0.4%
7	Ohio	7,753,839	4.0%
27	Oklahoma	2,359,878	1.2%
35	Oregon	1,534,999	0.8%
5	Pennsylvania	10,257,605	5.3%
44	Rhode Island	672,831	0.3%
24	South Carolina	3,006,247	1.5%
37	South Dakota	1,008,378	0.5%
12	Tennessee	5,372,297	2.8%
3	Texas	12,816,839	6.6%
38	Utah	1,003,917	0.5%
50	Vermont	337,004	0.2%
14	Virginia	4,354,340	2.2%
26	Washington	2,577,795	1.3%
33	West Virginia	1,656,614	0.9%
22	Wisconsin	3,168,542	1.6%
48	Wyoming	422,883	0.2%

RANK ORDER

RANK	STATE	DAYS	% of USA
1	New York	18,344,398	9.4%
2	California	17,154,514	8.8%
3	Texas	12,816,839	6.6%
4	Florida	12,351,368	6.3%
5	Pennsylvania	10,257,605	5.3%
6	Illinois	8,107,743	4.2%
7	Ohio	7,753,839	4.0%
8	Georgia	6,278,894	3.2%
9	Michigan	6,275,096	3.2%
10	North Carolina	6,069,660	3.1%
11	New Jersey	5,613,126	2.9%
12	Tennessee	5,372,297	2.8%
13	Massachusetts	4,391,528	2.3%
14	Virginia	4,354,340	2.2%
15	Missouri	4,310,130	2.2%
16	Minnesota	3,929,879	2.0%
17	Alabama	3,551,293	1.8%
18	Indiana	3,513,575	1.8%
19	Louisiana	3,448,099	1.8%
20	Maryland	3,243,033	1.7%
21	Kentucky	3,188,902	1.6%
22	Wisconsin	3,168,542	1.6%
23	Arizona	3,041,795	1.6%
24	South Carolina	3,006,247	1.5%
25	Mississippi	2,675,307	1.4%
26	Washington	2,577,795	1.3%
27	Oklahoma	2,359,878	1.2%
28	Iowa	2,266,094	1.2%
29	Colorado	2,169,902	1.1%
30	Connecticut	2,128,239	1.1%
31	Kansas	2,025,564	1.0%
32	Arkansas	1,908,909	1.0%
33	West Virginia	1,656,614	0.9%
34	Nebraska	1,619,546	0.8%
35	Oregon	1,534,999	0.8%
36	Nevada	1,275,671	0.7%
37	South Dakota	1,008,378	0.5%
38	Utah	1,003,917	0.5%
39	Montana	957,251	0.5%
40	Maine	839,900	0.4%
41	Hawaii	796,898	0.4%
42	North Dakota	772,643	0.4%
43	New Mexico	764,458	0.4%
44	Rhode Island	672,831	0.3%
45	Delaware	671,628	0.3%
46	New Hampshire	659,511	0.3%
47	Idaho	654,818	0.3%
48	Wyoming	422,883	0.2%
49	Alaska	337,028	0.2%
50	Vermont	337,004	0.2%
	District of Columbia	908,940	0.5%

Source: American Hospital Association (Chicago, IL)
   "Hospital Statistics" (2009 edition)
*Inpatient days in all nonfederal short-term general and other special hospitals, whose facilities and services are available to the public. Includes days in hospital and nursing home units.

Average Daily Census in Community Hospitals in 2007

National Average = 533,012 Inpatients*

ALPHA ORDER

RANK	STATE	INPATIENTS	% of USA
17	Alabama	9,730	1.8%
49	Alaska	923	0.2%
23	Arizona	8,334	1.6%
32	Arkansas	5,230	1.0%
2	California	46,999	8.8%
29	Colorado	5,945	1.1%
30	Connecticut	5,831	1.1%
45	Delaware	1,840	0.3%
4	Florida	33,839	6.3%
8	Georgia	17,202	3.2%
41	Hawaii	2,183	0.4%
47	Idaho	1,794	0.3%
6	Illinois	22,213	4.2%
18	Indiana	9,626	1.8%
28	Iowa	6,208	1.2%
31	Kansas	5,549	1.0%
21	Kentucky	8,737	1.6%
19	Louisiana	9,447	1.8%
40	Maine	2,301	0.4%
20	Maryland	8,885	1.7%
13	Massachusetts	12,032	2.3%
9	Michigan	17,192	3.2%
16	Minnesota	10,767	2.0%
25	Mississippi	7,330	1.4%
15	Missouri	11,809	2.2%
39	Montana	2,623	0.5%
34	Nebraska	4,437	0.8%
36	Nevada	3,495	0.7%
46	New Hampshire	1,807	0.3%
11	New Jersey	15,378	2.9%
43	New Mexico	2,094	0.4%
1	New York	50,259	9.4%
10	North Carolina	16,629	3.1%
42	North Dakota	2,117	0.4%
7	Ohio	21,243	4.0%
27	Oklahoma	6,465	1.2%
35	Oregon	4,205	0.8%
5	Pennsylvania	28,103	5.3%
44	Rhode Island	1,843	0.3%
24	South Carolina	8,236	1.5%
37	South Dakota	2,763	0.5%
12	Tennessee	14,719	2.8%
3	Texas	35,115	6.6%
38	Utah	2,750	0.5%
49	Vermont	923	0.2%
14	Virginia	11,930	2.2%
26	Washington	7,062	1.3%
33	West Virginia	4,539	0.9%
22	Wisconsin	8,681	1.6%
48	Wyoming	1,159	0.2%

RANK ORDER

RANK	STATE	INPATIENTS	% of USA
1	New York	50,259	9.4%
2	California	46,999	8.8%
3	Texas	35,115	6.6%
4	Florida	33,839	6.3%
5	Pennsylvania	28,103	5.3%
6	Illinois	22,213	4.2%
7	Ohio	21,243	4.0%
8	Georgia	17,202	3.2%
9	Michigan	17,192	3.2%
10	North Carolina	16,629	3.1%
11	New Jersey	15,378	2.9%
12	Tennessee	14,719	2.8%
13	Massachusetts	12,032	2.3%
14	Virginia	11,930	2.2%
15	Missouri	11,809	2.2%
16	Minnesota	10,767	2.0%
17	Alabama	9,730	1.8%
18	Indiana	9,626	1.8%
19	Louisiana	9,447	1.8%
20	Maryland	8,885	1.7%
21	Kentucky	8,737	1.6%
22	Wisconsin	8,681	1.6%
23	Arizona	8,334	1.6%
24	South Carolina	8,236	1.5%
25	Mississippi	7,330	1.4%
26	Washington	7,062	1.3%
27	Oklahoma	6,465	1.2%
28	Iowa	6,208	1.2%
29	Colorado	5,945	1.1%
30	Connecticut	5,831	1.1%
31	Kansas	5,549	1.0%
32	Arkansas	5,230	1.0%
33	West Virginia	4,539	0.9%
34	Nebraska	4,437	0.8%
35	Oregon	4,205	0.8%
36	Nevada	3,495	0.7%
37	South Dakota	2,763	0.5%
38	Utah	2,750	0.5%
39	Montana	2,623	0.5%
40	Maine	2,301	0.4%
41	Hawaii	2,183	0.4%
42	North Dakota	2,117	0.4%
43	New Mexico	2,094	0.4%
44	Rhode Island	1,843	0.3%
45	Delaware	1,840	0.3%
46	New Hampshire	1,807	0.3%
47	Idaho	1,794	0.3%
48	Wyoming	1,159	0.2%
49	Alaska	923	0.2%
49	Vermont	923	0.2%
	District of Columbia	2,490	0.5%

Source: CQ Press using data from American Hospital Association (Chicago, IL)
"Hospital Statistics" (2009 edition)
*Average total of inpatients receiving care in all nonfederal short-term general and other special hospitals, whose facilities and services are available to the public. Excludes newborns.

Average Stay in Community Hospitals in 2007

National Average = 5.5 Days*

ALPHA ORDER

RANK	STATE	DAYS
39	Alabama	5.1
15	Alaska	6.0
46	Arizona	4.5
26	Arkansas	5.2
26	California	5.2
39	Colorado	5.1
24	Connecticut	5.4
11	Delaware	6.3
26	Florida	5.2
9	Georgia	6.5
6	Hawaii	7.2
44	Idaho	4.9
42	Illinois	5.0
39	Indiana	5.1
12	Iowa	6.2
12	Kansas	6.2
26	Kentucky	5.2
19	Louisiana	5.5
19	Maine	5.5
45	Maryland	4.6
26	Massachusetts	5.2
26	Michigan	5.2
12	Minnesota	6.2
10	Mississippi	6.4
26	Missouri	5.2
2	Montana	9.0
5	Nebraska	7.5
26	Nevada	5.2
24	New Hampshire	5.4
26	New Jersey	5.2
46	New Mexico	4.5
6	New York	7.2
16	North Carolina	5.9
3	North Dakota	8.7
42	Ohio	5.0
26	Oklahoma	5.2
50	Oregon	4.4
19	Pennsylvania	5.5
26	Rhode Island	5.2
17	South Carolina	5.8
1	South Dakota	10.1
19	Tennessee	5.5
26	Texas	5.2
46	Utah	4.5
8	Vermont	6.8
19	Virginia	5.5
46	Washington	4.5
17	West Virginia	5.8
26	Wisconsin	5.2
4	Wyoming	8.0

RANK ORDER

RANK	STATE	DAYS
1	South Dakota	10.1
2	Montana	9.0
3	North Dakota	8.7
4	Wyoming	8.0
5	Nebraska	7.5
6	Hawaii	7.2
6	New York	7.2
8	Vermont	6.8
9	Georgia	6.5
10	Mississippi	6.4
11	Delaware	6.3
12	Iowa	6.2
12	Kansas	6.2
12	Minnesota	6.2
15	Alaska	6.0
16	North Carolina	5.9
17	South Carolina	5.8
17	West Virginia	5.8
19	Louisiana	5.5
19	Maine	5.5
19	Pennsylvania	5.5
19	Tennessee	5.5
19	Virginia	5.5
24	Connecticut	5.4
24	New Hampshire	5.4
26	Arkansas	5.2
26	California	5.2
26	Florida	5.2
26	Kentucky	5.2
26	Massachusetts	5.2
26	Michigan	5.2
26	Missouri	5.2
26	Nevada	5.2
26	New Jersey	5.2
26	Oklahoma	5.2
26	Rhode Island	5.2
26	Texas	5.2
26	Wisconsin	5.2
39	Alabama	5.1
39	Colorado	5.1
39	Indiana	5.1
42	Illinois	5.0
42	Ohio	5.0
44	Idaho	4.9
45	Maryland	4.6
46	Arizona	4.5
46	New Mexico	4.5
46	Utah	4.5
46	Washington	4.5
50	Oregon	4.4

District of Columbia	6.7

Source: American Hospital Association (Chicago, IL)
"Hospital Statistics" (2009 edition)
*All nonfederal short-term general and other special hospitals, whose facilities and services are available to the public.

Occupancy Rate in Community Hospitals in 2007

National Rate = 66.6% of Community Hospital Beds Occupied*

RANK	STATE (ALPHA ORDER)	PERCENT		RANK	STATE (RANK ORDER)	PERCENT
31	Alabama	62.0		1	New York	80.6
41	Alaska	59.4		2	Delaware	80.4
13	Arizona	68.6		3	Connecticut	77.9
49	Arkansas	55.0		4	Maryland	75.7
17	California	67.8		5	Rhode Island	75.3
33	Colorado	61.2		6	Hawaii	74.8
3	Connecticut	77.9		7	Massachusetts	72.9
2	Delaware	80.4		8	North Carolina	71.8
22	Florida	65.5		9	New Jersey	71.4
20	Georgia	67.5		10	Pennsylvania	70.7
6	Hawaii	74.8		11	Virginia	70.6
50	Idaho	54.4		12	Nevada	69.2
26	Illinois	64.3		13	Arizona	68.6
46	Indiana	56.4		14	South Carolina	68.5
43	Iowa	59.0		15	Minnesota	68.1
48	Kansas	55.1		16	Tennessee	67.9
37	Kentucky	60.6		17	California	67.8
35	Louisiana	60.9		17	Vermont	67.8
21	Maine	65.6		19	Michigan	67.7
4	Maryland	75.7		20	Georgia	67.5
7	Massachusetts	72.9		21	Maine	65.6
19	Michigan	67.7		22	Florida	65.5
15	Minnesota	68.1		22	Montana	65.5
44	Mississippi	57.7		24	South Dakota	65.1
27	Missouri	64.0		25	Ohio	64.6
22	Montana	65.5		26	Illinois	64.3
41	Nebraska	59.4		27	Missouri	64.0
12	Nevada	69.2		28	New Hampshire	63.6
28	New Hampshire	63.6		29	Washington	62.4
9	New Jersey	71.4		30	Wisconsin	62.1
45	New Mexico	56.7		31	Alabama	62.0
1	New York	80.6		32	Oregon	61.5
8	North Carolina	71.8		33	Colorado	61.2
36	North Dakota	60.7		34	West Virginia	61.0
25	Ohio	64.6		35	Louisiana	60.9
40	Oklahoma	59.5		36	North Dakota	60.7
32	Oregon	61.5		37	Kentucky	60.6
10	Pennsylvania	70.7		38	Texas	60.3
5	Rhode Island	75.3		39	Utah	60.0
14	South Carolina	68.5		40	Oklahoma	59.5
24	South Dakota	65.1		41	Alaska	59.4
16	Tennessee	67.9		41	Nebraska	59.4
38	Texas	60.3		43	Iowa	59.0
39	Utah	60.0		44	Mississippi	57.7
17	Vermont	67.8		45	New Mexico	56.7
11	Virginia	70.6		46	Indiana	56.4
29	Washington	62.4		47	Wyoming	56.0
34	West Virginia	61.0		48	Kansas	55.1
30	Wisconsin	62.1		49	Arkansas	55.0
47	Wyoming	56.0		50	Idaho	54.4

District of Columbia 72.8

Source: CQ Press using data from American Hospital Association (Chicago, IL)
"Hospital Statistics" (2009 edition)
*Average daily census compared to number of community hospital beds.

Outpatient Visits to Community Hospitals in 2007

National Total = 603,300,374 Visits*

ALPHA ORDER

RANK	STATE	VISITS	% of USA
23	Alabama	8,187,693	1.4%
48	Alaska	1,784,563	0.3%
27	Arizona	7,313,560	1.2%
33	Arkansas	5,236,516	0.9%
2	California	45,936,577	7.6%
25	Colorado	7,754,420	1.3%
26	Connecticut	7,550,938	1.3%
46	Delaware	1,838,749	0.3%
8	Florida	23,496,020	3.9%
14	Georgia	13,757,851	2.3%
45	Hawaii	1,877,991	0.3%
41	Idaho	2,868,062	0.5%
6	Illinois	30,647,460	5.1%
13	Indiana	16,721,388	2.8%
19	Iowa	10,555,885	1.7%
30	Kansas	6,397,805	1.1%
22	Kentucky	9,524,817	1.6%
20	Louisiana	10,428,195	1.7%
35	Maine	4,701,003	0.8%
28	Maryland	7,301,819	1.2%
9	Massachusetts	19,580,205	3.2%
7	Michigan	27,886,463	4.6%
21	Minnesota	9,853,482	1.6%
36	Mississippi	4,424,466	0.7%
12	Missouri	16,975,654	2.8%
40	Montana	3,035,030	0.5%
37	Nebraska	4,199,804	0.7%
43	Nevada	2,655,790	0.4%
39	New Hampshire	4,099,092	0.7%
11	New Jersey	17,189,615	2.8%
38	New Mexico	4,108,993	0.7%
1	New York	53,137,548	8.8%
10	North Carolina	17,768,346	2.9%
49	North Dakota	1,748,447	0.3%
4	Ohio	33,085,429	5.5%
32	Oklahoma	5,273,112	0.9%
24	Oregon	8,179,445	1.4%
3	Pennsylvania	36,784,412	6.1%
44	Rhode Island	2,567,803	0.4%
31	South Carolina	6,042,322	1.0%
47	South Dakota	1,788,725	0.3%
17	Tennessee	11,818,795	2.0%
5	Texas	32,499,012	5.4%
34	Utah	4,963,779	0.8%
42	Vermont	2,773,809	0.5%
16	Virginia	12,932,891	2.1%
18	Washington	11,195,681	1.9%
29	West Virginia	6,455,082	1.1%
15	Wisconsin	13,072,405	2.2%
50	Wyoming	956,713	0.2%

RANK ORDER

RANK	STATE	VISITS	% of USA
1	New York	53,137,548	8.8%
2	California	45,936,577	7.6%
3	Pennsylvania	36,784,412	6.1%
4	Ohio	33,085,429	5.5%
5	Texas	32,499,012	5.4%
6	Illinois	30,647,460	5.1%
7	Michigan	27,886,463	4.6%
8	Florida	23,496,020	3.9%
9	Massachusetts	19,580,205	3.2%
10	North Carolina	17,768,346	2.9%
11	New Jersey	17,189,615	2.8%
12	Missouri	16,975,654	2.8%
13	Indiana	16,721,388	2.8%
14	Georgia	13,757,851	2.3%
15	Wisconsin	13,072,405	2.2%
16	Virginia	12,932,891	2.1%
17	Tennessee	11,818,795	2.0%
18	Washington	11,195,681	1.9%
19	Iowa	10,555,885	1.7%
20	Louisiana	10,428,195	1.7%
21	Minnesota	9,853,482	1.6%
22	Kentucky	9,524,817	1.6%
23	Alabama	8,187,693	1.4%
24	Oregon	8,179,445	1.4%
25	Colorado	7,754,420	1.3%
26	Connecticut	7,550,938	1.3%
27	Arizona	7,313,560	1.2%
28	Maryland	7,301,819	1.2%
29	West Virginia	6,455,082	1.1%
30	Kansas	6,397,805	1.1%
31	South Carolina	6,042,322	1.0%
32	Oklahoma	5,273,112	0.9%
33	Arkansas	5,236,516	0.9%
34	Utah	4,963,779	0.8%
35	Maine	4,701,003	0.8%
36	Mississippi	4,424,466	0.7%
37	Nebraska	4,199,804	0.7%
38	New Mexico	4,108,993	0.7%
39	New Hampshire	4,099,092	0.7%
40	Montana	3,035,030	0.5%
41	Idaho	2,868,062	0.5%
42	Vermont	2,773,809	0.5%
43	Nevada	2,655,790	0.4%
44	Rhode Island	2,567,803	0.4%
45	Hawaii	1,877,991	0.3%
46	Delaware	1,838,749	0.3%
47	South Dakota	1,788,725	0.3%
48	Alaska	1,784,563	0.3%
49	North Dakota	1,748,447	0.3%
50	Wyoming	956,713	0.2%
	District of Columbia	2,366,712	0.4%

Source: American Hospital Association (Chicago, IL)
"Hospital Statistics" (2009 edition)
*All nonfederal short-term general and other special hospitals, whose facilities and services are available to the public. Includes emergency and other visits.

Emergency Outpatient Visits to Community Hospitals in 2007

National Total = 120,811,299 Visits*

RANK	STATE	VISITS	% of USA
20	Alabama	2,253,215	1.9%
46	Alaska	328,947	0.3%
22	Arizona	2,122,695	1.8%
31	Arkansas	1,294,119	1.1%
1	California	10,006,018	8.3%
28	Colorado	1,548,319	1.3%
29	Connecticut	1,461,985	1.2%
44	Delaware	343,713	0.3%
4	Florida	7,085,930	5.9%
10	Georgia	3,747,532	3.1%
45	Hawaii	339,004	0.3%
41	Idaho	521,382	0.4%
7	Illinois	5,068,338	4.2%
14	Indiana	3,080,110	2.5%
33	Iowa	1,165,305	1.0%
34	Kansas	1,003,181	0.8%
18	Kentucky	2,305,046	1.9%
21	Louisiana	2,194,465	1.8%
37	Maine	718,242	0.6%
19	Maryland	2,285,417	1.9%
12	Massachusetts	3,187,172	2.6%
8	Michigan	4,468,623	3.7%
26	Minnesota	1,727,682	1.4%
25	Mississippi	1,736,141	1.4%
16	Missouri	2,677,716	2.2%
43	Montana	354,943	0.3%
39	Nebraska	630,134	0.5%
36	Nevada	751,845	0.6%
40	New Hampshire	619,714	0.5%
13	New Jersey	3,175,910	2.6%
38	New Mexico	650,026	0.5%
3	New York	8,193,513	6.8%
9	North Carolina	4,068,389	3.4%
47	North Dakota	274,223	0.2%
5	Ohio	5,918,218	4.9%
27	Oklahoma	1,618,741	1.3%
30	Oregon	1,301,629	1.1%
6	Pennsylvania	5,771,876	4.8%
42	Rhode Island	485,624	0.4%
24	South Carolina	1,890,731	1.6%
50	South Dakota	226,131	0.2%
11	Tennessee	3,253,035	2.7%
2	Texas	8,444,299	7.0%
35	Utah	900,975	0.7%
48	Vermont	259,661	0.2%
15	Virginia	3,040,762	2.5%
17	Washington	2,343,863	1.9%
32	West Virginia	1,171,507	1.0%
23	Wisconsin	2,106,402	1.7%
49	Wyoming	227,386	0.2%

RANK	STATE	VISITS	% of USA
1	California	10,006,018	8.3%
2	Texas	8,444,299	7.0%
3	New York	8,193,513	6.8%
4	Florida	7,085,930	5.9%
5	Ohio	5,918,218	4.9%
6	Pennsylvania	5,771,876	4.8%
7	Illinois	5,068,338	4.2%
8	Michigan	4,468,623	3.7%
9	North Carolina	4,068,389	3.4%
10	Georgia	3,747,532	3.1%
11	Tennessee	3,253,035	2.7%
12	Massachusetts	3,187,172	2.6%
13	New Jersey	3,175,910	2.6%
14	Indiana	3,080,110	2.5%
15	Virginia	3,040,762	2.5%
16	Missouri	2,677,716	2.2%
17	Washington	2,343,863	1.9%
18	Kentucky	2,305,046	1.9%
19	Maryland	2,285,417	1.9%
20	Alabama	2,253,215	1.9%
21	Louisiana	2,194,465	1.8%
22	Arizona	2,122,695	1.8%
23	Wisconsin	2,106,402	1.7%
24	South Carolina	1,890,731	1.6%
25	Mississippi	1,736,141	1.4%
26	Minnesota	1,727,682	1.4%
27	Oklahoma	1,618,741	1.3%
28	Colorado	1,548,319	1.3%
29	Connecticut	1,461,985	1.2%
30	Oregon	1,301,629	1.1%
31	Arkansas	1,294,119	1.1%
32	West Virginia	1,171,507	1.0%
33	Iowa	1,165,305	1.0%
34	Kansas	1,003,181	0.8%
35	Utah	900,975	0.7%
36	Nevada	751,845	0.6%
37	Maine	718,242	0.6%
38	New Mexico	650,026	0.5%
39	Nebraska	630,134	0.5%
40	New Hampshire	619,714	0.5%
41	Idaho	521,382	0.4%
42	Rhode Island	485,624	0.4%
43	Montana	354,943	0.3%
44	Delaware	343,713	0.3%
45	Hawaii	339,004	0.3%
46	Alaska	328,947	0.3%
47	North Dakota	274,223	0.2%
48	Vermont	259,661	0.2%
49	Wyoming	227,386	0.2%
50	South Dakota	226,131	0.2%
	District of Columbia	461,465	0.4%

Source: American Hospital Association (Chicago, IL)
   "Hospital Statistics" (2009 edition)
*All nonfederal short-term general and other special hospitals, whose facilities and services are available to the public.

Medicare and Medicaid Certified Facilities in 2009

National Total = 272,480 Facilities*

ALPHA ORDER

RANK	STATE	FACILITIES	% of USA
19	Alabama	4,677	1.7%
48	Alaska	643	0.2%
17	Arizona	4,800	1.8%
33	Arkansas	2,913	1.1%
2	California	25,084	9.2%
28	Colorado	3,639	1.3%
30	Connecticut	3,318	1.2%
46	Delaware	912	0.3%
3	Florida	19,064	7.0%
9	Georgia	8,560	3.1%
44	Hawaii	989	0.4%
39	Idaho	1,384	0.5%
6	Illinois	11,766	4.3%
11	Indiana	6,963	2.6%
27	Iowa	4,091	1.5%
29	Kansas	3,481	1.3%
23	Kentucky	4,384	1.6%
16	Louisiana	5,696	2.1%
40	Maine	1,377	0.5%
21	Maryland	4,469	1.6%
18	Massachusetts	4,717	1.7%
8	Michigan	9,073	3.3%
20	Minnesota	4,489	1.6%
31	Mississippi	3,273	1.2%
12	Missouri	6,605	2.4%
43	Montana	1,016	0.4%
34	Nebraska	2,404	0.9%
37	Nevada	1,755	0.6%
42	New Hampshire	1,189	0.4%
13	New Jersey	6,550	2.4%
38	New Mexico	1,751	0.6%
4	New York	12,750	4.7%
10	North Carolina	8,227	3.0%
47	North Dakota	907	0.3%
5	Ohio	12,413	4.6%
26	Oklahoma	4,303	1.6%
32	Oregon	2,930	1.1%
7	Pennsylvania	10,466	3.8%
45	Rhode Island	977	0.4%
22	South Carolina	4,410	1.6%
41	South Dakota	1,199	0.4%
14	Tennessee	6,192	2.3%
1	Texas	25,930	9.5%
36	Utah	1,847	0.7%
49	Vermont	596	0.2%
15	Virginia	5,998	2.2%
25	Washington	4,356	1.6%
35	West Virginia	2,367	0.9%
24	Wisconsin	4,378	1.6%
50	Wyoming	546	0.2%

RANK ORDER

RANK	STATE	FACILITIES	% of USA
1	Texas	25,930	9.5%
2	California	25,084	9.2%
3	Florida	19,064	7.0%
4	New York	12,750	4.7%
5	Ohio	12,413	4.6%
6	Illinois	11,766	4.3%
7	Pennsylvania	10,466	3.8%
8	Michigan	9,073	3.3%
9	Georgia	8,560	3.1%
10	North Carolina	8,227	3.0%
11	Indiana	6,963	2.6%
12	Missouri	6,605	2.4%
13	New Jersey	6,550	2.4%
14	Tennessee	6,192	2.3%
15	Virginia	5,998	2.2%
16	Louisiana	5,696	2.1%
17	Arizona	4,800	1.8%
18	Massachusetts	4,717	1.7%
19	Alabama	4,677	1.7%
20	Minnesota	4,489	1.6%
21	Maryland	4,469	1.6%
22	South Carolina	4,410	1.6%
23	Kentucky	4,384	1.6%
24	Wisconsin	4,378	1.6%
25	Washington	4,356	1.6%
26	Oklahoma	4,303	1.6%
27	Iowa	4,091	1.5%
28	Colorado	3,639	1.3%
29	Kansas	3,481	1.3%
30	Connecticut	3,318	1.2%
31	Mississippi	3,273	1.2%
32	Oregon	2,930	1.1%
33	Arkansas	2,913	1.1%
34	Nebraska	2,404	0.9%
35	West Virginia	2,367	0.9%
36	Utah	1,847	0.7%
37	Nevada	1,755	0.6%
38	New Mexico	1,751	0.6%
39	Idaho	1,384	0.5%
40	Maine	1,377	0.5%
41	South Dakota	1,199	0.4%
42	New Hampshire	1,189	0.4%
43	Montana	1,016	0.4%
44	Hawaii	989	0.4%
45	Rhode Island	977	0.4%
46	Delaware	912	0.3%
47	North Dakota	907	0.3%
48	Alaska	643	0.2%
49	Vermont	596	0.2%
50	Wyoming	546	0.2%
	District of Columbia	656	0.2%

Source: U.S. Department of Health and Human Services, Centers for Medicare and Medicaid Services
    OSCAR Report 10 (January 05, 2009)
*Certified by CMS to participate in the Medicare/Medicaid programs. All provider groups including hospitals, home health agencies, rural health centers, community mental health centers, nursing facilities, outpatient physical therapy facilities, hospices, and laboratories. National total does not include 1,508 certified facilities in U.S. territories.

Medicare and Medicaid Certified Hospitals in 2009

National Total = 6,108 Hospitals*

ALPHA ORDER

RANK	STATE	HOSPITALS	% of USA
19	Alabama	130	2.1%
47	Alaska	25	0.4%
25	Arizona	102	1.7%
25	Arkansas	102	1.7%
2	California	423	6.9%
29	Colorado	97	1.6%
42	Connecticut	45	0.7%
50	Delaware	11	0.2%
3	Florida	238	3.9%
9	Georgia	178	2.9%
46	Hawaii	27	0.4%
37	Idaho	51	0.8%
8	Illinois	212	3.5%
11	Indiana	164	2.7%
20	Iowa	122	2.0%
12	Kansas	158	2.6%
21	Kentucky	119	1.9%
6	Louisiana	231	3.8%
43	Maine	43	0.7%
33	Maryland	64	1.0%
24	Massachusetts	112	1.8%
10	Michigan	174	2.8%
17	Minnesota	142	2.3%
23	Mississippi	114	1.9%
15	Missouri	146	2.4%
32	Montana	65	1.1%
30	Nebraska	96	1.6%
39	Nevada	50	0.8%
44	New Hampshire	30	0.5%
27	New Jersey	101	1.7%
37	New Mexico	51	0.8%
3	New York	238	3.9%
18	North Carolina	131	2.1%
39	North Dakota	50	0.8%
7	Ohio	222	3.6%
13	Oklahoma	152	2.5%
36	Oregon	61	1.0%
5	Pennsylvania	237	3.9%
48	Rhode Island	15	0.2%
31	South Carolina	80	1.3%
33	South Dakota	64	1.0%
14	Tennessee	151	2.5%
1	Texas	556	9.1%
41	Utah	48	0.8%
48	Vermont	15	0.2%
22	Virginia	115	1.9%
28	Washington	99	1.6%
35	West Virginia	63	1.0%
16	Wisconsin	144	2.4%
44	Wyoming	30	0.5%

RANK ORDER

RANK	STATE	HOSPITALS	% of USA
1	Texas	556	9.1%
2	California	423	6.9%
3	Florida	238	3.9%
3	New York	238	3.9%
5	Pennsylvania	237	3.9%
6	Louisiana	231	3.8%
7	Ohio	222	3.6%
8	Illinois	212	3.5%
9	Georgia	178	2.9%
10	Michigan	174	2.8%
11	Indiana	164	2.7%
12	Kansas	158	2.6%
13	Oklahoma	152	2.5%
14	Tennessee	151	2.5%
15	Missouri	146	2.4%
16	Wisconsin	144	2.4%
17	Minnesota	142	2.3%
18	North Carolina	131	2.1%
19	Alabama	130	2.1%
20	Iowa	122	2.0%
21	Kentucky	119	1.9%
22	Virginia	115	1.9%
23	Mississippi	114	1.9%
24	Massachusetts	112	1.8%
25	Arizona	102	1.7%
25	Arkansas	102	1.7%
27	New Jersey	101	1.7%
28	Washington	99	1.6%
29	Colorado	97	1.6%
30	Nebraska	96	1.6%
31	South Carolina	80	1.3%
32	Montana	65	1.1%
33	Maryland	64	1.0%
33	South Dakota	64	1.0%
35	West Virginia	63	1.0%
36	Oregon	61	1.0%
37	Idaho	51	0.8%
37	New Mexico	51	0.8%
39	Nevada	50	0.8%
39	North Dakota	50	0.8%
41	Utah	48	0.8%
42	Connecticut	45	0.7%
43	Maine	43	0.7%
44	New Hampshire	30	0.5%
44	Wyoming	30	0.5%
46	Hawaii	27	0.4%
47	Alaska	25	0.4%
48	Rhode Island	15	0.2%
48	Vermont	15	0.2%
50	Delaware	11	0.2%
	District of Columbia	14	0.2%

Source: U.S. Department of Health and Human Services, Centers for Medicare and Medicaid Services
   OSCAR Report 10 (January 05, 2009)

*Certified by CMS to participate in the Medicare/Medicaid programs. Excludes licensed facilities that do not accept federal funding and facilities managed by the Department of Veterans Affairs. National total does not include 64 certified hospitals in U.S. territories.

Beds in Medicare and Medicaid Certified Hospitals in 2009

National Total = 918,945 Beds*

ALPHA ORDER					RANK ORDER			
RANK	STATE	BEDS	% of USA		RANK	STATE	BEDS	% of USA
16	Alabama	20,035	2.2%		1	California	78,846	8.6%
49	Alaska	1,607	0.2%		2	New York	67,120	7.3%
21	Arizona	15,942	1.7%		3	Texas	66,366	7.2%
31	Arkansas	10,449	1.1%		4	Florida	57,976	6.3%
1	California	78,846	8.6%		5	Ohio	44,102	4.8%
28	Colorado	12,472	1.4%		6	Illinois	43,802	4.8%
32	Connecticut	10,255	1.1%		7	Pennsylvania	35,898	3.9%
47	Delaware	2,520	0.3%		8	Michigan	28,138	3.1%
4	Florida	57,976	6.3%		9	New Jersey	27,971	3.0%
11	Georgia	24,997	2.7%		10	North Carolina	25,224	2.7%
46	Hawaii	2,731	0.3%		11	Georgia	24,997	2.7%
42	Idaho	3,401	0.4%		12	Tennessee	24,638	2.7%
6	Illinois	43,802	4.8%		13	Missouri	23,558	2.6%
18	Indiana	18,804	2.0%		14	Louisiana	21,127	2.3%
30	Iowa	10,814	1.2%		15	Virginia	20,051	2.2%
29	Kansas	11,560	1.3%		16	Alabama	20,035	2.2%
20	Kentucky	17,337	1.9%		17	Massachusetts	19,864	2.2%
14	Louisiana	21,127	2.3%		18	Indiana	18,804	2.0%
39	Maine	4,081	0.4%		19	Wisconsin	17,565	1.9%
22	Maryland	15,562	1.7%		20	Kentucky	17,337	1.9%
17	Massachusetts	19,864	2.2%		21	Arizona	15,942	1.7%
8	Michigan	28,138	3.1%		22	Maryland	15,562	1.7%
23	Minnesota	15,389	1.7%		23	Minnesota	15,389	1.7%
26	Mississippi	13,256	1.4%		24	Oklahoma	14,713	1.6%
13	Missouri	23,558	2.6%		25	Washington	13,505	1.5%
45	Montana	3,151	0.3%		26	Mississippi	13,256	1.4%
35	Nebraska	6,578	0.7%		27	South Carolina	13,215	1.4%
36	Nevada	6,374	0.7%		28	Colorado	12,472	1.4%
41	New Hampshire	3,537	0.4%		29	Kansas	11,560	1.3%
9	New Jersey	27,971	3.0%		30	Iowa	10,814	1.2%
38	New Mexico	4,812	0.5%		31	Arkansas	10,449	1.1%
2	New York	67,120	7.3%		32	Connecticut	10,255	1.1%
10	North Carolina	25,224	2.7%		33	West Virginia	8,999	1.0%
44	North Dakota	3,195	0.3%		34	Oregon	7,886	0.9%
5	Ohio	44,102	4.8%		35	Nebraska	6,578	0.7%
24	Oklahoma	14,713	1.6%		36	Nevada	6,374	0.7%
34	Oregon	7,886	0.9%		37	Utah	5,011	0.5%
7	Pennsylvania	35,898	3.9%		38	New Mexico	4,812	0.5%
40	Rhode Island	3,657	0.4%		39	Maine	4,081	0.4%
27	South Carolina	13,215	1.4%		40	Rhode Island	3,657	0.4%
43	South Dakota	3,400	0.4%		41	New Hampshire	3,537	0.4%
12	Tennessee	24,638	2.7%		42	Idaho	3,401	0.4%
3	Texas	66,366	7.2%		43	South Dakota	3,400	0.4%
37	Utah	5,011	0.5%		44	North Dakota	3,195	0.3%
48	Vermont	1,808	0.2%		45	Montana	3,151	0.3%
15	Virginia	20,051	2.2%		46	Hawaii	2,731	0.3%
25	Washington	13,505	1.5%		47	Delaware	2,520	0.3%
33	West Virginia	8,999	1.0%		48	Vermont	1,808	0.2%
19	Wisconsin	17,565	1.9%		49	Alaska	1,607	0.2%
50	Wyoming	1,543	0.2%		50	Wyoming	1,543	0.2%
						District of Columbia	4,103	0.4%

Source: U.S. Department of Health and Human Services, Centers for Medicare and Medicaid Services
OSCAR Report 10 (January 05, 2009)
*Beds in hospitals certified by CMS to participate in the Medicare/Medicaid programs. Excludes licensed facilities that do not accept federal funding and facilities managed by the Department of Veterans Affairs. National total does not include 11,619 beds in U.S. territories.

Medicare and Medicaid Certified Children's Hospitals in 2009

National Total = 77 Hospitals*

ALPHA ORDER					RANK ORDER			
RANK	STATE		HOSPITALS	% of USA	RANK	STATE	HOSPITALS	% of USA
9	Alabama		2	2.6%	1	California	10	13.0%
32	Alaska		0	0.0%	2	Texas	8	10.4%
9	Arizona		2	2.6%	3	Ohio	6	7.8%
21	Arkansas		1	1.3%	4	Pennsylvania	5	6.5%
1	California		10	13.0%	5	Minnesota	3	3.9%
21	Colorado		1	1.3%	5	Missouri	3	3.9%
21	Connecticut		1	1.3%	5	Virginia	3	3.9%
21	Delaware		1	1.3%	5	Wisconsin	3	3.9%
9	Florida		2	2.6%	9	Alabama	2	2.6%
9	Georgia		2	2.6%	9	Arizona	2	2.6%
21	Hawaii		1	1.3%	9	Florida	2	2.6%
32	Idaho		0	0.0%	9	Georgia	2	2.6%
9	Illinois		2	2.6%	9	Illinois	2	2.6%
32	Indiana		0	0.0%	9	Maryland	2	2.6%
32	Iowa		0	0.0%	9	Massachusetts	2	2.6%
21	Kansas		1	1.3%	9	Nebraska	2	2.6%
32	Kentucky		0	0.0%	9	New Jersey	2	2.6%
21	Louisiana		1	1.3%	9	Oklahoma	2	2.6%
32	Maine		0	0.0%	9	Tennessee	2	2.6%
9	Maryland		2	2.6%	9	Washington	2	2.6%
9	Massachusetts		2	2.6%	21	Arkansas	1	1.3%
21	Michigan		1	1.3%	21	Colorado	1	1.3%
5	Minnesota		3	3.9%	21	Connecticut	1	1.3%
32	Mississippi		0	0.0%	21	Delaware	1	1.3%
5	Missouri		3	3.9%	21	Hawaii	1	1.3%
32	Montana		0	0.0%	21	Kansas	1	1.3%
9	Nebraska		2	2.6%	21	Louisiana	1	1.3%
32	Nevada		0	0.0%	21	Michigan	1	1.3%
32	New Hampshire		0	0.0%	21	New York	1	1.3%
9	New Jersey		2	2.6%	21	South Dakota	1	1.3%
32	New Mexico		0	0.0%	21	Utah	1	1.3%
21	New York		1	1.3%	32	Alaska	0	0.0%
32	North Carolina		0	0.0%	32	Idaho	0	0.0%
32	North Dakota		0	0.0%	32	Indiana	0	0.0%
3	Ohio		6	7.8%	32	Iowa	0	0.0%
9	Oklahoma		2	2.6%	32	Kentucky	0	0.0%
32	Oregon		0	0.0%	32	Maine	0	0.0%
4	Pennsylvania		5	6.5%	32	Mississippi	0	0.0%
32	Rhode Island		0	0.0%	32	Montana	0	0.0%
32	South Carolina		0	0.0%	32	Nevada	0	0.0%
21	South Dakota		1	1.3%	32	New Hampshire	0	0.0%
9	Tennessee		2	2.6%	32	New Mexico	0	0.0%
2	Texas		8	10.4%	32	North Carolina	0	0.0%
21	Utah		1	1.3%	32	North Dakota	0	0.0%
32	Vermont		0	0.0%	32	Oregon	0	0.0%
5	Virginia		3	3.9%	32	Rhode Island	0	0.0%
9	Washington		2	2.6%	32	South Carolina	0	0.0%
32	West Virginia		0	0.0%	32	Vermont	0	0.0%
5	Wisconsin		3	3.9%	32	West Virginia	0	0.0%
32	Wyoming		0	0.0%	32	Wyoming	0	0.0%
						District of Columbia	1	1.3%

Source: U.S. Department of Health and Human Services, Centers for Medicare and Medicaid Services
    OSCAR Report 10 (January 05, 2009)
*Certified by CMS to participate in the Medicare/Medicaid programs. National total does not include one facility in U.S. territories.
    Excludes licensed facilities that do not accept federal funding and facilities managed by the Department of Veterans Affairs.

Beds in Medicare and Medicaid Certified Children's Hospitals in 2009

National Total = 12,156 Beds*

<table>
<thead>
<tr><th colspan="4">ALPHA ORDER</th><th colspan="4">RANK ORDER</th></tr>
<tr><th>RANK</th><th>STATE</th><th>BEDS</th><th>% of USA</th><th>RANK</th><th>STATE</th><th>BEDS</th><th>% of USA</th></tr>
</thead>
<tbody>
<tr><td>6</td><td>Alabama</td><td>434</td><td>3.6%</td><td>1</td><td>California</td><td>1,722</td><td>14.2%</td></tr>
<tr><td>32</td><td>Alaska</td><td>0</td><td>0.0%</td><td>2</td><td>Texas</td><td>1,385</td><td>11.4%</td></tr>
<tr><td>17</td><td>Arizona</td><td>250</td><td>2.1%</td><td>3</td><td>Ohio</td><td>1,322</td><td>10.9%</td></tr>
<tr><td>13</td><td>Arkansas</td><td>280</td><td>2.3%</td><td>4</td><td>Pennsylvania</td><td>759</td><td>6.2%</td></tr>
<tr><td>1</td><td>California</td><td>1,722</td><td>14.2%</td><td>5</td><td>Georgia</td><td>483</td><td>4.0%</td></tr>
<tr><td>16</td><td>Colorado</td><td>253</td><td>2.1%</td><td>6</td><td>Alabama</td><td>434</td><td>3.6%</td></tr>
<tr><td>27</td><td>Connecticut</td><td>129</td><td>1.1%</td><td>7</td><td>Missouri</td><td>432</td><td>3.6%</td></tr>
<tr><td>24</td><td>Delaware</td><td>180</td><td>1.5%</td><td>8</td><td>Florida</td><td>424</td><td>3.5%</td></tr>
<tr><td>8</td><td>Florida</td><td>424</td><td>3.5%</td><td>9</td><td>Massachusetts</td><td>421</td><td>3.5%</td></tr>
<tr><td>5</td><td>Georgia</td><td>483</td><td>4.0%</td><td>10</td><td>Illinois</td><td>339</td><td>2.8%</td></tr>
<tr><td>20</td><td>Hawaii</td><td>201</td><td>1.7%</td><td>10</td><td>Minnesota</td><td>339</td><td>2.8%</td></tr>
<tr><td>32</td><td>Idaho</td><td>0</td><td>0.0%</td><td>12</td><td>Virginia</td><td>296</td><td>2.4%</td></tr>
<tr><td>10</td><td>Illinois</td><td>339</td><td>2.8%</td><td>13</td><td>Arkansas</td><td>280</td><td>2.3%</td></tr>
<tr><td>32</td><td>Indiana</td><td>0</td><td>0.0%</td><td>14</td><td>Washington</td><td>276</td><td>2.3%</td></tr>
<tr><td>32</td><td>Iowa</td><td>0</td><td>0.0%</td><td>14</td><td>Wisconsin</td><td>276</td><td>2.3%</td></tr>
<tr><td>31</td><td>Kansas</td><td>34</td><td>0.3%</td><td>16</td><td>Colorado</td><td>253</td><td>2.1%</td></tr>
<tr><td>32</td><td>Kentucky</td><td>0</td><td>0.0%</td><td>17</td><td>Arizona</td><td>250</td><td>2.1%</td></tr>
<tr><td>20</td><td>Louisiana</td><td>201</td><td>1.7%</td><td>18</td><td>Utah</td><td>232</td><td>1.9%</td></tr>
<tr><td>32</td><td>Maine</td><td>0</td><td>0.0%</td><td>19</td><td>Michigan</td><td>228</td><td>1.9%</td></tr>
<tr><td>26</td><td>Maryland</td><td>150</td><td>1.2%</td><td>20</td><td>Hawaii</td><td>201</td><td>1.7%</td></tr>
<tr><td>9</td><td>Massachusetts</td><td>421</td><td>3.5%</td><td>20</td><td>Louisiana</td><td>201</td><td>1.7%</td></tr>
<tr><td>19</td><td>Michigan</td><td>228</td><td>1.9%</td><td>22</td><td>Nebraska</td><td>200</td><td>1.6%</td></tr>
<tr><td>10</td><td>Minnesota</td><td>339</td><td>2.8%</td><td>23</td><td>Tennessee</td><td>197</td><td>1.6%</td></tr>
<tr><td>32</td><td>Mississippi</td><td>0</td><td>0.0%</td><td>24</td><td>Delaware</td><td>180</td><td>1.5%</td></tr>
<tr><td>7</td><td>Missouri</td><td>432</td><td>3.6%</td><td>25</td><td>Oklahoma</td><td>160</td><td>1.3%</td></tr>
<tr><td>32</td><td>Montana</td><td>0</td><td>0.0%</td><td>26</td><td>Maryland</td><td>150</td><td>1.2%</td></tr>
<tr><td>22</td><td>Nebraska</td><td>200</td><td>1.6%</td><td>27</td><td>Connecticut</td><td>129</td><td>1.1%</td></tr>
<tr><td>32</td><td>Nevada</td><td>0</td><td>0.0%</td><td>28</td><td>South Dakota</td><td>114</td><td>0.9%</td></tr>
<tr><td>32</td><td>New Hampshire</td><td>0</td><td>0.0%</td><td>29</td><td>New Jersey</td><td>104</td><td>0.9%</td></tr>
<tr><td>29</td><td>New Jersey</td><td>104</td><td>0.9%</td><td>30</td><td>New York</td><td>92</td><td>0.8%</td></tr>
<tr><td>32</td><td>New Mexico</td><td>0</td><td>0.0%</td><td>31</td><td>Kansas</td><td>34</td><td>0.3%</td></tr>
<tr><td>30</td><td>New York</td><td>92</td><td>0.8%</td><td>32</td><td>Alaska</td><td>0</td><td>0.0%</td></tr>
<tr><td>32</td><td>North Carolina</td><td>0</td><td>0.0%</td><td>32</td><td>Idaho</td><td>0</td><td>0.0%</td></tr>
<tr><td>32</td><td>North Dakota</td><td>0</td><td>0.0%</td><td>32</td><td>Indiana</td><td>0</td><td>0.0%</td></tr>
<tr><td>3</td><td>Ohio</td><td>1,322</td><td>10.9%</td><td>32</td><td>Iowa</td><td>0</td><td>0.0%</td></tr>
<tr><td>25</td><td>Oklahoma</td><td>160</td><td>1.3%</td><td>32</td><td>Kentucky</td><td>0</td><td>0.0%</td></tr>
<tr><td>32</td><td>Oregon</td><td>0</td><td>0.0%</td><td>32</td><td>Maine</td><td>0</td><td>0.0%</td></tr>
<tr><td>4</td><td>Pennsylvania</td><td>759</td><td>6.2%</td><td>32</td><td>Mississippi</td><td>0</td><td>0.0%</td></tr>
<tr><td>32</td><td>Rhode Island</td><td>0</td><td>0.0%</td><td>32</td><td>Montana</td><td>0</td><td>0.0%</td></tr>
<tr><td>32</td><td>South Carolina</td><td>0</td><td>0.0%</td><td>32</td><td>Nevada</td><td>0</td><td>0.0%</td></tr>
<tr><td>28</td><td>South Dakota</td><td>114</td><td>0.9%</td><td>32</td><td>New Hampshire</td><td>0</td><td>0.0%</td></tr>
<tr><td>23</td><td>Tennessee</td><td>197</td><td>1.6%</td><td>32</td><td>New Mexico</td><td>0</td><td>0.0%</td></tr>
<tr><td>2</td><td>Texas</td><td>1,385</td><td>11.4%</td><td>32</td><td>North Carolina</td><td>0</td><td>0.0%</td></tr>
<tr><td>18</td><td>Utah</td><td>232</td><td>1.9%</td><td>32</td><td>North Dakota</td><td>0</td><td>0.0%</td></tr>
<tr><td>32</td><td>Vermont</td><td>0</td><td>0.0%</td><td>32</td><td>Oregon</td><td>0</td><td>0.0%</td></tr>
<tr><td>12</td><td>Virginia</td><td>296</td><td>2.4%</td><td>32</td><td>Rhode Island</td><td>0</td><td>0.0%</td></tr>
<tr><td>14</td><td>Washington</td><td>276</td><td>2.3%</td><td>32</td><td>South Carolina</td><td>0</td><td>0.0%</td></tr>
<tr><td>32</td><td>West Virginia</td><td>0</td><td>0.0%</td><td>32</td><td>Vermont</td><td>0</td><td>0.0%</td></tr>
<tr><td>14</td><td>Wisconsin</td><td>276</td><td>2.3%</td><td>32</td><td>West Virginia</td><td>0</td><td>0.0%</td></tr>
<tr><td>32</td><td>Wyoming</td><td>0</td><td>0.0%</td><td>32</td><td>Wyoming</td><td>0</td><td>0.0%</td></tr>
<tr><td></td><td></td><td></td><td></td><td></td><td>District of Columbia</td><td>243</td><td>2.0%</td></tr>
</tbody>
</table>

Source: U.S. Department of Health and Human Services, Centers for Medicare and Medicaid Services
    OSCAR Database (January 05, 2009)

*Certified by CMS to participate in the Medicare/Medicaid programs. National total does not include 215 beds in one facility in U.S. territories. Excludes licensed facilities that do not accept federal funding and facilities managed by the Department of Veterans Affairs.

Medicare and Medicaid Certified Rehabilitation Hospitals in 2009

National Total = 221 Hospitals*

ALPHA ORDER

RANK	STATE	HOSPITALS	% of USA
9	Alabama	7	3.2%
41	Alaska	0	0.0%
11	Arizona	6	2.7%
5	Arkansas	8	3.6%
15	California	5	2.3%
21	Colorado	3	1.4%
30	Connecticut	1	0.5%
41	Delaware	0	0.0%
4	Florida	13	5.9%
21	Georgia	3	1.4%
30	Hawaii	1	0.5%
30	Idaho	1	0.5%
18	Illinois	4	1.8%
5	Indiana	8	3.6%
41	Iowa	0	0.0%
18	Kansas	4	1.8%
11	Kentucky	6	2.7%
2	Louisiana	22	10.0%
30	Maine	1	0.5%
26	Maryland	2	0.9%
5	Massachusetts	8	3.6%
18	Michigan	4	1.8%
30	Minnesota	1	0.5%
41	Mississippi	0	0.0%
21	Missouri	3	1.4%
41	Montana	0	0.0%
30	Nebraska	1	0.5%
21	Nevada	3	1.4%
26	New Hampshire	2	0.9%
5	New Jersey	8	3.6%
15	New Mexico	5	2.3%
41	New York	0	0.0%
26	North Carolina	2	0.9%
41	North Dakota	0	0.0%
21	Ohio	3	1.4%
26	Oklahoma	2	0.9%
41	Oregon	0	0.0%
3	Pennsylvania	17	7.7%
30	Rhode Island	1	0.5%
11	South Carolina	6	2.7%
41	South Dakota	0	0.0%
11	Tennessee	6	2.7%
1	Texas	37	16.7%
30	Utah	1	0.5%
41	Vermont	0	0.0%
9	Virginia	7	3.2%
30	Washington	1	0.5%
15	West Virginia	5	2.3%
30	Wisconsin	1	0.5%
30	Wyoming	1	0.5%

RANK ORDER

RANK	STATE	HOSPITALS	% of USA
1	Texas	37	16.7%
2	Louisiana	22	10.0%
3	Pennsylvania	17	7.7%
4	Florida	13	5.9%
5	Arkansas	8	3.6%
5	Indiana	8	3.6%
5	Massachusetts	8	3.6%
5	New Jersey	8	3.6%
9	Alabama	7	3.2%
9	Virginia	7	3.2%
11	Arizona	6	2.7%
11	Kentucky	6	2.7%
11	South Carolina	6	2.7%
11	Tennessee	6	2.7%
15	California	5	2.3%
15	New Mexico	5	2.3%
15	West Virginia	5	2.3%
18	Illinois	4	1.8%
18	Kansas	4	1.8%
18	Michigan	4	1.8%
21	Colorado	3	1.4%
21	Georgia	3	1.4%
21	Missouri	3	1.4%
21	Nevada	3	1.4%
21	Ohio	3	1.4%
26	Maryland	2	0.9%
26	New Hampshire	2	0.9%
26	North Carolina	2	0.9%
26	Oklahoma	2	0.9%
30	Connecticut	1	0.5%
30	Hawaii	1	0.5%
30	Idaho	1	0.5%
30	Maine	1	0.5%
30	Minnesota	1	0.5%
30	Nebraska	1	0.5%
30	Rhode Island	1	0.5%
30	Utah	1	0.5%
30	Washington	1	0.5%
30	Wisconsin	1	0.5%
30	Wyoming	1	0.5%
41	Alaska	0	0.0%
41	Delaware	0	0.0%
41	Iowa	0	0.0%
41	Mississippi	0	0.0%
41	Montana	0	0.0%
41	New York	0	0.0%
41	North Dakota	0	0.0%
41	Oregon	0	0.0%
41	South Dakota	0	0.0%
41	Vermont	0	0.0%
	District of Columbia	1	0.5%

Source: U.S. Department of Health and Human Services, Centers for Medicare and Medicaid Services
    OSCAR Database (January 05, 2009)
*Certified by CMS to participate in the Medicare/Medicaid programs. Excludes licensed facilities that do not accept federal funding and facilities managed by the Department of Veterans Affairs. National total does not include two certified hospitals in U.S. territories.

Beds in Medicare and Medicaid Certified Rehabilitation Hospitals in 2009

National Total = 14,152 Beds*

ALPHA ORDER						RANK ORDER			
RANK	STATE	BEDS	% of USA			RANK	STATE	BEDS	% of USA
9	Alabama	392	2.8%			1	Texas	2,152	15.2%
41	Alaska	0	0.0%			2	Pennsylvania	1,436	10.1%
14	Arizona	331	2.3%			3	Massachusetts	1,040	7.3%
7	Arkansas	463	3.3%			4	Florida	1,012	7.2%
11	California	367	2.6%			5	New Jersey	760	5.4%
20	Colorado	226	1.6%			6	Louisiana	578	4.1%
37	Connecticut	60	0.4%			7	Arkansas	463	3.3%
41	Delaware	0	0.0%			8	Illinois	448	3.2%
4	Florida	1,012	7.2%			9	Alabama	392	2.8%
26	Georgia	168	1.2%			10	Tennessee	370	2.6%
31	Hawaii	100	0.7%			11	California	367	2.6%
38	Idaho	46	0.3%			12	Indiana	366	2.6%
8	Illinois	448	3.2%			13	South Carolina	341	2.4%
12	Indiana	366	2.6%			14	Arizona	331	2.3%
41	Iowa	0	0.0%			15	Kentucky	328	2.3%
18	Kansas	257	1.8%			16	Virginia	288	2.0%
15	Kentucky	328	2.3%			17	West Virginia	270	1.9%
6	Louisiana	578	4.1%			18	Kansas	257	1.8%
31	Maine	100	0.7%			19	Michigan	240	1.7%
27	Maryland	131	0.9%			20	Colorado	226	1.6%
3	Massachusetts	1,040	7.3%			21	North Carolina	213	1.5%
19	Michigan	240	1.7%			22	New Mexico	212	1.5%
40	Minnesota	16	0.1%			23	Missouri	202	1.4%
41	Mississippi	0	0.0%			24	Ohio	199	1.4%
23	Missouri	202	1.4%			25	Nevada	181	1.3%
41	Montana	0	0.0%			26	Georgia	168	1.2%
36	Nebraska	72	0.5%			27	Maryland	131	0.9%
25	Nevada	181	1.3%			28	New Hampshire	130	0.9%
28	New Hampshire	130	0.9%			29	Oklahoma	107	0.8%
5	New Jersey	760	5.4%			30	Washington	102	0.7%
22	New Mexico	212	1.5%			31	Hawaii	100	0.7%
41	New York	0	0.0%			31	Maine	100	0.7%
21	North Carolina	213	1.5%			33	Utah	84	0.6%
41	North Dakota	0	0.0%			34	Rhode Island	82	0.6%
24	Ohio	199	1.4%			35	Wisconsin	81	0.6%
29	Oklahoma	107	0.8%			36	Nebraska	72	0.5%
41	Oregon	0	0.0%			37	Connecticut	60	0.4%
2	Pennsylvania	1,436	10.1%			38	Idaho	46	0.3%
34	Rhode Island	82	0.6%			39	Wyoming	41	0.3%
13	South Carolina	341	2.4%			40	Minnesota	16	0.1%
41	South Dakota	0	0.0%			41	Alaska	0	0.0%
10	Tennessee	370	2.6%			41	Delaware	0	0.0%
1	Texas	2,152	15.2%			41	Iowa	0	0.0%
33	Utah	84	0.6%			41	Mississippi	0	0.0%
41	Vermont	0	0.0%			41	Montana	0	0.0%
16	Virginia	288	2.0%			41	New York	0	0.0%
30	Washington	102	0.7%			41	North Dakota	0	0.0%
17	West Virginia	270	1.9%			41	Oregon	0	0.0%
35	Wisconsin	81	0.6%			41	South Dakota	0	0.0%
39	Wyoming	41	0.3%			41	Vermont	0	0.0%
							District of Columbia	160	1.1%

Source: U.S. Department of Health and Human Services, Centers for Medicare and Medicaid Services
    OSCAR Database (January 05, 2009)
*Beds in hospitals certified by CMS to participate in the Medicare/Medicaid programs. Excludes licensed facilities that do not accept federal funding and facilities managed by the Department of Veterans Affairs. National total does not include 72 beds in U.S. territories.

Medicare and Medicaid Certified Psychiatric Hospitals in 2009

National Total = 487 Psychiatric Hospitals*

ALPHA ORDER

RANK	STATE	HOSPITALS	% of USA
16	Alabama	10	2.1%
41	Alaska	2	0.4%
26	Arizona	7	1.4%
22	Arkansas	8	1.6%
3	California	31	6.4%
22	Colorado	8	1.6%
26	Connecticut	7	1.4%
32	Delaware	4	0.8%
6	Florida	22	4.5%
9	Georgia	15	3.1%
48	Hawaii	1	0.2%
29	Idaho	5	1.0%
12	Illinois	14	2.9%
7	Indiana	21	4.3%
32	Iowa	4	0.8%
32	Kansas	4	0.8%
14	Kentucky	11	2.3%
1	Louisiana	36	7.4%
32	Maine	4	0.8%
21	Maryland	9	1.8%
9	Massachusetts	15	3.1%
16	Michigan	10	2.1%
32	Minnesota	4	0.8%
29	Mississippi	5	1.0%
12	Missouri	14	2.9%
41	Montana	2	0.4%
38	Nebraska	3	0.6%
28	Nevada	6	1.2%
41	New Hampshire	2	0.4%
8	New Jersey	16	3.3%
41	New Mexico	2	0.4%
4	New York	28	5.7%
22	North Carolina	8	1.6%
38	North Dakota	3	0.6%
9	Ohio	15	3.1%
16	Oklahoma	10	2.1%
41	Oregon	2	0.4%
5	Pennsylvania	23	4.7%
41	Rhode Island	2	0.4%
22	South Carolina	8	1.6%
48	South Dakota	1	0.2%
16	Tennessee	10	2.1%
1	Texas	36	7.4%
38	Utah	3	0.6%
48	Vermont	1	0.2%
16	Virginia	10	2.1%
29	Washington	5	1.0%
32	West Virginia	4	0.8%
14	Wisconsin	11	2.3%
41	Wyoming	2	0.4%

RANK ORDER

RANK	STATE	HOSPITALS	% of USA
1	Louisiana	36	7.4%
1	Texas	36	7.4%
3	California	31	6.4%
4	New York	28	5.7%
5	Pennsylvania	23	4.7%
6	Florida	22	4.5%
7	Indiana	21	4.3%
8	New Jersey	16	3.3%
9	Georgia	15	3.1%
9	Massachusetts	15	3.1%
9	Ohio	15	3.1%
12	Illinois	14	2.9%
12	Missouri	14	2.9%
14	Kentucky	11	2.3%
14	Wisconsin	11	2.3%
16	Alabama	10	2.1%
16	Michigan	10	2.1%
16	Oklahoma	10	2.1%
16	Tennessee	10	2.1%
16	Virginia	10	2.1%
21	Maryland	9	1.8%
22	Arkansas	8	1.6%
22	Colorado	8	1.6%
22	North Carolina	8	1.6%
22	South Carolina	8	1.6%
26	Arizona	7	1.4%
26	Connecticut	7	1.4%
28	Nevada	6	1.2%
29	Idaho	5	1.0%
29	Mississippi	5	1.0%
29	Washington	5	1.0%
32	Delaware	4	0.8%
32	Iowa	4	0.8%
32	Kansas	4	0.8%
32	Maine	4	0.8%
32	Minnesota	4	0.8%
32	West Virginia	4	0.8%
38	Nebraska	3	0.6%
38	North Dakota	3	0.6%
38	Utah	3	0.6%
41	Alaska	2	0.4%
41	Montana	2	0.4%
41	New Hampshire	2	0.4%
41	New Mexico	2	0.4%
41	Oregon	2	0.4%
41	Rhode Island	2	0.4%
41	Wyoming	2	0.4%
48	Hawaii	1	0.2%
48	South Dakota	1	0.2%
48	Vermont	1	0.2%
	District of Columbia	3	0.6%

Source: U.S. Department of Health and Human Services, Centers for Medicare and Medicaid Services
    OSCAR Report 10 (January 05, 2009)
*Certified by CMS to participate in the Medicare/Medicaid programs. Excludes licensed facilities that do not accept federal
funding and facilities managed by the Department of Veterans Affairs. National total does not include four certified psychiatric
hospitals in U.S. territories.

Beds in Medicare and Medicaid Certified Psychiatric Hospitals in 2009

National Total = 53,584 Beds*

ALPHA ORDER

RANK	STATE	BEDS	% of USA
27	Alabama	732	1.4%
42	Alaska	205	0.4%
22	Arizona	937	1.7%
26	Arkansas	787	1.5%
6	California	2,378	4.4%
24	Colorado	865	1.6%
18	Connecticut	1,087	2.0%
39	Delaware	307	0.6%
5	Florida	2,663	5.0%
10	Georgia	1,657	3.1%
49	Hawaii	88	0.2%
41	Idaho	261	0.5%
13	Illinois	1,371	2.6%
19	Indiana	1,005	1.9%
36	Iowa	350	0.7%
30	Kansas	561	1.0%
14	Kentucky	1,360	2.5%
8	Louisiana	1,811	3.4%
34	Maine	386	0.7%
9	Maryland	1,731	3.2%
11	Massachusetts	1,557	2.9%
16	Michigan	1,221	2.3%
38	Minnesota	340	0.6%
29	Mississippi	585	1.1%
20	Missouri	958	1.8%
44	Montana	153	0.3%
35	Nebraska	369	0.7%
28	Nevada	589	1.1%
37	New Hampshire	341	0.6%
4	New Jersey	2,849	5.3%
45	New Mexico	151	0.3%
1	New York	6,245	11.7%
7	North Carolina	1,952	3.6%
40	North Dakota	303	0.6%
17	Ohio	1,206	2.3%
31	Oklahoma	536	1.0%
48	Oregon	90	0.2%
2	Pennsylvania	3,592	6.7%
43	Rhode Island	177	0.3%
23	South Carolina	880	1.6%
47	South Dakota	133	0.2%
21	Tennessee	954	1.8%
3	Texas	3,007	5.6%
33	Utah	391	0.7%
46	Vermont	149	0.3%
25	Virginia	807	1.5%
15	Washington	1,241	2.3%
32	West Virginia	485	0.9%
12	Wisconsin	1,407	2.6%
50	Wyoming	82	0.2%

RANK ORDER

RANK	STATE	BEDS	% of USA
1	New York	6,245	11.7%
2	Pennsylvania	3,592	6.7%
3	Texas	3,007	5.6%
4	New Jersey	2,849	5.3%
5	Florida	2,663	5.0%
6	California	2,378	4.4%
7	North Carolina	1,952	3.6%
8	Louisiana	1,811	3.4%
9	Maryland	1,731	3.2%
10	Georgia	1,657	3.1%
11	Massachusetts	1,557	2.9%
12	Wisconsin	1,407	2.6%
13	Illinois	1,371	2.6%
14	Kentucky	1,360	2.5%
15	Washington	1,241	2.3%
16	Michigan	1,221	2.3%
17	Ohio	1,206	2.3%
18	Connecticut	1,087	2.0%
19	Indiana	1,005	1.9%
20	Missouri	958	1.8%
21	Tennessee	954	1.8%
22	Arizona	937	1.7%
23	South Carolina	880	1.6%
24	Colorado	865	1.6%
25	Virginia	807	1.5%
26	Arkansas	787	1.5%
27	Alabama	732	1.4%
28	Nevada	589	1.1%
29	Mississippi	585	1.1%
30	Kansas	561	1.0%
31	Oklahoma	536	1.0%
32	West Virginia	485	0.9%
33	Utah	391	0.7%
34	Maine	386	0.7%
35	Nebraska	369	0.7%
36	Iowa	350	0.7%
37	New Hampshire	341	0.6%
38	Minnesota	340	0.6%
39	Delaware	307	0.6%
40	North Dakota	303	0.6%
41	Idaho	261	0.5%
42	Alaska	205	0.4%
43	Rhode Island	177	0.3%
44	Montana	153	0.3%
45	New Mexico	151	0.3%
46	Vermont	149	0.3%
47	South Dakota	133	0.2%
48	Oregon	90	0.2%
49	Hawaii	88	0.2%
50	Wyoming	82	0.2%
	District of Columbia	292	0.5%

Source: U.S. Department of Health and Human Services, Centers for Medicare and Medicaid Services
    OSCAR Database (January 05, 2009)
*Beds in hospitals certified by CMS to participate in the Medicare/Medicaid programs. Excludes licensed facilities that do not accept federal funding and facilities managed by the Department of Veterans Affairs. National total does not include 492 beds in U.S. territories.

Medicare and Medicaid Certified Outpatient Surgery Centers in 2009

National Total = 5,149 Centers*

ALPHA ORDER

RANK	STATE	CENTERS	% of USA
35	Alabama	36	0.7%
49	Alaska	9	0.2%
10	Arizona	151	2.9%
23	Arkansas	64	1.2%
1	California	694	13.5%
15	Colorado	103	2.0%
34	Connecticut	45	0.9%
37	Delaware	25	0.5%
2	Florida	387	7.5%
5	Georgia	263	5.1%
46	Hawaii	12	0.2%
26	Idaho	58	1.1%
13	Illinois	121	2.3%
12	Indiana	123	2.4%
37	Iowa	25	0.5%
23	Kansas	64	1.2%
36	Kentucky	35	0.7%
20	Louisiana	74	1.4%
42	Maine	17	0.3%
3	Maryland	353	6.9%
25	Massachusetts	61	1.2%
17	Michigan	86	1.7%
28	Minnesota	54	1.0%
22	Mississippi	65	1.3%
14	Missouri	106	2.1%
44	Montana	15	0.3%
32	Nebraska	47	0.9%
30	Nevada	51	1.0%
40	New Hampshire	21	0.4%
8	New Jersey	218	4.2%
39	New Mexico	22	0.4%
16	New York	91	1.8%
19	North Carolina	76	1.5%
43	North Dakota	16	0.3%
9	Ohio	201	3.9%
30	Oklahoma	51	1.0%
18	Oregon	78	1.5%
6	Pennsylvania	229	4.4%
47	Rhode Island	11	0.2%
21	South Carolina	66	1.3%
44	South Dakota	15	0.3%
11	Tennessee	147	2.9%
4	Texas	347	6.7%
32	Utah	47	0.9%
50	Vermont	0	0.0%
29	Virginia	52	1.0%
7	Washington	225	4.4%
47	West Virginia	11	0.2%
26	Wisconsin	58	1.1%
41	Wyoming	19	0.4%

RANK ORDER

RANK	STATE	CENTERS	% of USA
1	California	694	13.5%
2	Florida	387	7.5%
3	Maryland	353	6.9%
4	Texas	347	6.7%
5	Georgia	263	5.1%
6	Pennsylvania	229	4.4%
7	Washington	225	4.4%
8	New Jersey	218	4.2%
9	Ohio	201	3.9%
10	Arizona	151	2.9%
11	Tennessee	147	2.9%
12	Indiana	123	2.4%
13	Illinois	121	2.3%
14	Missouri	106	2.1%
15	Colorado	103	2.0%
16	New York	91	1.8%
17	Michigan	86	1.7%
18	Oregon	78	1.5%
19	North Carolina	76	1.5%
20	Louisiana	74	1.4%
21	South Carolina	66	1.3%
22	Mississippi	65	1.3%
23	Arkansas	64	1.2%
23	Kansas	64	1.2%
25	Massachusetts	61	1.2%
26	Idaho	58	1.1%
26	Wisconsin	58	1.1%
28	Minnesota	54	1.0%
29	Virginia	52	1.0%
30	Nevada	51	1.0%
30	Oklahoma	51	1.0%
32	Nebraska	47	0.9%
32	Utah	47	0.9%
34	Connecticut	45	0.9%
35	Alabama	36	0.7%
36	Kentucky	35	0.7%
37	Delaware	25	0.5%
37	Iowa	25	0.5%
39	New Mexico	22	0.4%
40	New Hampshire	21	0.4%
41	Wyoming	19	0.4%
42	Maine	17	0.3%
43	North Dakota	16	0.3%
44	Montana	15	0.3%
44	South Dakota	15	0.3%
46	Hawaii	12	0.2%
47	Rhode Island	11	0.2%
47	West Virginia	11	0.2%
49	Alaska	9	0.2%
50	Vermont	0	0.0%
	District of Columbia	4	0.1%

Source: U.S. Department of Health and Human Services, Centers for Medicare and Medicaid Services
OSCAR Report 10 (January 05, 2009)

*Certified by CMS to participate in the Medicare/Medicaid programs. Excludes licensed facilities that do not accept federal funding and facilities managed by the Department of Veterans Affairs. National total does not include 25 certified outpatient surgery centers in U.S. territories. Also known as Ambulatory Surgical Outpatient.

Medicare and Medicaid Certified Community Mental Health Centers in 2009

National Total = 631 Centers*

ALPHA ORDER

RANK	STATE	CENTERS	% of USA
2	Alabama	60	9.5%
40	Alaska	0	0.0%
30	Arizona	3	0.5%
15	Arkansas	13	2.1%
7	California	20	3.2%
11	Colorado	14	2.2%
27	Connecticut	5	0.8%
40	Delaware	0	0.0%
1	Florida	142	22.5%
20	Georgia	10	1.6%
40	Hawaii	0	0.0%
40	Idaho	0	0.0%
20	Illinois	10	1.6%
23	Indiana	8	1.3%
27	Iowa	5	0.8%
22	Kansas	9	1.4%
18	Kentucky	11	1.7%
3	Louisiana	51	8.1%
40	Maine	0	0.0%
33	Maryland	2	0.3%
11	Massachusetts	14	2.2%
26	Michigan	7	1.1%
11	Minnesota	14	2.2%
23	Mississippi	8	1.3%
18	Missouri	11	1.7%
40	Montana	0	0.0%
38	Nebraska	1	0.2%
33	Nevada	2	0.3%
40	New Hampshire	0	0.0%
5	New Jersey	28	4.4%
11	New Mexico	14	2.2%
29	New York	4	0.6%
7	North Carolina	20	3.2%
40	North Dakota	0	0.0%
15	Ohio	13	2.1%
23	Oklahoma	8	1.3%
17	Oregon	12	1.9%
10	Pennsylvania	16	2.5%
40	Rhode Island	0	0.0%
30	South Carolina	3	0.5%
38	South Dakota	1	0.2%
9	Tennessee	18	2.9%
4	Texas	40	6.3%
33	Utah	2	0.3%
40	Vermont	0	0.0%
33	Virginia	2	0.3%
6	Washington	25	4.0%
33	West Virginia	2	0.3%
40	Wisconsin	0	0.0%
30	Wyoming	3	0.5%

RANK ORDER

RANK	STATE	CENTERS	% of USA
1	Florida	142	22.5%
2	Alabama	60	9.5%
3	Louisiana	51	8.1%
4	Texas	40	6.3%
5	New Jersey	28	4.4%
6	Washington	25	4.0%
7	California	20	3.2%
7	North Carolina	20	3.2%
9	Tennessee	18	2.9%
10	Pennsylvania	16	2.5%
11	Colorado	14	2.2%
11	Massachusetts	14	2.2%
11	Minnesota	14	2.2%
11	New Mexico	14	2.2%
15	Arkansas	13	2.1%
15	Ohio	13	2.1%
17	Oregon	12	1.9%
18	Kentucky	11	1.7%
18	Missouri	11	1.7%
20	Georgia	10	1.6%
20	Illinois	10	1.6%
22	Kansas	9	1.4%
23	Indiana	8	1.3%
23	Mississippi	8	1.3%
23	Oklahoma	8	1.3%
26	Michigan	7	1.1%
27	Connecticut	5	0.8%
27	Iowa	5	0.8%
29	New York	4	0.6%
30	Arizona	3	0.5%
30	South Carolina	3	0.5%
30	Wyoming	3	0.5%
33	Maryland	2	0.3%
33	Nevada	2	0.3%
33	Utah	2	0.3%
33	Virginia	2	0.3%
33	West Virginia	2	0.3%
38	Nebraska	1	0.2%
38	South Dakota	1	0.2%
40	Alaska	0	0.0%
40	Delaware	0	0.0%
40	Hawaii	0	0.0%
40	Idaho	0	0.0%
40	Maine	0	0.0%
40	Montana	0	0.0%
40	New Hampshire	0	0.0%
40	North Dakota	0	0.0%
40	Rhode Island	0	0.0%
40	Vermont	0	0.0%
40	Wisconsin	0	0.0%
	District of Columbia	0	0.0%

Source: U.S. Department of Health and Human Services, Centers for Medicare and Medicaid Services
    OSCAR Report 10 (January 05, 2009)
*Certified by CMS to participate in the Medicare/Medicaid programs. Excludes licensed facilities that do not accept federal funding and facilities managed by the Department of Veterans Affairs. National total does not include 13 certified mental health centers in U.S. territories.

Medicare and Medicaid Certified Outpatient Physical Therapy Facilities in 2009

National Total = 2,779 Facilities*

ALPHA ORDER

RANK	STATE	FACILITIES	% of USA
25	Alabama	35	1.3%
36	Alaska	13	0.5%
28	Arizona	28	1.0%
30	Arkansas	25	0.9%
4	California	166	6.0%
17	Colorado	54	1.9%
23	Connecticut	36	1.3%
37	Delaware	12	0.4%
1	Florida	362	13.0%
10	Georgia	92	3.3%
44	Hawaii	5	0.2%
40	Idaho	9	0.3%
9	Illinois	93	3.3%
15	Indiana	59	2.1%
26	Iowa	34	1.2%
31	Kansas	24	0.9%
8	Kentucky	98	3.5%
19	Louisiana	49	1.8%
34	Maine	16	0.6%
11	Maryland	91	3.3%
34	Massachusetts	16	0.6%
3	Michigan	232	8.3%
21	Minnesota	42	1.5%
23	Mississippi	36	1.3%
13	Missouri	64	2.3%
47	Montana	1	0.0%
40	Nebraska	9	0.3%
33	Nevada	21	0.8%
38	New Hampshire	10	0.4%
14	New Jersey	60	2.2%
27	New Mexico	30	1.1%
31	New York	24	0.9%
16	North Carolina	56	2.0%
47	North Dakota	1	0.0%
5	Ohio	126	4.5%
18	Oklahoma	50	1.8%
38	Oregon	10	0.4%
7	Pennsylvania	112	4.0%
45	Rhode Island	3	0.1%
20	South Carolina	47	1.7%
46	South Dakota	2	0.1%
12	Tennessee	79	2.8%
2	Texas	239	8.6%
43	Utah	6	0.2%
47	Vermont	1	0.0%
6	Virginia	120	4.3%
29	Washington	26	0.9%
40	West Virginia	9	0.3%
21	Wisconsin	42	1.5%
47	Wyoming	1	0.0%

RANK ORDER

RANK	STATE	FACILITIES	% of USA
1	Florida	362	13.0%
2	Texas	239	8.6%
3	Michigan	232	8.3%
4	California	166	6.0%
5	Ohio	126	4.5%
6	Virginia	120	4.3%
7	Pennsylvania	112	4.0%
8	Kentucky	98	3.5%
9	Illinois	93	3.3%
10	Georgia	92	3.3%
11	Maryland	91	3.3%
12	Tennessee	79	2.8%
13	Missouri	64	2.3%
14	New Jersey	60	2.2%
15	Indiana	59	2.1%
16	North Carolina	56	2.0%
17	Colorado	54	1.9%
18	Oklahoma	50	1.8%
19	Louisiana	49	1.8%
20	South Carolina	47	1.7%
21	Minnesota	42	1.5%
21	Wisconsin	42	1.5%
23	Connecticut	36	1.3%
23	Mississippi	36	1.3%
25	Alabama	35	1.3%
26	Iowa	34	1.2%
27	New Mexico	30	1.1%
28	Arizona	28	1.0%
29	Washington	26	0.9%
30	Arkansas	25	0.9%
31	Kansas	24	0.9%
31	New York	24	0.9%
33	Nevada	21	0.8%
34	Maine	16	0.6%
34	Massachusetts	16	0.6%
36	Alaska	13	0.5%
37	Delaware	12	0.4%
38	New Hampshire	10	0.4%
38	Oregon	10	0.4%
40	Idaho	9	0.3%
40	Nebraska	9	0.3%
40	West Virginia	9	0.3%
43	Utah	6	0.2%
44	Hawaii	5	0.2%
45	Rhode Island	3	0.1%
46	South Dakota	2	0.1%
47	Montana	1	0.0%
47	North Dakota	1	0.0%
47	Vermont	1	0.0%
47	Wyoming	1	0.0%
	District of Columbia	3	0.1%

Source: U.S. Department of Health and Human Services, Centers for Medicare and Medicaid Services
OSCAR Report 10 (January 05, 2009)
*Certified by CMS to participate in the Medicare/Medicaid programs. Excludes licensed facilities that do not accept federal funding and facilities managed by the Department of Veterans Affairs. National total does not include two certified outpatient physical therapy facilities in U.S. territories.

Medicare and Medicaid Certified Rural Health Clinics in 2009

National Total = 3,760 Rural Health Clinics*

ALPHA ORDER

RANK	STATE	CLINICS	% of USA
18	Alabama	69	1.8%
43	Alaska	3	0.1%
37	Arizona	14	0.4%
18	Arkansas	69	1.8%
3	California	262	7.0%
29	Colorado	47	1.3%
46	Connecticut	0	0.0%
46	Delaware	0	0.0%
9	Florida	142	3.8%
16	Georgia	88	2.3%
44	Hawaii	2	0.1%
28	Idaho	48	1.3%
4	Illinois	226	6.0%
23	Indiana	59	1.6%
8	Iowa	144	3.8%
5	Kansas	173	4.6%
10	Kentucky	131	3.5%
14	Louisiana	107	2.8%
33	Maine	38	1.0%
46	Maryland	0	0.0%
45	Massachusetts	1	0.0%
6	Michigan	157	4.2%
17	Minnesota	80	2.1%
7	Mississippi	154	4.1%
1	Missouri	334	8.9%
31	Montana	45	1.2%
12	Nebraska	124	3.3%
42	Nevada	6	0.2%
38	New Hampshire	12	0.3%
46	New Jersey	0	0.0%
38	New Mexico	12	0.3%
41	New York	8	0.2%
15	North Carolina	92	2.4%
20	North Dakota	61	1.6%
40	Ohio	11	0.3%
32	Oklahoma	39	1.0%
23	Oregon	59	1.6%
26	Pennsylvania	54	1.4%
46	Rhode Island	0	0.0%
13	South Carolina	111	3.0%
22	South Dakota	60	1.6%
20	Tennessee	61	1.6%
2	Texas	315	8.4%
34	Utah	18	0.5%
34	Vermont	18	0.5%
27	Virginia	53	1.4%
10	Washington	131	3.5%
25	West Virginia	57	1.5%
29	Wisconsin	47	1.3%
34	Wyoming	18	0.5%

RANK ORDER

RANK	STATE	CLINICS	% of USA
1	Missouri	334	8.9%
2	Texas	315	8.4%
3	California	262	7.0%
4	Illinois	226	6.0%
5	Kansas	173	4.6%
6	Michigan	157	4.2%
7	Mississippi	154	4.1%
8	Iowa	144	3.8%
9	Florida	142	3.8%
10	Kentucky	131	3.5%
10	Washington	131	3.5%
12	Nebraska	124	3.3%
13	South Carolina	111	3.0%
14	Louisiana	107	2.8%
15	North Carolina	92	2.4%
16	Georgia	88	2.3%
17	Minnesota	80	2.1%
18	Alabama	69	1.8%
18	Arkansas	69	1.8%
20	North Dakota	61	1.6%
20	Tennessee	61	1.6%
22	South Dakota	60	1.6%
23	Indiana	59	1.6%
23	Oregon	59	1.6%
25	West Virginia	57	1.5%
26	Pennsylvania	54	1.4%
27	Virginia	53	1.4%
28	Idaho	48	1.3%
29	Colorado	47	1.3%
29	Wisconsin	47	1.3%
31	Montana	45	1.2%
32	Oklahoma	39	1.0%
33	Maine	38	1.0%
34	Utah	18	0.5%
34	Vermont	18	0.5%
34	Wyoming	18	0.5%
37	Arizona	14	0.4%
38	New Hampshire	12	0.3%
38	New Mexico	12	0.3%
40	Ohio	11	0.3%
41	New York	8	0.2%
42	Nevada	6	0.2%
43	Alaska	3	0.1%
44	Hawaii	2	0.1%
45	Massachusetts	1	0.0%
46	Connecticut	0	0.0%
46	Delaware	0	0.0%
46	Maryland	0	0.0%
46	New Jersey	0	0.0%
46	Rhode Island	0	0.0%
	District of Columbia	0	0.0%

Source: U.S. Department of Health and Human Services, Centers for Medicare and Medicaid Services
OSCAR Report 10 (January 05, 2009)
*Certified by CMS to participate in the Medicare/Medicaid programs. Excludes licensed facilities that do not accept federal funding and facilities managed by the Department of Veterans Affairs. There are no certified rural health centers in U.S. territories.

Medicare and Medicaid Certified Home Health Agencies in 2009

National Total = 9,731 Home Health Agencies*

ALPHA ORDER

RANK	STATE	AGENCIES	% of USA
18	Alabama	148	1.5%
48	Alaska	16	0.2%
26	Arizona	90	0.9%
15	Arkansas	174	1.8%
3	California	773	7.9%
20	Colorado	138	1.4%
27	Connecticut	85	0.9%
47	Delaware	19	0.2%
2	Florida	929	9.5%
25	Georgia	101	1.0%
49	Hawaii	14	0.1%
38	Idaho	49	0.5%
4	Illinois	513	5.3%
10	Indiana	217	2.2%
16	Iowa	173	1.8%
21	Kansas	131	1.3%
24	Kentucky	104	1.1%
9	Louisiana	220	2.3%
43	Maine	28	0.3%
38	Maryland	49	0.5%
21	Massachusetts	131	1.3%
6	Michigan	465	4.8%
11	Minnesota	215	2.2%
35	Mississippi	56	0.6%
14	Missouri	181	1.9%
41	Montana	36	0.4%
30	Nebraska	74	0.8%
29	Nevada	77	0.8%
41	New Hampshire	36	0.4%
37	New Jersey	51	0.5%
31	New Mexico	69	0.7%
12	New York	196	2.0%
17	North Carolina	170	1.7%
45	North Dakota	22	0.2%
5	Ohio	483	5.0%
8	Oklahoma	227	2.3%
35	Oregon	56	0.6%
7	Pennsylvania	343	3.5%
45	Rhode Island	22	0.2%
31	South Carolina	69	0.7%
40	South Dakota	42	0.4%
19	Tennessee	141	1.4%
1	Texas	2,009	20.6%
28	Utah	82	0.8%
50	Vermont	12	0.1%
13	Virginia	191	2.0%
34	Washington	60	0.6%
33	West Virginia	62	0.6%
23	Wisconsin	128	1.3%
44	Wyoming	27	0.3%

RANK ORDER

RANK	STATE	AGENCIES	% of USA
1	Texas	2,009	20.6%
2	Florida	929	9.5%
3	California	773	7.9%
4	Illinois	513	5.3%
5	Ohio	483	5.0%
6	Michigan	465	4.8%
7	Pennsylvania	343	3.5%
8	Oklahoma	227	2.3%
9	Louisiana	220	2.3%
10	Indiana	217	2.2%
11	Minnesota	215	2.2%
12	New York	196	2.0%
13	Virginia	191	2.0%
14	Missouri	181	1.9%
15	Arkansas	174	1.8%
16	Iowa	173	1.8%
17	North Carolina	170	1.7%
18	Alabama	148	1.5%
19	Tennessee	141	1.4%
20	Colorado	138	1.4%
21	Kansas	131	1.3%
21	Massachusetts	131	1.3%
23	Wisconsin	128	1.3%
24	Kentucky	104	1.1%
25	Georgia	101	1.0%
26	Arizona	90	0.9%
27	Connecticut	85	0.9%
28	Utah	82	0.8%
29	Nevada	77	0.8%
30	Nebraska	74	0.8%
31	New Mexico	69	0.7%
31	South Carolina	69	0.7%
33	West Virginia	62	0.6%
34	Washington	60	0.6%
35	Mississippi	56	0.6%
35	Oregon	56	0.6%
37	New Jersey	51	0.5%
38	Idaho	49	0.5%
38	Maryland	49	0.5%
40	South Dakota	42	0.4%
41	Montana	36	0.4%
41	New Hampshire	36	0.4%
43	Maine	28	0.3%
44	Wyoming	27	0.3%
45	North Dakota	22	0.2%
45	Rhode Island	22	0.2%
47	Delaware	19	0.2%
48	Alaska	16	0.2%
49	Hawaii	14	0.1%
50	Vermont	12	0.1%
	District of Columbia	27	0.3%

Source: U.S. Department of Health and Human Services, Centers for Medicare and Medicaid Services
  OSCAR Report 10 (January 05, 2009)

*Certified by CMS to participate in the Medicare/Medicaid programs. Excludes agencies that do not accept federal funding. National total does not include 56 certified home health agencies in U.S. territories. A home health agency provides health services to individuals in their homes for the purpose of promoting, maintaining, or restoring health or maximizing the level of independence, while minimizing the effects of disability and illness.

Medicare and Medicaid Certified Hospices in 2009

National Total = 3,306 Hospices*

ALPHA ORDER

RANK	STATE	HOSPICES	% of USA
7	Alabama	127	3.8%
50	Alaska	5	0.2%
22	Arizona	58	1.8%
26	Arkansas	51	1.5%
2	California	222	6.7%
26	Colorado	51	1.5%
35	Connecticut	31	0.9%
47	Delaware	8	0.2%
30	Florida	41	1.2%
4	Georgia	140	4.2%
47	Hawaii	8	0.2%
32	Idaho	37	1.1%
10	Illinois	106	3.2%
13	Indiana	84	2.5%
15	Iowa	75	2.3%
23	Kansas	56	1.7%
38	Kentucky	27	0.8%
6	Louisiana	129	3.9%
39	Maine	21	0.6%
36	Maryland	28	0.8%
19	Massachusetts	69	2.1%
12	Michigan	95	2.9%
21	Minnesota	64	1.9%
8	Mississippi	118	3.6%
11	Missouri	105	3.2%
36	Montana	28	0.8%
33	Nebraska	33	1.0%
42	Nevada	19	0.6%
39	New Hampshire	21	0.6%
25	New Jersey	55	1.7%
31	New Mexico	40	1.2%
26	New York	51	1.5%
14	North Carolina	81	2.5%
45	North Dakota	14	0.4%
9	Ohio	111	3.4%
5	Oklahoma	139	4.2%
29	Oregon	47	1.4%
3	Pennsylvania	167	5.1%
47	Rhode Island	8	0.2%
15	South Carolina	75	2.3%
44	South Dakota	15	0.5%
23	Tennessee	56	1.7%
1	Texas	298	9.0%
18	Utah	70	2.1%
46	Vermont	10	0.3%
15	Virginia	75	2.3%
34	Washington	32	1.0%
41	West Virginia	20	0.6%
20	Wisconsin	65	2.0%
43	Wyoming	17	0.5%

RANK ORDER

RANK	STATE	HOSPICES	% of USA
1	Texas	298	9.0%
2	California	222	6.7%
3	Pennsylvania	167	5.1%
4	Georgia	140	4.2%
5	Oklahoma	139	4.2%
6	Louisiana	129	3.9%
7	Alabama	127	3.8%
8	Mississippi	118	3.6%
9	Ohio	111	3.4%
10	Illinois	106	3.2%
11	Missouri	105	3.2%
12	Michigan	95	2.9%
13	Indiana	84	2.5%
14	North Carolina	81	2.5%
15	Iowa	75	2.3%
15	South Carolina	75	2.3%
15	Virginia	75	2.3%
18	Utah	70	2.1%
19	Massachusetts	69	2.1%
20	Wisconsin	65	2.0%
21	Minnesota	64	1.9%
22	Arizona	58	1.8%
23	Kansas	56	1.7%
23	Tennessee	56	1.7%
25	New Jersey	55	1.7%
26	Arkansas	51	1.5%
26	Colorado	51	1.5%
26	New York	51	1.5%
29	Oregon	47	1.4%
30	Florida	41	1.2%
31	New Mexico	40	1.2%
32	Idaho	37	1.1%
33	Nebraska	33	1.0%
34	Washington	32	1.0%
35	Connecticut	31	0.9%
36	Maryland	28	0.8%
36	Montana	28	0.8%
38	Kentucky	27	0.8%
39	Maine	21	0.6%
39	New Hampshire	21	0.6%
41	West Virginia	20	0.6%
42	Nevada	19	0.6%
43	Wyoming	17	0.5%
44	South Dakota	15	0.5%
45	North Dakota	14	0.4%
46	Vermont	10	0.3%
47	Delaware	8	0.2%
47	Hawaii	8	0.2%
47	Rhode Island	8	0.2%
50	Alaska	5	0.2%
	District of Columbia	3	0.1%

Source: U.S. Department of Health and Human Services, Centers for Medicare and Medicaid Services
   OSCAR Report 10 (January 05, 2009)
*Certified by CMS to participate in the Medicare/Medicaid programs. Excludes licensed facilities that do not accept federal
funding and facilities managed by the Department of Veterans Affairs. National total does not include 40 certified hospices in
U.S. territories.   A hospice provides specialized services for terminally ill people and their families.

Hospice Patients in Residential Facilities in 2009

National Total = 75,762 Patients*

ALPHA ORDER				RANK ORDER			
RANK	STATE	PATIENTS	% of USA	RANK	STATE	PATIENTS	% of USA
18	Alabama	1,387	1.8%	1	Florida	9,277	12.2%
50	Alaska	3	0.0%	2	Pennsylvania	6,919	9.1%
14	Arizona	1,841	2.4%	3	Texas	6,052	8.0%
35	Arkansas	492	0.6%	4	Ohio	3,658	4.8%
5	California	3,053	4.0%	5	California	3,053	4.0%
25	Colorado	1,120	1.5%	6	Massachusetts	2,956	3.9%
11	Connecticut	2,206	2.9%	7	Missouri	2,711	3.6%
41	Delaware	208	0.3%	8	Michigan	2,645	3.5%
1	Florida	9,277	12.2%	9	Illinois	2,559	3.4%
12	Georgia	2,202	2.9%	10	North Carolina	2,402	3.2%
47	Hawaii	56	0.1%	11	Connecticut	2,206	2.9%
45	Idaho	153	0.2%	12	Georgia	2,202	2.9%
9	Illinois	2,559	3.4%	13	Oregon	1,977	2.6%
17	Indiana	1,594	2.1%	14	Arizona	1,841	2.4%
26	Iowa	1,081	1.4%	15	Oklahoma	1,820	2.4%
33	Kansas	557	0.7%	16	Maine	1,634	2.2%
32	Kentucky	571	0.8%	17	Indiana	1,594	2.1%
30	Louisiana	678	0.9%	18	Alabama	1,387	1.8%
16	Maine	1,634	2.2%	19	Washington	1,355	1.8%
37	Maryland	458	0.6%	20	Tennessee	1,224	1.6%
6	Massachusetts	2,956	3.9%	21	New York	1,208	1.6%
8	Michigan	2,645	3.5%	22	Virginia	1,170	1.5%
23	Minnesota	1,163	1.5%	23	Minnesota	1,163	1.5%
36	Mississippi	462	0.6%	24	Rhode Island	1,143	1.5%
7	Missouri	2,711	3.6%	25	Colorado	1,120	1.5%
28	Montana	957	1.3%	26	Iowa	1,081	1.4%
38	Nebraska	423	0.6%	27	Wisconsin	967	1.3%
44	Nevada	160	0.2%	28	Montana	957	1.3%
34	New Hampshire	503	0.7%	29	New Jersey	890	1.2%
29	New Jersey	890	1.2%	30	Louisiana	678	0.9%
40	New Mexico	260	0.3%	31	South Carolina	614	0.8%
21	New York	1,208	1.6%	32	Kentucky	571	0.8%
10	North Carolina	2,402	3.2%	33	Kansas	557	0.7%
46	North Dakota	66	0.1%	34	New Hampshire	503	0.7%
4	Ohio	3,658	4.8%	35	Arkansas	492	0.6%
15	Oklahoma	1,820	2.4%	36	Mississippi	462	0.6%
13	Oregon	1,977	2.6%	37	Maryland	458	0.6%
2	Pennsylvania	6,919	9.1%	38	Nebraska	423	0.6%
24	Rhode Island	1,143	1.5%	39	Utah	384	0.5%
31	South Carolina	614	0.8%	40	New Mexico	260	0.3%
42	South Dakota	203	0.3%	41	Delaware	208	0.3%
20	Tennessee	1,224	1.6%	42	South Dakota	203	0.3%
3	Texas	6,052	8.0%	43	West Virginia	178	0.2%
39	Utah	384	0.5%	44	Nevada	160	0.2%
48	Vermont	49	0.1%	45	Idaho	153	0.2%
22	Virginia	1,170	1.5%	46	North Dakota	66	0.1%
19	Washington	1,355	1.8%	47	Hawaii	56	0.1%
43	West Virginia	178	0.2%	48	Vermont	49	0.1%
27	Wisconsin	967	1.3%	49	Wyoming	32	0.0%
49	Wyoming	32	0.0%	50	Alaska	3	0.0%
					District of Columbia	81	0.1%

Source: U.S. Department of Health and Human Services, Centers for Medicare and Medicaid Services
    OSCAR Database (January 05, 2009)

*Patients in facilities certified by CMS to participate in the Medicare/Medicaid programs. Excludes licensed facilities that do not accept federal funding and facilities managed by the Department of Veterans Affairs. National total does not include 30 patients in U.S. territories. A hospice provides specialized services for terminally ill people and their families.

Medicare and Medicaid Certified Nursing Care Facilities in 2009

National Total = 15,718 Nursing Care Facilities*

ALPHA ORDER

RANK	STATE	FACILITIES	% of USA
26	Alabama	232	1.5%
50	Alaska	15	0.1%
34	Arizona	133	0.8%
26	Arkansas	232	1.5%
1	California	1,255	8.0%
30	Colorado	211	1.3%
24	Connecticut	241	1.5%
47	Delaware	45	0.3%
6	Florida	677	4.3%
17	Georgia	358	2.3%
45	Hawaii	48	0.3%
43	Idaho	78	0.5%
4	Illinois	791	5.0%
9	Indiana	511	3.3%
10	Iowa	450	2.9%
18	Kansas	345	2.2%
21	Kentucky	287	1.8%
22	Louisiana	285	1.8%
37	Maine	109	0.7%
28	Maryland	230	1.5%
11	Massachusetts	433	2.8%
12	Michigan	425	2.7%
15	Minnesota	388	2.5%
31	Mississippi	202	1.3%
8	Missouri	515	3.3%
39	Montana	91	0.6%
29	Nebraska	225	1.4%
45	Nevada	48	0.3%
42	New Hampshire	80	0.5%
16	New Jersey	361	2.3%
44	New Mexico	70	0.4%
7	New York	651	4.1%
13	North Carolina	422	2.7%
41	North Dakota	83	0.5%
3	Ohio	956	6.1%
19	Oklahoma	321	2.0%
33	Oregon	138	0.9%
5	Pennsylvania	711	4.5%
40	Rhode Island	86	0.5%
32	South Carolina	175	1.1%
36	South Dakota	110	0.7%
20	Tennessee	319	2.0%
2	Texas	1,143	7.3%
38	Utah	93	0.6%
48	Vermont	40	0.3%
23	Virginia	281	1.8%
25	Washington	238	1.5%
35	West Virginia	130	0.8%
14	Wisconsin	393	2.5%
49	Wyoming	39	0.2%

RANK ORDER

RANK	STATE	FACILITIES	% of USA
1	California	1,255	8.0%
2	Texas	1,143	7.3%
3	Ohio	956	6.1%
4	Illinois	791	5.0%
5	Pennsylvania	711	4.5%
6	Florida	677	4.3%
7	New York	651	4.1%
8	Missouri	515	3.3%
9	Indiana	511	3.3%
10	Iowa	450	2.9%
11	Massachusetts	433	2.8%
12	Michigan	425	2.7%
13	North Carolina	422	2.7%
14	Wisconsin	393	2.5%
15	Minnesota	388	2.5%
16	New Jersey	361	2.3%
17	Georgia	358	2.3%
18	Kansas	345	2.2%
19	Oklahoma	321	2.0%
20	Tennessee	319	2.0%
21	Kentucky	287	1.8%
22	Louisiana	285	1.8%
23	Virginia	281	1.8%
24	Connecticut	241	1.5%
25	Washington	238	1.5%
26	Alabama	232	1.5%
26	Arkansas	232	1.5%
28	Maryland	230	1.5%
29	Nebraska	225	1.4%
30	Colorado	211	1.3%
31	Mississippi	202	1.3%
32	South Carolina	175	1.1%
33	Oregon	138	0.9%
34	Arizona	133	0.8%
35	West Virginia	130	0.8%
36	South Dakota	110	0.7%
37	Maine	109	0.7%
38	Utah	93	0.6%
39	Montana	91	0.6%
40	Rhode Island	86	0.5%
41	North Dakota	83	0.5%
42	New Hampshire	80	0.5%
43	Idaho	78	0.5%
44	New Mexico	70	0.4%
45	Hawaii	48	0.3%
45	Nevada	48	0.3%
47	Delaware	45	0.3%
48	Vermont	40	0.3%
49	Wyoming	39	0.2%
50	Alaska	15	0.1%
	District of Columbia	18	0.1%

Source: U.S. Department of Health and Human Services, Centers for Medicare and Medicaid Services
    OSCAR Database (January 05, 2009)
*Certified by CMS to participate in the Medicare/Medicaid programs. Excludes licensed facilities that do not accept federal funding and facilities managed by the Department of Veterans Affairs. National total does not include nine certified nursing facilities in U.S. territories.

Beds in Medicare and Medicaid Certified Nursing Care Facilities in 2009

National Total = 1,669,894 Beds*

ALPHA ORDER

RANK	STATE	BEDS	% of USA
24	Alabama	26,752	1.6%
50	Alaska	725	0.0%
33	Arizona	15,648	0.9%
26	Arkansas	24,395	1.5%
2	California	121,977	7.3%
29	Colorado	19,854	1.2%
22	Connecticut	29,235	1.8%
46	Delaware	4,787	0.3%
7	Florida	81,593	4.9%
14	Georgia	39,709	2.4%
47	Hawaii	4,142	0.2%
44	Idaho	6,034	0.4%
4	Illinois	96,280	5.8%
10	Indiana	49,224	2.9%
19	Iowa	32,244	1.9%
27	Kansas	22,973	1.4%
25	Kentucky	25,525	1.5%
17	Louisiana	35,425	2.1%
39	Maine	7,079	0.4%
23	Maryland	28,892	1.7%
11	Massachusetts	48,640	2.9%
12	Michigan	46,827	2.8%
18	Minnesota	33,755	2.0%
31	Mississippi	18,266	1.1%
8	Missouri	51,837	3.1%
40	Montana	7,055	0.4%
32	Nebraska	16,031	1.0%
45	Nevada	5,613	0.3%
38	New Hampshire	7,708	0.5%
9	New Jersey	51,153	3.1%
41	New Mexico	6,767	0.4%
3	New York	120,147	7.2%
13	North Carolina	43,186	2.6%
43	North Dakota	6,395	0.4%
5	Ohio	92,685	5.6%
21	Oklahoma	29,584	1.8%
34	Oregon	12,473	0.7%
6	Pennsylvania	87,874	5.3%
36	Rhode Island	8,850	0.5%
30	South Carolina	18,336	1.1%
42	South Dakota	6,529	0.4%
16	Tennessee	36,598	2.2%
1	Texas	122,434	7.3%
37	Utah	7,909	0.5%
48	Vermont	3,268	0.2%
20	Virginia	31,529	1.9%
28	Washington	22,203	1.3%
35	West Virginia	10,827	0.6%
15	Wisconsin	37,284	2.2%
49	Wyoming	2,993	0.2%

RANK ORDER

RANK	STATE	BEDS	% of USA
1	Texas	122,434	7.3%
2	California	121,977	7.3%
3	New York	120,147	7.2%
4	Illinois	96,280	5.8%
5	Ohio	92,685	5.6%
6	Pennsylvania	87,874	5.3%
7	Florida	81,593	4.9%
8	Missouri	51,837	3.1%
9	New Jersey	51,153	3.1%
10	Indiana	49,224	2.9%
11	Massachusetts	48,640	2.9%
12	Michigan	46,827	2.8%
13	North Carolina	43,186	2.6%
14	Georgia	39,709	2.4%
15	Wisconsin	37,284	2.2%
16	Tennessee	36,598	2.2%
17	Louisiana	35,425	2.1%
18	Minnesota	33,755	2.0%
19	Iowa	32,244	1.9%
20	Virginia	31,529	1.9%
21	Oklahoma	29,584	1.8%
22	Connecticut	29,235	1.8%
23	Maryland	28,892	1.7%
24	Alabama	26,752	1.6%
25	Kentucky	25,525	1.5%
26	Arkansas	24,395	1.5%
27	Kansas	22,973	1.4%
28	Washington	22,203	1.3%
29	Colorado	19,854	1.2%
30	South Carolina	18,336	1.1%
31	Mississippi	18,266	1.1%
32	Nebraska	16,031	1.0%
33	Arizona	15,648	0.9%
34	Oregon	12,473	0.7%
35	West Virginia	10,827	0.6%
36	Rhode Island	8,850	0.5%
37	Utah	7,909	0.5%
38	New Hampshire	7,708	0.5%
39	Maine	7,079	0.4%
40	Montana	7,055	0.4%
41	New Mexico	6,767	0.4%
42	South Dakota	6,529	0.4%
43	North Dakota	6,395	0.4%
44	Idaho	6,034	0.4%
45	Nevada	5,613	0.3%
46	Delaware	4,787	0.3%
47	Hawaii	4,142	0.2%
48	Vermont	3,268	0.2%
49	Wyoming	2,993	0.2%
50	Alaska	725	0.0%
	District of Columbia	2,645	0.2%

Source: U.S. Department of Health and Human Services, Centers for Medicare and Medicaid Services
  OSCAR Database (January 05, 2009)
*Beds in nursing care facilities certified by CMS to participate in the Medicare/Medicaid programs. National total does not include 349 beds in U.S. territories.

Rate of Beds in Medicare and Medicaid Certified Nursing Care Facilities in 2009

National Rate = 315 Beds per 1,000 Population 85 Years and Older*

ALPHA ORDER

RANK	STATE	RATE
22	Alabama	326
48	Alaska	160
50	Arizona	139
4	Arkansas	430
42	California	209
30	Colorado	307
12	Connecticut	376
28	Delaware	312
47	Florida	165
21	Georgia	336
49	Hawaii	141
41	Idaho	245
8	Illinois	412
5	Indiana	429
7	Iowa	417
11	Kansas	378
16	Kentucky	356
1	Louisiana	516
39	Maine	253
25	Maryland	323
20	Massachusetts	348
37	Michigan	258
26	Minnesota	322
14	Mississippi	360
2	Missouri	439
16	Montana	356
9	Nebraska	400
45	Nevada	188
26	New Hampshire	322
32	New Jersey	302
43	New Mexico	200
28	New York	312
31	North Carolina	303
13	North Dakota	366
6	Ohio	418
3	Oklahoma	433
46	Oregon	170
33	Pennsylvania	291
18	Rhode Island	349
39	South Carolina	253
23	South Dakota	325
15	Tennessee	358
10	Texas	385
38	Utah	255
35	Vermont	271
36	Virginia	269
44	Washington	199
34	West Virginia	289
24	Wisconsin	324
18	Wyoming	349

RANK ORDER

RANK	STATE	RATE
1	Louisiana	516
2	Missouri	439
3	Oklahoma	433
4	Arkansas	430
5	Indiana	429
6	Ohio	418
7	Iowa	417
8	Illinois	412
9	Nebraska	400
10	Texas	385
11	Kansas	378
12	Connecticut	376
13	North Dakota	366
14	Mississippi	360
15	Tennessee	358
16	Kentucky	356
16	Montana	356
18	Rhode Island	349
18	Wyoming	349
20	Massachusetts	348
21	Georgia	336
22	Alabama	326
23	South Dakota	325
24	Wisconsin	324
25	Maryland	323
26	Minnesota	322
26	New Hampshire	322
28	Delaware	312
28	New York	312
30	Colorado	307
31	North Carolina	303
32	New Jersey	302
33	Pennsylvania	291
34	West Virginia	289
35	Vermont	271
36	Virginia	269
37	Michigan	258
38	Utah	255
39	Maine	253
39	South Carolina	253
41	Idaho	245
42	California	209
43	New Mexico	200
44	Washington	199
45	Nevada	188
46	Oregon	170
47	Florida	165
48	Alaska	160
49	Hawaii	141
50	Arizona	139

| | District of Columbia | 248 |

Source: CQ Press using data from U.S. Department of Health and Human Services, Centers for Medicare and Medicaid Services OSCAR Database (January 05, 2009)

*Beds in nursing care facilities certified by CMS to participate in the Medicare/Medicaid programs. National rate does not include beds or population in U.S. territories. Calculated using 2007 Census population estimate.

Nursing Home Occupancy Rate in 2006

National Rate = 83.5% of Beds in Nursing Homes Occupied

ALPHA ORDER

RANK	STATE	RATE
25	Alabama	87.5
20	Alaska	88.3
38	Arizona	77.4
44	Arkansas	72.8
31	California	84.8
33	Colorado	83.0
8	Connecticut	90.9
35	Delaware	81.1
21	Florida	88.1
14	Georgia	89.6
3	Hawaii	92.8
40	Idaho	75.0
40	Illinois	75.0
47	Indiana	69.8
37	Iowa	77.8
39	Kansas	76.4
17	Kentucky	89.3
40	Louisiana	75.0
10	Maine	90.4
27	Maryland	87.1
16	Massachusetts	89.4
29	Michigan	86.6
6	Minnesota	91.4
14	Mississippi	89.6
48	Missouri	69.7
43	Montana	73.7
34	Nebraska	82.0
32	Nevada	83.1
12	New Hampshire	90.1
22	New Jersey	87.6
28	New Mexico	86.7
3	New York	92.8
22	North Carolina	87.6
5	North Dakota	91.8
26	Ohio	87.2
49	Oklahoma	65.8
50	Oregon	64.5
7	Pennsylvania	91.1
2	Rhode Island	93.0
11	South Carolina	90.3
1	South Dakota	99.5
22	Tennessee	87.6
45	Texas	72.2
46	Utah	70.9
9	Vermont	90.6
18	Virginia	89.2
29	Washington	86.6
13	West Virginia	89.9
19	Wisconsin	88.5
35	Wyoming	81.1

RANK ORDER

RANK	STATE	RATE
1	South Dakota	99.5
2	Rhode Island	93.0
3	Hawaii	92.8
3	New York	92.8
5	North Dakota	91.8
6	Minnesota	91.4
7	Pennsylvania	91.1
8	Connecticut	90.9
9	Vermont	90.6
10	Maine	90.4
11	South Carolina	90.3
12	New Hampshire	90.1
13	West Virginia	89.9
14	Georgia	89.6
14	Mississippi	89.6
16	Massachusetts	89.4
17	Kentucky	89.3
18	Virginia	89.2
19	Wisconsin	88.5
20	Alaska	88.3
21	Florida	88.1
22	New Jersey	87.6
22	North Carolina	87.6
22	Tennessee	87.6
25	Alabama	87.5
26	Ohio	87.2
27	Maryland	87.1
28	New Mexico	86.7
29	Michigan	86.6
29	Washington	86.6
31	California	84.8
32	Nevada	83.1
33	Colorado	83.0
34	Nebraska	82.0
35	Delaware	81.1
35	Wyoming	81.1
37	Iowa	77.8
38	Arizona	77.4
39	Kansas	76.4
40	Idaho	75.0
40	Illinois	75.0
40	Louisiana	75.0
43	Montana	73.7
44	Arkansas	72.8
45	Texas	72.2
46	Utah	70.9
47	Indiana	69.8
48	Missouri	69.7
49	Oklahoma	65.8
50	Oregon	64.5
	District of Columbia	92.4

Source: U.S. Department of Health and Human Services, Centers for Medicare and Medicaid Services
"Health, United States, 2007" (www.cdc.gov/nchs/data/hus/hus07.pdf)

Nursing Home Resident Rate in 2006

National Rate = 270.6 Residents per 1,000 Population Age 85 and Older*

ALPHA ORDER

RANK ORDER

RANK	STATE	RATE	RANK	STATE	RATE
26	Alabama	295.3	1	Louisiana	411.2
47	Alaska	154.3	2	Ohio	374.6
49	Arizona	121.5	3	Connecticut	358.2
17	Arkansas	327.4	4	Indiana	357.6
42	California	189.9	5	Iowa	357.4
33	Colorado	270.8	6	North Dakota	355.2
3	Connecticut	358.2	7	South Dakota	350.0
35	Delaware	264.9	8	Nebraska	340.6
46	Florida	156.9	9	Illinois	340.0
19	Georgia	315.4	10	Tennessee	335.9
48	Hawaii	142.4	11	Kentucky	334.9
40	Idaho	198.7	12	Missouri	334.0
9	Illinois	340.0	13	Kansas	332.4
4	Indiana	357.6	14	Mississippi	331.1
5	Iowa	357.4	15	Rhode Island	329.0
13	Kansas	332.4	16	Massachusetts	328.9
11	Kentucky	334.9	17	Arkansas	327.4
1	Louisiana	411.2	18	Minnesota	322.1
37	Maine	246.2	19	Georgia	315.4
27	Maryland	294.6	20	Oklahoma	308.7
16	Massachusetts	328.9	21	Wisconsin	306.9
39	Michigan	235.1	22	New Hampshire	305.0
18	Minnesota	322.1	23	New York	301.7
14	Mississippi	331.1	24	Texas	296.7
12	Missouri	334.0	25	Wyoming	295.7
28	Montana	284.5	26	Alabama	295.3
8	Nebraska	340.6	27	Maryland	294.6
45	Nevada	167.5	28	Montana	284.5
22	New Hampshire	305.0	29	North Carolina	281.6
30	New Jersey	274.2	30	New Jersey	274.2
41	New Mexico	192.2	31	Pennsylvania	273.6
23	New York	301.7	32	West Virginia	272.6
29	North Carolina	281.6	33	Colorado	270.8
6	North Dakota	355.2	34	Vermont	265.6
2	Ohio	374.6	35	Delaware	264.9
20	Oklahoma	308.7	36	Virginia	253.1
50	Oregon	114.2	37	Maine	246.2
31	Pennsylvania	273.6	38	South Carolina	242.1
15	Rhode Island	329.0	39	Michigan	235.1
38	South Carolina	242.1	40	Idaho	198.7
7	South Dakota	350.0	41	New Mexico	192.2
10	Tennessee	335.9	42	California	189.9
24	Texas	296.7	43	Utah	187.4
43	Utah	187.4	44	Washington	182.0
34	Vermont	265.6	45	Nevada	167.5
36	Virginia	253.1	46	Florida	156.9
44	Washington	182.0	47	Alaska	154.3
32	West Virginia	272.6	48	Hawaii	142.4
21	Wisconsin	306.9	49	Arizona	121.5
25	Wyoming	295.7	50	Oregon	114.2
				District of Columbia	256.3

Source: U.S. Department of Health and Human Services, Centers for Medicare and Medicaid Services
   "Health, United States, 2007" (www.cdc.gov/nchs/data/hus/hus07.pdf)
*Number of nursing home residents (all ages) per 1,000 resident population 85 years of age and over.

Nursing Home Population in 2006

National Total = 1,433,523

<u>ALPHA ORDER</u>

RANK	STATE	POPULATION	% of USA
23	Alabama	23,488	1.6%
50	Alaska	640	0.0%
33	Arizona	12,775	0.9%
28	Arkansas	17,970	1.3%
2	California	105,458	7.4%
30	Colorado	16,579	1.2%
20	Connecticut	27,364	1.9%
46	Delaware	3,855	0.3%
7	Florida	72,552	5.1%
14	Georgia	35,755	2.5%
47	Hawaii	3,828	0.3%
45	Idaho	4,646	0.3%
6	Illinois	77,204	5.4%
11	Indiana	39,758	2.8%
21	Iowa	26,866	1.9%
26	Kansas	19,785	1.4%
24	Kentucky	23,261	1.6%
19	Louisiana	27,800	1.9%
39	Maine	6,651	0.5%
22	Maryland	25,273	1.8%
9	Massachusetts	45,068	3.1%
10	Michigan	41,090	2.9%
17	Minnesota	32,738	2.3%
31	Mississippi	16,419	1.1%
13	Missouri	38,001	2.7%
43	Montana	5,405	0.4%
32	Nebraska	13,327	0.9%
44	Nevada	4,664	0.3%
37	New Hampshire	7,052	0.5%
8	New Jersey	45,667	3.2%
40	New Mexico	6,019	0.4%
1	New York	112,141	7.8%
12	North Carolina	38,362	2.7%
41	North Dakota	5,967	0.4%
4	Ohio	81,275	5.7%
25	Oklahoma	20,242	1.4%
36	Oregon	8,108	0.6%
5	Pennsylvania	80,660	5.6%
35	Rhode Island	8,265	0.6%
29	South Carolina	16,635	1.2%
38	South Dakota	6,677	0.5%
16	Tennessee	32,819	2.3%
3	Texas	89,788	6.3%
42	Utah	5,480	0.4%
48	Vermont	3,111	0.2%
18	Virginia	28,380	2.0%
27	Washington	19,478	1.4%
34	West Virginia	9,832	0.7%
15	Wisconsin	34,111	2.4%
49	Wyoming	2,474	0.2%

<u>RANK ORDER</u>

RANK	STATE	POPULATION	% of USA
1	New York	112,141	7.8%
2	California	105,458	7.4%
3	Texas	89,788	6.3%
4	Ohio	81,275	5.7%
5	Pennsylvania	80,660	5.6%
6	Illinois	77,204	5.4%
7	Florida	72,552	5.1%
8	New Jersey	45,667	3.2%
9	Massachusetts	45,068	3.1%
10	Michigan	41,090	2.9%
11	Indiana	39,758	2.8%
12	North Carolina	38,362	2.7%
13	Missouri	38,001	2.7%
14	Georgia	35,755	2.5%
15	Wisconsin	34,111	2.4%
16	Tennessee	32,819	2.3%
17	Minnesota	32,738	2.3%
18	Virginia	28,380	2.0%
19	Louisiana	27,800	1.9%
20	Connecticut	27,364	1.9%
21	Iowa	26,866	1.9%
22	Maryland	25,273	1.8%
23	Alabama	23,488	1.6%
24	Kentucky	23,261	1.6%
25	Oklahoma	20,242	1.4%
26	Kansas	19,785	1.4%
27	Washington	19,478	1.4%
28	Arkansas	17,970	1.3%
29	South Carolina	16,635	1.2%
30	Colorado	16,579	1.2%
31	Mississippi	16,419	1.1%
32	Nebraska	13,327	0.9%
33	Arizona	12,775	0.9%
34	West Virginia	9,832	0.7%
35	Rhode Island	8,265	0.6%
36	Oregon	8,108	0.6%
37	New Hampshire	7,052	0.5%
38	South Dakota	6,677	0.5%
39	Maine	6,651	0.5%
40	New Mexico	6,019	0.4%
41	North Dakota	5,967	0.4%
42	Utah	5,480	0.4%
43	Montana	5,405	0.4%
44	Nevada	4,664	0.3%
45	Idaho	4,646	0.3%
46	Delaware	3,855	0.3%
47	Hawaii	3,828	0.3%
48	Vermont	3,111	0.2%
49	Wyoming	2,474	0.2%
50	Alaska	640	0.0%
	District of Columbia	2,760	0.2%

Source: U.S. Department of Health and Human Services, Centers for Medicare and Medicaid Services
"Health, United States, 2007" (www.cdc.gov/nchs/data/hus/hus07.pdf)

Health Care Establishments in 2006

National Total = 611,626 Establishments*

ALPHA ORDER					RANK ORDER			
RANK	**STATE**	**ESTABLISH'S**	**% of USA**		**RANK**	**STATE**	**ESTABLISH'S**	**% of USA**
26	Alabama	7,932	1.3%		1	California	78,670	12.9%
47	Alaska	1,559	0.3%		2	Texas	43,981	7.2%
15	Arizona	12,512	2.0%		3	New York	42,587	7.0%
32	Arkansas	5,459	0.9%		4	Florida	42,256	6.9%
1	California	78,670	12.9%		5	Pennsylvania	27,607	4.5%
20	Colorado	10,652	1.7%		6	Illinois	24,328	4.0%
28	Connecticut	7,744	1.3%		7	Ohio	22,140	3.6%
45	Delaware	1,718	0.3%		8	New Jersey	21,119	3.5%
4	Florida	42,256	6.9%		9	Michigan	20,735	3.4%
10	Georgia	16,062	2.6%		10	Georgia	16,062	2.6%
41	Hawaii	2,853	0.5%		11	North Carolina	15,701	2.6%
40	Idaho	3,295	0.5%		12	Washington	13,572	2.2%
6	Illinois	24,328	4.0%		13	Massachusetts	13,335	2.2%
18	Indiana	11,571	1.9%		14	Virginia	13,244	2.2%
30	Iowa	5,862	1.0%		15	Arizona	12,512	2.0%
31	Kansas	5,704	0.9%		16	Maryland	12,246	2.0%
25	Kentucky	8,168	1.3%		17	Missouri	11,718	1.9%
23	Louisiana	8,875	1.5%		18	Indiana	11,571	1.9%
39	Maine	3,392	0.6%		19	Tennessee	11,192	1.8%
16	Maryland	12,246	2.0%		20	Colorado	10,652	1.7%
13	Massachusetts	13,335	2.2%		21	Wisconsin	10,437	1.7%
9	Michigan	20,735	3.4%		22	Minnesota	10,194	1.7%
22	Minnesota	10,194	1.7%		23	Louisiana	8,875	1.5%
35	Mississippi	4,334	0.7%		24	Oregon	8,799	1.4%
17	Missouri	11,718	1.9%		25	Kentucky	8,168	1.3%
44	Montana	2,323	0.4%		26	Alabama	7,932	1.3%
37	Nebraska	3,556	0.6%		27	Oklahoma	7,863	1.3%
34	Nevada	4,722	0.8%		28	Connecticut	7,744	1.3%
43	New Hampshire	2,424	0.4%		29	South Carolina	7,092	1.2%
8	New Jersey	21,119	3.5%		30	Iowa	5,862	1.0%
38	New Mexico	3,529	0.6%		31	Kansas	5,704	0.9%
3	New York	42,587	7.0%		32	Arkansas	5,459	0.9%
11	North Carolina	15,701	2.6%		33	Utah	5,256	0.9%
49	North Dakota	1,266	0.2%		34	Nevada	4,722	0.8%
7	Ohio	22,140	3.6%		35	Mississippi	4,334	0.7%
27	Oklahoma	7,863	1.3%		36	West Virginia	3,781	0.6%
24	Oregon	8,799	1.4%		37	Nebraska	3,556	0.6%
5	Pennsylvania	27,607	4.5%		38	New Mexico	3,529	0.6%
42	Rhode Island	2,579	0.4%		39	Maine	3,392	0.6%
29	South Carolina	7,092	1.2%		40	Idaho	3,295	0.5%
46	South Dakota	1,610	0.3%		41	Hawaii	2,853	0.5%
19	Tennessee	11,192	1.8%		42	Rhode Island	2,579	0.4%
2	Texas	43,981	7.2%		43	New Hampshire	2,424	0.4%
33	Utah	5,256	0.9%		44	Montana	2,323	0.4%
48	Vermont	1,457	0.2%		45	Delaware	1,718	0.3%
14	Virginia	13,244	2.2%		46	South Dakota	1,610	0.3%
12	Washington	13,572	2.2%		47	Alaska	1,559	0.3%
36	West Virginia	3,781	0.6%		48	Vermont	1,457	0.2%
21	Wisconsin	10,437	1.7%		49	North Dakota	1,266	0.2%
50	Wyoming	1,203	0.2%		50	Wyoming	1,203	0.2%
						District of Columbia	1,412	0.2%

Source: U.S. Bureau of the Census

"County Business Patterns 2006 (NAICS)" (http://censtats.census.gov/cbpnaic/cbpnaic.shtml)

*Includes establishments exempt from as well as subject to the federal income tax. Includes those establishments within the North American Industry Classification System (NAICS) classifications 621 (ambulatory health care services), 622 (hospitals), and 623 (nursing and residential care facilities). Does not include classification 624 (social assistance facilities).

IV. Finance

Average Medical Malpractice Payment in 2006

National Average = $311,965*

ALPHA ORDER				RANK ORDER		
RANK	STATE	AVERAGE PAYMENT		RANK	STATE	AVERAGE PAYMENT
7	Alabama	$453,665		1	Illinois	$619,205
39	Alaska	240,511		2	Wisconsin**	524,041
30	Arizona	286,898		3	Delaware	521,177
37	Arkansas	246,959		4	Connecticut	500,289
41	California	223,039		5	Minnesota	480,822
24	Colorado	312,138		6	Massachusetts	465,236
4	Connecticut	500,289		7	Alabama	453,665
3	Delaware	521,177		8	South Dakota	422,033
40	Florida**	240,363		9	Wyoming	413,553
29	Georgia	292,902		10	New York	405,558
14	Hawaii	342,316		11	New Jersey	401,144
31	Idaho	281,751		12	North Carolina	366,966
1	Illinois	619,205		13	Maryland	347,477
20	Indiana**	322,822		14	Hawaii	342,316
34	Iowa	274,281		15	Nevada	340,211
48	Kansas**	155,285		16	New Hampshire	336,032
32	Kentucky	280,599		17	Pennsylvania**	332,376
43	Louisiana**	207,878		18	Missouri	330,115
21	Maine	322,325		19	Rhode Island	326,542
13	Maryland	347,477		20	Indiana**	322,822
6	Massachusetts	465,236		21	Maine	322,325
49	Michigan	138,433		22	Montana	320,849
5	Minnesota	480,822		23	Tennessee	317,305
35	Mississippi	258,806		24	Colorado	312,138
18	Missouri	330,115		25	Ohio	310,573
22	Montana	320,849		26	Oregon	305,725
42	Nebraska**	213,081		27	North Dakota	301,422
15	Nevada	340,211		28	Virginia	295,840
16	New Hampshire	336,032		29	Georgia	292,902
11	New Jersey	401,144		30	Arizona	286,898
45	New Mexico**	199,917		31	Idaho	281,751
10	New York	405,558		32	Kentucky	280,599
12	North Carolina	366,966		33	Washington	277,493
27	North Dakota	301,422		34	Iowa	274,281
25	Ohio	310,573		35	Mississippi	258,806
38	Oklahoma	245,127		36	Utah	247,349
26	Oregon	305,725		37	Arkansas	246,959
17	Pennsylvania**	332,376		38	Oklahoma	245,127
19	Rhode Island	326,542		39	Alaska	240,511
47	South Carolina**	174,454		40	Florida**	240,363
8	South Dakota	422,033		41	California	223,039
23	Tennessee	317,305		42	Nebraska**	213,081
46	Texas	175,644		43	Louisiana**	207,878
36	Utah	247,349		44	West Virginia	204,794
50	Vermont	125,795		45	New Mexico**	199,917
28	Virginia	295,840		46	Texas	175,644
33	Washington	277,493		47	South Carolina**	174,454
44	West Virginia	204,794		48	Kansas**	155,285
2	Wisconsin**	524,041		49	Michigan	138,433
9	Wyoming	413,553		50	Vermont	125,795
					District of Columbia	331,628

Source: U.S. Department of Health and Human Services, Bureau of Health Professions
"National Practitioner Data Bank, 2006 Annual Report" (http://www.npdb-hipdb.com/annualrpt.html)
*National figure includes U.S. territories and U.S. Armed Forces locations overseas.
**The figures for these states have not been adjusted for payments by state compensation funds and other similar funds.
Average payments for these states understate the actual average amounts received by claimants.

Percent of Private-Sector Establishments That Offer Health Insurance: 2006

National Percent = 55.8%

ALPHA ORDER

RANK	STATE	PERCENT
8	Alabama	62.5
49	Alaska	40.3
37	Arizona	49.5
45	Arkansas	45.2
16	California	56.9
23	Colorado	55.3
5	Connecticut	65.1
13	Delaware	58.4
32	Florida	51.4
35	Georgia	49.9
1	Hawaii	89.6
46	Idaho	44.6
23	Illinois	55.3
28	Indiana	53.2
30	Iowa	52.1
29	Kansas	53.1
14	Kentucky	57.9
36	Louisiana	49.6
20	Maine	56.0
3	Maryland	65.7
2	Massachusetts	66.2
27	Michigan	53.4
31	Minnesota	52.0
43	Mississippi	46.4
22	Missouri	55.4
50	Montana	40.1
47	Nebraska	42.0
17	Nevada	56.7
10	New Hampshire	61.9
7	New Jersey	63.6
34	New Mexico	50.2
12	New York	59.7
18	North Carolina	56.6
41	North Dakota	46.7
11	Ohio	61.3
33	Oklahoma	51.3
19	Oregon	56.4
6	Pennsylvania	64.6
4	Rhode Island	65.3
38	South Carolina	49.4
48	South Dakota	41.1
21	Tennessee	55.5
39	Texas	49.1
44	Utah	46.1
14	Vermont	57.9
8	Virginia	62.5
26	Washington	53.8
40	West Virginia	48.6
25	Wisconsin	54.1
42	Wyoming	46.5

RANK ORDER

RANK	STATE	PERCENT
1	Hawaii	89.6
2	Massachusetts	66.2
3	Maryland	65.7
4	Rhode Island	65.3
5	Connecticut	65.1
6	Pennsylvania	64.6
7	New Jersey	63.6
8	Alabama	62.5
8	Virginia	62.5
10	New Hampshire	61.9
11	Ohio	61.3
12	New York	59.7
13	Delaware	58.4
14	Kentucky	57.9
14	Vermont	57.9
16	California	56.9
17	Nevada	56.7
18	North Carolina	56.6
19	Oregon	56.4
20	Maine	56.0
21	Tennessee	55.5
22	Missouri	55.4
23	Colorado	55.3
23	Illinois	55.3
25	Wisconsin	54.1
26	Washington	53.8
27	Michigan	53.4
28	Indiana	53.2
29	Kansas	53.1
30	Iowa	52.1
31	Minnesota	52.0
32	Florida	51.4
33	Oklahoma	51.3
34	New Mexico	50.2
35	Georgia	49.9
36	Louisiana	49.6
37	Arizona	49.5
38	South Carolina	49.4
39	Texas	49.1
40	West Virginia	48.6
41	North Dakota	46.7
42	Wyoming	46.5
43	Mississippi	46.4
44	Utah	46.1
45	Arkansas	45.2
46	Idaho	44.6
47	Nebraska	42.0
48	South Dakota	41.1
49	Alaska	40.3
50	Montana	40.1

District of Columbia	77.4

Source: U.S. Department of Health and Human Services, Agency for Healthcare Research and Quality
"Private-Sector Data by Firm Size and State" (Table II Series, Medical Expenditures Panel Survey)
(http://www.meps.ahrq.gov/mepsweb/survey_comp/Insurance.jsp)

Percent of Private-Sector Establishments with Fewer Than 50 Employees That Offer Health Insurance: 2006
National Percent = 42.6%

ALPHA ORDER

RANK	STATE	PERCENT
11	Alabama	48.3
50	Alaska	24.5
41	Arizona	32.3
46	Arkansas	29.3
15	California	45.5
19	Colorado	43.0
5	Connecticut	54.5
16	Delaware	44.9
29	Florida	38.9
38	Georgia	33.5
1	Hawaii	86.3
36	Idaho	34.2
23	Illinois	41.1
37	Indiana	34.0
30	Iowa	38.6
27	Kansas	39.6
22	Kentucky	42.0
39	Louisiana	32.7
17	Maine	44.8
3	Maryland	56.4
4	Massachusetts	55.5
25	Michigan	40.9
31	Minnesota	37.7
48	Mississippi	27.9
21	Missouri	42.4
45	Montana	30.6
49	Nebraska	27.2
18	Nevada	43.7
8	New Hampshire	50.7
6	New Jersey	52.7
35	New Mexico	34.6
9	New York	50.6
19	North Carolina	43.0
34	North Dakota	36.0
13	Ohio	46.9
28	Oklahoma	39.2
14	Oregon	45.9
7	Pennsylvania	51.2
2	Rhode Island	57.1
39	South Carolina	32.7
47	South Dakota	28.5
33	Tennessee	36.7
43	Texas	32.2
41	Utah	32.3
10	Vermont	48.6
12	Virginia	48.1
23	Washington	41.1
44	West Virginia	31.4
26	Wisconsin	40.8
32	Wyoming	36.8

RANK ORDER

RANK	STATE	PERCENT
1	Hawaii	86.3
2	Rhode Island	57.1
3	Maryland	56.4
4	Massachusetts	55.5
5	Connecticut	54.5
6	New Jersey	52.7
7	Pennsylvania	51.2
8	New Hampshire	50.7
9	New York	50.6
10	Vermont	48.6
11	Alabama	48.3
12	Virginia	48.1
13	Ohio	46.9
14	Oregon	45.9
15	California	45.5
16	Delaware	44.9
17	Maine	44.8
18	Nevada	43.7
19	Colorado	43.0
19	North Carolina	43.0
21	Missouri	42.4
22	Kentucky	42.0
23	Illinois	41.1
23	Washington	41.1
25	Michigan	40.9
26	Wisconsin	40.8
27	Kansas	39.6
28	Oklahoma	39.2
29	Florida	38.9
30	Iowa	38.6
31	Minnesota	37.7
32	Wyoming	36.8
33	Tennessee	36.7
34	North Dakota	36.0
35	New Mexico	34.6
36	Idaho	34.2
37	Indiana	34.0
38	Georgia	33.5
39	Louisiana	32.7
39	South Carolina	32.7
41	Arizona	32.3
41	Utah	32.3
43	Texas	32.2
44	West Virginia	31.4
45	Montana	30.6
46	Arkansas	29.3
47	South Dakota	28.5
48	Mississippi	27.9
49	Nebraska	27.2
50	Alaska	24.5

| | District of Columbia | 65.7 |

Source: U.S. Department of Health and Human Services, Agency for Healthcare Research and Quality
"Private-Sector Data by Firm Size and State" (Table II Series, Medical Expenditures Panel Survey)
(http://www.meps.ahrq.gov/mepsweb/survey_comp/Insurance.jsp)

Percent of Private-Sector Establishments with More Than 50 Employees That Offer Health Insurance: 2006
National Percent = 95.6%

ALPHA ORDER

RANK	STATE	PERCENT
23	Alabama	95.9
34	Alaska	94.7
33	Arizona	94.8
45	Arkansas	91.6
31	California	94.9
30	Colorado	95.0
3	Connecticut	98.3
49	Delaware	89.9
34	Florida	94.7
24	Georgia	95.5
10	Hawaii	97.8
45	Idaho	91.6
14	Illinois	97.6
17	Indiana	96.8
39	Iowa	93.8
28	Kansas	95.1
19	Kentucky	96.7
28	Louisiana	95.1
5	Maine	98.1
37	Maryland	94.0
16	Massachusetts	97.3
15	Michigan	97.4
4	Minnesota	98.2
31	Mississippi	94.9
21	Missouri	96.3
6	Montana	98.0
36	Nebraska	94.5
47	Nevada	91.3
24	New Hampshire	95.5
1	New Jersey	100.0
42	New Mexico	92.7
6	New York	98.0
19	North Carolina	96.7
42	North Dakota	92.7
13	Ohio	97.7
39	Oklahoma	93.8
26	Oregon	95.2
10	Pennsylvania	97.8
10	Rhode Island	97.8
41	South Carolina	92.9
26	South Dakota	95.2
17	Tennessee	96.8
50	Texas	88.9
48	Utah	90.7
2	Vermont	99.1
6	Virginia	98.0
22	Washington	96.0
44	West Virginia	92.1
9	Wisconsin	97.9
37	Wyoming	94.0

RANK ORDER

RANK	STATE	PERCENT
1	New Jersey	100.0
2	Vermont	99.1
3	Connecticut	98.3
4	Minnesota	98.2
5	Maine	98.1
6	Montana	98.0
6	New York	98.0
6	Virginia	98.0
9	Wisconsin	97.9
10	Hawaii	97.8
10	Pennsylvania	97.8
10	Rhode Island	97.8
13	Ohio	97.7
14	Illinois	97.6
15	Michigan	97.4
16	Massachusetts	97.3
17	Indiana	96.8
17	Tennessee	96.8
19	Kentucky	96.7
19	North Carolina	96.7
21	Missouri	96.3
22	Washington	96.0
23	Alabama	95.9
24	Georgia	95.5
24	New Hampshire	95.5
26	Oregon	95.2
26	South Dakota	95.2
28	Kansas	95.1
28	Louisiana	95.1
30	Colorado	95.0
31	California	94.9
31	Mississippi	94.9
33	Arizona	94.8
34	Alaska	94.7
34	Florida	94.7
36	Nebraska	94.5
37	Maryland	94.0
37	Wyoming	94.0
39	Iowa	93.8
39	Oklahoma	93.8
41	South Carolina	92.9
42	New Mexico	92.7
42	North Dakota	92.7
44	West Virginia	92.1
45	Arkansas	91.6
45	Idaho	91.6
47	Nevada	91.3
48	Utah	90.7
49	Delaware	89.9
50	Texas	88.9
	District of Columbia	96.0

Source: U.S. Department of Health and Human Services, Agency for Healthcare Research and Quality
"Private-Sector Data by Firm Size and State" (Table II Series, Medical Expenditures Panel Survey)
(http://www.meps.ahrq.gov/mepsweb/survey_comp/Insurance.jsp)

Average Annual Single Coverage Health Insurance Premium per Enrolled Employee in 2006
National Average = $4,118*

ALPHA ORDER				RANK ORDER		
RANK	STATE	PREMIUM		RANK	STATE	PREMIUM
33	Alabama	$3,943		1	Delaware	$4,712
7	Alaska	4,539		2	Maine	4,663
14	Arizona	4,280		3	New Hampshire	4,622
49	Arkansas	3,567		4	New York	4,605
25	California	4,036		4	Wyoming	4,605
27	Colorado	4,024		6	Rhode Island	4,595
11	Connecticut	4,402		7	Alaska	4,539
1	Delaware	4,712		8	New Jersey	4,471
36	Florida	3,936		9	Massachusetts	4,448
40	Georgia	3,873		10	Michigan	4,446
50	Hawaii	3,549		11	Connecticut	4,402
48	Idaho	3,573		12	West Virginia	4,349
16	Illinois	4,245		13	Vermont	4,322
29	Indiana	3,989		14	Arizona	4,280
38	Iowa	3,916		15	Pennsylvania	4,277
42	Kansas	3,833		16	Illinois	4,245
43	Kentucky	3,791		17	Wisconsin	4,241
34	Louisiana	3,938		18	Montana	4,144
2	Maine	4,663		19	Texas	4,133
37	Maryland	3,930		20	Oregon	4,122
9	Massachusetts	4,448		21	Virginia	4,091
10	Michigan	4,446		22	Washington	4,056
30	Minnesota	3,981		23	Ohio	4,054
46	Mississippi	3,704		24	New Mexico	4,037
32	Missouri	3,958		25	California	4,036
18	Montana	4,144		26	North Carolina	4,027
39	Nebraska	3,890		27	Colorado	4,024
47	Nevada	3,583		28	South Carolina	4,013
3	New Hampshire	4,622		29	Indiana	3,989
8	New Jersey	4,471		30	Minnesota	3,981
24	New Mexico	4,037		31	Oklahoma	3,967
4	New York	4,605		32	Missouri	3,958
26	North Carolina	4,027		33	Alabama	3,943
44	North Dakota	3,787		34	Louisiana	3,938
23	Ohio	4,054		34	South Dakota	3,938
31	Oklahoma	3,967		36	Florida	3,936
20	Oregon	4,122		37	Maryland	3,930
15	Pennsylvania	4,277		38	Iowa	3,916
6	Rhode Island	4,595		39	Nebraska	3,890
28	South Carolina	4,013		40	Georgia	3,873
34	South Dakota	3,938		41	Utah	3,849
45	Tennessee	3,747		42	Kansas	3,833
19	Texas	4,133		43	Kentucky	3,791
41	Utah	3,849		44	North Dakota	3,787
13	Vermont	4,322		45	Tennessee	3,747
21	Virginia	4,091		46	Mississippi	3,704
22	Washington	4,056		47	Nevada	3,583
12	West Virginia	4,349		48	Idaho	3,573
17	Wisconsin	4,241		49	Arkansas	3,567
4	Wyoming	4,605		50	Hawaii	3,549
					District of Columbia	4,540

Source: U.S. Department of Health and Human Services, Agency for Healthcare Research and Quality
"Private-Sector Data by Firm Size and State" (Table II Series, Medical Expenditures Panel Survey)
(http://www.meps.ahrq.gov/mepsweb/survey_comp/Insurance.jsp)
*Enrolled employees at private-sector establishments that offer health insurance coverage.

Average Annual Employee Contribution for
Single Coverage Health Insurance in 2006
National Average = $788*

ALPHA ORDER

RANK	STATE	CONTRIBUTION
8	Alabama	$891
35	Alaska	714
22	Arizona	803
38	Arkansas	699
42	California	658
34	Colorado	717
12	Connecticut	862
29	Delaware	735
15	Florida	860
12	Georgia	862
50	Hawaii	366
47	Idaho	565
19	Illinois	822
16	Indiana	833
23	Iowa	784
25	Kansas	765
39	Kentucky	691
26	Louisiana	755
1	Maine	1,072
7	Maryland	898
2	Massachusetts	1,011
40	Michigan	682
20	Minnesota	810
31	Mississippi	727
37	Missouri	703
46	Montana	598
11	Nebraska	873
48	Nevada	551
3	New Hampshire	1,004
6	New Jersey	902
32	New Mexico	726
5	New York	965
36	North Carolina	704
41	North Dakota	675
24	Ohio	781
44	Oklahoma	650
49	Oregon	547
10	Pennsylvania	881
12	Rhode Island	862
20	South Carolina	810
33	South Dakota	718
27	Tennessee	745
30	Texas	728
17	Utah	826
28	Vermont	738
4	Virginia	981
45	Washington	623
18	West Virginia	825
9	Wisconsin	885
43	Wyoming	655

RANK ORDER

RANK	STATE	CONTRIBUTION
1	Maine	$1,072
2	Massachusetts	1,011
3	New Hampshire	1,004
4	Virginia	981
5	New York	965
6	New Jersey	902
7	Maryland	898
8	Alabama	891
9	Wisconsin	885
10	Pennsylvania	881
11	Nebraska	873
12	Connecticut	862
12	Georgia	862
12	Rhode Island	862
15	Florida	860
16	Indiana	833
17	Utah	826
18	West Virginia	825
19	Illinois	822
20	Minnesota	810
20	South Carolina	810
22	Arizona	803
23	Iowa	784
24	Ohio	781
25	Kansas	765
26	Louisiana	755
27	Tennessee	745
28	Vermont	738
29	Delaware	735
30	Texas	728
31	Mississippi	727
32	New Mexico	726
33	South Dakota	718
34	Colorado	717
35	Alaska	714
36	North Carolina	704
37	Missouri	703
38	Arkansas	699
39	Kentucky	691
40	Michigan	682
41	North Dakota	675
42	California	658
43	Wyoming	655
44	Oklahoma	650
45	Washington	623
46	Montana	598
47	Idaho	565
48	Nevada	551
49	Oregon	547
50	Hawaii	366
	District of Columbia	699

Source: U.S. Department of Health and Human Services, Agency for Healthcare Research and Quality
"Private-Sector Data by Firm Size and State" (Table II Series, Medical Expenditures Panel Survey)
(http://www.meps.ahrq.gov/mepsweb/survey_comp/Insurance.jsp)
*Enrolled employees at private-sector establishments that offer health insurance coverage.

Percent of Total Premiums for Single Coverage
Health Insurance Paid by Employees in 2006
National Average = 19.1%*

ALPHA ORDER

RANK	STATE	PERCENT
5	Alabama	22.6
42	Alaska	15.7
28	Arizona	18.8
21	Arkansas	19.6
40	California	16.3
33	Colorado	17.8
21	Connecticut	19.6
43	Delaware	15.6
8	Florida	21.8
7	Georgia	22.3
50	Hawaii	10.3
41	Idaho	15.8
24	Illinois	19.4
12	Indiana	20.9
18	Iowa	20.0
18	Kansas	20.0
30	Kentucky	18.2
26	Louisiana	19.2
2	Maine	23.0
3	Maryland	22.9
4	Massachusetts	22.7
46	Michigan	15.3
15	Minnesota	20.3
21	Mississippi	19.6
33	Missouri	17.8
47	Montana	14.4
6	Nebraska	22.5
44	Nevada	15.4
9	New Hampshire	21.7
16	New Jersey	20.2
32	New Mexico	18.0
11	New York	21.0
37	North Carolina	17.5
33	North Dakota	17.8
25	Ohio	19.3
39	Oklahoma	16.4
49	Oregon	13.3
14	Pennsylvania	20.6
28	Rhode Island	18.8
16	South Carolina	20.2
30	South Dakota	18.2
20	Tennessee	19.9
36	Texas	17.6
10	Utah	21.5
38	Vermont	17.1
1	Virginia	24.0
44	Washington	15.4
27	West Virginia	19.0
12	Wisconsin	20.9
48	Wyoming	14.2

RANK ORDER

RANK	STATE	PERCENT
1	Virginia	24.0
2	Maine	23.0
3	Maryland	22.9
4	Massachusetts	22.7
5	Alabama	22.6
6	Nebraska	22.5
7	Georgia	22.3
8	Florida	21.8
9	New Hampshire	21.7
10	Utah	21.5
11	New York	21.0
12	Indiana	20.9
12	Wisconsin	20.9
14	Pennsylvania	20.6
15	Minnesota	20.3
16	New Jersey	20.2
16	South Carolina	20.2
18	Iowa	20.0
18	Kansas	20.0
20	Tennessee	19.9
21	Arkansas	19.6
21	Connecticut	19.6
21	Mississippi	19.6
24	Illinois	19.4
25	Ohio	19.3
26	Louisiana	19.2
27	West Virginia	19.0
28	Arizona	18.8
28	Rhode Island	18.8
30	Kentucky	18.2
30	South Dakota	18.2
32	New Mexico	18.0
33	Colorado	17.8
33	Missouri	17.8
33	North Dakota	17.8
36	Texas	17.6
37	North Carolina	17.5
38	Vermont	17.1
39	Oklahoma	16.4
40	California	16.3
41	Idaho	15.8
42	Alaska	15.7
43	Delaware	15.6
44	Nevada	15.4
44	Washington	15.4
46	Michigan	15.3
47	Montana	14.4
48	Wyoming	14.2
49	Oregon	13.3
50	Hawaii	10.3
	District of Columbia	15.4

Source: U.S. Department of Health and Human Services, Agency for Healthcare Research and Quality
  "Private-Sector Data by Firm Size and State" (Table II Series, Medical Expenditures Panel Survey)
  (http://www.meps.ahrq.gov/mepsweb/survey_comp/Insurance.jsp)
*Enrolled employees at private-sector establishments that offer health insurance coverage.

Average Annual Family Coverage Health Insurance Premium per Enrolled Employee in 2006
National Average = $11,381*

ALPHA ORDER

RANK	STATE	PREMIUM
41	Alabama	$10,571
7	Alaska	12,198
17	Arizona	11,549
45	Arkansas	9,928
19	California	11,493
27	Colorado	11,195
3	Connecticut	12,416
2	Delaware	12,601
31	Florida	11,046
37	Georgia	10,793
50	Hawaii	9,426
39	Idaho	10,775
12	Illinois	11,781
20	Indiana	11,454
42	Iowa	10,550
30	Kansas	11,048
47	Kentucky	9,864
36	Louisiana	10,796
4	Maine	12,363
26	Maryland	11,272
5	Massachusetts	12,290
21	Michigan	11,452
23	Minnesota	11,395
48	Mississippi	9,769
28	Missouri	11,171
29	Montana	11,068
38	Nebraska	10,777
49	Nevada	9,746
1	New Hampshire	12,686
6	New Jersey	12,233
25	New Mexico	11,279
9	New York	12,075
35	North Carolina	10,950
43	North Dakota	10,060
33	Ohio	10,967
40	Oklahoma	10,592
16	Oregon	11,613
11	Pennsylvania	11,794
10	Rhode Island	11,934
34	South Carolina	10,956
46	South Dakota	9,875
44	Tennessee	9,996
13	Texas	11,690
32	Utah	10,975
15	Vermont	11,631
18	Virginia	11,497
22	Washington	11,423
24	West Virginia	11,282
14	Wisconsin	11,658
8	Wyoming	12,087

RANK ORDER

RANK	STATE	PREMIUM
1	New Hampshire	$12,686
2	Delaware	12,601
3	Connecticut	12,416
4	Maine	12,363
5	Massachusetts	12,290
6	New Jersey	12,233
7	Alaska	12,198
8	Wyoming	12,087
9	New York	12,075
10	Rhode Island	11,934
11	Pennsylvania	11,794
12	Illinois	11,781
13	Texas	11,690
14	Wisconsin	11,658
15	Vermont	11,631
16	Oregon	11,613
17	Arizona	11,549
18	Virginia	11,497
19	California	11,493
20	Indiana	11,454
21	Michigan	11,452
22	Washington	11,423
23	Minnesota	11,395
24	West Virginia	11,282
25	New Mexico	11,279
26	Maryland	11,272
27	Colorado	11,195
28	Missouri	11,171
29	Montana	11,068
30	Kansas	11,048
31	Florida	11,046
32	Utah	10,975
33	Ohio	10,967
34	South Carolina	10,956
35	North Carolina	10,950
36	Louisiana	10,796
37	Georgia	10,793
38	Nebraska	10,777
39	Idaho	10,775
40	Oklahoma	10,592
41	Alabama	10,571
42	Iowa	10,550
43	North Dakota	10,060
44	Tennessee	9,996
45	Arkansas	9,928
46	South Dakota	9,875
47	Kentucky	9,864
48	Mississippi	9,769
49	Nevada	9,746
50	Hawaii	9,426

	District of Columbia	12,262

Source: U.S. Department of Health and Human Services, Agency for Healthcare Research and Quality
"Private-Sector Data by Firm Size and State" (Table II Series, Medical Expenditures Panel Survey)
(http://www.meps.ahrq.gov/mepsweb/survey_comp/Insurance.jsp)
*Enrolled employees at private-sector establishments that offer health insurance coverage.

Average Annual Employee Contribution for Family Coverage Health Insurance in 2006
National Average = $2,890*

<table>
<tr><td colspan="3">ALPHA ORDER</td><td colspan="3">RANK ORDER</td></tr>
<tr><td>RANK</td><td>STATE</td><td>CONTRIBUTION</td><td>RANK</td><td>STATE</td><td>CONTRIBUTION</td></tr>
<tr><td>21</td><td>Alabama</td><td>$2,958</td><td>1</td><td>Maine</td><td>$3,660</td></tr>
<tr><td>27</td><td>Alaska</td><td>2,870</td><td>2</td><td>Florida</td><td>3,600</td></tr>
<tr><td>6</td><td>Arizona</td><td>3,267</td><td>2</td><td>Virginia</td><td>3,600</td></tr>
<tr><td>7</td><td>Arkansas</td><td>3,183</td><td>4</td><td>New Hampshire</td><td>3,318</td></tr>
<tr><td>11</td><td>California</td><td>3,073</td><td>5</td><td>Oregon</td><td>3,294</td></tr>
<tr><td>28</td><td>Colorado</td><td>2,851</td><td>6</td><td>Arizona</td><td>3,267</td></tr>
<tr><td>22</td><td>Connecticut</td><td>2,947</td><td>7</td><td>Arkansas</td><td>3,183</td></tr>
<tr><td>40</td><td>Delaware</td><td>2,522</td><td>8</td><td>Massachusetts</td><td>3,128</td></tr>
<tr><td>2</td><td>Florida</td><td>3,600</td><td>9</td><td>Minnesota</td><td>3,099</td></tr>
<tr><td>24</td><td>Georgia</td><td>2,909</td><td>10</td><td>Oklahoma</td><td>3,081</td></tr>
<tr><td>42</td><td>Hawaii</td><td>2,480</td><td>11</td><td>California</td><td>3,073</td></tr>
<tr><td>49</td><td>Idaho</td><td>2,168</td><td>12</td><td>North Dakota</td><td>3,056</td></tr>
<tr><td>32</td><td>Illinois</td><td>2,743</td><td>13</td><td>Nebraska</td><td>3,041</td></tr>
<tr><td>33</td><td>Indiana</td><td>2,685</td><td>14</td><td>Louisiana</td><td>3,029</td></tr>
<tr><td>34</td><td>Iowa</td><td>2,651</td><td>15</td><td>Mississippi</td><td>3,028</td></tr>
<tr><td>23</td><td>Kansas</td><td>2,923</td><td>16</td><td>Texas</td><td>3,024</td></tr>
<tr><td>43</td><td>Kentucky</td><td>2,469</td><td>17</td><td>South Carolina</td><td>2,999</td></tr>
<tr><td>14</td><td>Louisiana</td><td>3,029</td><td>18</td><td>Maryland</td><td>2,990</td></tr>
<tr><td>1</td><td>Maine</td><td>3,660</td><td>19</td><td>New Jersey</td><td>2,981</td></tr>
<tr><td>18</td><td>Maryland</td><td>2,990</td><td>20</td><td>New Mexico</td><td>2,961</td></tr>
<tr><td>8</td><td>Massachusetts</td><td>3,128</td><td>21</td><td>Alabama</td><td>2,958</td></tr>
<tr><td>46</td><td>Michigan</td><td>2,411</td><td>22</td><td>Connecticut</td><td>2,947</td></tr>
<tr><td>9</td><td>Minnesota</td><td>3,099</td><td>23</td><td>Kansas</td><td>2,923</td></tr>
<tr><td>15</td><td>Mississippi</td><td>3,028</td><td>24</td><td>Georgia</td><td>2,909</td></tr>
<tr><td>39</td><td>Missouri</td><td>2,543</td><td>25</td><td>Washington</td><td>2,886</td></tr>
<tr><td>31</td><td>Montana</td><td>2,759</td><td>26</td><td>North Carolina</td><td>2,871</td></tr>
<tr><td>13</td><td>Nebraska</td><td>3,041</td><td>27</td><td>Alaska</td><td>2,870</td></tr>
<tr><td>50</td><td>Nevada</td><td>2,144</td><td>28</td><td>Colorado</td><td>2,851</td></tr>
<tr><td>4</td><td>New Hampshire</td><td>3,318</td><td>29</td><td>Pennsylvania</td><td>2,787</td></tr>
<tr><td>19</td><td>New Jersey</td><td>2,981</td><td>30</td><td>Tennessee</td><td>2,764</td></tr>
<tr><td>20</td><td>New Mexico</td><td>2,961</td><td>31</td><td>Montana</td><td>2,759</td></tr>
<tr><td>35</td><td>New York</td><td>2,620</td><td>32</td><td>Illinois</td><td>2,743</td></tr>
<tr><td>26</td><td>North Carolina</td><td>2,871</td><td>33</td><td>Indiana</td><td>2,685</td></tr>
<tr><td>12</td><td>North Dakota</td><td>3,056</td><td>34</td><td>Iowa</td><td>2,651</td></tr>
<tr><td>41</td><td>Ohio</td><td>2,488</td><td>35</td><td>New York</td><td>2,620</td></tr>
<tr><td>10</td><td>Oklahoma</td><td>3,081</td><td>36</td><td>Vermont</td><td>2,619</td></tr>
<tr><td>5</td><td>Oregon</td><td>3,294</td><td>37</td><td>Utah</td><td>2,617</td></tr>
<tr><td>29</td><td>Pennsylvania</td><td>2,787</td><td>38</td><td>South Dakota</td><td>2,552</td></tr>
<tr><td>47</td><td>Rhode Island</td><td>2,368</td><td>39</td><td>Missouri</td><td>2,543</td></tr>
<tr><td>17</td><td>South Carolina</td><td>2,999</td><td>40</td><td>Delaware</td><td>2,522</td></tr>
<tr><td>38</td><td>South Dakota</td><td>2,552</td><td>41</td><td>Ohio</td><td>2,488</td></tr>
<tr><td>30</td><td>Tennessee</td><td>2,764</td><td>42</td><td>Hawaii</td><td>2,480</td></tr>
<tr><td>16</td><td>Texas</td><td>3,024</td><td>43</td><td>Kentucky</td><td>2,469</td></tr>
<tr><td>37</td><td>Utah</td><td>2,617</td><td>44</td><td>West Virginia</td><td>2,426</td></tr>
<tr><td>36</td><td>Vermont</td><td>2,619</td><td>44</td><td>Wisconsin</td><td>2,426</td></tr>
<tr><td>2</td><td>Virginia</td><td>3,600</td><td>46</td><td>Michigan</td><td>2,411</td></tr>
<tr><td>25</td><td>Washington</td><td>2,886</td><td>47</td><td>Rhode Island</td><td>2,368</td></tr>
<tr><td>44</td><td>West Virginia</td><td>2,426</td><td>48</td><td>Wyoming</td><td>2,284</td></tr>
<tr><td>44</td><td>Wisconsin</td><td>2,426</td><td>49</td><td>Idaho</td><td>2,168</td></tr>
<tr><td>48</td><td>Wyoming</td><td>2,284</td><td>50</td><td>Nevada</td><td>2,144</td></tr>
<tr><td></td><td></td><td></td><td></td><td>District of Columbia</td><td>2,543</td></tr>
</table>

Source: U.S. Department of Health and Human Services, Agency for Healthcare Research and Quality
  "Private-Sector Data by Firm Size and State" (Table II Series, Medical Expenditures Panel Survey)
    (http://www.meps.ahrq.gov/mepsweb/survey_comp/Insurance.jsp)
*Enrolled employees at private-sector establishments that offer health insurance coverage.

Percent of Total Premiums for Family Coverage
Health Insurance Paid by Employees in 2006
National Average = 25.4%*

ALPHA ORDER

RANK	STATE	PERCENT
12	Alabama	28.0
36	Alaska	23.5
9	Arizona	28.3
2	Arkansas	32.1
17	California	26.7
26	Colorado	25.5
34	Connecticut	23.7
48	Delaware	20.0
1	Florida	32.6
16	Georgia	27.0
20	Hawaii	26.3
47	Idaho	20.1
38	Illinois	23.3
37	Indiana	23.4
29	Iowa	25.1
18	Kansas	26.5
30	Kentucky	25.0
11	Louisiana	28.1
6	Maine	29.6
18	Maryland	26.5
27	Massachusetts	25.4
45	Michigan	21.1
15	Minnesota	27.2
4	Mississippi	31.0
39	Missouri	22.8
31	Montana	24.9
10	Nebraska	28.2
42	Nevada	22.0
22	New Hampshire	26.2
32	New Jersey	24.4
20	New Mexico	26.3
43	New York	21.7
22	North Carolina	26.2
5	North Dakota	30.4
40	Ohio	22.7
7	Oklahoma	29.1
8	Oregon	28.4
35	Pennsylvania	23.6
49	Rhode Island	19.8
14	South Carolina	27.4
25	South Dakota	25.8
13	Tennessee	27.6
24	Texas	25.9
33	Utah	23.8
41	Vermont	22.5
3	Virginia	31.3
28	Washington	25.3
44	West Virginia	21.5
46	Wisconsin	20.8
50	Wyoming	18.9

RANK ORDER

RANK	STATE	PERCENT
1	Florida	32.6
2	Arkansas	32.1
3	Virginia	31.3
4	Mississippi	31.0
5	North Dakota	30.4
6	Maine	29.6
7	Oklahoma	29.1
8	Oregon	28.4
9	Arizona	28.3
10	Nebraska	28.2
11	Louisiana	28.1
12	Alabama	28.0
13	Tennessee	27.6
14	South Carolina	27.4
15	Minnesota	27.2
16	Georgia	27.0
17	California	26.7
18	Kansas	26.5
18	Maryland	26.5
20	Hawaii	26.3
20	New Mexico	26.3
22	New Hampshire	26.2
22	North Carolina	26.2
24	Texas	25.9
25	South Dakota	25.8
26	Colorado	25.5
27	Massachusetts	25.4
28	Washington	25.3
29	Iowa	25.1
30	Kentucky	25.0
31	Montana	24.9
32	New Jersey	24.4
33	Utah	23.8
34	Connecticut	23.7
35	Pennsylvania	23.6
36	Alaska	23.5
37	Indiana	23.4
38	Illinois	23.3
39	Missouri	22.8
40	Ohio	22.7
41	Vermont	22.5
42	Nevada	22.0
43	New York	21.7
44	West Virginia	21.5
45	Michigan	21.1
46	Wisconsin	20.8
47	Idaho	20.1
48	Delaware	20.0
49	Rhode Island	19.8
50	Wyoming	18.9
	District of Columbia	20.7

Source: U.S. Department of Health and Human Services, Agency for Healthcare Research and Quality
"Private-Sector Data by Firm Size and State" (Table II Series, Medical Expenditures Panel Survey)
(http://www.meps.ahrq.gov/mepsweb/survey_comp/Insurance.jsp)
*Enrolled employees at private-sector establishments that offer health insurance coverage.

Persons Not Covered by Health Insurance in 2007

National Total = 45,657,000 Uninsured

ALPHA ORDER					RANK ORDER			
RANK	STATE	UNINSURED	% of USA		RANK	STATE	UNINSURED	% of USA
25	Alabama	549,000	1.2%		1	California	6,613,000	14.5%
42	Alaska	123,000	0.3%		2	Texas	5,962,000	13.1%
11	Arizona	1,164,000	2.5%		3	Florida	3,648,000	8.0%
27	Arkansas	451,000	1.0%		4	New York	2,519,000	5.5%
1	California	6,613,000	14.5%		5	Illinois	1,700,000	3.7%
15	Colorado	801,000	1.8%		6	Georgia	1,662,000	3.6%
35	Connecticut	326,000	0.7%		7	North Carolina	1,510,000	3.3%
45	Delaware	96,000	0.2%		8	New Jersey	1,348,000	3.0%
3	Florida	3,648,000	8.0%		9	Ohio	1,322,000	2.9%
6	Georgia	1,662,000	3.6%		10	Pennsylvania	1,176,000	2.6%
45	Hawaii	96,000	0.2%		11	Arizona	1,164,000	2.5%
39	Idaho	209,000	0.5%		12	Michigan	1,151,000	2.5%
5	Illinois	1,700,000	3.7%		13	Virginia	1,135,000	2.5%
21	Indiana	717,000	1.6%		14	Tennessee	883,000	1.9%
36	Iowa	275,000	0.6%		15	Colorado	801,000	1.8%
32	Kansas	345,000	0.8%		16	Louisiana	776,000	1.7%
24	Kentucky	570,000	1.2%		17	Maryland	762,000	1.7%
16	Louisiana	776,000	1.7%		18	Washington	737,000	1.6%
43	Maine	115,000	0.3%		19	Missouri	729,000	1.6%
17	Maryland	762,000	1.7%		20	South Carolina	721,000	1.6%
33	Massachusetts	340,000	0.7%		21	Indiana	717,000	1.6%
12	Michigan	1,151,000	2.5%		22	Oregon	632,000	1.4%
31	Minnesota	433,000	0.9%		23	Oklahoma	631,000	1.4%
26	Mississippi	545,000	1.2%		24	Kentucky	570,000	1.2%
19	Missouri	729,000	1.6%		25	Alabama	549,000	1.2%
40	Montana	146,000	0.3%		26	Mississippi	545,000	1.2%
38	Nebraska	232,000	0.5%		27	Arkansas	451,000	1.0%
29	Nevada	441,000	1.0%		27	Wisconsin	451,000	1.0%
41	New Hampshire	137,000	0.3%		29	Nevada	441,000	1.0%
8	New Jersey	1,348,000	3.0%		30	New Mexico	437,000	1.0%
30	New Mexico	437,000	1.0%		31	Minnesota	433,000	0.9%
4	New York	2,519,000	5.5%		32	Kansas	345,000	0.8%
7	North Carolina	1,510,000	3.3%		33	Massachusetts	340,000	0.7%
50	North Dakota	61,000	0.1%		33	Utah	340,000	0.7%
9	Ohio	1,322,000	2.9%		35	Connecticut	326,000	0.7%
23	Oklahoma	631,000	1.4%		36	Iowa	275,000	0.6%
22	Oregon	632,000	1.4%		37	West Virginia	254,000	0.6%
10	Pennsylvania	1,176,000	2.6%		38	Nebraska	232,000	0.5%
44	Rhode Island	113,000	0.2%		39	Idaho	209,000	0.5%
20	South Carolina	721,000	1.6%		40	Montana	146,000	0.3%
47	South Dakota	80,000	0.2%		41	New Hampshire	137,000	0.3%
14	Tennessee	883,000	1.9%		42	Alaska	123,000	0.3%
2	Texas	5,962,000	13.1%		43	Maine	115,000	0.3%
33	Utah	340,000	0.7%		44	Rhode Island	113,000	0.2%
49	Vermont	69,000	0.2%		45	Delaware	96,000	0.2%
13	Virginia	1,135,000	2.5%		45	Hawaii	96,000	0.2%
18	Washington	737,000	1.6%		47	South Dakota	80,000	0.2%
37	West Virginia	254,000	0.6%		48	Wyoming	70,000	0.2%
27	Wisconsin	451,000	1.0%		49	Vermont	69,000	0.2%
48	Wyoming	70,000	0.2%		50	North Dakota	61,000	0.1%
						District of Columbia	55,000	0.1%

Source: U.S. Bureau of the Census
   "Health Insurance Coverage Status by State for All People: 2007" (http://www.census.gov/hhes/www/hlthins/hlthin07.html)

Percent of Population Not Covered by Health Insurance in 2007

National Percent = 15.4% of Population*

ALPHA ORDER

RANK	STATE	PERCENT
23	Alabama	13.9
12	Alaska	17.3
4	Arizona	19.6
11	Arkansas	17.5
7	California	18.6
14	Colorado	16.7
43	Connecticut	9.9
34	Delaware	11.8
3	Florida	20.5
10	Georgia	17.8
49	Hawaii	8.3
21	Idaho	14.7
26	Illinois	13.7
31	Indiana	12.3
46	Iowa	9.4
34	Kansas	11.8
25	Kentucky	13.8
5	Louisiana	19.4
45	Maine	9.5
27	Maryland	13.6
49	Massachusetts	8.3
40	Michigan	10.8
48	Minnesota	8.5
6	Mississippi	18.8
30	Missouri	12.5
17	Montana	16.1
33	Nebraska	12.0
9	Nevada	17.9
41	New Hampshire	10.5
19	New Jersey	15.2
2	New Mexico	21.9
29	New York	13.4
15	North Carolina	16.6
37	North Dakota	11.1
38	Ohio	11.0
8	Oklahoma	18.2
13	Oregon	16.8
44	Pennsylvania	9.8
42	Rhode Island	10.3
16	South Carolina	16.5
36	South Dakota	11.2
23	Tennessee	13.9
1	Texas	24.4
18	Utah	15.6
38	Vermont	11.0
27	Virginia	13.6
32	Washington	12.1
20	West Virginia	14.9
47	Wisconsin	8.8
22	Wyoming	14.3

RANK ORDER

RANK	STATE	PERCENT
1	Texas	24.4
2	New Mexico	21.9
3	Florida	20.5
4	Arizona	19.6
5	Louisiana	19.4
6	Mississippi	18.8
7	California	18.6
8	Oklahoma	18.2
9	Nevada	17.9
10	Georgia	17.8
11	Arkansas	17.5
12	Alaska	17.3
13	Oregon	16.8
14	Colorado	16.7
15	North Carolina	16.6
16	South Carolina	16.5
17	Montana	16.1
18	Utah	15.6
19	New Jersey	15.2
20	West Virginia	14.9
21	Idaho	14.7
22	Wyoming	14.3
23	Alabama	13.9
23	Tennessee	13.9
25	Kentucky	13.8
26	Illinois	13.7
27	Maryland	13.6
27	Virginia	13.6
29	New York	13.4
30	Missouri	12.5
31	Indiana	12.3
32	Washington	12.1
33	Nebraska	12.0
34	Delaware	11.8
34	Kansas	11.8
36	South Dakota	11.2
37	North Dakota	11.1
38	Ohio	11.0
38	Vermont	11.0
40	Michigan	10.8
41	New Hampshire	10.5
42	Rhode Island	10.3
43	Connecticut	9.9
44	Pennsylvania	9.8
45	Maine	9.5
46	Iowa	9.4
47	Wisconsin	8.8
48	Minnesota	8.5
49	Hawaii	8.3
49	Massachusetts	8.3
	District of Columbia	11.4

Source: U.S. Bureau of the Census
   "Health Insurance Coverage Status by State for All People: 2007" (http://www.census.gov/hhes/www/hlthins/hlthin07.html)
*Three-year average for 2005 through 2007.

Numerical Change in Persons Uninsured: 2003 to 2007

National Change = 696,000 Increase

ALPHA ORDER

RANK	STATE	UNINSURED
42	Alabama	(80,000)
25	Alaska	1,000
4	Arizona	213,000
32	Arkansas	(14,000)
8	California	114,000
17	Colorado	29,000
34	Connecticut	(31,000)
23	Delaware	5,000
2	Florida	577,000
3	Georgia	253,000
34	Hawaii	(31,000)
39	Idaho	(44,000)
43	Illinois	(118,000)
44	Indiana	(136,000)
40	Iowa	(54,000)
13	Kansas	51,000
27	Kentucky	(4,000)
44	Louisiana	(136,000)
33	Maine	(18,000)
26	Maryland	0
49	Massachusetts	(342,000)
12	Michigan	71,000
30	Minnesota	(11,000)
16	Mississippi	34,000
9	Missouri	109,000
34	Montana	(31,000)
15	Nebraska	37,000
20	Nevada	15,000
22	New Hampshire	6,000
6	New Jersey	147,000
18	New Mexico	23,000
50	New York	(347,000)
11	North Carolina	86,000
28	North Dakota	(8,000)
37	Ohio	(40,000)
41	Oklahoma	(70,000)
19	Oregon	19,000
48	Pennsylvania	(208,000)
23	Rhode Island	5,000
7	South Carolina	137,000
30	South Dakota	(11,000)
10	Tennessee	105,000
1	Texas	588,000
14	Utah	42,000
21	Vermont	11,000
5	Virginia	173,000
47	Washington	(207,000)
38	West Virginia	(42,000)
46	Wisconsin	(142,000)
28	Wyoming	(8,000)

RANK ORDER

RANK	STATE	UNINSURED
1	Texas	588,000
2	Florida	577,000
3	Georgia	253,000
4	Arizona	213,000
5	Virginia	173,000
6	New Jersey	147,000
7	South Carolina	137,000
8	California	114,000
9	Missouri	109,000
10	Tennessee	105,000
11	North Carolina	86,000
12	Michigan	71,000
13	Kansas	51,000
14	Utah	42,000
15	Nebraska	37,000
16	Mississippi	34,000
17	Colorado	29,000
18	New Mexico	23,000
19	Oregon	19,000
20	Nevada	15,000
21	Vermont	11,000
22	New Hampshire	6,000
23	Delaware	5,000
23	Rhode Island	5,000
25	Alaska	1,000
26	Maryland	0
27	Kentucky	(4,000)
28	North Dakota	(8,000)
28	Wyoming	(8,000)
30	Minnesota	(11,000)
30	South Dakota	(11,000)
32	Arkansas	(14,000)
33	Maine	(18,000)
34	Connecticut	(31,000)
34	Hawaii	(31,000)
34	Montana	(31,000)
37	Ohio	(40,000)
38	West Virginia	(42,000)
39	Idaho	(44,000)
40	Iowa	(54,000)
41	Oklahoma	(70,000)
42	Alabama	(80,000)
43	Illinois	(118,000)
44	Indiana	(136,000)
44	Louisiana	(136,000)
46	Wisconsin	(142,000)
47	Washington	(207,000)
48	Pennsylvania	(208,000)
49	Massachusetts	(342,000)
50	New York	(347,000)

District of Columbia (24,000)

Source: CQ Press using data from U.S. Bureau of the Census
"Health Insurance Coverage Status by State for All People: 2007" (http://www.census.gov/hhes/www/hlthins/hlthin07.html)
"Health Insurance Coverage Status by State for All People: 2003"

Percent Change in Persons Uninsured: 2003 to 2007

National Percent Change = 1.5% Increase

ALPHA ORDER				RANK ORDER		
RANK	STATE	PERCENT CHANGE		RANK	STATE	PERCENT CHANGE
38	Alabama	(12.7)		1	South Carolina	23.5
25	Alaska	0.8		2	Arizona	22.4
2	Arizona	22.4		3	Nebraska	19.0
30	Arkansas	(3.0)		3	Vermont	19.0
24	California	1.8		5	Florida	18.8
21	Colorado	3.8		6	Georgia	18.0
32	Connecticut	(8.7)		6	Virginia	18.0
18	Delaware	5.5		8	Missouri	17.6
5	Florida	18.8		9	Kansas	17.3
6	Georgia	18.0		10	Utah	14.1
49	Hawaii	(24.4)		11	Tennessee	13.5
45	Idaho	(17.4)		12	New Jersey	12.2
31	Illinois	(6.5)		13	Texas	10.9
43	Indiana	(15.9)		14	Mississippi	6.7
44	Iowa	(16.4)		15	Michigan	6.6
9	Kansas	17.3		16	North Carolina	6.0
27	Kentucky	(0.7)		17	New Mexico	5.6
41	Louisiana	(14.9)		18	Delaware	5.5
39	Maine	(13.5)		19	New Hampshire	4.6
26	Maryland	0.0		19	Rhode Island	4.6
50	Massachusetts	(50.1)		21	Colorado	3.8
15	Michigan	6.6		22	Nevada	3.5
28	Minnesota	(2.5)		23	Oregon	3.1
14	Mississippi	6.7		24	California	1.8
8	Missouri	17.6		25	Alaska	0.8
46	Montana	(17.5)		26	Maryland	0.0
3	Nebraska	19.0		27	Kentucky	(0.7)
22	Nevada	3.5		28	Minnesota	(2.5)
19	New Hampshire	4.6		29	Ohio	(2.9)
12	New Jersey	12.2		30	Arkansas	(3.0)
17	New Mexico	5.6		31	Illinois	(6.5)
36	New York	(12.1)		32	Connecticut	(8.7)
16	North Carolina	6.0		33	Oklahoma	(10.0)
35	North Dakota	(11.6)		34	Wyoming	(10.3)
29	Ohio	(2.9)		35	North Dakota	(11.6)
33	Oklahoma	(10.0)		36	New York	(12.1)
23	Oregon	3.1		36	South Dakota	(12.1)
42	Pennsylvania	(15.0)		38	Alabama	(12.7)
19	Rhode Island	4.6		39	Maine	(13.5)
1	South Carolina	23.5		40	West Virginia	(14.2)
36	South Dakota	(12.1)		41	Louisiana	(14.9)
11	Tennessee	13.5		42	Pennsylvania	(15.0)
13	Texas	10.9		43	Indiana	(15.9)
10	Utah	14.1		44	Iowa	(16.4)
3	Vermont	19.0		45	Idaho	(17.4)
6	Virginia	18.0		46	Montana	(17.5)
47	Washington	(21.9)		47	Washington	(21.9)
40	West Virginia	(14.2)		48	Wisconsin	(23.9)
48	Wisconsin	(23.9)		49	Hawaii	(24.4)
34	Wyoming	(10.3)		50	Massachusetts	(50.1)
				District of Columbia		(30.4)

Source: CQ Press using data from U.S. Bureau of the Census
"Health Insurance Coverage Status by State for All People: 2007" (http://www.census.gov/hhes/www/hlthins/hlthin07.html)
"Health Insurance Coverage Status by State for All People: 2003"

Change in Percent of Population Uninsured: 2003 to 2007

National Percent Change = 2.0% Increase*

ALPHA ORDER

RANK	STATE	PERCENT CHANGE
20	Alabama	4.5
38	Alaska	(2.8)
9	Arizona	13.3
19	Arkansas	5.4
31	California	(0.5)
26	Colorado	2.5
40	Connecticut	(4.8)
3	Delaware	16.8
4	Florida	16.5
15	Georgia	8.5
50	Hawaii	(16.2)
49	Idaho	(16.0)
35	Illinois	(2.1)
39	Indiana	(4.7)
33	Iowa	(1.1)
16	Kansas	8.3
21	Kentucky	3.8
29	Louisiana	0.0
44	Maine	(11.2)
24	Maryland	3.0
46	Massachusetts	(13.5)
34	Michigan	(1.8)
22	Minnesota	3.7
13	Mississippi	10.6
6	Missouri	14.7
29	Montana	0.0
4	Nebraska	16.5
36	Nevada	(2.2)
17	New Hampshire	6.1
11	New Jersey	10.9
25	New Mexico	2.8
46	New York	(13.5)
23	North Carolina	3.1
18	North Dakota	5.7
41	Ohio	(6.0)
37	Oklahoma	(2.7)
8	Oregon	13.5
43	Pennsylvania	(8.4)
12	Rhode Island	10.8
1	South Carolina	26.0
27	South Dakota	1.8
2	Tennessee	17.8
32	Texas	(0.8)
6	Utah	14.7
10	Vermont	11.1
14	Virginia	8.8
48	Washington	(15.4)
28	West Virginia	0.7
42	Wisconsin	(7.4)
45	Wyoming	(13.3)

RANK ORDER

RANK	STATE	PERCENT CHANGE
1	South Carolina	26.0
2	Tennessee	17.8
3	Delaware	16.8
4	Florida	16.5
4	Nebraska	16.5
6	Missouri	14.7
6	Utah	14.7
8	Oregon	13.5
9	Arizona	13.3
10	Vermont	11.1
11	New Jersey	10.9
12	Rhode Island	10.8
13	Mississippi	10.6
14	Virginia	8.8
15	Georgia	8.5
16	Kansas	8.3
17	New Hampshire	6.1
18	North Dakota	5.7
19	Arkansas	5.4
20	Alabama	4.5
21	Kentucky	3.8
22	Minnesota	3.7
23	North Carolina	3.1
24	Maryland	3.0
25	New Mexico	2.8
26	Colorado	2.5
27	South Dakota	1.8
28	West Virginia	0.7
29	Louisiana	0.0
29	Montana	0.0
31	California	(0.5)
32	Texas	(0.8)
33	Iowa	(1.1)
34	Michigan	(1.8)
35	Illinois	(2.1)
36	Nevada	(2.2)
37	Oklahoma	(2.7)
38	Alaska	(2.8)
39	Indiana	(4.7)
40	Connecticut	(4.8)
41	Ohio	(6.0)
42	Wisconsin	(7.4)
43	Pennsylvania	(8.4)
44	Maine	(11.2)
45	Wyoming	(13.3)
46	Massachusetts	(13.5)
46	New York	(13.5)
48	Washington	(15.4)
49	Idaho	(16.0)
50	Hawaii	(16.2)

District of Columbia   (14.3)

Source: CQ Press using data from U.S. Bureau of the Census
   "Health Insurance Coverage Status by State for All People: 2007" (http://www.census.gov/hhes/www/hlthins/hlthin07.html)
   "Health Insurance Coverage Status by State for All People: 2003"
*Based on three-year averages for 2004 through 2006 and 2000 through 2002.

Percent of Children Not Covered by Health Insurance in 2007

National Percent = 11.0% of Children*

ALPHA ORDER

RANK	STATE	PERCENT
36	Alabama	7.3
15	Alaska	11.4
6	Arizona	13.8
41	Arkansas	6.2
17	California	10.7
7	Colorado	13.0
44	Connecticut	5.2
34	Delaware	7.5
2	Florida	19.2
14	Georgia	11.5
47	Hawaii	4.8
16	Idaho	11.0
38	Illinois	6.6
44	Indiana	5.2
47	Iowa	4.8
33	Kansas	7.7
30	Kentucky	8.0
11	Louisiana	12.5
46	Maine	5.1
19	Maryland	10.5
50	Massachusetts	3.0
41	Michigan	6.2
40	Minnesota	6.4
12	Mississippi	12.1
20	Missouri	10.4
9	Montana	12.6
23	Nebraska	10.0
4	Nevada	14.3
39	New Hampshire	6.5
8	New Jersey	12.9
3	New Mexico	15.5
27	New York	8.9
12	North Carolina	12.1
32	North Dakota	7.9
29	Ohio	8.6
9	Oklahoma	12.6
18	Oregon	10.6
35	Pennsylvania	7.4
28	Rhode Island	8.8
5	South Carolina	14.2
30	South Dakota	8.0
26	Tennessee	9.1
1	Texas	21.4
20	Utah	10.4
25	Vermont	9.4
22	Virginia	10.2
37	Washington	6.8
49	West Virginia	4.6
43	Wisconsin	5.8
24	Wyoming	9.6

RANK ORDER

RANK	STATE	PERCENT
1	Texas	21.4
2	Florida	19.2
3	New Mexico	15.5
4	Nevada	14.3
5	South Carolina	14.2
6	Arizona	13.8
7	Colorado	13.0
8	New Jersey	12.9
9	Montana	12.6
9	Oklahoma	12.6
11	Louisiana	12.5
12	Mississippi	12.1
12	North Carolina	12.1
14	Georgia	11.5
15	Alaska	11.4
16	Idaho	11.0
17	California	10.7
18	Oregon	10.6
19	Maryland	10.5
20	Missouri	10.4
20	Utah	10.4
22	Virginia	10.2
23	Nebraska	10.0
24	Wyoming	9.6
25	Vermont	9.4
26	Tennessee	9.1
27	New York	8.9
28	Rhode Island	8.8
29	Ohio	8.6
30	Kentucky	8.0
30	South Dakota	8.0
32	North Dakota	7.9
33	Kansas	7.7
34	Delaware	7.5
35	Pennsylvania	7.4
36	Alabama	7.3
37	Washington	6.8
38	Illinois	6.6
39	New Hampshire	6.5
40	Minnesota	6.4
41	Arkansas	6.2
41	Michigan	6.2
43	Wisconsin	5.8
44	Connecticut	5.2
44	Indiana	5.2
46	Maine	5.1
47	Hawaii	4.8
47	Iowa	4.8
49	West Virginia	4.6
50	Massachusetts	3.0
	District of Columbia	6.2

Source: U.S. Bureau of the Census
    "Health Insurance Coverage Status by State for All People: 2007" (http://www.census.gov/hhes/www/hlthins/hlthin07.html)
*Children under 18 years old.

Persons Covered by Health Insurance in 2007

National Total = 253,449,000 Insured

ALPHA ORDER

RANK	STATE	INSURED	% of USA
23	Alabama	4,021,000	1.6%
48	Alaska	552,000	0.2%
17	Arizona	5,204,000	2.1%
33	Arkansas	2,354,000	0.9%
1	California	29,682,000	11.7%
22	Colorado	4,077,000	1.6%
27	Connecticut	3,150,000	1.2%
45	Delaware	766,000	0.3%
4	Florida	14,426,000	5.7%
9	Georgia	7,831,000	3.1%
42	Hawaii	1,172,000	0.5%
39	Idaho	1,292,000	0.5%
6	Illinois	10,988,000	4.3%
15	Indiana	5,546,000	2.2%
30	Iowa	2,695,000	1.1%
31	Kansas	2,376,000	0.9%
25	Kentucky	3,637,000	1.4%
26	Louisiana	3,421,000	1.3%
40	Maine	1,197,000	0.5%
20	Maryland	4,804,000	1.9%
13	Massachusetts	6,000,000	2.4%
8	Michigan	8,776,000	3.5%
21	Minnesota	4,758,000	1.9%
32	Mississippi	2,358,000	0.9%
18	Missouri	5,062,000	2.0%
44	Montana	793,000	0.3%
37	Nebraska	1,522,000	0.6%
35	Nevada	2,126,000	0.8%
41	New Hampshire	1,177,000	0.5%
11	New Jersey	7,208,000	2.8%
38	New Mexico	1,509,000	0.6%
3	New York	16,543,000	6.5%
10	North Carolina	7,673,000	3.0%
47	North Dakota	553,000	0.2%
7	Ohio	9,979,000	3.9%
29	Oklahoma	2,920,000	1.2%
28	Oregon	3,130,000	1.2%
5	Pennsylvania	11,138,000	4.4%
43	Rhode Island	931,000	0.4%
24	South Carolina	3,664,000	1.4%
46	South Dakota	708,000	0.3%
16	Tennessee	5,268,000	2.1%
2	Texas	17,742,000	7.0%
34	Utah	2,317,000	0.9%
49	Vermont	545,000	0.2%
12	Virginia	6,548,000	2.6%
14	Washington	5,773,000	2.3%
36	West Virginia	1,541,000	0.6%
19	Wisconsin	5,023,000	2.0%
50	Wyoming	447,000	0.2%

RANK ORDER

RANK	STATE	INSURED	% of USA
1	California	29,682,000	11.7%
2	Texas	17,742,000	7.0%
3	New York	16,543,000	6.5%
4	Florida	14,426,000	5.7%
5	Pennsylvania	11,138,000	4.4%
6	Illinois	10,988,000	4.3%
7	Ohio	9,979,000	3.9%
8	Michigan	8,776,000	3.5%
9	Georgia	7,831,000	3.1%
10	North Carolina	7,673,000	3.0%
11	New Jersey	7,208,000	2.8%
12	Virginia	6,548,000	2.6%
13	Massachusetts	6,000,000	2.4%
14	Washington	5,773,000	2.3%
15	Indiana	5,546,000	2.2%
16	Tennessee	5,268,000	2.1%
17	Arizona	5,204,000	2.1%
18	Missouri	5,062,000	2.0%
19	Wisconsin	5,023,000	2.0%
20	Maryland	4,804,000	1.9%
21	Minnesota	4,758,000	1.9%
22	Colorado	4,077,000	1.6%
23	Alabama	4,021,000	1.6%
24	South Carolina	3,664,000	1.4%
25	Kentucky	3,637,000	1.4%
26	Louisiana	3,421,000	1.3%
27	Connecticut	3,150,000	1.2%
28	Oregon	3,130,000	1.2%
29	Oklahoma	2,920,000	1.2%
30	Iowa	2,695,000	1.1%
31	Kansas	2,376,000	0.9%
32	Mississippi	2,358,000	0.9%
33	Arkansas	2,354,000	0.9%
34	Utah	2,317,000	0.9%
35	Nevada	2,126,000	0.8%
36	West Virginia	1,541,000	0.6%
37	Nebraska	1,522,000	0.6%
38	New Mexico	1,509,000	0.6%
39	Idaho	1,292,000	0.5%
40	Maine	1,197,000	0.5%
41	New Hampshire	1,177,000	0.5%
42	Hawaii	1,172,000	0.5%
43	Rhode Island	931,000	0.4%
44	Montana	793,000	0.3%
45	Delaware	766,000	0.3%
46	South Dakota	708,000	0.3%
47	North Dakota	553,000	0.2%
48	Alaska	552,000	0.2%
49	Vermont	545,000	0.2%
50	Wyoming	447,000	0.2%
	District of Columbia	526,000	0.2%

Source: U.S. Bureau of the Census

"Health Insurance Coverage Status by State for All People: 2007" (http://www.census.gov/hhes/www/hlthins/hlthin07.html)

Percent of Population Covered by Health Insurance in 2007

National Percent = 84.7% of Population

ALPHA ORDER

RANK	STATE	PERCENT
19	Alabama	88.0
43	Alaska	81.8
45	Arizona	81.7
35	Arkansas	83.9
43	California	81.8
36	Colorado	83.6
7	Connecticut	90.6
13	Delaware	88.8
48	Florida	79.8
41	Georgia	82.5
2	Hawaii	92.5
29	Idaho	86.1
25	Illinois	86.6
16	Indiana	88.6
6	Iowa	90.7
21	Kansas	87.3
26	Kentucky	86.4
46	Louisiana	81.5
5	Maine	91.2
28	Maryland	86.3
1	Massachusetts	94.6
17	Michigan	88.4
4	Minnesota	91.7
47	Mississippi	81.2
20	Missouri	87.4
33	Montana	84.4
23	Nebraska	86.8
40	Nevada	82.8
11	New Hampshire	89.5
34	New Jersey	84.2
49	New Mexico	77.5
23	New York	86.8
36	North Carolina	83.6
9	North Dakota	90.0
18	Ohio	88.3
42	Oklahoma	82.2
39	Oregon	83.2
8	Pennsylvania	90.5
12	Rhode Island	89.2
36	South Carolina	83.6
10	South Dakota	89.9
31	Tennessee	85.6
50	Texas	74.8
22	Utah	87.2
13	Vermont	88.8
32	Virginia	85.2
15	Washington	88.7
30	West Virginia	85.9
3	Wisconsin	91.8
26	Wyoming	86.4

RANK ORDER

RANK	STATE	PERCENT
1	Massachusetts	94.6
2	Hawaii	92.5
3	Wisconsin	91.8
4	Minnesota	91.7
5	Maine	91.2
6	Iowa	90.7
7	Connecticut	90.6
8	Pennsylvania	90.5
9	North Dakota	90.0
10	South Dakota	89.9
11	New Hampshire	89.5
12	Rhode Island	89.2
13	Delaware	88.8
13	Vermont	88.8
15	Washington	88.7
16	Indiana	88.6
17	Michigan	88.4
18	Ohio	88.3
19	Alabama	88.0
20	Missouri	87.4
21	Kansas	87.3
22	Utah	87.2
23	Nebraska	86.8
23	New York	86.8
25	Illinois	86.6
26	Kentucky	86.4
26	Wyoming	86.4
28	Maryland	86.3
29	Idaho	86.1
30	West Virginia	85.9
31	Tennessee	85.6
32	Virginia	85.2
33	Montana	84.4
34	New Jersey	84.2
35	Arkansas	83.9
36	Colorado	83.6
36	North Carolina	83.6
36	South Carolina	83.6
39	Oregon	83.2
40	Nevada	82.8
41	Georgia	82.5
42	Oklahoma	82.2
43	Alaska	81.8
43	California	81.8
45	Arizona	81.7
46	Louisiana	81.5
47	Mississippi	81.2
48	Florida	79.8
49	New Mexico	77.5
50	Texas	74.8

| | District of Columbia | 90.5 |

Source: U.S. Bureau of the Census
"Health Insurance Coverage Status by State for All People: 2007" (http://www.census.gov/hhes/www/hlthins/hlthin07.html)

Percent of Population Covered by Private Health Insurance in 2007

National Percent = 67.5% of Population*

ALPHA ORDER

RANK	STATE	PERCENT
27	Alabama	70.5
40	Alaska	63.4
44	Arizona	61.6
45	Arkansas	61.0
43	California	62.6
24	Colorado	71.5
6	Connecticut	76.3
18	Delaware	72.5
40	Florida	63.4
34	Georgia	66.5
11	Hawaii	75.0
20	Idaho	72.2
19	Illinois	72.3
16	Indiana	72.6
4	Iowa	78.1
22	Kansas	71.9
37	Kentucky	64.6
47	Louisiana	60.5
27	Maine	70.5
12	Maryland	74.6
10	Massachusetts	75.4
14	Michigan	73.2
1	Minnesota	79.9
49	Mississippi	56.6
29	Missouri	70.0
33	Montana	67.7
13	Nebraska	74.4
30	Nevada	69.9
2	New Hampshire	79.8
25	New Jersey	71.3
50	New Mexico	55.8
36	New York	64.9
39	North Carolina	64.1
3	North Dakota	78.2
15	Ohio	72.7
45	Oklahoma	61.0
31	Oregon	69.4
8	Pennsylvania	75.7
23	Rhode Island	71.6
35	South Carolina	65.0
7	South Dakota	76.0
42	Tennessee	63.1
48	Texas	56.9
9	Utah	75.6
26	Vermont	71.2
31	Virginia	69.4
20	Washington	72.2
38	West Virginia	64.4
5	Wisconsin	77.0
16	Wyoming	72.6

RANK ORDER

RANK	STATE	PERCENT
1	Minnesota	79.9
2	New Hampshire	79.8
3	North Dakota	78.2
4	Iowa	78.1
5	Wisconsin	77.0
6	Connecticut	76.3
7	South Dakota	76.0
8	Pennsylvania	75.7
9	Utah	75.6
10	Massachusetts	75.4
11	Hawaii	75.0
12	Maryland	74.6
13	Nebraska	74.4
14	Michigan	73.2
15	Ohio	72.7
16	Indiana	72.6
16	Wyoming	72.6
18	Delaware	72.5
19	Illinois	72.3
20	Idaho	72.2
20	Washington	72.2
22	Kansas	71.9
23	Rhode Island	71.6
24	Colorado	71.5
25	New Jersey	71.3
26	Vermont	71.2
27	Alabama	70.5
27	Maine	70.5
29	Missouri	70.0
30	Nevada	69.9
31	Oregon	69.4
31	Virginia	69.4
33	Montana	67.7
34	Georgia	66.5
35	South Carolina	65.0
36	New York	64.9
37	Kentucky	64.6
38	West Virginia	64.4
39	North Carolina	64.1
40	Alaska	63.4
40	Florida	63.4
42	Tennessee	63.1
43	California	62.6
44	Arizona	61.6
45	Arkansas	61.0
45	Oklahoma	61.0
47	Louisiana	60.5
48	Texas	56.9
49	Mississippi	56.6
50	New Mexico	55.8
	District of Columbia	67.7

Source: U.S. Bureau of the Census

"Health Insurance Coverage Status by State for All People: 2007" (http://www.census.gov/hhes/www/hlthins/hlthin07.html)

*Private health insurance is coverage by a health plan provided through an employer or union or purchased by an individual from a private health insurance company.

Percent of Population Covered by
Employment-Based Health Insurance in 2007
National Percent = 59.3% of Population*

<u>ALPHA ORDER</u>

RANK	STATE	PERCENT
20	Alabama	62.8
35	Alaska	58.4
40	Arizona	55.0
47	Arkansas	52.8
41	California	54.2
24	Colorado	61.7
4	Connecticut	68.0
7	Delaware	66.7
41	Florida	54.2
28	Georgia	60.4
2	Hawaii	70.3
31	Idaho	59.6
15	Illinois	64.1
11	Indiana	66.0
13	Iowa	65.0
32	Kansas	59.4
36	Kentucky	57.9
44	Louisiana	53.8
29	Maine	59.7
4	Maryland	68.0
7	Massachusetts	66.7
9	Michigan	66.3
3	Minnesota	68.4
49	Mississippi	49.2
27	Missouri	60.5
46	Montana	53.2
21	Nebraska	62.6
17	Nevada	63.8
1	New Hampshire	71.5
16	New Jersey	64.0
50	New Mexico	47.9
34	New York	58.6
39	North Carolina	55.7
25	North Dakota	61.2
12	Ohio	65.4
45	Oklahoma	53.5
37	Oregon	57.6
14	Pennsylvania	64.3
18	Rhode Island	63.4
38	South Carolina	57.2
29	South Dakota	59.7
41	Tennessee	54.2
48	Texas	50.4
10	Utah	66.2
19	Vermont	63.2
22	Virginia	61.9
23	Washington	61.8
33	West Virginia	58.8
6	Wisconsin	67.3
26	Wyoming	60.8

<u>RANK ORDER</u>

RANK	STATE	PERCENT
1	New Hampshire	71.5
2	Hawaii	70.3
3	Minnesota	68.4
4	Connecticut	68.0
4	Maryland	68.0
6	Wisconsin	67.3
7	Delaware	66.7
7	Massachusetts	66.7
9	Michigan	66.3
10	Utah	66.2
11	Indiana	66.0
12	Ohio	65.4
13	Iowa	65.0
14	Pennsylvania	64.3
15	Illinois	64.1
16	New Jersey	64.0
17	Nevada	63.8
18	Rhode Island	63.4
19	Vermont	63.2
20	Alabama	62.8
21	Nebraska	62.6
22	Virginia	61.9
23	Washington	61.8
24	Colorado	61.7
25	North Dakota	61.2
26	Wyoming	60.8
27	Missouri	60.5
28	Georgia	60.4
29	Maine	59.7
29	South Dakota	59.7
31	Idaho	59.6
32	Kansas	59.4
33	West Virginia	58.8
34	New York	58.6
35	Alaska	58.4
36	Kentucky	57.9
37	Oregon	57.6
38	South Carolina	57.2
39	North Carolina	55.7
40	Arizona	55.0
41	California	54.2
41	Florida	54.2
41	Tennessee	54.2
44	Louisiana	53.8
45	Oklahoma	53.5
46	Montana	53.2
47	Arkansas	52.8
48	Texas	50.4
49	Mississippi	49.2
50	New Mexico	47.9
	District of Columbia	60.4

Source: U.S. Bureau of the Census

"Health Insurance Coverage Status by State for All People: 2007" (http://www.census.gov/hhes/www/hlthins/hlthin07.html)

*Employment-based health insurance is private insurance coverage offered through one's own employment or a relative's. It may be offered by an employer or by a union.

Percent of Population Covered by Direct-Purchase Health Insurance in 2007

National Percent = 8.9% of Population*

ALPHA ORDER

RANK	STATE	PERCENT
24	Alabama	8.9
50	Alaska	5.3
42	Arizona	6.8
16	Arkansas	10.3
22	California	9.3
12	Colorado	11.6
21	Connecticut	9.4
43	Delaware	6.7
15	Florida	10.6
43	Georgia	6.7
47	Hawaii	6.3
5	Idaho	13.6
20	Illinois	9.9
37	Indiana	7.5
3	Iowa	14.2
6	Kansas	13.1
34	Kentucky	7.7
38	Louisiana	7.4
13	Maine	11.5
35	Maryland	7.6
28	Massachusetts	8.5
41	Michigan	7.1
8	Minnesota	12.0
24	Mississippi	8.9
16	Missouri	10.3
4	Montana	14.0
10	Nebraska	11.7
45	Nevada	6.4
26	New Hampshire	8.7
32	New Jersey	8.0
48	New Mexico	6.1
45	New York	6.4
30	North Carolina	8.3
2	North Dakota	17.0
33	Ohio	7.8
38	Oklahoma	7.4
7	Oregon	12.8
8	Pennsylvania	12.0
31	Rhode Island	8.2
27	South Carolina	8.6
1	South Dakota	17.7
22	Tennessee	9.3
40	Texas	7.2
19	Utah	10.0
28	Vermont	8.5
35	Virginia	7.6
14	Washington	11.3
49	West Virginia	5.8
18	Wisconsin	10.2
10	Wyoming	11.7

RANK ORDER

RANK	STATE	PERCENT
1	South Dakota	17.7
2	North Dakota	17.0
3	Iowa	14.2
4	Montana	14.0
5	Idaho	13.6
6	Kansas	13.1
7	Oregon	12.8
8	Minnesota	12.0
8	Pennsylvania	12.0
10	Nebraska	11.7
10	Wyoming	11.7
12	Colorado	11.6
13	Maine	11.5
14	Washington	11.3
15	Florida	10.6
16	Arkansas	10.3
16	Missouri	10.3
18	Wisconsin	10.2
19	Utah	10.0
20	Illinois	9.9
21	Connecticut	9.4
22	California	9.3
22	Tennessee	9.3
24	Alabama	8.9
24	Mississippi	8.9
26	New Hampshire	8.7
27	South Carolina	8.6
28	Massachusetts	8.5
28	Vermont	8.5
30	North Carolina	8.3
31	Rhode Island	8.2
32	New Jersey	8.0
33	Ohio	7.8
34	Kentucky	7.7
35	Maryland	7.6
35	Virginia	7.6
37	Indiana	7.5
38	Louisiana	7.4
38	Oklahoma	7.4
40	Texas	7.2
41	Michigan	7.1
42	Arizona	6.8
43	Delaware	6.7
43	Georgia	6.7
45	Nevada	6.4
45	New York	6.4
47	Hawaii	6.3
48	New Mexico	6.1
49	West Virginia	5.8
50	Alaska	5.3
	District of Columbia	8.1

Source: U.S. Bureau of the Census
"Health Insurance Coverage Status by State for All People: 2007" (http://www.census.gov/hhes/www/hlthins/hlthin07.html)
*Direct-purchase health insurance is private insurance coverage through a plan purchased by an individual from a private company.

Percent of Population Covered by Government Health Insurance in 2007

National Percent = 27.8% of Population*

ALPHA ORDER

RANK	STATE	PERCENT
18	Alabama	29.8
20	Alaska	29.3
15	Arizona	30.3
7	Arkansas	33.2
31	California	26.5
49	Colorado	20.3
37	Connecticut	25.8
27	Delaware	28.2
22	Florida	29.1
34	Georgia	26.2
9	Hawaii	32.7
39	Idaho	25.5
41	Illinois	25.0
35	Indiana	25.9
32	Iowa	26.4
25	Kansas	28.4
6	Kentucky	33.4
14	Louisiana	30.6
1	Maine	38.0
44	Maryland	24.1
12	Massachusetts	30.9
26	Michigan	28.3
43	Minnesota	24.4
2	Mississippi	35.1
23	Missouri	28.9
13	Montana	30.7
45	Nebraska	23.9
47	Nevada	20.7
48	New Hampshire	20.5
46	New Jersey	21.6
10	New Mexico	31.7
10	New York	31.7
16	North Carolina	30.2
42	North Dakota	24.9
33	Ohio	26.3
8	Oklahoma	32.9
39	Oregon	25.5
24	Pennsylvania	28.7
18	Rhode Island	29.8
17	South Carolina	29.9
29	South Dakota	28.1
5	Tennessee	33.7
38	Texas	25.7
50	Utah	18.8
4	Vermont	33.8
21	Virginia	29.2
27	Washington	28.2
3	West Virginia	34.8
35	Wisconsin	25.9
30	Wyoming	26.7

RANK ORDER

RANK	STATE	PERCENT
1	Maine	38.0
2	Mississippi	35.1
3	West Virginia	34.8
4	Vermont	33.8
5	Tennessee	33.7
6	Kentucky	33.4
7	Arkansas	33.2
8	Oklahoma	32.9
9	Hawaii	32.7
10	New Mexico	31.7
10	New York	31.7
12	Massachusetts	30.9
13	Montana	30.7
14	Louisiana	30.6
15	Arizona	30.3
16	North Carolina	30.2
17	South Carolina	29.9
18	Alabama	29.8
18	Rhode Island	29.8
20	Alaska	29.3
21	Virginia	29.2
22	Florida	29.1
23	Missouri	28.9
24	Pennsylvania	28.7
25	Kansas	28.4
26	Michigan	28.3
27	Delaware	28.2
27	Washington	28.2
29	South Dakota	28.1
30	Wyoming	26.7
31	California	26.5
32	Iowa	26.4
33	Ohio	26.3
34	Georgia	26.2
35	Indiana	25.9
35	Wisconsin	25.9
37	Connecticut	25.8
38	Texas	25.7
39	Idaho	25.5
39	Oregon	25.5
41	Illinois	25.0
42	North Dakota	24.9
43	Minnesota	24.4
44	Maryland	24.1
45	Nebraska	23.9
46	New Jersey	21.6
47	Nevada	20.7
48	New Hampshire	20.5
49	Colorado	20.3
50	Utah	18.8
	District of Columbia	31.6

Source: U.S. Bureau of the Census
"Health Insurance Coverage Status by State for All People: 2007" (http://www.census.gov/hhes/www/hlthins/hlthin07.html)
*Includes Medicaid, Medicare, State Children's Health Insurance Program (SCHIP) and military health care.

Percent of Population Covered by Military Health Care in 2007

National Percent = 3.7% of Population*

ALPHA ORDER

RANK	STATE	PERCENT
35	Alabama	3.2
1	Alaska	14.0
26	Arizona	4.0
14	Arkansas	5.2
42	California	2.3
23	Colorado	4.4
46	Connecticut	1.9
33	Delaware	3.3
16	Florida	4.9
18	Georgia	4.7
2	Hawaii	10.9
25	Idaho	4.1
46	Illinois	1.9
44	Indiana	2.2
32	Iowa	3.4
8	Kansas	6.2
26	Kentucky	4.0
36	Louisiana	3.1
9	Maine	6.1
18	Maryland	4.7
48	Massachusetts	1.3
38	Michigan	2.6
38	Minnesota	2.6
12	Mississippi	5.5
33	Missouri	3.3
13	Montana	5.4
18	Nebraska	4.7
28	Nevada	3.8
31	New Hampshire	3.7
48	New Jersey	1.3
11	New Mexico	6.0
50	New York	1.2
14	North Carolina	5.2
18	North Dakota	4.7
37	Ohio	3.0
4	Oklahoma	7.6
40	Oregon	2.5
45	Pennsylvania	2.0
28	Rhode Island	3.8
22	South Carolina	4.5
9	South Dakota	6.1
7	Tennessee	6.3
24	Texas	4.3
42	Utah	2.3
28	Vermont	3.8
3	Virginia	10.7
5	Washington	7.0
16	West Virginia	4.9
40	Wisconsin	2.5
6	Wyoming	6.5

RANK ORDER

RANK	STATE	PERCENT
1	Alaska	14.0
2	Hawaii	10.9
3	Virginia	10.7
4	Oklahoma	7.6
5	Washington	7.0
6	Wyoming	6.5
7	Tennessee	6.3
8	Kansas	6.2
9	Maine	6.1
9	South Dakota	6.1
11	New Mexico	6.0
12	Mississippi	5.5
13	Montana	5.4
14	Arkansas	5.2
14	North Carolina	5.2
16	Florida	4.9
16	West Virginia	4.9
18	Georgia	4.7
18	Maryland	4.7
18	Nebraska	4.7
18	North Dakota	4.7
22	South Carolina	4.5
23	Colorado	4.4
24	Texas	4.3
25	Idaho	4.1
26	Arizona	4.0
26	Kentucky	4.0
28	Nevada	3.8
28	Rhode Island	3.8
28	Vermont	3.8
31	New Hampshire	3.7
32	Iowa	3.4
33	Delaware	3.3
33	Missouri	3.3
35	Alabama	3.2
36	Louisiana	3.1
37	Ohio	3.0
38	Michigan	2.6
38	Minnesota	2.6
40	Oregon	2.5
40	Wisconsin	2.5
42	California	2.3
42	Utah	2.3
44	Indiana	2.2
45	Pennsylvania	2.0
46	Connecticut	1.9
46	Illinois	1.9
48	Massachusetts	1.3
48	New Jersey	1.3
50	New York	1.2
	District of Columbia	1.7

Source: U.S. Bureau of the Census
"Health Insurance Coverage Status by State for All People: 2007" (http://www.census.gov/hhes/www/hlthins/hlthin07.html)
*Includes CHAMPUS (Comprehensive Health and Medical Plan for Uniformed Services)/Tricare, Veterans, and military health care.

Percent of Children Covered by Health Insurance in 2007

National Percent = 89.0% of Children*

ALPHA ORDER

ALPHA ORDER

RANK	STATE	PERCENT		RANK	STATE	PERCENT
15	Alabama	92.7		1	Massachusetts	97.0
36	Alaska	88.6		2	West Virginia	95.4
45	Arizona	86.2		3	Hawaii	95.2
9	Arkansas	93.8		3	Iowa	95.2
34	California	89.3		5	Maine	94.9
44	Colorado	87.0		6	Connecticut	94.8
6	Connecticut	94.8		6	Indiana	94.8
17	Delaware	92.5		8	Wisconsin	94.2
49	Florida	80.8		9	Arkansas	93.8
37	Georgia	88.5		9	Michigan	93.8
3	Hawaii	95.2		11	Minnesota	93.6
35	Idaho	89.0		12	New Hampshire	93.5
13	Illinois	93.4		13	Illinois	93.4
6	Indiana	94.8		14	Washington	93.2
3	Iowa	95.2		15	Alabama	92.7
18	Kansas	92.3		16	Pennsylvania	92.6
20	Kentucky	92.0		17	Delaware	92.5
40	Louisiana	87.5		18	Kansas	92.3
5	Maine	94.9		19	North Dakota	92.1
32	Maryland	89.5		20	Kentucky	92.0
1	Massachusetts	97.0		20	South Dakota	92.0
9	Michigan	93.8		22	Ohio	91.4
11	Minnesota	93.6		23	Rhode Island	91.2
38	Mississippi	87.9		24	New York	91.1
30	Missouri	89.6		25	Tennessee	90.9
41	Montana	87.4		26	Vermont	90.6
28	Nebraska	90.0		27	Wyoming	90.4
47	Nevada	85.7		28	Nebraska	90.0
12	New Hampshire	93.5		29	Virginia	89.8
43	New Jersey	87.1		30	Missouri	89.6
48	New Mexico	84.5		30	Utah	89.6
24	New York	91.1		32	Maryland	89.5
38	North Carolina	87.9		33	Oregon	89.4
19	North Dakota	92.1		34	California	89.3
22	Ohio	91.4		35	Idaho	89.0
41	Oklahoma	87.4		36	Alaska	88.6
33	Oregon	89.4		37	Georgia	88.5
16	Pennsylvania	92.6		38	Mississippi	87.9
23	Rhode Island	91.2		38	North Carolina	87.9
46	South Carolina	85.8		40	Louisiana	87.5
20	South Dakota	92.0		41	Montana	87.4
25	Tennessee	90.9		41	Oklahoma	87.4
50	Texas	78.6		43	New Jersey	87.1
30	Utah	89.6		44	Colorado	87.0
26	Vermont	90.6		45	Arizona	86.2
29	Virginia	89.8		46	South Carolina	85.8
14	Washington	93.2		47	Nevada	85.7
2	West Virginia	95.4		48	New Mexico	84.5
8	Wisconsin	94.2		49	Florida	80.8
27	Wyoming	90.4		50	Texas	78.6
					District of Columbia	93.8

Source: U.S. Bureau of the Census
    "Health Insurance Coverage Status by State for All People: 2007" (http://www.census.gov/hhes/www/hlthins/hlthin07.html)
*Children under 18 covered by either private or government health insurance.

Percent of Children Covered by Private Health Insurance in 2007

National Percent = 64.2% of Children*

ALPHA ORDER

ALPHA ORDER

RANK ORDER

RANK	STATE	PERCENT		RANK	STATE	PERCENT
28	Alabama	67.3		1	New Hampshire	81.7
32	Alaska	64.0		2	Minnesota	78.3
39	Arizona	60.3		3	Iowa	76.9
47	Arkansas	51.5		4	Connecticut	76.0
41	California	60.0		5	Utah	75.3
16	Colorado	71.3		6	Wisconsin	74.8
4	Connecticut	76.0		7	Pennsylvania	74.0
21	Delaware	69.8		8	New Jersey	72.9
36	Florida	61.6		9	South Dakota	72.5
37	Georgia	61.4		10	North Dakota	72.4
20	Hawaii	70.2		11	Maryland	72.1
17	Idaho	71.1		11	Nevada	72.1
22	Illinois	69.7		13	Nebraska	72.0
19	Indiana	70.3		14	Massachusetts	71.6
3	Iowa	76.9		14	Wyoming	71.6
27	Kansas	67.8		16	Colorado	71.3
33	Kentucky	63.4		17	Idaho	71.1
45	Louisiana	57.5		18	Washington	70.8
29	Maine	67.0		19	Indiana	70.3
11	Maryland	72.1		20	Hawaii	70.2
14	Massachusetts	71.6		21	Delaware	69.8
25	Michigan	69.2		22	Illinois	69.7
2	Minnesota	78.3		23	Rhode Island	69.6
50	Mississippi	47.0		24	Ohio	69.3
34	Missouri	62.9		25	Michigan	69.2
42	Montana	59.0		26	Oregon	68.1
13	Nebraska	72.0		27	Kansas	67.8
11	Nevada	72.1		28	Alabama	67.3
1	New Hampshire	81.7		29	Maine	67.0
8	New Jersey	72.9		30	Vermont	66.5
49	New Mexico	49.5		31	Virginia	65.1
35	New York	62.3		32	Alaska	64.0
44	North Carolina	58.0		33	Kentucky	63.4
10	North Dakota	72.4		34	Missouri	62.9
24	Ohio	69.3		35	New York	62.3
46	Oklahoma	56.1		36	Florida	61.6
26	Oregon	68.1		37	Georgia	61.4
7	Pennsylvania	74.0		38	South Carolina	60.8
23	Rhode Island	69.6		39	Arizona	60.3
38	South Carolina	60.8		39	West Virginia	60.3
9	South Dakota	72.5		41	California	60.0
43	Tennessee	58.3		42	Montana	59.0
48	Texas	51.1		43	Tennessee	58.3
5	Utah	75.3		44	North Carolina	58.0
30	Vermont	66.5		45	Louisiana	57.5
31	Virginia	65.1		46	Oklahoma	56.1
18	Washington	70.8		47	Arkansas	51.5
39	West Virginia	60.3		48	Texas	51.1
6	Wisconsin	74.8		49	New Mexico	49.5
14	Wyoming	71.6		50	Mississippi	47.0
					District of Columbia	56.1

Source: U.S. Bureau of the Census

"Health Insurance Coverage Status by State for All People: 2007" (http://www.census.gov/hhes/www/hlthins/hlthin07.html)
*Children under 18. Private health insurance is coverage by a health plan provided through an employer or union or purchased by an individual from a private health insurance company.

Percent of Children Covered by Employment-Based Health Insurance in 2007

National Percent = 59.5% of Children*

ALPHA ORDER

RANK	STATE	PERCENT
21	Alabama	64.7
34	Alaska	59.0
40	Arizona	55.7
47	Arkansas	47.6
41	California	53.9
23	Colorado	64.5
3	Connecticut	71.6
15	Delaware	66.3
39	Florida	56.0
35	Georgia	58.3
13	Hawaii	66.9
19	Idaho	65.1
17	Illinois	65.9
12	Indiana	67.0
5	Iowa	70.3
28	Kansas	61.5
33	Kentucky	59.1
46	Louisiana	51.7
29	Maine	61.1
11	Maryland	67.1
7	Massachusetts	68.9
24	Michigan	64.1
2	Minnesota	72.8
50	Mississippi	42.8
37	Missouri	57.9
45	Montana	52.1
15	Nebraska	66.3
10	Nevada	67.7
1	New Hampshire	76.7
8	New Jersey	68.3
49	New Mexico	45.2
32	New York	59.4
43	North Carolina	53.0
22	North Dakota	64.6
18	Ohio	65.2
44	Oklahoma	52.5
31	Oregon	60.7
6	Pennsylvania	69.0
14	Rhode Island	66.6
38	South Carolina	57.2
27	South Dakota	62.5
42	Tennessee	53.3
48	Texas	47.2
9	Utah	67.8
26	Vermont	62.6
29	Virginia	61.1
20	Washington	64.9
36	West Virginia	58.1
4	Wisconsin	70.7
25	Wyoming	63.0

RANK ORDER

RANK	STATE	PERCENT
1	New Hampshire	76.7
2	Minnesota	72.8
3	Connecticut	71.6
4	Wisconsin	70.7
5	Iowa	70.3
6	Pennsylvania	69.0
7	Massachusetts	68.9
8	New Jersey	68.3
9	Utah	67.8
10	Nevada	67.7
11	Maryland	67.1
12	Indiana	67.0
13	Hawaii	66.9
14	Rhode Island	66.6
15	Delaware	66.3
15	Nebraska	66.3
17	Illinois	65.9
18	Ohio	65.2
19	Idaho	65.1
20	Washington	64.9
21	Alabama	64.7
22	North Dakota	64.6
23	Colorado	64.5
24	Michigan	64.1
25	Wyoming	63.0
26	Vermont	62.6
27	South Dakota	62.5
28	Kansas	61.5
29	Maine	61.1
29	Virginia	61.1
31	Oregon	60.7
32	New York	59.4
33	Kentucky	59.1
34	Alaska	59.0
35	Georgia	58.3
36	West Virginia	58.1
37	Missouri	57.9
38	South Carolina	57.2
39	Florida	56.0
40	Arizona	55.7
41	California	53.9
42	Tennessee	53.3
43	North Carolina	53.0
44	Oklahoma	52.5
45	Montana	52.1
46	Louisiana	51.7
47	Arkansas	47.6
48	Texas	47.2
49	New Mexico	45.2
50	Mississippi	42.8
	District of Columbia	52.6

Source: U.S. Bureau of the Census
    "Health Insurance Coverage Status by State for All People: 2007" (http://www.census.gov/hhes/www/hlthins/hlthin07.html)
*Children under 18. Employment-based health insurance is private insurance coverage offered through one's own employment or a relative's. It may be offered by an employer or by a union.

Percent of Children Covered by Direct-Purchase Health Insurance in 2007

National Percent = 5.3% of Children*

ALPHA ORDER

RANK	STATE	PERCENT
33	Alabama	4.5
33	Alaska	4.5
28	Arizona	4.7
12	Arkansas	6.5
7	California	7.4
2	Colorado	8.7
16	Connecticut	5.9
31	Delaware	4.6
11	Florida	6.6
42	Georgia	3.6
42	Hawaii	3.6
6	Idaho	7.6
23	Illinois	5.0
45	Indiana	3.2
14	Iowa	6.3
15	Kansas	6.1
37	Kentucky	4.2
8	Louisiana	7.2
26	Maine	4.8
24	Maryland	4.9
40	Massachusetts	3.9
26	Michigan	4.8
17	Minnesota	5.8
37	Mississippi	4.2
21	Missouri	5.1
9	Montana	7.1
36	Nebraska	4.4
31	Nevada	4.6
33	New Hampshire	4.5
20	New Jersey	5.2
46	New Mexico	3.1
50	New York	2.4
28	North Carolina	4.7
5	North Dakota	8.0
41	Ohio	3.7
48	Oklahoma	2.8
4	Oregon	8.1
19	Pennsylvania	5.3
44	Rhode Island	3.5
24	South Carolina	4.9
1	South Dakota	12.1
28	Tennessee	4.7
21	Texas	5.1
3	Utah	8.4
48	Vermont	2.8
37	Virginia	4.2
10	Washington	6.8
46	West Virginia	3.1
18	Wisconsin	5.4
12	Wyoming	6.5

RANK ORDER

RANK	STATE	PERCENT
1	South Dakota	12.1
2	Colorado	8.7
3	Utah	8.4
4	Oregon	8.1
5	North Dakota	8.0
6	Idaho	7.6
7	California	7.4
8	Louisiana	7.2
9	Montana	7.1
10	Washington	6.8
11	Florida	6.6
12	Arkansas	6.5
12	Wyoming	6.5
14	Iowa	6.3
15	Kansas	6.1
16	Connecticut	5.9
17	Minnesota	5.8
18	Wisconsin	5.4
19	Pennsylvania	5.3
20	New Jersey	5.2
21	Missouri	5.1
21	Texas	5.1
23	Illinois	5.0
24	Maryland	4.9
24	South Carolina	4.9
26	Maine	4.8
26	Michigan	4.8
28	Arizona	4.7
28	North Carolina	4.7
28	Tennessee	4.7
31	Delaware	4.6
31	Nevada	4.6
33	Alabama	4.5
33	Alaska	4.5
33	New Hampshire	4.5
36	Nebraska	4.4
37	Kentucky	4.2
37	Mississippi	4.2
37	Virginia	4.2
40	Massachusetts	3.9
41	Ohio	3.7
42	Georgia	3.6
42	Hawaii	3.6
44	Rhode Island	3.5
45	Indiana	3.2
46	New Mexico	3.1
46	West Virginia	3.1
48	Oklahoma	2.8
48	Vermont	2.8
50	New York	2.4
	District of Columbia	3.6

Source: U.S. Bureau of the Census

"Health Insurance Coverage Status by State for All People: 2007" (http://www.census.gov/hhes/www/hlthins/hlthin07.html)

*Children under 18. Direct-purchase health insurance is private insurance coverage through a plan purchased by an individual from a private company.

Percent of Children Covered by Government Health Insurance in 2007

National Percent = 31.0% of Children*

ALPHA ORDER

RANK	STATE	PERCENT
23	Alabama	30.7
11	Alaska	36.0
18	Arizona	32.9
2	Arkansas	48.6
16	California	34.1
47	Colorado	19.1
41	Connecticut	25.3
33	Delaware	28.2
36	Florida	26.8
13	Georgia	35.4
10	Hawaii	37.1
43	Idaho	24.1
26	Illinois	30.6
26	Indiana	30.6
34	Iowa	27.1
21	Kansas	32.2
12	Kentucky	35.8
8	Louisiana	38.8
6	Maine	40.4
43	Maryland	24.1
29	Massachusetts	29.7
23	Michigan	30.7
45	Minnesota	22.0
1	Mississippi	49.2
20	Missouri	32.4
14	Montana	35.3
41	Nebraska	25.3
50	Nevada	16.3
48	New Hampshire	17.8
49	New Jersey	16.7
3	New Mexico	42.3
17	New York	33.7
15	North Carolina	34.3
40	North Dakota	25.5
32	Ohio	28.8
4	Oklahoma	40.8
39	Oregon	25.6
38	Pennsylvania	26.0
28	Rhode Island	29.9
23	South Carolina	30.7
36	South Dakota	26.8
7	Tennessee	39.3
21	Texas	32.2
46	Utah	19.2
9	Vermont	38.1
19	Virginia	32.5
29	Washington	29.7
5	West Virginia	40.7
34	Wisconsin	27.1
31	Wyoming	28.9

RANK ORDER

RANK	STATE	PERCENT
1	Mississippi	49.2
2	Arkansas	48.6
3	New Mexico	42.3
4	Oklahoma	40.8
5	West Virginia	40.7
6	Maine	40.4
7	Tennessee	39.3
8	Louisiana	38.8
9	Vermont	38.1
10	Hawaii	37.1
11	Alaska	36.0
12	Kentucky	35.8
13	Georgia	35.4
14	Montana	35.3
15	North Carolina	34.3
16	California	34.1
17	New York	33.7
18	Arizona	32.9
19	Virginia	32.5
20	Missouri	32.4
21	Kansas	32.2
21	Texas	32.2
23	Alabama	30.7
23	Michigan	30.7
23	South Carolina	30.7
26	Illinois	30.6
26	Indiana	30.6
28	Rhode Island	29.9
29	Massachusetts	29.7
29	Washington	29.7
31	Wyoming	28.9
32	Ohio	28.8
33	Delaware	28.2
34	Iowa	27.1
34	Wisconsin	27.1
36	Florida	26.8
36	South Dakota	26.8
38	Pennsylvania	26.0
39	Oregon	25.6
40	North Dakota	25.5
41	Connecticut	25.3
41	Nebraska	25.3
43	Idaho	24.1
43	Maryland	24.1
45	Minnesota	22.0
46	Utah	19.2
47	Colorado	19.1
48	New Hampshire	17.8
49	New Jersey	16.7
50	Nevada	16.3
	District of Columbia	41.0

Source: U.S. Bureau of the Census
     "Health Insurance Coverage Status by State for All People: 2007" (http://www.census.gov/hhes/www/hlthins/hlthin07.html)
*Children under 18. Includes Medicaid, Medicare, State Children's Health Insurance Program (SCHIP) and military health care.

Percent of Children Covered by Military Health Care in 2007

National Percent = 2.8% of Children*

ALPHA ORDER

RANK	STATE	PERCENT
38	Alabama	1.8
1	Alaska	14.5
24	Arizona	3.0
29	Arkansas	2.7
38	California	1.8
19	Colorado	3.4
35	Connecticut	1.9
29	Delaware	2.7
22	Florida	3.3
15	Georgia	3.9
2	Hawaii	13.0
19	Idaho	3.4
41	Illinois	1.6
38	Indiana	1.8
35	Iowa	1.9
9	Kansas	5.2
23	Kentucky	3.1
35	Louisiana	1.9
8	Maine	5.3
12	Maryland	4.5
50	Massachusetts	0.2
31	Michigan	2.2
43	Minnesota	1.3
10	Mississippi	4.7
45	Missouri	0.9
28	Montana	2.8
15	Nebraska	3.9
32	Nevada	2.1
24	New Hampshire	3.0
47	New Jersey	0.7
14	New Mexico	4.0
49	New York	0.3
11	North Carolina	4.6
13	North Dakota	4.2
32	Ohio	2.1
4	Oklahoma	8.1
44	Oregon	1.2
46	Pennsylvania	0.8
26	Rhode Island	2.9
32	South Carolina	2.1
15	South Dakota	3.9
5	Tennessee	6.9
26	Texas	2.9
48	Utah	0.6
19	Vermont	3.4
3	Virginia	11.9
5	Washington	6.9
15	West Virginia	3.9
41	Wisconsin	1.6
5	Wyoming	6.9

RANK ORDER

RANK	STATE	PERCENT
1	Alaska	14.5
2	Hawaii	13.0
3	Virginia	11.9
4	Oklahoma	8.1
5	Tennessee	6.9
5	Washington	6.9
5	Wyoming	6.9
8	Maine	5.3
9	Kansas	5.2
10	Mississippi	4.7
11	North Carolina	4.6
12	Maryland	4.5
13	North Dakota	4.2
14	New Mexico	4.0
15	Georgia	3.9
15	Nebraska	3.9
15	South Dakota	3.9
15	West Virginia	3.9
19	Colorado	3.4
19	Idaho	3.4
19	Vermont	3.4
22	Florida	3.3
23	Kentucky	3.1
24	Arizona	3.0
24	New Hampshire	3.0
26	Rhode Island	2.9
26	Texas	2.9
28	Montana	2.8
29	Arkansas	2.7
29	Delaware	2.7
31	Michigan	2.2
32	Nevada	2.1
32	Ohio	2.1
32	South Carolina	2.1
35	Connecticut	1.9
35	Iowa	1.9
35	Louisiana	1.9
38	Alabama	1.8
38	California	1.8
38	Indiana	1.8
41	Illinois	1.6
41	Wisconsin	1.6
43	Minnesota	1.3
44	Oregon	1.2
45	Missouri	0.9
46	Pennsylvania	0.8
47	New Jersey	0.7
48	Utah	0.6
49	New York	0.3
50	Massachusetts	0.2
	District of Columbia	1.3

Source: U.S. Bureau of the Census
   "Health Insurance Coverage Status by State for All People: 2007" (http://www.census.gov/hhes/www/hlthins/hlthin07.html)
*Children under 18. Includes CHAMPUS (Comprehensive Health and Medical Plan for Uniformed Services)/Tricare, Veterans, and military health care.

Percent of Children Covered by Medicaid in 2007

National Percent = 28.1% of Children*

ALPHA ORDER

RANK	STATE	PERCENT
22	Alabama	28.7
36	Alaska	23.3
16	Arizona	30.5
1	Arkansas	47.1
13	California	32.0
48	Colorado	15.3
35	Connecticut	23.4
29	Delaware	25.4
38	Florida	23.2
15	Georgia	30.6
32	Hawaii	24.7
41	Idaho	20.9
23	Illinois	28.4
19	Indiana	29.3
31	Iowa	24.8
25	Kansas	28.1
12	Kentucky	32.8
5	Louisiana	37.1
7	Maine	35.6
45	Maryland	20.2
18	Massachusetts	29.5
20	Michigan	28.9
44	Minnesota	20.6
2	Mississippi	43.9
14	Missouri	31.2
9	Montana	33.2
40	Nebraska	21.6
50	Nevada	14.5
48	New Hampshire	15.3
47	New Jersey	15.8
3	New Mexico	38.2
8	New York	33.3
17	North Carolina	30.1
39	North Dakota	21.8
27	Ohio	26.7
10	Oklahoma	33.0
33	Oregon	24.4
30	Pennsylvania	24.9
26	Rhode Island	27.1
23	South Carolina	28.4
41	South Dakota	20.9
11	Tennessee	32.9
21	Texas	28.8
46	Utah	18.4
6	Vermont	35.8
41	Virginia	20.9
34	Washington	23.6
4	West Virginia	37.3
28	Wisconsin	25.8
36	Wyoming	23.3

RANK ORDER

RANK	STATE	PERCENT
1	Arkansas	47.1
2	Mississippi	43.9
3	New Mexico	38.2
4	West Virginia	37.3
5	Louisiana	37.1
6	Vermont	35.8
7	Maine	35.6
8	New York	33.3
9	Montana	33.2
10	Oklahoma	33.0
11	Tennessee	32.9
12	Kentucky	32.8
13	California	32.0
14	Missouri	31.2
15	Georgia	30.6
16	Arizona	30.5
17	North Carolina	30.1
18	Massachusetts	29.5
19	Indiana	29.3
20	Michigan	28.9
21	Texas	28.8
22	Alabama	28.7
23	Illinois	28.4
23	South Carolina	28.4
25	Kansas	28.1
26	Rhode Island	27.1
27	Ohio	26.7
28	Wisconsin	25.8
29	Delaware	25.4
30	Pennsylvania	24.9
31	Iowa	24.8
32	Hawaii	24.7
33	Oregon	24.4
34	Washington	23.6
35	Connecticut	23.4
36	Alaska	23.3
36	Wyoming	23.3
38	Florida	23.2
39	North Dakota	21.8
40	Nebraska	21.6
41	Idaho	20.9
41	South Dakota	20.9
41	Virginia	20.9
44	Minnesota	20.6
45	Maryland	20.2
46	Utah	18.4
47	New Jersey	15.8
48	Colorado	15.3
48	New Hampshire	15.3
50	Nevada	14.5

	District of Columbia	40.0

Source: U.S. Bureau of the Census
   "Health Insurance Coverage Status by State for All People: 2007" (http://www.census.gov/hhes/www/hlthins/hlthin07.html)
*Children under 18 years old. Medicaid is a form of government insurance.

State Children's Health Insurance Program (SCHIP) Enrollment in 2007

National Total = 7,144,794 Children*

ALPHA ORDER

RANK	STATE	ENROLLMENT	% of USA
18	Alabama	106,691	1.5%
41	Alaska	17,558	0.2%
19	Arizona	104,209	1.5%
20	Arkansas	89,642	1.3%
1	California	1,538,416	21.5%
21	Colorado	84,649	1.2%
39	Connecticut	23,632	0.3%
46	Delaware	11,143	0.2%
6	Florida	323,529	4.5%
4	Georgia	356,285	5.0%
38	Hawaii	23,958	0.3%
35	Idaho	33,060	0.5%
5	Illinois	345,576	4.8%
15	Indiana	130,368	1.8%
28	Iowa	50,238	0.7%
29	Kansas	49,536	0.7%
24	Kentucky	68,776	1.0%
11	Louisiana	153,663	2.2%
36	Maine	31,037	0.4%
14	Maryland	132,887	1.9%
10	Massachusetts	184,483	2.6%
17	Michigan	114,025	1.6%
50	Minnesota	5,408	0.1%
23	Mississippi	81,565	1.1%
22	Missouri	81,764	1.1%
40	Montana	20,115	0.3%
30	Nebraska	46,199	0.6%
32	Nevada	41,862	0.6%
45	New Hampshire	12,088	0.2%
12	New Jersey	150,277	2.1%
42	New Mexico	16,525	0.2%
3	New York	651,853	9.1%
7	North Carolina	240,152	3.4%
49	North Dakota	5,469	0.1%
8	Ohio	231,538	3.2%
16	Oklahoma	117,084	1.6%
25	Oregon	63,090	0.9%
9	Pennsylvania	227,367	3.2%
37	Rhode Island	26,067	0.4%
27	South Carolina	59,920	0.8%
43	South Dakota	14,982	0.2%
33	Tennessee	41,363	0.6%
2	Texas	710,690	9.9%
31	Utah	44,785	0.6%
48	Vermont	6,132	0.1%
13	Virginia	144,163	2.0%
44	Washington	14,734	0.2%
34	West Virginia	38,582	0.5%
26	Wisconsin	62,523	0.9%
47	Wyoming	8,570	0.1%

RANK ORDER

RANK	STATE	ENROLLMENT	% of USA
1	California	1,538,416	21.5%
2	Texas	710,690	9.9%
3	New York	651,853	9.1%
4	Georgia	356,285	5.0%
5	Illinois	345,576	4.8%
6	Florida	323,529	4.5%
7	North Carolina	240,152	3.4%
8	Ohio	231,538	3.2%
9	Pennsylvania	227,367	3.2%
10	Massachusetts	184,483	2.6%
11	Louisiana	153,663	2.2%
12	New Jersey	150,277	2.1%
13	Virginia	144,163	2.0%
14	Maryland	132,887	1.9%
15	Indiana	130,368	1.8%
16	Oklahoma	117,084	1.6%
17	Michigan	114,025	1.6%
18	Alabama	106,691	1.5%
19	Arizona	104,209	1.5%
20	Arkansas	89,642	1.3%
21	Colorado	84,649	1.2%
22	Missouri	81,764	1.1%
23	Mississippi	81,565	1.1%
24	Kentucky	68,776	1.0%
25	Oregon	63,090	0.9%
26	Wisconsin	62,523	0.9%
27	South Carolina	59,920	0.8%
28	Iowa	50,238	0.7%
29	Kansas	49,536	0.7%
30	Nebraska	46,199	0.6%
31	Utah	44,785	0.6%
32	Nevada	41,862	0.6%
33	Tennessee	41,363	0.6%
34	West Virginia	38,582	0.5%
35	Idaho	33,060	0.5%
36	Maine	31,037	0.4%
37	Rhode Island	26,067	0.4%
38	Hawaii	23,958	0.3%
39	Connecticut	23,632	0.3%
40	Montana	20,115	0.3%
41	Alaska	17,558	0.2%
42	New Mexico	16,525	0.2%
43	South Dakota	14,982	0.2%
44	Washington	14,734	0.2%
45	New Hampshire	12,088	0.2%
46	Delaware	11,143	0.2%
47	Wyoming	8,570	0.1%
48	Vermont	6,132	0.1%
49	North Dakota	5,469	0.1%
50	Minnesota	5,408	0.1%
	District of Columbia	6,566	0.1%

Source: U.S. Department of Health and Human Services, Centers for Medicare and Medicaid Services
"Children's Health Insurance Program Annual Enrollment Report" (http://www.cms.hhs.gov/NationalSCHIPPolicy/)
*Figures for fiscal year 2007. The State Children's Health Insurance Program (SCHIP) was created in 1997 to help states expand health insurance to children whose families earn too much to qualify for Medicaid, yet not enough to afford private health insurance.

Percent Change in State Children's Health Insurance Program (SCHIP) Enrollment: 2006 to 2007
National Percent Change = 5.9% Increase*

ALPHA ORDER

RANK	STATE	PERCENT CHANGE
2	Alabama	26.6
47	Alaska	(14.1)
13	Arizona	7.8
31	Arkansas	0.5
8	California	10.6
4	Colorado	20.9
26	Connecticut	1.4
22	Delaware	3.6
15	Florida	6.6
21	Georgia	3.7
11	Hawaii	8.7
1	Idaho	33.7
10	Illinois	9.1
36	Indiana	(2.5)
27	Iowa	1.3
28	Kansas	1.2
17	Kentucky	5.3
12	Louisiana	7.9
32	Maine	(0.2)
35	Maryland	(2.3)
43	Massachusetts	(8.2)
40	Michigan	(3.8)
28	Minnesota	1.2
34	Mississippi	(2.2)
48	Missouri	(23.3)
6	Montana	16.2
23	Nebraska	2.7
16	Nevada	6.5
36	New Hampshire	(2.5)
18	New Jersey	5.2
49	New Mexico	(34.3)
41	New York	(5.3)
39	North Carolina	(3.3)
45	North Dakota	(13.4)
20	Ohio	4.5
30	Oklahoma	0.9
14	Oregon	6.9
5	Pennsylvania	20.4
25	Rhode Island	2.3
44	South Carolina	(13.0)
23	South Dakota	2.7
NA	Tennessee**	NA
3	Texas	21.4
46	Utah	(13.8)
42	Vermont	(5.9)
19	Virginia	5.1
33	Washington	(1.8)
38	West Virginia	(3.2)
9	Wisconsin	9.6
7	Wyoming	11.1

RANK ORDER

RANK	STATE	PERCENT CHANGE
1	Idaho	33.7
2	Alabama	26.6
3	Texas	21.4
4	Colorado	20.9
5	Pennsylvania	20.4
6	Montana	16.2
7	Wyoming	11.1
8	California	10.6
9	Wisconsin	9.6
10	Illinois	9.1
11	Hawaii	8.7
12	Louisiana	7.9
13	Arizona	7.8
14	Oregon	6.9
15	Florida	6.6
16	Nevada	6.5
17	Kentucky	5.3
18	New Jersey	5.2
19	Virginia	5.1
20	Ohio	4.5
21	Georgia	3.7
22	Delaware	3.6
23	Nebraska	2.7
23	South Dakota	2.7
25	Rhode Island	2.3
26	Connecticut	1.4
27	Iowa	1.3
28	Kansas	1.2
28	Minnesota	1.2
30	Oklahoma	0.9
31	Arkansas	0.5
32	Maine	(0.2)
33	Washington	(1.8)
34	Mississippi	(2.2)
35	Maryland	(2.3)
36	Indiana	(2.5)
36	New Hampshire	(2.5)
38	West Virginia	(3.2)
39	North Carolina	(3.3)
40	Michigan	(3.8)
41	New York	(5.3)
42	Vermont	(5.9)
43	Massachusetts	(8.2)
44	South Carolina	(13.0)
45	North Dakota	(13.4)
46	Utah	(13.8)
47	Alaska	(14.1)
48	Missouri	(23.3)
49	New Mexico	(34.3)
NA	Tennessee**	NA

District of Columbia   3.7

Source: CQ Press using data from U.S. Department of Health and Human Services, Centers for Medicare and Medicaid Services "Children's Health Insurance Program Annual Enrollment Report" (http://www.cms.hhs.gov/NationalSCHIPPolicy/)
*Figures for fiscal years. The State Children's Health Insurance Program (SCHIP) was created in 1997 to help states expand health insurance to children whose families earn too much to qualify for Medicaid, yet not enough to afford private health insurance.
**Not available.

Percent of Children Enrolled in State Children's
Health Insurance Program (SCHIP) in 2007
National Percent = 9.7% of Children 17 Years and Younger*

ALPHA ORDER

RANK	STATE	PERCENT
18	Alabama	9.5
17	Alaska	9.6
36	Arizona	6.2
7	Arkansas	12.8
1	California	16.4
30	Colorado	7.1
47	Connecticut	2.9
40	Delaware	5.4
25	Florida	8.0
4	Georgia	14.1
20	Hawaii	8.4
24	Idaho	8.1
10	Illinois	10.8
22	Indiana	8.2
30	Iowa	7.1
30	Kansas	7.1
33	Kentucky	6.9
3	Louisiana	14.2
9	Maine	11.1
16	Maryland	9.8
6	Massachusetts	12.9
41	Michigan	4.7
50	Minnesota	0.4
13	Mississippi	10.6
37	Missouri	5.7
19	Montana	9.2
14	Nebraska	10.4
35	Nevada	6.3
44	New Hampshire	4.1
28	New Jersey	7.3
46	New Mexico	3.3
2	New York	14.8
10	North Carolina	10.8
45	North Dakota	3.8
20	Ohio	8.4
5	Oklahoma	13.0
28	Oregon	7.3
22	Pennsylvania	8.2
8	Rhode Island	11.2
37	South Carolina	5.7
27	South Dakota	7.6
48	Tennessee	2.8
12	Texas	10.7
39	Utah	5.5
41	Vermont	4.7
26	Virginia	7.9
49	Washington	1.0
15	West Virginia	10.0
41	Wisconsin	4.7
34	Wyoming	6.8

RANK ORDER

RANK	STATE	PERCENT
1	California	16.4
2	New York	14.8
3	Louisiana	14.2
4	Georgia	14.1
5	Oklahoma	13.0
6	Massachusetts	12.9
7	Arkansas	12.8
8	Rhode Island	11.2
9	Maine	11.1
10	Illinois	10.8
10	North Carolina	10.8
12	Texas	10.7
13	Mississippi	10.6
14	Nebraska	10.4
15	West Virginia	10.0
16	Maryland	9.8
17	Alaska	9.6
18	Alabama	9.5
19	Montana	9.2
20	Hawaii	8.4
20	Ohio	8.4
22	Indiana	8.2
22	Pennsylvania	8.2
24	Idaho	8.1
25	Florida	8.0
26	Virginia	7.9
27	South Dakota	7.6
28	New Jersey	7.3
28	Oregon	7.3
30	Colorado	7.1
30	Iowa	7.1
30	Kansas	7.1
33	Kentucky	6.9
34	Wyoming	6.8
35	Nevada	6.3
36	Arizona	6.2
37	Missouri	5.7
37	South Carolina	5.7
39	Utah	5.5
40	Delaware	5.4
41	Michigan	4.7
41	Vermont	4.7
41	Wisconsin	4.7
44	New Hampshire	4.1
45	North Dakota	3.8
46	New Mexico	3.3
47	Connecticut	2.9
48	Tennessee	2.8
49	Washington	1.0
50	Minnesota	0.4

District of Columbia   5.8

Source: CQ Press using data from U.S. Department of Health and Human Services, Centers for Medicare and Medicaid Services
"Children's Health Insurance Program Annual Enrollment Report" (http://www.cms.hhs.gov/NationalSCHIPPolicy/)
*Figures for fiscal year 2007. The State Children's Health Insurance Program (SCHIP) was created in 1997 to help states expand
health insurance to children whose families earn too much to qualify for Medicaid, yet not enough to afford private health
insurance. Calculated using 2007 Census estimates for 17 and younger for reporting states.

Expenditures for State Children's Health Insurance Program (SCHIP) in 2007

National Total = $5,931,570,000*

ALPHA ORDER

RANK	STATE	EXPENDITURES	% of USA
19	Alabama	$95,200,000	1.6%
43	Alaska	16,200,000	0.3%
15	Arizona	117,700,000	2.0%
24	Arkansas	68,800,000	1.2%
1	California	980,700,000	16.5%
26	Colorado	65,900,000	1.1%
39	Connecticut	30,100,000	0.5%
47	Delaware	8,600,000	0.1%
7	Florida	261,700,000	4.4%
4	Georgia	328,100,000	5.5%
41	Hawaii	18,700,000	0.3%
40	Idaho	27,400,000	0.5%
2	Illinois	448,500,000	7.6%
20	Indiana	92,100,000	1.6%
28	Iowa	51,300,000	0.9%
31	Kansas	45,100,000	0.8%
22	Kentucky	81,200,000	1.4%
14	Louisiana	119,900,000	2.0%
37	Maine	31,200,000	0.5%
13	Maryland	138,400,000	2.3%
8	Massachusetts	211,500,000	3.6%
11	Michigan	171,600,000	2.9%
27	Minnesota	64,400,000	1.1%
17	Mississippi	107,500,000	1.8%
23	Missouri	79,400,000	1.3%
42	Montana	18,200,000	0.3%
35	Nebraska	33,200,000	0.6%
38	Nevada	30,300,000	0.5%
44	New Hampshire	11,100,000	0.2%
6	New Jersey	280,000,000	4.7%
29	New Mexico	49,900,000	0.8%
5	New York	324,400,000	5.5%
12	North Carolina	166,600,000	2.8%
45	North Dakota	10,500,000	0.2%
10	Ohio	186,900,000	3.2%
18	Oklahoma	96,400,000	1.6%
25	Oregon	66,600,000	1.1%
9	Pennsylvania	190,000,000	3.2%
30	Rhode Island	47,700,000	0.8%
36	South Carolina	31,400,000	0.5%
46	South Dakota	9,800,000	0.2%
50	Tennessee	4,100,000	0.1%
3	Texas	385,700,000	6.5%
32	Utah	38,900,000	0.7%
49	Vermont	5,900,000	0.1%
16	Virginia	110,700,000	1.9%
33	Washington	36,800,000	0.6%
34	West Virginia	35,400,000	0.6%
21	Wisconsin	84,500,000	1.4%
48	Wyoming	7,800,000	0.1%

RANK ORDER

RANK	STATE	EXPENDITURES	% of USA
1	California	$980,700,000	16.5%
2	Illinois	448,500,000	7.6%
3	Texas	385,700,000	6.5%
4	Georgia	328,100,000	5.5%
5	New York	324,400,000	5.5%
6	New Jersey	280,000,000	4.7%
7	Florida	261,700,000	4.4%
8	Massachusetts	211,500,000	3.6%
9	Pennsylvania	190,000,000	3.2%
10	Ohio	186,900,000	3.2%
11	Michigan	171,600,000	2.9%
12	North Carolina	166,600,000	2.8%
13	Maryland	138,400,000	2.3%
14	Louisiana	119,900,000	2.0%
15	Arizona	117,700,000	2.0%
16	Virginia	110,700,000	1.9%
17	Mississippi	107,500,000	1.8%
18	Oklahoma	96,400,000	1.6%
19	Alabama	95,200,000	1.6%
20	Indiana	92,100,000	1.6%
21	Wisconsin	84,500,000	1.4%
22	Kentucky	81,200,000	1.4%
23	Missouri	79,400,000	1.3%
24	Arkansas	68,800,000	1.2%
25	Oregon	66,600,000	1.1%
26	Colorado	65,900,000	1.1%
27	Minnesota	64,400,000	1.1%
28	Iowa	51,300,000	0.9%
29	New Mexico	49,900,000	0.8%
30	Rhode Island	47,700,000	0.8%
31	Kansas	45,100,000	0.8%
32	Utah	38,900,000	0.7%
33	Washington	36,800,000	0.6%
34	West Virginia	35,400,000	0.6%
35	Nebraska	33,200,000	0.6%
36	South Carolina	31,400,000	0.5%
37	Maine	31,200,000	0.5%
38	Nevada	30,300,000	0.5%
39	Connecticut	30,100,000	0.5%
40	Idaho	27,400,000	0.5%
41	Hawaii	18,700,000	0.3%
42	Montana	18,200,000	0.3%
43	Alaska	16,200,000	0.3%
44	New Hampshire	11,100,000	0.2%
45	North Dakota	10,500,000	0.2%
46	South Dakota	9,800,000	0.2%
47	Delaware	8,600,000	0.1%
48	Wyoming	7,800,000	0.1%
49	Vermont	5,900,000	0.1%
50	Tennessee	4,100,000	0.1%
	District of Columbia	7,200,000	0.1%

Source: U.S. Department of Health and Human Services, Centers for Medicare and Medicaid Services
"Statement of Expenditures for the SCHIP Program" (CMS-21 Report, http://www.cms.hhs.gov)
*Federal and state expenditures for fiscal year 2007. National total does not include funds spent in U.S. territories. The State Children's Health Insurance Program (SCHIP) was created in 1997 to help states expand health insurance to children whose families earn too much to qualify for Medicaid, yet not enough to afford private health insurance.

Per Capita Expenditures for State Children's
Health Insurance Program (SCHIP) in 2007
National Per Capita = $19.69*

ALPHA ORDER

RANK	STATE	PER CAPITA
15	Alabama	$20.58
13	Alaska	23.78
20	Arizona	18.53
12	Arkansas	24.31
8	California	26.96
39	Colorado	13.61
46	Connecticut	8.62
44	Delaware	9.98
37	Florida	14.38
4	Georgia	34.45
34	Hawaii	14.64
22	Idaho	18.31
3	Illinois	34.97
36	Indiana	14.54
24	Iowa	17.20
29	Kansas	16.24
17	Kentucky	19.17
7	Louisiana	27.42
14	Maine	23.72
11	Maryland	24.63
5	Massachusetts	32.70
25	Michigan	17.07
41	Minnesota	12.43
2	Mississippi	36.80
40	Missouri	13.51
18	Montana	19.03
19	Nebraska	18.76
43	Nevada	11.86
47	New Hampshire	8.46
6	New Jersey	32.36
10	New Mexico	25.40
26	New York	16.70
21	North Carolina	18.43
27	North Dakota	16.46
28	Ohio	16.28
9	Oklahoma	26.72
23	Oregon	17.83
31	Pennsylvania	15.30
1	Rhode Island	45.29
48	South Carolina	7.13
42	South Dakota	12.32
50	Tennessee	0.67
30	Texas	16.18
35	Utah	14.58
45	Vermont	9.50
37	Virginia	14.38
49	Washington	5.71
16	West Virginia	19.56
32	Wisconsin	15.09
33	Wyoming	14.91

RANK ORDER

RANK	STATE	PER CAPITA
1	Rhode Island	$45.29
2	Mississippi	36.80
3	Illinois	34.97
4	Georgia	34.45
5	Massachusetts	32.70
6	New Jersey	32.36
7	Louisiana	27.42
8	California	26.96
9	Oklahoma	26.72
10	New Mexico	25.40
11	Maryland	24.63
12	Arkansas	24.31
13	Alaska	23.78
14	Maine	23.72
15	Alabama	20.58
16	West Virginia	19.56
17	Kentucky	19.17
18	Montana	19.03
19	Nebraska	18.76
20	Arizona	18.53
21	North Carolina	18.43
22	Idaho	18.31
23	Oregon	17.83
24	Iowa	17.20
25	Michigan	17.07
26	New York	16.70
27	North Dakota	16.46
28	Ohio	16.28
29	Kansas	16.24
30	Texas	16.18
31	Pennsylvania	15.30
32	Wisconsin	15.09
33	Wyoming	14.91
34	Hawaii	14.64
35	Utah	14.58
36	Indiana	14.54
37	Florida	14.38
37	Virginia	14.38
39	Colorado	13.61
40	Missouri	13.51
41	Minnesota	12.43
42	South Dakota	12.32
43	Nevada	11.86
44	Delaware	9.98
45	Vermont	9.50
46	Connecticut	8.62
47	New Hampshire	8.46
48	South Carolina	7.13
49	Washington	5.71
50	Tennessee	0.67

| | District of Columbia | 12.25 |

Source: CQ Press using data from U.S. Department of Health and Human Services, Centers for Medicare and Medicaid Services
"Statement of Expenditures for the SCHIP Program" (CMS-21 Report, http://www.cms.hhs.gov)
*Federal and state expenditures for fiscal year 2007. National figure does not include funds spent in U.S. territories. The State
Children's Health Insurance Program (SCHIP) was created in 1997 to help states expand health insurance to children whose
families earn too much to qualify for Medicaid, yet not enough to afford private health insurance.

Expenditures per State Children's Health Insurance Program (SCHIP) Participant in 2007
National Per Participant = $830*

ALPHA ORDER

RANK	STATE	PER PARTICIPANT
28	Alabama	$892
21	Alaska	923
14	Arizona	1,129
40	Arkansas	767
46	California	637
37	Colorado	779
11	Connecticut	1,274
38	Delaware	772
33	Florida	809
22	Georgia	921
35	Hawaii	781
31	Idaho	829
10	Illinois	1,298
43	Indiana	706
17	Iowa	1,021
25	Kansas	910
12	Kentucky	1,181
36	Louisiana	780
18	Maine	1,005
16	Maryland	1,041
13	Massachusetts	1,146
7	Michigan	1,505
1	Minnesota	11,908
9	Mississippi	1,318
19	Missouri	971
27	Montana	905
42	Nebraska	719
41	Nevada	724
23	New Hampshire	918
5	New Jersey	1,863
2	New Mexico	3,020
49	New York	498
44	North Carolina	694
4	North Dakota	1,920
34	Ohio	807
32	Oklahoma	823
15	Oregon	1,056
30	Pennsylvania	836
6	Rhode Island	1,830
48	South Carolina	524
45	South Dakota	654
50	Tennessee	99
47	Texas	543
29	Utah	869
20	Vermont	962
39	Virginia	768
3	Washington	2,498
23	West Virginia	918
8	Wisconsin	1,352
25	Wyoming	910

RANK ORDER

RANK	STATE	PER PARTICIPANT
1	Minnesota	$11,908
2	New Mexico	3,020
3	Washington	2,498
4	North Dakota	1,920
5	New Jersey	1,863
6	Rhode Island	1,830
7	Michigan	1,505
8	Wisconsin	1,352
9	Mississippi	1,318
10	Illinois	1,298
11	Connecticut	1,274
12	Kentucky	1,181
13	Massachusetts	1,146
14	Arizona	1,129
15	Oregon	1,056
16	Maryland	1,041
17	Iowa	1,021
18	Maine	1,005
19	Missouri	971
20	Vermont	962
21	Alaska	923
22	Georgia	921
23	New Hampshire	918
23	West Virginia	918
25	Kansas	910
25	Wyoming	910
27	Montana	905
28	Alabama	892
29	Utah	869
30	Pennsylvania	836
31	Idaho	829
32	Oklahoma	823
33	Florida	809
34	Ohio	807
35	Hawaii	781
36	Louisiana	780
37	Colorado	779
38	Delaware	772
39	Virginia	768
40	Arkansas	767
41	Nevada	724
42	Nebraska	719
43	Indiana	706
44	North Carolina	694
45	South Dakota	654
46	California	637
47	Texas	543
48	South Carolina	524
49	New York	498
50	Tennessee	99
	District of Columbia	1,097

Source: CQ Press using data from U.S. Department of Health and Human Services, Centers for Medicare and Medicaid Services "Statement of Expenditures for the SCHIP Program" (CMS-21 Report, http://www.cms.hhs.gov)

*Federal and state expenditures for fiscal year 2007. National figure does not include funds spent in U.S. territories. The State Children's Health Insurance Program (SCHIP) was created in 1997 to help states expand health insurance to children whose families earn too much to qualify for Medicaid, yet not enough to afford private health insurance.

Health Maintenance Organizations (HMOs) in 2008

National Total = 477 HMOs*

ALPHA ORDER

RANK	STATE	HMOs	% of USA
33	Alabama	30	6.3%
50	Alaska	14	2.9%
5	Arizona	63	13.2%
31	Arkansas	33	6.9%
1	California	90	18.9%
24	Colorado	37	7.8%
29	Connecticut	34	7.1%
33	Delaware	30	6.3%
2	Florida	77	16.1%
18	Georgia	44	9.2%
42	Hawaii	23	4.8%
37	Idaho	27	5.7%
7	Illinois	52	10.9%
16	Indiana	45	9.4%
36	Iowa	28	5.9%
24	Kansas	37	7.8%
26	Kentucky	35	7.3%
26	Louisiana	35	7.3%
42	Maine	23	4.8%
22	Maryland	38	8.0%
8	Massachusetts	49	10.3%
11	Michigan	48	10.1%
26	Minnesota	35	7.3%
37	Mississippi	27	5.7%
8	Missouri	49	10.3%
49	Montana	16	3.4%
42	Nebraska	23	4.8%
19	Nevada	43	9.0%
40	New Hampshire	25	5.2%
21	New Jersey	39	8.2%
35	New Mexico	29	6.1%
3	New York	76	15.9%
22	North Carolina	38	8.0%
48	North Dakota	19	4.0%
11	Ohio	48	10.1%
32	Oklahoma	31	6.5%
14	Oregon	46	9.6%
6	Pennsylvania	58	12.2%
46	Rhode Island	20	4.2%
16	South Carolina	45	9.4%
40	South Dakota	25	5.2%
13	Tennessee	47	9.9%
4	Texas	69	14.5%
29	Utah	34	7.1%
45	Vermont	21	4.4%
20	Virginia	42	8.8%
14	Washington	46	9.6%
37	West Virginia	27	5.7%
8	Wisconsin	49	10.3%
46	Wyoming	20	4.2%

RANK ORDER

RANK	STATE	HMOs	% of USA
1	California	90	18.9%
2	Florida	77	16.1%
3	New York	76	15.9%
4	Texas	69	14.5%
5	Arizona	63	13.2%
6	Pennsylvania	58	12.2%
7	Illinois	52	10.9%
8	Massachusetts	49	10.3%
8	Missouri	49	10.3%
8	Wisconsin	49	10.3%
11	Michigan	48	10.1%
11	Ohio	48	10.1%
13	Tennessee	47	9.9%
14	Oregon	46	9.6%
14	Washington	46	9.6%
16	Indiana	45	9.4%
16	South Carolina	45	9.4%
18	Georgia	44	9.2%
19	Nevada	43	9.0%
20	Virginia	42	8.8%
21	New Jersey	39	8.2%
22	Maryland	38	8.0%
22	North Carolina	38	8.0%
24	Colorado	37	7.8%
24	Kansas	37	7.8%
26	Kentucky	35	7.3%
26	Louisiana	35	7.3%
26	Minnesota	35	7.3%
29	Connecticut	34	7.1%
29	Utah	34	7.1%
31	Arkansas	33	6.9%
32	Oklahoma	31	6.5%
33	Alabama	30	6.3%
33	Delaware	30	6.3%
35	New Mexico	29	6.1%
36	Iowa	28	5.9%
37	Idaho	27	5.7%
37	Mississippi	27	5.7%
37	West Virginia	27	5.7%
40	New Hampshire	25	5.2%
40	South Dakota	25	5.2%
42	Hawaii	23	4.8%
42	Maine	23	4.8%
42	Nebraska	23	4.8%
45	Vermont	21	4.4%
46	Rhode Island	20	4.2%
46	Wyoming	20	4.2%
48	North Dakota	19	4.0%
49	Montana	16	3.4%
50	Alaska	14	2.9%
	District of Columbia	24	5.0%

Source: Lance Wolkenbrod, Data Analyst
    HealthLeaders - InterStudy (Nashville, TN, http://home.healthleaders-interstudy.com)
*As of January 2008. National total reflects the total HMOs nationwide and does not count HMOs in more than one state as multiple HMOs. The total for all HMO programs by state is 1,963.

Enrollees in Health Maintenance Organizations (HMOs) in 2008

National Total = 75,394,587 Enrollees*

ALPHA ORDER

RANK	STATE	ENROLLEES	% of USA
38	Alabama	235,163	0.3%
50	Alaska	8,631	0.0%
11	Arizona	1,967,152	2.6%
43	Arkansas	98,941	0.1%
1	California	16,449,040	21.7%
21	Colorado	1,059,851	1.4%
24	Connecticut	933,678	1.2%
39	Delaware	194,544	0.3%
3	Florida	4,562,758	6.0%
9	Georgia	2,228,626	2.9%
26	Hawaii	613,521	0.8%
42	Idaho	101,318	0.1%
13	Illinois	1,842,489	2.4%
18	Indiana	1,164,900	1.5%
35	Iowa	264,452	0.3%
30	Kansas	459,930	0.6%
31	Kentucky	428,953	0.6%
32	Louisiana	388,398	0.5%
40	Maine	174,807	0.2%
14	Maryland	1,736,280	2.3%
6	Massachusetts	2,855,836	3.8%
7	Michigan	2,855,371	3.8%
19	Minnesota	1,121,732	1.5%
46	Mississippi	65,868	0.1%
22	Missouri	1,028,669	1.4%
47	Montana	57,053	0.1%
44	Nebraska	91,385	0.1%
28	Nevada	549,283	0.7%
33	New Hampshire	312,819	0.4%
10	New Jersey	2,206,566	2.9%
27	New Mexico	608,771	0.8%
2	New York	5,814,842	7.7%
25	North Carolina	850,216	1.1%
49	North Dakota	18,511	0.0%
8	Ohio	2,363,413	3.1%
36	Oklahoma	262,597	0.3%
20	Oregon	1,080,408	1.4%
4	Pennsylvania	4,018,501	5.3%
37	Rhode Island	255,065	0.3%
29	South Carolina	512,298	0.7%
41	South Dakota	147,987	0.2%
12	Tennessee	1,891,758	2.5%
5	Texas	3,853,568	5.1%
23	Utah	947,743	1.2%
45	Vermont	85,945	0.1%
15	Virginia	1,691,854	2.2%
17	Washington	1,298,269	1.7%
34	West Virginia	288,507	0.4%
16	Wisconsin	1,522,782	2.0%
48	Wyoming	24,434	0.0%

RANK ORDER

RANK	STATE	ENROLLEES	% of USA
1	California	16,449,040	21.7%
2	New York	5,814,842	7.7%
3	Florida	4,562,758	6.0%
4	Pennsylvania	4,018,501	5.3%
5	Texas	3,853,568	5.1%
6	Massachusetts	2,855,836	3.8%
7	Michigan	2,855,371	3.8%
8	Ohio	2,363,413	3.1%
9	Georgia	2,228,626	2.9%
10	New Jersey	2,206,566	2.9%
11	Arizona	1,967,152	2.6%
12	Tennessee	1,891,758	2.5%
13	Illinois	1,842,489	2.4%
14	Maryland	1,736,280	2.3%
15	Virginia	1,691,854	2.2%
16	Wisconsin	1,522,782	2.0%
17	Washington	1,298,269	1.7%
18	Indiana	1,164,900	1.5%
19	Minnesota	1,121,732	1.5%
20	Oregon	1,080,408	1.4%
21	Colorado	1,059,851	1.4%
22	Missouri	1,028,669	1.4%
23	Utah	947,743	1.2%
24	Connecticut	933,678	1.2%
25	North Carolina	850,216	1.1%
26	Hawaii	613,521	0.8%
27	New Mexico	608,771	0.8%
28	Nevada	549,283	0.7%
29	South Carolina	512,298	0.7%
30	Kansas	459,930	0.6%
31	Kentucky	428,953	0.6%
32	Louisiana	388,398	0.5%
33	New Hampshire	312,819	0.4%
34	West Virginia	288,507	0.4%
35	Iowa	264,452	0.3%
36	Oklahoma	262,597	0.3%
37	Rhode Island	255,065	0.3%
38	Alabama	235,163	0.3%
39	Delaware	194,544	0.3%
40	Maine	174,807	0.2%
41	South Dakota	147,987	0.2%
42	Idaho	101,318	0.1%
43	Arkansas	98,941	0.1%
44	Nebraska	91,385	0.1%
45	Vermont	85,945	0.1%
46	Mississippi	65,868	0.1%
47	Montana	57,053	0.1%
48	Wyoming	24,434	0.0%
49	North Dakota	18,511	0.0%
50	Alaska	8,631	0.0%
	District of Columbia	313,264	0.4%

Source: Lance Wolkenbrod, Data Analyst
    HealthLeaders - InterStudy (Nashville, TN, http://home.healthleaders-interstudy.com)
*As of January 2008.

Percent Change in Enrollees in Health Maintenance Organizations (HMOs): 2007 to 2008
National Percent Change = 13.7% Increase*

ALPHA ORDER

RANK	STATE	PERCENT CHANGE
7	Alabama	84.8
1	Alaska	15,312.5
21	Arizona	25.5
39	Arkansas	7.5
45	California	(2.9)
34	Colorado	12.9
49	Connecticut	(20.8)
31	Delaware	13.4
17	Florida	30.2
38	Georgia	7.7
42	Hawaii	3.9
12	Idaho	53.9
36	Illinois	10.9
26	Indiana	21.8
44	Iowa	(1.1)
31	Kansas	13.4
13	Kentucky	46.0
19	Louisiana	27.1
50	Maine	(51.1)
27	Maryland	21.4
20	Massachusetts	25.6
43	Michigan	3.1
10	Minnesota	56.6
2	Mississippi	1,393.3
41	Missouri	5.6
29	Montana	17.2
46	Nebraska	(4.9)
48	Nevada	(10.2)
9	New Hampshire	60.5
33	New Jersey	13.0
24	New Mexico	23.6
47	New York	(9.8)
5	North Carolina	100.2
3	North Dakota	867.1
37	Ohio	9.4
30	Oklahoma	15.2
27	Oregon	21.4
25	Pennsylvania	22.4
16	Rhode Island	31.6
8	South Carolina	63.6
4	South Dakota	113.4
23	Tennessee	24.3
15	Texas	32.7
22	Utah	24.4
11	Vermont	55.9
18	Virginia	27.7
40	Washington	6.5
14	West Virginia	38.0
35	Wisconsin	11.5
6	Wyoming	89.2

RANK ORDER

RANK	STATE	PERCENT CHANGE
1	Alaska	15,312.5
2	Mississippi	1,393.3
3	North Dakota	867.1
4	South Dakota	113.4
5	North Carolina	100.2
6	Wyoming	89.2
7	Alabama	84.8
8	South Carolina	63.6
9	New Hampshire	60.5
10	Minnesota	56.6
11	Vermont	55.9
12	Idaho	53.9
13	Kentucky	46.0
14	West Virginia	38.0
15	Texas	32.7
16	Rhode Island	31.6
17	Florida	30.2
18	Virginia	27.7
19	Louisiana	27.1
20	Massachusetts	25.6
21	Arizona	25.5
22	Utah	24.4
23	Tennessee	24.3
24	New Mexico	23.6
25	Pennsylvania	22.4
26	Indiana	21.8
27	Maryland	21.4
27	Oregon	21.4
29	Montana	17.2
30	Oklahoma	15.2
31	Delaware	13.4
31	Kansas	13.4
33	New Jersey	13.0
34	Colorado	12.9
35	Wisconsin	11.5
36	Illinois	10.9
37	Ohio	9.4
38	Georgia	7.7
39	Arkansas	7.5
40	Washington	6.5
41	Missouri	5.6
42	Hawaii	3.9
43	Michigan	3.1
44	Iowa	(1.1)
45	California	(2.9)
46	Nebraska	(4.9)
47	New York	(9.8)
48	Nevada	(10.2)
49	Connecticut	(20.8)
50	Maine	(51.1)
	District of Columbia	(11.0)

Source: CQ Press using data from Lance Wolkenbrod, Data Analyst
   HealthLeaders - InterStudy (Nashville, TN, http://home.healthleaders-interstudy.com)
*As of January 2008. National figure does not include enrollees in U.S. territories.

Percent of Population Enrolled in Health Maintenance Organizations (HMOs) in 2008
National Percent = 24.8% Enrolled in HMOs*

ALPHA ORDER

RANK	STATE	PERCENT
44	Alabama	5.1
50	Alaska	1.3
6	Arizona	31.0
47	Arkansas	3.5
2	California	45.0
22	Colorado	21.8
14	Connecticut	26.7
20	Delaware	22.5
16	Florida	25.0
19	Georgia	23.3
1	Hawaii	47.8
42	Idaho	6.8
33	Illinois	14.3
28	Indiana	18.4
40	Iowa	8.9
30	Kansas	16.6
37	Kentucky	10.1
39	Louisiana	9.0
35	Maine	13.3
7	Maryland	30.9
3	Massachusetts	44.3
12	Michigan	28.4
23	Minnesota	21.6
49	Mississippi	2.3
29	Missouri	17.5
43	Montana	6.0
44	Nebraska	5.1
24	Nevada	21.4
18	New Hampshire	23.8
15	New Jersey	25.4
7	New Mexico	30.9
10	New York	30.1
38	North Carolina	9.4
48	North Dakota	2.9
25	Ohio	20.6
41	Oklahoma	7.3
11	Oregon	28.8
5	Pennsylvania	32.3
17	Rhode Island	24.1
36	South Carolina	11.6
27	South Dakota	18.6
9	Tennessee	30.7
31	Texas	16.1
4	Utah	35.8
34	Vermont	13.8
21	Virginia	21.9
26	Washington	20.1
32	West Virginia	15.9
13	Wisconsin	27.2
46	Wyoming	4.7

RANK ORDER

RANK	STATE	PERCENT
1	Hawaii	47.8
2	California	45.0
3	Massachusetts	44.3
4	Utah	35.8
5	Pennsylvania	32.3
6	Arizona	31.0
7	Maryland	30.9
7	New Mexico	30.9
9	Tennessee	30.7
10	New York	30.1
11	Oregon	28.8
12	Michigan	28.4
13	Wisconsin	27.2
14	Connecticut	26.7
15	New Jersey	25.4
16	Florida	25.0
17	Rhode Island	24.1
18	New Hampshire	23.8
19	Georgia	23.3
20	Delaware	22.5
21	Virginia	21.9
22	Colorado	21.8
23	Minnesota	21.6
24	Nevada	21.4
25	Ohio	20.6
26	Washington	20.1
27	South Dakota	18.6
28	Indiana	18.4
29	Missouri	17.5
30	Kansas	16.6
31	Texas	16.1
32	West Virginia	15.9
33	Illinois	14.3
34	Vermont	13.8
35	Maine	13.3
36	South Carolina	11.6
37	Kentucky	10.1
38	North Carolina	9.4
39	Louisiana	9.0
40	Iowa	8.9
41	Oklahoma	7.3
42	Idaho	6.8
43	Montana	6.0
44	Alabama	5.1
44	Nebraska	5.1
46	Wyoming	4.7
47	Arkansas	3.5
48	North Dakota	2.9
49	Mississippi	2.3
50	Alaska	1.3
	District of Columbia	53.2

Source: Lance Wolkenbrod, Data Analyst
    HealthLeaders - InterStudy (Nashville, TN, http://home.healthleaders-interstudy.com)
*As of January 2008.

Percent of Insured Population Enrolled in
Health Maintenance Organizations (HMOs) in 2008
National Percent = 30.4% of Insured Are Enrolled in HMOs*

ALPHA ORDER

RANK	STATE	PERCENT
44	Alabama	6.1
50	Alaska	1.6
6	Arizona	39.7
47	Arkansas	4.4
1	California	55.9
20	Colorado	26.6
16	Connecticut	29.8
23	Delaware	25.7
12	Florida	32.1
17	Georgia	29.0
2	Hawaii	53.6
42	Idaho	8.1
33	Illinois	17.0
29	Indiana	20.8
40	Iowa	10.1
31	Kansas	19.3
37	Kentucky	12.4
38	Louisiana	11.8
35	Maine	14.7
9	Maryland	35.9
3	Massachusetts	50.3
13	Michigan	32.0
24	Minnesota	24.0
49	Mississippi	2.9
30	Missouri	20.5
43	Montana	7.4
45	Nebraska	5.9
19	Nevada	26.9
18	New Hampshire	27.0
15	New Jersey	30.1
5	New Mexico	40.6
10	New York	35.5
39	North Carolina	11.7
48	North Dakota	3.4
26	Ohio	23.2
41	Oklahoma	9.3
11	Oregon	35.4
8	Pennsylvania	36.2
21	Rhode Island	26.5
36	South Carolina	14.4
28	South Dakota	21.8
7	Tennessee	37.0
27	Texas	22.0
4	Utah	45.3
34	Vermont	15.4
22	Virginia	25.9
25	Washington	23.3
32	West Virginia	18.4
14	Wisconsin	30.5
46	Wyoming	5.5

RANK ORDER

RANK	STATE	PERCENT
1	California	55.9
2	Hawaii	53.6
3	Massachusetts	50.3
4	Utah	45.3
5	New Mexico	40.6
6	Arizona	39.7
7	Tennessee	37.0
8	Pennsylvania	36.2
9	Maryland	35.9
10	New York	35.5
11	Oregon	35.4
12	Florida	32.1
13	Michigan	32.0
14	Wisconsin	30.5
15	New Jersey	30.1
16	Connecticut	29.8
17	Georgia	29.0
18	New Hampshire	27.0
19	Nevada	26.9
20	Colorado	26.6
21	Rhode Island	26.5
22	Virginia	25.9
23	Delaware	25.7
24	Minnesota	24.0
25	Washington	23.3
26	Ohio	23.2
27	Texas	22.0
28	South Dakota	21.8
29	Indiana	20.8
30	Missouri	20.5
31	Kansas	19.3
32	West Virginia	18.4
33	Illinois	17.0
34	Vermont	15.4
35	Maine	14.7
36	South Carolina	14.4
37	Kentucky	12.4
38	Louisiana	11.8
39	North Carolina	11.7
40	Iowa	10.1
41	Oklahoma	9.3
42	Idaho	8.1
43	Montana	7.4
44	Alabama	6.1
45	Nebraska	5.9
46	Wyoming	5.5
47	Arkansas	4.4
48	North Dakota	3.4
49	Mississippi	2.9
50	Alaska	1.6
	District of Columbia	62.3

Source: CQ Press using data from Lance Wolkenbrod, Data Analyst
 HealthLeaders - InterStudy (Nashville, TN, http://home.healthleaders-interstudy.com)
*As of January 2008. Calculated using estimated number of insured as of 2007 from the U.S. Census Bureau.

Medicare Enrollees in 2007

National Total = 44,263,111 Enrollees*

ALPHA ORDER

RANK	STATE	ENROLLEES	% of USA
20	Alabama	789,250	1.8%
50	Alaska	56,803	0.1%
19	Arizona	840,527	1.9%
31	Arkansas	496,335	1.1%
1	California	4,368,858	9.9%
28	Colorado	558,222	1.3%
29	Connecticut	537,064	1.2%
45	Delaware	136,206	0.3%
2	Florida	3,132,634	7.1%
11	Georgia	1,110,510	2.5%
42	Hawaii	189,385	0.4%
40	Idaho	206,570	0.5%
7	Illinois	1,740,751	3.9%
16	Indiana	940,825	2.1%
30	Iowa	500,056	1.1%
33	Kansas	411,660	0.9%
23	Kentucky	710,977	1.6%
25	Louisiana	639,499	1.4%
39	Maine	246,571	0.6%
22	Maryland	723,302	1.6%
13	Massachusetts	996,741	2.3%
8	Michigan	1,540,827	3.5%
21	Minnesota	729,147	1.6%
32	Mississippi	469,402	1.1%
15	Missouri	946,284	2.1%
44	Montana	155,753	0.4%
37	Nebraska	267,588	0.6%
35	Nevada	317,741	0.7%
41	New Hampshire	204,313	0.5%
10	New Jersey	1,257,125	2.8%
36	New Mexico	284,910	0.6%
3	New York	2,840,560	6.4%
9	North Carolina	1,358,548	3.1%
47	North Dakota	105,324	0.2%
6	Ohio	1,805,235	4.1%
27	Oklahoma	565,079	1.3%
26	Oregon	566,960	1.3%
5	Pennsylvania	2,183,604	4.9%
43	Rhode Island	175,012	0.4%
24	South Carolina	697,189	1.6%
46	South Dakota	129,381	0.3%
14	Tennessee	974,803	2.2%
4	Texas	2,708,229	6.1%
38	Utah	254,060	0.6%
48	Vermont	101,593	0.2%
12	Virginia	1,044,603	2.4%
17	Washington	873,385	2.0%
34	West Virginia	367,338	0.8%
18	Wisconsin	854,343	1.9%
49	Wyoming	74,113	0.2%

RANK ORDER

RANK	STATE	ENROLLEES	% of USA
1	California	4,368,858	9.9%
2	Florida	3,132,634	7.1%
3	New York	2,840,560	6.4%
4	Texas	2,708,229	6.1%
5	Pennsylvania	2,183,604	4.9%
6	Ohio	1,805,235	4.1%
7	Illinois	1,740,751	3.9%
8	Michigan	1,540,827	3.5%
9	North Carolina	1,358,548	3.1%
10	New Jersey	1,257,125	2.8%
11	Georgia	1,110,510	2.5%
12	Virginia	1,044,603	2.4%
13	Massachusetts	996,741	2.3%
14	Tennessee	974,803	2.2%
15	Missouri	946,284	2.1%
16	Indiana	940,825	2.1%
17	Washington	873,385	2.0%
18	Wisconsin	854,343	1.9%
19	Arizona	840,527	1.9%
20	Alabama	789,250	1.8%
21	Minnesota	729,147	1.6%
22	Maryland	723,302	1.6%
23	Kentucky	710,977	1.6%
24	South Carolina	697,189	1.6%
25	Louisiana	639,499	1.4%
26	Oregon	566,960	1.3%
27	Oklahoma	565,079	1.3%
28	Colorado	558,222	1.3%
29	Connecticut	537,064	1.2%
30	Iowa	500,056	1.1%
31	Arkansas	496,335	1.1%
32	Mississippi	469,402	1.1%
33	Kansas	411,660	0.9%
34	West Virginia	367,338	0.8%
35	Nevada	317,741	0.7%
36	New Mexico	284,910	0.6%
37	Nebraska	267,588	0.6%
38	Utah	254,060	0.6%
39	Maine	246,571	0.6%
40	Idaho	206,570	0.5%
41	New Hampshire	204,313	0.5%
42	Hawaii	189,385	0.4%
43	Rhode Island	175,012	0.4%
44	Montana	155,753	0.4%
45	Delaware	136,206	0.3%
46	South Dakota	129,381	0.3%
47	North Dakota	105,324	0.2%
48	Vermont	101,593	0.2%
49	Wyoming	74,113	0.2%
50	Alaska	56,803	0.1%
	District of Columbia	74,085	0.2%

Source: U.S. Department of Health and Human Services, Centers for Medicare and Medicaid Services
"2008 Data Compendium" (http://www.cms.hhs.gov/DataCompendium/)
*Includes aged and disabled enrollees. Total includes 622,826 enrollees in Puerto Rico and other outlying areas, foreign countries
or whose address is unknown.

Percent Change in Medicare Enrollees: 2006 to 2007

National Percent Change = 2.0% Increase*

ALPHA ORDER				RANK ORDER		
RANK	STATE	PERCENT CHANGE		RANK	STATE	PERCENT CHANGE
25	Alabama	2.2		1	Alaska	4.6
1	Alaska	4.6		2	Nevada	3.6
11	Arizona	3.1		3	Idaho	3.5
22	Arkansas	2.4		4	Colorado	3.4
25	California	2.2		4	South Carolina	3.4
4	Colorado	3.4		6	Delaware	3.3
42	Connecticut	1.3		6	Georgia	3.3
6	Delaware	3.3		6	New Hampshire	3.3
35	Florida	1.7		6	New Mexico	3.3
6	Georgia	3.3		6	Utah	3.3
29	Hawaii	2.1		11	Arizona	3.1
3	Idaho	3.5		11	North Carolina	3.1
39	Illinois	1.6		11	Texas	3.1
31	Indiana	2.0		11	Washington	3.1
48	Iowa	1.1		15	Tennessee	2.7
42	Kansas	1.3		16	Montana	2.6
24	Kentucky	2.3		16	Oregon	2.6
19	Louisiana	2.5		16	Virginia	2.6
19	Maine	2.5		19	Louisiana	2.5
25	Maryland	2.2		19	Maine	2.5
40	Massachusetts	1.5		19	Vermont	2.5
31	Michigan	2.0		22	Arkansas	2.4
25	Minnesota	2.2		22	Wyoming	2.4
35	Mississippi	1.7		24	Kentucky	2.3
33	Missouri	1.8		25	Alabama	2.2
16	Montana	2.6		25	California	2.2
46	Nebraska	1.2		25	Maryland	2.2
2	Nevada	3.6		25	Minnesota	2.2
6	New Hampshire	3.3		29	Hawaii	2.1
46	New Jersey	1.2		29	Oklahoma	2.1
6	New Mexico	3.3		31	Indiana	2.0
42	New York	1.3		31	Michigan	2.0
11	North Carolina	3.1		33	Missouri	1.8
49	North Dakota	0.9		33	South Dakota	1.8
40	Ohio	1.5		35	Florida	1.7
29	Oklahoma	2.1		35	Mississippi	1.7
16	Oregon	2.6		35	West Virginia	1.7
42	Pennsylvania	1.3		35	Wisconsin	1.7
50	Rhode Island	0.7		39	Illinois	1.6
4	South Carolina	3.4		40	Massachusetts	1.5
33	South Dakota	1.8		40	Ohio	1.5
15	Tennessee	2.7		42	Connecticut	1.3
11	Texas	3.1		42	Kansas	1.3
6	Utah	3.3		42	New York	1.3
19	Vermont	2.5		42	Pennsylvania	1.3
16	Virginia	2.6		46	Nebraska	1.2
11	Washington	3.1		46	New Jersey	1.2
35	West Virginia	1.7		48	Iowa	1.1
35	Wisconsin	1.7		49	North Dakota	0.9
22	Wyoming	2.4		50	Rhode Island	0.7

District of Columbia   0.7

Source: CQ Press using data from U.S. Department of Health and Human Services, Centers for Medicare and Medicaid Services
   "2008 Data Compendium" (http://www.cms.hhs.gov/DataCompendium/)
*Includes aged and disabled enrollees. National rate includes enrollees in Puerto Rico and other outlying areas, foreign countries
or whose address is unknown.

Percent of Population Enrolled in Medicare in 2007

National Percent = 14.3% of Population*

ALPHA ORDER

RANK	STATE	PERCENT
6	Alabama	17.1
50	Alaska	8.3
42	Arizona	13.3
4	Arkansas	17.5
45	California	12.0
47	Colorado	11.5
23	Connecticut	15.3
18	Delaware	15.8
5	Florida	17.2
46	Georgia	11.6
32	Hawaii	14.8
38	Idaho	13.8
40	Illinois	13.5
31	Indiana	14.8
8	Iowa	16.7
30	Kansas	14.8
7	Kentucky	16.8
29	Louisiana	14.9
2	Maine	18.7
43	Maryland	12.9
22	Massachusetts	15.5
24	Michigan	15.3
37	Minnesota	14.0
15	Mississippi	16.1
14	Missouri	16.1
12	Montana	16.3
27	Nebraska	15.1
44	Nevada	12.4
21	New Hampshire	15.5
34	New Jersey	14.5
35	New Mexico	14.5
33	New York	14.7
28	North Carolina	15.0
10	North Dakota	16.5
19	Ohio	15.7
20	Oklahoma	15.6
26	Oregon	15.1
3	Pennsylvania	17.6
9	Rhode Island	16.5
17	South Carolina	15.8
13	South Dakota	16.2
16	Tennessee	15.8
48	Texas	11.3
49	Utah	9.6
11	Vermont	16.4
39	Virginia	13.5
41	Washington	13.5
1	West Virginia	20.3
25	Wisconsin	15.3
36	Wyoming	14.2

RANK ORDER

RANK	STATE	PERCENT
1	West Virginia	20.3
2	Maine	18.7
3	Pennsylvania	17.6
4	Arkansas	17.5
5	Florida	17.2
6	Alabama	17.1
7	Kentucky	16.8
8	Iowa	16.7
9	Rhode Island	16.5
10	North Dakota	16.5
11	Vermont	16.4
12	Montana	16.3
13	South Dakota	16.2
14	Missouri	16.1
15	Mississippi	16.1
16	Tennessee	15.8
17	South Carolina	15.8
18	Delaware	15.8
19	Ohio	15.7
20	Oklahoma	15.6
21	New Hampshire	15.5
22	Massachusetts	15.5
23	Connecticut	15.3
24	Michigan	15.3
25	Wisconsin	15.3
26	Oregon	15.1
27	Nebraska	15.1
28	North Carolina	15.0
29	Louisiana	14.9
30	Kansas	14.8
31	Indiana	14.8
32	Hawaii	14.8
33	New York	14.7
34	New Jersey	14.5
35	New Mexico	14.5
36	Wyoming	14.2
37	Minnesota	14.0
38	Idaho	13.8
39	Virginia	13.5
40	Illinois	13.5
41	Washington	13.5
42	Arizona	13.3
43	Maryland	12.9
44	Nevada	12.4
45	California	12.0
46	Georgia	11.6
47	Colorado	11.5
48	Texas	11.3
49	Utah	9.6
50	Alaska	8.3
	District of Columbia	12.6

Source: U.S. Department of Health and Human Services, Centers for Medicare and Medicaid Services
   "2008 Data Compendium" (http://www.cms.hhs.gov/DataCompendium/)
*Includes aged and disabled enrollees. National rate includes only residents of the 50 states and the District of Columbia.

Percent of Medicare Enrollees in Managed Care Programs in 2007

National Percent = 19.7% of Medicare Enrollees*

ALPHA ORDER

RANK	STATE	PERCENT
25	Alabama	14.9
50	Alaska	0.5
4	Arizona	34.8
34	Arkansas	10.5
5	California	33.4
7	Colorado	30.9
32	Connecticut	11.0
46	Delaware	2.8
10	Florida	25.1
31	Georgia	11.1
2	Hawaii	36.1
14	Idaho	21.4
39	Illinois	8.3
35	Indiana	10.1
29	Iowa	11.6
40	Kansas	7.6
30	Kentucky	11.5
20	Louisiana	17.6
46	Maine	2.8
43	Maryland	6.4
20	Massachusetts	17.6
23	Michigan	15.7
8	Minnesota	30.4
42	Mississippi	6.8
22	Missouri	16.5
27	Montana	12.2
37	Nebraska	9.7
9	Nevada	29.8
46	New Hampshire	2.8
38	New Jersey	9.4
13	New Mexico	21.5
11	New York	24.8
26	North Carolina	14.2
43	North Dakota	6.4
19	Ohio	17.9
28	Oklahoma	12.0
1	Oregon	39.3
6	Pennsylvania	32.9
3	Rhode Island	35.0
32	South Carolina	11.0
41	South Dakota	7.1
18	Tennessee	18.0
24	Texas	15.1
12	Utah	22.5
49	Vermont	1.8
36	Virginia	9.8
17	Washington	19.9
16	West Virginia	20.4
15	Wisconsin	20.8
45	Wyoming	4.4

RANK ORDER

RANK	STATE	PERCENT
1	Oregon	39.3
2	Hawaii	36.1
3	Rhode Island	35.0
4	Arizona	34.8
5	California	33.4
6	Pennsylvania	32.9
7	Colorado	30.9
8	Minnesota	30.4
9	Nevada	29.8
10	Florida	25.1
11	New York	24.8
12	Utah	22.5
13	New Mexico	21.5
14	Idaho	21.4
15	Wisconsin	20.8
16	West Virginia	20.4
17	Washington	19.9
18	Tennessee	18.0
19	Ohio	17.9
20	Louisiana	17.6
20	Massachusetts	17.6
22	Missouri	16.5
23	Michigan	15.7
24	Texas	15.1
25	Alabama	14.9
26	North Carolina	14.2
27	Montana	12.2
28	Oklahoma	12.0
29	Iowa	11.6
30	Kentucky	11.5
31	Georgia	11.1
32	Connecticut	11.0
32	South Carolina	11.0
34	Arkansas	10.5
35	Indiana	10.1
36	Virginia	9.8
37	Nebraska	9.7
38	New Jersey	9.4
39	Illinois	8.3
40	Kansas	7.6
41	South Dakota	7.1
42	Mississippi	6.8
43	Maryland	6.4
43	North Dakota	6.4
45	Wyoming	4.4
46	Delaware	2.8
46	Maine	2.8
46	New Hampshire	2.8
49	Vermont	1.8
50	Alaska	0.5

	District of Columbia	8.7

Source: U.S. Department of Health and Human Services, Centers for Medicare and Medicaid Services
   "Health Care Financing Review, 2008 Statistical Supplement" (http://www.cms.hhs.gov/MedicareMedicaidStatSupp)
*As of December 2007. National rate is a weighted average calculated by the editors. Includes Medicare Advantage and Employer Direct Plans. Regional Preferred Provider Organizations, Special Needs Plans, and employer only plans are also included.

Percent of Physicians Participating in Medicare in 2008

National Percent = 94.7% of Physicians Participate in Medicare*

ALPHA ORDER

RANK	STATE	PERCENT
6	Alabama	97.6
48	Alaska	90.2
41	Arizona	93.5
12	Arkansas	97.4
49	California	89.3
44	Colorado	93.2
34	Connecticut	95.3
6	Delaware	97.6
32	Florida	95.6
38	Georgia	94.0
29	Hawaii	96.2
47	Idaho	91.1
31	Illinois	95.9
26	Indiana	96.3
30	Iowa	96.1
12	Kansas	97.4
26	Kentucky	96.3
33	Louisiana	95.4
3	Maine	98.2
24	Maryland	96.4
1	Massachusetts	99.0
4	Michigan	98.0
50	Minnesota	81.5
41	Mississippi	93.5
36	Missouri	95.1
37	Montana	94.9
17	Nebraska	97.1
15	Nevada	97.2
14	New Hampshire	97.3
46	New Jersey	92.5
22	New Mexico	96.5
38	New York	94.0
22	North Carolina	96.5
9	North Dakota	97.5
9	Ohio	97.5
26	Oklahoma	96.3
35	Oregon	95.2
5	Pennsylvania	97.8
2	Rhode Island	98.5
19	South Carolina	96.7
43	South Dakota	93.3
20	Tennessee	96.6
40	Texas	93.8
6	Utah	97.6
15	Vermont	97.2
24	Virginia	96.4
18	Washington	96.8
9	West Virginia	97.5
20	Wisconsin	96.6
45	Wyoming	93.0

RANK ORDER

RANK	STATE	PERCENT
1	Massachusetts	99.0
2	Rhode Island	98.5
3	Maine	98.2
4	Michigan	98.0
5	Pennsylvania	97.8
6	Alabama	97.6
6	Delaware	97.6
6	Utah	97.6
9	North Dakota	97.5
9	Ohio	97.5
9	West Virginia	97.5
12	Arkansas	97.4
12	Kansas	97.4
14	New Hampshire	97.3
15	Nevada	97.2
15	Vermont	97.2
17	Nebraska	97.1
18	Washington	96.8
19	South Carolina	96.7
20	Tennessee	96.6
20	Wisconsin	96.6
22	New Mexico	96.5
22	North Carolina	96.5
24	Maryland	96.4
24	Virginia	96.4
26	Indiana	96.3
26	Kentucky	96.3
26	Oklahoma	96.3
29	Hawaii	96.2
30	Iowa	96.1
31	Illinois	95.9
32	Florida	95.6
33	Louisiana	95.4
34	Connecticut	95.3
35	Oregon	95.2
36	Missouri	95.1
37	Montana	94.9
38	Georgia	94.0
38	New York	94.0
40	Texas	93.8
41	Arizona	93.5
41	Mississippi	93.5
43	South Dakota	93.3
44	Colorado	93.2
45	Wyoming	93.0
46	New Jersey	92.5
47	Idaho	91.1
48	Alaska	90.2
49	California	89.3
50	Minnesota	81.5

	District of Columbia	94.3

Source: U.S. Department of Health and Human Services, Centers for Medicare and Medicaid Services
"2008 Data Compendium" (http://www.cms.hhs.gov/DataCompendium/)
*As of January 2008. Refers to Medicare Part B. Physicians include MDs, DOs, limited license practitioners, and non-physician practitioners. National average is a weighted average based on state population.

Enrollees in Medicare Prescription Drug Program in 2008

National Total = 25,935,144 Enrollees*

ALPHA ORDER

RANK	STATE	ENROLLEES	% of USA
19	Alabama	466,116	1.8%
50	Alaska	23,681	0.1%
16	Arizona	520,327	2.0%
31	Arkansas	301,784	1.2%
1	California	3,071,720	11.8%
27	Colorado	334,471	1.3%
32	Connecticut	294,441	1.1%
47	Delaware	68,787	0.3%
2	Florida	1,854,340	7.1%
10	Georgia	671,522	2.6%
40	Hawaii	125,672	0.5%
41	Idaho	120,086	0.5%
6	Illinois	968,978	3.7%
17	Indiana	506,588	2.0%
28	Iowa	331,453	1.3%
33	Kansas	250,665	1.0%
22	Kentucky	402,396	1.6%
23	Louisiana	393,897	1.5%
38	Maine	146,431	0.6%
29	Maryland	319,081	1.2%
14	Massachusetts	576,340	2.2%
9	Michigan	783,760	3.0%
18	Minnesota	499,965	1.9%
30	Mississippi	304,148	1.2%
13	Missouri	583,180	2.2%
44	Montana	90,540	0.3%
37	Nebraska	173,499	0.7%
35	Nevada	180,745	0.7%
43	New Hampshire	92,478	0.4%
11	New Jersey	656,900	2.5%
36	New Mexico	179,464	0.7%
3	New York	1,644,012	6.3%
8	North Carolina	814,813	3.1%
46	North Dakota	74,158	0.3%
7	Ohio	909,150	3.5%
26	Oklahoma	334,889	1.3%
25	Oregon	367,338	1.4%
5	Pennsylvania	1,356,759	5.2%
42	Rhode Island	117,083	0.5%
24	South Carolina	381,843	1.5%
45	South Dakota	86,410	0.3%
12	Tennessee	625,679	2.4%
4	Texas	1,552,002	6.0%
39	Utah	141,922	0.5%
48	Vermont	57,524	0.2%
15	Virginia	544,351	2.1%
20	Washington	463,426	1.8%
34	West Virginia	221,566	0.9%
21	Wisconsin	446,391	1.7%
49	Wyoming	40,927	0.2%

RANK ORDER

RANK	STATE	ENROLLEES	% of USA
1	California	3,071,720	11.8%
2	Florida	1,854,340	7.1%
3	New York	1,644,012	6.3%
4	Texas	1,552,002	6.0%
5	Pennsylvania	1,356,759	5.2%
6	Illinois	968,978	3.7%
7	Ohio	909,150	3.5%
8	North Carolina	814,813	3.1%
9	Michigan	783,760	3.0%
10	Georgia	671,522	2.6%
11	New Jersey	656,900	2.5%
12	Tennessee	625,679	2.4%
13	Missouri	583,180	2.2%
14	Massachusetts	576,340	2.2%
15	Virginia	544,351	2.1%
16	Arizona	520,327	2.0%
17	Indiana	506,588	2.0%
18	Minnesota	499,965	1.9%
19	Alabama	466,116	1.8%
20	Washington	463,426	1.8%
21	Wisconsin	446,391	1.7%
22	Kentucky	402,396	1.6%
23	Louisiana	393,897	1.5%
24	South Carolina	381,843	1.5%
25	Oregon	367,338	1.4%
26	Oklahoma	334,889	1.3%
27	Colorado	334,471	1.3%
28	Iowa	331,453	1.3%
29	Maryland	319,081	1.2%
30	Mississippi	304,148	1.2%
31	Arkansas	301,784	1.2%
32	Connecticut	294,441	1.1%
33	Kansas	250,665	1.0%
34	West Virginia	221,566	0.9%
35	Nevada	180,745	0.7%
36	New Mexico	179,464	0.7%
37	Nebraska	173,499	0.7%
38	Maine	146,431	0.6%
39	Utah	141,922	0.5%
40	Hawaii	125,672	0.5%
41	Idaho	120,086	0.5%
42	Rhode Island	117,083	0.5%
43	New Hampshire	92,478	0.4%
44	Montana	90,540	0.3%
45	South Dakota	86,410	0.3%
46	North Dakota	74,158	0.3%
47	Delaware	68,787	0.3%
48	Vermont	57,524	0.2%
49	Wyoming	40,927	0.2%
50	Alaska	23,681	0.1%
	District of Columbia	34,592	0.1%

Source: U.S. Department of Health and Human Services, Centers for Medicare and Medicaid Services
   "2008 Data Compendium" (http://www.cms.hhs.gov/DataCompendium/)
*Total includes 411,161 enrollees in U.S. territories.

Percent of Medicare Enrollees Participating in the Medicare Prescription Drug Program: 2008
National Percent = 57.0%*

ALPHA ORDER				RANK ORDER		
RANK	STATE	PERCENT		RANK	STATE	PERCENT
24	Alabama	57.5		1	North Dakota	69.6
50	Alaska	39.2		2	California	68.1
17	Arizona	59.8		3	Minnesota	66.4
19	Arkansas	59.2		4	Rhode Island	65.7
2	California	68.1		5	Iowa	65.3
24	Colorado	57.5		6	South Dakota	65.2
37	Connecticut	53.5		7	Hawaii	64.4
47	Delaware	48.8		8	Nebraska	63.8
22	Florida	57.8		9	Mississippi	63.4
20	Georgia	57.9		10	Oregon	62.7
7	Hawaii	64.4		11	Tennessee	62.3
30	Idaho	56.0		12	Pennsylvania	60.9
35	Illinois	54.4		13	New Mexico	60.8
40	Indiana	52.5		14	Missouri	60.2
5	Iowa	65.3		15	Kansas	59.9
15	Kansas	59.9		15	Louisiana	59.9
32	Kentucky	55.1		17	Arizona	59.8
15	Louisiana	59.9		18	West Virginia	59.3
24	Maine	57.5		19	Arkansas	59.2
49	Maryland	42.7		20	Georgia	57.9
28	Massachusetts	56.4		20	North Carolina	57.9
45	Michigan	49.5		22	Florida	57.8
3	Minnesota	66.4		23	Oklahoma	57.7
9	Mississippi	63.4		24	Alabama	57.5
14	Missouri	60.2		24	Colorado	57.5
29	Montana	56.2		24	Maine	57.5
8	Nebraska	63.8		27	New York	56.6
34	Nevada	54.5		28	Massachusetts	56.4
48	New Hampshire	44.9		29	Montana	56.2
42	New Jersey	51.0		30	Idaho	56.0
13	New Mexico	60.8		31	Texas	55.2
27	New York	56.6		32	Kentucky	55.1
20	North Carolina	57.9		33	Vermont	54.6
1	North Dakota	69.6		34	Nevada	54.5
46	Ohio	49.3		35	Illinois	54.4
23	Oklahoma	57.7		36	Wyoming	53.6
10	Oregon	62.7		37	Connecticut	53.5
12	Pennsylvania	60.9		37	Utah	53.5
4	Rhode Island	65.7		39	South Carolina	52.8
39	South Carolina	52.8		40	Indiana	52.5
6	South Dakota	65.2		41	Washington	51.1
11	Tennessee	62.3		42	New Jersey	51.0
31	Texas	55.2		43	Wisconsin	50.9
37	Utah	53.5		44	Virginia	50.2
33	Vermont	54.6		45	Michigan	49.5
44	Virginia	50.2		46	Ohio	49.3
41	Washington	51.1		47	Delaware	48.8
18	West Virginia	59.3		48	New Hampshire	44.9
43	Wisconsin	50.9		49	Maryland	42.7
36	Wyoming	53.6		50	Alaska	39.2
					District of Columbia	46.0

Source: U.S. Department of Health and Human Services, Centers for Medicare and Medicaid Services
   "2008 Data Compendium" (http://www.cms.hhs.gov/DataCompendium/)
*National figure includes enrollees in U.S. territories.

Medicare Program Payments in 2007

National Total = $287,442,000,000*

ALPHA ORDER

RANK	STATE	PAYMENTS	% of USA
18	Alabama	$5,246,000,000	1.8%
50	Alaska	370,000,000	0.1%
25	Arizona	4,114,000,000	1.4%
29	Arkansas	3,200,000,000	1.1%
1	California	24,275,000,000	8.4%
32	Colorado	2,770,000,000	1.0%
24	Connecticut	4,394,000,000	1.5%
41	Delaware	1,098,000,000	0.4%
2	Florida	22,494,000,000	7.8%
11	Georgia	7,562,000,000	2.6%
47	Hawaii	652,000,000	0.2%
42	Idaho	977,000,000	0.3%
5	Illinois	13,710,000,000	4.8%
15	Indiana	6,425,000,000	2.2%
30	Iowa	2,888,000,000	1.0%
31	Kansas	2,838,000,000	1.0%
21	Kentucky	4,801,000,000	1.7%
19	Louisiana	4,968,000,000	1.7%
37	Maine	1,568,000,000	0.5%
13	Maryland	6,560,000,000	2.3%
12	Massachusetts	7,166,000,000	2.5%
8	Michigan	11,685,000,000	4.1%
27	Minnesota	3,769,000,000	1.3%
28	Mississippi	3,654,000,000	1.3%
17	Missouri	6,224,000,000	2.2%
44	Montana	829,000,000	0.3%
35	Nebraska	1,783,000,000	0.6%
36	Nevada	1,736,000,000	0.6%
39	New Hampshire	1,358,000,000	0.5%
9	New Jersey	10,932,000,000	3.8%
38	New Mexico	1,429,000,000	0.5%
4	New York	19,663,000,000	6.8%
10	North Carolina	8,915,000,000	3.1%
48	North Dakota	602,000,000	0.2%
6	Ohio	12,294,000,000	4.3%
26	Oklahoma	4,065,000,000	1.4%
33	Oregon	2,241,000,000	0.8%
7	Pennsylvania	12,140,000,000	4.2%
43	Rhode Island	854,000,000	0.3%
21	South Carolina	4,801,000,000	1.7%
45	South Dakota	734,000,000	0.3%
16	Tennessee	6,303,000,000	2.2%
3	Texas	21,983,000,000	7.6%
40	Utah	1,338,000,000	0.5%
46	Vermont	679,000,000	0.2%
14	Virginia	6,525,000,000	2.3%
23	Washington	4,644,000,000	1.6%
34	West Virginia	2,235,000,000	0.8%
20	Wisconsin	4,833,000,000	1.7%
49	Wyoming	451,000,000	0.2%

RANK ORDER

RANK	STATE	PAYMENTS	% of USA
1	California	$24,275,000,000	8.4%
2	Florida	22,494,000,000	7.8%
3	Texas	21,983,000,000	7.6%
4	New York	19,663,000,000	6.8%
5	Illinois	13,710,000,000	4.8%
6	Ohio	12,294,000,000	4.3%
7	Pennsylvania	12,140,000,000	4.2%
8	Michigan	11,685,000,000	4.1%
9	New Jersey	10,932,000,000	3.8%
10	North Carolina	8,915,000,000	3.1%
11	Georgia	7,562,000,000	2.6%
12	Massachusetts	7,166,000,000	2.5%
13	Maryland	6,560,000,000	2.3%
14	Virginia	6,525,000,000	2.3%
15	Indiana	6,425,000,000	2.2%
16	Tennessee	6,303,000,000	2.2%
17	Missouri	6,224,000,000	2.2%
18	Alabama	5,246,000,000	1.8%
19	Louisiana	4,968,000,000	1.7%
20	Wisconsin	4,833,000,000	1.7%
21	Kentucky	4,801,000,000	1.7%
21	South Carolina	4,801,000,000	1.7%
23	Washington	4,644,000,000	1.6%
24	Connecticut	4,394,000,000	1.5%
25	Arizona	4,114,000,000	1.4%
26	Oklahoma	4,065,000,000	1.4%
27	Minnesota	3,769,000,000	1.3%
28	Mississippi	3,654,000,000	1.3%
29	Arkansas	3,200,000,000	1.1%
30	Iowa	2,888,000,000	1.0%
31	Kansas	2,838,000,000	1.0%
32	Colorado	2,770,000,000	1.0%
33	Oregon	2,241,000,000	0.8%
34	West Virginia	2,235,000,000	0.8%
35	Nebraska	1,783,000,000	0.6%
36	Nevada	1,736,000,000	0.6%
37	Maine	1,568,000,000	0.5%
38	New Mexico	1,429,000,000	0.5%
39	New Hampshire	1,358,000,000	0.5%
40	Utah	1,338,000,000	0.5%
41	Delaware	1,098,000,000	0.4%
42	Idaho	977,000,000	0.3%
43	Rhode Island	854,000,000	0.3%
44	Montana	829,000,000	0.3%
45	South Dakota	734,000,000	0.3%
46	Vermont	679,000,000	0.2%
47	Hawaii	652,000,000	0.2%
48	North Dakota	602,000,000	0.2%
49	Wyoming	451,000,000	0.2%
50	Alaska	370,000,000	0.1%
	District of Columbia	670,000,000	0.2%

Source: U.S. Department of Health and Human Services, Centers for Medicare and Medicaid Services
"Health Care Financing Review, 2008 Statistical Supplement" (http://cms.hhs.gov/MedicareMedicaidStatSupp)
*Figures for calendar year 2007. Includes payments to aged and disabled enrollees. Total does not include payments to beneficiaries in Puerto Rico and other outlying areas.

Per Capita Medicare Program Payments in 2007

National Per Capita = $954*

ALPHA ORDER

RANK	STATE	PER CAPITA
11	Alabama	$1,134
48	Alaska	543
45	Arizona	648
13	Arkansas	1,131
43	California	667
47	Colorado	572
3	Connecticut	1,259
1	Delaware	1,274
5	Florida	1,236
38	Georgia	794
49	Hawaii	510
44	Idaho	653
19	Illinois	1,069
24	Indiana	1,014
29	Iowa	968
23	Kansas	1,022
12	Kentucky	1,133
10	Louisiana	1,136
7	Maine	1,192
8	Maryland	1,167
15	Massachusetts	1,108
9	Michigan	1,163
39	Minnesota	727
4	Mississippi	1,251
20	Missouri	1,059
33	Montana	867
26	Nebraska	1,008
42	Nevada	680
21	New Hampshire	1,035
2	New Jersey	1,263
39	New Mexico	727
25	New York	1,012
27	North Carolina	986
30	North Dakota	944
18	Ohio	1,071
14	Oklahoma	1,127
46	Oregon	600
28	Pennsylvania	977
37	Rhode Island	811
17	South Carolina	1,090
31	South Dakota	922
22	Tennessee	1,025
31	Texas	922
50	Utah	501
16	Vermont	1,094
36	Virginia	848
41	Washington	720
6	West Virginia	1,235
34	Wisconsin	863
35	Wyoming	862

RANK ORDER

RANK	STATE	PER CAPITA
1	Delaware	$1,274
2	New Jersey	1,263
3	Connecticut	1,259
4	Mississippi	1,251
5	Florida	1,236
6	West Virginia	1,235
7	Maine	1,192
8	Maryland	1,167
9	Michigan	1,163
10	Louisiana	1,136
11	Alabama	1,134
12	Kentucky	1,133
13	Arkansas	1,131
14	Oklahoma	1,127
15	Massachusetts	1,108
16	Vermont	1,094
17	South Carolina	1,090
18	Ohio	1,071
19	Illinois	1,069
20	Missouri	1,059
21	New Hampshire	1,035
22	Tennessee	1,025
23	Kansas	1,022
24	Indiana	1,014
25	New York	1,012
26	Nebraska	1,008
27	North Carolina	986
28	Pennsylvania	977
29	Iowa	968
30	North Dakota	944
31	South Dakota	922
31	Texas	922
33	Montana	867
34	Wisconsin	863
35	Wyoming	862
36	Virginia	848
37	Rhode Island	811
38	Georgia	794
39	Minnesota	727
39	New Mexico	727
41	Washington	720
42	Nevada	680
43	California	667
44	Idaho	653
45	Arizona	648
46	Oregon	600
47	Colorado	572
48	Alaska	543
49	Hawaii	510
50	Utah	501

District of Columbia 1,140

Source: CQ Press using data from U.S. Department of Health and Human Services, Centers for Medicare and Medicaid Services
"Health Care Financing Review, 2008 Statistical Supplement" (http://www.cms.hhs.gov/MedicareMedicaidStatSupp)
*Figures for calendar year 2007. Includes payments to aged and disabled enrollees. National rate does not include payments or enrollees in Puerto Rico and other outlying areas.

Medicare Program Payments per Enrollee in 2007

National Rate = $8,246*

ALPHA ORDER

RANK	STATE	PER ENROLLEE
18	Alabama	$7,815
39	Alaska	6,720
26	Arizona	7,576
31	Arkansas	7,313
12	California	8,332
34	Colorado	7,159
7	Connecticut	9,093
15	Delaware	8,197
2	Florida	9,594
25	Georgia	7,577
50	Hawaii	5,292
49	Idaho	6,014
10	Illinois	8,561
23	Indiana	7,658
41	Iowa	6,619
29	Kansas	7,514
24	Kentucky	7,625
5	Louisiana	9,388
42	Maine	6,553
1	Maryland	9,628
9	Massachusetts	8,684
8	Michigan	8,974
30	Minnesota	7,396
11	Mississippi	8,440
19	Missouri	7,795
48	Montana	6,026
32	Nebraska	7,279
21	Nevada	7,705
35	New Hampshire	6,947
4	New Jersey	9,520
43	New Mexico	6,472
6	New York	9,128
22	North Carolina	7,694
47	North Dakota	6,029
13	Ohio	8,245
16	Oklahoma	8,191
44	Oregon	6,451
14	Pennsylvania	8,239
28	Rhode Island	7,544
20	South Carolina	7,746
46	South Dakota	6,081
17	Tennessee	7,847
3	Texas	9,542
37	Utah	6,807
38	Vermont	6,740
36	Virginia	6,907
40	Washington	6,658
27	West Virginia	7,557
33	Wisconsin	7,187
45	Wyoming	6,234

RANK ORDER

RANK	STATE	PER ENROLLEE
1	Maryland	$9,628
2	Florida	9,594
3	Texas	9,542
4	New Jersey	9,520
5	Louisiana	9,388
6	New York	9,128
7	Connecticut	9,093
8	Michigan	8,974
9	Massachusetts	8,684
10	Illinois	8,561
11	Mississippi	8,440
12	California	8,332
13	Ohio	8,245
14	Pennsylvania	8,239
15	Delaware	8,197
16	Oklahoma	8,191
17	Tennessee	7,847
18	Alabama	7,815
19	Missouri	7,795
20	South Carolina	7,746
21	Nevada	7,705
22	North Carolina	7,694
23	Indiana	7,658
24	Kentucky	7,625
25	Georgia	7,577
26	Arizona	7,576
27	West Virginia	7,557
28	Rhode Island	7,544
29	Kansas	7,514
30	Minnesota	7,396
31	Arkansas	7,313
32	Nebraska	7,279
33	Wisconsin	7,187
34	Colorado	7,159
35	New Hampshire	6,947
36	Virginia	6,907
37	Utah	6,807
38	Vermont	6,740
39	Alaska	6,720
40	Washington	6,658
41	Iowa	6,619
42	Maine	6,553
43	New Mexico	6,472
44	Oregon	6,451
45	Wyoming	6,234
46	South Dakota	6,081
47	North Dakota	6,029
48	Montana	6,026
49	Idaho	6,014
50	Hawaii	5,292

	District of Columbia	9,732

Source: U.S. Department of Health and Human Services, Centers for Medicare and Medicaid Services
"Health Care Financing Review, 2008 Statistical Supplement" (http://cms.hhs.gov/MedicareMedicaidStatSupp)
*Figures for calendar year 2007. Includes payments to aged and disabled enrollees. National figure does not include enrollees in managed care plans in the denominator used to calculate average payments. National rate also does not include payments or enrollees in Puerto Rico and other outlying areas.

Medicaid Enrollment in 2007

National Total = 45,962,000 Enrollees*

ALPHA ORDER					RANK ORDER			
RANK	STATE	ENROLLMENT	% of USA		RANK	STATE	ENROLLMENT	% of USA
20	Alabama	724,000	1.6%		1	California	6,465,000	14.1%
47	Alaska	96,000	0.2%		2	New York	4,120,000	9.0%
14	Arizona	990,000	2.2%		3	Texas	3,002,000	6.5%
25	Arkansas	626,000	1.4%		4	Florida	2,195,000	4.8%
1	California	6,465,000	14.1%		5	Illinois	2,003,000	4.4%
32	Colorado	381,000	0.8%		6	Pennsylvania	1,773,000	3.9%
30	Connecticut	405,000	0.9%		7	Ohio	1,719,000	3.7%
44	Delaware	144,000	0.3%		8	Michigan	1,520,000	3.3%
4	Florida	2,195,000	4.8%		9	Georgia	1,502,000	3.3%
9	Georgia	1,502,000	3.3%		10	North Carolina	1,317,000	2.9%
38	Hawaii	202,000	0.4%		11	Tennessee	1,182,000	2.6%
41	Idaho	180,000	0.4%		12	Massachusetts	1,082,000	2.4%
5	Illinois	2,003,000	4.4%		13	Washington	993,000	2.2%
18	Indiana	826,000	1.8%		14	Arizona	990,000	2.2%
33	Iowa	366,000	0.8%		15	Louisiana	935,000	2.0%
35	Kansas	272,000	0.6%		16	New Jersey	878,000	1.9%
21	Kentucky	714,000	1.6%		17	Wisconsin	852,000	1.9%
15	Louisiana	935,000	2.0%		18	Indiana	826,000	1.8%
36	Maine	254,000	0.6%		19	Missouri	823,000	1.8%
23	Maryland	693,000	1.5%		20	Alabama	724,000	1.6%
12	Massachusetts	1,082,000	2.4%		21	Kentucky	714,000	1.6%
8	Michigan	1,520,000	3.3%		22	Virginia	695,000	1.5%
26	Minnesota	594,000	1.3%		23	Maryland	693,000	1.5%
28	Mississippi	548,000	1.2%		24	South Carolina	655,000	1.4%
19	Missouri	823,000	1.8%		25	Arkansas	626,000	1.4%
48	Montana	80,000	0.2%		26	Minnesota	594,000	1.3%
37	Nebraska	210,000	0.5%		27	Oklahoma	592,000	1.3%
42	Nevada	170,000	0.4%		28	Mississippi	548,000	1.2%
45	New Hampshire	109,000	0.2%		29	New Mexico	414,000	0.9%
16	New Jersey	878,000	1.9%		30	Connecticut	405,000	0.9%
29	New Mexico	414,000	0.9%		31	Oregon	396,000	0.9%
2	New York	4,120,000	9.0%		32	Colorado	381,000	0.8%
10	North Carolina	1,317,000	2.9%		33	Iowa	366,000	0.8%
50	North Dakota	52,000	0.1%		34	West Virginia	304,000	0.7%
7	Ohio	1,719,000	3.7%		35	Kansas	272,000	0.6%
27	Oklahoma	592,000	1.3%		36	Maine	254,000	0.6%
31	Oregon	396,000	0.9%		37	Nebraska	210,000	0.5%
6	Pennsylvania	1,773,000	3.9%		38	Hawaii	202,000	0.4%
40	Rhode Island	181,000	0.4%		39	Utah	201,000	0.4%
24	South Carolina	655,000	1.4%		40	Rhode Island	181,000	0.4%
46	South Dakota	101,000	0.2%		41	Idaho	180,000	0.4%
11	Tennessee	1,182,000	2.6%		42	Nevada	170,000	0.4%
3	Texas	3,002,000	6.5%		43	Vermont	146,000	0.3%
39	Utah	201,000	0.4%		44	Delaware	144,000	0.3%
43	Vermont	146,000	0.3%		45	New Hampshire	109,000	0.2%
22	Virginia	695,000	1.5%		46	South Dakota	101,000	0.2%
13	Washington	993,000	2.2%		47	Alaska	96,000	0.2%
34	West Virginia	304,000	0.7%		48	Montana	80,000	0.2%
17	Wisconsin	852,000	1.9%		49	Wyoming	61,000	0.1%
49	Wyoming	61,000	0.1%		50	North Dakota	52,000	0.1%
						District of Columbia	142,000	0.3%

Source: U.S. Department of Health and Human Services, Centers for Medicare and Medicaid Services
"2007 Medicaid Managed Care Enrollment Report" (http://www.cms.hhs.gov/MedicaidDataSourcesGenInfo/)
*Unduplicated enrollment as of June 30, 2007. National total includes 1,074,000 Medicaid enrollees in Puerto Rico and the Virgin Islands.

Percent of Population Enrolled in Medicaid in 2007

National Percent = 14.9% of Population*

ALPHA ORDER

RANK	STATE	PERCENT
18	Alabama	15.6
28	Alaska	14.1
18	Arizona	15.6
2	Arkansas	22.1
9	California	17.8
48	Colorado	7.9
39	Connecticut	11.6
13	Delaware	16.7
35	Florida	12.1
16	Georgia	15.8
16	Hawaii	15.8
36	Idaho	12.0
18	Illinois	15.6
30	Indiana	13.0
33	Iowa	12.3
43	Kansas	9.8
11	Kentucky	16.9
3	Louisiana	21.4
6	Maine	19.3
33	Maryland	12.3
13	Massachusetts	16.7
23	Michigan	15.1
40	Minnesota	11.5
8	Mississippi	18.8
29	Missouri	14.0
45	Montana	8.4
37	Nebraska	11.9
50	Nevada	6.7
46	New Hampshire	8.3
42	New Jersey	10.1
5	New Mexico	21.1
4	New York	21.2
26	North Carolina	14.6
47	North Dakota	8.2
24	Ohio	15.0
15	Oklahoma	16.4
41	Oregon	10.6
27	Pennsylvania	14.3
10	Rhode Island	17.2
25	South Carolina	14.9
31	South Dakota	12.7
7	Tennessee	19.2
32	Texas	12.6
49	Utah	7.5
1	Vermont	23.5
44	Virginia	9.0
21	Washington	15.4
12	West Virginia	16.8
22	Wisconsin	15.2
38	Wyoming	11.7

RANK ORDER

RANK	STATE	PERCENT
1	Vermont	23.5
2	Arkansas	22.1
3	Louisiana	21.4
4	New York	21.2
5	New Mexico	21.1
6	Maine	19.3
7	Tennessee	19.2
8	Mississippi	18.8
9	California	17.8
10	Rhode Island	17.2
11	Kentucky	16.9
12	West Virginia	16.8
13	Delaware	16.7
13	Massachusetts	16.7
15	Oklahoma	16.4
16	Georgia	15.8
16	Hawaii	15.8
18	Alabama	15.6
18	Arizona	15.6
18	Illinois	15.6
21	Washington	15.4
22	Wisconsin	15.2
23	Michigan	15.1
24	Ohio	15.0
25	South Carolina	14.9
26	North Carolina	14.6
27	Pennsylvania	14.3
28	Alaska	14.1
29	Missouri	14.0
30	Indiana	13.0
31	South Dakota	12.7
32	Texas	12.6
33	Iowa	12.3
33	Maryland	12.3
35	Florida	12.1
36	Idaho	12.0
37	Nebraska	11.9
38	Wyoming	11.7
39	Connecticut	11.6
40	Minnesota	11.5
41	Oregon	10.6
42	New Jersey	10.1
43	Kansas	9.8
44	Virginia	9.0
45	Montana	8.4
46	New Hampshire	8.3
47	North Dakota	8.2
48	Colorado	7.9
49	Utah	7.5
50	Nevada	6.7

District of Columbia   24.2

Source: CQ Press using data from U.S. Department of Health and Human Services, Centers for Medicare and Medicaid Services
"2007 Medicaid Managed Care Enrollment Report" (http://www.cms.hhs.gov/MedicaidDataSourcesGenInfo/)
*Unduplicated enrollment as of June 30, 2007. National percent does not include recipients or population in U.S. territories.

Medicaid Managed Care Enrollment in 2007

National Total = 29,463,000 Enrollees*

ALPHA ORDER

RANK	STATE	ENROLLMENT	% of USA
20	Alabama	472,000	1.6%
48	Alaska	0	0.0%
10	Arizona	890,000	3.0%
18	Arkansas	511,000	1.7%
1	California	3,286,000	11.2%
26	Colorado	359,000	1.2%
29	Connecticut	299,000	1.0%
44	Delaware	96,000	0.3%
5	Florida	1,355,000	4.6%
9	Georgia	965,000	3.3%
35	Hawaii	161,000	0.5%
36	Idaho	152,000	0.5%
17	Illinois	568,000	1.9%
16	Indiana	600,000	2.0%
30	Iowa	283,000	1.0%
39	Kansas	139,000	0.5%
21	Kentucky	448,000	1.5%
14	Louisiana	636,000	2.2%
32	Maine	172,000	0.6%
19	Maryland	502,000	1.7%
13	Massachusetts	642,000	2.2%
6	Michigan	1,343,000	4.6%
25	Minnesota	367,000	1.2%
48	Mississippi	0	0.0%
28	Missouri	345,000	1.2%
46	Montana	45,000	0.2%
33	Nebraska	170,000	0.6%
38	Nevada	144,000	0.5%
45	New Hampshire	84,000	0.3%
15	New Jersey	620,000	2.1%
31	New Mexico	256,000	0.9%
2	New York	2,559,000	8.7%
12	North Carolina	848,000	2.9%
47	North Dakota	29,000	0.1%
7	Ohio	1,194,000	4.1%
23	Oklahoma	412,000	1.4%
26	Oregon	359,000	1.2%
4	Pennsylvania	1,439,000	4.9%
42	Rhode Island	114,000	0.4%
37	South Carolina	150,000	0.5%
43	South Dakota	99,000	0.3%
8	Tennessee	1,182,000	4.0%
3	Texas	2,021,000	6.9%
34	Utah	165,000	0.6%
41	Vermont	123,000	0.4%
22	Virginia	446,000	1.5%
11	Washington	849,000	2.9%
40	West Virginia	135,000	0.5%
24	Wisconsin	411,000	1.4%
48	Wyoming	0	0.0%

RANK ORDER

RANK	STATE	ENROLLMENT	% of USA
1	California	3,286,000	11.2%
2	New York	2,559,000	8.7%
3	Texas	2,021,000	6.9%
4	Pennsylvania	1,439,000	4.9%
5	Florida	1,355,000	4.6%
6	Michigan	1,343,000	4.6%
7	Ohio	1,194,000	4.1%
8	Tennessee	1,182,000	4.0%
9	Georgia	965,000	3.3%
10	Arizona	890,000	3.0%
11	Washington	849,000	2.9%
12	North Carolina	848,000	2.9%
13	Massachusetts	642,000	2.2%
14	Louisiana	636,000	2.2%
15	New Jersey	620,000	2.1%
16	Indiana	600,000	2.0%
17	Illinois	568,000	1.9%
18	Arkansas	511,000	1.7%
19	Maryland	502,000	1.7%
20	Alabama	472,000	1.6%
21	Kentucky	448,000	1.5%
22	Virginia	446,000	1.5%
23	Oklahoma	412,000	1.4%
24	Wisconsin	411,000	1.4%
25	Minnesota	367,000	1.2%
26	Colorado	359,000	1.2%
26	Oregon	359,000	1.2%
28	Missouri	345,000	1.2%
29	Connecticut	299,000	1.0%
30	Iowa	283,000	1.0%
31	New Mexico	256,000	0.9%
32	Maine	172,000	0.6%
33	Nebraska	170,000	0.6%
34	Utah	165,000	0.6%
35	Hawaii	161,000	0.5%
36	Idaho	152,000	0.5%
37	South Carolina	150,000	0.5%
38	Nevada	144,000	0.5%
39	Kansas	139,000	0.5%
40	West Virginia	135,000	0.5%
41	Vermont	123,000	0.4%
42	Rhode Island	114,000	0.4%
43	South Dakota	99,000	0.3%
44	Delaware	96,000	0.3%
45	New Hampshire	84,000	0.3%
46	Montana	45,000	0.2%
47	North Dakota	29,000	0.1%
48	Alaska	0	0.0%
48	Mississippi	0	0.0%
48	Wyoming	0	0.0%
	District of Columbia	92,000	0.3%

Source: U.S. Department of Health and Human Services, Centers for Medicare and Medicaid Services
"2007 Medicaid Managed Care Enrollment Report" (http://www.cms.hhs.gov/MedicaidDataSourcesGenInfo/)
*Unduplicated enrollment as of June 30, 2007. Enrollment in state health care reform programs that expand eligibility beyond traditional Medicaid standards. National total includes 922,000 Medicaid managed care enrollees in Puerto Rico.

Percent of Medicaid Enrollees in Managed Care in 2007

National Percent = 64.1% of Medicaid Enrollees*

ALPHA ORDER

RANK	STATE	PERCENT
28	Alabama	65.1
48	Alaska	0.0
5	Arizona	89.9
12	Arkansas	81.7
42	California	50.8
3	Colorado	94.1
18	Connecticut	73.7
27	Delaware	66.9
37	Florida	61.7
30	Georgia	64.2
15	Hawaii	79.9
8	Idaho	84.8
46	Illinois	28.4
19	Indiana	72.6
16	Iowa	77.4
41	Kansas	51.1
33	Kentucky	62.8
24	Louisiana	68.1
25	Maine	67.4
20	Maryland	72.4
38	Massachusetts	59.3
6	Michigan	88.4
36	Minnesota	61.8
48	Mississippi	0.0
45	Missouri	41.9
40	Montana	55.7
13	Nebraska	81.2
8	Nevada	84.8
17	New Hampshire	77.2
21	New Jersey	70.6
35	New Mexico	61.9
34	New York	62.1
29	North Carolina	64.4
39	North Dakota	56.0
22	Ohio	69.5
22	Oklahoma	69.5
4	Oregon	90.8
13	Pennsylvania	81.2
32	Rhode Island	63.1
47	South Carolina	22.9
2	South Dakota	98.6
1	Tennessee	100.0
26	Texas	67.3
11	Utah	82.3
10	Vermont	84.3
30	Virginia	64.2
7	Washington	85.5
44	West Virginia	44.6
43	Wisconsin	48.2
48	Wyoming	0.0

RANK ORDER

RANK	STATE	PERCENT
1	Tennessee	100.0
2	South Dakota	98.6
3	Colorado	94.1
4	Oregon	90.8
5	Arizona	89.9
6	Michigan	88.4
7	Washington	85.5
8	Idaho	84.8
8	Nevada	84.8
10	Vermont	84.3
11	Utah	82.3
12	Arkansas	81.7
13	Nebraska	81.2
13	Pennsylvania	81.2
15	Hawaii	79.9
16	Iowa	77.4
17	New Hampshire	77.2
18	Connecticut	73.7
19	Indiana	72.6
20	Maryland	72.4
21	New Jersey	70.6
22	Ohio	69.5
22	Oklahoma	69.5
24	Louisiana	68.1
25	Maine	67.4
26	Texas	67.3
27	Delaware	66.9
28	Alabama	65.1
29	North Carolina	64.4
30	Georgia	64.2
30	Virginia	64.2
32	Rhode Island	63.1
33	Kentucky	62.8
34	New York	62.1
35	New Mexico	61.9
36	Minnesota	61.8
37	Florida	61.7
38	Massachusetts	59.3
39	North Dakota	56.0
40	Montana	55.7
41	Kansas	51.1
42	California	50.8
43	Wisconsin	48.2
44	West Virginia	44.6
45	Missouri	41.9
46	Illinois	28.4
47	South Carolina	22.9
48	Alaska	0.0
48	Mississippi	0.0
48	Wyoming	0.0

| | District of Columbia | 64.7 |

Source: U.S. Department of Health and Human Services, Centers for Medicare and Medicaid Services
 "2007 Medicaid Managed Care Enrollment Report" (http://www.cms.hhs.gov/MedicaidDataSourcesGenInfo/)
*Unduplicated enrollment as of June 30, 2007. Enrollment in state health care reform programs that expand eligibility beyond traditional Medicaid standards. National percent includes Medicaid enrollees in Puerto Rico and the Virgin Islands.

Estimated Medicaid Expenditures in 2008

National Total = $322,027,000,000*

ALPHA ORDER

RANK	STATE	EXPENDITURES	% of USA
25	Alabama	$4,325,000,000	1.3%
41	Alaska	1,212,000,000	0.4%
15	Arizona	6,786,000,000	2.1%
28	Arkansas	3,573,000,000	1.1%
1	California	36,639,000,000	11.4%
32	Colorado	2,746,000,000	0.9%
26	Connecticut	4,304,000,000	1.3%
45	Delaware	1,059,000,000	0.3%
5	Florida	14,913,000,000	4.6%
12	Georgia	7,735,000,000	2.4%
44	Hawaii	1,161,000,000	0.4%
42	Idaho	1,208,000,000	0.4%
7	Illinois	13,958,000,000	4.3%
21	Indiana	5,252,000,000	1.6%
33	Iowa	2,731,000,000	0.8%
35	Kansas	2,379,000,000	0.7%
24	Kentucky	4,837,000,000	1.5%
17	Louisiana	6,006,000,000	1.9%
34	Maine	2,401,000,000	0.7%
19	Maryland	5,553,000,000	1.7%
11	Massachusetts	8,248,000,000	2.6%
9	Michigan	10,143,000,000	3.1%
16	Minnesota	6,469,000,000	2.0%
30	Mississippi	3,158,000,000	1.0%
13	Missouri	7,633,000,000	2.4%
47	Montana	787,000,000	0.2%
38	Nebraska	1,719,000,000	0.5%
43	Nevada	1,167,000,000	0.4%
40	New Hampshire	1,250,000,000	0.4%
10	New Jersey	8,899,000,000	2.8%
31	New Mexico	2,971,000,000	0.9%
2	New York	31,040,000,000	9.6%
8	North Carolina	10,994,000,000	3.4%
49	North Dakota	557,000,000	0.2%
6	Ohio	14,090,000,000	4.4%
27	Oklahoma	3,716,000,000	1.2%
29	Oregon	3,368,000,000	1.0%
4	Pennsylvania	18,096,000,000	5.6%
37	Rhode Island	1,820,000,000	0.6%
22	South Carolina	4,925,000,000	1.5%
48	South Dakota	717,000,000	0.2%
14	Tennessee	7,611,000,000	2.4%
3	Texas	22,187,000,000	6.9%
39	Utah	1,603,000,000	0.5%
46	Vermont	952,000,000	0.3%
20	Virginia	5,346,000,000	1.7%
18	Washington	5,989,000,000	1.9%
36	West Virginia	2,369,000,000	0.7%
23	Wisconsin	4,921,000,000	1.5%
50	Wyoming	504,000,000	0.2%

RANK ORDER

RANK	STATE	EXPENDITURES	% of USA
1	California	$36,639,000,000	11.4%
2	New York	31,040,000,000	9.6%
3	Texas	22,187,000,000	6.9%
4	Pennsylvania	18,096,000,000	5.6%
5	Florida	14,913,000,000	4.6%
6	Ohio	14,090,000,000	4.4%
7	Illinois	13,958,000,000	4.3%
8	North Carolina	10,994,000,000	3.4%
9	Michigan	10,143,000,000	3.1%
10	New Jersey	8,899,000,000	2.8%
11	Massachusetts	8,248,000,000	2.6%
12	Georgia	7,735,000,000	2.4%
13	Missouri	7,633,000,000	2.4%
14	Tennessee	7,611,000,000	2.4%
15	Arizona	6,786,000,000	2.1%
16	Minnesota	6,469,000,000	2.0%
17	Louisiana	6,006,000,000	1.9%
18	Washington	5,989,000,000	1.9%
19	Maryland	5,553,000,000	1.7%
20	Virginia	5,346,000,000	1.7%
21	Indiana	5,252,000,000	1.6%
22	South Carolina	4,925,000,000	1.5%
23	Wisconsin	4,921,000,000	1.5%
24	Kentucky	4,837,000,000	1.5%
25	Alabama	4,325,000,000	1.3%
26	Connecticut	4,304,000,000	1.3%
27	Oklahoma	3,716,000,000	1.2%
28	Arkansas	3,573,000,000	1.1%
29	Oregon	3,368,000,000	1.0%
30	Mississippi	3,158,000,000	1.0%
31	New Mexico	2,971,000,000	0.9%
32	Colorado	2,746,000,000	0.9%
33	Iowa	2,731,000,000	0.8%
34	Maine	2,401,000,000	0.7%
35	Kansas	2,379,000,000	0.7%
36	West Virginia	2,369,000,000	0.7%
37	Rhode Island	1,820,000,000	0.6%
38	Nebraska	1,719,000,000	0.5%
39	Utah	1,603,000,000	0.5%
40	New Hampshire	1,250,000,000	0.4%
41	Alaska	1,212,000,000	0.4%
42	Idaho	1,208,000,000	0.4%
43	Nevada	1,167,000,000	0.4%
44	Hawaii	1,161,000,000	0.4%
45	Delaware	1,059,000,000	0.3%
46	Vermont	952,000,000	0.3%
47	Montana	787,000,000	0.2%
48	South Dakota	717,000,000	0.2%
49	North Dakota	557,000,000	0.2%
50	Wyoming	504,000,000	0.2%
	District of Columbia**	NA	NA

Source: National Association of State Budget Officers
"2007 State Expenditure Report" (http://www.nasbo.org)
*Estimates for fiscal year 2008.
**Not available.

Estimated Per Capita Medicaid Expenditures in 2008

National Per Capita = $1,059*

<table>
<tr><td colspan="3">ALPHA ORDER</td><td colspan="3">RANK ORDER</td></tr>
<tr><td>RANK</td><td>STATE</td><td>PER CAPITA</td><td>RANK</td><td>STATE</td><td>PER CAPITA</td></tr>
<tr><td>32</td><td>Alabama</td><td>$928</td><td>1</td><td>Maine</td><td>$1,824</td></tr>
<tr><td>2</td><td>Alaska</td><td>1,766</td><td>2</td><td>Alaska</td><td>1,766</td></tr>
<tr><td>23</td><td>Arizona</td><td>1,044</td><td>3</td><td>Rhode Island</td><td>1,732</td></tr>
<tr><td>12</td><td>Arkansas</td><td>1,251</td><td>4</td><td>New York</td><td>1,593</td></tr>
<tr><td>27</td><td>California</td><td>997</td><td>5</td><td>Vermont</td><td>1,532</td></tr>
<tr><td>49</td><td>Colorado</td><td>556</td><td>6</td><td>New Mexico</td><td>1,497</td></tr>
<tr><td>14</td><td>Connecticut</td><td>1,229</td><td>7</td><td>Pennsylvania</td><td>1,454</td></tr>
<tr><td>17</td><td>Delaware</td><td>1,213</td><td>8</td><td>Louisiana</td><td>1,362</td></tr>
<tr><td>43</td><td>Florida</td><td>814</td><td>9</td><td>West Virginia</td><td>1,306</td></tr>
<tr><td>45</td><td>Georgia</td><td>799</td><td>10</td><td>Missouri</td><td>1,291</td></tr>
<tr><td>36</td><td>Hawaii</td><td>901</td><td>11</td><td>Massachusetts</td><td>1,269</td></tr>
<tr><td>46</td><td>Idaho</td><td>793</td><td>12</td><td>Arkansas</td><td>1,251</td></tr>
<tr><td>21</td><td>Illinois</td><td>1,082</td><td>13</td><td>Minnesota</td><td>1,239</td></tr>
<tr><td>42</td><td>Indiana</td><td>824</td><td>14</td><td>Connecticut</td><td>1,229</td></tr>
<tr><td>35</td><td>Iowa</td><td>910</td><td>15</td><td>Ohio</td><td>1,227</td></tr>
<tr><td>41</td><td>Kansas</td><td>849</td><td>16</td><td>Tennessee</td><td>1,225</td></tr>
<tr><td>19</td><td>Kentucky</td><td>1,133</td><td>17</td><td>Delaware</td><td>1,213</td></tr>
<tr><td>8</td><td>Louisiana</td><td>1,362</td><td>18</td><td>North Carolina</td><td>1,192</td></tr>
<tr><td>1</td><td>Maine</td><td>1,824</td><td>19</td><td>Kentucky</td><td>1,133</td></tr>
<tr><td>28</td><td>Maryland</td><td>986</td><td>20</td><td>South Carolina</td><td>1,099</td></tr>
<tr><td>11</td><td>Massachusetts</td><td>1,269</td><td>21</td><td>Illinois</td><td>1,082</td></tr>
<tr><td>26</td><td>Michigan</td><td>1,014</td><td>22</td><td>Mississippi</td><td>1,075</td></tr>
<tr><td>13</td><td>Minnesota</td><td>1,239</td><td>23</td><td>Arizona</td><td>1,044</td></tr>
<tr><td>22</td><td>Mississippi</td><td>1,075</td><td>24</td><td>New Jersey</td><td>1,025</td></tr>
<tr><td>10</td><td>Missouri</td><td>1,291</td><td>25</td><td>Oklahoma</td><td>1,020</td></tr>
<tr><td>44</td><td>Montana</td><td>813</td><td>26</td><td>Michigan</td><td>1,014</td></tr>
<tr><td>29</td><td>Nebraska</td><td>964</td><td>27</td><td>California</td><td>997</td></tr>
<tr><td>50</td><td>Nevada</td><td>449</td><td>28</td><td>Maryland</td><td>986</td></tr>
<tr><td>30</td><td>New Hampshire</td><td>950</td><td>29</td><td>Nebraska</td><td>964</td></tr>
<tr><td>24</td><td>New Jersey</td><td>1,025</td><td>30</td><td>New Hampshire</td><td>950</td></tr>
<tr><td>6</td><td>New Mexico</td><td>1,497</td><td>31</td><td>Wyoming</td><td>946</td></tr>
<tr><td>4</td><td>New York</td><td>1,593</td><td>32</td><td>Alabama</td><td>928</td></tr>
<tr><td>18</td><td>North Carolina</td><td>1,192</td><td>33</td><td>Washington</td><td>914</td></tr>
<tr><td>40</td><td>North Dakota</td><td>868</td><td>34</td><td>Texas</td><td>912</td></tr>
<tr><td>15</td><td>Ohio</td><td>1,227</td><td>35</td><td>Iowa</td><td>910</td></tr>
<tr><td>25</td><td>Oklahoma</td><td>1,020</td><td>36</td><td>Hawaii</td><td>901</td></tr>
<tr><td>38</td><td>Oregon</td><td>889</td><td>37</td><td>South Dakota</td><td>892</td></tr>
<tr><td>7</td><td>Pennsylvania</td><td>1,454</td><td>38</td><td>Oregon</td><td>889</td></tr>
<tr><td>3</td><td>Rhode Island</td><td>1,732</td><td>39</td><td>Wisconsin</td><td>874</td></tr>
<tr><td>20</td><td>South Carolina</td><td>1,099</td><td>40</td><td>North Dakota</td><td>868</td></tr>
<tr><td>37</td><td>South Dakota</td><td>892</td><td>41</td><td>Kansas</td><td>849</td></tr>
<tr><td>16</td><td>Tennessee</td><td>1,225</td><td>42</td><td>Indiana</td><td>824</td></tr>
<tr><td>34</td><td>Texas</td><td>912</td><td>43</td><td>Florida</td><td>814</td></tr>
<tr><td>48</td><td>Utah</td><td>586</td><td>44</td><td>Montana</td><td>813</td></tr>
<tr><td>5</td><td>Vermont</td><td>1,532</td><td>45</td><td>Georgia</td><td>799</td></tr>
<tr><td>47</td><td>Virginia</td><td>688</td><td>46</td><td>Idaho</td><td>793</td></tr>
<tr><td>33</td><td>Washington</td><td>914</td><td>47</td><td>Virginia</td><td>688</td></tr>
<tr><td>9</td><td>West Virginia</td><td>1,306</td><td>48</td><td>Utah</td><td>586</td></tr>
<tr><td>39</td><td>Wisconsin</td><td>874</td><td>49</td><td>Colorado</td><td>556</td></tr>
<tr><td>31</td><td>Wyoming</td><td>946</td><td>50</td><td>Nevada</td><td>449</td></tr>
<tr><td></td><td></td><td></td><td></td><td>District of Columbia**</td><td>NA</td></tr>
</table>

Source: CQ Press using data from National Association of State Budget Officers
   "2007 State Expenditure Report" (http://www.nasbo.org)
*Estimates for fiscal year 2008.
**Not available.

Estimated Medicaid Expenditures as a Percent of Total Expenditures in 2008

National Percent = 20.7%*

ALPHA ORDER

RANK	STATE	PERCENT
48	Alabama	10.0
49	Alaska	9.7
11	Arizona	23.7
25	Arkansas	18.6
31	California	18.0
37	Colorado	15.3
27	Connecticut	18.4
44	Delaware	13.1
17	Florida	21.2
20	Georgia	20.0
50	Hawaii	9.2
24	Idaho	18.8
4	Illinois	29.2
16	Indiana	21.8
35	Iowa	16.7
28	Kansas	18.2
22	Kentucky	18.9
40	Louisiana	14.8
2	Maine	31.9
31	Maryland	18.0
20	Massachusetts	20.0
13	Michigan	23.1
15	Minnesota	22.4
22	Mississippi	18.9
1	Missouri	33.2
42	Montana	13.9
31	Nebraska	18.0
38	Nevada	15.1
6	New Hampshire	26.8
30	New Jersey	18.1
19	New Mexico	20.9
7	New York	26.7
12	North Carolina	23.3
36	North Dakota	15.5
8	Ohio	25.7
34	Oklahoma	17.8
41	Oregon	14.4
3	Pennsylvania	30.2
9	Rhode Island	24.9
13	South Carolina	23.1
18	South Dakota	21.1
5	Tennessee	27.9
10	Texas	24.7
45	Utah	12.7
28	Vermont	18.2
38	Virginia	15.1
26	Washington	18.5
46	West Virginia	12.5
43	Wisconsin	13.6
47	Wyoming	10.2

RANK ORDER

RANK	STATE	PERCENT
1	Missouri	33.2
2	Maine	31.9
3	Pennsylvania	30.2
4	Illinois	29.2
5	Tennessee	27.9
6	New Hampshire	26.8
7	New York	26.7
8	Ohio	25.7
9	Rhode Island	24.9
10	Texas	24.7
11	Arizona	23.7
12	North Carolina	23.3
13	Michigan	23.1
13	South Carolina	23.1
15	Minnesota	22.4
16	Indiana	21.8
17	Florida	21.2
18	South Dakota	21.1
19	New Mexico	20.9
20	Georgia	20.0
20	Massachusetts	20.0
22	Kentucky	18.9
22	Mississippi	18.9
24	Idaho	18.8
25	Arkansas	18.6
26	Washington	18.5
27	Connecticut	18.4
28	Kansas	18.2
28	Vermont	18.2
30	New Jersey	18.1
31	California	18.0
31	Maryland	18.0
31	Nebraska	18.0
34	Oklahoma	17.8
35	Iowa	16.7
36	North Dakota	15.5
37	Colorado	15.3
38	Nevada	15.1
38	Virginia	15.1
40	Louisiana	14.8
41	Oregon	14.4
42	Montana	13.9
43	Wisconsin	13.6
44	Delaware	13.1
45	Utah	12.7
46	West Virginia	12.5
47	Wyoming	10.2
48	Alabama	10.0
49	Alaska	9.7
50	Hawaii	9.2

District of Columbia**   NA

Source: National Association of State Budget Officers
    "2007 State Expenditure Report" (http://www.nasbo.org)
*Estimates for fiscal year 2008.
**Not available.

Percent Change in Medicaid Expenditures: 2007 to 2008

National Percent Change = 5.5% Increase*

<table>
<tr><th colspan="3">ALPHA ORDER</th><th colspan="3">RANK ORDER</th></tr>
<tr><th>RANK</th><th>STATE</th><th>PERCENT CHANGE</th><th>RANK</th><th>STATE</th><th>PERCENT CHANGE</th></tr>
<tr><td>47</td><td>Alabama</td><td>(3.8)</td><td>1</td><td>Louisiana</td><td>15.9</td></tr>
<tr><td>2</td><td>Alaska</td><td>14.7</td><td>2</td><td>Alaska</td><td>14.7</td></tr>
<tr><td>37</td><td>Arizona</td><td>4.3</td><td>3</td><td>Nebraska</td><td>12.5</td></tr>
<tr><td>7</td><td>Arkansas</td><td>11.5</td><td>3</td><td>North Dakota</td><td>12.5</td></tr>
<tr><td>17</td><td>California</td><td>9.5</td><td>5</td><td>South Dakota</td><td>12.2</td></tr>
<tr><td>34</td><td>Colorado</td><td>5.0</td><td>6</td><td>Oklahoma</td><td>11.9</td></tr>
<tr><td>16</td><td>Connecticut</td><td>9.6</td><td>7</td><td>Arkansas</td><td>11.5</td></tr>
<tr><td>21</td><td>Delaware</td><td>8.5</td><td>7</td><td>Wyoming</td><td>11.5</td></tr>
<tr><td>39</td><td>Florida</td><td>4.0</td><td>9</td><td>Illinois</td><td>11.2</td></tr>
<tr><td>37</td><td>Georgia</td><td>4.3</td><td>10</td><td>Rhode Island</td><td>10.7</td></tr>
<tr><td>19</td><td>Hawaii</td><td>9.3</td><td>11</td><td>Maine</td><td>10.6</td></tr>
<tr><td>23</td><td>Idaho</td><td>8.0</td><td>12</td><td>Ohio</td><td>10.5</td></tr>
<tr><td>9</td><td>Illinois</td><td>11.2</td><td>13</td><td>South Carolina</td><td>10.1</td></tr>
<tr><td>33</td><td>Indiana</td><td>5.2</td><td>14</td><td>Michigan</td><td>9.8</td></tr>
<tr><td>39</td><td>Iowa</td><td>4.0</td><td>14</td><td>West Virginia</td><td>9.8</td></tr>
<tr><td>29</td><td>Kansas</td><td>6.6</td><td>16</td><td>Connecticut</td><td>9.6</td></tr>
<tr><td>28</td><td>Kentucky</td><td>6.8</td><td>17</td><td>California</td><td>9.5</td></tr>
<tr><td>1</td><td>Louisiana</td><td>15.9</td><td>17</td><td>Montana</td><td>9.5</td></tr>
<tr><td>11</td><td>Maine</td><td>10.6</td><td>19</td><td>Hawaii</td><td>9.3</td></tr>
<tr><td>44</td><td>Maryland</td><td>1.9</td><td>20</td><td>Massachusetts</td><td>9.2</td></tr>
<tr><td>20</td><td>Massachusetts</td><td>9.2</td><td>21</td><td>Delaware</td><td>8.5</td></tr>
<tr><td>14</td><td>Michigan</td><td>9.8</td><td>22</td><td>New Mexico</td><td>8.1</td></tr>
<tr><td>26</td><td>Minnesota</td><td>7.4</td><td>23</td><td>Idaho</td><td>8.0</td></tr>
<tr><td>49</td><td>Mississippi</td><td>(4.7)</td><td>24</td><td>Utah</td><td>7.9</td></tr>
<tr><td>43</td><td>Missouri</td><td>2.2</td><td>25</td><td>Texas</td><td>7.7</td></tr>
<tr><td>17</td><td>Montana</td><td>9.5</td><td>26</td><td>Minnesota</td><td>7.4</td></tr>
<tr><td>3</td><td>Nebraska</td><td>12.5</td><td>27</td><td>Tennessee</td><td>7.3</td></tr>
<tr><td>50</td><td>Nevada</td><td>(6.1)</td><td>28</td><td>Kentucky</td><td>6.8</td></tr>
<tr><td>30</td><td>New Hampshire</td><td>6.2</td><td>29</td><td>Kansas</td><td>6.6</td></tr>
<tr><td>46</td><td>New Jersey</td><td>(1.8)</td><td>30</td><td>New Hampshire</td><td>6.2</td></tr>
<tr><td>22</td><td>New Mexico</td><td>8.1</td><td>31</td><td>Virginia</td><td>6.0</td></tr>
<tr><td>48</td><td>New York</td><td>(4.2)</td><td>32</td><td>Washington</td><td>5.5</td></tr>
<tr><td>35</td><td>North Carolina</td><td>4.8</td><td>33</td><td>Indiana</td><td>5.2</td></tr>
<tr><td>3</td><td>North Dakota</td><td>12.5</td><td>34</td><td>Colorado</td><td>5.0</td></tr>
<tr><td>12</td><td>Ohio</td><td>10.5</td><td>35</td><td>North Carolina</td><td>4.8</td></tr>
<tr><td>6</td><td>Oklahoma</td><td>11.9</td><td>36</td><td>Oregon</td><td>4.6</td></tr>
<tr><td>36</td><td>Oregon</td><td>4.6</td><td>37</td><td>Arizona</td><td>4.3</td></tr>
<tr><td>41</td><td>Pennsylvania</td><td>3.4</td><td>37</td><td>Georgia</td><td>4.3</td></tr>
<tr><td>10</td><td>Rhode Island</td><td>10.7</td><td>39</td><td>Florida</td><td>4.0</td></tr>
<tr><td>13</td><td>South Carolina</td><td>10.1</td><td>39</td><td>Iowa</td><td>4.0</td></tr>
<tr><td>5</td><td>South Dakota</td><td>12.2</td><td>41</td><td>Pennsylvania</td><td>3.4</td></tr>
<tr><td>27</td><td>Tennessee</td><td>7.3</td><td>42</td><td>Wisconsin</td><td>3.2</td></tr>
<tr><td>25</td><td>Texas</td><td>7.7</td><td>43</td><td>Missouri</td><td>2.2</td></tr>
<tr><td>24</td><td>Utah</td><td>7.9</td><td>44</td><td>Maryland</td><td>1.9</td></tr>
<tr><td>45</td><td>Vermont</td><td>1.2</td><td>45</td><td>Vermont</td><td>1.2</td></tr>
<tr><td>31</td><td>Virginia</td><td>6.0</td><td>46</td><td>New Jersey</td><td>(1.8)</td></tr>
<tr><td>32</td><td>Washington</td><td>5.5</td><td>47</td><td>Alabama</td><td>(3.8)</td></tr>
<tr><td>14</td><td>West Virginia</td><td>9.8</td><td>48</td><td>New York</td><td>(4.2)</td></tr>
<tr><td>42</td><td>Wisconsin</td><td>3.2</td><td>49</td><td>Mississippi</td><td>(4.7)</td></tr>
<tr><td>7</td><td>Wyoming</td><td>11.5</td><td>50</td><td>Nevada</td><td>(6.1)</td></tr>
<tr><td></td><td></td><td></td><td colspan="2">District of Columbia**</td><td>NA</td></tr>
</table>

Source: National Association of State Budget Officers
"2007 State Expenditure Report" (http://www.nasbo.org)
*Estimates for fiscal year 2008.
**Not available.

Medicaid Expenditures in 2007

National Total = $315,771,772,844*

ALPHA ORDER

RANK	STATE	EXPENDITURES	% of USA
25	Alabama	$4,099,163,829	1.3%
46	Alaska	947,339,783	0.3%
14	Arizona	6,609,346,183	2.1%
29	Arkansas	3,060,407,830	1.0%
2	California	34,884,518,837	11.0%
30	Colorado	2,911,647,539	0.9%
24	Connecticut	4,229,689,762	1.3%
45	Delaware	990,683,309	0.3%
5	Florida	13,450,490,934	4.3%
13	Georgia	6,844,102,301	2.2%
42	Hawaii	1,089,577,939	0.3%
43	Idaho	1,078,074,833	0.3%
7	Illinois	12,508,958,330	4.0%
20	Indiana	5,080,277,554	1.6%
33	Iowa	2,465,590,698	0.8%
35	Kansas	2,121,598,065	0.7%
23	Kentucky	4,513,988,817	1.4%
19	Louisiana	5,207,246,125	1.6%
36	Maine	1,977,693,124	0.6%
18	Maryland	5,383,477,265	1.7%
8	Massachusetts	10,166,110,000	3.2%
10	Michigan	9,213,679,007	2.9%
16	Minnesota	6,327,281,799	2.0%
28	Mississippi	3,256,111,556	1.0%
15	Missouri	6,515,259,281	2.1%
47	Montana	724,679,158	0.2%
38	Nebraska	1,495,709,937	0.5%
40	Nevada	1,241,248,471	0.4%
41	New Hampshire	1,153,993,168	0.4%
11	New Jersey	8,855,366,275	2.8%
32	New Mexico	2,626,097,407	0.8%
1	New York	43,564,119,806	13.8%
9	North Carolina	9,397,798,245	3.0%
49	North Dakota	503,564,400	0.2%
6	Ohio	12,821,041,986	4.1%
27	Oklahoma	3,263,204,924	1.0%
31	Oregon	2,851,153,656	0.9%
4	Pennsylvania	15,825,480,891	5.0%
37	Rhode Island	1,687,169,653	0.5%
26	South Carolina	4,039,243,153	1.3%
48	South Dakota	616,113,377	0.2%
12	Tennessee	7,070,169,782	2.2%
3	Texas	20,278,820,695	6.4%
39	Utah	1,365,289,240	0.4%
44	Vermont	1,056,251,605	0.3%
21	Virginia	4,882,347,418	1.5%
17	Washington	5,722,427,414	1.8%
34	West Virginia	2,158,876,640	0.7%
22	Wisconsin	4,875,516,535	1.5%
50	Wyoming	424,952,159	0.1%

RANK ORDER

RANK	STATE	EXPENDITURES	% of USA
1	New York	$43,564,119,806	13.8%
2	California	34,884,518,837	11.0%
3	Texas	20,278,820,695	6.4%
4	Pennsylvania	15,825,480,891	5.0%
5	Florida	13,450,490,934	4.3%
6	Ohio	12,821,041,986	4.1%
7	Illinois	12,508,958,330	4.0%
8	Massachusetts	10,166,110,000	3.2%
9	North Carolina	9,397,798,245	3.0%
10	Michigan	9,213,679,007	2.9%
11	New Jersey	8,855,366,275	2.8%
12	Tennessee	7,070,169,782	2.2%
13	Georgia	6,844,102,301	2.2%
14	Arizona	6,609,346,183	2.1%
15	Missouri	6,515,259,281	2.1%
16	Minnesota	6,327,281,799	2.0%
17	Washington	5,722,427,414	1.8%
18	Maryland	5,383,477,265	1.7%
19	Louisiana	5,207,246,125	1.6%
20	Indiana	5,080,277,554	1.6%
21	Virginia	4,882,347,418	1.5%
22	Wisconsin	4,875,516,535	1.5%
23	Kentucky	4,513,988,817	1.4%
24	Connecticut	4,229,689,762	1.3%
25	Alabama	4,099,163,829	1.3%
26	South Carolina	4,039,243,153	1.3%
27	Oklahoma	3,263,204,924	1.0%
28	Mississippi	3,256,111,556	1.0%
29	Arkansas	3,060,407,830	1.0%
30	Colorado	2,911,647,539	0.9%
31	Oregon	2,851,153,656	0.9%
32	New Mexico	2,626,097,407	0.8%
33	Iowa	2,465,590,698	0.8%
34	West Virginia	2,158,876,640	0.7%
35	Kansas	2,121,598,065	0.7%
36	Maine	1,977,693,124	0.6%
37	Rhode Island	1,687,169,653	0.5%
38	Nebraska	1,495,709,937	0.5%
39	Utah	1,365,289,240	0.4%
40	Nevada	1,241,248,471	0.4%
41	New Hampshire	1,153,993,168	0.4%
42	Hawaii	1,089,577,939	0.3%
43	Idaho	1,078,074,833	0.3%
44	Vermont	1,056,251,605	0.3%
45	Delaware	990,683,309	0.3%
46	Alaska	947,339,783	0.3%
47	Montana	724,679,158	0.2%
48	South Dakota	616,113,377	0.2%
49	North Dakota	503,564,400	0.2%
50	Wyoming	424,952,159	0.1%
	District of Columbia	1,378,323,404	0.4%

Source: U.S. Department of Health and Human Services, Centers for Medicare and Medicaid Services
    "2008 Data Compendium" (http://www.cms.hhs.gov/DataCompendium/)
*For fiscal year 2007. National total includes $960,498,745 in expenditures in U.S. territories. Net expenditures reported from Form CMS-64. Excludes ADM, Medicaid SCHIP expansions and CMS adjustments.

Per Capita Medicaid Expenditures in 2007

National Per Capita = $1,045*

ALPHA ORDER				RANK ORDER		
RANK	STATE	PER CAPITA		RANK	STATE	PER CAPITA
30	Alabama	$886		1	New York	$2,242
6	Alaska	1,391		2	Vermont	1,702
20	Arizona	1,040		3	Rhode Island	1,602
18	Arkansas	1,081		4	Massachusetts	1,572
24	California	959		5	Maine	1,503
48	Colorado	601		6	Alaska	1,391
10	Connecticut	1,212		7	New Mexico	1,337
14	Delaware	1,149		8	Pennsylvania	1,274
44	Florida	739		9	Minnesota	1,221
46	Georgia	719		10	Connecticut	1,212
33	Hawaii	853		11	West Virginia	1,193
45	Idaho	721		12	Louisiana	1,191
23	Illinois	975		13	Tennessee	1,150
38	Indiana	802		14	Delaware	1,149
36	Iowa	826		15	Ohio	1,117
41	Kansas	764		16	Mississippi	1,115
19	Kentucky	1,066		17	Missouri	1,108
12	Louisiana	1,191		18	Arkansas	1,081
5	Maine	1,503		19	Kentucky	1,066
25	Maryland	958		20	Arizona	1,040
4	Massachusetts	1,572		21	North Carolina	1,039
26	Michigan	917		22	New Jersey	1,023
9	Minnesota	1,221		23	Illinois	975
16	Mississippi	1,115		24	California	959
17	Missouri	1,108		25	Maryland	958
43	Montana	758		26	Michigan	917
35	Nebraska	845		26	South Carolina	917
50	Nevada	486		28	Oklahoma	904
31	New Hampshire	879		29	Washington	887
22	New Jersey	1,023		30	Alabama	886
7	New Mexico	1,337		31	New Hampshire	879
1	New York	2,242		32	Wisconsin	871
21	North Carolina	1,039		33	Hawaii	853
39	North Dakota	789		34	Texas	850
15	Ohio	1,117		35	Nebraska	845
28	Oklahoma	904		36	Iowa	826
42	Oregon	763		37	Wyoming	812
8	Pennsylvania	1,274		38	Indiana	802
3	Rhode Island	1,602		39	North Dakota	789
26	South Carolina	917		40	South Dakota	774
40	South Dakota	774		41	Kansas	764
13	Tennessee	1,150		42	Oregon	763
34	Texas	850		43	Montana	758
49	Utah	512		44	Florida	739
2	Vermont	1,702		45	Idaho	721
47	Virginia	634		46	Georgia	719
29	Washington	887		47	Virginia	634
11	West Virginia	1,193		48	Colorado	601
32	Wisconsin	871		49	Utah	512
37	Wyoming	812		50	Nevada	486
					District of Columbia	2,345

Source: CQ Press using data from U.S. Department of Health and Human Services, Centers for Medicare and Medicaid Services
   "2008 Data Compendium" (http://www.cms.hhs.gov/DataCompendium/)
*Figures for fiscal year 2007. National figure does not include expenditures or population in U.S. territories. Net expenditures
reported from Form CMS-64. Excludes ADM, Medicaid SCHIP expansions and CMS adjustments.

Medicaid Expenditures per Beneficiary in 2007

National Rate = $7,014 per Beneficiary*

ALPHA ORDER

RANK	STATE	PER BENEFICIARY
44	Alabama	$5,662
6	Alaska	9,868
30	Arizona	6,676
49	Arkansas	4,889
47	California	5,396
16	Colorado	7,642
4	Connecticut	10,444
26	Delaware	6,880
36	Florida	6,128
50	Georgia	4,557
48	Hawaii	5,394
39	Idaho	5,989
33	Illinois	6,245
35	Indiana	6,150
29	Iowa	6,737
13	Kansas	7,800
32	Kentucky	6,322
45	Louisiana	5,569
14	Maine	7,786
15	Maryland	7,768
8	Massachusetts	9,396
38	Michigan	6,062
1	Minnesota	10,652
41	Mississippi	5,942
12	Missouri	7,916
10	Montana	9,058
22	Nebraska	7,122
18	Nevada	7,301
2	New Hampshire	10,587
5	New Jersey	10,086
31	New Mexico	6,343
3	New York	10,574
21	North Carolina	7,136
7	North Dakota	9,684
17	Ohio	7,458
46	Oklahoma	5,512
20	Oregon	7,200
11	Pennsylvania	8,926
9	Rhode Island	9,321
34	South Carolina	6,167
37	South Dakota	6,100
40	Tennessee	5,982
28	Texas	6,755
27	Utah	6,792
19	Vermont	7,235
24	Virginia	7,025
42	Washington	5,763
23	West Virginia	7,102
43	Wisconsin	5,722
25	Wyoming	6,966

RANK ORDER

RANK	STATE	PER BENEFICIARY
1	Minnesota	$10,652
2	New Hampshire	10,587
3	New York	10,574
4	Connecticut	10,444
5	New Jersey	10,086
6	Alaska	9,868
7	North Dakota	9,684
8	Massachusetts	9,396
9	Rhode Island	9,321
10	Montana	9,058
11	Pennsylvania	8,926
12	Missouri	7,916
13	Kansas	7,800
14	Maine	7,786
15	Maryland	7,768
16	Colorado	7,642
17	Ohio	7,458
18	Nevada	7,301
19	Vermont	7,235
20	Oregon	7,200
21	North Carolina	7,136
22	Nebraska	7,122
23	West Virginia	7,102
24	Virginia	7,025
25	Wyoming	6,966
26	Delaware	6,880
27	Utah	6,792
28	Texas	6,755
29	Iowa	6,737
30	Arizona	6,676
31	New Mexico	6,343
32	Kentucky	6,322
33	Illinois	6,245
34	South Carolina	6,167
35	Indiana	6,150
36	Florida	6,128
37	South Dakota	6,100
38	Michigan	6,062
39	Idaho	5,989
40	Tennessee	5,982
41	Mississippi	5,942
42	Washington	5,763
43	Wisconsin	5,722
44	Alabama	5,662
45	Louisiana	5,569
46	Oklahoma	5,512
47	California	5,396
48	Hawaii	5,394
49	Arkansas	4,889
50	Georgia	4,557

District of Columbia   9,707

Source: CQ Press using data from U.S. Department of Health and Human Services, Centers for Medicare and Medicaid Services
"2008 Data Compendium" (http://www.cms.hhs.gov/DataCompendium/)

*Figures for fiscal year 2007. National figure does not include expenditures or enrollees in U.S. territories. Net expenditures reported from Form CMS-64. Excludes ADM, Medicaid SCHIP expansions and CMS adjustments.

Federal Medicaid Matching Fund Rate for 2009

National Average = 71.99% of States' Funds Matched by Federal Government*

ALPHA ORDER

RANK	STATE	RATE
11	Alabama	77.59
36	Alaska	65.37
13	Arizona	76.04
3	Arkansas	80.97
38	California	65.00
38	Colorado	65.00
38	Connecticut	65.00
38	Delaware	65.00
31	Florida	68.78
15	Georgia	75.14
32	Hawaii	68.58
9	Idaho	78.84
37	Illinois	65.22
18	Indiana	74.98
21	Iowa	73.83
26	Kansas	72.06
7	Kentucky	79.09
4	Louisiana	79.92
16	Maine	75.09
38	Maryland	65.00
38	Massachusetts	65.00
25	Michigan	72.19
38	Minnesota	65.00
1	Mississippi	83.09
19	Missouri	74.23
10	Montana	77.63
27	Nebraska	71.68
38	Nevada	65.00
38	New Hampshire	65.00
38	New Jersey	65.00
5	New Mexico	79.62
38	New York	65.00
14	North Carolina	75.22
20	North Dakota	74.21
24	Ohio	73.50
12	Oklahoma	76.13
23	Oregon	73.72
33	Pennsylvania	68.16
34	Rhode Island	66.81
8	South Carolina	79.05
22	South Dakota	73.79
17	Tennessee	75.00
29	Texas	71.61
6	Utah	79.50
28	Vermont	71.62
38	Virginia	65.00
35	Washington	65.66
2	West Virginia	81.61
30	Wisconsin	71.57
38	Wyoming	65.00

RANK ORDER

RANK	STATE	RATE
1	Mississippi	83.09
2	West Virginia	81.61
3	Arkansas	80.97
4	Louisiana	79.92
5	New Mexico	79.62
6	Utah	79.50
7	Kentucky	79.09
8	South Carolina	79.05
9	Idaho	78.84
10	Montana	77.63
11	Alabama	77.59
12	Oklahoma	76.13
13	Arizona	76.04
14	North Carolina	75.22
15	Georgia	75.14
16	Maine	75.09
17	Tennessee	75.00
18	Indiana	74.98
19	Missouri	74.23
20	North Dakota	74.21
21	Iowa	73.83
22	South Dakota	73.79
23	Oregon	73.72
24	Ohio	73.50
25	Michigan	72.19
26	Kansas	72.06
27	Nebraska	71.68
28	Vermont	71.62
29	Texas	71.61
30	Wisconsin	71.57
31	Florida	68.78
32	Hawaii	68.58
33	Pennsylvania	68.16
34	Rhode Island	66.81
35	Washington	65.66
36	Alaska	65.37
37	Illinois	65.22
38	California	65.00
38	Colorado	65.00
38	Connecticut	65.00
38	Delaware	65.00
38	Maryland	65.00
38	Massachusetts	65.00
38	Minnesota	65.00
38	Nevada	65.00
38	New Hampshire	65.00
38	New Jersey	65.00
38	New York	65.00
38	Virginia	65.00
38	Wyoming	65.00

District of Columbia	79.00

Source: U.S. Department of Health and Human Services, Centers for Medicare and Medicaid Services
"Enhanced Federal Medical Assistance Percentages" (http://aspe.hhs.gov/health/fmap09.htm)
*For fiscal year 2009. These are "enhanced" matching rates established by the Children's Health Insurance Program, signed into law in August 1997. Sixty-five percent is the minimum. National average is a simple average of the 51 individual rates and is not weighted for population or funds.

State and Local Government Expenditures for Hospitals in 2006

National Total = $110,455,082,000*

ALPHA ORDER

RANK	STATE	EXPENDITURES	% of USA
6	Alabama	$3,762,417,000	3.4%
42	Alaska	133,521,000	0.1%
29	Arizona	882,105,000	0.8%
30	Arkansas	868,447,000	0.8%
1	California	14,715,283,000	13.3%
23	Colorado	1,537,013,000	1.4%
26	Connecticut	1,215,481,000	1.1%
47	Delaware	60,712,000	0.1%
4	Florida	6,137,946,000	5.6%
8	Georgia	3,712,025,000	3.4%
40	Hawaii	407,814,000	0.4%
37	Idaho	654,213,000	0.6%
16	Illinois	2,352,600,000	2.1%
12	Indiana	3,052,267,000	2.8%
20	Iowa	1,914,428,000	1.7%
34	Kansas	722,420,000	0.7%
27	Kentucky	1,172,567,000	1.1%
11	Louisiana	3,122,466,000	2.8%
43	Maine	120,645,000	0.1%
39	Maryland	452,995,000	0.4%
25	Massachusetts	1,331,711,000	1.2%
13	Michigan	2,990,320,000	2.7%
22	Minnesota	1,567,186,000	1.4%
17	Mississippi	2,331,634,000	2.1%
18	Missouri	2,280,185,000	2.1%
45	Montana	90,952,000	0.1%
38	Nebraska	598,743,000	0.5%
33	Nevada	763,116,000	0.7%
48	New Hampshire	54,845,000	0.0%
21	New Jersey	1,749,946,000	1.6%
32	New Mexico	833,062,000	0.8%
2	New York	13,186,993,000	11.9%
5	North Carolina	4,358,535,000	3.9%
49	North Dakota	22,622,000	0.0%
9	Ohio	3,290,784,000	3.0%
31	Oklahoma	837,004,000	0.8%
24	Oregon	1,352,159,000	1.2%
19	Pennsylvania	2,253,238,000	2.0%
44	Rhode Island	115,164,000	0.1%
7	South Carolina	3,733,631,000	3.4%
46	South Dakota	85,562,000	0.1%
14	Tennessee	2,667,273,000	2.4%
3	Texas	8,268,785,000	7.5%
35	Utah	702,004,000	0.6%
50	Vermont	5,363,000	0.0%
15	Virginia	2,626,634,000	2.4%
10	Washington	3,128,792,000	2.8%
41	West Virginia	288,288,000	0.3%
28	Wisconsin	1,121,839,000	1.0%
36	Wyoming	659,849,000	0.6%

RANK ORDER

RANK	STATE	EXPENDITURES	% of USA
1	California	$14,715,283,000	13.3%
2	New York	13,186,993,000	11.9%
3	Texas	8,268,785,000	7.5%
4	Florida	6,137,946,000	5.6%
5	North Carolina	4,358,535,000	3.9%
6	Alabama	3,762,417,000	3.4%
7	South Carolina	3,733,631,000	3.4%
8	Georgia	3,712,025,000	3.4%
9	Ohio	3,290,784,000	3.0%
10	Washington	3,128,792,000	2.8%
11	Louisiana	3,122,466,000	2.8%
12	Indiana	3,052,267,000	2.8%
13	Michigan	2,990,320,000	2.7%
14	Tennessee	2,667,273,000	2.4%
15	Virginia	2,626,634,000	2.4%
16	Illinois	2,352,600,000	2.1%
17	Mississippi	2,331,634,000	2.1%
18	Missouri	2,280,185,000	2.1%
19	Pennsylvania	2,253,238,000	2.0%
20	Iowa	1,914,428,000	1.7%
21	New Jersey	1,749,946,000	1.6%
22	Minnesota	1,567,186,000	1.4%
23	Colorado	1,537,013,000	1.4%
24	Oregon	1,352,159,000	1.2%
25	Massachusetts	1,331,711,000	1.2%
26	Connecticut	1,215,481,000	1.1%
27	Kentucky	1,172,567,000	1.1%
28	Wisconsin	1,121,839,000	1.0%
29	Arizona	882,105,000	0.8%
30	Arkansas	868,447,000	0.8%
31	Oklahoma	837,004,000	0.8%
32	New Mexico	833,062,000	0.8%
33	Nevada	763,116,000	0.7%
34	Kansas	722,420,000	0.7%
35	Utah	702,004,000	0.6%
36	Wyoming	659,849,000	0.6%
37	Idaho	654,213,000	0.6%
38	Nebraska	598,743,000	0.5%
39	Maryland	452,995,000	0.4%
40	Hawaii	407,814,000	0.4%
41	West Virginia	288,288,000	0.3%
42	Alaska	133,521,000	0.1%
43	Maine	120,645,000	0.1%
44	Rhode Island	115,164,000	0.1%
45	Montana	90,952,000	0.1%
46	South Dakota	85,562,000	0.1%
47	Delaware	60,712,000	0.1%
48	New Hampshire	54,845,000	0.0%
49	North Dakota	22,622,000	0.0%
50	Vermont	5,363,000	0.0%
	District of Columbia	161,498,000	0.1%

Source: U.S. Bureau of the Census, Governments Division
"State and Local Government Finances 2005-2006" (http://www.census.gov/govs/www/estimate06.html)
*Financing, construction, acquisition, maintenance or operation of hospital facilities, provision of hospital care, and support of public or private hospitals.

Per Capita State and Local Government Expenditures for Hospitals in 2006

National Per Capita = $370*

ALPHA ORDER

RANK	STATE	PER CAPITA
3	Alabama	$820
37	Alaska	197
41	Arizona	143
25	Arkansas	310
14	California	407
23	Colorado	323
19	Connecticut	348
47	Delaware	71
21	Florida	341
15	Georgia	398
24	Hawaii	320
11	Idaho	448
38	Illinois	184
10	Indiana	485
7	Iowa	645
32	Kansas	262
30	Kentucky	279
5	Louisiana	736
45	Maine	92
46	Maryland	81
34	Massachusetts	207
28	Michigan	297
27	Minnesota	305
4	Mississippi	805
16	Missouri	391
44	Montana	96
22	Nebraska	340
26	Nevada	307
48	New Hampshire	42
35	New Jersey	203
13	New Mexico	430
6	New York	681
8	North Carolina	493
49	North Dakota	36
29	Ohio	287
33	Oklahoma	235
17	Oregon	367
39	Pennsylvania	182
42	Rhode Island	109
2	South Carolina	863
42	South Dakota	109
12	Tennessee	440
18	Texas	354
31	Utah	272
50	Vermont	9
20	Virginia	344
9	Washington	492
40	West Virginia	160
36	Wisconsin	201
1	Wyoming	1,287

RANK ORDER

RANK	STATE	PER CAPITA
1	Wyoming	$1,287
2	South Carolina	863
3	Alabama	820
4	Mississippi	805
5	Louisiana	736
6	New York	681
7	Iowa	645
8	North Carolina	493
9	Washington	492
10	Indiana	485
11	Idaho	448
12	Tennessee	440
13	New Mexico	430
14	California	407
15	Georgia	398
16	Missouri	391
17	Oregon	367
18	Texas	354
19	Connecticut	348
20	Virginia	344
21	Florida	341
22	Nebraska	340
23	Colorado	323
24	Hawaii	320
25	Arkansas	310
26	Nevada	307
27	Minnesota	305
28	Michigan	297
29	Ohio	287
30	Kentucky	279
31	Utah	272
32	Kansas	262
33	Oklahoma	235
34	Massachusetts	207
35	New Jersey	203
36	Wisconsin	201
37	Alaska	197
38	Illinois	184
39	Pennsylvania	182
40	West Virginia	160
41	Arizona	143
42	Rhode Island	109
42	South Dakota	109
44	Montana	96
45	Maine	92
46	Maryland	81
47	Delaware	71
48	New Hampshire	42
49	North Dakota	36
50	Vermont	9
	District of Columbia	276

Source: CQ Press using data from U.S. Bureau of the Census, Governments Division
"State and Local Government Finances 2005-2006" (http://www.census.gov/govs/www/estimate06.html)
*Financing, construction, acquisition, maintenance or operation of hospital facilities, provision of hospital care, and support of public or private hospitals.

Percent of State and Local Government Expenditures
Used for Hospitals in 2006
National Percent = 5.2%*

ALPHA ORDER

RANK	STATE	PERCENT
3	Alabama	12.2
43	Alaska	1.4
36	Arizona	2.5
18	Arkansas	5.2
21	California	5.0
21	Colorado	5.0
28	Connecticut	4.4
47	Delaware	0.8
21	Florida	5.0
12	Georgia	6.8
29	Hawaii	4.1
7	Idaho	7.8
34	Illinois	2.8
10	Indiana	7.7
6	Iowa	9.3
30	Kansas	4.0
25	Kentucky	4.6
5	Louisiana	10.2
45	Maine	1.2
45	Maryland	1.2
36	Massachusetts	2.5
26	Michigan	4.5
30	Minnesota	4.0
4	Mississippi	12.1
14	Missouri	6.6
42	Montana	1.5
20	Nebraska	5.1
24	Nevada	4.7
48	New Hampshire	0.7
36	New Jersey	2.5
16	New Mexico	5.6
12	New York	6.8
7	North Carolina	7.8
49	North Dakota	0.5
30	Ohio	4.0
30	Oklahoma	4.0
17	Oregon	5.3
36	Pennsylvania	2.5
43	Rhode Island	1.4
1	South Carolina	12.8
41	South Dakota	1.8
7	Tennessee	7.8
15	Texas	6.0
26	Utah	4.5
50	Vermont	0.1
18	Virginia	5.2
11	Washington	6.9
36	West Virginia	2.5
34	Wisconsin	2.8
2	Wyoming	12.3

RANK ORDER

RANK	STATE	PERCENT
1	South Carolina	12.8
2	Wyoming	12.3
3	Alabama	12.2
4	Mississippi	12.1
5	Louisiana	10.2
6	Iowa	9.3
7	Idaho	7.8
7	North Carolina	7.8
7	Tennessee	7.8
10	Indiana	7.7
11	Washington	6.9
12	Georgia	6.8
12	New York	6.8
14	Missouri	6.6
15	Texas	6.0
16	New Mexico	5.6
17	Oregon	5.3
18	Arkansas	5.2
18	Virginia	5.2
20	Nebraska	5.1
21	California	5.0
21	Colorado	5.0
21	Florida	5.0
24	Nevada	4.7
25	Kentucky	4.6
26	Michigan	4.5
26	Utah	4.5
28	Connecticut	4.4
29	Hawaii	4.1
30	Kansas	4.0
30	Minnesota	4.0
30	Ohio	4.0
30	Oklahoma	4.0
34	Illinois	2.8
34	Wisconsin	2.8
36	Arizona	2.5
36	Massachusetts	2.5
36	New Jersey	2.5
36	Pennsylvania	2.5
36	West Virginia	2.5
41	South Dakota	1.8
42	Montana	1.5
43	Alaska	1.4
43	Rhode Island	1.4
45	Maine	1.2
45	Maryland	1.2
47	Delaware	0.8
48	New Hampshire	0.7
49	North Dakota	0.5
50	Vermont	0.1

District of Columbia 2.0

Source: CQ Press using data from U.S. Bureau of the Census, Governments Division
"State and Local Government Finances 2005-2006" (http://www.census.gov/govs/www/estimate06.html)
*As a percent of direct general expenditures. Financing, construction, acquisition, maintenance or operation of hospital facilities, provision of hospital care, and support of public or private hospitals.

State and Local Government Expenditures for Health Programs in 2006

National Total = $71,109,591,000*

ALPHA ORDER

RANK	STATE	EXPENDITURES	% of USA
18	Alabama	$1,392,316,000	2.0%
45	Alaska	212,569,000	0.3%
14	Arizona	1,510,920,000	2.1%
37	Arkansas	382,779,000	0.5%
1	California	11,523,754,000	16.2%
21	Colorado	941,131,000	1.3%
27	Connecticut	657,466,000	0.9%
40	Delaware	339,544,000	0.5%
5	Florida	3,874,421,000	5.4%
11	Georgia	1,847,548,000	2.6%
30	Hawaii	517,047,000	0.7%
44	Idaho	214,283,000	0.3%
8	Illinois	2,578,166,000	3.6%
25	Indiana	740,961,000	1.0%
33	Iowa	444,149,000	0.6%
35	Kansas	408,157,000	0.6%
28	Kentucky	643,284,000	0.9%
26	Louisiana	715,209,000	1.0%
31	Maine	495,633,000	0.7%
15	Maryland	1,493,256,000	2.1%
24	Massachusetts	846,630,000	1.2%
3	Michigan	4,163,136,000	5.9%
22	Minnesota	931,746,000	1.3%
38	Mississippi	363,893,000	0.5%
17	Missouri	1,393,628,000	2.0%
39	Montana	361,403,000	0.5%
34	Nebraska	409,482,000	0.6%
42	Nevada	306,120,000	0.4%
48	New Hampshire	125,043,000	0.2%
19	New Jersey	1,165,312,000	1.6%
36	New Mexico	391,731,000	0.6%
2	New York	5,194,732,000	7.3%
7	North Carolina	3,101,656,000	4.4%
50	North Dakota	78,697,000	0.1%
4	Ohio	3,986,118,000	5.6%
29	Oklahoma	579,390,000	0.8%
23	Oregon	894,114,000	1.3%
6	Pennsylvania	3,771,864,000	5.3%
46	Rhode Island	162,046,000	0.2%
20	South Carolina	972,866,000	1.4%
49	South Dakota	122,315,000	0.2%
16	Tennessee	1,437,804,000	2.0%
9	Texas	2,463,388,000	3.5%
32	Utah	465,884,000	0.7%
47	Vermont	140,252,000	0.2%
12	Virginia	1,674,253,000	2.4%
10	Washington	2,101,105,000	3.0%
41	West Virginia	313,028,000	0.4%
13	Wisconsin	1,512,750,000	2.1%
43	Wyoming	238,911,000	0.3%

RANK ORDER

RANK	STATE	EXPENDITURES	% of USA
1	California	$11,523,754,000	16.2%
2	New York	5,194,732,000	7.3%
3	Michigan	4,163,136,000	5.9%
4	Ohio	3,986,118,000	5.6%
5	Florida	3,874,421,000	5.4%
6	Pennsylvania	3,771,864,000	5.3%
7	North Carolina	3,101,656,000	4.4%
8	Illinois	2,578,166,000	3.6%
9	Texas	2,463,388,000	3.5%
10	Washington	2,101,105,000	3.0%
11	Georgia	1,847,548,000	2.6%
12	Virginia	1,674,253,000	2.4%
13	Wisconsin	1,512,750,000	2.1%
14	Arizona	1,510,920,000	2.1%
15	Maryland	1,493,256,000	2.1%
16	Tennessee	1,437,804,000	2.0%
17	Missouri	1,393,628,000	2.0%
18	Alabama	1,392,316,000	2.0%
19	New Jersey	1,165,312,000	1.6%
20	South Carolina	972,866,000	1.4%
21	Colorado	941,131,000	1.3%
22	Minnesota	931,746,000	1.3%
23	Oregon	894,114,000	1.3%
24	Massachusetts	846,630,000	1.2%
25	Indiana	740,961,000	1.0%
26	Louisiana	715,209,000	1.0%
27	Connecticut	657,466,000	0.9%
28	Kentucky	643,284,000	0.9%
29	Oklahoma	579,390,000	0.8%
30	Hawaii	517,047,000	0.7%
31	Maine	495,633,000	0.7%
32	Utah	465,884,000	0.7%
33	Iowa	444,149,000	0.6%
34	Nebraska	409,482,000	0.6%
35	Kansas	408,157,000	0.6%
36	New Mexico	391,731,000	0.6%
37	Arkansas	382,779,000	0.5%
38	Mississippi	363,893,000	0.5%
39	Montana	361,403,000	0.5%
40	Delaware	339,544,000	0.5%
41	West Virginia	313,028,000	0.4%
42	Nevada	306,120,000	0.4%
43	Wyoming	238,911,000	0.3%
44	Idaho	214,283,000	0.3%
45	Alaska	212,569,000	0.3%
46	Rhode Island	162,046,000	0.2%
47	Vermont	140,252,000	0.2%
48	New Hampshire	125,043,000	0.2%
49	South Dakota	122,315,000	0.2%
50	North Dakota	78,697,000	0.1%
	District of Columbia	507,701,000	0.7%

Source: U.S. Bureau of the Census, Governments Division
"State and Local Government Finances 2005-2006" (http://www.census.gov/govs/www/estimate06.html)
*Includes outpatient health services other than hospital care, research and education, categorical health programs, treatment and immunization clinics, nursing, and environmental health activities. Includes capital expenditures.

Per Capita State and Local Government Expenditures for Health Programs in 2006
National Per Capita = $238*

ALPHA ORDER

RANK	STATE	PER CAPITA
13	Alabama	$303
11	Alaska	314
17	Arizona	245
42	Arkansas	137
10	California	319
28	Colorado	198
30	Connecticut	188
4	Delaware	399
25	Florida	215
28	Georgia	198
3	Hawaii	405
41	Idaho	147
26	Illinois	202
48	Indiana	118
39	Iowa	150
40	Kansas	148
37	Kentucky	153
34	Louisiana	169
6	Maine	377
16	Maryland	267
44	Massachusetts	131
2	Michigan	413
31	Minnesota	181
45	Mississippi	126
19	Missouri	239
5	Montana	382
21	Nebraska	233
47	Nevada	123
50	New Hampshire	96
43	New Jersey	135
26	New Mexico	202
15	New York	268
7	North Carolina	351
46	North Dakota	124
8	Ohio	348
35	Oklahoma	162
18	Oregon	243
12	Pennsylvania	304
37	Rhode Island	153
23	South Carolina	225
36	South Dakota	155
20	Tennessee	237
49	Texas	105
32	Utah	180
22	Vermont	226
24	Virginia	219
9	Washington	330
33	West Virginia	173
14	Wisconsin	272
1	Wyoming	466

RANK ORDER

RANK	STATE	PER CAPITA
1	Wyoming	$466
2	Michigan	413
3	Hawaii	405
4	Delaware	399
5	Montana	382
6	Maine	377
7	North Carolina	351
8	Ohio	348
9	Washington	330
10	California	319
11	Alaska	314
12	Pennsylvania	304
13	Alabama	303
14	Wisconsin	272
15	New York	268
16	Maryland	267
17	Arizona	245
18	Oregon	243
19	Missouri	239
20	Tennessee	237
21	Nebraska	233
22	Vermont	226
23	South Carolina	225
24	Virginia	219
25	Florida	215
26	Illinois	202
26	New Mexico	202
28	Colorado	198
28	Georgia	198
30	Connecticut	188
31	Minnesota	181
32	Utah	180
33	West Virginia	173
34	Louisiana	169
35	Oklahoma	162
36	South Dakota	155
37	Kentucky	153
37	Rhode Island	153
39	Iowa	150
40	Kansas	148
41	Idaho	147
42	Arkansas	137
43	New Jersey	135
44	Massachusetts	131
45	Mississippi	126
46	North Dakota	124
47	Nevada	123
48	Indiana	118
49	Texas	105
50	New Hampshire	96

| | District of Columbia | 867 |

Source: CQ Press using data from U.S. Bureau of the Census, Governments Division
"State and Local Government Finances 2005-2006" (http://www.census.gov/govs/www/estimate06.html)
*Includes outpatient health services other than hospital care, research and education, categorical health programs, treatment and immunization clinics, nursing, and environmental health activities. Includes capital expenditures.

Percent of State and Local Government Expenditures
Used for Health Programs in 2006
National Percent = 3.4%*

ALPHA ORDER

RANK	STATE	PERCENT
9	Alabama	4.5
37	Alaska	2.3
11	Arizona	4.2
37	Arkansas	2.3
15	California	3.9
24	Colorado	3.1
35	Connecticut	2.4
8	Delaware	4.6
23	Florida	3.2
20	Georgia	3.4
4	Hawaii	5.3
33	Idaho	2.5
24	Illinois	3.1
43	Indiana	1.9
41	Iowa	2.2
37	Kansas	2.3
33	Kentucky	2.5
37	Louisiana	2.3
5	Maine	5.0
16	Maryland	3.8
48	Massachusetts	1.6
1	Michigan	6.3
35	Minnesota	2.4
43	Mississippi	1.9
14	Missouri	4.0
2	Montana	5.8
18	Nebraska	3.5
43	Nevada	1.9
50	New Hampshire	1.5
48	New Jersey	1.6
31	New Mexico	2.6
29	New York	2.7
3	North Carolina	5.5
47	North Dakota	1.7
6	Ohio	4.9
28	Oklahoma	2.8
18	Oregon	3.5
11	Pennsylvania	4.2
42	Rhode Island	2.0
21	South Carolina	3.3
31	South Dakota	2.6
11	Tennessee	4.2
46	Texas	1.8
26	Utah	3.0
27	Vermont	2.9
21	Virginia	3.3
7	Washington	4.7
29	West Virginia	2.7
16	Wisconsin	3.8
9	Wyoming	4.5

RANK ORDER

RANK	STATE	PERCENT
1	Michigan	6.3
2	Montana	5.8
3	North Carolina	5.5
4	Hawaii	5.3
5	Maine	5.0
6	Ohio	4.9
7	Washington	4.7
8	Delaware	4.6
9	Alabama	4.5
9	Wyoming	4.5
11	Arizona	4.2
11	Pennsylvania	4.2
11	Tennessee	4.2
14	Missouri	4.0
15	California	3.9
16	Maryland	3.8
16	Wisconsin	3.8
18	Nebraska	3.5
18	Oregon	3.5
20	Georgia	3.4
21	South Carolina	3.3
21	Virginia	3.3
23	Florida	3.2
24	Colorado	3.1
24	Illinois	3.1
26	Utah	3.0
27	Vermont	2.9
28	Oklahoma	2.8
29	New York	2.7
29	West Virginia	2.7
31	New Mexico	2.6
31	South Dakota	2.6
33	Idaho	2.5
33	Kentucky	2.5
35	Connecticut	2.4
35	Minnesota	2.4
37	Alaska	2.3
37	Arkansas	2.3
37	Kansas	2.3
37	Louisiana	2.3
41	Iowa	2.2
42	Rhode Island	2.0
43	Indiana	1.9
43	Mississippi	1.9
43	Nevada	1.9
46	Texas	1.8
47	North Dakota	1.7
48	Massachusetts	1.6
48	New Jersey	1.6
50	New Hampshire	1.5

District of Columbia	6.3

Source: CQ Press using data from U.S. Bureau of the Census, Governments Division
   "State and Local Government Finances 2005-2006" (http://www.census.gov/govs/www/estimate06.html)
*As a percent of direct general expenditures. Includes outpatient health services other than hospital care, research and education, categorical health programs, treatment and immunization clinics, nursing, and environmental health activities. Includes capital expenditures.

Estimated Tobacco Settlement Revenues in Fiscal Year 2009

National Total = $8,000,000,000*

ALPHA ORDER

RANK	STATE	REVENUE	% of USA
26	Alabama	$105,000,000	1.3%
45	Alaska	34,000,000	0.4%
24	Arizona	115,000,000	1.4%
35	Arkansas	57,000,000	0.7%
2	California	827,000,000	10.3%
27	Colorado	103,000,000	1.3%
21	Connecticut	141,000,000	1.8%
47	Delaware	30,000,000	0.4%
4	Florida	389,000,000	4.9%
16	Georgia	158,000,000	2.0%
36	Hawaii	56,000,000	0.7%
48	Idaho	28,000,000	0.4%
7	Illinois	308,000,000	3.9%
20	Indiana	147,000,000	1.8%
31	Iowa	75,000,000	0.9%
33	Kansas	66,000,000	0.8%
25	Kentucky	114,000,000	1.4%
14	Louisiana	160,000,000	2.0%
34	Maine	58,000,000	0.7%
13	Maryland	165,000,000	2.1%
9	Massachusetts	287,000,000	3.6%
8	Michigan	288,000,000	3.6%
11	Minnesota	180,000,000	2.3%
23	Mississippi	121,000,000	1.5%
18	Missouri	152,000,000	1.9%
45	Montana	34,000,000	0.4%
41	Nebraska	42,000,000	0.5%
39	Nevada	45,000,000	0.6%
38	New Hampshire	48,000,000	0.6%
10	New Jersey	261,000,000	3.3%
40	New Mexico	44,000,000	0.6%
1	New York	830,000,000	10.4%
15	North Carolina	159,000,000	2.0%
44	North Dakota	36,000,000	0.5%
6	Ohio	332,000,000	4.2%
29	Oklahoma	89,000,000	1.1%
28	Oregon	90,000,000	1.1%
5	Pennsylvania	380,000,000	4.8%
37	Rhode Island	53,000,000	0.7%
30	South Carolina	83,000,000	1.0%
49	South Dakota	27,000,000	0.3%
17	Tennessee	156,000,000	2.0%
3	Texas	505,000,000	6.3%
41	Utah	42,000,000	0.5%
43	Vermont	39,000,000	0.5%
22	Virginia	132,000,000	1.7%
12	Washington	173,000,000	2.2%
32	West Virginia	72,000,000	0.9%
19	Wisconsin	148,000,000	1.9%
50	Wyoming	21,000,000	0.3%

RANK ORDER

RANK	STATE	REVENUE	% of USA
1	New York	$830,000,000	10.4%
2	California	827,000,000	10.3%
3	Texas	505,000,000	6.3%
4	Florida	389,000,000	4.9%
5	Pennsylvania	380,000,000	4.8%
6	Ohio	332,000,000	4.2%
7	Illinois	308,000,000	3.9%
8	Michigan	288,000,000	3.6%
9	Massachusetts	287,000,000	3.6%
10	New Jersey	261,000,000	3.3%
11	Minnesota	180,000,000	2.3%
12	Washington	173,000,000	2.2%
13	Maryland	165,000,000	2.1%
14	Louisiana	160,000,000	2.0%
15	North Carolina	159,000,000	2.0%
16	Georgia	158,000,000	2.0%
17	Tennessee	156,000,000	2.0%
18	Missouri	152,000,000	1.9%
19	Wisconsin	148,000,000	1.9%
20	Indiana	147,000,000	1.8%
21	Connecticut	141,000,000	1.8%
22	Virginia	132,000,000	1.7%
23	Mississippi	121,000,000	1.5%
24	Arizona	115,000,000	1.4%
25	Kentucky	114,000,000	1.4%
26	Alabama	105,000,000	1.3%
27	Colorado	103,000,000	1.3%
28	Oregon	90,000,000	1.1%
29	Oklahoma	89,000,000	1.1%
30	South Carolina	83,000,000	1.0%
31	Iowa	75,000,000	0.9%
32	West Virginia	72,000,000	0.9%
33	Kansas	66,000,000	0.8%
34	Maine	58,000,000	0.7%
35	Arkansas	57,000,000	0.7%
36	Hawaii	56,000,000	0.7%
37	Rhode Island	53,000,000	0.7%
38	New Hampshire	48,000,000	0.6%
39	Nevada	45,000,000	0.6%
40	New Mexico	44,000,000	0.6%
41	Nebraska	42,000,000	0.5%
41	Utah	42,000,000	0.5%
43	Vermont	39,000,000	0.5%
44	North Dakota	36,000,000	0.5%
45	Alaska	34,000,000	0.4%
45	Montana	34,000,000	0.4%
47	Delaware	30,000,000	0.4%
48	Idaho	28,000,000	0.4%
49	South Dakota	27,000,000	0.3%
50	Wyoming	21,000,000	0.3%
	District of Columbia	43,000,000	0.5%

Source: Campaign for Tobacco-Free Kids
   "A Decade of Broken Promises" (http://tobaccofreekids.org/reports/settlements/)
*For fiscal year 2009. Settlement originally reached in November 1998 and called for an estimated 25 years of payments.

Annual Smoking-Related Health Costs in 2009

National Estimate = $95,900,000,000*

RANK	STATE	COSTS	% of USA
23	Alabama	$1,490,000,000	1.6%
49	Alaska	169,000,000	0.2%
26	Arizona	1,300,000,000	1.4%
32	Arkansas	812,000,000	0.8%
1	California	9,140,000,000	9.5%
25	Colorado	1,310,000,000	1.4%
21	Connecticut	1,630,000,000	1.7%
44	Delaware	284,000,000	0.3%
3	Florida	6,320,000,000	6.6%
12	Georgia	2,250,000,000	2.3%
42	Hawaii	336,000,000	0.4%
43	Idaho	319,000,000	0.3%
7	Illinois	4,100,000,000	4.3%
15	Indiana	2,080,000,000	2.2%
30	Iowa	1,010,000,000	1.1%
31	Kansas	927,000,000	1.0%
22	Kentucky	1,500,000,000	1.6%
24	Louisiana	1,470,000,000	1.5%
35	Maine	602,000,000	0.6%
19	Maryland	1,960,000,000	2.0%
8	Massachusetts	3,540,000,000	3.7%
9	Michigan	3,400,000,000	3.5%
17	Minnesota	2,060,000,000	2.1%
33	Mississippi	719,000,000	0.7%
14	Missouri	2,130,000,000	2.2%
45	Montana	277,000,000	0.3%
38	Nebraska	537,000,000	0.6%
36	Nevada	565,000,000	0.6%
37	New Hampshire	564,000,000	0.6%
10	New Jersey	3,170,000,000	3.3%
40	New Mexico	461,000,000	0.5%
2	New York	8,170,000,000	8.5%
11	North Carolina	2,460,000,000	2.6%
47	North Dakota	247,000,000	0.3%
6	Ohio	4,370,000,000	4.6%
27	Oklahoma	1,160,000,000	1.2%
28	Oregon	1,110,000,000	1.2%
5	Pennsylvania	5,190,000,000	5.4%
39	Rhode Island	506,000,000	0.5%
29	South Carolina	1,090,000,000	1.1%
46	South Dakota	274,000,000	0.3%
13	Tennessee	2,160,000,000	2.3%
4	Texas	5,830,000,000	6.1%
41	Utah	345,000,000	0.4%
48	Vermont	233,000,000	0.2%
15	Virginia	2,080,000,000	2.2%
20	Washington	1,950,000,000	2.0%
34	West Virginia	690,000,000	0.7%
18	Wisconsin	2,020,000,000	2.1%
50	Wyoming	136,000,000	0.1%

RANK	STATE	COSTS	% of USA
1	California	$9,140,000,000	9.5%
2	New York	8,170,000,000	8.5%
3	Florida	6,320,000,000	6.6%
4	Texas	5,830,000,000	6.1%
5	Pennsylvania	5,190,000,000	5.4%
6	Ohio	4,370,000,000	4.6%
7	Illinois	4,100,000,000	4.3%
8	Massachusetts	3,540,000,000	3.7%
9	Michigan	3,400,000,000	3.5%
10	New Jersey	3,170,000,000	3.3%
11	North Carolina	2,460,000,000	2.6%
12	Georgia	2,250,000,000	2.3%
13	Tennessee	2,160,000,000	2.3%
14	Missouri	2,130,000,000	2.2%
15	Indiana	2,080,000,000	2.2%
15	Virginia	2,080,000,000	2.2%
17	Minnesota	2,060,000,000	2.1%
18	Wisconsin	2,020,000,000	2.1%
19	Maryland	1,960,000,000	2.0%
20	Washington	1,950,000,000	2.0%
21	Connecticut	1,630,000,000	1.7%
22	Kentucky	1,500,000,000	1.6%
23	Alabama	1,490,000,000	1.6%
24	Louisiana	1,470,000,000	1.5%
25	Colorado	1,310,000,000	1.4%
26	Arizona	1,300,000,000	1.4%
27	Oklahoma	1,160,000,000	1.2%
28	Oregon	1,110,000,000	1.2%
29	South Carolina	1,090,000,000	1.1%
30	Iowa	1,010,000,000	1.1%
31	Kansas	927,000,000	1.0%
32	Arkansas	812,000,000	0.8%
33	Mississippi	719,000,000	0.7%
34	West Virginia	690,000,000	0.7%
35	Maine	602,000,000	0.6%
36	Nevada	565,000,000	0.6%
37	New Hampshire	564,000,000	0.6%
38	Nebraska	537,000,000	0.6%
39	Rhode Island	506,000,000	0.5%
40	New Mexico	461,000,000	0.5%
41	Utah	345,000,000	0.4%
42	Hawaii	336,000,000	0.4%
43	Idaho	319,000,000	0.3%
44	Delaware	284,000,000	0.3%
45	Montana	277,000,000	0.3%
46	South Dakota	274,000,000	0.3%
47	North Dakota	247,000,000	0.3%
48	Vermont	233,000,000	0.2%
49	Alaska	169,000,000	0.2%
50	Wyoming	136,000,000	0.1%
	District of Columbia	243,000,000	0.3%

Source: Campaign for Tobacco-Free Kids
  "A Decade of Broken Promises" (http://tobaccofreekids.org/reports/settlements/)
*Estimate based on figures from Centers for Disease Control and Prevention.

Personal Health Care Expenditures in 2004

National Total = $1,551,255,000,000*

RANK	STATE	EXPENDITURES	% of USA
22	Alabama	$23,199,000,000	1.5%
46	Alaska	4,237,000,000	0.3%
21	Arizona	23,576,000,000	1.5%
33	Arkansas	13,357,000,000	0.9%
1	California	166,236,000,000	10.7%
26	Colorado	21,691,000,000	1.4%
25	Connecticut	22,167,000,000	1.4%
44	Delaware	5,226,000,000	0.3%
4	Florida	95,223,000,000	6.1%
12	Georgia	41,097,000,000	2.6%
42	Hawaii	6,222,000,000	0.4%
43	Idaho	6,197,000,000	0.4%
6	Illinois	67,292,000,000	4.3%
14	Indiana	32,951,000,000	2.1%
30	Iowa	15,892,000,000	1.0%
31	Kansas	14,736,000,000	0.9%
23	Kentucky	22,662,000,000	1.5%
24	Louisiana	22,658,000,000	1.5%
38	Maine	8,593,000,000	0.6%
19	Maryland	31,044,000,000	2.0%
11	Massachusetts	43,009,000,000	2.8%
8	Michigan	51,048,000,000	3.3%
20	Minnesota	29,524,000,000	1.9%
32	Mississippi	14,634,000,000	0.9%
17	Missouri	31,317,000,000	2.0%
45	Montana	4,706,000,000	0.3%
36	Nebraska	9,782,000,000	0.6%
35	Nevada	10,656,000,000	0.7%
40	New Hampshire	7,050,000,000	0.5%
9	New Jersey	50,384,000,000	3.2%
39	New Mexico	8,498,000,000	0.5%
2	New York	126,076,000,000	8.1%
10	North Carolina	44,281,000,000	2.9%
49	North Dakota	3,693,000,000	0.2%
7	Ohio	65,622,000,000	4.2%
29	Oklahoma	17,323,000,000	1.1%
28	Oregon	17,516,000,000	1.1%
5	Pennsylvania	73,441,000,000	4.7%
41	Rhode Island	6,682,000,000	0.4%
27	South Carolina	21,450,000,000	1.4%
47	South Dakota	4,103,000,000	0.3%
15	Tennessee	32,161,000,000	2.1%
3	Texas	103,600,000,000	6.7%
37	Utah	9,618,000,000	0.6%
48	Vermont	3,768,000,000	0.2%
13	Virginia	36,032,000,000	2.3%
16	Washington	31,600,000,000	2.0%
34	West Virginia	10,783,000,000	0.7%
18	Wisconsin	31,177,000,000	2.0%
50	Wyoming	2,662,000,000	0.2%

RANK	STATE	EXPENDITURES	% of USA
1	California	$166,236,000,000	10.7%
2	New York	126,076,000,000	8.1%
3	Texas	103,600,000,000	6.7%
4	Florida	95,223,000,000	6.1%
5	Pennsylvania	73,441,000,000	4.7%
6	Illinois	67,292,000,000	4.3%
7	Ohio	65,622,000,000	4.2%
8	Michigan	51,048,000,000	3.3%
9	New Jersey	50,384,000,000	3.2%
10	North Carolina	44,281,000,000	2.9%
11	Massachusetts	43,009,000,000	2.8%
12	Georgia	41,097,000,000	2.6%
13	Virginia	36,032,000,000	2.3%
14	Indiana	32,951,000,000	2.1%
15	Tennessee	32,161,000,000	2.1%
16	Washington	31,600,000,000	2.0%
17	Missouri	31,317,000,000	2.0%
18	Wisconsin	31,177,000,000	2.0%
19	Maryland	31,044,000,000	2.0%
20	Minnesota	29,524,000,000	1.9%
21	Arizona	23,576,000,000	1.5%
22	Alabama	23,199,000,000	1.5%
23	Kentucky	22,662,000,000	1.5%
24	Louisiana	22,658,000,000	1.5%
25	Connecticut	22,167,000,000	1.4%
26	Colorado	21,691,000,000	1.4%
27	South Carolina	21,450,000,000	1.4%
28	Oregon	17,516,000,000	1.1%
29	Oklahoma	17,323,000,000	1.1%
30	Iowa	15,892,000,000	1.0%
31	Kansas	14,736,000,000	0.9%
32	Mississippi	14,634,000,000	0.9%
33	Arkansas	13,357,000,000	0.9%
34	West Virginia	10,783,000,000	0.7%
35	Nevada	10,656,000,000	0.7%
36	Nebraska	9,782,000,000	0.6%
37	Utah	9,618,000,000	0.6%
38	Maine	8,593,000,000	0.6%
39	New Mexico	8,498,000,000	0.5%
40	New Hampshire	7,050,000,000	0.5%
41	Rhode Island	6,682,000,000	0.4%
42	Hawaii	6,222,000,000	0.4%
43	Idaho	6,197,000,000	0.4%
44	Delaware	5,226,000,000	0.3%
45	Montana	4,706,000,000	0.3%
46	Alaska	4,237,000,000	0.3%
47	South Dakota	4,103,000,000	0.3%
48	Vermont	3,768,000,000	0.2%
49	North Dakota	3,693,000,000	0.2%
50	Wyoming	2,662,000,000	0.2%
	District of Columbia	4,809,000,000	0.3%

Source: U.S. Department of Health and Human Services, Centers for Medicare and Medicaid Services
"State Health Care Expenditures" (http://www.cms.hhs.gov/NationalHealthExpendData/)
*By state of residence. Includes hospital care, physician services, dental services, home health care, drugs, vision products, nursing home care, and other personal health care services and products.

Health Care Expenditures as a Percent of Gross State Product in 2004

National Percent = 13.3% of Total Gross State Product*

ALPHA ORDER				RANK ORDER		
RANK	STATE	PERCENT		RANK	STATE	PERCENT
7	Alabama	16.2		1	West Virginia	20.3
44	Alaska	11.6		2	Maine	19.4
36	Arizona	12.5		3	Mississippi	18.1
16	Arkansas	15.4		4	North Dakota	17.6
46	California	11.0		5	Kentucky	16.9
45	Colorado	11.1		6	Montana	16.7
40	Connecticut	12.1		7	Alabama	16.2
49	Delaware	9.7		7	Rhode Island	16.2
13	Florida	15.6		7	Vermont	16.2
38	Georgia	12.2		10	Pennsylvania	16.1
36	Hawaii	12.5		11	Missouri	15.7
32	Idaho	13.0		11	South Carolina	15.7
38	Illinois	12.2		13	Florida	15.6
20	Indiana	14.4		13	Tennessee	15.6
27	Iowa	13.7		15	Ohio	15.5
20	Kansas	14.4		16	Arkansas	15.4
5	Kentucky	16.9		17	Oklahoma	14.8
23	Louisiana	14.2		17	Wisconsin	14.8
2	Maine	19.4		19	Nebraska	14.5
31	Maryland	13.3		20	Indiana	14.4
24	Massachusetts	14.1		20	Kansas	14.4
29	Michigan	13.5		20	South Dakota	14.4
27	Minnesota	13.7		23	Louisiana	14.2
3	Mississippi	18.1		24	Massachusetts	14.1
11	Missouri	15.7		25	New York	13.9
6	Montana	16.7		26	North Carolina	13.8
19	Nebraska	14.5		27	Iowa	13.7
46	Nevada	11.0		27	Minnesota	13.7
29	New Hampshire	13.5		29	Michigan	13.5
42	New Jersey	11.8		29	New Hampshire	13.5
34	New Mexico	12.6		31	Maryland	13.3
25	New York	13.9		32	Idaho	13.0
26	North Carolina	13.8		32	Oregon	13.0
4	North Dakota	17.6		34	New Mexico	12.6
15	Ohio	15.5		34	Washington	12.6
17	Oklahoma	14.8		36	Arizona	12.5
32	Oregon	13.0		36	Hawaii	12.5
10	Pennsylvania	16.1		38	Georgia	12.2
7	Rhode Island	16.2		38	Illinois	12.2
11	South Carolina	15.7		40	Connecticut	12.1
20	South Dakota	14.4		40	Utah	12.1
13	Tennessee	15.6		42	New Jersey	11.8
43	Texas	11.7		43	Texas	11.7
40	Utah	12.1		44	Alaska	11.6
7	Vermont	16.2		45	Colorado	11.1
48	Virginia	10.9		46	California	11.0
34	Washington	12.6		46	Nevada	11.0
1	West Virginia	20.3		48	Virginia	10.9
17	Wisconsin	14.8		49	Delaware	9.7
50	Wyoming	9.4		50	Wyoming	9.4
					District of Columbia	8.1

Source: U.S. Department of Health and Human Services, Centers for Medicare and Medicaid Services
   "State Health Care Expenditures" (http://www.cms.hhs.gov/NationalHealthExpendData/)
*By state of provider. Includes hospital care, physician services, dental services, home health care, drugs, vision products, nursing home care, and other personal health care services and products.

Per Capita Personal Health Care Expenditures in 2004

National Per Capita = $5,283*

ALPHA ORDER				RANK ORDER		
RANK	STATE	PER CAPITA		RANK	STATE	PER CAPITA
30	Alabama	$5,135		1	Massachusetts	$6,683
4	Alaska	6,450		2	Maine	6,540
49	Arizona	4,103		3	New York	6,535
40	Arkansas	4,863		4	Alaska	6,450
43	California	4,638		5	Connecticut	6,344
42	Colorado	4,717		6	Delaware	6,306
5	Connecticut	6,344		7	Rhode Island	6,193
6	Delaware	6,306		8	Vermont	6,069
18	Florida	5,483		9	West Virginia	5,954
45	Georgia	4,600		10	Pennsylvania	5,933
37	Hawaii	4,941		11	North Dakota	5,808
48	Idaho	4,444		12	New Jersey	5,807
27	Illinois	5,293		13	Minnesota	5,795
26	Indiana	5,295		14	Ohio	5,725
24	Iowa	5,380		15	Wisconsin	5,670
23	Kansas	5,382		16	Nebraska	5,599
19	Kentucky	5,473		17	Maryland	5,590
36	Louisiana	5,040		18	Florida	5,483
2	Maine	6,540		19	Kentucky	5,473
17	Maryland	5,590		20	Tennessee	5,464
1	Massachusetts	6,683		21	Missouri	5,444
35	Michigan	5,058		22	New Hampshire	5,432
13	Minnesota	5,795		23	Kansas	5,382
34	Mississippi	5,059		24	Iowa	5,380
21	Missouri	5,444		25	South Dakota	5,327
33	Montana	5,080		26	Indiana	5,295
16	Nebraska	5,599		27	Illinois	5,293
46	Nevada	4,569		28	Wyoming	5,265
22	New Hampshire	5,432		29	North Carolina	5,191
12	New Jersey	5,807		30	Alabama	5,135
47	New Mexico	4,471		31	South Carolina	5,114
3	New York	6,535		32	Washington	5,092
29	North Carolina	5,191		33	Montana	5,080
11	North Dakota	5,808		34	Mississippi	5,059
14	Ohio	5,725		35	Michigan	5,058
38	Oklahoma	4,917		36	Louisiana	5,040
39	Oregon	4,880		37	Hawaii	4,941
10	Pennsylvania	5,933		38	Oklahoma	4,917
7	Rhode Island	6,193		39	Oregon	4,880
31	South Carolina	5,114		40	Arkansas	4,863
25	South Dakota	5,327		41	Virginia	4,822
20	Tennessee	5,464		42	Colorado	4,717
44	Texas	4,601		43	California	4,638
50	Utah	3,972		44	Texas	4,601
8	Vermont	6,069		45	Georgia	4,600
41	Virginia	4,822		46	Nevada	4,569
32	Washington	5,092		47	New Mexico	4,471
9	West Virginia	5,954		48	Idaho	4,444
15	Wisconsin	5,670		49	Arizona	4,103
28	Wyoming	5,265		50	Utah	3,972
					District of Columbia	8,295

Source: U.S. Department of Health and Human Services, Centers for Medicare and Medicaid Services
   "State Health Care Expenditures" (http://www.cms.hhs.gov/NationalHealthExpendData/)
*By state of provider. Includes hospital care, physician services, dental services, home health care, drugs, vision products,
nursing home care, and other personal health care services and products.

Average Annual Growth in Personal Health Care Expenditures: 1991 to 2004

National Average = 6.7% Annual Growth*

ALPHA ORDER				RANK ORDER		
RANK	STATE	ANNUAL GROWTH		RANK	STATE	ANNUAL GROWTH
37	Alabama	6.4		1	Nevada	10.0
3	Alaska	8.4		2	North Carolina	8.6
10	Arizona	7.7		3	Alaska	8.4
30	Arkansas	6.9		3	Idaho	8.4
48	California	5.7		3	Vermont	8.4
10	Colorado	7.7		6	Maine	8.3
48	Connecticut	5.7		6	Utah	8.3
8	Delaware	8.0		8	Delaware	8.0
26	Florida	7.1		9	South Carolina	7.8
23	Georgia	7.2		10	Arizona	7.7
45	Hawaii	5.9		10	Colorado	7.7
3	Idaho	8.4		10	Oregon	7.7
44	Illinois	6.1		10	Wyoming	7.7
31	Indiana	6.8		14	Minnesota	7.6
37	Iowa	6.4		14	Mississippi	7.6
34	Kansas	6.6		14	Nebraska	7.6
18	Kentucky	7.5		14	New Hampshire	7.6
48	Louisiana	5.7		18	Kentucky	7.5
6	Maine	8.3		19	Tennessee	7.4
34	Maryland	6.6		19	Texas	7.4
40	Massachusetts	6.3		21	Montana	7.3
46	Michigan	5.8		21	Washington	7.3
14	Minnesota	7.6		23	Georgia	7.2
14	Mississippi	7.6		23	New Mexico	7.2
27	Missouri	7.0		23	Wisconsin	7.2
21	Montana	7.3		26	Florida	7.1
14	Nebraska	7.6		27	Missouri	7.0
1	Nevada	10.0		27	South Dakota	7.0
14	New Hampshire	7.6		27	Virginia	7.0
40	New Jersey	6.3		30	Arkansas	6.9
23	New Mexico	7.2		31	Indiana	6.8
40	New York	6.3		31	West Virginia	6.8
2	North Carolina	8.6		33	Oklahoma	6.7
40	North Dakota	6.3		34	Kansas	6.6
37	Ohio	6.4		34	Maryland	6.6
33	Oklahoma	6.7		34	Rhode Island	6.6
10	Oregon	7.7		37	Alabama	6.4
46	Pennsylvania	5.8		37	Iowa	6.4
34	Rhode Island	6.6		37	Ohio	6.4
9	South Carolina	7.8		40	Massachusetts	6.3
27	South Dakota	7.0		40	New Jersey	6.3
19	Tennessee	7.4		40	New York	6.3
19	Texas	7.4		40	North Dakota	6.3
6	Utah	8.3		44	Illinois	6.1
3	Vermont	8.4		45	Hawaii	5.9
27	Virginia	7.0		46	Michigan	5.8
21	Washington	7.3		46	Pennsylvania	5.8
31	West Virginia	6.8		48	California	5.7
23	Wisconsin	7.2		48	Connecticut	5.7
10	Wyoming	7.7		48	Louisiana	5.7
					District of Columbia	4.1

Source: U.S. Department of Health and Human Services, Centers for Medicare and Medicaid Services
"State Health Care Expenditures" (http://www.cms.hhs.gov/NationalHealthExpendData/)
*By state of residence. Includes hospital care, physician services, dental services, home health care, drugs, vision products, nursing home care, and other personal health care services and products.

Expenditures for Hospital Care in 2004

National Total = $566,886,000,000*

<table>
<tr><td colspan="4">ALPHA ORDER</td><td colspan="4">RANK ORDER</td></tr>
<tr><th>RANK</th><th>STATE</th><th>EXPENDITURES</th><th>% of USA</th><th>RANK</th><th>STATE</th><th>EXPENDITURES</th><th>% of USA</th></tr>
<tr><td>25</td><td>Alabama</td><td>$7,938,000,000</td><td>1.4%</td><td>1</td><td>California</td><td>$57,805,000,000</td><td>10.2%</td></tr>
<tr><td>47</td><td>Alaska</td><td>1,704,000,000</td><td>0.3%</td><td>2</td><td>New York</td><td>45,569,000,000</td><td>8.0%</td></tr>
<tr><td>22</td><td>Arizona</td><td>8,499,000,000</td><td>1.5%</td><td>3</td><td>Texas</td><td>38,910,000,000</td><td>6.9%</td></tr>
<tr><td>33</td><td>Arkansas</td><td>5,092,000,000</td><td>0.9%</td><td>4</td><td>Florida</td><td>31,494,000,000</td><td>5.6%</td></tr>
<tr><td>1</td><td>California</td><td>57,805,000,000</td><td>10.2%</td><td>5</td><td>Pennsylvania</td><td>26,715,000,000</td><td>4.7%</td></tr>
<tr><td>26</td><td>Colorado</td><td>7,624,000,000</td><td>1.3%</td><td>6</td><td>Illinois</td><td>25,801,000,000</td><td>4.6%</td></tr>
<tr><td>27</td><td>Connecticut</td><td>7,029,000,000</td><td>1.2%</td><td>7</td><td>Ohio</td><td>24,822,000,000</td><td>4.4%</td></tr>
<tr><td>45</td><td>Delaware</td><td>1,917,000,000</td><td>0.3%</td><td>8</td><td>Michigan</td><td>20,206,000,000</td><td>3.6%</td></tr>
<tr><td>4</td><td>Florida</td><td>31,494,000,000</td><td>5.6%</td><td>9</td><td>New Jersey</td><td>17,024,000,000</td><td>3.0%</td></tr>
<tr><td>12</td><td>Georgia</td><td>14,613,000,000</td><td>2.6%</td><td>10</td><td>Massachusetts</td><td>16,865,000,000</td><td>3.0%</td></tr>
<tr><td>42</td><td>Hawaii</td><td>2,310,000,000</td><td>0.4%</td><td>11</td><td>North Carolina</td><td>16,294,000,000</td><td>2.9%</td></tr>
<tr><td>43</td><td>Idaho</td><td>2,298,000,000</td><td>0.4%</td><td>12</td><td>Georgia</td><td>14,613,000,000</td><td>2.6%</td></tr>
<tr><td>6</td><td>Illinois</td><td>25,801,000,000</td><td>4.6%</td><td>13</td><td>Virginia</td><td>13,361,000,000</td><td>2.4%</td></tr>
<tr><td>15</td><td>Indiana</td><td>12,761,000,000</td><td>2.3%</td><td>14</td><td>Missouri</td><td>12,993,000,000</td><td>2.3%</td></tr>
<tr><td>29</td><td>Iowa</td><td>6,179,000,000</td><td>1.1%</td><td>15</td><td>Indiana</td><td>12,761,000,000</td><td>2.3%</td></tr>
<tr><td>32</td><td>Kansas</td><td>5,157,000,000</td><td>0.9%</td><td>16</td><td>Wisconsin</td><td>11,625,000,000</td><td>2.1%</td></tr>
<tr><td>24</td><td>Kentucky</td><td>8,283,000,000</td><td>1.5%</td><td>17</td><td>Maryland</td><td>11,559,000,000</td><td>2.0%</td></tr>
<tr><td>21</td><td>Louisiana</td><td>9,145,000,000</td><td>1.6%</td><td>18</td><td>Tennessee</td><td>10,744,000,000</td><td>1.9%</td></tr>
<tr><td>39</td><td>Maine</td><td>3,035,000,000</td><td>0.5%</td><td>19</td><td>Washington</td><td>10,702,000,000</td><td>1.9%</td></tr>
<tr><td>17</td><td>Maryland</td><td>11,559,000,000</td><td>2.0%</td><td>20</td><td>Minnesota</td><td>10,009,000,000</td><td>1.8%</td></tr>
<tr><td>10</td><td>Massachusetts</td><td>16,865,000,000</td><td>3.0%</td><td>21</td><td>Louisiana</td><td>9,145,000,000</td><td>1.6%</td></tr>
<tr><td>8</td><td>Michigan</td><td>20,206,000,000</td><td>3.6%</td><td>22</td><td>Arizona</td><td>8,499,000,000</td><td>1.5%</td></tr>
<tr><td>20</td><td>Minnesota</td><td>10,009,000,000</td><td>1.8%</td><td>23</td><td>South Carolina</td><td>8,316,000,000</td><td>1.5%</td></tr>
<tr><td>30</td><td>Mississippi</td><td>6,129,000,000</td><td>1.1%</td><td>24</td><td>Kentucky</td><td>8,283,000,000</td><td>1.5%</td></tr>
<tr><td>14</td><td>Missouri</td><td>12,993,000,000</td><td>2.3%</td><td>25</td><td>Alabama</td><td>7,938,000,000</td><td>1.4%</td></tr>
<tr><td>44</td><td>Montana</td><td>1,944,000,000</td><td>0.3%</td><td>26</td><td>Colorado</td><td>7,624,000,000</td><td>1.3%</td></tr>
<tr><td>35</td><td>Nebraska</td><td>3,938,000,000</td><td>0.7%</td><td>27</td><td>Connecticut</td><td>7,029,000,000</td><td>1.2%</td></tr>
<tr><td>37</td><td>Nevada</td><td>3,459,000,000</td><td>0.6%</td><td>28</td><td>Oklahoma</td><td>6,659,000,000</td><td>1.2%</td></tr>
<tr><td>40</td><td>New Hampshire</td><td>2,519,000,000</td><td>0.4%</td><td>29</td><td>Iowa</td><td>6,179,000,000</td><td>1.1%</td></tr>
<tr><td>9</td><td>New Jersey</td><td>17,024,000,000</td><td>3.0%</td><td>30</td><td>Mississippi</td><td>6,129,000,000</td><td>1.1%</td></tr>
<tr><td>38</td><td>New Mexico</td><td>3,315,000,000</td><td>0.6%</td><td>31</td><td>Oregon</td><td>5,998,000,000</td><td>1.1%</td></tr>
<tr><td>2</td><td>New York</td><td>45,569,000,000</td><td>8.0%</td><td>32</td><td>Kansas</td><td>5,157,000,000</td><td>0.9%</td></tr>
<tr><td>11</td><td>North Carolina</td><td>16,294,000,000</td><td>2.9%</td><td>33</td><td>Arkansas</td><td>5,092,000,000</td><td>0.9%</td></tr>
<tr><td>48</td><td>North Dakota</td><td>1,533,000,000</td><td>0.3%</td><td>34</td><td>West Virginia</td><td>4,432,000,000</td><td>0.8%</td></tr>
<tr><td>7</td><td>Ohio</td><td>24,822,000,000</td><td>4.4%</td><td>35</td><td>Nebraska</td><td>3,938,000,000</td><td>0.7%</td></tr>
<tr><td>28</td><td>Oklahoma</td><td>6,659,000,000</td><td>1.2%</td><td>36</td><td>Utah</td><td>3,468,000,000</td><td>0.6%</td></tr>
<tr><td>31</td><td>Oregon</td><td>5,998,000,000</td><td>1.1%</td><td>37</td><td>Nevada</td><td>3,459,000,000</td><td>0.6%</td></tr>
<tr><td>5</td><td>Pennsylvania</td><td>26,715,000,000</td><td>4.7%</td><td>38</td><td>New Mexico</td><td>3,315,000,000</td><td>0.6%</td></tr>
<tr><td>41</td><td>Rhode Island</td><td>2,437,000,000</td><td>0.4%</td><td>39</td><td>Maine</td><td>3,035,000,000</td><td>0.5%</td></tr>
<tr><td>23</td><td>South Carolina</td><td>8,316,000,000</td><td>1.5%</td><td>40</td><td>New Hampshire</td><td>2,519,000,000</td><td>0.4%</td></tr>
<tr><td>46</td><td>South Dakota</td><td>1,753,000,000</td><td>0.3%</td><td>41</td><td>Rhode Island</td><td>2,437,000,000</td><td>0.4%</td></tr>
<tr><td>18</td><td>Tennessee</td><td>10,744,000,000</td><td>1.9%</td><td>42</td><td>Hawaii</td><td>2,310,000,000</td><td>0.4%</td></tr>
<tr><td>3</td><td>Texas</td><td>38,910,000,000</td><td>6.9%</td><td>43</td><td>Idaho</td><td>2,298,000,000</td><td>0.4%</td></tr>
<tr><td>36</td><td>Utah</td><td>3,468,000,000</td><td>0.6%</td><td>44</td><td>Montana</td><td>1,944,000,000</td><td>0.3%</td></tr>
<tr><td>49</td><td>Vermont</td><td>1,446,000,000</td><td>0.3%</td><td>45</td><td>Delaware</td><td>1,917,000,000</td><td>0.3%</td></tr>
<tr><td>13</td><td>Virginia</td><td>13,361,000,000</td><td>2.4%</td><td>46</td><td>South Dakota</td><td>1,753,000,000</td><td>0.3%</td></tr>
<tr><td>19</td><td>Washington</td><td>10,702,000,000</td><td>1.9%</td><td>47</td><td>Alaska</td><td>1,704,000,000</td><td>0.3%</td></tr>
<tr><td>34</td><td>West Virginia</td><td>4,432,000,000</td><td>0.8%</td><td>48</td><td>North Dakota</td><td>1,533,000,000</td><td>0.3%</td></tr>
<tr><td>16</td><td>Wisconsin</td><td>11,625,000,000</td><td>2.1%</td><td>49</td><td>Vermont</td><td>1,446,000,000</td><td>0.3%</td></tr>
<tr><td>50</td><td>Wyoming</td><td>1,095,000,000</td><td>0.2%</td><td>50</td><td>Wyoming</td><td>1,095,000,000</td><td>0.2%</td></tr>
<tr><td></td><td></td><td></td><td></td><td></td><td>District of Columbia</td><td>2,366,000,000</td><td>0.4%</td></tr>
</table>

Source: U.S. Department of Health and Human Services, Centers for Medicare and Medicaid Services
"State Health Care Expenditures" (http://www.cms.hhs.gov/NationalHealthExpendData/)
*By state of residence.

Percent of Total Personal Health Care Expenditures
Spent on Hospital Care in 2004
National Percent = 36.5%*

ALPHA ORDER

RANK	STATE	PERCENT
42	Alabama	34.2
10	Alaska	40.2
35	Arizona	36.0
20	Arkansas	38.1
41	California	34.8
39	Colorado	35.1
50	Connecticut	31.7
29	Delaware	36.7
48	Florida	33.1
37	Georgia	35.6
25	Hawaii	37.1
25	Idaho	37.1
19	Illinois	38.3
16	Indiana	38.7
14	Iowa	38.9
40	Kansas	35.0
30	Kentucky	36.6
8	Louisiana	40.4
38	Maine	35.3
24	Maryland	37.2
12	Massachusetts	39.2
11	Michigan	39.6
44	Minnesota	33.9
2	Mississippi	41.9
3	Missouri	41.5
5	Montana	41.3
9	Nebraska	40.3
49	Nevada	32.5
36	New Hampshire	35.7
46	New Jersey	33.8
13	New Mexico	39.0
33	New York	36.1
28	North Carolina	36.8
3	North Dakota	41.5
21	Ohio	37.8
17	Oklahoma	38.4
42	Oregon	34.2
32	Pennsylvania	36.4
31	Rhode Island	36.5
15	South Carolina	38.8
1	South Dakota	42.7
47	Tennessee	33.4
22	Texas	37.6
33	Utah	36.1
17	Vermont	38.4
25	Virginia	37.1
44	Washington	33.9
6	West Virginia	41.1
23	Wisconsin	37.3
6	Wyoming	41.1

RANK ORDER

RANK	STATE	PERCENT
1	South Dakota	42.7
2	Mississippi	41.9
3	Missouri	41.5
3	North Dakota	41.5
5	Montana	41.3
6	West Virginia	41.1
6	Wyoming	41.1
8	Louisiana	40.4
9	Nebraska	40.3
10	Alaska	40.2
11	Michigan	39.6
12	Massachusetts	39.2
13	New Mexico	39.0
14	Iowa	38.9
15	South Carolina	38.8
16	Indiana	38.7
17	Oklahoma	38.4
17	Vermont	38.4
19	Illinois	38.3
20	Arkansas	38.1
21	Ohio	37.8
22	Texas	37.6
23	Wisconsin	37.3
24	Maryland	37.2
25	Hawaii	37.1
25	Idaho	37.1
25	Virginia	37.1
28	North Carolina	36.8
29	Delaware	36.7
30	Kentucky	36.6
31	Rhode Island	36.5
32	Pennsylvania	36.4
33	New York	36.1
33	Utah	36.1
35	Arizona	36.0
36	New Hampshire	35.7
37	Georgia	35.6
38	Maine	35.3
39	Colorado	35.1
40	Kansas	35.0
41	California	34.8
42	Alabama	34.2
42	Oregon	34.2
44	Minnesota	33.9
44	Washington	33.9
46	New Jersey	33.8
47	Tennessee	33.4
48	Florida	33.1
49	Nevada	32.5
50	Connecticut	31.7

| | District of Columbia | 49.2 |

Source: CQ Press using data from U.S. Department of Health and Human Services, Centers for Medicare and Medicaid Services
"State Health Care Expenditures" (http://www.cms.hhs.gov/NationalHealthExpendData/)
*By state of residence.

Per Capita Expenditures for Hospital Care in 2004

National Per Capita = $1,931*

ALPHA ORDER

RANK	STATE	PER CAPITA
39	Alabama	$1,757
2	Alaska	2,594
49	Arizona	1,479
34	Arkansas	1,854
47	California	1,613
44	Colorado	1,658
24	Connecticut	2,012
7	Delaware	2,313
37	Florida	1,813
46	Georgia	1,635
35	Hawaii	1,834
45	Idaho	1,648
23	Illinois	2,029
21	Indiana	2,051
19	Iowa	2,092
33	Kansas	1,883
26	Kentucky	2,001
22	Louisiana	2,034
8	Maine	2,310
20	Maryland	2,081
1	Massachusetts	2,620
25	Michigan	2,002
28	Minnesota	1,965
16	Mississippi	2,119
10	Missouri	2,259
18	Montana	2,099
12	Nebraska	2,254
48	Nevada	1,483
30	New Hampshire	1,941
29	New Jersey	1,962
40	New Mexico	1,744
5	New York	2,362
31	North Carolina	1,910
4	North Dakota	2,411
13	Ohio	2,166
32	Oklahoma	1,890
43	Oregon	1,671
15	Pennsylvania	2,158
10	Rhode Island	2,259
27	South Carolina	1,982
9	South Dakota	2,276
36	Tennessee	1,826
41	Texas	1,728
50	Utah	1,432
6	Vermont	2,329
38	Virginia	1,788
42	Washington	1,725
3	West Virginia	2,447
17	Wisconsin	2,114
14	Wyoming	2,165

RANK ORDER

RANK	STATE	PER CAPITA
1	Massachusetts	$2,620
2	Alaska	2,594
3	West Virginia	2,447
4	North Dakota	2,411
5	New York	2,362
6	Vermont	2,329
7	Delaware	2,313
8	Maine	2,310
9	South Dakota	2,276
10	Missouri	2,259
10	Rhode Island	2,259
12	Nebraska	2,254
13	Ohio	2,166
14	Wyoming	2,165
15	Pennsylvania	2,158
16	Mississippi	2,119
17	Wisconsin	2,114
18	Montana	2,099
19	Iowa	2,092
20	Maryland	2,081
21	Indiana	2,051
22	Louisiana	2,034
23	Illinois	2,029
24	Connecticut	2,012
25	Michigan	2,002
26	Kentucky	2,001
27	South Carolina	1,982
28	Minnesota	1,965
29	New Jersey	1,962
30	New Hampshire	1,941
31	North Carolina	1,910
32	Oklahoma	1,890
33	Kansas	1,883
34	Arkansas	1,854
35	Hawaii	1,834
36	Tennessee	1,826
37	Florida	1,813
38	Virginia	1,788
39	Alabama	1,757
40	New Mexico	1,744
41	Texas	1,728
42	Washington	1,725
43	Oregon	1,671
44	Colorado	1,658
45	Idaho	1,648
46	Georgia	1,635
47	California	1,613
48	Nevada	1,483
49	Arizona	1,479
50	Utah	1,432
	District of Columbia	4,081

Source: U.S. Department of Health and Human Services, Centers for Medicare and Medicaid Services
"State Health Care Expenditures" (http://www.cms.hhs.gov/NationalHealthExpendData/)
*By state of residence.

Expenditures for Physician and Clinical Services in 2004

National Total = $393,713,000,000*

ALPHA ORDER

RANK	STATE	EXPENDITURES	% of USA
23	Alabama	$6,200,000,000	1.6%
45	Alaska	1,220,000,000	0.3%
21	Arizona	6,855,000,000	1.7%
33	Arkansas	3,316,000,000	0.8%
1	California	49,417,000,000	12.6%
22	Colorado	6,375,000,000	1.6%
27	Connecticut	5,155,000,000	1.3%
44	Delaware	1,228,000,000	0.3%
3	Florida	26,439,000,000	6.7%
10	Georgia	11,227,000,000	2.9%
41	Hawaii	1,587,000,000	0.4%
42	Idaho	1,466,000,000	0.4%
5	Illinois	16,984,000,000	4.3%
18	Indiana	7,869,000,000	2.0%
31	Iowa	3,719,000,000	0.9%
30	Kansas	4,144,000,000	1.1%
24	Kentucky	5,748,000,000	1.5%
26	Louisiana	5,271,000,000	1.3%
38	Maine	2,075,000,000	0.5%
17	Maryland	7,891,000,000	2.0%
13	Massachusetts	9,116,000,000	2.3%
9	Michigan	11,757,000,000	3.0%
19	Minnesota	7,757,000,000	2.0%
34	Mississippi	3,219,000,000	0.8%
20	Missouri	6,891,000,000	1.8%
46	Montana	1,157,000,000	0.3%
37	Nebraska	2,287,000,000	0.6%
32	Nevada	3,386,000,000	0.9%
40	New Hampshire	1,757,000,000	0.4%
8	New Jersey	12,265,000,000	3.1%
39	New Mexico	1,925,000,000	0.5%
4	New York	25,643,000,000	6.5%
11	North Carolina	10,248,000,000	2.6%
49	North Dakota	763,000,000	0.2%
7	Ohio	15,322,000,000	3.9%
29	Oklahoma	4,305,000,000	1.1%
28	Oregon	5,142,000,000	1.3%
6	Pennsylvania	16,942,000,000	4.3%
43	Rhode Island	1,325,000,000	0.3%
25	South Carolina	5,491,000,000	1.4%
47	South Dakota	920,000,000	0.2%
14	Tennessee	9,069,000,000	2.3%
2	Texas	28,769,000,000	7.3%
36	Utah	2,393,000,000	0.6%
48	Vermont	874,000,000	0.2%
12	Virginia	9,220,000,000	2.3%
15	Washington	9,004,000,000	2.3%
35	West Virginia	2,444,000,000	0.6%
16	Wisconsin	8,441,000,000	2.1%
50	Wyoming	670,000,000	0.2%

RANK ORDER

RANK	STATE	EXPENDITURES	% of USA
1	California	$49,417,000,000	12.6%
2	Texas	28,769,000,000	7.3%
3	Florida	26,439,000,000	6.7%
4	New York	25,643,000,000	6.5%
5	Illinois	16,984,000,000	4.3%
6	Pennsylvania	16,942,000,000	4.3%
7	Ohio	15,322,000,000	3.9%
8	New Jersey	12,265,000,000	3.1%
9	Michigan	11,757,000,000	3.0%
10	Georgia	11,227,000,000	2.9%
11	North Carolina	10,248,000,000	2.6%
12	Virginia	9,220,000,000	2.3%
13	Massachusetts	9,116,000,000	2.3%
14	Tennessee	9,069,000,000	2.3%
15	Washington	9,004,000,000	2.3%
16	Wisconsin	8,441,000,000	2.1%
17	Maryland	7,891,000,000	2.0%
18	Indiana	7,869,000,000	2.0%
19	Minnesota	7,757,000,000	2.0%
20	Missouri	6,891,000,000	1.8%
21	Arizona	6,855,000,000	1.7%
22	Colorado	6,375,000,000	1.6%
23	Alabama	6,200,000,000	1.6%
24	Kentucky	5,748,000,000	1.5%
25	South Carolina	5,491,000,000	1.4%
26	Louisiana	5,271,000,000	1.3%
27	Connecticut	5,155,000,000	1.3%
28	Oregon	5,142,000,000	1.3%
29	Oklahoma	4,305,000,000	1.1%
30	Kansas	4,144,000,000	1.1%
31	Iowa	3,719,000,000	0.9%
32	Nevada	3,386,000,000	0.9%
33	Arkansas	3,316,000,000	0.8%
34	Mississippi	3,219,000,000	0.8%
35	West Virginia	2,444,000,000	0.6%
36	Utah	2,393,000,000	0.6%
37	Nebraska	2,287,000,000	0.6%
38	Maine	2,075,000,000	0.5%
39	New Mexico	1,925,000,000	0.5%
40	New Hampshire	1,757,000,000	0.4%
41	Hawaii	1,587,000,000	0.4%
42	Idaho	1,466,000,000	0.4%
43	Rhode Island	1,325,000,000	0.3%
44	Delaware	1,228,000,000	0.3%
45	Alaska	1,220,000,000	0.3%
46	Montana	1,157,000,000	0.3%
47	South Dakota	920,000,000	0.2%
48	Vermont	874,000,000	0.2%
49	North Dakota	763,000,000	0.2%
50	Wyoming	670,000,000	0.2%
	District of Columbia	1,024,000,000	0.3%

Source: U.S. Department of Health and Human Services, Centers for Medicare and Medicaid Services
  "State Health Care Expenditures" (http://www.cms.hhs.gov/NationalHealthExpendData/)
*By state of residence. Includes private physician offices and clinics, independently billing laboratories and clinics run by U.S. Department of Veteran Affairs and the U.S. Indian Health Service.

Percent of Total Personal Health Care Expenditures
Spent on Physician and Clinical Services in 2004
National Percent = 25.4%*

ALPHA ORDER

RANK	STATE	PERCENT
14	Alabama	26.7
6	Alaska	28.8
5	Arizona	29.1
26	Arkansas	24.8
2	California	29.7
3	Colorado	29.4
35	Connecticut	23.3
32	Delaware	23.5
10	Florida	27.8
12	Georgia	27.3
18	Hawaii	25.5
31	Idaho	23.7
21	Illinois	25.2
30	Indiana	23.9
33	Iowa	23.4
9	Kansas	28.1
19	Kentucky	25.4
35	Louisiana	23.3
29	Maine	24.1
19	Maryland	25.4
47	Massachusetts	21.2
41	Michigan	23.0
15	Minnesota	26.3
45	Mississippi	22.0
45	Missouri	22.0
27	Montana	24.6
33	Nebraska	23.4
1	Nevada	31.8
23	New Hampshire	24.9
28	New Jersey	24.3
42	New Mexico	22.7
49	New York	20.3
39	North Carolina	23.1
48	North Dakota	20.7
35	Ohio	23.3
23	Oklahoma	24.9
3	Oregon	29.4
39	Pennsylvania	23.1
50	Rhode Island	19.8
16	South Carolina	25.6
44	South Dakota	22.4
8	Tennessee	28.2
10	Texas	27.8
23	Utah	24.9
38	Vermont	23.2
16	Virginia	25.6
7	Washington	28.5
42	West Virginia	22.7
13	Wisconsin	27.1
21	Wyoming	25.2

RANK ORDER

RANK	STATE	PERCENT
1	Nevada	31.8
2	California	29.7
3	Colorado	29.4
3	Oregon	29.4
5	Arizona	29.1
6	Alaska	28.8
7	Washington	28.5
8	Tennessee	28.2
9	Kansas	28.1
10	Florida	27.8
10	Texas	27.8
12	Georgia	27.3
13	Wisconsin	27.1
14	Alabama	26.7
15	Minnesota	26.3
16	South Carolina	25.6
16	Virginia	25.6
18	Hawaii	25.5
19	Kentucky	25.4
19	Maryland	25.4
21	Illinois	25.2
21	Wyoming	25.2
23	New Hampshire	24.9
23	Oklahoma	24.9
23	Utah	24.9
26	Arkansas	24.8
27	Montana	24.6
28	New Jersey	24.3
29	Maine	24.1
30	Indiana	23.9
31	Idaho	23.7
32	Delaware	23.5
33	Iowa	23.4
33	Nebraska	23.4
35	Connecticut	23.3
35	Louisiana	23.3
35	Ohio	23.3
38	Vermont	23.2
39	North Carolina	23.1
39	Pennsylvania	23.1
41	Michigan	23.0
42	New Mexico	22.7
42	West Virginia	22.7
44	South Dakota	22.4
45	Mississippi	22.0
45	Missouri	22.0
47	Massachusetts	21.2
48	North Dakota	20.7
49	New York	20.3
50	Rhode Island	19.8

| | District of Columbia | 21.3 |

Source: CQ Press using data from U.S. Department of Health and Human Services, Centers for Medicare and Medicaid Services
"State Health Care Expenditures" (http://www.cms.hhs.gov/NationalHealthExpendData/)
*By state of residence. Includes private physician offices and clinics, independently billing laboratories and clinics run by U.S.
Department of Veteran Affairs and the U.S. Indian Health Service.

Per Capita Expenditures for Physician and Clinical Services in 2004

National Per Capita = $1,341*

ALPHA ORDER

RANK	STATE	PER CAPITA
20	Alabama	$1,372
1	Alaska	1,858
44	Arizona	1,193
39	Arkansas	1,207
19	California	1,379
18	Colorado	1,386
9	Connecticut	1,475
8	Delaware	1,482
6	Florida	1,522
34	Georgia	1,257
32	Hawaii	1,260
48	Idaho	1,051
25	Illinois	1,336
31	Indiana	1,264
33	Iowa	1,259
7	Kansas	1,513
17	Kentucky	1,388
45	Louisiana	1,173
2	Maine	1,579
13	Maryland	1,421
14	Massachusetts	1,416
46	Michigan	1,165
5	Minnesota	1,523
47	Mississippi	1,113
42	Missouri	1,198
35	Montana	1,249
28	Nebraska	1,309
10	Nevada	1,451
22	New Hampshire	1,354
15	New Jersey	1,414
49	New Mexico	1,013
26	New York	1,329
40	North Carolina	1,201
41	North Dakota	1,200
24	Ohio	1,337
38	Oklahoma	1,222
12	Oregon	1,433
21	Pennsylvania	1,369
37	Rhode Island	1,228
28	South Carolina	1,309
43	South Dakota	1,195
3	Tennessee	1,541
30	Texas	1,278
50	Utah	988
16	Vermont	1,408
36	Virginia	1,234
10	Washington	1,451
23	West Virginia	1,350
4	Wisconsin	1,535
27	Wyoming	1,326

RANK ORDER

RANK	STATE	PER CAPITA
1	Alaska	$1,858
2	Maine	1,579
3	Tennessee	1,541
4	Wisconsin	1,535
5	Minnesota	1,523
6	Florida	1,522
7	Kansas	1,513
8	Delaware	1,482
9	Connecticut	1,475
10	Nevada	1,451
10	Washington	1,451
12	Oregon	1,433
13	Maryland	1,421
14	Massachusetts	1,416
15	New Jersey	1,414
16	Vermont	1,408
17	Kentucky	1,388
18	Colorado	1,386
19	California	1,379
20	Alabama	1,372
21	Pennsylvania	1,369
22	New Hampshire	1,354
23	West Virginia	1,350
24	Ohio	1,337
25	Illinois	1,336
26	New York	1,329
27	Wyoming	1,326
28	Nebraska	1,309
28	South Carolina	1,309
30	Texas	1,278
31	Indiana	1,264
32	Hawaii	1,260
33	Iowa	1,259
34	Georgia	1,257
35	Montana	1,249
36	Virginia	1,234
37	Rhode Island	1,228
38	Oklahoma	1,222
39	Arkansas	1,207
40	North Carolina	1,201
41	North Dakota	1,200
42	Missouri	1,198
43	South Dakota	1,195
44	Arizona	1,193
45	Louisiana	1,173
46	Michigan	1,165
47	Mississippi	1,113
48	Idaho	1,051
49	New Mexico	1,013
50	Utah	988
	District of Columbia	1,767

Source: U.S. Department of Health and Human Services, Centers for Medicare and Medicaid Services
"State Health Care Expenditures" (http://www.cms.hhs.gov/NationalHealthExpendData/)
*By state of residence. Includes private physician offices and clinics, independently billing laboratories and clinics run by U.S. Department of Veteran Affairs and the U.S. Indian Health Service.

Expenditures for Dental Services in 2004

National Total = $81,476,000,000*

<table>
<tr><td colspan="4">ALPHA ORDER</td><td colspan="4">RANK ORDER</td></tr>
<tr><td>RANK</td><td>STATE</td><td>EXPENDITURES</td><td>% of USA</td><td>RANK</td><td>STATE</td><td>EXPENDITURES</td><td>% of USA</td></tr>
<tr><td>26</td><td>Alabama</td><td>$977,000,000</td><td>1.2%</td><td>1</td><td>California</td><td>$11,625,000,000</td><td>14.3%</td></tr>
<tr><td>46</td><td>Alaska</td><td>241,000,000</td><td>0.3%</td><td>2</td><td>New York</td><td>5,445,000,000</td><td>6.7%</td></tr>
<tr><td>20</td><td>Arizona</td><td>1,457,000,000</td><td>1.8%</td><td>3</td><td>Texas</td><td>4,749,000,000</td><td>5.8%</td></tr>
<tr><td>34</td><td>Arkansas</td><td>601,000,000</td><td>0.7%</td><td>4</td><td>Florida</td><td>4,494,000,000</td><td>5.5%</td></tr>
<tr><td>1</td><td>California</td><td>11,625,000,000</td><td>14.3%</td><td>5</td><td>Illinois</td><td>3,488,000,000</td><td>4.3%</td></tr>
<tr><td>19</td><td>Colorado</td><td>1,537,000,000</td><td>1.9%</td><td>6</td><td>Pennsylvania</td><td>3,189,000,000</td><td>3.9%</td></tr>
<tr><td>22</td><td>Connecticut</td><td>1,336,000,000</td><td>1.6%</td><td>7</td><td>Michigan</td><td>3,147,000,000</td><td>3.9%</td></tr>
<tr><td>44</td><td>Delaware</td><td>279,000,000</td><td>0.3%</td><td>8</td><td>New Jersey</td><td>2,903,000,000</td><td>3.6%</td></tr>
<tr><td>4</td><td>Florida</td><td>4,494,000,000</td><td>5.5%</td><td>9</td><td>Ohio</td><td>2,901,000,000</td><td>3.6%</td></tr>
<tr><td>12</td><td>Georgia</td><td>2,257,000,000</td><td>2.8%</td><td>10</td><td>Washington</td><td>2,505,000,000</td><td>3.1%</td></tr>
<tr><td>41</td><td>Hawaii</td><td>382,000,000</td><td>0.5%</td><td>11</td><td>Massachusetts</td><td>2,276,000,000</td><td>2.8%</td></tr>
<tr><td>37</td><td>Idaho</td><td>468,000,000</td><td>0.6%</td><td>12</td><td>Georgia</td><td>2,257,000,000</td><td>2.8%</td></tr>
<tr><td>5</td><td>Illinois</td><td>3,488,000,000</td><td>4.3%</td><td>13</td><td>North Carolina</td><td>2,253,000,000</td><td>2.8%</td></tr>
<tr><td>17</td><td>Indiana</td><td>1,606,000,000</td><td>2.0%</td><td>14</td><td>Virginia</td><td>2,043,000,000</td><td>2.5%</td></tr>
<tr><td>30</td><td>Iowa</td><td>735,000,000</td><td>0.9%</td><td>15</td><td>Wisconsin</td><td>1,694,000,000</td><td>2.1%</td></tr>
<tr><td>31</td><td>Kansas</td><td>723,000,000</td><td>0.9%</td><td>16</td><td>Minnesota</td><td>1,678,000,000</td><td>2.1%</td></tr>
<tr><td>27</td><td>Kentucky</td><td>876,000,000</td><td>1.1%</td><td>17</td><td>Indiana</td><td>1,606,000,000</td><td>2.0%</td></tr>
<tr><td>29</td><td>Louisiana</td><td>781,000,000</td><td>1.0%</td><td>18</td><td>Maryland</td><td>1,553,000,000</td><td>1.9%</td></tr>
<tr><td>42</td><td>Maine</td><td>363,000,000</td><td>0.4%</td><td>19</td><td>Colorado</td><td>1,537,000,000</td><td>1.9%</td></tr>
<tr><td>18</td><td>Maryland</td><td>1,553,000,000</td><td>1.9%</td><td>20</td><td>Arizona</td><td>1,457,000,000</td><td>1.8%</td></tr>
<tr><td>11</td><td>Massachusetts</td><td>2,276,000,000</td><td>2.8%</td><td>21</td><td>Tennessee</td><td>1,428,000,000</td><td>1.8%</td></tr>
<tr><td>7</td><td>Michigan</td><td>3,147,000,000</td><td>3.9%</td><td>22</td><td>Connecticut</td><td>1,336,000,000</td><td>1.6%</td></tr>
<tr><td>16</td><td>Minnesota</td><td>1,678,000,000</td><td>2.1%</td><td>22</td><td>Missouri</td><td>1,336,000,000</td><td>1.6%</td></tr>
<tr><td>35</td><td>Mississippi</td><td>507,000,000</td><td>0.6%</td><td>24</td><td>Oregon</td><td>1,269,000,000</td><td>1.6%</td></tr>
<tr><td>22</td><td>Missouri</td><td>1,336,000,000</td><td>1.6%</td><td>25</td><td>South Carolina</td><td>1,003,000,000</td><td>1.2%</td></tr>
<tr><td>45</td><td>Montana</td><td>249,000,000</td><td>0.3%</td><td>26</td><td>Alabama</td><td>977,000,000</td><td>1.2%</td></tr>
<tr><td>39</td><td>Nebraska</td><td>423,000,000</td><td>0.5%</td><td>27</td><td>Kentucky</td><td>876,000,000</td><td>1.1%</td></tr>
<tr><td>33</td><td>Nevada</td><td>679,000,000</td><td>0.8%</td><td>28</td><td>Oklahoma</td><td>842,000,000</td><td>1.0%</td></tr>
<tr><td>36</td><td>New Hampshire</td><td>471,000,000</td><td>0.6%</td><td>29</td><td>Louisiana</td><td>781,000,000</td><td>1.0%</td></tr>
<tr><td>8</td><td>New Jersey</td><td>2,903,000,000</td><td>3.6%</td><td>30</td><td>Iowa</td><td>735,000,000</td><td>0.9%</td></tr>
<tr><td>38</td><td>New Mexico</td><td>425,000,000</td><td>0.5%</td><td>31</td><td>Kansas</td><td>723,000,000</td><td>0.9%</td></tr>
<tr><td>2</td><td>New York</td><td>5,445,000,000</td><td>6.7%</td><td>32</td><td>Utah</td><td>718,000,000</td><td>0.9%</td></tr>
<tr><td>13</td><td>North Carolina</td><td>2,253,000,000</td><td>2.8%</td><td>33</td><td>Nevada</td><td>679,000,000</td><td>0.8%</td></tr>
<tr><td>49</td><td>North Dakota</td><td>174,000,000</td><td>0.2%</td><td>34</td><td>Arkansas</td><td>601,000,000</td><td>0.7%</td></tr>
<tr><td>9</td><td>Ohio</td><td>2,901,000,000</td><td>3.6%</td><td>35</td><td>Mississippi</td><td>507,000,000</td><td>0.6%</td></tr>
<tr><td>28</td><td>Oklahoma</td><td>842,000,000</td><td>1.0%</td><td>36</td><td>New Hampshire</td><td>471,000,000</td><td>0.6%</td></tr>
<tr><td>24</td><td>Oregon</td><td>1,269,000,000</td><td>1.6%</td><td>37</td><td>Idaho</td><td>468,000,000</td><td>0.6%</td></tr>
<tr><td>6</td><td>Pennsylvania</td><td>3,189,000,000</td><td>3.9%</td><td>38</td><td>New Mexico</td><td>425,000,000</td><td>0.5%</td></tr>
<tr><td>43</td><td>Rhode Island</td><td>294,000,000</td><td>0.4%</td><td>39</td><td>Nebraska</td><td>423,000,000</td><td>0.5%</td></tr>
<tr><td>25</td><td>South Carolina</td><td>1,003,000,000</td><td>1.2%</td><td>40</td><td>West Virginia</td><td>384,000,000</td><td>0.5%</td></tr>
<tr><td>48</td><td>South Dakota</td><td>195,000,000</td><td>0.2%</td><td>41</td><td>Hawaii</td><td>382,000,000</td><td>0.5%</td></tr>
<tr><td>21</td><td>Tennessee</td><td>1,428,000,000</td><td>1.8%</td><td>42</td><td>Maine</td><td>363,000,000</td><td>0.4%</td></tr>
<tr><td>3</td><td>Texas</td><td>4,749,000,000</td><td>5.8%</td><td>43</td><td>Rhode Island</td><td>294,000,000</td><td>0.4%</td></tr>
<tr><td>32</td><td>Utah</td><td>718,000,000</td><td>0.9%</td><td>44</td><td>Delaware</td><td>279,000,000</td><td>0.3%</td></tr>
<tr><td>47</td><td>Vermont</td><td>198,000,000</td><td>0.2%</td><td>45</td><td>Montana</td><td>249,000,000</td><td>0.3%</td></tr>
<tr><td>14</td><td>Virginia</td><td>2,043,000,000</td><td>2.5%</td><td>46</td><td>Alaska</td><td>241,000,000</td><td>0.3%</td></tr>
<tr><td>10</td><td>Washington</td><td>2,505,000,000</td><td>3.1%</td><td>47</td><td>Vermont</td><td>198,000,000</td><td>0.2%</td></tr>
<tr><td>40</td><td>West Virginia</td><td>384,000,000</td><td>0.5%</td><td>48</td><td>South Dakota</td><td>195,000,000</td><td>0.2%</td></tr>
<tr><td>15</td><td>Wisconsin</td><td>1,694,000,000</td><td>2.1%</td><td>49</td><td>North Dakota</td><td>174,000,000</td><td>0.2%</td></tr>
<tr><td>50</td><td>Wyoming</td><td>134,000,000</td><td>0.2%</td><td>50</td><td>Wyoming</td><td>134,000,000</td><td>0.2%</td></tr>
<tr><td></td><td></td><td></td><td></td><td></td><td>District of Columbia</td><td>183,000,000</td><td>0.2%</td></tr>
</table>

Source: U.S. Department of Health and Human Services, Centers for Medicare and Medicaid Services
   "State Health Care Expenditures" (http://www.cms.hhs.gov/NationalHealthExpendData/)
*By state of residence.

Percent of Total Personal Health Care Expenditures
Spent on Dental Services in 2004
National Percent = 5.3%*

ALPHA ORDER

RANK	STATE	PERCENT
45	Alabama	4.2
14	Alaska	5.7
9	Arizona	6.2
37	Arkansas	4.5
6	California	7.0
5	Colorado	7.1
12	Connecticut	6.0
19	Delaware	5.3
32	Florida	4.7
17	Georgia	5.5
11	Hawaii	6.1
2	Idaho	7.6
23	Illinois	5.2
28	Indiana	4.9
35	Iowa	4.6
28	Kansas	4.9
47	Kentucky	3.9
50	Louisiana	3.4
45	Maine	4.2
25	Maryland	5.0
19	Massachusetts	5.3
9	Michigan	6.2
14	Minnesota	5.7
49	Mississippi	3.5
41	Missouri	4.3
19	Montana	5.3
41	Nebraska	4.3
8	Nevada	6.4
7	New Hampshire	6.7
13	New Jersey	5.8
25	New Mexico	5.0
41	New York	4.3
24	North Carolina	5.1
32	North Dakota	4.7
38	Ohio	4.4
28	Oklahoma	4.9
4	Oregon	7.2
41	Pennsylvania	4.3
38	Rhode Island	4.4
32	South Carolina	4.7
31	South Dakota	4.8
38	Tennessee	4.4
35	Texas	4.6
3	Utah	7.5
19	Vermont	5.3
14	Virginia	5.7
1	Washington	7.9
48	West Virginia	3.6
18	Wisconsin	5.4
25	Wyoming	5.0

RANK ORDER

RANK	STATE	PERCENT
1	Washington	7.9
2	Idaho	7.6
3	Utah	7.5
4	Oregon	7.2
5	Colorado	7.1
6	California	7.0
7	New Hampshire	6.7
8	Nevada	6.4
9	Arizona	6.2
9	Michigan	6.2
11	Hawaii	6.1
12	Connecticut	6.0
13	New Jersey	5.8
14	Alaska	5.7
14	Minnesota	5.7
14	Virginia	5.7
17	Georgia	5.5
18	Wisconsin	5.4
19	Delaware	5.3
19	Massachusetts	5.3
19	Montana	5.3
19	Vermont	5.3
23	Illinois	5.2
24	North Carolina	5.1
25	Maryland	5.0
25	New Mexico	5.0
25	Wyoming	5.0
28	Indiana	4.9
28	Kansas	4.9
28	Oklahoma	4.9
31	South Dakota	4.8
32	Florida	4.7
32	North Dakota	4.7
32	South Carolina	4.7
35	Iowa	4.6
35	Texas	4.6
37	Arkansas	4.5
38	Ohio	4.4
38	Rhode Island	4.4
38	Tennessee	4.4
41	Missouri	4.3
41	Nebraska	4.3
41	New York	4.3
41	Pennsylvania	4.3
45	Alabama	4.2
45	Maine	4.2
47	Kentucky	3.9
48	West Virginia	3.6
49	Mississippi	3.5
50	Louisiana	3.4
	District of Columbia	3.8

Source: CQ Press using data from U.S. Department of Health and Human Services, Centers for Medicare and Medicaid Services
   "State Health Care Expenditures" (http://www.cms.hhs.gov/NationalHealthExpendData/)
*By state of residence.

Per Capita Expenditures for Dental Care in 2004

National Per Capita = $277*

ALPHA ORDER

RANK	STATE	PER CAPITA
45	Alabama	$216
3	Alaska	366
33	Arizona	254
44	Arkansas	219
12	California	324
10	Colorado	334
2	Connecticut	382
7	Delaware	337
30	Florida	259
34	Georgia	253
16	Hawaii	303
8	Idaho	336
22	Illinois	274
31	Indiana	258
37	Iowa	249
28	Kansas	264
46	Kentucky	212
50	Louisiana	174
21	Maine	276
20	Maryland	280
5	Massachusetts	354
14	Michigan	312
11	Minnesota	329
49	Mississippi	175
42	Missouri	232
26	Montana	269
39	Nebraska	242
18	Nevada	291
4	New Hampshire	363
9	New Jersey	335
43	New Mexico	224
19	New York	282
28	North Carolina	264
22	North Dakota	274
34	Ohio	253
40	Oklahoma	239
5	Oregon	354
31	Pennsylvania	258
25	Rhode Island	272
40	South Carolina	239
34	South Dakota	253
38	Tennessee	243
48	Texas	211
17	Utah	297
13	Vermont	319
24	Virginia	273
1	Washington	404
46	West Virginia	212
15	Wisconsin	308
27	Wyoming	265

RANK ORDER

RANK	STATE	PER CAPITA
1	Washington	$404
2	Connecticut	382
3	Alaska	366
4	New Hampshire	363
5	Massachusetts	354
5	Oregon	354
7	Delaware	337
8	Idaho	336
9	New Jersey	335
10	Colorado	334
11	Minnesota	329
12	California	324
13	Vermont	319
14	Michigan	312
15	Wisconsin	308
16	Hawaii	303
17	Utah	297
18	Nevada	291
19	New York	282
20	Maryland	280
21	Maine	276
22	Illinois	274
22	North Dakota	274
24	Virginia	273
25	Rhode Island	272
26	Montana	269
27	Wyoming	265
28	Kansas	264
28	North Carolina	264
30	Florida	259
31	Indiana	258
31	Pennsylvania	258
33	Arizona	254
34	Georgia	253
34	Ohio	253
34	South Dakota	253
37	Iowa	249
38	Tennessee	243
39	Nebraska	242
40	Oklahoma	239
40	South Carolina	239
42	Missouri	232
43	New Mexico	224
44	Arkansas	219
45	Alabama	216
46	Kentucky	212
46	West Virginia	212
48	Texas	211
49	Mississippi	175
50	Louisiana	174
	District of Columbia	315

Source: U.S. Department of Health and Human Services, Centers for Medicare and Medicaid Services
   "State Health Care Expenditures" (http://www.cms.hhs.gov/NationalHealthExpendData/)
*By state of residence.

Expenditures for Other Professional Health Care Services in 2004

National Total = $52,636,000,000*

ALPHA ORDER				RANK ORDER			
RANK	STATE	EXPENDITURES	% of USA	RANK	STATE	EXPENDITURES	% of USA
27	Alabama	$681,000,000	1.3%	1	California	$6,178,000,000	11.7%
46	Alaska	164,000,000	0.3%	2	New York	3,587,000,000	6.8%
22	Arizona	932,000,000	1.8%	3	Florida	3,529,000,000	6.7%
32	Arkansas	463,000,000	0.9%	4	Texas	3,177,000,000	6.0%
1	California	6,178,000,000	11.7%	5	Pennsylvania	2,613,000,000	5.0%
21	Colorado	939,000,000	1.8%	6	Illinois	2,365,000,000	4.5%
23	Connecticut	855,000,000	1.6%	7	Ohio	2,285,000,000	4.3%
43	Delaware	210,000,000	0.4%	8	New Jersey	1,919,000,000	3.6%
3	Florida	3,529,000,000	6.7%	9	Michigan	1,896,000,000	3.6%
13	Georgia	1,252,000,000	2.4%	10	Washington	1,363,000,000	2.6%
42	Hawaii	224,000,000	0.4%	11	North Carolina	1,336,000,000	2.5%
40	Idaho	303,000,000	0.6%	12	Massachusetts	1,289,000,000	2.4%
6	Illinois	2,365,000,000	4.5%	13	Georgia	1,252,000,000	2.4%
19	Indiana	1,002,000,000	1.9%	14	Virginia	1,123,000,000	2.1%
29	Iowa	557,000,000	1.1%	15	Tennessee	1,035,000,000	2.0%
31	Kansas	499,000,000	0.9%	16	Maryland	1,034,000,000	2.0%
24	Kentucky	796,000,000	1.5%	17	Wisconsin	1,031,000,000	2.0%
26	Louisiana	705,000,000	1.3%	18	Minnesota	1,005,000,000	1.9%
38	Maine	305,000,000	0.6%	19	Indiana	1,002,000,000	1.9%
16	Maryland	1,034,000,000	2.0%	20	Missouri	958,000,000	1.8%
12	Massachusetts	1,289,000,000	2.4%	21	Colorado	939,000,000	1.8%
9	Michigan	1,896,000,000	3.6%	22	Arizona	932,000,000	1.8%
18	Minnesota	1,005,000,000	1.9%	23	Connecticut	855,000,000	1.6%
35	Mississippi	351,000,000	0.7%	24	Kentucky	796,000,000	1.5%
20	Missouri	958,000,000	1.8%	25	Oregon	715,000,000	1.4%
45	Montana	172,000,000	0.3%	26	Louisiana	705,000,000	1.3%
39	Nebraska	304,000,000	0.6%	27	Alabama	681,000,000	1.3%
33	Nevada	370,000,000	0.7%	28	Oklahoma	561,000,000	1.1%
41	New Hampshire	229,000,000	0.4%	29	Iowa	557,000,000	1.1%
8	New Jersey	1,919,000,000	3.6%	30	South Carolina	534,000,000	1.0%
37	New Mexico	321,000,000	0.6%	31	Kansas	499,000,000	0.9%
2	New York	3,587,000,000	6.8%	32	Arkansas	463,000,000	0.9%
11	North Carolina	1,336,000,000	2.5%	33	Nevada	370,000,000	0.7%
50	North Dakota	103,000,000	0.2%	34	West Virginia	361,000,000	0.7%
7	Ohio	2,285,000,000	4.3%	35	Mississippi	351,000,000	0.7%
28	Oklahoma	561,000,000	1.1%	36	Utah	332,000,000	0.6%
25	Oregon	715,000,000	1.4%	37	New Mexico	321,000,000	0.6%
5	Pennsylvania	2,613,000,000	5.0%	38	Maine	305,000,000	0.6%
44	Rhode Island	193,000,000	0.4%	39	Nebraska	304,000,000	0.6%
30	South Carolina	534,000,000	1.0%	40	Idaho	303,000,000	0.6%
47	South Dakota	135,000,000	0.3%	41	New Hampshire	229,000,000	0.4%
15	Tennessee	1,035,000,000	2.0%	42	Hawaii	224,000,000	0.4%
4	Texas	3,177,000,000	6.0%	43	Delaware	210,000,000	0.4%
36	Utah	332,000,000	0.6%	44	Rhode Island	193,000,000	0.4%
48	Vermont	132,000,000	0.3%	45	Montana	172,000,000	0.3%
14	Virginia	1,123,000,000	2.1%	46	Alaska	164,000,000	0.3%
10	Washington	1,363,000,000	2.6%	47	South Dakota	135,000,000	0.3%
34	West Virginia	361,000,000	0.7%	48	Vermont	132,000,000	0.3%
17	Wisconsin	1,031,000,000	2.0%	49	Wyoming	117,000,000	0.2%
49	Wyoming	117,000,000	0.2%	50	North Dakota	103,000,000	0.2%
					District of Columbia	98,000,000	0.2%

Source: U.S. Department of Health and Human Services, Centers for Medicare and Medicaid Services
"State Health Care Expenditures" (http://www.cms.hhs.gov/NationalHealthExpendData/)
*By state of residence. Includes services of licensed professionals such as chiropractors, optometrists, podiatrists, and independently practicing nurses. Also includes Medicare ambulance services.

Percent of Total Personal Health Care Expenditures
Spent on Other Professional Health Care Services in 2004
National Percent = 3.4%*

ALPHA ORDER

RANK	STATE	PERCENT
45	Alabama	2.9
8	Alaska	3.9
6	Arizona	4.0
18	Arkansas	3.5
12	California	3.7
3	Colorado	4.3
8	Connecticut	3.9
6	Delaware	4.0
12	Florida	3.7
41	Georgia	3.0
16	Hawaii	3.6
1	Idaho	4.9
18	Illinois	3.5
41	Indiana	3.0
18	Iowa	3.5
27	Kansas	3.4
18	Kentucky	3.5
36	Louisiana	3.1
18	Maine	3.5
29	Maryland	3.3
41	Massachusetts	3.0
12	Michigan	3.7
27	Minnesota	3.4
50	Mississippi	2.4
36	Missouri	3.1
12	Montana	3.7
36	Nebraska	3.1
18	Nevada	3.5
33	New Hampshire	3.2
10	New Jersey	3.8
10	New Mexico	3.8
47	New York	2.8
41	North Carolina	3.0
47	North Dakota	2.8
18	Ohio	3.5
33	Oklahoma	3.2
5	Oregon	4.1
16	Pennsylvania	3.6
45	Rhode Island	2.9
49	South Carolina	2.5
29	South Dakota	3.3
33	Tennessee	3.2
36	Texas	3.1
18	Utah	3.5
18	Vermont	3.5
36	Virginia	3.1
3	Washington	4.3
29	West Virginia	3.3
29	Wisconsin	3.3
2	Wyoming	4.4

RANK ORDER

RANK	STATE	PERCENT
1	Idaho	4.9
2	Wyoming	4.4
3	Colorado	4.3
3	Washington	4.3
5	Oregon	4.1
6	Arizona	4.0
6	Delaware	4.0
8	Alaska	3.9
8	Connecticut	3.9
10	New Jersey	3.8
10	New Mexico	3.8
12	California	3.7
12	Florida	3.7
12	Michigan	3.7
12	Montana	3.7
16	Hawaii	3.6
16	Pennsylvania	3.6
18	Arkansas	3.5
18	Illinois	3.5
18	Iowa	3.5
18	Kentucky	3.5
18	Maine	3.5
18	Nevada	3.5
18	Ohio	3.5
18	Utah	3.5
18	Vermont	3.5
27	Kansas	3.4
27	Minnesota	3.4
29	Maryland	3.3
29	South Dakota	3.3
29	West Virginia	3.3
29	Wisconsin	3.3
33	New Hampshire	3.2
33	Oklahoma	3.2
33	Tennessee	3.2
36	Louisiana	3.1
36	Missouri	3.1
36	Nebraska	3.1
36	Texas	3.1
36	Virginia	3.1
41	Georgia	3.0
41	Indiana	3.0
41	Massachusetts	3.0
41	North Carolina	3.0
45	Alabama	2.9
45	Rhode Island	2.9
47	New York	2.8
47	North Dakota	2.8
49	South Carolina	2.5
50	Mississippi	2.4

District of Columbia 2.0

Source: CQ Press using data from U.S. Department of Health and Human Services, Centers for Medicare and Medicaid Services
"State Health Care Expenditures" (http://www.cms.hhs.gov/NationalHealthExpendData/)
*By state of residence. Includes services of licensed professionals such as chiropractors, optometrists, podiatrists, and independently practicing nurses. Also includes Medicare ambulance services.

Per Capita Expenditures for Other Professional Health Care Services in 2004

National Per Capita = $179*

ALPHA ORDER

RANK	STATE	PER CAPITA
44	Alabama	$151
2	Alaska	249
37	Arizona	162
35	Arkansas	168
33	California	172
11	Colorado	204
3	Connecticut	245
1	Delaware	253
12	Florida	203
47	Georgia	140
27	Hawaii	178
8	Idaho	217
22	Illinois	186
39	Indiana	161
19	Iowa	188
26	Kansas	182
18	Kentucky	192
42	Louisiana	157
4	Maine	232
22	Maryland	186
13	Massachusetts	200
19	Michigan	188
17	Minnesota	197
50	Mississippi	121
36	Missouri	167
22	Montana	186
32	Nebraska	174
40	Nevada	159
29	New Hampshire	176
6	New Jersey	221
34	New Mexico	169
22	New York	186
42	North Carolina	157
37	North Dakota	162
14	Ohio	199
40	Oklahoma	159
14	Oregon	199
10	Pennsylvania	211
27	Rhode Island	178
49	South Carolina	127
29	South Dakota	176
29	Tennessee	176
46	Texas	141
48	Utah	137
9	Vermont	212
45	Virginia	150
7	Washington	220
14	West Virginia	199
21	Wisconsin	187
5	Wyoming	231

RANK ORDER

RANK	STATE	PER CAPITA
1	Delaware	$253
2	Alaska	249
3	Connecticut	245
4	Maine	232
5	Wyoming	231
6	New Jersey	221
7	Washington	220
8	Idaho	217
9	Vermont	212
10	Pennsylvania	211
11	Colorado	204
12	Florida	203
13	Massachusetts	200
14	Ohio	199
14	Oregon	199
14	West Virginia	199
17	Minnesota	197
18	Kentucky	192
19	Iowa	188
19	Michigan	188
21	Wisconsin	187
22	Illinois	186
22	Maryland	186
22	Montana	186
22	New York	186
26	Kansas	182
27	Hawaii	178
27	Rhode Island	178
29	New Hampshire	176
29	South Dakota	176
29	Tennessee	176
32	Nebraska	174
33	California	172
34	New Mexico	169
35	Arkansas	168
36	Missouri	167
37	Arizona	162
37	North Dakota	162
39	Indiana	161
40	Nevada	159
40	Oklahoma	159
42	Louisiana	157
42	North Carolina	157
44	Alabama	151
45	Virginia	150
46	Texas	141
47	Georgia	140
48	Utah	137
49	South Carolina	127
50	Mississippi	121

District of Columbia	170

Source: U.S. Department of Health and Human Services, Centers for Medicare and Medicaid Services
"State Health Care Expenditures" (http://www.cms.hhs.gov/NationalHealthExpendData/)
*By state of residence. Includes services of licensed professionals such as chiropractors, optometrists, podiatrists, and independently practicing nurses. Also includes Medicare ambulance services.

Expenditures for Nursing Home Care in 2004

National Total = $115,015,000,000*

ALPHA ORDER					RANK ORDER			
RANK	STATE	EXPENDITURES	% of USA		RANK	STATE	EXPENDITURES	% of USA
25	Alabama	$1,475,000,000	1.3%		1	New York	$13,364,000,000	11.6%
50	Alaska	80,000,000	0.1%		2	California	8,424,000,000	7.3%
32	Arizona	1,023,000,000	0.9%		3	Pennsylvania	7,562,000,000	6.6%
31	Arkansas	1,040,000,000	0.9%		4	Ohio	6,834,000,000	5.9%
2	California	8,424,000,000	7.3%		5	Florida	6,503,000,000	5.7%
27	Colorado	1,178,000,000	1.0%		6	Texas	5,600,000,000	4.9%
13	Connecticut	2,711,000,000	2.4%		7	Illinois	5,173,000,000	4.5%
40	Delaware	409,000,000	0.4%		8	New Jersey	4,261,000,000	3.7%
5	Florida	6,503,000,000	5.7%		9	Massachusetts	4,124,000,000	3.6%
19	Georgia	2,272,000,000	2.0%		10	North Carolina	3,354,000,000	2.9%
47	Hawaii	293,000,000	0.3%		11	Michigan	3,193,000,000	2.8%
44	Idaho	361,000,000	0.3%		12	Indiana	2,871,000,000	2.5%
7	Illinois	5,173,000,000	4.5%		13	Connecticut	2,711,000,000	2.4%
12	Indiana	2,871,000,000	2.5%		14	Missouri	2,479,000,000	2.2%
22	Iowa	1,623,000,000	1.4%		15	Virginia	2,448,000,000	2.1%
29	Kansas	1,110,000,000	1.0%		16	Maryland	2,419,000,000	2.1%
24	Kentucky	1,526,000,000	1.3%		17	Wisconsin	2,405,000,000	2.1%
23	Louisiana	1,617,000,000	1.4%		18	Minnesota	2,367,000,000	2.1%
36	Maine	630,000,000	0.5%		19	Georgia	2,272,000,000	2.0%
16	Maryland	2,419,000,000	2.1%		20	Tennessee	2,211,000,000	1.9%
9	Massachusetts	4,124,000,000	3.6%		21	Washington	1,860,000,000	1.6%
11	Michigan	3,193,000,000	2.8%		22	Iowa	1,623,000,000	1.4%
18	Minnesota	2,367,000,000	2.1%		23	Louisiana	1,617,000,000	1.4%
30	Mississippi	1,094,000,000	1.0%		24	Kentucky	1,526,000,000	1.3%
14	Missouri	2,479,000,000	2.2%		25	Alabama	1,475,000,000	1.3%
46	Montana	322,000,000	0.3%		26	South Carolina	1,236,000,000	1.1%
34	Nebraska	860,000,000	0.7%		27	Colorado	1,178,000,000	1.0%
45	Nevada	341,000,000	0.3%		28	Oklahoma	1,157,000,000	1.0%
38	New Hampshire	548,000,000	0.5%		29	Kansas	1,110,000,000	1.0%
8	New Jersey	4,261,000,000	3.7%		30	Mississippi	1,094,000,000	1.0%
43	New Mexico	372,000,000	0.3%		31	Arkansas	1,040,000,000	0.9%
1	New York	13,364,000,000	11.6%		32	Arizona	1,023,000,000	0.9%
10	North Carolina	3,354,000,000	2.9%		33	Oregon	897,000,000	0.8%
42	North Dakota	387,000,000	0.3%		34	Nebraska	860,000,000	0.7%
4	Ohio	6,834,000,000	5.9%		35	West Virginia	716,000,000	0.6%
28	Oklahoma	1,157,000,000	1.0%		36	Maine	630,000,000	0.5%
33	Oregon	897,000,000	0.8%		37	Rhode Island	616,000,000	0.5%
3	Pennsylvania	7,562,000,000	6.6%		38	New Hampshire	548,000,000	0.5%
37	Rhode Island	616,000,000	0.5%		39	Utah	428,000,000	0.4%
26	South Carolina	1,236,000,000	1.1%		40	Delaware	409,000,000	0.4%
41	South Dakota	406,000,000	0.4%		41	South Dakota	406,000,000	0.4%
20	Tennessee	2,211,000,000	1.9%		42	North Dakota	387,000,000	0.3%
6	Texas	5,600,000,000	4.9%		43	New Mexico	372,000,000	0.3%
39	Utah	428,000,000	0.4%		44	Idaho	361,000,000	0.3%
48	Vermont	235,000,000	0.2%		45	Nevada	341,000,000	0.3%
15	Virginia	2,448,000,000	2.1%		46	Montana	322,000,000	0.3%
21	Washington	1,860,000,000	1.6%		47	Hawaii	293,000,000	0.3%
35	West Virginia	716,000,000	0.6%		48	Vermont	235,000,000	0.2%
17	Wisconsin	2,405,000,000	2.1%		49	Wyoming	150,000,000	0.1%
49	Wyoming	150,000,000	0.1%		50	Alaska	80,000,000	0.1%
						District of Columbia	452,000,000	0.4%

Source: U.S. Department of Health and Human Services, Centers for Medicare and Medicaid Services
"State Health Care Expenditures" (http://www.cms.hhs.gov/NationalHealthExpendData/)
*By state of residence. Includes all freestanding nursing homes. Does not include nursing home services provided in long-term care units of hospitals.

Percent of Total Personal Health Care Expenditures
Spent on Nursing Home Care in 2004
National Percent = 7.4%*

ALPHA ORDER

RANK	STATE	PERCENT
33	Alabama	6.4
50	Alaska	1.9
48	Arizona	4.3
15	Arkansas	7.8
43	California	5.1
41	Colorado	5.4
1	Connecticut	12.2
15	Delaware	7.8
27	Florida	6.8
40	Georgia	5.5
45	Hawaii	4.7
37	Idaho	5.8
19	Illinois	7.7
11	Indiana	8.7
6	Iowa	10.2
22	Kansas	7.5
30	Kentucky	6.7
25	Louisiana	7.1
24	Maine	7.3
15	Maryland	7.8
8	Massachusetts	9.6
34	Michigan	6.3
13	Minnesota	8.0
22	Mississippi	7.5
14	Missouri	7.9
27	Montana	6.8
10	Nebraska	8.8
49	Nevada	3.2
15	New Hampshire	7.8
12	New Jersey	8.5
46	New Mexico	4.4
2	New York	10.6
21	North Carolina	7.6
3	North Dakota	10.5
4	Ohio	10.4
30	Oklahoma	6.7
43	Oregon	5.1
5	Pennsylvania	10.3
9	Rhode Island	9.2
37	South Carolina	5.8
7	South Dakota	9.9
26	Tennessee	6.9
41	Texas	5.4
46	Utah	4.4
35	Vermont	6.2
27	Virginia	6.8
36	Washington	5.9
32	West Virginia	6.6
19	Wisconsin	7.7
39	Wyoming	5.6

RANK ORDER

RANK	STATE	PERCENT
1	Connecticut	12.2
2	New York	10.6
3	North Dakota	10.5
4	Ohio	10.4
5	Pennsylvania	10.3
6	Iowa	10.2
7	South Dakota	9.9
8	Massachusetts	9.6
9	Rhode Island	9.2
10	Nebraska	8.8
11	Indiana	8.7
12	New Jersey	8.5
13	Minnesota	8.0
14	Missouri	7.9
15	Arkansas	7.8
15	Delaware	7.8
15	Maryland	7.8
15	New Hampshire	7.8
19	Illinois	7.7
19	Wisconsin	7.7
21	North Carolina	7.6
22	Kansas	7.5
22	Mississippi	7.5
24	Maine	7.3
25	Louisiana	7.1
26	Tennessee	6.9
27	Florida	6.8
27	Montana	6.8
27	Virginia	6.8
30	Kentucky	6.7
30	Oklahoma	6.7
32	West Virginia	6.6
33	Alabama	6.4
34	Michigan	6.3
35	Vermont	6.2
36	Washington	5.9
37	Idaho	5.8
37	South Carolina	5.8
39	Wyoming	5.6
40	Georgia	5.5
41	Colorado	5.4
41	Texas	5.4
43	California	5.1
43	Oregon	5.1
45	Hawaii	4.7
46	New Mexico	4.4
46	Utah	4.4
48	Arizona	4.3
49	Nevada	3.2
50	Alaska	1.9

District of Columbia 9.4

Source: CQ Press using data from U.S. Department of Health and Human Services, Centers for Medicare and Medicaid Services
"State Health Care Expenditures" (http://www.cms.hhs.gov/NationalHealthExpendData/)
*By state of residence. Includes all freestanding nursing homes. Does not include nursing home services provided in long-term care units of hospitals.

Per Capita Expenditures for Nursing Home Care in 2004

National Per Capita = $392*

ALPHA ORDER

RANK	STATE	PER CAPITA
34	Alabama	$326
50	Alaska	122
47	Arizona	178
24	Arkansas	378
44	California	235
40	Colorado	256
1	Connecticut	776
10	Delaware	493
28	Florida	374
41	Georgia	254
45	Hawaii	233
39	Idaho	259
20	Illinois	407
15	Indiana	461
8	Iowa	549
21	Kansas	406
29	Kentucky	369
30	Louisiana	360
13	Maine	480
17	Maryland	436
3	Massachusetts	641
35	Michigan	316
14	Minnesota	465
24	Mississippi	378
18	Missouri	431
31	Montana	348
11	Nebraska	492
49	Nevada	146
19	New Hampshire	422
12	New Jersey	491
46	New Mexico	196
2	New York	693
23	North Carolina	393
5	North Dakota	608
6	Ohio	596
32	Oklahoma	329
42	Oregon	250
4	Pennsylvania	611
7	Rhode Island	570
38	South Carolina	295
9	South Dakota	527
27	Tennessee	376
43	Texas	249
48	Utah	177
24	Vermont	378
33	Virginia	328
36	Washington	300
22	West Virginia	395
16	Wisconsin	437
37	Wyoming	297

RANK ORDER

RANK	STATE	PER CAPITA
1	Connecticut	$776
2	New York	693
3	Massachusetts	641
4	Pennsylvania	611
5	North Dakota	608
6	Ohio	596
7	Rhode Island	570
8	Iowa	549
9	South Dakota	527
10	Delaware	493
11	Nebraska	492
12	New Jersey	491
13	Maine	480
14	Minnesota	465
15	Indiana	461
16	Wisconsin	437
17	Maryland	436
18	Missouri	431
19	New Hampshire	422
20	Illinois	407
21	Kansas	406
22	West Virginia	395
23	North Carolina	393
24	Arkansas	378
24	Mississippi	378
24	Vermont	378
27	Tennessee	376
28	Florida	374
29	Kentucky	369
30	Louisiana	360
31	Montana	348
32	Oklahoma	329
33	Virginia	328
34	Alabama	326
35	Michigan	316
36	Washington	300
37	Wyoming	297
38	South Carolina	295
39	Idaho	259
40	Colorado	256
41	Georgia	254
42	Oregon	250
43	Texas	249
44	California	235
45	Hawaii	233
46	New Mexico	196
47	Arizona	178
48	Utah	177
49	Nevada	146
50	Alaska	122
	District of Columbia	780

Source: U.S. Department of Health and Human Services, Centers for Medicare and Medicaid Services
    "State Health Care Expenditures" (http://www.cms.hhs.gov/NationalHealthExpendData/)
*By state of residence. Includes all freestanding nursing homes. Does not include nursing home services provided in long-term care units of hospitals.

Expenditures for Home Health Care in 2004

National Total = $42,710,000,000*

ALPHA ORDER

RANK	STATE	EXPENDITURES	% of USA
18	Alabama	$661,000,000	1.5%
47	Alaska	64,000,000	0.1%
19	Arizona	656,000,000	1.5%
31	Arkansas	325,000,000	0.8%
2	California	5,537,000,000	13.0%
30	Colorado	367,000,000	0.9%
15	Connecticut	708,000,000	1.7%
43	Delaware	94,000,000	0.2%
4	Florida	2,876,000,000	6.7%
12	Georgia	876,000,000	2.1%
42	Hawaii	105,000,000	0.2%
41	Idaho	115,000,000	0.3%
11	Illinois	1,269,000,000	3.0%
25	Indiana	509,000,000	1.2%
32	Iowa	310,000,000	0.7%
34	Kansas	241,000,000	0.6%
23	Kentucky	531,000,000	1.2%
21	Louisiana	624,000,000	1.5%
38	Maine	173,000,000	0.4%
24	Maryland	511,000,000	1.2%
5	Massachusetts	1,743,000,000	4.1%
10	Michigan	1,326,000,000	3.1%
17	Minnesota	679,000,000	1.6%
26	Mississippi	484,000,000	1.1%
15	Missouri	708,000,000	1.7%
45	Montana	89,000,000	0.2%
46	Nebraska	79,000,000	0.2%
35	Nevada	231,000,000	0.5%
39	New Hampshire	168,000,000	0.4%
8	New Jersey	1,427,000,000	3.3%
28	New Mexico	451,000,000	1.1%
1	New York	6,021,000,000	14.1%
9	North Carolina	1,413,000,000	3.3%
50	North Dakota	18,000,000	0.0%
7	Ohio	1,519,000,000	3.6%
27	Oklahoma	464,000,000	1.1%
36	Oregon	201,000,000	0.5%
6	Pennsylvania	1,527,000,000	3.6%
40	Rhode Island	116,000,000	0.3%
29	South Carolina	422,000,000	1.0%
49	South Dakota	20,000,000	0.0%
14	Tennessee	738,000,000	1.7%
3	Texas	3,604,000,000	8.4%
33	Utah	245,000,000	0.6%
43	Vermont	94,000,000	0.2%
22	Virginia	605,000,000	1.4%
13	Washington	823,000,000	1.9%
37	West Virginia	197,000,000	0.5%
20	Wisconsin	642,000,000	1.5%
48	Wyoming	28,000,000	0.1%

RANK ORDER

RANK	STATE	EXPENDITURES	% of USA
1	New York	$6,021,000,000	14.1%
2	California	5,537,000,000	13.0%
3	Texas	3,604,000,000	8.4%
4	Florida	2,876,000,000	6.7%
5	Massachusetts	1,743,000,000	4.1%
6	Pennsylvania	1,527,000,000	3.6%
7	Ohio	1,519,000,000	3.6%
8	New Jersey	1,427,000,000	3.3%
9	North Carolina	1,413,000,000	3.3%
10	Michigan	1,326,000,000	3.1%
11	Illinois	1,269,000,000	3.0%
12	Georgia	876,000,000	2.1%
13	Washington	823,000,000	1.9%
14	Tennessee	738,000,000	1.7%
15	Connecticut	708,000,000	1.7%
15	Missouri	708,000,000	1.7%
17	Minnesota	679,000,000	1.6%
18	Alabama	661,000,000	1.5%
19	Arizona	656,000,000	1.5%
20	Wisconsin	642,000,000	1.5%
21	Louisiana	624,000,000	1.5%
22	Virginia	605,000,000	1.4%
23	Kentucky	531,000,000	1.2%
24	Maryland	511,000,000	1.2%
25	Indiana	509,000,000	1.2%
26	Mississippi	484,000,000	1.1%
27	Oklahoma	464,000,000	1.1%
28	New Mexico	451,000,000	1.1%
29	South Carolina	422,000,000	1.0%
30	Colorado	367,000,000	0.9%
31	Arkansas	325,000,000	0.8%
32	Iowa	310,000,000	0.7%
33	Utah	245,000,000	0.6%
34	Kansas	241,000,000	0.6%
35	Nevada	231,000,000	0.5%
36	Oregon	201,000,000	0.5%
37	West Virginia	197,000,000	0.5%
38	Maine	173,000,000	0.4%
39	New Hampshire	168,000,000	0.4%
40	Rhode Island	116,000,000	0.3%
41	Idaho	115,000,000	0.3%
42	Hawaii	105,000,000	0.2%
43	Delaware	94,000,000	0.2%
43	Vermont	94,000,000	0.2%
45	Montana	89,000,000	0.2%
46	Nebraska	79,000,000	0.2%
47	Alaska	64,000,000	0.1%
48	Wyoming	28,000,000	0.1%
49	South Dakota	20,000,000	0.0%
50	North Dakota	18,000,000	0.0%
	District of Columbia	78,000,000	0.2%

Source: U.S. Department of Health and Human Services, Centers for Medicare and Medicaid Services
   "State Health Care Expenditures" (http://www.cms.hhs.gov/NationalHealthExpendData/)
*By state of residence. Includes spending for services and products by public and private freestanding home health agencies.
Excludes home health care services provided by hospital-based agencies which are included in hospital expenditures.

Percent of Total Personal Health Care Expenditures
Spent on Home Health Care in 2004
National Percent = 2.8%*

RANK	STATE	PERCENT
10	Alabama	2.8
44	Alaska	1.5
10	Arizona	2.8
19	Arkansas	2.4
5	California	3.3
38	Colorado	1.7
7	Connecticut	3.2
36	Delaware	1.8
9	Florida	3.0
27	Georgia	2.1
38	Hawaii	1.7
33	Idaho	1.9
33	Illinois	1.9
44	Indiana	1.5
30	Iowa	2.0
42	Kansas	1.6
21	Kentucky	2.3
10	Louisiana	2.8
30	Maine	2.0
42	Maryland	1.6
3	Massachusetts	4.1
15	Michigan	2.6
21	Minnesota	2.3
5	Mississippi	3.3
21	Missouri	2.3
33	Montana	1.9
48	Nebraska	0.8
26	Nevada	2.2
19	New Hampshire	2.4
10	New Jersey	2.8
1	New Mexico	5.3
2	New York	4.8
7	North Carolina	3.2
49	North Dakota	0.5
21	Ohio	2.3
14	Oklahoma	2.7
46	Oregon	1.1
27	Pennsylvania	2.1
38	Rhode Island	1.7
30	South Carolina	2.0
49	South Dakota	0.5
21	Tennessee	2.3
4	Texas	3.5
17	Utah	2.5
17	Vermont	2.5
38	Virginia	1.7
15	Washington	2.6
36	West Virginia	1.8
27	Wisconsin	2.1
46	Wyoming	1.1

RANK	STATE	PERCENT
1	New Mexico	5.3
2	New York	4.8
3	Massachusetts	4.1
4	Texas	3.5
5	California	3.3
5	Mississippi	3.3
7	Connecticut	3.2
7	North Carolina	3.2
9	Florida	3.0
10	Alabama	2.8
10	Arizona	2.8
10	Louisiana	2.8
10	New Jersey	2.8
14	Oklahoma	2.7
15	Michigan	2.6
15	Washington	2.6
17	Utah	2.5
17	Vermont	2.5
19	Arkansas	2.4
19	New Hampshire	2.4
21	Kentucky	2.3
21	Minnesota	2.3
21	Missouri	2.3
21	Ohio	2.3
21	Tennessee	2.3
26	Nevada	2.2
27	Georgia	2.1
27	Pennsylvania	2.1
27	Wisconsin	2.1
30	Iowa	2.0
30	Maine	2.0
30	South Carolina	2.0
33	Idaho	1.9
33	Illinois	1.9
33	Montana	1.9
36	Delaware	1.8
36	West Virginia	1.8
38	Colorado	1.7
38	Hawaii	1.7
38	Rhode Island	1.7
38	Virginia	1.7
42	Kansas	1.6
42	Maryland	1.6
44	Alaska	1.5
44	Indiana	1.5
46	Oregon	1.1
46	Wyoming	1.1
48	Nebraska	0.8
49	North Dakota	0.5
49	South Dakota	0.5

| | District of Columbia | 1.6 |

Source: CQ Press using data from U.S. Department of Health and Human Services, Centers for Medicare and Medicaid Services
"State Health Care Expenditures" (http://www.cms.hhs.gov/NationalHealthExpendData/)
*By state of residence. Includes spending for services and products by public and private freestanding home health agencies.
Excludes home health care services provided by hospital-based agencies which are included in hospital expenditures.

Per Capita Expenditures for Home Health Care in 2004

National Per Capita = $145*

ALPHA ORDER				RANK ORDER		
RANK	STATE	PER CAPITA		RANK	STATE	PER CAPITA
12	Alabama	$146		1	New York	$312
36	Alaska	98		2	Massachusetts	271
27	Arizona	114		3	New Mexico	237
25	Arkansas	118		4	Connecticut	203
10	California	154		5	Mississippi	167
45	Colorado	80		6	Florida	166
4	Connecticut	203		6	North Carolina	166
28	Delaware	113		8	New Jersey	164
6	Florida	166		9	Texas	160
36	Georgia	98		10	California	154
41	Hawaii	84		11	Vermont	152
42	Idaho	82		12	Alabama	146
34	Illinois	100		13	Louisiana	139
42	Indiana	82		14	Minnesota	133
31	Iowa	105		14	Ohio	133
40	Kansas	88		14	Washington	133
21	Kentucky	128		17	Maine	132
13	Louisiana	139		17	Oklahoma	132
17	Maine	132		19	Michigan	131
39	Maryland	92		20	New Hampshire	130
2	Massachusetts	271		21	Kentucky	128
19	Michigan	131		22	Tennessee	125
14	Minnesota	133		23	Missouri	123
5	Mississippi	167		23	Pennsylvania	123
23	Missouri	123		25	Arkansas	118
38	Montana	96		26	Wisconsin	117
48	Nebraska	45		27	Arizona	114
35	Nevada	99		28	Delaware	113
20	New Hampshire	130		29	West Virginia	109
8	New Jersey	164		30	Rhode Island	107
3	New Mexico	237		31	Iowa	105
1	New York	312		32	South Carolina	101
6	North Carolina	166		32	Utah	101
49	North Dakota	28		34	Illinois	100
14	Ohio	133		35	Nevada	99
17	Oklahoma	132		36	Alaska	98
46	Oregon	56		36	Georgia	98
23	Pennsylvania	123		38	Montana	96
30	Rhode Island	107		39	Maryland	92
32	South Carolina	101		40	Kansas	88
50	South Dakota	26		41	Hawaii	84
22	Tennessee	125		42	Idaho	82
9	Texas	160		42	Indiana	82
32	Utah	101		44	Virginia	81
11	Vermont	152		45	Colorado	80
44	Virginia	81		46	Oregon	56
14	Washington	133		47	Wyoming	55
29	West Virginia	109		48	Nebraska	45
26	Wisconsin	117		49	North Dakota	28
47	Wyoming	55		50	South Dakota	26
					District of Columbia	134

Source: U.S. Department of Health and Human Services, Centers for Medicare and Medicaid Services
"State Health Care Expenditures" (http://www.cms.hhs.gov/NationalHealthExpendData/)
*By state of residence. Includes spending for services and products by public and private freestanding home health agencies.
Excludes home health care services provided by hospital-based agencies which are included in hospital expenditures.

Expenditures for Drugs and Other Medical Nondurables in 2004

National Total = $222,412,000,000*

ALPHA ORDER				RANK ORDER			
RANK	STATE	EXPENDITURES	% of USA	RANK	STATE	EXPENDITURES	% of USA
18	Alabama	$4,241,000,000	1.9%	1	California	$20,799,000,000	9.4%
49	Alaska	418,000,000	0.2%	2	New York	17,722,000,000	8.0%
24	Arizona	3,378,000,000	1.5%	3	Florida	15,545,000,000	7.0%
32	Arkansas	1,938,000,000	0.9%	4	Texas	13,870,000,000	6.2%
1	California	20,799,000,000	9.4%	5	Pennsylvania	11,086,000,000	5.0%
28	Colorado	2,346,000,000	1.1%	6	Ohio	9,205,000,000	4.1%
26	Connecticut	3,246,000,000	1.5%	7	Illinois	9,098,000,000	4.1%
44	Delaware	769,000,000	0.3%	8	New Jersey	8,317,000,000	3.7%
3	Florida	15,545,000,000	7.0%	9	Michigan	7,790,000,000	3.5%
11	Georgia	6,493,000,000	2.9%	10	North Carolina	7,445,000,000	3.3%
42	Hawaii	925,000,000	0.4%	11	Georgia	6,493,000,000	2.9%
43	Idaho	834,000,000	0.4%	12	Tennessee	5,785,000,000	2.6%
7	Illinois	9,098,000,000	4.1%	13	Virginia	5,651,000,000	2.5%
15	Indiana	4,951,000,000	2.2%	14	Massachusetts	5,462,000,000	2.5%
31	Iowa	2,021,000,000	0.9%	15	Indiana	4,951,000,000	2.2%
33	Kansas	1,897,000,000	0.9%	16	Missouri	4,664,000,000	2.1%
19	Kentucky	3,917,000,000	1.8%	17	Maryland	4,595,000,000	2.1%
23	Louisiana	3,586,000,000	1.6%	18	Alabama	4,241,000,000	1.9%
40	Maine	1,052,000,000	0.5%	19	Kentucky	3,917,000,000	1.8%
17	Maryland	4,595,000,000	2.1%	20	Wisconsin	3,831,000,000	1.7%
14	Massachusetts	5,462,000,000	2.5%	21	Washington	3,792,000,000	1.7%
9	Michigan	7,790,000,000	3.5%	22	Minnesota	3,639,000,000	1.6%
22	Minnesota	3,639,000,000	1.6%	23	Louisiana	3,586,000,000	1.6%
29	Mississippi	2,208,000,000	1.0%	24	Arizona	3,378,000,000	1.5%
16	Missouri	4,664,000,000	2.1%	25	South Carolina	3,369,000,000	1.5%
46	Montana	499,000,000	0.2%	26	Connecticut	3,246,000,000	1.5%
37	Nebraska	1,288,000,000	0.6%	27	Oklahoma	2,472,000,000	1.1%
34	Nevada	1,786,000,000	0.8%	28	Colorado	2,346,000,000	1.1%
41	New Hampshire	962,000,000	0.4%	29	Mississippi	2,208,000,000	1.0%
8	New Jersey	8,317,000,000	3.7%	30	Oregon	2,042,000,000	0.9%
38	New Mexico	1,127,000,000	0.5%	31	Iowa	2,021,000,000	0.9%
2	New York	17,722,000,000	8.0%	32	Arkansas	1,938,000,000	0.9%
10	North Carolina	7,445,000,000	3.3%	33	Kansas	1,897,000,000	0.9%
45	North Dakota	537,000,000	0.2%	34	Nevada	1,786,000,000	0.8%
6	Ohio	9,205,000,000	4.1%	35	West Virginia	1,627,000,000	0.7%
27	Oklahoma	2,472,000,000	1.1%	36	Utah	1,592,000,000	0.7%
30	Oregon	2,042,000,000	0.9%	37	Nebraska	1,288,000,000	0.6%
5	Pennsylvania	11,086,000,000	5.0%	38	New Mexico	1,127,000,000	0.5%
39	Rhode Island	1,066,000,000	0.5%	39	Rhode Island	1,066,000,000	0.5%
25	South Carolina	3,369,000,000	1.5%	40	Maine	1,052,000,000	0.5%
48	South Dakota	440,000,000	0.2%	41	New Hampshire	962,000,000	0.4%
12	Tennessee	5,785,000,000	2.6%	42	Hawaii	925,000,000	0.4%
4	Texas	13,870,000,000	6.2%	43	Idaho	834,000,000	0.4%
36	Utah	1,592,000,000	0.7%	44	Delaware	769,000,000	0.3%
47	Vermont	444,000,000	0.2%	45	North Dakota	537,000,000	0.2%
13	Virginia	5,651,000,000	2.5%	46	Montana	499,000,000	0.2%
21	Washington	3,792,000,000	1.7%	47	Vermont	444,000,000	0.2%
35	West Virginia	1,627,000,000	0.7%	48	South Dakota	440,000,000	0.2%
20	Wisconsin	3,831,000,000	1.7%	49	Alaska	418,000,000	0.2%
50	Wyoming	302,000,000	0.1%	50	Wyoming	302,000,000	0.1%
					District of Columbia	345,000,000	0.2%

Source: U.S. Department of Health and Human Services, Centers for Medicare and Medicaid Services
  "State Health Care Expenditures" (http://www.cms.hhs.gov/NationalHealthExpendData/)
*Purchases in retail outlets. By state of residence. Includes prescription drugs, over-the-counter drugs, and sundries.

Percent of Total Personal Health Care Expenditures
Spent on Drugs and Other Medical Nondurables in 2004
National Percent = 14.3%*

ALPHA ORDER

RANK	STATE	PERCENT
1	Alabama	18.3
50	Alaska	9.9
26	Arizona	14.3
24	Arkansas	14.5
39	California	12.5
47	Colorado	10.8
23	Connecticut	14.6
22	Delaware	14.7
8	Florida	16.3
10	Georgia	15.8
19	Hawaii	14.9
31	Idaho	13.5
31	Illinois	13.5
18	Indiana	15.0
37	Iowa	12.7
36	Kansas	12.9
3	Kentucky	17.3
10	Louisiana	15.8
42	Maine	12.2
21	Maryland	14.8
37	Massachusetts	12.7
14	Michigan	15.3
40	Minnesota	12.3
15	Mississippi	15.1
19	Missouri	14.9
49	Montana	10.6
35	Nebraska	13.2
4	Nevada	16.8
30	New Hampshire	13.6
7	New Jersey	16.5
34	New Mexico	13.3
28	New York	14.1
4	North Carolina	16.8
24	North Dakota	14.5
29	Ohio	14.0
26	Oklahoma	14.3
45	Oregon	11.7
15	Pennsylvania	15.1
9	Rhode Island	16.0
12	South Carolina	15.7
48	South Dakota	10.7
2	Tennessee	18.0
33	Texas	13.4
6	Utah	16.6
44	Vermont	11.8
12	Virginia	15.7
43	Washington	12.0
15	West Virginia	15.1
40	Wisconsin	12.3
46	Wyoming	11.3

RANK ORDER

RANK	STATE	PERCENT
1	Alabama	18.3
2	Tennessee	18.0
3	Kentucky	17.3
4	Nevada	16.8
4	North Carolina	16.8
6	Utah	16.6
7	New Jersey	16.5
8	Florida	16.3
9	Rhode Island	16.0
10	Georgia	15.8
10	Louisiana	15.8
12	South Carolina	15.7
12	Virginia	15.7
14	Michigan	15.3
15	Mississippi	15.1
15	Pennsylvania	15.1
15	West Virginia	15.1
18	Indiana	15.0
19	Hawaii	14.9
19	Missouri	14.9
21	Maryland	14.8
22	Delaware	14.7
23	Connecticut	14.6
24	Arkansas	14.5
24	North Dakota	14.5
26	Arizona	14.3
26	Oklahoma	14.3
28	New York	14.1
29	Ohio	14.0
30	New Hampshire	13.6
31	Idaho	13.5
31	Illinois	13.5
33	Texas	13.4
34	New Mexico	13.3
35	Nebraska	13.2
36	Kansas	12.9
37	Iowa	12.7
37	Massachusetts	12.7
39	California	12.5
40	Minnesota	12.3
40	Wisconsin	12.3
42	Maine	12.2
43	Washington	12.0
44	Vermont	11.8
45	Oregon	11.7
46	Wyoming	11.3
47	Colorado	10.8
48	South Dakota	10.7
49	Montana	10.6
50	Alaska	9.9

District of Columbia   7.2

Source: CQ Press using data from U.S. Department of Health and Human Services, Centers for Medicare and Medicaid Services
"State Health Care Expenditures" (http://www.cms.hhs.gov/NationalHealthExpendData/)
*Purchases in retail outlets. By state of residence. Includes prescription drugs, over-the-counter drugs, and sundries.

Per Capita Expenditures for Drugs and Other Medical Nondurables in 2004

National Per Capita = $757*

ALPHA ORDER

RANK	STATE	PER CAPITA
5	Alabama	$939
39	Alaska	636
45	Arizona	588
33	Arkansas	705
46	California	580
50	Colorado	510
6	Connecticut	929
7	Delaware	928
11	Florida	895
29	Georgia	727
28	Hawaii	734
42	Idaho	598
30	Illinois	716
21	Indiana	796
37	Iowa	684
36	Kansas	693
4	Kentucky	946
20	Louisiana	798
19	Maine	800
15	Maryland	827
13	Massachusetts	849
22	Michigan	772
32	Minnesota	714
24	Mississippi	763
16	Missouri	811
49	Montana	539
27	Nebraska	737
23	Nevada	766
26	New Hampshire	741
3	New Jersey	959
44	New Mexico	593
8	New York	919
12	North Carolina	873
14	North Dakota	845
17	Ohio	803
34	Oklahoma	702
48	Oregon	569
10	Pennsylvania	896
1	Rhode Island	988
17	South Carolina	803
47	South Dakota	572
2	Tennessee	983
40	Texas	616
38	Utah	658
31	Vermont	715
25	Virginia	756
41	Washington	611
9	West Virginia	898
35	Wisconsin	697
43	Wyoming	597

RANK ORDER

RANK	STATE	PER CAPITA
1	Rhode Island	$988
2	Tennessee	983
3	New Jersey	959
4	Kentucky	946
5	Alabama	939
6	Connecticut	929
7	Delaware	928
8	New York	919
9	West Virginia	898
10	Pennsylvania	896
11	Florida	895
12	North Carolina	873
13	Massachusetts	849
14	North Dakota	845
15	Maryland	827
16	Missouri	811
17	Ohio	803
17	South Carolina	803
19	Maine	800
20	Louisiana	798
21	Indiana	796
22	Michigan	772
23	Nevada	766
24	Mississippi	763
25	Virginia	756
26	New Hampshire	741
27	Nebraska	737
28	Hawaii	734
29	Georgia	727
30	Illinois	716
31	Vermont	715
32	Minnesota	714
33	Arkansas	705
34	Oklahoma	702
35	Wisconsin	697
36	Kansas	693
37	Iowa	684
38	Utah	658
39	Alaska	636
40	Texas	616
41	Washington	611
42	Idaho	598
43	Wyoming	597
44	New Mexico	593
45	Arizona	588
46	California	580
47	South Dakota	572
48	Oregon	569
49	Montana	539
50	Colorado	510
	District of Columbia	594

Source: U.S. Department of Health and Human Services, Centers for Medicare and Medicaid Services
   "State Health Care Expenditures" (http://www.cms.hhs.gov/NationalHealthExpendData/)
*Purchases in retail outlets. By state of residence. Includes prescription drugs, over-the-counter drugs, and sundries.

Expenditures for Durable Medical Products in 2004

National Total = $23,128,000,000*

ALPHA ORDER

RANK	STATE	EXPENDITURES	% of USA
24	Alabama	$316,000,000	1.4%
46	Alaska	61,000,000	0.3%
21	Arizona	422,000,000	1.8%
36	Arkansas	164,000,000	0.7%
1	California	2,552,000,000	11.0%
18	Colorado	440,000,000	1.9%
23	Connecticut	317,000,000	1.4%
44	Delaware	78,000,000	0.3%
4	Florida	1,574,000,000	6.8%
11	Georgia	619,000,000	2.7%
39	Hawaii	118,000,000	0.5%
41	Idaho	101,000,000	0.4%
6	Illinois	987,000,000	4.3%
16	Indiana	470,000,000	2.0%
29	Iowa	261,000,000	1.1%
32	Kansas	215,000,000	0.9%
25	Kentucky	281,000,000	1.2%
28	Louisiana	272,000,000	1.2%
42	Maine	92,000,000	0.4%
13	Maryland	503,000,000	2.2%
14	Massachusetts	501,000,000	2.2%
9	Michigan	779,000,000	3.4%
17	Minnesota	456,000,000	2.0%
34	Mississippi	172,000,000	0.7%
20	Missouri	424,000,000	1.8%
43	Montana	85,000,000	0.4%
29	Nebraska	261,000,000	1.1%
33	Nevada	211,000,000	0.9%
40	New Hampshire	116,000,000	0.5%
7	New Jersey	964,000,000	4.2%
37	New Mexico	141,000,000	0.6%
2	New York	1,685,000,000	7.3%
12	North Carolina	524,000,000	2.3%
48	North Dakota	55,000,000	0.2%
8	Ohio	880,000,000	3.8%
31	Oklahoma	239,000,000	1.0%
26	Oregon	279,000,000	1.2%
5	Pennsylvania	1,026,000,000	4.4%
45	Rhode Island	62,000,000	0.3%
27	South Carolina	275,000,000	1.2%
47	South Dakota	60,000,000	0.3%
19	Tennessee	431,000,000	1.9%
3	Texas	1,678,000,000	7.3%
35	Utah	171,000,000	0.7%
50	Vermont	44,000,000	0.2%
10	Virginia	630,000,000	2.7%
15	Washington	485,000,000	2.1%
38	West Virginia	129,000,000	0.6%
22	Wisconsin	419,000,000	1.8%
49	Wyoming	47,000,000	0.2%

RANK ORDER

RANK	STATE	EXPENDITURES	% of USA
1	California	$2,552,000,000	11.0%
2	New York	1,685,000,000	7.3%
3	Texas	1,678,000,000	7.3%
4	Florida	1,574,000,000	6.8%
5	Pennsylvania	1,026,000,000	4.4%
6	Illinois	987,000,000	4.3%
7	New Jersey	964,000,000	4.2%
8	Ohio	880,000,000	3.8%
9	Michigan	779,000,000	3.4%
10	Virginia	630,000,000	2.7%
11	Georgia	619,000,000	2.7%
12	North Carolina	524,000,000	2.3%
13	Maryland	503,000,000	2.2%
14	Massachusetts	501,000,000	2.2%
15	Washington	485,000,000	2.1%
16	Indiana	470,000,000	2.0%
17	Minnesota	456,000,000	2.0%
18	Colorado	440,000,000	1.9%
19	Tennessee	431,000,000	1.9%
20	Missouri	424,000,000	1.8%
21	Arizona	422,000,000	1.8%
22	Wisconsin	419,000,000	1.8%
23	Connecticut	317,000,000	1.4%
24	Alabama	316,000,000	1.4%
25	Kentucky	281,000,000	1.2%
26	Oregon	279,000,000	1.2%
27	South Carolina	275,000,000	1.2%
28	Louisiana	272,000,000	1.2%
29	Iowa	261,000,000	1.1%
29	Nebraska	261,000,000	1.1%
31	Oklahoma	239,000,000	1.0%
32	Kansas	215,000,000	0.9%
33	Nevada	211,000,000	0.9%
34	Mississippi	172,000,000	0.7%
35	Utah	171,000,000	0.7%
36	Arkansas	164,000,000	0.7%
37	New Mexico	141,000,000	0.6%
38	West Virginia	129,000,000	0.6%
39	Hawaii	118,000,000	0.5%
40	New Hampshire	116,000,000	0.5%
41	Idaho	101,000,000	0.4%
42	Maine	92,000,000	0.4%
43	Montana	85,000,000	0.4%
44	Delaware	78,000,000	0.3%
45	Rhode Island	62,000,000	0.3%
46	Alaska	61,000,000	0.3%
47	South Dakota	60,000,000	0.3%
48	North Dakota	55,000,000	0.2%
49	Wyoming	47,000,000	0.2%
50	Vermont	44,000,000	0.2%
	District of Columbia	59,000,000	0.3%

Source: U.S. Department of Health and Human Services, Centers for Medicare and Medicaid Services
    "State Health Care Expenditures" (http://www.cms.hhs.gov/NationalHealthExpendData/)
*By state of residence. Includes eyeglasses, hearing aids, surgical appliances and supplies, bulk and cylinder oxygen, and medical equipment rentals.

Percent of Total Personal Health Care Expenditures
Spent on Durable Medical Products in 2004
National Percent = 1.5%*

ALPHA ORDER

RANK	STATE	PERCENT
29	Alabama	1.4
29	Alaska	1.4
6	Arizona	1.8
41	Arkansas	1.2
19	California	1.5
2	Colorado	2.0
29	Connecticut	1.4
19	Delaware	1.5
10	Florida	1.7
19	Georgia	1.5
4	Hawaii	1.9
13	Idaho	1.6
19	Illinois	1.5
29	Indiana	1.4
13	Iowa	1.6
19	Kansas	1.5
41	Kentucky	1.2
41	Louisiana	1.2
49	Maine	1.1
13	Maryland	1.6
41	Massachusetts	1.2
19	Michigan	1.5
19	Minnesota	1.5
41	Mississippi	1.2
29	Missouri	1.4
6	Montana	1.8
1	Nebraska	2.7
2	Nevada	2.0
13	New Hampshire	1.6
4	New Jersey	1.9
10	New Mexico	1.7
36	New York	1.3
41	North Carolina	1.2
19	North Dakota	1.5
36	Ohio	1.3
29	Oklahoma	1.4
13	Oregon	1.6
29	Pennsylvania	1.4
50	Rhode Island	0.9
36	South Carolina	1.3
19	South Dakota	1.5
36	Tennessee	1.3
13	Texas	1.6
6	Utah	1.8
41	Vermont	1.2
10	Virginia	1.7
19	Washington	1.5
41	West Virginia	1.2
36	Wisconsin	1.3
6	Wyoming	1.8

RANK ORDER

RANK	STATE	PERCENT
1	Nebraska	2.7
2	Colorado	2.0
2	Nevada	2.0
4	Hawaii	1.9
4	New Jersey	1.9
6	Arizona	1.8
6	Montana	1.8
6	Utah	1.8
6	Wyoming	1.8
10	Florida	1.7
10	New Mexico	1.7
10	Virginia	1.7
13	Idaho	1.6
13	Iowa	1.6
13	Maryland	1.6
13	New Hampshire	1.6
13	Oregon	1.6
13	Texas	1.6
19	California	1.5
19	Delaware	1.5
19	Georgia	1.5
19	Illinois	1.5
19	Kansas	1.5
19	Michigan	1.5
19	Minnesota	1.5
19	North Dakota	1.5
19	South Dakota	1.5
19	Washington	1.5
29	Alabama	1.4
29	Alaska	1.4
29	Connecticut	1.4
29	Indiana	1.4
29	Missouri	1.4
29	Oklahoma	1.4
29	Pennsylvania	1.4
36	New York	1.3
36	Ohio	1.3
36	South Carolina	1.3
36	Tennessee	1.3
36	Wisconsin	1.3
41	Arkansas	1.2
41	Kentucky	1.2
41	Louisiana	1.2
41	Massachusetts	1.2
41	Mississippi	1.2
41	North Carolina	1.2
41	Vermont	1.2
41	West Virginia	1.2
49	Maine	1.1
50	Rhode Island	0.9

District of Columbia   1.2

Source: CQ Press using data from U.S. Department of Health and Human Services, Centers for Medicare and Medicaid Services
"State Health Care Expenditures" (http://www.cms.hhs.gov/NationalHealthExpendData/)
*By state of residence. Includes eyeglasses, hearing aids, surgical appliances and supplies, bulk and cylinder oxygen, and medical equipment rentals.

Per Capita Expenditures for Durable Medical Products in 2004

National Per Capita = $79*

ALPHA ORDER

RANK	STATE	PER CAPITA
40	Alabama	$70
6	Alaska	93
30	Arizona	74
47	Arkansas	60
37	California	71
3	Colorado	96
9	Connecticut	91
4	Delaware	95
9	Florida	91
42	Georgia	69
5	Hawaii	94
35	Idaho	72
20	Illinois	78
28	Indiana	76
15	Iowa	88
20	Kansas	78
43	Kentucky	68
47	Louisiana	60
40	Maine	70
9	Maryland	91
20	Massachusetts	78
25	Michigan	77
14	Minnesota	89
47	Mississippi	60
30	Missouri	74
7	Montana	92
1	Nebraska	149
12	Nevada	90
12	New Hampshire	90
2	New Jersey	111
30	New Mexico	74
16	New York	87
46	North Carolina	61
17	North Dakota	86
25	Ohio	77
43	Oklahoma	68
20	Oregon	78
19	Pennsylvania	83
50	Rhode Island	57
45	South Carolina	66
25	South Dakota	77
34	Tennessee	73
30	Texas	74
37	Utah	71
35	Vermont	72
18	Virginia	84
20	Washington	78
37	West Virginia	71
28	Wisconsin	76
7	Wyoming	92

RANK ORDER

RANK	STATE	PER CAPITA
1	Nebraska	$149
2	New Jersey	111
3	Colorado	96
4	Delaware	95
5	Hawaii	94
6	Alaska	93
7	Montana	92
7	Wyoming	92
9	Connecticut	91
9	Florida	91
9	Maryland	91
12	Nevada	90
12	New Hampshire	90
14	Minnesota	89
15	Iowa	88
16	New York	87
17	North Dakota	86
18	Virginia	84
19	Pennsylvania	83
20	Illinois	78
20	Kansas	78
20	Massachusetts	78
20	Oregon	78
20	Washington	78
25	Michigan	77
25	Ohio	77
25	South Dakota	77
28	Indiana	76
28	Wisconsin	76
30	Arizona	74
30	Missouri	74
30	New Mexico	74
30	Texas	74
34	Tennessee	73
35	Idaho	72
35	Vermont	72
37	California	71
37	Utah	71
37	West Virginia	71
40	Alabama	70
40	Maine	70
42	Georgia	69
43	Kentucky	68
43	Oklahoma	68
45	South Carolina	66
46	North Carolina	61
47	Arkansas	60
47	Louisiana	60
47	Mississippi	60
50	Rhode Island	57

	District of Columbia	102

Source: U.S. Department of Health and Human Services, Centers for Medicare and Medicaid Services
   "State Health Care Expenditures" (http://www.cms.hhs.gov/NationalHealthExpendData/)
*By state of residence. Includes eyeglasses, hearing aids, surgical appliances and supplies, bulk and cylinder oxygen, and medical equipment rentals.

Projected National Health Care Expenditures in 2009

Total Health Care Expenditures = $2,555,060,000,000*

The 2004 health care expenditures broken down to the state level and shown on pages 305 to 332 were released in February of 2007 and are the most recent state health expenditure data available from the Centers for Medicare and Medicaid Services (CMS).

Given the high level of interest in health care finance data, we have assembled a table showing the most recent national level health care expenditure projections.

	PROJECTED EXPENDITURES IN 2009	PROJECTED PERCENT CHANGE: 2008 TO 2009
Total Health Care Expenditures	$2,555,060,000,000	6.7
Per Capita Total Health Care Expenditures	$8,403	
Personal Health Care Expenditures	$2,130,561,000,000	6.6
Per Capita Personal Health Care Expenditures	$7,007	
Hospital Care Expenditures	$799,989,000,000	7.1
Per Capita Hospital Care Expenditures	$2,631	
Physician Services Expenditures	$532,783,000,000	6.2
Per Capita Physician Services Expenditures	$1,752	
Dental Services Expenditures	$108,190,000,000	5.6
Per Capita Dental Services Expenditures	$356	
Other Professional Services	$68,500,000,000	5.2
Per Capita Other Professional Services	$225	
Home Health Care Expenditures	$66,732,000,000	7.6
Per Capita Home Health Care Expenditures	$219	
Prescription Drugs	$264,489,000,000	7.1
Per Capita Prescription Drugs	$870	
Nursing Home Care	$143,503,000,000	5.2
Per Capita Nursing Home Care	$472	
Other Personal Care Expenditures	$81,082,000,000	9.6
Per Capita Other Personal Care Expenditures	$267	

Source: U.S. Department of Health and Human Services, Centers for Medicare and Medicaid Services
    "National Health Care Expenditures Projections: 2002-2017"
    (http://www.cms.hhs.gov/NationalHealthExpendData/downloads/proj2007.pdf)
*Per Capita figures calculated by CQ Press using 2008 Census population estimates. For definitions see the corresponding 2004 state tables in this chapter.

V. Incidence of Disease

Estimated New Cancer Cases in 2008

National Estimated Total = 1,437,180 New Cases*

ALPHA ORDER

RANK	STATE	CASES	% of USA
24	Alabama	22,340	1.6%
49	Alaska	2,650	0.2%
20	Arizona	25,540	1.8%
31	Arkansas	14,840	1.0%
1	California	156,530	10.9%
28	Colorado	18,900	1.3%
27	Connecticut	19,190	1.3%
45	Delaware	4,590	0.3%
2	Florida	101,920	7.1%
11	Georgia	36,980	2.6%
42	Hawaii	6,310	0.4%
41	Idaho	6,430	0.4%
6	Illinois	59,130	4.1%
15	Indiana	29,550	2.1%
30	Iowa	16,150	1.1%
33	Kansas	12,520	0.9%
22	Kentucky	23,270	1.6%
21	Louisiana	23,360	1.6%
38	Maine	8,140	0.6%
19	Maryland	27,380	1.9%
13	Massachusetts	34,470	2.4%
8	Michigan	51,150	3.6%
23	Minnesota	23,160	1.6%
32	Mississippi	13,400	0.9%
16	Missouri	29,390	2.0%
44	Montana	5,090	0.4%
36	Nebraska	8,710	0.6%
34	Nevada	11,370	0.8%
40	New Hampshire	7,030	0.5%
9	New Jersey	45,900	3.2%
37	New Mexico	8,260	0.6%
3	New York	97,130	6.8%
10	North Carolina	40,420	2.8%
48	North Dakota	3,090	0.2%
7	Ohio	56,840	4.0%
29	Oklahoma	17,860	1.2%
26	Oregon	19,230	1.3%
5	Pennsylvania	70,110	4.9%
43	Rhode Island	6,120	0.4%
25	South Carolina	20,740	1.4%
46	South Dakota	4,080	0.3%
16	Tennessee	29,390	2.0%
4	Texas	96,320	6.7%
39	Utah	7,760	0.5%
47	Vermont	3,530	0.2%
12	Virginia	35,590	2.5%
14	Washington	32,380	2.3%
35	West Virginia	10,250	0.7%
18	Wisconsin	27,590	1.9%
50	Wyoming	2,570	0.2%

RANK ORDER

RANK	STATE	CASES	% of USA
1	California	156,530	10.9%
2	Florida	101,920	7.1%
3	New York	97,130	6.8%
4	Texas	96,320	6.7%
5	Pennsylvania	70,110	4.9%
6	Illinois	59,130	4.1%
7	Ohio	56,840	4.0%
8	Michigan	51,150	3.6%
9	New Jersey	45,900	3.2%
10	North Carolina	40,420	2.8%
11	Georgia	36,980	2.6%
12	Virginia	35,590	2.5%
13	Massachusetts	34,470	2.4%
14	Washington	32,380	2.3%
15	Indiana	29,550	2.1%
16	Missouri	29,390	2.0%
16	Tennessee	29,390	2.0%
18	Wisconsin	27,590	1.9%
19	Maryland	27,380	1.9%
20	Arizona	25,540	1.8%
21	Louisiana	23,360	1.6%
22	Kentucky	23,270	1.6%
23	Minnesota	23,160	1.6%
24	Alabama	22,340	1.6%
25	South Carolina	20,740	1.4%
26	Oregon	19,230	1.3%
27	Connecticut	19,190	1.3%
28	Colorado	18,900	1.3%
29	Oklahoma	17,860	1.2%
30	Iowa	16,150	1.1%
31	Arkansas	14,840	1.0%
32	Mississippi	13,400	0.9%
33	Kansas	12,520	0.9%
34	Nevada	11,370	0.8%
35	West Virginia	10,250	0.7%
36	Nebraska	8,710	0.6%
37	New Mexico	8,260	0.6%
38	Maine	8,140	0.6%
39	Utah	7,760	0.5%
40	New Hampshire	7,030	0.5%
41	Idaho	6,430	0.4%
42	Hawaii	6,310	0.4%
43	Rhode Island	6,120	0.4%
44	Montana	5,090	0.4%
45	Delaware	4,590	0.3%
46	South Dakota	4,080	0.3%
47	Vermont	3,530	0.2%
48	North Dakota	3,090	0.2%
49	Alaska	2,650	0.2%
50	Wyoming	2,570	0.2%
	District of Columbia	2,560	0.2%

Source: American Cancer Society

"Cancer Facts & Figures 2008" (Copyright 2008, American Cancer Society, http://www.cancer.org/docroot/stt/stt_0.asp)
*These estimates are offered as a rough guide and should not be regarded as definitive. They are calculated according to the distribution of estimated 2008 cancer deaths by state. Totals do not include basal and squamous cell skin cancers or in situ carcinomas except urinary bladder.

Estimated Rate of New Cancer Cases in 2008

National Estimated Rate = 472.7 New Cases per 100,000 Population*

ALPHA ORDER

RANK	STATE	RATE
31	Alabama	479.2
47	Alaska	386.1
46	Arizona	392.9
16	Arkansas	519.7
42	California	425.9
48	Colorado	382.6
7	Connecticut	548.1
15	Delaware	525.7
6	Florida	556.1
49	Georgia	381.8
26	Hawaii	489.8
43	Idaho	422.0
35	Illinois	458.3
33	Indiana	463.4
9	Iowa	537.9
38	Kansas	446.8
8	Kentucky	545.1
12	Louisiana	529.6
1	Maine	618.3
28	Maryland	486.0
11	Massachusetts	530.5
17	Michigan	511.3
39	Minnesota	443.6
37	Mississippi	456.0
21	Missouri	497.2
14	Montana	526.1
27	Nebraska	488.4
41	Nevada	437.3
10	New Hampshire	534.3
13	New Jersey	528.6
44	New Mexico	416.3
20	New York	498.4
40	North Carolina	438.3
30	North Dakota	481.7
22	Ohio	494.9
24	Oklahoma	490.3
18	Oregon	507.4
5	Pennsylvania	563.2
2	Rhode Island	582.4
34	South Carolina	463.0
19	South Dakota	507.3
32	Tennessee	472.9
45	Texas	395.9
50	Utah	283.6
3	Vermont	568.2
36	Virginia	458.1
23	Washington	494.4
4	West Virginia	564.9
25	Wisconsin	490.2
29	Wyoming	482.5

RANK ORDER

RANK	STATE	RATE
1	Maine	618.3
2	Rhode Island	582.4
3	Vermont	568.2
4	West Virginia	564.9
5	Pennsylvania	563.2
6	Florida	556.1
7	Connecticut	548.1
8	Kentucky	545.1
9	Iowa	537.9
10	New Hampshire	534.3
11	Massachusetts	530.5
12	Louisiana	529.6
13	New Jersey	528.6
14	Montana	526.1
15	Delaware	525.7
16	Arkansas	519.7
17	Michigan	511.3
18	Oregon	507.4
19	South Dakota	507.3
20	New York	498.4
21	Missouri	497.2
22	Ohio	494.9
23	Washington	494.4
24	Oklahoma	490.3
25	Wisconsin	490.2
26	Hawaii	489.8
27	Nebraska	488.4
28	Maryland	486.0
29	Wyoming	482.5
30	North Dakota	481.7
31	Alabama	479.2
32	Tennessee	472.9
33	Indiana	463.4
34	South Carolina	463.0
35	Illinois	458.3
36	Virginia	458.1
37	Mississippi	456.0
38	Kansas	446.8
39	Minnesota	443.6
40	North Carolina	438.3
41	Nevada	437.3
42	California	425.9
43	Idaho	422.0
44	New Mexico	416.3
45	Texas	395.9
46	Arizona	392.9
47	Alaska	386.1
48	Colorado	382.6
49	Georgia	381.8
50	Utah	283.6

| | District of Columbia | 432.6 |

Source: CQ Press using data from American Cancer Society
   "Cancer Facts & Figures 2008" (Copyright 2008, American Cancer Society, http://www.cancer.org/docroot/stt/stt_0.asp)
*These estimates are offered as a rough guide and should not be regarded as definitive. They are calculated according to the distribution of estimated 2008 cancer deaths by state. Totals do not include basal and squamous cell skin cancers or in situ carcinomas except urinary bladder. Rates calculated using 2008 Census resident population estimates.

Age-Adjusted Cancer Incidence Rates for Males in 2004

National Rate = 557.8 New Cases per 100,000 Male Population*

ALPHA ORDER

RANK	STATE	RATE
31	Alabama	540.4
20	Alaska	556.1
44	Arizona	464.1
27	Arkansas	547.1
38	California	517.3
40	Colorado	510.2
8	Connecticut	588.7
7	Delaware	589.9
22	Florida	553.0
17	Georgia	568.4
43	Hawaii	482.0
35	Idaho	533.6
12	Illinois	578.2
23	Indiana	551.7
24	Iowa	551.6
NA	Kansas**	NA
5	Kentucky	611.2
2	Louisiana	615.7
4	Maine	612.4
NA	Maryland**	NA
10	Massachusetts	586.9
6	Michigan	606.0
NA	Minnesota**	NA
28	Mississippi	546.7
34	Missouri	535.4
19	Montana	557.1
25	Nebraska	550.3
21	Nevada	555.6
14	New Hampshire	575.8
3	New Jersey	613.9
42	New Mexico	485.4
16	New York	570.3
NA	North Carolina**	NA
37	North Dakota	518.6
30	Ohio	542.0
26	Oklahoma	547.3
32	Oregon	538.9
9	Pennsylvania	588.5
1	Rhode Island	620.2
11	South Carolina	586.6
13	South Dakota	577.0
45	Tennessee	459.2
33	Texas	535.9
41	Utah	487.6
NA	Vermont**	NA
39	Virginia	511.6
18	Washington	567.1
15	West Virginia	570.6
29	Wisconsin	543.4
36	Wyoming	519.2

RANK ORDER

RANK	STATE	RATE
1	Rhode Island	620.2
2	Louisiana	615.7
3	New Jersey	613.9
4	Maine	612.4
5	Kentucky	611.2
6	Michigan	606.0
7	Delaware	589.9
8	Connecticut	588.7
9	Pennsylvania	588.5
10	Massachusetts	586.9
11	South Carolina	586.6
12	Illinois	578.2
13	South Dakota	577.0
14	New Hampshire	575.8
15	West Virginia	570.6
16	New York	570.3
17	Georgia	568.4
18	Washington	567.1
19	Montana	557.1
20	Alaska	556.1
21	Nevada	555.6
22	Florida	553.0
23	Indiana	551.7
24	Iowa	551.6
25	Nebraska	550.3
26	Oklahoma	547.3
27	Arkansas	547.1
28	Mississippi	546.7
29	Wisconsin	543.4
30	Ohio	542.0
31	Alabama	540.4
32	Oregon	538.9
33	Texas	535.9
34	Missouri	535.4
35	Idaho	533.6
36	Wyoming	519.2
37	North Dakota	518.6
38	California	517.3
39	Virginia	511.6
40	Colorado	510.2
41	Utah	487.6
42	New Mexico	485.4
43	Hawaii	482.0
44	Arizona	464.1
45	Tennessee	459.2
NA	Kansas**	NA
NA	Maryland**	NA
NA	Minnesota**	NA
NA	North Carolina**	NA
NA	Vermont**	NA

District of Columbia   611.5

Source: American Cancer Society
"Cancer Facts & Figures 2008" (Copyright 2008, American Cancer Society, http://www.cancer.org/docroot/stt/stt_0.asp)
*For 2000 to 2004. Age-adjusted to the 2000 U.S. standard population.
**Not available.

Age-Adjusted Cancer Incidence Rates for Females in 2004

National Rate = 413.1 New Cases per 100,000 Female Population*

ALPHA ORDER

RANK	STATE	RATE
40	Alabama	370.1
18	Alaska	416.8
41	Arizona	364.6
37	Arkansas	376.9
31	California	393.5
29	Colorado	400.1
4	Connecticut	445.2
12	Delaware	430.2
22	Florida	411.2
30	Georgia	394.5
39	Hawaii	372.1
32	Idaho	393.4
16	Illinois	423.1
19	Indiana	414.5
17	Iowa	422.3
NA	Kansas**	NA
7	Kentucky	441.6
27	Louisiana	402.4
2	Maine	451.9
NA	Maryland**	NA
1	Massachusetts	452.1
11	Michigan	431.7
NA	Minnesota**	NA
43	Mississippi	359.8
23	Missouri	408.9
25	Montana	407.3
20	Nebraska	413.9
15	Nevada	425.8
8	New Hampshire	440.8
3	New Jersey	446.4
44	New Mexico	359.4
13	New York	427.0
NA	North Carolina**	NA
36	North Dakota	378.8
23	Ohio	408.9
26	Oklahoma	403.1
10	Oregon	433.8
9	Pennsylvania	436.3
6	Rhode Island	443.0
34	South Carolina	391.1
28	South Dakota	400.9
42	Tennessee	361.3
35	Texas	385.1
45	Utah	345.2
NA	Vermont**	NA
38	Virginia	372.8
5	Washington	444.3
14	West Virginia	426.5
21	Wisconsin	413.4
33	Wyoming	392.2

RANK ORDER

RANK	STATE	RATE
1	Massachusetts	452.1
2	Maine	451.9
3	New Jersey	446.4
4	Connecticut	445.2
5	Washington	444.3
6	Rhode Island	443.0
7	Kentucky	441.6
8	New Hampshire	440.8
9	Pennsylvania	436.3
10	Oregon	433.8
11	Michigan	431.7
12	Delaware	430.2
13	New York	427.0
14	West Virginia	426.5
15	Nevada	425.8
16	Illinois	423.1
17	Iowa	422.3
18	Alaska	416.8
19	Indiana	414.5
20	Nebraska	413.9
21	Wisconsin	413.4
22	Florida	411.2
23	Missouri	408.9
23	Ohio	408.9
25	Montana	407.3
26	Oklahoma	403.1
27	Louisiana	402.4
28	South Dakota	400.9
29	Colorado	400.1
30	Georgia	394.5
31	California	393.5
32	Idaho	393.4
33	Wyoming	392.2
34	South Carolina	391.1
35	Texas	385.1
36	North Dakota	378.8
37	Arkansas	376.9
38	Virginia	372.8
39	Hawaii	372.1
40	Alabama	370.1
41	Arizona	364.6
42	Tennessee	361.3
43	Mississippi	359.8
44	New Mexico	359.4
45	Utah	345.2
NA	Kansas**	NA
NA	Maryland**	NA
NA	Minnesota**	NA
NA	North Carolina**	NA
NA	Vermont**	NA

District of Columbia 421.2

Source: American Cancer Society
"Cancer Facts & Figures 2008" (Copyright 2008, American Cancer Society, http://www.cancer.org/docroot/stt/stt_0.asp)
*For 2000 to 2004. Age-adjusted to the 2000 U.S. standard population.
**Not available.

Estimated New Cases of Bladder Cancer in 2008

National Estimated Total = 68,810 New Cases*

ALPHA ORDER

RANK	STATE	CASES	% of USA
26	Alabama	890	1.3%
49	Alaska	120	0.2%
14	Arizona	1,380	2.0%
31	Arkansas	610	0.9%
1	California	6,940	10.1%
26	Colorado	890	1.3%
22	Connecticut	1,080	1.6%
44	Delaware	220	0.3%
3	Florida	5,390	7.8%
14	Georgia	1,380	2.0%
45	Hawaii	210	0.3%
42	Idaho	320	0.5%
6	Illinois	2,840	4.1%
14	Indiana	1,380	2.0%
29	Iowa	830	1.2%
32	Kansas	570	0.8%
24	Kentucky	990	1.4%
25	Louisiana	920	1.3%
36	Maine	490	0.7%
20	Maryland	1,120	1.6%
10	Massachusetts	1,950	2.8%
9	Michigan	2,510	3.6%
21	Minnesota	1,110	1.6%
35	Mississippi	500	0.7%
14	Missouri	1,380	2.0%
43	Montana	270	0.4%
37	Nebraska	420	0.6%
32	Nevada	570	0.8%
38	New Hampshire	390	0.6%
8	New Jersey	2,620	3.8%
40	New Mexico	350	0.5%
2	New York	5,460	7.9%
11	North Carolina	1,740	2.5%
48	North Dakota	170	0.2%
7	Ohio	2,810	4.1%
30	Oklahoma	750	1.1%
23	Oregon	1,000	1.5%
4	Pennsylvania	4,290	6.2%
39	Rhode Island	370	0.5%
28	South Carolina	850	1.2%
45	South Dakota	210	0.3%
19	Tennessee	1,250	1.8%
5	Texas	3,610	5.2%
41	Utah	340	0.5%
47	Vermont	180	0.3%
13	Virginia	1,460	2.1%
12	Washington	1,580	2.3%
34	West Virginia	530	0.8%
18	Wisconsin	1,360	2.0%
49	Wyoming	120	0.2%

RANK ORDER

RANK	STATE	CASES	% of USA
1	California	6,940	10.1%
2	New York	5,460	7.9%
3	Florida	5,390	7.8%
4	Pennsylvania	4,290	6.2%
5	Texas	3,610	5.2%
6	Illinois	2,840	4.1%
7	Ohio	2,810	4.1%
8	New Jersey	2,620	3.8%
9	Michigan	2,510	3.6%
10	Massachusetts	1,950	2.8%
11	North Carolina	1,740	2.5%
12	Washington	1,580	2.3%
13	Virginia	1,460	2.1%
14	Arizona	1,380	2.0%
14	Georgia	1,380	2.0%
14	Indiana	1,380	2.0%
14	Missouri	1,380	2.0%
18	Wisconsin	1,360	2.0%
19	Tennessee	1,250	1.8%
20	Maryland	1,120	1.6%
21	Minnesota	1,110	1.6%
22	Connecticut	1,080	1.6%
23	Oregon	1,000	1.5%
24	Kentucky	990	1.4%
25	Louisiana	920	1.3%
26	Alabama	890	1.3%
26	Colorado	890	1.3%
28	South Carolina	850	1.2%
29	Iowa	830	1.2%
30	Oklahoma	750	1.1%
31	Arkansas	610	0.9%
32	Kansas	570	0.8%
32	Nevada	570	0.8%
34	West Virginia	530	0.8%
35	Mississippi	500	0.7%
36	Maine	490	0.7%
37	Nebraska	420	0.6%
38	New Hampshire	390	0.6%
39	Rhode Island	370	0.5%
40	New Mexico	350	0.5%
41	Utah	340	0.5%
42	Idaho	320	0.5%
43	Montana	270	0.4%
44	Delaware	220	0.3%
45	Hawaii	210	0.3%
45	South Dakota	210	0.3%
47	Vermont	180	0.3%
48	North Dakota	170	0.2%
49	Alaska	120	0.2%
49	Wyoming	120	0.2%
	District of Columbia	80	0.1%

Source: American Cancer Society
    "Cancer Facts & Figures 2008" (Copyright 2008, American Cancer Society, http://www.cancer.org/docroot/stt/stt_0.asp)
*These estimates are offered as a rough guide and should be interpreted with caution. They are calculated according to the distribution of estimated 2008 cancer deaths by state.

Estimated Rate of New Bladder Cancer Cases in 2008

National Estimated Rate = 22.6 New Cases per 100,000 Population*

ALPHA ORDER

RANK	STATE	RATE
38	Alabama	19.1
45	Alaska	17.5
31	Arizona	21.2
29	Arkansas	21.4
40	California	18.9
43	Colorado	18.0
4	Connecticut	30.8
17	Delaware	25.2
8	Florida	29.4
49	Georgia	14.2
47	Hawaii	16.3
32	Idaho	21.0
26	Illinois	22.0
28	Indiana	21.6
13	Iowa	27.6
35	Kansas	20.3
24	Kentucky	23.2
33	Louisiana	20.9
1	Maine	37.2
37	Maryland	19.9
6	Massachusetts	30.0
18	Michigan	25.1
30	Minnesota	21.3
46	Mississippi	17.0
23	Missouri	23.3
12	Montana	27.9
22	Nebraska	23.6
27	Nevada	21.9
7	New Hampshire	29.6
5	New Jersey	30.2
44	New Mexico	17.6
11	New York	28.0
40	North Carolina	18.9
14	North Dakota	26.5
19	Ohio	24.5
34	Oklahoma	20.6
15	Oregon	26.4
3	Pennsylvania	34.5
2	Rhode Island	35.2
39	South Carolina	19.0
16	South Dakota	26.1
36	Tennessee	20.1
48	Texas	14.8
50	Utah	12.4
10	Vermont	29.0
42	Virginia	18.8
21	Washington	24.1
9	West Virginia	29.2
20	Wisconsin	24.2
25	Wyoming	22.5

RANK ORDER

RANK	STATE	RATE
1	Maine	37.2
2	Rhode Island	35.2
3	Pennsylvania	34.5
4	Connecticut	30.8
5	New Jersey	30.2
6	Massachusetts	30.0
7	New Hampshire	29.6
8	Florida	29.4
9	West Virginia	29.2
10	Vermont	29.0
11	New York	28.0
12	Montana	27.9
13	Iowa	27.6
14	North Dakota	26.5
15	Oregon	26.4
16	South Dakota	26.1
17	Delaware	25.2
18	Michigan	25.1
19	Ohio	24.5
20	Wisconsin	24.2
21	Washington	24.1
22	Nebraska	23.6
23	Missouri	23.3
24	Kentucky	23.2
25	Wyoming	22.5
26	Illinois	22.0
27	Nevada	21.9
28	Indiana	21.6
29	Arkansas	21.4
30	Minnesota	21.3
31	Arizona	21.2
32	Idaho	21.0
33	Louisiana	20.9
34	Oklahoma	20.6
35	Kansas	20.3
36	Tennessee	20.1
37	Maryland	19.9
38	Alabama	19.1
39	South Carolina	19.0
40	California	18.9
40	North Carolina	18.9
42	Virginia	18.8
43	Colorado	18.0
44	New Mexico	17.6
45	Alaska	17.5
46	Mississippi	17.0
47	Hawaii	16.3
48	Texas	14.8
49	Georgia	14.2
50	Utah	12.4

District of Columbia   13.5

Source: CQ Press using data from American Cancer Society
    "Cancer Facts & Figures 2008" (Copyright 2008, American Cancer Society, http://www.cancer.org/docroot/stt/stt_0.asp)
*These estimates are offered as a rough guide and should be interpreted with caution. They are calculated according to the
distribution of estimated 2008 cancer deaths by state. Rates calculated using 2008 Census resident population estimates.

Estimated New Female Breast Cancer Cases in 2008

National Estimated Total = 182,460 New Cases*

ALPHA ORDER

RANK	STATE	CASES	% of USA
23	Alabama	2,750	1.5%
49	Alaska	350	0.2%
20	Arizona	3,220	1.8%
31	Arkansas	1,790	1.0%
1	California	20,080	11.0%
26	Colorado	2,520	1.4%
24	Connecticut	2,640	1.4%
45	Delaware	580	0.3%
4	Florida	11,850	6.5%
11	Georgia	4,910	2.7%
41	Hawaii	840	0.5%
43	Idaho	760	0.4%
6	Illinois	7,190	3.9%
18	Indiana	3,660	2.0%
30	Iowa	1,990	1.1%
32	Kansas	1,730	0.9%
25	Kentucky	2,600	1.4%
22	Louisiana	2,840	1.6%
39	Maine	990	0.5%
17	Maryland	3,670	2.0%
13	Massachusetts	4,480	2.5%
9	Michigan	6,120	3.4%
21	Minnesota	3,090	1.7%
33	Mississippi	1,630	0.9%
15	Missouri	3,810	2.1%
44	Montana	620	0.3%
35	Nebraska	1,160	0.6%
34	Nevada	1,270	0.7%
40	New Hampshire	950	0.5%
8	New Jersey	6,310	3.5%
37	New Mexico	1,060	0.6%
2	New York	13,310	7.3%
10	North Carolina	5,000	2.7%
48	North Dakota	410	0.2%
7	Ohio	6,990	3.8%
29	Oklahoma	2,270	1.2%
28	Oregon	2,430	1.3%
5	Pennsylvania	9,410	5.2%
42	Rhode Island	770	0.4%
27	South Carolina	2,510	1.4%
46	South Dakota	520	0.3%
16	Tennessee	3,720	2.0%
3	Texas	12,210	6.7%
38	Utah	1,010	0.6%
47	Vermont	470	0.3%
12	Virginia	4,680	2.6%
14	Washington	4,140	2.3%
36	West Virginia	1,150	0.6%
19	Wisconsin	3,400	1.9%
50	Wyoming	310	0.2%

RANK ORDER

RANK	STATE	CASES	% of USA
1	California	20,080	11.0%
2	New York	13,310	7.3%
3	Texas	12,210	6.7%
4	Florida	11,850	6.5%
5	Pennsylvania	9,410	5.2%
6	Illinois	7,190	3.9%
7	Ohio	6,990	3.8%
8	New Jersey	6,310	3.5%
9	Michigan	6,120	3.4%
10	North Carolina	5,000	2.7%
11	Georgia	4,910	2.7%
12	Virginia	4,680	2.6%
13	Massachusetts	4,480	2.5%
14	Washington	4,140	2.3%
15	Missouri	3,810	2.1%
16	Tennessee	3,720	2.0%
17	Maryland	3,670	2.0%
18	Indiana	3,660	2.0%
19	Wisconsin	3,400	1.9%
20	Arizona	3,220	1.8%
21	Minnesota	3,090	1.7%
22	Louisiana	2,840	1.6%
23	Alabama	2,750	1.5%
24	Connecticut	2,640	1.4%
25	Kentucky	2,600	1.4%
26	Colorado	2,520	1.4%
27	South Carolina	2,510	1.4%
28	Oregon	2,430	1.3%
29	Oklahoma	2,270	1.2%
30	Iowa	1,990	1.1%
31	Arkansas	1,790	1.0%
32	Kansas	1,730	0.9%
33	Mississippi	1,630	0.9%
34	Nevada	1,270	0.7%
35	Nebraska	1,160	0.6%
36	West Virginia	1,150	0.6%
37	New Mexico	1,060	0.6%
38	Utah	1,010	0.6%
39	Maine	990	0.5%
40	New Hampshire	950	0.5%
41	Hawaii	840	0.5%
42	Rhode Island	770	0.4%
43	Idaho	760	0.4%
44	Montana	620	0.3%
45	Delaware	580	0.3%
46	South Dakota	520	0.3%
47	Vermont	470	0.3%
48	North Dakota	410	0.2%
49	Alaska	350	0.2%
50	Wyoming	310	0.2%
	District of Columbia	300	0.2%

Source: American Cancer Society
"Cancer Facts & Figures 2008" (Copyright 2008, American Cancer Society, http://www.cancer.org/docroot/stt/stt_0.asp)
*These estimates are offered as a rough guide and should be interpreted with caution. They are calculated according to the distribution of estimated 2008 cancer deaths by state.

Age-Adjusted Incidence Rate of Female Breast Cancer Cases in 2004

National Rate = 125.3 New Cases per 100,000 Female Population*

ALPHA ORDER

RANK	STATE	RATE
42	Alabama	113.9
6	Alaska	132.0
41	Arizona	114.4
38	Arkansas	117.1
17	California	126.5
11	Colorado	129.3
3	Connecticut	137.3
19	Delaware	126.1
36	Florida	119.7
25	Georgia	123.9
23	Hawaii	124.2
28	Idaho	123.1
18	Illinois	126.2
34	Indiana	121.0
21	Iowa	125.9
NA	Kansas**	NA
29	Kentucky	122.1
30	Louisiana	122.0
8	Maine	130.8
NA	Maryland**	NA
4	Massachusetts	136.7
13	Michigan	128.8
NA	Minnesota**	NA
45	Mississippi	105.4
23	Missouri	124.2
22	Montana	124.5
9	Nebraska	130.4
33	Nevada	121.5
5	New Hampshire	133.9
7	New Jersey	131.7
44	New Mexico	112.2
20	New York	126.0
NA	North Carolina**	NA
27	North Dakota	123.4
26	Ohio	123.5
15	Oklahoma	127.0
2	Oregon	138.8
14	Pennsylvania	127.1
10	Rhode Island	129.9
34	South Carolina	121.0
16	South Dakota	126.6
42	Tennessee	113.9
37	Texas	117.2
39	Utah	115.7
NA	Vermont**	NA
31	Virginia	121.6
1	Washington	142.2
40	West Virginia	115.5
12	Wisconsin	129.0
31	Wyoming	121.6

RANK ORDER

RANK	STATE	RATE
1	Washington	142.2
2	Oregon	138.8
3	Connecticut	137.3
4	Massachusetts	136.7
5	New Hampshire	133.9
6	Alaska	132.0
7	New Jersey	131.7
8	Maine	130.8
9	Nebraska	130.4
10	Rhode Island	129.9
11	Colorado	129.3
12	Wisconsin	129.0
13	Michigan	128.8
14	Pennsylvania	127.1
15	Oklahoma	127.0
16	South Dakota	126.6
17	California	126.5
18	Illinois	126.2
19	Delaware	126.1
20	New York	126.0
21	Iowa	125.9
22	Montana	124.5
23	Hawaii	124.2
23	Missouri	124.2
25	Georgia	123.9
26	Ohio	123.5
27	North Dakota	123.4
28	Idaho	123.1
29	Kentucky	122.1
30	Louisiana	122.0
31	Virginia	121.6
31	Wyoming	121.6
33	Nevada	121.5
34	Indiana	121.0
34	South Carolina	121.0
36	Florida	119.7
37	Texas	117.2
38	Arkansas	117.1
39	Utah	115.7
40	West Virginia	115.5
41	Arizona	114.4
42	Alabama	113.9
42	Tennessee	113.9
44	New Mexico	112.2
45	Mississippi	105.4
NA	Kansas**	NA
NA	Maryland**	NA
NA	Minnesota**	NA
NA	North Carolina**	NA
NA	Vermont**	NA

District of Columbia   134.8

Source: American Cancer Society
    "Cancer Facts & Figures 2008" (Copyright 2008, American Cancer Society, http://www.cancer.org/docroot/stt/stt_0.asp)
*For 2000 to 2004. Age-adjusted to the 2000 U.S. standard population.
**Not available.

Percent of Women 40 and Older Who Have Had a Mammogram in the Past Two Years: 2006
National Median = 76.5% of Women*

<table>
<tr><td colspan="3">ALPHA ORDER</td><td colspan="3">RANK ORDER</td></tr>
<tr><td>RANK</td><td>STATE</td><td>PERCENT</td><td>RANK</td><td>STATE</td><td>PERCENT</td></tr>
<tr><td>22</td><td>Alabama</td><td>77.2</td><td>1</td><td>Massachusetts</td><td>84.8</td></tr>
<tr><td>36</td><td>Alaska</td><td>73.4</td><td>2</td><td>Rhode Island</td><td>84.5</td></tr>
<tr><td>20</td><td>Arizona</td><td>77.4</td><td>3</td><td>Delaware</td><td>83.7</td></tr>
<tr><td>44</td><td>Arkansas</td><td>70.0</td><td>4</td><td>Connecticut</td><td>82.0</td></tr>
<tr><td>15</td><td>California</td><td>78.5</td><td>5</td><td>Maine</td><td>81.8</td></tr>
<tr><td>39</td><td>Colorado</td><td>72.0</td><td>6</td><td>Minnesota</td><td>81.4</td></tr>
<tr><td>4</td><td>Connecticut</td><td>82.0</td><td>7</td><td>Michigan</td><td>79.9</td></tr>
<tr><td>3</td><td>Delaware</td><td>83.7</td><td>8</td><td>Maryland</td><td>79.8</td></tr>
<tr><td>16</td><td>Florida</td><td>78.0</td><td>9</td><td>Tennessee</td><td>79.4</td></tr>
<tr><td>14</td><td>Georgia</td><td>78.6</td><td>10</td><td>New York</td><td>79.3</td></tr>
<tr><td>21</td><td>Hawaii</td><td>77.3</td><td>10</td><td>Vermont</td><td>79.3</td></tr>
<tr><td>50</td><td>Idaho</td><td>67.3</td><td>12</td><td>North Carolina</td><td>79.2</td></tr>
<tr><td>31</td><td>Illinois</td><td>74.6</td><td>13</td><td>New Hampshire</td><td>79.0</td></tr>
<tr><td>40</td><td>Indiana</td><td>71.6</td><td>14</td><td>Georgia</td><td>78.6</td></tr>
<tr><td>19</td><td>Iowa</td><td>77.5</td><td>15</td><td>California</td><td>78.5</td></tr>
<tr><td>31</td><td>Kansas</td><td>74.6</td><td>16</td><td>Florida</td><td>78.0</td></tr>
<tr><td>30</td><td>Kentucky</td><td>75.1</td><td>17</td><td>New Jersey</td><td>77.9</td></tr>
<tr><td>28</td><td>Louisiana</td><td>75.8</td><td>17</td><td>Wisconsin</td><td>77.9</td></tr>
<tr><td>5</td><td>Maine</td><td>81.8</td><td>19</td><td>Iowa</td><td>77.5</td></tr>
<tr><td>8</td><td>Maryland</td><td>79.8</td><td>20</td><td>Arizona</td><td>77.4</td></tr>
<tr><td>1</td><td>Massachusetts</td><td>84.8</td><td>21</td><td>Hawaii</td><td>77.3</td></tr>
<tr><td>7</td><td>Michigan</td><td>79.9</td><td>22</td><td>Alabama</td><td>77.2</td></tr>
<tr><td>6</td><td>Minnesota</td><td>81.4</td><td>22</td><td>North Dakota</td><td>77.2</td></tr>
<tr><td>48</td><td>Mississippi</td><td>67.8</td><td>24</td><td>Ohio</td><td>76.7</td></tr>
<tr><td>41</td><td>Missouri</td><td>71.1</td><td>25</td><td>Oregon</td><td>76.5</td></tr>
<tr><td>38</td><td>Montana</td><td>72.2</td><td>25</td><td>Virginia</td><td>76.5</td></tr>
<tr><td>37</td><td>Nebraska</td><td>73.3</td><td>27</td><td>Washington</td><td>76.0</td></tr>
<tr><td>43</td><td>Nevada</td><td>70.7</td><td>28</td><td>Louisiana</td><td>75.8</td></tr>
<tr><td>13</td><td>New Hampshire</td><td>79.0</td><td>29</td><td>Pennsylvania</td><td>75.7</td></tr>
<tr><td>17</td><td>New Jersey</td><td>77.9</td><td>30</td><td>Kentucky</td><td>75.1</td></tr>
<tr><td>44</td><td>New Mexico</td><td>70.0</td><td>31</td><td>Illinois</td><td>74.6</td></tr>
<tr><td>10</td><td>New York</td><td>79.3</td><td>31</td><td>Kansas</td><td>74.6</td></tr>
<tr><td>12</td><td>North Carolina</td><td>79.2</td><td>33</td><td>South Carolina</td><td>74.5</td></tr>
<tr><td>22</td><td>North Dakota</td><td>77.2</td><td>33</td><td>West Virginia</td><td>74.5</td></tr>
<tr><td>24</td><td>Ohio</td><td>76.7</td><td>35</td><td>South Dakota</td><td>74.2</td></tr>
<tr><td>49</td><td>Oklahoma</td><td>67.7</td><td>36</td><td>Alaska</td><td>73.4</td></tr>
<tr><td>25</td><td>Oregon</td><td>76.5</td><td>37</td><td>Nebraska</td><td>73.3</td></tr>
<tr><td>29</td><td>Pennsylvania</td><td>75.7</td><td>38</td><td>Montana</td><td>72.2</td></tr>
<tr><td>2</td><td>Rhode Island</td><td>84.5</td><td>39</td><td>Colorado</td><td>72.0</td></tr>
<tr><td>33</td><td>South Carolina</td><td>74.5</td><td>40</td><td>Indiana</td><td>71.6</td></tr>
<tr><td>35</td><td>South Dakota</td><td>74.2</td><td>41</td><td>Missouri</td><td>71.1</td></tr>
<tr><td>9</td><td>Tennessee</td><td>79.4</td><td>42</td><td>Texas</td><td>71.0</td></tr>
<tr><td>42</td><td>Texas</td><td>71.0</td><td>43</td><td>Nevada</td><td>70.7</td></tr>
<tr><td>47</td><td>Utah</td><td>68.2</td><td>44</td><td>Arkansas</td><td>70.0</td></tr>
<tr><td>10</td><td>Vermont</td><td>79.3</td><td>44</td><td>New Mexico</td><td>70.0</td></tr>
<tr><td>25</td><td>Virginia</td><td>76.5</td><td>46</td><td>Wyoming</td><td>68.6</td></tr>
<tr><td>27</td><td>Washington</td><td>76.0</td><td>47</td><td>Utah</td><td>68.2</td></tr>
<tr><td>33</td><td>West Virginia</td><td>74.5</td><td>48</td><td>Mississippi</td><td>67.8</td></tr>
<tr><td>17</td><td>Wisconsin</td><td>77.9</td><td>49</td><td>Oklahoma</td><td>67.7</td></tr>
<tr><td>46</td><td>Wyoming</td><td>68.6</td><td>50</td><td>Idaho</td><td>67.3</td></tr>
<tr><td></td><td></td><td></td><td></td><td>District of Columbia</td><td>81.8</td></tr>
</table>

Source: U.S. Department of Health and Human Services, Centers for Disease Control and Prevention
"2006 Behavioral Risk Factor Surveillance Summary Prevalence Data" (http://apps.nccd.cdc.gov/brfss/)
*Percent of women 40 years and older.

Estimated New Colon and Rectum Cancer Cases in 2008

National Estimated Total = 148,810 New Cases*

ALPHA ORDER

RANK	STATE	CASES	% of USA
24	Alabama	2,390	1.6%
50	Alaska	250	0.2%
20	Arizona	2,620	1.8%
31	Arkansas	1,690	1.1%
1	California	14,500	9.7%
28	Colorado	1,840	1.2%
26	Connecticut	2,090	1.4%
45	Delaware	480	0.3%
2	Florida	10,920	7.3%
11	Georgia	3,760	2.5%
41	Hawaii	700	0.5%
43	Idaho	620	0.4%
6	Illinois	6,570	4.4%
14	Indiana	3,350	2.3%
29	Iowa	1,810	1.2%
33	Kansas	1,270	0.9%
21	Kentucky	2,560	1.7%
22	Louisiana	2,490	1.7%
37	Maine	860	0.6%
18	Maryland	2,920	2.0%
13	Massachusetts	3,560	2.4%
8	Michigan	5,150	3.5%
23	Minnesota	2,430	1.6%
32	Mississippi	1,470	1.0%
16	Missouri	3,090	2.1%
44	Montana	530	0.4%
36	Nebraska	910	0.6%
35	Nevada	1,160	0.8%
39	New Hampshire	760	0.5%
9	New Jersey	4,600	3.1%
38	New Mexico	830	0.6%
3	New York	10,060	6.8%
10	North Carolina	4,380	2.9%
48	North Dakota	350	0.2%
7	Ohio	6,270	4.2%
27	Oklahoma	1,860	1.2%
30	Oregon	1,740	1.2%
5	Pennsylvania	7,560	5.1%
42	Rhode Island	650	0.4%
25	South Carolina	2,170	1.5%
46	South Dakota	430	0.3%
15	Tennessee	3,290	2.2%
4	Texas	9,570	6.4%
40	Utah	750	0.5%
47	Vermont	360	0.2%
12	Virginia	3,690	2.5%
19	Washington	2,850	1.9%
34	West Virginia	1,200	0.8%
17	Wisconsin	2,930	2.0%
49	Wyoming	260	0.2%

RANK ORDER

RANK	STATE	CASES	% of USA
1	California	14,500	9.7%
2	Florida	10,920	7.3%
3	New York	10,060	6.8%
4	Texas	9,570	6.4%
5	Pennsylvania	7,560	5.1%
6	Illinois	6,570	4.4%
7	Ohio	6,270	4.2%
8	Michigan	5,150	3.5%
9	New Jersey	4,600	3.1%
10	North Carolina	4,380	2.9%
11	Georgia	3,760	2.5%
12	Virginia	3,690	2.5%
13	Massachusetts	3,560	2.4%
14	Indiana	3,350	2.3%
15	Tennessee	3,290	2.2%
16	Missouri	3,090	2.1%
17	Wisconsin	2,930	2.0%
18	Maryland	2,920	2.0%
19	Washington	2,850	1.9%
20	Arizona	2,620	1.8%
21	Kentucky	2,560	1.7%
22	Louisiana	2,490	1.7%
23	Minnesota	2,430	1.6%
24	Alabama	2,390	1.6%
25	South Carolina	2,170	1.5%
26	Connecticut	2,090	1.4%
27	Oklahoma	1,860	1.2%
28	Colorado	1,840	1.2%
29	Iowa	1,810	1.2%
30	Oregon	1,740	1.2%
31	Arkansas	1,690	1.1%
32	Mississippi	1,470	1.0%
33	Kansas	1,270	0.9%
34	West Virginia	1,200	0.8%
35	Nevada	1,160	0.8%
36	Nebraska	910	0.6%
37	Maine	860	0.6%
38	New Mexico	830	0.6%
39	New Hampshire	760	0.5%
40	Utah	750	0.5%
41	Hawaii	700	0.5%
42	Rhode Island	650	0.4%
43	Idaho	620	0.4%
44	Montana	530	0.4%
45	Delaware	480	0.3%
46	South Dakota	430	0.3%
47	Vermont	360	0.2%
48	North Dakota	350	0.2%
49	Wyoming	260	0.2%
50	Alaska	250	0.2%
	District of Columbia	270	0.2%

Source: American Cancer Society
"Cancer Facts & Figures 2008" (Copyright 2008, American Cancer Society, http://www.cancer.org/docroot/stt/stt_0.asp)
*These estimates are offered as a rough guide and should be interpreted with caution. They are calculated according to the distribution of estimated 2008 cancer deaths by state.

Estimated Rate of New Colon and Rectum Cancer Cases in 2008

National Estimated Rate = 48.9 New Cases per 100,000 Population*

ALPHA ORDER

RANK	STATE	RATE
28	Alabama	51.3
49	Alaska	36.4
44	Arizona	40.3
9	Arkansas	59.2
45	California	39.4
48	Colorado	37.3
7	Connecticut	59.7
13	Delaware	55.0
8	Florida	59.6
47	Georgia	38.8
18	Hawaii	54.3
43	Idaho	40.7
31	Illinois	50.9
22	Indiana	52.5
5	Iowa	60.3
39	Kansas	45.3
6	Kentucky	60.0
12	Louisiana	56.5
2	Maine	65.3
25	Maryland	51.8
14	Massachusetts	54.8
27	Michigan	51.5
37	Minnesota	46.5
32	Mississippi	50.0
23	Missouri	52.3
14	Montana	54.8
30	Nebraska	51.0
40	Nevada	44.6
11	New Hampshire	57.8
20	New Jersey	53.0
42	New Mexico	41.8
26	New York	51.6
35	North Carolina	47.5
16	North Dakota	54.6
16	Ohio	54.6
29	Oklahoma	51.1
38	Oregon	45.9
4	Pennsylvania	60.7
3	Rhode Island	61.9
34	South Carolina	48.4
19	South Dakota	53.5
21	Tennessee	52.9
46	Texas	39.3
50	Utah	27.4
10	Vermont	57.9
35	Virginia	47.5
41	Washington	43.5
1	West Virginia	66.1
24	Wisconsin	52.1
33	Wyoming	48.8

RANK ORDER

RANK	STATE	RATE
1	West Virginia	66.1
2	Maine	65.3
3	Rhode Island	61.9
4	Pennsylvania	60.7
5	Iowa	60.3
6	Kentucky	60.0
7	Connecticut	59.7
8	Florida	59.6
9	Arkansas	59.2
10	Vermont	57.9
11	New Hampshire	57.8
12	Louisiana	56.5
13	Delaware	55.0
14	Massachusetts	54.8
14	Montana	54.8
16	North Dakota	54.6
16	Ohio	54.6
18	Hawaii	54.3
19	South Dakota	53.5
20	New Jersey	53.0
21	Tennessee	52.9
22	Indiana	52.5
23	Missouri	52.3
24	Wisconsin	52.1
25	Maryland	51.8
26	New York	51.6
27	Michigan	51.5
28	Alabama	51.3
29	Oklahoma	51.1
30	Nebraska	51.0
31	Illinois	50.9
32	Mississippi	50.0
33	Wyoming	48.8
34	South Carolina	48.4
35	North Carolina	47.5
35	Virginia	47.5
37	Minnesota	46.5
38	Oregon	45.9
39	Kansas	45.3
40	Nevada	44.6
41	Washington	43.5
42	New Mexico	41.8
43	Idaho	40.7
44	Arizona	40.3
45	California	39.4
46	Texas	39.3
47	Georgia	38.8
48	Colorado	37.3
49	Alaska	36.4
50	Utah	27.4

District of Columbia	45.6

Source: CQ Press using data from American Cancer Society
"Cancer Facts & Figures 2008" (Copyright 2008, American Cancer Society, http://www.cancer.org/docroot/stt/stt_0.asp)
*These estimates are offered as a rough guide and should be interpreted with caution. They are calculated according to the distribution of estimated 2008 cancer deaths by state. Rates calculated using 2008 Census resident population estimates.

Percent of Adults Who Have Ever Had a Sigmoidoscopy or Colonoscopy Exam: 2006
National Median = 57.1% of Adults*

ALPHA ORDER

RANK	STATE	PERCENT
42	Alabama	53.3
37	Alaska	55.2
28	Arizona	56.6
45	Arkansas	52.6
25	California	57.1
24	Colorado	57.2
2	Connecticut	68.7
3	Delaware	68.4
19	Florida	58.9
27	Georgia	57.0
40	Hawaii	54.1
39	Idaho	54.2
36	Illinois	55.6
31	Indiana	56.4
35	Iowa	55.8
29	Kansas	56.5
21	Kentucky	58.6
50	Louisiana	49.8
10	Maine	64.2
5	Maryland	66.7
6	Massachusetts	66.3
7	Michigan	66.1
4	Minnesota	68.2
49	Mississippi	50.4
23	Missouri	57.8
43	Montana	52.9
48	Nebraska	51.4
37	Nevada	55.2
14	New Hampshire	63.6
22	New Jersey	58.3
43	New Mexico	52.9
12	New York	63.9
16	North Carolina	61.8
29	North Dakota	56.5
25	Ohio	57.1
47	Oklahoma	51.7
17	Oregon	60.7
20	Pennsylvania	58.8
1	Rhode Island	69.2
18	South Carolina	59.5
34	South Dakota	55.9
33	Tennessee	56.2
32	Texas	56.3
15	Utah	62.7
9	Vermont	64.8
8	Virginia	65.3
13	Washington	63.7
41	West Virginia	53.4
11	Wisconsin	64.0
45	Wyoming	52.6

RANK ORDER

RANK	STATE	PERCENT
1	Rhode Island	69.2
2	Connecticut	68.7
3	Delaware	68.4
4	Minnesota	68.2
5	Maryland	66.7
6	Massachusetts	66.3
7	Michigan	66.1
8	Virginia	65.3
9	Vermont	64.8
10	Maine	64.2
11	Wisconsin	64.0
12	New York	63.9
13	Washington	63.7
14	New Hampshire	63.6
15	Utah	62.7
16	North Carolina	61.8
17	Oregon	60.7
18	South Carolina	59.5
19	Florida	58.9
20	Pennsylvania	58.8
21	Kentucky	58.6
22	New Jersey	58.3
23	Missouri	57.8
24	Colorado	57.2
25	California	57.1
25	Ohio	57.1
27	Georgia	57.0
28	Arizona	56.6
29	Kansas	56.5
29	North Dakota	56.5
31	Indiana	56.4
32	Texas	56.3
33	Tennessee	56.2
34	South Dakota	55.9
35	Iowa	55.8
36	Illinois	55.6
37	Alaska	55.2
37	Nevada	55.2
39	Idaho	54.2
40	Hawaii	54.1
41	West Virginia	53.4
42	Alabama	53.3
43	Montana	52.9
43	New Mexico	52.9
45	Arkansas	52.6
45	Wyoming	52.6
47	Oklahoma	51.7
48	Nebraska	51.4
49	Mississippi	50.4
50	Louisiana	49.8
	District of Columbia	64.7

Source: U.S. Department of Health and Human Services, Centers for Disease Control and Prevention
    "2006 Behavioral Risk Factor Surveillance Summary Prevalence Data" (http://apps.nccd.cdc.gov/brfss/)
*Persons 50 and older.

Estimated New Leukemia Cases in 2008

National Estimated Total = 44,270 New Cases*

ALPHA ORDER

RANK	STATE	CASES	% of USA
25	Alabama	630	1.4%
50	Alaska	70	0.2%
20	Arizona	760	1.7%
30	Arkansas	520	1.2%
1	California	4,530	10.2%
21	Colorado	720	1.6%
28	Connecticut	570	1.3%
46	Delaware	110	0.2%
3	Florida	3,190	7.2%
11	Georgia	1,030	2.3%
42	Hawaii	170	0.4%
40	Idaho	240	0.5%
6	Illinois	1,890	4.3%
15	Indiana	910	2.1%
25	Iowa	630	1.4%
32	Kansas	410	0.9%
22	Kentucky	700	1.6%
23	Louisiana	690	1.6%
39	Maine	260	0.6%
24	Maryland	640	1.4%
12	Massachusetts	1,000	2.3%
8	Michigan	1,630	3.7%
15	Minnesota	910	2.1%
33	Mississippi	380	0.9%
18	Missouri	870	2.0%
44	Montana	160	0.4%
37	Nebraska	290	0.7%
34	Nevada	370	0.8%
41	New Hampshire	200	0.5%
9	New Jersey	1,440	3.3%
35	New Mexico	320	0.7%
4	New York	3,140	7.1%
10	North Carolina	1,110	2.5%
47	North Dakota	100	0.2%
7	Ohio	1,660	3.7%
28	Oklahoma	570	1.3%
31	Oregon	490	1.1%
5	Pennsylvania	2,220	5.0%
42	Rhode Island	170	0.4%
27	South Carolina	590	1.3%
45	South Dakota	130	0.3%
17	Tennessee	880	2.0%
2	Texas	3,330	7.5%
35	Utah	320	0.7%
47	Vermont	100	0.2%
19	Virginia	850	1.9%
14	Washington	970	2.2%
37	West Virginia	290	0.7%
13	Wisconsin	980	2.2%
49	Wyoming	80	0.2%

RANK ORDER

RANK	STATE	CASES	% of USA
1	California	4,530	10.2%
2	Texas	3,330	7.5%
3	Florida	3,190	7.2%
4	New York	3,140	7.1%
5	Pennsylvania	2,220	5.0%
6	Illinois	1,890	4.3%
7	Ohio	1,660	3.7%
8	Michigan	1,630	3.7%
9	New Jersey	1,440	3.3%
10	North Carolina	1,110	2.5%
11	Georgia	1,030	2.3%
12	Massachusetts	1,000	2.3%
13	Wisconsin	980	2.2%
14	Washington	970	2.2%
15	Indiana	910	2.1%
15	Minnesota	910	2.1%
17	Tennessee	880	2.0%
18	Missouri	870	2.0%
19	Virginia	850	1.9%
20	Arizona	760	1.7%
21	Colorado	720	1.6%
22	Kentucky	700	1.6%
23	Louisiana	690	1.6%
24	Maryland	640	1.4%
25	Alabama	630	1.4%
25	Iowa	630	1.4%
27	South Carolina	590	1.3%
28	Connecticut	570	1.3%
28	Oklahoma	570	1.3%
30	Arkansas	520	1.2%
31	Oregon	490	1.1%
32	Kansas	410	0.9%
33	Mississippi	380	0.9%
34	Nevada	370	0.8%
35	New Mexico	320	0.7%
35	Utah	320	0.7%
37	Nebraska	290	0.7%
37	West Virginia	290	0.7%
39	Maine	260	0.6%
40	Idaho	240	0.5%
41	New Hampshire	200	0.5%
42	Hawaii	170	0.4%
42	Rhode Island	170	0.4%
44	Montana	160	0.4%
45	South Dakota	130	0.3%
46	Delaware	110	0.2%
47	North Dakota	100	0.2%
47	Vermont	100	0.2%
49	Wyoming	80	0.2%
50	Alaska	70	0.2%
	District of Columbia	50	0.1%

Source: American Cancer Society
"Cancer Facts & Figures 2008" (Copyright 2008, American Cancer Society, http://www.cancer.org/docroot/stt/stt_0.asp)
*These estimates are offered as a rough guide and should be interpreted with caution. They are calculated according to the distribution of estimated 2008 cancer deaths by state.

Estimated Rate of New Leukemia Cases in 2008

National Estimated Rate = 14.6 New Cases per 100,000 Population*

ALPHA ORDER

RANK	STATE	RATE
37	Alabama	13.5
50	Alaska	10.2
45	Arizona	11.7
3	Arkansas	18.2
43	California	12.3
29	Colorado	14.6
11	Connecticut	16.3
42	Delaware	12.6
5	Florida	17.4
49	Georgia	10.6
38	Hawaii	13.2
20	Idaho	15.7
29	Illinois	14.6
33	Indiana	14.3
1	Iowa	21.0
29	Kansas	14.6
10	Kentucky	16.4
21	Louisiana	15.6
2	Maine	19.7
47	Maryland	11.4
24	Massachusetts	15.4
11	Michigan	16.3
5	Minnesota	17.4
40	Mississippi	12.9
28	Missouri	14.7
9	Montana	16.5
11	Nebraska	16.3
34	Nevada	14.2
25	New Hampshire	15.2
8	New Jersey	16.6
16	New Mexico	16.1
16	New York	16.1
44	North Carolina	12.0
21	North Dakota	15.6
32	Ohio	14.5
21	Oklahoma	15.6
40	Oregon	12.9
4	Pennsylvania	17.8
14	Rhode Island	16.2
38	South Carolina	13.2
14	South Dakota	16.2
34	Tennessee	14.2
36	Texas	13.7
45	Utah	11.7
16	Vermont	16.1
48	Virginia	10.9
27	Washington	14.8
19	West Virginia	16.0
5	Wisconsin	17.4
26	Wyoming	15.0

RANK ORDER

RANK	STATE	RATE
1	Iowa	21.0
2	Maine	19.7
3	Arkansas	18.2
4	Pennsylvania	17.8
5	Florida	17.4
5	Minnesota	17.4
5	Wisconsin	17.4
8	New Jersey	16.6
9	Montana	16.5
10	Kentucky	16.4
11	Connecticut	16.3
11	Michigan	16.3
11	Nebraska	16.3
14	Rhode Island	16.2
14	South Dakota	16.2
16	New Mexico	16.1
16	New York	16.1
16	Vermont	16.1
19	West Virginia	16.0
20	Idaho	15.7
21	Louisiana	15.6
21	North Dakota	15.6
21	Oklahoma	15.6
24	Massachusetts	15.4
25	New Hampshire	15.2
26	Wyoming	15.0
27	Washington	14.8
28	Missouri	14.7
29	Colorado	14.6
29	Illinois	14.6
29	Kansas	14.6
32	Ohio	14.5
33	Indiana	14.3
34	Nevada	14.2
34	Tennessee	14.2
36	Texas	13.7
37	Alabama	13.5
38	Hawaii	13.2
38	South Carolina	13.2
40	Mississippi	12.9
40	Oregon	12.9
42	Delaware	12.6
43	California	12.3
44	North Carolina	12.0
45	Arizona	11.7
45	Utah	11.7
47	Maryland	11.4
48	Virginia	10.9
49	Georgia	10.6
50	Alaska	10.2
	District of Columbia	8.4

Source: CQ Press using data from American Cancer Society

"Cancer Facts & Figures 2008" (Copyright 2008, American Cancer Society, http://www.cancer.org/docroot/stt/stt_0.asp)
*These estimates are offered as a rough guide and should be interpreted with caution. They are calculated according to the distribution of estimated 2008 cancer deaths by state. Rates calculated using 2008 Census resident population estimates.

Estimated New Lung Cancer Cases in 2008

National Estimated Total = 215,020 New Cases*

ALPHA ORDER

RANK	STATE	CASES	% of USA
21	Alabama	3,900	1.8%
49	Alaska	340	0.2%
22	Arizona	3,850	1.8%
28	Arkansas	2,640	1.2%
1	California	18,060	8.4%
32	Colorado	2,210	1.0%
27	Connecticut	2,680	1.2%
42	Delaware	760	0.4%
2	Florida	17,360	8.1%
11	Georgia	5,980	2.8%
43	Hawaii	710	0.3%
41	Idaho	800	0.4%
7	Illinois	9,340	4.3%
14	Indiana	5,140	2.4%
29	Iowa	2,590	1.2%
34	Kansas	1,910	0.9%
17	Kentucky	4,580	2.1%
23	Louisiana	3,730	1.7%
36	Maine	1,330	0.6%
19	Maryland	4,100	1.9%
16	Massachusetts	4,930	2.3%
8	Michigan	8,020	3.7%
25	Minnesota	3,330	1.5%
31	Mississippi	2,290	1.1%
12	Missouri	5,560	2.6%
43	Montana	710	0.3%
37	Nebraska	1,240	0.6%
35	Nevada	1,850	0.9%
38	New Hampshire	1,040	0.5%
10	New Jersey	6,210	2.9%
39	New Mexico	940	0.4%
4	New York	13,500	6.3%
9	North Carolina	6,510	3.0%
48	North Dakota	390	0.2%
6	Ohio	9,510	4.4%
26	Oklahoma	3,150	1.5%
30	Oregon	2,580	1.2%
5	Pennsylvania	10,320	4.8%
40	Rhode Island	880	0.4%
24	South Carolina	3,550	1.7%
46	South Dakota	500	0.2%
15	Tennessee	5,070	2.4%
3	Texas	13,840	6.4%
45	Utah	580	0.3%
47	Vermont	460	0.2%
13	Virginia	5,340	2.5%
18	Washington	4,110	1.9%
33	West Virginia	2,000	0.9%
20	Wisconsin	3,920	1.8%
50	Wyoming	320	0.1%

RANK ORDER

RANK	STATE	CASES	% of USA
1	California	18,060	8.4%
2	Florida	17,360	8.1%
3	Texas	13,840	6.4%
4	New York	13,500	6.3%
5	Pennsylvania	10,320	4.8%
6	Ohio	9,510	4.4%
7	Illinois	9,340	4.3%
8	Michigan	8,020	3.7%
9	North Carolina	6,510	3.0%
10	New Jersey	6,210	2.9%
11	Georgia	5,980	2.8%
12	Missouri	5,560	2.6%
13	Virginia	5,340	2.5%
14	Indiana	5,140	2.4%
15	Tennessee	5,070	2.4%
16	Massachusetts	4,930	2.3%
17	Kentucky	4,580	2.1%
18	Washington	4,110	1.9%
19	Maryland	4,100	1.9%
20	Wisconsin	3,920	1.8%
21	Alabama	3,900	1.8%
22	Arizona	3,850	1.8%
23	Louisiana	3,730	1.7%
24	South Carolina	3,550	1.7%
25	Minnesota	3,330	1.5%
26	Oklahoma	3,150	1.5%
27	Connecticut	2,680	1.2%
28	Arkansas	2,640	1.2%
29	Iowa	2,590	1.2%
30	Oregon	2,580	1.2%
31	Mississippi	2,290	1.1%
32	Colorado	2,210	1.0%
33	West Virginia	2,000	0.9%
34	Kansas	1,910	0.9%
35	Nevada	1,850	0.9%
36	Maine	1,330	0.6%
37	Nebraska	1,240	0.6%
38	New Hampshire	1,040	0.5%
39	New Mexico	940	0.4%
40	Rhode Island	880	0.4%
41	Idaho	800	0.4%
42	Delaware	760	0.4%
43	Hawaii	710	0.3%
43	Montana	710	0.3%
45	Utah	580	0.3%
46	South Dakota	500	0.2%
47	Vermont	460	0.2%
48	North Dakota	390	0.2%
49	Alaska	340	0.2%
50	Wyoming	320	0.1%
	District of Columbia	350	0.2%

Source: American Cancer Society
"Cancer Facts & Figures 2008" (Copyright 2008, American Cancer Society, http://www.cancer.org/docroot/stt/stt_0.asp)
*These estimates are offered as a rough guide and should be interpreted with caution. They are calculated according to the distribution of estimated 2008 cancer deaths by state.

Estimated Rate of New Lung Cancer Cases in 2008

National Estimated Rate = 70.7 New Cases per 100,000 Population*

ALPHA ORDER

RANK	STATE	RATE
11	Alabama	83.7
46	Alaska	49.5
42	Arizona	59.2
6	Arkansas	92.5
47	California	49.1
49	Colorado	44.7
21	Connecticut	76.5
7	Delaware	87.0
4	Florida	94.7
39	Georgia	61.7
44	Hawaii	55.1
45	Idaho	52.5
26	Illinois	72.4
16	Indiana	80.6
9	Iowa	86.3
34	Kansas	68.2
2	Kentucky	107.3
10	Louisiana	84.6
3	Maine	101.0
25	Maryland	72.8
22	Massachusetts	75.9
17	Michigan	80.2
36	Minnesota	63.8
20	Mississippi	77.9
5	Missouri	94.1
24	Montana	73.4
31	Nebraska	69.5
28	Nevada	71.1
19	New Hampshire	79.0
27	New Jersey	71.5
48	New Mexico	47.4
32	New York	69.3
29	North Carolina	70.6
40	North Dakota	60.8
14	Ohio	82.8
8	Oklahoma	86.5
35	Oregon	68.1
13	Pennsylvania	82.9
11	Rhode Island	83.7
18	South Carolina	79.2
38	South Dakota	62.2
15	Tennessee	81.6
43	Texas	56.9
50	Utah	21.2
23	Vermont	74.0
33	Virginia	68.7
37	Washington	62.8
1	West Virginia	110.2
30	Wisconsin	69.7
41	Wyoming	60.1

RANK ORDER

RANK	STATE	RATE
1	West Virginia	110.2
2	Kentucky	107.3
3	Maine	101.0
4	Florida	94.7
5	Missouri	94.1
6	Arkansas	92.5
7	Delaware	87.0
8	Oklahoma	86.5
9	Iowa	86.3
10	Louisiana	84.6
11	Alabama	83.7
11	Rhode Island	83.7
13	Pennsylvania	82.9
14	Ohio	82.8
15	Tennessee	81.6
16	Indiana	80.6
17	Michigan	80.2
18	South Carolina	79.2
19	New Hampshire	79.0
20	Mississippi	77.9
21	Connecticut	76.5
22	Massachusetts	75.9
23	Vermont	74.0
24	Montana	73.4
25	Maryland	72.8
26	Illinois	72.4
27	New Jersey	71.5
28	Nevada	71.1
29	North Carolina	70.6
30	Wisconsin	69.7
31	Nebraska	69.5
32	New York	69.3
33	Virginia	68.7
34	Kansas	68.2
35	Oregon	68.1
36	Minnesota	63.8
37	Washington	62.8
38	South Dakota	62.2
39	Georgia	61.7
40	North Dakota	60.8
41	Wyoming	60.1
42	Arizona	59.2
43	Texas	56.9
44	Hawaii	55.1
45	Idaho	52.5
46	Alaska	49.5
47	California	49.1
48	New Mexico	47.4
49	Colorado	44.7
50	Utah	21.2
	District of Columbia	59.1

Source: CQ Press using data from American Cancer Society
    "Cancer Facts & Figures 2008" (Copyright 2008, American Cancer Society, http://www.cancer.org/docroot/stt/stt_0.asp)
*These estimates are offered as a rough guide and should be interpreted with caution. They are calculated according to the distribution of estimated 2008 cancer deaths by state. Rates calculated using 2008 Census resident population estimates.

Estimated New Non-Hodgkin's Lymphoma Cases in 2008

National Estimated Total = 66,120 New Cases*

ALPHA ORDER

RANK	STATE	CASES	% of USA
23	Alabama	970	1.5%
49	Alaska	120	0.2%
19	Arizona	1,180	1.8%
31	Arkansas	650	1.0%
1	California	7,560	11.4%
26	Colorado	920	1.4%
27	Connecticut	910	1.4%
45	Delaware	190	0.3%
2	Florida	4,750	7.2%
13	Georgia	1,550	2.3%
42	Hawaii	250	0.4%
39	Idaho	340	0.5%
6	Illinois	2,870	4.3%
16	Indiana	1,340	2.0%
30	Iowa	730	1.1%
32	Kansas	600	0.9%
23	Kentucky	970	1.5%
22	Louisiana	1,020	1.5%
39	Maine	340	0.5%
21	Maryland	1,080	1.6%
12	Massachusetts	1,580	2.4%
8	Michigan	2,360	3.6%
20	Minnesota	1,110	1.7%
33	Mississippi	540	0.8%
17	Missouri	1,330	2.0%
44	Montana	230	0.3%
37	Nebraska	390	0.6%
34	Nevada	480	0.7%
41	New Hampshire	320	0.5%
9	New Jersey	2,210	3.3%
38	New Mexico	350	0.5%
4	New York	4,460	6.7%
10	North Carolina	1,610	2.4%
48	North Dakota	140	0.2%
7	Ohio	2,790	4.2%
28	Oklahoma	840	1.3%
25	Oregon	930	1.4%
5	Pennsylvania	3,300	5.0%
42	Rhode Island	250	0.4%
29	South Carolina	780	1.2%
46	South Dakota	170	0.3%
18	Tennessee	1,320	2.0%
3	Texas	4,650	7.0%
35	Utah	420	0.6%
47	Vermont	160	0.2%
14	Virginia	1,410	2.1%
11	Washington	1,590	2.4%
36	West Virginia	410	0.6%
15	Wisconsin	1,390	2.1%
50	Wyoming	110	0.2%

RANK ORDER

RANK	STATE	CASES	% of USA
1	California	7,560	11.4%
2	Florida	4,750	7.2%
3	Texas	4,650	7.0%
4	New York	4,460	6.7%
5	Pennsylvania	3,300	5.0%
6	Illinois	2,870	4.3%
7	Ohio	2,790	4.2%
8	Michigan	2,360	3.6%
9	New Jersey	2,210	3.3%
10	North Carolina	1,610	2.4%
11	Washington	1,590	2.4%
12	Massachusetts	1,580	2.4%
13	Georgia	1,550	2.3%
14	Virginia	1,410	2.1%
15	Wisconsin	1,390	2.1%
16	Indiana	1,340	2.0%
17	Missouri	1,330	2.0%
18	Tennessee	1,320	2.0%
19	Arizona	1,180	1.8%
20	Minnesota	1,110	1.7%
21	Maryland	1,080	1.6%
22	Louisiana	1,020	1.5%
23	Alabama	970	1.5%
23	Kentucky	970	1.5%
25	Oregon	930	1.4%
26	Colorado	920	1.4%
27	Connecticut	910	1.4%
28	Oklahoma	840	1.3%
29	South Carolina	780	1.2%
30	Iowa	730	1.1%
31	Arkansas	650	1.0%
32	Kansas	600	0.9%
33	Mississippi	540	0.8%
34	Nevada	480	0.7%
35	Utah	420	0.6%
36	West Virginia	410	0.6%
37	Nebraska	390	0.6%
38	New Mexico	350	0.5%
39	Idaho	340	0.5%
39	Maine	340	0.5%
41	New Hampshire	320	0.5%
42	Hawaii	250	0.4%
42	Rhode Island	250	0.4%
44	Montana	230	0.3%
45	Delaware	190	0.3%
46	South Dakota	170	0.3%
47	Vermont	160	0.2%
48	North Dakota	140	0.2%
49	Alaska	120	0.2%
50	Wyoming	110	0.2%
	District of Columbia	100	0.2%

Source: American Cancer Society
"Cancer Facts & Figures 2008" (Copyright 2008, American Cancer Society, http://www.cancer.org/docroot/stt/stt_0.asp)
*These estimates are offered as a rough guide and should be interpreted with caution. They are calculated according to the distribution of estimated 2008 cancer deaths by state.

Estimated Rate of New Non-Hodgkin's Lymphoma Cases in 2008

National Estimated Rate = 21.7 New Cases per 100,000 Population*

ALPHA ORDER

RANK	STATE	RATE
34	Alabama	20.8
46	Alaska	17.5
43	Arizona	18.2
20	Arkansas	22.8
36	California	20.6
40	Colorado	18.6
2	Connecticut	26.0
27	Delaware	21.8
3	Florida	25.9
49	Georgia	16.0
37	Hawaii	19.4
24	Idaho	22.3
25	Illinois	22.2
33	Indiana	21.0
9	Iowa	24.3
29	Kansas	21.4
21	Kentucky	22.7
17	Louisiana	23.1
4	Maine	25.8
38	Maryland	19.2
9	Massachusetts	24.3
16	Michigan	23.6
30	Minnesota	21.3
42	Mississippi	18.4
23	Missouri	22.5
14	Montana	23.8
26	Nebraska	21.9
41	Nevada	18.5
9	New Hampshire	24.3
6	New Jersey	25.5
45	New Mexico	17.6
19	New York	22.9
46	North Carolina	17.5
27	North Dakota	21.8
9	Ohio	24.3
17	Oklahoma	23.1
8	Oregon	24.5
1	Pennsylvania	26.5
14	Rhode Island	23.8
48	South Carolina	17.4
32	South Dakota	21.1
31	Tennessee	21.2
39	Texas	19.1
50	Utah	15.3
4	Vermont	25.8
44	Virginia	18.1
9	Washington	24.3
22	West Virginia	22.6
7	Wisconsin	24.7
35	Wyoming	20.7

RANK ORDER

RANK	STATE	RATE
1	Pennsylvania	26.5
2	Connecticut	26.0
3	Florida	25.9
4	Maine	25.8
4	Vermont	25.8
6	New Jersey	25.5
7	Wisconsin	24.7
8	Oregon	24.5
9	Iowa	24.3
9	Massachusetts	24.3
9	New Hampshire	24.3
9	Ohio	24.3
9	Washington	24.3
14	Montana	23.8
14	Rhode Island	23.8
16	Michigan	23.6
17	Louisiana	23.1
17	Oklahoma	23.1
19	New York	22.9
20	Arkansas	22.8
21	Kentucky	22.7
22	West Virginia	22.6
23	Missouri	22.5
24	Idaho	22.3
25	Illinois	22.2
26	Nebraska	21.9
27	Delaware	21.8
27	North Dakota	21.8
29	Kansas	21.4
30	Minnesota	21.3
31	Tennessee	21.2
32	South Dakota	21.1
33	Indiana	21.0
34	Alabama	20.8
35	Wyoming	20.7
36	California	20.6
37	Hawaii	19.4
38	Maryland	19.2
39	Texas	19.1
40	Colorado	18.6
41	Nevada	18.5
42	Mississippi	18.4
43	Arizona	18.2
44	Virginia	18.1
45	New Mexico	17.6
46	Alaska	17.5
46	North Carolina	17.5
48	South Carolina	17.4
49	Georgia	16.0
50	Utah	15.3

District of Columbia   16.9

Source: CQ Press using data from American Cancer Society
"Cancer Facts & Figures 2008" (Copyright 2008, American Cancer Society, http://www.cancer.org/docroot/stt/stt_0.asp)
*These estimates are offered as a rough guide and should be interpreted with caution. They are calculated according to the distribution of estimated 2008 cancer deaths by state. Rates calculated using 2008 Census resident population estimates.

Estimated New Prostate Cancer Cases in 2008

National Estimated Total = 186,320 New Cases*

ALPHA ORDER

RANK	STATE	CASES	% of USA
25	Alabama	2,850	1.5%
49	Alaska	450	0.2%
17	Arizona	3,610	1.9%
31	Arkansas	1,980	1.1%
1	California	24,380	13.1%
22	Colorado	3,210	1.7%
29	Connecticut	2,280	1.2%
46	Delaware	530	0.3%
3	Florida	11,380	6.1%
12	Georgia	4,700	2.5%
41	Hawaii	930	0.5%
39	Idaho	1,160	0.6%
5	Illinois	7,790	4.2%
18	Indiana	3,550	1.9%
32	Iowa	1,910	1.0%
36	Kansas	1,350	0.7%
23	Kentucky	3,140	1.7%
19	Louisiana	3,430	1.8%
40	Maine	1,110	0.6%
20	Maryland	3,420	1.8%
16	Massachusetts	3,800	2.0%
6	Michigan	7,180	3.9%
21	Minnesota	3,400	1.8%
30	Mississippi	2,010	1.1%
24	Missouri	3,050	1.6%
42	Montana	900	0.5%
37	Nebraska	1,260	0.7%
33	Nevada	1,710	0.9%
43	New Hampshire	850	0.5%
9	New Jersey	5,090	2.7%
35	New Mexico	1,470	0.8%
4	New York	10,500	5.6%
10	North Carolina	5,050	2.7%
48	North Dakota	480	0.3%
7	Ohio	6,650	3.6%
27	Oklahoma	2,530	1.4%
26	Oregon	2,730	1.5%
8	Pennsylvania	6,510	3.5%
44	Rhode Island	650	0.3%
28	South Carolina	2,520	1.4%
45	South Dakota	580	0.3%
14	Tennessee	3,980	2.1%
2	Texas	12,960	7.0%
34	Utah	1,510	0.8%
47	Vermont	490	0.3%
13	Virginia	4,430	2.4%
11	Washington	4,990	2.7%
38	West Virginia	1,180	0.6%
15	Wisconsin	3,970	2.1%
50	Wyoming	400	0.2%

RANK ORDER

RANK	STATE	CASES	% of USA
1	California	24,380	13.1%
2	Texas	12,960	7.0%
3	Florida	11,380	6.1%
4	New York	10,500	5.6%
5	Illinois	7,790	4.2%
6	Michigan	7,180	3.9%
7	Ohio	6,650	3.6%
8	Pennsylvania	6,510	3.5%
9	New Jersey	5,090	2.7%
10	North Carolina	5,050	2.7%
11	Washington	4,990	2.7%
12	Georgia	4,700	2.5%
13	Virginia	4,430	2.4%
14	Tennessee	3,980	2.1%
15	Wisconsin	3,970	2.1%
16	Massachusetts	3,800	2.0%
17	Arizona	3,610	1.9%
18	Indiana	3,550	1.9%
19	Louisiana	3,430	1.8%
20	Maryland	3,420	1.8%
21	Minnesota	3,400	1.8%
22	Colorado	3,210	1.7%
23	Kentucky	3,140	1.7%
24	Missouri	3,050	1.6%
25	Alabama	2,850	1.5%
26	Oregon	2,730	1.5%
27	Oklahoma	2,530	1.4%
28	South Carolina	2,520	1.4%
29	Connecticut	2,280	1.2%
30	Mississippi	2,010	1.1%
31	Arkansas	1,980	1.1%
32	Iowa	1,910	1.0%
33	Nevada	1,710	0.9%
34	Utah	1,510	0.8%
35	New Mexico	1,470	0.8%
36	Kansas	1,350	0.7%
37	Nebraska	1,260	0.7%
38	West Virginia	1,180	0.6%
39	Idaho	1,160	0.6%
40	Maine	1,110	0.6%
41	Hawaii	930	0.5%
42	Montana	900	0.5%
43	New Hampshire	850	0.5%
44	Rhode Island	650	0.3%
45	South Dakota	580	0.3%
46	Delaware	530	0.3%
47	Vermont	490	0.3%
48	North Dakota	480	0.3%
49	Alaska	450	0.2%
50	Wyoming	400	0.2%
	District of Columbia	330	0.2%

Source: American Cancer Society
  "Cancer Facts & Figures 2008" (Copyright 2008, American Cancer Society, http://www.cancer.org/docroot/stt/stt_0.asp)
*These estimates are offered as a rough guide and should be interpreted with caution. They are calculated according to the distribution of estimated 2008 cancer deaths by state.

Age-Adjusted Incidence Rate of Prostate Cancer Cases in 2004

National Rate = 160.8 New Cases per 100,000 Male Population*

ALPHA ORDER

RANK	STATE	RATE
39	Alabama	146.3
19	Alaska	166.2
44	Arizona	118.6
31	Arkansas	154.6
30	California	156.9
25	Colorado	160.1
11	Connecticut	174.1
10	Delaware	174.7
38	Florida	147.4
21	Georgia	165.7
43	Hawaii	131.8
14	Idaho	172.3
23	Illinois	163.4
41	Indiana	140.0
32	Iowa	151.1
NA	Kansas**	NA
35	Kentucky	149.2
7	Louisiana	179.7
15	Maine	172.0
NA	Maryland**	NA
12	Massachusetts	173.1
1	Michigan	194.5
NA	Minnesota**	NA
26	Mississippi	158.7
42	Missouri	132.8
5	Montana	184.3
24	Nebraska	160.4
27	Nevada	158.4
20	New Hampshire	166.1
2	New Jersey	192.8
33	New Mexico	150.7
17	New York	170.1
NA	North Carolina**	NA
8	North Dakota	175.2
34	Ohio	149.3
36	Oklahoma	148.1
28	Oregon	157.7
18	Pennsylvania	166.7
16	Rhode Island	170.6
9	South Carolina	175.1
3	South Dakota	191.4
45	Tennessee	110.8
37	Texas	147.9
4	Utah	186.3
NA	Vermont**	NA
29	Virginia	157.3
13	Washington	172.6
40	West Virginia	144.2
22	Wisconsin	163.9
6	Wyoming	179.9

RANK ORDER

RANK	STATE	RATE
1	Michigan	194.5
2	New Jersey	192.8
3	South Dakota	191.4
4	Utah	186.3
5	Montana	184.3
6	Wyoming	179.9
7	Louisiana	179.7
8	North Dakota	175.2
9	South Carolina	175.1
10	Delaware	174.7
11	Connecticut	174.1
12	Massachusetts	173.1
13	Washington	172.6
14	Idaho	172.3
15	Maine	172.0
16	Rhode Island	170.6
17	New York	170.1
18	Pennsylvania	166.7
19	Alaska	166.2
20	New Hampshire	166.1
21	Georgia	165.7
22	Wisconsin	163.9
23	Illinois	163.4
24	Nebraska	160.4
25	Colorado	160.1
26	Mississippi	158.7
27	Nevada	158.4
28	Oregon	157.7
29	Virginia	157.3
30	California	156.9
31	Arkansas	154.6
32	Iowa	151.1
33	New Mexico	150.7
34	Ohio	149.3
35	Kentucky	149.2
36	Oklahoma	148.1
37	Texas	147.9
38	Florida	147.4
39	Alabama	146.3
40	West Virginia	144.2
41	Indiana	140.0
42	Missouri	132.8
43	Hawaii	131.8
44	Arizona	118.6
45	Tennessee	110.8
NA	Kansas**	NA
NA	Maryland**	NA
NA	Minnesota**	NA
NA	North Carolina**	NA
NA	Vermont**	NA

District of Columbia   215.0

Source: American Cancer Society

"Cancer Facts & Figures 2008" (Copyright 2008, American Cancer Society, http://www.cancer.org/docroot/stt/stt_0.asp)

*For 2000 to 2004. Age-adjusted to the 2000 U.S. standard population.

**Not available.

Percent of Males Receiving PSA Test for Prostate Cancer: 2006

National Median = 53.5% of Men*

ALPHA ORDER

RANK	STATE	PERCENT
7	Alabama	56.6
49	Alaska	45.9
10	Arizona	56.1
28	Arkansas	52.8
39	California	49.3
24	Colorado	53.8
18	Connecticut	54.7
5	Delaware	56.9
3	Florida	60.1
4	Georgia	57.2
50	Hawaii	40.0
35	Idaho	51.3
46	Illinois	47.9
38	Indiana	49.6
29	Iowa	52.7
17	Kansas	54.8
26	Kentucky	53.0
13	Louisiana	55.8
44	Maine	48.0
14	Maryland	55.7
10	Massachusetts	56.1
5	Michigan	56.9
41	Minnesota	48.8
18	Mississippi	54.7
33	Missouri	51.7
8	Montana	56.3
32	Nebraska	51.9
29	Nevada	52.7
36	New Hampshire	50.2
16	New Jersey	55.4
40	New Mexico	49.0
20	New York	54.5
14	North Carolina	55.7
31	North Dakota	52.2
10	Ohio	56.1
33	Oklahoma	51.7
37	Oregon	50.0
26	Pennsylvania	53.0
2	Rhode Island	61.0
8	South Carolina	56.3
21	South Dakota	54.4
22	Tennessee	54.3
42	Texas	48.4
48	Utah	46.6
47	Vermont	47.7
25	Virginia	53.5
44	Washington	48.0
23	West Virginia	54.1
42	Wisconsin	48.4
1	Wyoming	63.0

RANK ORDER

RANK	STATE	PERCENT
1	Wyoming	63.0
2	Rhode Island	61.0
3	Florida	60.1
4	Georgia	57.2
5	Delaware	56.9
5	Michigan	56.9
7	Alabama	56.6
8	Montana	56.3
8	South Carolina	56.3
10	Arizona	56.1
10	Massachusetts	56.1
10	Ohio	56.1
13	Louisiana	55.8
14	Maryland	55.7
14	North Carolina	55.7
16	New Jersey	55.4
17	Kansas	54.8
18	Connecticut	54.7
18	Mississippi	54.7
20	New York	54.5
21	South Dakota	54.4
22	Tennessee	54.3
23	West Virginia	54.1
24	Colorado	53.8
25	Virginia	53.5
26	Kentucky	53.0
26	Pennsylvania	53.0
28	Arkansas	52.8
29	Iowa	52.7
29	Nevada	52.7
31	North Dakota	52.2
32	Nebraska	51.9
33	Missouri	51.7
33	Oklahoma	51.7
35	Idaho	51.3
36	New Hampshire	50.2
37	Oregon	50.0
38	Indiana	49.6
39	California	49.3
40	New Mexico	49.0
41	Minnesota	48.8
42	Texas	48.4
42	Wisconsin	48.4
44	Maine	48.0
44	Washington	48.0
46	Illinois	47.9
47	Vermont	47.7
48	Utah	46.6
49	Alaska	45.9
50	Hawaii	40.0

| | District of Columbia | 58.8 |

Source: U.S. Department of Health and Human Services, Centers for Disease Control and Prevention
"2006 Behavioral Risk Factor Surveillance Summary Prevalence Data" (http://apps.nccd.cdc.gov/brfss/)
*Men 40 and older receiving prostate-specific antigen (PSA) test within the past two years.

Estimated New Skin Melanoma Cases in 2008

National Estimated Total = 62,480 New Cases*

<u>ALPHA ORDER</u>				<u>RANK ORDER</u>			
RANK	STATE	CASES	% of USA	RANK	STATE	CASES	% of USA
27	Alabama	820	1.3%	1	California	7,620	12.2%
50	Alaska	80	0.1%	2	Florida	4,430	7.1%
15	Arizona	1,380	2.2%	3	Texas	3,940	6.3%
32	Arkansas	540	0.9%	4	New York	3,440	5.5%
1	California	7,620	12.2%	5	Pennsylvania	3,280	5.2%
16	Colorado	1,180	1.9%	6	New Jersey	2,300	3.7%
23	Connecticut	1,060	1.7%	7	Michigan	2,140	3.4%
45	Delaware	180	0.3%	8	Ohio	2,110	3.4%
2	Florida	4,430	7.1%	9	Illinois	1,930	3.1%
14	Georgia	1,600	2.6%	10	Washington	1,900	3.0%
43	Hawaii	300	0.5%	11	North Carolina	1,830	2.9%
40	Idaho	360	0.6%	12	Massachusetts	1,810	2.9%
9	Illinois	1,930	3.1%	13	Virginia	1,620	2.6%
18	Indiana	1,130	1.8%	14	Georgia	1,600	2.6%
28	Iowa	790	1.3%	15	Arizona	1,380	2.2%
31	Kansas	550	0.9%	16	Colorado	1,180	1.9%
22	Kentucky	1,080	1.7%	17	Tennessee	1,150	1.8%
30	Louisiana	690	1.1%	18	Indiana	1,130	1.8%
36	Maine	410	0.7%	19	Oregon	1,120	1.8%
20	Maryland	1,110	1.8%	20	Maryland	1,110	1.8%
12	Massachusetts	1,810	2.9%	20	Missouri	1,110	1.8%
7	Michigan	2,140	3.4%	22	Kentucky	1,080	1.7%
26	Minnesota	830	1.3%	23	Connecticut	1,060	1.7%
41	Mississippi	310	0.5%	24	Wisconsin	1,010	1.6%
20	Missouri	1,110	1.8%	25	South Carolina	940	1.5%
44	Montana	200	0.3%	26	Minnesota	830	1.3%
39	Nebraska	380	0.6%	27	Alabama	820	1.3%
35	Nevada	430	0.7%	28	Iowa	790	1.3%
38	New Hampshire	400	0.6%	29	Oklahoma	700	1.1%
6	New Jersey	2,300	3.7%	30	Louisiana	690	1.1%
36	New Mexico	410	0.7%	31	Kansas	550	0.9%
4	New York	3,440	5.5%	32	Arkansas	540	0.9%
11	North Carolina	1,830	2.9%	33	Utah	500	0.8%
49	North Dakota	110	0.2%	34	West Virginia	440	0.7%
8	Ohio	2,110	3.4%	35	Nevada	430	0.7%
29	Oklahoma	700	1.1%	36	Maine	410	0.7%
19	Oregon	1,120	1.8%	36	New Mexico	410	0.7%
5	Pennsylvania	3,280	5.2%	38	New Hampshire	400	0.6%
41	Rhode Island	310	0.5%	39	Nebraska	380	0.6%
25	South Carolina	940	1.5%	40	Idaho	360	0.6%
47	South Dakota	160	0.3%	41	Mississippi	310	0.5%
17	Tennessee	1,150	1.8%	41	Rhode Island	310	0.5%
3	Texas	3,940	6.3%	43	Hawaii	300	0.5%
33	Utah	500	0.8%	44	Montana	200	0.3%
45	Vermont	180	0.3%	45	Delaware	180	0.3%
13	Virginia	1,620	2.6%	45	Vermont	180	0.3%
10	Washington	1,900	3.0%	47	South Dakota	160	0.3%
34	West Virginia	440	0.7%	48	Wyoming	120	0.2%
24	Wisconsin	1,010	1.6%	49	North Dakota	110	0.2%
48	Wyoming	120	0.2%	50	Alaska	80	0.1%
					District of Columbia	50	0.1%

Source: American Cancer Society
   "Cancer Facts & Figures 2008" (Copyright 2008, American Cancer Society, http://www.cancer.org/docroot/stt/stt_0.asp)
*These estimates are offered as a rough guide and should be interpreted with caution. They are calculated according to the distribution of estimated 2008 cancer deaths by state.

Estimated Rate of New Skin Melanoma Cases in 2008

National Estimated Rate = 20.5 New Cases per 100,000 Population*

ALPHA ORDER

RANK	STATE	RATE
40	Alabama	17.6
49	Alaska	11.7
21	Arizona	21.2
33	Arkansas	18.9
24	California	20.7
15	Colorado	23.9
3	Connecticut	30.3
27	Delaware	20.6
13	Florida	24.2
43	Georgia	16.5
17	Hawaii	23.3
16	Idaho	23.6
48	Illinois	15.0
39	Indiana	17.7
10	Iowa	26.3
31	Kansas	19.6
12	Kentucky	25.3
47	Louisiana	15.6
1	Maine	31.1
30	Maryland	19.7
8	Massachusetts	27.9
19	Michigan	21.4
46	Minnesota	15.9
50	Mississippi	10.5
34	Missouri	18.8
24	Montana	20.7
20	Nebraska	21.3
43	Nevada	16.5
2	New Hampshire	30.4
9	New Jersey	26.5
24	New Mexico	20.7
40	New York	17.6
29	North Carolina	19.8
42	North Dakota	17.1
36	Ohio	18.4
32	Oklahoma	19.2
4	Oregon	29.6
10	Pennsylvania	26.3
5	Rhode Island	29.5
22	South Carolina	21.0
28	South Dakota	19.9
35	Tennessee	18.5
45	Texas	16.2
37	Utah	18.3
6	Vermont	29.0
23	Virginia	20.9
6	Washington	29.0
13	West Virginia	24.2
38	Wisconsin	17.9
18	Wyoming	22.5

RANK ORDER

RANK	STATE	RATE
1	Maine	31.1
2	New Hampshire	30.4
3	Connecticut	30.3
4	Oregon	29.6
5	Rhode Island	29.5
6	Vermont	29.0
6	Washington	29.0
8	Massachusetts	27.9
9	New Jersey	26.5
10	Iowa	26.3
10	Pennsylvania	26.3
12	Kentucky	25.3
13	Florida	24.2
13	West Virginia	24.2
15	Colorado	23.9
16	Idaho	23.6
17	Hawaii	23.3
18	Wyoming	22.5
19	Michigan	21.4
20	Nebraska	21.3
21	Arizona	21.2
22	South Carolina	21.0
23	Virginia	20.9
24	California	20.7
24	Montana	20.7
24	New Mexico	20.7
27	Delaware	20.6
28	South Dakota	19.9
29	North Carolina	19.8
30	Maryland	19.7
31	Kansas	19.6
32	Oklahoma	19.2
33	Arkansas	18.9
34	Missouri	18.8
35	Tennessee	18.5
36	Ohio	18.4
37	Utah	18.3
38	Wisconsin	17.9
39	Indiana	17.7
40	Alabama	17.6
40	New York	17.6
42	North Dakota	17.1
43	Georgia	16.5
43	Nevada	16.5
45	Texas	16.2
46	Minnesota	15.9
47	Louisiana	15.6
48	Illinois	15.0
49	Alaska	11.7
50	Mississippi	10.5

	District of Columbia	8.4

Source: CQ Press using data from American Cancer Society
"Cancer Facts & Figures 2008" (Copyright 2008, American Cancer Society, http://www.cancer.org/docroot/stt/stt_0.asp)
*These estimates are offered as a rough guide and should be interpreted with caution. They are calculated according to the distribution of estimated 2008 cancer deaths by state. Rates calculated using 2008 Census resident population estimates.

Estimated New Cervical Cancer Cases in 2008

National Estimated Total = 11,070 New Cases*

ALPHA ORDER

RANK	STATE	CASES	% of USA
23	Alabama	170	1.5%
NA	Alaska**	NA	NA
18	Arizona	200	1.8%
28	Arkansas	130	1.2%
1	California	1,280	11.6%
26	Colorado	140	1.3%
30	Connecticut	120	1.1%
NA	Delaware**	NA	NA
4	Florida	770	7.0%
9	Georgia	340	3.1%
39	Hawaii	50	0.5%
NA	Idaho**	NA	NA
5	Illinois	500	4.5%
14	Indiana	230	2.1%
31	Iowa	100	0.9%
34	Kansas	80	0.7%
20	Kentucky	190	1.7%
15	Louisiana	210	1.9%
39	Maine	50	0.5%
15	Maryland	210	1.9%
18	Massachusetts	200	1.8%
11	Michigan	330	3.0%
26	Minnesota	140	1.3%
28	Mississippi	130	1.2%
15	Missouri	210	1.9%
NA	Montana**	NA	NA
37	Nebraska	60	0.5%
32	Nevada	90	0.8%
NA	New Hampshire**	NA	NA
8	New Jersey	370	3.3%
36	New Mexico	70	0.6%
3	New York	830	7.5%
9	North Carolina	340	3.1%
NA	North Dakota**	NA	NA
7	Ohio	380	3.4%
25	Oklahoma	150	1.4%
32	Oregon	90	0.8%
6	Pennsylvania	440	4.0%
NA	Rhode Island**	NA	NA
22	South Carolina	180	1.6%
NA	South Dakota**	NA	NA
13	Tennessee	250	2.3%
2	Texas	970	8.8%
37	Utah	60	0.5%
NA	Vermont**	NA	NA
12	Virginia	260	2.3%
23	Washington	170	1.5%
34	West Virginia	80	0.7%
20	Wisconsin	190	1.7%
NA	Wyoming**	NA	NA

RANK ORDER

RANK	STATE	CASES	% of USA
1	California	1,280	11.6%
2	Texas	970	8.8%
3	New York	830	7.5%
4	Florida	770	7.0%
5	Illinois	500	4.5%
6	Pennsylvania	440	4.0%
7	Ohio	380	3.4%
8	New Jersey	370	3.3%
9	Georgia	340	3.1%
9	North Carolina	340	3.1%
11	Michigan	330	3.0%
12	Virginia	260	2.3%
13	Tennessee	250	2.3%
14	Indiana	230	2.1%
15	Louisiana	210	1.9%
15	Maryland	210	1.9%
15	Missouri	210	1.9%
18	Arizona	200	1.8%
18	Massachusetts	200	1.8%
20	Kentucky	190	1.7%
20	Wisconsin	190	1.7%
22	South Carolina	180	1.6%
23	Alabama	170	1.5%
23	Washington	170	1.5%
25	Oklahoma	150	1.4%
26	Colorado	140	1.3%
26	Minnesota	140	1.3%
28	Arkansas	130	1.2%
28	Mississippi	130	1.2%
30	Connecticut	120	1.1%
31	Iowa	100	0.9%
32	Nevada	90	0.8%
32	Oregon	90	0.8%
34	Kansas	80	0.7%
34	West Virginia	80	0.7%
36	New Mexico	70	0.6%
37	Nebraska	60	0.5%
37	Utah	60	0.5%
39	Hawaii	50	0.5%
39	Maine	50	0.5%
NA	Alaska**	NA	NA
NA	Delaware**	NA	NA
NA	Idaho**	NA	NA
NA	Montana**	NA	NA
NA	New Hampshire**	NA	NA
NA	North Dakota**	NA	NA
NA	Rhode Island**	NA	NA
NA	South Dakota**	NA	NA
NA	Vermont**	NA	NA
NA	Wyoming**	NA	NA
	District of Columbia**	NA	NA

Source: American Cancer Society
   "Cancer Facts & Figures 2008" (Copyright 2008, American Cancer Society, http://www.cancer.org/docroot/stt/stt_0.asp)
*These estimates are offered as a rough guide and should be interpreted with caution. They are calculated according to the distribution of estimated 2008 cancer deaths by state.
**Not available.

Estimated Rate of New Cervical Cancer Cases in 2008

National Estimated Rate = 7.2 New Cases per 100,000 Female Population*

ALPHA ORDER			RANK ORDER		
RANK	STATE	RATE	RANK	STATE	RATE
19	Alabama	7.1	1	Louisiana	9.5
NA	Alaska**	NA	2	Arkansas	9.0
33	Arizona	6.3	3	Kentucky	8.8
2	Arkansas	9.0	4	West Virginia	8.7
21	California	7.0	5	Mississippi	8.6
35	Colorado	5.8	6	New York	8.4
26	Connecticut	6.7	7	Florida	8.3
NA	Delaware**	NA	7	New Jersey	8.3
7	Florida	8.3	9	Oklahoma	8.2
21	Georgia	7.0	10	Texas	8.1
13	Hawaii	7.8	11	South Carolina	8.0
NA	Idaho**	NA	12	Tennessee	7.9
14	Illinois	7.7	13	Hawaii	7.8
19	Indiana	7.1	14	Illinois	7.7
29	Iowa	6.6	15	Maine	7.4
36	Kansas	5.7	16	North Carolina	7.3
3	Kentucky	8.8	17	Maryland	7.2
1	Louisiana	9.5	17	Nevada	7.2
15	Maine	7.4	19	Alabama	7.1
17	Maryland	7.2	19	Indiana	7.1
34	Massachusetts	6.0	21	California	7.0
31	Michigan	6.5	21	Georgia	7.0
37	Minnesota	5.4	21	Missouri	7.0
5	Mississippi	8.6	21	New Mexico	7.0
21	Missouri	7.0	25	Pennsylvania	6.9
NA	Montana**	NA	26	Connecticut	6.7
26	Nebraska	6.7	26	Nebraska	6.7
17	Nevada	7.2	26	Wisconsin	6.7
NA	New Hampshire**	NA	29	Iowa	6.6
7	New Jersey	8.3	29	Virginia	6.6
21	New Mexico	7.0	31	Michigan	6.5
6	New York	8.4	31	Ohio	6.5
16	North Carolina	7.3	33	Arizona	6.3
NA	North Dakota**	NA	34	Massachusetts	6.0
31	Ohio	6.5	35	Colorado	5.8
9	Oklahoma	8.2	36	Kansas	5.7
39	Oregon	4.8	37	Minnesota	5.4
25	Pennsylvania	6.9	38	Washington	5.2
NA	Rhode Island**	NA	39	Oregon	4.8
11	South Carolina	8.0	40	Utah	4.6
NA	South Dakota**	NA	NA	Alaska**	NA
12	Tennessee	7.9	NA	Delaware**	NA
10	Texas	8.1	NA	Idaho**	NA
40	Utah	4.6	NA	Montana**	NA
NA	Vermont**	NA	NA	New Hampshire**	NA
29	Virginia	6.6	NA	North Dakota**	NA
38	Washington	5.2	NA	Rhode Island**	NA
4	West Virginia	8.7	NA	South Dakota**	NA
26	Wisconsin	6.7	NA	Vermont**	NA
NA	Wyoming**	NA	NA	Wyoming**	NA
				District of Columbia**	NA

Source: CQ Press using data from American Cancer Society
"Cancer Facts & Figures 2008" (Copyright 2008, American Cancer Society, http://www.cancer.org/docroot/stt/stt_0.asp)
*These estimates are offered as a rough guide and should be interpreted with caution. They are calculated according to the distribution of estimated 2008 cancer deaths by state. Rates calculated using 2007 Census female population estimates.
**Not available.

Percent of Women 18 Years Old and Older
Who Had a Pap Smear within the Past Three Years: 2006
National Median = 84.0% of Women 18 Years and Older*

ALPHA ORDER

RANK	STATE	PERCENT
32	Alabama	83.4
9	Alaska	87.0
24	Arizona	84.1
45	Arkansas	80.5
25	California	84.0
19	Colorado	85.3
10	Connecticut	86.8
2	Delaware	89.0
37	Florida	82.8
7	Georgia	87.4
41	Hawaii	82.0
49	Idaho	77.6
30	Illinois	83.6
43	Indiana	81.0
14	Iowa	86.1
30	Kansas	83.6
35	Kentucky	83.1
22	Louisiana	84.5
1	Maine	89.1
4	Maryland	87.8
6	Massachusetts	87.7
17	Michigan	85.8
13	Minnesota	86.2
25	Mississippi	84.0
47	Missouri	79.9
39	Montana	82.1
42	Nebraska	81.6
39	Nevada	82.1
3	New Hampshire	88.0
25	New Jersey	84.0
35	New Mexico	83.1
20	New York	85.1
10	North Carolina	86.8
22	North Dakota	84.5
32	Ohio	83.4
48	Oklahoma	79.4
32	Oregon	83.4
37	Pennsylvania	82.8
4	Rhode Island	87.8
10	South Carolina	86.8
20	South Dakota	85.1
16	Tennessee	85.9
46	Texas	80.2
50	Utah	74.3
8	Vermont	87.1
18	Virginia	85.6
25	Washington	84.0
29	West Virginia	83.8
15	Wisconsin	86.0
44	Wyoming	80.9

RANK ORDER

RANK	STATE	PERCENT
1	Maine	89.1
2	Delaware	89.0
3	New Hampshire	88.0
4	Maryland	87.8
4	Rhode Island	87.8
6	Massachusetts	87.7
7	Georgia	87.4
8	Vermont	87.1
9	Alaska	87.0
10	Connecticut	86.8
10	North Carolina	86.8
10	South Carolina	86.8
13	Minnesota	86.2
14	Iowa	86.1
15	Wisconsin	86.0
16	Tennessee	85.9
17	Michigan	85.8
18	Virginia	85.6
19	Colorado	85.3
20	New York	85.1
20	South Dakota	85.1
22	Louisiana	84.5
22	North Dakota	84.5
24	Arizona	84.1
25	California	84.0
25	Mississippi	84.0
25	New Jersey	84.0
25	Washington	84.0
29	West Virginia	83.8
30	Illinois	83.6
30	Kansas	83.6
32	Alabama	83.4
32	Ohio	83.4
32	Oregon	83.4
35	Kentucky	83.1
35	New Mexico	83.1
37	Florida	82.8
37	Pennsylvania	82.8
39	Montana	82.1
39	Nevada	82.1
41	Hawaii	82.0
42	Nebraska	81.6
43	Indiana	81.0
44	Wyoming	80.9
45	Arkansas	80.5
46	Texas	80.2
47	Missouri	79.9
48	Oklahoma	79.4
49	Idaho	77.6
50	Utah	74.3

| | District of Columbia | 89.4 |

Source: U.S. Department of Health and Human Services, Centers for Disease Control and Prevention
   "2006 Behavioral Risk Factor Surveillance Summary Prevalence Data" (http://apps.nccd.cdc.gov/brfss/)
*A Pap test is a test for cancer, especially of the female genital tract such as cancer of the cervix. Named after George Papanicolaou (1883-1962), American anatomist.

Estimated New Uterine Cancer Cases in 2008

National Estimated Total = 40,100 New Cases*

ALPHA ORDER

RANK	STATE	CASES	% of USA
28	Alabama	490	1.2%
50	Alaska	60	0.1%
22	Arizona	610	1.5%
32	Arkansas	330	0.8%
1	California	4,020	10.0%
24	Colorado	510	1.3%
21	Connecticut	660	1.6%
44	Delaware	130	0.3%
4	Florida	2,450	6.1%
16	Georgia	840	2.1%
42	Hawaii	180	0.4%
43	Idaho	160	0.4%
7	Illinois	1,790	4.5%
13	Indiana	890	2.2%
24	Iowa	510	1.3%
30	Kansas	390	1.0%
23	Kentucky	580	1.4%
29	Louisiana	430	1.1%
34	Maine	270	0.7%
18	Maryland	810	2.0%
10	Massachusetts	1,120	2.8%
8	Michigan	1,620	4.0%
19	Minnesota	750	1.9%
39	Mississippi	230	0.6%
14	Missouri	860	2.1%
44	Montana	130	0.3%
34	Nebraska	270	0.7%
36	Nevada	240	0.6%
36	New Hampshire	240	0.6%
9	New Jersey	1,590	4.0%
40	New Mexico	220	0.5%
2	New York	3,340	8.3%
11	North Carolina	1,050	2.6%
48	North Dakota	90	0.2%
6	Ohio	1,830	4.6%
30	Oklahoma	390	1.0%
26	Oregon	500	1.2%
3	Pennsylvania	2,460	6.1%
41	Rhode Island	200	0.5%
26	South Carolina	500	1.2%
46	South Dakota	120	0.3%
20	Tennessee	680	1.7%
5	Texas	2,100	5.2%
36	Utah	240	0.6%
47	Vermont	110	0.3%
12	Virginia	1,000	2.5%
15	Washington	850	2.1%
33	West Virginia	320	0.8%
17	Wisconsin	830	2.1%
49	Wyoming	70	0.2%

RANK ORDER

RANK	STATE	CASES	% of USA
1	California	4,020	10.0%
2	New York	3,340	8.3%
3	Pennsylvania	2,460	6.1%
4	Florida	2,450	6.1%
5	Texas	2,100	5.2%
6	Ohio	1,830	4.6%
7	Illinois	1,790	4.5%
8	Michigan	1,620	4.0%
9	New Jersey	1,590	4.0%
10	Massachusetts	1,120	2.8%
11	North Carolina	1,050	2.6%
12	Virginia	1,000	2.5%
13	Indiana	890	2.2%
14	Missouri	860	2.1%
15	Washington	850	2.1%
16	Georgia	840	2.1%
17	Wisconsin	830	2.1%
18	Maryland	810	2.0%
19	Minnesota	750	1.9%
20	Tennessee	680	1.7%
21	Connecticut	660	1.6%
22	Arizona	610	1.5%
23	Kentucky	580	1.4%
24	Colorado	510	1.3%
24	Iowa	510	1.3%
26	Oregon	500	1.2%
26	South Carolina	500	1.2%
28	Alabama	490	1.2%
29	Louisiana	430	1.1%
30	Kansas	390	1.0%
30	Oklahoma	390	1.0%
32	Arkansas	330	0.8%
33	West Virginia	320	0.8%
34	Maine	270	0.7%
34	Nebraska	270	0.7%
36	Nevada	240	0.6%
36	New Hampshire	240	0.6%
36	Utah	240	0.6%
39	Mississippi	230	0.6%
40	New Mexico	220	0.5%
41	Rhode Island	200	0.5%
42	Hawaii	180	0.4%
43	Idaho	160	0.4%
44	Delaware	130	0.3%
44	Montana	130	0.3%
46	South Dakota	120	0.3%
47	Vermont	110	0.3%
48	North Dakota	90	0.2%
49	Wyoming	70	0.2%
50	Alaska	60	0.1%
	District of Columbia	60	0.1%

Source: American Cancer Society
    "Cancer Facts & Figures 2008" (Copyright 2008, American Cancer Society, http://www.cancer.org/docroot/stt/stt_0.asp)
*These estimates are offered as a rough guide and should be interpreted with caution. They are calculated according to the distribution of estimated 2008 cancer deaths by state.

Estimated Rate of New Uterine Cancer Cases in 2008

National Estimated Rate = 26.2 New Cases per 100,000 Female Population*

ALPHA ORDER

RANK	STATE	RATE
42	Alabama	20.5
46	Alaska	18.3
44	Arizona	19.3
33	Arkansas	22.8
36	California	22.0
41	Colorado	21.2
3	Connecticut	36.8
17	Delaware	29.2
30	Florida	26.4
49	Georgia	17.3
20	Hawaii	28.2
39	Idaho	21.5
25	Illinois	27.5
24	Indiana	27.7
9	Iowa	33.7
22	Kansas	27.9
28	Kentucky	26.8
43	Louisiana	19.5
1	Maine	40.0
22	Maryland	27.9
9	Massachusetts	33.7
12	Michigan	31.7
18	Minnesota	28.7
50	Mississippi	15.3
19	Missouri	28.6
26	Montana	27.2
14	Nebraska	30.2
45	Nevada	19.1
5	New Hampshire	36.0
6	New Jersey	35.8
36	New Mexico	22.0
11	New York	33.6
34	North Carolina	22.7
20	North Dakota	28.2
13	Ohio	31.1
40	Oklahoma	21.3
29	Oregon	26.5
2	Pennsylvania	38.5
4	Rhode Island	36.6
35	South Carolina	22.1
15	South Dakota	30.0
38	Tennessee	21.6
48	Texas	17.5
46	Utah	18.3
7	Vermont	34.9
32	Virginia	25.5
31	Washington	26.2
8	West Virginia	34.6
16	Wisconsin	29.5
26	Wyoming	27.2

RANK ORDER

RANK	STATE	RATE
1	Maine	40.0
2	Pennsylvania	38.5
3	Connecticut	36.8
4	Rhode Island	36.6
5	New Hampshire	36.0
6	New Jersey	35.8
7	Vermont	34.9
8	West Virginia	34.6
9	Iowa	33.7
9	Massachusetts	33.7
11	New York	33.6
12	Michigan	31.7
13	Ohio	31.1
14	Nebraska	30.2
15	South Dakota	30.0
16	Wisconsin	29.5
17	Delaware	29.2
18	Minnesota	28.7
19	Missouri	28.6
20	Hawaii	28.2
20	North Dakota	28.2
22	Kansas	27.9
22	Maryland	27.9
24	Indiana	27.7
25	Illinois	27.5
26	Montana	27.2
26	Wyoming	27.2
28	Kentucky	26.8
29	Oregon	26.5
30	Florida	26.4
31	Washington	26.2
32	Virginia	25.5
33	Arkansas	22.8
34	North Carolina	22.7
35	South Carolina	22.1
36	California	22.0
36	New Mexico	22.0
38	Tennessee	21.6
39	Idaho	21.5
40	Oklahoma	21.3
41	Colorado	21.2
42	Alabama	20.5
43	Louisiana	19.5
44	Arizona	19.3
45	Nevada	19.1
46	Alaska	18.3
46	Utah	18.3
48	Texas	17.5
49	Georgia	17.3
50	Mississippi	15.3
	District of Columbia	19.3

Source: CQ Press using data from American Cancer Society
"Cancer Facts & Figures 2008" (Copyright 2008, American Cancer Society, http://www.cancer.org/docroot/stt/stt_0.asp)
*These estimates are offered as a rough guide and should be interpreted with caution. They are calculated according to the distribution of estimated 2008 cancer deaths by state. Rates calculated using 2007 Census female population estimates.

AIDS Cases Reported in 2006

National Total = 37,911 New AIDS Cases*

ALPHA ORDER

RANK	STATE	CASES	% of USA
20	Alabama	462	1.2%
44	Alaska	38	0.1%
17	Arizona	539	1.4%
28	Arkansas	252	0.7%
3	California	3,960	10.4%
25	Colorado	322	0.8%
21	Connecticut	422	1.1%
35	Delaware	116	0.3%
2	Florida	4,932	13.0%
7	Georgia	1,605	4.2%
37	Hawaii	93	0.2%
45	Idaho	26	0.1%
8	Illinois	1,382	3.6%
24	Indiana	346	0.9%
39	Iowa	86	0.2%
33	Kansas	120	0.3%
31	Kentucky	207	0.5%
11	Louisiana	824	2.2%
40	Maine	68	0.2%
6	Maryland	1,626	4.3%
18	Massachusetts	533	1.4%
15	Michigan	672	1.8%
30	Minnesota	212	0.6%
23	Mississippi	365	1.0%
19	Missouri	469	1.2%
49	Montana	7	0.0%
34	Nebraska	118	0.3%
26	Nevada	294	0.8%
43	New Hampshire	55	0.1%
10	New Jersey	1,065	2.8%
37	New Mexico	93	0.2%
1	New York	5,495	14.5%
9	North Carolina	1,229	3.2%
50	North Dakota	6	0.0%
12	Ohio	767	2.0%
32	Oklahoma	205	0.5%
27	Oregon	281	0.7%
5	Pennsylvania	1,893	5.0%
36	Rhode Island	111	0.3%
13	South Carolina	705	1.9%
46	South Dakota	18	0.0%
14	Tennessee	680	1.8%
4	Texas	2,998	7.9%
42	Utah	57	0.2%
46	Vermont	18	0.0%
16	Virginia	605	1.6%
22	Washington	389	1.0%
41	West Virginia	67	0.2%
29	Wisconsin	217	0.6%
48	Wyoming	8	0.0%

RANK ORDER

RANK	STATE	CASES	% of USA
1	New York	5,495	14.5%
2	Florida	4,932	13.0%
3	California	3,960	10.4%
4	Texas	2,998	7.9%
5	Pennsylvania	1,893	5.0%
6	Maryland	1,626	4.3%
7	Georgia	1,605	4.2%
8	Illinois	1,382	3.6%
9	North Carolina	1,229	3.2%
10	New Jersey	1,065	2.8%
11	Louisiana	824	2.2%
12	Ohio	767	2.0%
13	South Carolina	705	1.9%
14	Tennessee	680	1.8%
15	Michigan	672	1.8%
16	Virginia	605	1.6%
17	Arizona	539	1.4%
18	Massachusetts	533	1.4%
19	Missouri	469	1.2%
20	Alabama	462	1.2%
21	Connecticut	422	1.1%
22	Washington	389	1.0%
23	Mississippi	365	1.0%
24	Indiana	346	0.9%
25	Colorado	322	0.8%
26	Nevada	294	0.8%
27	Oregon	281	0.7%
28	Arkansas	252	0.7%
29	Wisconsin	217	0.6%
30	Minnesota	212	0.6%
31	Kentucky	207	0.5%
32	Oklahoma	205	0.5%
33	Kansas	120	0.3%
34	Nebraska	118	0.3%
35	Delaware	116	0.3%
36	Rhode Island	111	0.3%
37	Hawaii	93	0.2%
37	New Mexico	93	0.2%
39	Iowa	86	0.2%
40	Maine	68	0.2%
41	West Virginia	67	0.2%
42	Utah	57	0.2%
43	New Hampshire	55	0.1%
44	Alaska	38	0.1%
45	Idaho	26	0.1%
46	South Dakota	18	0.0%
46	Vermont	18	0.0%
48	Wyoming	8	0.0%
49	Montana	7	0.0%
50	North Dakota	6	0.0%
	District of Columbia	853	2.3%

Source: U.S. Department of Health and Human Services, Centers for Disease Control and Prevention
"HIV/AIDS Surveillance Report, 2006" (Vol. 18, http://www.cdc.gov/hiv/topics/surveillance/resources/reports/index.htm)
*AIDS is Acquired Immunodeficiency Syndrome. It is a specific group of diseases or conditions which are indicative of severe immunosuppression related to infection with the Human Immunodeficiency Virus (HIV). National total does not include 850 new cases in Puerto Rico and 32 in the Virgin Islands.

AIDS Rate in 2006

National Rate = 12.7 New AIDS Cases Reported per 100,000 Population*

ALPHA ORDER

RANK	STATE	RATE
19	Alabama	10.0
32	Alaska	5.7
21	Arizona	8.7
20	Arkansas	9.0
16	California	10.9
27	Colorado	6.8
13	Connecticut	12.0
9	Delaware	13.6
3	Florida	27.3
5	Georgia	17.1
26	Hawaii	7.2
47	Idaho	1.8
17	Illinois	10.8
34	Indiana	5.5
43	Iowa	2.9
38	Kansas	4.3
36	Kentucky	4.9
4	Louisiana	19.2
35	Maine	5.1
1	Maryland	29.0
22	Massachusetts	8.3
28	Michigan	6.7
40	Minnesota	4.1
11	Mississippi	12.5
23	Missouri	8.0
50	Montana	0.7
28	Nebraska	6.7
14	Nevada	11.8
39	New Hampshire	4.2
12	New Jersey	12.2
37	New Mexico	4.8
2	New York	28.5
8	North Carolina	13.9
49	North Dakota	0.9
28	Ohio	6.7
32	Oklahoma	5.7
25	Oregon	7.6
7	Pennsylvania	15.2
18	Rhode Island	10.4
6	South Carolina	16.3
45	South Dakota	2.3
15	Tennessee	11.3
10	Texas	12.8
46	Utah	2.2
43	Vermont	2.9
24	Virginia	7.9
31	Washington	6.1
42	West Virginia	3.7
41	Wisconsin	3.9
48	Wyoming	1.6

RANK ORDER

RANK	STATE	RATE
1	Maryland	29.0
2	New York	28.5
3	Florida	27.3
4	Louisiana	19.2
5	Georgia	17.1
6	South Carolina	16.3
7	Pennsylvania	15.2
8	North Carolina	13.9
9	Delaware	13.6
10	Texas	12.8
11	Mississippi	12.5
12	New Jersey	12.2
13	Connecticut	12.0
14	Nevada	11.8
15	Tennessee	11.3
16	California	10.9
17	Illinois	10.8
18	Rhode Island	10.4
19	Alabama	10.0
20	Arkansas	9.0
21	Arizona	8.7
22	Massachusetts	8.3
23	Missouri	8.0
24	Virginia	7.9
25	Oregon	7.6
26	Hawaii	7.2
27	Colorado	6.8
28	Michigan	6.7
28	Nebraska	6.7
28	Ohio	6.7
31	Washington	6.1
32	Alaska	5.7
32	Oklahoma	5.7
34	Indiana	5.5
35	Maine	5.1
36	Kentucky	4.9
37	New Mexico	4.8
38	Kansas	4.3
39	New Hampshire	4.2
40	Minnesota	4.1
41	Wisconsin	3.9
42	West Virginia	3.7
43	Iowa	2.9
43	Vermont	2.9
45	South Dakota	2.3
46	Utah	2.2
47	Idaho	1.8
48	Wyoming	1.6
49	North Dakota	0.9
50	Montana	0.7

District of Columbia	146.7

Source: U.S. Department of Health and Human Services, Centers for Disease Control and Prevention
    "HIV/AIDS Surveillance Report, 2006" (Vol. 18, http://www.cdc.gov/hiv/topics/surveillance/resources/reports/index.htm)
*AIDS is Acquired Immunodeficiency Syndrome. It is a specific group of diseases or conditions which are indicative of severe immunosuppression related to infection with the Human Immunodeficiency Virus (HIV). National rate does not include cases or population in U.S. territories.

AIDS Cases Reported through December 2006

National Total = 961,315 Reported AIDS Cases*

ALPHA ORDER

RANK	STATE	CASES	% of USA
23	Alabama	8,702	0.9%
44	Alaska	655	0.1%
21	Arizona	10,442	1.1%
32	Arkansas	3,927	0.4%
2	California	142,918	14.9%
22	Colorado	8,773	0.9%
16	Connecticut	14,899	1.5%
33	Delaware	3,573	0.4%
3	Florida	105,614	11.0%
8	Georgia	31,965	3.3%
34	Hawaii	2,944	0.3%
45	Idaho	606	0.1%
6	Illinois	33,902	3.5%
24	Indiana	8,295	0.9%
39	Iowa	1,740	0.2%
35	Kansas	2,795	0.3%
30	Kentucky	4,632	0.5%
11	Louisiana	17,740	1.8%
42	Maine	1,118	0.1%
9	Maryland	30,571	3.2%
10	Massachusetts	19,395	2.0%
15	Michigan	15,054	1.6%
29	Minnesota	4,845	0.5%
25	Mississippi	6,698	0.7%
20	Missouri	11,077	1.2%
47	Montana	376	0.0%
41	Nebraska	1,490	0.2%
27	Nevada	5,762	0.6%
43	New Hampshire	1,084	0.1%
5	New Jersey	49,528	5.2%
36	New Mexico	2,610	0.3%
1	New York	177,262	18.4%
13	North Carolina	16,072	1.7%
50	North Dakota	145	0.0%
14	Ohio	15,095	1.6%
28	Oklahoma	4,862	0.5%
26	Oregon	6,015	0.6%
7	Pennsylvania	33,782	3.5%
37	Rhode Island	2,608	0.3%
17	South Carolina	13,406	1.4%
48	South Dakota	260	0.0%
18	Tennessee	12,516	1.3%
4	Texas	70,127	7.3%
38	Utah	2,315	0.2%
46	Vermont	467	0.0%
12	Virginia	16,979	1.8%
19	Washington	11,826	1.2%
40	West Virginia	1,511	0.2%
31	Wisconsin	4,546	0.5%
49	Wyoming	230	0.0%

RANK ORDER

RANK	STATE	CASES	% of USA
1	New York	177,262	18.4%
2	California	142,918	14.9%
3	Florida	105,614	11.0%
4	Texas	70,127	7.3%
5	New Jersey	49,528	5.2%
6	Illinois	33,902	3.5%
7	Pennsylvania	33,782	3.5%
8	Georgia	31,965	3.3%
9	Maryland	30,571	3.2%
10	Massachusetts	19,395	2.0%
11	Louisiana	17,740	1.8%
12	Virginia	16,979	1.8%
13	North Carolina	16,072	1.7%
14	Ohio	15,095	1.6%
15	Michigan	15,054	1.6%
16	Connecticut	14,899	1.5%
17	South Carolina	13,406	1.4%
18	Tennessee	12,516	1.3%
19	Washington	11,826	1.2%
20	Missouri	11,077	1.2%
21	Arizona	10,442	1.1%
22	Colorado	8,773	0.9%
23	Alabama	8,702	0.9%
24	Indiana	8,295	0.9%
25	Mississippi	6,698	0.7%
26	Oregon	6,015	0.6%
27	Nevada	5,762	0.6%
28	Oklahoma	4,862	0.5%
29	Minnesota	4,845	0.5%
30	Kentucky	4,632	0.5%
31	Wisconsin	4,546	0.5%
32	Arkansas	3,927	0.4%
33	Delaware	3,573	0.4%
34	Hawaii	2,944	0.3%
35	Kansas	2,795	0.3%
36	New Mexico	2,610	0.3%
37	Rhode Island	2,608	0.3%
38	Utah	2,315	0.2%
39	Iowa	1,740	0.2%
40	West Virginia	1,511	0.2%
41	Nebraska	1,490	0.2%
42	Maine	1,118	0.1%
43	New Hampshire	1,084	0.1%
44	Alaska	655	0.1%
45	Idaho	606	0.1%
46	Vermont	467	0.0%
47	Montana	376	0.0%
48	South Dakota	260	0.0%
49	Wyoming	230	0.0%
50	North Dakota	145	0.0%
	District of Columbia	17,561	1.8%

Source: U.S. Department of Health and Human Services, Centers for Disease Control and Prevention
   "HIV/AIDS Surveillance Report, 2006" (Vol. 18, http://www.cdc.gov/hiv/topics/surveillance/resources/reports/index.htm)
*Cumulative through December 2006. AIDS is Acquired Immunodeficiency Syndrome. It is a specific group of diseases or conditions which are indicative of severe immunosuppression related to infection with the Human Immunodeficiency Virus (HIV). National total does not include 29,911 cases in Puerto Rico, 647 cases in the Virgin Islands and 76 cases in other U.S. territories.

AIDS Cases in Children 12 Years and Younger through December 2006

National Total = 9,094 Juvenile AIDS Cases*

ALPHA ORDER

RANK	STATE	CASES	% of USA
18	Alabama	76	0.8%
43	Alaska	7	0.1%
23	Arizona	46	0.5%
24	Arkansas	36	0.4%
4	California	664	7.3%
28	Colorado	31	0.3%
11	Connecticut	183	2.0%
32	Delaware	26	0.3%
2	Florida	1,530	16.8%
9	Georgia	231	2.5%
36	Hawaii	17	0.2%
48	Idaho	2	0.0%
8	Illinois	282	3.1%
21	Indiana	56	0.6%
38	Iowa	13	0.1%
37	Kansas	14	0.2%
27	Kentucky	32	0.4%
14	Louisiana	128	1.4%
42	Maine	8	0.1%
7	Maryland	319	3.5%
10	Massachusetts	214	2.4%
16	Michigan	113	1.2%
30	Minnesota	28	0.3%
21	Mississippi	56	0.6%
19	Missouri	61	0.7%
47	Montana	3	0.0%
39	Nebraska	11	0.1%
29	Nevada	29	0.3%
41	New Hampshire	10	0.1%
3	New Jersey	778	8.6%
43	New Mexico	7	0.1%
1	New York	2,354	25.9%
15	North Carolina	118	1.3%
50	North Dakota	1	0.0%
13	Ohio	138	1.5%
32	Oklahoma	26	0.3%
34	Oregon	20	0.2%
6	Pennsylvania	365	4.0%
30	Rhode Island	28	0.3%
17	South Carolina	105	1.2%
46	South Dakota	5	0.1%
20	Tennessee	59	0.6%
5	Texas	392	4.3%
34	Utah	20	0.2%
45	Vermont	6	0.1%
12	Virginia	177	1.9%
25	Washington	34	0.4%
39	West Virginia	11	0.1%
26	Wisconsin	33	0.4%
48	Wyoming	2	0.0%

RANK ORDER

RANK	STATE	CASES	% of USA
1	New York	2,354	25.9%
2	Florida	1,530	16.8%
3	New Jersey	778	8.6%
4	California	664	7.3%
5	Texas	392	4.3%
6	Pennsylvania	365	4.0%
7	Maryland	319	3.5%
8	Illinois	282	3.1%
9	Georgia	231	2.5%
10	Massachusetts	214	2.4%
11	Connecticut	183	2.0%
12	Virginia	177	1.9%
13	Ohio	138	1.5%
14	Louisiana	128	1.4%
15	North Carolina	118	1.3%
16	Michigan	113	1.2%
17	South Carolina	105	1.2%
18	Alabama	76	0.8%
19	Missouri	61	0.7%
20	Tennessee	59	0.6%
21	Indiana	56	0.6%
21	Mississippi	56	0.6%
23	Arizona	46	0.5%
24	Arkansas	36	0.4%
25	Washington	34	0.4%
26	Wisconsin	33	0.4%
27	Kentucky	32	0.4%
28	Colorado	31	0.3%
29	Nevada	29	0.3%
30	Minnesota	28	0.3%
30	Rhode Island	28	0.3%
32	Delaware	26	0.3%
32	Oklahoma	26	0.3%
34	Oregon	20	0.2%
34	Utah	20	0.2%
36	Hawaii	17	0.2%
37	Kansas	14	0.2%
38	Iowa	13	0.1%
39	Nebraska	11	0.1%
39	West Virginia	11	0.1%
41	New Hampshire	10	0.1%
42	Maine	8	0.1%
43	Alaska	7	0.1%
43	New Mexico	7	0.1%
45	Vermont	6	0.1%
46	South Dakota	5	0.1%
47	Montana	3	0.0%
48	Idaho	2	0.0%
48	Wyoming	2	0.0%
50	North Dakota	1	0.0%
	District of Columbia	189	2.1%

Source: U.S. Department of Health and Human Services, Centers for Disease Control and Prevention
   "HIV/AIDS Surveillance Report, 2006" (Vol. 18, http://www.cdc.gov/hiv/topics/surveillance/resources/reports/index.htm)
*Cumulative through December 2006. AIDS is Acquired Immunodeficiency Syndrome. It is a specific group of diseases or conditions which are indicative of severe immunosuppression related to infection with the Human Immunodeficiency Virus (HIV). National total does not include 400 cases in Puerto Rico, 18 cases in the Virgin Islands and one case in Guam.

Chickenpox (Varicella) Cases Reported in 2008

National Total = 26,924 Cases*

RANK	STATE	CASES	% of USA
8	Alabama	1,081	4.0%
21	Alaska	74	0.3%
30	Arizona	0	0.0%
14	Arkansas	557	2.1%
30	California	0	0.0%
10	Colorado	842	3.1%
30	Connecticut	0	0.0%
25	Delaware	45	0.2%
5	Florida	1,708	6.3%
NA	Georgia**	NA	NA
23	Hawaii	64	0.2%
NA	Idaho**	NA	NA
6	Illinois	1,369	5.1%
30	Indiana	0	0.0%
NA	Iowa**	NA	NA
16	Kansas	471	1.7%
NA	Kentucky**	NA	NA
22	Louisiana	70	0.3%
30	Maine	0	0.0%
NA	Maryland**	NA	NA
29	Massachusetts	1	0.0%
2	Michigan	2,824	10.5%
30	Minnesota	0	0.0%
27	Mississippi	13	0.0%
11	Missouri	766	2.8%
17	Montana	340	1.3%
NA	Nebraska**	NA	NA
NA	Nevada**	NA	NA
19	New Hampshire	264	1.0%
NA	New Jersey**	NA	NA
20	New Mexico	209	0.8%
NA	New York**	NA	NA
NA	North Carolina**	NA	NA
24	North Dakota	49	0.2%
3	Ohio	2,406	8.9%
NA	Oklahoma**	NA	NA
NA	Oregon**	NA	NA
4	Pennsylvania	2,272	8.4%
30	Rhode Island	0	0.0%
9	South Carolina	851	3.2%
26	South Dakota	20	0.1%
NA	Tennessee**	NA	NA
1	Texas	7,106	26.4%
12	Utah	740	2.7%
18	Vermont	283	1.1%
7	Virginia	1,296	4.8%
NA	Washington**	NA	NA
13	West Virginia	682	2.5%
15	Wisconsin	488	1.8%
28	Wyoming	10	0.0%

RANK	STATE	CASES	% of USA
1	Texas	7,106	26.4%
2	Michigan	2,824	10.5%
3	Ohio	2,406	8.9%
4	Pennsylvania	2,272	8.4%
5	Florida	1,708	6.3%
6	Illinois	1,369	5.1%
7	Virginia	1,296	4.8%
8	Alabama	1,081	4.0%
9	South Carolina	851	3.2%
10	Colorado	842	3.1%
11	Missouri	766	2.8%
12	Utah	740	2.7%
13	West Virginia	682	2.5%
14	Arkansas	557	2.1%
15	Wisconsin	488	1.8%
16	Kansas	471	1.7%
17	Montana	340	1.3%
18	Vermont	283	1.1%
19	New Hampshire	264	1.0%
20	New Mexico	209	0.8%
21	Alaska	74	0.3%
22	Louisiana	70	0.3%
23	Hawaii	64	0.2%
24	North Dakota	49	0.2%
25	Delaware	45	0.2%
26	South Dakota	20	0.1%
27	Mississippi	13	0.0%
28	Wyoming	10	0.0%
29	Massachusetts	1	0.0%
30	Arizona	0	0.0%
30	California	0	0.0%
30	Connecticut	0	0.0%
30	Indiana	0	0.0%
30	Maine	0	0.0%
30	Minnesota	0	0.0%
30	Rhode Island	0	0.0%
NA	Georgia**	NA	NA
NA	Idaho**	NA	NA
NA	Iowa**	NA	NA
NA	Kentucky**	NA	NA
NA	Maryland**	NA	NA
NA	Nebraska**	NA	NA
NA	Nevada**	NA	NA
NA	New Jersey**	NA	NA
NA	New York**	NA	NA
NA	North Carolina**	NA	NA
NA	Oklahoma**	NA	NA
NA	Oregon**	NA	NA
NA	Tennessee**	NA	NA
NA	Washington**	NA	NA
	District of Columbia	23	0.1%

Source: U.S. Department of Health and Human Services, National Center for Health Statistics
"Morbidity and Mortality Weekly Report" (January 9, 2009, Vol. 57, No. 53, http://www.cdc.gov/mmwr/)
*Provisional data. An illness with acute onset of generalized maculo-papulovesicular rash without other apparent cause.
**Not notifiable.

Chickenpox (Varicella) Rate in 2008

National Rate = 8.9 Cases per 100,000 Population*

ALPHA ORDER

RANK	STATE	RATE
7	Alabama	23.2
17	Alaska	10.8
29	Arizona	0.0
10	Arkansas	19.5
29	California	0.0
13	Colorado	17.0
29	Connecticut	0.0
23	Delaware	5.2
20	Florida	9.3
NA	Georgia**	NA
24	Hawaii	5.0
NA	Idaho**	NA
18	Illinois	10.6
29	Indiana	0.0
NA	Iowa**	NA
14	Kansas	16.8
NA	Kentucky**	NA
27	Louisiana	1.6
29	Maine	0.0
NA	Maryland**	NA
29	Massachusetts	0.0
5	Michigan	28.2
29	Minnesota	0.0
28	Mississippi	0.4
16	Missouri	13.0
3	Montana	35.1
NA	Nebraska**	NA
NA	Nevada**	NA
9	New Hampshire	20.1
NA	New Jersey**	NA
19	New Mexico	10.5
NA	New York**	NA
NA	North Carolina**	NA
22	North Dakota	7.6
8	Ohio	20.9
NA	Oklahoma**	NA
NA	Oregon**	NA
12	Pennsylvania	18.3
29	Rhode Island	0.0
11	South Carolina	19.0
25	South Dakota	2.5
NA	Tennessee**	NA
4	Texas	29.2
6	Utah	27.0
1	Vermont	45.6
15	Virginia	16.7
NA	Washington**	NA
2	West Virginia	37.6
21	Wisconsin	8.7
26	Wyoming	1.9

RANK ORDER

RANK	STATE	RATE
1	Vermont	45.6
2	West Virginia	37.6
3	Montana	35.1
4	Texas	29.2
5	Michigan	28.2
6	Utah	27.0
7	Alabama	23.2
8	Ohio	20.9
9	New Hampshire	20.1
10	Arkansas	19.5
11	South Carolina	19.0
12	Pennsylvania	18.3
13	Colorado	17.0
14	Kansas	16.8
15	Virginia	16.7
16	Missouri	13.0
17	Alaska	10.8
18	Illinois	10.6
19	New Mexico	10.5
20	Florida	9.3
21	Wisconsin	8.7
22	North Dakota	7.6
23	Delaware	5.2
24	Hawaii	5.0
25	South Dakota	2.5
26	Wyoming	1.9
27	Louisiana	1.6
28	Mississippi	0.4
29	Arizona	0.0
29	California	0.0
29	Connecticut	0.0
29	Indiana	0.0
29	Maine	0.0
29	Massachusetts	0.0
29	Minnesota	0.0
29	Rhode Island	0.0
NA	Georgia**	NA
NA	Idaho**	NA
NA	Iowa**	NA
NA	Kentucky**	NA
NA	Maryland**	NA
NA	Nebraska**	NA
NA	Nevada**	NA
NA	New Jersey**	NA
NA	New York**	NA
NA	North Carolina**	NA
NA	Oklahoma**	NA
NA	Oregon**	NA
NA	Tennessee**	NA
NA	Washington**	NA

District of Columbia   3.9

Source: CQ Press using data from U.S. Department of Health and Human Services, National Center for Health Statistics
"Morbidity and Mortality Weekly Report" (January 9, 2009, Vol. 57, No. 53, http://www.cdc.gov/mmwr/)
*Provisional data. An illness with acute onset of generalized maculo-papulovesicular rash without other apparent cause.
**Not notifiable.

E. Coli Cases Reported in 2008

National Total = 5,164 Cases*

ALPHA ORDER

RANK	STATE	CASES	% of USA
28	Alabama	60	1.2%
46	Alaska	7	0.1%
26	Arizona	70	1.4%
34	Arkansas	43	0.8%
2	California	327	6.3%
10	Colorado	189	3.7%
33	Connecticut	44	0.9%
42	Delaware	14	0.3%
14	Florida	148	2.9%
23	Georgia	89	1.7%
43	Hawaii	13	0.3%
14	Idaho	148	2.9%
19	Illinois	112	2.2%
21	Indiana	93	1.8%
8	Iowa	203	3.9%
29	Kansas	54	1.0%
20	Kentucky	100	1.9%
50	Louisiana	2	0.0%
41	Maine	25	0.5%
17	Maryland	122	2.4%
25	Massachusetts	80	1.5%
4	Michigan	235	4.6%
8	Minnesota	203	3.9%
47	Mississippi	6	0.1%
12	Missouri	149	2.9%
37	Montana	37	0.7%
12	Nebraska	149	2.9%
44	Nevada	10	0.2%
35	New Hampshire	41	0.8%
38	New Jersey	30	0.6%
32	New Mexico	49	0.9%
1	New York	474	9.2%
16	North Carolina	140	2.7%
49	North Dakota	3	0.1%
7	Ohio	204	4.0%
29	Oklahoma	54	1.0%
27	Oregon	68	1.3%
22	Pennsylvania	91	1.8%
45	Rhode Island	9	0.2%
36	South Carolina	40	0.8%
31	South Dakota	51	1.0%
18	Tennessee	116	2.2%
5	Texas	227	4.4%
23	Utah	89	1.7%
40	Vermont	27	0.5%
6	Virginia	210	4.1%
11	Washington	183	3.5%
39	West Virginia	29	0.6%
3	Wisconsin	280	5.4%
48	Wyoming	5	0.1%

RANK ORDER

RANK	STATE	CASES	% of USA
1	New York	474	9.2%
2	California	327	6.3%
3	Wisconsin	280	5.4%
4	Michigan	235	4.6%
5	Texas	227	4.4%
6	Virginia	210	4.1%
7	Ohio	204	4.0%
8	Iowa	203	3.9%
8	Minnesota	203	3.9%
10	Colorado	189	3.7%
11	Washington	183	3.5%
12	Missouri	149	2.9%
12	Nebraska	149	2.9%
14	Florida	148	2.9%
14	Idaho	148	2.9%
16	North Carolina	140	2.7%
17	Maryland	122	2.4%
18	Tennessee	116	2.2%
19	Illinois	112	2.2%
20	Kentucky	100	1.9%
21	Indiana	93	1.8%
22	Pennsylvania	91	1.8%
23	Georgia	89	1.7%
23	Utah	89	1.7%
25	Massachusetts	80	1.5%
26	Arizona	70	1.4%
27	Oregon	68	1.3%
28	Alabama	60	1.2%
29	Kansas	54	1.0%
29	Oklahoma	54	1.0%
31	South Dakota	51	1.0%
32	New Mexico	49	0.9%
33	Connecticut	44	0.9%
34	Arkansas	43	0.8%
35	New Hampshire	41	0.8%
36	South Carolina	40	0.8%
37	Montana	37	0.7%
38	New Jersey	30	0.6%
39	West Virginia	29	0.6%
40	Vermont	27	0.5%
41	Maine	25	0.5%
42	Delaware	14	0.3%
43	Hawaii	13	0.3%
44	Nevada	10	0.2%
45	Rhode Island	9	0.2%
46	Alaska	7	0.1%
47	Mississippi	6	0.1%
48	Wyoming	5	0.1%
49	North Dakota	3	0.1%
50	Louisiana	2	0.0%
	District of Columbia	12	0.2%

Source: U.S. Department of Health and Human Services, National Center for Health Statistics
    "Morbidity and Mortality Weekly Report" (January 9, 2009, Vol. 57, No. 53, http://www.cdc.gov/mmwr/)
*Escherichia Coli is a common bacterium that normally inhabits the intestinal tracts of humans and animals but can cause infection in other parts of the body, especially the urinary tract. One strain, sometimes transmitted in hamburger meat, can cause serious infection resulting in sickness and death.

E. Coli Rate in 2008

National Rate = 1.7 Cases per 100,000 Population*

ALPHA ORDER

RANK	STATE	RATE
31	Alabama	1.3
35	Alaska	1.0
34	Arizona	1.1
27	Arkansas	1.5
37	California	0.9
8	Colorado	3.8
31	Connecticut	1.3
25	Delaware	1.6
44	Florida	0.8
37	Georgia	0.9
35	Hawaii	1.0
1	Idaho	9.7
37	Illinois	0.9
27	Indiana	1.5
3	Iowa	6.8
20	Kansas	1.9
17	Kentucky	2.3
50	Louisiana	0.0
20	Maine	1.9
19	Maryland	2.2
33	Massachusetts	1.2
17	Michigan	2.3
7	Minnesota	3.9
49	Mississippi	0.2
14	Missouri	2.5
8	Montana	3.8
2	Nebraska	8.4
47	Nevada	0.4
11	New Hampshire	3.1
48	New Jersey	0.3
14	New Mexico	2.5
16	New York	2.4
27	North Carolina	1.5
46	North Dakota	0.5
23	Ohio	1.8
27	Oklahoma	1.5
23	Oregon	1.8
45	Pennsylvania	0.7
37	Rhode Island	0.9
37	South Carolina	0.9
4	South Dakota	6.3
20	Tennessee	1.9
37	Texas	0.9
10	Utah	3.3
6	Vermont	4.3
13	Virginia	2.7
12	Washington	2.8
25	West Virginia	1.6
5	Wisconsin	5.0
37	Wyoming	0.9

RANK ORDER

RANK	STATE	RATE
1	Idaho	9.7
2	Nebraska	8.4
3	Iowa	6.8
4	South Dakota	6.3
5	Wisconsin	5.0
6	Vermont	4.3
7	Minnesota	3.9
8	Colorado	3.8
8	Montana	3.8
10	Utah	3.3
11	New Hampshire	3.1
12	Washington	2.8
13	Virginia	2.7
14	Missouri	2.5
14	New Mexico	2.5
16	New York	2.4
17	Kentucky	2.3
17	Michigan	2.3
19	Maryland	2.2
20	Kansas	1.9
20	Maine	1.9
20	Tennessee	1.9
23	Ohio	1.8
23	Oregon	1.8
25	Delaware	1.6
25	West Virginia	1.6
27	Arkansas	1.5
27	Indiana	1.5
27	North Carolina	1.5
27	Oklahoma	1.5
31	Alabama	1.3
31	Connecticut	1.3
33	Massachusetts	1.2
34	Arizona	1.1
35	Alaska	1.0
35	Hawaii	1.0
37	California	0.9
37	Georgia	0.9
37	Illinois	0.9
37	Rhode Island	0.9
37	South Carolina	0.9
37	Texas	0.9
37	Wyoming	0.9
44	Florida	0.8
45	Pennsylvania	0.7
46	North Dakota	0.5
47	Nevada	0.4
48	New Jersey	0.3
49	Mississippi	0.2
50	Louisiana	0.0

District of Columbia	2.0

Source: CQ Press using data from U.S. Department of Health and Human Services, National Center for Health Statistics
"Morbidity and Mortality Weekly Report" (January 9, 2009, Vol. 57, No. 53, http://www.cdc.gov/mmwr/)

*Escherichia Coli is a common bacterium that normally inhabits the intestinal tracts of humans and animals but can cause infection in other parts of the body, especially the urinary tract. One strain, sometimes transmitted in hamburger meat, can cause serious infection resulting in sickness and death.

Hepatitis A and B Cases Reported in 2008

National Total = 5,853 Cases*

ALPHA ORDER

RANK	STATE	CASES	% of USA
19	Alabama	115	2.0%
45	Alaska	12	0.2%
9	Arizona	177	3.0%
36	Arkansas	35	0.6%
1	California	711	12.1%
26	Colorado	65	1.1%
30	Connecticut	49	0.8%
43	Delaware	18	0.3%
3	Florida	486	8.3%
8	Georgia	191	3.3%
39	Hawaii	24	0.4%
38	Idaho	27	0.5%
7	Illinois	212	3.6%
24	Indiana	75	1.3%
15	Iowa	126	2.2%
42	Kansas	21	0.4%
17	Kentucky	121	2.1%
22	Louisiana	90	1.5%
39	Maine	24	0.4%
17	Maryland	121	2.1%
32	Massachusetts	47	0.8%
5	Michigan	246	4.2%
28	Minnesota	57	1.0%
29	Mississippi	51	0.9%
20	Missouri	102	1.7%
49	Montana	3	0.1%
30	Nebraska	49	0.8%
33	Nevada	43	0.7%
39	New Hampshire	24	0.4%
10	New Jersey	174	3.0%
37	New Mexico	28	0.5%
4	New York	364	6.2%
14	North Carolina	145	2.5%
50	North Dakota	1	0.0%
12	Ohio	163	2.8%
16	Oklahoma	124	2.1%
27	Oregon	64	1.1%
6	Pennsylvania	220	3.8%
44	Rhode Island	16	0.3%
23	South Carolina	81	1.4%
47	South Dakota	4	0.1%
11	Tennessee	168	2.9%
2	Texas	590	10.1%
33	Utah	43	0.7%
47	Vermont	4	0.1%
13	Virginia	158	2.7%
21	Washington	97	1.7%
25	West Virginia	74	1.3%
35	Wisconsin	37	0.6%
46	Wyoming	7	0.1%

RANK ORDER

RANK	STATE	CASES	% of USA
1	California	711	12.1%
2	Texas	590	10.1%
3	Florida	486	8.3%
4	New York	364	6.2%
5	Michigan	246	4.2%
6	Pennsylvania	220	3.8%
7	Illinois	212	3.6%
8	Georgia	191	3.3%
9	Arizona	177	3.0%
10	New Jersey	174	3.0%
11	Tennessee	168	2.9%
12	Ohio	163	2.8%
13	Virginia	158	2.7%
14	North Carolina	145	2.5%
15	Iowa	126	2.2%
16	Oklahoma	124	2.1%
17	Kentucky	121	2.1%
17	Maryland	121	2.1%
19	Alabama	115	2.0%
20	Missouri	102	1.7%
21	Washington	97	1.7%
22	Louisiana	90	1.5%
23	South Carolina	81	1.4%
24	Indiana	75	1.3%
25	West Virginia	74	1.3%
26	Colorado	65	1.1%
27	Oregon	64	1.1%
28	Minnesota	57	1.0%
29	Mississippi	51	0.9%
30	Connecticut	49	0.8%
30	Nebraska	49	0.8%
32	Massachusetts	47	0.8%
33	Nevada	43	0.7%
33	Utah	43	0.7%
35	Wisconsin	37	0.6%
36	Arkansas	35	0.6%
37	New Mexico	28	0.5%
38	Idaho	27	0.5%
39	Hawaii	24	0.4%
39	Maine	24	0.4%
39	New Hampshire	24	0.4%
42	Kansas	21	0.4%
43	Delaware	18	0.3%
44	Rhode Island	16	0.3%
45	Alaska	12	0.2%
46	Wyoming	7	0.1%
47	South Dakota	4	0.1%
47	Vermont	4	0.1%
49	Montana	3	0.1%
50	North Dakota	1	0.0%
	District of Columbia**	NA	NA

Source: U.S. Department of Health and Human Services, National Center for Health Statistics
   "Morbidity and Mortality Weekly Report" (January 9, 2009, Vol. 57, No. 53, http://www.cdc.gov/mmwr/)
*Provisional data. An inflammation of the liver.
**Not available.

Hepatitis A and B Rate in 2008

National Rate = 1.9 Cases per 100,000 Population*

ALPHA ORDER				RANK ORDER		
RANK	STATE	RATE		RANK	STATE	RATE
9	Alabama	2.5		1	Iowa	4.2
26	Alaska	1.7		2	West Virginia	4.1
5	Arizona	2.7		3	Oklahoma	3.4
41	Arkansas	1.2		4	Kentucky	2.8
18	California	1.9		5	Arizona	2.7
39	Colorado	1.3		5	Florida	2.7
36	Connecticut	1.4		5	Nebraska	2.7
12	Delaware	2.1		5	Tennessee	2.7
5	Florida	2.7		9	Alabama	2.5
14	Georgia	2.0		9	Michigan	2.5
18	Hawaii	1.9		11	Texas	2.4
21	Idaho	1.8		12	Delaware	2.1
31	Illinois	1.6		12	Maryland	2.1
41	Indiana	1.2		14	Georgia	2.0
1	Iowa	4.2		14	Louisiana	2.0
44	Kansas	0.7		14	New Jersey	2.0
4	Kentucky	2.8		14	Virginia	2.0
14	Louisiana	2.0		18	California	1.9
21	Maine	1.8		18	Hawaii	1.9
12	Maryland	2.1		18	New York	1.9
44	Massachusetts	0.7		21	Idaho	1.8
9	Michigan	2.5		21	Maine	1.8
43	Minnesota	1.1		21	New Hampshire	1.8
26	Mississippi	1.7		21	Pennsylvania	1.8
26	Missouri	1.7		21	South Carolina	1.8
49	Montana	0.3		26	Alaska	1.7
5	Nebraska	2.7		26	Mississippi	1.7
26	Nevada	1.7		26	Missouri	1.7
21	New Hampshire	1.8		26	Nevada	1.7
14	New Jersey	2.0		26	Oregon	1.7
36	New Mexico	1.4		31	Illinois	1.6
18	New York	1.9		31	North Carolina	1.6
31	North Carolina	1.6		31	Utah	1.6
50	North Dakota	0.2		34	Rhode Island	1.5
36	Ohio	1.4		34	Washington	1.5
3	Oklahoma	3.4		36	Connecticut	1.4
26	Oregon	1.7		36	New Mexico	1.4
21	Pennsylvania	1.8		36	Ohio	1.4
34	Rhode Island	1.5		39	Colorado	1.3
21	South Carolina	1.8		39	Wyoming	1.3
48	South Dakota	0.5		41	Arkansas	1.2
5	Tennessee	2.7		41	Indiana	1.2
11	Texas	2.4		43	Minnesota	1.1
31	Utah	1.6		44	Kansas	0.7
47	Vermont	0.6		44	Massachusetts	0.7
14	Virginia	2.0		44	Wisconsin	0.7
34	Washington	1.5		47	Vermont	0.6
2	West Virginia	4.1		48	South Dakota	0.5
44	Wisconsin	0.7		49	Montana	0.3
39	Wyoming	1.3		50	North Dakota	0.2
				District of Columbia**		NA

Source: CQ Press using data from U.S. Department of Health and Human Services, National Center for Health Statistics
   "Morbidity and Mortality Weekly Report" (January 9, 2009, Vol. 57, No. 53, http://www.cdc.gov/mmwr/)
*Provisional data. An inflammation of the liver.
**Not available.

Legionellosis Cases Reported in 2008

National Total = 2,815 Cases*

ALPHA ORDER

RANK	STATE	CASES	% of USA
29	Alabama	16	0.6%
44	Alaska	3	0.1%
23	Arizona	23	0.8%
34	Arkansas	11	0.4%
4	California	190	6.7%
35	Colorado	10	0.4%
15	Connecticut	46	1.6%
31	Delaware	13	0.5%
6	Florida	149	5.3%
19	Georgia	32	1.1%
40	Hawaii	8	0.3%
44	Idaho	3	0.1%
9	Illinois	89	3.2%
14	Indiana	53	1.9%
27	Iowa	19	0.7%
47	Kansas	2	0.1%
12	Kentucky	56	2.0%
39	Louisiana	9	0.3%
35	Maine	10	0.4%
7	Maryland	126	4.5%
31	Massachusetts	13	0.5%
5	Michigan	158	5.6%
23	Minnesota	23	0.8%
48	Mississippi	1	0.0%
10	Missouri	70	2.5%
43	Montana	4	0.1%
26	Nebraska	21	0.7%
35	Nevada	10	0.4%
21	New Hampshire	30	1.1%
8	New Jersey	103	3.7%
41	New Mexico	7	0.2%
1	New York	455	16.2%
18	North Carolina	37	1.3%
49	North Dakota	0	0.0%
3	Ohio	269	9.6%
35	Oklahoma	10	0.4%
29	Oregon	16	0.6%
2	Pennsylvania	392	13.9%
16	Rhode Island	40	1.4%
31	South Carolina	13	0.5%
44	South Dakota	3	0.1%
16	Tennessee	40	1.4%
12	Texas	56	2.0%
20	Utah	31	1.1%
42	Vermont	5	0.2%
11	Virginia	60	2.1%
28	Washington	17	0.6%
23	West Virginia	23	0.8%
22	Wisconsin	25	0.9%
49	Wyoming	0	0.0%

RANK ORDER

RANK	STATE	CASES	% of USA
1	New York	455	16.2%
2	Pennsylvania	392	13.9%
3	Ohio	269	9.6%
4	California	190	6.7%
5	Michigan	158	5.6%
6	Florida	149	5.3%
7	Maryland	126	4.5%
8	New Jersey	103	3.7%
9	Illinois	89	3.2%
10	Missouri	70	2.5%
11	Virginia	60	2.1%
12	Kentucky	56	2.0%
12	Texas	56	2.0%
14	Indiana	53	1.9%
15	Connecticut	46	1.6%
16	Rhode Island	40	1.4%
16	Tennessee	40	1.4%
18	North Carolina	37	1.3%
19	Georgia	32	1.1%
20	Utah	31	1.1%
21	New Hampshire	30	1.1%
22	Wisconsin	25	0.9%
23	Arizona	23	0.8%
23	Minnesota	23	0.8%
23	West Virginia	23	0.8%
26	Nebraska	21	0.7%
27	Iowa	19	0.7%
28	Washington	17	0.6%
29	Alabama	16	0.6%
29	Oregon	16	0.6%
31	Delaware	13	0.5%
31	Massachusetts	13	0.5%
31	South Carolina	13	0.5%
34	Arkansas	11	0.4%
35	Colorado	10	0.4%
35	Maine	10	0.4%
35	Nevada	10	0.4%
35	Oklahoma	10	0.4%
39	Louisiana	9	0.3%
40	Hawaii	8	0.3%
41	New Mexico	7	0.2%
42	Vermont	5	0.2%
43	Montana	4	0.1%
44	Alaska	3	0.1%
44	Idaho	3	0.1%
44	South Dakota	3	0.1%
47	Kansas	2	0.1%
48	Mississippi	1	0.0%
49	North Dakota	0	0.0%
49	Wyoming	0	0.0%
	District of Columbia	15	0.5%

Source: U.S. Department of Health and Human Services, National Center for Health Statistics
"Morbidity and Mortality Weekly Report" (January 9, 2009, Vol. 57, No. 53, http://www.cdc.gov/mmwr/)
*Provisional data. A pneumonia-like disease (Legionnaire's Disease).

Legionellosis Rate in 2008

National Rate = 0.9 Cases per 100,000 Population*

ALPHA ORDER				RANK ORDER		
RANK	STATE	RATE		RANK	STATE	RATE
37	Alabama	0.3		1	Rhode Island	3.8
26	Alaska	0.4		2	Pennsylvania	3.1
26	Arizona	0.4		3	New Hampshire	2.3
26	Arkansas	0.4		3	New York	2.3
25	California	0.5		3	Ohio	2.3
42	Colorado	0.2		6	Maryland	2.2
9	Connecticut	1.3		7	Michigan	1.6
8	Delaware	1.5		8	Delaware	1.5
16	Florida	0.8		9	Connecticut	1.3
37	Georgia	0.3		9	Kentucky	1.3
22	Hawaii	0.6		9	West Virginia	1.3
42	Idaho	0.2		12	Missouri	1.2
21	Illinois	0.7		12	Nebraska	1.2
16	Indiana	0.8		12	New Jersey	1.2
22	Iowa	0.6		15	Utah	1.1
47	Kansas	0.1		16	Florida	0.8
9	Kentucky	1.3		16	Indiana	0.8
42	Louisiana	0.2		16	Maine	0.8
16	Maine	0.8		16	Vermont	0.8
6	Maryland	2.2		16	Virginia	0.8
42	Massachusetts	0.2		21	Illinois	0.7
7	Michigan	1.6		22	Hawaii	0.6
26	Minnesota	0.4		22	Iowa	0.6
48	Mississippi	0.0		22	Tennessee	0.6
12	Missouri	1.2		25	California	0.5
26	Montana	0.4		26	Alaska	0.4
12	Nebraska	1.2		26	Arizona	0.4
26	Nevada	0.4		26	Arkansas	0.4
3	New Hampshire	2.3		26	Minnesota	0.4
12	New Jersey	1.2		26	Montana	0.4
26	New Mexico	0.4		26	Nevada	0.4
3	New York	2.3		26	New Mexico	0.4
26	North Carolina	0.4		26	North Carolina	0.4
48	North Dakota	0.0		26	Oregon	0.4
3	Ohio	2.3		26	South Dakota	0.4
37	Oklahoma	0.3		26	Wisconsin	0.4
26	Oregon	0.4		37	Alabama	0.3
2	Pennsylvania	3.1		37	Georgia	0.3
1	Rhode Island	3.8		37	Oklahoma	0.3
37	South Carolina	0.3		37	South Carolina	0.3
26	South Dakota	0.4		37	Washington	0.3
22	Tennessee	0.6		42	Colorado	0.2
42	Texas	0.2		42	Idaho	0.2
15	Utah	1.1		42	Louisiana	0.2
16	Vermont	0.8		42	Massachusetts	0.2
16	Virginia	0.8		42	Texas	0.2
37	Washington	0.3		47	Kansas	0.1
9	West Virginia	1.3		48	Mississippi	0.0
26	Wisconsin	0.4		48	North Dakota	0.0
48	Wyoming	0.0		48	Wyoming	0.0
					District of Columbia	2.5

Source: CQ Press using data from U.S. Department of Health and Human Services, National Center for Health Statistics
    "Morbidity and Mortality Weekly Report" (January 9, 2009, Vol. 57, No. 53, http://www.cdc.gov/mmwr/)
*Provisional data. A pneumonia-like disease (Legionnaire's Disease).

Lyme Disease Cases in 2008

National Total = 26,739 Cases*

ALPHA ORDER

RANK	STATE	CASES	% of USA
29	Alabama	10	0.0%
35	Alaska	5	0.0%
31	Arizona	8	0.0%
46	Arkansas	0	0.0%
13	California	205	0.8%
33	Colorado	7	0.0%
46	Connecticut	0	0.0%
11	Delaware	766	2.9%
14	Florida	115	0.4%
25	Georgia	24	0.1%
NA	Hawaii**	NA	NA
30	Idaho	9	0.0%
19	Illinois	96	0.4%
23	Indiana	41	0.2%
15	Iowa	103	0.4%
35	Kansas	5	0.0%
35	Kentucky	5	0.0%
41	Louisiana	3	0.0%
9	Maine	868	3.2%
4	Maryland	2,076	7.8%
8	Massachusetts	1,039	3.9%
16	Michigan	100	0.4%
6	Minnesota	1,183	4.4%
44	Mississippi	1	0.0%
31	Missouri	8	0.0%
39	Montana	4	0.0%
27	Nebraska	14	0.1%
35	Nevada	5	0.0%
5	New Hampshire	1,465	5.5%
3	New Jersey	2,801	10.5%
34	New Mexico	6	0.0%
2	New York	5,914	22.1%
20	North Carolina	51	0.2%
44	North Dakota	1	0.0%
21	Ohio	48	0.2%
46	Oklahoma	0	0.0%
21	Oregon	48	0.2%
1	Pennsylvania	6,958	26.0%
46	Rhode Island	0	0.0%
25	South Carolina	24	0.1%
41	South Dakota	3	0.0%
24	Tennessee	31	0.1%
17	Texas	98	0.4%
39	Utah	4	0.0%
12	Vermont	362	1.4%
10	Virginia	809	3.0%
28	Washington	11	0.0%
17	West Virginia	98	0.4%
7	Wisconsin	1,146	4.3%
41	Wyoming	3	0.0%

RANK ORDER

RANK	STATE	CASES	% of USA
1	Pennsylvania	6,958	26.0%
2	New York	5,914	22.1%
3	New Jersey	2,801	10.5%
4	Maryland	2,076	7.8%
5	New Hampshire	1,465	5.5%
6	Minnesota	1,183	4.4%
7	Wisconsin	1,146	4.3%
8	Massachusetts	1,039	3.9%
9	Maine	868	3.2%
10	Virginia	809	3.0%
11	Delaware	766	2.9%
12	Vermont	362	1.4%
13	California	205	0.8%
14	Florida	115	0.4%
15	Iowa	103	0.4%
16	Michigan	100	0.4%
17	Texas	98	0.4%
17	West Virginia	98	0.4%
19	Illinois	96	0.4%
20	North Carolina	51	0.2%
21	Ohio	48	0.2%
21	Oregon	48	0.2%
23	Indiana	41	0.2%
24	Tennessee	31	0.1%
25	Georgia	24	0.1%
25	South Carolina	24	0.1%
27	Nebraska	14	0.1%
28	Washington	11	0.0%
29	Alabama	10	0.0%
30	Idaho	9	0.0%
31	Arizona	8	0.0%
31	Missouri	8	0.0%
33	Colorado	7	0.0%
34	New Mexico	6	0.0%
35	Alaska	5	0.0%
35	Kansas	5	0.0%
35	Kentucky	5	0.0%
35	Nevada	5	0.0%
39	Montana	4	0.0%
39	Utah	4	0.0%
41	Louisiana	3	0.0%
41	South Dakota	3	0.0%
41	Wyoming	3	0.0%
44	Mississippi	1	0.0%
44	North Dakota	1	0.0%
46	Arkansas	0	0.0%
46	Connecticut	0	0.0%
46	Oklahoma	0	0.0%
46	Rhode Island	0	0.0%
NA	Hawaii**	NA	NA

District of Columbia   158   0.6%

Source: U.S. Department of Health and Human Services, National Center for Health Statistics
   "Morbidity and Mortality Weekly Report" (January 9, 2009, Vol. 57, No. 53, http://www.cdc.gov/mmwr/)
*Provisional data. Caused by ticks-lesions, followed by arthritis of large joints, myalgia, malaise, and neurologic and cardiac manifestations. Named after Old Lyme, CT, where the disease was first reported.
**Not notifiable.

Lyme Disease Rate in 2008

National Rate = 8.8 Cases per 100,000 Population*

ALPHA ORDER

RANK	STATE	RATE
33	Alabama	0.2
18	Alaska	0.7
39	Arizona	0.1
45	Arkansas	0.0
20	California	0.6
39	Colorado	0.1
45	Connecticut	0.0
2	Delaware	87.7
20	Florida	0.6
33	Georgia	0.2
NA	Hawaii**	NA
20	Idaho	0.6
18	Illinois	0.7
20	Indiana	0.6
14	Iowa	3.4
33	Kansas	0.2
39	Kentucky	0.1
39	Louisiana	0.1
3	Maine	65.9
6	Maryland	36.9
11	Massachusetts	16.0
16	Michigan	1.0
9	Minnesota	22.7
45	Mississippi	0.0
39	Missouri	0.1
28	Montana	0.4
17	Nebraska	0.8
33	Nevada	0.2
1	New Hampshire	111.3
7	New Jersey	32.3
32	New Mexico	0.3
8	New York	30.3
20	North Carolina	0.6
33	North Dakota	0.2
28	Ohio	0.4
45	Oklahoma	0.0
15	Oregon	1.3
5	Pennsylvania	55.9
45	Rhode Island	0.0
26	South Carolina	0.5
28	South Dakota	0.4
26	Tennessee	0.5
28	Texas	0.4
39	Utah	0.1
4	Vermont	58.3
12	Virginia	10.4
33	Washington	0.2
13	West Virginia	5.4
10	Wisconsin	20.4
20	Wyoming	0.6

RANK ORDER

RANK	STATE	RATE
1	New Hampshire	111.3
2	Delaware	87.7
3	Maine	65.9
4	Vermont	58.3
5	Pennsylvania	55.9
6	Maryland	36.9
7	New Jersey	32.3
8	New York	30.3
9	Minnesota	22.7
10	Wisconsin	20.4
11	Massachusetts	16.0
12	Virginia	10.4
13	West Virginia	5.4
14	Iowa	3.4
15	Oregon	1.3
16	Michigan	1.0
17	Nebraska	0.8
18	Alaska	0.7
18	Illinois	0.7
20	California	0.6
20	Florida	0.6
20	Idaho	0.6
20	Indiana	0.6
20	North Carolina	0.6
20	Wyoming	0.6
26	South Carolina	0.5
26	Tennessee	0.5
28	Montana	0.4
28	Ohio	0.4
28	South Dakota	0.4
28	Texas	0.4
32	New Mexico	0.3
33	Alabama	0.2
33	Georgia	0.2
33	Kansas	0.2
33	Nevada	0.2
33	North Dakota	0.2
33	Washington	0.2
39	Arizona	0.1
39	Colorado	0.1
39	Kentucky	0.1
39	Louisiana	0.1
39	Missouri	0.1
39	Utah	0.1
45	Arkansas	0.0
45	Connecticut	0.0
45	Mississippi	0.0
45	Oklahoma	0.0
45	Rhode Island	0.0
NA	Hawaii**	NA

District of Columbia 26.7

Source: CQ Press using data from U.S. Department of Health and Human Services, National Center for Health Statistics
    "Morbidity and Mortality Weekly Report" (January 9, 2009, Vol. 57, No. 53, http://www.cdc.gov/mmwr/)
*Provisional data. Caused by ticks-lesions, followed by arthritis of large joints, myalgia, malaise, and neurologic and cardiac
manifestations. Named after Old Lyme, CT, where the disease was first reported.
**Not notifiable.

Malaria Cases Reported in 2008

National Total = 1,075 Cases*

ALPHA ORDER

RANK	STATE	CASES	% of USA
31	Alabama	4	0.4%
25	Alaska	6	0.6%
16	Arizona	14	1.3%
44	Arkansas	0	0.0%
2	California	123	11.4%
31	Colorado	4	0.4%
21	Connecticut	11	1.0%
36	Delaware	3	0.3%
6	Florida	64	6.0%
7	Georgia	53	4.9%
36	Hawaii	3	0.3%
36	Idaho	3	0.3%
4	Illinois	70	6.5%
28	Indiana	5	0.5%
20	Iowa	12	1.1%
22	Kansas	9	0.8%
25	Kentucky	6	0.6%
31	Louisiana	4	0.4%
41	Maine	1	0.1%
5	Maryland	68	6.3%
16	Massachusetts	14	1.3%
14	Michigan	18	1.7%
13	Minnesota	28	2.6%
41	Mississippi	1	0.1%
16	Missouri	14	1.3%
44	Montana	0	0.0%
24	Nebraska	8	0.7%
36	Nevada	3	0.3%
25	New Hampshire	6	0.6%
44	New Jersey	0	0.0%
36	New Mexico	3	0.3%
1	New York	207	19.3%
10	North Carolina	31	2.9%
44	North Dakota	0	0.0%
11	Ohio	30	2.8%
31	Oklahoma	4	0.4%
31	Oregon	4	0.4%
9	Pennsylvania	40	3.7%
41	Rhode Island	1	0.1%
22	South Carolina	9	0.8%
44	South Dakota	0	0.0%
19	Tennessee	13	1.2%
3	Texas	74	6.9%
28	Utah	5	0.5%
28	Vermont	5	0.5%
8	Virginia	43	4.0%
12	Washington	29	2.7%
44	West Virginia	0	0.0%
14	Wisconsin	18	1.7%
44	Wyoming	0	0.0%

RANK ORDER

RANK	STATE	CASES	% of USA
1	New York	207	19.3%
2	California	123	11.4%
3	Texas	74	6.9%
4	Illinois	70	6.5%
5	Maryland	68	6.3%
6	Florida	64	6.0%
7	Georgia	53	4.9%
8	Virginia	43	4.0%
9	Pennsylvania	40	3.7%
10	North Carolina	31	2.9%
11	Ohio	30	2.8%
12	Washington	29	2.7%
13	Minnesota	28	2.6%
14	Michigan	18	1.7%
14	Wisconsin	18	1.7%
16	Arizona	14	1.3%
16	Massachusetts	14	1.3%
16	Missouri	14	1.3%
19	Tennessee	13	1.2%
20	Iowa	12	1.1%
21	Connecticut	11	1.0%
22	Kansas	9	0.8%
22	South Carolina	9	0.8%
24	Nebraska	8	0.7%
25	Alaska	6	0.6%
25	Kentucky	6	0.6%
25	New Hampshire	6	0.6%
28	Indiana	5	0.5%
28	Utah	5	0.5%
28	Vermont	5	0.5%
31	Alabama	4	0.4%
31	Colorado	4	0.4%
31	Louisiana	4	0.4%
31	Oklahoma	4	0.4%
31	Oregon	4	0.4%
36	Delaware	3	0.3%
36	Hawaii	3	0.3%
36	Idaho	3	0.3%
36	Nevada	3	0.3%
36	New Mexico	3	0.3%
41	Maine	1	0.1%
41	Mississippi	1	0.1%
41	Rhode Island	1	0.1%
44	Arkansas	0	0.0%
44	Montana	0	0.0%
44	New Jersey	0	0.0%
44	North Dakota	0	0.0%
44	South Dakota	0	0.0%
44	West Virginia	0	0.0%
44	Wyoming	0	0.0%
	District of Columbia	4	0.4%

Source: U.S. Department of Health and Human Services, National Center for Health Statistics
"Morbidity and Mortality Weekly Report" (January 9, 2009, Vol. 57, No. 53, http://www.cdc.gov/mmwr/)
*Provisional data. Infectious disease usually transmitted by bites of infected mosquitoes. Symptoms include high fever, shaking chills, sweating, and anemia.

Malaria Rate in 2008

National Rate = 0.4 Cases per 100,000 Population*

ALPHA ORDER

RANK	STATE	RATE
33	Alabama	0.1
3	Alaska	0.9
23	Arizona	0.2
43	Arkansas	0.0
13	California	0.3
33	Colorado	0.1
13	Connecticut	0.3
13	Delaware	0.3
13	Florida	0.3
6	Georgia	0.5
23	Hawaii	0.2
23	Idaho	0.2
6	Illinois	0.5
33	Indiana	0.1
10	Iowa	0.4
13	Kansas	0.3
33	Kentucky	0.1
33	Louisiana	0.1
33	Maine	0.1
1	Maryland	1.2
23	Massachusetts	0.2
23	Michigan	0.2
6	Minnesota	0.5
43	Mississippi	0.0
23	Missouri	0.2
43	Montana	0.0
10	Nebraska	0.4
33	Nevada	0.1
6	New Hampshire	0.5
43	New Jersey	0.0
23	New Mexico	0.2
2	New York	1.1
13	North Carolina	0.3
43	North Dakota	0.0
13	Ohio	0.3
33	Oklahoma	0.1
33	Oregon	0.1
13	Pennsylvania	0.3
33	Rhode Island	0.1
23	South Carolina	0.2
43	South Dakota	0.0
23	Tennessee	0.2
13	Texas	0.3
23	Utah	0.2
4	Vermont	0.8
5	Virginia	0.6
10	Washington	0.4
43	West Virginia	0.0
13	Wisconsin	0.3
43	Wyoming	0.0

RANK ORDER

RANK	STATE	RATE
1	Maryland	1.2
2	New York	1.1
3	Alaska	0.9
4	Vermont	0.8
5	Virginia	0.6
6	Georgia	0.5
6	Illinois	0.5
6	Minnesota	0.5
6	New Hampshire	0.5
10	Iowa	0.4
10	Nebraska	0.4
10	Washington	0.4
13	California	0.3
13	Connecticut	0.3
13	Delaware	0.3
13	Florida	0.3
13	Kansas	0.3
13	North Carolina	0.3
13	Ohio	0.3
13	Pennsylvania	0.3
13	Texas	0.3
13	Wisconsin	0.3
23	Arizona	0.2
23	Hawaii	0.2
23	Idaho	0.2
23	Massachusetts	0.2
23	Michigan	0.2
23	Missouri	0.2
23	New Mexico	0.2
23	South Carolina	0.2
23	Tennessee	0.2
23	Utah	0.2
33	Alabama	0.1
33	Colorado	0.1
33	Indiana	0.1
33	Kentucky	0.1
33	Louisiana	0.1
33	Maine	0.1
33	Nevada	0.1
33	Oklahoma	0.1
33	Oregon	0.1
33	Rhode Island	0.1
43	Arkansas	0.0
43	Mississippi	0.0
43	Montana	0.0
43	New Jersey	0.0
43	North Dakota	0.0
43	South Dakota	0.0
43	West Virginia	0.0
43	Wyoming	0.0

District of Columbia   0.7

Source: CQ Press using data from U.S. Department of Health and Human Services, National Center for Health Statistics
"Morbidity and Mortality Weekly Report" (January 9, 2009, Vol. 57, No. 53, http://www.cdc.gov/mmwr/)
*Provisional data. Infectious disease usually transmitted by bites of infected mosquitoes. Symptoms include high fever,
shaking chills, sweating, and anemia.

Meningococcal Infections Reported in 2008

National Total = 1,057 Cases*

ALPHA ORDER

RANK	STATE	CASES	% of USA
29	Alabama	10	0.9%
37	Alaska	5	0.5%
32	Arizona	9	0.9%
25	Arkansas	14	1.3%
1	California	186	17.6%
22	Colorado	16	1.5%
47	Connecticut	1	0.1%
45	Delaware	2	0.2%
5	Florida	50	4.7%
18	Georgia	18	1.7%
37	Hawaii	5	0.5%
37	Idaho	5	0.5%
2	Illinois	66	6.2%
11	Indiana	27	2.6%
18	Iowa	18	1.7%
35	Kansas	7	0.7%
29	Kentucky	10	0.9%
14	Louisiana	24	2.3%
36	Maine	6	0.6%
18	Maryland	18	1.7%
24	Massachusetts	15	1.4%
9	Michigan	30	2.8%
11	Minnesota	27	2.6%
27	Mississippi	12	1.1%
13	Missouri	26	2.5%
37	Montana	5	0.5%
27	Nebraska	12	1.1%
42	Nevada	4	0.4%
48	New Hampshire	0	0.0%
29	New Jersey	10	0.9%
34	New Mexico	8	0.8%
3	New York	60	5.7%
22	North Carolina	16	1.5%
43	North Dakota	3	0.3%
7	Ohio	40	3.8%
18	Oklahoma	18	1.7%
8	Oregon	39	3.7%
6	Pennsylvania	49	4.6%
48	Rhode Island	0	0.0%
15	South Carolina	22	2.1%
43	South Dakota	3	0.3%
15	Tennessee	22	2.1%
4	Texas	59	5.6%
32	Utah	9	0.9%
48	Vermont	0	0.0%
15	Virginia	22	2.1%
10	Washington	28	2.6%
37	West Virginia	5	0.5%
25	Wisconsin	14	1.3%
45	Wyoming	2	0.2%

RANK ORDER

RANK	STATE	CASES	% of USA
1	California	186	17.6%
2	Illinois	66	6.2%
3	New York	60	5.7%
4	Texas	59	5.6%
5	Florida	50	4.7%
6	Pennsylvania	49	4.6%
7	Ohio	40	3.8%
8	Oregon	39	3.7%
9	Michigan	30	2.8%
10	Washington	28	2.6%
11	Indiana	27	2.6%
11	Minnesota	27	2.6%
13	Missouri	26	2.5%
14	Louisiana	24	2.3%
15	South Carolina	22	2.1%
15	Tennessee	22	2.1%
15	Virginia	22	2.1%
18	Georgia	18	1.7%
18	Iowa	18	1.7%
18	Maryland	18	1.7%
18	Oklahoma	18	1.7%
22	Colorado	16	1.5%
22	North Carolina	16	1.5%
24	Massachusetts	15	1.4%
25	Arkansas	14	1.3%
25	Wisconsin	14	1.3%
27	Mississippi	12	1.1%
27	Nebraska	12	1.1%
29	Alabama	10	0.9%
29	Kentucky	10	0.9%
29	New Jersey	10	0.9%
32	Arizona	9	0.9%
32	Utah	9	0.9%
34	New Mexico	8	0.8%
35	Kansas	7	0.7%
36	Maine	6	0.6%
37	Alaska	5	0.5%
37	Hawaii	5	0.5%
37	Idaho	5	0.5%
37	Montana	5	0.5%
37	West Virginia	5	0.5%
42	Nevada	4	0.4%
43	North Dakota	3	0.3%
43	South Dakota	3	0.3%
45	Delaware	2	0.2%
45	Wyoming	2	0.2%
47	Connecticut	1	0.1%
48	New Hampshire	0	0.0%
48	Rhode Island	0	0.0%
48	Vermont	0	0.0%
	District of Columbia	0	0.0%

Source: U.S. Department of Health and Human Services, National Center for Health Statistics
    "Morbidity and Mortality Weekly Report" (January 9, 2009, Vol. 57, No. 53, http://www.cdc.gov/mmwr/)
*Provisional data. A bacterium (Neisseria meningitidis) that causes cerebrospinal meningitis.

Meningococcal Infection Rate in 2008

National Rate = 0.3 Cases per 100,000 Population*

ALPHA ORDER

RANK	STATE	RATE
35	Alabama	0.2
2	Alaska	0.7
45	Arizona	0.1
5	Arkansas	0.5
5	California	0.5
25	Colorado	0.3
47	Connecticut	0.0
35	Delaware	0.2
25	Florida	0.3
35	Georgia	0.2
15	Hawaii	0.4
25	Idaho	0.3
5	Illinois	0.5
15	Indiana	0.4
4	Iowa	0.6
35	Kansas	0.2
35	Kentucky	0.2
5	Louisiana	0.5
5	Maine	0.5
25	Maryland	0.3
35	Massachusetts	0.2
25	Michigan	0.3
5	Minnesota	0.5
15	Mississippi	0.4
15	Missouri	0.4
5	Montana	0.5
2	Nebraska	0.7
35	Nevada	0.2
47	New Hampshire	0.0
45	New Jersey	0.1
15	New Mexico	0.4
25	New York	0.3
35	North Carolina	0.2
5	North Dakota	0.5
25	Ohio	0.3
5	Oklahoma	0.5
1	Oregon	1.0
15	Pennsylvania	0.4
47	Rhode Island	0.0
5	South Carolina	0.5
15	South Dakota	0.4
15	Tennessee	0.4
35	Texas	0.2
25	Utah	0.3
47	Vermont	0.0
25	Virginia	0.3
15	Washington	0.4
25	West Virginia	0.3
35	Wisconsin	0.2
15	Wyoming	0.4

RANK ORDER

RANK	STATE	RATE
1	Oregon	1.0
2	Alaska	0.7
2	Nebraska	0.7
4	Iowa	0.6
5	Arkansas	0.5
5	California	0.5
5	Illinois	0.5
5	Louisiana	0.5
5	Maine	0.5
5	Minnesota	0.5
5	Montana	0.5
5	North Dakota	0.5
5	Oklahoma	0.5
5	South Carolina	0.5
15	Hawaii	0.4
15	Indiana	0.4
15	Mississippi	0.4
15	Missouri	0.4
15	New Mexico	0.4
15	Pennsylvania	0.4
15	South Dakota	0.4
15	Tennessee	0.4
15	Washington	0.4
15	Wyoming	0.4
25	Colorado	0.3
25	Florida	0.3
25	Idaho	0.3
25	Maryland	0.3
25	Michigan	0.3
25	New York	0.3
25	Ohio	0.3
25	Utah	0.3
25	Virginia	0.3
25	West Virginia	0.3
35	Alabama	0.2
35	Delaware	0.2
35	Georgia	0.2
35	Kansas	0.2
35	Kentucky	0.2
35	Massachusetts	0.2
35	Nevada	0.2
35	North Carolina	0.2
35	Texas	0.2
35	Wisconsin	0.2
45	Arizona	0.1
45	New Jersey	0.1
47	Connecticut	0.0
47	New Hampshire	0.0
47	Rhode Island	0.0
47	Vermont	0.0
	District of Columbia	0.0

Source: CQ Press using data from U.S. Department of Health and Human Services, National Center for Health Statistics
   "Morbidity and Mortality Weekly Report" (January 9, 2009, Vol. 57, No. 53, http://www.cdc.gov/mmwr/)
*Provisional data. A bacterium (Neisseria meningitidis) that causes cerebrospinal meningitis.

Rabies (Animal) Cases Reported in 2008

National Total = 4,911 Cases*

ALPHA ORDER

RANK	STATE	CASES	% of USA
36	Alabama	0	0.0%
28	Alaska	15	0.3%
NA	Arizona**	NA	NA
19	Arkansas	48	1.0%
8	California	163	3.3%
36	Colorado	0	0.0%
7	Connecticut	203	4.1%
36	Delaware	0	0.0%
9	Florida	139	2.8%
6	Georgia	339	6.9%
36	Hawaii	0	0.0%
36	Idaho	0	0.0%
11	Illinois	103	2.1%
31	Indiana	10	0.2%
23	Iowa	29	0.6%
36	Kansas	0	0.0%
20	Kentucky	45	0.9%
36	Louisiana	0	0.0%
17	Maine	64	1.3%
5	Maryland	420	8.6%
NA	Massachusetts**	NA	NA
13	Michigan	73	1.5%
15	Minnesota	65	1.3%
34	Mississippi	2	0.0%
15	Missouri	65	1.3%
32	Montana	9	0.2%
36	Nebraska	0	0.0%
33	Nevada	5	0.1%
22	New Hampshire	35	0.7%
36	New Jersey	0	0.0%
24	New Mexico	25	0.5%
3	New York	519	10.6%
4	North Carolina	454	9.2%
25	North Dakota	24	0.5%
18	Ohio	61	1.2%
21	Oklahoma	42	0.9%
29	Oregon	14	0.3%
1	Pennsylvania	1,017	20.7%
NA	Rhode Island**	NA	NA
36	South Carolina	0	0.0%
27	South Dakota	23	0.5%
10	Tennessee	118	2.4%
34	Texas	2	0.0%
29	Utah	14	0.3%
14	Vermont	70	1.4%
2	Virginia	591	12.0%
36	Washington	0	0.0%
12	West Virginia	81	1.6%
NA	Wisconsin**	NA	NA
25	Wyoming	24	0.5%

RANK ORDER

RANK	STATE	CASES	% of USA
1	Pennsylvania	1,017	20.7%
2	Virginia	591	12.0%
3	New York	519	10.6%
4	North Carolina	454	9.2%
5	Maryland	420	8.6%
6	Georgia	339	6.9%
7	Connecticut	203	4.1%
8	California	163	3.3%
9	Florida	139	2.8%
10	Tennessee	118	2.4%
11	Illinois	103	2.1%
12	West Virginia	81	1.6%
13	Michigan	73	1.5%
14	Vermont	70	1.4%
15	Minnesota	65	1.3%
15	Missouri	65	1.3%
17	Maine	64	1.3%
18	Ohio	61	1.2%
19	Arkansas	48	1.0%
20	Kentucky	45	0.9%
21	Oklahoma	42	0.9%
22	New Hampshire	35	0.7%
23	Iowa	29	0.6%
24	New Mexico	25	0.5%
25	North Dakota	24	0.5%
25	Wyoming	24	0.5%
27	South Dakota	23	0.5%
28	Alaska	15	0.3%
29	Oregon	14	0.3%
29	Utah	14	0.3%
31	Indiana	10	0.2%
32	Montana	9	0.2%
33	Nevada	5	0.1%
34	Mississippi	2	0.0%
34	Texas	2	0.0%
36	Alabama	0	0.0%
36	Colorado	0	0.0%
36	Delaware	0	0.0%
36	Hawaii	0	0.0%
36	Idaho	0	0.0%
36	Kansas	0	0.0%
36	Louisiana	0	0.0%
36	Nebraska	0	0.0%
36	New Jersey	0	0.0%
36	South Carolina	0	0.0%
36	Washington	0	0.0%
NA	Arizona**	NA	NA
NA	Massachusetts**	NA	NA
NA	Rhode Island**	NA	NA
NA	Wisconsin**	NA	NA
	District of Columbia	0	0.0%

Source: U.S. Department of Health and Human Services, National Center for Health Statistics
"Morbidity and Mortality Weekly Report" (January 9, 2009, Vol. 57, No. 53, http://www.cdc.gov/mmwr/)
*Provisional data. An acute, infectious, often fatal viral disease of most warm-blooded animals, especially wolves, cats, and dogs, that attacks the central nervous system and is transmitted by the bite of infected animals.
**Not notifiable.

Rabies (Animal) Rate in 2008

National Rate = 1.6 Cases per 100,000 Human Population*

ALPHA ORDER

RANK	STATE	RATE
35	Alabama	0.0
15	Alaska	2.2
NA	Arizona**	NA
17	Arkansas	1.7
30	California	0.4
35	Colorado	0.0
5	Connecticut	5.8
35	Delaware	0.0
25	Florida	0.8
11	Georgia	3.5
35	Hawaii	0.0
35	Idaho	0.0
25	Illinois	0.8
32	Indiana	0.2
23	Iowa	1.0
35	Kansas	0.0
21	Kentucky	1.1
35	Louisiana	0.0
6	Maine	4.9
4	Maryland	7.5
NA	Massachusetts**	NA
27	Michigan	0.7
19	Minnesota	1.2
34	Mississippi	0.1
21	Missouri	1.1
24	Montana	0.9
35	Nebraska	0.0
32	Nevada	0.2
13	New Hampshire	2.7
35	New Jersey	0.0
18	New Mexico	1.3
13	New York	2.7
6	North Carolina	4.9
10	North Dakota	3.7
28	Ohio	0.5
19	Oklahoma	1.2
30	Oregon	0.4
2	Pennsylvania	8.2
NA	Rhode Island**	NA
35	South Carolina	0.0
12	South Dakota	2.9
16	Tennessee	1.9
35	Texas	0.0
28	Utah	0.5
1	Vermont	11.3
3	Virginia	7.6
35	Washington	0.0
8	West Virginia	4.5
NA	Wisconsin**	NA
8	Wyoming	4.5

RANK ORDER

RANK	STATE	RATE
1	Vermont	11.3
2	Pennsylvania	8.2
3	Virginia	7.6
4	Maryland	7.5
5	Connecticut	5.8
6	Maine	4.9
6	North Carolina	4.9
8	West Virginia	4.5
8	Wyoming	4.5
10	North Dakota	3.7
11	Georgia	3.5
12	South Dakota	2.9
13	New Hampshire	2.7
13	New York	2.7
15	Alaska	2.2
16	Tennessee	1.9
17	Arkansas	1.7
18	New Mexico	1.3
19	Minnesota	1.2
19	Oklahoma	1.2
21	Kentucky	1.1
21	Missouri	1.1
23	Iowa	1.0
24	Montana	0.9
25	Florida	0.8
25	Illinois	0.8
27	Michigan	0.7
28	Ohio	0.5
28	Utah	0.5
30	California	0.4
30	Oregon	0.4
32	Indiana	0.2
32	Nevada	0.2
34	Mississippi	0.1
35	Alabama	0.0
35	Colorado	0.0
35	Delaware	0.0
35	Hawaii	0.0
35	Idaho	0.0
35	Kansas	0.0
35	Louisiana	0.0
35	Nebraska	0.0
35	New Jersey	0.0
35	South Carolina	0.0
35	Texas	0.0
35	Washington	0.0
NA	Arizona**	NA
NA	Massachusetts**	NA
NA	Rhode Island**	NA
NA	Wisconsin**	NA

District of Columbia 0.0

Source: CQ Press using data from U.S. Department of Health and Human Services, National Center for Health Statistics
"Morbidity and Mortality Weekly Report" (January 9, 2009, Vol. 57, No. 53, http://www.cdc.gov/mmwr/)
*Provisional data. An acute, infectious, often fatal viral disease of most warm-blooded animals, especially wolves, cats, and dogs, that attacks the central nervous system and is transmitted by the bite of infected animals.
**Not notifiable.

Rocky Mountain Spotted Fever Cases Reported in 2008

National Total = 2,276 Cases*

ALPHA ORDER

RANK	STATE	CASES	% of USA
7	Alabama	90	4.0%
NA	Alaska**	NA	NA
19	Arizona	17	0.7%
10	Arkansas	68	3.0%
32	California	2	0.1%
36	Colorado	1	0.0%
42	Connecticut	0	0.0%
15	Delaware	33	1.4%
17	Florida	20	0.9%
8	Georgia	73	3.2%
NA	Hawaii**	NA	NA
36	Idaho	1	0.0%
6	Illinois	104	4.6%
23	Indiana	8	0.4%
24	Iowa	7	0.3%
42	Kansas	0	0.0%
36	Kentucky	1	0.0%
27	Louisiana	5	0.2%
NA	Maine**	NA	NA
9	Maryland	72	3.2%
36	Massachusetts	1	0.0%
28	Michigan	3	0.1%
42	Minnesota	0	0.0%
20	Mississippi	12	0.5%
2	Missouri	426	18.7%
28	Montana	3	0.1%
17	Nebraska	20	0.9%
32	Nevada	2	0.1%
36	New Hampshire	1	0.0%
20	New Jersey	12	0.5%
32	New Mexico	2	0.1%
13	New York	41	1.8%
1	North Carolina	511	22.5%
42	North Dakota	0	0.0%
14	Ohio	34	1.5%
4	Oklahoma	170	7.5%
28	Oregon	3	0.1%
16	Pennsylvania	27	1.2%
32	Rhode Island	2	0.1%
11	South Carolina	55	2.4%
28	South Dakota	3	0.1%
3	Tennessee	221	9.7%
12	Texas	43	1.9%
24	Utah	7	0.3%
42	Vermont	0	0.0%
5	Virginia	149	6.5%
NA	Washington**	NA	NA
24	West Virginia	7	0.3%
36	Wisconsin	1	0.0%
22	Wyoming	10	0.4%

RANK ORDER

RANK	STATE	CASES	% of USA
1	North Carolina	511	22.5%
2	Missouri	426	18.7%
3	Tennessee	221	9.7%
4	Oklahoma	170	7.5%
5	Virginia	149	6.5%
6	Illinois	104	4.6%
7	Alabama	90	4.0%
8	Georgia	73	3.2%
9	Maryland	72	3.2%
10	Arkansas	68	3.0%
11	South Carolina	55	2.4%
12	Texas	43	1.9%
13	New York	41	1.8%
14	Ohio	34	1.5%
15	Delaware	33	1.4%
16	Pennsylvania	27	1.2%
17	Florida	20	0.9%
17	Nebraska	20	0.9%
19	Arizona	17	0.7%
20	Mississippi	12	0.5%
20	New Jersey	12	0.5%
22	Wyoming	10	0.4%
23	Indiana	8	0.4%
24	Iowa	7	0.3%
24	Utah	7	0.3%
24	West Virginia	7	0.3%
27	Louisiana	5	0.2%
28	Michigan	3	0.1%
28	Montana	3	0.1%
28	Oregon	3	0.1%
28	South Dakota	3	0.1%
32	California	2	0.1%
32	Nevada	2	0.1%
32	New Mexico	2	0.1%
32	Rhode Island	2	0.1%
36	Colorado	1	0.0%
36	Idaho	1	0.0%
36	Kentucky	1	0.0%
36	Massachusetts	1	0.0%
36	New Hampshire	1	0.0%
36	Wisconsin	1	0.0%
42	Connecticut	0	0.0%
42	Kansas	0	0.0%
42	Minnesota	0	0.0%
42	North Dakota	0	0.0%
42	Vermont	0	0.0%
NA	Alaska**	NA	NA
NA	Hawaii**	NA	NA
NA	Maine**	NA	NA
NA	Washington**	NA	NA

| | District of Columbia | 8 | 0.4% |

Source: U.S. Department of Health and Human Services, National Center for Health Statistics
    "Morbidity and Mortality Weekly Report" (January 9, 2009, Vol. 57, No. 53, http://www.cdc.gov/mmwr/)
*Provisional data. An illness caused by Rickettsia rickettsii, a bacterial pathogen transmitted to humans through contact with ticks. Characterized by acute onset of fever, and may be accompanied by headache, malaise, myalgia, nausea/vomiting, or neurologic signs. A rash is often present on the palms and soles.
**Not notifiable.

Rocky Mountain Spotted Fever Rate in 2008

National Rate = 0.7 Cases per 100,000 Population*

ALPHA ORDER

RANK	STATE	RATE
7	Alabama	1.9
NA	Alaska**	NA
18	Arizona	0.3
6	Arkansas	2.4
36	California	0.0
36	Colorado	0.0
36	Connecticut	0.0
4	Delaware	3.8
27	Florida	0.1
13	Georgia	0.8
NA	Hawaii**	NA
27	Idaho	0.1
13	Illinois	0.8
27	Indiana	0.1
22	Iowa	0.2
36	Kansas	0.0
36	Kentucky	0.0
27	Louisiana	0.1
NA	Maine**	NA
10	Maryland	1.3
36	Massachusetts	0.0
36	Michigan	0.0
36	Minnesota	0.0
15	Mississippi	0.4
1	Missouri	7.2
18	Montana	0.3
12	Nebraska	1.1
27	Nevada	0.1
27	New Hampshire	0.1
27	New Jersey	0.1
27	New Mexico	0.1
22	New York	0.2
2	North Carolina	5.5
36	North Dakota	0.0
18	Ohio	0.3
3	Oklahoma	4.7
27	Oregon	0.1
22	Pennsylvania	0.2
22	Rhode Island	0.2
11	South Carolina	1.2
15	South Dakota	0.4
5	Tennessee	3.6
22	Texas	0.2
18	Utah	0.3
36	Vermont	0.0
7	Virginia	1.9
NA	Washington**	NA
15	West Virginia	0.4
36	Wisconsin	0.0
7	Wyoming	1.9

RANK ORDER

RANK	STATE	RATE
1	Missouri	7.2
2	North Carolina	5.5
3	Oklahoma	4.7
4	Delaware	3.8
5	Tennessee	3.6
6	Arkansas	2.4
7	Alabama	1.9
7	Virginia	1.9
7	Wyoming	1.9
10	Maryland	1.3
11	South Carolina	1.2
12	Nebraska	1.1
13	Georgia	0.8
13	Illinois	0.8
15	Mississippi	0.4
15	South Dakota	0.4
15	West Virginia	0.4
18	Arizona	0.3
18	Montana	0.3
18	Ohio	0.3
18	Utah	0.3
22	Iowa	0.2
22	New York	0.2
22	Pennsylvania	0.2
22	Rhode Island	0.2
22	Texas	0.2
27	Florida	0.1
27	Idaho	0.1
27	Indiana	0.1
27	Louisiana	0.1
27	Nevada	0.1
27	New Hampshire	0.1
27	New Jersey	0.1
27	New Mexico	0.1
27	Oregon	0.1
36	California	0.0
36	Colorado	0.0
36	Connecticut	0.0
36	Kansas	0.0
36	Kentucky	0.0
36	Massachusetts	0.0
36	Michigan	0.0
36	Minnesota	0.0
36	North Dakota	0.0
36	Vermont	0.0
36	Wisconsin	0.0
NA	Alaska**	NA
NA	Hawaii**	NA
NA	Maine**	NA
NA	Washington**	NA

District of Columbia 1.4

Source: CQ Press using data from U.S. Department of Health and Human Services, National Center for Health Statistics
   "Morbidity and Mortality Weekly Report" (January 9, 2009, Vol. 57, No. 53, http://www.cdc.gov/mmwr/)
*Provisional data. An illness caused by Rickettsia rickettsii, a bacterial pathogen transmitted to humans through contact with ticks. Characterized by acute onset of fever, and may be accompanied by headache, malaise, myalgia, nausea/vomiting, or neurologic signs. A rash is often present on the palms and soles.
**Not notifiable.

Salmonellosis Cases Reported in 2008

National Total = 46,151 Cases*

ALPHA ORDER

RANK	STATE	CASES	% of USA
15	Alabama	940	2.0%
48	Alaska	57	0.1%
11	Arizona	1,122	2.4%
22	Arkansas	777	1.7%
2	California	4,810	10.4%
26	Colorado	703	1.5%
29	Connecticut	484	1.0%
43	Delaware	146	0.3%
1	Florida	5,242	11.4%
5	Georgia	2,239	4.9%
36	Hawaii	264	0.6%
38	Idaho	192	0.4%
9	Illinois	1,315	2.8%
28	Indiana	613	1.3%
33	Iowa	424	0.9%
32	Kansas	474	1.0%
31	Kentucky	480	1.0%
14	Louisiana	983	2.1%
41	Maine	153	0.3%
19	Maryland	792	1.7%
24	Massachusetts	741	1.6%
17	Michigan	914	2.0%
25	Minnesota	710	1.5%
12	Mississippi	1,054	2.3%
23	Missouri	772	1.7%
45	Montana	122	0.3%
37	Nebraska	239	0.5%
40	Nevada	178	0.4%
43	New Hampshire	146	0.3%
27	New Jersey	671	1.5%
30	New Mexico	482	1.0%
4	New York	2,700	5.9%
7	North Carolina	1,563	3.4%
50	North Dakota	45	0.1%
8	Ohio	1,369	3.0%
18	Oklahoma	814	1.8%
33	Oregon	424	0.9%
6	Pennsylvania	1,721	3.7%
46	Rhode Island	106	0.2%
10	South Carolina	1,133	2.5%
42	South Dakota	151	0.3%
16	Tennessee	920	2.0%
3	Texas	3,647	7.9%
35	Utah	359	0.8%
47	Vermont	83	0.2%
13	Virginia	1,015	2.2%
21	Washington	786	1.7%
39	West Virginia	181	0.4%
20	Wisconsin	791	1.7%
49	Wyoming	52	0.1%

RANK ORDER

RANK	STATE	CASES	% of USA
1	Florida	5,242	11.4%
2	California	4,810	10.4%
3	Texas	3,647	7.9%
4	New York	2,700	5.9%
5	Georgia	2,239	4.9%
6	Pennsylvania	1,721	3.7%
7	North Carolina	1,563	3.4%
8	Ohio	1,369	3.0%
9	Illinois	1,315	2.8%
10	South Carolina	1,133	2.5%
11	Arizona	1,122	2.4%
12	Mississippi	1,054	2.3%
13	Virginia	1,015	2.2%
14	Louisiana	983	2.1%
15	Alabama	940	2.0%
16	Tennessee	920	2.0%
17	Michigan	914	2.0%
18	Oklahoma	814	1.8%
19	Maryland	792	1.7%
20	Wisconsin	791	1.7%
21	Washington	786	1.7%
22	Arkansas	777	1.7%
23	Missouri	772	1.7%
24	Massachusetts	741	1.6%
25	Minnesota	710	1.5%
26	Colorado	703	1.5%
27	New Jersey	671	1.5%
28	Indiana	613	1.3%
29	Connecticut	484	1.0%
30	New Mexico	482	1.0%
31	Kentucky	480	1.0%
32	Kansas	474	1.0%
33	Iowa	424	0.9%
33	Oregon	424	0.9%
35	Utah	359	0.8%
36	Hawaii	264	0.6%
37	Nebraska	239	0.5%
38	Idaho	192	0.4%
39	West Virginia	181	0.4%
40	Nevada	178	0.4%
41	Maine	153	0.3%
42	South Dakota	151	0.3%
43	Delaware	146	0.3%
43	New Hampshire	146	0.3%
45	Montana	122	0.3%
46	Rhode Island	106	0.2%
47	Vermont	83	0.2%
48	Alaska	57	0.1%
49	Wyoming	52	0.1%
50	North Dakota	45	0.1%
	District of Columbia	52	0.1%

Source: U.S. Department of Health and Human Services, National Center for Health Statistics
    "Morbidity and Mortality Weekly Report" (January 9, 2009, Vol. 57, No. 53, http://www.cdc.gov/mmwr/)
*Provisional data. Any disease caused by a salmonella infection, which may be manifested as food poisoning with acute gastroenteritis, vomiting, and diarrhea.

Salmonellosis Rate in 2008

National Rate = 15.2 Cases per 100,000 Population*

ALPHA ORDER

RANK	STATE	RATE
10	Alabama	20.2
47	Alaska	8.3
12	Arizona	17.3
3	Arkansas	27.2
28	California	13.1
18	Colorado	14.2
23	Connecticut	13.8
15	Delaware	16.7
2	Florida	28.6
6	Georgia	23.1
9	Hawaii	20.5
32	Idaho	12.6
41	Illinois	10.2
45	Indiana	9.6
19	Iowa	14.1
13	Kansas	16.9
38	Kentucky	11.2
7	Louisiana	22.3
36	Maine	11.6
19	Maryland	14.1
37	Massachusetts	11.4
46	Michigan	9.1
25	Minnesota	13.6
1	Mississippi	35.9
28	Missouri	13.1
32	Montana	12.6
26	Nebraska	13.4
50	Nevada	6.8
40	New Hampshire	11.1
48	New Jersey	7.7
5	New Mexico	24.3
22	New York	13.9
13	North Carolina	16.9
49	North Dakota	7.0
35	Ohio	11.9
7	Oklahoma	22.3
38	Oregon	11.2
23	Pennsylvania	13.8
42	Rhode Island	10.1
4	South Carolina	25.3
11	South Dakota	18.8
17	Tennessee	14.8
16	Texas	15.0
28	Utah	13.1
26	Vermont	13.4
28	Virginia	13.1
34	Washington	12.0
43	West Virginia	10.0
19	Wisconsin	14.1
44	Wyoming	9.8

RANK ORDER

RANK	STATE	RATE
1	Mississippi	35.9
2	Florida	28.6
3	Arkansas	27.2
4	South Carolina	25.3
5	New Mexico	24.3
6	Georgia	23.1
7	Louisiana	22.3
7	Oklahoma	22.3
9	Hawaii	20.5
10	Alabama	20.2
11	South Dakota	18.8
12	Arizona	17.3
13	Kansas	16.9
13	North Carolina	16.9
15	Delaware	16.7
16	Texas	15.0
17	Tennessee	14.8
18	Colorado	14.2
19	Iowa	14.1
19	Maryland	14.1
19	Wisconsin	14.1
22	New York	13.9
23	Connecticut	13.8
23	Pennsylvania	13.8
25	Minnesota	13.6
26	Nebraska	13.4
26	Vermont	13.4
28	California	13.1
28	Missouri	13.1
28	Utah	13.1
28	Virginia	13.1
32	Idaho	12.6
32	Montana	12.6
34	Washington	12.0
35	Ohio	11.9
36	Maine	11.6
37	Massachusetts	11.4
38	Kentucky	11.2
38	Oregon	11.2
40	New Hampshire	11.1
41	Illinois	10.2
42	Rhode Island	10.1
43	West Virginia	10.0
44	Wyoming	9.8
45	Indiana	9.6
46	Michigan	9.1
47	Alaska	8.3
48	New Jersey	7.7
49	North Dakota	7.0
50	Nevada	6.8

	District of Columbia	8.8

Source: CQ Press using data from U.S. Department of Health and Human Services, National Center for Health Statistics
"Morbidity and Mortality Weekly Report" (January 9, 2009, Vol. 57, No. 53, http://www.cdc.gov/mmwr/)
*Provisional data. Any disease caused by a salmonella infection, which may be manifested as food poisoning with acute gastroenteritis, vomiting, and diarrhea.

Shigellosis Cases Reported in 2008

National Total = 20,444 Cases*

ALPHA ORDER

RANK	STATE	CASES	% of USA
16	Alabama	395	1.9%
50	Alaska	1	0.0%
10	Arizona	655	3.2%
13	Arkansas	573	2.8%
3	California	1,590	7.8%
28	Colorado	145	0.7%
38	Connecticut	38	0.2%
44	Delaware	12	0.1%
8	Florida	796	3.9%
5	Georgia	1,091	5.3%
36	Hawaii	42	0.2%
43	Idaho	14	0.1%
7	Illinois	896	4.4%
11	Indiana	596	2.9%
26	Iowa	201	1.0%
35	Kansas	68	0.3%
21	Kentucky	260	1.3%
12	Louisiana	594	2.9%
40	Maine	21	0.1%
30	Maryland	118	0.6%
33	Massachusetts	78	0.4%
25	Michigan	214	1.0%
17	Minnesota	308	1.5%
18	Mississippi	291	1.4%
23	Missouri	223	1.1%
46	Montana	8	0.0%
42	Nebraska	15	0.1%
24	Nevada	217	1.1%
49	New Hampshire	4	0.0%
9	New Jersey	764	3.7%
29	New Mexico	122	0.6%
4	New York	1,284	6.3%
19	North Carolina	275	1.3%
39	North Dakota	37	0.2%
2	Ohio	1,927	9.4%
27	Oklahoma	178	0.9%
32	Oregon	92	0.5%
20	Pennsylvania	261	1.3%
44	Rhode Island	12	0.1%
14	South Carolina	539	2.6%
34	South Dakota	76	0.4%
6	Tennessee	940	4.6%
1	Texas	3,583	17.5%
37	Utah	39	0.2%
48	Vermont	5	0.0%
22	Virginia	249	1.2%
31	Washington	109	0.5%
40	West Virginia	21	0.1%
15	Wisconsin	440	2.2%
46	Wyoming	8	0.0%

RANK ORDER

RANK	STATE	CASES	% of USA
1	Texas	3,583	17.5%
2	Ohio	1,927	9.4%
3	California	1,590	7.8%
4	New York	1,284	6.3%
5	Georgia	1,091	5.3%
6	Tennessee	940	4.6%
7	Illinois	896	4.4%
8	Florida	796	3.9%
9	New Jersey	764	3.7%
10	Arizona	655	3.2%
11	Indiana	596	2.9%
12	Louisiana	594	2.9%
13	Arkansas	573	2.8%
14	South Carolina	539	2.6%
15	Wisconsin	440	2.2%
16	Alabama	395	1.9%
17	Minnesota	308	1.5%
18	Mississippi	291	1.4%
19	North Carolina	275	1.3%
20	Pennsylvania	261	1.3%
21	Kentucky	260	1.3%
22	Virginia	249	1.2%
23	Missouri	223	1.1%
24	Nevada	217	1.1%
25	Michigan	214	1.0%
26	Iowa	201	1.0%
27	Oklahoma	178	0.9%
28	Colorado	145	0.7%
29	New Mexico	122	0.6%
30	Maryland	118	0.6%
31	Washington	109	0.5%
32	Oregon	92	0.5%
33	Massachusetts	78	0.4%
34	South Dakota	76	0.4%
35	Kansas	68	0.3%
36	Hawaii	42	0.2%
37	Utah	39	0.2%
38	Connecticut	38	0.2%
39	North Dakota	37	0.2%
40	Maine	21	0.1%
40	West Virginia	21	0.1%
42	Nebraska	15	0.1%
43	Idaho	14	0.1%
44	Delaware	12	0.1%
44	Rhode Island	12	0.1%
46	Montana	8	0.0%
46	Wyoming	8	0.0%
48	Vermont	5	0.0%
49	New Hampshire	4	0.0%
50	Alaska	1	0.0%
	District of Columbia	19	0.1%

Source: U.S. Department of Health and Human Services, National Center for Health Statistics
   "Morbidity and Mortality Weekly Report" (January 9, 2009, Vol. 57, No. 53, http://www.cdc.gov/mmwr/)
*Provisional data. Dysentery caused by any of various species of shigellae, occurring most frequently in areas where poor sanitation and malnutrition are prevalent, and commonly affecting children and infants.

Shigellosis Rate in 2008

National Rate = 6.7 Cases per 100,000 Population*

ALPHA ORDER				RANK ORDER		
RANK	**STATE**	**RATE**		**RANK**	**STATE**	**RATE**
13	Alabama	8.5		1	Arkansas	20.1
50	Alaska	0.1		2	Ohio	16.8
8	Arizona	10.1		3	Tennessee	15.1
1	Arkansas	20.1		4	Texas	14.7
24	California	4.3		5	Louisiana	13.5
30	Colorado	2.9		6	South Carolina	12.0
43	Connecticut	1.1		7	Georgia	11.3
39	Delaware	1.4		8	Arizona	10.1
24	Florida	4.3		9	Mississippi	9.9
7	Georgia	11.3		10	South Dakota	9.5
27	Hawaii	3.3		11	Indiana	9.3
45	Idaho	0.9		12	New Jersey	8.8
16	Illinois	6.9		13	Alabama	8.5
11	Indiana	9.3		14	Nevada	8.3
17	Iowa	6.7		15	Wisconsin	7.8
31	Kansas	2.4		16	Illinois	6.9
19	Kentucky	6.1		17	Iowa	6.7
5	Louisiana	13.5		18	New York	6.6
37	Maine	1.6		19	Kentucky	6.1
33	Maryland	2.1		19	New Mexico	6.1
41	Massachusetts	1.2		21	Minnesota	5.9
33	Michigan	2.1		22	North Dakota	5.8
21	Minnesota	5.9		23	Oklahoma	4.9
9	Mississippi	9.9		24	California	4.3
26	Missouri	3.8		24	Florida	4.3
46	Montana	0.8		26	Missouri	3.8
46	Nebraska	0.8		27	Hawaii	3.3
14	Nevada	8.3		28	Virginia	3.2
49	New Hampshire	0.3		29	North Carolina	3.0
12	New Jersey	8.8		30	Colorado	2.9
19	New Mexico	6.1		31	Kansas	2.4
18	New York	6.6		31	Oregon	2.4
29	North Carolina	3.0		33	Maryland	2.1
22	North Dakota	5.8		33	Michigan	2.1
2	Ohio	16.8		33	Pennsylvania	2.1
23	Oklahoma	4.9		36	Washington	1.7
31	Oregon	2.4		37	Maine	1.6
33	Pennsylvania	2.1		38	Wyoming	1.5
43	Rhode Island	1.1		39	Delaware	1.4
6	South Carolina	12.0		39	Utah	1.4
10	South Dakota	9.5		41	Massachusetts	1.2
3	Tennessee	15.1		41	West Virginia	1.2
4	Texas	14.7		43	Connecticut	1.1
39	Utah	1.4		43	Rhode Island	1.1
46	Vermont	0.8		45	Idaho	0.9
28	Virginia	3.2		46	Montana	0.8
36	Washington	1.7		46	Nebraska	0.8
41	West Virginia	1.2		46	Vermont	0.8
15	Wisconsin	7.8		49	New Hampshire	0.3
38	Wyoming	1.5		50	Alaska	0.1

	District of Columbia	3.2

Source: U.S. Department of Health and Human Services, National Center for Health Statistics
 "Morbidity and Mortality Weekly Report" (January 9, 2009, Vol. 57, No. 53, http://www.cdc.gov/mmwr/)
*Provisional data. Dysentery caused by any of various species of shigellae, occurring most frequently in areas where poor sanitation and malnutrition are prevalent, and commonly affecting children and infants.

West Nile Virus Disease Cases Reported in 2008

National Total = 1,328 Cases*

ALPHA ORDER

RANK	STATE	CASES	% of USA
14	Alabama	21	1.6%
44	Alaska	0	0.0%
2	Arizona	111	8.4%
25	Arkansas	9	0.7%
1	California	427	32.2%
3	Colorado	95	7.2%
27	Connecticut	8	0.6%
39	Delaware	1	0.1%
38	Florida	2	0.2%
27	Georgia	8	0.6%
44	Hawaii	0	0.0%
12	Idaho	33	2.5%
15	Illinois	19	1.4%
35	Indiana	3	0.2%
33	Iowa	6	0.5%
9	Kansas	38	2.9%
35	Kentucky	3	0.2%
11	Louisiana	36	2.7%
44	Maine	0	0.0%
22	Maryland	14	1.1%
44	Massachusetts	0	0.0%
17	Michigan	17	1.3%
24	Minnesota	10	0.8%
4	Mississippi	63	4.7%
15	Missouri	19	1.4%
34	Montana	5	0.4%
6	Nebraska	49	3.7%
19	Nevada	16	1.2%
44	New Hampshire	0	0.0%
30	New Jersey	7	0.5%
25	New Mexico	9	0.7%
7	New York	44	3.3%
44	North Carolina	0	0.0%
10	North Dakota	37	2.8%
21	Ohio	15	1.1%
30	Oklahoma	7	0.5%
19	Oregon	16	1.2%
22	Pennsylvania	14	1.1%
39	Rhode Island	1	0.1%
39	South Carolina	1	0.1%
8	South Dakota	39	2.9%
17	Tennessee	17	1.3%
5	Texas	62	4.7%
13	Utah	26	2.0%
44	Vermont	0	0.0%
39	Virginia	1	0.1%
35	Washington	3	0.2%
39	West Virginia	1	0.1%
30	Wisconsin	7	0.5%
27	Wyoming	8	0.6%

RANK ORDER

RANK	STATE	CASES	% of USA
1	California	427	32.2%
2	Arizona	111	8.4%
3	Colorado	95	7.2%
4	Mississippi	63	4.7%
5	Texas	62	4.7%
6	Nebraska	49	3.7%
7	New York	44	3.3%
8	South Dakota	39	2.9%
9	Kansas	38	2.9%
10	North Dakota	37	2.8%
11	Louisiana	36	2.7%
12	Idaho	33	2.5%
13	Utah	26	2.0%
14	Alabama	21	1.6%
15	Illinois	19	1.4%
15	Missouri	19	1.4%
17	Michigan	17	1.3%
17	Tennessee	17	1.3%
19	Nevada	16	1.2%
19	Oregon	16	1.2%
21	Ohio	15	1.1%
22	Maryland	14	1.1%
22	Pennsylvania	14	1.1%
24	Minnesota	10	0.8%
25	Arkansas	9	0.7%
25	New Mexico	9	0.7%
27	Connecticut	8	0.6%
27	Georgia	8	0.6%
27	Wyoming	8	0.6%
30	New Jersey	7	0.5%
30	Oklahoma	7	0.5%
30	Wisconsin	7	0.5%
33	Iowa	6	0.5%
34	Montana	5	0.4%
35	Indiana	3	0.2%
35	Kentucky	3	0.2%
35	Washington	3	0.2%
38	Florida	2	0.2%
39	Delaware	1	0.1%
39	Rhode Island	1	0.1%
39	South Carolina	1	0.1%
39	Virginia	1	0.1%
39	West Virginia	1	0.1%
44	Alaska	0	0.0%
44	Hawaii	0	0.0%
44	Maine	0	0.0%
44	Massachusetts	0	0.0%
44	New Hampshire	0	0.0%
44	North Carolina	0	0.0%
44	Vermont	0	0.0%
	District of Columbia	0	0.0%

Source: U.S. Department of Health and Human Services, National Center for Health Statistics
"Morbidity and Mortality Weekly Report" (January 9, 2009, Vol. 57, No. 53, http://www.cdc.gov/mmwr/)
*Provisional data. A flavivirus typically carried by mosquitoes.

West Nile Disease Rate in 2008

National Rate = 0.4 Cases per 100,000 Population*

ALPHA ORDER			RANK ORDER		
RANK	STATE	RATE	RANK	STATE	RATE
14	Alabama	0.5	1	North Dakota	5.8
39	Alaska	0.0	2	South Dakota	4.8
7	Arizona	1.7	3	Nebraska	2.7
18	Arkansas	0.3	4	Idaho	2.2
10	California	1.2	5	Mississippi	2.1
6	Colorado	1.9	6	Colorado	1.9
22	Connecticut	0.2	7	Arizona	1.7
29	Delaware	0.1	8	Wyoming	1.5
39	Florida	0.0	9	Kansas	1.4
29	Georgia	0.1	10	California	1.2
39	Hawaii	0.0	11	Utah	1.0
4	Idaho	2.2	12	Louisiana	0.8
29	Illinois	0.1	13	Nevada	0.6
39	Indiana	0.0	14	Alabama	0.5
22	Iowa	0.2	14	Montana	0.5
9	Kansas	1.4	14	New Mexico	0.5
29	Kentucky	0.1	17	Oregon	0.4
12	Louisiana	0.8	18	Arkansas	0.3
39	Maine	0.0	18	Missouri	0.3
22	Maryland	0.2	18	Tennessee	0.3
39	Massachusetts	0.0	18	Texas	0.3
22	Michigan	0.2	22	Connecticut	0.2
22	Minnesota	0.2	22	Iowa	0.2
5	Mississippi	2.1	22	Maryland	0.2
18	Missouri	0.3	22	Michigan	0.2
14	Montana	0.5	22	Minnesota	0.2
3	Nebraska	2.7	22	New York	0.2
13	Nevada	0.6	22	Oklahoma	0.2
39	New Hampshire	0.0	29	Delaware	0.1
29	New Jersey	0.1	29	Georgia	0.1
14	New Mexico	0.5	29	Illinois	0.1
22	New York	0.2	29	Kentucky	0.1
39	North Carolina	0.0	29	New Jersey	0.1
1	North Dakota	5.8	29	Ohio	0.1
29	Ohio	0.1	29	Pennsylvania	0.1
22	Oklahoma	0.2	29	Rhode Island	0.1
17	Oregon	0.4	29	West Virginia	0.1
29	Pennsylvania	0.1	29	Wisconsin	0.1
29	Rhode Island	0.1	39	Alaska	0.0
39	South Carolina	0.0	39	Florida	0.0
2	South Dakota	4.8	39	Hawaii	0.0
18	Tennessee	0.3	39	Indiana	0.0
18	Texas	0.3	39	Maine	0.0
11	Utah	1.0	39	Massachusetts	0.0
39	Vermont	0.0	39	New Hampshire	0.0
39	Virginia	0.0	39	North Carolina	0.0
39	Washington	0.0	39	South Carolina	0.0
29	West Virginia	0.1	39	Vermont	0.0
29	Wisconsin	0.1	39	Virginia	0.0
8	Wyoming	1.5	39	Washington	0.0
				District of Columbia	0.0

Source: CQ Press using data from U.S. Department of Health and Human Services, National Center for Health Statistics
"Morbidity and Mortality Weekly Report" (January 9, 2009, Vol. 57, No. 53, http://www.cdc.gov/mmwr/)
*Provisional data. A flavivirus typically carried by mosquitoes.

Whooping Cough (Pertussis) Cases Reported in 2008

National Total = 10,007 Cases*

ALPHA ORDER

RANK	STATE	CASES	% of USA
36	Alabama	59	0.6%
13	Alaska	258	2.6%
17	Arizona	204	2.0%
28	Arkansas	93	0.9%
9	California	392	3.9%
19	Colorado	160	1.6%
43	Connecticut	34	0.3%
45	Delaware	18	0.2%
10	Florida	306	3.1%
30	Georgia	91	0.9%
46	Hawaii	17	0.2%
42	Idaho	38	0.4%
4	Illinois	517	5.2%
21	Indiana	139	1.4%
16	Iowa	209	2.1%
32	Kansas	78	0.8%
22	Kentucky	136	1.4%
33	Louisiana	77	0.8%
41	Maine	47	0.5%
23	Maryland	130	1.3%
7	Massachusetts	420	4.2%
11	Michigan	294	2.9%
15	Minnesota	224	2.2%
29	Mississippi	92	0.9%
3	Missouri	535	5.3%
31	Montana	83	0.8%
12	Nebraska	281	2.8%
44	Nevada	19	0.2%
40	New Hampshire	48	0.5%
34	New Jersey	71	0.7%
35	New Mexico	68	0.7%
6	New York	472	4.7%
27	North Carolina	94	0.9%
50	North Dakota	1	0.0%
2	Ohio	846	8.5%
38	Oklahoma	56	0.6%
18	Oregon	176	1.8%
5	Pennsylvania	508	5.1%
36	Rhode Island	59	0.6%
24	South Carolina	129	1.3%
39	South Dakota	50	0.5%
26	Tennessee	108	1.1%
1	Texas	1,405	14.0%
14	Utah	226	2.3%
48	Vermont	12	0.1%
20	Virginia	152	1.5%
8	Washington	419	4.2%
49	West Virginia	10	0.1%
25	Wisconsin	123	1.2%
47	Wyoming	16	0.2%

RANK ORDER

RANK	STATE	CASES	% of USA
1	Texas	1,405	14.0%
2	Ohio	846	8.5%
3	Missouri	535	5.3%
4	Illinois	517	5.2%
5	Pennsylvania	508	5.1%
6	New York	472	4.7%
7	Massachusetts	420	4.2%
8	Washington	419	4.2%
9	California	392	3.9%
10	Florida	306	3.1%
11	Michigan	294	2.9%
12	Nebraska	281	2.8%
13	Alaska	258	2.6%
14	Utah	226	2.3%
15	Minnesota	224	2.2%
16	Iowa	209	2.1%
17	Arizona	204	2.0%
18	Oregon	176	1.8%
19	Colorado	160	1.6%
20	Virginia	152	1.5%
21	Indiana	139	1.4%
22	Kentucky	136	1.4%
23	Maryland	130	1.3%
24	South Carolina	129	1.3%
25	Wisconsin	123	1.2%
26	Tennessee	108	1.1%
27	North Carolina	94	0.9%
28	Arkansas	93	0.9%
29	Mississippi	92	0.9%
30	Georgia	91	0.9%
31	Montana	83	0.8%
32	Kansas	78	0.8%
33	Louisiana	77	0.8%
34	New Jersey	71	0.7%
35	New Mexico	68	0.7%
36	Alabama	59	0.6%
36	Rhode Island	59	0.6%
38	Oklahoma	56	0.6%
39	South Dakota	50	0.5%
40	New Hampshire	48	0.5%
41	Maine	47	0.5%
42	Idaho	38	0.4%
43	Connecticut	34	0.3%
44	Nevada	19	0.2%
45	Delaware	18	0.2%
46	Hawaii	17	0.2%
47	Wyoming	16	0.2%
48	Vermont	12	0.1%
49	West Virginia	10	0.1%
50	North Dakota	1	0.0%
	District of Columbia	7	0.1%

Source: U.S. Department of Health and Human Services, National Center for Health Statistics
   "Morbidity and Mortality Weekly Report" (January 9, 2009, Vol. 57, No. 53, http://www.cdc.gov/mmwr/)
*Provisional data. Acute, highly contagious infection of respiratory tract.

Whooping Cough (Pertussis) Rate in 2008

National Rate = 3.3 Cases per 100,000 Population*

<table>
<tr><td colspan="3">ALPHA ORDER</td><td colspan="3">RANK ORDER</td></tr>
<tr><td>RANK</td><td>STATE</td><td>RATE</td><td>RANK</td><td>STATE</td><td>RATE</td></tr>
<tr><td>41</td><td>Alabama</td><td>1.3</td><td>1</td><td>Alaska</td><td>37.6</td></tr>
<tr><td>1</td><td>Alaska</td><td>37.6</td><td>2</td><td>Nebraska</td><td>15.8</td></tr>
<tr><td>23</td><td>Arizona</td><td>3.1</td><td>3</td><td>Missouri</td><td>9.0</td></tr>
<tr><td>20</td><td>Arkansas</td><td>3.3</td><td>4</td><td>Montana</td><td>8.6</td></tr>
<tr><td>43</td><td>California</td><td>1.1</td><td>5</td><td>Utah</td><td>8.3</td></tr>
<tr><td>21</td><td>Colorado</td><td>3.2</td><td>6</td><td>Ohio</td><td>7.4</td></tr>
<tr><td>44</td><td>Connecticut</td><td>1.0</td><td>7</td><td>Iowa</td><td>7.0</td></tr>
<tr><td>34</td><td>Delaware</td><td>2.1</td><td>8</td><td>Massachusetts</td><td>6.5</td></tr>
<tr><td>37</td><td>Florida</td><td>1.7</td><td>9</td><td>Washington</td><td>6.4</td></tr>
<tr><td>46</td><td>Georgia</td><td>0.9</td><td>10</td><td>South Dakota</td><td>6.2</td></tr>
<tr><td>41</td><td>Hawaii</td><td>1.3</td><td>11</td><td>Texas</td><td>5.8</td></tr>
<tr><td>29</td><td>Idaho</td><td>2.5</td><td>12</td><td>Rhode Island</td><td>5.6</td></tr>
<tr><td>16</td><td>Illinois</td><td>4.0</td><td>13</td><td>Oregon</td><td>4.6</td></tr>
<tr><td>32</td><td>Indiana</td><td>2.2</td><td>14</td><td>Minnesota</td><td>4.3</td></tr>
<tr><td>7</td><td>Iowa</td><td>7.0</td><td>15</td><td>Pennsylvania</td><td>4.1</td></tr>
<tr><td>28</td><td>Kansas</td><td>2.8</td><td>16</td><td>Illinois</td><td>4.0</td></tr>
<tr><td>21</td><td>Kentucky</td><td>3.2</td><td>17</td><td>Maine</td><td>3.6</td></tr>
<tr><td>37</td><td>Louisiana</td><td>1.7</td><td>17</td><td>New Hampshire</td><td>3.6</td></tr>
<tr><td>17</td><td>Maine</td><td>3.6</td><td>19</td><td>New Mexico</td><td>3.4</td></tr>
<tr><td>31</td><td>Maryland</td><td>2.3</td><td>20</td><td>Arkansas</td><td>3.3</td></tr>
<tr><td>8</td><td>Massachusetts</td><td>6.5</td><td>21</td><td>Colorado</td><td>3.2</td></tr>
<tr><td>26</td><td>Michigan</td><td>2.9</td><td>21</td><td>Kentucky</td><td>3.2</td></tr>
<tr><td>14</td><td>Minnesota</td><td>4.3</td><td>23</td><td>Arizona</td><td>3.1</td></tr>
<tr><td>23</td><td>Mississippi</td><td>3.1</td><td>23</td><td>Mississippi</td><td>3.1</td></tr>
<tr><td>3</td><td>Missouri</td><td>9.0</td><td>25</td><td>Wyoming</td><td>3.0</td></tr>
<tr><td>4</td><td>Montana</td><td>8.6</td><td>26</td><td>Michigan</td><td>2.9</td></tr>
<tr><td>2</td><td>Nebraska</td><td>15.8</td><td>26</td><td>South Carolina</td><td>2.9</td></tr>
<tr><td>48</td><td>Nevada</td><td>0.7</td><td>28</td><td>Kansas</td><td>2.8</td></tr>
<tr><td>17</td><td>New Hampshire</td><td>3.6</td><td>29</td><td>Idaho</td><td>2.5</td></tr>
<tr><td>47</td><td>New Jersey</td><td>0.8</td><td>30</td><td>New York</td><td>2.4</td></tr>
<tr><td>19</td><td>New Mexico</td><td>3.4</td><td>31</td><td>Maryland</td><td>2.3</td></tr>
<tr><td>30</td><td>New York</td><td>2.4</td><td>32</td><td>Indiana</td><td>2.2</td></tr>
<tr><td>44</td><td>North Carolina</td><td>1.0</td><td>32</td><td>Wisconsin</td><td>2.2</td></tr>
<tr><td>50</td><td>North Dakota</td><td>0.2</td><td>34</td><td>Delaware</td><td>2.1</td></tr>
<tr><td>6</td><td>Ohio</td><td>7.4</td><td>35</td><td>Virginia</td><td>2.0</td></tr>
<tr><td>40</td><td>Oklahoma</td><td>1.5</td><td>36</td><td>Vermont</td><td>1.9</td></tr>
<tr><td>13</td><td>Oregon</td><td>4.6</td><td>37</td><td>Florida</td><td>1.7</td></tr>
<tr><td>15</td><td>Pennsylvania</td><td>4.1</td><td>37</td><td>Louisiana</td><td>1.7</td></tr>
<tr><td>12</td><td>Rhode Island</td><td>5.6</td><td>37</td><td>Tennessee</td><td>1.7</td></tr>
<tr><td>26</td><td>South Carolina</td><td>2.9</td><td>40</td><td>Oklahoma</td><td>1.5</td></tr>
<tr><td>10</td><td>South Dakota</td><td>6.2</td><td>41</td><td>Alabama</td><td>1.3</td></tr>
<tr><td>37</td><td>Tennessee</td><td>1.7</td><td>41</td><td>Hawaii</td><td>1.3</td></tr>
<tr><td>11</td><td>Texas</td><td>5.8</td><td>43</td><td>California</td><td>1.1</td></tr>
<tr><td>5</td><td>Utah</td><td>8.3</td><td>44</td><td>Connecticut</td><td>1.0</td></tr>
<tr><td>36</td><td>Vermont</td><td>1.9</td><td>44</td><td>North Carolina</td><td>1.0</td></tr>
<tr><td>35</td><td>Virginia</td><td>2.0</td><td>46</td><td>Georgia</td><td>0.9</td></tr>
<tr><td>9</td><td>Washington</td><td>6.4</td><td>47</td><td>New Jersey</td><td>0.8</td></tr>
<tr><td>49</td><td>West Virginia</td><td>0.6</td><td>48</td><td>Nevada</td><td>0.7</td></tr>
<tr><td>32</td><td>Wisconsin</td><td>2.2</td><td>49</td><td>West Virginia</td><td>0.6</td></tr>
<tr><td>25</td><td>Wyoming</td><td>3.0</td><td>50</td><td>North Dakota</td><td>0.2</td></tr>
<tr><td colspan="3"></td><td colspan="2">District of Columbia</td><td>1.2</td></tr>
</table>

Source: CQ Press using data from U.S. Department of Health and Human Services, National Center for Health Statistics
"Morbidity and Mortality Weekly Report" (January 9, 2009, Vol. 57, No. 53, http://www.cdc.gov/mmwr/)
*Provisional data. Acute, highly contagious infection of respiratory tract.

Percent of Children Aged 19 to 35 Months Fully Immunized in 2007

National Percent = 77.4%*

ALPHA ORDER			RANK ORDER		
RANK	STATE	PERCENT	RANK	STATE	PERCENT
16	Alabama	78.2	1	Maryland	91.3
45	Alaska	70.1	2	New Hampshire	90.6
36	Arizona	75.2	3	Hawaii	87.5
42	Arkansas	72.3	4	Connecticut	86.8
25	California	77.1	5	Nebraska	82.9
18	Colorado	78.0	6	Minnesota	80.5
4	Connecticut	86.8	6	New Jersey	80.5
8	Delaware	80.3	8	Delaware	80.3
8	Florida	80.3	8	Florida	80.3
10	Georgia	79.6	10	Georgia	79.6
3	Hawaii	87.5	11	South Carolina	79.5
48	Idaho	65.6	12	Michigan	78.8
40	Illinois	73.5	12	Pennsylvania	78.8
38	Indiana	74.0	14	Tennessee	78.7
33	Iowa	75.9	15	Oklahoma	78.5
31	Kansas	76.0	16	Alabama	78.2
16	Kentucky	78.2	16	Kentucky	78.2
28	Louisiana	77.0	18	Colorado	78.0
41	Maine	72.9	19	Massachusetts	77.9
1	Maryland	91.3	20	New York	77.8
19	Massachusetts	77.9	21	Ohio	77.7
12	Michigan	78.8	22	North Carolina	77.3
6	Minnesota	80.5	22	Texas	77.3
25	Mississippi	77.1	24	North Dakota	77.2
30	Missouri	76.1	25	California	77.1
49	Montana	65.3	25	Mississippi	77.1
5	Nebraska	82.9	25	Wisconsin	77.1
50	Nevada	63.1	28	Louisiana	77.0
2	New Hampshire	90.6	29	South Dakota	76.9
6	New Jersey	80.5	30	Missouri	76.1
31	New Mexico	76.0	31	Kansas	76.0
20	New York	77.8	31	New Mexico	76.0
22	North Carolina	77.3	33	Iowa	75.9
24	North Dakota	77.2	34	Virginia	75.5
21	Ohio	77.7	34	West Virginia	75.5
15	Oklahoma	78.5	36	Arizona	75.2
43	Oregon	70.5	37	Rhode Island	75.0
12	Pennsylvania	78.8	38	Indiana	74.0
37	Rhode Island	75.0	39	Utah	73.6
11	South Carolina	79.5	40	Illinois	73.5
29	South Dakota	76.9	41	Maine	72.9
14	Tennessee	78.7	42	Arkansas	72.3
22	Texas	77.3	43	Oregon	70.5
39	Utah	73.6	44	Wyoming	70.2
47	Vermont	67.3	45	Alaska	70.1
34	Virginia	75.5	46	Washington	69.0
46	Washington	69.0	47	Vermont	67.3
34	West Virginia	75.5	48	Idaho	65.6
25	Wisconsin	77.1	49	Montana	65.3
44	Wyoming	70.2	50	Nevada	63.1
				District of Columbia	81.6

Source: U.S. Department of Health and Human Services, Centers for Disease Control and Prevention
"State Vaccination Coverage Levels" (MMWR, Vol. 57, No. 35, 09/05/08, http://www.cdc.gov/mmwr/)
*Fully immunized (4:3:1:3:3:1 series) children received four doses of DTP/DT/DTaP (Diphtheria, Tetanus, Pertussis [Whooping Cough], Acellular Pertussis), three doses of OPV (Oral Poliovirus Vaccine), one dose of MCV (Measles-Containing Vaccine), three doses of Hib (Haemophilus influenzae type b), three doses of Hepatitis B vaccine and one dose of Varicella (chickenpox) vaccine. This differs from previous "fully" immunized tables.

Percent of Adults Aged 65 Years and Older Who Received Flu Shots in 2007

National Median = 72.0%*

ALPHA ORDER

RANK ORDER

RANK	STATE	PERCENT
42	Alabama	69.0
49	Alaska	64.4
42	Arizona	69.0
33	Arkansas	70.5
40	California	69.3
9	Colorado	76.4
14	Connecticut	74.7
18	Delaware	73.8
48	Florida	64.7
46	Georgia	67.6
3	Hawaii	78.5
41	Idaho	69.1
45	Illinois	68.1
27	Indiana	71.9
16	Iowa	74.6
19	Kansas	73.5
20	Kentucky	73.2
44	Louisiana	68.4
7	Maine	77.2
28	Maryland	71.3
4	Massachusetts	77.9
30	Michigan	70.9
2	Minnesota	79.6
38	Mississippi	69.6
39	Missouri	69.5
22	Montana	72.8
8	Nebraska	76.8
50	Nevada	61.9
5	New Hampshire	77.6
32	New Jersey	70.6
37	New Mexico	70.0
33	New York	70.5
28	North Carolina	71.3
25	North Dakota	72.4
24	Ohio	72.5
12	Oklahoma	76.1
21	Oregon	73.1
23	Pennsylvania	72.6
1	Rhode Island	80.0
35	South Carolina	70.2
6	South Dakota	77.4
36	Tennessee	70.1
47	Texas	66.7
11	Utah	76.2
14	Vermont	74.7
13	Virginia	75.3
26	Washington	72.0
31	West Virginia	70.7
17	Wisconsin	74.1
10	Wyoming	76.3

RANK	STATE	PERCENT
1	Rhode Island	80.0
2	Minnesota	79.6
3	Hawaii	78.5
4	Massachusetts	77.9
5	New Hampshire	77.6
6	South Dakota	77.4
7	Maine	77.2
8	Nebraska	76.8
9	Colorado	76.4
10	Wyoming	76.3
11	Utah	76.2
12	Oklahoma	76.1
13	Virginia	75.3
14	Connecticut	74.7
14	Vermont	74.7
16	Iowa	74.6
17	Wisconsin	74.1
18	Delaware	73.8
19	Kansas	73.5
20	Kentucky	73.2
21	Oregon	73.1
22	Montana	72.8
23	Pennsylvania	72.6
24	Ohio	72.5
25	North Dakota	72.4
26	Washington	72.0
27	Indiana	71.9
28	Maryland	71.3
28	North Carolina	71.3
30	Michigan	70.9
31	West Virginia	70.7
32	New Jersey	70.6
33	Arkansas	70.5
33	New York	70.5
35	South Carolina	70.2
36	Tennessee	70.1
37	New Mexico	70.0
38	Mississippi	69.6
39	Missouri	69.5
40	California	69.3
41	Idaho	69.1
42	Alabama	69.0
42	Arizona	69.0
44	Louisiana	68.4
45	Illinois	68.1
46	Georgia	67.6
47	Texas	66.7
48	Florida	64.7
49	Alaska	64.4
50	Nevada	61.9

District of Columbia 60.2

Source: U.S. Department of Health and Human Services, Centers for Disease Control and Prevention
"2007 Behavioral Risk Factor Surveillance Summary Prevalence Data" (http://apps.nccd.cdc.gov/brfss/)
*Percent of adults 65 years old and older who reported receiving influenza vaccine during the preceding 12 months.

Percent of Adults Aged 65 Years and Older
Who Have Had a Pneumonia Vaccine: 2007
National Median = 67.3%*

ALPHA ORDER

RANK	STATE	PERCENT
35	Alabama	65.3
32	Alaska	66.0
27	Arizona	67.2
40	Arkansas	63.9
50	California	60.4
3	Colorado	72.5
38	Connecticut	64.9
5	Delaware	72.2
48	Florida	63.0
42	Georgia	63.6
19	Hawaii	69.4
31	Idaho	66.1
49	Illinois	61.4
25	Indiana	68.4
21	Iowa	69.3
24	Kansas	68.7
32	Kentucky	66.0
29	Louisiana	66.6
11	Maine	71.1
34	Maryland	65.6
10	Massachusetts	71.2
43	Michigan	63.5
12	Minnesota	70.9
35	Mississippi	65.3
30	Missouri	66.4
2	Montana	72.6
8	Nebraska	71.8
28	Nevada	66.7
7	New Hampshire	71.9
44	New Jersey	63.4
47	New Mexico	63.2
44	New York	63.4
22	North Carolina	69.2
14	North Dakota	70.5
15	Ohio	69.9
9	Oklahoma	71.7
1	Oregon	74.0
17	Pennsylvania	69.7
4	Rhode Island	72.4
39	South Carolina	64.2
41	South Dakota	63.7
35	Tennessee	65.3
44	Texas	63.4
23	Utah	68.8
16	Vermont	69.8
17	Virginia	69.7
13	Washington	70.7
26	West Virginia	67.3
19	Wisconsin	69.4
5	Wyoming	72.2

RANK ORDER

RANK	STATE	PERCENT
1	Oregon	74.0
2	Montana	72.6
3	Colorado	72.5
4	Rhode Island	72.4
5	Delaware	72.2
5	Wyoming	72.2
7	New Hampshire	71.9
8	Nebraska	71.8
9	Oklahoma	71.7
10	Massachusetts	71.2
11	Maine	71.1
12	Minnesota	70.9
13	Washington	70.7
14	North Dakota	70.5
15	Ohio	69.9
16	Vermont	69.8
17	Pennsylvania	69.7
17	Virginia	69.7
19	Hawaii	69.4
19	Wisconsin	69.4
21	Iowa	69.3
22	North Carolina	69.2
23	Utah	68.8
24	Kansas	68.7
25	Indiana	68.4
26	West Virginia	67.3
27	Arizona	67.2
28	Nevada	66.7
29	Louisiana	66.6
30	Missouri	66.4
31	Idaho	66.1
32	Alaska	66.0
32	Kentucky	66.0
34	Maryland	65.6
35	Alabama	65.3
35	Mississippi	65.3
35	Tennessee	65.3
38	Connecticut	64.9
39	South Carolina	64.2
40	Arkansas	63.9
41	South Dakota	63.7
42	Georgia	63.6
43	Michigan	63.5
44	New Jersey	63.4
44	New York	63.4
44	Texas	63.4
47	New Mexico	63.2
48	Florida	63.0
49	Illinois	61.4
50	California	60.4

| | District of Columbia | 55.9 |

Source: U.S. Department of Health and Human Services, Centers for Disease Control and Prevention
"2007 Behavioral Risk Factor Surveillance Summary Prevalence Data" (http://apps.nccd.cdc.gov/brfss/)
*Percent of adults 65 years old and older who reported ever receiving a pneumonia vaccine.

Sexually Transmitted Diseases in 2007

National Total = 1,475,854 Cases*

ALPHA ORDER

ALPHA ORDER

RANK	STATE	CASES	% of USA
13	Alabama	36,418	2.5%
39	Alaska	5,497	0.4%
18	Arizona	30,224	2.0%
28	Arkansas	14,244	1.0%
1	California	175,261	11.9%
24	Colorado	20,619	1.4%
29	Connecticut	13,820	0.9%
40	Delaware	4,790	0.3%
4	Florida	81,818	5.5%
7	Georgia	61,428	4.2%
38	Hawaii	6,327	0.4%
42	Idaho	3,992	0.3%
5	Illinois	76,747	5.2%
20	Indiana	29,556	2.0%
34	Iowa	10,592	0.7%
35	Kansas	10,490	0.7%
30	Kentucky	12,303	0.8%
16	Louisiana	31,036	2.1%
46	Maine	2,668	0.2%
17	Maryland	30,263	2.1%
25	Massachusetts	18,996	1.3%
9	Michigan	52,958	3.6%
27	Minnesota	16,931	1.1%
19	Mississippi	30,133	2.0%
14	Missouri	33,423	2.3%
45	Montana	2,878	0.2%
36	Nebraska	6,570	0.4%
31	Nevada	11,982	0.8%
47	New Hampshire	2,223	0.2%
21	New Jersey	27,839	1.9%
32	New Mexico	11,302	0.8%
3	New York	99,487	6.7%
10	North Carolina	47,602	3.2%
48	North Dakota	1,906	0.1%
6	Ohio	68,694	4.7%
26	Oklahoma	17,421	1.2%
33	Oregon	11,103	0.8%
8	Pennsylvania	55,438	3.8%
43	Rhode Island	3,615	0.2%
11	South Carolina	36,848	2.5%
44	South Dakota	2,888	0.2%
12	Tennessee	36,797	2.5%
2	Texas	119,024	8.1%
37	Utah	6,562	0.4%
50	Vermont	1,131	0.1%
15	Virginia	31,078	2.1%
23	Washington	22,591	1.5%
41	West Virginia	4,104	0.3%
22	Wisconsin	26,375	1.8%
49	Wyoming	1,282	0.1%

RANK ORDER

RANK	STATE	CASES	% of USA
1	California	175,261	11.9%
2	Texas	119,024	8.1%
3	New York	99,487	6.7%
4	Florida	81,818	5.5%
5	Illinois	76,747	5.2%
6	Ohio	68,694	4.7%
7	Georgia	61,428	4.2%
8	Pennsylvania	55,438	3.8%
9	Michigan	52,958	3.6%
10	North Carolina	47,602	3.2%
11	South Carolina	36,848	2.5%
12	Tennessee	36,797	2.5%
13	Alabama	36,418	2.5%
14	Missouri	33,423	2.3%
15	Virginia	31,078	2.1%
16	Louisiana	31,036	2.1%
17	Maryland	30,263	2.1%
18	Arizona	30,224	2.0%
19	Mississippi	30,133	2.0%
20	Indiana	29,556	2.0%
21	New Jersey	27,839	1.9%
22	Wisconsin	26,375	1.8%
23	Washington	22,591	1.5%
24	Colorado	20,619	1.4%
25	Massachusetts	18,996	1.3%
26	Oklahoma	17,421	1.2%
27	Minnesota	16,931	1.1%
28	Arkansas	14,244	1.0%
29	Connecticut	13,820	0.9%
30	Kentucky	12,303	0.8%
31	Nevada	11,982	0.8%
32	New Mexico	11,302	0.8%
33	Oregon	11,103	0.8%
34	Iowa	10,592	0.7%
35	Kansas	10,490	0.7%
36	Nebraska	6,570	0.4%
37	Utah	6,562	0.4%
38	Hawaii	6,327	0.4%
39	Alaska	5,497	0.4%
40	Delaware	4,790	0.3%
41	West Virginia	4,104	0.3%
42	Idaho	3,992	0.3%
43	Rhode Island	3,615	0.2%
44	South Dakota	2,888	0.2%
45	Montana	2,878	0.2%
46	Maine	2,668	0.2%
47	New Hampshire	2,223	0.2%
48	North Dakota	1,906	0.1%
49	Wyoming	1,282	0.1%
50	Vermont	1,131	0.1%

	District of Columbia	8,580	0.6%

Source: CQ Press using data from U.S. Dept. of Health and Human Services, Nat'l Center for Health Statistics
"Sexually Transmitted Disease Surveillance 2007" (http://www.cdc.gov/std/stats/TOC2007.htm)
*Includes chancroid, chlamydia, gonorrhea, and primary and secondary syphilis.

Sexually Transmitted Disease Rate in 2007

National Rate = 492.9 Cases per 100,000 Population*

ALPHA ORDER

RANK	STATE	RATE
4	Alabama	791.9
3	Alaska	820.3
20	Arizona	490.2
17	Arkansas	506.7
22	California	480.7
28	Colorado	433.8
30	Connecticut	394.3
12	Delaware	561.2
26	Florida	452.3
6	Georgia	656.1
19	Hawaii	492.2
44	Idaho	272.2
9	Illinois	598.1
25	Indiana	468.2
34	Iowa	355.2
31	Kansas	379.5
43	Kentucky	292.5
5	Louisiana	723.8
48	Maine	201.9
13	Maryland	538.8
42	Massachusetts	295.1
15	Michigan	524.6
37	Minnesota	327.6
1	Mississippi	1,035.4
11	Missouri	572.0
39	Montana	304.6
32	Nebraska	371.5
23	Nevada	480.0
50	New Hampshire	169.1
38	New Jersey	319.0
10	New Mexico	578.3
16	New York	515.3
14	North Carolina	537.4
41	North Dakota	299.7
8	Ohio	598.5
21	Oklahoma	486.7
40	Oregon	300.0
27	Pennsylvania	445.6
36	Rhode Island	338.7
2	South Carolina	852.8
33	South Dakota	369.4
7	Tennessee	609.4
18	Texas	506.2
45	Utah	257.3
49	Vermont	181.3
29	Virginia	406.6
35	Washington	353.2
47	West Virginia	225.6
24	Wisconsin	474.6
46	Wyoming	248.9

RANK ORDER

RANK	STATE	RATE
1	Mississippi	1,035.4
2	South Carolina	852.8
3	Alaska	820.3
4	Alabama	791.9
5	Louisiana	723.8
6	Georgia	656.1
7	Tennessee	609.4
8	Ohio	598.5
9	Illinois	598.1
10	New Mexico	578.3
11	Missouri	572.0
12	Delaware	561.2
13	Maryland	538.8
14	North Carolina	537.4
15	Michigan	524.6
16	New York	515.3
17	Arkansas	506.7
18	Texas	506.2
19	Hawaii	492.2
20	Arizona	490.2
21	Oklahoma	486.7
22	California	480.7
23	Nevada	480.0
24	Wisconsin	474.6
25	Indiana	468.2
26	Florida	452.3
27	Pennsylvania	445.6
28	Colorado	433.8
29	Virginia	406.6
30	Connecticut	394.3
31	Kansas	379.5
32	Nebraska	371.5
33	South Dakota	369.4
34	Iowa	355.2
35	Washington	353.2
36	Rhode Island	338.7
37	Minnesota	327.6
38	New Jersey	319.0
39	Montana	304.6
40	Oregon	300.0
41	North Dakota	299.7
42	Massachusetts	295.1
43	Kentucky	292.5
44	Idaho	272.2
45	Utah	257.3
46	Wyoming	248.9
47	West Virginia	225.6
48	Maine	201.9
49	Vermont	181.3
50	New Hampshire	169.1

| | District of Columbia | 1,475.4 |

Source: CQ Press using data from U.S. Dept. of Health and Human Services, Nat'l Center for Health Statistics
"Sexually Transmitted Disease Surveillance 2007" (http://www.cdc.gov/std/stats/TOC2007.htm)
*Includes chancroid, chlamydia, gonorrhea, and primary and secondary syphilis.

Chlamydia Cases Reported in 2007

National Total = 1,108,374 Cases*

ALPHA ORDER

RANK	STATE	CASES	% of USA
13	Alabama	25,153	2.3%
39	Alaska	4,911	0.4%
14	Arizona	24,866	2.2%
29	Arkansas	9,954	0.9%
1	California	141,928	12.8%
24	Colorado	17,186	1.6%
28	Connecticut	11,454	1.0%
41	Delaware	3,479	0.3%
4	Florida	57,575	5.2%
7	Georgia	42,913	3.9%
37	Hawaii	5,659	0.5%
40	Idaho	3,722	0.3%
5	Illinois	55,470	5.0%
20	Indiana	20,712	1.9%
34	Iowa	8,643	0.8%
35	Kansas	8,180	0.7%
33	Kentucky	8,798	0.8%
22	Louisiana	19,362	1.7%
46	Maine	2,541	0.2%
17	Maryland	23,150	2.1%
25	Massachusetts	16,145	1.5%
9	Michigan	37,353	3.4%
26	Minnesota	13,413	1.2%
18	Mississippi	21,686	2.0%
16	Missouri	23,308	2.1%
44	Montana	2,748	0.2%
38	Nebraska	5,132	0.5%
31	Nevada	9,514	0.9%
47	New Hampshire	2,055	0.2%
19	New Jersey	21,536	1.9%
32	New Mexico	9,460	0.9%
3	New York	80,717	7.3%
10	North Carolina	30,611	2.8%
48	North Dakota	1,789	0.2%
6	Ohio	47,434	4.3%
27	Oklahoma	12,529	1.1%
30	Oregon	9,849	0.9%
8	Pennsylvania	42,469	3.8%
42	Rhode Island	3,177	0.3%
12	South Carolina	26,431	2.4%
45	South Dakota	2,620	0.2%
11	Tennessee	26,866	2.4%
2	Texas	85,786	7.7%
36	Utah	5,721	0.5%
50	Vermont	1,057	0.1%
15	Virginia	24,579	2.2%
23	Washington	18,784	1.7%
43	West Virginia	3,168	0.3%
21	Wisconsin	19,555	1.8%
49	Wyoming	1,197	0.1%

RANK ORDER

RANK	STATE	CASES	% of USA
1	California	141,928	12.8%
2	Texas	85,786	7.7%
3	New York	80,717	7.3%
4	Florida	57,575	5.2%
5	Illinois	55,470	5.0%
6	Ohio	47,434	4.3%
7	Georgia	42,913	3.9%
8	Pennsylvania	42,469	3.8%
9	Michigan	37,353	3.4%
10	North Carolina	30,611	2.8%
11	Tennessee	26,866	2.4%
12	South Carolina	26,431	2.4%
13	Alabama	25,153	2.3%
14	Arizona	24,866	2.2%
15	Virginia	24,579	2.2%
16	Missouri	23,308	2.1%
17	Maryland	23,150	2.1%
18	Mississippi	21,686	2.0%
19	New Jersey	21,536	1.9%
20	Indiana	20,712	1.9%
21	Wisconsin	19,555	1.8%
22	Louisiana	19,362	1.7%
23	Washington	18,784	1.7%
24	Colorado	17,186	1.6%
25	Massachusetts	16,145	1.5%
26	Minnesota	13,413	1.2%
27	Oklahoma	12,529	1.1%
28	Connecticut	11,454	1.0%
29	Arkansas	9,954	0.9%
30	Oregon	9,849	0.9%
31	Nevada	9,514	0.9%
32	New Mexico	9,460	0.9%
33	Kentucky	8,798	0.8%
34	Iowa	8,643	0.8%
35	Kansas	8,180	0.7%
36	Utah	5,721	0.5%
37	Hawaii	5,659	0.5%
38	Nebraska	5,132	0.5%
39	Alaska	4,911	0.4%
40	Idaho	3,722	0.3%
41	Delaware	3,479	0.3%
42	Rhode Island	3,177	0.3%
43	West Virginia	3,168	0.3%
44	Montana	2,748	0.2%
45	South Dakota	2,620	0.2%
46	Maine	2,541	0.2%
47	New Hampshire	2,055	0.2%
48	North Dakota	1,789	0.2%
49	Wyoming	1,197	0.1%
50	Vermont	1,057	0.1%
	District of Columbia	6,029	0.5%

Source: U.S. Department of Health and Human Services, National Center for Health Statistics
    "Sexually Transmitted Disease Surveillance 2007" (http://www.cdc.gov/std/stats/TOC2007.htm)
*Any of several common, often asymptomatic, sexually transmitted diseases caused by the microorganism Chlamydia
trachomatis, including nonspecific urethritis in men.

Chlamydia Rate in 2007

National Rate = 370.2 Cases per 100,000 Population*

ALPHA ORDER

RANK	STATE	RATE
4	Alabama	546.9
2	Alaska	732.9
15	Arizona	403.3
22	Arkansas	354.1
17	California	389.3
21	Colorado	361.6
29	Connecticut	326.8
14	Delaware	407.6
31	Florida	318.3
6	Georgia	458.3
9	Hawaii	440.2
41	Idaho	253.8
10	Illinois	432.3
28	Indiana	328.1
37	Iowa	289.8
33	Kansas	295.9
46	Kentucky	209.2
7	Louisiana	451.6
47	Maine	192.3
13	Maryland	412.2
42	Massachusetts	250.8
19	Michigan	370.0
40	Minnesota	259.6
1	Mississippi	745.1
16	Missouri	398.9
35	Montana	290.9
36	Nebraska	290.2
18	Nevada	381.2
50	New Hampshire	156.3
43	New Jersey	246.8
5	New Mexico	484.0
11	New York	418.1
25	North Carolina	345.6
38	North Dakota	281.3
12	Ohio	413.3
24	Oklahoma	350.0
39	Oregon	266.1
26	Pennsylvania	341.4
32	Rhode Island	297.6
3	South Carolina	611.7
27	South Dakota	335.1
8	Tennessee	444.9
20	Texas	364.9
45	Utah	224.3
49	Vermont	169.4
30	Virginia	321.6
34	Washington	293.7
48	West Virginia	174.2
23	Wisconsin	351.9
44	Wyoming	232.4

RANK ORDER

RANK	STATE	RATE
1	Mississippi	745.1
2	Alaska	732.9
3	South Carolina	611.7
4	Alabama	546.9
5	New Mexico	484.0
6	Georgia	458.3
7	Louisiana	451.6
8	Tennessee	444.9
9	Hawaii	440.2
10	Illinois	432.3
11	New York	418.1
12	Ohio	413.3
13	Maryland	412.2
14	Delaware	407.6
15	Arizona	403.3
16	Missouri	398.9
17	California	389.3
18	Nevada	381.2
19	Michigan	370.0
20	Texas	364.9
21	Colorado	361.6
22	Arkansas	354.1
23	Wisconsin	351.9
24	Oklahoma	350.0
25	North Carolina	345.6
26	Pennsylvania	341.4
27	South Dakota	335.1
28	Indiana	328.1
29	Connecticut	326.8
30	Virginia	321.6
31	Florida	318.3
32	Rhode Island	297.6
33	Kansas	295.9
34	Washington	293.7
35	Montana	290.9
36	Nebraska	290.2
37	Iowa	289.8
38	North Dakota	281.3
39	Oregon	266.1
40	Minnesota	259.6
41	Idaho	253.8
42	Massachusetts	250.8
43	New Jersey	246.8
44	Wyoming	232.4
45	Utah	224.3
46	Kentucky	209.2
47	Maine	192.3
48	West Virginia	174.2
49	Vermont	169.4
50	New Hampshire	156.3

District of Columbia 1,036.7

Source: U.S. Department of Health and Human Services, National Center for Health Statistics
    "Sexually Transmitted Disease Surveillance 2007" (http://www.cdc.gov/std/stats/TOC2007.htm)
*Any of several common, often asymptomatic, sexually transmitted diseases caused by the microorganism Chlamydia trachomatis, including nonspecific urethritis in men.

Gonorrhea Cases Reported in 2007

National Total = 355,991 Cases*

ALPHA ORDER

RANK	STATE	CASES	% of USA
12	Alabama	10,885	3.1%
41	Alaska	579	0.2%
22	Arizona	5,062	1.4%
24	Arkansas	4,168	1.2%
2	California	31,294	8.8%
28	Colorado	3,376	0.9%
31	Connecticut	2,327	0.7%
36	Delaware	1,293	0.4%
3	Florida	23,327	6.6%
6	Georgia	17,835	5.0%
40	Hawaii	659	0.2%
43	Idaho	269	0.1%
5	Illinois	20,813	5.8%
16	Indiana	8,790	2.5%
33	Iowa	1,928	0.5%
32	Kansas	2,282	0.6%
27	Kentucky	3,449	1.0%
11	Louisiana	11,137	3.1%
47	Maine	118	0.0%
18	Maryland	6,768	1.9%
29	Massachusetts	2,695	0.8%
9	Michigan	15,482	4.3%
26	Minnesota	3,459	1.0%
17	Mississippi	8,314	2.3%
14	Missouri	9,876	2.8%
46	Montana	122	0.0%
35	Nebraska	1,434	0.4%
30	Nevada	2,357	0.7%
45	New Hampshire	138	0.0%
21	New Jersey	6,076	1.7%
34	New Mexico	1,796	0.5%
7	New York	17,697	5.0%
8	North Carolina	16,666	4.7%
48	North Dakota	116	0.0%
4	Ohio	21,066	5.9%
23	Oklahoma	4,827	1.4%
37	Oregon	1,236	0.3%
10	Pennsylvania	12,706	3.6%
42	Rhode Island	402	0.1%
13	South Carolina	10,326	2.9%
44	South Dakota	261	0.1%
15	Tennessee	9,564	2.7%
1	Texas	32,073	9.0%
39	Utah	821	0.2%
50	Vermont	64	0.0%
20	Virginia	6,269	1.8%
25	Washington	3,653	1.0%
38	West Virginia	930	0.3%
19	Wisconsin	6,752	1.9%
49	Wyoming	81	0.0%

RANK ORDER

RANK	STATE	CASES	% of USA
1	Texas	32,073	9.0%
2	California	31,294	8.8%
3	Florida	23,327	6.6%
4	Ohio	21,066	5.9%
5	Illinois	20,813	5.8%
6	Georgia	17,835	5.0%
7	New York	17,697	5.0%
8	North Carolina	16,666	4.7%
9	Michigan	15,482	4.3%
10	Pennsylvania	12,706	3.6%
11	Louisiana	11,137	3.1%
12	Alabama	10,885	3.1%
13	South Carolina	10,326	2.9%
14	Missouri	9,876	2.8%
15	Tennessee	9,564	2.7%
16	Indiana	8,790	2.5%
17	Mississippi	8,314	2.3%
18	Maryland	6,768	1.9%
19	Wisconsin	6,752	1.9%
20	Virginia	6,269	1.8%
21	New Jersey	6,076	1.7%
22	Arizona	5,062	1.4%
23	Oklahoma	4,827	1.4%
24	Arkansas	4,168	1.2%
25	Washington	3,653	1.0%
26	Minnesota	3,459	1.0%
27	Kentucky	3,449	1.0%
28	Colorado	3,376	0.9%
29	Massachusetts	2,695	0.8%
30	Nevada	2,357	0.7%
31	Connecticut	2,327	0.7%
32	Kansas	2,282	0.6%
33	Iowa	1,928	0.5%
34	New Mexico	1,796	0.5%
35	Nebraska	1,434	0.4%
36	Delaware	1,293	0.4%
37	Oregon	1,236	0.3%
38	West Virginia	930	0.3%
39	Utah	821	0.2%
40	Hawaii	659	0.2%
41	Alaska	579	0.2%
42	Rhode Island	402	0.1%
43	Idaho	269	0.1%
44	South Dakota	261	0.1%
45	New Hampshire	138	0.0%
46	Montana	122	0.0%
47	Maine	118	0.0%
48	North Dakota	116	0.0%
49	Wyoming	81	0.0%
50	Vermont	64	0.0%
	District of Columbia	2,373	0.7%

Source: U.S. Department of Health and Human Services, National Center for Health Statistics
"Sexually Transmitted Disease Surveillance 2007" (http://www.cdc.gov/std/stats/TOC2007.htm)
*Gonorrhea is a sexually transmitted disease caused by gonococcal bacteria that affects the mucous membrane chiefly of the genital and urinary tracts and is characterized by an acute purulent discharge and painful or difficult urination, though women often have no symptoms.

Gonorrhea Rate in 2007

National Rate = 118.9 Cases per 100,000 Population*

ALPHA ORDER

RANK	STATE	RATE
4	Alabama	236.7
24	Alaska	86.4
27	Arizona	82.1
13	Arkansas	148.3
25	California	85.8
31	Colorado	71.0
34	Connecticut	66.4
12	Delaware	151.5
17	Florida	129.0
5	Georgia	190.5
37	Hawaii	51.3
44	Idaho	18.3
9	Illinois	162.2
14	Indiana	139.2
35	Iowa	64.7
26	Kansas	82.6
28	Kentucky	82.0
2	Louisiana	259.7
50	Maine	8.9
19	Maryland	120.5
39	Massachusetts	41.9
11	Michigan	153.4
33	Minnesota	66.9
1	Mississippi	285.7
8	Missouri	169.0
47	Montana	12.9
30	Nebraska	81.1
21	Nevada	94.4
48	New Hampshire	10.5
32	New Jersey	69.6
22	New Mexico	91.9
23	New York	91.7
6	North Carolina	188.2
45	North Dakota	18.2
7	Ohio	183.5
16	Oklahoma	134.9
41	Oregon	33.4
20	Pennsylvania	102.1
40	Rhode Island	37.7
3	South Carolina	239.0
41	South Dakota	33.4
10	Tennessee	158.4
15	Texas	136.4
43	Utah	32.2
49	Vermont	10.3
28	Virginia	82.0
36	Washington	57.1
38	West Virginia	51.1
18	Wisconsin	121.5
46	Wyoming	15.7

RANK ORDER

RANK	STATE	RATE
1	Mississippi	285.7
2	Louisiana	259.7
3	South Carolina	239.0
4	Alabama	236.7
5	Georgia	190.5
6	North Carolina	188.2
7	Ohio	183.5
8	Missouri	169.0
9	Illinois	162.2
10	Tennessee	158.4
11	Michigan	153.4
12	Delaware	151.5
13	Arkansas	148.3
14	Indiana	139.2
15	Texas	136.4
16	Oklahoma	134.9
17	Florida	129.0
18	Wisconsin	121.5
19	Maryland	120.5
20	Pennsylvania	102.1
21	Nevada	94.4
22	New Mexico	91.9
23	New York	91.7
24	Alaska	86.4
25	California	85.8
26	Kansas	82.6
27	Arizona	82.1
28	Kentucky	82.0
28	Virginia	82.0
30	Nebraska	81.1
31	Colorado	71.0
32	New Jersey	69.6
33	Minnesota	66.9
34	Connecticut	66.4
35	Iowa	64.7
36	Washington	57.1
37	Hawaii	51.3
38	West Virginia	51.1
39	Massachusetts	41.9
40	Rhode Island	37.7
41	Oregon	33.4
41	South Dakota	33.4
43	Utah	32.2
44	Idaho	18.3
45	North Dakota	18.2
46	Wyoming	15.7
47	Montana	12.9
48	New Hampshire	10.5
49	Vermont	10.3
50	Maine	8.9

| | District of Columbia | 408.1 |

Source: U.S. Department of Health and Human Services, National Center for Health Statistics
    "Sexually Transmitted Disease Surveillance 2007" (http://www.cdc.gov/std/stats/TOC2007.htm)
*Gonorrhea is a sexually transmitted disease caused by gonococcal bacteria that affects the mucous membrane chiefly of the genital and urinary tracts and is characterized by an acute purulent discharge and painful or difficult urination, though women often have no symptoms.

Syphilis Cases Reported in 2007

National Total = 11,466 Cases*

RANK	STATE	CASES	% of USA
8	Alabama	380	3.3%
44	Alaska	7	0.1%
12	Arizona	296	2.6%
22	Arkansas	122	1.1%
1	California	2,038	17.8%
28	Colorado	57	0.5%
32	Connecticut	39	0.3%
38	Delaware	18	0.2%
4	Florida	913	8.0%
5	Georgia	680	5.9%
41	Hawaii	9	0.1%
49	Idaho	1	0.0%
7	Illinois	464	4.0%
30	Indiana	54	0.5%
36	Iowa	21	0.2%
35	Kansas	28	0.2%
29	Kentucky	56	0.5%
6	Louisiana	533	4.6%
41	Maine	9	0.1%
10	Maryland	345	3.0%
18	Massachusetts	155	1.4%
21	Michigan	123	1.1%
27	Minnesota	59	0.5%
20	Mississippi	133	1.2%
14	Missouri	239	2.1%
43	Montana	8	0.1%
47	Nebraska	4	0.0%
23	Nevada	111	1.0%
34	New Hampshire	30	0.3%
16	New Jersey	227	2.0%
31	New Mexico	46	0.4%
3	New York	1,068	9.3%
11	North Carolina	323	2.8%
49	North Dakota	1	0.0%
17	Ohio	194	1.7%
26	Oklahoma	65	0.6%
38	Oregon	18	0.2%
13	Pennsylvania	263	2.3%
33	Rhode Island	36	0.3%
24	South Carolina	91	0.8%
44	South Dakota	7	0.1%
9	Tennessee	367	3.2%
2	Texas	1,160	10.1%
37	Utah	20	0.2%
40	Vermont	10	0.1%
15	Virginia	230	2.0%
19	Washington	154	1.3%
46	West Virginia	6	0.1%
25	Wisconsin	66	0.6%
47	Wyoming	4	0.0%

RANK	STATE	CASES	% of USA
1	California	2,038	17.8%
2	Texas	1,160	10.1%
3	New York	1,068	9.3%
4	Florida	913	8.0%
5	Georgia	680	5.9%
6	Louisiana	533	4.6%
7	Illinois	464	4.0%
8	Alabama	380	3.3%
9	Tennessee	367	3.2%
10	Maryland	345	3.0%
11	North Carolina	323	2.8%
12	Arizona	296	2.6%
13	Pennsylvania	263	2.3%
14	Missouri	239	2.1%
15	Virginia	230	2.0%
16	New Jersey	227	2.0%
17	Ohio	194	1.7%
18	Massachusetts	155	1.4%
19	Washington	154	1.3%
20	Mississippi	133	1.2%
21	Michigan	123	1.1%
22	Arkansas	122	1.1%
23	Nevada	111	1.0%
24	South Carolina	91	0.8%
25	Wisconsin	66	0.6%
26	Oklahoma	65	0.6%
27	Minnesota	59	0.5%
28	Colorado	57	0.5%
29	Kentucky	56	0.5%
30	Indiana	54	0.5%
31	New Mexico	46	0.4%
32	Connecticut	39	0.3%
33	Rhode Island	36	0.3%
34	New Hampshire	30	0.3%
35	Kansas	28	0.2%
36	Iowa	21	0.2%
37	Utah	20	0.2%
38	Delaware	18	0.2%
38	Oregon	18	0.2%
40	Vermont	10	0.1%
41	Hawaii	9	0.1%
41	Maine	9	0.1%
43	Montana	8	0.1%
44	Alaska	7	0.1%
44	South Dakota	7	0.1%
46	West Virginia	6	0.1%
47	Nebraska	4	0.0%
47	Wyoming	4	0.0%
49	Idaho	1	0.0%
49	North Dakota	1	0.0%
	District of Columbia	178	1.6%

Source: U.S. Department of Health and Human Services, National Center for Health Statistics
"Sexually Transmitted Disease Surveillance 2007" (http://www.cdc.gov/std/stats/TOC2007.htm)
*Includes only primary and secondary cases. Does not include 29,454 cases in other stages. A chronic infectious disease caused by a spirochete (Treponema pallidum), either transmitted by direct contact, usually in sexual intercourse, or passed from mother to child in utero, and progressing through three stages characterized respectively by local formation of chancres, ulcerous skin eruptions, and systemic infection leading to general paresis.

Syphilis Rate in 2007

National Rate = 3.8 Cases per 100,000 Population*

ALPHA ORDER				RANK ORDER		
RANK	**STATE**	**RATE**		**RANK**	**STATE**	**RATE**
2	Alabama	8.3		1	Louisiana	12.4
36	Alaska	1.0		2	Alabama	8.3
10	Arizona	4.8		3	Georgia	7.3
13	Arkansas	4.3		4	Maryland	6.1
6	California	5.6		4	Tennessee	6.1
31	Colorado	1.2		6	California	5.6
34	Connecticut	1.1		7	New York	5.5
24	Delaware	2.1		8	Florida	5.0
8	Florida	5.0		9	Texas	4.9
3	Georgia	7.3		10	Arizona	4.8
43	Hawaii	0.7		11	Mississippi	4.6
50	Idaho	0.1		12	Nevada	4.4
15	Illinois	3.6		13	Arkansas	4.3
38	Indiana	0.9		14	Missouri	4.1
43	Iowa	0.7		15	Illinois	3.6
36	Kansas	1.0		15	North Carolina	3.6
30	Kentucky	1.3		17	Rhode Island	3.4
1	Louisiana	12.4		18	Virginia	3.0
43	Maine	0.7		19	New Jersey	2.6
4	Maryland	6.1		20	Massachusetts	2.4
20	Massachusetts	2.4		20	New Mexico	2.4
31	Michigan	1.2		20	Washington	2.4
34	Minnesota	1.1		23	New Hampshire	2.3
11	Mississippi	4.6		24	Delaware	2.1
14	Missouri	4.1		24	Pennsylvania	2.1
40	Montana	0.8		24	South Carolina	2.1
48	Nebraska	0.2		27	Oklahoma	1.8
12	Nevada	4.4		28	Ohio	1.7
23	New Hampshire	2.3		29	Vermont	1.6
19	New Jersey	2.6		30	Kentucky	1.3
20	New Mexico	2.4		31	Colorado	1.2
7	New York	5.5		31	Michigan	1.2
15	North Carolina	3.6		31	Wisconsin	1.2
48	North Dakota	0.2		34	Connecticut	1.1
28	Ohio	1.7		34	Minnesota	1.1
27	Oklahoma	1.8		36	Alaska	1.0
46	Oregon	0.5		36	Kansas	1.0
24	Pennsylvania	2.1		38	Indiana	0.9
17	Rhode Island	3.4		38	South Dakota	0.9
24	South Carolina	2.1		40	Montana	0.8
38	South Dakota	0.9		40	Utah	0.8
4	Tennessee	6.1		40	Wyoming	0.8
9	Texas	4.9		43	Hawaii	0.7
40	Utah	0.8		43	Iowa	0.7
29	Vermont	1.6		43	Maine	0.7
18	Virginia	3.0		46	Oregon	0.5
20	Washington	2.4		47	West Virginia	0.3
47	West Virginia	0.3		48	Nebraska	0.2
31	Wisconsin	1.2		48	North Dakota	0.2
40	Wyoming	0.8		50	Idaho	0.1
					District of Columbia	30.6

Source: U.S. Department of Health and Human Services, National Center for Health Statistics
"Sexually Transmitted Disease Surveillance 2007" (http://www.cdc.gov/std/stats/TOC2007.htm)
*Includes only primary and secondary cases. Does not include 29,454 cases in other stages. A chronic infectious disease caused by a spirochete (Treponema pallidum), either transmitted by direct contact, usually in sexual intercourse, or passed from mother to child in utero, and progressing through three stages characterized respectively by local formation of chancres, ulcerous skin eruptions, and systemic infection leading to general paresis.

Percent of Adults Who Have Asthma: 2007

National Median = 8.4% of Adults*

ALPHA ORDER

RANK	STATE	PERCENT
16	Alabama	8.8
35	Alaska	7.8
18	Arizona	8.7
45	Arkansas	7.0
42	California	7.5
35	Colorado	7.8
8	Connecticut	9.3
35	Delaware	7.8
50	Florida	6.2
41	Georgia	7.6
33	Hawaii	8.0
18	Idaho	8.7
26	Illinois	8.3
16	Indiana	8.8
45	Iowa	7.0
25	Kansas	8.4
13	Kentucky	9.0
49	Louisiana	6.3
1	Maine	10.3
26	Maryland	8.3
3	Massachusetts	9.9
7	Michigan	9.5
39	Minnesota	7.7
48	Mississippi	6.6
24	Missouri	8.5
8	Montana	9.3
30	Nebraska	8.1
47	Nevada	6.9
2	New Hampshire	10.2
26	New Jersey	8.3
18	New Mexico	8.7
18	New York	8.7
35	North Carolina	7.8
39	North Dakota	7.7
15	Ohio	8.9
23	Oklahoma	8.6
5	Oregon	9.7
8	Pennsylvania	9.3
3	Rhode Island	9.9
42	South Carolina	7.5
44	South Dakota	7.1
18	Tennessee	8.7
29	Texas	8.2
30	Utah	8.1
6	Vermont	9.6
33	Virginia	8.0
8	Washington	9.3
13	West Virginia	9.0
12	Wisconsin	9.2
30	Wyoming	8.1

RANK ORDER

RANK	STATE	PERCENT
1	Maine	10.3
2	New Hampshire	10.2
3	Massachusetts	9.9
3	Rhode Island	9.9
5	Oregon	9.7
6	Vermont	9.6
7	Michigan	9.5
8	Connecticut	9.3
8	Montana	9.3
8	Pennsylvania	9.3
8	Washington	9.3
12	Wisconsin	9.2
13	Kentucky	9.0
13	West Virginia	9.0
15	Ohio	8.9
16	Alabama	8.8
16	Indiana	8.8
18	Arizona	8.7
18	Idaho	8.7
18	New Mexico	8.7
18	New York	8.7
18	Tennessee	8.7
23	Oklahoma	8.6
24	Missouri	8.5
25	Kansas	8.4
26	Illinois	8.3
26	Maryland	8.3
26	New Jersey	8.3
29	Texas	8.2
30	Nebraska	8.1
30	Utah	8.1
30	Wyoming	8.1
33	Hawaii	8.0
33	Virginia	8.0
35	Alaska	7.8
35	Colorado	7.8
35	Delaware	7.8
35	North Carolina	7.8
39	Minnesota	7.7
39	North Dakota	7.7
41	Georgia	7.6
42	California	7.5
42	South Carolina	7.5
44	South Dakota	7.1
45	Arkansas	7.0
45	Iowa	7.0
47	Nevada	6.9
48	Mississippi	6.6
49	Louisiana	6.3
50	Florida	6.2
	District of Columbia	9.4

Source: U.S. Department of Health and Human Services, Centers for Disease Control and Prevention
"2007 Behavioral Risk Factor Surveillance Summary Prevalence Data" (http://apps.nccd.cdc.gov/brfss/)
*Percent of adults who answered yes to the questions "Have you ever been told by a doctor, nurse or other health professional that you had asthma?" and "Do you still have asthma?"

Percent of Adults Who Have Been Told They Have Arthritis: 2007

National Median = 27.5%*

ALPHA ORDER

RANK	STATE	PERCENT
2	Alabama	34.7
43	Alaska	24.9
41	Arizona	25.3
11	Arkansas	30.7
50	California	20.8
46	Colorado	23.9
39	Connecticut	25.5
10	Delaware	31.0
44	Florida	24.3
26	Georgia	27.5
45	Hawaii	24.1
38	Idaho	25.8
32	Illinois	26.9
13	Indiana	30.4
31	Iowa	27.1
26	Kansas	27.5
8	Kentucky	31.6
40	Louisiana	25.4
4	Maine	32.2
24	Maryland	27.8
26	Massachusetts	27.5
9	Michigan	31.4
48	Minnesota	22.9
12	Mississippi	30.5
7	Missouri	31.9
18	Montana	29.0
22	Nebraska	28.0
42	Nevada	25.2
19	New Hampshire	28.7
36	New Jersey	26.7
30	New Mexico	27.2
21	New York	28.1
17	North Carolina	29.1
32	North Dakota	26.9
4	Ohio	32.2
14	Oklahoma	30.3
37	Oregon	26.4
6	Pennsylvania	32.1
16	Rhode Island	29.3
15	South Carolina	29.5
34	South Dakota	26.8
3	Tennessee	34.0
47	Texas	23.7
49	Utah	21.8
20	Vermont	28.4
34	Virginia	26.8
29	Washington	27.4
1	West Virginia	35.5
24	Wisconsin	27.8
23	Wyoming	27.9

RANK ORDER

RANK	STATE	PERCENT
1	West Virginia	35.5
2	Alabama	34.7
3	Tennessee	34.0
4	Maine	32.2
4	Ohio	32.2
6	Pennsylvania	32.1
7	Missouri	31.9
8	Kentucky	31.6
9	Michigan	31.4
10	Delaware	31.0
11	Arkansas	30.7
12	Mississippi	30.5
13	Indiana	30.4
14	Oklahoma	30.3
15	South Carolina	29.5
16	Rhode Island	29.3
17	North Carolina	29.1
18	Montana	29.0
19	New Hampshire	28.7
20	Vermont	28.4
21	New York	28.1
22	Nebraska	28.0
23	Wyoming	27.9
24	Maryland	27.8
24	Wisconsin	27.8
26	Georgia	27.5
26	Kansas	27.5
26	Massachusetts	27.5
29	Washington	27.4
30	New Mexico	27.2
31	Iowa	27.1
32	Illinois	26.9
32	North Dakota	26.9
34	South Dakota	26.8
34	Virginia	26.8
36	New Jersey	26.7
37	Oregon	26.4
38	Idaho	25.8
39	Connecticut	25.5
40	Louisiana	25.4
41	Arizona	25.3
42	Nevada	25.2
43	Alaska	24.9
44	Florida	24.3
45	Hawaii	24.1
46	Colorado	23.9
47	Texas	23.7
48	Minnesota	22.9
49	Utah	21.8
50	California	20.8
	District of Columbia	23.6

Source: U.S. Department of Health and Human Services, Centers for Disease Control and Prevention
"2007 Behavioral Risk Factor Surveillance Summary Prevalence Data" (http://apps.nccd.cdc.gov/brfss/)
*Of population 18 years old and older.

Percent of Adults Who Have Been Told They Have Diabetes: 2007

National Median = 8.0% of Adults*

ALPHA ORDER

RANK	STATE	PERCENT
4	Alabama	10.3
47	Alaska	6.1
21	Arizona	8.4
12	Arkansas	9.2
31	California	7.6
50	Colorado	5.3
33	Connecticut	7.3
17	Delaware	8.7
17	Florida	8.7
8	Georgia	10.1
30	Hawaii	7.7
27	Idaho	7.9
15	Illinois	8.8
20	Indiana	8.5
42	Iowa	6.8
33	Kansas	7.3
9	Kentucky	9.9
6	Louisiana	10.2
28	Maine	7.8
21	Maryland	8.4
32	Massachusetts	7.4
15	Michigan	8.8
49	Minnesota	5.7
2	Mississippi	11.1
24	Missouri	8.0
44	Montana	6.6
37	Nebraska	7.1
24	Nevada	8.0
35	New Hampshire	7.2
12	New Jersey	9.2
28	New Mexico	7.8
23	New York	8.2
14	North Carolina	9.1
46	North Dakota	6.3
11	Ohio	9.5
6	Oklahoma	10.2
41	Oregon	6.9
17	Pennsylvania	8.7
35	Rhode Island	7.2
10	South Carolina	9.6
43	South Dakota	6.7
1	Tennessee	11.9
4	Texas	10.3
48	Utah	5.8
39	Vermont	7.0
24	Virginia	8.0
37	Washington	7.1
3	West Virginia	10.8
45	Wisconsin	6.5
39	Wyoming	7.0

RANK ORDER

RANK	STATE	PERCENT
1	Tennessee	11.9
2	Mississippi	11.1
3	West Virginia	10.8
4	Alabama	10.3
4	Texas	10.3
6	Louisiana	10.2
6	Oklahoma	10.2
8	Georgia	10.1
9	Kentucky	9.9
10	South Carolina	9.6
11	Ohio	9.5
12	Arkansas	9.2
12	New Jersey	9.2
14	North Carolina	9.1
15	Illinois	8.8
15	Michigan	8.8
17	Delaware	8.7
17	Florida	8.7
17	Pennsylvania	8.7
20	Indiana	8.5
21	Arizona	8.4
21	Maryland	8.4
23	New York	8.2
24	Missouri	8.0
24	Nevada	8.0
24	Virginia	8.0
27	Idaho	7.9
28	Maine	7.8
28	New Mexico	7.8
30	Hawaii	7.7
31	California	7.6
32	Massachusetts	7.4
33	Connecticut	7.3
33	Kansas	7.3
35	New Hampshire	7.2
35	Rhode Island	7.2
37	Nebraska	7.1
37	Washington	7.1
39	Vermont	7.0
39	Wyoming	7.0
41	Oregon	6.9
42	Iowa	6.8
43	South Dakota	6.7
44	Montana	6.6
45	Wisconsin	6.5
46	North Dakota	6.3
47	Alaska	6.1
48	Utah	5.8
49	Minnesota	5.7
50	Colorado	5.3
	District of Columbia	8.1

Source: U.S. Department of Health and Human Services, Centers for Disease Control and Prevention
 "2007 Behavioral Risk Factor Surveillance Summary Prevalence Data" (http://apps.nccd.cdc.gov/brfss/)
*Of population 18 years old and older. Does not include pregnancy-related diabetes.

Percent of Adults Reporting Serious Psychological Distress: 2006

National Percent = 11.3% of Population*

ALPHA ORDER				RANK ORDER		
RANK	STATE	PERCENT		RANK	STATE	PERCENT
33	Alabama	11.2		1	Utah	14.4
29	Alaska	11.3		2	West Virginia	14.0
24	Arizona	11.7		3	Kansas	13.8
7	Arkansas	13.3		3	Missouri	13.8
47	California	10.2		5	Rhode Island	13.5
29	Colorado	11.3		6	Kentucky	13.4
43	Connecticut	10.6		7	Arkansas	13.3
40	Delaware	10.7		7	Oklahoma	13.3
45	Florida	10.3		7	Tennessee	13.3
22	Georgia	11.8		10	Wyoming	13.2
50	Hawaii	8.8		11	Nebraska	12.9
20	Idaho	12.0		12	Indiana	12.7
45	Illinois	10.3		13	Louisiana	12.5
12	Indiana	12.7		13	Montana	12.5
29	Iowa	11.3		15	Mississippi	12.4
3	Kansas	13.8		15	Vermont	12.4
6	Kentucky	13.4		17	South Carolina	12.3
13	Louisiana	12.5		18	Maine	12.2
18	Maine	12.2		18	New Mexico	12.2
49	Maryland	10.0		20	Idaho	12.0
40	Massachusetts	10.7		21	Ohio	11.9
24	Michigan	11.7		22	Georgia	11.8
29	Minnesota	11.3		22	Nevada	11.8
15	Mississippi	12.4		24	Arizona	11.7
3	Missouri	13.8		24	Michigan	11.7
13	Montana	12.5		26	North Carolina	11.6
11	Nebraska	12.9		26	North Dakota	11.6
22	Nevada	11.8		26	Wisconsin	11.6
33	New Hampshire	11.2		29	Alaska	11.3
48	New Jersey	10.1		29	Colorado	11.3
18	New Mexico	12.2		29	Iowa	11.3
37	New York	10.9		29	Minnesota	11.3
26	North Carolina	11.6		33	Alabama	11.2
26	North Dakota	11.6		33	New Hampshire	11.2
21	Ohio	11.9		33	Oregon	11.2
7	Oklahoma	13.3		36	Texas	11.0
33	Oregon	11.2		37	New York	10.9
37	Pennsylvania	10.9		37	Pennsylvania	10.9
5	Rhode Island	13.5		39	Washington	10.8
17	South Carolina	12.3		40	Delaware	10.7
40	South Dakota	10.7		40	Massachusetts	10.7
7	Tennessee	13.3		40	South Dakota	10.7
36	Texas	11.0		43	Connecticut	10.6
1	Utah	14.4		43	Virginia	10.6
15	Vermont	12.4		45	Florida	10.3
43	Virginia	10.6		45	Illinois	10.3
39	Washington	10.8		47	California	10.2
2	West Virginia	14.0		48	New Jersey	10.1
26	Wisconsin	11.6		49	Maryland	10.0
10	Wyoming	13.2		50	Hawaii	8.8

District of Columbia   11.2

Source: U.S. Department of Health and Human Services, Substance Abuse and Mental Health Services Administration
    "2005-2006 National Surveys on Drug Use and Health" (March 2008, http://www.oas.samhsa.gov/2k6state/toc.cfm)
*Population 18 years and older. Serious psychological distress was previously referred to as serious mental illness. It is defined as having a diagnosable mental, behavioral or emotional disorder that resulted in functional impairment that substantially interfered with or limited one or more major life activities.

VI. Providers

Health Care Practitioners and Technicians in 2007

National Total = 6,753,650 Practitioners and Technicians*

ALPHA ORDER

RANK	STATE	PRACTITIONERS	% of USA
22	Alabama	109,990	1.6%
49	Alaska	13,050	0.2%
21	Arizona	112,090	1.7%
32	Arkansas	65,430	1.0%
1	California	622,290	9.2%
25	Colorado	99,340	1.5%
27	Connecticut	88,190	1.3%
45	Delaware	22,520	0.3%
4	Florida	409,740	6.1%
12	Georgia	185,530	2.7%
43	Hawaii	24,870	0.4%
42	Idaho	28,030	0.4%
7	Illinois	297,110	4.4%
16	Indiana	154,790	2.3%
30	Iowa	72,100	1.1%
31	Kansas	65,880	1.0%
24	Kentucky	102,350	1.5%
23	Louisiana	106,900	1.6%
39	Maine	34,770	0.5%
19	Maryland	134,980	2.0%
10	Massachusetts	203,050	3.0%
8	Michigan	233,910	3.5%
17	Minnesota	144,860	2.1%
33	Mississippi	65,220	1.0%
14	Missouri	159,990	2.4%
46	Montana	21,690	0.3%
34	Nebraska	49,420	0.7%
37	Nevada	40,900	0.6%
40	New Hampshire	32,210	0.5%
11	New Jersey	195,900	2.9%
38	New Mexico	38,850	0.6%
3	New York	447,040	6.6%
9	North Carolina	205,670	3.0%
47	North Dakota	19,410	0.3%
6	Ohio	304,560	4.5%
28	Oklahoma	83,460	1.2%
29	Oregon	73,520	1.1%
5	Pennsylvania	337,010	5.0%
41	Rhode Island	29,350	0.4%
26	South Carolina	95,350	1.4%
44	South Dakota	23,250	0.3%
15	Tennessee	157,950	2.3%
2	Texas	462,400	6.8%
35	Utah	48,040	0.7%
48	Vermont	15,600	0.2%
13	Virginia	162,780	2.4%
20	Washington	129,050	1.9%
36	West Virginia	47,330	0.7%
18	Wisconsin	139,230	2.1%
50	Wyoming	11,240	0.2%

RANK ORDER

RANK	STATE	PRACTITIONERS	% of USA
1	California	622,290	9.2%
2	Texas	462,400	6.8%
3	New York	447,040	6.6%
4	Florida	409,740	6.1%
5	Pennsylvania	337,010	5.0%
6	Ohio	304,560	4.5%
7	Illinois	297,110	4.4%
8	Michigan	233,910	3.5%
9	North Carolina	205,670	3.0%
10	Massachusetts	203,050	3.0%
11	New Jersey	195,900	2.9%
12	Georgia	185,530	2.7%
13	Virginia	162,780	2.4%
14	Missouri	159,990	2.4%
15	Tennessee	157,950	2.3%
16	Indiana	154,790	2.3%
17	Minnesota	144,860	2.1%
18	Wisconsin	139,230	2.1%
19	Maryland	134,980	2.0%
20	Washington	129,050	1.9%
21	Arizona	112,090	1.7%
22	Alabama	109,990	1.6%
23	Louisiana	106,900	1.6%
24	Kentucky	102,350	1.5%
25	Colorado	99,340	1.5%
26	South Carolina	95,350	1.4%
27	Connecticut	88,190	1.3%
28	Oklahoma	83,460	1.2%
29	Oregon	73,520	1.1%
30	Iowa	72,100	1.1%
31	Kansas	65,880	1.0%
32	Arkansas	65,430	1.0%
33	Mississippi	65,220	1.0%
34	Nebraska	49,420	0.7%
35	Utah	48,040	0.7%
36	West Virginia	47,330	0.7%
37	Nevada	40,900	0.6%
38	New Mexico	38,850	0.6%
39	Maine	34,770	0.5%
40	New Hampshire	32,210	0.5%
41	Rhode Island	29,350	0.4%
42	Idaho	28,030	0.4%
43	Hawaii	24,870	0.4%
44	South Dakota	23,250	0.3%
45	Delaware	22,520	0.3%
46	Montana	21,690	0.3%
47	North Dakota	19,410	0.3%
48	Vermont	15,600	0.2%
49	Alaska	13,050	0.2%
50	Wyoming	11,240	0.2%
	District of Columbia	25,480	0.4%

Source: U.S. Department of Labor, Bureau of Labor Statistics
   "Occupational Employment and Wages, 2007" (http://www.bls.gov/oes/)
*Does not include self-employed. Includes various doctors, dentists, nurses, therapists, optometrists, paramedics, and technicians. Does not include assistants and aides listed under health care support occupations. Veterinarians and veterinarian technicians have been subtracted from the totals.

Rate of Health Care Practitioners and Technicians in 2007

National Rate = 2,242 Practitioners and Technicians per 100,000 Population*

ALPHA ORDER

RANK	STATE	RATE
23	Alabama	2,377
45	Alaska	1,916
48	Arizona	1,764
28	Arkansas	2,312
49	California	1,711
38	Colorado	2,051
14	Connecticut	2,527
12	Delaware	2,613
33	Florida	2,251
42	Georgia	1,948
43	Hawaii	1,947
46	Idaho	1,873
26	Illinois	2,317
19	Indiana	2,443
20	Iowa	2,417
24	Kansas	2,372
21	Kentucky	2,416
18	Louisiana	2,444
10	Maine	2,643
22	Maryland	2,402
1	Massachusetts	3,139
25	Michigan	2,328
4	Minnesota	2,795
34	Mississippi	2,233
7	Missouri	2,722
31	Montana	2,267
5	Nebraska	2,793
50	Nevada	1,601
17	New Hampshire	2,455
32	New Jersey	2,264
40	New Mexico	1,978
29	New York	2,301
30	North Carolina	2,275
2	North Dakota	3,043
9	Ohio	2,654
27	Oklahoma	2,313
41	Oregon	1,968
8	Pennsylvania	2,713
6	Rhode Island	2,787
35	South Carolina	2,165
3	South Dakota	2,922
13	Tennessee	2,569
44	Texas	1,939
47	Utah	1,800
15	Vermont	2,513
37	Virginia	2,114
39	Washington	2,001
11	West Virginia	2,615
16	Wisconsin	2,487
36	Wyoming	2,148

RANK ORDER

RANK	STATE	RATE
1	Massachusetts	3,139
2	North Dakota	3,043
3	South Dakota	2,922
4	Minnesota	2,795
5	Nebraska	2,793
6	Rhode Island	2,787
7	Missouri	2,722
8	Pennsylvania	2,713
9	Ohio	2,654
10	Maine	2,643
11	West Virginia	2,615
12	Delaware	2,613
13	Tennessee	2,569
14	Connecticut	2,527
15	Vermont	2,513
16	Wisconsin	2,487
17	New Hampshire	2,455
18	Louisiana	2,444
19	Indiana	2,443
20	Iowa	2,417
21	Kentucky	2,416
22	Maryland	2,402
23	Alabama	2,377
24	Kansas	2,372
25	Michigan	2,328
26	Illinois	2,317
27	Oklahoma	2,313
28	Arkansas	2,312
29	New York	2,301
30	North Carolina	2,275
31	Montana	2,267
32	New Jersey	2,264
33	Florida	2,251
34	Mississippi	2,233
35	South Carolina	2,165
36	Wyoming	2,148
37	Virginia	2,114
38	Colorado	2,051
39	Washington	2,001
40	New Mexico	1,978
41	Oregon	1,968
42	Georgia	1,948
43	Hawaii	1,947
44	Texas	1,939
45	Alaska	1,916
46	Idaho	1,873
47	Utah	1,800
48	Arizona	1,764
49	California	1,711
50	Nevada	1,601

District of Columbia 4,334

Source: CQ Press using data from U.S. Department of Labor, Bureau of Labor Statistics
   "Occupational Employment and Wages, 2007" (http://www.bls.gov/oes/)
*Does not include self-employed. Includes various doctors, dentists, nurses, therapists, optometrists, paramedics, and technicians. Does not include assistants and aides listed under health care support occupations. Veterinarians and veterinarian technicians have been subtracted from the totals.

Average Annual Wages of Health Care Practitioners and Technicians in 2007

National Average = $65,020*

ALPHA ORDER				RANK ORDER		
RANK	STATE	WAGES		RANK	STATE	WAGES
41	Alabama	$55,600		1	New Jersey	$76,180
2	Alaska	75,580		2	Alaska	75,580
22	Arizona	63,170		3	California	75,480
45	Arkansas	55,020		4	Maryland	74,390
3	California	75,480		5	Hawaii	73,690
16	Colorado	65,930		6	Massachusetts	73,360
10	Connecticut	71,200		7	Oregon	72,720
13	Delaware	69,600		8	New York	72,420
26	Florida	62,530		9	Nevada	72,100
28	Georgia	61,820		10	Connecticut	71,200
5	Hawaii	73,690		11	Washington	71,190
34	Idaho	59,420		12	Minnesota	70,080
27	Illinois	62,120		13	Delaware	69,600
35	Indiana	59,310		14	Rhode Island	69,010
44	Iowa	55,030		15	New Hampshire	66,580
37	Kansas	58,430		16	Colorado	65,930
36	Kentucky	58,770		17	Michigan	65,250
47	Louisiana	54,550		18	Maine	65,220
18	Maine	65,220		19	Wisconsin	65,080
4	Maryland	74,390		20	Virginia	64,240
6	Massachusetts	73,360		21	New Mexico	63,260
17	Michigan	65,250		22	Arizona	63,170
12	Minnesota	70,080		23	Vermont	63,110
43	Mississippi	55,250		24	North Carolina	62,930
40	Missouri	56,930		25	Ohio	62,860
46	Montana	54,570		26	Florida	62,530
39	Nebraska	57,360		27	Illinois	62,120
9	Nevada	72,100		28	Georgia	61,820
15	New Hampshire	66,580		29	Texas	61,780
1	New Jersey	76,180		30	Utah	61,610
21	New Mexico	63,260		31	Pennsylvania	61,050
8	New York	72,420		32	Wyoming	60,770
24	North Carolina	62,930		33	South Carolina	59,460
49	North Dakota	54,520		34	Idaho	59,420
25	Ohio	62,860		35	Indiana	59,310
50	Oklahoma	54,010		36	Kentucky	58,770
7	Oregon	72,720		37	Kansas	58,430
31	Pennsylvania	61,050		38	Tennessee	57,580
14	Rhode Island	69,010		39	Nebraska	57,360
33	South Carolina	59,460		40	Missouri	56,930
42	South Dakota	55,520		41	Alabama	55,600
38	Tennessee	57,580		42	South Dakota	55,520
29	Texas	61,780		43	Mississippi	55,250
30	Utah	61,610		44	Iowa	55,030
23	Vermont	63,110		45	Arkansas	55,020
20	Virginia	64,240		46	Montana	54,570
11	Washington	71,190		47	Louisiana	54,550
47	West Virginia	54,550		47	West Virginia	54,550
19	Wisconsin	65,080		49	North Dakota	54,520
32	Wyoming	60,770		50	Oklahoma	54,010
					District of Columbia	67,810

Source: U.S. Department of Labor, Bureau of Labor Statistics
   "Occupational Employment and Wages, 2007" (http://www.bls.gov/oes/)
*Does not include self-employed. Includes various doctors, dentists, nurses, therapists, optometrists, paramedics and,
technicians. Does not include assistants and aides listed under health care support occupations.

Physicians in 2007

National Total = 927,395 Physicians*

RANK	STATE	PHYSICIANS	% of USA
27	Alabama	11,239	1.2%
49	Alaska	1,717	0.2%
20	Arizona	15,710	1.7%
31	Arkansas	6,548	0.7%
1	California	112,776	12.2%
23	Colorado	14,515	1.6%
22	Connecticut	14,753	1.6%
46	Delaware	2,456	0.3%
4	Florida	55,037	5.9%
14	Georgia	23,239	2.5%
39	Hawaii	4,665	0.5%
43	Idaho	2,993	0.3%
6	Illinois	39,986	4.3%
21	Indiana	15,478	1.7%
32	Iowa	6,536	0.7%
30	Kansas	7,180	0.8%
28	Kentucky	11,024	1.2%
24	Louisiana	12,741	1.4%
41	Maine	4,305	0.5%
11	Maryland	26,402	2.8%
8	Massachusetts	33,313	3.6%
10	Michigan	28,356	3.1%
17	Minnesota	17,178	1.9%
34	Mississippi	5,961	0.6%
19	Missouri	15,968	1.7%
45	Montana	2,580	0.3%
37	Nebraska	4,942	0.5%
35	Nevada	5,591	0.6%
42	New Hampshire	4,232	0.5%
9	New Jersey	30,595	3.3%
36	New Mexico	5,533	0.6%
2	New York	85,304	9.2%
12	North Carolina	26,046	2.8%
48	North Dakota	1,769	0.2%
7	Ohio	34,472	3.7%
29	Oklahoma	7,245	0.8%
25	Oregon	12,048	1.3%
5	Pennsylvania	43,257	4.7%
40	Rhode Island	4,430	0.5%
26	South Carolina	11,514	1.2%
47	South Dakota	2,012	0.2%
16	Tennessee	18,137	2.0%
3	Texas	56,531	6.1%
33	Utah	6,269	0.7%
44	Vermont	2,735	0.3%
13	Virginia	24,162	2.6%
15	Washington	20,353	2.2%
38	West Virginia	4,760	0.5%
18	Wisconsin	16,485	1.8%
50	Wyoming	1,165	0.1%

RANK	STATE	PHYSICIANS	% of USA
1	California	112,776	12.2%
2	New York	85,304	9.2%
3	Texas	56,531	6.1%
4	Florida	55,037	5.9%
5	Pennsylvania	43,257	4.7%
6	Illinois	39,986	4.3%
7	Ohio	34,472	3.7%
8	Massachusetts	33,313	3.6%
9	New Jersey	30,595	3.3%
10	Michigan	28,356	3.1%
11	Maryland	26,402	2.8%
12	North Carolina	26,046	2.8%
13	Virginia	24,162	2.6%
14	Georgia	23,239	2.5%
15	Washington	20,353	2.2%
16	Tennessee	18,137	2.0%
17	Minnesota	17,178	1.9%
18	Wisconsin	16,485	1.8%
19	Missouri	15,968	1.7%
20	Arizona	15,710	1.7%
21	Indiana	15,478	1.7%
22	Connecticut	14,753	1.6%
23	Colorado	14,515	1.6%
24	Louisiana	12,741	1.4%
25	Oregon	12,048	1.3%
26	South Carolina	11,514	1.2%
27	Alabama	11,239	1.2%
28	Kentucky	11,024	1.2%
29	Oklahoma	7,245	0.8%
30	Kansas	7,180	0.8%
31	Arkansas	6,548	0.7%
32	Iowa	6,536	0.7%
33	Utah	6,269	0.7%
34	Mississippi	5,961	0.6%
35	Nevada	5,591	0.6%
36	New Mexico	5,533	0.6%
37	Nebraska	4,942	0.5%
38	West Virginia	4,760	0.5%
39	Hawaii	4,665	0.5%
40	Rhode Island	4,430	0.5%
41	Maine	4,305	0.5%
42	New Hampshire	4,232	0.5%
43	Idaho	2,993	0.3%
44	Vermont	2,735	0.3%
45	Montana	2,580	0.3%
46	Delaware	2,456	0.3%
47	South Dakota	2,012	0.2%
48	North Dakota	1,769	0.2%
49	Alaska	1,717	0.2%
50	Wyoming	1,165	0.1%
	District of Columbia	5,152	0.6%

Source: American Medical Association (Chicago, Illinois)
    "Physician Characteristics and Distribution in the U.S." (2009 Edition)
*As of December 31, 2007. Total does not include 13,909 physicians in the U.S. territories and possessions, at APO's and FPO's, or whose addresses are unknown.

Rate of Physicians in 2007

National Rate = 308 Physicians per 100,000 Population*

<table>
<tr><td colspan="3">ALPHA ORDER</td><td colspan="3">RANK ORDER</td></tr>
<tr><th>RANK</th><th>STATE</th><th>RATE</th><th>RANK</th><th>STATE</th><th>RATE</th></tr>
<tr><td>41</td><td>Alabama</td><td>243</td><td>1</td><td>Massachusetts</td><td>515</td></tr>
<tr><td>37</td><td>Alaska</td><td>252</td><td>2</td><td>Maryland</td><td>470</td></tr>
<tr><td>38</td><td>Arizona</td><td>247</td><td>3</td><td>Vermont</td><td>441</td></tr>
<tr><td>44</td><td>Arkansas</td><td>231</td><td>4</td><td>New York</td><td>439</td></tr>
<tr><td>17</td><td>California</td><td>310</td><td>5</td><td>Connecticut</td><td>423</td></tr>
<tr><td>19</td><td>Colorado</td><td>300</td><td>6</td><td>Rhode Island</td><td>421</td></tr>
<tr><td>5</td><td>Connecticut</td><td>423</td><td>7</td><td>Hawaii</td><td>365</td></tr>
<tr><td>25</td><td>Delaware</td><td>285</td><td>8</td><td>New Jersey</td><td>354</td></tr>
<tr><td>18</td><td>Florida</td><td>302</td><td>9</td><td>Pennsylvania</td><td>348</td></tr>
<tr><td>39</td><td>Georgia</td><td>244</td><td>10</td><td>Minnesota</td><td>331</td></tr>
<tr><td>7</td><td>Hawaii</td><td>365</td><td>11</td><td>Maine</td><td>327</td></tr>
<tr><td>50</td><td>Idaho</td><td>200</td><td>12</td><td>Oregon</td><td>323</td></tr>
<tr><td>16</td><td>Illinois</td><td>312</td><td>13</td><td>New Hampshire</td><td>322</td></tr>
<tr><td>39</td><td>Indiana</td><td>244</td><td>14</td><td>Washington</td><td>316</td></tr>
<tr><td>46</td><td>Iowa</td><td>219</td><td>15</td><td>Virginia</td><td>314</td></tr>
<tr><td>35</td><td>Kansas</td><td>259</td><td>16</td><td>Illinois</td><td>312</td></tr>
<tr><td>34</td><td>Kentucky</td><td>260</td><td>17</td><td>California</td><td>310</td></tr>
<tr><td>23</td><td>Louisiana</td><td>291</td><td>18</td><td>Florida</td><td>302</td></tr>
<tr><td>11</td><td>Maine</td><td>327</td><td>19</td><td>Colorado</td><td>300</td></tr>
<tr><td>2</td><td>Maryland</td><td>470</td><td>19</td><td>Ohio</td><td>300</td></tr>
<tr><td>1</td><td>Massachusetts</td><td>515</td><td>21</td><td>Tennessee</td><td>295</td></tr>
<tr><td>26</td><td>Michigan</td><td>282</td><td>22</td><td>Wisconsin</td><td>294</td></tr>
<tr><td>10</td><td>Minnesota</td><td>331</td><td>23</td><td>Louisiana</td><td>291</td></tr>
<tr><td>48</td><td>Mississippi</td><td>204</td><td>24</td><td>North Carolina</td><td>288</td></tr>
<tr><td>30</td><td>Missouri</td><td>272</td><td>25</td><td>Delaware</td><td>285</td></tr>
<tr><td>31</td><td>Montana</td><td>270</td><td>26</td><td>Michigan</td><td>282</td></tr>
<tr><td>28</td><td>Nebraska</td><td>279</td><td>26</td><td>New Mexico</td><td>282</td></tr>
<tr><td>46</td><td>Nevada</td><td>219</td><td>28</td><td>Nebraska</td><td>279</td></tr>
<tr><td>13</td><td>New Hampshire</td><td>322</td><td>29</td><td>North Dakota</td><td>277</td></tr>
<tr><td>8</td><td>New Jersey</td><td>354</td><td>30</td><td>Missouri</td><td>272</td></tr>
<tr><td>26</td><td>New Mexico</td><td>282</td><td>31</td><td>Montana</td><td>270</td></tr>
<tr><td>4</td><td>New York</td><td>439</td><td>32</td><td>West Virginia</td><td>263</td></tr>
<tr><td>24</td><td>North Carolina</td><td>288</td><td>33</td><td>South Carolina</td><td>261</td></tr>
<tr><td>29</td><td>North Dakota</td><td>277</td><td>34</td><td>Kentucky</td><td>260</td></tr>
<tr><td>19</td><td>Ohio</td><td>300</td><td>35</td><td>Kansas</td><td>259</td></tr>
<tr><td>49</td><td>Oklahoma</td><td>201</td><td>36</td><td>South Dakota</td><td>253</td></tr>
<tr><td>12</td><td>Oregon</td><td>323</td><td>37</td><td>Alaska</td><td>252</td></tr>
<tr><td>9</td><td>Pennsylvania</td><td>348</td><td>38</td><td>Arizona</td><td>247</td></tr>
<tr><td>6</td><td>Rhode Island</td><td>421</td><td>39</td><td>Georgia</td><td>244</td></tr>
<tr><td>33</td><td>South Carolina</td><td>261</td><td>39</td><td>Indiana</td><td>244</td></tr>
<tr><td>36</td><td>South Dakota</td><td>253</td><td>41</td><td>Alabama</td><td>243</td></tr>
<tr><td>21</td><td>Tennessee</td><td>295</td><td>42</td><td>Texas</td><td>237</td></tr>
<tr><td>42</td><td>Texas</td><td>237</td><td>43</td><td>Utah</td><td>235</td></tr>
<tr><td>43</td><td>Utah</td><td>235</td><td>44</td><td>Arkansas</td><td>231</td></tr>
<tr><td>3</td><td>Vermont</td><td>441</td><td>45</td><td>Wyoming</td><td>223</td></tr>
<tr><td>15</td><td>Virginia</td><td>314</td><td>46</td><td>Iowa</td><td>219</td></tr>
<tr><td>14</td><td>Washington</td><td>316</td><td>46</td><td>Nevada</td><td>219</td></tr>
<tr><td>32</td><td>West Virginia</td><td>263</td><td>48</td><td>Mississippi</td><td>204</td></tr>
<tr><td>22</td><td>Wisconsin</td><td>294</td><td>49</td><td>Oklahoma</td><td>201</td></tr>
<tr><td>45</td><td>Wyoming</td><td>223</td><td>50</td><td>Idaho</td><td>200</td></tr>
<tr><td></td><td></td><td></td><td></td><td>District of Columbia</td><td>876</td></tr>
</table>

Source: CQ Press using data from American Medical Association (Chicago, Illinois)
"Physician Characteristics and Distribution in the U.S." (2009 Edition)
*As of December 31, 2007. National rate does not include physicians in the U.S. territories and possessions, at APO's and FPO's, or whose addresses are unknown.

Percent of Physicians Who Are Female: 2007

National Percent = 28.3% of Physicians*

ALPHA ORDER

RANK	STATE	PERCENT
40	Alabama	22.7
8	Alaska	30.8
29	Arizona	25.8
43	Arkansas	22.0
15	California	28.8
13	Colorado	29.5
11	Connecticut	29.9
10	Delaware	30.1
42	Florida	22.2
25	Georgia	27.3
21	Hawaii	27.7
50	Idaho	18.8
3	Illinois	32.4
30	Indiana	25.5
36	Iowa	23.3
30	Kansas	25.5
32	Kentucky	25.2
33	Louisiana	24.7
24	Maine	27.4
2	Maryland	32.9
1	Massachusetts	34.6
14	Michigan	29.3
15	Minnesota	28.8
48	Mississippi	20.1
22	Missouri	27.5
46	Montana	21.6
34	Nebraska	24.6
38	Nevada	23.1
27	New Hampshire	26.9
6	New Jersey	31.7
7	New Mexico	31.4
3	New York	32.4
22	North Carolina	27.5
44	North Dakota	21.9
20	Ohio	28.2
39	Oklahoma	22.8
19	Oregon	28.4
15	Pennsylvania	28.8
5	Rhode Island	32.3
36	South Carolina	23.3
44	South Dakota	21.9
35	Tennessee	23.7
25	Texas	27.3
47	Utah	20.7
9	Vermont	30.7
12	Virginia	29.7
18	Washington	28.5
41	West Virginia	22.6
27	Wisconsin	26.9
49	Wyoming	20.0

RANK ORDER

RANK	STATE	PERCENT
1	Massachusetts	34.6
2	Maryland	32.9
3	Illinois	32.4
3	New York	32.4
5	Rhode Island	32.3
6	New Jersey	31.7
7	New Mexico	31.4
8	Alaska	30.8
9	Vermont	30.7
10	Delaware	30.1
11	Connecticut	29.9
12	Virginia	29.7
13	Colorado	29.5
14	Michigan	29.3
15	California	28.8
15	Minnesota	28.8
15	Pennsylvania	28.8
18	Washington	28.5
19	Oregon	28.4
20	Ohio	28.2
21	Hawaii	27.7
22	Missouri	27.5
22	North Carolina	27.5
24	Maine	27.4
25	Georgia	27.3
25	Texas	27.3
27	New Hampshire	26.9
27	Wisconsin	26.9
29	Arizona	25.8
30	Indiana	25.5
30	Kansas	25.5
32	Kentucky	25.2
33	Louisiana	24.7
34	Nebraska	24.6
35	Tennessee	23.7
36	Iowa	23.3
36	South Carolina	23.3
38	Nevada	23.1
39	Oklahoma	22.8
40	Alabama	22.7
41	West Virginia	22.6
42	Florida	22.2
43	Arkansas	22.0
44	North Dakota	21.9
44	South Dakota	21.9
46	Montana	21.6
47	Utah	20.7
48	Mississippi	20.1
49	Wyoming	20.0
50	Idaho	18.8
	District of Columbia	37.3

Source: CQ Press using data from American Medical Association (Chicago, Illinois)
"Physician Characteristics and Distribution in the U.S." (2009 Edition)
*As of December 31, 2007. National percent does not include physicians in the U.S. territories and possessions, at APO's and FPO's, or whose addresses are unknown.

Percent of Physicians Under 35 Years Old in 2007

National Percent = 15.1% of Physicians*

ALPHA ORDER

RANK	STATE	PERCENT
16	Alabama	15.3
47	Alaska	7.1
37	Arizona	11.4
25	Arkansas	14.1
32	California	12.8
35	Colorado	12.0
13	Connecticut	16.1
17	Delaware	15.1
44	Florida	9.3
30	Georgia	13.3
37	Hawaii	11.4
48	Idaho	6.2
2	Illinois	19.4
29	Indiana	13.9
20	Iowa	14.9
25	Kansas	14.1
18	Kentucky	15.0
10	Louisiana	16.7
46	Maine	8.5
21	Maryland	14.8
4	Massachusetts	19.2
6	Michigan	18.9
12	Minnesota	16.2
34	Mississippi	12.1
2	Missouri	19.4
50	Montana	4.2
9	Nebraska	18.1
45	Nevada	8.9
41	New Hampshire	10.6
32	New Jersey	12.8
35	New Mexico	12.0
4	New York	19.2
15	North Carolina	15.4
40	North Dakota	10.9
7	Ohio	18.4
31	Oklahoma	12.9
41	Oregon	10.6
7	Pennsylvania	18.4
1	Rhode Island	20.1
14	South Carolina	15.5
43	South Dakota	10.3
22	Tennessee	14.7
11	Texas	16.3
22	Utah	14.7
27	Vermont	14.0
24	Virginia	14.3
39	Washington	11.1
18	West Virginia	15.0
27	Wisconsin	14.0
49	Wyoming	6.0

RANK ORDER

RANK	STATE	PERCENT
1	Rhode Island	20.1
2	Illinois	19.4
2	Missouri	19.4
4	Massachusetts	19.2
4	New York	19.2
6	Michigan	18.9
7	Ohio	18.4
7	Pennsylvania	18.4
9	Nebraska	18.1
10	Louisiana	16.7
11	Texas	16.3
12	Minnesota	16.2
13	Connecticut	16.1
14	South Carolina	15.5
15	North Carolina	15.4
16	Alabama	15.3
17	Delaware	15.1
18	Kentucky	15.0
18	West Virginia	15.0
20	Iowa	14.9
21	Maryland	14.8
22	Tennessee	14.7
22	Utah	14.7
24	Virginia	14.3
25	Arkansas	14.1
25	Kansas	14.1
27	Vermont	14.0
27	Wisconsin	14.0
29	Indiana	13.9
30	Georgia	13.3
31	Oklahoma	12.9
32	California	12.8
32	New Jersey	12.8
34	Mississippi	12.1
35	Colorado	12.0
35	New Mexico	12.0
37	Arizona	11.4
37	Hawaii	11.4
39	Washington	11.1
40	North Dakota	10.9
41	New Hampshire	10.6
41	Oregon	10.6
43	South Dakota	10.3
44	Florida	9.3
45	Nevada	8.9
46	Maine	8.5
47	Alaska	7.1
48	Idaho	6.2
49	Wyoming	6.0
50	Montana	4.2

District of Columbia 25.3

Source: CQ Press using data from American Medical Association (Chicago, Illinois)
"Physician Characteristics and Distribution in the U.S." (2009 Edition)
*As of December 31, 2007. National percent does not include physicians in the U.S. territories and possessions, at APO's and FPO's, or whose addresses are unknown.

Percent of Physicians 65 Years Old and Older in 2007

National Percent = 19.9% of Physicians*

ALPHA ORDER				RANK ORDER		
RANK	STATE	PERCENT		RANK	STATE	PERCENT
47	Alabama	16.7		1	Florida	26.9
50	Alaska	15.4		2	Montana	24.2
8	Arizona	21.9		3	California	23.4
30	Arkansas	18.5		4	Maine	23.3
3	California	23.4		5	Wyoming	23.2
27	Colorado	19.2		6	Hawaii	22.0
20	Connecticut	20.2		6	Idaho	22.0
17	Delaware	20.4		8	Arizona	21.9
1	Florida	26.9		8	Vermont	21.9
41	Georgia	17.1		10	Nevada	21.2
6	Hawaii	22.0		11	New Hampshire	21.1
6	Idaho	22.0		12	Oregon	21.0
35	Illinois	17.5		12	West Virginia	21.0
39	Indiana	17.2		14	Kansas	20.7
31	Iowa	18.3		15	Washington	20.6
14	Kansas	20.7		16	Oklahoma	20.5
41	Kentucky	17.1		17	Delaware	20.4
32	Louisiana	18.1		17	New Mexico	20.4
4	Maine	23.3		17	New York	20.4
22	Maryland	20.1		20	Connecticut	20.2
37	Massachusetts	17.4		20	New Jersey	20.2
28	Michigan	18.9		22	Maryland	20.1
48	Minnesota	16.5		23	Mississippi	19.8
23	Mississippi	19.8		24	Virginia	19.7
48	Missouri	16.5		25	Rhode Island	19.4
2	Montana	24.2		26	Pennsylvania	19.3
39	Nebraska	17.2		27	Colorado	19.2
10	Nevada	21.2		28	Michigan	18.9
11	New Hampshire	21.1		29	South Carolina	18.7
20	New Jersey	20.2		30	Arkansas	18.5
17	New Mexico	20.4		31	Iowa	18.3
17	New York	20.4		32	Louisiana	18.1
41	North Carolina	17.1		32	Ohio	18.1
35	North Dakota	17.5		34	South Dakota	17.6
32	Ohio	18.1		35	Illinois	17.5
16	Oklahoma	20.5		35	North Dakota	17.5
12	Oregon	21.0		37	Massachusetts	17.4
26	Pennsylvania	19.3		38	Wisconsin	17.3
25	Rhode Island	19.4		39	Indiana	17.2
29	South Carolina	18.7		39	Nebraska	17.2
34	South Dakota	17.6		41	Georgia	17.1
46	Tennessee	16.9		41	Kentucky	17.1
45	Texas	17.0		41	North Carolina	17.1
41	Utah	17.1		41	Utah	17.1
8	Vermont	21.9		45	Texas	17.0
24	Virginia	19.7		46	Tennessee	16.9
15	Washington	20.6		47	Alabama	16.7
12	West Virginia	21.0		48	Minnesota	16.5
38	Wisconsin	17.3		48	Missouri	16.5
5	Wyoming	23.2		50	Alaska	15.4
				District of Columbia		20.4

Source: CQ Press using data from American Medical Association (Chicago, Illinois)
   "Physician Characteristics and Distribution in the U.S." (2009 Edition)
*As of December 31, 2007. National percent does not include physicians in the U.S. territories and possessions, at APO's and FPO's, or whose addresses are unknown.

Physicians in Patient Care in 2007

National Total = 721,781 Physicians*

ALPHA ORDER

RANK	STATE	PHYSICIANS	% of USA
26	Alabama	9,208	1.3%
49	Alaska	1,447	0.2%
21	Arizona	12,008	1.7%
31	Arkansas	5,311	0.7%
1	California	86,182	11.9%
22	Colorado	11,331	1.6%
23	Connecticut	11,323	1.6%
46	Delaware	1,944	0.3%
4	Florida	41,042	5.7%
14	Georgia	18,608	2.6%
39	Hawaii	3,665	0.5%
43	Idaho	2,399	0.3%
6	Illinois	31,569	4.4%
20	Indiana	12,621	1.7%
32	Iowa	4,988	0.7%
30	Kansas	5,655	0.8%
28	Kentucky	8,941	1.2%
24	Louisiana	10,410	1.4%
41	Maine	3,319	0.5%
12	Maryland	19,327	2.7%
8	Massachusetts	24,903	3.5%
10	Michigan	22,166	3.1%
17	Minnesota	13,541	1.9%
34	Mississippi	4,796	0.7%
19	Missouri	12,814	1.8%
45	Montana	2,010	0.3%
37	Nebraska	3,906	0.5%
35	Nevada	4,442	0.6%
42	New Hampshire	3,273	0.5%
9	New Jersey	24,209	3.4%
36	New Mexico	4,212	0.6%
2	New York	65,637	9.1%
11	North Carolina	20,473	2.8%
48	North Dakota	1,452	0.2%
7	Ohio	26,970	3.7%
29	Oklahoma	5,734	0.8%
27	Oregon	9,183	1.3%
5	Pennsylvania	32,963	4.6%
40	Rhode Island	3,482	0.5%
25	South Carolina	9,349	1.3%
47	South Dakota	1,633	0.2%
16	Tennessee	14,695	2.0%
3	Texas	45,597	6.3%
33	Utah	4,963	0.7%
44	Vermont	2,022	0.3%
13	Virginia	18,874	2.6%
15	Washington	15,524	2.2%
38	West Virginia	3,773	0.5%
18	Wisconsin	13,251	1.8%
50	Wyoming	912	0.1%

RANK ORDER

RANK	STATE	PHYSICIANS	% of USA
1	California	86,182	11.9%
2	New York	65,637	9.1%
3	Texas	45,597	6.3%
4	Florida	41,042	5.7%
5	Pennsylvania	32,963	4.6%
6	Illinois	31,569	4.4%
7	Ohio	26,970	3.7%
8	Massachusetts	24,903	3.5%
9	New Jersey	24,209	3.4%
10	Michigan	22,166	3.1%
11	North Carolina	20,473	2.8%
12	Maryland	19,327	2.7%
13	Virginia	18,874	2.6%
14	Georgia	18,608	2.6%
15	Washington	15,524	2.2%
16	Tennessee	14,695	2.0%
17	Minnesota	13,541	1.9%
18	Wisconsin	13,251	1.8%
19	Missouri	12,814	1.8%
20	Indiana	12,621	1.7%
21	Arizona	12,008	1.7%
22	Colorado	11,331	1.6%
23	Connecticut	11,323	1.6%
24	Louisiana	10,410	1.4%
25	South Carolina	9,349	1.3%
26	Alabama	9,208	1.3%
27	Oregon	9,183	1.3%
28	Kentucky	8,941	1.2%
29	Oklahoma	5,734	0.8%
30	Kansas	5,655	0.8%
31	Arkansas	5,311	0.7%
32	Iowa	4,988	0.7%
33	Utah	4,963	0.7%
34	Mississippi	4,796	0.7%
35	Nevada	4,442	0.6%
36	New Mexico	4,212	0.6%
37	Nebraska	3,906	0.5%
38	West Virginia	3,773	0.5%
39	Hawaii	3,665	0.5%
40	Rhode Island	3,482	0.5%
41	Maine	3,319	0.5%
42	New Hampshire	3,273	0.5%
43	Idaho	2,399	0.3%
44	Vermont	2,022	0.3%
45	Montana	2,010	0.3%
46	Delaware	1,944	0.3%
47	South Dakota	1,633	0.2%
48	North Dakota	1,452	0.2%
49	Alaska	1,447	0.2%
50	Wyoming	912	0.1%
	District of Columbia	3,724	0.5%

Source: American Medical Association (Chicago, Illinois)
     "Physician Characteristics and Distribution in the U.S." (2009 Edition)
*As of December 31, 2007. Total does not include 10,453 physicians in U.S. territories and possessions.

Rate of Physicians in Patient Care in 2007

National Rate = 240 Physicians per 100,000 Population*

ALPHA ORDER

RANK	STATE	RATE
38	Alabama	199
31	Alaska	212
42	Arizona	189
43	Arkansas	188
19	California	237
22	Colorado	234
6	Connecticut	324
24	Delaware	226
24	Florida	226
40	Georgia	195
7	Hawaii	287
49	Idaho	160
13	Illinois	246
38	Indiana	199
47	Iowa	167
37	Kansas	204
33	Kentucky	211
18	Louisiana	238
11	Maine	252
2	Maryland	344
1	Massachusetts	385
27	Michigan	221
10	Minnesota	261
48	Mississippi	164
29	Missouri	218
34	Montana	210
27	Nebraska	221
45	Nevada	174
12	New Hampshire	249
8	New Jersey	280
30	New Mexico	214
3	New York	338
24	North Carolina	226
23	North Dakota	228
21	Ohio	235
50	Oklahoma	159
13	Oregon	246
9	Pennsylvania	265
4	Rhode Island	331
31	South Carolina	212
36	South Dakota	205
17	Tennessee	239
41	Texas	191
44	Utah	186
5	Vermont	326
15	Virginia	245
16	Washington	241
35	West Virginia	208
19	Wisconsin	237
45	Wyoming	174

RANK ORDER

RANK	STATE	RATE
1	Massachusetts	385
2	Maryland	344
3	New York	338
4	Rhode Island	331
5	Vermont	326
6	Connecticut	324
7	Hawaii	287
8	New Jersey	280
9	Pennsylvania	265
10	Minnesota	261
11	Maine	252
12	New Hampshire	249
13	Illinois	246
13	Oregon	246
15	Virginia	245
16	Washington	241
17	Tennessee	239
18	Louisiana	238
19	California	237
19	Wisconsin	237
21	Ohio	235
22	Colorado	234
23	North Dakota	228
24	Delaware	226
24	Florida	226
24	North Carolina	226
27	Michigan	221
27	Nebraska	221
29	Missouri	218
30	New Mexico	214
31	Alaska	212
31	South Carolina	212
33	Kentucky	211
34	Montana	210
35	West Virginia	208
36	South Dakota	205
37	Kansas	204
38	Alabama	199
38	Indiana	199
40	Georgia	195
41	Texas	191
42	Arizona	189
43	Arkansas	188
44	Utah	186
45	Nevada	174
45	Wyoming	174
47	Iowa	167
48	Mississippi	164
49	Idaho	160
50	Oklahoma	159

District of Columbia	633

Source: CQ Press using data from American Medical Association (Chicago, Illinois)
   "Physician Characteristics and Distribution in the U.S." (2009 Edition)
*As of December 31, 2006. National rate does not include physicians in the U.S. territories and possessions.

Physicians in Primary Care in 2007

National Total = 298,267 Physicians*

ALPHA ORDER

RANK	STATE	PHYSICIANS	% of USA
27	Alabama	3,912	1.3%
48	Alaska	699	0.2%
21	Arizona	4,838	1.6%
31	Arkansas	2,325	0.8%
1	California	36,419	12.2%
22	Colorado	4,667	1.6%
23	Connecticut	4,500	1.5%
47	Delaware	738	0.2%
4	Florida	15,934	5.3%
12	Georgia	8,071	2.7%
38	Hawaii	1,630	0.5%
43	Idaho	1,031	0.3%
5	Illinois	13,789	4.6%
19	Indiana	5,313	1.8%
32	Iowa	2,134	0.7%
30	Kansas	2,377	0.8%
28	Kentucky	3,652	1.2%
24	Louisiana	4,182	1.4%
40	Maine	1,472	0.5%
14	Maryland	7,788	2.6%
10	Massachusetts	9,352	3.1%
9	Michigan	9,431	3.2%
17	Minnesota	5,919	2.0%
33	Mississippi	2,012	0.7%
20	Missouri	4,946	1.7%
45	Montana	854	0.3%
37	Nebraska	1,760	0.6%
36	Nevada	1,877	0.6%
42	New Hampshire	1,406	0.5%
8	New Jersey	10,078	3.4%
35	New Mexico	1,913	0.6%
2	New York	26,575	8.9%
11	North Carolina	8,488	2.8%
49	North Dakota	682	0.2%
7	Ohio	11,044	3.7%
29	Oklahoma	2,457	0.8%
25	Oregon	4,018	1.3%
6	Pennsylvania	12,564	4.2%
41	Rhode Island	1,418	0.5%
26	South Carolina	3,953	1.3%
46	South Dakota	739	0.2%
16	Tennessee	6,093	2.0%
3	Texas	18,425	6.2%
34	Utah	1,958	0.7%
44	Vermont	907	0.3%
12	Virginia	8,071	2.7%
15	Washington	6,781	2.3%
39	West Virginia	1,588	0.5%
18	Wisconsin	5,661	1.9%
50	Wyoming	439	0.1%

RANK ORDER

RANK	STATE	PHYSICIANS	% of USA
1	California	36,419	12.2%
2	New York	26,575	8.9%
3	Texas	18,425	6.2%
4	Florida	15,934	5.3%
5	Illinois	13,789	4.6%
6	Pennsylvania	12,564	4.2%
7	Ohio	11,044	3.7%
8	New Jersey	10,078	3.4%
9	Michigan	9,431	3.2%
10	Massachusetts	9,352	3.1%
11	North Carolina	8,488	2.8%
12	Georgia	8,071	2.7%
12	Virginia	8,071	2.7%
14	Maryland	7,788	2.6%
15	Washington	6,781	2.3%
16	Tennessee	6,093	2.0%
17	Minnesota	5,919	2.0%
18	Wisconsin	5,661	1.9%
19	Indiana	5,313	1.8%
20	Missouri	4,946	1.7%
21	Arizona	4,838	1.6%
22	Colorado	4,667	1.6%
23	Connecticut	4,500	1.5%
24	Louisiana	4,182	1.4%
25	Oregon	4,018	1.3%
26	South Carolina	3,953	1.3%
27	Alabama	3,912	1.3%
28	Kentucky	3,652	1.2%
29	Oklahoma	2,457	0.8%
30	Kansas	2,377	0.8%
31	Arkansas	2,325	0.8%
32	Iowa	2,134	0.7%
33	Mississippi	2,012	0.7%
34	Utah	1,958	0.7%
35	New Mexico	1,913	0.6%
36	Nevada	1,877	0.6%
37	Nebraska	1,760	0.6%
38	Hawaii	1,630	0.5%
39	West Virginia	1,588	0.5%
40	Maine	1,472	0.5%
41	Rhode Island	1,418	0.5%
42	New Hampshire	1,406	0.5%
43	Idaho	1,031	0.3%
44	Vermont	907	0.3%
45	Montana	854	0.3%
46	South Dakota	739	0.2%
47	Delaware	738	0.2%
48	Alaska	699	0.2%
49	North Dakota	682	0.2%
50	Wyoming	439	0.1%
	District of Columbia	1,387	0.5%

Source: American Medical Association (Chicago, Illinois)
    "Physician Characteristics and Distribution in the U.S." (2009 Edition)
*As of December 31, 2007. National total does not include 5,482 physicians in U.S. territories and possessions. Primary Care Specialties include Family Practice, General Practice, Internal Medicine, Obstetrics/Gynecology, and Pediatrics excluding subspecialties within each category.

Rate of Physicians in Primary Care in 2007

National Rate = 99 Physicians per 100,000 Population*

ALPHA ORDER			RANK ORDER		
RANK	STATE	RATE	RANK	STATE	RATE
37	Alabama	85	1	Vermont	146
17	Alaska	103	2	Massachusetts	145
44	Arizona	76	3	Maryland	139
42	Arkansas	82	4	New York	137
20	California	100	5	Rhode Island	135
24	Colorado	96	6	Connecticut	129
6	Connecticut	129	7	Hawaii	128
34	Delaware	86	8	New Jersey	116
32	Florida	88	9	Minnesota	114
37	Georgia	85	10	Maine	112
7	Hawaii	128	11	Illinois	108
48	Idaho	69	11	Oregon	108
11	Illinois	108	13	New Hampshire	107
39	Indiana	84	13	North Dakota	107
47	Iowa	72	15	Virginia	105
34	Kansas	86	15	Washington	105
34	Kentucky	86	17	Alaska	103
24	Louisiana	96	18	Pennsylvania	101
10	Maine	112	18	Wisconsin	101
3	Maryland	139	20	California	100
2	Massachusetts	145	21	Nebraska	99
27	Michigan	94	21	Tennessee	99
9	Minnesota	114	23	New Mexico	97
48	Mississippi	69	24	Colorado	96
39	Missouri	84	24	Louisiana	96
31	Montana	89	24	Ohio	96
21	Nebraska	99	27	Michigan	94
45	Nevada	73	27	North Carolina	94
13	New Hampshire	107	29	South Dakota	93
8	New Jersey	116	30	South Carolina	90
23	New Mexico	97	31	Montana	89
4	New York	137	32	Florida	88
27	North Carolina	94	32	West Virginia	88
13	North Dakota	107	34	Delaware	86
24	Ohio	96	34	Kansas	86
50	Oklahoma	68	34	Kentucky	86
11	Oregon	108	37	Alabama	85
18	Pennsylvania	101	37	Georgia	85
5	Rhode Island	135	39	Indiana	84
30	South Carolina	90	39	Missouri	84
29	South Dakota	93	39	Wyoming	84
21	Tennessee	99	42	Arkansas	82
43	Texas	77	43	Texas	77
45	Utah	73	44	Arizona	76
1	Vermont	146	45	Nevada	73
15	Virginia	105	45	Utah	73
15	Washington	105	47	Iowa	72
32	West Virginia	88	48	Idaho	69
18	Wisconsin	101	48	Mississippi	69
39	Wyoming	84	50	Oklahoma	68

District of Columbia   236

Source: CQ Press using data from American Medical Association (Chicago, Illinois)
"Physician Characteristics and Distribution in the U.S." (2009 Edition)
*As of December 31, 2007. National rate does not include physicians in U.S. territories and possessions. Primary Care Specialties include Family Practice, General Practice, Internal Medicine, Obstetrics/Gynecology, and Pediatrics excluding subspecialties within each category.

Percent of Physicians in Primary Care in 2007

National Percent = 32.2% of Physicians*

ALPHA ORDER

RANK	STATE	PERCENT
8	Alabama	34.8
1	Alaska	40.7
44	Arizona	30.8
6	Arkansas	35.5
37	California	32.3
38	Colorado	32.2
45	Connecticut	30.5
46	Delaware	30.0
48	Florida	29.0
9	Georgia	34.7
7	Hawaii	34.9
13	Idaho	34.4
11	Illinois	34.5
14	Indiana	34.3
34	Iowa	32.6
29	Kansas	33.1
29	Kentucky	33.1
33	Louisiana	32.8
17	Maine	34.2
47	Maryland	29.5
50	Massachusetts	28.1
24	Michigan	33.3
11	Minnesota	34.5
19	Mississippi	33.8
43	Missouri	31.0
29	Montana	33.1
5	Nebraska	35.6
20	Nevada	33.6
27	New Hampshire	33.2
32	New Jersey	32.9
10	New Mexico	34.6
41	New York	31.2
34	North Carolina	32.6
2	North Dakota	38.6
39	Ohio	32.0
18	Oklahoma	33.9
24	Oregon	33.3
48	Pennsylvania	29.0
39	Rhode Island	32.0
14	South Carolina	34.3
4	South Dakota	36.7
20	Tennessee	33.6
34	Texas	32.6
41	Utah	31.2
27	Vermont	33.2
22	Virginia	33.4
24	Washington	33.3
22	West Virginia	33.4
14	Wisconsin	34.3
3	Wyoming	37.7

RANK ORDER

RANK	STATE	PERCENT
1	Alaska	40.7
2	North Dakota	38.6
3	Wyoming	37.7
4	South Dakota	36.7
5	Nebraska	35.6
6	Arkansas	35.5
7	Hawaii	34.9
8	Alabama	34.8
9	Georgia	34.7
10	New Mexico	34.6
11	Illinois	34.5
11	Minnesota	34.5
13	Idaho	34.4
14	Indiana	34.3
14	South Carolina	34.3
14	Wisconsin	34.3
17	Maine	34.2
18	Oklahoma	33.9
19	Mississippi	33.8
20	Nevada	33.6
20	Tennessee	33.6
22	Virginia	33.4
22	West Virginia	33.4
24	Michigan	33.3
24	Oregon	33.3
24	Washington	33.3
27	New Hampshire	33.2
27	Vermont	33.2
29	Kansas	33.1
29	Kentucky	33.1
29	Montana	33.1
32	New Jersey	32.9
33	Louisiana	32.8
34	Iowa	32.6
34	North Carolina	32.6
34	Texas	32.6
37	California	32.3
38	Colorado	32.2
39	Ohio	32.0
39	Rhode Island	32.0
41	New York	31.2
41	Utah	31.2
43	Missouri	31.0
44	Arizona	30.8
45	Connecticut	30.5
46	Delaware	30.0
47	Maryland	29.5
48	Florida	29.0
48	Pennsylvania	29.0
50	Massachusetts	28.1

District of Columbia   26.9

Source: CQ Press using data from American Medical Association (Chicago, Illinois)
   "Physician Characteristics and Distribution in the U.S." (2009 Edition)
*As of December 31, 2007. National percent does not include physicians in U.S. territories and possessions. Primary Care Specialties include Family Practice, General Practice, Internal Medicine, Obstetrics/Gynecology, and Pediatrics excluding subspecialties within each category.

Percent of Population Lacking Access to Primary Care in 2008

National Percent = 11.3% of Population*

ALPHA ORDER				RANK ORDER		
RANK	STATE	PERCENT		RANK	STATE	PERCENT
8	Alabama	19.0		1	Louisiana	34.4
20	Alaska	12.1		2	New Mexico	32.0
12	Arizona	16.1		3	Mississippi	31.9
28	Arkansas	9.8		4	South Dakota	26.8
32	California	9.0		5	Montana	23.1
30	Colorado	9.3		6	North Dakota	22.0
33	Connecticut	8.9		7	Wyoming	20.3
16	Delaware	13.8		8	Alabama	19.0
14	Florida	15.3		9	Missouri	18.6
15	Georgia	15.2		10	Idaho	17.4
49	Hawaii	2.6		11	Illinois	16.9
10	Idaho	17.4		12	Arizona	16.1
11	Illinois	16.9		13	Oklahoma	15.4
36	Indiana	7.8		14	Florida	15.3
35	Iowa	8.2		15	Georgia	15.2
19	Kansas	12.3		16	Delaware	13.8
22	Kentucky	11.3		17	South Carolina	13.7
1	Louisiana	34.4		18	Nevada	13.3
41	Maine	5.9		19	Kansas	12.3
46	Maryland	4.7		20	Alaska	12.1
37	Massachusetts	7.1		21	Texas	12.0
26	Michigan	10.7		22	Kentucky	11.3
44	Minnesota	5.3		23	New York	11.0
3	Mississippi	31.9		24	Utah	10.9
9	Missouri	18.6		25	Wisconsin	10.8
5	Montana	23.1		26	Michigan	10.7
46	Nebraska	4.7		27	Tennessee	10.6
18	Nevada	13.3		28	Arkansas	9.8
45	New Hampshire	5.0		29	Washington	9.5
50	New Jersey	1.7		30	Colorado	9.3
2	New Mexico	32.0		30	West Virginia	9.3
23	New York	11.0		32	California	9.0
43	North Carolina	5.4		33	Connecticut	8.9
6	North Dakota	22.0		34	Virginia	8.6
39	Ohio	6.8		35	Iowa	8.2
13	Oklahoma	15.4		36	Indiana	7.8
37	Oregon	7.1		37	Massachusetts	7.1
41	Pennsylvania	5.9		37	Oregon	7.1
40	Rhode Island	6.3		39	Ohio	6.8
17	South Carolina	13.7		40	Rhode Island	6.3
4	South Dakota	26.8		41	Maine	5.9
27	Tennessee	10.6		41	Pennsylvania	5.9
21	Texas	12.0		43	North Carolina	5.4
24	Utah	10.9		44	Minnesota	5.3
48	Vermont	2.7		45	New Hampshire	5.0
34	Virginia	8.6		46	Maryland	4.7
29	Washington	9.5		46	Nebraska	4.7
30	West Virginia	9.3		48	Vermont	2.7
25	Wisconsin	10.8		49	Hawaii	2.6
7	Wyoming	20.3		50	New Jersey	1.7

District of Columbia   25.5

Source: CQ Press using data from U.S. Dept. of Health and Human Services, Div. of Shortage Designation
  "Selected Statistics on Health Professional Shortage Areas" (as of September 30, 2008)
*Percent of population considered under-served by primary medical practitioners (Family & General Practice doctors, Internists, Ob/Gyns, and Pediatricians). An under-served population does not have primary medical care within reasonable economic and geographic bounds.

Physicians in General/Family Practice in 2007

National Total = 91,983 Physicians*

ALPHA ORDER

RANK	STATE	PHYSICIANS	% of USA
25	Alabama	1,349	1.5%
45	Alaska	392	0.4%
20	Arizona	1,547	1.7%
28	Arkansas	1,245	1.4%
1	California	10,980	11.9%
17	Colorado	1,856	2.0%
38	Connecticut	602	0.7%
49	Delaware	252	0.3%
3	Florida	4,992	5.4%
15	Georgia	2,362	2.6%
43	Hawaii	423	0.5%
39	Idaho	587	0.6%
4	Illinois	3,929	4.3%
14	Indiana	2,427	2.6%
29	Iowa	1,149	1.2%
30	Kansas	1,135	1.2%
23	Kentucky	1,368	1.5%
26	Louisiana	1,336	1.5%
37	Maine	625	0.7%
24	Maryland	1,367	1.5%
26	Massachusetts	1,336	1.5%
10	Michigan	2,849	3.1%
11	Minnesota	2,842	3.1%
33	Mississippi	803	0.9%
22	Missouri	1,388	1.5%
42	Montana	446	0.5%
32	Nebraska	888	1.0%
40	Nevada	568	0.6%
41	New Hampshire	503	0.5%
18	New Jersey	1,628	1.8%
34	New Mexico	790	0.9%
5	New York	3,886	4.2%
9	North Carolina	2,941	3.2%
46	North Dakota	382	0.4%
7	Ohio	3,498	3.8%
31	Oklahoma	1,081	1.2%
21	Oregon	1,437	1.6%
6	Pennsylvania	3,793	4.1%
50	Rhode Island	226	0.2%
19	South Carolina	1,619	1.8%
44	South Dakota	395	0.4%
16	Tennessee	1,960	2.1%
2	Texas	6,439	7.0%
35	Utah	750	0.8%
47	Vermont	324	0.4%
12	Virginia	2,728	3.0%
8	Washington	3,010	3.3%
36	West Virginia	652	0.7%
13	Wisconsin	2,449	2.7%
48	Wyoming	253	0.3%

RANK ORDER

RANK	STATE	PHYSICIANS	% of USA
1	California	10,980	11.9%
2	Texas	6,439	7.0%
3	Florida	4,992	5.4%
4	Illinois	3,929	4.3%
5	New York	3,886	4.2%
6	Pennsylvania	3,793	4.1%
7	Ohio	3,498	3.8%
8	Washington	3,010	3.3%
9	North Carolina	2,941	3.2%
10	Michigan	2,849	3.1%
11	Minnesota	2,842	3.1%
12	Virginia	2,728	3.0%
13	Wisconsin	2,449	2.7%
14	Indiana	2,427	2.6%
15	Georgia	2,362	2.6%
16	Tennessee	1,960	2.1%
17	Colorado	1,856	2.0%
18	New Jersey	1,628	1.8%
19	South Carolina	1,619	1.8%
20	Arizona	1,547	1.7%
21	Oregon	1,437	1.6%
22	Missouri	1,388	1.5%
23	Kentucky	1,368	1.5%
24	Maryland	1,367	1.5%
25	Alabama	1,349	1.5%
26	Louisiana	1,336	1.5%
26	Massachusetts	1,336	1.5%
28	Arkansas	1,245	1.4%
29	Iowa	1,149	1.2%
30	Kansas	1,135	1.2%
31	Oklahoma	1,081	1.2%
32	Nebraska	888	1.0%
33	Mississippi	803	0.9%
34	New Mexico	790	0.9%
35	Utah	750	0.8%
36	West Virginia	652	0.7%
37	Maine	625	0.7%
38	Connecticut	602	0.7%
39	Idaho	587	0.6%
40	Nevada	568	0.6%
41	New Hampshire	503	0.5%
42	Montana	446	0.5%
43	Hawaii	423	0.5%
44	South Dakota	395	0.4%
45	Alaska	392	0.4%
46	North Dakota	382	0.4%
47	Vermont	324	0.4%
48	Wyoming	253	0.3%
49	Delaware	252	0.3%
50	Rhode Island	226	0.2%
	District of Columbia	196	0.2%

Source: American Medical Association (Chicago, Illinois)
   "Physician Characteristics and Distribution in the U.S." (2009 Edition)
*As of December 31, 2007. Total does not include 2,479 physicians in U.S. territories and possessions.

Rate of Physicians in General/Family Practice in 2007

National Rate = 31 Physicians per 100,000 Population*

ALPHA ORDER

RANK	STATE	RATE
34	Alabama	29
2	Alaska	58
42	Arizona	24
11	Arkansas	44
31	California	30
17	Colorado	38
50	Connecticut	17
34	Delaware	29
38	Florida	27
41	Georgia	25
24	Hawaii	33
15	Idaho	39
28	Illinois	31
17	Indiana	38
15	Iowa	39
13	Kansas	41
26	Kentucky	32
28	Louisiana	31
7	Maine	48
42	Maryland	24
46	Massachusetts	21
36	Michigan	28
3	Minnesota	55
38	Mississippi	27
42	Missouri	24
9	Montana	47
5	Nebraska	50
45	Nevada	22
17	New Hampshire	38
49	New Jersey	19
14	New Mexico	40
48	New York	20
24	North Carolina	33
1	North Dakota	60
31	Ohio	30
31	Oklahoma	30
17	Oregon	38
28	Pennsylvania	31
46	Rhode Island	21
21	South Carolina	37
5	South Dakota	50
26	Tennessee	32
38	Texas	27
36	Utah	28
4	Vermont	52
23	Virginia	35
9	Washington	47
22	West Virginia	36
11	Wisconsin	44
7	Wyoming	48

RANK ORDER

RANK	STATE	RATE
1	North Dakota	60
2	Alaska	58
3	Minnesota	55
4	Vermont	52
5	Nebraska	50
5	South Dakota	50
7	Maine	48
7	Wyoming	48
9	Montana	47
9	Washington	47
11	Arkansas	44
11	Wisconsin	44
13	Kansas	41
14	New Mexico	40
15	Idaho	39
15	Iowa	39
17	Colorado	38
17	Indiana	38
17	New Hampshire	38
17	Oregon	38
21	South Carolina	37
22	West Virginia	36
23	Virginia	35
24	Hawaii	33
24	North Carolina	33
26	Kentucky	32
26	Tennessee	32
28	Illinois	31
28	Louisiana	31
28	Pennsylvania	31
31	California	30
31	Ohio	30
31	Oklahoma	30
34	Alabama	29
34	Delaware	29
36	Michigan	28
36	Utah	28
38	Florida	27
38	Mississippi	27
38	Texas	27
41	Georgia	25
42	Arizona	24
42	Maryland	24
42	Missouri	24
45	Nevada	22
46	Massachusetts	21
46	Rhode Island	21
48	New York	20
49	New Jersey	19
50	Connecticut	17

	District of Columbia	33

Source: CQ Press using data from American Medical Association (Chicago, Illinois)
"Physician Characteristics and Distribution in the U.S." (2009 Edition)
*As of December 31, 2007. National rate does not include physicians in the U.S. territories and possessions.

Average Annual Wages of Family and General Practitioners in 2007

National Average = $153,640*

ALPHA ORDER

RANK	STATE	WAGES
37	Alabama	$145,680
48	Alaska	135,790
44	Arizona	140,220
3	Arkansas	176,760
46	California	139,130
43	Colorado	141,900
24	Connecticut	155,300
20	Delaware	157,820
30	Florida	152,080
7	Georgia	173,160
36	Hawaii	146,190
29	Idaho	152,780
45	Illinois	139,770
32	Indiana	151,480
11	Iowa	166,850
2	Kansas	180,440
23	Kentucky	155,790
12	Louisiana	164,450
39	Maine	144,270
21	Maryland	157,680
5	Massachusetts	175,650
25	Michigan	154,850
15	Minnesota	161,560
10	Mississippi	170,790
41	Missouri	143,870
49	Montana	130,580
18	Nebraska	160,640
22	Nevada	156,350
38	New Hampshire	145,210
31	New Jersey	151,950
28	New Mexico	153,120
27	New York	153,230
9	North Carolina	171,340
34	North Dakota	149,460
17	Ohio	160,840
14	Oklahoma	162,270
40	Oregon	144,090
26	Pennsylvania	153,980
4	Rhode Island	175,820
19	South Carolina	160,120
35	South Dakota	147,550
42	Tennessee	142,070
47	Texas	137,810
16	Utah	161,020
50	Vermont	129,570
13	Virginia	162,790
33	Washington	150,940
8	West Virginia	171,830
1	Wisconsin	183,790
6	Wyoming	174,130

RANK ORDER

RANK	STATE	WAGES
1	Wisconsin	$183,790
2	Kansas	180,440
3	Arkansas	176,760
4	Rhode Island	175,820
5	Massachusetts	175,650
6	Wyoming	174,130
7	Georgia	173,160
8	West Virginia	171,830
9	North Carolina	171,340
10	Mississippi	170,790
11	Iowa	166,850
12	Louisiana	164,450
13	Virginia	162,790
14	Oklahoma	162,270
15	Minnesota	161,560
16	Utah	161,020
17	Ohio	160,840
18	Nebraska	160,640
19	South Carolina	160,120
20	Delaware	157,820
21	Maryland	157,680
22	Nevada	156,350
23	Kentucky	155,790
24	Connecticut	155,300
25	Michigan	154,850
26	Pennsylvania	153,980
27	New York	153,230
28	New Mexico	153,120
29	Idaho	152,780
30	Florida	152,080
31	New Jersey	151,950
32	Indiana	151,480
33	Washington	150,940
34	North Dakota	149,460
35	South Dakota	147,550
36	Hawaii	146,190
37	Alabama	145,680
38	New Hampshire	145,210
39	Maine	144,270
40	Oregon	144,090
41	Missouri	143,870
42	Tennessee	142,070
43	Colorado	141,900
44	Arizona	140,220
45	Illinois	139,770
46	California	139,130
47	Texas	137,810
48	Alaska	135,790
49	Montana	130,580
50	Vermont	129,570
	District of Columbia	84,960

Source: U.S. Department of Labor, Bureau of Labor Statistics
"Occupational Employment and Wages, 2007" (http://www.bls.gov/oes/)
*Does not include self-employed.

Percent of Physicians Who Are Specialists in 2007

National Percent = 72.6% of Physicians*

ALPHA ORDER

RANK	STATE	PERCENT
12	Alabama	73.5
44	Alaska	65.4
26	Arizona	70.5
42	Arkansas	65.6
23	California	71.5
28	Colorado	70.1
1	Connecticut	78.8
15	Delaware	72.9
33	Florida	68.9
9	Georgia	74.6
10	Hawaii	74.3
49	Idaho	62.9
13	Illinois	73.4
29	Indiana	69.8
47	Iowa	63.4
41	Kansas	66.6
18	Kentucky	72.2
8	Louisiana	74.7
37	Maine	67.4
6	Maryland	77.5
4	Massachusetts	77.8
17	Michigan	72.5
39	Minnesota	66.8
27	Mississippi	70.4
7	Missouri	76.1
48	Montana	63.1
43	Nebraska	65.5
22	Nevada	71.9
32	New Hampshire	69.4
1	New Jersey	78.8
38	New Mexico	67.0
5	New York	77.6
18	North Carolina	72.2
46	North Dakota	63.7
18	Ohio	72.2
35	Oklahoma	68.0
34	Oregon	68.6
16	Pennsylvania	72.8
3	Rhode Island	78.2
25	South Carolina	70.7
45	South Dakota	64.4
10	Tennessee	74.3
14	Texas	73.3
21	Utah	72.0
36	Vermont	67.9
24	Virginia	71.1
39	Washington	66.8
31	West Virginia	69.5
30	Wisconsin	69.7
50	Wyoming	59.5

RANK ORDER

RANK	STATE	PERCENT
1	Connecticut	78.8
1	New Jersey	78.8
3	Rhode Island	78.2
4	Massachusetts	77.8
5	New York	77.6
6	Maryland	77.5
7	Missouri	76.1
8	Louisiana	74.7
9	Georgia	74.6
10	Hawaii	74.3
10	Tennessee	74.3
12	Alabama	73.5
13	Illinois	73.4
14	Texas	73.3
15	Delaware	72.9
16	Pennsylvania	72.8
17	Michigan	72.5
18	Kentucky	72.2
18	North Carolina	72.2
18	Ohio	72.2
21	Utah	72.0
22	Nevada	71.9
23	California	71.5
24	Virginia	71.1
25	South Carolina	70.7
26	Arizona	70.5
27	Mississippi	70.4
28	Colorado	70.1
29	Indiana	69.8
30	Wisconsin	69.7
31	West Virginia	69.5
32	New Hampshire	69.4
33	Florida	68.9
34	Oregon	68.6
35	Oklahoma	68.0
36	Vermont	67.9
37	Maine	67.4
38	New Mexico	67.0
39	Minnesota	66.8
39	Washington	66.8
41	Kansas	66.6
42	Arkansas	65.6
43	Nebraska	65.5
44	Alaska	65.4
45	South Dakota	64.4
46	North Dakota	63.7
47	Iowa	63.4
48	Montana	63.1
49	Idaho	62.9
50	Wyoming	59.5

District of Columbia	78.5

Source: CQ Press using data from American Medical Association (Chicago, Illinois)
"Physician Characteristics and Distribution in the U.S." (2009 Edition)
*As of December 31, 2007. National percent does not include physicians in the U.S. territories and possessions. Includes physicians in medical, surgical, and other specialties.

Physicians in Medical Specialties in 2007

National Total = 291,570 Physicians*

ALPHA ORDER				RANK ORDER			
RANK	STATE	PHYSICIANS	% of USA	RANK	STATE	PHYSICIANS	% of USA
25	Alabama	3,524	1.2%	1	California	34,334	11.8%
49	Alaska	353	0.1%	2	New York	31,221	10.7%
21	Arizona	4,612	1.6%	3	Texas	17,142	5.9%
33	Arkansas	1,686	0.6%	4	Florida	16,548	5.7%
1	California	34,334	11.8%	5	Pennsylvania	13,574	4.7%
24	Colorado	3,986	1.4%	6	Illinois	13,353	4.6%
16	Connecticut	5,437	1.9%	7	Massachusetts	12,236	4.2%
43	Delaware	767	0.3%	8	New Jersey	11,725	4.0%
4	Florida	16,548	5.7%	9	Ohio	10,876	3.7%
13	Georgia	7,401	2.5%	10	Maryland	9,384	3.2%
38	Hawaii	1,459	0.5%	11	Michigan	8,986	3.1%
45	Idaho	616	0.2%	12	North Carolina	8,016	2.7%
6	Illinois	13,353	4.6%	13	Georgia	7,401	2.5%
22	Indiana	4,329	1.5%	14	Virginia	7,129	2.4%
36	Iowa	1,559	0.5%	15	Tennessee	5,914	2.0%
30	Kansas	1,810	0.6%	16	Connecticut	5,437	1.9%
27	Kentucky	3,248	1.1%	17	Washington	5,434	1.9%
23	Louisiana	3,996	1.4%	18	Missouri	5,383	1.8%
42	Maine	1,138	0.4%	19	Minnesota	4,895	1.7%
10	Maryland	9,384	3.2%	20	Wisconsin	4,637	1.6%
7	Massachusetts	12,236	4.2%	21	Arizona	4,612	1.6%
11	Michigan	8,986	3.1%	22	Indiana	4,329	1.5%
19	Minnesota	4,895	1.7%	23	Louisiana	3,996	1.4%
35	Mississippi	1,654	0.6%	24	Colorado	3,986	1.4%
18	Missouri	5,383	1.8%	25	Alabama	3,524	1.2%
46	Montana	553	0.2%	26	Oregon	3,314	1.1%
40	Nebraska	1,258	0.4%	27	Kentucky	3,248	1.1%
32	Nevada	1,711	0.6%	28	South Carolina	3,210	1.1%
41	New Hampshire	1,217	0.4%	29	Oklahoma	1,957	0.7%
8	New Jersey	11,725	4.0%	30	Kansas	1,810	0.6%
37	New Mexico	1,520	0.5%	31	Utah	1,715	0.6%
2	New York	31,221	10.7%	32	Nevada	1,711	0.6%
12	North Carolina	8,016	2.7%	33	Arkansas	1,686	0.6%
48	North Dakota	432	0.1%	34	Rhode Island	1,680	0.6%
9	Ohio	10,876	3.7%	35	Mississippi	1,654	0.6%
29	Oklahoma	1,957	0.7%	36	Iowa	1,559	0.5%
26	Oregon	3,314	1.1%	37	New Mexico	1,520	0.5%
5	Pennsylvania	13,574	4.7%	38	Hawaii	1,459	0.5%
34	Rhode Island	1,680	0.6%	39	West Virginia	1,347	0.5%
28	South Carolina	3,210	1.1%	40	Nebraska	1,258	0.4%
47	South Dakota	496	0.2%	41	New Hampshire	1,217	0.4%
15	Tennessee	5,914	2.0%	42	Maine	1,138	0.4%
3	Texas	17,142	5.9%	43	Delaware	767	0.3%
31	Utah	1,715	0.6%	44	Vermont	758	0.3%
44	Vermont	758	0.3%	45	Idaho	616	0.2%
14	Virginia	7,129	2.4%	46	Montana	553	0.2%
17	Washington	5,434	1.9%	47	South Dakota	496	0.2%
39	West Virginia	1,347	0.5%	48	North Dakota	432	0.1%
20	Wisconsin	4,637	1.6%	49	Alaska	353	0.1%
50	Wyoming	201	0.1%	50	Wyoming	201	0.1%
					District of Columbia	1,839	0.6%

Source: American Medical Association (Chicago, Illinois)
   "Physician Characteristics and Distribution in the U.S." (2009 Edition)
*As of December 31, 2007. Total does not include 3,541 physicians in U.S. territories and possessions. Medical Specialties are Allergy/Immunology, Cardiovascular Diseases, Dermatology, Gastroenterology, Internal Medicine, Pediatrics, Pediatric Cardiology, and Pulmonary Diseases.

Rate of Nonfederal Physicians in Medical Specialties in 2007

National Rate = 97 Physicians per 100,000 Population*

ALPHA ORDER

RANK	STATE	RATE
31	Alabama	76
47	Alaska	52
33	Arizona	73
43	Arkansas	60
13	California	94
27	Colorado	82
5	Connecticut	156
20	Delaware	89
18	Florida	91
28	Georgia	78
8	Hawaii	114
49	Idaho	41
10	Illinois	104
37	Indiana	68
47	Iowa	52
40	Kansas	65
29	Kentucky	77
18	Louisiana	91
24	Maine	87
2	Maryland	167
1	Massachusetts	189
20	Michigan	89
13	Minnesota	94
45	Mississippi	57
17	Missouri	92
44	Montana	58
36	Nebraska	71
39	Nevada	67
15	New Hampshire	93
6	New Jersey	136
29	New Mexico	77
3	New York	161
20	North Carolina	89
37	North Dakota	68
12	Ohio	95
46	Oklahoma	54
20	Oregon	89
9	Pennsylvania	109
4	Rhode Island	160
33	South Carolina	73
42	South Dakota	62
11	Tennessee	96
35	Texas	72
41	Utah	64
7	Vermont	122
15	Virginia	93
25	Washington	84
32	West Virginia	74
26	Wisconsin	83
50	Wyoming	38

RANK ORDER

RANK	STATE	RATE
1	Massachusetts	189
2	Maryland	167
3	New York	161
4	Rhode Island	160
5	Connecticut	156
6	New Jersey	136
7	Vermont	122
8	Hawaii	114
9	Pennsylvania	109
10	Illinois	104
11	Tennessee	96
12	Ohio	95
13	California	94
13	Minnesota	94
15	New Hampshire	93
15	Virginia	93
17	Missouri	92
18	Florida	91
18	Louisiana	91
20	Delaware	89
20	Michigan	89
20	North Carolina	89
20	Oregon	89
24	Maine	87
25	Washington	84
26	Wisconsin	83
27	Colorado	82
28	Georgia	78
29	Kentucky	77
29	New Mexico	77
31	Alabama	76
32	West Virginia	74
33	Arizona	73
33	South Carolina	73
35	Texas	72
36	Nebraska	71
37	Indiana	68
37	North Dakota	68
39	Nevada	67
40	Kansas	65
41	Utah	64
42	South Dakota	62
43	Arkansas	60
44	Montana	58
45	Mississippi	57
46	Oklahoma	54
47	Alaska	52
47	Iowa	52
49	Idaho	41
50	Wyoming	38

District of Columbia — 313

Source: CQ Press using data from American Medical Association (Chicago, Illinois)
"Physician Characteristics and Distribution in the U.S." (2009 Edition)
*As of December 31, 2007. National rate does not include physicians in U.S. territories and possessions. Medical Specialties are Allergy/Immunology, Cardiovascular Diseases, Dermatology, Gastroenterology, Internal Medicine, Pediatrics, Pediatric Cardiology, and Pulmonary Diseases.

Physicians in Internal Medicine in 2007

National Total = 156,272 Physicians*

ALPHA ORDER

RANK	STATE	PHYSICIANS	% of USA
26	Alabama	1,896	1.2%
49	Alaska	169	0.1%
21	Arizona	2,416	1.5%
36	Arkansas	765	0.5%
1	California	18,330	11.7%
23	Colorado	2,053	1.3%
15	Connecticut	3,164	2.0%
44	Delaware	361	0.2%
3	Florida	8,416	5.4%
13	Georgia	3,902	2.5%
35	Hawaii	811	0.5%
45	Idaho	317	0.2%
5	Illinois	7,640	4.9%
22	Indiana	2,177	1.4%
37	Iowa	754	0.5%
32	Kansas	895	0.6%
27	Kentucky	1,608	1.0%
25	Louisiana	1,969	1.3%
42	Maine	633	0.4%
10	Maryland	5,309	3.4%
7	Massachusetts	7,097	4.5%
11	Michigan	5,070	3.2%
19	Minnesota	2,604	1.7%
33	Mississippi	847	0.5%
18	Missouri	2,805	1.8%
46	Montana	298	0.2%
41	Nebraska	643	0.4%
30	Nevada	988	0.6%
40	New Hampshire	673	0.4%
8	New Jersey	6,293	4.0%
34	New Mexico	827	0.5%
2	New York	17,842	11.4%
12	North Carolina	4,131	2.6%
48	North Dakota	264	0.2%
9	Ohio	5,636	3.6%
29	Oklahoma	1,033	0.7%
24	Oregon	1,980	1.3%
6	Pennsylvania	7,381	4.7%
31	Rhode Island	938	0.6%
28	South Carolina	1,587	1.0%
47	South Dakota	280	0.2%
16	Tennessee	3,048	2.0%
4	Texas	8,335	5.3%
38	Utah	751	0.5%
43	Vermont	422	0.3%
14	Virginia	3,708	2.4%
17	Washington	2,916	1.9%
39	West Virginia	696	0.4%
20	Wisconsin	2,475	1.6%
50	Wyoming	114	0.1%

RANK ORDER

RANK	STATE	PHYSICIANS	% of USA
1	California	18,330	11.7%
2	New York	17,842	11.4%
3	Florida	8,416	5.4%
4	Texas	8,335	5.3%
5	Illinois	7,640	4.9%
6	Pennsylvania	7,381	4.7%
7	Massachusetts	7,097	4.5%
8	New Jersey	6,293	4.0%
9	Ohio	5,636	3.6%
10	Maryland	5,309	3.4%
11	Michigan	5,070	3.2%
12	North Carolina	4,131	2.6%
13	Georgia	3,902	2.5%
14	Virginia	3,708	2.4%
15	Connecticut	3,164	2.0%
16	Tennessee	3,048	2.0%
17	Washington	2,916	1.9%
18	Missouri	2,805	1.8%
19	Minnesota	2,604	1.7%
20	Wisconsin	2,475	1.6%
21	Arizona	2,416	1.5%
22	Indiana	2,177	1.4%
23	Colorado	2,053	1.3%
24	Oregon	1,980	1.3%
25	Louisiana	1,969	1.3%
26	Alabama	1,896	1.2%
27	Kentucky	1,608	1.0%
28	South Carolina	1,587	1.0%
29	Oklahoma	1,033	0.7%
30	Nevada	988	0.6%
31	Rhode Island	938	0.6%
32	Kansas	895	0.6%
33	Mississippi	847	0.5%
34	New Mexico	827	0.5%
35	Hawaii	811	0.5%
36	Arkansas	765	0.5%
37	Iowa	754	0.5%
38	Utah	751	0.5%
39	West Virginia	696	0.4%
40	New Hampshire	673	0.4%
41	Nebraska	643	0.4%
42	Maine	633	0.4%
43	Vermont	422	0.3%
44	Delaware	361	0.2%
45	Idaho	317	0.2%
46	Montana	298	0.2%
47	South Dakota	280	0.2%
48	North Dakota	264	0.2%
49	Alaska	169	0.1%
50	Wyoming	114	0.1%
	District of Columbia	1,005	0.6%

Source: American Medical Association (Chicago, Illinois)
   "Physician Characteristics and Distribution in the U.S." (2009 Edition)
*As of December 31, 2007. Total does not include 1,747 physicians in U.S. territories and possessions. Internal Medicine includes Diabetes, Endocrinology, Geriatrics, Hematology, Infectious Diseases, Nephrology, Nutrition, Medical Oncology, and Rheumatology.

Rate of Physicians in Internal Medicine in 2007

National Rate = 52 Physicians per 100,000 Population*

ALPHA ORDER				RANK ORDER		
RANK	STATE	RATE		RANK	STATE	RATE
29	Alabama	41		1	Massachusetts	110
47	Alaska	25		2	Maryland	94
33	Arizona	38		3	New York	92
46	Arkansas	27		4	Connecticut	91
13	California	50		5	Rhode Island	89
26	Colorado	42		6	New Jersey	73
4	Connecticut	91		7	Vermont	68
26	Delaware	42		8	Hawaii	63
21	Florida	46		9	Illinois	60
29	Georgia	41		10	Pennsylvania	59
8	Hawaii	63		11	Oregon	53
50	Idaho	21		12	New Hampshire	51
9	Illinois	60		13	California	50
40	Indiana	34		13	Michigan	50
47	Iowa	25		13	Minnesota	50
41	Kansas	32		13	Tennessee	50
33	Kentucky	38		17	Ohio	49
23	Louisiana	45		18	Maine	48
18	Maine	48		18	Missouri	48
2	Maryland	94		18	Virginia	48
1	Massachusetts	110		21	Florida	46
13	Michigan	50		21	North Carolina	46
13	Minnesota	50		23	Louisiana	45
43	Mississippi	29		23	Washington	45
18	Missouri	48		25	Wisconsin	44
42	Montana	31		26	Colorado	42
36	Nebraska	36		26	Delaware	42
32	Nevada	39		26	New Mexico	42
12	New Hampshire	51		29	Alabama	41
6	New Jersey	73		29	Georgia	41
26	New Mexico	42		29	North Dakota	41
3	New York	92		32	Nevada	39
21	North Carolina	46		33	Arizona	38
29	North Dakota	41		33	Kentucky	38
17	Ohio	49		33	West Virginia	38
43	Oklahoma	29		36	Nebraska	36
11	Oregon	53		36	South Carolina	36
10	Pennsylvania	59		38	South Dakota	35
5	Rhode Island	89		38	Texas	35
36	South Carolina	36		40	Indiana	34
38	South Dakota	35		41	Kansas	32
13	Tennessee	50		42	Montana	31
38	Texas	35		43	Mississippi	29
45	Utah	28		43	Oklahoma	29
7	Vermont	68		45	Utah	28
18	Virginia	48		46	Arkansas	27
23	Washington	45		47	Alaska	25
33	West Virginia	38		47	Iowa	25
25	Wisconsin	44		49	Wyoming	22
49	Wyoming	22		50	Idaho	21

District of Columbia   171

Source: CQ Press using data from American Medical Association (Chicago, Illinois)
"Physician Characteristics and Distribution in the U.S." (2009 Edition)
*As of December 31, 2007. National rate does not include physicians in U.S. territories and possessions. Internal Medicine includes Diabetes, Endocrinology, Geriatrics, Hematology, Infectious Diseases, Nephrology, Nutrition, Medical Oncology, and Rheumatology.

Physicians in Pediatrics in 2007

National Total = 73,145 Physicians*

ALPHA ORDER

RANK	STATE	PHYSICIANS	% of USA
27	Alabama	845	1.2%
46	Alaska	120	0.2%
22	Arizona	1,134	1.6%
30	Arkansas	510	0.7%
1	California	8,861	12.1%
24	Colorado	1,038	1.4%
21	Connecticut	1,141	1.6%
43	Delaware	251	0.3%
4	Florida	3,901	5.3%
13	Georgia	1,982	2.7%
33	Hawaii	422	0.6%
45	Idaho	131	0.2%
5	Illinois	3,136	4.3%
20	Indiana	1,146	1.6%
36	Iowa	391	0.5%
31	Kansas	488	0.7%
25	Kentucky	908	1.2%
23	Louisiana	1,084	1.5%
42	Maine	272	0.4%
10	Maryland	2,264	3.1%
9	Massachusetts	2,739	3.7%
11	Michigan	2,200	3.0%
18	Minnesota	1,158	1.6%
35	Mississippi	407	0.6%
16	Missouri	1,370	1.9%
47	Montana	118	0.2%
40	Nebraska	331	0.5%
38	Nevada	376	0.5%
41	New Hampshire	297	0.4%
6	New Jersey	3,020	4.1%
36	New Mexico	391	0.5%
2	New York	7,424	10.1%
12	North Carolina	2,096	2.9%
49	North Dakota	86	0.1%
6	Ohio	3,020	4.1%
32	Oklahoma	464	0.6%
28	Oregon	710	1.0%
8	Pennsylvania	2,984	4.1%
34	Rhode Island	418	0.6%
26	South Carolina	878	1.2%
48	South Dakota	106	0.1%
15	Tennessee	1,587	2.2%
3	Texas	4,870	6.7%
29	Utah	559	0.8%
44	Vermont	189	0.3%
14	Virginia	1,943	2.7%
17	Washington	1,360	1.9%
39	West Virginia	345	0.5%
19	Wisconsin	1,156	1.6%
50	Wyoming	47	0.1%

RANK ORDER

RANK	STATE	PHYSICIANS	% of USA
1	California	8,861	12.1%
2	New York	7,424	10.1%
3	Texas	4,870	6.7%
4	Florida	3,901	5.3%
5	Illinois	3,136	4.3%
6	New Jersey	3,020	4.1%
6	Ohio	3,020	4.1%
8	Pennsylvania	2,984	4.1%
9	Massachusetts	2,739	3.7%
10	Maryland	2,264	3.1%
11	Michigan	2,200	3.0%
12	North Carolina	2,096	2.9%
13	Georgia	1,982	2.7%
14	Virginia	1,943	2.7%
15	Tennessee	1,587	2.2%
16	Missouri	1,370	1.9%
17	Washington	1,360	1.9%
18	Minnesota	1,158	1.6%
19	Wisconsin	1,156	1.6%
20	Indiana	1,146	1.6%
21	Connecticut	1,141	1.6%
22	Arizona	1,134	1.6%
23	Louisiana	1,084	1.5%
24	Colorado	1,038	1.4%
25	Kentucky	908	1.2%
26	South Carolina	878	1.2%
27	Alabama	845	1.2%
28	Oregon	710	1.0%
29	Utah	559	0.8%
30	Arkansas	510	0.7%
31	Kansas	488	0.7%
32	Oklahoma	464	0.6%
33	Hawaii	422	0.6%
34	Rhode Island	418	0.6%
35	Mississippi	407	0.6%
36	Iowa	391	0.5%
36	New Mexico	391	0.5%
38	Nevada	376	0.5%
39	West Virginia	345	0.5%
40	Nebraska	331	0.5%
41	New Hampshire	297	0.4%
42	Maine	272	0.4%
43	Delaware	251	0.3%
44	Vermont	189	0.3%
45	Idaho	131	0.2%
46	Alaska	120	0.2%
47	Montana	118	0.2%
48	South Dakota	106	0.1%
49	North Dakota	86	0.1%
50	Wyoming	47	0.1%
	District of Columbia	471	0.6%

Source: American Medical Association (Chicago, Illinois)
"Physician Characteristics and Distribution in the U.S." (2009 Edition)
*As of December 31, 2007. Total does not include 1,205 physicians in U.S. territories and possessions. Pediatrics includes Adolescent Medicine, Neonatal-Perinatal, Pediatric Allergy, Pediatric Endocrinology, Pediatric Pulmonology, Pediatric Hematology-Oncology, and Pediatric Nephrology.

Rate of Physicians in Pediatrics in 2007

National Rate = 99 Physicians per 100,000 Population 17 Years and Younger*

ALPHA ORDER

RANK	STATE	RATE
33	Alabama	75
41	Alaska	66
39	Arizona	68
36	Arkansas	73
21	California	94
27	Colorado	87
8	Connecticut	139
9	Delaware	122
18	Florida	96
31	Georgia	78
5	Hawaii	148
50	Idaho	32
16	Illinois	98
37	Indiana	72
44	Iowa	55
38	Kansas	70
23	Kentucky	90
14	Louisiana	100
17	Maine	97
4	Maryland	167
1	Massachusetts	191
23	Michigan	90
22	Minnesota	92
47	Mississippi	53
18	Missouri	96
45	Montana	54
34	Nebraska	74
43	Nevada	57
14	New Hampshire	100
6	New Jersey	146
31	New Mexico	78
3	New York	168
20	North Carolina	95
42	North Dakota	60
10	Ohio	110
48	Oklahoma	52
30	Oregon	82
12	Pennsylvania	107
2	Rhode Island	179
29	South Carolina	83
45	South Dakota	54
11	Tennessee	108
34	Texas	74
39	Utah	68
7	Vermont	144
13	Virginia	106
25	Washington	89
25	West Virginia	89
27	Wisconsin	87
49	Wyoming	37

RANK ORDER

RANK	STATE	RATE
1	Massachusetts	191
2	Rhode Island	179
3	New York	168
4	Maryland	167
5	Hawaii	148
6	New Jersey	146
7	Vermont	144
8	Connecticut	139
9	Delaware	122
10	Ohio	110
11	Tennessee	108
12	Pennsylvania	107
13	Virginia	106
14	Louisiana	100
14	New Hampshire	100
16	Illinois	98
17	Maine	97
18	Florida	96
18	Missouri	96
20	North Carolina	95
21	California	94
22	Minnesota	92
23	Kentucky	90
23	Michigan	90
25	Washington	89
25	West Virginia	89
27	Colorado	87
27	Wisconsin	87
29	South Carolina	83
30	Oregon	82
31	Georgia	78
31	New Mexico	78
33	Alabama	75
34	Nebraska	74
34	Texas	74
36	Arkansas	73
37	Indiana	72
38	Kansas	70
39	Arizona	68
39	Utah	68
41	Alaska	66
42	North Dakota	60
43	Nevada	57
44	Iowa	55
45	Montana	54
45	South Dakota	54
47	Mississippi	53
48	Oklahoma	52
49	Wyoming	37
50	Idaho	32

District of Columbia	414

Source: CQ Press using data from American Medical Association (Chicago, Illinois)
   "Physician Characteristics and Distribution in the U.S." (2009 Edition)
*As of December 31, 2007. National rate does not include physicians in U.S. territories and possessions. Pediatrics includes Adolescent Medicine, Neonatal-Perinatal, Pediatric Allergy, Pediatric Endocrinology, Pediatric Pulmonology, Pediatric Hematology-Oncology, and Pediatric Nephrology.

Physicians in Surgical Specialties in 2007

National Total = 160,301 Physicians*

ALPHA ORDER

RANK	STATE	PHYSICIANS	% of USA
25	Alabama	2,285	1.4%
48	Alaska	342	0.2%
22	Arizona	2,624	1.6%
33	Arkansas	1,160	0.7%
1	California	18,772	11.7%
23	Colorado	2,538	1.6%
24	Connecticut	2,489	1.6%
45	Delaware	429	0.3%
4	Florida	9,296	5.8%
12	Georgia	4,461	2.8%
39	Hawaii	819	0.5%
43	Idaho	587	0.4%
6	Illinois	6,574	4.1%
20	Indiana	2,698	1.7%
34	Iowa	1,142	0.7%
30	Kansas	1,291	0.8%
27	Kentucky	2,100	1.3%
21	Louisiana	2,682	1.7%
42	Maine	707	0.4%
14	Maryland	4,244	2.6%
11	Massachusetts	4,729	3.0%
9	Michigan	4,880	3.0%
19	Minnesota	2,723	1.7%
31	Mississippi	1,255	0.8%
17	Missouri	2,935	1.8%
44	Montana	498	0.3%
36	Nebraska	909	0.6%
35	Nevada	953	0.6%
40	New Hampshire	747	0.5%
8	New Jersey	5,266	3.3%
38	New Mexico	841	0.5%
2	New York	13,908	8.7%
10	North Carolina	4,738	3.0%
49	North Dakota	298	0.2%
7	Ohio	6,064	3.8%
29	Oklahoma	1,359	0.8%
28	Oregon	2,068	1.3%
5	Pennsylvania	7,310	4.6%
40	Rhode Island	747	0.5%
26	South Carolina	2,260	1.4%
47	South Dakota	385	0.2%
15	Tennessee	3,550	2.2%
3	Texas	10,761	6.7%
32	Utah	1,197	0.7%
46	Vermont	424	0.3%
13	Virginia	4,257	2.7%
16	Washington	3,199	2.0%
37	West Virginia	893	0.6%
18	Wisconsin	2,812	1.8%
50	Wyoming	233	0.1%

RANK ORDER

RANK	STATE	PHYSICIANS	% of USA
1	California	18,772	11.7%
2	New York	13,908	8.7%
3	Texas	10,761	6.7%
4	Florida	9,296	5.8%
5	Pennsylvania	7,310	4.6%
6	Illinois	6,574	4.1%
7	Ohio	6,064	3.8%
8	New Jersey	5,266	3.3%
9	Michigan	4,880	3.0%
10	North Carolina	4,738	3.0%
11	Massachusetts	4,729	3.0%
12	Georgia	4,461	2.8%
13	Virginia	4,257	2.7%
14	Maryland	4,244	2.6%
15	Tennessee	3,550	2.2%
16	Washington	3,199	2.0%
17	Missouri	2,935	1.8%
18	Wisconsin	2,812	1.8%
19	Minnesota	2,723	1.7%
20	Indiana	2,698	1.7%
21	Louisiana	2,682	1.7%
22	Arizona	2,624	1.6%
23	Colorado	2,538	1.6%
24	Connecticut	2,489	1.6%
25	Alabama	2,285	1.4%
26	South Carolina	2,260	1.4%
27	Kentucky	2,100	1.3%
28	Oregon	2,068	1.3%
29	Oklahoma	1,359	0.8%
30	Kansas	1,291	0.8%
31	Mississippi	1,255	0.8%
32	Utah	1,197	0.7%
33	Arkansas	1,160	0.7%
34	Iowa	1,142	0.7%
35	Nevada	953	0.6%
36	Nebraska	909	0.6%
37	West Virginia	893	0.6%
38	New Mexico	841	0.5%
39	Hawaii	819	0.5%
40	New Hampshire	747	0.5%
40	Rhode Island	747	0.5%
42	Maine	707	0.4%
43	Idaho	587	0.4%
44	Montana	498	0.3%
45	Delaware	429	0.3%
46	Vermont	424	0.3%
47	South Dakota	385	0.2%
48	Alaska	342	0.2%
49	North Dakota	298	0.2%
50	Wyoming	233	0.1%
	District of Columbia	862	0.5%

Source: American Medical Association (Chicago, Illinois)
    "Physician Characteristics and Distribution in the U.S." (2009 Edition)

*As of December 31, 2007. Total does not include 1,767 physicians in U.S. territories and possessions. Surgical Specialties include Colon and Rectal, General, Neurological, Obstetrics and Gynecology, Ophthalmology, Orthopedic, Otolaryngology, Plastic, Thoracic, and Urological Surgeries.

Rate of Physicians in Surgical Specialties in 2007

National Rate = 52 Physicians per 100,000 Population*

ALPHA ORDER			RANK ORDER		
RANK	STATE	RATE	RANK	STATE	RATE
32	Alabama	49	1	Maryland	76
26	Alaska	50	2	Massachusetts	73
45	Arizona	41	3	New York	72
45	Arkansas	41	4	Connecticut	71
18	California	52	4	Rhode Island	71
18	Colorado	52	6	Vermont	68
4	Connecticut	71	7	Hawaii	64
26	Delaware	50	8	Louisiana	61
22	Florida	51	8	New Jersey	61
36	Georgia	47	10	Pennsylvania	59
7	Hawaii	64	11	Tennessee	58
47	Idaho	39	12	New Hampshire	57
22	Illinois	51	13	Oregon	55
42	Indiana	43	13	Virginia	55
48	Iowa	38	15	Maine	54
38	Kansas	46	16	Minnesota	53
26	Kentucky	50	16	Ohio	53
8	Louisiana	61	18	California	52
15	Maine	54	18	Colorado	52
1	Maryland	76	18	Montana	52
2	Massachusetts	73	18	North Carolina	52
32	Michigan	49	22	Florida	51
16	Minnesota	53	22	Illinois	51
42	Mississippi	43	22	Nebraska	51
26	Missouri	50	22	South Carolina	51
18	Montana	52	26	Alaska	50
22	Nebraska	51	26	Delaware	50
50	Nevada	37	26	Kentucky	50
12	New Hampshire	57	26	Missouri	50
8	New Jersey	61	26	Washington	50
42	New Mexico	43	26	Wisconsin	50
3	New York	72	32	Alabama	49
18	North Carolina	52	32	Michigan	49
36	North Dakota	47	32	West Virginia	49
16	Ohio	53	35	South Dakota	48
48	Oklahoma	38	36	Georgia	47
13	Oregon	55	36	North Dakota	47
10	Pennsylvania	59	38	Kansas	46
4	Rhode Island	71	39	Texas	45
22	South Carolina	51	39	Utah	45
35	South Dakota	48	39	Wyoming	45
11	Tennessee	58	42	Indiana	43
39	Texas	45	42	Mississippi	43
39	Utah	45	42	New Mexico	43
6	Vermont	68	45	Arizona	41
13	Virginia	55	45	Arkansas	41
26	Washington	50	47	Idaho	39
32	West Virginia	49	48	Iowa	38
26	Wisconsin	50	48	Oklahoma	38
39	Wyoming	45	50	Nevada	37

District of Columbia   147

Source: CQ Press using data from American Medical Association (Chicago, Illinois)
"Physician Characteristics and Distribution in the U.S." (2009 Edition)

*As of December 31, 2007. National rate does not include physicians in U.S. territories and possessions. Surgical Specialties include Colon and Rectal, General, Neurological, Obstetrics and Gynecology, Ophthalmology, Orthopedic, Otolaryngology, Plastic, Thoracic, and Urological Surgeries.

Average Annual Wages of Surgeons in 2007

National Average = $191,410*

<table>
<tr><td colspan="3">ALPHA ORDER</td><td colspan="3">RANK ORDER</td></tr>
<tr><td>RANK</td><td>STATE</td><td>WAGES</td><td>RANK</td><td>STATE</td><td>WAGES</td></tr>
<tr><td>22</td><td>Alabama</td><td>$195,370</td><td>1</td><td>New Mexico</td><td>$212,230</td></tr>
<tr><td>NA</td><td>Alaska**</td><td>NA</td><td>2</td><td>Georgia</td><td>207,600</td></tr>
<tr><td>31</td><td>Arizona</td><td>176,180</td><td>3</td><td>Massachusetts</td><td>207,580</td></tr>
<tr><td>11</td><td>Arkansas</td><td>201,270</td><td>4</td><td>Mississippi</td><td>203,650</td></tr>
<tr><td>34</td><td>California</td><td>171,200</td><td>5</td><td>Maryland</td><td>203,500</td></tr>
<tr><td>16</td><td>Colorado</td><td>199,390</td><td>6</td><td>Washington</td><td>203,250</td></tr>
<tr><td>23</td><td>Connecticut</td><td>194,190</td><td>7</td><td>Oklahoma</td><td>202,810</td></tr>
<tr><td>29</td><td>Delaware</td><td>182,860</td><td>8</td><td>Missouri</td><td>202,230</td></tr>
<tr><td>35</td><td>Florida</td><td>170,170</td><td>9</td><td>Michigan</td><td>201,350</td></tr>
<tr><td>2</td><td>Georgia</td><td>207,600</td><td>10</td><td>South Carolina</td><td>201,320</td></tr>
<tr><td>38</td><td>Hawaii</td><td>157,100</td><td>11</td><td>Arkansas</td><td>201,270</td></tr>
<tr><td>NA</td><td>Idaho**</td><td>NA</td><td>12</td><td>Indiana</td><td>201,090</td></tr>
<tr><td>37</td><td>Illinois</td><td>164,250</td><td>13</td><td>Utah</td><td>201,030</td></tr>
<tr><td>12</td><td>Indiana</td><td>201,090</td><td>14</td><td>Ohio</td><td>200,760</td></tr>
<tr><td>25</td><td>Iowa</td><td>191,610</td><td>15</td><td>Nevada</td><td>200,630</td></tr>
<tr><td>NA</td><td>Kansas**</td><td>NA</td><td>16</td><td>Colorado</td><td>199,390</td></tr>
<tr><td>17</td><td>Kentucky</td><td>199,120</td><td>17</td><td>Kentucky</td><td>199,120</td></tr>
<tr><td>19</td><td>Louisiana</td><td>197,540</td><td>18</td><td>South Dakota</td><td>198,380</td></tr>
<tr><td>NA</td><td>Maine**</td><td>NA</td><td>19</td><td>Louisiana</td><td>197,540</td></tr>
<tr><td>5</td><td>Maryland</td><td>203,500</td><td>20</td><td>Oregon</td><td>196,450</td></tr>
<tr><td>3</td><td>Massachusetts</td><td>207,580</td><td>21</td><td>West Virginia</td><td>196,200</td></tr>
<tr><td>9</td><td>Michigan</td><td>201,350</td><td>22</td><td>Alabama</td><td>195,370</td></tr>
<tr><td>NA</td><td>Minnesota**</td><td>NA</td><td>23</td><td>Connecticut</td><td>194,190</td></tr>
<tr><td>4</td><td>Mississippi</td><td>203,650</td><td>24</td><td>Texas</td><td>192,570</td></tr>
<tr><td>8</td><td>Missouri</td><td>202,230</td><td>25</td><td>Iowa</td><td>191,610</td></tr>
<tr><td>NA</td><td>Montana**</td><td>NA</td><td>26</td><td>Tennessee</td><td>190,010</td></tr>
<tr><td>36</td><td>Nebraska</td><td>164,520</td><td>27</td><td>Virginia</td><td>186,360</td></tr>
<tr><td>15</td><td>Nevada</td><td>200,630</td><td>28</td><td>New York</td><td>184,810</td></tr>
<tr><td>NA</td><td>New Hampshire**</td><td>NA</td><td>29</td><td>Delaware</td><td>182,860</td></tr>
<tr><td>NA</td><td>New Jersey**</td><td>NA</td><td>30</td><td>North Dakota</td><td>179,310</td></tr>
<tr><td>1</td><td>New Mexico</td><td>212,230</td><td>31</td><td>Arizona</td><td>176,180</td></tr>
<tr><td>28</td><td>New York</td><td>184,810</td><td>32</td><td>Pennsylvania</td><td>175,240</td></tr>
<tr><td>NA</td><td>North Carolina**</td><td>NA</td><td>33</td><td>Vermont</td><td>172,410</td></tr>
<tr><td>30</td><td>North Dakota</td><td>179,310</td><td>34</td><td>California</td><td>171,200</td></tr>
<tr><td>14</td><td>Ohio</td><td>200,760</td><td>35</td><td>Florida</td><td>170,170</td></tr>
<tr><td>7</td><td>Oklahoma</td><td>202,810</td><td>36</td><td>Nebraska</td><td>164,520</td></tr>
<tr><td>20</td><td>Oregon</td><td>196,450</td><td>37</td><td>Illinois</td><td>164,250</td></tr>
<tr><td>32</td><td>Pennsylvania</td><td>175,240</td><td>38</td><td>Hawaii</td><td>157,100</td></tr>
<tr><td>NA</td><td>Rhode Island**</td><td>NA</td><td>NA</td><td>Alaska**</td><td>NA</td></tr>
<tr><td>10</td><td>South Carolina</td><td>201,320</td><td>NA</td><td>Idaho**</td><td>NA</td></tr>
<tr><td>18</td><td>South Dakota</td><td>198,380</td><td>NA</td><td>Kansas**</td><td>NA</td></tr>
<tr><td>26</td><td>Tennessee</td><td>190,010</td><td>NA</td><td>Maine**</td><td>NA</td></tr>
<tr><td>24</td><td>Texas</td><td>192,570</td><td>NA</td><td>Minnesota**</td><td>NA</td></tr>
<tr><td>13</td><td>Utah</td><td>201,030</td><td>NA</td><td>Montana**</td><td>NA</td></tr>
<tr><td>33</td><td>Vermont</td><td>172,410</td><td>NA</td><td>New Hampshire**</td><td>NA</td></tr>
<tr><td>27</td><td>Virginia</td><td>186,360</td><td>NA</td><td>New Jersey**</td><td>NA</td></tr>
<tr><td>6</td><td>Washington</td><td>203,250</td><td>NA</td><td>North Carolina**</td><td>NA</td></tr>
<tr><td>21</td><td>West Virginia</td><td>196,200</td><td>NA</td><td>Rhode Island**</td><td>NA</td></tr>
<tr><td>NA</td><td>Wisconsin**</td><td>NA</td><td>NA</td><td>Wisconsin**</td><td>NA</td></tr>
<tr><td>NA</td><td>Wyoming**</td><td>NA</td><td>NA</td><td>Wyoming**</td><td>NA</td></tr>
<tr><td></td><td></td><td></td><td></td><td>District of Columbia</td><td>127,360</td></tr>
</table>

Source: U.S. Department of Labor, Bureau of Labor Statistics
    "Occupational Employment and Wages, 2007" (http://www.bls.gov/oes/)
*Does not include self-employed.
**Not available.

Physicians in General Surgery in 2007

National Total = 37,073 Physicians*

ALPHA ORDER

RANK	STATE	PHYSICIANS	% of USA
27	Alabama	538	1.5%
49	Alaska	77	0.2%
20	Arizona	611	1.6%
32	Arkansas	275	0.7%
1	California	4,059	10.9%
23	Colorado	566	1.5%
26	Connecticut	543	1.5%
45	Delaware	112	0.3%
5	Florida	1,862	5.0%
12	Georgia	1,016	2.7%
41	Hawaii	177	0.5%
43	Idaho	136	0.4%
6	Illinois	1,529	4.1%
21	Indiana	595	1.6%
30	Iowa	298	0.8%
31	Kansas	293	0.8%
25	Kentucky	548	1.5%
22	Louisiana	586	1.6%
39	Maine	189	0.5%
13	Maryland	956	2.6%
8	Massachusetts	1,246	3.4%
9	Michigan	1,241	3.3%
19	Minnesota	617	1.7%
33	Mississippi	271	0.7%
17	Missouri	649	1.8%
46	Montana	107	0.3%
35	Nebraska	240	0.6%
37	Nevada	212	0.6%
40	New Hampshire	188	0.5%
10	New Jersey	1,193	3.2%
38	New Mexico	198	0.5%
2	New York	3,308	8.9%
11	North Carolina	1,096	3.0%
48	North Dakota	84	0.2%
7	Ohio	1,518	4.1%
29	Oklahoma	306	0.8%
28	Oregon	480	1.3%
4	Pennsylvania	1,895	5.1%
42	Rhode Island	175	0.5%
24	South Carolina	553	1.5%
47	South Dakota	104	0.3%
15	Tennessee	891	2.4%
3	Texas	2,313	6.2%
36	Utah	237	0.6%
44	Vermont	120	0.3%
14	Virginia	943	2.5%
16	Washington	748	2.0%
34	West Virginia	246	0.7%
18	Wisconsin	639	1.7%
50	Wyoming	56	0.2%

RANK ORDER

RANK	STATE	PHYSICIANS	% of USA
1	California	4,059	10.9%
2	New York	3,308	8.9%
3	Texas	2,313	6.2%
4	Pennsylvania	1,895	5.1%
5	Florida	1,862	5.0%
6	Illinois	1,529	4.1%
7	Ohio	1,518	4.1%
8	Massachusetts	1,246	3.4%
9	Michigan	1,241	3.3%
10	New Jersey	1,193	3.2%
11	North Carolina	1,096	3.0%
12	Georgia	1,016	2.7%
13	Maryland	956	2.6%
14	Virginia	943	2.5%
15	Tennessee	891	2.4%
16	Washington	748	2.0%
17	Missouri	649	1.8%
18	Wisconsin	639	1.7%
19	Minnesota	617	1.7%
20	Arizona	611	1.6%
21	Indiana	595	1.6%
22	Louisiana	586	1.6%
23	Colorado	566	1.5%
24	South Carolina	553	1.5%
25	Kentucky	548	1.5%
26	Connecticut	543	1.5%
27	Alabama	538	1.5%
28	Oregon	480	1.3%
29	Oklahoma	306	0.8%
30	Iowa	298	0.8%
31	Kansas	293	0.8%
32	Arkansas	275	0.7%
33	Mississippi	271	0.7%
34	West Virginia	246	0.7%
35	Nebraska	240	0.6%
36	Utah	237	0.6%
37	Nevada	212	0.6%
38	New Mexico	198	0.5%
39	Maine	189	0.5%
40	New Hampshire	188	0.5%
41	Hawaii	177	0.5%
42	Rhode Island	175	0.5%
43	Idaho	136	0.4%
44	Vermont	120	0.3%
45	Delaware	112	0.3%
46	Montana	107	0.3%
47	South Dakota	104	0.3%
48	North Dakota	84	0.2%
49	Alaska	77	0.2%
50	Wyoming	56	0.2%
	District of Columbia	233	0.6%

Source: American Medical Association (Chicago, Illinois)
   "Physician Characteristics and Distribution in the U.S." (2009 Edition)
*As of December 31, 2007. Total does not include 451 physicians in U.S. territories and possessions. General Surgery includes Abdominal, Cardiovascular, Hand, Head and Neck, Pediatric, Traumatic, and Vascular Surgeries.

Rate of Physicians in General Surgery in 2007

National Rate = 12 Physicians per 100,000 Population*

ALPHA ORDER

RANK	STATE	RATE
23	Alabama	12
31	Alaska	11
39	Arizona	10
39	Arkansas	10
31	California	11
23	Colorado	12
6	Connecticut	16
15	Delaware	13
39	Florida	10
31	Georgia	11
8	Hawaii	14
45	Idaho	9
23	Illinois	12
45	Indiana	9
39	Iowa	10
31	Kansas	11
15	Kentucky	13
15	Louisiana	13
8	Maine	14
3	Maryland	17
1	Massachusetts	19
23	Michigan	12
23	Minnesota	12
45	Mississippi	9
31	Missouri	11
31	Montana	11
8	Nebraska	14
49	Nevada	8
8	New Hampshire	14
8	New Jersey	14
39	New Mexico	10
3	New York	17
23	North Carolina	12
15	North Dakota	13
15	Ohio	13
49	Oklahoma	8
15	Oregon	13
7	Pennsylvania	15
3	Rhode Island	17
15	South Carolina	13
15	South Dakota	13
8	Tennessee	14
39	Texas	10
45	Utah	9
1	Vermont	19
23	Virginia	12
23	Washington	12
8	West Virginia	14
31	Wisconsin	11
31	Wyoming	11

RANK ORDER

RANK	STATE	RATE
1	Massachusetts	19
1	Vermont	19
3	Maryland	17
3	New York	17
3	Rhode Island	17
6	Connecticut	16
7	Pennsylvania	15
8	Hawaii	14
8	Maine	14
8	Nebraska	14
8	New Hampshire	14
8	New Jersey	14
8	Tennessee	14
8	West Virginia	14
15	Delaware	13
15	Kentucky	13
15	Louisiana	13
15	North Dakota	13
15	Ohio	13
15	Oregon	13
15	South Carolina	13
15	South Dakota	13
23	Alabama	12
23	Colorado	12
23	Illinois	12
23	Michigan	12
23	Minnesota	12
23	North Carolina	12
23	Virginia	12
23	Washington	12
31	Alaska	11
31	California	11
31	Georgia	11
31	Kansas	11
31	Missouri	11
31	Montana	11
31	Wisconsin	11
31	Wyoming	11
39	Arizona	10
39	Arkansas	10
39	Florida	10
39	Iowa	10
39	New Mexico	10
39	Texas	10
45	Idaho	9
45	Indiana	9
45	Mississippi	9
45	Utah	9
49	Nevada	8
49	Oklahoma	8
	District of Columbia	40

Source: CQ Press using data from American Medical Association (Chicago, Illinois)
"Physician Characteristics and Distribution in the U.S." (2009 Edition)

*As of December 31, 2007. National rate does not include physicians in U.S. territories and possessions. General Surgery includes Abdominal, Cardiovascular, Hand, Head and Neck, Pediatric, Traumatic, and Vascular Surgeries.

Physicians in Obstetrics and Gynecology in 2007

National Total = 41,947 Physicians*

<table>
<tr><td colspan="4"><u>ALPHA ORDER</u></td><td colspan="4"><u>RANK ORDER</u></td></tr>
<tr><th>RANK</th><th>STATE</th><th>PHYSICIANS</th><th>% of USA</th><th>RANK</th><th>STATE</th><th>PHYSICIANS</th><th>% of USA</th></tr>
<tr><td>26</td><td>Alabama</td><td>568</td><td>1.4%</td><td>1</td><td>California</td><td>5,012</td><td>11.9%</td></tr>
<tr><td>47</td><td>Alaska</td><td>84</td><td>0.2%</td><td>2</td><td>New York</td><td>3,765</td><td>9.0%</td></tr>
<tr><td>18</td><td>Arizona</td><td>711</td><td>1.7%</td><td>3</td><td>Texas</td><td>3,005</td><td>7.2%</td></tr>
<tr><td>34</td><td>Arkansas</td><td>268</td><td>0.6%</td><td>4</td><td>Florida</td><td>2,264</td><td>5.4%</td></tr>
<tr><td>1</td><td>California</td><td>5,012</td><td>11.9%</td><td>5</td><td>Illinois</td><td>1,853</td><td>4.4%</td></tr>
<tr><td>22</td><td>Colorado</td><td>675</td><td>1.6%</td><td>6</td><td>Pennsylvania</td><td>1,708</td><td>4.1%</td></tr>
<tr><td>19</td><td>Connecticut</td><td>709</td><td>1.7%</td><td>7</td><td>New Jersey</td><td>1,531</td><td>3.6%</td></tr>
<tr><td>46</td><td>Delaware</td><td>98</td><td>0.2%</td><td>8</td><td>Ohio</td><td>1,497</td><td>3.6%</td></tr>
<tr><td>4</td><td>Florida</td><td>2,264</td><td>5.4%</td><td>9</td><td>Georgia</td><td>1,390</td><td>3.3%</td></tr>
<tr><td>9</td><td>Georgia</td><td>1,390</td><td>3.3%</td><td>10</td><td>Michigan</td><td>1,362</td><td>3.2%</td></tr>
<tr><td>35</td><td>Hawaii</td><td>253</td><td>0.6%</td><td>11</td><td>North Carolina</td><td>1,286</td><td>3.1%</td></tr>
<tr><td>43</td><td>Idaho</td><td>134</td><td>0.3%</td><td>12</td><td>Virginia</td><td>1,241</td><td>3.0%</td></tr>
<tr><td>5</td><td>Illinois</td><td>1,853</td><td>4.4%</td><td>13</td><td>Maryland</td><td>1,156</td><td>2.8%</td></tr>
<tr><td>20</td><td>Indiana</td><td>703</td><td>1.7%</td><td>14</td><td>Massachusetts</td><td>1,120</td><td>2.7%</td></tr>
<tr><td>37</td><td>Iowa</td><td>208</td><td>0.5%</td><td>15</td><td>Tennessee</td><td>908</td><td>2.2%</td></tr>
<tr><td>31</td><td>Kansas</td><td>292</td><td>0.7%</td><td>16</td><td>Washington</td><td>777</td><td>1.9%</td></tr>
<tr><td>28</td><td>Kentucky</td><td>530</td><td>1.3%</td><td>17</td><td>Missouri</td><td>728</td><td>1.7%</td></tr>
<tr><td>21</td><td>Louisiana</td><td>687</td><td>1.6%</td><td>18</td><td>Arizona</td><td>711</td><td>1.7%</td></tr>
<tr><td>42</td><td>Maine</td><td>171</td><td>0.4%</td><td>19</td><td>Connecticut</td><td>709</td><td>1.7%</td></tr>
<tr><td>13</td><td>Maryland</td><td>1,156</td><td>2.8%</td><td>20</td><td>Indiana</td><td>703</td><td>1.7%</td></tr>
<tr><td>14</td><td>Massachusetts</td><td>1,120</td><td>2.7%</td><td>21</td><td>Louisiana</td><td>687</td><td>1.6%</td></tr>
<tr><td>10</td><td>Michigan</td><td>1,362</td><td>3.2%</td><td>22</td><td>Colorado</td><td>675</td><td>1.6%</td></tr>
<tr><td>24</td><td>Minnesota</td><td>627</td><td>1.5%</td><td>23</td><td>Wisconsin</td><td>641</td><td>1.5%</td></tr>
<tr><td>30</td><td>Mississippi</td><td>327</td><td>0.8%</td><td>24</td><td>Minnesota</td><td>627</td><td>1.5%</td></tr>
<tr><td>17</td><td>Missouri</td><td>728</td><td>1.7%</td><td>25</td><td>South Carolina</td><td>581</td><td>1.4%</td></tr>
<tr><td>45</td><td>Montana</td><td>112</td><td>0.3%</td><td>26</td><td>Alabama</td><td>568</td><td>1.4%</td></tr>
<tr><td>40</td><td>Nebraska</td><td>199</td><td>0.5%</td><td>27</td><td>Oregon</td><td>537</td><td>1.3%</td></tr>
<tr><td>33</td><td>Nevada</td><td>284</td><td>0.7%</td><td>28</td><td>Kentucky</td><td>530</td><td>1.3%</td></tr>
<tr><td>41</td><td>New Hampshire</td><td>194</td><td>0.5%</td><td>29</td><td>Oklahoma</td><td>332</td><td>0.8%</td></tr>
<tr><td>7</td><td>New Jersey</td><td>1,531</td><td>3.6%</td><td>30</td><td>Mississippi</td><td>327</td><td>0.8%</td></tr>
<tr><td>36</td><td>New Mexico</td><td>226</td><td>0.5%</td><td>31</td><td>Kansas</td><td>292</td><td>0.7%</td></tr>
<tr><td>2</td><td>New York</td><td>3,765</td><td>9.0%</td><td>32</td><td>Utah</td><td>286</td><td>0.7%</td></tr>
<tr><td>11</td><td>North Carolina</td><td>1,286</td><td>3.1%</td><td>33</td><td>Nevada</td><td>284</td><td>0.7%</td></tr>
<tr><td>50</td><td>North Dakota</td><td>51</td><td>0.1%</td><td>34</td><td>Arkansas</td><td>268</td><td>0.6%</td></tr>
<tr><td>8</td><td>Ohio</td><td>1,497</td><td>3.6%</td><td>35</td><td>Hawaii</td><td>253</td><td>0.6%</td></tr>
<tr><td>29</td><td>Oklahoma</td><td>332</td><td>0.8%</td><td>36</td><td>New Mexico</td><td>226</td><td>0.5%</td></tr>
<tr><td>27</td><td>Oregon</td><td>537</td><td>1.3%</td><td>37</td><td>Iowa</td><td>208</td><td>0.5%</td></tr>
<tr><td>6</td><td>Pennsylvania</td><td>1,708</td><td>4.1%</td><td>38</td><td>Rhode Island</td><td>204</td><td>0.5%</td></tr>
<tr><td>38</td><td>Rhode Island</td><td>204</td><td>0.5%</td><td>39</td><td>West Virginia</td><td>201</td><td>0.5%</td></tr>
<tr><td>25</td><td>South Carolina</td><td>581</td><td>1.4%</td><td>40</td><td>Nebraska</td><td>199</td><td>0.5%</td></tr>
<tr><td>48</td><td>South Dakota</td><td>74</td><td>0.2%</td><td>41</td><td>New Hampshire</td><td>194</td><td>0.5%</td></tr>
<tr><td>15</td><td>Tennessee</td><td>908</td><td>2.2%</td><td>42</td><td>Maine</td><td>171</td><td>0.4%</td></tr>
<tr><td>3</td><td>Texas</td><td>3,005</td><td>7.2%</td><td>43</td><td>Idaho</td><td>134</td><td>0.3%</td></tr>
<tr><td>32</td><td>Utah</td><td>286</td><td>0.7%</td><td>44</td><td>Vermont</td><td>113</td><td>0.3%</td></tr>
<tr><td>44</td><td>Vermont</td><td>113</td><td>0.3%</td><td>45</td><td>Montana</td><td>112</td><td>0.3%</td></tr>
<tr><td>12</td><td>Virginia</td><td>1,241</td><td>3.0%</td><td>46</td><td>Delaware</td><td>98</td><td>0.2%</td></tr>
<tr><td>16</td><td>Washington</td><td>777</td><td>1.9%</td><td>47</td><td>Alaska</td><td>84</td><td>0.2%</td></tr>
<tr><td>39</td><td>West Virginia</td><td>201</td><td>0.5%</td><td>48</td><td>South Dakota</td><td>74</td><td>0.2%</td></tr>
<tr><td>23</td><td>Wisconsin</td><td>641</td><td>1.5%</td><td>49</td><td>Wyoming</td><td>55</td><td>0.1%</td></tr>
<tr><td>49</td><td>Wyoming</td><td>55</td><td>0.1%</td><td>50</td><td>North Dakota</td><td>51</td><td>0.1%</td></tr>
<tr><td></td><td></td><td></td><td></td><td></td><td>District of Columbia</td><td>209</td><td>0.5%</td></tr>
</table>

Source: American Medical Association (Chicago, Illinois)
   "Physician Characteristics and Distribution in the U.S." (2009 Edition)
*As of December 31, 2007. Total does not include 647 physicians in U.S. territories and possessions. Obstetrics and Gynecology includes Gynecology and Oncology, Maternal and Fetal Medicine, and Reproductive Endocrinology.

Rate of Physicians in Obstetrics and Gynecology in 2007

National Rate = 27 Physicians per 100,000 Female Population*

ALPHA ORDER

RANK	STATE	RATE
27	Alabama	24
21	Alaska	26
36	Arizona	22
45	Arkansas	19
18	California	27
14	Colorado	28
3	Connecticut	39
36	Delaware	22
27	Florida	24
11	Georgia	29
1	Hawaii	40
47	Idaho	18
14	Illinois	28
36	Indiana	22
50	Iowa	14
43	Kansas	21
23	Kentucky	25
10	Louisiana	31
23	Maine	25
1	Maryland	40
8	Massachusetts	34
18	Michigan	27
27	Minnesota	24
36	Mississippi	22
27	Missouri	24
32	Montana	23
36	Nebraska	22
32	Nevada	23
11	New Hampshire	29
7	New Jersey	35
32	New Mexico	23
4	New York	38
14	North Carolina	28
49	North Dakota	16
23	Ohio	25
47	Oklahoma	18
14	Oregon	28
18	Pennsylvania	27
5	Rhode Island	37
21	South Carolina	26
45	South Dakota	19
11	Tennessee	29
23	Texas	25
36	Utah	22
6	Vermont	36
9	Virginia	32
27	Washington	24
36	West Virginia	22
32	Wisconsin	23
43	Wyoming	21

RANK ORDER

RANK	STATE	RATE
1	Hawaii	40
1	Maryland	40
3	Connecticut	39
4	New York	38
5	Rhode Island	37
6	Vermont	36
7	New Jersey	35
8	Massachusetts	34
9	Virginia	32
10	Louisiana	31
11	Georgia	29
11	New Hampshire	29
11	Tennessee	29
14	Colorado	28
14	Illinois	28
14	North Carolina	28
14	Oregon	28
18	California	27
18	Michigan	27
18	Pennsylvania	27
21	Alaska	26
21	South Carolina	26
23	Kentucky	25
23	Maine	25
23	Ohio	25
23	Texas	25
27	Alabama	24
27	Florida	24
27	Minnesota	24
27	Missouri	24
27	Washington	24
32	Montana	23
32	Nevada	23
32	New Mexico	23
32	Wisconsin	23
36	Arizona	22
36	Delaware	22
36	Indiana	22
36	Mississippi	22
36	Nebraska	22
36	Utah	22
36	West Virginia	22
43	Kansas	21
43	Wyoming	21
45	Arkansas	19
45	South Dakota	19
47	Idaho	18
47	Oklahoma	18
49	North Dakota	16
50	Iowa	14

District of Columbia   67

Source: CQ Press using data from American Medical Association (Chicago, Illinois)
"Physician Characteristics and Distribution in the U.S." (2009 Edition)
*As of December 31, 2007. National rate does not include physicians in U.S. territories and possessions. Obstetrics and Gynecology includes Gynecology and Oncology, Maternal and Fetal Medicine, and Reproductive Endocrinology.

Physicians in Ophthalmology in 2007

National Total = 17,999 Physicians*

<table>
<tr><td colspan="4">ALPHA ORDER</td><td colspan="4">RANK ORDER</td></tr>
<tr><th>RANK</th><th>STATE</th><th>PHYSICIANS</th><th>% of USA</th><th>RANK</th><th>STATE</th><th>PHYSICIANS</th><th>% of USA</th></tr>
<tr><td>27</td><td>Alabama</td><td>221</td><td>1.2%</td><td>1</td><td>California</td><td>2,198</td><td>12.2%</td></tr>
<tr><td>49</td><td>Alaska</td><td>30</td><td>0.2%</td><td>2</td><td>New York</td><td>1,766</td><td>9.8%</td></tr>
<tr><td>24</td><td>Arizona</td><td>274</td><td>1.5%</td><td>3</td><td>Florida</td><td>1,177</td><td>6.5%</td></tr>
<tr><td>34</td><td>Arkansas</td><td>134</td><td>0.7%</td><td>4</td><td>Texas</td><td>1,129</td><td>6.3%</td></tr>
<tr><td>1</td><td>California</td><td>2,198</td><td>12.2%</td><td>5</td><td>Pennsylvania</td><td>856</td><td>4.8%</td></tr>
<tr><td>23</td><td>Colorado</td><td>277</td><td>1.5%</td><td>6</td><td>Illinois</td><td>734</td><td>4.1%</td></tr>
<tr><td>20</td><td>Connecticut</td><td>304</td><td>1.7%</td><td>7</td><td>Ohio</td><td>638</td><td>3.5%</td></tr>
<tr><td>45</td><td>Delaware</td><td>41</td><td>0.2%</td><td>8</td><td>New Jersey</td><td>614</td><td>3.4%</td></tr>
<tr><td>3</td><td>Florida</td><td>1,177</td><td>6.5%</td><td>9</td><td>Michigan</td><td>567</td><td>3.2%</td></tr>
<tr><td>14</td><td>Georgia</td><td>422</td><td>2.3%</td><td>10</td><td>Maryland</td><td>530</td><td>2.9%</td></tr>
<tr><td>35</td><td>Hawaii</td><td>100</td><td>0.6%</td><td>11</td><td>Massachusetts</td><td>523</td><td>2.9%</td></tr>
<tr><td>43</td><td>Idaho</td><td>57</td><td>0.3%</td><td>12</td><td>North Carolina</td><td>478</td><td>2.7%</td></tr>
<tr><td>6</td><td>Illinois</td><td>734</td><td>4.1%</td><td>13</td><td>Virginia</td><td>464</td><td>2.6%</td></tr>
<tr><td>22</td><td>Indiana</td><td>278</td><td>1.5%</td><td>14</td><td>Georgia</td><td>422</td><td>2.3%</td></tr>
<tr><td>29</td><td>Iowa</td><td>157</td><td>0.9%</td><td>15</td><td>Tennessee</td><td>338</td><td>1.9%</td></tr>
<tr><td>30</td><td>Kansas</td><td>151</td><td>0.8%</td><td>15</td><td>Washington</td><td>338</td><td>1.9%</td></tr>
<tr><td>28</td><td>Kentucky</td><td>188</td><td>1.0%</td><td>17</td><td>Wisconsin</td><td>326</td><td>1.8%</td></tr>
<tr><td>21</td><td>Louisiana</td><td>293</td><td>1.6%</td><td>18</td><td>Missouri</td><td>323</td><td>1.8%</td></tr>
<tr><td>41</td><td>Maine</td><td>72</td><td>0.4%</td><td>19</td><td>Minnesota</td><td>305</td><td>1.7%</td></tr>
<tr><td>10</td><td>Maryland</td><td>530</td><td>2.9%</td><td>20</td><td>Connecticut</td><td>304</td><td>1.7%</td></tr>
<tr><td>11</td><td>Massachusetts</td><td>523</td><td>2.9%</td><td>21</td><td>Louisiana</td><td>293</td><td>1.6%</td></tr>
<tr><td>9</td><td>Michigan</td><td>567</td><td>3.2%</td><td>22</td><td>Indiana</td><td>278</td><td>1.5%</td></tr>
<tr><td>19</td><td>Minnesota</td><td>305</td><td>1.7%</td><td>23</td><td>Colorado</td><td>277</td><td>1.5%</td></tr>
<tr><td>32</td><td>Mississippi</td><td>138</td><td>0.8%</td><td>24</td><td>Arizona</td><td>274</td><td>1.5%</td></tr>
<tr><td>18</td><td>Missouri</td><td>323</td><td>1.8%</td><td>25</td><td>South Carolina</td><td>245</td><td>1.4%</td></tr>
<tr><td>44</td><td>Montana</td><td>48</td><td>0.3%</td><td>26</td><td>Oregon</td><td>236</td><td>1.3%</td></tr>
<tr><td>38</td><td>Nebraska</td><td>94</td><td>0.5%</td><td>27</td><td>Alabama</td><td>221</td><td>1.2%</td></tr>
<tr><td>37</td><td>Nevada</td><td>95</td><td>0.5%</td><td>28</td><td>Kentucky</td><td>188</td><td>1.0%</td></tr>
<tr><td>42</td><td>New Hampshire</td><td>67</td><td>0.4%</td><td>29</td><td>Iowa</td><td>157</td><td>0.9%</td></tr>
<tr><td>8</td><td>New Jersey</td><td>614</td><td>3.4%</td><td>30</td><td>Kansas</td><td>151</td><td>0.8%</td></tr>
<tr><td>40</td><td>New Mexico</td><td>77</td><td>0.4%</td><td>31</td><td>Oklahoma</td><td>148</td><td>0.8%</td></tr>
<tr><td>2</td><td>New York</td><td>1,766</td><td>9.8%</td><td>32</td><td>Mississippi</td><td>138</td><td>0.8%</td></tr>
<tr><td>12</td><td>North Carolina</td><td>478</td><td>2.7%</td><td>32</td><td>Utah</td><td>138</td><td>0.8%</td></tr>
<tr><td>48</td><td>North Dakota</td><td>32</td><td>0.2%</td><td>34</td><td>Arkansas</td><td>134</td><td>0.7%</td></tr>
<tr><td>7</td><td>Ohio</td><td>638</td><td>3.5%</td><td>35</td><td>Hawaii</td><td>100</td><td>0.6%</td></tr>
<tr><td>31</td><td>Oklahoma</td><td>148</td><td>0.8%</td><td>36</td><td>West Virginia</td><td>96</td><td>0.5%</td></tr>
<tr><td>26</td><td>Oregon</td><td>236</td><td>1.3%</td><td>37</td><td>Nevada</td><td>95</td><td>0.5%</td></tr>
<tr><td>5</td><td>Pennsylvania</td><td>856</td><td>4.8%</td><td>38</td><td>Nebraska</td><td>94</td><td>0.5%</td></tr>
<tr><td>39</td><td>Rhode Island</td><td>80</td><td>0.4%</td><td>39</td><td>Rhode Island</td><td>80</td><td>0.4%</td></tr>
<tr><td>25</td><td>South Carolina</td><td>245</td><td>1.4%</td><td>40</td><td>New Mexico</td><td>77</td><td>0.4%</td></tr>
<tr><td>46</td><td>South Dakota</td><td>40</td><td>0.2%</td><td>41</td><td>Maine</td><td>72</td><td>0.4%</td></tr>
<tr><td>15</td><td>Tennessee</td><td>338</td><td>1.9%</td><td>42</td><td>New Hampshire</td><td>67</td><td>0.4%</td></tr>
<tr><td>4</td><td>Texas</td><td>1,129</td><td>6.3%</td><td>43</td><td>Idaho</td><td>57</td><td>0.3%</td></tr>
<tr><td>32</td><td>Utah</td><td>138</td><td>0.8%</td><td>44</td><td>Montana</td><td>48</td><td>0.3%</td></tr>
<tr><td>47</td><td>Vermont</td><td>37</td><td>0.2%</td><td>45</td><td>Delaware</td><td>41</td><td>0.2%</td></tr>
<tr><td>13</td><td>Virginia</td><td>464</td><td>2.6%</td><td>46</td><td>South Dakota</td><td>40</td><td>0.2%</td></tr>
<tr><td>15</td><td>Washington</td><td>338</td><td>1.9%</td><td>47</td><td>Vermont</td><td>37</td><td>0.2%</td></tr>
<tr><td>36</td><td>West Virginia</td><td>96</td><td>0.5%</td><td>48</td><td>North Dakota</td><td>32</td><td>0.2%</td></tr>
<tr><td>17</td><td>Wisconsin</td><td>326</td><td>1.8%</td><td>49</td><td>Alaska</td><td>30</td><td>0.2%</td></tr>
<tr><td>50</td><td>Wyoming</td><td>17</td><td>0.1%</td><td>50</td><td>Wyoming</td><td>17</td><td>0.1%</td></tr>
<tr><td></td><td></td><td></td><td></td><td colspan="2">District of Columbia</td><td>108</td><td>0.6%</td></tr>
</table>

Source: American Medical Association (Chicago, Illinois)
"Physician Characteristics and Distribution in the U.S." (2009 Edition)
*As of December 31, 2007. Total does not include 185 physicians in U.S. territories and possessions. Ophthalmology is the branch of medicine dealing with the anatomy, functions, and diseases of the eye.

Rate of Physicians in Ophthalmology in 2007

National Rate = 6 Physicians per 100,000 Population*

ALPHA ORDER

RANK	STATE	RATE
22	Alabama	5
41	Alaska	4
41	Arizona	4
22	Arkansas	5
10	California	6
10	Colorado	6
1	Connecticut	9
22	Delaware	5
10	Florida	6
41	Georgia	4
4	Hawaii	8
41	Idaho	4
10	Illinois	6
41	Indiana	4
22	Iowa	5
22	Kansas	5
41	Kentucky	4
7	Louisiana	7
22	Maine	5
1	Maryland	9
4	Massachusetts	8
10	Michigan	6
10	Minnesota	6
22	Mississippi	5
22	Missouri	5
22	Montana	5
22	Nebraska	5
41	Nevada	4
22	New Hampshire	5
7	New Jersey	7
41	New Mexico	4
1	New York	9
22	North Carolina	5
22	North Dakota	5
10	Ohio	6
41	Oklahoma	4
10	Oregon	6
7	Pennsylvania	7
4	Rhode Island	8
10	South Carolina	6
22	South Dakota	5
22	Tennessee	5
22	Texas	5
22	Utah	5
10	Vermont	6
10	Virginia	6
22	Washington	5
22	West Virginia	5
10	Wisconsin	6
50	Wyoming	3

RANK ORDER

RANK	STATE	RATE
1	Connecticut	9
1	Maryland	9
1	New York	9
4	Hawaii	8
4	Massachusetts	8
4	Rhode Island	8
7	Louisiana	7
7	New Jersey	7
7	Pennsylvania	7
10	California	6
10	Colorado	6
10	Florida	6
10	Illinois	6
10	Michigan	6
10	Minnesota	6
10	Ohio	6
10	Oregon	6
10	South Carolina	6
10	Vermont	6
10	Virginia	6
10	Wisconsin	6
22	Alabama	5
22	Arkansas	5
22	Delaware	5
22	Iowa	5
22	Kansas	5
22	Maine	5
22	Mississippi	5
22	Missouri	5
22	Montana	5
22	Nebraska	5
22	New Hampshire	5
22	North Carolina	5
22	North Dakota	5
22	South Dakota	5
22	Tennessee	5
22	Texas	5
22	Utah	5
22	Washington	5
22	West Virginia	5
41	Alaska	4
41	Arizona	4
41	Georgia	4
41	Idaho	4
41	Indiana	4
41	Kentucky	4
41	Nevada	4
41	New Mexico	4
41	Oklahoma	4
50	Wyoming	3
	District of Columbia	18

Source: CQ Press using data from American Medical Association (Chicago, Illinois)
"Physician Characteristics and Distribution in the U.S." (2009 Edition)
*As of December 31, 2007. National rate does not include physicians in U.S. territories and possessions. Ophthalmology is the branch of medicine dealing with the anatomy, functions, and diseases of the eye.

Physicians in Orthopedic Surgery in 2007

National Total = 24,316 Physicians*

ALPHA ORDER

RANK	STATE	PHYSICIANS	% of USA	RANK	STATE	PHYSICIANS	% of USA
24	Alabama	380	1.6%	1	California	2,918	12.0%
45	Alaska	76	0.3%	2	New York	1,860	7.6%
23	Arizona	383	1.6%	3	Texas	1,591	6.5%
34	Arkansas	179	0.7%	4	Florida	1,334	5.5%
1	California	2,918	12.0%	5	Pennsylvania	1,063	4.4%
20	Colorado	449	1.8%	6	Illinois	943	3.9%
26	Connecticut	366	1.5%	7	Ohio	899	3.7%
47	Delaware	67	0.3%	8	Massachusetts	759	3.1%
4	Florida	1,334	5.5%	9	North Carolina	737	3.0%
13	Georgia	614	2.5%	10	New Jersey	721	3.0%
40	Hawaii	126	0.5%	11	Virginia	622	2.6%
40	Idaho	126	0.5%	12	Michigan	616	2.5%
6	Illinois	943	3.9%	13	Georgia	614	2.5%
21	Indiana	447	1.8%	14	Maryland	600	2.5%
32	Iowa	193	0.8%	15	Washington	553	2.3%
30	Kansas	226	0.9%	16	Tennessee	538	2.2%
28	Kentucky	319	1.3%	17	Minnesota	516	2.1%
22	Louisiana	392	1.6%	18	Wisconsin	504	2.1%
39	Maine	130	0.5%	19	Missouri	463	1.9%
14	Maryland	600	2.5%	20	Colorado	449	1.8%
8	Massachusetts	759	3.1%	21	Indiana	447	1.8%
12	Michigan	616	2.5%	22	Louisiana	392	1.6%
17	Minnesota	516	2.1%	23	Arizona	383	1.6%
33	Mississippi	180	0.7%	24	Alabama	380	1.6%
19	Missouri	463	1.9%	25	South Carolina	368	1.5%
44	Montana	113	0.5%	26	Connecticut	366	1.5%
35	Nebraska	161	0.7%	27	Oregon	322	1.3%
38	Nevada	136	0.6%	28	Kentucky	319	1.3%
37	New Hampshire	138	0.6%	29	Oklahoma	227	0.9%
10	New Jersey	721	3.0%	30	Kansas	226	0.9%
36	New Mexico	148	0.6%	31	Utah	214	0.9%
2	New York	1,860	7.6%	32	Iowa	193	0.8%
9	North Carolina	737	3.0%	33	Mississippi	180	0.7%
50	North Dakota	51	0.2%	34	Arkansas	179	0.7%
7	Ohio	899	3.7%	35	Nebraska	161	0.7%
29	Oklahoma	227	0.9%	36	New Mexico	148	0.6%
27	Oregon	322	1.3%	37	New Hampshire	138	0.6%
5	Pennsylvania	1,063	4.4%	38	Nevada	136	0.6%
43	Rhode Island	119	0.5%	39	Maine	130	0.5%
25	South Carolina	368	1.5%	40	Hawaii	126	0.5%
47	South Dakota	67	0.3%	40	Idaho	126	0.5%
16	Tennessee	538	2.2%	42	West Virginia	123	0.5%
3	Texas	1,591	6.5%	43	Rhode Island	119	0.5%
31	Utah	214	0.9%	44	Montana	113	0.5%
45	Vermont	76	0.3%	45	Alaska	76	0.3%
11	Virginia	622	2.6%	45	Vermont	76	0.3%
15	Washington	553	2.3%	47	Delaware	67	0.3%
42	West Virginia	123	0.5%	47	South Dakota	67	0.3%
18	Wisconsin	504	2.1%	49	Wyoming	60	0.2%
49	Wyoming	60	0.2%	50	North Dakota	51	0.2%
					District of Columbia	103	0.4%

Source: American Medical Association (Chicago, Illinois)
    "Physician Characteristics and Distribution in the U.S." (2009 Edition)
*As of December 31, 2007. Total does not include 169 physicians in U.S. territories and possessions. Orthopedics is the branch of medicine dealing with the skeletal system.

Rate of Physicians in Orthopedic Surgery in 2007

National Rate = 8 Physicians per 100,000 Population*

ALPHA ORDER

RANK	STATE	RATE
22	Alabama	8
4	Alaska	11
43	Arizona	6
43	Arkansas	6
22	California	8
14	Colorado	9
9	Connecticut	10
22	Delaware	8
38	Florida	7
43	Georgia	6
9	Hawaii	10
22	Idaho	8
38	Illinois	7
38	Indiana	7
43	Iowa	6
22	Kansas	8
22	Kentucky	8
14	Louisiana	9
9	Maine	10
4	Maryland	11
1	Massachusetts	12
43	Michigan	6
9	Minnesota	10
43	Mississippi	6
22	Missouri	8
1	Montana	12
14	Nebraska	9
50	Nevada	5
4	New Hampshire	11
22	New Jersey	8
22	New Mexico	8
9	New York	10
22	North Carolina	8
22	North Dakota	8
22	Ohio	8
43	Oklahoma	6
14	Oregon	9
14	Pennsylvania	9
4	Rhode Island	11
22	South Carolina	8
22	South Dakota	8
14	Tennessee	9
38	Texas	7
22	Utah	8
1	Vermont	12
22	Virginia	8
14	Washington	9
38	West Virginia	7
14	Wisconsin	9
4	Wyoming	11

RANK ORDER

RANK	STATE	RATE
1	Massachusetts	12
1	Montana	12
1	Vermont	12
4	Alaska	11
4	Maryland	11
4	New Hampshire	11
4	Rhode Island	11
4	Wyoming	11
9	Connecticut	10
9	Hawaii	10
9	Maine	10
9	Minnesota	10
9	New York	10
14	Colorado	9
14	Louisiana	9
14	Nebraska	9
14	Oregon	9
14	Pennsylvania	9
14	Tennessee	9
14	Washington	9
14	Wisconsin	9
22	Alabama	8
22	California	8
22	Delaware	8
22	Idaho	8
22	Kansas	8
22	Kentucky	8
22	Missouri	8
22	New Jersey	8
22	New Mexico	8
22	North Carolina	8
22	North Dakota	8
22	Ohio	8
22	South Carolina	8
22	South Dakota	8
22	Utah	8
22	Virginia	8
38	Florida	7
38	Illinois	7
38	Indiana	7
38	Texas	7
38	West Virginia	7
43	Arizona	6
43	Arkansas	6
43	Georgia	6
43	Iowa	6
43	Michigan	6
43	Mississippi	6
43	Oklahoma	6
50	Nevada	5
	District of Columbia	18

Source: CQ Press using data from American Medical Association (Chicago, Illinois)
"Physician Characteristics and Distribution in the U.S." (2009 Edition)
*As of December 31, 2007. National rate does not include physicians in U.S. territories and possessions. Orthopedics is the branch of medicine dealing with the skeletal system.

Physicians in Plastic Surgery in 2007

National Total = 7,131 Physicians*

RANK	STATE	PHYSICIANS	% of USA
27	Alabama	81	1.1%
49	Alaska	7	0.1%
17	Arizona	137	1.9%
35	Arkansas	31	0.4%
1	California	1,094	15.3%
19	Colorado	110	1.5%
23	Connecticut	95	1.3%
41	Delaware	24	0.3%
3	Florida	599	8.4%
10	Georgia	192	2.7%
38	Hawaii	29	0.4%
43	Idaho	18	0.3%
6	Illinois	258	3.6%
20	Indiana	104	1.5%
35	Iowa	31	0.4%
30	Kansas	65	0.9%
24	Kentucky	92	1.3%
25	Louisiana	90	1.3%
44	Maine	17	0.2%
12	Maryland	179	2.5%
10	Massachusetts	192	2.7%
9	Michigan	210	2.9%
22	Minnesota	96	1.3%
31	Mississippi	47	0.7%
16	Missouri	139	1.9%
45	Montana	16	0.2%
38	Nebraska	29	0.4%
32	Nevada	45	0.6%
41	New Hampshire	24	0.3%
7	New Jersey	226	3.2%
34	New Mexico	35	0.5%
2	New York	625	8.8%
12	North Carolina	179	2.5%
47	North Dakota	12	0.2%
8	Ohio	220	3.1%
33	Oklahoma	44	0.6%
29	Oregon	67	0.9%
5	Pennsylvania	276	3.9%
35	Rhode Island	31	0.4%
26	South Carolina	86	1.2%
46	South Dakota	13	0.2%
15	Tennessee	143	2.0%
4	Texas	559	7.8%
28	Utah	79	1.1%
48	Vermont	9	0.1%
14	Virginia	176	2.5%
18	Washington	125	1.8%
38	West Virginia	29	0.4%
21	Wisconsin	101	1.4%
50	Wyoming	4	0.1%

RANK	STATE	PHYSICIANS	% of USA
1	California	1,094	15.3%
2	New York	625	8.8%
3	Florida	599	8.4%
4	Texas	559	7.8%
5	Pennsylvania	276	3.9%
6	Illinois	258	3.6%
7	New Jersey	226	3.2%
8	Ohio	220	3.1%
9	Michigan	210	2.9%
10	Georgia	192	2.7%
10	Massachusetts	192	2.7%
12	Maryland	179	2.5%
12	North Carolina	179	2.5%
14	Virginia	176	2.5%
15	Tennessee	143	2.0%
16	Missouri	139	1.9%
17	Arizona	137	1.9%
18	Washington	125	1.8%
19	Colorado	110	1.5%
20	Indiana	104	1.5%
21	Wisconsin	101	1.4%
22	Minnesota	96	1.3%
23	Connecticut	95	1.3%
24	Kentucky	92	1.3%
25	Louisiana	90	1.3%
26	South Carolina	86	1.2%
27	Alabama	81	1.1%
28	Utah	79	1.1%
29	Oregon	67	0.9%
30	Kansas	65	0.9%
31	Mississippi	47	0.7%
32	Nevada	45	0.6%
33	Oklahoma	44	0.6%
34	New Mexico	35	0.5%
35	Arkansas	31	0.4%
35	Iowa	31	0.4%
35	Rhode Island	31	0.4%
38	Hawaii	29	0.4%
38	Nebraska	29	0.4%
38	West Virginia	29	0.4%
41	Delaware	24	0.3%
41	New Hampshire	24	0.3%
43	Idaho	18	0.3%
44	Maine	17	0.2%
45	Montana	16	0.2%
46	South Dakota	13	0.2%
47	North Dakota	12	0.2%
48	Vermont	9	0.1%
49	Alaska	7	0.1%
50	Wyoming	4	0.1%
	District of Columbia	41	0.6%

Source: American Medical Association (Chicago, Illinois)
"Physician Characteristics and Distribution in the U.S." (2009 Edition)
*As of December 31, 2007. Total does not include 30 physicians in U.S. territories and possessions.

Rate of Physicians in Plastic Surgery in 2007

National Rate = 2 Physicians per 100,000 Population*

<table>
<tr><td colspan="3">ALPHA ORDER</td><td colspan="3">RANK ORDER</td></tr>
<tr><th>RANK</th><th>STATE</th><th>RATE</th><th>RANK</th><th>STATE</th><th>RATE</th></tr>
<tr><td>11</td><td>Alabama</td><td>2</td><td>1</td><td>California</td><td>3</td></tr>
<tr><td>43</td><td>Alaska</td><td>1</td><td>1</td><td>Connecticut</td><td>3</td></tr>
<tr><td>11</td><td>Arizona</td><td>2</td><td>1</td><td>Delaware</td><td>3</td></tr>
<tr><td>43</td><td>Arkansas</td><td>1</td><td>1</td><td>Florida</td><td>3</td></tr>
<tr><td>1</td><td>California</td><td>3</td><td>1</td><td>Maryland</td><td>3</td></tr>
<tr><td>11</td><td>Colorado</td><td>2</td><td>1</td><td>Massachusetts</td><td>3</td></tr>
<tr><td>1</td><td>Connecticut</td><td>3</td><td>1</td><td>New Jersey</td><td>3</td></tr>
<tr><td>1</td><td>Delaware</td><td>3</td><td>1</td><td>New York</td><td>3</td></tr>
<tr><td>1</td><td>Florida</td><td>3</td><td>1</td><td>Rhode Island</td><td>3</td></tr>
<tr><td>11</td><td>Georgia</td><td>2</td><td>1</td><td>Utah</td><td>3</td></tr>
<tr><td>11</td><td>Hawaii</td><td>2</td><td>11</td><td>Alabama</td><td>2</td></tr>
<tr><td>43</td><td>Idaho</td><td>1</td><td>11</td><td>Arizona</td><td>2</td></tr>
<tr><td>11</td><td>Illinois</td><td>2</td><td>11</td><td>Colorado</td><td>2</td></tr>
<tr><td>11</td><td>Indiana</td><td>2</td><td>11</td><td>Georgia</td><td>2</td></tr>
<tr><td>43</td><td>Iowa</td><td>1</td><td>11</td><td>Hawaii</td><td>2</td></tr>
<tr><td>11</td><td>Kansas</td><td>2</td><td>11</td><td>Illinois</td><td>2</td></tr>
<tr><td>11</td><td>Kentucky</td><td>2</td><td>11</td><td>Indiana</td><td>2</td></tr>
<tr><td>11</td><td>Louisiana</td><td>2</td><td>11</td><td>Kansas</td><td>2</td></tr>
<tr><td>43</td><td>Maine</td><td>1</td><td>11</td><td>Kentucky</td><td>2</td></tr>
<tr><td>1</td><td>Maryland</td><td>3</td><td>11</td><td>Louisiana</td><td>2</td></tr>
<tr><td>1</td><td>Massachusetts</td><td>3</td><td>11</td><td>Michigan</td><td>2</td></tr>
<tr><td>11</td><td>Michigan</td><td>2</td><td>11</td><td>Minnesota</td><td>2</td></tr>
<tr><td>11</td><td>Minnesota</td><td>2</td><td>11</td><td>Mississippi</td><td>2</td></tr>
<tr><td>11</td><td>Mississippi</td><td>2</td><td>11</td><td>Missouri</td><td>2</td></tr>
<tr><td>11</td><td>Missouri</td><td>2</td><td>11</td><td>Montana</td><td>2</td></tr>
<tr><td>11</td><td>Montana</td><td>2</td><td>11</td><td>Nebraska</td><td>2</td></tr>
<tr><td>11</td><td>Nebraska</td><td>2</td><td>11</td><td>Nevada</td><td>2</td></tr>
<tr><td>11</td><td>Nevada</td><td>2</td><td>11</td><td>New Hampshire</td><td>2</td></tr>
<tr><td>11</td><td>New Hampshire</td><td>2</td><td>11</td><td>New Mexico</td><td>2</td></tr>
<tr><td>1</td><td>New Jersey</td><td>3</td><td>11</td><td>North Carolina</td><td>2</td></tr>
<tr><td>11</td><td>New Mexico</td><td>2</td><td>11</td><td>North Dakota</td><td>2</td></tr>
<tr><td>1</td><td>New York</td><td>3</td><td>11</td><td>Ohio</td><td>2</td></tr>
<tr><td>11</td><td>North Carolina</td><td>2</td><td>11</td><td>Oregon</td><td>2</td></tr>
<tr><td>11</td><td>North Dakota</td><td>2</td><td>11</td><td>Pennsylvania</td><td>2</td></tr>
<tr><td>11</td><td>Ohio</td><td>2</td><td>11</td><td>South Carolina</td><td>2</td></tr>
<tr><td>43</td><td>Oklahoma</td><td>1</td><td>11</td><td>South Dakota</td><td>2</td></tr>
<tr><td>11</td><td>Oregon</td><td>2</td><td>11</td><td>Tennessee</td><td>2</td></tr>
<tr><td>11</td><td>Pennsylvania</td><td>2</td><td>11</td><td>Texas</td><td>2</td></tr>
<tr><td>1</td><td>Rhode Island</td><td>3</td><td>11</td><td>Virginia</td><td>2</td></tr>
<tr><td>11</td><td>South Carolina</td><td>2</td><td>11</td><td>Washington</td><td>2</td></tr>
<tr><td>11</td><td>South Dakota</td><td>2</td><td>11</td><td>West Virginia</td><td>2</td></tr>
<tr><td>11</td><td>Tennessee</td><td>2</td><td>11</td><td>Wisconsin</td><td>2</td></tr>
<tr><td>11</td><td>Texas</td><td>2</td><td>43</td><td>Alaska</td><td>1</td></tr>
<tr><td>1</td><td>Utah</td><td>3</td><td>43</td><td>Arkansas</td><td>1</td></tr>
<tr><td>43</td><td>Vermont</td><td>1</td><td>43</td><td>Idaho</td><td>1</td></tr>
<tr><td>11</td><td>Virginia</td><td>2</td><td>43</td><td>Iowa</td><td>1</td></tr>
<tr><td>11</td><td>Washington</td><td>2</td><td>43</td><td>Maine</td><td>1</td></tr>
<tr><td>11</td><td>West Virginia</td><td>2</td><td>43</td><td>Oklahoma</td><td>1</td></tr>
<tr><td>11</td><td>Wisconsin</td><td>2</td><td>43</td><td>Vermont</td><td>1</td></tr>
<tr><td>43</td><td>Wyoming</td><td>1</td><td>43</td><td>Wyoming</td><td>1</td></tr>
<tr><td></td><td></td><td></td><td></td><td>District of Columbia</td><td>7</td></tr>
</table>

Source: CQ Press using data from American Medical Association (Chicago, Illinois)
   "Physician Characteristics and Distribution in the U.S." (2009 Edition)
*As of December 31, 2005. National rate does not include physicians in U.S. territories and possessions.

Physicians in Other Specialties in 2007

National Total = 221,743 Physicians*

ALPHA ORDER

RANK	STATE	PHYSICIANS	% of USA
28	Alabama	2,450	1.1%
47	Alaska	428	0.2%
19	Arizona	3,841	1.7%
32	Arkansas	1,452	0.7%
1	California	27,474	12.4%
23	Colorado	3,652	1.6%
22	Connecticut	3,700	1.7%
45	Delaware	595	0.3%
4	Florida	12,088	5.5%
14	Georgia	5,466	2.5%
37	Hawaii	1,187	0.5%
43	Idaho	681	0.3%
6	Illinois	9,427	4.3%
21	Indiana	3,775	1.7%
33	Iowa	1,445	0.7%
29	Kansas	1,678	0.8%
27	Kentucky	2,613	1.2%
25	Louisiana	2,839	1.3%
40	Maine	1,055	0.5%
10	Maryland	6,825	3.1%
7	Massachusetts	8,938	4.0%
11	Michigan	6,683	3.0%
18	Minnesota	3,858	1.7%
36	Mississippi	1,285	0.6%
20	Missouri	3,840	1.7%
46	Montana	576	0.3%
38	Nebraska	1,069	0.5%
34	Nevada	1,356	0.6%
42	New Hampshire	971	0.4%
9	New Jersey	7,128	3.2%
35	New Mexico	1,344	0.6%
2	New York	21,104	9.5%
12	North Carolina	6,047	2.7%
49	North Dakota	397	0.2%
8	Ohio	7,938	3.6%
30	Oklahoma	1,614	0.7%
24	Oregon	2,880	1.3%
5	Pennsylvania	10,628	4.8%
41	Rhode Island	1,039	0.5%
26	South Carolina	2,670	1.2%
48	South Dakota	414	0.2%
17	Tennessee	4,009	1.8%
3	Texas	13,553	6.1%
31	Utah	1,601	0.7%
44	Vermont	674	0.3%
13	Virginia	5,785	2.6%
15	Washington	4,964	2.2%
38	West Virginia	1,069	0.5%
16	Wisconsin	4,035	1.8%
50	Wyoming	259	0.1%

RANK ORDER

RANK	STATE	PHYSICIANS	% of USA
1	California	27,474	12.4%
2	New York	21,104	9.5%
3	Texas	13,553	6.1%
4	Florida	12,088	5.5%
5	Pennsylvania	10,628	4.8%
6	Illinois	9,427	4.3%
7	Massachusetts	8,938	4.0%
8	Ohio	7,938	3.6%
9	New Jersey	7,128	3.2%
10	Maryland	6,825	3.1%
11	Michigan	6,683	3.0%
12	North Carolina	6,047	2.7%
13	Virginia	5,785	2.6%
14	Georgia	5,466	2.5%
15	Washington	4,964	2.2%
16	Wisconsin	4,035	1.8%
17	Tennessee	4,009	1.8%
18	Minnesota	3,858	1.7%
19	Arizona	3,841	1.7%
20	Missouri	3,840	1.7%
21	Indiana	3,775	1.7%
22	Connecticut	3,700	1.7%
23	Colorado	3,652	1.6%
24	Oregon	2,880	1.3%
25	Louisiana	2,839	1.3%
26	South Carolina	2,670	1.2%
27	Kentucky	2,613	1.2%
28	Alabama	2,450	1.1%
29	Kansas	1,678	0.8%
30	Oklahoma	1,614	0.7%
31	Utah	1,601	0.7%
32	Arkansas	1,452	0.7%
33	Iowa	1,445	0.7%
34	Nevada	1,356	0.6%
35	New Mexico	1,344	0.6%
36	Mississippi	1,285	0.6%
37	Hawaii	1,187	0.5%
38	Nebraska	1,069	0.5%
38	West Virginia	1,069	0.5%
40	Maine	1,055	0.5%
41	Rhode Island	1,039	0.5%
42	New Hampshire	971	0.4%
43	Idaho	681	0.3%
44	Vermont	674	0.3%
45	Delaware	595	0.3%
46	Montana	576	0.3%
47	Alaska	428	0.2%
48	South Dakota	414	0.2%
49	North Dakota	397	0.2%
50	Wyoming	259	0.1%
	District of Columbia	1,344	0.6%

Source: American Medical Association (Chicago, Illinois)
"Physician Characteristics and Distribution in the U.S." (2009 Edition)
*As of December 31, 2007. Total does not include 3,170 physicians in U.S. territories and possessions. Other Specialties include Aerospace Medicine, Anatomic/Clinical Pathology, Anesthesiology, Child Psychiatry, Diagnostic Radiology, Emergency Medicine, Forensic Pathology, Nuclear Medicine, Occupational Medicine, Neurology, Psychiatry, Public Health, Radiation Oncology, Radiology, and other specialties.

Rate of Physicians in Other Specialties in 2007

National Rate = 74 Physicians per 100,000 Population*

ALPHA ORDER

RANK	STATE	RATE
42	Alabama	53
29	Alaska	63
33	Arizona	60
45	Arkansas	51
13	California	76
14	Colorado	75
5	Connecticut	106
20	Delaware	69
24	Florida	66
40	Georgia	57
7	Hawaii	93
48	Idaho	46
16	Illinois	74
33	Indiana	60
47	Iowa	48
33	Kansas	60
30	Kentucky	62
26	Louisiana	65
10	Maine	80
2	Maryland	121
1	Massachusetts	138
24	Michigan	66
16	Minnesota	74
50	Mississippi	44
26	Missouri	65
33	Montana	60
33	Nebraska	60
42	Nevada	53
16	New Hampshire	74
9	New Jersey	82
22	New Mexico	68
3	New York	109
23	North Carolina	67
30	North Dakota	62
20	Ohio	69
49	Oklahoma	45
11	Oregon	77
8	Pennsylvania	86
6	Rhode Island	99
32	South Carolina	61
44	South Dakota	52
26	Tennessee	65
40	Texas	57
33	Utah	60
3	Vermont	109
14	Virginia	75
11	Washington	77
39	West Virginia	59
19	Wisconsin	72
46	Wyoming	49

RANK ORDER

RANK	STATE	RATE
1	Massachusetts	138
2	Maryland	121
3	New York	109
3	Vermont	109
5	Connecticut	106
6	Rhode Island	99
7	Hawaii	93
8	Pennsylvania	86
9	New Jersey	82
10	Maine	80
11	Oregon	77
11	Washington	77
13	California	76
14	Colorado	75
14	Virginia	75
16	Illinois	74
16	Minnesota	74
16	New Hampshire	74
19	Wisconsin	72
20	Delaware	69
20	Ohio	69
22	New Mexico	68
23	North Carolina	67
24	Florida	66
24	Michigan	66
26	Louisiana	65
26	Missouri	65
26	Tennessee	65
29	Alaska	63
30	Kentucky	62
30	North Dakota	62
32	South Carolina	61
33	Arizona	60
33	Indiana	60
33	Kansas	60
33	Montana	60
33	Nebraska	60
33	Utah	60
39	West Virginia	59
40	Georgia	57
40	Texas	57
42	Alabama	53
42	Nevada	53
44	South Dakota	52
45	Arkansas	51
46	Wyoming	49
47	Iowa	48
48	Idaho	46
49	Oklahoma	45
50	Mississippi	44

District of Columbia   229

Source: CQ Press using data from American Medical Association (Chicago, Illinois)
   "Physician Characteristics and Distribution in the U.S." (2009 Edition)
*As of December 31, 2007. National rate does not include physicians in U.S. territories and possessions. Other Specialties include Aerospace Medicine, Anatomic/Clinical Pathology, Anesthesiology, Child Psychiatry, Diagnostic Radiology, Emergency Medicine, Forensic Pathology, Nuclear Medicine, Occupational Medicine, Neurology, Psychiatry, Public Health, Radiation Oncology, Radiology, and other specialties.

Physicians in Anesthesiology in 2007

National Total = 41,346 Physicians*

ALPHA ORDER

RANK	STATE	PHYSICIANS	% of USA
27	Alabama	483	1.2%
46	Alaska	85	0.2%
17	Arizona	893	2.2%
34	Arkansas	302	0.7%
1	California	5,226	12.6%
20	Colorado	736	1.8%
23	Connecticut	575	1.4%
45	Delaware	90	0.2%
4	Florida	2,608	6.3%
15	Georgia	968	2.3%
40	Hawaii	156	0.4%
43	Idaho	112	0.3%
5	Illinois	1,861	4.5%
16	Indiana	951	2.3%
33	Iowa	312	0.8%
32	Kansas	335	0.8%
25	Kentucky	555	1.3%
26	Louisiana	508	1.2%
39	Maine	178	0.4%
10	Maryland	1,053	2.5%
9	Massachusetts	1,385	3.3%
14	Michigan	978	2.4%
24	Minnesota	564	1.4%
35	Mississippi	246	0.6%
21	Missouri	709	1.7%
50	Montana	14	0.0%
36	Nebraska	226	0.5%
30	Nevada	365	0.9%
38	New Hampshire	181	0.4%
7	New Jersey	1,524	3.7%
37	New Mexico	218	0.5%
2	New York	3,487	8.4%
13	North Carolina	979	2.4%
48	North Dakota	59	0.1%
8	Ohio	1,507	3.6%
29	Oklahoma	367	0.9%
22	Oregon	587	1.4%
6	Pennsylvania	1,755	4.2%
42	Rhode Island	120	0.3%
28	South Carolina	470	1.1%
47	South Dakota	69	0.2%
19	Tennessee	774	1.9%
3	Texas	3,140	7.6%
31	Utah	362	0.9%
44	Vermont	107	0.3%
12	Virginia	983	2.4%
11	Washington	984	2.4%
41	West Virginia	150	0.4%
18	Wisconsin	844	2.0%
49	Wyoming	52	0.1%

RANK ORDER

RANK	STATE	PHYSICIANS	% of USA
1	California	5,226	12.6%
2	New York	3,487	8.4%
3	Texas	3,140	7.6%
4	Florida	2,608	6.3%
5	Illinois	1,861	4.5%
6	Pennsylvania	1,755	4.2%
7	New Jersey	1,524	3.7%
8	Ohio	1,507	3.6%
9	Massachusetts	1,385	3.3%
10	Maryland	1,053	2.5%
11	Washington	984	2.4%
12	Virginia	983	2.4%
13	North Carolina	979	2.4%
14	Michigan	978	2.4%
15	Georgia	968	2.3%
16	Indiana	951	2.3%
17	Arizona	893	2.2%
18	Wisconsin	844	2.0%
19	Tennessee	774	1.9%
20	Colorado	736	1.8%
21	Missouri	709	1.7%
22	Oregon	587	1.4%
23	Connecticut	575	1.4%
24	Minnesota	564	1.4%
25	Kentucky	555	1.3%
26	Louisiana	508	1.2%
27	Alabama	483	1.2%
28	South Carolina	470	1.1%
29	Oklahoma	367	0.9%
30	Nevada	365	0.9%
31	Utah	362	0.9%
32	Kansas	335	0.8%
33	Iowa	312	0.8%
34	Arkansas	302	0.7%
35	Mississippi	246	0.6%
36	Nebraska	226	0.5%
37	New Mexico	218	0.5%
38	New Hampshire	181	0.4%
39	Maine	178	0.4%
40	Hawaii	156	0.4%
41	West Virginia	150	0.4%
42	Rhode Island	120	0.3%
43	Idaho	112	0.3%
44	Vermont	107	0.3%
45	Delaware	90	0.2%
46	Alaska	85	0.2%
47	South Dakota	69	0.2%
48	North Dakota	59	0.1%
49	Wyoming	52	0.1%
50	Montana	14	0.0%
	District of Columbia	153	0.4%

Source: American Medical Association (Chicago, Illinois)
"Physician Characteristics and Distribution in the U.S." (2009 Edition)
*As of December 31, 2007. Total does not include 353 physicians in U.S. territories and possessions.

Rate of Physicians in Anesthesiology in 2007

National Rate = 14 Physicians per 100,000 Population*

ALPHA ORDER

RANK	STATE	RATE
38	Alabama	10
27	Alaska	12
13	Arizona	14
32	Arkansas	11
13	California	14
8	Colorado	15
6	Connecticut	16
38	Delaware	10
13	Florida	14
38	Georgia	10
27	Hawaii	12
49	Idaho	7
8	Illinois	15
8	Indiana	15
38	Iowa	10
27	Kansas	12
21	Kentucky	13
27	Louisiana	12
13	Maine	14
2	Maryland	19
1	Massachusetts	21
38	Michigan	10
32	Minnesota	11
47	Mississippi	8
27	Missouri	12
50	Montana	1
21	Nebraska	13
13	Nevada	14
13	New Hampshire	14
3	New Jersey	18
32	New Mexico	11
3	New York	18
32	North Carolina	11
45	North Dakota	9
21	Ohio	13
38	Oklahoma	10
6	Oregon	16
13	Pennsylvania	14
32	Rhode Island	11
32	South Carolina	11
45	South Dakota	9
21	Tennessee	13
21	Texas	13
13	Utah	14
5	Vermont	17
21	Virginia	13
8	Washington	15
47	West Virginia	8
8	Wisconsin	15
38	Wyoming	10

RANK ORDER

RANK	STATE	RATE
1	Massachusetts	21
2	Maryland	19
3	New Jersey	18
3	New York	18
5	Vermont	17
6	Connecticut	16
6	Oregon	16
8	Colorado	15
8	Illinois	15
8	Indiana	15
8	Washington	15
8	Wisconsin	15
13	Arizona	14
13	California	14
13	Florida	14
13	Maine	14
13	Nevada	14
13	New Hampshire	14
13	Pennsylvania	14
13	Utah	14
21	Kentucky	13
21	Nebraska	13
21	Ohio	13
21	Tennessee	13
21	Texas	13
21	Virginia	13
27	Alaska	12
27	Hawaii	12
27	Kansas	12
27	Louisiana	12
27	Missouri	12
32	Arkansas	11
32	Minnesota	11
32	New Mexico	11
32	North Carolina	11
32	Rhode Island	11
32	South Carolina	11
38	Alabama	10
38	Delaware	10
38	Georgia	10
38	Iowa	10
38	Michigan	10
38	Oklahoma	10
38	Wyoming	10
45	North Dakota	9
45	South Dakota	9
47	Mississippi	8
47	West Virginia	8
49	Idaho	7
50	Montana	1

District of Columbia	26

Source: CQ Press using data from American Medical Association (Chicago, Illinois)
"Physician Characteristics and Distribution in the U.S." (2009 Edition)
*As of December 31, 2007. National rate does not include physicians in U.S. territories and possessions.

Physicians in Psychiatry in 2007

National Total = 40,732 Physicians*

ALPHA ORDER					RANK ORDER			

RANK	STATE	PHYSICIANS	% of USA		RANK	STATE	PHYSICIANS	% of USA
27	Alabama	353	0.9%		1	California	5,668	13.9%
44	Alaska	81	0.2%		2	New York	5,596	13.7%
21	Arizona	582	1.4%		3	Massachusetts	2,151	5.3%
34	Arkansas	232	0.6%		4	Pennsylvania	1,968	4.8%
1	California	5,668	13.9%		5	Texas	1,892	4.6%
17	Colorado	624	1.5%		6	Florida	1,788	4.4%
14	Connecticut	940	2.3%		7	Illinois	1,587	3.9%
43	Delaware	97	0.2%		8	New Jersey	1,448	3.6%
6	Florida	1,788	4.4%		9	Maryland	1,409	3.5%
15	Georgia	933	2.3%		10	Ohio	1,196	2.9%
31	Hawaii	261	0.6%		11	Virginia	1,103	2.7%
46	Idaho	80	0.2%		12	Michigan	1,091	2.7%
7	Illinois	1,587	3.9%		13	North Carolina	1,071	2.6%
25	Indiana	470	1.2%		14	Connecticut	940	2.3%
35	Iowa	210	0.5%		15	Georgia	933	2.3%
29	Kansas	297	0.7%		16	Washington	815	2.0%
50	Kentucky	31	0.1%		17	Colorado	624	1.5%
26	Louisiana	468	1.1%		18	Tennessee	612	1.5%
33	Maine	238	0.6%		19	Wisconsin	610	1.5%
9	Maryland	1,409	3.5%		20	Missouri	605	1.5%
3	Massachusetts	2,151	5.3%		21	Arizona	582	1.4%
12	Michigan	1,091	2.7%		22	Minnesota	573	1.4%
22	Minnesota	573	1.4%		23	South Carolina	484	1.2%
36	Mississippi	201	0.5%		24	Oregon	480	1.2%
20	Missouri	605	1.5%		25	Indiana	470	1.2%
44	Montana	81	0.2%		26	Louisiana	468	1.1%
40	Nebraska	178	0.4%		27	Alabama	353	0.9%
38	Nevada	182	0.4%		28	Oklahoma	302	0.7%
39	New Hampshire	179	0.4%		29	Kansas	297	0.7%
8	New Jersey	1,448	3.6%		30	New Mexico	274	0.7%
30	New Mexico	274	0.7%		31	Hawaii	261	0.6%
2	New York	5,596	13.7%		32	Rhode Island	242	0.6%
13	North Carolina	1,071	2.6%		33	Maine	238	0.6%
46	North Dakota	80	0.2%		34	Arkansas	232	0.6%
10	Ohio	1,196	2.9%		35	Iowa	210	0.5%
28	Oklahoma	302	0.7%		36	Mississippi	201	0.5%
24	Oregon	480	1.2%		37	Utah	192	0.5%
4	Pennsylvania	1,968	4.8%		38	Nevada	182	0.4%
32	Rhode Island	242	0.6%		39	New Hampshire	179	0.4%
23	South Carolina	484	1.2%		40	Nebraska	178	0.4%
48	South Dakota	58	0.1%		41	Vermont	170	0.4%
18	Tennessee	612	1.5%		41	West Virginia	170	0.4%
5	Texas	1,892	4.6%		43	Delaware	97	0.2%
37	Utah	192	0.5%		44	Alaska	81	0.2%
41	Vermont	170	0.4%		44	Montana	81	0.2%
11	Virginia	1,103	2.7%		46	Idaho	80	0.2%
16	Washington	815	2.0%		46	North Dakota	80	0.2%
41	West Virginia	170	0.4%		48	South Dakota	58	0.1%
19	Wisconsin	610	1.5%		49	Wyoming	44	0.1%
49	Wyoming	44	0.1%		50	Kentucky	31	0.1%
						District of Columbia	335	0.8%

Source: American Medical Association (Chicago, Illinois)
   "Physician Characteristics and Distribution in the U.S." (2009 Edition)
*As of December 31, 2007. Total does not include 860 physicians in U.S. territories and possessions. Psychiatry includes psychoanalysis.

Rate of Physicians in Psychiatry in 2007

National Rate = 14 Physicians per 100,000 Population*

ALPHA ORDER

RANK	STATE	RATE
37	Alabama	8
19	Alaska	12
35	Arizona	9
37	Arkansas	8
10	California	16
15	Colorado	13
3	Connecticut	27
22	Delaware	11
29	Florida	10
29	Georgia	10
7	Hawaii	20
49	Idaho	5
19	Illinois	12
43	Indiana	7
43	Iowa	7
22	Kansas	11
50	Kentucky	1
22	Louisiana	11
8	Maine	18
5	Maryland	25
1	Massachusetts	33
22	Michigan	11
22	Minnesota	11
43	Mississippi	7
29	Missouri	10
37	Montana	8
29	Nebraska	10
43	Nevada	7
12	New Hampshire	14
9	New Jersey	17
12	New Mexico	14
2	New York	29
19	North Carolina	12
15	North Dakota	13
29	Ohio	10
37	Oklahoma	8
15	Oregon	13
10	Pennsylvania	16
6	Rhode Island	23
22	South Carolina	11
43	South Dakota	7
29	Tennessee	10
37	Texas	8
43	Utah	7
3	Vermont	27
12	Virginia	14
15	Washington	13
35	West Virginia	9
22	Wisconsin	11
37	Wyoming	8

RANK ORDER

RANK	STATE	RATE
1	Massachusetts	33
2	New York	29
3	Connecticut	27
3	Vermont	27
5	Maryland	25
6	Rhode Island	23
7	Hawaii	20
8	Maine	18
9	New Jersey	17
10	California	16
10	Pennsylvania	16
12	New Hampshire	14
12	New Mexico	14
12	Virginia	14
15	Colorado	13
15	North Dakota	13
15	Oregon	13
15	Washington	13
19	Alaska	12
19	Illinois	12
19	North Carolina	12
22	Delaware	11
22	Kansas	11
22	Louisiana	11
22	Michigan	11
22	Minnesota	11
22	South Carolina	11
22	Wisconsin	11
29	Florida	10
29	Georgia	10
29	Missouri	10
29	Nebraska	10
29	Ohio	10
29	Tennessee	10
35	Arizona	9
35	West Virginia	9
37	Alabama	8
37	Arkansas	8
37	Montana	8
37	Oklahoma	8
37	Texas	8
37	Wyoming	8
43	Indiana	7
43	Iowa	7
43	Mississippi	7
43	Nevada	7
43	South Dakota	7
43	Utah	7
49	Idaho	5
50	Kentucky	1
	District of Columbia	57

Source: CQ Press using data from American Medical Association (Chicago, Illinois)
"Physician Characteristics and Distribution in the U.S." (2009 Edition)

*As of December 31, 2007. National rate does not include physicians in U.S. territories and possessions. Psychiatry includes psychoanalysis.

Percent of Population Lacking Access to Mental Health Care in 2008

National Percent = 17.7% of Population*

ALPHA ORDER

RANK	STATE	PERCENT
8	Alabama	41.6
32	Alaska	13.9
33	Arizona	13.7
5	Arkansas	46.2
38	California	9.2
37	Colorado	9.3
47	Connecticut	1.9
50	Delaware	0.0
39	Florida	9.0
20	Georgia	29.2
45	Hawaii	4.7
2	Idaho	62.0
24	Illinois	21.4
30	Indiana	15.0
11	Iowa	38.4
14	Kansas	35.7
12	Kentucky	37.5
4	Louisiana	48.1
36	Maine	9.5
44	Maryland	5.7
49	Massachusetts	0.7
34	Michigan	13.6
21	Minnesota	26.6
10	Mississippi	40.2
13	Missouri	36.5
7	Montana	41.9
9	Nebraska	41.4
43	Nevada	6.9
46	New Hampshire	3.7
48	New Jersey	1.3
6	New Mexico	44.6
42	New York	7.2
40	North Carolina	7.7
15	North Dakota	34.4
31	Ohio	14.2
29	Oklahoma	15.1
25	Oregon	19.2
35	Pennsylvania	9.8
28	Rhode Island	15.6
16	South Carolina	33.4
3	South Dakota	49.3
17	Tennessee	32.3
26	Texas	19.1
18	Utah	31.5
41	Vermont	7.4
27	Virginia	15.8
22	Washington	25.1
23	West Virginia	24.9
19	Wisconsin	29.9
1	Wyoming	70.7

RANK ORDER

RANK	STATE	PERCENT
1	Wyoming	70.7
2	Idaho	62.0
3	South Dakota	49.3
4	Louisiana	48.1
5	Arkansas	46.2
6	New Mexico	44.6
7	Montana	41.9
8	Alabama	41.6
9	Nebraska	41.4
10	Mississippi	40.2
11	Iowa	38.4
12	Kentucky	37.5
13	Missouri	36.5
14	Kansas	35.7
15	North Dakota	34.4
16	South Carolina	33.4
17	Tennessee	32.3
18	Utah	31.5
19	Wisconsin	29.9
20	Georgia	29.2
21	Minnesota	26.6
22	Washington	25.1
23	West Virginia	24.9
24	Illinois	21.4
25	Oregon	19.2
26	Texas	19.1
27	Virginia	15.8
28	Rhode Island	15.6
29	Oklahoma	15.1
30	Indiana	15.0
31	Ohio	14.2
32	Alaska	13.9
33	Arizona	13.7
34	Michigan	13.6
35	Pennsylvania	9.8
36	Maine	9.5
37	Colorado	9.3
38	California	9.2
39	Florida	9.0
40	North Carolina	7.7
41	Vermont	7.4
42	New York	7.2
43	Nevada	6.9
44	Maryland	5.7
45	Hawaii	4.7
46	New Hampshire	3.7
47	Connecticut	1.9
48	New Jersey	1.3
49	Massachusetts	0.7
50	Delaware	0.0

District of Columbia	13.3

Source: CQ Press using data from U.S. Dept. of Health and Human Services, Div. of Shortage Designation
"Selected Statistics on Health Professional Shortage Areas" (as of September 30, 2008)
*Percent of population considered under-served by mental health practitioners. An under-served population does not have primary medical care within reasonable economic and geographic bounds.

International Medical School Graduates in 2007

National Total = 236,437 Nonfederal Physicians*

ALPHA ORDER

RANK	STATE	PHYSICIANS	% of USA
25	Alabama	1,817	0.8%
48	Alaska	124	0.1%
16	Arizona	3,461	1.5%
35	Arkansas	1,039	0.4%
2	California	26,209	11.1%
34	Colorado	1,084	0.5%
14	Connecticut	4,339	1.8%
38	Delaware	765	0.3%
3	Florida	20,243	8.6%
13	Georgia	4,597	1.9%
39	Hawaii	708	0.3%
50	Idaho	115	0.0%
6	Illinois	13,698	5.8%
18	Indiana	3,238	1.4%
31	Iowa	1,276	0.5%
30	Kansas	1,333	0.6%
24	Kentucky	2,289	1.0%
23	Louisiana	2,403	1.0%
41	Maine	634	0.3%
11	Maryland	7,262	3.1%
10	Massachusetts	7,377	3.1%
9	Michigan	9,749	4.1%
21	Minnesota	2,592	1.1%
37	Mississippi	798	0.3%
15	Missouri	3,600	1.5%
49	Montana	118	0.0%
40	Nebraska	704	0.3%
27	Nevada	1,693	0.7%
42	New Hampshire	626	0.3%
4	New Jersey	13,824	5.8%
36	New Mexico	961	0.4%
1	New York	35,934	15.2%
17	North Carolina	3,393	1.4%
44	North Dakota	468	0.2%
8	Ohio	10,046	4.2%
29	Oklahoma	1,423	0.6%
33	Oregon	1,085	0.5%
7	Pennsylvania	11,231	4.8%
32	Rhode Island	1,172	0.5%
28	South Carolina	1,485	0.6%
45	South Dakota	272	0.1%
20	Tennessee	3,069	1.3%
5	Texas	13,705	5.8%
43	Utah	530	0.2%
46	Vermont	245	0.1%
12	Virginia	5,197	2.2%
22	Washington	2,531	1.1%
26	West Virginia	1,698	0.7%
19	Wisconsin	3,075	1.3%
47	Wyoming	126	0.1%

RANK ORDER

RANK	STATE	PHYSICIANS	% of USA
1	New York	35,934	15.2%
2	California	26,209	11.1%
3	Florida	20,243	8.6%
4	New Jersey	13,824	5.8%
5	Texas	13,705	5.8%
6	Illinois	13,698	5.8%
7	Pennsylvania	11,231	4.8%
8	Ohio	10,046	4.2%
9	Michigan	9,749	4.1%
10	Massachusetts	7,377	3.1%
11	Maryland	7,262	3.1%
12	Virginia	5,197	2.2%
13	Georgia	4,597	1.9%
14	Connecticut	4,339	1.8%
15	Missouri	3,600	1.5%
16	Arizona	3,461	1.5%
17	North Carolina	3,393	1.4%
18	Indiana	3,238	1.4%
19	Wisconsin	3,075	1.3%
20	Tennessee	3,069	1.3%
21	Minnesota	2,592	1.1%
22	Washington	2,531	1.1%
23	Louisiana	2,403	1.0%
24	Kentucky	2,289	1.0%
25	Alabama	1,817	0.8%
26	West Virginia	1,698	0.7%
27	Nevada	1,693	0.7%
28	South Carolina	1,485	0.6%
29	Oklahoma	1,423	0.6%
30	Kansas	1,333	0.6%
31	Iowa	1,276	0.5%
32	Rhode Island	1,172	0.5%
33	Oregon	1,085	0.5%
34	Colorado	1,084	0.5%
35	Arkansas	1,039	0.4%
36	New Mexico	961	0.4%
37	Mississippi	798	0.3%
38	Delaware	765	0.3%
39	Hawaii	708	0.3%
40	Nebraska	704	0.3%
41	Maine	634	0.3%
42	New Hampshire	626	0.3%
43	Utah	530	0.2%
44	North Dakota	468	0.2%
45	South Dakota	272	0.1%
46	Vermont	245	0.1%
47	Wyoming	126	0.1%
48	Alaska	124	0.1%
49	Montana	118	0.0%
50	Idaho	115	0.0%
	District of Columbia	1,076	0.5%

Source: American Medical Association (Chicago, Illinois)
   "Physician Characteristics and Distribution in the U.S." (2009 Edition)
*As of December 31, 2007. Total does not include 7,020 physicians in U.S. territories and possessions.

International Medical School Graduates as a Percent of Physicians in 2007

National Percent = 25.5% of Physicians*

ALPHA ORDER

ALPHA ORDER

RANK	STATE	PERCENT
31	Alabama	16.2
48	Alaska	7.2
19	Arizona	22.0
32	Arkansas	15.9
16	California	23.2
47	Colorado	7.5
9	Connecticut	29.4
7	Delaware	31.1
3	Florida	36.8
23	Georgia	19.8
33	Hawaii	15.2
50	Idaho	3.8
6	Illinois	34.3
21	Indiana	20.9
25	Iowa	19.5
28	Kansas	18.6
22	Kentucky	20.8
26	Louisiana	18.9
36	Maine	14.7
11	Maryland	27.5
18	Massachusetts	22.1
5	Michigan	34.4
34	Minnesota	15.1
39	Mississippi	13.4
17	Missouri	22.5
49	Montana	4.6
37	Nebraska	14.2
8	Nevada	30.3
35	New Hampshire	14.8
1	New Jersey	45.2
29	New Mexico	17.4
2	New York	42.1
40	North Carolina	13.0
12	North Dakota	26.5
10	Ohio	29.1
24	Oklahoma	19.6
44	Oregon	9.0
14	Pennsylvania	26.0
12	Rhode Island	26.5
41	South Carolina	12.9
38	South Dakota	13.5
30	Tennessee	16.9
15	Texas	24.2
46	Utah	8.5
44	Vermont	9.0
20	Virginia	21.5
42	Washington	12.4
4	West Virginia	35.7
27	Wisconsin	18.7
43	Wyoming	10.8

RANK ORDER

RANK	STATE	PERCENT
1	New Jersey	45.2
2	New York	42.1
3	Florida	36.8
4	West Virginia	35.7
5	Michigan	34.4
6	Illinois	34.3
7	Delaware	31.1
8	Nevada	30.3
9	Connecticut	29.4
10	Ohio	29.1
11	Maryland	27.5
12	North Dakota	26.5
12	Rhode Island	26.5
14	Pennsylvania	26.0
15	Texas	24.2
16	California	23.2
17	Missouri	22.5
18	Massachusetts	22.1
19	Arizona	22.0
20	Virginia	21.5
21	Indiana	20.9
22	Kentucky	20.8
23	Georgia	19.8
24	Oklahoma	19.6
25	Iowa	19.5
26	Louisiana	18.9
27	Wisconsin	18.7
28	Kansas	18.6
29	New Mexico	17.4
30	Tennessee	16.9
31	Alabama	16.2
32	Arkansas	15.9
33	Hawaii	15.2
34	Minnesota	15.1
35	New Hampshire	14.8
36	Maine	14.7
37	Nebraska	14.2
38	South Dakota	13.5
39	Mississippi	13.4
40	North Carolina	13.0
41	South Carolina	12.9
42	Washington	12.4
43	Wyoming	10.8
44	Oregon	9.0
44	Vermont	9.0
46	Utah	8.5
47	Colorado	7.5
48	Alaska	7.2
49	Montana	4.6
50	Idaho	3.8

District of Columbia 20.9

Source: CQ Press using data from American Medical Association (Chicago, Illinois)
"Physician Characteristics and Distribution in the U.S." (2009 Edition)
*As of December 31, 2007. National rate does not include physicians in the U.S. territories and possessions.

Osteopathic Physicians in 2008

National Total = 56,754 Osteopathic Physicians*

ALPHA ORDER

RANK	STATE	OSTEOPATHS	% of USA
33	Alabama	385	0.7%
44	Alaska	147	0.3%
11	Arizona	1,561	2.8%
36	Arkansas	248	0.4%
3	California	3,891	6.9%
14	Colorado	935	1.6%
31	Connecticut	430	0.8%
37	Delaware	245	0.4%
6	Florida	3,760	6.6%
18	Georgia	765	1.3%
42	Hawaii	199	0.4%
39	Idaho	235	0.4%
9	Illinois	2,406	4.2%
16	Indiana	814	1.4%
13	Iowa	1,105	1.9%
23	Kansas	643	1.1%
30	Kentucky	457	0.8%
46	Louisiana	125	0.2%
25	Maine	630	1.1%
21	Maryland	700	1.2%
23	Massachusetts	643	1.1%
2	Michigan	4,978	8.8%
28	Minnesota	469	0.8%
34	Mississippi	314	0.6%
10	Missouri	1,829	3.2%
45	Montana	140	0.2%
43	Nebraska	181	0.3%
29	Nevada	467	0.8%
38	New Hampshire	237	0.4%
8	New Jersey	2,972	5.2%
40	New Mexico	215	0.4%
4	New York	3,871	6.8%
19	North Carolina	753	1.3%
49	North Dakota	60	0.1%
5	Ohio	3,854	6.8%
12	Oklahoma	1,531	2.7%
26	Oregon	564	1.0%
1	Pennsylvania	5,675	10.0%
41	Rhode Island	203	0.4%
32	South Carolina	391	0.7%
47	South Dakota	106	0.2%
27	Tennessee	556	1.0%
7	Texas	3,346	5.9%
35	Utah	307	0.5%
50	Vermont	59	0.1%
15	Virginia	907	1.6%
17	Washington	788	1.4%
22	West Virginia	685	1.2%
20	Wisconsin	732	1.3%
48	Wyoming	80	0.1%

RANK ORDER

RANK	STATE	OSTEOPATHS	% of USA
1	Pennsylvania	5,675	10.0%
2	Michigan	4,978	8.8%
3	California	3,891	6.9%
4	New York	3,871	6.8%
5	Ohio	3,854	6.8%
6	Florida	3,760	6.6%
7	Texas	3,346	5.9%
8	New Jersey	2,972	5.2%
9	Illinois	2,406	4.2%
10	Missouri	1,829	3.2%
11	Arizona	1,561	2.8%
12	Oklahoma	1,531	2.7%
13	Iowa	1,105	1.9%
14	Colorado	935	1.6%
15	Virginia	907	1.6%
16	Indiana	814	1.4%
17	Washington	788	1.4%
18	Georgia	765	1.3%
19	North Carolina	753	1.3%
20	Wisconsin	732	1.3%
21	Maryland	700	1.2%
22	West Virginia	685	1.2%
23	Kansas	643	1.1%
23	Massachusetts	643	1.1%
25	Maine	630	1.1%
26	Oregon	564	1.0%
27	Tennessee	556	1.0%
28	Minnesota	469	0.8%
29	Nevada	467	0.8%
30	Kentucky	457	0.8%
31	Connecticut	430	0.8%
32	South Carolina	391	0.7%
33	Alabama	385	0.7%
34	Mississippi	314	0.6%
35	Utah	307	0.5%
36	Arkansas	248	0.4%
37	Delaware	245	0.4%
38	New Hampshire	237	0.4%
39	Idaho	235	0.4%
40	New Mexico	215	0.4%
41	Rhode Island	203	0.4%
42	Hawaii	199	0.4%
43	Nebraska	181	0.3%
44	Alaska	147	0.3%
45	Montana	140	0.2%
46	Louisiana	125	0.2%
47	South Dakota	106	0.2%
48	Wyoming	80	0.1%
49	North Dakota	60	0.1%
50	Vermont	59	0.1%
	District of Columbia	70	0.1%

Source: American Osteopathic Association
   "Osteopathic Medical Profession Report" (https://www.do-online.org/index.cfm?PageID=aoa_ompreport_us)
*Active osteopaths under age 65 as of May 31, 2008. National total does not include 224 osteopaths not shown by state.
Osteopaths practice a system of medicine based on the theory that disturbances in the musculoskeletal system affect other body parts, causing many disorders that can be corrected by various manipulative techniques in conjunction with conventional medical, surgical, pharmacological, and other therapeutic procedures.

Rate of Osteopathic Physicians in 2008

National Rate = 19 Osteopaths per 100,000 Population*

ALPHA ORDER

RANK	STATE	RATE
47	Alabama	8
13	Alaska	21
11	Arizona	24
41	Arkansas	9
34	California	11
16	Colorado	19
30	Connecticut	12
10	Delaware	28
13	Florida	21
47	Georgia	8
21	Hawaii	15
21	Idaho	15
16	Illinois	19
27	Indiana	13
6	Iowa	37
12	Kansas	23
34	Kentucky	11
50	Louisiana	3
2	Maine	48
30	Maryland	12
39	Massachusetts	10
1	Michigan	50
41	Minnesota	9
34	Mississippi	11
9	Missouri	31
25	Montana	14
39	Nebraska	10
19	Nevada	18
19	New Hampshire	18
7	New Jersey	34
34	New Mexico	11
15	New York	20
47	North Carolina	8
41	North Dakota	9
7	Ohio	34
4	Oklahoma	42
21	Oregon	15
3	Pennsylvania	46
16	Rhode Island	19
41	South Carolina	9
27	South Dakota	13
41	Tennessee	9
25	Texas	14
34	Utah	11
41	Vermont	9
30	Virginia	12
30	Washington	12
5	West Virginia	38
27	Wisconsin	13
21	Wyoming	15

RANK ORDER

RANK	STATE	RATE
1	Michigan	50
2	Maine	48
3	Pennsylvania	46
4	Oklahoma	42
5	West Virginia	38
6	Iowa	37
7	New Jersey	34
7	Ohio	34
9	Missouri	31
10	Delaware	28
11	Arizona	24
12	Kansas	23
13	Alaska	21
13	Florida	21
15	New York	20
16	Colorado	19
16	Illinois	19
16	Rhode Island	19
19	Nevada	18
19	New Hampshire	18
21	Hawaii	15
21	Idaho	15
21	Oregon	15
21	Wyoming	15
25	Montana	14
25	Texas	14
27	Indiana	13
27	South Dakota	13
27	Wisconsin	13
30	Connecticut	12
30	Maryland	12
30	Virginia	12
30	Washington	12
34	California	11
34	Kentucky	11
34	Mississippi	11
34	New Mexico	11
34	Utah	11
39	Massachusetts	10
39	Nebraska	10
41	Arkansas	9
41	Minnesota	9
41	North Dakota	9
41	South Carolina	9
41	Tennessee	9
41	Vermont	9
47	Alabama	8
47	Georgia	8
47	North Carolina	8
50	Louisiana	3

District of Columbia   12

Source: CQ Press using data from American Osteopathic Association
"Osteopathic Medical Profession Report" (https://www.do-online.org/index.cfm?PageID=aoa_ompreport_us)
*Active osteopaths under age 65 as of May 31, 2008. National rate does not include osteopaths not shown by state.
Osteopaths practice a system of medicine based on the theory that disturbances in the musculoskeletal system affect other body parts, causing many disorders that can be corrected by various manipulative techniques in conjunction with conventional medical, surgical, pharmacological, and other therapeutic procedures.

Podiatrists in 2007

National Total = 9,320 Podiatrists*

ALPHA ORDER

RANK	STATE	PODIATRISTS	% of USA
28	Alabama	70	0.8%
NA	Alaska**	NA	NA
9	Arizona	350	3.8%
NA	Arkansas**	NA	NA
2	California	870	9.3%
30	Colorado	60	0.6%
16	Connecticut	130	1.4%
26	Delaware	80	0.9%
5	Florida	540	5.8%
13	Georgia	200	2.1%
NA	Hawaii**	NA	NA
NA	Idaho**	NA	NA
11	Illinois	300	3.2%
21	Indiana	110	1.2%
22	Iowa	100	1.1%
32	Kansas	50	0.5%
28	Kentucky	70	0.8%
32	Louisiana	50	0.5%
35	Maine	40	0.4%
10	Maryland	310	3.3%
14	Massachusetts	190	2.0%
8	Michigan	430	4.6%
22	Minnesota	100	1.1%
NA	Mississippi**	NA	NA
16	Missouri	130	1.4%
35	Montana	40	0.4%
32	Nebraska	50	0.5%
30	Nevada	60	0.6%
NA	New Hampshire**	NA	NA
6	New Jersey	470	5.0%
16	New Mexico	130	1.4%
1	New York	1,010	10.8%
16	North Carolina	130	1.4%
NA	North Dakota**	NA	NA
4	Ohio	570	6.1%
20	Oklahoma	120	1.3%
NA	Oregon**	NA	NA
3	Pennsylvania	770	8.3%
35	Rhode Island	40	0.4%
22	South Carolina	100	1.1%
NA	South Dakota**	NA	NA
15	Tennessee	150	1.6%
7	Texas	440	4.7%
NA	Utah**	NA	NA
NA	Vermont**	NA	NA
12	Virginia	220	2.4%
22	Washington	100	1.1%
NA	West Virginia**	NA	NA
26	Wisconsin	80	0.9%
NA	Wyoming**	NA	NA

RANK ORDER

RANK	STATE	PODIATRISTS	% of USA
1	New York	1,010	10.8%
2	California	870	9.3%
3	Pennsylvania	770	8.3%
4	Ohio	570	6.1%
5	Florida	540	5.8%
6	New Jersey	470	5.0%
7	Texas	440	4.7%
8	Michigan	430	4.6%
9	Arizona	350	3.8%
10	Maryland	310	3.3%
11	Illinois	300	3.2%
12	Virginia	220	2.4%
13	Georgia	200	2.1%
14	Massachusetts	190	2.0%
15	Tennessee	150	1.6%
16	Connecticut	130	1.4%
16	Missouri	130	1.4%
16	New Mexico	130	1.4%
16	North Carolina	130	1.4%
20	Oklahoma	120	1.3%
21	Indiana	110	1.2%
22	Iowa	100	1.1%
22	Minnesota	100	1.1%
22	South Carolina	100	1.1%
22	Washington	100	1.1%
26	Delaware	80	0.9%
26	Wisconsin	80	0.9%
28	Alabama	70	0.8%
28	Kentucky	70	0.8%
30	Colorado	60	0.6%
30	Nevada	60	0.6%
32	Kansas	50	0.5%
32	Louisiana	50	0.5%
32	Nebraska	50	0.5%
35	Maine	40	0.4%
35	Montana	40	0.4%
35	Rhode Island	40	0.4%
NA	Alaska**	NA	NA
NA	Arkansas**	NA	NA
NA	Hawaii**	NA	NA
NA	Idaho**	NA	NA
NA	Mississippi**	NA	NA
NA	New Hampshire**	NA	NA
NA	North Dakota**	NA	NA
NA	Oregon**	NA	NA
NA	South Dakota**	NA	NA
NA	Utah**	NA	NA
NA	Vermont**	NA	NA
NA	West Virginia**	NA	NA
NA	Wyoming**	NA	NA
	District of Columbia**	NA	NA

Source: U.S. Department of Labor, Bureau of Labor Statistics
"Occupational Employment and Wages, 2007" (http://www.bls.gov/oes/)
*Does not include self-employed.
**Not available.

Rate of Podiatrists in 2007

National Rate = 3 Podiatrists per 100,000 Population*

ALPHA ORDER

RANK	STATE	RATE
20	Alabama	2
NA	Alaska**	NA
3	Arizona	6
NA	Arkansas**	NA
20	California	2
34	Colorado	1
9	Connecticut	4
1	Delaware	9
13	Florida	3
20	Georgia	2
NA	Hawaii**	NA
NA	Idaho**	NA
20	Illinois	2
20	Indiana	2
13	Iowa	3
20	Kansas	2
20	Kentucky	2
34	Louisiana	1
13	Maine	3
3	Maryland	6
13	Massachusetts	3
9	Michigan	4
20	Minnesota	2
NA	Mississippi**	NA
20	Missouri	2
9	Montana	4
13	Nebraska	3
20	Nevada	2
NA	New Hampshire**	NA
6	New Jersey	5
2	New Mexico	7
6	New York	5
34	North Carolina	1
NA	North Dakota**	NA
6	Ohio	5
13	Oklahoma	3
NA	Oregon**	NA
3	Pennsylvania	6
9	Rhode Island	4
20	South Carolina	2
NA	South Dakota**	NA
20	Tennessee	2
20	Texas	2
NA	Utah**	NA
NA	Vermont**	NA
13	Virginia	3
20	Washington	2
NA	West Virginia**	NA
34	Wisconsin	1
NA	Wyoming**	NA

RANK ORDER

RANK	STATE	RATE
1	Delaware	9
2	New Mexico	7
3	Arizona	6
3	Maryland	6
3	Pennsylvania	6
6	New Jersey	5
6	New York	5
6	Ohio	5
9	Connecticut	4
9	Michigan	4
9	Montana	4
9	Rhode Island	4
13	Florida	3
13	Iowa	3
13	Maine	3
13	Massachusetts	3
13	Nebraska	3
13	Oklahoma	3
13	Virginia	3
20	Alabama	2
20	California	2
20	Georgia	2
20	Illinois	2
20	Indiana	2
20	Kansas	2
20	Kentucky	2
20	Minnesota	2
20	Missouri	2
20	Nevada	2
20	South Carolina	2
20	Tennessee	2
20	Texas	2
20	Washington	2
34	Colorado	1
34	Louisiana	1
34	North Carolina	1
34	Wisconsin	1
NA	Alaska**	NA
NA	Arkansas**	NA
NA	Hawaii**	NA
NA	Idaho**	NA
NA	Mississippi**	NA
NA	New Hampshire**	NA
NA	North Dakota**	NA
NA	Oregon**	NA
NA	South Dakota**	NA
NA	Utah**	NA
NA	Vermont**	NA
NA	West Virginia**	NA
NA	Wyoming**	NA
	District of Columbia**	NA

Source: CQ Press using data from U.S. Department of Labor, Bureau of Labor Statistics
"Occupational Employment and Wages, 2007" (http://www.bls.gov/oes/)
*Does not include self-employed.
**Not available.

Average Annual Wages of Podiatrists in 2006

National Average = $119,790*

ALPHA ORDER

RANK	STATE	WAGES
10	Alabama	$147,350
NA	Alaska**	NA
35	Arizona	100,380
NA	Arkansas**	NA
34	California	102,850
23	Colorado	122,660
22	Connecticut	123,170
37	Delaware	94,530
32	Florida	105,650
5	Georgia	162,220
NA	Hawaii**	NA
NA	Idaho**	NA
30	Illinois	108,050
17	Indiana	130,220
28	Iowa	110,590
6	Kansas	159,180
3	Kentucky	163,250
4	Louisiana	162,920
27	Maine	111,300
9	Maryland	148,640
25	Massachusetts	115,400
2	Michigan	169,690
7	Minnesota	157,700
NA	Mississippi**	NA
11	Missouri	141,580
8	Montana	152,720
15	Nebraska	135,810
31	Nevada	107,150
NA	New Hampshire**	NA
19	New Jersey	126,210
33	New Mexico	103,240
18	New York	129,030
12	North Carolina	138,390
NA	North Dakota**	NA
26	Ohio	111,780
20	Oklahoma	125,250
1	Oregon	177,790
36	Pennsylvania	97,300
NA	Rhode Island**	NA
29	South Carolina	109,060
NA	South Dakota**	NA
21	Tennessee	124,740
24	Texas	115,750
38	Utah	60,630
NA	Vermont**	NA
16	Virginia	130,460
14	Washington	136,730
NA	West Virginia**	NA
13	Wisconsin	137,350
NA	Wyoming**	NA

RANK ORDER

RANK	STATE	WAGES
1	Oregon	$177,790
2	Michigan	169,690
3	Kentucky	163,250
4	Louisiana	162,920
5	Georgia	162,220
6	Kansas	159,180
7	Minnesota	157,700
8	Montana	152,720
9	Maryland	148,640
10	Alabama	147,350
11	Missouri	141,580
12	North Carolina	138,390
13	Wisconsin	137,350
14	Washington	136,730
15	Nebraska	135,810
16	Virginia	130,460
17	Indiana	130,220
18	New York	129,030
19	New Jersey	126,210
20	Oklahoma	125,250
21	Tennessee	124,740
22	Connecticut	123,170
23	Colorado	122,660
24	Texas	115,750
25	Massachusetts	115,400
26	Ohio	111,780
27	Maine	111,300
28	Iowa	110,590
29	South Carolina	109,060
30	Illinois	108,050
31	Nevada	107,150
32	Florida	105,650
33	New Mexico	103,240
34	California	102,850
35	Arizona	100,380
36	Pennsylvania	97,300
37	Delaware	94,530
38	Utah	60,630
NA	Alaska**	NA
NA	Arkansas**	NA
NA	Hawaii**	NA
NA	Idaho**	NA
NA	Mississippi**	NA
NA	New Hampshire**	NA
NA	North Dakota**	NA
NA	Rhode Island**	NA
NA	South Dakota**	NA
NA	Vermont**	NA
NA	West Virginia**	NA
NA	Wyoming**	NA
	District of Columbia**	NA

Source: U.S. Department of Labor, Bureau of Labor Statistics
"Occupational Employment and Wages, 2007" (http://www.bls.gov/oes/)
*Does not include self-employed.
**Not available.

Doctors of Chiropractic in 2007

National Total = 88,761 Chiropractors*

ALPHA ORDER

RANK	STATE	CHIROPRACTORS	% of USA
30	Alabama	784	0.9%
49	Alaska	240	0.3%
10	Arizona	2,578	2.9%
34	Arkansas	556	0.6%
1	California	13,851	15.6%
12	Colorado	2,495	2.8%
24	Connecticut	1,003	1.1%
45	Delaware	300	0.3%
3	Florida	4,909	5.5%
8	Georgia	3,045	3.4%
38	Hawaii	473	0.5%
35	Idaho	519	0.6%
5	Illinois	4,167	4.7%
23	Indiana	1,124	1.3%
20	Iowa	1,555	1.8%
26	Kansas	904	1.0%
27	Kentucky	862	1.0%
32	Louisiana	606	0.7%
40	Maine	370	0.4%
31	Maryland	771	0.9%
15	Massachusetts	2,185	2.5%
9	Michigan	2,841	3.2%
11	Minnesota	2,532	2.9%
44	Mississippi	330	0.4%
16	Missouri	2,120	2.4%
40	Montana	370	0.4%
37	Nebraska	492	0.6%
33	Nevada	602	0.7%
39	New Hampshire	433	0.5%
7	New Jersey	3,392	3.8%
36	New Mexico	504	0.6%
2	New York	5,830	6.6%
18	North Carolina	1,904	2.1%
47	North Dakota	263	0.3%
14	Ohio	2,234	2.5%
29	Oklahoma	785	0.9%
22	Oregon	1,372	1.5%
6	Pennsylvania	4,164	4.7%
46	Rhode Island	269	0.3%
19	South Carolina	1,557	1.8%
43	South Dakota	336	0.4%
25	Tennessee	995	1.1%
4	Texas	4,580	5.2%
28	Utah	816	0.9%
48	Vermont	250	0.3%
21	Virginia	1,472	1.7%
13	Washington	2,305	2.6%
42	West Virginia	338	0.4%
17	Wisconsin	2,106	2.4%
50	Wyoming	202	0.2%

RANK ORDER

RANK	STATE	CHIROPRACTORS	% of USA
1	California	13,851	15.6%
2	New York	5,830	6.6%
3	Florida	4,909	5.5%
4	Texas	4,580	5.2%
5	Illinois	4,167	4.7%
6	Pennsylvania	4,164	4.7%
7	New Jersey	3,392	3.8%
8	Georgia	3,045	3.4%
9	Michigan	2,841	3.2%
10	Arizona	2,578	2.9%
11	Minnesota	2,532	2.9%
12	Colorado	2,495	2.8%
13	Washington	2,305	2.6%
14	Ohio	2,234	2.5%
15	Massachusetts	2,185	2.5%
16	Missouri	2,120	2.4%
17	Wisconsin	2,106	2.4%
18	North Carolina	1,904	2.1%
19	South Carolina	1,557	1.8%
20	Iowa	1,555	1.8%
21	Virginia	1,472	1.7%
22	Oregon	1,372	1.5%
23	Indiana	1,124	1.3%
24	Connecticut	1,003	1.1%
25	Tennessee	995	1.1%
26	Kansas	904	1.0%
27	Kentucky	862	1.0%
28	Utah	816	0.9%
29	Oklahoma	785	0.9%
30	Alabama	784	0.9%
31	Maryland	771	0.9%
32	Louisiana	606	0.7%
33	Nevada	602	0.7%
34	Arkansas	556	0.6%
35	Idaho	519	0.6%
36	New Mexico	504	0.6%
37	Nebraska	492	0.6%
38	Hawaii	473	0.5%
39	New Hampshire	433	0.5%
40	Maine	370	0.4%
40	Montana	370	0.4%
42	West Virginia	338	0.4%
43	South Dakota	336	0.4%
44	Mississippi	330	0.4%
45	Delaware	300	0.3%
46	Rhode Island	269	0.3%
47	North Dakota	263	0.3%
48	Vermont	250	0.3%
49	Alaska	240	0.3%
50	Wyoming	202	0.2%

District of Columbia	70	0.1%

Source: Federation of Chiropractic Licensing Boards
   "Official Directory" (http://www.fclb.org/directory/index.htm)
*As of December 2007. Licensed active doctors. There is some duplication as some doctors are licensed in more than one state.

Rate of Doctors of Chiropractic in 2007

National Rate = 29 Chiropractors per 100,000 Population*

ALPHA ORDER

ALPHA ORDER

RANK ORDER

RANK	STATE	RATE
46	Alabama	17
17	Alaska	35
5	Arizona	41
39	Arkansas	20
11	California	38
1	Colorado	52
29	Connecticut	29
17	Delaware	35
33	Florida	27
25	Georgia	32
13	Hawaii	37
17	Idaho	35
25	Illinois	32
45	Indiana	18
1	Iowa	52
23	Kansas	33
39	Kentucky	20
48	Louisiana	14
30	Maine	28
48	Maryland	14
21	Massachusetts	34
30	Michigan	28
3	Minnesota	49
50	Mississippi	11
15	Missouri	36
8	Montana	39
30	Nebraska	28
36	Nevada	24
23	New Hampshire	33
8	New Jersey	39
34	New Mexico	26
28	New York	30
38	North Carolina	21
5	North Dakota	41
41	Ohio	19
37	Oklahoma	22
13	Oregon	37
21	Pennsylvania	34
34	Rhode Island	26
17	South Carolina	35
4	South Dakota	42
47	Tennessee	16
41	Texas	19
27	Utah	31
7	Vermont	40
41	Virginia	19
15	Washington	36
41	West Virginia	19
11	Wisconsin	38
8	Wyoming	39

RANK	STATE	RATE
1	Colorado	52
1	Iowa	52
3	Minnesota	49
4	South Dakota	42
5	Arizona	41
5	North Dakota	41
7	Vermont	40
8	Montana	39
8	New Jersey	39
8	Wyoming	39
11	California	38
11	Wisconsin	38
13	Hawaii	37
13	Oregon	37
15	Missouri	36
15	Washington	36
17	Alaska	35
17	Delaware	35
17	Idaho	35
17	South Carolina	35
21	Massachusetts	34
21	Pennsylvania	34
23	Kansas	33
23	New Hampshire	33
25	Georgia	32
25	Illinois	32
27	Utah	31
28	New York	30
29	Connecticut	29
30	Maine	28
30	Michigan	28
30	Nebraska	28
33	Florida	27
34	New Mexico	26
34	Rhode Island	26
36	Nevada	24
37	Oklahoma	22
38	North Carolina	21
39	Arkansas	20
39	Kentucky	20
41	Ohio	19
41	Texas	19
41	Virginia	19
41	West Virginia	19
45	Indiana	18
46	Alabama	17
47	Tennessee	16
48	Louisiana	14
48	Maryland	14
50	Mississippi	11
	District of Columbia	12

Source: CQ Press using data from Federation of Chiropractic Licensing Boards
   "Official Directory" (http://www.fclb.org/directory/index.htm)
*As of December 2007. Licensed active doctors. There is some duplication as some doctors are licensed in more than one state.

Average Annual Wages of Chiropractors in 2007

National Average = $81,390*

RANK	STATE	WAGES
2	Alabama	$129,720
16	Alaska	87,130
44	Arizona	62,040
10	Arkansas	101,010
36	California	71,310
32	Colorado	76,470
15	Connecticut	91,470
19	Delaware	86,220
35	Florida	72,730
45	Georgia	58,780
47	Hawaii	46,470
34	Idaho	73,350
14	Illinois	92,540
22	Indiana	83,520
28	Iowa	78,150
20	Kansas	86,030
7	Kentucky	105,870
30	Louisiana	77,750
37	Maine	70,460
3	Maryland	117,660
18	Massachusetts	86,460
29	Michigan	78,140
31	Minnesota	77,560
41	Mississippi	67,410
33	Missouri	74,000
48	Montana	41,550
9	Nebraska	104,760
1	Nevada	132,920
21	New Hampshire	83,550
23	New Jersey	81,500
42	New Mexico	64,980
27	New York	79,240
6	North Carolina	110,390
43	North Dakota	63,710
8	Ohio	105,820
25	Oklahoma	79,530
46	Oregon	52,560
38	Pennsylvania	70,130
17	Rhode Island	86,860
39	South Carolina	69,790
11	South Dakota	100,640
12	Tennessee	98,850
40	Texas	67,540
26	Utah	79,510
NA	Vermont**	NA
NA	Virginia**	NA
5	Washington	111,150
13	West Virginia	93,370
4	Wisconsin	113,560
24	Wyoming	79,740

RANK	STATE	WAGES
1	Nevada	$132,920
2	Alabama	129,720
3	Maryland	117,660
4	Wisconsin	113,560
5	Washington	111,150
6	North Carolina	110,390
7	Kentucky	105,870
8	Ohio	105,820
9	Nebraska	104,760
10	Arkansas	101,010
11	South Dakota	100,640
12	Tennessee	98,850
13	West Virginia	93,370
14	Illinois	92,540
15	Connecticut	91,470
16	Alaska	87,130
17	Rhode Island	86,860
18	Massachusetts	86,460
19	Delaware	86,220
20	Kansas	86,030
21	New Hampshire	83,550
22	Indiana	83,520
23	New Jersey	81,500
24	Wyoming	79,740
25	Oklahoma	79,530
26	Utah	79,510
27	New York	79,240
28	Iowa	78,150
29	Michigan	78,140
30	Louisiana	77,750
31	Minnesota	77,560
32	Colorado	76,470
33	Missouri	74,000
34	Idaho	73,350
35	Florida	72,730
36	California	71,310
37	Maine	70,460
38	Pennsylvania	70,130
39	South Carolina	69,790
40	Texas	67,540
41	Mississippi	67,410
42	New Mexico	64,980
43	North Dakota	63,710
44	Arizona	62,040
45	Georgia	58,780
46	Oregon	52,560
47	Hawaii	46,470
48	Montana	41,550
NA	Vermont**	NA
NA	Virginia**	NA
	District of Columbia**	NA

Source: U.S. Department of Labor, Bureau of Labor Statistics
"Occupational Employment and Wages, 2007" (http://www.bls.gov/oes/)
*Does not include self-employed.
**Not available.

Physician Assistants in Clinical Practice in 2008

National Total = 73,506 Physician Assistants*

ALPHA ORDER

RANK	STATE	PAs	% of USA
38	Alabama	485	0.7%
41	Alaska	376	0.5%
15	Arizona	1,668	2.3%
49	Arkansas	155	0.2%
2	California	7,115	9.7%
13	Colorado	1,792	2.4%
19	Connecticut	1,375	1.9%
46	Delaware	215	0.3%
5	Florida	4,324	5.9%
8	Georgia	2,369	3.2%
48	Hawaii	158	0.2%
37	Idaho	511	0.7%
12	Illinois	1,950	2.7%
32	Indiana	621	0.8%
26	Iowa	765	1.0%
25	Kansas	796	1.1%
23	Kentucky	866	1.2%
34	Louisiana	545	0.7%
33	Maine	555	0.8%
9	Maryland	1,978	2.7%
14	Massachusetts	1,725	2.3%
7	Michigan	3,015	4.1%
20	Minnesota	1,251	1.7%
50	Mississippi	86	0.1%
31	Missouri	635	0.9%
42	Montana	353	0.5%
28	Nebraska	731	1.0%
35	Nevada	517	0.7%
39	New Hampshire	420	0.6%
18	New Jersey	1,434	2.0%
36	New Mexico	516	0.7%
1	New York	7,916	10.8%
6	North Carolina	3,586	4.9%
43	North Dakota	243	0.3%
11	Ohio	1,960	2.7%
21	Oklahoma	1,072	1.5%
24	Oregon	853	1.2%
4	Pennsylvania	4,357	5.9%
44	Rhode Island	226	0.3%
27	South Carolina	743	1.0%
40	South Dakota	409	0.6%
22	Tennessee	954	1.3%
3	Texas	4,696	6.4%
30	Utah	693	0.9%
45	Vermont	219	0.3%
16	Virginia	1,611	2.2%
10	Washington	1,967	2.7%
29	West Virginia	719	1.0%
17	Wisconsin	1,557	2.1%
47	Wyoming	192	0.3%

RANK ORDER

RANK	STATE	PAs	% of USA
1	New York	7,916	10.8%
2	California	7,115	9.7%
3	Texas	4,696	6.4%
4	Pennsylvania	4,357	5.9%
5	Florida	4,324	5.9%
6	North Carolina	3,586	4.9%
7	Michigan	3,015	4.1%
8	Georgia	2,369	3.2%
9	Maryland	1,978	2.7%
10	Washington	1,967	2.7%
11	Ohio	1,960	2.7%
12	Illinois	1,950	2.7%
13	Colorado	1,792	2.4%
14	Massachusetts	1,725	2.3%
15	Arizona	1,668	2.3%
16	Virginia	1,611	2.2%
17	Wisconsin	1,557	2.1%
18	New Jersey	1,434	2.0%
19	Connecticut	1,375	1.9%
20	Minnesota	1,251	1.7%
21	Oklahoma	1,072	1.5%
22	Tennessee	954	1.3%
23	Kentucky	866	1.2%
24	Oregon	853	1.2%
25	Kansas	796	1.1%
26	Iowa	765	1.0%
27	South Carolina	743	1.0%
28	Nebraska	731	1.0%
29	West Virginia	719	1.0%
30	Utah	693	0.9%
31	Missouri	635	0.9%
32	Indiana	621	0.8%
33	Maine	555	0.8%
34	Louisiana	545	0.7%
35	Nevada	517	0.7%
36	New Mexico	516	0.7%
37	Idaho	511	0.7%
38	Alabama	485	0.7%
39	New Hampshire	420	0.6%
40	South Dakota	409	0.6%
41	Alaska	376	0.5%
42	Montana	353	0.5%
43	North Dakota	243	0.3%
44	Rhode Island	226	0.3%
45	Vermont	219	0.3%
46	Delaware	215	0.3%
47	Wyoming	192	0.3%
48	Hawaii	158	0.2%
49	Arkansas	155	0.2%
50	Mississippi	86	0.1%
	District of Columbia	231	0.3%

Source: The American Academy of Physician Assistants

"Projected Number of People in Clinical Practice as PAs as of December 31, 2008" (http://www.aapa.org/research/)

*Projected. National total does not include 387 physician assistants who work outside the United States or whose location is unknown.

Rate of Physician Assistants in Clinical Practice in 2008

National Rate = 24 PAs per 100,000 Population*

ALPHA ORDER

RANK	STATE	RATE
47	Alabama	10
1	Alaska	55
24	Arizona	26
49	Arkansas	5
37	California	19
10	Colorado	36
7	Connecticut	39
26	Delaware	25
29	Florida	24
29	Georgia	24
44	Hawaii	12
16	Idaho	34
42	Illinois	15
47	Indiana	10
26	Iowa	25
21	Kansas	28
35	Kentucky	20
44	Louisiana	12
3	Maine	42
13	Maryland	35
23	Massachusetts	27
18	Michigan	30
29	Minnesota	24
50	Mississippi	3
46	Missouri	11
10	Montana	36
4	Nebraska	41
35	Nevada	20
17	New Hampshire	32
39	New Jersey	17
24	New Mexico	26
4	New York	41
7	North Carolina	39
9	North Dakota	38
39	Ohio	17
20	Oklahoma	29
32	Oregon	23
13	Pennsylvania	35
33	Rhode Island	22
39	South Carolina	17
2	South Dakota	51
42	Tennessee	15
37	Texas	19
26	Utah	25
13	Vermont	35
34	Virginia	21
18	Washington	30
6	West Virginia	40
21	Wisconsin	28
10	Wyoming	36

RANK ORDER

RANK	STATE	RATE
1	Alaska	55
2	South Dakota	51
3	Maine	42
4	Nebraska	41
4	New York	41
6	West Virginia	40
7	Connecticut	39
7	North Carolina	39
9	North Dakota	38
10	Colorado	36
10	Montana	36
10	Wyoming	36
13	Maryland	35
13	Pennsylvania	35
13	Vermont	35
16	Idaho	34
17	New Hampshire	32
18	Michigan	30
18	Washington	30
20	Oklahoma	29
21	Kansas	28
21	Wisconsin	28
23	Massachusetts	27
24	Arizona	26
24	New Mexico	26
26	Delaware	25
26	Iowa	25
26	Utah	25
29	Florida	24
29	Georgia	24
29	Minnesota	24
32	Oregon	23
33	Rhode Island	22
34	Virginia	21
35	Kentucky	20
35	Nevada	20
37	California	19
37	Texas	19
39	New Jersey	17
39	Ohio	17
39	South Carolina	17
42	Illinois	15
42	Tennessee	15
44	Hawaii	12
44	Louisiana	12
46	Missouri	11
47	Alabama	10
47	Indiana	10
49	Arkansas	5
50	Mississippi	3

	District of Columbia	39

Source: CQ Press using data from The American Academy of Physician Assistants
   "Projected Number of People in Clinical Practice as PAs as of December 31, 2008" (http://www.aapa.org/research/)
*Projected. Rates calculated using 2008 Census population figures.

Average Annual Wages of Physician Assistants in 2007

National Average = $77,800*

ALPHA ORDER

RANK	STATE	WAGES
37	Alabama	$68,720
2	Alaska	89,460
28	Arizona	77,690
41	Arkansas	66,490
26	California	78,120
31	Colorado	76,050
1	Connecticut	91,010
17	Delaware	80,710
13	Florida	81,600
25	Georgia	78,170
44	Hawaii	64,040
46	Idaho	62,700
38	Illinois	68,680
39	Indiana	68,190
30	Iowa	76,130
22	Kansas	79,170
32	Kentucky	75,160
48	Louisiana	56,650
10	Maine	82,960
8	Maryland	83,190
12	Massachusetts	81,720
21	Michigan	79,240
7	Minnesota	83,280
50	Mississippi	42,160
47	Missouri	61,240
43	Montana	64,440
23	Nebraska	79,010
6	Nevada	83,820
16	New Hampshire	80,920
3	New Jersey	88,800
49	New Mexico	50,320
9	New York	83,160
24	North Carolina	78,760
36	North Dakota	70,080
20	Ohio	79,280
18	Oklahoma	80,600
14	Oregon	81,460
40	Pennsylvania	67,370
29	Rhode Island	76,400
35	South Carolina	73,450
27	South Dakota	77,920
34	Tennessee	73,590
11	Texas	81,960
4	Utah	86,360
15	Vermont	81,340
45	Virginia	63,350
5	Washington	86,210
33	West Virginia	74,950
19	Wisconsin	80,140
42	Wyoming	65,080

RANK ORDER

RANK	STATE	WAGES
1	Connecticut	$91,010
2	Alaska	89,460
3	New Jersey	88,800
4	Utah	86,360
5	Washington	86,210
6	Nevada	83,820
7	Minnesota	83,280
8	Maryland	83,190
9	New York	83,160
10	Maine	82,960
11	Texas	81,960
12	Massachusetts	81,720
13	Florida	81,600
14	Oregon	81,460
15	Vermont	81,340
16	New Hampshire	80,920
17	Delaware	80,710
18	Oklahoma	80,600
19	Wisconsin	80,140
20	Ohio	79,280
21	Michigan	79,240
22	Kansas	79,170
23	Nebraska	79,010
24	North Carolina	78,760
25	Georgia	78,170
26	California	78,120
27	South Dakota	77,920
28	Arizona	77,690
29	Rhode Island	76,400
30	Iowa	76,130
31	Colorado	76,050
32	Kentucky	75,160
33	West Virginia	74,950
34	Tennessee	73,590
35	South Carolina	73,450
36	North Dakota	70,080
37	Alabama	68,720
38	Illinois	68,680
39	Indiana	68,190
40	Pennsylvania	67,370
41	Arkansas	66,490
42	Wyoming	65,080
43	Montana	64,440
44	Hawaii	64,040
45	Virginia	63,350
46	Idaho	62,700
47	Missouri	61,240
48	Louisiana	56,650
49	New Mexico	50,320
50	Mississippi	42,160
	District of Columbia	76,880

Source: U.S. Department of Labor, Bureau of Labor Statistics
   "Occupational Employment and Wages, 2007" (http://www.bls.gov/oes/)
*Does not include self-employed.

Registered Nurses in 2007

National Total = 2,468,340 Registered Nurses*

ALPHA ORDER

RANK	STATE	NURSES	% of USA
21	Alabama	42,180	1.7%
49	Alaska	5,150	0.2%
27	Arizona	34,580	1.4%
33	Arkansas	21,920	0.9%
1	California	233,200	9.4%
24	Colorado	36,850	1.5%
26	Connecticut	34,690	1.4%
45	Delaware	8,420	0.3%
4	Florida	148,180	6.0%
12	Georgia	62,230	2.5%
43	Hawaii	9,620	0.4%
44	Idaho	9,600	0.4%
7	Illinois	104,130	4.2%
16	Indiana	54,770	2.2%
29	Iowa	29,550	1.2%
32	Kansas	24,070	1.0%
22	Kentucky	39,120	1.6%
23	Louisiana	39,090	1.6%
38	Maine	13,850	0.6%
20	Maryland	48,840	2.0%
11	Massachusetts	78,280	3.2%
8	Michigan	84,480	3.4%
17	Minnesota	52,690	2.1%
31	Mississippi	25,350	1.0%
14	Missouri	56,290	2.3%
46	Montana	7,160	0.3%
34	Nebraska	17,870	0.7%
37	Nevada	14,670	0.6%
39	New Hampshire	12,730	0.5%
10	New Jersey	78,510	3.2%
40	New Mexico	11,400	0.5%
2	New York	166,990	6.8%
9	North Carolina	80,090	3.2%
47	North Dakota	7,000	0.3%
6	Ohio	114,920	4.7%
30	Oklahoma	25,700	1.0%
28	Oregon	29,700	1.2%
5	Pennsylvania	126,370	5.1%
41	Rhode Island	10,600	0.4%
25	South Carolina	35,040	1.4%
42	South Dakota	9,670	0.4%
15	Tennessee	54,960	2.2%
3	Texas	157,870	6.4%
36	Utah	16,670	0.7%
48	Vermont	5,660	0.2%
13	Virginia	57,740	2.3%
19	Washington	49,910	2.0%
35	West Virginia	16,970	0.7%
18	Wisconsin	50,690	2.1%
50	Wyoming	4,250	0.2%

RANK ORDER

RANK	STATE	NURSES	% of USA
1	California	233,200	9.4%
2	New York	166,990	6.8%
3	Texas	157,870	6.4%
4	Florida	148,180	6.0%
5	Pennsylvania	126,370	5.1%
6	Ohio	114,920	4.7%
7	Illinois	104,130	4.2%
8	Michigan	84,480	3.4%
9	North Carolina	80,090	3.2%
10	New Jersey	78,510	3.2%
11	Massachusetts	78,280	3.2%
12	Georgia	62,230	2.5%
13	Virginia	57,740	2.3%
14	Missouri	56,290	2.3%
15	Tennessee	54,960	2.2%
16	Indiana	54,770	2.2%
17	Minnesota	52,690	2.1%
18	Wisconsin	50,690	2.1%
19	Washington	49,910	2.0%
20	Maryland	48,840	2.0%
21	Alabama	42,180	1.7%
22	Kentucky	39,120	1.6%
23	Louisiana	39,090	1.6%
24	Colorado	36,850	1.5%
25	South Carolina	35,040	1.4%
26	Connecticut	34,690	1.4%
27	Arizona	34,580	1.4%
28	Oregon	29,700	1.2%
29	Iowa	29,550	1.2%
30	Oklahoma	25,700	1.0%
31	Mississippi	25,350	1.0%
32	Kansas	24,070	1.0%
33	Arkansas	21,920	0.9%
34	Nebraska	17,870	0.7%
35	West Virginia	16,970	0.7%
36	Utah	16,670	0.7%
37	Nevada	14,670	0.6%
38	Maine	13,850	0.6%
39	New Hampshire	12,730	0.5%
40	New Mexico	11,400	0.5%
41	Rhode Island	10,600	0.4%
42	South Dakota	9,670	0.4%
43	Hawaii	9,620	0.4%
44	Idaho	9,600	0.4%
45	Delaware	8,420	0.3%
46	Montana	7,160	0.3%
47	North Dakota	7,000	0.3%
48	Vermont	5,660	0.2%
49	Alaska	5,150	0.2%
50	Wyoming	4,250	0.2%
	District of Columbia	8,110	0.3%

Source: U.S. Department of Labor, Bureau of Labor Statistics
"Occupational Employment and Wages, 2007" (http://www.bls.gov/oes/)
*Does not include self-employed.

Rate of Registered Nurses in 2007

National Rate = 819 Nurses per 100,000 Population*

ALPHA ORDER			RANK ORDER		
RANK	STATE	RATE	RANK	STATE	RATE
17	Alabama	912	1	South Dakota	1,215
38	Alaska	756	2	Massachusetts	1,210
50	Arizona	544	3	North Dakota	1,097
35	Arkansas	774	4	Maine	1,053
46	California	641	5	Minnesota	1,017
37	Colorado	761	5	Pennsylvania	1,017
10	Connecticut	994	7	Nebraska	1,010
12	Delaware	977	8	Rhode Island	1,007
30	Florida	814	9	Ohio	1,001
44	Georgia	653	10	Connecticut	994
39	Hawaii	753	11	Iowa	990
45	Idaho	642	12	Delaware	977
31	Illinois	812	13	New Hampshire	970
27	Indiana	864	14	Missouri	958
11	Iowa	990	15	West Virginia	938
26	Kansas	867	16	Kentucky	923
16	Kentucky	923	17	Alabama	912
21	Louisiana	894	17	Vermont	912
4	Maine	1,053	19	New Jersey	907
24	Maryland	869	20	Wisconsin	905
2	Massachusetts	1,210	21	Louisiana	894
29	Michigan	841	21	Tennessee	894
5	Minnesota	1,017	23	North Carolina	886
25	Mississippi	868	24	Maryland	869
14	Missouri	958	25	Mississippi	868
41	Montana	748	26	Kansas	867
7	Nebraska	1,010	27	Indiana	864
49	Nevada	574	28	New York	859
13	New Hampshire	970	29	Michigan	841
19	New Jersey	907	30	Florida	814
48	New Mexico	580	31	Illinois	812
28	New York	859	31	Wyoming	812
23	North Carolina	886	33	Oregon	795
3	North Dakota	1,097	33	South Carolina	795
9	Ohio	1,001	35	Arkansas	774
42	Oklahoma	712	35	Washington	774
33	Oregon	795	37	Colorado	761
5	Pennsylvania	1,017	38	Alaska	756
8	Rhode Island	1,007	39	Hawaii	753
33	South Carolina	795	40	Virginia	750
1	South Dakota	1,215	41	Montana	748
21	Tennessee	894	42	Oklahoma	712
43	Texas	662	43	Texas	662
47	Utah	625	44	Georgia	653
17	Vermont	912	45	Idaho	642
40	Virginia	750	46	California	641
35	Washington	774	47	Utah	625
15	West Virginia	938	48	New Mexico	580
20	Wisconsin	905	49	Nevada	574
31	Wyoming	812	50	Arizona	544
				District of Columbia	1,380

Source: CQ Press using data from U.S. Department of Labor, Bureau of Labor Statistics
"Occupational Employment and Wages, 2007" (http://www.bls.gov/oes/)
*Does not include self-employed.

Average Annual Wages of Registered Nurses in 2007

National Average = $62,480*

ALPHA ORDER			RANK ORDER		
RANK	STATE	WAGES	RANK	STATE	WAGES
38	Alabama	$54,370	1	California	$78,550
6	Alaska	70,300	2	Massachusetts	74,940
18	Arizona	60,670	3	Hawaii	74,220
44	Arkansas	52,600	4	New Jersey	70,900
1	California	78,550	5	Maryland	70,480
15	Colorado	61,890	6	Alaska	70,300
12	Connecticut	66,890	7	New York	69,620
13	Delaware	65,550	8	Minnesota	67,510
22	Florida	59,450	9	Nevada	67,430
28	Georgia	57,350	9	Washington	67,430
3	Hawaii	74,220	11	Oregon	67,250
39	Idaho	53,960	12	Connecticut	66,890
16	Illinois	61,060	13	Delaware	65,550
36	Indiana	54,990	14	Rhode Island	65,190
50	Iowa	49,140	15	Colorado	61,890
46	Kansas	52,420	16	Illinois	61,060
34	Kentucky	55,800	17	Michigan	61,030
35	Louisiana	55,670	18	Arizona	60,670
27	Maine	58,010	19	Wisconsin	59,980
5	Maryland	70,480	20	Texas	59,720
2	Massachusetts	74,940	21	New Mexico	59,570
17	Michigan	61,030	22	Florida	59,450
8	Minnesota	67,510	23	Virginia	59,350
41	Mississippi	53,400	24	Pennsylvania	59,280
37	Missouri	54,710	25	Vermont	58,950
42	Montana	53,320	26	New Hampshire	58,900
45	Nebraska	52,520	27	Maine	58,010
9	Nevada	67,430	28	Georgia	57,350
26	New Hampshire	58,900	29	Ohio	57,320
4	New Jersey	70,900	30	Utah	56,180
21	New Mexico	59,570	31	North Carolina	55,920
7	New York	69,620	32	Tennessee	55,910
31	North Carolina	55,920	33	South Carolina	55,820
40	North Dakota	53,610	34	Kentucky	55,800
29	Ohio	57,320	35	Louisiana	55,670
49	Oklahoma	50,330	36	Indiana	54,990
11	Oregon	67,250	37	Missouri	54,710
24	Pennsylvania	59,280	38	Alabama	54,370
14	Rhode Island	65,190	39	Idaho	53,960
33	South Carolina	55,820	40	North Dakota	53,610
48	South Dakota	50,830	41	Mississippi	53,400
32	Tennessee	55,910	42	Montana	53,320
20	Texas	59,720	43	Wyoming	52,800
30	Utah	56,180	44	Arkansas	52,600
25	Vermont	58,950	45	Nebraska	52,520
23	Virginia	59,350	46	Kansas	52,420
9	Washington	67,430	47	West Virginia	51,020
47	West Virginia	51,020	48	South Dakota	50,830
19	Wisconsin	59,980	49	Oklahoma	50,330
43	Wyoming	52,800	50	Iowa	49,140
				District of Columbia	66,750

Source: U.S. Department of Labor, Bureau of Labor Statistics
  "Occupational Employment and Wages, 2007" (http://www.bls.gov/oes/)
*Does not include self-employed.

Licensed Practical and Licensed Vocational Nurses in 2007

National Total = 719,240 LPN/LVNs*

ALPHA ORDER

RANK	STATE	NURSES	% of USA
19	Alabama	14,960	2.1%
50	Alaska	430	0.1%
24	Arizona	10,430	1.5%
21	Arkansas	11,710	1.6%
2	California	57,350	8.0%
32	Colorado	6,930	1.0%
29	Connecticut	7,930	1.1%
43	Delaware	2,160	0.3%
3	Florida	49,350	6.9%
8	Georgia	24,210	3.4%
47	Hawaii	1,770	0.2%
37	Idaho	2,820	0.4%
7	Illinois	24,760	3.4%
12	Indiana	19,160	2.7%
31	Iowa	7,170	1.0%
30	Kansas	7,370	1.0%
22	Kentucky	10,930	1.5%
14	Louisiana	18,490	2.6%
46	Maine	1,780	0.2%
25	Maryland	10,380	1.4%
16	Massachusetts	17,420	2.4%
13	Michigan	18,650	2.6%
10	Minnesota	19,640	2.7%
28	Mississippi	9,700	1.3%
15	Missouri	17,750	2.5%
38	Montana	2,750	0.4%
34	Nebraska	5,720	0.8%
39	Nevada	2,600	0.4%
40	New Hampshire	2,500	0.3%
17	New Jersey	16,680	2.3%
35	New Mexico	4,910	0.7%
4	New York	47,120	6.6%
18	North Carolina	16,250	2.3%
36	North Dakota	2,910	0.4%
5	Ohio	38,880	5.4%
20	Oklahoma	13,440	1.9%
40	Oregon	2,500	0.3%
6	Pennsylvania	35,580	4.9%
45	Rhode Island	1,790	0.2%
26	South Carolina	10,310	1.4%
44	South Dakota	1,980	0.3%
9	Tennessee	23,080	3.2%
1	Texas	64,560	9.0%
42	Utah	2,440	0.3%
48	Vermont	1,460	0.2%
11	Virginia	19,270	2.7%
27	Washington	9,810	1.4%
33	West Virginia	6,300	0.9%
23	Wisconsin	10,660	1.5%
49	Wyoming	700	0.1%

RANK ORDER

RANK	STATE	NURSES	% of USA
1	Texas	64,560	9.0%
2	California	57,350	8.0%
3	Florida	49,350	6.9%
4	New York	47,120	6.6%
5	Ohio	38,880	5.4%
6	Pennsylvania	35,580	4.9%
7	Illinois	24,760	3.4%
8	Georgia	24,210	3.4%
9	Tennessee	23,080	3.2%
10	Minnesota	19,640	2.7%
11	Virginia	19,270	2.7%
12	Indiana	19,160	2.7%
13	Michigan	18,650	2.6%
14	Louisiana	18,490	2.6%
15	Missouri	17,750	2.5%
16	Massachusetts	17,420	2.4%
17	New Jersey	16,680	2.3%
18	North Carolina	16,250	2.3%
19	Alabama	14,960	2.1%
20	Oklahoma	13,440	1.9%
21	Arkansas	11,710	1.6%
22	Kentucky	10,930	1.5%
23	Wisconsin	10,660	1.5%
24	Arizona	10,430	1.5%
25	Maryland	10,380	1.4%
26	South Carolina	10,310	1.4%
27	Washington	9,810	1.4%
28	Mississippi	9,700	1.3%
29	Connecticut	7,930	1.1%
30	Kansas	7,370	1.0%
31	Iowa	7,170	1.0%
32	Colorado	6,930	1.0%
33	West Virginia	6,300	0.9%
34	Nebraska	5,720	0.8%
35	New Mexico	4,910	0.7%
36	North Dakota	2,910	0.4%
37	Idaho	2,820	0.4%
38	Montana	2,750	0.4%
39	Nevada	2,600	0.4%
40	New Hampshire	2,500	0.3%
40	Oregon	2,500	0.3%
42	Utah	2,440	0.3%
43	Delaware	2,160	0.3%
44	South Dakota	1,980	0.3%
45	Rhode Island	1,790	0.2%
46	Maine	1,780	0.2%
47	Hawaii	1,770	0.2%
48	Vermont	1,460	0.2%
49	Wyoming	700	0.1%
50	Alaska	430	0.1%
	District of Columbia	1,810	0.3%

Source: U.S. Department of Labor, Bureau of Labor Statistics
   "Occupational Employment and Wages, 2007" (http://www.bls.gov/oes/)
*Does not include self-employed.

Rate of Licensed Practical and Licensed Vocational Nurses in 2007

National Rate = 239 LPN/LVNs per 100,000 Population*

<table>
<tr><td colspan="3">ALPHA ORDER</td><td colspan="3">RANK ORDER</td></tr>
<tr><td>RANK</td><td>STATE</td><td>RATE</td><td>RANK</td><td>STATE</td><td>RATE</td></tr>
<tr><td>10</td><td>Alabama</td><td>323</td><td>1</td><td>North Dakota</td><td>456</td></tr>
<tr><td>50</td><td>Alaska</td><td>63</td><td>2</td><td>Louisiana</td><td>423</td></tr>
<tr><td>40</td><td>Arizona</td><td>164</td><td>3</td><td>Arkansas</td><td>414</td></tr>
<tr><td>3</td><td>Arkansas</td><td>414</td><td>4</td><td>Minnesota</td><td>379</td></tr>
<tr><td>41</td><td>California</td><td>158</td><td>5</td><td>Tennessee</td><td>375</td></tr>
<tr><td>43</td><td>Colorado</td><td>143</td><td>6</td><td>Oklahoma</td><td>372</td></tr>
<tr><td>30</td><td>Connecticut</td><td>227</td><td>7</td><td>West Virginia</td><td>348</td></tr>
<tr><td>22</td><td>Delaware</td><td>251</td><td>8</td><td>Ohio</td><td>339</td></tr>
<tr><td>16</td><td>Florida</td><td>271</td><td>9</td><td>Mississippi</td><td>332</td></tr>
<tr><td>21</td><td>Georgia</td><td>254</td><td>10</td><td>Alabama</td><td>323</td></tr>
<tr><td>44</td><td>Hawaii</td><td>139</td><td>10</td><td>Nebraska</td><td>323</td></tr>
<tr><td>35</td><td>Idaho</td><td>188</td><td>12</td><td>Indiana</td><td>302</td></tr>
<tr><td>31</td><td>Illinois</td><td>193</td><td>12</td><td>Missouri</td><td>302</td></tr>
<tr><td>12</td><td>Indiana</td><td>302</td><td>14</td><td>Montana</td><td>287</td></tr>
<tr><td>27</td><td>Iowa</td><td>240</td><td>15</td><td>Pennsylvania</td><td>286</td></tr>
<tr><td>19</td><td>Kansas</td><td>265</td><td>16</td><td>Florida</td><td>271</td></tr>
<tr><td>20</td><td>Kentucky</td><td>258</td><td>16</td><td>Texas</td><td>271</td></tr>
<tr><td>2</td><td>Louisiana</td><td>423</td><td>18</td><td>Massachusetts</td><td>269</td></tr>
<tr><td>45</td><td>Maine</td><td>135</td><td>19</td><td>Kansas</td><td>265</td></tr>
<tr><td>37</td><td>Maryland</td><td>185</td><td>20</td><td>Kentucky</td><td>258</td></tr>
<tr><td>18</td><td>Massachusetts</td><td>269</td><td>21</td><td>Georgia</td><td>254</td></tr>
<tr><td>36</td><td>Michigan</td><td>186</td><td>22</td><td>Delaware</td><td>251</td></tr>
<tr><td>4</td><td>Minnesota</td><td>379</td><td>23</td><td>New Mexico</td><td>250</td></tr>
<tr><td>9</td><td>Mississippi</td><td>332</td><td>23</td><td>Virginia</td><td>250</td></tr>
<tr><td>12</td><td>Missouri</td><td>302</td><td>25</td><td>South Dakota</td><td>249</td></tr>
<tr><td>14</td><td>Montana</td><td>287</td><td>26</td><td>New York</td><td>243</td></tr>
<tr><td>10</td><td>Nebraska</td><td>323</td><td>27</td><td>Iowa</td><td>240</td></tr>
<tr><td>47</td><td>Nevada</td><td>102</td><td>28</td><td>Vermont</td><td>235</td></tr>
<tr><td>33</td><td>New Hampshire</td><td>191</td><td>29</td><td>South Carolina</td><td>234</td></tr>
<tr><td>31</td><td>New Jersey</td><td>193</td><td>30</td><td>Connecticut</td><td>227</td></tr>
<tr><td>23</td><td>New Mexico</td><td>250</td><td>31</td><td>Illinois</td><td>193</td></tr>
<tr><td>26</td><td>New York</td><td>243</td><td>31</td><td>New Jersey</td><td>193</td></tr>
<tr><td>38</td><td>North Carolina</td><td>180</td><td>33</td><td>New Hampshire</td><td>191</td></tr>
<tr><td>1</td><td>North Dakota</td><td>456</td><td>34</td><td>Wisconsin</td><td>190</td></tr>
<tr><td>8</td><td>Ohio</td><td>339</td><td>35</td><td>Idaho</td><td>188</td></tr>
<tr><td>6</td><td>Oklahoma</td><td>372</td><td>36</td><td>Michigan</td><td>186</td></tr>
<tr><td>49</td><td>Oregon</td><td>67</td><td>37</td><td>Maryland</td><td>185</td></tr>
<tr><td>15</td><td>Pennsylvania</td><td>286</td><td>38</td><td>North Carolina</td><td>180</td></tr>
<tr><td>39</td><td>Rhode Island</td><td>170</td><td>39</td><td>Rhode Island</td><td>170</td></tr>
<tr><td>29</td><td>South Carolina</td><td>234</td><td>40</td><td>Arizona</td><td>164</td></tr>
<tr><td>25</td><td>South Dakota</td><td>249</td><td>41</td><td>California</td><td>158</td></tr>
<tr><td>5</td><td>Tennessee</td><td>375</td><td>42</td><td>Washington</td><td>152</td></tr>
<tr><td>16</td><td>Texas</td><td>271</td><td>43</td><td>Colorado</td><td>143</td></tr>
<tr><td>48</td><td>Utah</td><td>91</td><td>44</td><td>Hawaii</td><td>139</td></tr>
<tr><td>28</td><td>Vermont</td><td>235</td><td>45</td><td>Maine</td><td>135</td></tr>
<tr><td>23</td><td>Virginia</td><td>250</td><td>46</td><td>Wyoming</td><td>134</td></tr>
<tr><td>42</td><td>Washington</td><td>152</td><td>47</td><td>Nevada</td><td>102</td></tr>
<tr><td>7</td><td>West Virginia</td><td>348</td><td>48</td><td>Utah</td><td>91</td></tr>
<tr><td>34</td><td>Wisconsin</td><td>190</td><td>49</td><td>Oregon</td><td>67</td></tr>
<tr><td>46</td><td>Wyoming</td><td>134</td><td>50</td><td>Alaska</td><td>63</td></tr>
</table>

District of Columbia   308

Source: CQ Press using data from U.S. Department of Labor, Bureau of Labor Statistics
 "Occupational Employment and Wages, 2007" (http://www.bls.gov/oes/)
*Does not include self-employed.

Average Annual Wages of Licensed Practical and Licensed Vocational Nurses in 2007
National Average = $38,940*

ALPHA ORDER				RANK ORDER		
RANK	STATE	WAGES		RANK	STATE	WAGES
47	Alabama	$31,560		1	Connecticut	$50,950
7	Alaska	46,330		2	Massachusetts	48,790
14	Arizona	41,170		3	New Jersey	48,750
45	Arkansas	32,290		4	Rhode Island	47,090
5	California	46,990		5	California	46,990
19	Colorado	39,880		6	Maryland	46,760
1	Connecticut	50,950		7	Alaska	46,330
9	Delaware	45,110		8	New Mexico	45,810
24	Florida	38,570		9	Delaware	45,110
37	Georgia	34,700		10	Nevada	43,610
17	Hawaii	40,040		11	Washington	42,290
32	Idaho	36,250		12	New Hampshire	42,230
18	Illinois	39,980		13	Oregon	42,150
29	Indiana	37,220		14	Arizona	41,170
40	Iowa	34,450		15	Michigan	40,400
36	Kansas	34,950		16	New York	40,150
35	Kentucky	35,130		17	Hawaii	40,040
41	Louisiana	33,750		18	Illinois	39,980
26	Maine	37,940		19	Colorado	39,880
6	Maryland	46,760		20	Pennsylvania	39,490
2	Massachusetts	48,790		21	Wisconsin	39,460
15	Michigan	40,400		22	Vermont	38,700
25	Minnesota	38,010		23	Ohio	38,630
48	Mississippi	31,370		24	Florida	38,570
43	Missouri	33,170		25	Minnesota	38,010
44	Montana	32,590		26	Maine	37,940
39	Nebraska	34,520		27	North Carolina	37,900
10	Nevada	43,610		28	Texas	37,360
12	New Hampshire	42,230		29	Indiana	37,220
3	New Jersey	48,750		30	Virginia	36,610
8	New Mexico	45,810		31	Wyoming	36,310
16	New York	40,150		32	Idaho	36,250
27	North Carolina	37,900		33	Utah	35,890
42	North Dakota	33,410		34	South Carolina	35,860
23	Ohio	38,630		35	Kentucky	35,130
46	Oklahoma	31,680		36	Kansas	34,950
13	Oregon	42,150		37	Georgia	34,700
20	Pennsylvania	39,490		38	Tennessee	34,540
4	Rhode Island	47,090		39	Nebraska	34,520
34	South Carolina	35,860		40	Iowa	34,450
49	South Dakota	31,290		41	Louisiana	33,750
38	Tennessee	34,540		42	North Dakota	33,410
28	Texas	37,360		43	Missouri	33,170
33	Utah	35,890		44	Montana	32,590
22	Vermont	38,700		45	Arkansas	32,290
30	Virginia	36,610		46	Oklahoma	31,680
11	Washington	42,290		47	Alabama	31,560
50	West Virginia	30,680		48	Mississippi	31,370
21	Wisconsin	39,460		49	South Dakota	31,290
31	Wyoming	36,310		50	West Virginia	30,680
				District of Columbia		49,620

Source: U.S. Department of Labor, Bureau of Labor Statistics
   "Occupational Employment and Wages, 2007" (http://www.bls.gov/oes/)
*Does not include self-employed.

Physical Therapists in 2007

National Total = 161,850 Physical Therapists*

ALPHA ORDER					RANK ORDER			

RANK	STATE	THERAPISTS	% of USA		RANK	STATE	THERAPISTS	% of USA
29	Alabama	1,710	1.1%		1	California	14,110	8.7%
49	Alaska	310	0.2%		2	New York	11,790	7.3%
23	Arizona	2,670	1.6%		3	Florida	10,620	6.6%
32	Arkansas	1,410	0.9%		4	Texas	9,840	6.1%
1	California	14,110	8.7%		5	Pennsylvania	8,790	5.4%
20	Colorado	3,260	2.0%		6	Illinois	6,710	4.1%
21	Connecticut	3,220	2.0%		7	Ohio	6,650	4.1%
47	Delaware	470	0.3%		8	Massachusetts	5,970	3.7%
3	Florida	10,620	6.6%		9	Michigan	5,890	3.6%
17	Georgia	3,600	2.2%		10	New Jersey	5,570	3.4%
40	Hawaii	860	0.5%		11	Maryland	3,950	2.4%
42	Idaho	810	0.5%		11	North Carolina	3,950	2.4%
6	Illinois	6,710	4.1%		13	Wisconsin	3,900	2.4%
16	Indiana	3,640	2.2%		14	Missouri	3,870	2.4%
30	Iowa	1,550	1.0%		15	Virginia	3,670	2.3%
31	Kansas	1,490	0.9%		16	Indiana	3,640	2.2%
28	Kentucky	1,810	1.1%		17	Georgia	3,600	2.2%
24	Louisiana	2,200	1.4%		18	Washington	3,540	2.2%
39	Maine	900	0.6%		19	Tennessee	3,300	2.0%
11	Maryland	3,950	2.4%		20	Colorado	3,260	2.0%
8	Massachusetts	5,970	3.7%		21	Connecticut	3,220	2.0%
9	Michigan	5,890	3.6%		22	Minnesota	2,920	1.8%
22	Minnesota	2,920	1.8%		23	Arizona	2,670	1.6%
33	Mississippi	1,320	0.8%		24	Louisiana	2,200	1.4%
14	Missouri	3,870	2.4%		25	South Carolina	2,110	1.3%
44	Montana	650	0.4%		26	Oregon	2,090	1.3%
34	Nebraska	1,070	0.7%		27	Oklahoma	1,850	1.1%
41	Nevada	850	0.5%		28	Kentucky	1,810	1.1%
35	New Hampshire	1,060	0.7%		29	Alabama	1,710	1.1%
10	New Jersey	5,570	3.4%		30	Iowa	1,550	1.0%
38	New Mexico	920	0.6%		31	Kansas	1,490	0.9%
2	New York	11,790	7.3%		32	Arkansas	1,410	0.9%
11	North Carolina	3,950	2.4%		33	Mississippi	1,320	0.8%
48	North Dakota	420	0.3%		34	Nebraska	1,070	0.7%
7	Ohio	6,650	4.1%		35	New Hampshire	1,060	0.7%
27	Oklahoma	1,850	1.1%		36	West Virginia	1,040	0.6%
26	Oregon	2,090	1.3%		37	Utah	990	0.6%
5	Pennsylvania	8,790	5.4%		38	New Mexico	920	0.6%
43	Rhode Island	770	0.5%		39	Maine	900	0.6%
25	South Carolina	2,110	1.3%		40	Hawaii	860	0.5%
46	South Dakota	500	0.3%		41	Nevada	850	0.5%
19	Tennessee	3,300	2.0%		42	Idaho	810	0.5%
4	Texas	9,840	6.1%		43	Rhode Island	770	0.5%
37	Utah	990	0.6%		44	Montana	650	0.4%
45	Vermont	570	0.4%		45	Vermont	570	0.4%
15	Virginia	3,670	2.3%		46	South Dakota	500	0.3%
18	Washington	3,540	2.2%		47	Delaware	470	0.3%
36	West Virginia	1,040	0.6%		48	North Dakota	420	0.3%
13	Wisconsin	3,900	2.4%		49	Alaska	310	0.2%
50	Wyoming	290	0.2%		50	Wyoming	290	0.2%
					District of Columbia		420	0.3%

Source: U.S. Department of Labor, Bureau of Labor Statistics
    "Occupational Employment and Wages, 2007" (http://www.bls.gov/oes/)
*Does not include self-employed.

Rate of Physical Therapists in 2007

National Rate = 54 Physical Therapists per 100,000 Population*

ALPHA ORDER

RANK	STATE	RATE
48	Alabama	37
40	Alaska	46
44	Arizona	42
35	Arkansas	50
46	California	39
11	Colorado	67
1	Connecticut	92
26	Delaware	55
20	Florida	58
47	Georgia	38
11	Hawaii	67
29	Idaho	54
32	Illinois	52
22	Indiana	57
32	Iowa	52
29	Kansas	54
43	Kentucky	43
35	Louisiana	50
9	Maine	68
7	Maryland	70
1	Massachusetts	92
19	Michigan	59
24	Minnesota	56
41	Mississippi	45
13	Missouri	66
9	Montana	68
18	Nebraska	60
50	Nevada	33
4	New Hampshire	81
15	New Jersey	64
39	New Mexico	47
17	New York	61
42	North Carolina	44
13	North Dakota	66
20	Ohio	58
34	Oklahoma	51
24	Oregon	56
6	Pennsylvania	71
5	Rhode Island	73
37	South Carolina	48
16	South Dakota	63
29	Tennessee	54
45	Texas	41
48	Utah	37
1	Vermont	92
37	Virginia	48
26	Washington	55
22	West Virginia	57
7	Wisconsin	70
26	Wyoming	55

RANK ORDER

RANK	STATE	RATE
1	Connecticut	92
1	Massachusetts	92
1	Vermont	92
4	New Hampshire	81
5	Rhode Island	73
6	Pennsylvania	71
7	Maryland	70
7	Wisconsin	70
9	Maine	68
9	Montana	68
11	Colorado	67
11	Hawaii	67
13	Missouri	66
13	North Dakota	66
15	New Jersey	64
16	South Dakota	63
17	New York	61
18	Nebraska	60
19	Michigan	59
20	Florida	58
20	Ohio	58
22	Indiana	57
22	West Virginia	57
24	Minnesota	56
24	Oregon	56
26	Delaware	55
26	Washington	55
26	Wyoming	55
29	Idaho	54
29	Kansas	54
29	Tennessee	54
32	Illinois	52
32	Iowa	52
34	Oklahoma	51
35	Arkansas	50
35	Louisiana	50
37	South Carolina	48
37	Virginia	48
39	New Mexico	47
40	Alaska	46
41	Mississippi	45
42	North Carolina	44
43	Kentucky	43
44	Arizona	42
45	Texas	41
46	California	39
47	Georgia	38
48	Alabama	37
48	Utah	37
50	Nevada	33
	District of Columbia	71

Source: CQ Press using data from U.S. Department of Labor, Bureau of Labor Statistics
   "Occupational Employment and Wages, 2007" (http://www.bls.gov/oes/)
*Does not include self-employed.

Average Annual Wages of Physical Therapists in 2007

National Average = $71,520*

ALPHA ORDER

RANK	STATE	WAGES
19	Alabama	$71,590
7	Alaska	76,650
38	Arizona	65,450
27	Arkansas	68,920
2	California	78,940
42	Colorado	63,110
14	Connecticut	72,010
26	Delaware	69,730
12	Florida	72,540
15	Georgia	71,780
49	Hawaii	55,470
32	Idaho	68,070
8	Illinois	75,480
30	Indiana	68,360
37	Iowa	65,770
34	Kansas	67,230
17	Kentucky	71,630
10	Louisiana	73,950
46	Maine	60,400
9	Maryland	74,370
28	Massachusetts	68,590
23	Michigan	70,720
39	Minnesota	65,310
16	Mississippi	71,680
43	Missouri	62,660
50	Montana	54,460
41	Nebraska	63,260
1	Nevada	80,960
36	New Hampshire	66,800
4	New Jersey	78,130
44	New Mexico	62,480
21	New York	71,120
20	North Carolina	71,390
47	North Dakota	60,190
13	Ohio	72,380
29	Oklahoma	68,480
35	Oregon	66,990
24	Pennsylvania	70,340
3	Rhode Island	78,430
22	South Carolina	70,810
45	South Dakota	61,250
11	Tennessee	72,740
5	Texas	77,290
31	Utah	68,270
48	Vermont	59,950
18	Virginia	71,600
25	Washington	69,890
6	West Virginia	77,050
33	Wisconsin	67,820
40	Wyoming	64,250

RANK ORDER

RANK	STATE	WAGES
1	Nevada	$80,960
2	California	78,940
3	Rhode Island	78,430
4	New Jersey	78,130
5	Texas	77,290
6	West Virginia	77,050
7	Alaska	76,650
8	Illinois	75,480
9	Maryland	74,370
10	Louisiana	73,950
11	Tennessee	72,740
12	Florida	72,540
13	Ohio	72,380
14	Connecticut	72,010
15	Georgia	71,780
16	Mississippi	71,680
17	Kentucky	71,630
18	Virginia	71,600
19	Alabama	71,590
20	North Carolina	71,390
21	New York	71,120
22	South Carolina	70,810
23	Michigan	70,720
24	Pennsylvania	70,340
25	Washington	69,890
26	Delaware	69,730
27	Arkansas	68,920
28	Massachusetts	68,590
29	Oklahoma	68,480
30	Indiana	68,360
31	Utah	68,270
32	Idaho	68,070
33	Wisconsin	67,820
34	Kansas	67,230
35	Oregon	66,990
36	New Hampshire	66,800
37	Iowa	65,770
38	Arizona	65,450
39	Minnesota	65,310
40	Wyoming	64,250
41	Nebraska	63,260
42	Colorado	63,110
43	Missouri	62,660
44	New Mexico	62,480
45	South Dakota	61,250
46	Maine	60,400
47	North Dakota	60,190
48	Vermont	59,950
49	Hawaii	55,470
50	Montana	54,460

District of Columbia   66,290

Source: U.S. Department of Labor, Bureau of Labor Statistics
   "Occupational Employment and Wages, 2007" (http://www.bls.gov/oes/)
*Does not include self-employed.

Dentists in 2006

National Total = 179,594 Dentists*

<table>
<tr><td colspan="4">ALPHA ORDER</td></tr>
<tr><td>RANK</td><td>STATE</td><td>DENTISTS</td><td>% of USA</td></tr>
<tr><td>27</td><td>Alabama</td><td>2,032</td><td>1.1%</td></tr>
<tr><td>45</td><td>Alaska</td><td>513</td><td>0.3%</td></tr>
<tr><td>19</td><td>Arizona</td><td>3,107</td><td>1.7%</td></tr>
<tr><td>35</td><td>Arkansas</td><td>1,146</td><td>0.6%</td></tr>
<tr><td>1</td><td>California</td><td>26,887</td><td>15.0%</td></tr>
<tr><td>17</td><td>Colorado</td><td>3,139</td><td>1.7%</td></tr>
<tr><td>23</td><td>Connecticut</td><td>2,694</td><td>1.5%</td></tr>
<tr><td>46</td><td>Delaware</td><td>395</td><td>0.2%</td></tr>
<tr><td>4</td><td>Florida</td><td>9,450</td><td>5.3%</td></tr>
<tr><td>13</td><td>Georgia</td><td>4,167</td><td>2.3%</td></tr>
<tr><td>37</td><td>Hawaii</td><td>1,046</td><td>0.6%</td></tr>
<tr><td>40</td><td>Idaho</td><td>834</td><td>0.5%</td></tr>
<tr><td>5</td><td>Illinois</td><td>8,249</td><td>4.6%</td></tr>
<tr><td>21</td><td>Indiana</td><td>3,013</td><td>1.7%</td></tr>
<tr><td>31</td><td>Iowa</td><td>1,583</td><td>0.9%</td></tr>
<tr><td>32</td><td>Kansas</td><td>1,417</td><td>0.8%</td></tr>
<tr><td>25</td><td>Kentucky</td><td>2,340</td><td>1.3%</td></tr>
<tr><td>26</td><td>Louisiana</td><td>2,102</td><td>1.2%</td></tr>
<tr><td>42</td><td>Maine</td><td>650</td><td>0.4%</td></tr>
<tr><td>14</td><td>Maryland</td><td>4,132</td><td>2.3%</td></tr>
<tr><td>10</td><td>Massachusetts</td><td>5,299</td><td>3.0%</td></tr>
<tr><td>8</td><td>Michigan</td><td>6,141</td><td>3.4%</td></tr>
<tr><td>18</td><td>Minnesota</td><td>3,137</td><td>1.7%</td></tr>
<tr><td>34</td><td>Mississippi</td><td>1,173</td><td>0.7%</td></tr>
<tr><td>22</td><td>Missouri</td><td>2,803</td><td>1.6%</td></tr>
<tr><td>44</td><td>Montana</td><td>525</td><td>0.3%</td></tr>
<tr><td>36</td><td>Nebraska</td><td>1,116</td><td>0.6%</td></tr>
<tr><td>33</td><td>Nevada</td><td>1,185</td><td>0.7%</td></tr>
<tr><td>41</td><td>New Hampshire</td><td>821</td><td>0.5%</td></tr>
<tr><td>7</td><td>New Jersey</td><td>7,113</td><td>4.0%</td></tr>
<tr><td>38</td><td>New Mexico</td><td>871</td><td>0.5%</td></tr>
<tr><td>2</td><td>New York</td><td>15,110</td><td>8.4%</td></tr>
<tr><td>15</td><td>North Carolina</td><td>4,031</td><td>2.2%</td></tr>
<tr><td>49</td><td>North Dakota</td><td>323</td><td>0.2%</td></tr>
<tr><td>9</td><td>Ohio</td><td>6,081</td><td>3.4%</td></tr>
<tr><td>29</td><td>Oklahoma</td><td>1,774</td><td>1.0%</td></tr>
<tr><td>24</td><td>Oregon</td><td>2,506</td><td>1.4%</td></tr>
<tr><td>6</td><td>Pennsylvania</td><td>7,907</td><td>4.4%</td></tr>
<tr><td>43</td><td>Rhode Island</td><td>596</td><td>0.3%</td></tr>
<tr><td>28</td><td>South Carolina</td><td>2,006</td><td>1.1%</td></tr>
<tr><td>47</td><td>South Dakota</td><td>387</td><td>0.2%</td></tr>
<tr><td>20</td><td>Tennessee</td><td>3,031</td><td>1.7%</td></tr>
<tr><td>3</td><td>Texas</td><td>10,758</td><td>6.0%</td></tr>
<tr><td>30</td><td>Utah</td><td>1,671</td><td>0.9%</td></tr>
<tr><td>48</td><td>Vermont</td><td>360</td><td>0.2%</td></tr>
<tr><td>12</td><td>Virginia</td><td>4,489</td><td>2.5%</td></tr>
<tr><td>11</td><td>Washington</td><td>4,510</td><td>2.5%</td></tr>
<tr><td>39</td><td>West Virginia</td><td>854</td><td>0.5%</td></tr>
<tr><td>16</td><td>Wisconsin</td><td>3,199</td><td>1.8%</td></tr>
<tr><td>50</td><td>Wyoming</td><td>281</td><td>0.2%</td></tr>
</table>

<table>
<tr><td colspan="4">RANK ORDER</td></tr>
<tr><td>RANK</td><td>STATE</td><td>DENTISTS</td><td>% of USA</td></tr>
<tr><td>1</td><td>California</td><td>26,887</td><td>15.0%</td></tr>
<tr><td>2</td><td>New York</td><td>15,110</td><td>8.4%</td></tr>
<tr><td>3</td><td>Texas</td><td>10,758</td><td>6.0%</td></tr>
<tr><td>4</td><td>Florida</td><td>9,450</td><td>5.3%</td></tr>
<tr><td>5</td><td>Illinois</td><td>8,249</td><td>4.6%</td></tr>
<tr><td>6</td><td>Pennsylvania</td><td>7,907</td><td>4.4%</td></tr>
<tr><td>7</td><td>New Jersey</td><td>7,113</td><td>4.0%</td></tr>
<tr><td>8</td><td>Michigan</td><td>6,141</td><td>3.4%</td></tr>
<tr><td>9</td><td>Ohio</td><td>6,081</td><td>3.4%</td></tr>
<tr><td>10</td><td>Massachusetts</td><td>5,299</td><td>3.0%</td></tr>
<tr><td>11</td><td>Washington</td><td>4,510</td><td>2.5%</td></tr>
<tr><td>12</td><td>Virginia</td><td>4,489</td><td>2.5%</td></tr>
<tr><td>13</td><td>Georgia</td><td>4,167</td><td>2.3%</td></tr>
<tr><td>14</td><td>Maryland</td><td>4,132</td><td>2.3%</td></tr>
<tr><td>15</td><td>North Carolina</td><td>4,031</td><td>2.2%</td></tr>
<tr><td>16</td><td>Wisconsin</td><td>3,199</td><td>1.8%</td></tr>
<tr><td>17</td><td>Colorado</td><td>3,139</td><td>1.7%</td></tr>
<tr><td>18</td><td>Minnesota</td><td>3,137</td><td>1.7%</td></tr>
<tr><td>19</td><td>Arizona</td><td>3,107</td><td>1.7%</td></tr>
<tr><td>20</td><td>Tennessee</td><td>3,031</td><td>1.7%</td></tr>
<tr><td>21</td><td>Indiana</td><td>3,013</td><td>1.7%</td></tr>
<tr><td>22</td><td>Missouri</td><td>2,803</td><td>1.6%</td></tr>
<tr><td>23</td><td>Connecticut</td><td>2,694</td><td>1.5%</td></tr>
<tr><td>24</td><td>Oregon</td><td>2,506</td><td>1.4%</td></tr>
<tr><td>25</td><td>Kentucky</td><td>2,340</td><td>1.3%</td></tr>
<tr><td>26</td><td>Louisiana</td><td>2,102</td><td>1.2%</td></tr>
<tr><td>27</td><td>Alabama</td><td>2,032</td><td>1.1%</td></tr>
<tr><td>28</td><td>South Carolina</td><td>2,006</td><td>1.1%</td></tr>
<tr><td>29</td><td>Oklahoma</td><td>1,774</td><td>1.0%</td></tr>
<tr><td>30</td><td>Utah</td><td>1,671</td><td>0.9%</td></tr>
<tr><td>31</td><td>Iowa</td><td>1,583</td><td>0.9%</td></tr>
<tr><td>32</td><td>Kansas</td><td>1,417</td><td>0.8%</td></tr>
<tr><td>33</td><td>Nevada</td><td>1,185</td><td>0.7%</td></tr>
<tr><td>34</td><td>Mississippi</td><td>1,173</td><td>0.7%</td></tr>
<tr><td>35</td><td>Arkansas</td><td>1,146</td><td>0.6%</td></tr>
<tr><td>36</td><td>Nebraska</td><td>1,116</td><td>0.6%</td></tr>
<tr><td>37</td><td>Hawaii</td><td>1,046</td><td>0.6%</td></tr>
<tr><td>38</td><td>New Mexico</td><td>871</td><td>0.5%</td></tr>
<tr><td>39</td><td>West Virginia</td><td>854</td><td>0.5%</td></tr>
<tr><td>40</td><td>Idaho</td><td>834</td><td>0.5%</td></tr>
<tr><td>41</td><td>New Hampshire</td><td>821</td><td>0.5%</td></tr>
<tr><td>42</td><td>Maine</td><td>650</td><td>0.4%</td></tr>
<tr><td>43</td><td>Rhode Island</td><td>596</td><td>0.3%</td></tr>
<tr><td>44</td><td>Montana</td><td>525</td><td>0.3%</td></tr>
<tr><td>45</td><td>Alaska</td><td>513</td><td>0.3%</td></tr>
<tr><td>46</td><td>Delaware</td><td>395</td><td>0.2%</td></tr>
<tr><td>47</td><td>South Dakota</td><td>387</td><td>0.2%</td></tr>
<tr><td>48</td><td>Vermont</td><td>360</td><td>0.2%</td></tr>
<tr><td>49</td><td>North Dakota</td><td>323</td><td>0.2%</td></tr>
<tr><td>50</td><td>Wyoming</td><td>281</td><td>0.2%</td></tr>
<tr><td></td><td>District of Columbia</td><td>609</td><td>0.3%</td></tr>
</table>

Source: American Dental Association
   "Distribution of Dentists, by Region and State, 2006"
*Professionally active dentists. Total includes 31 dentists for whom state is not known.

Rate of Dentists in 2006

National Rate = 60 Dentists per 100,000 Population*

RANK	STATE	RATE
48	Alabama	44
6	Alaska	76
32	Arizona	50
49	Arkansas	41
7	California	74
11	Colorado	66
5	Connecticut	77
42	Delaware	46
29	Florida	52
46	Georgia	45
1	Hawaii	82
21	Idaho	57
12	Illinois	65
38	Indiana	48
27	Iowa	53
30	Kansas	51
23	Kentucky	56
32	Louisiana	50
36	Maine	49
7	Maryland	74
1	Massachusetts	82
17	Michigan	61
17	Minnesota	61
50	Mississippi	40
38	Missouri	48
23	Montana	56
15	Nebraska	63
38	Nevada	48
15	New Hampshire	63
1	New Jersey	82
46	New Mexico	45
4	New York	78
42	North Carolina	46
30	North Dakota	51
27	Ohio	53
32	Oklahoma	50
10	Oregon	68
14	Pennsylvania	64
23	Rhode Island	56
42	South Carolina	46
36	South Dakota	49
32	Tennessee	50
42	Texas	46
12	Utah	65
20	Vermont	58
19	Virginia	59
9	Washington	71
41	West Virginia	47
21	Wisconsin	57
26	Wyoming	55

RANK	STATE	RATE
1	Hawaii	82
1	Massachusetts	82
1	New Jersey	82
4	New York	78
5	Connecticut	77
6	Alaska	76
7	California	74
7	Maryland	74
9	Washington	71
10	Oregon	68
11	Colorado	66
12	Illinois	65
12	Utah	65
14	Pennsylvania	64
15	Nebraska	63
15	New Hampshire	63
17	Michigan	61
17	Minnesota	61
19	Virginia	59
20	Vermont	58
21	Idaho	57
21	Wisconsin	57
23	Kentucky	56
23	Montana	56
23	Rhode Island	56
26	Wyoming	55
27	Iowa	53
27	Ohio	53
29	Florida	52
30	Kansas	51
30	North Dakota	51
32	Arizona	50
32	Louisiana	50
32	Oklahoma	50
32	Tennessee	50
36	Maine	49
36	South Dakota	49
38	Indiana	48
38	Missouri	48
38	Nevada	48
41	West Virginia	47
42	Delaware	46
42	North Carolina	46
42	South Carolina	46
42	Texas	46
46	Georgia	45
46	New Mexico	45
48	Alabama	44
49	Arkansas	41
50	Mississippi	40

District of Columbia 104

Source: CQ Press using data from American Dental Association
   "Distribution of Dentists, by Region and State, 2006"
*Professionally active dentists. Total includes 31 dentists for whom state is not known.

Average Annual Wages of Dentists in 2007

National Average = $147,010*

ALPHA ORDER				RANK ORDER		
RANK	STATE	WAGES		RANK	STATE	WAGES
24	Alabama	$149,640		1	Delaware	$184,690
5	Alaska	168,820		2	North Carolina	178,180
42	Arizona	135,340		3	Washington	173,490
36	Arkansas	142,300		4	Connecticut	169,230
40	California	138,280		5	Alaska	168,820
8	Colorado	164,470		6	Maine	167,400
4	Connecticut	169,230		7	Missouri	165,630
1	Delaware	184,690		8	Colorado	164,470
32	Florida	144,850		9	Nevada	164,250
13	Georgia	160,290		10	South Dakota	164,220
41	Hawaii	136,880		11	Virginia	161,580
NA	Idaho**	NA		12	Rhode Island	160,880
38	Illinois	139,150		13	Georgia	160,290
30	Indiana	145,630		14	Wisconsin	159,510
28	Iowa	146,350		15	Vermont	159,310
35	Kansas	143,970		16	Ohio	158,380
37	Kentucky	139,430		17	Michigan	155,920
49	Louisiana	101,900		18	West Virginia	155,110
6	Maine	167,400		19	Minnesota	154,820
43	Maryland	131,970		20	Nebraska	153,360
25	Massachusetts	148,220		21	South Carolina	152,750
17	Michigan	155,920		22	New Hampshire	150,500
19	Minnesota	154,820		23	Tennessee	149,980
34	Mississippi	144,170		24	Alabama	149,640
7	Missouri	165,630		25	Massachusetts	148,220
47	Montana	117,980		26	Texas	147,900
20	Nebraska	153,360		27	Oregon	147,210
9	Nevada	164,250		28	Iowa	146,350
22	New Hampshire	150,500		29	North Dakota	145,640
39	New Jersey	138,470		30	Indiana	145,630
31	New Mexico	145,430		31	New Mexico	145,430
33	New York	144,660		32	Florida	144,850
2	North Carolina	178,180		33	New York	144,660
29	North Dakota	145,640		34	Mississippi	144,170
16	Ohio	158,380		35	Kansas	143,970
48	Oklahoma	114,920		36	Arkansas	142,300
27	Oregon	147,210		37	Kentucky	139,430
46	Pennsylvania	126,700		38	Illinois	139,150
12	Rhode Island	160,880		39	New Jersey	138,470
21	South Carolina	152,750		40	California	138,280
10	South Dakota	164,220		41	Hawaii	136,880
23	Tennessee	149,980		42	Arizona	135,340
26	Texas	147,900		43	Maryland	131,970
44	Utah	128,980		44	Utah	128,980
15	Vermont	159,310		45	Wyoming	128,530
11	Virginia	161,580		46	Pennsylvania	126,700
3	Washington	173,490		47	Montana	117,980
18	West Virginia	155,110		48	Oklahoma	114,920
14	Wisconsin	159,510		49	Louisiana	101,900
45	Wyoming	128,530		NA	Idaho**	NA
					District of Columbia	146,960

Source: U.S. Department of Labor, Bureau of Labor Statistics
    "Occupational Employment and Wages, 2007" (http://www.bls.gov/oes/)
*Does not include self-employed.
**Not available.

Percent of Population Lacking Access to Dental Care in 2008

National Percent = 9.8% of Population*

<table>
<tr><td colspan="3">ALPHA ORDER</td><td colspan="3">RANK ORDER</td></tr>
<tr><th>RANK</th><th>STATE</th><th>PERCENT</th><th>RANK</th><th>STATE</th><th>PERCENT</th></tr>
<tr><td>3</td><td>Alabama</td><td>26.6</td><td>1</td><td>Mississippi</td><td>31.8</td></tr>
<tr><td>27</td><td>Alaska</td><td>8.1</td><td>2</td><td>Louisiana</td><td>31.6</td></tr>
<tr><td>34</td><td>Arizona</td><td>7.2</td><td>3</td><td>Alabama</td><td>26.6</td></tr>
<tr><td>43</td><td>Arkansas</td><td>4.5</td><td>4</td><td>New Mexico</td><td>25.0</td></tr>
<tr><td>45</td><td>California</td><td>3.5</td><td>5</td><td>South Carolina</td><td>20.9</td></tr>
<tr><td>40</td><td>Colorado</td><td>5.1</td><td>6</td><td>Tennessee</td><td>19.8</td></tr>
<tr><td>30</td><td>Connecticut</td><td>7.9</td><td>7</td><td>Kansas</td><td>18.9</td></tr>
<tr><td>12</td><td>Delaware</td><td>16.4</td><td>8</td><td>Montana</td><td>18.3</td></tr>
<tr><td>13</td><td>Florida</td><td>15.8</td><td>9</td><td>Missouri</td><td>17.9</td></tr>
<tr><td>22</td><td>Georgia</td><td>9.6</td><td>10</td><td>Idaho</td><td>17.2</td></tr>
<tr><td>39</td><td>Hawaii</td><td>5.6</td><td>11</td><td>Maine</td><td>16.9</td></tr>
<tr><td>10</td><td>Idaho</td><td>17.2</td><td>12</td><td>Delaware</td><td>16.4</td></tr>
<tr><td>16</td><td>Illinois</td><td>13.1</td><td>13</td><td>Florida</td><td>15.8</td></tr>
<tr><td>47</td><td>Indiana</td><td>3.0</td><td>14</td><td>Oregon</td><td>14.6</td></tr>
<tr><td>26</td><td>Iowa</td><td>8.3</td><td>15</td><td>Nevada</td><td>14.1</td></tr>
<tr><td>7</td><td>Kansas</td><td>18.9</td><td>16</td><td>Illinois</td><td>13.1</td></tr>
<tr><td>42</td><td>Kentucky</td><td>4.8</td><td>17</td><td>Michigan</td><td>12.0</td></tr>
<tr><td>2</td><td>Louisiana</td><td>31.6</td><td>17</td><td>South Dakota</td><td>12.0</td></tr>
<tr><td>11</td><td>Maine</td><td>16.9</td><td>19</td><td>Rhode Island</td><td>10.7</td></tr>
<tr><td>36</td><td>Maryland</td><td>6.3</td><td>19</td><td>Texas</td><td>10.7</td></tr>
<tr><td>25</td><td>Massachusetts</td><td>8.4</td><td>21</td><td>North Carolina</td><td>10.6</td></tr>
<tr><td>17</td><td>Michigan</td><td>12.0</td><td>22</td><td>Georgia</td><td>9.6</td></tr>
<tr><td>44</td><td>Minnesota</td><td>3.7</td><td>23</td><td>Pennsylvania</td><td>8.7</td></tr>
<tr><td>1</td><td>Mississippi</td><td>31.8</td><td>23</td><td>Virginia</td><td>8.7</td></tr>
<tr><td>9</td><td>Missouri</td><td>17.9</td><td>25</td><td>Massachusetts</td><td>8.4</td></tr>
<tr><td>8</td><td>Montana</td><td>18.3</td><td>26</td><td>Iowa</td><td>8.3</td></tr>
<tr><td>49</td><td>Nebraska</td><td>1.6</td><td>27</td><td>Alaska</td><td>8.1</td></tr>
<tr><td>15</td><td>Nevada</td><td>14.1</td><td>27</td><td>Washington</td><td>8.1</td></tr>
<tr><td>46</td><td>New Hampshire</td><td>3.2</td><td>27</td><td>Wisconsin</td><td>8.1</td></tr>
<tr><td>50</td><td>New Jersey</td><td>0.9</td><td>30</td><td>Connecticut</td><td>7.9</td></tr>
<tr><td>4</td><td>New Mexico</td><td>25.0</td><td>31</td><td>North Dakota</td><td>7.6</td></tr>
<tr><td>37</td><td>New York</td><td>6.1</td><td>32</td><td>Ohio</td><td>7.4</td></tr>
<tr><td>21</td><td>North Carolina</td><td>10.6</td><td>33</td><td>West Virginia</td><td>7.3</td></tr>
<tr><td>31</td><td>North Dakota</td><td>7.6</td><td>34</td><td>Arizona</td><td>7.2</td></tr>
<tr><td>32</td><td>Ohio</td><td>7.4</td><td>35</td><td>Wyoming</td><td>6.9</td></tr>
<tr><td>41</td><td>Oklahoma</td><td>5.0</td><td>36</td><td>Maryland</td><td>6.3</td></tr>
<tr><td>14</td><td>Oregon</td><td>14.6</td><td>37</td><td>New York</td><td>6.1</td></tr>
<tr><td>23</td><td>Pennsylvania</td><td>8.7</td><td>38</td><td>Utah</td><td>5.7</td></tr>
<tr><td>19</td><td>Rhode Island</td><td>10.7</td><td>39</td><td>Hawaii</td><td>5.6</td></tr>
<tr><td>5</td><td>South Carolina</td><td>20.9</td><td>40</td><td>Colorado</td><td>5.1</td></tr>
<tr><td>17</td><td>South Dakota</td><td>12.0</td><td>41</td><td>Oklahoma</td><td>5.0</td></tr>
<tr><td>6</td><td>Tennessee</td><td>19.8</td><td>42</td><td>Kentucky</td><td>4.8</td></tr>
<tr><td>19</td><td>Texas</td><td>10.7</td><td>43</td><td>Arkansas</td><td>4.5</td></tr>
<tr><td>38</td><td>Utah</td><td>5.7</td><td>44</td><td>Minnesota</td><td>3.7</td></tr>
<tr><td>48</td><td>Vermont</td><td>2.5</td><td>45</td><td>California</td><td>3.5</td></tr>
<tr><td>23</td><td>Virginia</td><td>8.7</td><td>46</td><td>New Hampshire</td><td>3.2</td></tr>
<tr><td>27</td><td>Washington</td><td>8.1</td><td>47</td><td>Indiana</td><td>3.0</td></tr>
<tr><td>33</td><td>West Virginia</td><td>7.3</td><td>48</td><td>Vermont</td><td>2.5</td></tr>
<tr><td>27</td><td>Wisconsin</td><td>8.1</td><td>49</td><td>Nebraska</td><td>1.6</td></tr>
<tr><td>35</td><td>Wyoming</td><td>6.9</td><td>50</td><td>New Jersey</td><td>0.9</td></tr>
<tr><td></td><td></td><td></td><td></td><td>District of Columbia</td><td>3.8</td></tr>
</table>

Source: CQ Press using data from U.S. Dept. of Health and Human Services, Div. of Shortage Designation
"Selected Statistics on Health Professional Shortage Areas" (as of September 30, 2008)
*Percent of population considered under-served by dental practitioners. An under-served population does not have primary medical care within reasonable economic and geographic bounds.

Pharmacists in 2007

National Total = 253,110 Pharmacists*

RANK	STATE	PHARMACISTS	% of USA
22	Alabama	4,440	1.8%
50	Alaska	360	0.1%
20	Arizona	4,940	2.0%
31	Arkansas	2,580	1.0%
1	California	23,030	9.1%
23	Colorado	4,080	1.6%
29	Connecticut	2,820	1.1%
47	Delaware	780	0.3%
2	Florida	17,690	7.0%
11	Georgia	7,530	3.0%
40	Hawaii	1,310	0.5%
39	Idaho	1,410	0.6%
7	Illinois	9,250	3.7%
15	Indiana	5,680	2.2%
29	Iowa	2,820	1.1%
32	Kansas	2,480	1.0%
24	Kentucky	4,000	1.6%
26	Louisiana	3,820	1.5%
41	Maine	1,190	0.5%
21	Maryland	4,640	1.8%
12	Massachusetts	6,780	2.7%
8	Michigan	8,640	3.4%
19	Minnesota	4,990	2.0%
33	Mississippi	2,250	0.9%
16	Missouri	5,360	2.1%
45	Montana	1,020	0.4%
35	Nebraska	1,980	0.8%
34	Nevada	2,240	0.9%
43	New Hampshire	1,140	0.5%
9	New Jersey	7,900	3.1%
38	New Mexico	1,510	0.6%
4	New York	15,310	6.0%
10	North Carolina	7,590	3.0%
46	North Dakota	810	0.3%
6	Ohio	11,260	4.4%
27	Oklahoma	3,280	1.3%
28	Oregon	3,100	1.2%
5	Pennsylvania	11,810	4.7%
42	Rhode Island	1,150	0.5%
25	South Carolina	3,950	1.6%
44	South Dakota	1,040	0.4%
13	Tennessee	6,130	2.4%
3	Texas	17,660	7.0%
37	Utah	1,840	0.7%
49	Vermont	450	0.2%
14	Virginia	5,790	2.3%
17	Washington	5,250	2.1%
36	West Virginia	1,890	0.7%
18	Wisconsin	5,060	2.0%
48	Wyoming	480	0.2%

RANK ORDER

RANK	STATE	PHARMACISTS	% of USA
1	California	23,030	9.1%
2	Florida	17,690	7.0%
3	Texas	17,660	7.0%
4	New York	15,310	6.0%
5	Pennsylvania	11,810	4.7%
6	Ohio	11,260	4.4%
7	Illinois	9,250	3.7%
8	Michigan	8,640	3.4%
9	New Jersey	7,900	3.1%
10	North Carolina	7,590	3.0%
11	Georgia	7,530	3.0%
12	Massachusetts	6,780	2.7%
13	Tennessee	6,130	2.4%
14	Virginia	5,790	2.3%
15	Indiana	5,680	2.2%
16	Missouri	5,360	2.1%
17	Washington	5,250	2.1%
18	Wisconsin	5,060	2.0%
19	Minnesota	4,990	2.0%
20	Arizona	4,940	2.0%
21	Maryland	4,640	1.8%
22	Alabama	4,440	1.8%
23	Colorado	4,080	1.6%
24	Kentucky	4,000	1.6%
25	South Carolina	3,950	1.6%
26	Louisiana	3,820	1.5%
27	Oklahoma	3,280	1.3%
28	Oregon	3,100	1.2%
29	Connecticut	2,820	1.1%
29	Iowa	2,820	1.1%
31	Arkansas	2,580	1.0%
32	Kansas	2,480	1.0%
33	Mississippi	2,250	0.9%
34	Nevada	2,240	0.9%
35	Nebraska	1,980	0.8%
36	West Virginia	1,890	0.7%
37	Utah	1,840	0.7%
38	New Mexico	1,510	0.6%
39	Idaho	1,410	0.6%
40	Hawaii	1,310	0.5%
41	Maine	1,190	0.5%
42	Rhode Island	1,150	0.5%
43	New Hampshire	1,140	0.5%
44	South Dakota	1,040	0.4%
45	Montana	1,020	0.4%
46	North Dakota	810	0.3%
47	Delaware	780	0.3%
48	Wyoming	480	0.2%
49	Vermont	450	0.2%
50	Alaska	360	0.1%
	District of Columbia	590	0.2%

Source: U.S. Department of Labor, Bureau of Labor Statistics
    "Occupational Employment and Wages, 2007" (http://www.bls.gov/oes/)
*Does not include self-employed.

Rate of Pharmacists in 2007

National Rate = 84 Pharmacists per 100,000 Population*

ALPHA ORDER

RANK	STATE	RATE
12	Alabama	96
50	Alaska	53
41	Arizona	78
19	Arkansas	91
49	California	63
33	Colorado	84
37	Connecticut	81
23	Delaware	90
11	Florida	97
39	Georgia	79
8	Hawaii	103
16	Idaho	94
46	Illinois	72
23	Indiana	90
14	Iowa	95
28	Kansas	89
16	Kentucky	94
30	Louisiana	87
23	Maine	90
35	Maryland	83
6	Massachusetts	105
32	Michigan	86
12	Minnesota	96
42	Mississippi	77
19	Missouri	91
5	Montana	107
3	Nebraska	112
29	Nevada	88
30	New Hampshire	87
19	New Jersey	91
42	New Mexico	77
39	New York	79
33	North Carolina	84
2	North Dakota	127
10	Ohio	98
19	Oklahoma	91
35	Oregon	83
14	Pennsylvania	95
4	Rhode Island	109
23	South Carolina	90
1	South Dakota	131
9	Tennessee	100
45	Texas	74
48	Utah	69
46	Vermont	72
44	Virginia	75
37	Washington	81
7	West Virginia	104
23	Wisconsin	90
18	Wyoming	92

RANK ORDER

RANK	STATE	RATE
1	South Dakota	131
2	North Dakota	127
3	Nebraska	112
4	Rhode Island	109
5	Montana	107
6	Massachusetts	105
7	West Virginia	104
8	Hawaii	103
9	Tennessee	100
10	Ohio	98
11	Florida	97
12	Alabama	96
12	Minnesota	96
14	Iowa	95
14	Pennsylvania	95
16	Idaho	94
16	Kentucky	94
18	Wyoming	92
19	Arkansas	91
19	Missouri	91
19	New Jersey	91
19	Oklahoma	91
23	Delaware	90
23	Indiana	90
23	Maine	90
23	South Carolina	90
23	Wisconsin	90
28	Kansas	89
29	Nevada	88
30	Louisiana	87
30	New Hampshire	87
32	Michigan	86
33	Colorado	84
33	North Carolina	84
35	Maryland	83
35	Oregon	83
37	Connecticut	81
37	Washington	81
39	Georgia	79
39	New York	79
41	Arizona	78
42	Mississippi	77
42	New Mexico	77
44	Virginia	75
45	Texas	74
46	Illinois	72
46	Vermont	72
48	Utah	69
49	California	63
50	Alaska	53
	District of Columbia	100

Source: CQ Press using data from U.S. Department of Labor, Bureau of Labor Statistics
   "Occupational Employment and Wages, 2007" (http://www.bls.gov/oes/)
*Does not include self-employed.

Average Annual Wages of Pharmacists in 2007

National Average = $98,960*

ALPHA ORDER

RANK	STATE	WAGES
13	Alabama	$101,140
2	Alaska	109,810
28	Arizona	97,570
37	Arkansas	94,410
1	California	112,020
19	Colorado	98,570
12	Connecticut	101,850
40	Delaware	93,360
24	Florida	98,190
25	Georgia	98,070
35	Hawaii	95,000
16	Idaho	99,870
30	Illinois	96,730
39	Indiana	93,400
45	Iowa	89,150
38	Kansas	94,130
7	Kentucky	103,800
43	Louisiana	90,150
3	Maine	108,930
36	Maryland	94,460
47	Massachusetts	88,920
27	Michigan	97,640
4	Minnesota	105,440
33	Mississippi	95,630
22	Missouri	98,500
49	Montana	87,260
46	Nebraska	89,120
17	Nevada	99,760
10	New Hampshire	102,170
23	New Jersey	98,200
31	New Mexico	95,980
29	New York	97,270
9	North Carolina	102,480
50	North Dakota	83,710
32	Ohio	95,750
41	Oklahoma	92,210
18	Oregon	99,410
44	Pennsylvania	89,650
34	Rhode Island	95,500
21	South Carolina	98,540
48	South Dakota	88,650
5	Tennessee	105,280
6	Texas	103,820
14	Utah	100,440
11	Vermont	102,100
19	Virginia	98,570
26	Washington	97,860
15	West Virginia	100,080
8	Wisconsin	102,910
42	Wyoming	91,320

RANK ORDER

RANK	STATE	WAGES
1	California	$112,020
2	Alaska	109,810
3	Maine	108,930
4	Minnesota	105,440
5	Tennessee	105,280
6	Texas	103,820
7	Kentucky	103,800
8	Wisconsin	102,910
9	North Carolina	102,480
10	New Hampshire	102,170
11	Vermont	102,100
12	Connecticut	101,850
13	Alabama	101,140
14	Utah	100,440
15	West Virginia	100,080
16	Idaho	99,870
17	Nevada	99,760
18	Oregon	99,410
19	Colorado	98,570
19	Virginia	98,570
21	South Carolina	98,540
22	Missouri	98,500
23	New Jersey	98,200
24	Florida	98,190
25	Georgia	98,070
26	Washington	97,860
27	Michigan	97,640
28	Arizona	97,570
29	New York	97,270
30	Illinois	96,730
31	New Mexico	95,980
32	Ohio	95,750
33	Mississippi	95,630
34	Rhode Island	95,500
35	Hawaii	95,000
36	Maryland	94,460
37	Arkansas	94,410
38	Kansas	94,130
39	Indiana	93,400
40	Delaware	93,360
41	Oklahoma	92,210
42	Wyoming	91,320
43	Louisiana	90,150
44	Pennsylvania	89,650
45	Iowa	89,150
46	Nebraska	89,120
47	Massachusetts	88,920
48	South Dakota	88,650
49	Montana	87,260
50	North Dakota	83,710
	District of Columbia	83,870

Source: U.S. Department of Labor, Bureau of Labor Statistics
   "Occupational Employment and Wages, 2007" (http://www.bls.gov/oes/)
*Does not include self-employed.

Optometrists in 2007

National Total = 24,900 Optometrists*

ALPHA ORDER

RANK	STATE	OPTOMETRISTS	% of USA
24	Alabama	330	1.3%
47	Alaska	80	0.3%
15	Arizona	600	2.4%
24	Arkansas	330	1.3%
1	California	2,410	9.7%
16	Colorado	570	2.3%
33	Connecticut	200	0.8%
NA	Delaware**	NA	NA
8	Florida	990	4.0%
18	Georgia	550	2.2%
40	Hawaii	150	0.6%
37	Idaho	190	0.8%
2	Illinois	1,730	6.9%
14	Indiana	610	2.4%
28	Iowa	300	1.2%
22	Kansas	400	1.6%
30	Kentucky	250	1.0%
33	Louisiana	200	0.8%
45	Maine	90	0.4%
19	Maryland	420	1.7%
17	Massachusetts	560	2.2%
5	Michigan	1,260	5.1%
10	Minnesota	670	2.7%
32	Mississippi	210	0.8%
12	Missouri	640	2.6%
45	Montana	90	0.4%
33	Nebraska	200	0.8%
37	Nevada	190	0.8%
41	New Hampshire	120	0.5%
11	New Jersey	650	2.6%
39	New Mexico	180	0.7%
4	New York	1,450	5.8%
9	North Carolina	690	2.8%
33	North Dakota	200	0.8%
7	Ohio	1,020	4.1%
19	Oklahoma	420	1.7%
23	Oregon	350	1.4%
6	Pennsylvania	1,180	4.7%
42	Rhode Island	110	0.4%
31	South Carolina	230	0.9%
43	South Dakota	100	0.4%
27	Tennessee	310	1.2%
3	Texas	1,620	6.5%
29	Utah	260	1.0%
49	Vermont	60	0.2%
13	Virginia	630	2.5%
24	Washington	330	1.3%
43	West Virginia	100	0.4%
19	Wisconsin	420	1.7%
47	Wyoming	80	0.3%

RANK ORDER

RANK	STATE	OPTOMETRISTS	% of USA
1	California	2,410	9.7%
2	Illinois	1,730	6.9%
3	Texas	1,620	6.5%
4	New York	1,450	5.8%
5	Michigan	1,260	5.1%
6	Pennsylvania	1,180	4.7%
7	Ohio	1,020	4.1%
8	Florida	990	4.0%
9	North Carolina	690	2.8%
10	Minnesota	670	2.7%
11	New Jersey	650	2.6%
12	Missouri	640	2.6%
13	Virginia	630	2.5%
14	Indiana	610	2.4%
15	Arizona	600	2.4%
16	Colorado	570	2.3%
17	Massachusetts	560	2.2%
18	Georgia	550	2.2%
19	Maryland	420	1.7%
19	Oklahoma	420	1.7%
19	Wisconsin	420	1.7%
22	Kansas	400	1.6%
23	Oregon	350	1.4%
24	Alabama	330	1.3%
24	Arkansas	330	1.3%
24	Washington	330	1.3%
27	Tennessee	310	1.2%
28	Iowa	300	1.2%
29	Utah	260	1.0%
30	Kentucky	250	1.0%
31	South Carolina	230	0.9%
32	Mississippi	210	0.8%
33	Connecticut	200	0.8%
33	Louisiana	200	0.8%
33	Nebraska	200	0.8%
33	North Dakota	200	0.8%
37	Idaho	190	0.8%
37	Nevada	190	0.8%
39	New Mexico	180	0.7%
40	Hawaii	150	0.6%
41	New Hampshire	120	0.5%
42	Rhode Island	110	0.4%
43	South Dakota	100	0.4%
43	West Virginia	100	0.4%
45	Maine	90	0.4%
45	Montana	90	0.4%
47	Alaska	80	0.3%
47	Wyoming	80	0.3%
49	Vermont	60	0.2%
NA	Delaware**	NA	NA
	District of Columbia	100	0.4%

Source: U.S. Department of Labor, Bureau of Labor Statistics
"Occupational Employment and Wages, 2007" (http://www.bls.gov/oes/)
*Does not include self-employed.
**Not available.

Rate of Optometrists in 2007

National Rate = 8 Optometrists per 100,000 Population*

ALPHA ORDER

RANK	STATE	RATE
33	Alabama	7
9	Alaska	12
22	Arizona	9
9	Arkansas	12
33	California	7
9	Colorado	12
41	Connecticut	6
NA	Delaware**	NA
45	Florida	5
41	Georgia	6
9	Hawaii	12
4	Idaho	13
4	Illinois	13
16	Indiana	10
16	Iowa	10
3	Kansas	14
41	Kentucky	6
45	Louisiana	5
33	Maine	7
33	Maryland	7
22	Massachusetts	9
4	Michigan	13
4	Minnesota	13
33	Mississippi	7
14	Missouri	11
22	Montana	9
14	Nebraska	11
33	Nevada	7
22	New Hampshire	9
29	New Jersey	8
22	New Mexico	9
33	New York	7
29	North Carolina	8
1	North Dakota	31
22	Ohio	9
9	Oklahoma	12
22	Oregon	9
16	Pennsylvania	10
16	Rhode Island	10
45	South Carolina	5
4	South Dakota	13
45	Tennessee	5
33	Texas	7
16	Utah	10
16	Vermont	10
29	Virginia	8
45	Washington	5
41	West Virginia	6
29	Wisconsin	8
2	Wyoming	15

RANK ORDER

RANK	STATE	RATE
1	North Dakota	31
2	Wyoming	15
3	Kansas	14
4	Idaho	13
4	Illinois	13
4	Michigan	13
4	Minnesota	13
4	South Dakota	13
9	Alaska	12
9	Arkansas	12
9	Colorado	12
9	Hawaii	12
9	Oklahoma	12
14	Missouri	11
14	Nebraska	11
16	Indiana	10
16	Iowa	10
16	Pennsylvania	10
16	Rhode Island	10
16	Utah	10
16	Vermont	10
22	Arizona	9
22	Massachusetts	9
22	Montana	9
22	New Hampshire	9
22	New Mexico	9
22	Ohio	9
22	Oregon	9
29	New Jersey	8
29	North Carolina	8
29	Virginia	8
29	Wisconsin	8
33	Alabama	7
33	California	7
33	Maine	7
33	Maryland	7
33	Mississippi	7
33	Nevada	7
33	New York	7
33	Texas	7
41	Connecticut	6
41	Georgia	6
41	Kentucky	6
41	West Virginia	6
45	Florida	5
45	Louisiana	5
45	South Carolina	5
45	Tennessee	5
45	Washington	5
NA	Delaware**	NA
	District of Columbia	17

Source: CQ Press using data from U.S. Department of Labor, Bureau of Labor Statistics
"Occupational Employment and Wages, 2007" (http://www.bls.gov/oes/)
*Does not include self-employed.
**Not available.

Average Annual Wages of Optometrists in 2007

National Average = $101,840*

ALPHA ORDER

RANK	STATE	WAGES
44	Alabama	$86,290
5	Alaska	122,560
10	Arizona	113,100
13	Arkansas	110,940
34	California	93,570
49	Colorado	72,140
23	Connecticut	105,590
21	Delaware	106,310
32	Florida	96,070
4	Georgia	124,260
37	Hawaii	92,900
50	Idaho	52,550
27	Illinois	100,670
24	Indiana	104,510
38	Iowa	91,810
25	Kansas	101,850
14	Kentucky	109,950
2	Louisiana	147,070
16	Maine	107,930
30	Maryland	98,300
39	Massachusetts	91,480
20	Michigan	106,560
8	Minnesota	120,110
47	Mississippi	78,870
42	Missouri	87,550
48	Montana	75,500
26	Nebraska	101,020
17	Nevada	107,760
15	New Hampshire	109,610
31	New Jersey	97,230
18	New Mexico	107,130
11	New York	112,990
3	North Carolina	125,100
33	North Dakota	95,610
19	Ohio	106,950
41	Oklahoma	89,640
45	Oregon	84,310
40	Pennsylvania	91,320
6	Rhode Island	120,420
43	South Carolina	87,310
12	South Dakota	111,340
29	Tennessee	98,440
9	Texas	113,800
22	Utah	106,250
1	Vermont	165,930
28	Virginia	98,720
7	Washington	120,290
36	West Virginia	93,270
35	Wisconsin	93,280
46	Wyoming	82,690

RANK ORDER

RANK	STATE	WAGES
1	Vermont	$165,930
2	Louisiana	147,070
3	North Carolina	125,100
4	Georgia	124,260
5	Alaska	122,560
6	Rhode Island	120,420
7	Washington	120,290
8	Minnesota	120,110
9	Texas	113,800
10	Arizona	113,100
11	New York	112,990
12	South Dakota	111,340
13	Arkansas	110,940
14	Kentucky	109,950
15	New Hampshire	109,610
16	Maine	107,930
17	Nevada	107,760
18	New Mexico	107,130
19	Ohio	106,950
20	Michigan	106,560
21	Delaware	106,310
22	Utah	106,250
23	Connecticut	105,590
24	Indiana	104,510
25	Kansas	101,850
26	Nebraska	101,020
27	Illinois	100,670
28	Virginia	98,720
29	Tennessee	98,440
30	Maryland	98,300
31	New Jersey	97,230
32	Florida	96,070
33	North Dakota	95,610
34	California	93,570
35	Wisconsin	93,280
36	West Virginia	93,270
37	Hawaii	92,900
38	Iowa	91,810
39	Massachusetts	91,480
40	Pennsylvania	91,320
41	Oklahoma	89,640
42	Missouri	87,550
43	South Carolina	87,310
44	Alabama	86,290
45	Oregon	84,310
46	Wyoming	82,690
47	Mississippi	78,870
48	Montana	75,500
49	Colorado	72,140
50	Idaho	52,550
	District of Columbia	84,100

Source: U.S. Department of Labor, Bureau of Labor Statistics
    "Occupational Employment and Wages, 2007" (http://www.bls.gov/oes/)
*Does not include self-employed.

Emergency Medical Technicians and Paramedics in 2007

National Total = 201,200 Technicians and Paramedics*

ALPHA ORDER

RANK	STATE	PARAMEDICS	% of USA
23	Alabama	3,150	1.6%
50	Alaska	150	0.1%
19	Arizona	3,810	1.9%
33	Arkansas	1,740	0.9%
3	California	12,950	6.4%
25	Colorado	2,910	1.4%
28	Connecticut	2,640	1.3%
41	Delaware	700	0.3%
7	Florida	8,160	4.1%
9	Georgia	6,440	3.2%
46	Hawaii	510	0.3%
40	Idaho	750	0.4%
5	Illinois	11,030	5.5%
16	Indiana	5,090	2.5%
30	Iowa	2,170	1.1%
29	Kansas	2,340	1.2%
17	Kentucky	4,130	2.1%
24	Louisiana	2,990	1.5%
36	Maine	1,380	0.7%
22	Maryland	3,340	1.7%
15	Massachusetts	5,600	2.8%
11	Michigan	6,200	3.1%
18	Minnesota	4,090	2.0%
34	Mississippi	1,570	0.8%
13	Missouri	6,140	3.1%
43	Montana	630	0.3%
47	Nebraska	500	0.2%
37	Nevada	1,200	0.6%
38	New Hampshire	1,050	0.5%
10	New Jersey	6,260	3.1%
39	New Mexico	920	0.5%
2	New York	13,140	6.5%
8	North Carolina	8,150	4.1%
45	North Dakota	600	0.3%
6	Ohio	9,740	4.8%
26	Oklahoma	2,740	1.4%
35	Oregon	1,510	0.8%
1	Pennsylvania	13,330	6.6%
43	Rhode Island	630	0.3%
20	South Carolina	3,770	1.9%
42	South Dakota	690	0.3%
12	Tennessee	6,170	3.1%
4	Texas	12,280	6.1%
32	Utah	1,810	0.9%
48	Vermont	490	0.2%
21	Virginia	3,350	1.7%
27	Washington	2,650	1.3%
31	West Virginia	1,970	1.0%
14	Wisconsin	5,970	3.0%
49	Wyoming	470	0.2%

RANK ORDER

RANK	STATE	PARAMEDICS	% of USA
1	Pennsylvania	13,330	6.6%
2	New York	13,140	6.5%
3	California	12,950	6.4%
4	Texas	12,280	6.1%
5	Illinois	11,030	5.5%
6	Ohio	9,740	4.8%
7	Florida	8,160	4.1%
8	North Carolina	8,150	4.1%
9	Georgia	6,440	3.2%
10	New Jersey	6,260	3.1%
11	Michigan	6,200	3.1%
12	Tennessee	6,170	3.1%
13	Missouri	6,140	3.1%
14	Wisconsin	5,970	3.0%
15	Massachusetts	5,600	2.8%
16	Indiana	5,090	2.5%
17	Kentucky	4,130	2.1%
18	Minnesota	4,090	2.0%
19	Arizona	3,810	1.9%
20	South Carolina	3,770	1.9%
21	Virginia	3,350	1.7%
22	Maryland	3,340	1.7%
23	Alabama	3,150	1.6%
24	Louisiana	2,990	1.5%
25	Colorado	2,910	1.4%
26	Oklahoma	2,740	1.4%
27	Washington	2,650	1.3%
28	Connecticut	2,640	1.3%
29	Kansas	2,340	1.2%
30	Iowa	2,170	1.1%
31	West Virginia	1,970	1.0%
32	Utah	1,810	0.9%
33	Arkansas	1,740	0.9%
34	Mississippi	1,570	0.8%
35	Oregon	1,510	0.8%
36	Maine	1,380	0.7%
37	Nevada	1,200	0.6%
38	New Hampshire	1,050	0.5%
39	New Mexico	920	0.5%
40	Idaho	750	0.4%
41	Delaware	700	0.3%
42	South Dakota	690	0.3%
43	Montana	630	0.3%
43	Rhode Island	630	0.3%
45	North Dakota	600	0.3%
46	Hawaii	510	0.3%
47	Nebraska	500	0.2%
48	Vermont	490	0.2%
49	Wyoming	470	0.2%
50	Alaska	150	0.1%
	District of Columbia	1,240	0.6%

Source: U.S. Department of Labor, Bureau of Labor Statistics
"Occupational Employment and Wages, 2007" (http://www.bls.gov/oes/)
*Does not include self-employed.

Rate of Emergency Medical Technicians and Paramedics in 2007

National Rate = 67 Technicians and Paramedics per 100,000 Population*

ALPHA ORDER

RANK	STATE	RATE
26	Alabama	68
50	Alaska	22
34	Arizona	60
33	Arkansas	61
48	California	36
34	Colorado	60
22	Connecticut	76
17	Delaware	81
43	Florida	45
26	Georgia	68
46	Hawaii	40
40	Idaho	50
13	Illinois	86
18	Indiana	80
24	Iowa	73
16	Kansas	84
7	Kentucky	97
26	Louisiana	68
4	Maine	105
37	Maryland	59
11	Massachusetts	87
32	Michigan	62
20	Minnesota	79
38	Mississippi	54
5	Missouri	104
31	Montana	66
49	Nebraska	28
41	Nevada	47
18	New Hampshire	80
25	New Jersey	72
41	New Mexico	47
26	New York	68
9	North Carolina	90
8	North Dakota	94
15	Ohio	85
22	Oklahoma	76
46	Oregon	40
2	Pennsylvania	107
34	Rhode Island	60
13	South Carolina	86
11	South Dakota	87
6	Tennessee	100
39	Texas	52
26	Utah	68
20	Vermont	79
44	Virginia	44
45	Washington	41
1	West Virginia	109
2	Wisconsin	107
9	Wyoming	90

RANK ORDER

RANK	STATE	RATE
1	West Virginia	109
2	Pennsylvania	107
2	Wisconsin	107
4	Maine	105
5	Missouri	104
6	Tennessee	100
7	Kentucky	97
8	North Dakota	94
9	North Carolina	90
9	Wyoming	90
11	Massachusetts	87
11	South Dakota	87
13	Illinois	86
13	South Carolina	86
15	Ohio	85
16	Kansas	84
17	Delaware	81
18	Indiana	80
18	New Hampshire	80
20	Minnesota	79
20	Vermont	79
22	Connecticut	76
22	Oklahoma	76
24	Iowa	73
25	New Jersey	72
26	Alabama	68
26	Georgia	68
26	Louisiana	68
26	New York	68
26	Utah	68
31	Montana	66
32	Michigan	62
33	Arkansas	61
34	Arizona	60
34	Colorado	60
34	Rhode Island	60
37	Maryland	59
38	Mississippi	54
39	Texas	52
40	Idaho	50
41	Nevada	47
41	New Mexico	47
43	Florida	45
44	Virginia	44
45	Washington	41
46	Hawaii	40
46	Oregon	40
48	California	36
49	Nebraska	28
50	Alaska	22

| | District of Columbia | 211 |

Source: CQ Press using data from U.S. Department of Labor, Bureau of Labor Statistics
"Occupational Employment and Wages, 2007" (http://www.bls.gov/oes/)
*Does not include self-employed.

Average Annual Wages of
Emergency Medical Technicians and Paramedics in 2007
National Average = $30,870*

ALPHA ORDER

RANK	STATE	WAGES
39	Alabama	$26,350
1	Alaska	53,090
37	Arizona	27,470
47	Arkansas	24,500
19	California	31,550
12	Colorado	34,470
10	Connecticut	35,670
9	Delaware	36,630
18	Florida	31,580
22	Georgia	30,350
3	Hawaii	41,980
13	Idaho	33,740
16	Illinois	32,420
32	Indiana	29,010
43	Iowa	25,950
41	Kansas	26,290
40	Kentucky	26,310
45	Louisiana	25,900
36	Maine	27,640
4	Maryland	41,530
6	Massachusetts	37,690
24	Michigan	29,930
25	Minnesota	29,870
43	Mississippi	25,950
17	Missouri	32,260
48	Montana	23,750
28	Nebraska	29,650
2	Nevada	42,540
11	New Hampshire	35,570
14	New Jersey	33,660
27	New Mexico	29,770
7	New York	37,470
30	North Carolina	29,420
42	North Dakota	26,030
38	Ohio	27,010
50	Oklahoma	23,040
8	Oregon	37,280
33	Pennsylvania	28,350
15	Rhode Island	33,550
23	South Carolina	29,980
46	South Dakota	25,530
20	Tennessee	31,050
34	Texas	27,740
26	Utah	29,800
29	Vermont	29,480
21	Virginia	31,010
5	Washington	38,790
49	West Virginia	23,370
35	Wisconsin	27,710
31	Wyoming	29,330

RANK ORDER

RANK	STATE	WAGES
1	Alaska	$53,090
2	Nevada	42,540
3	Hawaii	41,980
4	Maryland	41,530
5	Washington	38,790
6	Massachusetts	37,690
7	New York	37,470
8	Oregon	37,280
9	Delaware	36,630
10	Connecticut	35,670
11	New Hampshire	35,570
12	Colorado	34,470
13	Idaho	33,740
14	New Jersey	33,660
15	Rhode Island	33,550
16	Illinois	32,420
17	Missouri	32,260
18	Florida	31,580
19	California	31,550
20	Tennessee	31,050
21	Virginia	31,010
22	Georgia	30,350
23	South Carolina	29,980
24	Michigan	29,930
25	Minnesota	29,870
26	Utah	29,800
27	New Mexico	29,770
28	Nebraska	29,650
29	Vermont	29,480
30	North Carolina	29,420
31	Wyoming	29,330
32	Indiana	29,010
33	Pennsylvania	28,350
34	Texas	27,740
35	Wisconsin	27,710
36	Maine	27,640
37	Arizona	27,470
38	Ohio	27,010
39	Alabama	26,350
40	Kentucky	26,310
41	Kansas	26,290
42	North Dakota	26,030
43	Iowa	25,950
43	Mississippi	25,950
45	Louisiana	25,900
46	South Dakota	25,530
47	Arkansas	24,500
48	Montana	23,750
49	West Virginia	23,370
50	Oklahoma	23,040
	District of Columbia	43,370

Source: U.S. Department of Labor, Bureau of Labor Statistics
   "Occupational Employment and Wages, 2007" (http://www.bls.gov/oes/)
*Does not include self-employed.

Employment in Health Care Support Industries in 2007

National Total = 3,625,240 Aides and Assistants*

ALPHA ORDER

RANK	STATE	EMPLOYEES	% of USA
25	Alabama	48,300	1.3%
50	Alaska	6,090	0.2%
21	Arizona	60,460	1.7%
33	Arkansas	31,160	0.9%
1	California	331,290	9.1%
29	Colorado	44,880	1.2%
22	Connecticut	53,400	1.5%
46	Delaware	10,840	0.3%
4	Florida	207,440	5.7%
14	Georgia	78,720	2.2%
43	Hawaii	14,670	0.4%
41	Idaho	16,430	0.5%
7	Illinois	140,220	3.9%
17	Indiana	71,220	2.0%
28	Iowa	45,300	1.2%
31	Kansas	40,780	1.1%
24	Kentucky	48,330	1.3%
23	Louisiana	52,250	1.4%
38	Maine	21,180	0.6%
20	Maryland	65,350	1.8%
11	Massachusetts	97,660	2.7%
9	Michigan	133,250	3.7%
13	Minnesota	84,010	2.3%
32	Mississippi	31,610	0.9%
16	Missouri	73,780	2.0%
45	Montana	11,430	0.3%
35	Nebraska	26,250	0.7%
39	Nevada	20,390	0.6%
42	New Hampshire	15,990	0.4%
10	New Jersey	109,660	3.0%
37	New Mexico	21,960	0.6%
2	New York	324,310	8.9%
8	North Carolina	136,020	3.8%
44	North Dakota	11,710	0.3%
6	Ohio	182,050	5.0%
27	Oklahoma	46,080	1.3%
30	Oregon	41,730	1.2%
5	Pennsylvania	185,990	5.1%
40	Rhode Island	19,130	0.5%
26	South Carolina	48,240	1.3%
47	South Dakota	9,930	0.3%
18	Tennessee	68,790	1.9%
3	Texas	237,740	6.6%
34	Utah	26,270	0.7%
48	Vermont	7,860	0.2%
15	Virginia	75,590	2.1%
19	Washington	67,300	1.9%
36	West Virginia	23,130	0.6%
12	Wisconsin	85,300	2.4%
49	Wyoming	6,300	0.2%

RANK ORDER

RANK	STATE	EMPLOYEES	% of USA
1	California	331,290	9.1%
2	New York	324,310	8.9%
3	Texas	237,740	6.6%
4	Florida	207,440	5.7%
5	Pennsylvania	185,990	5.1%
6	Ohio	182,050	5.0%
7	Illinois	140,220	3.9%
8	North Carolina	136,020	3.8%
9	Michigan	133,250	3.7%
10	New Jersey	109,660	3.0%
11	Massachusetts	97,660	2.7%
12	Wisconsin	85,300	2.4%
13	Minnesota	84,010	2.3%
14	Georgia	78,720	2.2%
15	Virginia	75,590	2.1%
16	Missouri	73,780	2.0%
17	Indiana	71,220	2.0%
18	Tennessee	68,790	1.9%
19	Washington	67,300	1.9%
20	Maryland	65,350	1.8%
21	Arizona	60,460	1.7%
22	Connecticut	53,400	1.5%
23	Louisiana	52,250	1.4%
24	Kentucky	48,330	1.3%
25	Alabama	48,300	1.3%
26	South Carolina	48,240	1.3%
27	Oklahoma	46,080	1.3%
28	Iowa	45,300	1.2%
29	Colorado	44,880	1.2%
30	Oregon	41,730	1.2%
31	Kansas	40,780	1.1%
32	Mississippi	31,610	0.9%
33	Arkansas	31,160	0.9%
34	Utah	26,270	0.7%
35	Nebraska	26,250	0.7%
36	West Virginia	23,130	0.6%
37	New Mexico	21,960	0.6%
38	Maine	21,180	0.6%
39	Nevada	20,390	0.6%
40	Rhode Island	19,130	0.5%
41	Idaho	16,430	0.5%
42	New Hampshire	15,990	0.4%
43	Hawaii	14,670	0.4%
44	North Dakota	11,710	0.3%
45	Montana	11,430	0.3%
46	Delaware	10,840	0.3%
47	South Dakota	9,930	0.3%
48	Vermont	7,860	0.2%
49	Wyoming	6,300	0.2%
50	Alaska	6,090	0.2%
	District of Columbia	7,470	0.2%

Source: U.S. Department of Labor, Bureau of Labor Statistics
"Occupational Employment and Wages, 2007" (http://www.bls.gov/oes/)
*Does not include self-employed. Includes various health care assistants and aides not included in the category of health care practitioners and technicians. Among the included occupations are home health aides, nursing aides, psychiatric aides, dental assistants, and pharmacy aides.

Rate of Employees in Health Care Support Industries in 2007

National Rate = 1,203 Aides and Assistants per 100,000 Population*

ALPHA ORDER

RANK ORDER

RANK	STATE	RATE	RANK	STATE	RATE
40	Alabama	1,044	1	North Dakota	1,836
48	Alaska	894	2	Rhode Island	1,816
45	Arizona	952	3	New York	1,669
35	Arkansas	1,101	4	Minnesota	1,621
47	California	911	5	Maine	1,610
46	Colorado	927	6	Ohio	1,586
7	Connecticut	1,530	7	Connecticut	1,530
20	Delaware	1,258	8	Wisconsin	1,524
30	Florida	1,140	9	Iowa	1,518
49	Georgia	827	10	Massachusetts	1,510
28	Hawaii	1,148	11	North Carolina	1,504
36	Idaho	1,098	12	Pennsylvania	1,498
38	Illinois	1,093	13	Nebraska	1,483
31	Indiana	1,124	14	Kansas	1,468
9	Iowa	1,518	15	Michigan	1,326
14	Kansas	1,468	16	West Virginia	1,278
29	Kentucky	1,141	17	Oklahoma	1,277
25	Louisiana	1,195	18	New Jersey	1,267
5	Maine	1,610	19	Vermont	1,266
27	Maryland	1,163	20	Delaware	1,258
10	Massachusetts	1,510	21	Missouri	1,255
15	Michigan	1,326	22	South Dakota	1,248
4	Minnesota	1,621	23	New Hampshire	1,219
39	Mississippi	1,082	24	Wyoming	1,204
21	Missouri	1,255	25	Louisiana	1,195
25	Montana	1,195	25	Montana	1,195
13	Nebraska	1,483	27	Maryland	1,163
50	Nevada	798	28	Hawaii	1,148
23	New Hampshire	1,219	29	Kentucky	1,141
18	New Jersey	1,267	30	Florida	1,140
33	New Mexico	1,118	31	Indiana	1,124
3	New York	1,669	32	Tennessee	1,119
11	North Carolina	1,504	33	New Mexico	1,118
1	North Dakota	1,836	34	Oregon	1,117
6	Ohio	1,586	35	Arkansas	1,101
17	Oklahoma	1,277	36	Idaho	1,098
34	Oregon	1,117	37	South Carolina	1,095
12	Pennsylvania	1,498	38	Illinois	1,093
2	Rhode Island	1,816	39	Mississippi	1,082
37	South Carolina	1,095	40	Alabama	1,044
22	South Dakota	1,248	41	Washington	1,043
32	Tennessee	1,119	42	Texas	997
42	Texas	997	43	Utah	984
43	Utah	984	44	Virginia	982
19	Vermont	1,266	45	Arizona	952
44	Virginia	982	46	Colorado	927
41	Washington	1,043	47	California	911
16	West Virginia	1,278	48	Alaska	894
8	Wisconsin	1,524	49	Georgia	827
24	Wyoming	1,204	50	Nevada	798

District of Columbia   1,271

Source: CQ Press using data from U.S. Department of Labor, Bureau of Labor Statistics
"Occupational Employment and Wages, 2007" (http://www.bls.gov/oes/)

*Does not include self-employed. Includes various health care assistants and aides not included in the category of health care practitioners and technicians. Among the included occupations are home health aides, nursing aides, psychiatric aides, dental assistants, and pharmacy aides.

Average Annual Wages of Employees in Health Care Support Industries in 2007

National Average = $25,600*

ALPHA ORDER

RANK	STATE	WAGES
46	Alabama	$21,310
1	Alaska	34,290
21	Arizona	25,260
47	Arkansas	21,150
5	California	29,110
9	Colorado	28,370
2	Connecticut	30,470
12	Delaware	28,190
23	Florida	24,980
34	Georgia	23,700
6	Hawaii	28,840
33	Idaho	23,800
18	Illinois	26,160
22	Indiana	25,240
29	Iowa	24,210
36	Kansas	23,350
31	Kentucky	23,900
50	Louisiana	19,850
26	Maine	24,650
11	Maryland	28,260
3	Massachusetts	29,760
17	Michigan	26,430
15	Minnesota	27,280
49	Mississippi	20,170
40	Missouri	23,020
44	Montana	22,500
30	Nebraska	24,000
7	Nevada	28,740
8	New Hampshire	28,530
13	New Jersey	28,040
35	New Mexico	23,510
16	New York	26,830
42	North Carolina	22,940
38	North Dakota	23,260
27	Ohio	24,440
45	Oklahoma	21,910
14	Oregon	27,400
24	Pennsylvania	24,920
10	Rhode Island	28,310
41	South Carolina	22,950
39	South Dakota	23,100
31	Tennessee	23,900
43	Texas	22,810
37	Utah	23,310
20	Vermont	25,730
25	Virginia	24,910
4	Washington	29,400
48	West Virginia	20,310
19	Wisconsin	26,000
28	Wyoming	24,310

RANK ORDER

RANK	STATE	WAGES
1	Alaska	$34,290
2	Connecticut	30,470
3	Massachusetts	29,760
4	Washington	29,400
5	California	29,110
6	Hawaii	28,840
7	Nevada	28,740
8	New Hampshire	28,530
9	Colorado	28,370
10	Rhode Island	28,310
11	Maryland	28,260
12	Delaware	28,190
13	New Jersey	28,040
14	Oregon	27,400
15	Minnesota	27,280
16	New York	26,830
17	Michigan	26,430
18	Illinois	26,160
19	Wisconsin	26,000
20	Vermont	25,730
21	Arizona	25,260
22	Indiana	25,240
23	Florida	24,980
24	Pennsylvania	24,920
25	Virginia	24,910
26	Maine	24,650
27	Ohio	24,440
28	Wyoming	24,310
29	Iowa	24,210
30	Nebraska	24,000
31	Kentucky	23,900
31	Tennessee	23,900
33	Idaho	23,800
34	Georgia	23,700
35	New Mexico	23,510
36	Kansas	23,350
37	Utah	23,310
38	North Dakota	23,260
39	South Dakota	23,100
40	Missouri	23,020
41	South Carolina	22,950
42	North Carolina	22,940
43	Texas	22,810
44	Montana	22,500
45	Oklahoma	21,910
46	Alabama	21,310
47	Arkansas	21,150
48	West Virginia	20,310
49	Mississippi	20,170
50	Louisiana	19,850
	District of Columbia	29,820

Source: U.S. Department of Labor, Bureau of Labor Statistics
"Occupational Employment and Wages, 2007" (http://www.bls.gov/oes/)
*Does not include self-employed. Includes various health care assistants and aides not included in the category of health care practitioners and technicians. Among the included occupations are home health aides, nursing aides, psychiatric aides, dental assistants, and pharmacy aides.

VII. Physical Fitness

Users of Exercise Equipment in 2007

National Total = 52,827,000 Users

ALPHA ORDER

RANK	STATE	USERS	% of USA
25	Alabama	666,000	1.3%
NA	Alaska*	NA	NA
13	Arizona	1,381,000	2.6%
34	Arkansas	336,000	0.6%
1	California	6,077,000	11.5%
18	Colorado	1,177,000	2.2%
28	Connecticut	553,000	1.0%
46	Delaware	110,000	0.2%
4	Florida	2,877,000	5.5%
14	Georgia	1,357,000	2.6%
NA	Hawaii*	NA	NA
43	Idaho	144,000	0.3%
6	Illinois	2,377,000	4.5%
15	Indiana	1,296,000	2.5%
33	Iowa	361,000	0.7%
23	Kansas	728,000	1.4%
20	Kentucky	1,074,000	2.0%
26	Louisiana	621,000	1.2%
40	Maine	214,000	0.4%
17	Maryland	1,245,000	2.4%
12	Massachusetts	1,533,000	2.9%
8	Michigan	1,822,000	3.5%
19	Minnesota	1,164,000	2.2%
39	Mississippi	219,000	0.4%
22	Missouri	938,000	1.8%
41	Montana	175,000	0.3%
36	Nebraska	284,000	0.5%
27	Nevada	588,000	1.1%
38	New Hampshire	235,000	0.4%
9	New Jersey	1,688,000	3.2%
37	New Mexico	244,000	0.5%
3	New York	3,455,000	6.5%
10	North Carolina	1,668,000	3.2%
44	North Dakota	142,000	0.3%
7	Ohio	2,096,000	4.0%
32	Oklahoma	401,000	0.8%
35	Oregon	331,000	0.6%
5	Pennsylvania	2,576,000	4.9%
48	Rhode Island	93,000	0.2%
24	South Carolina	699,000	1.3%
41	South Dakota	175,000	0.3%
29	Tennessee	552,000	1.0%
2	Texas	4,131,000	7.8%
31	Utah	433,000	0.8%
47	Vermont	108,000	0.2%
11	Virginia	1,583,000	3.0%
16	Washington	1,254,000	2.4%
30	West Virginia	446,000	0.8%
21	Wisconsin	1,017,000	1.9%
45	Wyoming	140,000	0.3%

RANK ORDER

RANK	STATE	USERS	% of USA
1	California	6,077,000	11.5%
2	Texas	4,131,000	7.8%
3	New York	3,455,000	6.5%
4	Florida	2,877,000	5.5%
5	Pennsylvania	2,576,000	4.9%
6	Illinois	2,377,000	4.5%
7	Ohio	2,096,000	4.0%
8	Michigan	1,822,000	3.5%
9	New Jersey	1,688,000	3.2%
10	North Carolina	1,668,000	3.2%
11	Virginia	1,583,000	3.0%
12	Massachusetts	1,533,000	2.9%
13	Arizona	1,381,000	2.6%
14	Georgia	1,357,000	2.6%
15	Indiana	1,296,000	2.5%
16	Washington	1,254,000	2.4%
17	Maryland	1,245,000	2.4%
18	Colorado	1,177,000	2.2%
19	Minnesota	1,164,000	2.2%
20	Kentucky	1,074,000	2.0%
21	Wisconsin	1,017,000	1.9%
22	Missouri	938,000	1.8%
23	Kansas	728,000	1.4%
24	South Carolina	699,000	1.3%
25	Alabama	666,000	1.3%
26	Louisiana	621,000	1.2%
27	Nevada	588,000	1.1%
28	Connecticut	553,000	1.0%
29	Tennessee	552,000	1.0%
30	West Virginia	446,000	0.8%
31	Utah	433,000	0.8%
32	Oklahoma	401,000	0.8%
33	Iowa	361,000	0.7%
34	Arkansas	336,000	0.6%
35	Oregon	331,000	0.6%
36	Nebraska	284,000	0.5%
37	New Mexico	244,000	0.5%
38	New Hampshire	235,000	0.4%
39	Mississippi	219,000	0.4%
40	Maine	214,000	0.4%
41	Montana	175,000	0.3%
41	South Dakota	175,000	0.3%
43	Idaho	144,000	0.3%
44	North Dakota	142,000	0.3%
45	Wyoming	140,000	0.3%
46	Delaware	110,000	0.2%
47	Vermont	108,000	0.2%
48	Rhode Island	93,000	0.2%
NA	Alaska*	NA	NA
NA	Hawaii*	NA	NA
	District of Columbia*	NA	NA

Source: The National Sporting Goods Association
"NSGA Sports Participation Survey, January-December 2007" (Copyright 2008, reprinted with permission)
*Not available.

Participants in Golf in 2007

National Total = 22,729,000 Golfers

ALPHA ORDER

RANK	STATE	GOLFERS	% of USA
26	Alabama	245,000	1.1%
NA	Alaska*	NA	NA
18	Arizona	401,000	1.8%
35	Arkansas	139,000	0.6%
1	California	2,340,000	10.3%
21	Colorado	318,000	1.4%
33	Connecticut	160,000	0.7%
47	Delaware	12,000	0.1%
4	Florida	1,545,000	6.8%
12	Georgia	572,000	2.5%
NA	Hawaii*	NA	NA
24	Idaho	267,000	1.2%
5	Illinois	1,464,000	6.4%
17	Indiana	431,000	1.9%
38	Iowa	90,000	0.4%
27	Kansas	235,000	1.0%
22	Kentucky	295,000	1.3%
29	Louisiana	195,000	0.9%
46	Maine	50,000	0.2%
19	Maryland	392,000	1.7%
13	Massachusetts	570,000	2.5%
3	Michigan	1,557,000	6.9%
14	Minnesota	518,000	2.3%
40	Mississippi	76,000	0.3%
15	Missouri	479,000	2.1%
45	Montana	52,000	0.2%
41	Nebraska	75,000	0.3%
34	Nevada	154,000	0.7%
42	New Hampshire	63,000	0.3%
10	New Jersey	808,000	3.6%
25	New Mexico	246,000	1.1%
2	New York	1,685,000	7.4%
11	North Carolina	599,000	2.6%
NA	North Dakota*	NA	NA
7	Ohio	1,159,000	5.1%
37	Oklahoma	117,000	0.5%
28	Oregon	204,000	0.9%
8	Pennsylvania	1,056,000	4.6%
36	Rhode Island	134,000	0.6%
23	South Carolina	271,000	1.2%
39	South Dakota	81,000	0.4%
32	Tennessee	186,000	0.8%
6	Texas	1,296,000	5.7%
31	Utah	191,000	0.8%
44	Vermont	58,000	0.3%
20	Virginia	348,000	1.5%
16	Washington	435,000	1.9%
30	West Virginia	193,000	0.8%
9	Wisconsin	900,000	4.0%
42	Wyoming	63,000	0.3%

RANK ORDER

RANK	STATE	GOLFERS	% of USA
1	California	2,340,000	10.3%
2	New York	1,685,000	7.4%
3	Michigan	1,557,000	6.9%
4	Florida	1,545,000	6.8%
5	Illinois	1,464,000	6.4%
6	Texas	1,296,000	5.7%
7	Ohio	1,159,000	5.1%
8	Pennsylvania	1,056,000	4.6%
9	Wisconsin	900,000	4.0%
10	New Jersey	808,000	3.6%
11	North Carolina	599,000	2.6%
12	Georgia	572,000	2.5%
13	Massachusetts	570,000	2.5%
14	Minnesota	518,000	2.3%
15	Missouri	479,000	2.1%
16	Washington	435,000	1.9%
17	Indiana	431,000	1.9%
18	Arizona	401,000	1.8%
19	Maryland	392,000	1.7%
20	Virginia	348,000	1.5%
21	Colorado	318,000	1.4%
22	Kentucky	295,000	1.3%
23	South Carolina	271,000	1.2%
24	Idaho	267,000	1.2%
25	New Mexico	246,000	1.1%
26	Alabama	245,000	1.1%
27	Kansas	235,000	1.0%
28	Oregon	204,000	0.9%
29	Louisiana	195,000	0.9%
30	West Virginia	193,000	0.8%
31	Utah	191,000	0.8%
32	Tennessee	186,000	0.8%
33	Connecticut	160,000	0.7%
34	Nevada	154,000	0.7%
35	Arkansas	139,000	0.6%
36	Rhode Island	134,000	0.6%
37	Oklahoma	117,000	0.5%
38	Iowa	90,000	0.4%
39	South Dakota	81,000	0.4%
40	Mississippi	76,000	0.3%
41	Nebraska	75,000	0.3%
42	New Hampshire	63,000	0.3%
42	Wyoming	63,000	0.3%
44	Vermont	58,000	0.3%
45	Montana	52,000	0.2%
46	Maine	50,000	0.2%
47	Delaware	12,000	0.1%
NA	Alaska*	NA	NA
NA	Hawaii*	NA	NA
NA	North Dakota*	NA	NA
	District of Columbia*	NA	NA

Source: The National Sporting Goods Association
"NSGA Sports Participation Survey, January-December 2007" (Copyright 2008, reprinted with permission)
*Not available.

Participants in Running/Jogging in 2007

National Total = 30,372,000 Runners/Joggers

ALPHA ORDER

RANK	STATE	RUNNERS	% of USA
19	Alabama	494,000	1.6%
NA	Alaska*	NA	NA
13	Arizona	694,000	2.3%
35	Arkansas	200,000	0.7%
1	California	4,563,000	15.0%
16	Colorado	578,000	1.9%
31	Connecticut	275,000	0.9%
40	Delaware	101,000	0.3%
5	Florida	1,520,000	5.0%
4	Georgia	1,633,000	5.4%
NA	Hawaii*	NA	NA
36	Idaho	187,000	0.6%
6	Illinois	1,347,000	4.4%
14	Indiana	679,000	2.2%
28	Iowa	369,000	1.2%
32	Kansas	242,000	0.8%
27	Kentucky	372,000	1.2%
29	Louisiana	363,000	1.2%
42	Maine	95,000	0.3%
15	Maryland	656,000	2.2%
25	Massachusetts	432,000	1.4%
8	Michigan	1,193,000	3.9%
23	Minnesota	453,000	1.5%
38	Mississippi	116,000	0.4%
24	Missouri	440,000	1.4%
37	Montana	156,000	0.5%
43	Nebraska	88,000	0.3%
33	Nevada	223,000	0.7%
45	New Hampshire	71,000	0.2%
11	New Jersey	911,000	3.0%
34	New Mexico	207,000	0.7%
3	New York	1,930,000	6.4%
12	North Carolina	757,000	2.5%
39	North Dakota	110,000	0.4%
9	Ohio	1,099,000	3.6%
46	Oklahoma	59,000	0.2%
18	Oregon	527,000	1.7%
7	Pennsylvania	1,287,000	4.2%
47	Rhode Island	30,000	0.1%
26	South Carolina	380,000	1.3%
44	South Dakota	80,000	0.3%
22	Tennessee	464,000	1.5%
2	Texas	2,142,000	7.1%
20	Utah	487,000	1.6%
48	Vermont	24,000	0.1%
10	Virginia	914,000	3.0%
17	Washington	565,000	1.9%
30	West Virginia	287,000	0.9%
21	Wisconsin	470,000	1.5%
40	Wyoming	101,000	0.3%

RANK ORDER

RANK	STATE	RUNNERS	% of USA
1	California	4,563,000	15.0%
2	Texas	2,142,000	7.1%
3	New York	1,930,000	6.4%
4	Georgia	1,633,000	5.4%
5	Florida	1,520,000	5.0%
6	Illinois	1,347,000	4.4%
7	Pennsylvania	1,287,000	4.2%
8	Michigan	1,193,000	3.9%
9	Ohio	1,099,000	3.6%
10	Virginia	914,000	3.0%
11	New Jersey	911,000	3.0%
12	North Carolina	757,000	2.5%
13	Arizona	694,000	2.3%
14	Indiana	679,000	2.2%
15	Maryland	656,000	2.2%
16	Colorado	578,000	1.9%
17	Washington	565,000	1.9%
18	Oregon	527,000	1.7%
19	Alabama	494,000	1.6%
20	Utah	487,000	1.6%
21	Wisconsin	470,000	1.5%
22	Tennessee	464,000	1.5%
23	Minnesota	453,000	1.5%
24	Missouri	440,000	1.4%
25	Massachusetts	432,000	1.4%
26	South Carolina	380,000	1.3%
27	Kentucky	372,000	1.2%
28	Iowa	369,000	1.2%
29	Louisiana	363,000	1.2%
30	West Virginia	287,000	0.9%
31	Connecticut	275,000	0.9%
32	Kansas	242,000	0.8%
33	Nevada	223,000	0.7%
34	New Mexico	207,000	0.7%
35	Arkansas	200,000	0.7%
36	Idaho	187,000	0.6%
37	Montana	156,000	0.5%
38	Mississippi	116,000	0.4%
39	North Dakota	110,000	0.4%
40	Delaware	101,000	0.3%
40	Wyoming	101,000	0.3%
42	Maine	95,000	0.3%
43	Nebraska	88,000	0.3%
44	South Dakota	80,000	0.3%
45	New Hampshire	71,000	0.2%
46	Oklahoma	59,000	0.2%
47	Rhode Island	30,000	0.1%
48	Vermont	24,000	0.1%
NA	Alaska*	NA	NA
NA	Hawaii*	NA	NA
	District of Columbia*	NA	NA

Source: The National Sporting Goods Association
"NSGA Sports Participation Survey, January-December 2007" (Copyright 2008, reprinted with permission)
*Not available.

Participants in Swimming in 2007

National Total = 52,346,000 Swimmers

ALPHA ORDER

RANK	STATE	SWIMMERS	% of USA
25	Alabama	746,000	1.4%
NA	Alaska*	NA	NA
16	Arizona	1,142,000	2.2%
40	Arkansas	256,000	0.5%
1	California	5,651,000	10.8%
23	Colorado	772,000	1.5%
35	Connecticut	341,000	0.7%
44	Delaware	124,000	0.2%
4	Florida	2,889,000	5.5%
13	Georgia	1,510,000	2.9%
NA	Hawaii*	NA	NA
34	Idaho	434,000	0.8%
6	Illinois	2,538,000	4.8%
21	Indiana	866,000	1.7%
26	Iowa	703,000	1.3%
32	Kansas	520,000	1.0%
20	Kentucky	867,000	1.7%
29	Louisiana	608,000	1.2%
37	Maine	285,000	0.5%
14	Maryland	1,505,000	2.9%
15	Massachusetts	1,323,000	2.5%
7	Michigan	2,142,000	4.1%
19	Minnesota	975,000	1.9%
38	Mississippi	284,000	0.5%
17	Missouri	1,061,000	2.0%
42	Montana	158,000	0.3%
48	Nebraska	62,000	0.1%
31	Nevada	534,000	1.0%
36	New Hampshire	304,000	0.6%
10	New Jersey	1,673,000	3.2%
41	New Mexico	160,000	0.3%
2	New York	4,016,000	7.7%
9	North Carolina	1,684,000	3.2%
43	North Dakota	129,000	0.2%
8	Ohio	1,897,000	3.6%
22	Oklahoma	822,000	1.6%
24	Oregon	762,000	1.5%
3	Pennsylvania	2,918,000	5.6%
47	Rhode Island	95,000	0.2%
28	South Carolina	620,000	1.2%
45	South Dakota	99,000	0.2%
27	Tennessee	647,000	1.2%
5	Texas	2,657,000	5.1%
30	Utah	592,000	1.1%
45	Vermont	99,000	0.2%
12	Virginia	1,526,000	2.9%
11	Washington	1,563,000	3.0%
33	West Virginia	505,000	1.0%
18	Wisconsin	978,000	1.9%
39	Wyoming	261,000	0.5%

RANK ORDER

RANK	STATE	SWIMMERS	% of USA
1	California	5,651,000	10.8%
2	New York	4,016,000	7.7%
3	Pennsylvania	2,918,000	5.6%
4	Florida	2,889,000	5.5%
5	Texas	2,657,000	5.1%
6	Illinois	2,538,000	4.8%
7	Michigan	2,142,000	4.1%
8	Ohio	1,897,000	3.6%
9	North Carolina	1,684,000	3.2%
10	New Jersey	1,673,000	3.2%
11	Washington	1,563,000	3.0%
12	Virginia	1,526,000	2.9%
13	Georgia	1,510,000	2.9%
14	Maryland	1,505,000	2.9%
15	Massachusetts	1,323,000	2.5%
16	Arizona	1,142,000	2.2%
17	Missouri	1,061,000	2.0%
18	Wisconsin	978,000	1.9%
19	Minnesota	975,000	1.9%
20	Kentucky	867,000	1.7%
21	Indiana	866,000	1.7%
22	Oklahoma	822,000	1.6%
23	Colorado	772,000	1.5%
24	Oregon	762,000	1.5%
25	Alabama	746,000	1.4%
26	Iowa	703,000	1.3%
27	Tennessee	647,000	1.2%
28	South Carolina	620,000	1.2%
29	Louisiana	608,000	1.2%
30	Utah	592,000	1.1%
31	Nevada	534,000	1.0%
32	Kansas	520,000	1.0%
33	West Virginia	505,000	1.0%
34	Idaho	434,000	0.8%
35	Connecticut	341,000	0.7%
36	New Hampshire	304,000	0.6%
37	Maine	285,000	0.5%
38	Mississippi	284,000	0.5%
39	Wyoming	261,000	0.5%
40	Arkansas	256,000	0.5%
41	New Mexico	160,000	0.3%
42	Montana	158,000	0.3%
43	North Dakota	129,000	0.2%
44	Delaware	124,000	0.2%
45	South Dakota	99,000	0.2%
45	Vermont	99,000	0.2%
47	Rhode Island	95,000	0.2%
48	Nebraska	62,000	0.1%
NA	Alaska*	NA	NA
NA	Hawaii*	NA	NA
	District of Columbia*	NA	NA

Source: The National Sporting Goods Association
   "NSGA Sports Participation Survey, January-December 2007" (Copyright 2008, reprinted with permission)
*Not available.

Participants in Tennis in 2007

National Total = 12,290,000 Tennis Players

ALPHA ORDER

RANK	STATE	PLAYERS	% of USA
24	Alabama	132,000	1.1%
NA	Alaska*	NA	NA
20	Arizona	171,000	1.4%
31	Arkansas	67,000	0.5%
1	California	2,527,000	20.6%
14	Colorado	300,000	2.4%
19	Connecticut	176,000	1.4%
34	Delaware	44,000	0.4%
6	Florida	575,000	4.7%
3	Georgia	831,000	6.8%
NA	Hawaii*	NA	NA
43	Idaho	9,000	0.1%
7	Illinois	544,000	4.4%
15	Indiana	261,000	2.1%
23	Iowa	134,000	1.1%
22	Kansas	135,000	1.1%
27	Kentucky	104,000	0.8%
35	Louisiana	39,000	0.3%
37	Maine	32,000	0.3%
33	Maryland	52,000	0.4%
17	Massachusetts	199,000	1.6%
10	Michigan	428,000	3.5%
25	Minnesota	128,000	1.0%
30	Mississippi	70,000	0.6%
16	Missouri	218,000	1.8%
NA	Montana*	NA	NA
42	Nebraska	11,000	0.1%
40	Nevada	16,000	0.1%
NA	New Hampshire*	NA	NA
9	New Jersey	485,000	3.9%
36	New Mexico	38,000	0.3%
5	New York	579,000	4.7%
8	North Carolina	521,000	4.2%
28	North Dakota	87,000	0.7%
4	Ohio	673,000	5.5%
NA	Oklahoma*	NA	NA
29	Oregon	79,000	0.6%
11	Pennsylvania	354,000	2.9%
38	Rhode Island	31,000	0.3%
18	South Carolina	181,000	1.5%
NA	South Dakota*	NA	NA
39	Tennessee	26,000	0.2%
2	Texas	1,003,000	8.2%
32	Utah	65,000	0.5%
NA	Vermont*	NA	NA
13	Virginia	328,000	2.7%
26	Washington	121,000	1.0%
12	West Virginia	337,000	2.7%
21	Wisconsin	167,000	1.4%
41	Wyoming	13,000	0.1%

RANK ORDER

RANK	STATE	PLAYERS	% of USA
1	California	2,527,000	20.6%
2	Texas	1,003,000	8.2%
3	Georgia	831,000	6.8%
4	Ohio	673,000	5.5%
5	New York	579,000	4.7%
6	Florida	575,000	4.7%
7	Illinois	544,000	4.4%
8	North Carolina	521,000	4.2%
9	New Jersey	485,000	3.9%
10	Michigan	428,000	3.5%
11	Pennsylvania	354,000	2.9%
12	West Virginia	337,000	2.7%
13	Virginia	328,000	2.7%
14	Colorado	300,000	2.4%
15	Indiana	261,000	2.1%
16	Missouri	218,000	1.8%
17	Massachusetts	199,000	1.6%
18	South Carolina	181,000	1.5%
19	Connecticut	176,000	1.4%
20	Arizona	171,000	1.4%
21	Wisconsin	167,000	1.4%
22	Kansas	135,000	1.1%
23	Iowa	134,000	1.1%
24	Alabama	132,000	1.1%
25	Minnesota	128,000	1.0%
26	Washington	121,000	1.0%
27	Kentucky	104,000	0.8%
28	North Dakota	87,000	0.7%
29	Oregon	79,000	0.6%
30	Mississippi	70,000	0.6%
31	Arkansas	67,000	0.5%
32	Utah	65,000	0.5%
33	Maryland	52,000	0.4%
34	Delaware	44,000	0.4%
35	Louisiana	39,000	0.3%
36	New Mexico	38,000	0.3%
37	Maine	32,000	0.3%
38	Rhode Island	31,000	0.3%
39	Tennessee	26,000	0.2%
40	Nevada	16,000	0.1%
41	Wyoming	13,000	0.1%
42	Nebraska	11,000	0.1%
43	Idaho	9,000	0.1%
NA	Alaska*	NA	NA
NA	Hawaii*	NA	NA
NA	Montana*	NA	NA
NA	New Hampshire*	NA	NA
NA	Oklahoma*	NA	NA
NA	South Dakota*	NA	NA
NA	Vermont*	NA	NA
	District of Columbia*	NA	NA

Source: The National Sporting Goods Association
"NSGA Sports Participation Survey, January-December 2007" (Copyright 2008, reprinted with permission)
*Not available.

Alcohol Consumption in 2006

National Total = 550,808,000 Gallons*

ALPHA ORDER

RANK	STATE	GALLONS	% of USA
27	Alabama	7,370,000	1.3%
47	Alaska	1,473,000	0.3%
15	Arizona	12,065,000	2.2%
35	Arkansas	4,142,000	0.8%
1	California	66,439,000	12.1%
18	Colorado	10,377,000	1.9%
28	Connecticut	6,655,000	1.2%
43	Delaware	2,299,000	0.4%
3	Florida	40,855,000	7.4%
10	Georgia	15,302,000	2.8%
40	Hawaii	2,719,000	0.5%
38	Idaho	2,920,000	0.5%
5	Illinois	23,992,000	4.4%
19	Indiana	10,193,000	1.9%
30	Iowa	5,315,000	1.0%
34	Kansas	4,305,000	0.8%
29	Kentucky	6,284,000	1.1%
23	Louisiana	9,110,000	1.7%
39	Maine	2,729,000	0.5%
21	Maryland	10,007,000	1.8%
12	Massachusetts	13,590,000	2.5%
8	Michigan	17,873,000	3.2%
20	Minnesota	10,061,000	1.8%
31	Mississippi	5,196,000	0.9%
17	Missouri	11,331,000	2.1%
45	Montana	2,149,000	0.4%
37	Nebraska	3,347,000	0.6%
26	Nevada	7,378,000	1.3%
32	New Hampshire	4,567,000	0.8%
9	New Jersey	16,430,000	3.0%
36	New Mexico	3,727,000	0.7%
4	New York	31,622,000	5.7%
11	North Carolina	14,145,000	2.6%
48	North Dakota	1,451,000	0.3%
7	Ohio	18,681,000	3.4%
33	Oklahoma	4,378,000	0.8%
25	Oregon	7,689,000	1.4%
6	Pennsylvania	21,793,000	4.0%
44	Rhode Island	2,226,000	0.4%
24	South Carolina	8,699,000	1.6%
46	South Dakota	1,586,000	0.3%
22	Tennessee	9,367,000	1.7%
2	Texas	41,034,000	7.4%
42	Utah	2,526,000	0.5%
49	Vermont	1,370,000	0.2%
14	Virginia	13,081,000	2.4%
16	Washington	11,698,000	2.1%
41	West Virginia	2,636,000	0.5%
13	Wisconsin	13,540,000	2.5%
50	Wyoming	1,152,000	0.2%

RANK ORDER

RANK	STATE	GALLONS	% of USA
1	California	66,439,000	12.1%
2	Texas	41,034,000	7.4%
3	Florida	40,855,000	7.4%
4	New York	31,622,000	5.7%
5	Illinois	23,992,000	4.4%
6	Pennsylvania	21,793,000	4.0%
7	Ohio	18,681,000	3.4%
8	Michigan	17,873,000	3.2%
9	New Jersey	16,430,000	3.0%
10	Georgia	15,302,000	2.8%
11	North Carolina	14,145,000	2.6%
12	Massachusetts	13,590,000	2.5%
13	Wisconsin	13,540,000	2.5%
14	Virginia	13,081,000	2.4%
15	Arizona	12,065,000	2.2%
16	Washington	11,698,000	2.1%
17	Missouri	11,331,000	2.1%
18	Colorado	10,377,000	1.9%
19	Indiana	10,193,000	1.9%
20	Minnesota	10,061,000	1.8%
21	Maryland	10,007,000	1.8%
22	Tennessee	9,367,000	1.7%
23	Louisiana	9,110,000	1.7%
24	South Carolina	8,699,000	1.6%
25	Oregon	7,689,000	1.4%
26	Nevada	7,378,000	1.3%
27	Alabama	7,370,000	1.3%
28	Connecticut	6,655,000	1.2%
29	Kentucky	6,284,000	1.1%
30	Iowa	5,315,000	1.0%
31	Mississippi	5,196,000	0.9%
32	New Hampshire	4,567,000	0.8%
33	Oklahoma	4,378,000	0.8%
34	Kansas	4,305,000	0.8%
35	Arkansas	4,142,000	0.8%
36	New Mexico	3,727,000	0.7%
37	Nebraska	3,347,000	0.6%
38	Idaho	2,920,000	0.5%
39	Maine	2,729,000	0.5%
40	Hawaii	2,719,000	0.5%
41	West Virginia	2,636,000	0.5%
42	Utah	2,526,000	0.5%
43	Delaware	2,299,000	0.4%
44	Rhode Island	2,226,000	0.4%
45	Montana	2,149,000	0.4%
46	South Dakota	1,586,000	0.3%
47	Alaska	1,473,000	0.3%
48	North Dakota	1,451,000	0.3%
49	Vermont	1,370,000	0.2%
50	Wyoming	1,152,000	0.2%
	District of Columbia	1,932,000	0.4%

Source: U.S. Department of Health and Human Services, National Institute on Alcohol Abuse and Alcoholism
"Volume Beverage and Ethanol Consumption for States" (http://www.niaaa.nih.gov/Resources/)
*This is apparent consumption of actual alcohol, not entire volume of an alcoholic beverage (for example, wine is roughly 11% absolute alcohol content). Apparent consumption is based on several sources which together approximate sales but do not actually measure consumption. Accordingly, figures for some states may be skewed by purchases by nonresidents.

Adult Per Capita Alcohol Consumption in 2006

National Per Capita = 2.6 Gallons Consumed per Adult 21 Years and Older*

ALPHA ORDER

RANK	STATE	PER CAPITA
42	Alabama	2.2
5	Alaska	3.2
18	Arizona	2.8
45	Arkansas	2.1
27	California	2.6
11	Colorado	3.0
27	Connecticut	2.6
3	Delaware	3.8
7	Florida	3.1
36	Georgia	2.4
13	Hawaii	2.9
13	Idaho	2.9
22	Illinois	2.7
39	Indiana	2.3
32	Iowa	2.5
42	Kansas	2.2
45	Kentucky	2.1
7	Louisiana	3.1
18	Maine	2.8
32	Maryland	2.5
13	Massachusetts	2.9
32	Michigan	2.5
22	Minnesota	2.7
27	Mississippi	2.6
22	Missouri	2.7
7	Montana	3.1
22	Nebraska	2.7
2	Nevada	4.2
1	New Hampshire	4.8
27	New Jersey	2.6
22	New Mexico	2.7
39	New York	2.3
42	North Carolina	2.2
5	North Dakota	3.2
39	Ohio	2.3
49	Oklahoma	1.7
13	Oregon	2.9
36	Pennsylvania	2.4
13	Rhode Island	2.9
18	South Carolina	2.8
18	South Dakota	2.8
45	Tennessee	2.1
27	Texas	2.6
50	Utah	1.5
11	Vermont	3.0
36	Virginia	2.4
32	Washington	2.5
48	West Virginia	2.0
4	Wisconsin	3.4
7	Wyoming	3.1

RANK ORDER

RANK	STATE	PER CAPITA
1	New Hampshire	4.8
2	Nevada	4.2
3	Delaware	3.8
4	Wisconsin	3.4
5	Alaska	3.2
5	North Dakota	3.2
7	Florida	3.1
7	Louisiana	3.1
7	Montana	3.1
7	Wyoming	3.1
11	Colorado	3.0
11	Vermont	3.0
13	Hawaii	2.9
13	Idaho	2.9
13	Massachusetts	2.9
13	Oregon	2.9
13	Rhode Island	2.9
18	Arizona	2.8
18	Maine	2.8
18	South Carolina	2.8
18	South Dakota	2.8
22	Illinois	2.7
22	Minnesota	2.7
22	Missouri	2.7
22	Nebraska	2.7
22	New Mexico	2.7
27	California	2.6
27	Connecticut	2.6
27	Mississippi	2.6
27	New Jersey	2.6
27	Texas	2.6
32	Iowa	2.5
32	Maryland	2.5
32	Michigan	2.5
32	Washington	2.5
36	Georgia	2.4
36	Pennsylvania	2.4
36	Virginia	2.4
39	Indiana	2.3
39	New York	2.3
39	Ohio	2.3
42	Alabama	2.2
42	Kansas	2.2
42	North Carolina	2.2
45	Arkansas	2.1
45	Kentucky	2.1
45	Tennessee	2.1
48	West Virginia	2.0
49	Oklahoma	1.7
50	Utah	1.5

| | District of Columbia | 4.4 |

Source: CQ Press using data from U.S. Dept of Health and Human Services, National Institute on Alcohol Abuse and Alcoholism
"Volume Beverage and Ethanol Consumption for States" (http://www.niaaa.nih.gov/Resources/)
*This is apparent consumption of actual alcohol, not entire volume of an alcoholic beverage (for example, wine is roughly 11% absolute alcohol content). Apparent consumption is based on several sources which together approximate sales but do not actually measure consumption. Accordingly, figures for some states may be skewed by purchases by nonresidents.

Apparent Beer Consumption in 2006

National Total = 6,431,869,000 Gallons of Beer Consumed*

<table>
<tr><td colspan="4">ALPHA ORDER</td><td colspan="4">RANK ORDER</td></tr>
<tr><th>RANK</th><th>STATE</th><th>GALLONS</th><th>% of USA</th><th>RANK</th><th>STATE</th><th>GALLONS</th><th>% of USA</th></tr>
<tr><td>25</td><td>Alabama</td><td>101,025,000</td><td>1.6%</td><td>1</td><td>California</td><td>675,608,000</td><td>10.5%</td></tr>
<tr><td>49</td><td>Alaska</td><td>14,917,000</td><td>0.2%</td><td>2</td><td>Texas</td><td>581,767,000</td><td>9.0%</td></tr>
<tr><td>14</td><td>Arizona</td><td>142,756,000</td><td>2.2%</td><td>3</td><td>Florida</td><td>442,518,000</td><td>6.9%</td></tr>
<tr><td>33</td><td>Arkansas</td><td>53,843,000</td><td>0.8%</td><td>4</td><td>New York</td><td>312,574,000</td><td>4.9%</td></tr>
<tr><td>1</td><td>California</td><td>675,608,000</td><td>10.5%</td><td>5</td><td>Pennsylvania</td><td>298,350,000</td><td>4.6%</td></tr>
<tr><td>22</td><td>Colorado</td><td>108,981,000</td><td>1.7%</td><td>6</td><td>Illinois</td><td>281,239,000</td><td>4.4%</td></tr>
<tr><td>31</td><td>Connecticut</td><td>59,047,000</td><td>0.9%</td><td>7</td><td>Ohio</td><td>274,140,000</td><td>4.3%</td></tr>
<tr><td>45</td><td>Delaware</td><td>22,070,000</td><td>0.3%</td><td>8</td><td>Michigan</td><td>205,142,000</td><td>3.2%</td></tr>
<tr><td>3</td><td>Florida</td><td>442,518,000</td><td>6.9%</td><td>9</td><td>Georgia</td><td>192,848,000</td><td>3.0%</td></tr>
<tr><td>9</td><td>Georgia</td><td>192,848,000</td><td>3.0%</td><td>10</td><td>North Carolina</td><td>183,372,000</td><td>2.9%</td></tr>
<tr><td>41</td><td>Hawaii</td><td>30,688,000</td><td>0.5%</td><td>11</td><td>Wisconsin</td><td>157,950,000</td><td>2.5%</td></tr>
<tr><td>42</td><td>Idaho</td><td>29,240,000</td><td>0.5%</td><td>12</td><td>Virginia</td><td>157,404,000</td><td>2.4%</td></tr>
<tr><td>6</td><td>Illinois</td><td>281,239,000</td><td>4.4%</td><td>13</td><td>New Jersey</td><td>148,555,000</td><td>2.3%</td></tr>
<tr><td>18</td><td>Indiana</td><td>123,749,000</td><td>1.9%</td><td>14</td><td>Arizona</td><td>142,756,000</td><td>2.2%</td></tr>
<tr><td>30</td><td>Iowa</td><td>74,385,000</td><td>1.2%</td><td>15</td><td>Missouri</td><td>142,009,000</td><td>2.2%</td></tr>
<tr><td>32</td><td>Kansas</td><td>56,433,000</td><td>0.9%</td><td>16</td><td>Massachusetts</td><td>130,122,000</td><td>2.0%</td></tr>
<tr><td>27</td><td>Kentucky</td><td>79,340,000</td><td>1.2%</td><td>17</td><td>Tennessee</td><td>125,438,000</td><td>2.0%</td></tr>
<tr><td>19</td><td>Louisiana</td><td>122,400,000</td><td>1.9%</td><td>18</td><td>Indiana</td><td>123,749,000</td><td>1.9%</td></tr>
<tr><td>39</td><td>Maine</td><td>30,938,000</td><td>0.5%</td><td>19</td><td>Louisiana</td><td>122,400,000</td><td>1.9%</td></tr>
<tr><td>24</td><td>Maryland</td><td>103,038,000</td><td>1.6%</td><td>20</td><td>Washington</td><td>121,275,000</td><td>1.9%</td></tr>
<tr><td>16</td><td>Massachusetts</td><td>130,122,000</td><td>2.0%</td><td>21</td><td>South Carolina</td><td>114,345,000</td><td>1.8%</td></tr>
<tr><td>8</td><td>Michigan</td><td>205,142,000</td><td>3.2%</td><td>22</td><td>Colorado</td><td>108,981,000</td><td>1.7%</td></tr>
<tr><td>23</td><td>Minnesota</td><td>107,021,000</td><td>1.7%</td><td>23</td><td>Minnesota</td><td>107,021,000</td><td>1.7%</td></tr>
<tr><td>29</td><td>Mississippi</td><td>74,813,000</td><td>1.2%</td><td>24</td><td>Maryland</td><td>103,038,000</td><td>1.6%</td></tr>
<tr><td>15</td><td>Missouri</td><td>142,009,000</td><td>2.2%</td><td>25</td><td>Alabama</td><td>101,025,000</td><td>1.6%</td></tr>
<tr><td>43</td><td>Montana</td><td>27,293,000</td><td>0.4%</td><td>26</td><td>Oregon</td><td>85,275,000</td><td>1.3%</td></tr>
<tr><td>36</td><td>Nebraska</td><td>45,088,000</td><td>0.7%</td><td>27</td><td>Kentucky</td><td>79,340,000</td><td>1.2%</td></tr>
<tr><td>28</td><td>Nevada</td><td>77,182,000</td><td>1.2%</td><td>28</td><td>Nevada</td><td>77,182,000</td><td>1.2%</td></tr>
<tr><td>37</td><td>New Hampshire</td><td>41,639,000</td><td>0.6%</td><td>29</td><td>Mississippi</td><td>74,813,000</td><td>1.2%</td></tr>
<tr><td>13</td><td>New Jersey</td><td>148,555,000</td><td>2.3%</td><td>30</td><td>Iowa</td><td>74,385,000</td><td>1.2%</td></tr>
<tr><td>35</td><td>New Mexico</td><td>48,024,000</td><td>0.7%</td><td>31</td><td>Connecticut</td><td>59,047,000</td><td>0.9%</td></tr>
<tr><td>4</td><td>New York</td><td>312,574,000</td><td>4.9%</td><td>32</td><td>Kansas</td><td>56,433,000</td><td>0.9%</td></tr>
<tr><td>10</td><td>North Carolina</td><td>183,372,000</td><td>2.9%</td><td>33</td><td>Arkansas</td><td>53,843,000</td><td>0.8%</td></tr>
<tr><td>47</td><td>North Dakota</td><td>17,903,000</td><td>0.3%</td><td>34</td><td>Oklahoma</td><td>50,090,000</td><td>0.8%</td></tr>
<tr><td>7</td><td>Ohio</td><td>274,140,000</td><td>4.3%</td><td>35</td><td>New Mexico</td><td>48,024,000</td><td>0.7%</td></tr>
<tr><td>34</td><td>Oklahoma</td><td>50,090,000</td><td>0.8%</td><td>36</td><td>Nebraska</td><td>45,088,000</td><td>0.7%</td></tr>
<tr><td>26</td><td>Oregon</td><td>85,275,000</td><td>1.3%</td><td>37</td><td>New Hampshire</td><td>41,639,000</td><td>0.6%</td></tr>
<tr><td>5</td><td>Pennsylvania</td><td>298,350,000</td><td>4.6%</td><td>38</td><td>West Virginia</td><td>41,130,000</td><td>0.6%</td></tr>
<tr><td>44</td><td>Rhode Island</td><td>22,275,000</td><td>0.3%</td><td>39</td><td>Maine</td><td>30,938,000</td><td>0.5%</td></tr>
<tr><td>21</td><td>South Carolina</td><td>114,345,000</td><td>1.8%</td><td>40</td><td>Utah</td><td>30,780,000</td><td>0.5%</td></tr>
<tr><td>46</td><td>South Dakota</td><td>21,420,000</td><td>0.3%</td><td>41</td><td>Hawaii</td><td>30,688,000</td><td>0.5%</td></tr>
<tr><td>17</td><td>Tennessee</td><td>125,438,000</td><td>2.0%</td><td>42</td><td>Idaho</td><td>29,240,000</td><td>0.5%</td></tr>
<tr><td>2</td><td>Texas</td><td>581,767,000</td><td>9.0%</td><td>43</td><td>Montana</td><td>27,293,000</td><td>0.4%</td></tr>
<tr><td>40</td><td>Utah</td><td>30,780,000</td><td>0.5%</td><td>44</td><td>Rhode Island</td><td>22,275,000</td><td>0.3%</td></tr>
<tr><td>48</td><td>Vermont</td><td>15,728,000</td><td>0.2%</td><td>45</td><td>Delaware</td><td>22,070,000</td><td>0.3%</td></tr>
<tr><td>12</td><td>Virginia</td><td>157,404,000</td><td>2.4%</td><td>46</td><td>South Dakota</td><td>21,420,000</td><td>0.3%</td></tr>
<tr><td>20</td><td>Washington</td><td>121,275,000</td><td>1.9%</td><td>47</td><td>North Dakota</td><td>17,903,000</td><td>0.3%</td></tr>
<tr><td>38</td><td>West Virginia</td><td>41,130,000</td><td>0.6%</td><td>48</td><td>Vermont</td><td>15,728,000</td><td>0.2%</td></tr>
<tr><td>11</td><td>Wisconsin</td><td>157,950,000</td><td>2.5%</td><td>49</td><td>Alaska</td><td>14,917,000</td><td>0.2%</td></tr>
<tr><td>50</td><td>Wyoming</td><td>13,673,000</td><td>0.2%</td><td>50</td><td>Wyoming</td><td>13,673,000</td><td>0.2%</td></tr>
<tr><td></td><td></td><td></td><td></td><td></td><td>District of Columbia</td><td>15,030,000</td><td>0.2%</td></tr>
</table>

Source: U.S. Department of Health and Human Services, National Institute on Alcohol Abuse and Alcoholism
"Volume Beverage and Ethanol Consumption for States" (http://www.niaaa.nih.gov/Resources/)
*This is apparent consumption and is based on several sources which together approximate sales but do not actually measure consumption. Reported state volumes reflect only in-state purchases. Accordingly, figures for some states may be skewed by purchases by nonresidents.

Adult Per Capita Beer Consumption in 2006

National Per Capita = 30.3 Gallons Consumed per Adult 21 Years and Older*

ALPHA ORDER

RANK	STATE	PER CAPITA
28	Alabama	30.8
23	Alaska	32.0
19	Arizona	33.2
41	Arkansas	26.9
42	California	26.8
23	Colorado	32.0
47	Connecticut	23.4
13	Delaware	36.1
20	Florida	33.1
30	Georgia	29.7
22	Hawaii	32.5
31	Idaho	29.1
27	Illinois	31.2
39	Indiana	27.8
15	Iowa	35.0
31	Kansas	29.1
44	Kentucky	26.1
3	Louisiana	41.1
26	Maine	31.5
45	Maryland	25.8
40	Massachusetts	27.6
38	Michigan	28.5
31	Minnesota	29.1
8	Mississippi	37.3
17	Missouri	34.0
4	Montana	39.6
12	Nebraska	36.4
2	Nevada	43.5
1	New Hampshire	43.6
46	New Jersey	23.7
14	New Mexico	35.4
48	New York	22.4
34	North Carolina	28.9
6	North Dakota	39.1
18	Ohio	33.3
49	Oklahoma	19.8
25	Oregon	31.6
21	Pennsylvania	33.0
34	Rhode Island	28.9
10	South Carolina	37.0
7	South Dakota	38.5
36	Tennessee	28.6
11	Texas	36.6
50	Utah	18.5
16	Vermont	34.3
36	Virginia	28.6
43	Washington	26.4
29	West Virginia	30.5
5	Wisconsin	39.4
9	Wyoming	37.2

RANK ORDER

RANK	STATE	PER CAPITA
1	New Hampshire	43.6
2	Nevada	43.5
3	Louisiana	41.1
4	Montana	39.6
5	Wisconsin	39.4
6	North Dakota	39.1
7	South Dakota	38.5
8	Mississippi	37.3
9	Wyoming	37.2
10	South Carolina	37.0
11	Texas	36.6
12	Nebraska	36.4
13	Delaware	36.1
14	New Mexico	35.4
15	Iowa	35.0
16	Vermont	34.3
17	Missouri	34.0
18	Ohio	33.3
19	Arizona	33.2
20	Florida	33.1
21	Pennsylvania	33.0
22	Hawaii	32.5
23	Alaska	32.0
23	Colorado	32.0
25	Oregon	31.6
26	Maine	31.5
27	Illinois	31.2
28	Alabama	30.8
29	West Virginia	30.5
30	Georgia	29.7
31	Idaho	29.1
31	Kansas	29.1
31	Minnesota	29.1
34	North Carolina	28.9
34	Rhode Island	28.9
36	Tennessee	28.6
36	Virginia	28.6
38	Michigan	28.5
39	Indiana	27.8
40	Massachusetts	27.6
41	Arkansas	26.9
42	California	26.8
43	Washington	26.4
44	Kentucky	26.1
45	Maryland	25.8
46	New Jersey	23.7
47	Connecticut	23.4
48	New York	22.4
49	Oklahoma	19.8
50	Utah	18.5

District of Columbia   34.1

Source: CQ Press using data from U.S. Dept of Health and Human Services, National Institute on Alcohol Abuse and Alcoholism
"Volume Beverage and Ethanol Consumption for States" (http://www.niaaa.nih.gov/Resources/)
*This is apparent consumption and is based on several sources which together approximate sales but do not actually measure consumption. Reported state volumes reflect only in-state purchases. Accordingly, figures for some states may be skewed by purchases by nonresidents.

Wine Consumption in 2006

National Total = 687,317,000 Gallons of Wine Consumed*

ALPHA ORDER

RANK	STATE	GALLONS	% of USA
29	Alabama	6,091,000	0.9%
46	Alaska	1,935,000	0.3%
15	Arizona	14,194,000	2.1%
40	Arkansas	2,910,000	0.4%
1	California	121,560,000	17.7%
16	Colorado	13,311,000	1.9%
17	Connecticut	12,258,000	1.8%
37	Delaware	3,215,000	0.5%
2	Florida	55,595,000	8.1%
14	Georgia	14,724,000	2.1%
32	Hawaii	3,914,000	0.6%
27	Idaho	6,606,000	1.0%
5	Illinois	29,333,000	4.3%
24	Indiana	9,847,000	1.4%
39	Iowa	3,074,000	0.4%
38	Kansas	3,144,000	0.5%
31	Kentucky	4,536,000	0.7%
26	Louisiana	6,740,000	1.0%
35	Maine	3,615,000	0.5%
18	Maryland	12,156,000	1.8%
7	Massachusetts	25,085,000	3.6%
11	Michigan	18,246,000	2.7%
21	Minnesota	10,477,000	1.5%
44	Mississippi	2,154,000	0.3%
22	Missouri	10,465,000	1.5%
45	Montana	2,112,000	0.3%
42	Nebraska	2,366,000	0.3%
23	Nevada	10,193,000	1.5%
30	New Hampshire	6,073,000	0.9%
6	New Jersey	29,296,000	4.3%
34	New Mexico	3,707,000	0.5%
3	New York	55,565,000	8.1%
13	North Carolina	15,192,000	2.2%
49	North Dakota	851,000	0.1%
12	Ohio	17,232,000	2.5%
33	Oklahoma	3,751,000	0.5%
19	Oregon	11,493,000	1.7%
9	Pennsylvania	19,117,000	2.8%
36	Rhode Island	3,604,000	0.5%
28	South Carolina	6,594,000	1.0%
48	South Dakota	934,000	0.1%
25	Tennessee	7,382,000	1.1%
4	Texas	36,525,000	5.3%
41	Utah	2,372,000	0.3%
43	Vermont	2,350,000	0.3%
10	Virginia	19,090,000	2.8%
8	Washington	19,498,000	2.8%
47	West Virginia	1,208,000	0.2%
20	Wisconsin	11,222,000	1.6%
50	Wyoming	748,000	0.1%

RANK ORDER

RANK	STATE	GALLONS	% of USA
1	California	121,560,000	17.7%
2	Florida	55,595,000	8.1%
3	New York	55,565,000	8.1%
4	Texas	36,525,000	5.3%
5	Illinois	29,333,000	4.3%
6	New Jersey	29,296,000	4.3%
7	Massachusetts	25,085,000	3.6%
8	Washington	19,498,000	2.8%
9	Pennsylvania	19,117,000	2.8%
10	Virginia	19,090,000	2.8%
11	Michigan	18,246,000	2.7%
12	Ohio	17,232,000	2.5%
13	North Carolina	15,192,000	2.2%
14	Georgia	14,724,000	2.1%
15	Arizona	14,194,000	2.1%
16	Colorado	13,311,000	1.9%
17	Connecticut	12,258,000	1.8%
18	Maryland	12,156,000	1.8%
19	Oregon	11,493,000	1.7%
20	Wisconsin	11,222,000	1.6%
21	Minnesota	10,477,000	1.5%
22	Missouri	10,465,000	1.5%
23	Nevada	10,193,000	1.5%
24	Indiana	9,847,000	1.4%
25	Tennessee	7,382,000	1.1%
26	Louisiana	6,740,000	1.0%
27	Idaho	6,606,000	1.0%
28	South Carolina	6,594,000	1.0%
29	Alabama	6,091,000	0.9%
30	New Hampshire	6,073,000	0.9%
31	Kentucky	4,536,000	0.7%
32	Hawaii	3,914,000	0.6%
33	Oklahoma	3,751,000	0.5%
34	New Mexico	3,707,000	0.5%
35	Maine	3,615,000	0.5%
36	Rhode Island	3,604,000	0.5%
37	Delaware	3,215,000	0.5%
38	Kansas	3,144,000	0.5%
39	Iowa	3,074,000	0.4%
40	Arkansas	2,910,000	0.4%
41	Utah	2,372,000	0.3%
42	Nebraska	2,366,000	0.3%
43	Vermont	2,350,000	0.3%
44	Mississippi	2,154,000	0.3%
45	Montana	2,112,000	0.3%
46	Alaska	1,935,000	0.3%
47	West Virginia	1,208,000	0.2%
48	South Dakota	934,000	0.1%
49	North Dakota	851,000	0.1%
50	Wyoming	748,000	0.1%
	District of Columbia	3,657,000	0.5%

Source: U.S. Department of Health and Human Services, National Institute on Alcohol Abuse and Alcoholism
"Volume Beverage and Ethanol Consumption for States" (http://www.niaaa.nih.gov/Resources/)
*This is apparent consumption and is based on several sources which together approximate sales but do not actually measure consumption. Reported state volumes reflect only in-state purchases. Accordingly, figures for some states may be skewed by purchases by nonresidents.

Adult Per Capita Wine Consumption in 2006

National Per Capita = 3.2 Gallons Consumed per Adult 21 Years and Older*

ALPHA ORDER

RANK	STATE	PER CAPITA
38	Alabama	1.9
12	Alaska	4.2
20	Arizona	3.3
44	Arkansas	1.5
8	California	4.8
17	Colorado	3.9
7	Connecticut	4.9
4	Delaware	5.3
12	Florida	4.2
30	Georgia	2.3
15	Hawaii	4.1
1	Idaho	6.6
20	Illinois	3.3
33	Indiana	2.2
47	Iowa	1.4
43	Kansas	1.6
44	Kentucky	1.5
30	Louisiana	2.3
18	Maine	3.7
23	Maryland	3.0
4	Massachusetts	5.3
27	Michigan	2.5
24	Minnesota	2.9
49	Mississippi	1.1
27	Missouri	2.5
22	Montana	3.1
38	Nebraska	1.9
3	Nevada	5.7
2	New Hampshire	6.4
9	New Jersey	4.7
26	New Mexico	2.7
16	New York	4.0
29	North Carolina	2.4
38	North Dakota	1.9
34	Ohio	2.1
44	Oklahoma	1.5
11	Oregon	4.3
34	Pennsylvania	2.1
9	Rhode Island	4.7
34	South Carolina	2.1
41	South Dakota	1.7
41	Tennessee	1.7
30	Texas	2.3
47	Utah	1.4
6	Vermont	5.1
19	Virginia	3.5
12	Washington	4.2
50	West Virginia	0.9
25	Wisconsin	2.8
37	Wyoming	2.0

RANK ORDER

RANK	STATE	PER CAPITA
1	Idaho	6.6
2	New Hampshire	6.4
3	Nevada	5.7
4	Delaware	5.3
4	Massachusetts	5.3
6	Vermont	5.1
7	Connecticut	4.9
8	California	4.8
9	New Jersey	4.7
9	Rhode Island	4.7
11	Oregon	4.3
12	Alaska	4.2
12	Florida	4.2
12	Washington	4.2
15	Hawaii	4.1
16	New York	4.0
17	Colorado	3.9
18	Maine	3.7
19	Virginia	3.5
20	Arizona	3.3
20	Illinois	3.3
22	Montana	3.1
23	Maryland	3.0
24	Minnesota	2.9
25	Wisconsin	2.8
26	New Mexico	2.7
27	Michigan	2.5
27	Missouri	2.5
29	North Carolina	2.4
30	Georgia	2.3
30	Louisiana	2.3
30	Texas	2.3
33	Indiana	2.2
34	Ohio	2.1
34	Pennsylvania	2.1
34	South Carolina	2.1
37	Wyoming	2.0
38	Alabama	1.9
38	Nebraska	1.9
38	North Dakota	1.9
41	South Dakota	1.7
41	Tennessee	1.7
43	Kansas	1.6
44	Arkansas	1.5
44	Kentucky	1.5
44	Oklahoma	1.5
47	Iowa	1.4
47	Utah	1.4
49	Mississippi	1.1
50	West Virginia	0.9

District of Columbia — 8.3

Source: CQ Press using data from U.S. Dept of Health and Human Services, National Institute on Alcohol Abuse and Alcoholism
"Volume Beverage and Ethanol Consumption for States" (http://www.niaaa.nih.gov/Resources/)
*This is apparent consumption and is based on several sources which together approximate sales but do not actually measure consumption. Reported state volumes reflect only in-state purchases. Accordingly, figures for some states may be skewed by purchases by nonresidents.

Distilled Spirits Consumption in 2006

National Total = 420,219,000 Gallons of Distilled Spirits Consumed*

ALPHA ORDER

RANK	STATE	GALLONS	% of USA
29	Alabama	4,960,000	1.2%
46	Alaska	1,344,000	0.3%
15	Arizona	9,271,000	2.2%
35	Arkansas	3,270,000	0.8%
1	California	49,526,000	11.8%
17	Colorado	9,138,000	2.2%
26	Connecticut	5,880,000	1.4%
38	Delaware	2,167,000	0.5%
2	Florida	33,505,000	8.0%
10	Georgia	11,494,000	2.7%
41	Hawaii	2,028,000	0.5%
43	Idaho	1,829,000	0.4%
5	Illinois	18,375,000	4.4%
21	Indiana	8,162,000	1.9%
32	Iowa	3,823,000	0.9%
34	Kansas	3,308,000	0.8%
28	Kentucky	5,178,000	1.2%
23	Louisiana	6,650,000	1.6%
39	Maine	2,118,000	0.5%
16	Maryland	9,251,000	2.2%
11	Massachusetts	10,947,000	2.6%
6	Michigan	15,299,000	3.6%
14	Minnesota	9,474,000	2.3%
33	Mississippi	3,776,000	0.9%
19	Missouri	8,736,000	2.1%
44	Montana	1,578,000	0.4%
37	Nebraska	2,465,000	0.6%
25	Nevada	6,300,000	1.5%
30	New Hampshire	4,647,000	1.1%
7	New Jersey	14,516,000	3.5%
36	New Mexico	2,646,000	0.6%
3	New York	25,277,000	6.0%
13	North Carolina	9,570,000	2.3%
47	North Dakota	1,304,000	0.3%
12	Ohio	10,029,000	2.4%
31	Oklahoma	3,990,000	0.9%
27	Oregon	5,764,000	1.4%
8	Pennsylvania	14,358,000	3.4%
42	Rhode Island	1,847,000	0.4%
24	South Carolina	6,576,000	1.6%
48	South Dakota	1,221,000	0.3%
22	Tennessee	6,740,000	1.6%
4	Texas	24,678,000	5.9%
40	Utah	2,031,000	0.5%
50	Vermont	874,000	0.2%
20	Virginia	8,601,000	2.0%
18	Washington	9,065,000	2.2%
45	West Virginia	1,530,000	0.4%
9	Wisconsin	12,129,000	2.9%
49	Wyoming	1,070,000	0.3%

RANK ORDER

RANK	STATE	GALLONS	% of USA
1	California	49,526,000	11.8%
2	Florida	33,505,000	8.0%
3	New York	25,277,000	6.0%
4	Texas	24,678,000	5.9%
5	Illinois	18,375,000	4.4%
6	Michigan	15,299,000	3.6%
7	New Jersey	14,516,000	3.5%
8	Pennsylvania	14,358,000	3.4%
9	Wisconsin	12,129,000	2.9%
10	Georgia	11,494,000	2.7%
11	Massachusetts	10,947,000	2.6%
12	Ohio	10,029,000	2.4%
13	North Carolina	9,570,000	2.3%
14	Minnesota	9,474,000	2.3%
15	Arizona	9,271,000	2.2%
16	Maryland	9,251,000	2.2%
17	Colorado	9,138,000	2.2%
18	Washington	9,065,000	2.2%
19	Missouri	8,736,000	2.1%
20	Virginia	8,601,000	2.0%
21	Indiana	8,162,000	1.9%
22	Tennessee	6,740,000	1.6%
23	Louisiana	6,650,000	1.6%
24	South Carolina	6,576,000	1.6%
25	Nevada	6,300,000	1.5%
26	Connecticut	5,880,000	1.4%
27	Oregon	5,764,000	1.4%
28	Kentucky	5,178,000	1.2%
29	Alabama	4,960,000	1.2%
30	New Hampshire	4,647,000	1.1%
31	Oklahoma	3,990,000	0.9%
32	Iowa	3,823,000	0.9%
33	Mississippi	3,776,000	0.9%
34	Kansas	3,308,000	0.8%
35	Arkansas	3,270,000	0.8%
36	New Mexico	2,646,000	0.6%
37	Nebraska	2,465,000	0.6%
38	Delaware	2,167,000	0.5%
39	Maine	2,118,000	0.5%
40	Utah	2,031,000	0.5%
41	Hawaii	2,028,000	0.5%
42	Rhode Island	1,847,000	0.4%
43	Idaho	1,829,000	0.4%
44	Montana	1,578,000	0.4%
45	West Virginia	1,530,000	0.4%
46	Alaska	1,344,000	0.3%
47	North Dakota	1,304,000	0.3%
48	South Dakota	1,221,000	0.3%
49	Wyoming	1,070,000	0.3%
50	Vermont	874,000	0.2%
	District of Columbia	1,907,000	0.5%

Source: U.S. Department of Health and Human Services, National Institute on Alcohol Abuse and Alcoholism
"Volume Beverage and Ethanol Consumption for States" (http://www.niaaa.nih.gov/Resources/)
*This is apparent consumption and is based on several sources which together approximate sales but do not actually measure consumption. Reported state volumes reflect only in-state purchases. Accordingly, figures for some states may be skewed by purchases by nonresidents.

Adult Per Capita Distilled Spirits Consumption in 2006

National Per Capita = 2.0 Gallons Consumed per Adult 21 Years and Older*

ALPHA ORDER

RANK	STATE	PER CAPITA
45	Alabama	1.5
5	Alaska	2.9
17	Arizona	2.2
40	Arkansas	1.6
26	California	2.0
8	Colorado	2.7
12	Connecticut	2.3
3	Delaware	3.5
10	Florida	2.5
33	Georgia	1.8
21	Hawaii	2.1
33	Idaho	1.8
26	Illinois	2.0
33	Indiana	1.8
33	Iowa	1.8
38	Kansas	1.7
38	Kentucky	1.7
17	Louisiana	2.2
17	Maine	2.2
12	Maryland	2.3
12	Massachusetts	2.3
21	Michigan	2.1
9	Minnesota	2.6
30	Mississippi	1.9
21	Missouri	2.1
12	Montana	2.3
26	Nebraska	2.0
2	Nevada	3.6
1	New Hampshire	4.9
12	New Jersey	2.3
30	New Mexico	1.9
33	New York	1.8
45	North Carolina	1.5
7	North Dakota	2.8
48	Ohio	1.2
40	Oklahoma	1.6
21	Oregon	2.1
40	Pennsylvania	1.6
11	Rhode Island	2.4
21	South Carolina	2.1
17	South Dakota	2.2
45	Tennessee	1.5
40	Texas	1.6
48	Utah	1.2
30	Vermont	1.9
40	Virginia	1.6
26	Washington	2.0
50	West Virginia	1.1
4	Wisconsin	3.0
5	Wyoming	2.9

RANK ORDER

RANK	STATE	PER CAPITA
1	New Hampshire	4.9
2	Nevada	3.6
3	Delaware	3.5
4	Wisconsin	3.0
5	Alaska	2.9
5	Wyoming	2.9
7	North Dakota	2.8
8	Colorado	2.7
9	Minnesota	2.6
10	Florida	2.5
11	Rhode Island	2.4
12	Connecticut	2.3
12	Maryland	2.3
12	Massachusetts	2.3
12	Montana	2.3
12	New Jersey	2.3
17	Arizona	2.2
17	Louisiana	2.2
17	Maine	2.2
17	South Dakota	2.2
21	Hawaii	2.1
21	Michigan	2.1
21	Missouri	2.1
21	Oregon	2.1
21	South Carolina	2.1
26	California	2.0
26	Illinois	2.0
26	Nebraska	2.0
26	Washington	2.0
30	Mississippi	1.9
30	New Mexico	1.9
30	Vermont	1.9
33	Georgia	1.8
33	Idaho	1.8
33	Indiana	1.8
33	Iowa	1.8
33	New York	1.8
38	Kansas	1.7
38	Kentucky	1.7
40	Arkansas	1.6
40	Oklahoma	1.6
40	Pennsylvania	1.6
40	Texas	1.6
40	Virginia	1.6
45	Alabama	1.5
45	North Carolina	1.5
45	Tennessee	1.5
48	Ohio	1.2
48	Utah	1.2
50	West Virginia	1.1

District of Columbia   4.3

Source: CQ Press using data from U.S. Dept of Health and Human Services, National Institute on Alcohol Abuse and Alcoholism
"Volume Beverage and Ethanol Consumption for States" (http://www.niaaa.nih.gov/Resources/)
*This is apparent consumption and is based on several sources which together approximate sales but do not actually measure consumption. Reported state volumes reflect only in-state purchases. Accordingly, figures for some states may be skewed by purchases by nonresidents.

Percent of Adults Who Do Not Drink Alcohol: 2007

National Median = 45.2% of Adults*

ALPHA ORDER

RANK	STATE	PERCENT
6	Alabama	61.8
25	Alaska	45.2
20	Arizona	46.4
7	Arkansas	59.9
23	California	45.4
44	Colorado	37.4
49	Connecticut	34.2
38	Delaware	41.6
22	Florida	45.6
13	Georgia	51.6
18	Hawaii	49.0
11	Idaho	53.4
37	Illinois	41.9
16	Indiana	49.6
33	Iowa	43.3
15	Kansas	50.3
2	Kentucky	68.6
10	Louisiana	53.8
35	Maine	42.7
27	Maryland	44.7
48	Massachusetts	34.7
39	Michigan	40.6
42	Minnesota	40.0
5	Mississippi	61.9
19	Missouri	48.1
32	Montana	43.6
31	Nebraska	44.0
25	Nevada	45.2
45	New Hampshire	36.3
30	New Jersey	44.3
17	New Mexico	49.3
36	New York	42.3
9	North Carolina	55.7
43	North Dakota	38.0
21	Ohio	46.2
8	Oklahoma	59.1
41	Oregon	40.2
23	Pennsylvania	45.4
46	Rhode Island	35.7
12	South Carolina	52.5
34	South Dakota	42.8
3	Tennessee	67.1
14	Texas	51.4
1	Utah	72.5
46	Vermont	35.7
29	Virginia	44.5
40	Washington	40.3
4	West Virginia	65.7
50	Wisconsin	31.7
28	Wyoming	44.6

RANK ORDER

RANK	STATE	PERCENT
1	Utah	72.5
2	Kentucky	68.6
3	Tennessee	67.1
4	West Virginia	65.7
5	Mississippi	61.9
6	Alabama	61.8
7	Arkansas	59.9
8	Oklahoma	59.1
9	North Carolina	55.7
10	Louisiana	53.8
11	Idaho	53.4
12	South Carolina	52.5
13	Georgia	51.6
14	Texas	51.4
15	Kansas	50.3
16	Indiana	49.6
17	New Mexico	49.3
18	Hawaii	49.0
19	Missouri	48.1
20	Arizona	46.4
21	Ohio	46.2
22	Florida	45.6
23	California	45.4
23	Pennsylvania	45.4
25	Alaska	45.2
25	Nevada	45.2
27	Maryland	44.7
28	Wyoming	44.6
29	Virginia	44.5
30	New Jersey	44.3
31	Nebraska	44.0
32	Montana	43.6
33	Iowa	43.3
34	South Dakota	42.8
35	Maine	42.7
36	New York	42.3
37	Illinois	41.9
38	Delaware	41.6
39	Michigan	40.6
40	Washington	40.3
41	Oregon	40.2
42	Minnesota	40.0
43	North Dakota	38.0
44	Colorado	37.4
45	New Hampshire	36.3
46	Rhode Island	35.7
46	Vermont	35.7
48	Massachusetts	34.7
49	Connecticut	34.2
50	Wisconsin	31.7

District of Columbia	38.5

Source: U.S. Department of Health and Human Services, Centers for Disease Control and Prevention
"2007 Behavioral Risk Factor Surveillance Summary Prevalence Data" (http://apps.nccd.cdc.gov/brfss/)
*Persons 18 and older reporting not having at least one drink of alcohol in the past 30 days.

Percent of Adults Who Are Binge Drinkers: 2007

National Median = 15.8% of Adults*

ALPHA ORDER

RANK	STATE	PERCENT
45	Alabama	11.0
5	Alaska	19.2
31	Arizona	15.0
46	Arkansas	10.4
18	California	16.9
14	Colorado	17.3
12	Connecticut	17.8
6	Delaware	18.6
35	Florida	14.2
39	Georgia	12.6
6	Hawaii	18.6
32	Idaho	14.7
4	Illinois	19.5
26	Indiana	15.6
3	Iowa	19.9
33	Kansas	14.6
50	Kentucky	8.2
38	Louisiana	13.4
23	Maine	15.9
39	Maryland	12.6
13	Massachusetts	17.6
9	Michigan	18.5
34	Minnesota	14.3
44	Mississippi	11.3
21	Missouri	16.2
16	Montana	17.1
10	Nebraska	18.0
18	Nevada	16.9
28	New Hampshire	15.5
37	New Jersey	13.6
42	New Mexico	12.3
30	New York	15.2
42	North Carolina	12.3
2	North Dakota	23.2
16	Ohio	17.1
41	Oklahoma	12.5
26	Oregon	15.6
21	Pennsylvania	16.2
6	Rhode Island	18.6
36	South Carolina	13.9
14	South Dakota	17.3
49	Tennessee	9.2
29	Texas	15.3
47	Utah	9.8
11	Vermont	17.9
23	Virginia	15.9
25	Washington	15.8
47	West Virginia	9.8
1	Wisconsin	23.4
20	Wyoming	16.8

RANK ORDER

RANK	STATE	PERCENT
1	Wisconsin	23.4
2	North Dakota	23.2
3	Iowa	19.9
4	Illinois	19.5
5	Alaska	19.2
6	Delaware	18.6
6	Hawaii	18.6
6	Rhode Island	18.6
9	Michigan	18.5
10	Nebraska	18.0
11	Vermont	17.9
12	Connecticut	17.8
13	Massachusetts	17.6
14	Colorado	17.3
14	South Dakota	17.3
16	Montana	17.1
16	Ohio	17.1
18	California	16.9
18	Nevada	16.9
20	Wyoming	16.8
21	Missouri	16.2
21	Pennsylvania	16.2
23	Maine	15.9
23	Virginia	15.9
25	Washington	15.8
26	Indiana	15.6
26	Oregon	15.6
28	New Hampshire	15.5
29	Texas	15.3
30	New York	15.2
31	Arizona	15.0
32	Idaho	14.7
33	Kansas	14.6
34	Minnesota	14.3
35	Florida	14.2
36	South Carolina	13.9
37	New Jersey	13.6
38	Louisiana	13.4
39	Georgia	12.6
39	Maryland	12.6
41	Oklahoma	12.5
42	New Mexico	12.3
42	North Carolina	12.3
44	Mississippi	11.3
45	Alabama	11.0
46	Arkansas	10.4
47	Utah	9.8
47	West Virginia	9.8
49	Tennessee	9.2
50	Kentucky	8.2
	District of Columbia	16.1

Source: U.S. Department of Health and Human Services, Centers for Disease Control and Prevention
  "2007 Behavioral Risk Factor Surveillance Summary Prevalence Data" (http://apps.nccd.cdc.gov/brfss/)
*Persons 18 and older reporting consumption of five or more alcoholic drinks on one or more occasions during the previous month.

Percent of Adults Who Smoke: 2007

National Median = 19.8% of Adults*

ALPHA ORDER

RANK	STATE	PERCENT
11	Alabama	22.5
13	Alaska	22.2
24	Arizona	19.8
12	Arkansas	22.4
49	California	14.3
36	Colorado	18.7
48	Connecticut	15.4
34	Delaware	18.9
30	Florida	19.3
29	Georgia	19.4
42	Hawaii	17.0
33	Idaho	19.1
22	Illinois	20.1
6	Indiana	24.1
24	Iowa	19.8
38	Kansas	17.9
1	Kentucky	28.2
10	Louisiana	22.6
21	Maine	20.2
40	Maryland	17.1
47	Massachusetts	16.4
17	Michigan	21.1
46	Minnesota	16.5
7	Mississippi	23.9
4	Missouri	24.5
28	Montana	19.5
23	Nebraska	19.9
16	Nevada	21.5
30	New Hampshire	19.3
40	New Jersey	17.1
20	New Mexico	20.8
34	New York	18.9
9	North Carolina	22.9
19	North Dakota	20.9
8	Ohio	23.1
3	Oklahoma	25.8
44	Oregon	16.9
18	Pennsylvania	21.0
42	Rhode Island	17.0
15	South Carolina	21.9
24	South Dakota	19.8
5	Tennessee	24.3
30	Texas	19.3
50	Utah	11.7
39	Vermont	17.6
37	Virginia	18.5
45	Washington	16.8
2	West Virginia	26.9
27	Wisconsin	19.6
14	Wyoming	22.1

RANK ORDER

RANK	STATE	PERCENT
1	Kentucky	28.2
2	West Virginia	26.9
3	Oklahoma	25.8
4	Missouri	24.5
5	Tennessee	24.3
6	Indiana	24.1
7	Mississippi	23.9
8	Ohio	23.1
9	North Carolina	22.9
10	Louisiana	22.6
11	Alabama	22.5
12	Arkansas	22.4
13	Alaska	22.2
14	Wyoming	22.1
15	South Carolina	21.9
16	Nevada	21.5
17	Michigan	21.1
18	Pennsylvania	21.0
19	North Dakota	20.9
20	New Mexico	20.8
21	Maine	20.2
22	Illinois	20.1
23	Nebraska	19.9
24	Arizona	19.8
24	Iowa	19.8
24	South Dakota	19.8
27	Wisconsin	19.6
28	Montana	19.5
29	Georgia	19.4
30	Florida	19.3
30	New Hampshire	19.3
30	Texas	19.3
33	Idaho	19.1
34	Delaware	18.9
34	New York	18.9
36	Colorado	18.7
37	Virginia	18.5
38	Kansas	17.9
39	Vermont	17.6
40	Maryland	17.1
40	New Jersey	17.1
42	Hawaii	17.0
42	Rhode Island	17.0
44	Oregon	16.9
45	Washington	16.8
46	Minnesota	16.5
47	Massachusetts	16.4
48	Connecticut	15.4
49	California	14.3
50	Utah	11.7

District of Columbia	17.2

Source: U.S. Department of Health and Human Services, Centers for Disease Control and Prevention
   "2007 Behavioral Risk Factor Surveillance Summary Prevalence Data" (http://apps.nccd.cdc.gov/brfss/)
*Persons 18 and older who have smoked more than 100 cigarettes during their lifetime and who currently smoke every day or some days.

Percent of Men Who Smoke: 2007

National Median = 21.2% of Men*

ALPHA ORDER

RANK	STATE	PERCENT
8	Alabama	25.7
13	Alaska	24.7
18	Arizona	23.3
12	Arkansas	24.8
44	California	18.1
34	Colorado	19.7
49	Connecticut	16.5
47	Delaware	17.5
26	Florida	21.2
26	Georgia	21.2
34	Hawaii	19.7
29	Idaho	20.9
22	Illinois	22.1
6	Indiana	25.9
25	Iowa	21.3
41	Kansas	18.6
1	Kentucky	28.7
5	Louisiana	26.4
28	Maine	21.1
42	Maryland	18.3
48	Massachusetts	17.3
16	Michigan	23.4
42	Minnesota	18.3
4	Mississippi	27.8
6	Missouri	25.9
34	Montana	19.7
19	Nebraska	23.2
16	Nevada	23.4
32	New Hampshire	20.1
39	New Jersey	19.3
15	New Mexico	23.6
24	New York	21.6
11	North Carolina	25.2
21	North Dakota	22.2
14	Ohio	24.3
3	Oklahoma	27.9
40	Oregon	18.9
30	Pennsylvania	20.8
46	Rhode Island	17.8
10	South Carolina	25.3
32	South Dakota	20.1
8	Tennessee	25.7
23	Texas	21.9
50	Utah	15.5
38	Vermont	19.4
31	Virginia	20.2
45	Washington	18.0
2	West Virginia	28.4
34	Wisconsin	19.7
20	Wyoming	22.9

RANK ORDER

RANK	STATE	PERCENT
1	Kentucky	28.7
2	West Virginia	28.4
3	Oklahoma	27.9
4	Mississippi	27.8
5	Louisiana	26.4
6	Indiana	25.9
6	Missouri	25.9
8	Alabama	25.7
8	Tennessee	25.7
10	South Carolina	25.3
11	North Carolina	25.2
12	Arkansas	24.8
13	Alaska	24.7
14	Ohio	24.3
15	New Mexico	23.6
16	Michigan	23.4
16	Nevada	23.4
18	Arizona	23.3
19	Nebraska	23.2
20	Wyoming	22.9
21	North Dakota	22.2
22	Illinois	22.1
23	Texas	21.9
24	New York	21.6
25	Iowa	21.3
26	Florida	21.2
26	Georgia	21.2
28	Maine	21.1
29	Idaho	20.9
30	Pennsylvania	20.8
31	Virginia	20.2
32	New Hampshire	20.1
32	South Dakota	20.1
34	Colorado	19.7
34	Hawaii	19.7
34	Montana	19.7
34	Wisconsin	19.7
38	Vermont	19.4
39	New Jersey	19.3
40	Oregon	18.9
41	Kansas	18.6
42	Maryland	18.3
42	Minnesota	18.3
44	California	18.1
45	Washington	18.0
46	Rhode Island	17.8
47	Delaware	17.5
48	Massachusetts	17.3
49	Connecticut	16.5
50	Utah	15.5
	District of Columbia	19.1

Source: U.S. Department of Health and Human Services, Centers for Disease Control and Prevention
"2007 Behavioral Risk Factor Surveillance Summary Prevalence Data" (http://apps.nccd.cdc.gov/brfss/)
*Males 18 and older who have smoked more than 100 cigarettes during their lifetime and who currently smoke every day or some days.

Percent of Women Who Smoke: 2007

National Median = 18.4% of Women*

ALPHA ORDER				RANK ORDER		
RANK	STATE	PERCENT		RANK	STATE	PERCENT
15	Alabama	19.6		1	Kentucky	27.7
15	Alaska	19.6		2	West Virginia	25.4
38	Arizona	16.3		3	Oklahoma	23.8
13	Arkansas	20.2		4	Missouri	23.2
49	California	10.6		5	Tennessee	22.9
29	Colorado	17.6		6	Indiana	22.5
47	Connecticut	14.4		7	Ohio	22.0
12	Delaware	20.3		8	Wyoming	21.4
31	Florida	17.5		9	Pennsylvania	21.1
29	Georgia	17.6		10	North Carolina	20.7
48	Hawaii	14.3		11	Mississippi	20.4
32	Idaho	17.4		12	Delaware	20.3
27	Illinois	18.3		13	Arkansas	20.2
6	Indiana	22.5		14	North Dakota	19.7
26	Iowa	18.4		15	Alabama	19.6
33	Kansas	17.1		15	Alaska	19.6
1	Kentucky	27.7		15	South Dakota	19.6
22	Louisiana	19.2		18	Nevada	19.5
20	Maine	19.3		18	Wisconsin	19.5
40	Maryland	15.9		20	Maine	19.3
43	Massachusetts	15.5		20	Montana	19.3
23	Michigan	19.0		22	Louisiana	19.2
46	Minnesota	14.7		23	Michigan	19.0
11	Mississippi	20.4		24	South Carolina	18.7
4	Missouri	23.2		25	New Hampshire	18.6
20	Montana	19.3		26	Iowa	18.4
35	Nebraska	16.8		27	Illinois	18.3
18	Nevada	19.5		28	New Mexico	18.1
25	New Hampshire	18.6		29	Colorado	17.6
44	New Jersey	15.2		29	Georgia	17.6
28	New Mexico	18.1		31	Florida	17.5
37	New York	16.5		32	Idaho	17.4
10	North Carolina	20.7		33	Kansas	17.1
14	North Dakota	19.7		34	Texas	16.9
7	Ohio	22.0		35	Nebraska	16.8
3	Oklahoma	23.8		35	Virginia	16.8
45	Oregon	14.9		37	New York	16.5
9	Pennsylvania	21.1		38	Arizona	16.3
38	Rhode Island	16.3		38	Rhode Island	16.3
24	South Carolina	18.7		40	Maryland	15.9
15	South Dakota	19.6		41	Vermont	15.8
5	Tennessee	22.9		42	Washington	15.7
34	Texas	16.9		43	Massachusetts	15.5
50	Utah	8.0		44	New Jersey	15.2
41	Vermont	15.8		45	Oregon	14.9
35	Virginia	16.8		46	Minnesota	14.7
42	Washington	15.7		47	Connecticut	14.4
2	West Virginia	25.4		48	Hawaii	14.3
18	Wisconsin	19.5		49	California	10.6
8	Wyoming	21.4		50	Utah	8.0
				District of Columbia		15.6

Source: U.S. Department of Health and Human Services, Centers for Disease Control and Prevention
   "2007 Behavioral Risk Factor Surveillance Summary Prevalence Data" (http://apps.nccd.cdc.gov/brfss/)
*Females 18 and older who have smoked more than 100 cigarettes during their lifetime and who currently smoke every day
or some days.

Percent of Adults Who Are Former Smokers: 2007

National Median = 24.6% of Adults*

ALPHA ORDER

RANK	STATE	PERCENT
41	Alabama	23.2
9	Alaska	27.1
29	Arizona	24.0
34	Arkansas	23.7
43	California	22.9
26	Colorado	24.6
3	Connecticut	30.5
13	Delaware	26.1
11	Florida	26.2
45	Georgia	22.7
14	Hawaii	26.0
46	Idaho	22.6
36	Illinois	23.5
44	Indiana	22.8
36	Iowa	23.5
40	Kansas	23.3
31	Kentucky	23.9
49	Louisiana	20.2
1	Maine	30.8
34	Maryland	23.7
5	Massachusetts	28.5
20	Michigan	24.8
8	Minnesota	27.6
47	Mississippi	21.2
39	Missouri	23.4
10	Montana	26.6
33	Nebraska	23.8
17	Nevada	25.4
4	New Hampshire	30.3
25	New Jersey	24.7
20	New Mexico	24.8
16	New York	25.5
20	North Carolina	24.8
18	North Dakota	25.3
20	Ohio	24.8
41	Oklahoma	23.2
7	Oregon	28.2
31	Pennsylvania	23.9
6	Rhode Island	28.4
19	South Carolina	25.0
28	South Dakota	24.3
29	Tennessee	24.0
48	Texas	20.7
50	Utah	15.8
2	Vermont	30.7
36	Virginia	23.5
11	Washington	26.2
27	West Virginia	24.5
15	Wisconsin	25.9
20	Wyoming	24.8

RANK ORDER

RANK	STATE	PERCENT
1	Maine	30.8
2	Vermont	30.7
3	Connecticut	30.5
4	New Hampshire	30.3
5	Massachusetts	28.5
6	Rhode Island	28.4
7	Oregon	28.2
8	Minnesota	27.6
9	Alaska	27.1
10	Montana	26.6
11	Florida	26.2
11	Washington	26.2
13	Delaware	26.1
14	Hawaii	26.0
15	Wisconsin	25.9
16	New York	25.5
17	Nevada	25.4
18	North Dakota	25.3
19	South Carolina	25.0
20	Michigan	24.8
20	New Mexico	24.8
20	North Carolina	24.8
20	Ohio	24.8
20	Wyoming	24.8
25	New Jersey	24.7
26	Colorado	24.6
27	West Virginia	24.5
28	South Dakota	24.3
29	Arizona	24.0
29	Tennessee	24.0
31	Kentucky	23.9
31	Pennsylvania	23.9
33	Nebraska	23.8
34	Arkansas	23.7
34	Maryland	23.7
36	Illinois	23.5
36	Iowa	23.5
36	Virginia	23.5
39	Missouri	23.4
40	Kansas	23.3
41	Alabama	23.2
41	Oklahoma	23.2
43	California	22.9
44	Indiana	22.8
45	Georgia	22.7
46	Idaho	22.6
47	Mississippi	21.2
48	Texas	20.7
49	Louisiana	20.2
50	Utah	15.8

District of Columbia — 22.4

Source: U.S. Department of Health and Human Services, Centers for Disease Control and Prevention
"2007 Behavioral Risk Factor Surveillance Summary Prevalence Data" (http://apps.nccd.cdc.gov/brfss/)
*Persons 18 and older who have smoked more than 100 cigarettes during their lifetime and who currently do not smoke.

Percent of Adults Who Have Never Smoked: 2007

National Median = 54.8% of Adults*

ALPHA ORDER			RANK ORDER		
RANK	STATE	PERCENT	RANK	STATE	PERCENT
30	Alabama	54.3	1	Utah	72.5
46	Alaska	50.7	2	California	62.8
16	Arizona	56.2	3	Texas	60.0
33	Arkansas	53.9	4	Maryland	59.3
2	California	62.8	5	Kansas	58.8
13	Colorado	56.7	6	Idaho	58.3
31	Connecticut	54.1	7	New Jersey	58.2
23	Delaware	54.9	8	Virginia	58.0
27	Florida	54.5	9	Georgia	57.9
9	Georgia	57.9	10	Louisiana	57.1
11	Hawaii	57.0	11	Hawaii	57.0
6	Idaho	58.3	11	Washington	57.0
15	Illinois	56.4	13	Colorado	56.7
39	Indiana	53.0	13	Iowa	56.7
13	Iowa	56.7	15	Illinois	56.4
5	Kansas	58.8	16	Arizona	56.2
50	Kentucky	47.9	16	Nebraska	56.2
10	Louisiana	57.1	18	Minnesota	55.9
48	Maine	49.1	18	South Dakota	55.9
4	Maryland	59.3	20	New York	55.6
21	Massachusetts	55.1	21	Massachusetts	55.1
31	Michigan	54.1	21	Pennsylvania	55.1
18	Minnesota	55.9	23	Delaware	54.9
25	Mississippi	54.8	23	Oregon	54.9
41	Missouri	52.1	25	Mississippi	54.8
33	Montana	53.9	26	Rhode Island	54.6
16	Nebraska	56.2	27	Florida	54.5
36	Nevada	53.1	27	Wisconsin	54.5
47	New Hampshire	50.4	29	New Mexico	54.4
7	New Jersey	58.2	30	Alabama	54.3
29	New Mexico	54.4	31	Connecticut	54.1
20	New York	55.6	31	Michigan	54.1
40	North Carolina	52.3	33	Arkansas	53.9
35	North Dakota	53.8	33	Montana	53.9
41	Ohio	52.1	35	North Dakota	53.8
45	Oklahoma	51.0	36	Nevada	53.1
23	Oregon	54.9	36	South Carolina	53.1
21	Pennsylvania	55.1	36	Wyoming	53.1
26	Rhode Island	54.6	39	Indiana	53.0
36	South Carolina	53.1	40	North Carolina	52.3
18	South Dakota	55.9	41	Missouri	52.1
43	Tennessee	51.8	41	Ohio	52.1
3	Texas	60.0	43	Tennessee	51.8
1	Utah	72.5	44	Vermont	51.7
44	Vermont	51.7	45	Oklahoma	51.0
8	Virginia	58.0	46	Alaska	50.7
11	Washington	57.0	47	New Hampshire	50.4
49	West Virginia	48.6	48	Maine	49.1
27	Wisconsin	54.5	49	West Virginia	48.6
36	Wyoming	53.1	50	Kentucky	47.9

District of Columbia   60.4

Source: U.S. Department of Health and Human Services, Centers for Disease Control and Prevention
"2007 Behavioral Risk Factor Surveillance Summary Prevalence Data" (http://apps.nccd.cdc.gov/brfss/)
*Persons 18 and older who have not smoked more than 100 cigarettes during their lifetime.

Percent of Population Who Are Illicit Drug Users: 2006

National Percent = 8.2% of Population*

ALPHA ORDER

RANK	STATE	PERCENT
36	Alabama	7.4
2	Alaska	11.1
23	Arizona	8.1
18	Arkansas	8.4
13	California	9.1
5	Colorado	10.0
12	Connecticut	9.2
23	Delaware	8.1
23	Florida	8.1
32	Georgia	7.8
27	Hawaii	8.0
41	Idaho	7.2
36	Illinois	7.4
23	Indiana	8.1
48	Iowa	6.3
30	Kansas	7.9
44	Kentucky	7.0
18	Louisiana	8.4
5	Maine	10.0
49	Maryland	6.2
5	Massachusetts	10.0
16	Michigan	8.8
22	Minnesota	8.2
35	Mississippi	7.5
27	Missouri	8.0
4	Montana	10.7
43	Nebraska	7.1
10	Nevada	9.4
14	New Hampshire	8.9
36	New Jersey	7.4
21	New Mexico	8.3
10	New York	9.4
33	North Carolina	7.7
50	North Dakota	5.7
30	Ohio	7.9
18	Oklahoma	8.4
9	Oregon	9.6
33	Pennsylvania	7.7
1	Rhode Island	11.2
39	South Carolina	7.3
45	South Dakota	6.9
14	Tennessee	8.9
46	Texas	6.8
46	Utah	6.8
3	Vermont	11.0
39	Virginia	7.3
5	Washington	10.0
27	West Virginia	8.0
41	Wisconsin	7.2
17	Wyoming	8.7

RANK ORDER

RANK	STATE	PERCENT
1	Rhode Island	11.2
2	Alaska	11.1
3	Vermont	11.0
4	Montana	10.7
5	Colorado	10.0
5	Maine	10.0
5	Massachusetts	10.0
5	Washington	10.0
9	Oregon	9.6
10	Nevada	9.4
10	New York	9.4
12	Connecticut	9.2
13	California	9.1
14	New Hampshire	8.9
14	Tennessee	8.9
16	Michigan	8.8
17	Wyoming	8.7
18	Arkansas	8.4
18	Louisiana	8.4
18	Oklahoma	8.4
21	New Mexico	8.3
22	Minnesota	8.2
23	Arizona	8.1
23	Delaware	8.1
23	Florida	8.1
23	Indiana	8.1
27	Hawaii	8.0
27	Missouri	8.0
27	West Virginia	8.0
30	Kansas	7.9
30	Ohio	7.9
32	Georgia	7.8
33	North Carolina	7.7
33	Pennsylvania	7.7
35	Mississippi	7.5
36	Alabama	7.4
36	Illinois	7.4
36	New Jersey	7.4
39	South Carolina	7.3
39	Virginia	7.3
41	Idaho	7.2
41	Wisconsin	7.2
43	Nebraska	7.1
44	Kentucky	7.0
45	South Dakota	6.9
46	Texas	6.8
46	Utah	6.8
48	Iowa	6.3
49	Maryland	6.2
50	North Dakota	5.7

District of Columbia 11.1

Source: U.S. Department of Health and Human Services, Substance Abuse and Mental Health Services Administration
   "2005-2006 National Surveys on Drug Use and Health" (February 2008, http://www.oas.samhsa.gov/2k6state/toc.cfm)
*Population 12 years and older who used any illicit drug at least once within month of survey.

Percent of Adults Overweight: 2007

National Median = 36.6% of Adults*

RANK	STATE	PERCENT		RANK	STATE	PERCENT
40	Alabama	35.7		1	Kentucky	40.4
20	Alaska	36.9		2	Montana	39.2
22	Arizona	36.8		3	Rhode Island	39.1
30	Arkansas	36.3		4	Nevada	38.4
40	California	35.7		5	South Dakota	38.3
27	Colorado	36.4		6	Nebraska	38.2
14	Connecticut	37.5		6	New Jersey	38.2
22	Delaware	36.8		8	Florida	38.0
8	Florida	38.0		8	Idaho	38.0
30	Georgia	36.3		10	North Dakota	37.9
47	Hawaii	35.1		11	Maine	37.7
8	Idaho	38.0		11	West Virginia	37.7
15	Illinois	37.4		11	Wyoming	37.7
39	Indiana	35.8		14	Connecticut	37.5
18	Iowa	37.0		15	Illinois	37.4
35	Kansas	36.1		16	Massachusetts	37.2
1	Kentucky	40.4		16	Texas	37.2
50	Louisiana	34.5		18	Iowa	37.0
11	Maine	37.7		18	Wisconsin	37.0
27	Maryland	36.4		20	Alaska	36.9
16	Massachusetts	37.2		20	Vermont	36.9
35	Michigan	36.1		22	Arizona	36.8
37	Minnesota	36.0		22	Delaware	36.8
45	Mississippi	35.5		24	New Hampshire	36.7
47	Missouri	35.1		24	Tennessee	36.7
2	Montana	39.2		26	Virginia	36.6
6	Nebraska	38.2		27	Colorado	36.4
4	Nevada	38.4		27	Maryland	36.4
24	New Hampshire	36.7		27	New York	36.4
6	New Jersey	38.2		30	Arkansas	36.3
40	New Mexico	35.7		30	Georgia	36.3
27	New York	36.4		30	Oklahoma	36.3
38	North Carolina	35.9		30	South Carolina	36.3
10	North Dakota	37.9		34	Washington	36.2
46	Ohio	35.4		35	Kansas	36.1
30	Oklahoma	36.3		35	Michigan	36.1
40	Oregon	35.7		37	Minnesota	36.0
49	Pennsylvania	34.9		38	North Carolina	35.9
3	Rhode Island	39.1		39	Indiana	35.8
30	South Carolina	36.3		40	Alabama	35.7
5	South Dakota	38.3		40	California	35.7
24	Tennessee	36.7		40	New Mexico	35.7
16	Texas	37.2		40	Oregon	35.7
44	Utah	35.6		44	Utah	35.6
20	Vermont	36.9		45	Mississippi	35.5
26	Virginia	36.6		46	Ohio	35.4
34	Washington	36.2		47	Hawaii	35.1
11	West Virginia	37.7		47	Missouri	35.1
18	Wisconsin	37.0		49	Pennsylvania	34.9
11	Wyoming	37.7		50	Louisiana	34.5
					District of Columbia	33.1

Source: U.S. Department of Health and Human Services, Centers for Disease Control and Prevention
"2007 Behavioral Risk Factor Surveillance Summary Prevalence Data" (http://apps.nccd.cdc.gov/brfss/)
*Persons 18 and older. Does not include obese adults. Overweight is defined as a Body Mass Index (BMI) of 25.0 to 29.9 regardless of sex. BMI is a ratio of height to weight. As an example, a person 5' 8" and weighing 171 pounds has a BMI of 26. See http://www.cdc.gov/nccdphp/dnpa/bmi/bmi-adult.htm.

Percent of Adults Obese: 2007

National Median = 26.3% of Adults*

RANK	STATE	PERCENT		RANK	STATE	PERCENT
2	Alabama	30.9		1	Mississippi	32.6
13	Alaska	28.2		2	Alabama	30.9
29	Arizona	25.8		3	Louisiana	30.7
6	Arkansas	29.3		3	Tennessee	30.7
42	California	23.3		5	West Virginia	30.3
50	Colorado	19.3		6	Arkansas	29.3
46	Connecticut	21.7		7	South Carolina	29.0
13	Delaware	28.2		8	Oklahoma	28.8
40	Florida	24.1		9	Georgia	28.7
9	Georgia	28.7		9	Kentucky	28.7
46	Hawaii	21.7		9	North Carolina	28.7
35	Idaho	25.1		12	Texas	28.6
30	Illinois	25.6		13	Alaska	28.2
21	Indiana	27.4		13	Delaware	28.2
19	Iowa	27.7		13	Michigan	28.2
19	Kansas	27.7		13	Missouri	28.2
9	Kentucky	28.7		17	Ohio	28.1
3	Louisiana	30.7		18	Pennsylvania	27.8
34	Maine	25.2		19	Iowa	27.7
25	Maryland	26.3		19	Kansas	27.7
46	Massachusetts	21.7		21	Indiana	27.4
13	Michigan	28.2		22	South Dakota	27.2
27	Minnesota	26.0		23	North Dakota	27.0
1	Mississippi	32.6		24	Nebraska	26.5
13	Missouri	28.2		25	Maryland	26.3
43	Montana	22.6		25	Oregon	26.3
24	Nebraska	26.5		27	Minnesota	26.0
38	Nevada	24.6		28	Washington	25.9
35	New Hampshire	25.1		29	Arizona	25.8
40	New Jersey	24.1		30	Illinois	25.6
35	New Mexico	25.1		31	New York	25.5
31	New York	25.5		32	Virginia	25.3
9	North Carolina	28.7		32	Wisconsin	25.3
23	North Dakota	27.0		34	Maine	25.2
17	Ohio	28.1		35	Idaho	25.1
8	Oklahoma	28.8		35	New Hampshire	25.1
25	Oregon	26.3		35	New Mexico	25.1
18	Pennsylvania	27.8		38	Nevada	24.6
46	Rhode Island	21.7		39	Wyoming	24.5
7	South Carolina	29.0		40	Florida	24.1
22	South Dakota	27.2		40	New Jersey	24.1
3	Tennessee	30.7		42	California	23.3
12	Texas	28.6		43	Montana	22.6
44	Utah	22.4		44	Utah	22.4
45	Vermont	21.9		45	Vermont	21.9
32	Virginia	25.3		46	Connecticut	21.7
28	Washington	25.9		46	Hawaii	21.7
5	West Virginia	30.3		46	Massachusetts	21.7
32	Wisconsin	25.3		46	Rhode Island	21.7
39	Wyoming	24.5		50	Colorado	19.3
					District of Columbia	22.2

Source: U.S. Department of Health and Human Services, Centers for Disease Control and Prevention
  "2007 Behavioral Risk Factor Surveillance Summary Prevalence Data" (http://apps.nccd.cdc.gov/brfss/)
*Persons 18 and older. Obese is defined as a Body Mass Index (BMI) of 30.0 or more regardless of sex. BMI is a ratio of height to weight. As an example, a person 5' 8" and weighing 197 pounds has a BMI of 30. See http://www.cdc.gov/nccdphp/dnpa/bmi/bmi-adult.htm.

Percent of Adults Overweight or Obese: 2007

National Median = 62.9% of Adults*

ALPHA ORDER

RANK	STATE	PERCENT
5	Alabama	66.6
11	Alaska	65.1
30	Arizona	62.6
7	Arkansas	65.6
45	California	59.0
50	Colorado	55.7
44	Connecticut	59.2
13	Delaware	65.0
34	Florida	62.1
13	Georgia	65.0
49	Hawaii	56.8
24	Idaho	63.1
25	Illinois	63.0
23	Indiana	63.2
16	Iowa	64.7
20	Kansas	63.8
1	Kentucky	69.1
10	Louisiana	65.2
27	Maine	62.9
28	Maryland	62.7
46	Massachusetts	58.9
19	Michigan	64.3
36	Minnesota	62.0
2	Mississippi	68.1
22	Missouri	63.3
40	Montana	61.8
16	Nebraska	64.7
25	Nevada	63.0
40	New Hampshire	61.8
31	New Jersey	62.3
42	New Mexico	60.8
38	New York	61.9
18	North Carolina	64.6
15	North Dakota	64.9
21	Ohio	63.5
11	Oklahoma	65.1
36	Oregon	62.0
28	Pennsylvania	62.7
42	Rhode Island	60.8
9	South Carolina	65.3
8	South Dakota	65.5
4	Tennessee	67.4
6	Texas	65.8
48	Utah	58.0
47	Vermont	58.8
38	Virginia	61.9
34	Washington	62.1
3	West Virginia	68.0
31	Wisconsin	62.3
33	Wyoming	62.2

RANK ORDER

RANK	STATE	PERCENT
1	Kentucky	69.1
2	Mississippi	68.1
3	West Virginia	68.0
4	Tennessee	67.4
5	Alabama	66.6
6	Texas	65.8
7	Arkansas	65.6
8	South Dakota	65.5
9	South Carolina	65.3
10	Louisiana	65.2
11	Alaska	65.1
11	Oklahoma	65.1
13	Delaware	65.0
13	Georgia	65.0
15	North Dakota	64.9
16	Iowa	64.7
16	Nebraska	64.7
18	North Carolina	64.6
19	Michigan	64.3
20	Kansas	63.8
21	Ohio	63.5
22	Missouri	63.3
23	Indiana	63.2
24	Idaho	63.1
25	Illinois	63.0
25	Nevada	63.0
27	Maine	62.9
28	Maryland	62.7
28	Pennsylvania	62.7
30	Arizona	62.6
31	New Jersey	62.3
31	Wisconsin	62.3
33	Wyoming	62.2
34	Florida	62.1
34	Washington	62.1
36	Minnesota	62.0
36	Oregon	62.0
38	New York	61.9
38	Virginia	61.9
40	Montana	61.8
40	New Hampshire	61.8
42	New Mexico	60.8
42	Rhode Island	60.8
44	Connecticut	59.2
45	California	59.0
46	Massachusetts	58.9
47	Vermont	58.8
48	Utah	58.0
49	Hawaii	56.8
50	Colorado	55.7

| | District of Columbia | 55.3 |

Source: CQ Press using data from U.S. Department of Health and Human Services, Centers for Disease Control and Prevention
"2007 Behavioral Risk Factor Surveillance Summary Prevalence Data" (http://apps.nccd.cdc.gov/brfss/)
*Persons 18 and older. Overweight is defined as a Body Mass Index (BMI) of 25.0 to 29.9 regardless of sex. Obese is a BMI of 30.0 or greater. BMI is a ratio of height to weight. As an example, a person 5' 8" and weighing 165 pounds has a BMI of 25. The same height at 197 pounds has a BMI of 30. See http://www.cdc.gov/nccdphp/dnpa/bmi/bmi-adult.htm.

Percent of Adults Who Do Not Exercise: 2007

National Median = 22.6% of Adults*

ALPHA ORDER

RANK	STATE	PERCENT
5	Alabama	29.8
38	Alaska	20.0
28	Arizona	22.4
9	Arkansas	28.1
22	California	23.1
48	Colorado	17.3
39	Connecticut	19.7
30	Delaware	22.1
12	Florida	25.4
14	Georgia	24.7
46	Hawaii	18.0
40	Idaho	19.6
23	Illinois	23.0
19	Indiana	24.2
30	Iowa	22.1
23	Kansas	23.0
3	Kentucky	30.3
4	Louisiana	30.0
37	Maine	20.3
23	Maryland	23.0
35	Massachusetts	21.1
36	Michigan	20.8
50	Minnesota	16.7
1	Mississippi	31.8
11	Missouri	25.5
40	Montana	19.6
29	Nebraska	22.2
15	Nevada	24.4
44	New Hampshire	19.1
10	New Jersey	26.1
32	New Mexico	21.7
15	New York	24.4
17	North Carolina	24.3
27	North Dakota	22.5
17	Ohio	24.3
6	Oklahoma	29.6
48	Oregon	17.3
20	Pennsylvania	23.4
20	Rhode Island	23.4
13	South Carolina	24.8
26	South Dakota	22.6
2	Tennessee	31.5
7	Texas	28.3
42	Utah	19.5
45	Vermont	18.3
34	Virginia	21.6
47	Washington	17.6
8	West Virginia	28.2
43	Wisconsin	19.4
32	Wyoming	21.7

RANK ORDER

RANK	STATE	PERCENT
1	Mississippi	31.8
2	Tennessee	31.5
3	Kentucky	30.3
4	Louisiana	30.0
5	Alabama	29.8
6	Oklahoma	29.6
7	Texas	28.3
8	West Virginia	28.2
9	Arkansas	28.1
10	New Jersey	26.1
11	Missouri	25.5
12	Florida	25.4
13	South Carolina	24.8
14	Georgia	24.7
15	Nevada	24.4
15	New York	24.4
17	North Carolina	24.3
17	Ohio	24.3
19	Indiana	24.2
20	Pennsylvania	23.4
20	Rhode Island	23.4
22	California	23.1
23	Illinois	23.0
23	Kansas	23.0
23	Maryland	23.0
26	South Dakota	22.6
27	North Dakota	22.5
28	Arizona	22.4
29	Nebraska	22.2
30	Delaware	22.1
30	Iowa	22.1
32	New Mexico	21.7
32	Wyoming	21.7
34	Virginia	21.6
35	Massachusetts	21.1
36	Michigan	20.8
37	Maine	20.3
38	Alaska	20.0
39	Connecticut	19.7
40	Idaho	19.6
40	Montana	19.6
42	Utah	19.5
43	Wisconsin	19.4
44	New Hampshire	19.1
45	Vermont	18.3
46	Hawaii	18.0
47	Washington	17.6
48	Colorado	17.3
48	Oregon	17.3
50	Minnesota	16.7

	District of Columbia	21.3

Source: U.S. Department of Health and Human Services, Centers for Disease Control and Prevention
   "2007 Behavioral Risk Factor Surveillance Summary Prevalence Data" (http://apps.nccd.cdc.gov/brfss/)
*Persons 18 and older who, in the previous month, did not participate in any physical activities.

Percent of Adults Who Exercise Vigorously: 2007

National Median = 28.3% of Adults*

ALPHA ORDER				RANK ORDER		
RANK	STATE	PERCENT		RANK	STATE	PERCENT
45	Alabama	21.7		1	Alaska	39.5
1	Alaska	39.5		2	Utah	35.8
19	Arizona	29.5		3	Idaho	33.4
42	Arkansas	24.3		4	Vermont	33.2
11	California	31.3		5	Colorado	33.0
5	Colorado	33.0		6	Montana	32.8
16	Connecticut	30.2		7	Wyoming	32.7
32	Delaware	26.7		8	Wisconsin	32.1
34	Florida	26.0		9	Maine	31.9
26	Georgia	28.1		10	Oregon	31.5
15	Hawaii	30.4		11	California	31.3
3	Idaho	33.4		12	New Hampshire	31.2
24	Illinois	28.3		13	Washington	30.8
33	Indiana	26.5		14	Nebraska	30.6
40	Iowa	25.0		15	Hawaii	30.4
35	Kansas	25.8		16	Connecticut	30.2
45	Kentucky	21.7		17	Virginia	30.0
47	Louisiana	20.5		18	Massachusetts	29.7
9	Maine	31.9		19	Arizona	29.5
28	Maryland	27.7		19	Michigan	29.5
18	Massachusetts	29.7		21	New Mexico	29.2
19	Michigan	29.5		22	North Dakota	28.9
44	Minnesota	22.8		23	Pennsylvania	28.6
48	Mississippi	19.7		24	Illinois	28.3
36	Missouri	25.5		24	Nevada	28.3
6	Montana	32.8		26	Georgia	28.1
14	Nebraska	30.6		27	Ohio	28.0
24	Nevada	28.3		28	Maryland	27.7
12	New Hampshire	31.2		28	Rhode Island	27.7
31	New Jersey	27.3		30	New York	27.5
21	New Mexico	29.2		31	New Jersey	27.3
30	New York	27.5		32	Delaware	26.7
43	North Carolina	23.4		33	Indiana	26.5
22	North Dakota	28.9		34	Florida	26.0
27	Ohio	28.0		35	Kansas	25.8
41	Oklahoma	24.9		36	Missouri	25.5
10	Oregon	31.5		36	Texas	25.5
23	Pennsylvania	28.6		38	South Carolina	25.4
28	Rhode Island	27.7		38	South Dakota	25.4
38	South Carolina	25.4		40	Iowa	25.0
38	South Dakota	25.4		41	Oklahoma	24.9
50	Tennessee	18.5		42	Arkansas	24.3
36	Texas	25.5		43	North Carolina	23.4
2	Utah	35.8		44	Minnesota	22.8
4	Vermont	33.2		45	Alabama	21.7
17	Virginia	30.0		45	Kentucky	21.7
13	Washington	30.8		47	Louisiana	20.5
49	West Virginia	19.2		48	Mississippi	19.7
8	Wisconsin	32.1		49	West Virginia	19.2
7	Wyoming	32.7		50	Tennessee	18.5
					District of Columbia	30.9

Source: U.S. Department of Health and Human Services, Centers for Disease Control and Prevention
    "2007 Behavioral Risk Factor Surveillance Summary Prevalence Data" (http://apps.nccd.cdc.gov/brfss/)
*Persons 18 and older.   Vigorous exercise is activity that caused large increases in breathing or heart rate at least 20 minutes three or more times per week (such as running, aerobics, or heavy yard work).

Percent of Adults Who Are Disabled: 2007

National Median = 18.9%*

ALPHA ORDER				RANK ORDER		
RANK	STATE	PERCENT		RANK	STATE	PERCENT
5	Alabama	23.2		1	West Virginia	25.9
12	Alaska	21.1		2	Kentucky	23.5
30	Arizona	18.4		2	Oklahoma	23.5
6	Arkansas	23.1		4	Oregon	23.4
47	California	16.0		5	Alabama	23.2
43	Colorado	16.7		6	Arkansas	23.1
45	Connecticut	16.5		7	Washington	22.8
14	Delaware	20.8		8	Mississippi	22.5
35	Florida	17.8		9	Maine	21.8
17	Georgia	20.5		10	Montana	21.5
49	Hawaii	15.3		11	Missouri	21.4
19	Idaho	20.0		12	Alaska	21.1
41	Illinois	17.1		13	Michigan	21.0
27	Indiana	18.8		14	Delaware	20.8
37	Iowa	17.4		15	New Mexico	20.7
25	Kansas	18.9		15	Ohio	20.7
2	Kentucky	23.5		17	Georgia	20.5
32	Louisiana	18.2		18	Tennessee	20.3
9	Maine	21.8		19	Idaho	20.0
37	Maryland	17.4		19	South Carolina	20.0
35	Massachusetts	17.8		21	New Hampshire	19.9
13	Michigan	21.0		22	Rhode Island	19.8
46	Minnesota	16.4		23	North Carolina	19.6
8	Mississippi	22.5		24	Pennsylvania	19.2
11	Missouri	21.4		25	Kansas	18.9
10	Montana	21.5		25	Vermont	18.9
37	Nebraska	17.4		27	Indiana	18.8
27	Nevada	18.8		27	Nevada	18.8
21	New Hampshire	19.9		29	Wyoming	18.7
40	New Jersey	17.3		30	Arizona	18.4
15	New Mexico	20.7		31	Texas	18.3
32	New York	18.2		32	Louisiana	18.2
23	North Carolina	19.6		32	New York	18.2
50	North Dakota	15.0		32	South Dakota	18.2
15	Ohio	20.7		35	Florida	17.8
2	Oklahoma	23.5		35	Massachusetts	17.8
4	Oregon	23.4		37	Iowa	17.4
24	Pennsylvania	19.2		37	Maryland	17.4
22	Rhode Island	19.8		37	Nebraska	17.4
19	South Carolina	20.0		40	New Jersey	17.3
32	South Dakota	18.2		41	Illinois	17.1
18	Tennessee	20.3		42	Utah	17.0
31	Texas	18.3		43	Colorado	16.7
42	Utah	17.0		44	Virginia	16.6
25	Vermont	18.9		45	Connecticut	16.5
44	Virginia	16.6		46	Minnesota	16.4
7	Washington	22.8		47	California	16.0
1	West Virginia	25.9		47	Wisconsin	16.0
47	Wisconsin	16.0		49	Hawaii	15.3
29	Wyoming	18.7		50	North Dakota	15.0
					District of Columbia	16.1

Source: U.S. Department of Health and Human Services, Centers for Disease Control and Prevention
"2007 Behavioral Risk Factor Surveillance Summary Prevalence Data" (http://apps.nccd.cdc.gov/brfss/)
*Persons 18 and older. Adults who are limited in any activities because of physical, mental, or emotional problems.

Percent of Adults with High Blood Pressure: 2007

National Median = 27.8% of Adults*

ALPHA ORDER

RANK	STATE	PERCENT
4	Alabama	33.1
45	Alaska	24.9
46	Arizona	24.8
7	Arkansas	31.3
42	California	25.2
49	Colorado	21.2
36	Connecticut	26.2
12	Delaware	29.3
20	Florida	28.2
8	Georgia	30.4
14	Hawaii	28.8
38	Idaho	25.9
23	Illinois	28.0
24	Indiana	27.9
29	Iowa	26.8
29	Kansas	26.8
10	Kentucky	30.0
5	Louisiana	32.1
16	Maine	28.7
13	Maryland	29.1
33	Massachusetts	26.4
17	Michigan	28.6
48	Minnesota	21.4
2	Mississippi	33.7
11	Missouri	29.4
42	Montana	25.2
31	Nebraska	26.5
28	Nevada	27.0
34	New Hampshire	26.3
20	New Jersey	28.2
39	New Mexico	25.6
26	New York	27.2
14	North Carolina	28.8
37	North Dakota	26.0
18	Ohio	28.4
6	Oklahoma	31.5
31	Oregon	26.5
22	Pennsylvania	28.1
18	Rhode Island	28.4
8	South Carolina	30.4
40	South Dakota	25.5
1	Tennessee	33.8
25	Texas	27.8
50	Utah	19.7
46	Vermont	24.8
27	Virginia	27.1
41	Washington	25.4
3	West Virginia	33.3
34	Wisconsin	26.3
44	Wyoming	25.1

RANK ORDER

RANK	STATE	PERCENT
1	Tennessee	33.8
2	Mississippi	33.7
3	West Virginia	33.3
4	Alabama	33.1
5	Louisiana	32.1
6	Oklahoma	31.5
7	Arkansas	31.3
8	Georgia	30.4
8	South Carolina	30.4
10	Kentucky	30.0
11	Missouri	29.4
12	Delaware	29.3
13	Maryland	29.1
14	Hawaii	28.8
14	North Carolina	28.8
16	Maine	28.7
17	Michigan	28.6
18	Ohio	28.4
18	Rhode Island	28.4
20	Florida	28.2
20	New Jersey	28.2
22	Pennsylvania	28.1
23	Illinois	28.0
24	Indiana	27.9
25	Texas	27.8
26	New York	27.2
27	Virginia	27.1
28	Nevada	27.0
29	Iowa	26.8
29	Kansas	26.8
31	Nebraska	26.5
31	Oregon	26.5
33	Massachusetts	26.4
34	New Hampshire	26.3
34	Wisconsin	26.3
36	Connecticut	26.2
37	North Dakota	26.0
38	Idaho	25.9
39	New Mexico	25.6
40	South Dakota	25.5
41	Washington	25.4
42	California	25.2
42	Montana	25.2
44	Wyoming	25.1
45	Alaska	24.9
46	Arizona	24.8
46	Vermont	24.8
48	Minnesota	21.4
49	Colorado	21.2
50	Utah	19.7

District of Columbia	28.6

Source: U.S. Department of Health and Human Services, Centers for Disease Control and Prevention
   "2007 Behavioral Risk Factor Surveillance Summary Prevalence Data" (http://apps.nccd.cdc.gov/brfss/)
*Persons 18 and older who have been told by a doctor, nurse, or other health professional that they have high blood pressure.

Percent of Adults with High Cholesterol: 2007

National Median = 37.6% of Adults*

ALPHA ORDER

RANK	STATE	PERCENT
10	Alabama	39.4
25	Alaska	37.6
18	Arizona	38.3
4	Arkansas	40.1
41	California	34.9
48	Colorado	33.5
18	Connecticut	38.3
18	Delaware	38.3
30	Florida	37.1
28	Georgia	37.4
37	Hawaii	36.3
25	Idaho	37.6
37	Illinois	36.3
14	Indiana	38.5
23	Iowa	37.8
35	Kansas	36.6
14	Kentucky	38.5
47	Louisiana	33.7
3	Maine	40.2
33	Maryland	36.9
39	Massachusetts	35.6
5	Michigan	39.9
50	Minnesota	32.4
14	Mississippi	38.5
9	Missouri	39.5
43	Montana	34.6
35	Nebraska	36.6
30	Nevada	37.1
12	New Hampshire	38.7
13	New Jersey	38.6
44	New Mexico	34.5
24	New York	37.7
7	North Carolina	39.6
30	North Dakota	37.1
7	Ohio	39.6
2	Oklahoma	41.0
25	Oregon	37.6
6	Pennsylvania	39.7
22	Rhode Island	38.0
11	South Carolina	39.2
46	South Dakota	34.0
45	Tennessee	34.2
14	Texas	38.5
49	Utah	32.6
40	Vermont	35.1
28	Virginia	37.4
34	Washington	36.7
1	West Virginia	42.4
41	Wisconsin	34.9
21	Wyoming	38.1

RANK ORDER

RANK	STATE	PERCENT
1	West Virginia	42.4
2	Oklahoma	41.0
3	Maine	40.2
4	Arkansas	40.1
5	Michigan	39.9
6	Pennsylvania	39.7
7	North Carolina	39.6
7	Ohio	39.6
9	Missouri	39.5
10	Alabama	39.4
11	South Carolina	39.2
12	New Hampshire	38.7
13	New Jersey	38.6
14	Indiana	38.5
14	Kentucky	38.5
14	Mississippi	38.5
14	Texas	38.5
18	Arizona	38.3
18	Connecticut	38.3
18	Delaware	38.3
21	Wyoming	38.1
22	Rhode Island	38.0
23	Iowa	37.8
24	New York	37.7
25	Alaska	37.6
25	Idaho	37.6
25	Oregon	37.6
28	Georgia	37.4
28	Virginia	37.4
30	Florida	37.1
30	Nevada	37.1
30	North Dakota	37.1
33	Maryland	36.9
34	Washington	36.7
35	Kansas	36.6
35	Nebraska	36.6
37	Hawaii	36.3
37	Illinois	36.3
39	Massachusetts	35.6
40	Vermont	35.1
41	California	34.9
41	Wisconsin	34.9
43	Montana	34.6
44	New Mexico	34.5
45	Tennessee	34.2
46	South Dakota	34.0
47	Louisiana	33.7
48	Colorado	33.5
49	Utah	32.6
50	Minnesota	32.4
	District of Columbia	34.1

Source: U.S. Department of Health and Human Services, Centers for Disease Control and Prevention
 "2007 Behavioral Risk Factor Surveillance Summary Prevalence Data" (http://apps.nccd.cdc.gov/brfss/)
*Persons 18 and older who have had their cholesterol checked and have been told that they have high blood cholesterol.

Percent of Adults Who Have Visited a Dentist or Dental Clinic: 2006

National Median = 70.3%*

ALPHA ORDER

RANK	STATE	PERCENT
34	Alabama	68.0
37	Alaska	66.9
30	Arizona	68.5
48	Arkansas	60.2
30	California	68.5
25	Colorado	70.3
1	Connecticut	80.5
6	Delaware	76.3
28	Florida	68.7
22	Georgia	70.7
11	Hawaii	73.7
37	Idaho	66.9
27	Illinois	68.8
34	Indiana	68.0
11	Iowa	73.7
24	Kansas	70.4
45	Kentucky	63.3
43	Louisiana	63.5
21	Maine	70.9
9	Maryland	75.0
4	Massachusetts	78.1
8	Michigan	75.1
3	Minnesota	78.7
49	Mississippi	59.4
46	Missouri	61.7
32	Montana	68.3
16	Nebraska	72.6
39	Nevada	66.2
5	New Hampshire	77.1
10	New Jersey	74.5
41	New Mexico	64.9
18	New York	71.8
36	North Carolina	67.0
17	North Dakota	72.2
14	Ohio	73.4
50	Oklahoma	58.0
29	Oregon	68.6
20	Pennsylvania	71.3
2	Rhode Island	80.4
39	South Carolina	66.2
26	South Dakota	69.5
42	Tennessee	64.8
43	Texas	63.5
23	Utah	70.6
13	Vermont	73.5
15	Virginia	73.2
19	Washington	71.6
47	West Virginia	61.4
6	Wisconsin	76.3
33	Wyoming	68.2

RANK ORDER

RANK	STATE	PERCENT
1	Connecticut	80.5
2	Rhode Island	80.4
3	Minnesota	78.7
4	Massachusetts	78.1
5	New Hampshire	77.1
6	Delaware	76.3
6	Wisconsin	76.3
8	Michigan	75.1
9	Maryland	75.0
10	New Jersey	74.5
11	Hawaii	73.7
11	Iowa	73.7
13	Vermont	73.5
14	Ohio	73.4
15	Virginia	73.2
16	Nebraska	72.6
17	North Dakota	72.2
18	New York	71.8
19	Washington	71.6
20	Pennsylvania	71.3
21	Maine	70.9
22	Georgia	70.7
23	Utah	70.6
24	Kansas	70.4
25	Colorado	70.3
26	South Dakota	69.5
27	Illinois	68.8
28	Florida	68.7
29	Oregon	68.6
30	Arizona	68.5
30	California	68.5
32	Montana	68.3
33	Wyoming	68.2
34	Alabama	68.0
34	Indiana	68.0
36	North Carolina	67.0
37	Alaska	66.9
37	Idaho	66.9
39	Nevada	66.2
39	South Carolina	66.2
41	New Mexico	64.9
42	Tennessee	64.8
43	Louisiana	63.5
43	Texas	63.5
45	Kentucky	63.3
46	Missouri	61.7
47	West Virginia	61.4
48	Arkansas	60.2
49	Mississippi	59.4
50	Oklahoma	58.0

| | District of Columbia | 71.4 |

Source: U.S. Department of Health and Human Services, Centers for Disease Control and Prevention
"2006 Behavioral Risk Factor Surveillance Summary Prevalence Data" (http://apps.nccd.cdc.gov/brfss/)
*Persons 18 and older who have visited a dentist within the past year for any reason.

Percent of Adults 65 Years Old and Older
Who Have Lost All Their Natural Teeth: 2006
National Median = 19.3%*

ALPHA ORDER

RANK	STATE	PERCENT
7	Alabama	27.2
12	Alaska	23.6
46	Arizona	14.3
15	Arkansas	22.7
47	California	14.0
48	Colorado	12.9
49	Connecticut	12.8
35	Delaware	17.8
37	Florida	17.4
18	Georgia	21.5
50	Hawaii	9.6
23	Idaho	19.7
25	Illinois	19.3
20	Indiana	21.2
22	Iowa	19.8
26	Kansas	19.1
2	Kentucky	38.9
5	Louisiana	28.9
8	Maine	26.2
41	Maryland	16.2
39	Massachusetts	17.2
38	Michigan	17.3
27	Minnesota	18.6
4	Mississippi	31.5
9	Missouri	24.1
32	Montana	18.2
27	Nebraska	18.6
31	Nevada	18.4
27	New Hampshire	18.6
32	New Jersey	18.2
11	New Mexico	23.8
36	New York	17.5
16	North Carolina	22.6
14	North Dakota	22.9
17	Ohio	21.6
6	Oklahoma	28.3
42	Oregon	15.9
10	Pennsylvania	23.9
34	Rhode Island	17.9
13	South Carolina	23.0
19	South Dakota	21.4
3	Tennessee	34.9
27	Texas	18.6
44	Utah	14.8
23	Vermont	19.7
45	Virginia	14.4
43	Washington	15.4
1	West Virginia	40.5
40	Wisconsin	16.9
21	Wyoming	20.1

RANK ORDER

RANK	STATE	PERCENT
1	West Virginia	40.5
2	Kentucky	38.9
3	Tennessee	34.9
4	Mississippi	31.5
5	Louisiana	28.9
6	Oklahoma	28.3
7	Alabama	27.2
8	Maine	26.2
9	Missouri	24.1
10	Pennsylvania	23.9
11	New Mexico	23.8
12	Alaska	23.6
13	South Carolina	23.0
14	North Dakota	22.9
15	Arkansas	22.7
16	North Carolina	22.6
17	Ohio	21.6
18	Georgia	21.5
19	South Dakota	21.4
20	Indiana	21.2
21	Wyoming	20.1
22	Iowa	19.8
23	Idaho	19.7
23	Vermont	19.7
25	Illinois	19.3
26	Kansas	19.1
27	Minnesota	18.6
27	Nebraska	18.6
27	New Hampshire	18.6
27	Texas	18.6
31	Nevada	18.4
32	Montana	18.2
32	New Jersey	18.2
34	Rhode Island	17.9
35	Delaware	17.8
36	New York	17.5
37	Florida	17.4
38	Michigan	17.3
39	Massachusetts	17.2
40	Wisconsin	16.9
41	Maryland	16.2
42	Oregon	15.9
43	Washington	15.4
44	Utah	14.8
45	Virginia	14.4
46	Arizona	14.3
47	California	14.0
48	Colorado	12.9
49	Connecticut	12.8
50	Hawaii	9.6
	District of Columbia	20.8

Source: U.S. Department of Health and Human Services, Centers for Disease Control and Prevention
"2006 Behavioral Risk Factor Surveillance Summary Prevalence Data" (http://apps.nccd.cdc.gov/brfss/)
*Those who have had all their natural teeth extracted.

Percent of Adults Who Average Five or More Servings of Fruits and Vegetables Each Day: 2007
National Median = 24.4%*

ALPHA ORDER

RANK	STATE	PERCENT
39	Alabama	20.6
26	Alaska	24.2
7	Arizona	28.3
34	Arkansas	21.8
2	California	28.9
17	Colorado	25.8
5	Connecticut	28.5
36	Delaware	21.4
15	Florida	26.2
22	Georgia	25.0
3	Hawaii	28.7
31	Idaho	22.3
23	Illinois	24.6
28	Indiana	22.8
41	Iowa	19.9
45	Kansas	18.8
48	Kentucky	18.4
43	Louisiana	19.6
4	Maine	28.6
12	Maryland	26.6
8	Massachusetts	27.5
37	Michigan	21.3
44	Minnesota	19.4
49	Mississippi	18.1
40	Missouri	20.2
20	Montana	25.3
27	Nebraska	24.1
32	Nevada	21.9
5	New Hampshire	28.5
8	New Jersey	27.5
30	New Mexico	22.4
10	New York	27.4
35	North Carolina	21.6
32	North Dakota	21.9
38	Ohio	20.8
50	Oklahoma	16.3
11	Oregon	27.0
19	Pennsylvania	25.4
18	Rhode Island	25.6
46	South Carolina	18.7
47	South Dakota	18.6
13	Tennessee	26.4
21	Texas	25.2
28	Utah	22.8
1	Vermont	30.0
14	Virginia	26.3
16	Washington	26.0
42	West Virginia	19.7
24	Wisconsin	24.4
24	Wyoming	24.4

RANK ORDER

RANK	STATE	PERCENT
1	Vermont	30.0
2	California	28.9
3	Hawaii	28.7
4	Maine	28.6
5	Connecticut	28.5
5	New Hampshire	28.5
7	Arizona	28.3
8	Massachusetts	27.5
8	New Jersey	27.5
10	New York	27.4
11	Oregon	27.0
12	Maryland	26.6
13	Tennessee	26.4
14	Virginia	26.3
15	Florida	26.2
16	Washington	26.0
17	Colorado	25.8
18	Rhode Island	25.6
19	Pennsylvania	25.4
20	Montana	25.3
21	Texas	25.2
22	Georgia	25.0
23	Illinois	24.6
24	Wisconsin	24.4
24	Wyoming	24.4
26	Alaska	24.2
27	Nebraska	24.1
28	Indiana	22.8
28	Utah	22.8
30	New Mexico	22.4
31	Idaho	22.3
32	Nevada	21.9
32	North Dakota	21.9
34	Arkansas	21.8
35	North Carolina	21.6
36	Delaware	21.4
37	Michigan	21.3
38	Ohio	20.8
39	Alabama	20.6
40	Missouri	20.2
41	Iowa	19.9
42	West Virginia	19.7
43	Louisiana	19.6
44	Minnesota	19.4
45	Kansas	18.8
46	South Carolina	18.7
47	South Dakota	18.6
48	Kentucky	18.4
49	Mississippi	18.1
50	Oklahoma	16.3

District of Columbia	32.5

Source: U.S. Department of Health and Human Services, Centers for Disease Control and Prevention
"2007 Behavioral Risk Factor Surveillance Summary Prevalence Data" (http://apps.nccd.cdc.gov/brfss/)
*Persons 18 and older.

Percent of Adults Rating Their Health as Fair or Poor in 2007

National Median = 14.9% of Adults*

ALPHA ORDER

RANK	STATE	PERCENT
3	Alabama	21.4
32	Alaska	13.8
13	Arizona	17.3
6	Arkansas	20.1
11	California	17.9
35	Colorado	13.2
46	Connecticut	12.2
37	Delaware	13.0
19	Florida	16.6
21	Georgia	15.8
27	Hawaii	14.7
26	Idaho	14.9
13	Illinois	17.3
21	Indiana	15.8
45	Iowa	12.4
37	Kansas	13.0
1	Kentucky	23.1
9	Louisiana	19.0
33	Maine	13.5
31	Maryland	14.1
39	Massachusetts	12.7
28	Michigan	14.4
49	Minnesota	11.0
3	Mississippi	21.4
17	Missouri	17.1
28	Montana	14.4
47	Nebraska	12.1
13	Nevada	17.3
39	New Hampshire	12.7
17	New Jersey	17.1
12	New Mexico	17.5
16	New York	17.2
10	North Carolina	18.7
42	North Dakota	12.5
21	Ohio	15.8
8	Oklahoma	19.2
36	Oregon	13.1
24	Pennsylvania	15.2
25	Rhode Island	15.1
20	South Carolina	16.3
42	South Dakota	12.5
5	Tennessee	20.5
7	Texas	19.6
50	Utah	10.9
48	Vermont	11.6
30	Virginia	14.2
34	Washington	13.3
2	West Virginia	21.6
42	Wisconsin	12.5
39	Wyoming	12.7

RANK ORDER

RANK	STATE	PERCENT
1	Kentucky	23.1
2	West Virginia	21.6
3	Alabama	21.4
3	Mississippi	21.4
5	Tennessee	20.5
6	Arkansas	20.1
7	Texas	19.6
8	Oklahoma	19.2
9	Louisiana	19.0
10	North Carolina	18.7
11	California	17.9
12	New Mexico	17.5
13	Arizona	17.3
13	Illinois	17.3
13	Nevada	17.3
16	New York	17.2
17	Missouri	17.1
17	New Jersey	17.1
19	Florida	16.6
20	South Carolina	16.3
21	Georgia	15.8
21	Indiana	15.8
21	Ohio	15.8
24	Pennsylvania	15.2
25	Rhode Island	15.1
26	Idaho	14.9
27	Hawaii	14.7
28	Michigan	14.4
28	Montana	14.4
30	Virginia	14.2
31	Maryland	14.1
32	Alaska	13.8
33	Maine	13.5
34	Washington	13.3
35	Colorado	13.2
36	Oregon	13.1
37	Delaware	13.0
37	Kansas	13.0
39	Massachusetts	12.7
39	New Hampshire	12.7
39	Wyoming	12.7
42	North Dakota	12.5
42	South Dakota	12.5
42	Wisconsin	12.5
45	Iowa	12.4
46	Connecticut	12.2
47	Nebraska	12.1
48	Vermont	11.6
49	Minnesota	11.0
50	Utah	10.9
	District of Columbia	13.5

Source: U.S. Department of Health and Human Services, Centers for Disease Control and Prevention
"2007 Behavioral Risk Factor Surveillance Summary Prevalence Data" (http://apps.nccd.cdc.gov/brfss/)
*Persons 18 and older.

Safety Belt Usage Rate in 2007

National Rate = 82.0% Use Safety Belts

ALPHA ORDER				RANK ORDER		
RANK	STATE	PERCENT		RANK	STATE	PERCENT
26	Alabama	82.3		1	Hawaii	97.6
25	Alaska	82.4		2	Washington	96.4
30	Arizona	80.9		3	Oregon	95.3
48	Arkansas	69.9		4	California	94.6
4	California	94.6		5	Michigan	93.7
29	Colorado	81.1		6	Maryland	93.1
22	Connecticut	85.8		7	Nevada	92.2
21	Delaware	86.6		8	Texas	91.8
35	Florida	79.1		9	New Mexico	91.5
14	Georgia	89.0		10	New Jersey	91.4
1	Hawaii	97.6		11	Iowa	91.3
38	Idaho	78.5		12	Illinois	90.1
12	Illinois	90.1		13	West Virginia	89.6
16	Indiana	87.9		14	Georgia	89.0
11	Iowa	91.3		15	North Carolina	88.8
42	Kansas	75.0		16	Indiana	87.9
46	Kentucky	71.8		17	Minnesota	87.8
41	Louisiana	75.2		18	Vermont	87.1
33	Maine	79.8		19	Utah	86.8
6	Maryland	93.1		20	Pennsylvania	86.7
49	Massachusetts	68.7		21	Delaware	86.6
5	Michigan	93.7		22	Connecticut	85.8
17	Minnesota	87.8		23	New York	83.5
46	Mississippi	71.8		24	Oklahoma	83.1
39	Missouri	77.2		25	Alaska	82.4
34	Montana	79.6		26	Alabama	82.3
37	Nebraska	78.7		27	North Dakota	82.2
7	Nevada	92.2		28	Ohio	81.6
50	New Hampshire	63.8		29	Colorado	81.1
10	New Jersey	91.4		30	Arizona	80.9
9	New Mexico	91.5		31	Tennessee	80.2
23	New York	83.5		32	Virginia	79.9
15	North Carolina	88.8		33	Maine	79.8
27	North Dakota	82.2		34	Montana	79.6
28	Ohio	81.6		35	Florida	79.1
24	Oklahoma	83.1		35	Rhode Island	79.1
3	Oregon	95.3		37	Nebraska	78.7
20	Pennsylvania	86.7		38	Idaho	78.5
35	Rhode Island	79.1		39	Missouri	77.2
43	South Carolina	74.5		40	Wisconsin	75.3
44	South Dakota	73.0		41	Louisiana	75.2
31	Tennessee	80.2		42	Kansas	75.0
8	Texas	91.8		43	South Carolina	74.5
19	Utah	86.8		44	South Dakota	73.0
18	Vermont	87.1		45	Wyoming	72.2
32	Virginia	79.9		46	Kentucky	71.8
2	Washington	96.4		46	Mississippi	71.8
13	West Virginia	89.6		48	Arkansas	69.9
40	Wisconsin	75.3		49	Massachusetts	68.7
45	Wyoming	72.2		50	New Hampshire	63.8
				District of Columbia		87.1

Source: U.S. Department of Transportation, National Highway Traffic Safety Administration
   "Seat Belt Use in 2007" (http://www-nrd.nhtsa.dot.gov/Pubs/810949.pdf)

VIII. Appendix

Population in 2008

National Total = 304,059,724*

ALPHA ORDER

RANK	STATE	POPULATION	% of USA
23	Alabama	4,661,900	1.5%
47	Alaska	686,293	0.2%
14	Arizona	6,500,180	2.1%
32	Arkansas	2,855,390	0.9%
1	California	36,756,666	12.1%
22	Colorado	4,939,456	1.6%
29	Connecticut	3,501,252	1.2%
45	Delaware	873,092	0.3%
4	Florida	18,328,340	6.0%
9	Georgia	9,685,744	3.2%
42	Hawaii	1,288,198	0.4%
39	Idaho	1,523,816	0.5%
5	Illinois	12,901,563	4.2%
16	Indiana	6,376,792	2.1%
30	Iowa	3,002,555	1.0%
33	Kansas	2,802,134	0.9%
26	Kentucky	4,269,245	1.4%
25	Louisiana	4,410,796	1.5%
40	Maine	1,316,456	0.4%
19	Maryland	5,633,597	1.9%
15	Massachusetts	6,497,967	2.1%
8	Michigan	10,003,422	3.3%
21	Minnesota	5,220,393	1.7%
31	Mississippi	2,938,618	1.0%
18	Missouri	5,911,605	1.9%
44	Montana	967,440	0.3%
38	Nebraska	1,783,432	0.6%
35	Nevada	2,600,167	0.9%
41	New Hampshire	1,315,809	0.4%
11	New Jersey	8,682,661	2.9%
36	New Mexico	1,984,356	0.7%
3	New York	19,490,297	6.4%
10	North Carolina	9,222,414	3.0%
48	North Dakota	641,481	0.2%
7	Ohio	11,485,910	3.8%
28	Oklahoma	3,642,361	1.2%
27	Oregon	3,790,060	1.2%
6	Pennsylvania	12,448,279	4.1%
43	Rhode Island	1,050,788	0.3%
24	South Carolina	4,479,800	1.5%
46	South Dakota	804,194	0.3%
17	Tennessee	6,214,888	2.0%
2	Texas	24,326,974	8.0%
34	Utah	2,736,424	0.9%
49	Vermont	621,270	0.2%
12	Virginia	7,769,089	2.6%
13	Washington	6,549,224	2.2%
37	West Virginia	1,814,468	0.6%
20	Wisconsin	5,627,967	1.9%
50	Wyoming	532,668	0.2%

RANK ORDER

RANK	STATE	POPULATION	% of USA
1	California	36,756,666	12.1%
2	Texas	24,326,974	8.0%
3	New York	19,490,297	6.4%
4	Florida	18,328,340	6.0%
5	Illinois	12,901,563	4.2%
6	Pennsylvania	12,448,279	4.1%
7	Ohio	11,485,910	3.8%
8	Michigan	10,003,422	3.3%
9	Georgia	9,685,744	3.2%
10	North Carolina	9,222,414	3.0%
11	New Jersey	8,682,661	2.9%
12	Virginia	7,769,089	2.6%
13	Washington	6,549,224	2.2%
14	Arizona	6,500,180	2.1%
15	Massachusetts	6,497,967	2.1%
16	Indiana	6,376,792	2.1%
17	Tennessee	6,214,888	2.0%
18	Missouri	5,911,605	1.9%
19	Maryland	5,633,597	1.9%
20	Wisconsin	5,627,967	1.9%
21	Minnesota	5,220,393	1.7%
22	Colorado	4,939,456	1.6%
23	Alabama	4,661,900	1.5%
24	South Carolina	4,479,800	1.5%
25	Louisiana	4,410,796	1.5%
26	Kentucky	4,269,245	1.4%
27	Oregon	3,790,060	1.2%
28	Oklahoma	3,642,361	1.2%
29	Connecticut	3,501,252	1.2%
30	Iowa	3,002,555	1.0%
31	Mississippi	2,938,618	1.0%
32	Arkansas	2,855,390	0.9%
33	Kansas	2,802,134	0.9%
34	Utah	2,736,424	0.9%
35	Nevada	2,600,167	0.9%
36	New Mexico	1,984,356	0.7%
37	West Virginia	1,814,468	0.6%
38	Nebraska	1,783,432	0.6%
39	Idaho	1,523,816	0.5%
40	Maine	1,316,456	0.4%
41	New Hampshire	1,315,809	0.4%
42	Hawaii	1,288,198	0.4%
43	Rhode Island	1,050,788	0.3%
44	Montana	967,440	0.3%
45	Delaware	873,092	0.3%
46	South Dakota	804,194	0.3%
47	Alaska	686,293	0.2%
48	North Dakota	641,481	0.2%
49	Vermont	621,270	0.2%
50	Wyoming	532,668	0.2%
	District of Columbia	591,833	0.2%

Source: U.S. Bureau of the Census
   "Population Estimates" (December 22, 2008, http://www.census.gov/popest/estimates.php)
*Resident population.

Population in 2007

National Total = 301,290,332*

RANK	STATE	POPULATION	% of USA
23	Alabama	4,626,595	1.5%
47	Alaska	681,111	0.2%
15	Arizona	6,353,421	2.1%
32	Arkansas	2,830,557	0.9%
1	California	36,377,534	12.1%
22	Colorado	4,842,770	1.6%
29	Connecticut	3,489,868	1.2%
45	Delaware	861,953	0.3%
4	Florida	18,199,526	6.0%
9	Georgia	9,523,297	3.2%
42	Hawaii	1,277,356	0.4%
39	Idaho	1,496,145	0.5%
5	Illinois	12,825,809	4.3%
16	Indiana	6,335,862	2.1%
30	Iowa	2,983,360	1.0%
33	Kansas	2,777,382	0.9%
26	Kentucky	4,236,308	1.4%
25	Louisiana	4,373,310	1.5%
40	Maine	1,315,398	0.4%
19	Maryland	5,618,899	1.9%
13	Massachusetts	6,467,915	2.1%
8	Michigan	10,049,790	3.3%
21	Minnesota	5,182,360	1.7%
31	Mississippi	2,921,030	1.0%
18	Missouri	5,878,399	2.0%
44	Montana	956,624	0.3%
38	Nebraska	1,769,473	0.6%
35	Nevada	2,554,344	0.8%
41	New Hampshire	1,312,256	0.4%
11	New Jersey	8,653,126	2.9%
36	New Mexico	1,964,402	0.7%
3	New York	19,429,316	6.4%
10	North Carolina	9,041,594	3.0%
48	North Dakota	637,904	0.2%
7	Ohio	11,477,641	3.8%
28	Oklahoma	3,608,123	1.2%
27	Oregon	3,735,549	1.2%
6	Pennsylvania	12,419,930	4.1%
43	Rhode Island	1,053,136	0.3%
24	South Carolina	4,404,914	1.5%
46	South Dakota	795,689	0.3%
17	Tennessee	6,149,116	2.0%
2	Texas	23,843,432	7.9%
34	Utah	2,668,925	0.9%
49	Vermont	620,748	0.2%
12	Virginia	7,698,775	2.6%
14	Washington	6,449,511	2.1%
37	West Virginia	1,809,836	0.6%
20	Wisconsin	5,598,893	1.9%
50	Wyoming	523,252	0.2%

RANK	STATE	POPULATION	% of USA
1	California	36,377,534	12.1%
2	Texas	23,843,432	7.9%
3	New York	19,429,316	6.4%
4	Florida	18,199,526	6.0%
5	Illinois	12,825,809	4.3%
6	Pennsylvania	12,419,930	4.1%
7	Ohio	11,477,641	3.8%
8	Michigan	10,049,790	3.3%
9	Georgia	9,523,297	3.2%
10	North Carolina	9,041,594	3.0%
11	New Jersey	8,653,126	2.9%
12	Virginia	7,698,775	2.6%
13	Massachusetts	6,467,915	2.1%
14	Washington	6,449,511	2.1%
15	Arizona	6,353,421	2.1%
16	Indiana	6,335,862	2.1%
17	Tennessee	6,149,116	2.0%
18	Missouri	5,878,399	2.0%
19	Maryland	5,618,899	1.9%
20	Wisconsin	5,598,893	1.9%
21	Minnesota	5,182,360	1.7%
22	Colorado	4,842,770	1.6%
23	Alabama	4,626,595	1.5%
24	South Carolina	4,404,914	1.5%
25	Louisiana	4,373,310	1.5%
26	Kentucky	4,236,308	1.4%
27	Oregon	3,735,549	1.2%
28	Oklahoma	3,608,123	1.2%
29	Connecticut	3,489,868	1.2%
30	Iowa	2,983,360	1.0%
31	Mississippi	2,921,030	1.0%
32	Arkansas	2,830,557	0.9%
33	Kansas	2,777,382	0.9%
34	Utah	2,668,925	0.9%
35	Nevada	2,554,344	0.8%
36	New Mexico	1,964,402	0.7%
37	West Virginia	1,809,836	0.6%
38	Nebraska	1,769,473	0.6%
39	Idaho	1,496,145	0.5%
40	Maine	1,315,398	0.4%
41	New Hampshire	1,312,256	0.4%
42	Hawaii	1,277,356	0.4%
43	Rhode Island	1,053,136	0.3%
44	Montana	956,624	0.3%
45	Delaware	861,953	0.3%
46	South Dakota	795,689	0.3%
47	Alaska	681,111	0.2%
48	North Dakota	637,904	0.2%
49	Vermont	620,748	0.2%
50	Wyoming	523,252	0.2%
	District of Columbia	587,868	0.2%

Source: U.S. Bureau of the Census
   "Population Estimates" (December 22, 2008, http://www.census.gov/popest/estimates.php)
*Resident population. Revised estimates.

Male Population in 2007

National Total = 148,658,898

<table>
<tr><td colspan="4">ALPHA ORDER</td></tr>
<tr><th>RANK</th><th>STATE</th><th>MALES</th><th>% of USA</th></tr>
<tr><td>23</td><td>Alabama</td><td>2,242,125</td><td>1.5%</td></tr>
<tr><td>47</td><td>Alaska</td><td>354,840</td><td>0.2%</td></tr>
<tr><td>14</td><td>Arizona</td><td>3,173,144</td><td>2.1%</td></tr>
<tr><td>32</td><td>Arkansas</td><td>1,389,199</td><td>0.9%</td></tr>
<tr><td>1</td><td>California</td><td>18,277,795</td><td>12.3%</td></tr>
<tr><td>22</td><td>Colorado</td><td>2,450,582</td><td>1.6%</td></tr>
<tr><td>29</td><td>Connecticut</td><td>1,706,987</td><td>1.1%</td></tr>
<tr><td>45</td><td>Delaware</td><td>419,294</td><td>0.3%</td></tr>
<tr><td>4</td><td>Florida</td><td>8,968,843</td><td>6.0%</td></tr>
<tr><td>9</td><td>Georgia</td><td>4,693,704</td><td>3.2%</td></tr>
<tr><td>41</td><td>Hawaii</td><td>645,820</td><td>0.4%</td></tr>
<tr><td>39</td><td>Idaho</td><td>754,499</td><td>0.5%</td></tr>
<tr><td>5</td><td>Illinois</td><td>6,333,402</td><td>4.3%</td></tr>
<tr><td>15</td><td>Indiana</td><td>3,126,580</td><td>2.1%</td></tr>
<tr><td>30</td><td>Iowa</td><td>1,474,541</td><td>1.0%</td></tr>
<tr><td>33</td><td>Kansas</td><td>1,376,311</td><td>0.9%</td></tr>
<tr><td>26</td><td>Kentucky</td><td>2,078,507</td><td>1.4%</td></tr>
<tr><td>25</td><td>Louisiana</td><td>2,085,445</td><td>1.4%</td></tr>
<tr><td>42</td><td>Maine</td><td>642,799</td><td>0.4%</td></tr>
<tr><td>20</td><td>Maryland</td><td>2,718,590</td><td>1.8%</td></tr>
<tr><td>16</td><td>Massachusetts</td><td>3,126,493</td><td>2.1%</td></tr>
<tr><td>8</td><td>Michigan</td><td>4,959,730</td><td>3.3%</td></tr>
<tr><td>21</td><td>Minnesota</td><td>2,588,258</td><td>1.7%</td></tr>
<tr><td>31</td><td>Mississippi</td><td>1,413,709</td><td>1.0%</td></tr>
<tr><td>18</td><td>Missouri</td><td>2,871,022</td><td>1.9%</td></tr>
<tr><td>44</td><td>Montana</td><td>479,633</td><td>0.3%</td></tr>
<tr><td>38</td><td>Nebraska</td><td>879,391</td><td>0.6%</td></tr>
<tr><td>35</td><td>Nevada</td><td>1,306,749</td><td>0.9%</td></tr>
<tr><td>40</td><td>New Hampshire</td><td>649,299</td><td>0.4%</td></tr>
<tr><td>11</td><td>New Jersey</td><td>4,248,866</td><td>2.9%</td></tr>
<tr><td>36</td><td>New Mexico</td><td>971,773</td><td>0.7%</td></tr>
<tr><td>3</td><td>New York</td><td>9,360,736</td><td>6.3%</td></tr>
<tr><td>10</td><td>North Carolina</td><td>4,427,561</td><td>3.0%</td></tr>
<tr><td>48</td><td>North Dakota</td><td>321,060</td><td>0.2%</td></tr>
<tr><td>7</td><td>Ohio</td><td>5,591,161</td><td>3.8%</td></tr>
<tr><td>28</td><td>Oklahoma</td><td>1,787,488</td><td>1.2%</td></tr>
<tr><td>27</td><td>Oregon</td><td>1,862,139</td><td>1.3%</td></tr>
<tr><td>6</td><td>Pennsylvania</td><td>6,048,989</td><td>4.1%</td></tr>
<tr><td>43</td><td>Rhode Island</td><td>511,857</td><td>0.3%</td></tr>
<tr><td>24</td><td>South Carolina</td><td>2,147,146</td><td>1.4%</td></tr>
<tr><td>46</td><td>South Dakota</td><td>396,812</td><td>0.3%</td></tr>
<tr><td>17</td><td>Tennessee</td><td>3,006,118</td><td>2.0%</td></tr>
<tr><td>2</td><td>Texas</td><td>11,925,864</td><td>8.0%</td></tr>
<tr><td>34</td><td>Utah</td><td>1,335,747</td><td>0.9%</td></tr>
<tr><td>49</td><td>Vermont</td><td>305,785</td><td>0.2%</td></tr>
<tr><td>12</td><td>Virginia</td><td>3,785,039</td><td>2.5%</td></tr>
<tr><td>13</td><td>Washington</td><td>3,222,926</td><td>2.2%</td></tr>
<tr><td>37</td><td>West Virginia</td><td>887,218</td><td>0.6%</td></tr>
<tr><td>19</td><td>Wisconsin</td><td>2,784,170</td><td>1.9%</td></tr>
<tr><td>50</td><td>Wyoming</td><td>265,045</td><td>0.2%</td></tr>
</table>

<table>
<tr><td colspan="4">RANK ORDER</td></tr>
<tr><th>RANK</th><th>STATE</th><th>MALES</th><th>% of USA</th></tr>
<tr><td>1</td><td>California</td><td>18,277,795</td><td>12.3%</td></tr>
<tr><td>2</td><td>Texas</td><td>11,925,864</td><td>8.0%</td></tr>
<tr><td>3</td><td>New York</td><td>9,360,736</td><td>6.3%</td></tr>
<tr><td>4</td><td>Florida</td><td>8,968,843</td><td>6.0%</td></tr>
<tr><td>5</td><td>Illinois</td><td>6,333,402</td><td>4.3%</td></tr>
<tr><td>6</td><td>Pennsylvania</td><td>6,048,989</td><td>4.1%</td></tr>
<tr><td>7</td><td>Ohio</td><td>5,591,161</td><td>3.8%</td></tr>
<tr><td>8</td><td>Michigan</td><td>4,959,730</td><td>3.3%</td></tr>
<tr><td>9</td><td>Georgia</td><td>4,693,704</td><td>3.2%</td></tr>
<tr><td>10</td><td>North Carolina</td><td>4,427,561</td><td>3.0%</td></tr>
<tr><td>11</td><td>New Jersey</td><td>4,248,866</td><td>2.9%</td></tr>
<tr><td>12</td><td>Virginia</td><td>3,785,039</td><td>2.5%</td></tr>
<tr><td>13</td><td>Washington</td><td>3,222,926</td><td>2.2%</td></tr>
<tr><td>14</td><td>Arizona</td><td>3,173,144</td><td>2.1%</td></tr>
<tr><td>15</td><td>Indiana</td><td>3,126,580</td><td>2.1%</td></tr>
<tr><td>16</td><td>Massachusetts</td><td>3,126,493</td><td>2.1%</td></tr>
<tr><td>17</td><td>Tennessee</td><td>3,006,118</td><td>2.0%</td></tr>
<tr><td>18</td><td>Missouri</td><td>2,871,022</td><td>1.9%</td></tr>
<tr><td>19</td><td>Wisconsin</td><td>2,784,170</td><td>1.9%</td></tr>
<tr><td>20</td><td>Maryland</td><td>2,718,590</td><td>1.8%</td></tr>
<tr><td>21</td><td>Minnesota</td><td>2,588,258</td><td>1.7%</td></tr>
<tr><td>22</td><td>Colorado</td><td>2,450,582</td><td>1.6%</td></tr>
<tr><td>23</td><td>Alabama</td><td>2,242,125</td><td>1.5%</td></tr>
<tr><td>24</td><td>South Carolina</td><td>2,147,146</td><td>1.4%</td></tr>
<tr><td>25</td><td>Louisiana</td><td>2,085,445</td><td>1.4%</td></tr>
<tr><td>26</td><td>Kentucky</td><td>2,078,507</td><td>1.4%</td></tr>
<tr><td>27</td><td>Oregon</td><td>1,862,139</td><td>1.3%</td></tr>
<tr><td>28</td><td>Oklahoma</td><td>1,787,488</td><td>1.2%</td></tr>
<tr><td>29</td><td>Connecticut</td><td>1,706,987</td><td>1.1%</td></tr>
<tr><td>30</td><td>Iowa</td><td>1,474,541</td><td>1.0%</td></tr>
<tr><td>31</td><td>Mississippi</td><td>1,413,709</td><td>1.0%</td></tr>
<tr><td>32</td><td>Arkansas</td><td>1,389,199</td><td>0.9%</td></tr>
<tr><td>33</td><td>Kansas</td><td>1,376,311</td><td>0.9%</td></tr>
<tr><td>34</td><td>Utah</td><td>1,335,747</td><td>0.9%</td></tr>
<tr><td>35</td><td>Nevada</td><td>1,306,749</td><td>0.9%</td></tr>
<tr><td>36</td><td>New Mexico</td><td>971,773</td><td>0.7%</td></tr>
<tr><td>37</td><td>West Virginia</td><td>887,218</td><td>0.6%</td></tr>
<tr><td>38</td><td>Nebraska</td><td>879,391</td><td>0.6%</td></tr>
<tr><td>39</td><td>Idaho</td><td>754,499</td><td>0.5%</td></tr>
<tr><td>40</td><td>New Hampshire</td><td>649,299</td><td>0.4%</td></tr>
<tr><td>41</td><td>Hawaii</td><td>645,820</td><td>0.4%</td></tr>
<tr><td>42</td><td>Maine</td><td>642,799</td><td>0.4%</td></tr>
<tr><td>43</td><td>Rhode Island</td><td>511,857</td><td>0.3%</td></tr>
<tr><td>44</td><td>Montana</td><td>479,633</td><td>0.3%</td></tr>
<tr><td>45</td><td>Delaware</td><td>419,294</td><td>0.3%</td></tr>
<tr><td>46</td><td>South Dakota</td><td>396,812</td><td>0.3%</td></tr>
<tr><td>47</td><td>Alaska</td><td>354,840</td><td>0.2%</td></tr>
<tr><td>48</td><td>North Dakota</td><td>321,060</td><td>0.2%</td></tr>
<tr><td>49</td><td>Vermont</td><td>305,785</td><td>0.2%</td></tr>
<tr><td>50</td><td>Wyoming</td><td>265,045</td><td>0.2%</td></tr>
<tr><td></td><td>District of Columbia</td><td>278,107</td><td>0.2%</td></tr>
</table>

Source: CQ Press using data from U.S. Bureau of the Census
"SC-EST2007-AGESEX_RES - State Characteristic Estimates" (http://www.census.gov/popest/datasets.html)

Female Population in 2007

National Total = 152,962,259 Females

ALPHA ORDER

RANK	STATE	FEMALES	% of USA
23	Alabama	2,385,726	1.6%
47	Alaska	328,638	0.2%
16	Arizona	3,165,611	2.1%
32	Arkansas	1,445,598	0.9%
1	California	18,275,420	11.9%
22	Colorado	2,410,933	1.6%
29	Connecticut	1,795,322	1.2%
45	Delaware	445,470	0.3%
4	Florida	9,282,400	6.1%
9	Georgia	4,851,046	3.2%
42	Hawaii	637,568	0.4%
39	Idaho	744,903	0.5%
5	Illinois	6,519,146	4.3%
15	Indiana	3,218,709	2.1%
30	Iowa	1,513,505	1.0%
33	Kansas	1,399,686	0.9%
26	Kentucky	2,162,967	1.4%
25	Louisiana	2,207,759	1.4%
40	Maine	674,408	0.4%
19	Maryland	2,899,754	1.9%
13	Massachusetts	3,323,262	2.2%
8	Michigan	5,112,092	3.3%
21	Minnesota	2,609,363	1.7%
31	Mississippi	1,505,076	1.0%
18	Missouri	3,007,393	2.0%
44	Montana	478,228	0.3%
38	Nebraska	895,180	0.6%
35	Nevada	1,258,633	0.8%
41	New Hampshire	666,529	0.4%
11	New Jersey	4,437,054	2.9%
36	New Mexico	998,142	0.7%
3	New York	9,936,993	6.5%
10	North Carolina	4,633,471	3.0%
48	North Dakota	318,655	0.2%
7	Ohio	5,875,756	3.8%
28	Oklahoma	1,829,828	1.2%
27	Oregon	1,885,316	1.2%
6	Pennsylvania	6,383,803	4.2%
43	Rhode Island	545,975	0.4%
24	South Carolina	2,260,563	1.5%
46	South Dakota	399,402	0.3%
17	Tennessee	3,150,601	2.1%
2	Texas	11,978,516	7.8%
34	Utah	1,309,583	0.9%
49	Vermont	315,469	0.2%
12	Virginia	3,927,052	2.6%
14	Washington	3,245,498	2.1%
37	West Virginia	924,817	0.6%
20	Wisconsin	2,817,470	1.8%
50	Wyoming	257,785	0.2%

RANK ORDER

RANK	STATE	FEMALES	% of USA
1	California	18,275,420	11.9%
2	Texas	11,978,516	7.8%
3	New York	9,936,993	6.5%
4	Florida	9,282,400	6.1%
5	Illinois	6,519,146	4.3%
6	Pennsylvania	6,383,803	4.2%
7	Ohio	5,875,756	3.8%
8	Michigan	5,112,092	3.3%
9	Georgia	4,851,046	3.2%
10	North Carolina	4,633,471	3.0%
11	New Jersey	4,437,054	2.9%
12	Virginia	3,927,052	2.6%
13	Massachusetts	3,323,262	2.2%
14	Washington	3,245,498	2.1%
15	Indiana	3,218,709	2.1%
16	Arizona	3,165,611	2.1%
17	Tennessee	3,150,601	2.1%
18	Missouri	3,007,393	2.0%
19	Maryland	2,899,754	1.9%
20	Wisconsin	2,817,470	1.8%
21	Minnesota	2,609,363	1.7%
22	Colorado	2,410,933	1.6%
23	Alabama	2,385,726	1.6%
24	South Carolina	2,260,563	1.5%
25	Louisiana	2,207,759	1.4%
26	Kentucky	2,162,967	1.4%
27	Oregon	1,885,316	1.2%
28	Oklahoma	1,829,828	1.2%
29	Connecticut	1,795,322	1.2%
30	Iowa	1,513,505	1.0%
31	Mississippi	1,505,076	1.0%
32	Arkansas	1,445,598	0.9%
33	Kansas	1,399,686	0.9%
34	Utah	1,309,583	0.9%
35	Nevada	1,258,633	0.8%
36	New Mexico	998,142	0.7%
37	West Virginia	924,817	0.6%
38	Nebraska	895,180	0.6%
39	Idaho	744,903	0.5%
40	Maine	674,408	0.4%
41	New Hampshire	666,529	0.4%
42	Hawaii	637,568	0.4%
43	Rhode Island	545,975	0.4%
44	Montana	478,228	0.3%
45	Delaware	445,470	0.3%
46	South Dakota	399,402	0.3%
47	Alaska	328,638	0.2%
48	North Dakota	318,655	0.2%
49	Vermont	315,469	0.2%
50	Wyoming	257,785	0.2%
	District of Columbia	310,185	0.2%

Source: CQ Press using data from U.S. Bureau of the Census
"SC-EST2007-AGESEX_RES - State Characteristic Estimates" (http://www.census.gov/popest/datasets.html)

Sources

American Academy of Physicians Assistants
950 North Washington Street
Alexandria, VA 22314-1552
703-836-2272
www.aapa.org

American Cancer Society, Inc.
1599 Clifton Road, NE
Atlanta, GA 30329-4251
800-227-2345
www.cancer.org

American Dental Association
211 E. Chicago Ave.
Chicago, IL 60611-2678
312-440-2500
www.ada.org

American Hospital Association
One North Franklin
Chicago, IL 60606-3421
312-422-3000
www.aha.org

American Medical Association
515 North State Street
Chicago, IL 60610
800-621-8335
www.ama-assn.org

American Osteopathic Association
142 East Ontario Street
Chicago, IL 60611
800-621-1773
www.osteopathic.org

Bureau of Labor Statistics
2 Massachusetts Ave., NE
Washington, DC 20212-0001
202-691-5200
www.bls.gov

Bureau of the Census
4700 Silver Hill Road
Washington, DC 20233-0001
301-457-2800
www.census.gov

Centers for Disease Control and Prevention
1600 Clifton Road
Atlanta, GA 30333
800-232-4636
www.cdc.gov

Centers for Medicare and Medicaid Services
7500 Security Boulevard
Baltimore, MD 21244-1850
877-267-2323
www.cms.hhs.gov

Federation of Chiropractic Licensing Boards
5401 W 10th Street, Ste 101
Greeley, CO 80634-4400
970-356-3500
www.fclb.org

HealthLeaders/InterStudy
One Vantage Way, B-300
Nashville, TN 37228
615-385-4131
http://home.healthleaders-interstudy.com

Health Resources and Services Admin
Division of Practitioner Data Banks
5600 Fishers Lane
Rockville, MD 20857
800-767-6732
www.hrsa.gov

Medical Expenditure Panel Survey
Agency for Healthcare Research and Quality
540 Gaither Road
Rockville, MD 20850
301-427-1364
www.meps.ahrq.gov

National Association of State Budget Officers
444 N Capitol St., NW, Ste 642
Washington, DC 20001-1551
202-624-5382
www.nasbo.org

National Center for Health Statistics
U.S. Department of Health and Human Services
3311 Toledo Road
Hyattsville, MD   20782
301-458-4000
www.cdc.gov/nchs/

National Highway Traffic Safety Admin.
1200 New Jersey Ave., SE
West Building
Washington, DC 20590
888-327-4236
www.nhtsa.dot.gov

**National Institute on Alcohol Abuse
and Alcoholism**
National Institutes of Health
5635 Fishers Lane, MSC 9304
Bethesda, MD 20892-9304
301-443-3860
www.niaaa.nih.gov/

National Sporting Goods Association
1601 Feehanville Drive, Ste 300
Mt. Prospect, IL 60056
800-815-5422
www.nsga.org

Substance Abuse and Mental Health Services Admin.
U.S. Department of Health and Human Services
P.O. Box 2345
Rockville, MD 20847
877-726-4727
www.samhsa.gov

Index